# Lecture Notes in Computer Science　1969

Edited by G. Goos, J. Hartmanis and J. van Leeuwen

T0189574

**Springer**
Berlin
Heidelberg
New York
Barcelona
Hong Kong
London
Milan
Paris
Tokyo

D.T. Lee   Shang-Hua Teng (Eds.)

# Algorithms
# and Computation

11th International Conference, ISAAC 2000
Taipei, Taiwan, December 18-20, 2000
Proceedings

 Springer

Series Editors

Gerhard Goos, Karlsruhe University, Germany
Juris Hartmanis, Cornell University, NY, USA
Jan van Leeuwen, Utrecht University, The Netherlands

Volume Editors

D.T. Lee
Academia Sinica
Institute of Information Science
128 Academia Road, Section 2, Nankang, Taipei 115, Taiwan, R.O.C.
E-mail: dtlee@iis.sinica.edu.tw

Shang-Hua Teng
University of Illinois at Urbana Champaign
Department of Computer Science
and
Akamai Technologies
500 Technology Square, Cambridge, MA 02139, USA
E-mail: steng@akamai.com

Cataloging-in-Publication Data applied for

Die Deutsche Bibliothek - CIP-Einheitsaufnahme

Algorithms and computation : 11th international conference ;
proceedings / ISAAC 2000, Taipei, Taiwan, December 18 - 20, 2000.
D. T. Lee ; Shang-Hua Teng (ed.). - Berlin ; Heidelberg ; New York ;
Barcelona ; Hong Kong ; London ; Milan ; Paris ; Singapore ; Tokyo :
Springer, 2000
   (Lecture notes in computer science ; Vol. 1969)
   ISBN 3-540-41255-7


CR Subject Classification (1998): F.2, F.1, C.2, G.2-3, I.3.5, E.1

ISSN 0302-9743
ISBN 3-540-41255-7 Springer-Verlag Berlin Heidelberg New York

Springer-Verlag Berlin Heidelberg New York
a member of BertelsmannSpringer Science+Business Media GmbH
© Springer-Verlag Berlin Heidelberg 2000
Printed in Germany

Typesetting: Camera-ready by author, data conversion by PTP-Berlin, Stefan Sossna
Printed on acid-free paper      SPIN: 10781373      06/3142      5 4 3 2 1 0

# Preface

The papers in this volume were selected for presentation at the *Eleventh Annual International Symposium on Algorithms and Computation* (ISAAC 2000), held on 18–20 December, 2000 at the Institute of Information Science, Academia Sinica, Taipei, Taiwan. Previous meetings were held in Tokyo (1990), Taipei (1991), Nagoya (1992), Hong Kong (1993), Beijing (1994), Cairns (1995), Osaka (1996), Singapore (1997), Taejon (1998), and Chennai (1999).

Submissions to the conference this year were conducted entirely electronically. Thanks to the excellent software developed by the Institute of Information Science, Academia Sinica, we were able to carry out virtually all communication via the World Wide Web.

In response to the call for papers, a total of 87 extended abstracts were submitted from 25 countries. Each submitted paper was handled by at least three program committee members, with the assistance of a number of external reviewers, as indicated by the referee list found in the proceedings. There were many more acceptable papers than there was space available in the symposium program, which made the program committee's task extremely difficult. Finally 46 papers were selected for presentation at the Symposium. In addition to these contributed papers, the conference also included two invited presentations by Dr. Jean-Daniel Boissonnat, INRIA Sophia-Antipolis, France and Professor Jin-Yi Cai, University of Wisconsin at Madison, Wisconsin, USA. It is expected that most of the accepted papers will appear in a more complete form in scientific journals.

We thank all program committee members and the external reviewers for their excellent work, especially given the demanding time constraints; they gave the symposium its distinctive character. We thank all authors who submitted papers for consideration: they all contributed to the high quality of the symposium. Finally, we thank all our colleagues who worked hard to put in place the logistical arrangements of the symposium.


December 2000                                                    D. T. Lee
                                                          Shang-Hua Teng

# Organization

ISAAC 2000 was organized by the Institute of Information Science, Academia Sinica, Taipei, Taiwan, R.O.C. and in cooperation with the Institute of Information and Computing Machinery (IICM), Taiwan, R.O.C.

## Program Committee

| | |
|---|---|
| D. T. Lee (Symposium Chair) | Academia Sinica, Taiwan (Co-chair) |
| Shang-Hua Teng | University of Illinois, USA (Co-chair) |
| Helmut Alt | Free University of Berlin, Germany |
| Nina Amenta | University of Texas at Austin, USA |
| Gen-Huey Chen | National Taiwan University, Taiwan |
| Jeff Erickson | University of Illinois, USA |
| Giuseppe Italiano | University of Rome, Italy |
| Kazuo Iwama | Kyoto University, Japan |
| Marcos Kiwi | University of Chile, Chile |
| Ming-Tat Ko | Academia Sinica, Taiwan |
| Kurt Mehlhorn | Max Planck Institute, Germany |
| Michael D. Mitzenmacher | Harvard University, USA |
| Kunsoo Park | Seoul National University, Korea |
| Tadao Takaoka | University of Canterbury, New Zealand |
| Takeshi Tokuyama | Sendi University, Japan |
| Peng-Jun Wan | Illinois Institute of Technology, USA |
| Derick Wood | Hong Kong Univ. of Sci. & Tech., Hong Kong |

## Organizing Committee

| | |
|---|---|
| Local arrangements | Tsan-sheng Hsu (Academia Sinica) |
| Web pages | Ming-Tat Ko (Academia Sinica) |
| Submission | Chi-Jen Lu (Academia Sinica) |
| Publication | Hsueh-I Lu (Academia Sinica) |
| Treasurer | Ting-Yi Sung (Academia Sinica) |
| Technical support | Chiou-Feng Wang (Academia Sinica) |
| Publicity | Da-Wei Wang (Academia Sinica) |

# Referees

| | | |
|---|---|---|
| Ricardo Baeza | Frank Hoffmann | Chi-Jen Lu |
| Peter Brass | Sun-Yuan Hsieh | Hsueh-I Lu |
| Massimiliano Caramia | Fang-Rong Hsu | Lutz Meissner |
| Marco Cesati | Tsan-sheng Hsu | Shuichi Miyazaki |
| Wei-Mei Chen | Valentine Kabanets | Gonzalo Navarro |
| Hsin-Hung Chou | Astrid Kaffanke | Rossella Petreschi |
| Kyung-Yong Chwa | Adam Klivans | Guenter Rote |
| Josep Diaz | Christian Knauer | Kunihiko Sadakane |
| Stefan Felsner | Ulrich Kortenkamp | Ting-Yi Sung |
| Qian Ping Gu | Klaus Kriegel | Da-Wei Wang |
| Cluadio Gutierrez | Cheng-Nan Lai | Jeng-Jung Wang |
| Xin He | Stefano Leonardi | Carola Wenk |
| Laura Heinrich-Litan | Yaw-Ling Lin | Chang-Wu Yu |
| Alejandro Hevia | Giuseppe Liotta | Moti Yung |
| Chin-Wen Ho | Martin Loebl | Xiao Zhou |

# Sponsoring Institutions

National Science Council of the Republic of China
Institute of Information Science, Academia Sinica, Taipei, Taiwan
ACM Taipei/Taiwan Chapter
The Institute of Information and Computing Machinery (IICM)

# Table of Contents

## Approximation and Randomized Algorithms (II)

## Graph Drawing and Algorithms

## Automata, Cryptography, and Complexity Theory

## Algorithms and Data Structures (IV)

## Parallel and Distributed Algorithms

## Algorithms and Data Structures (V)

# Computational Geometry (I)

# Algorithms and Data Structures (VI)

# Computational Geometry (II)

# Computational Biology

# Computational Geometry (III)

# Voronoi-Based Systems of Coordinates and Surface Reconstruction

Jean-Daniel Boissonnat

INRIA, Unité de Sophia Antipolis
Jean-Daniel.Boissonnat@sophia.inria.fr

**Abstract.** This talk will focus on systems of coordinates associated with scattered points. A first example of such a system of coordinates has been proposed by Sibson in 1980. It is defined geometrically from the Voronoi diagram of the points and has nice properties that make it suitable for scattered data interpolation. Since then, other systems of coordinates have been proposed, resulting in new theoretical insights and new applications. The case where the points are scattered on a surface is of particular interest since it occurs in various contexts, most notably in reverse engineering when one wants to reconstruct a surface from a set of points measured on the surface. The behaviour of the Voronoi-based systems of coordinates associated with points on a surface is closely related to the way the Voronoi diagram of the sample points approaches the medial axis of the surface when the sampling density increases. Elucidating the question of approximating the medial axis of a surface leads to new theoretical results in surface reconstruction and new algorithms with provable guarantees.

D.T. Lee and S.-H. Teng (Eds.): ISAAC 2000, LNCS 1969, p. 1, 2000.
© Springer-Verlag Berlin Heidelberg 2000

# Essentially Every Unimodular Matrix Defines an Expander

Jin-Yi Cai*

[1] Department of Computer Science and Engineering, State University of New York
at Buffalo, NY 14260.
[2] Computer Sciences Department, University of Wisconsin, Madison, WI 53706
jyc@cs.wisc.edu

**Abstract.** We generalize the construction of Gabber and Galil to essentially every unimodular matrix in $SL_2(\mathbf{Z})$. It is shown that every parabolic or hyperbolic fractional linear transformation explicitly defines an expander of bounded degree and constant expansion. Thus all but a vanishingly small fraction of unimodular matrices define expanders.

## 1 Introduction

It has been recognized in the last 25 years that certain combinatorial objects called expanders are extremely useful in a number of computer science applications. These include sorting networks, superconcentrators and sparse connection networks in general, pseudorandom generators and amplifications and deterministic simulations, to name just a few.

An $(n, k, d)$ *expander* is a bipartite graph $G = (L, R, E)$, with $|L| = |R| = n$ and at most $kn$ edges, such that for every subset $X$ of $L$, the neighbor set in $R$ has $|\Gamma(X)| \geq [1 + d(1 - |X|/n)]|X|$. Thus, for every subset of input vertices of cardinality at most, say, $n/2$, its neighbor set *expands*, having cardinality at least a constant multiple more than $|X|$. It is generally desired to have $k$ and $d$ fixed and $n$ grows to infinity.

The first existence theorems on expanders were provided by probabilistic counting argument [7][16]. Roughly speaking, such a proof starts by defining a certain probability space of graphs, and then one shows that the probability of such graphs is non-zero. In fact it is usually shown that such probability tends to 1. Thus not only such graphs exist, but they exist in *abundance*. The weakness of such a proof is that it is not explicit.

Margulis [12] was the first to give an explicit construction of a sequence of graphs $\{G_n\}$. This major achievement uses group representation theory. However, while his construction is explicit, the constant of expansion was not explicitly known. Gabber and Galil [10] in a beautiful paper gave an explicit construction of graphs $\{G_n\}$ with an explicitly stated constant of expansion. The Gabber-Galil proof also has the added advantage of being relatively elementary. We will

---

* Research supported in part by NSF grant CCR-9820806 and by a Guggenheim Fellowship.

D.T. Lee and S.-H. Teng (Eds.): ISAAC 2000, LNCS 1969, pp. 2–22, 2000.
© Springer-Verlag Berlin Heidelberg 2000

follow the proofs of [10] closely. There is an extensive literature on expanders and their applications to the theory of computing [1][2][4][5][6] [8][9][14][15]. It was realized that expansion properties are closely related to the second largest eigenvalues of the graph $\lambda(G)$ (see [6]), and for $d$-regular graphs the gap between $d$ and $\lambda(G)$ provides estimates for both upper and lower bound for the expansion constant. The best construction was given by Lubotsky, Phillip and Sarnak [11] and by Margulis [13], where asymptotically optimal $\lambda(G)$ was achieved. The proofs in [11] use deep results from number theory, especially results of Eichler and Igusa concerning the Ramanujan conjecture.

In this paper, we generalize the construction of Gabber and Galil [10] to essentially every unimodular matrix in $SL_2(\mathbf{Z})$. Our proofs are relatively elementary. They do provide a certain "abundance" as well as being explicit, with the same expansion constant $2 - \sqrt{3}$ as in [10]. It is shown that *every* parabolic or hyperbolic fractional linear transformation explicitly defines an expander of bounded degree and constant expansion.

## 2  Preliminary Remarks

Let $A = \begin{pmatrix} a & b \\ c & d \end{pmatrix}$ be an integral unimodular matrix, i.e., $A \in SL_2(\mathbf{Z})$, where $a, b, c, d \in \mathbf{Z}$ and $\det A = ad - bc = 1$.

We define a companion matrix $\tilde{A}$ to be $\begin{pmatrix} d & c \\ b & a \end{pmatrix}$. Note that in terms of the mappings they define on $\mathbf{R}^2$, $\tilde{A}$ is merely an exchange of the $x$ and $y$ coordinates. More formally, let $R = \begin{pmatrix} 0 & 1 \\ 1 & 0 \end{pmatrix}$. Then $R = R^{-1}$ is the matrix form of the permutation (12). Thus $\tilde{A} = RAR$.

We are going to consider the set $\Sigma = \{A, \tilde{A}, A^{-1}, \tilde{A}^{-1}\}$. We will use this set to define a constant degree expander. To this end we want all 4 matrices in $\Sigma$ to be distinct.

**Lemma 1.** $A = \tilde{A}$ *iff* $A = \pm I$.
$A = A^{-1}$ *iff* $A = \pm I$.
$A = \tilde{A}^{-1}$ *iff* $b + c = 0$.

For the other $\binom{4}{2}$ possibilities, we note that $\tilde{A} = RAR$, and thus

**Lemma 2.** $\tilde{A} = A^{-1}$ *iff* $A = \tilde{A}^{-1}$ *iff* $b + c = 0$.
$\tilde{A} = \tilde{A}^{-1}$ *iff* $A = A^{-1}$ *iff* $A = \pm I$.
$A^{-1} = \tilde{A}^{-1}$ *iff* $A = \tilde{A}$ *iff* $A = \pm I$.

There is also the possibility of choosing the transpose $A^T = \begin{pmatrix} a & c \\ b & d \end{pmatrix}$ as the companion matrix. However there are examples where Theorem 3 is not valid for this choice.

We will henceforth assume $A \neq \pm I$ and $b + c \neq 0$.

## 3    One Less, Three More

We will assume none of $a, b, c, d$ is zero, and deal with the case where $abcd = 0$ just prior to Theorem 3.

Let $p = (x, y)$. Define the max (or $\infty$-) norm $||p|| = \max\{|x|, |y|\}$. The goal in this section is to show that, under a mild condition, if one of the norms

$$\{||Ap||, ||\tilde{A}p||, ||A^{-1}p||, ||\tilde{A}^{-1}p||\}$$

is strictly less than the corresponding norm $||p||$, then the three other norms are all strictly greater than $||p||$. The proof involves an examination of all the cases with reductions using suitable symmetries.

Let us start with the following Lemma:

**Lemma 3.** $||Ap|| < ||p|| \implies ||\tilde{A}p|| > ||p||$.

Given $A = \begin{pmatrix} a & b \\ c & d \end{pmatrix}$, for a contradiction assume $||Ap|| < ||p||$ and $||\tilde{A}p|| \leq ||p||$, where $p = (x, y)$. First let's assume $|y| \geq |x|$, thus $||p|| = |y|$. We have

$$|ax + by| < |y|$$
$$|cx + dy| < |y|$$
$$|dx + cy| \leq |y|$$
$$|bx + ay| \leq |y|$$

Let $\xi = -\frac{x}{y}$. We note that since the strict inequality $||Ap|| < ||p||$ holds, $y \neq 0$. Dividing through by $y$ and $a, b, c, d$ respectively, we get the rational approximations of $\xi$

$$|\xi - \frac{b}{a}| < \frac{1}{|a|}$$

$$|\xi - \frac{d}{c}| < \frac{1}{|c|}$$

$$|\xi - \frac{a}{b}| \leq \frac{1}{|b|}$$

$$|\xi - \frac{c}{d}| \leq \frac{1}{|d|}$$

(We recall that none of $a, b, c, d$ is zero as assumed.) It follows that

$$\left||\xi| - |\frac{b}{a}|\right| < \frac{1}{|a|}$$

$$\left||\xi| - |\frac{d}{c}|\right| < \frac{1}{|c|}$$

$$\left||\xi| - |\frac{a}{b}|\right| \leq \frac{1}{|b|}$$

$$\left||\xi| - |\frac{c}{d}|\right| \leq \frac{1}{|d|}$$

Then

$$\frac{|b| - 1}{|a|} < |\xi| < \frac{|b| + 1}{|a|}$$

$$\frac{|a| - 1}{|b|} \leq |\xi| \leq \frac{|a| + 1}{|b|}$$

Thus,

$$\frac{|a| - 1}{|b|} < \frac{|b| + 1}{|a|}$$

and

$$\frac{|b| - 1}{|a|} < \frac{|a| + 1}{|b|}.$$

If $|b| < |a|$ then, being integral, we get $|b| + 1 \leq |a|$ and $|b| \leq |a| - 1$, and so the following contradiction follows

$$1 \leq \frac{|a| - 1}{|b|} < \frac{|b| + 1}{|a|} \leq 1.$$

If $|a| < |b|$ then $|a| + 1 \leq |b|$, $|a| \leq |b| - 1$, and the following contradiction arises

$$1 \leq \frac{|b| - 1}{|a|} < \frac{|a| + 1}{|b|} \leq 1.$$

Hence it follows that $|a| = |b|$. Being a row of a unimodular matrix $A$, the gcd of $(a, b)$ is 1. Thus $|a| = |b| = 1$.

The exact same argument can be made for the pair $(c, d)$. We conclude that $|c| = |d| = 1$ as well. Hence

$$a, b, c, d = 1 \pmod 2.$$

However, taken modulo 2 in $\det A = 1$, we arrive at the contradiction

$$ad - bc = 0 \pmod 2.$$

Next we consider the case $|x| \geq |y|$. This is essentially symmetric. We have

$$|ax + by| < |x|$$
$$|cx + dy| < |x|$$
$$|dx + cy| \leq |x|$$
$$|bx + ay| \leq |x|$$

Let $\eta = -\frac{y}{x}$. Since $x \neq 0$ in this case, $\eta$ is well defined. Dividing through by $x$ and $a, b, c, d$ respectively, we get the rational approximations of $\eta$

$$\left|\eta - \frac{a}{b}\right| < \frac{1}{|b|}$$

$$\left|\eta - \frac{c}{d}\right| < \frac{1}{|d|}$$

$$\left|\eta - \frac{b}{a}\right| \leq \frac{1}{|a|}$$

$$\left|\eta - \frac{d}{c}\right| \leq \frac{1}{|c|}$$

Then

$$\frac{|a| - 1}{|b|} < |\eta| < \frac{|a| + 1}{|b|}$$

$$\frac{|b| - 1}{|a|} \leq |\eta| \leq \frac{|b| + 1}{|a|}$$

and thus

$$\frac{|b| - 1}{|a|} < \frac{|a| + 1}{|b|}$$

$$\frac{|a| - 1}{|b|} < \frac{|b| + 1}{|a|}$$

The rest is the same.

This concludes the proof of Lemma 3.

By the symmetry of $a \leftrightarrow d$ and $b \leftrightarrow c$, which effects $A \leftrightarrow \tilde{A}$ we also have the following Lemma,

**Lemma 4.** $||\tilde{A}p|| < ||p|| \implies ||Ap|| > ||p||$.

We next consider the pair $(||Ap||, ||A^{-1}p||)$.

**Lemma 5.** *Suppose* $|\text{tr}(A)| = |a + d| \geq 2$, *then*

$$||Ap|| < ||p|| \implies ||A^{-1}p|| > ||p||.$$

Before we give the proof of this lemma, we shall discuss briefly the condition on the trace.

The elements in $SL_2(\mathbf{Z})$ with trace $|a + d| < 2$ are called elliptic elements, $|a + d| = 2$ parabolic elements, and $|a + d| > 2$ hyperbolic elements. (A final class called loxodromic elements for complex linear fractional transformations $z \mapsto \frac{az+b}{cz+d}$ do not occur here since our matrix $A$ is real.) We note that for integral matrix $A$, these classes are more simply stated as

- Elliptic elements: $a + d = 0, \pm1$.
- Parabolic elements: $|a + d| = 2$.
- Hyperbolic elements: $|a + d| > 2$.

In view of the mapping properties of these classes, it is not surprising that we needed, for the construction of expanders, the condition that the mappings be parabolic or hyperbolic, and not elliptic. We also note that except for a vanishingly small fraction, virtually all elements are hyperbolic.

We now turn to the proof of Lemma 5.

Assume for a contradiction that

$$||Ap|| < ||p|| \text{ and yet } ||A^{-1}p|| \leq ||p||.$$

First let's assume that $|y| \geq |x|$. Then we have the inequalities

$$|ax + by| < |y|$$
$$|cx + dy| < |y|$$
$$|dx - by| \leq |y|$$
$$|-cx + ay| \leq |y|.$$

With the second and the fourth inequalities we get

$$|(a + d)y| \leq |cx + dy| + |-cx + ay| < 2|y|,$$

and thus

$$|a + d| < 2,$$

where we have also used the fact that $y \neq 0$ as implied by the strict inequality $||Ap|| < ||p|| = |y|$. This is a contradiction to the assumption that $A$ is not elliptic.

The remaining case for Lemma 5 is when $|x| \geq |y|$. Then

$$|ax + by| < |x|$$
$$|cx + dy| < |x|$$
$$|dx - by| \leq |x|$$
$$|-cx + ay| \leq |x|.$$

This time with the first and the third inequalities we again get

$$|a + d| < 2.$$

The proof of Lemma 5 is complete.

Exactly the same argument gives us the following

**Lemma 6.** *Suppose* $|\text{tr}(A)| = |a+d| \geq 2$, *then* $||A^{-1}p|| < ||p|| \implies ||Ap|| > ||p||$.

We next consider the pair $(||Ap||, ||\tilde{A}^{-1}p||)$. We now require the condition $|b + c| \geq 2$. This condition is the same as requiring the trace of the permuted matrix $RA$ to be at least 2 in absolute value: $|\text{tr}(RA)| = |b + c| \geq 2$. In terms of the symmetry involved for $x$ and $y$, this is quite natural.

**Lemma 7.** *Suppose* $|\text{tr}(RA)| = |c + d| \geq 2$, *then*

$$||Ap|| < ||p|| \implies ||\tilde{A}^{-1}p|| > ||p||.$$

For the proof of Lemma 7, again we assume for a contradiction that

$$||Ap|| < ||p|| \text{ and yet } ||\tilde{A}^{-1}p|| \le ||p||.$$

First assume that $|y| \ge |x|$. Then

$$|ax + by| < |y|$$
$$|cx + dy| < |y|$$
$$|ax - cy| \le |y|$$
$$|-bx + dy| \le |y|.$$

With the first and the third inequalities we get

$$|(b + c)y| = |(ax + by) - (ax - cy)| \le |ax + by| + |ax - cy| < 2|y|,$$

and thus

$$|b + c| < 2,$$

just as before.

Similarly if $|x| \ge |y|$, then we use the second and the fourth inequalities to get the same contradiction

$$|b + c| < 2.$$

This completes the proof of Lemma 7.

Exactly the same argument gives us the following

**Lemma 8.** *Suppose* $|\text{tr}(RA)| = |c + d| \ge 2$, *then*

$$||\tilde{A}^{-1}p|| < ||p|| \implies ||Ap|| > ||p||.$$

Combining the 6 Lemmata above (Lemma 3 to Lemma 8), we conclude that under the condition $|\text{tr}(A)| = |a + d| \ge 2$ and $|\text{tr}(RA)| = |c + d| \ge 2$, for each of the 3 pairs

$$(||Ap||, ||\tilde{A}p||), (||Ap||, ||A^{-1}p||), (||Ap||, ||\tilde{A}^{-1}p||),$$

involving $||Ap||$ from the following set

$$\{||Ap||, ||\tilde{A}p||, ||A^{-1}p||, ||\tilde{A}^{-1}p||\}$$

there can be at most one of the entry to be strictly less than $||p||$, and in that case the other entry of the pair is strictly greater than $||p||$.

This is not quite enough for the goal of this section as stated, which include the remaining 3 pairs not involving $||Ap||$ (and corresponding 6 Lemmata above). However we will handle the remaining proof by symmetry.

For the pair $(||\tilde{A}p||, ||A^{-1}p||)$ we apply the symmetry $a \leftrightarrow d$, $b \leftrightarrow c$, thus $A \leftrightarrow \tilde{A}$. This reduces the pair $(||\tilde{A}p||, ||A^{-1}p||)$ to the pair $(||Ap||, ||\tilde{A}^{-1}p||)$ and Lemma 7, Lemma 8 give us respectively

**Lemma 9.** *Suppose* $|\text{tr}(RA)| = |c + d| \ge 2$, *then* $||\tilde{A}p|| < ||p|| \implies ||A^{-1}p|| > ||p||$.

and

**Lemma 10.** *Suppose* $|\mathrm{tr}(RA)| = |c + d| \geq 2$, *then* $||A^{-1}p|| < ||p|| \implies ||\tilde{A}p|| > ||p||$.

For the pair $(||\tilde{A}p||, ||\tilde{A}^{-1}p||)$ we apply the symmetry $b \leftrightarrow -c$, (and $c \leftrightarrow -b$, $a \leftrightarrow a$, and $d \leftrightarrow d$), thus, $A \leftrightarrow \tilde{A}^{-1}$ and $\tilde{A} \leftrightarrow A^{-1}$. Thus this reduces the pair $(||\tilde{A}p||, ||\tilde{A}^{-1}p||)$ to the pair $(||A^{-1}p||, ||Ap||)$. Now Lemma 6, Lemma 5 give us respectively

**Lemma 11.** *Suppose* $|\mathrm{tr}(A)| = |a + d| \geq 2$, *then* $||\tilde{A}p|| < ||p|| \implies ||\tilde{A}^{-1}p|| > ||p||$.

and

**Lemma 12.** *Suppose* $|\mathrm{tr}(A)| = |a + d| \geq 2$, *then* $||\tilde{A}^{-1}p|| < ||p|| \implies ||\tilde{A}p|| > ||p||$.

Finally for the pair $(||A^{-1}p||, ||\tilde{A}^{-1}p||)$ we apply the same symmetry $b \leftrightarrow -c$ as above, which transforms it to the pair $(||\tilde{A}p||, ||Ap||)$. Then we apply Lemma 4, Lemma 3 respectively,

**Lemma 13.** $||A^{-1}p|| < ||p|| \implies ||\tilde{A}^{-1}p|| > ||p||$.

and

**Lemma 14.** $||\tilde{A}^{-1}p|| < ||p|| \implies ||A^{-1}p|| > ||p||$.

Combining Lemma 3 to Lemma 14 we have

**Theorem 1.** *For any* $A \in SL_2(\mathbf{Z})$, *where* $abcd \neq 0$ *and* $A$, $RA$ *not elliptic, then if any one of the following 4 entries*

$$\{||Ap||, ||\tilde{A}p||, ||A^{-1}p||, ||\tilde{A}^{-1}p||\}$$

*is strictly less than the corresponding norm* $||p||$, *then the three other norms are all strictly greater than* $||p||$.

We note that the condition that none of $a, b, c, d$ is zero is only technical, and will be handled later. Only the conditions on the trace are real restrictions.

## 4    At Most Two Equalities

As shown in Section 3 if there is any one among

$$\{||Ap||, ||\tilde{A}p||, ||A^{-1}p||, ||\tilde{A}^{-1}p||\}$$

to be strictly less than $||p||$, then the three other norms are all strictly greater than $||p||$. In particular there are no equalities in this case. Suppose now, for this section, that there are no one among the four to be strictly less than $||p||$, i.e.,

$$||Ap|| \geq ||p||$$
$$||\tilde{A}p|| \geq ||p||$$
$$||A^{-1}p|| \geq ||p||$$
$$||\tilde{A}^{-1}p|| \geq ||p||$$

We count the number of equalities among these 4. The goal in this section is to show that, for $p \neq 0$, there can be at most two among the four to be equalities. It follows that the other terms, at least 2 among 4, are all strictly greater than $||p||$. Clearly the condition that $p \neq 0$ is necessary for handling the equalities.

We prove this by contradiction. Suppose there are at least three among the four are equalities. Then there are the following *two alternatives. EITHER*

$$||Ap|| = ||p||$$
$$||\tilde{A}p|| = ||p||$$

both hold and at least one of the following holds

$$||A^{-1}p|| = ||p||$$
$$||\tilde{A}^{-1}p|| = ||p||$$

*OR* vice versa.

We will assume the first alternative. Without loss of generality (wolog) we also assume that $|y| \geq |x|$. Since $p \neq 0$, $y \neq 0$. We note that the symmetry $x \leftrightarrow y$ exchanges and permutes the equalities

$$||Ap|| = ||p|| \leftrightarrow ||\tilde{A}p|| = ||p||$$
$$||A^{-1}p|| = ||p|| \leftrightarrow ||\tilde{A}^{-1}p|| = ||p||$$

respectively, and thus the assumption $|y| \geq |x|$ is indeed without loss of generality. Since there are no strict inequalities $<$ by assumption, the first alternative leads to

$$|ax + by| \leq |y|$$
$$|cx + dy| \leq |y|$$
$$|dx + cy| \leq |y|$$
$$|bx + ay| \leq |y|$$

and at least one of the following holds

$$|dx - by| \leq |y|$$
$$|-cx + ay| \leq |y|$$

or

$$|ax - cy| \leq |y|$$
$$|-bx + dy| \leq |y|.$$

As in the proof of Lemma 3, denoting $\xi = -\frac{x}{y}$, and dividing through by $y$ and $a, b, c, d$ respectively, we get the rational approximations of $\xi$

$$\left|\xi - \frac{b}{a}\right| \leq \frac{1}{|a|} \tag{1}$$

$$\left|\xi - \frac{d}{c}\right| \le \frac{1}{|c|} \tag{2}$$

$$\left|\xi - \frac{a}{b}\right| \le \frac{1}{|b|} \tag{3}$$

$$\left|\xi - \frac{c}{d}\right| \le \frac{1}{|d|} \tag{4}$$

**Lemma 15.** *Either $|a| \ne |b|$ or $|c| \ne |d|$.*

To prove this Lemma, we assume instead both equalities hold $|a| = |b|$ and $|c| = |d|$. Since they form the rows of a unimodular matrix, the gcd of both $(a, b)$ and $(c, d)$ are 1. Thus

$$|a| = |b| = |c| = |d| = 1,$$

and taken modulo 2

$$a = b = c = d = 1 \pmod 2.$$

However this leads to

$$\det(A) = ad - bc = 0 \pmod 2$$

which contradicts the unimodularity again. Lemma 15 is proved.

Hence we have two possibilities:

1. $|a| \ne |b|$

   Suppose $ab > 0$, i.e., they are of the same sign, then $\frac{b}{a} = \frac{|b|}{|a|}$, and

   $$\frac{|b| - 1}{|a|} \le \xi \le \frac{|b| + 1}{|a|},$$

   and also

   $$\frac{|a| - 1}{|b|} \le \xi \le \frac{|a| + 1}{|b|}.$$

   Note that these two bounds on $\xi$ are symmetric for $a$ and $b$. Thus, without loss of generality $|a| > |b|$. Then, by being integral, $|a| \ge |b| + 1$, it follows that

   $$1 \le \frac{|a| - 1}{|b|} \le \xi \le \frac{|b| + 1}{|a|} \le 1,$$

   which means that these inequalities are in fact all equalities, and $\xi = 1$. By definition of $\xi$, $x = -y$. This is true regardless $|a| > |b|$ or $|a| < |b|$, as long as $ab > 0$.

   The case where $a$ and $b$ are of opposite signs, i.e., $ab < 0$, is handled similarly with $\frac{b}{a} = -\frac{|b|}{|a|}$, and the corresponding rational approximations of $-\xi$. So we obtain $-\xi = 1$. Hence $x = y$.

   We conclude in this case that $|x| = |y|$.

2. $|c| \neq |d|$

This case is handled by the symmetry $a \leftrightarrow d$ and $b \leftrightarrow c$. Note that the rational approximations in Eqn. (1) to Eqn. (4) is invariant under this substitution. Hence we also get $|x| = |y|$.

We now proceed to deal with the possibility $|x| = |y|$, which is $\neq 0$, under the assumption that

$$|ax + by| \leq |y|$$
$$|cx + dy| \leq |y|$$
$$|dx + cy| \leq |y|$$
$$|bx + ay| \leq |y|$$

and at least one of the following holds

$$|dx - by| \leq |y|$$
$$|-cx + ay| \leq |y|$$

or

$$|ax - cy| \leq |y|$$
$$|-bx + dy| \leq |y|.$$

1. $x = -y$

Dividing through by $|y|$ we have

$$|a - b| \leq 1$$
$$|c - d| \leq 1$$

and

$$|d + b| \leq 1$$
$$|c + a| \leq 1.$$

From these we obtain

$$|a + d| \leq 2$$
$$|b + c| \leq 2.$$

By our condition on the trace of $A$ and $RA$, i.e., they are not elliptic, we get

$$|a + d| = |b + c| = 2.$$

Hence we get

$$|a - b| = 1$$
$$|c - d| = 1$$
$$|d + b| = 1$$
$$|c + a| = 1$$

Thus we can write

$$\begin{pmatrix} b & b \\ c & c \end{pmatrix} = \begin{pmatrix} a & -d \\ d & -a \end{pmatrix} + \mathcal{E}, \tag{5}$$

where we let

$$\mathcal{E} = \begin{pmatrix} \epsilon_{11} & \epsilon_{12} \\ \epsilon_{21} & \epsilon_{22} \end{pmatrix},$$

and $\epsilon_{ij} = \pm 1$ for $i, j = 1, 2$.

In $\mathcal{E}$ the top row cannot be of the same sign, otherwise $a + d = 0$. Similarly the bottom row cannot be of the same sign, otherwise $a + d = 0$ as well. Furthermore, we observe that

$$a + d + (\epsilon_{11} - \epsilon_{12}) = 0$$

and

$$a + d + (\epsilon_{21} - \epsilon_{22}) = 0.$$

Thus the trace $a + d = -2$ iff

$$\mathcal{E} = \begin{pmatrix} +1 & -1 \\ +1 & -1 \end{pmatrix},$$

and the trace $a + d = +2$ iff

$$\mathcal{E} = \begin{pmatrix} -1 & +1 \\ -1 & +1 \end{pmatrix}.$$

However in either cases we obtain

$$b + c = 0,$$

by adding the diagonal entries in the matrix equation Eqn.( 5).

So under $|a + d| \geq 2, |b + c| \geq 2$ we conclude that $x = -y$ is impossible.

2. $x = y$

This case is handled by the symmetry $b \leftrightarrow -b$ and $c \leftrightarrow -c$ in the above argument for $x = -y$. Thus $x = y$ is also impossible.

Finally we consider the second alternative: $|y| \geq |x|$ and,

$$|dx - by| \leq |y|$$
$$|-cx + ay| \leq |y|$$
$$|ax - cy| \leq |y|$$
$$|-bx + dy| \leq |y|$$

and at least one of the following holds

$$|ax + by| \leq |y|$$
$$|cx + dy| \leq |y|$$

or

$$|dx + cy| \le |y|$$
$$|bx + ay| \le |y|.$$

Use $\eta = -\xi = \frac{x}{y}$, and the symmetry $a \leftrightarrow d$, and $b \leftrightarrow b$, $c \leftrightarrow c$, we conclude that the second alternative is also impossible.

**Theorem 2.** *For any $A \in SL_2(\mathbf{Z})$, where $abcd \ne 0$ and $A$, $RA$ not elliptic, then for $p \ne 0$, among*

$$\{||Ap||, ||\tilde{A}p||, ||A^{-1}p||, ||\tilde{A}^{-1}p||\}$$

*there cannot be more than two of them equal to $||p||$.*

We now briefly handle the case with $abcd = 0$. Suppose $a = 0$. Then $bc = -1$ by unimodularity. Being both integral, $b = -c = \pm 1$. Then $b + c = 0$. This is excluded.

By the symmetry $a \leftrightarrow d$ and $b \leftrightarrow c$, which effects $A \leftrightarrow \tilde{A}$, we see that $d = 0$ is the same.

Suppose $b = 0$, then $ad = 1$ and being integral, $a = d = \pm 1$. Thus the matrix we are dealing with is $A = \pm \begin{pmatrix} 1 & 0 \\ c & 1 \end{pmatrix}$.

The case of $c = \pm 1$ with $b = 0$ is *the* matrix dealt with by Gabber and Galil [10]. (They show that $\begin{pmatrix} 1 & 0 \\ 1 & 1 \end{pmatrix}$ does define an expander with a smaller expansion constant. However the condition in Theorem 3 of $RA$ being non-elliptic technically excludes this case.) It is not difficult to see that the mapping properties stated in Theorem 3 are valid for $|c| \ge 2$ and $b = 0$. This is quite clear if we consider the mapping on the set of lattice points with $||(x, y)||_\infty = r$ for any $r \ge 1$. ([10] also contained a discussion of $c = \pm 2$.) By symmetry, the same is true for the case $|b| \ge 2$ and $c = 0$.

Combining Theorem 1, Theorem 2, and the above comments regarding $abcd \ne 0$, we have

**Theorem 3.** *For any $A \in SL_2(\mathbf{Z})$, where $A$, $RA$ not elliptic, and $p \ne 0$, then among*

$$\{||Ap||, ||\tilde{A}p||, ||A^{-1}p||, ||\tilde{A}^{-1}p||\},$$

- *Either one is less than $||p||$ and three others are greater than $||p||$,*
- *Or no more than two are equal to $||p||$ and the rest are all greater than $||p||$.*

## 5   Analytic Proof of Expansion

In this section we prove some explicit estimates using Fourier analysis. We will follow [10] and adapt their proof for special matrices to general matrices.

Let $B = A$ or $\tilde{A}$ and let $U = [0,1)^2$. $B$ defines a measure preserving automorphism $\beta = \beta_B$ of $U$ as follows:

$$\beta : (x,y) \mapsto (x,y)B \bmod 1.$$

We will denote $\alpha = \beta_A$ and $\tilde{\alpha} = \beta_{\tilde{A}}$. It is easy to check that $\beta$ is a bijection on $U$ with inverse map $\beta^{-1}(x,y) = (x,y)B^{-1} \bmod 1$. That it is measure preserving follows from the fact that the Jacobi of the map is $\det B = 1$.

For any function $\phi$ on $U$, we can define the function

$$B^*(\phi)(x,y) = \phi(\beta^{-1}(x,y)).$$

We will restrict our discussion to square integrable functions $\phi$. For such $\phi$ the Fourier coefficients are defined as follows

$$a_{\binom{m}{n}}(\phi) = \int_U \phi(x,y)e^{-2\pi i(mx+ny)}d\mu(x,y),$$

where $m,n \in \mathbf{Z}$. The next lemma relates the Fourier coefficients of $\phi$ with that of $B^*(\phi)$.

**Lemma 16.**

$$a_{\binom{m}{n}}(B^*(\phi)) = a_{B\binom{m}{n}}(\phi).$$

*Proof.*

$$a_{\binom{m}{n}}(B^*(\phi)) = \int_U \phi(\beta^{-1}(x,y))e^{-2\pi i(x,y)\cdot\binom{m}{n}}d\mu(x,y)$$

$$= \int_U \phi(\beta^{-1}(x,y))e^{-2\pi i(x,y)B^{-1}B\binom{m}{n}}d\mu(x,y)$$

We can replace $(x,y)B^{-1}$ by $\beta^{-1}(x,y)$ in the exponent since the function $\exp[-2\pi iX]$ has integral period 1. Hence, by a substitution of variables $(x',y') = \beta^{-1}(x,y)$, and note that the Jacobi is 1, we get

$$a_{\binom{m}{n}}(B^*(\phi)) = \int_U \phi(x',y')e^{-2\pi i(x',y')B\binom{m}{n}}d\mu(x',y')$$

$$= a_{B\binom{m}{n}}(\phi).$$

Our goal is to obtain a non-trivial estimate for

$$\sum_q \left[ |a_{Aq} - a_q|^2 + |a_{\tilde{A}q} - a_q|^2 \right],$$

where $q$ ranges over $\mathbf{Z}^2$, and $\{a_q\}$ is square summable $\sum_q |a_q|^2 < \infty$. Note that $A$ and $\tilde{A}$ define permutations on $\mathbf{Z}^2 - \{0\}$ while $A0 = \tilde{A}0 = 0$. Thus the above sum can also range over $\mathbf{Z}^2 - \{0\}$.

Let $f, g$ be any complex square summable functions on $\mathbf{Z}^2 - \{0\}$. The inner product is defined as

$$\langle f, g \rangle = \sum_{q \neq 0} f(q) \cdot \overline{g(q)},$$

and the norm is

$$||f|| = \langle f, f \rangle^{1/2} = \sum_{q \neq 0} |f(q)|^2.$$

It follows that

$$||f - f \circ A||^2 + ||f - f \circ \tilde{A}||^2 = 4||f||^2 - C,$$

where the *cross terms*

$$C = \langle f, f \circ A \rangle + \langle f \circ A, f \rangle + \langle f, f \circ \tilde{A} \rangle + \langle f \circ \tilde{A}, f \rangle,$$

thus $|C| \leq 2 \left[ \langle |f|, |f \circ A| \rangle + \langle |f|, |f \circ \tilde{A}| \rangle \right]$.

**Lemma 17.**

$$||f - f \circ A||^2 + ||f - f \circ \tilde{A}||^2 \geq (4 - 2\sqrt{3}) \, ||f||^2.$$

*Proof.* We only need to show an upper bound $|C| \leq 2\sqrt{3} \, ||f||^2$. Define

$$\lambda(p, q) = \begin{cases} \sqrt{3} & \text{if } ||q|| < ||p|| \\ 1 & \text{if } ||q|| = ||p|| \\ 1/\sqrt{3} & \text{if } ||q|| > ||p|| \end{cases}$$

By Cauchy-Schwarz, $2|XY| \leq \lambda |X|^2 + \frac{1}{\lambda} |Y|^2$. Note that $\lambda(p, q) = \lambda(q, p)^{-1}$, and thus for $\sigma = A$ or $\tilde{A}$,

$$2 \sum_{q \neq 0} |f(q)||f(\sigma(q))| \leq \sum_{q \neq 0} \left[ \lambda(q, \sigma(q))|f(q)|^2 + \lambda(\sigma(q), q)|f(\sigma(q))|^2 \right]$$

$$= \sum_{q \neq 0} |f(q)|^2 \left[ \lambda(q, \sigma(q)) + \lambda(q, \sigma^{-1}(q)) \right].$$

Hence

$$|C| \leq \sum_{q \neq 0} |f(q)|^2 \left[ \sum_{\sigma \in \Sigma} \lambda(q, \sigma(q)) \right].$$

By Theorem 3, the sum of four terms $\sum_{\sigma \in \Sigma} \lambda(q, \sigma(q)) \leq 2\sqrt{3}$ in all cases (being either $\leq \sqrt{3} + 3/\sqrt{3}$, or $\leq 4/\sqrt{3}$, or $\leq 1 + 3/\sqrt{3}$, or $\leq 2 + 2/\sqrt{3}$.) It follows that $|C| \leq 2\sqrt{3} \, ||f||^2$.

Stated for $\{a_q\}$ we have

**Lemma 18.** *If $a_0 = 0$ and $\sum_{q \neq 0} |a_q|^2 < \infty$, then*

$$\sum_q \left[ |a_{Aq} - a_q|^2 + |a_{\tilde{A}q} - a_q|^2 \right] \geq (4 - 2\sqrt{3}) \sum_{q \neq 0} |a_q|^2.$$

We next translate this lemma to integrals via Parseval equality.

**Lemma 19.** *For square integrable function $\phi$ on $U$ with $\int_U \phi = 0$,*

$$\int_U |A^*(\phi) - \phi|^2 + \int_U |\tilde{A}^*(\phi) - \phi|^2 \geq (4 - 2\sqrt{3}) \int_U |\phi|^2.$$

*Proof.* By Parseval equality, for square integrable $\psi$,

$$\int_U |\psi|^2 = \sum_q |a_q(\psi)|^2,$$

where $a_q(\psi)$ are the Fourier coefficients. Note that $a_0(\phi) = \int_U \phi = 0$. By linearity and Lemma 16, $a_q(A^*(\phi) - \phi) = a_q(A^*(\phi)) - a_q(\phi) = a_{Aq}(\phi) - a_q(\phi)$. Lemma 19 follows from Lemma 18.

Recall the definition of $\beta = \beta_B$ for $B \in \Sigma$, $\beta_B(\xi) = \xi B \mod 1$.

**Lemma 20.** *For measurable set $Z \subseteq U$,*

$$\sum_{B=A,\tilde{A}} \mu[Z - \beta_B^{-1}(Z)] \geq (2 - \sqrt{3})\, \mu(Z)\mu(Z^c).$$

*Proof.* Define $\phi = \chi_Z - \mu(Z) = \begin{cases} \mu(Z^c) & \text{on } Z \\ -\mu(Z) & \text{on } Z^c \end{cases}$. Then $\int_U \phi = 0$, and

$$\int_U |\phi|^2 = \mu(Z)\mu(Z^c) < \infty.$$

Let $\xi \in U$, and denote $\beta_A$ by $\alpha$, i.e., $\alpha(\xi) = \xi A \mod 1$. We observe that

$$\begin{aligned}
A^*(\phi)(\xi) &= \phi(\alpha^{-1}(\xi)) \\
&= \begin{cases} \mu(Z^c) & \text{for } \xi \in \alpha(Z) \\ -\mu(Z) & \text{for } \xi \notin \alpha(Z) \end{cases} \\
&= \chi_{\alpha(Z)} - \mu(Z)
\end{aligned}$$

It follows that

$$A^*(\phi) - \phi = \chi_{\alpha(Z)} - \chi_Z.$$

Hence for $\int_U |A^*(\phi) - \phi|^2$, the integrand is 1 on the symmetric difference $\alpha(Z)\Delta Z$, and 0 elsewhere. So

$$\int_U |A^*(\phi) - \phi|^2 = \mu[\alpha(Z)\Delta Z].$$

However, $\alpha(Z)\Delta Z = [\alpha(Z) - Z] \cup [Z - \alpha(Z)]$. Since $\alpha$ is bijective and measure preserving,

$$\begin{aligned}
\mu[Z - \alpha(Z)] &= \mu[Z] - \mu[Z \cap \alpha(Z)] \\
&= \mu[\alpha(Z)] - \mu[Z \cap \alpha(Z)] \\
&= \mu[\alpha(Z) - Z] \\
&= \mu[Z - \alpha^{-1}(Z)]
\end{aligned}$$

Thus

$$\int_U |A^*(\phi) - \phi|^2 = 2\mu[Z - \alpha^{-1}(Z)].$$

Similarly, denote $\tilde{\alpha} = \beta_{\tilde{A}}$, we have

$$\int_U |\tilde{A}^*(\phi) - \phi|^2 = 2\mu[Z - \tilde{\alpha}^{-1}(Z)].$$

Then by Lemma 19,

$$\sum_{B=A,\tilde{A}} \mu[Z - \beta_B^{-1}(Z)] = \frac{1}{2} \sum_{B=A,\tilde{A}} \int_U |B^*(\phi) - \phi|^2 \geq (2 - \sqrt{3}) \int_U |\phi|^2 = (2 - \sqrt{3})$$

$$\mu(Z)\mu(Z^c).$$

## 6  The Graph

In this section we prove an explicit expansion constant for a family of bipartite graphs, constructed from every matrix $A$ considered in Theorem 3.

We will first define the family of graphs. Denote the unit square by $U = [0,1)^2$. For $p = (i,j) \in \mathbf{Z}^2$, the translated square by $p$ is denoted by $U_p = p + U$. We define a set of "neighborhood" points as follows: For $B = A, \tilde{A}$,

$$N_B = \{q \in \mathbf{Z}^2 \mid \mu[UB \cap U_q] \neq 0\},$$

where $\mu$ denotes the Lebesgue measure, and $UB = \{\xi B \mid \xi \in U\}$ is the image of $U$ under $B$.

For $k \geq 1$, let the mod $k$ "neighborhood" be $N_{B,k} = N_B$ mod $k$. Note that the cardinality of $N_{B,k}$ is at most that of $N_B$ for every $k$. In particular since $|N_B|$ is independent of $k$, $|N_{B,k}|$ is bounded in $k$. For any measurable set $V \subseteq \mathbf{R}^2$, denote its mod $k$ fold in the torus $(\mathbf{R}/k\mathbf{Z})^2$ by $(V)_k = V$ mod $k$. We claim that

$$N_{B,k} = \{q \in (\mathbf{Z}/k\mathbf{Z})^2 \mid \mu_k[(UB)_k \cap (U_q)_k] \neq 0\}.$$

where $\mu_k$ is the Lebesgue measure on the torus $(\mathbf{R}/k\mathbf{Z})^2$. This is fairly obvious. To carry out the detail, let $q \in N_{B,k}$. Then there exists an integral vector $v$ such that $q + kv \in N_B$. Thus $\mu[UB \cap U_{q+kv}] \neq 0$. Note that $(U_{q+kv})_k = (U_q)_k$, it follows that $\mu_k[(UB)_k \cap (U_q)_k] \neq 0$. Conversely, if the above holds for $q$, then there exist integral vectors $v$ and $v'$ such that $\mu[\,[UB + kv] \cap [U + q + kv']\,] \neq 0$. So $\mu[UB \cap U_{q'}] \neq 0$, for $q' = q + k(v' - v)$. Hence $q' \in N_B$, and $q \equiv q'$ mod $k$.

We now define the family of graphs. For every $k \geq 1$, the bipartite graph $G_k = (L, R, E)$ has $n = k^2$ vertices on both sides, $L = R = (\mathbf{Z}/k\mathbf{Z})^2$. The vertex $p \in L$ is connected to $p \in R$ and every $p' = pB + q$ mod $k$, for $q \in N_{B,k}$, $B = A, \tilde{A}$. Thus, the maximum degree of $G_k$ is bounded, being at most $d = 1 + |N_A| + |N_{\tilde{A}}|$. We note that the neighbors $p' = pB + q$ mod $k$ of $p$ are precisely those satisfying

$$\mu_k[(U_p B)_k \cap (U_{p'})_k] \neq 0.$$

We will denote by $\sigma_0 = \mathrm{id}$, and $\sigma_\ell$ the permutations $p \mapsto pB + q \bmod k$, for $1 \le \ell < d_k$, where $d_k = 1 + |N_{A,k}| + |N_{\tilde{A},k}|$. Thus for $p \in L$ the neighbor set of $p$ in $R$ is $\Gamma(p) = \{\sigma_i(p) \mid 0 \le \ell < d_k\}$.

The next Lemma discretizes Lemma 20.

**Lemma 21.** *Let $X \subseteq L$. There exists $\ell$, $1 \le \ell < d_k$, such that*

$$|\sigma_\ell(X) - X| \ge (2 - \sqrt{3})|X||X^c|/n,$$

*where $n = k^2$.*

*Proof.* For $X$, define a subset of the torus $(\mathbf{R}/k\mathbf{Z})^2$ by $Y = \bigcup_{p \in X} U_p$. Thus each point $p = (i,j) \in X$ is replaced by the translated square $U_p$. Clearly $\mu_k(Y) = |X|$ and $\mu_k(Y^c) = |X^c|$. If we shrink $Y$ by a factor of $k$, we may consider $Z = \frac{1}{k}Y \subseteq U$, in which we can identify $U$ with the unit torus $(\mathbf{R}/\mathbf{Z})^2$. Clearly $\mu(Z) = \frac{|X|}{n}$ and $\mu(Z^c) = \frac{|X^c|}{n}$.

We next consider where does the small square $\frac{1}{k}U_p$ get mapped to under $\alpha$; more specifically, which $\frac{1}{k}U_q$ contains images of $\frac{1}{k}U_p$ with non-zero measure. For $\xi = [(i,j) + (u,v)]/k$,

$$\alpha(\xi) = \xi A \bmod 1 = \frac{(i+u, j+v)A \bmod k}{k}.$$

So $\alpha(\xi) \in \frac{1}{k}U_q$ iff $(i+u, j+v)A \bmod k \in U_q$. Hence $\mu[\alpha(\frac{1}{k}U_p) \cap \frac{1}{k}U_q] \ne 0$ iff $\mu_k[(U_pA)_k \cap (U_q)_k] \ne 0$. Thus, $q$ is a neighbor $\sigma_\ell(p)$ of $p$ in the graph $G_k$ for some $1 \le \ell < d_k$. Similarly for $\tilde{\alpha}(\xi)$.

Let $w_\ell = \mu[\alpha(\frac{1}{k}U_p) \cap \frac{1}{k}U_{\sigma_\ell(p)}] > 0$ be the weight of intersection, then since $\alpha$ is measure preserving, $\sum_{1 \le \ell < d_k} w_\ell = 1$.

By definition, $Z = \bigcup_{p \in X} \frac{1}{k}U_p$. Within each $\frac{1}{k}U_p$, divide it according to

$$\left[\frac{1}{k}U_p\right] \cap \alpha^{-1}\left(\frac{1}{k}U_{\sigma_\ell(p)}\right),$$

each with weight $w_\ell$.

$\xi \in Z - \alpha^{-1}(Z)$ iff $[\xi \in Z \ \& \ \alpha(\xi) \notin Z]$. For $\xi \in Z$, $\xi \in \frac{1}{k}U_p$ for a unique $p \in X$, and within $\frac{1}{k}U_p$ those $\xi \in (\frac{1}{k}U_p) \cap \alpha^{-1}(\frac{1}{k}U_{\sigma_\ell(p)})$ are mapped to $U_{\sigma_\ell(p)}$. For those $\xi$, $\alpha(\xi) \notin Z$ iff $\sigma_\ell(p) \notin X$. Similarly for $\tilde{\alpha}$. It follows that

$$\mu[Z - \alpha^{-1}(Z)] + \mu[Z - \tilde{\alpha}^{-1}(Z)] = \sum_{p \in X} \frac{1}{n} \sum_{1 \le \ell < d_k} w_\ell \mathbf{1}_{[\sigma_\ell(p) \notin X]}$$

$$= \frac{1}{n} \sum_{1 \le \ell < d_k} w_\ell \sum_{p \in L} \mathbf{1}_{[p \in X \text{ and } \sigma_\ell(p) \notin X]}$$

$$= \frac{1}{n} \sum_{1 \le \ell < d_k} w_\ell |X - \sigma_\ell^{-1}(X)|$$

By Lemma 20,

$$\mu[Z - \alpha^{-1}(Z)] + \mu[Z - \tilde{\alpha}^{-1}(Z)] \ge (2 - \sqrt{3})\frac{|X|}{n}\frac{|X^c|}{n}.$$

Hence,

$$\sum_{1 \le \ell < d_k} w_\ell |X - \sigma_\ell^{-1}(X)| \ge (2 - \sqrt{3})|X||X^c|/n.$$

It follows that there exists $\ell_0$, such that

$$|X - \sigma_{\ell_0}^{-1}(X)| \ge (2 - \sqrt{3})|X||X^c|/n.$$

Since $\sigma_{\ell_0}$ is a permutation, $|X - \sigma_{\ell_0}^{-1}(X)| = |\sigma_{\ell_0}(X) - X|$, and thus

$$|\sigma_{\ell_0}(X) - X| \ge (2 - \sqrt{3})|X||X^c|/n.$$

Lemma 21 is proved.

Now the neighbor set $\Gamma(X) \supseteq X \cup \sigma_{\ell_0}(X)$, it follows that

$$\begin{aligned}
|\Gamma(X)| &= |X| + |\Gamma(X) - X| \\
&\ge |X| + |\sigma_{\ell_0}(X) - X| \\
&\ge \left[ 1 + (2 - \sqrt{3})\left(1 - \frac{|X|}{n}\right) \right] |X|.
\end{aligned}$$

**Acknowledgements.** I thank Pavan Aduri, Charles Denis and especially Samit Sengupta for valuable discussions and comments. I also thank Venkat Chakaravarthy for help in handling the lncs latex package.

# References

1. M. Ajtai, J. Komlos and E. Szemeredi, Sorting in $c \log n$ parallel steps, *Combinatorica*, **3**, (1983) 1–19.
2. M. Ajtai, J. Komlos and E. Szemeredi, Deterministic simulation in LOGSPACE, Proc. of the *19th ACM STOC*, 132–140, 1987.
3. M. Ajtai, J. Komlós and E. Szemerédi, Generating expanders from two permutations. In *A tribute to Paul Erdös*, edited by A. Baker, B. Bollobás & A. Hajnal. pp. 1–12. Cambridge University Press, 1990.
4. N. Alon, Eigenvalues, geometric expanders, sorting in rounds and Ramsey Theory, *Combinatorica* **6**, 207–219.
5. N. Alon, Eigenvalues and Expanders, *Combinatorica* **6**, 83–96.
6. N. Alon and V. D. Milman, Eigenvalues, expanders and superconcentrators. Proc of the *25th ACM STOC*, 320–322. 1984.
7. N. Alon and J. Spencer, with an appendix by P. Erdös, The Probabilistic Method. John Wiley and Sons, Inc.1992.
8. D. Angulin, A note on a construction of Margulis, *Information Processing Letters*, **8**, pp 17–19, (1979).
9. F. R. K. Chung, On Concentrators, superconcentrators, generalized, and non-blocking networks, *Bell Sys. Tech J.* **58**, pp 1765–1777, (1978).
10. O. Gabber and Z. Galil, Explicit construction of linear size superconcentrators. *JCSS* **22**, pp 407–420 (1981).
11. A. Lubotsky, R. Phillip and P. Sarnak, Explicit expanders and the Ramanujan conjectures. Proceedings of the *18th ACM STOC*, 1986, 240–246. *Combinatorica*, **8**, 1988, 261–277.

12. G. A. Margulis, Explicit construction of concentrators. *Problems Inform. Transmission* **9**, 1973, 325–332.
13. G. A. Margulis, Explicit group-theoretic constructions for combinatorial designs with applications expanders and concentrators. *Problems Inform. Transmission* **24**, 1988, 39–46.
14. J. Naor and M. Naor, Small bias probability spaces: efficient constructions and applications. Proc. of *22nd ACM STOC*, 1990. 213–223.
15. N. Pippenger, Superconcentrators. *SIAM J. Computing* **6**, pp 298–304, (1972)
16. M. Pinsker, On the complexity of a concentrator, The *7th International Teletraffic Conference*, Stockholm, 318/1–318/4, 1973.
17. L. Valiant, Graph-theoretic properties in computational complexity, *JCSS*, **13**, 1976, 278–285.

# Appendix

In this appendix we give some further concrete geometric description of the neighbor set

$$N_B = \{q \in \mathbf{Z}^2 \mid \mu[UB \cap U_q] \neq 0\}$$

used to define the expander graph.

Consider the parallelogram $UB$. We are to collect all lattice points $q \in \mathbf{Z}^2$ such that there is $\xi \in U$, with $z = q + \xi \in UB$. We can reverse this process and start with an arbitrary $z \in UB$, and "cover" with a square $z + (-U) = \{z - \xi \mid \xi \in U\}$. As $z$ runs through $UB$, we get a region as the union

$$UB + (-U) = \{z - \xi \mid z \in UB, \xi \in U\}.$$

We look for all lattice points in this region. Since we are only interested in non-zero measure intersections, we can actually restrict the above to open interior sets $(U^o)B + (-U^o)$.

The more interesting claim in this appendix is the following: It suffices to trace the point $z$ along the boundary of $UB$ only, i.e., there is no need to place $z$ in the interior of $UB$.

$$N_B = \{q \in \mathbf{Z}^2 \mid \mu[(\partial U)B \cap U_q] \neq 0\}$$
$$= \{q \in \mathbf{Z}^2 \mid q \in (\partial U)B + (-U^o)\}$$

Let $B = \begin{pmatrix} a & b \\ c & d \end{pmatrix}$ be an integral unimodular matrix. The vertices of $UB$ are $(0,0)$, $(a,b)$, $(c,d)$ and $(a+c, b+d)$ respectively. First we note that being unimodular, there are no integral points in the interior of $UB$.

We claim that the interior of $UB$ is entirely placed inside one of the four quadrants. Suppose not, say, $(a,b)$ is in the first quadrant $(b > 0)$, and $(c,d)$ is in the fourth quadrant $(d < 0)$. (The other cases are similar.) Wolog $c \geq a$. Then draw a vertical line from $(a,b)$ to the $x$-axis, we get a lattice point $(a,0)$ in the interior of $UB$. By geometric symmetry, it is clear that wolog we may assume $UB$ is entirely placed inside the first quadrant.

There are two cases: $a \le c$ or $a > c$. We will only consider $a \le c$; the other case is similar. Cut the parallelogram $UB$ into 3 parts by drawing vertical lines at $x = a$ and $x = c$. (If $a = c$ the middle section is empty.) Thus $UB$ consists of a triangle $\Delta$ from $x = 0$ to $x = a$, a parallelogram from $x = a$ to $x = c$ (possibly empty); and another triangle $\Delta'$ which is geometrically $\Delta$ rotated by $\pi$.

Since $UB$ has no lattice point to its interior, the length of the vertical line segment at $x = a$ is at most 1, otherwise $(a, b+1)$ is an interior lattice point. Being a triangle, the length of the vertical line segment on $\Delta$ at any $x$, $0 \le x \le a$, is at most 1.

Start at an interior point $z = (x, y) \in \Delta$, and consider the square $z + (-U)$. If we slide this square vertically, there are points $z' = (x, y')$ and $z'' = (x, y'')$ both on the boundary of $UB$, where $y' < y < y''$, and $y'' - y' \le 1$, such that $z + (-U)$ is covered by the union of the two corresponding squares based at $z'$ and $z''$, namely,

$$z + (-U) \subset [z' + (-U)] \cup [z'' + (-U)].$$

Thus if a lattice point $q \in \mathbf{Z}^2$ is found in $z + (-U)$, it is also found in $z' + (-U)$ or $z'' + (-U)$. (Being of non-zero measure, we can also restrict them to $z' + (-U^o)$ and $z'' + (-U^o)$.)

For the parallelogram from $x = a$ to $x = c$ the line segments at $a \le x \le c$ are of the same length, all $\le 1$. Finally for $\Delta'$ the situation is the same as $\Delta$ by symmetry.

Thus to collect all lattice points in $N_B$, it suffices to trace the point $z$ with an attached square $-U$ on the boundary of $UB$.

Still placing the parallelogram $UB$ in the first quadrant, we can see that the region is the interior of the convex hull of

$(-1, -1), (0, -1), (a, b-1), (a+c, b+d-1), (a+c, b+d), (a+c-1, b+d), (c-1, d),$

$(-1, 0)$.

# Strategies for Hotlink Assignments[*]

Prosenjit Bose[1], Jurek Czyzowicz[2], Leszek Gąsieniec[3], Evangelos Kranakis[1],
Danny Krizanc[1], Andrzej Pelc[2], and Miguel Vargas Martin[1]

[1] School of Computer Science, Carleton University,
1125 Colonel By Drive, Ottawa, Ontario, Canada, K1S 5B6.
{jit,kranakis,krizanc,mvargas}@scs.carleton.ca
[2] Dept. Informatique, Univ. du Québec à Hull,
Hull, Québec J8X 3X7, Canada.
{jurek,pelc}@uqah.uquebec.ca
[3] Department of Computer Science, University of Liverpool,
Peach Street, L69 7ZF, Liverpool, UK.
leszek@csc.liv.ac.uk

**Abstract.** Consider a DAG (directed acyclic graph) $G = (V, E)$ representing a collection $V$ of web pages connected via links $E$. All web pages can be reached from a designated source page, represented by a source node $s$ of $G$. Each web page carries a weight representative of the frequency with which it is visited. By adding hotlinks, at most one per page, we are interested in minimizing the expected number of steps needed to visit a selected set of web pages from the source page. For arbitrary DAGs we show that the problem is NP-complete.

We also give algorithms for assigning hotlinks, as well as upper and lower bounds on the expected number of steps to reach the leaves from the source page $s$ located at the root of a complete binary tree. Depending on the probability distribution (arbitrary, uniform, Zipf) the expected number of steps is at most $c \cdot n$, where $c$ is a constant less than 1. For the geometric distribution we show how to obtain a constant average number of steps.

## 1 Introduction

Imposing and exploiting topological structure of the internet is often a key step in improving performance ([4,6,2,9,10]). In this paper we show how to improve web design by taking advantage of the knowledge of the network topology. Consider a DAG (directed acyclic graph) $G = (V, E)$ representing a collection $V$ of web pages connected via links $E$. All web pages can be reached from a designated source page, $s$ of $G$. Each web page carries a weight representative of the frequency with which it is visited. By adding at most one hotlink per page (i.e. at most one directed edge per node), we are interested in minimizing the weighted

---

[*] Research supported in part by NSERC (Natural Sciences and Engineering Research Council of Canada) grants, by MITACS (Mathematics of Information Technology and Complex Systems) and a CONACYT fellowship from the Mexican government.

D.T. Lee and S.-H. Teng (Eds.): ISAAC 2000, LNCS 1969, pp. 23–34, 2000.

average number of steps needed to visit from the source page a selected set of web pages. In the case of trees, this webpage is found by searching through a *tree* of nodes each including a set of possible choices. Thus the leaves of the tree are *sought web sites* that we want to link to the root of the tree with hotlinks. A naive way to do this is to add a hotlink from the root for each leaf. If the tree is large, this is unreasonable as it will exceed the space capacity of the web page at the root. An alternate approach (considered in [3,9,10]) is to connect the source node $s$ with $k$ hotlinks to $k$ specially selected nodes so as to maximize the gain. An optimal solution to this problem on trees was given in [9] and the problem was shown to be NP-Hard in [3]. This approach is limited by the desired size $k$ of the web page at the source node.

A more practical approach is to distribute hotlinks over the nodes of the tree to minimize the average number of hops required to visit the web sites. The question is *How do we distribute the hotlinks to minimize the expected number of steps from the root needed to reach a web page located at a leaf?* We consider collections of web pages organized as full binary trees and allow at most one hotlink going from a node $v$ to some other node of the subtree rooted at $v$. Web sites situated at leaves of the tree are visited with a certain frequency depending on their *popularity*. This yields a probability distribution on the leaves of the tree. The hotlink assignment chosen depends on the frequency with which web pages are visited, i.e. on this probability distribution.[1]

## 1.1 Results of the Paper

For arbitrary DAGs we show that the problem is NP-complete. We then prove upper and lower bounds on the expected number of steps to reach a web page located at a leaf of the full binary tree from the root when the weights on the leaves are drawn from one of the following distributions.

- **Arbitrary:** $p_1 + p_2 + \cdots + p_N = 1$.
- **Uniform:** $p_1 = p_2 = \cdots = p_N = 1/N$,
- **Geometric:** $p_i = a^{-i}$, for $i = 1, \ldots, N-1$, and $p_N = 2 - (1 - a^{-N})/(1 - a^{-1})$, where $a > 1$.
- **Zipf:** $p_i = \frac{1}{iH_N}$, where $H_N = \sum_{i=1}^{N} 1/i$ is the harmonic number.

The table below summarizes the upper and lower bounds in this paper.

| Ditribution | Upper Bound | Lower Bound |
|---|---|---|
| **Uniform** | $(3n+1)/4$ | $(3n+1)/4$ |
| **Geometric** | $O(1)$ | $\Omega(1)$ |
| **Arbitrary** | $(3n+1)/4$ | $H(p)/\log 3$ |
| **Zipf** | $(3n+1)/4$ | $n/(2\log 3)$ |
| **Zipf** (Sorted) | $n/3 + O(\sqrt{n}\log n)$ | $n/(2\log 3)$ |

---

[1] We note that a similar problem occurs with Integrated Voice Registers (also called IVRs) used by service providers, phone companies, government agencies, etc. Here the desired piece of information is located at a leaf of a tree. We want to find an assignment of *hyperlinks* that will improve the overall expected number of steps.

The Zipf distribution was popularized by Zipf [11] and is related to the *80-20* rule of thumb stating that 80 percent of transactions are dealing with the most active 20 percent of a list of items [8]. In fact, the Zipf distribution has been shown to be related to the relative access of pages at websites and is therefore important in this context.

For the sorted Zipf distribution (i.e. the $i$-th leaf of the tree is assigned probability $\frac{1}{iH_N}$) we can prove the stronger upper bound $n/3 + O(\sqrt{n}\log n)$. Here $H(p)$ is the Entropy (see [1]) of the probability distribution $p =< p_i : i = 1, \ldots, N >$, which is defined by the formula[2]

$$H(p) = \sum_{i=1}^{N} p_i \log(1/p_i). \tag{1}$$

Note that the lower bounds are valid under any permutation of the distribution on the leaves of the tree.

Due to space restrictions, certain proofs have been omitted from this version and can be found in the full version of the paper.

## 1.2   Notation and Preliminaries

In this paper we consider full binary trees with $n$ levels (not counting the root), $N = 2^n$ leaves, and a total of $2^{n+1} - 1$ nodes. Without hotlinks a leaf can be reached from the root in $n$ steps, which is also the height of the tree.

We give algorithms for assigning hotlinks to the nodes of the full binary tree. A hotlink is an additional directed edge from any node of the tree to a descendant node. We are restricting ourselves to the case where at most one hotlink can be added per node.

Let $r$ be the root (i.e., source page) of the tree. For any node $u$ let $d(u)$ be the distance of $u$ from the root. Let $T^A$ be the graph resulting from an assignment $A$ of hotlinks. The expected number of steps from the root to find a web page is defined by

$$E[T^A, p] = \sum_{x \text{ is a leaf}} d_A(x)p_x,$$

where $d_A(x)$ is the distance of the node $x$ from the root in $T^A$, and $p =< p_x : x = 1, \ldots, N >$ is the probability distribution on the leaves of the original tree $T$. In order to estimate the value of a given set $A$ of hotlinks we associate with $A$ a gain function $g(A)$ such that

$$g(A) = E[T, p] - E[T^A, p] = \sum_{x \text{ is a leaf}} (d(x) - d_A(x))p_x, \tag{2}$$

i.e., $g(A)$ is the difference between the expected number of steps to find a web page in the original tree $T$ and in the graph $T^A$. A set of hotlinks is optimal if it offers the greatest gain over all sets of hotlinks, where at most one hotlink

---

[2] Unless otherwise indicated, throughout this paper all logarithms are in base 2.

can be added per node. We will sometimes refer to $g(\{h\})$ as the gain of a single hotlink $h$. Observe that for a hotlink $h$ joining vertex $u$ to vertex $v$ the gain $g(\{h\})$ comes from the descendants of $v$ and in fact $g(\{h\}) = (d(u,v) - 1)q_v$, where $d(u,v)$ is the distance from $u$ to $v$ and $q_v$ the weight at $v$, i.e., the sum of the probabilities of the leaves descendant to $v$.

The reader may note that for balanced distributions short hotlinks offer better gain than long ones, while for unbalanced distributions long hyperlinks are better. For example, for the uniform distribution and a hotlink $h$ joining vertex $v$ to its descendant at distance $d$ we have that $g(\{h\})$, obtains its maximum value for $d = 2$ or $d = 3$ (see Section 3.3). On the other hand for the degenerate distribution $p_1 = 1, p_2 = p_3 = \cdots = p_N = 0$ the hotlink from the root to the leaf of weight $p_1$ leads to the greatest gain.

It is useful to assume that the probability distribution $p$ is extended to the internal nodes of the tree so that the weight at a node equals the sum of the probabilities of its descendant leaves. Moreover, it is easy to see that these weights can be computed in $O(N)$ time.

In the sequel we assume the leaves of the tree are numbered $1, 2, \ldots, N$ from left to right and for some permutation $\pi$ of the set $1, 2, \ldots, N$ the $i$-th node is assigned probability $p_{\pi(i)}$, for each $i = 1, 2, \ldots, N$. If $\pi$ is the identity permutation and $p_1 \geq p_2 \geq \cdots \geq p_N$ then we say that the distribution is sorted.

## 2   Arbitrary Directed Acyclic Graphs

In this section we prove that the problem of optimal assignment of hotlinks in arbitrary directed acyclic graphs is NP-hard, even for uniform distributions. More precisely, consider the following optimization problem.

**HOTLINK ASSIGNMENT**

**Instance:** Directed acyclic graph $G = (V, E)$, a source node $s \in V$ which can reach every node of the graph, and positive integer $g$.

**Question:** Is there a hotlink assignment from the source node $s$ for which the average length of a path from $s$ to the nodes of $G$ is reduced by at least $g$?

**Theorem 1.** *The problem HOTLINK ASSIGNMENT is NP-hard.*

*Proof.* The transformation is from the following NP-complete problem [5]:

**EXACT COVER BY 3-SETS (X3C)**

**Instance:** Set $S$ with $|S| = 3k$ and a collection $C$ of 3-element subsets of $S$.

**Question:** Does $C$ contain an exact cover for $S$, i.e., a subset $C' \subseteq C$ such that every element of $S$ belongs to exactly one member of $C'$?

Given an instance $C, S$ of X3C we construct an instance $G, g$ of HOTLINK ASSIGNMENT as follows. Let the set $S = \{s_1, s_2, \ldots, s_m\}$ be of size $m = 3k$, and the set $C$ of size $t$. The graph $G = (V, E)$ is defined as follows.

- The vertex set $V$ consists of the vertices below:
  1. $A_0$ is the source node of the graph,
  2. $A_1, \ldots, A_{k-1}, B_1, B_2, \ldots, B_{k-1}$, and $C_1, C_2, \ldots, C_t$,

3. $s_{i,1}, s_{i,2}, \ldots, s_{i,k}$, for $i = 1, 2, \ldots, m$, are $m$ rows of vertices each row of size $k$.

- The edge set $E$ consists of the directed edges below:
  1. $(A_0, A_i)$, and $(A_i, B_i)$, for all $i = 1, \ldots, k - 1$,
  2. $(B_i, C_j)$, for all $i = 1, \ldots, k - 1$, and $j = 1, 2, \ldots, t$,
  3. if $s_i \in C_j$ then there exist directed edges $(C_j, s_{i,1}), (C_j, s_{i,2}), \ldots,$ $(C_j, s_{i,k})$.

We can prove the following lemma.

**Lemma 1.** *There is a set cover of size at most $k$ if and only if the directed graph $G$ has a hotlink assignment which attains a gain of at least $mk + 3k$.*

Clearly the lemma implies the theorem. To prove the lemma it is enough to prove the following two claims.

**Claim 1:** If there is an exact cover of $S$ by 3-sets then there is a hotlink assignment for the graph $G$ whose gain is at least $mk + 3k$.
Indeed, let $C_{i_0}, C_{i_1}, \ldots, C_{i_{k-1}}$ be such a set cover of the set $S$. Consider the hotlinks:
$$A_0 \to C_{i_0}, A_1 \to C_{i_1}, \ldots, A_{k-1} \to C_{i_{k-1}}.$$
The gain resulting from the hotlink $A_0 \to C_{i_0}$ is $2(3k)$ and the gain resulting from the remaining $k - 1$ hotlinks is $(m - 3)k$. Hence the total gain is $mk + 3k$.

**Claim 2:** If there is no set cover of size $k$ then the gain from any hotlink assignment on the graph $G$ is less than $mk + 3k$.
Indeed, consider any hotlink assignment of $G$. On the one hand, if this hotlink assignment is using a hotlink from $A_0$ to some vertex $B_i$, for some $i = 1, 2, \ldots, k - 1$, then the maximum gain that can be attained is at most $mk + 2(k-1) + (k-1) < mk + 3k$. On the other hand, if this hotlink assignment is never using a hotlink from $A_0$ to any vertex $B_i$, for any $i = 1, 2, \ldots, k - 1$, then again the maximum gain that can be attained is at most $2(3k) + (m - 4)k + k - 1 < mk + 3k$. This completes the proof of the lemma and hence also of the theorem.

## 3    Full Binary Trees

In this section we consider the hotlink assignment problem on full binary trees.

### 3.1    Geometric Distribution

We can assign hotlinks by a simple bottom-up heuristic. The idea is to sort the leaves by weight and assign to each leaf a previously unassigned internal node that is its furthest ancestor. In this way, the heaviest leaf is assigned to the root. This simple heuristic will assign at most one leaf per node and can be efficient if the probability distribution is heavily weighted towards a few nodes. The algorithm we consider is the following.

**Bottom-up Strategy:**

1. Sort the $N$ leaves by the size of the probability distribution, i.e., if $u$ precedes $v$ then $p_u \leq p_v$.

2. Assign the highest probability leaf to the root.

3. Assign the remaining leaves recursively as follows. Consider an unassigned leaf, say $l$, of highest probability. Find its furthest unassigned ancestor, say $u$. Assign $l$ to $u$.

A simple analysis of the performance of the algorithm is as follows. Let $u_1, u_2, \ldots, u_{n-1}$ be the $n-1$ leaves of the 1st, 2nd,..., $(n-1)$st highest probability in the given probability distribution $p$. It is easy to see that the resulting gain

$$\geq (n-1)p_{u_1} + (n-2)p_{u_2} + \cdots + (n-(n-1))p_{u_{n-1}}$$
$$= n \sum_{i=1}^{n-1} p_{u_i} - \sum_{i=1}^{n-1} i p_{u_i}.$$

In particular, the expected number of steps satisfies

$$E[T^A, p] \leq n - n \sum_{i=1}^{n-1} p_{u_i} + \sum_{i=1}^{n-1} i p_{u_i}$$
$$= n \left( 1 - \sum_{i=1}^{n-1} p_{u_i} \right) + \sum_{i=1}^{n-1} i p_{u_i} \tag{3}$$

Inequality (3) can already provide good bounds for probability distributions which are heavily weighted on *a few* nodes. In particular, we have the following result.

**Theorem 2.** *Consider a rooted full binary tree on $n$ levels. In time linear in the number of vertices of the tree, an assignment of at most one hotlink per node can be computed for the geometric probability distribution on the leaves such that the expected number of steps to reach a leaf of the tree is $O(1)$.*

*Proof.* This follows easily from Inequality (3). In particular, we have that

$$E[T^A, p] \leq n \left( 1 - \sum_{i=1}^{n-1} p_{u_i} \right) + \sum_{i=1}^{n-1} i p_{u_i}$$
$$= n \left( 1 - \sum_{i=1}^{n-1} 2^{-i} \right) + \sum_{i=1}^{n-1} i 2^{-i}$$
$$= O(1)$$

This completes the proof of the theorem.

A similar argument works for the general geometric distribution.

## 3.2   Arbitrary Distributions

In this section we give an algorithm for arbitrary distributions.

**Theorem 3.** *Consider a rooted full binary tree on $n$ levels. There is an algorithm, running in time linear in the number of vertices of the tree, that assigns one hotlink per node in such a way that the expected number of steps to reach a leaf of the tree is at most $(3n + 1)/4$ for any probability distribution on the leaves.*

*Proof.* As mentioned before in $O(N)$ time we can propagate the original weights on the leaves of the tree through the entire tree using a bottom-up process. Once all these internal node weights are assigned we use a top-down method to assign hotlinks. Each hotlink is assigned from a node at level $i \leq n-2$ to a node at level $i+2$. The root is assigned the hotlink to the level two node of highest weight. By symmetry we can suppose that this hotlink is to the leftmost descendant at distance two from the root (see tree $T_n$ in Figure 1).

The assignment of hotlinks is done recursively. The recursive process assigns hotlinks to the two subtrees $T_n$ and $S_n$ as depicted in Figure 1. Let $a, b, c, d$ be

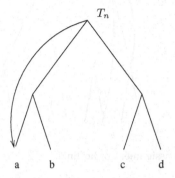
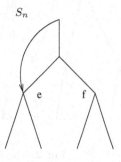

**Fig. 1.** Assignment of hotlinks to subtrees. The leftmost tree is $T_n$ and the rightmost tree is $S_n$.

the probabilities at the second level of the tree $T_n$ and $e, f$ the probabilities at the second level of the tree $S_n$. Without loss of generality assume that

$$a \geq b, c, d \text{ and } e \geq f,$$

We select the hotlinks from the root to the node with highest probability at the second level of $T_n$ and $S_n$, respectively. This leads to the hotlink assignment depicted in Figure 1. The overall algorithm is illustrated in Figure 2. Notice that by assumption we have that

$$a + b + c + d = 1$$
$$e + f = 1$$

Let $s_n$ (resp., $t_n$) be the expected number of steps to reach the leaves of the tree $T_n$ (resp. $S_n$), We now have the recurrences

$$t_n = 1 + (c+d)t_{n-1} + at_{n-2} + bs_{n-1}$$
$$s_n = 1 + et_{n-2} + fs_{n-2},$$

where $t_n$ and $s_n$ are the weights of the subtrees $T_n$ and $S_n$, respectively. We can prove the following claim.

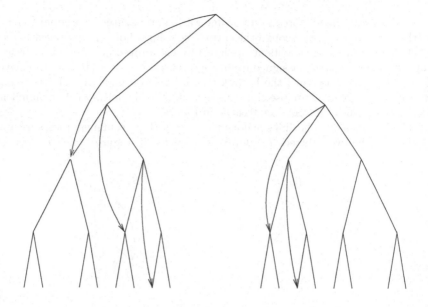

**Fig. 2.** The iteration of the assignment of hotlinks

**Claim:**

$$t_n \leq 3n/4 + 1/4$$
$$s_n \leq 3n/4$$

**Proof of the claim:** The proof is by induction on $n$. Cases $n = 2, 3, 4$ can be proved by inspection. First we consider $s_n$.

$$s_n = 1 + et_{n-2} + fs_{n-2}$$
$$\leq 1 + e(3(n-2)/4 + 1/4) + f3(n-1)/4$$
$$\leq 3n/4,$$

the last inequality being true because by assumption $e \geq 1/2$.

Next we consider $t_n$.

$$t_n = 1 + at_{n-2} + (c+d)t_{n-1} + bs_{n-1}$$
$$\leq 1 + a(3(n-2)/4 + 1/4) + (c+d)(3(n-1)/4 + 1/4) + 3(n-1)/4$$
$$= 1/2 + 3n/4 - 3a/4 - b/4$$

Now we have two cases depending on the size of $a$.

**Case 1:** $a \geq 1/3$.

In this case, the claim follows from the inequalities

$$t_n \leq 1/2 + 3n/4 - 3a/4 - b/4$$
$$\leq 1/2 + 3n/4 - 1/4$$
$$\leq 1/4 + 3n/4$$

**Case 2:** $a < 1/3$.

In this case, write $a = 1/3 - x$, where $x > 0$, and notice that

$$b + c + d = 1 - a = 2/3 + x$$

and

$$c \leq a = 1/3 - x$$
$$d \leq a = 1/3 - x$$

Consequently,

$$b = 2/3 + x - c - d \geq 3x.$$

It follows that

$$\begin{aligned} t_n &\leq 1/2 + 3n/4 - 3a/4 - b/4 \\ &\leq 1/2 + 3n/4 - 3/4(1/3 - x) - 3x/4 \\ &= 1/4 + 3n/4. \end{aligned}$$

This completes the proof of Case 2 and hence also of the claim. The proof of Theorem 3 is now complete.

### 3.3  Uniform Distribution

Consider the uniform distribution in a full binary tree. It is easy to see that adding a link from the root to a node at distance $k$ will save exactly a fraction of $(k-1)2^{-k}$ of the total weight of the tree. Moreover this saving is maximized at $k = 2$ or $k = 3$ and the maximum value is $1/4$. Similarly, any hotlink we add to a node can save at most $1/4$ of the total weight of the subtree rooted at this node. This indicates that the maximal gain attained by a hotlink on a given node is at most $1/4$ of the weight of the subtree rooted at this node. Therefore it is not difficult to see that by adding one hotlink per node on a tree with the uniform distribution we can never attain a gain higher than $(n-1)/4$. The previous discussion and Theorem 3 imply the following result.

**Theorem 4.** *Consider a rooted full binary tree on $n$ levels. There is an algorithm linear in the number of vertices of the tree which for the uniform distribution on the leaves of the tree assigns at most one hotlink per node in such a way that the expected number of steps to reach a leaf of the tree is at most $(3n+1)/4$. Moreover, $(3n+1)/4$ is a lower bound on any such algorithm.*

### 3.4  Zipf Distribution

In this section we consider the sorted Zipf distribution, i.e. the $i$-th leaf of the tree is assigned probability $\frac{1}{iH_N}$, and prove an $n/3 + O(\sqrt{n}\log n)$ upper bound on the expected number of steps to reach a leaf.

Recall the following estimate for the harmonic number $H_m = \sum_{i=1}^{m} 1/i$ from [7][page 75]:

$$H_m = \ln m + \gamma + \frac{1}{2m} - \frac{1}{12m^2} + \frac{1}{120m^4} - \epsilon,$$

where $0 < \epsilon < \frac{1}{252m^6}$ and $\gamma = 0.5772\ldots$ is Euler's constant. Consequently we have that

$$\gamma + \ln m < H_m < 1 + \ln m.$$

It follows that for $l \leq n$ we have the Inequalities

$$\frac{l}{n} + \frac{1}{n} \geq \sum_{i=1}^{2^l} p_i = \sum_{i=1}^{2^l} \frac{1}{iH_N} = \frac{1}{H_N} \sum_{i=1}^{2^l} \frac{1}{i} = \frac{H_{2^l}}{H_{2^n}} \geq \frac{l}{n} \cdot \left(\frac{n}{n+2}\right). \tag{4}$$

Let $r$ be the root of the tree. Define the sequence $r_0, r_1, \ldots, r_i, \ldots$ of tree nodes, where $i \leq n$, as follows: $r := r_0$ and for each $i$, $r_i$ is the left child of $r_{i-1}$. Next we assign hotlinks rooted to these nodes in the following manner. Assign to $r_i$ a hotlink to the node $r_{\lceil n/2^{i+1} \rceil}$, provided that $i < \lceil n/2^{i+1} \rceil$.

The weight of the subtree rooted at $r_{\lceil n/2^{i+1} \rceil}$ is equal to $\sum_{i=1}^{2^{l_{i+1}}} p_i$, where $l_{i+1} = n - \lceil n/2^{i+1} \rceil$. Since $n/2^{i+1} \leq \lceil n/2^{i+1} \rceil \leq 1 + n/2^{i+1}$ we can use Inequality (4) to obtain that

$$\left(1 - \frac{1}{2^{i+1}}\right) \frac{n}{n+2} - \frac{1}{n+2} \leq \sum_{i=1}^{2^{l_{i+1}}} p_i \leq \left(1 - \frac{1}{2^{i+1}}\right) + \frac{2}{n}. \tag{5}$$

In view of Inequality (5) it is not difficult to see that the gain resulting from adding a single hotlink from the node $r_i$ to the node $r_{\lceil n/2^{i+1} \rceil}$ is at least

$$\left(\frac{n}{2^{i+1}} - i - 1\right) \sum_{i=1+2^{l_i}}^{2^{l_{i+1}}} p_i \geq \left(\frac{n}{2^{i+1}} - i - 1\right) \cdot \frac{1}{2^{i+1}} \cdot \left(\frac{1}{2^{i+1}} - \frac{5}{n}\right). \tag{6}$$

By summing the terms in Formula (6) for $i$ such that $i < \lceil n/2^{i+1} \rceil$ we obtain that the gain resulting from all these hyperlinks is at least

$$\left(\frac{n}{2} - 1\right) \cdot \left(\frac{1}{2} - \frac{5}{n}\right) + \left(\frac{n}{4} - 2\right) \cdot \left(\frac{1}{4} - \frac{5}{n}\right) + \left(\frac{n}{8} - 3\right) \cdot \left(\frac{1}{8} - \frac{5}{n}\right) + \cdots. \tag{7}$$

Let $k := \lceil (\log n)/3 \rceil - 1$. Clearly, $k$ satisfies $k2^{k+1} \leq \sqrt{n} < n$. Summing Formula (7) we obtain that the total gain achieved from all these hotlinks is at least

$$n \sum_{i=1}^{k} \frac{1}{2^{2i}} - \sum_{i=1}^{k} \left(\frac{i}{2^i} - \frac{5}{n}\right) - \frac{5k}{2} \geq \frac{n}{3} - O(\sqrt{n}). \tag{8}$$

Let $c > 0$ be the constant in Inequality (8). We now apply the previous hotlink assignment recursively to each subtree rooted at the node $r_{\lceil n/2^i \rceil}$, respectively, for $i \leq l = \lfloor \log n \rfloor$. Using Inequality (8) it is easy to see that the total gain achieved must be at least

$$\sum_{i=0}^{l-1} \left(\frac{n2^{-i}}{3} - c\sqrt{n/2^i}\right) \geq \frac{n}{3} \sum_{i=0}^{k-1} 2^{-i} - c\sqrt{n} \log n \geq \frac{2n}{3} - O(\sqrt{n} \log n).$$

It follows that after adding these hotlinks to the tree the expected length of a path to reach a leaf is at most

$$n - \frac{2n}{3} + O(\sqrt{n}\log n)) = \frac{n}{3} + O(\sqrt{n}\log n).$$

Therefore we have proved the following result.

**Theorem 5.** *Consider a rooted full binary tree on n levels. There is an algorithm linear in the number of vertices of the tree which for the sorted Zipf distribution on the leaves of the tree assigns at most one hotlink per node in such a way that the expected number of steps to reach a leaf of the tree is at most $n/3 + O(\sqrt{n}\log n)$.*

## 4  Lower Bounds

A *code-alphabet* is any nonempty set. A *code-word* in the code-alphabet is a word (i.e., any concatenation) formed from letters of the code-alphabet; the number of letters in the code-word is the length of the code-word. A *code* is any set of code-words. The code is called a *prefix-code* if no code-word in the code is a prefix of any other code-word in the same code.

To prove lower bounds we use Shannon Theory and the Entropy [1] $H(p)$ of the probability distribution $p$, which is defined by Equation (1). Shannon's theorem states the following:

**Theorem 6.** *Let $p_1, p_2, \ldots, p_N$ be a probability distribution. Given a prefix code $w_1, w_2, \ldots, w_N$ of respective lengths $l_1, l_2, \ldots, l_N$ in an alphabet of size $k$, the expected length $\sum_{i=1}^{N} l_i p_i$ of the code is at least $H(p)/\log k$.*

A binary tree can be thought of as the encoding of the leaves with the two symbol alphabet $0, 1$. Adding a hotlink increments the alphabet by a single symbol to form a three symbol alphabet.

For a given hotlink assignment $A$, the distance of the $i$-th leaf from the root, previously denoted by $d_A(i)$, is the length of the encoding of the $i$-th leaf in this new alphabet. Notice that if two hotlinks are targeting the same node then the shortest one can be omitted without changing the value of $E[T^A, p]$. As a consequence, $E[T^A, p]$ is also the expected length of the *encoding* of the leaves of the tree $T^A$ represented as code words in a three letter alphabet. Moreover, the resulting encoding is a prefix code. In particular, Shannon's theorem applies and we have that

$$E[T^A, p] \geq \frac{1}{\log 3} \cdot H(p) = \frac{1}{\log 3} \cdot \sum_{i=1}^{N} p_i \log(1/p_i). \tag{9}$$

We have proved the following theorem.

**Theorem 7.** *For any probability distribution $p$ on the leaves of a full binary tree and any assignment of at most one hotlink per source node the expected number of steps to reach a webpage located at a leaf from the root of the tree is at least $H(p)/\log 3$, where $H(p)$ is the entropy of $p$.*

Theorem 7 is directly applicable. Straightforward calculations give lower bounds for several distributions. For the uniform distribution it is easily seen that $H(p) = n$. For the Zipf distribution,

$$
\begin{aligned}
H(p) &= \sum_{i=1}^{N} p_i \log(1/p_i) \\
&= \frac{1}{H_N} \sum_{i=1}^{N} \frac{\log i}{i} + \log(H_N) \\
&\geq \frac{1}{2} \cdot \log N + \Omega(\log \log N) \\
&= \frac{n}{2} + \Omega(\log n).
\end{aligned}
$$

In particular, this implies the $n/(2 \log 3)$ lower bound on the expected number of steps for the Zipf distribution.

## 5    Conclusions

In this paper we have considered the problem of assigning hotlinks to the nodes of a DAG in order to minimize the number of steps from a designated source node to a collection of nodes in the DAG. We have shown this problem to be NP-hard. However, when the underlying graph is a complete binary tree, with the source being the root of the tree, we provide linear time algorithms to assign hotlinks and compute the upper and lower bounds on the expected number of steps from root to leaf for various probability distributions on the leaves. Interesting open problems include: considering other topologies, and providing approximation algorithms for DAGs.

## References

1. N. Abramson, "Information Theory and Coding", McGraw Hill, 1963.
2. W. Aiello, F. Chung, L. Lu, "A random graph model for massive graphs". To appear in Proc. of the 32nd ACM Symp. on the Theory of Computing, 2000.
3. J. Czyzowicz, E. Kranakis, A. Pelc, M. Vargas Martin, "Optimal Assignment of Bookmarks to Web Pages", to appear.
4. M. Faloutsos, P. Faloutsos, C. Faloutsos, "On Power-Law Relationships of the Internet Topology", In proceedings of SIGCOM: IEEE Conference on Communication, 1999.
5. M.R. Garey and D.S. Johnson, "Computers and Intractability: A Guide to the Theory of NP-Completeness", Freeman and Co., New York, 1979.
6. J. M. Kleinberg, R. Kumar, P. Raghavan, S. Rajagopalan, A. S. Tomkins, "The Web as a graph: measurements, models, and methods. In Proc. of the Fifth Int. Conf. on Computing and Combinatorics", Springer-Verlag, pages 1-17, 1999.
7. D. Knuth, "The Art of Computer Programming: Volume 1, Fundamental Algorithms", Addison Wesley, 2nd ed., 1997.
8. D. Knuth, "The Art of Computer Programming: Volume 3, Sorting and Searching", Addison Wesley, 3rd ed., 1998.
9. B. Li, M. Golin, G. Italiano, X. Deng and K. Sohraby, "On the Optimal Placement of Web Proxies in the Internet", IEEE InfoCom'99, pp.1282–1290, 1999.
10. B. Li, X. Deng, M. Golin, and K. Sohraby, "On the Optimal Placement of Web Proxies in the Internet", 8th IFIP Conf. on High Performance Networking, 1998.
11. C. K. Zipf. "Human Behavior and the Principle of Least Effort", Reading Mass., Addison Wesley, 1949.

# A New Competitive Analysis of Randomized Caching

## (Extended Abstract)

Ching Law and Charles E. Leiserson

MIT Laboratory for Computer Science, 545 Technology Square, Cambridge, Massachusetts 02139, {ching,cel}@mit.edu

**Abstract.** We provide new competitive upper bounds on the performance of the memoryless, randomized caching algorithm RAND. Our bounds are expressed in terms of the *inherent hit rate* $\alpha$ of the sequence of memory references, which is the highest possible hit rate that any algorithm can achieve on the sequence for a cache of a given size. Our results show that RAND is $(1 - \alpha e^{-1/\alpha})/(1 - \alpha)$-competitive on any reference sequence with inherent hit rate $\alpha$. Since our new competitive bound does not scale up with the size $k$ of the cache, it beats the putative $\Omega(\lg k)$ lower bound on the competitiveness of randomized caching algorithms.

## 1 Introduction

Fiat *et al.* [11] show that no on-line cache replacement algorithm[1] on size-$k$ caches can be better than $H_k$-competitive, where $H_k = \Theta(\lg k)$ is the $k$th harmonic number. Moreover, subsequent research [1,21] has demonstrated the existence of $H_k$-competitive algorithms for this problem. Despite the apparent meeting of these upper and lower bounds, we show in this paper that much better competitive upper bounds can be obtained.

Before discussing our new upper bounds, we first present some background definitions. A cache-replacement algorithm is said to be *on-line* if at each point in time, the algorithm responds to a memory request based only on past information and with no knowledge whatsoever about any future requests. An *off-line* cache-replacement algorithm, on the other hand, assumes the availability of an entire input sequence of memory requests. In this paper, replacement algorithms will be denoted in Sans Serif font, for example, A, sometimes subscripted with the size of its cache, as in $\mathsf{A}_k$. We say that an algorithm $\mathsf{A}_k$ $\rho$-*competes* with another algorithm $\mathsf{B}_h$ if the number of cache misses incurred by $\mathsf{A}_k$ on any input

---

[1] Fiat *et al.* actually discuss paging algorithms, instead of cache replacement algorithms, but the basic issues are the same. We use caching terminology, because our results are more appropriate for the domain of caches than for virtual memory.

D.T. Lee and S.-H. Teng (Eds.): ISAAC 2000, LNCS 1969, pp. 35–46, 2000.

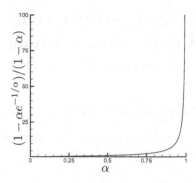

**Fig. 1.** The graph of $(1 - \alpha e^{-1/\alpha})/(1 - \alpha)$ for $\alpha \in (0, 1)$.

is at most $\rho$ times the number of cache misses incurred by $\mathsf{B}_h$. We say an algorithm $\mathsf{A}_k$ is $\rho$-*competitive* if $\mathsf{A}_k$ $\rho$-competes with $\mathsf{OPT}_k$, where $\mathsf{OPT}_k$ is the optimal off-line algorithm.

Fiat *et al.*'s $H_k$ lower bound for size-$k$ caches uses an adversarial argument to construct a sequence of memory requests that causes a given randomized caching algorithm to be at least $H_k$-competitive on the sequence. Their construction produces sequences whose *inherent miss rate* $\beta$, the fraction of requests on which the optimal off-line algorithm $\mathsf{OPT}_k$ misses, is at most $1/k$. Consequently, for sequences of requests with $\beta > 1/k$, their argument provides no lower bound on how efficiently a caching algorithm can serve these sequences. Indeed, we show in this paper that for a constant miss rate, an $O(1)$-competitive upper bound can be obtained by the memoryless, randomized caching algorithm RAND introduced by Raghavan and Snir [22].

As with Fiat *et al.*'s lower bound, previous upper bounds on the competitiveness of caching algorithms apply most aptly to low miss rates. For example, Raghavan and Snir's analysis of RAND, which shows that $\mathsf{RAND}_k$ is $k$-competitive, leads to a trivial upper bound for $\beta \geq 1/k$. Analysis of the least-recently used algorithm LRU [23] likewise shows that $\mathsf{LRU}_k$ is $k$-competitive, which is a trivial upper bound if $\beta \geq 1/k$. The $\mathsf{MARKING}_k$ algorithm [11] is $2H_k$-competitive, offering trivial upper bounds for $\beta \geq 1/2H_k$; and the $\mathsf{PARTITION}_k$ algorithm [21] and the $\mathsf{EQUITABLE}_k$ algorithm [1] are $H_k$-competitive, providing trivial upper bounds for $\beta \geq 1/H_k$.

In comparison, our new analysis of RAND provides nontrivial upper bounds for all $0 < \beta < 1$. In particular we show that $\mathsf{RAND}_k$ is $(1 - (1 - \beta)e^{-1/(1-\beta)})/\beta$-competitive on request sequences with inherent miss rate $\beta$. This result, because of its derivation, is more naturally expressed in terms of the *inherent hit rate* $\alpha = 1 - \beta$; so $\mathsf{RAND}_k$ is $(1 - \alpha e^{-1/\alpha})/(1 - \alpha)$-competitive on a request sequences with inherent hit rate $\alpha$. Figure 1 graphs $(1 - \alpha e^{-1/\alpha})/(1 - \alpha)$ for $\alpha \in (0, 1)$. Although the competitive ratio approaches $\infty$ as the inherent hit rate approaches 1, it is reasonably small for moderate hit rates. For example, when the inherent hit rate $\alpha$ is 90%, the competitive ratio $(1 - \alpha e^{-1/\alpha})/(1 - \alpha)$ is 7.04. Thus, for a

90% hit rate on any cache with more than 7 entries, our competitive bound for RAND improves Raghavan and Snir's bound of $k$.

Our new bounds do not subsume previous upper bounds, however. In particular, the previous bounds work well for miss rates in ranges that are normally associated with virtual-memory paging (and for which these algorithms were designed), whereas our new bounds are more applicable to the typical miss rates of certain hardware caches. Figure 2 shows the previous upper bounds together with our new bounds for RAND. As can be seen from Fig. 2, the bounds for PARTITION and EQUITABLE are the best to date for small inherent miss rates, while our new bounds for RAND are best for larger inherent miss rates. Therefore, our new results can be considered as a complement to previous results for nonnegligible miss rates.

Unlike previous bounds, our new bound for RAND is novel in two ways: it is independent of the cache size, and it applies throughout the entire range of inherent miss rates. An anonymous reviewer of an earlier version of our paper noted that one can, in fact, use our ideas to adapt the analysis of MARKING by Fiat *et al.* [11] to obtain the upper bound $2\beta(1 + \ln(1/2\beta))$ on miss rate, which is independent of cache size. Like previous bounds, however, this bound is trivial for certain miss rates, specifically greater than 50%. In contrast, our new bound not only is independent of cache size, it is meaningful for all inherent miss rates. Figure 3 illustrates a comparison of our new bound of RAND with the adapted bound of MARKING.

The remainder of this paper is organized as follows. Section 2 reviews related works on competitive analysis for caching algorithms. Section 3 states the essential definitions for describing replacement algorithms. Section 4 introduces a new framework for describing the adversary's strategy. Section 5 gives a competitive ratio for RAND using a convexity argument based on the strategy framework. Section 6 concludes with a discussion of possible extensions to this work.

## 2 Related Work

This section reviews previous results on competitive analysis for on-line replacement algorithms, both deterministic and randomized. We discuss criticisms of the common framework for competitive analysis that have been proposed in the literature. We conclude the section by observing that previous lower bounds involve request sequences with extremely low inherent miss rates, thus providing no information on many request sequences seen in practice that have moderate or high miss rates.

**Deterministic Algorithms.** Deterministic replacement algorithms were the first to be analyzed. Comparing on-line algorithms running on size-$k$ caches with the optimal off-line algorithm running on size-$h$ caches, where $h \le k$, Sleator and Tarjan showed in their seminal paper [23] that both $LRU_k$ (Least-Recently-Used) and $FIFO_k$ (First-In-First-Out) are $k/(k - h + 1)$-competitive with $OPT_h$. They also showed that this competitive ratio is the best possible for any deterministic algorithm. Karlin *et al.* [15] proved that $FWF_k$ (Flush-When-Full) is also $k/(k - h + 1)$-competitive with $OPT_h$.

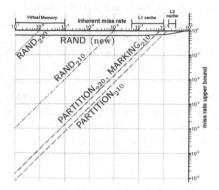

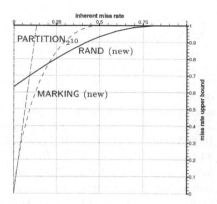

**Fig. 2.** Upper bounds on the miss rate for various on-line algorithms as a function of inherent miss rate across a range from $10^{-7}$ to 1 using a logarithmic scale. Since cache size influences the previous bounds in the literature, the upper bounds for cache sizes of $2^{10}$ and $2^{20}$ are shown. The upper bound for our new analysis is labeled "RAND(new)," and as can be seen from the figure, is the first bound that applies across the entire range of inherent miss rates.

**Fig. 3.** Upper bounds on the miss rate for various on-line algorithms as a function of inherent miss rate. The upper bound of MARKING is adapted from the analysis of Fiat *et al.* [11]. The new bounds are stronger for inherent miss rates of between 21% and 100%.

**Randomized Algorithms.** Competitive analysis for randomized algorithms generally assumes (as shall we) that the adversary is *oblivious* [22], meaning that the adversary generates a request sequence given only the description of the on-line algorithm, but not the random choices made by during the execution of the algorithm. Manasse *et al.* [19] studied competitive analysis for randomized replacement algorithms, in which context the *expected* miss rates are compared to the miss rates of OPT. Fiat *et al.* [11] showed that randomized replacement algorithms are at least $H_k$-competitive, where $H_k$ is the $k$th harmonic number. They also gave a simple $2H_k$-competitive algorithm $\text{MARKING}_k$. Also $H_k$-competitive are the algorithms $\text{PARTITION}_k$ [21] and $\text{EQUITABLE}_k$ [1]. Considering memoryless algorithms, Borodin and El-Yaniv [4] showed that $\text{RAND}_k$ $k/(k-h+1)$-competes with $\text{OPT}_h$. Moreover, Raghavan and Snir [22] demonstrated that no memoryless randomized algorithm can be better than $k$-competitive.

Since on-line algorithms are handicapped with imperfect information of the future, it is useful to investigate how the competitive ratio improves if they are compensated with larger caches. Although such results are known for FIFO, LRU and RAND, the corresponding knowledge for other randomized algorithms is limited. Young [25] showed that any randomized algorithm $A_k$ at most roughly $\ln(k/(k-h))$-competes with $\text{OPT}_h$ when $k/(k-h) \geq e$. He also showed that

$\mathsf{MARKING}_k$ roughly $2\ln(k/(k-h))$-competes with $\mathsf{OPT}_h$ under the same condition. It is not known in general how other randomized algorithms perform with varying cache sizes.

**Criticisms.** The literature includes criticisms against competitive analysis as an evaluation tool for on-line algorithms. Some researchers have complained that the adversary is too powerful, leading to weak competitive ratios of on-line algorithms, and consequently have suggested curbing the power of the adversary. For example, the access graph model [5,14,10] restricts the possible choices of the next request as the function of the current request, so as to model locality of reference. In contrast, some researchers have tried to enhance the power of the on-line algorithm, for example, with lookaheads [24,16].

Other researchers have suggested alternative evaluation criteria. For example, Ben-David and Borodin [3] indicate that some competitive algorithms require unbounded memory, and that finite lookahead is useless for improving the competitive ratio. They suggested the max/max ratio as an alternative measure for online algorithms. An online algorithm's max/max ratio is defined as its worst-case amortized cost over the worst-case amortized cost of the off-line algorithm. Dichterman [8] showed that the algorithm $\mathsf{UNIFORM}$ achieves the optimal max/max ratio, but is not competitive at all. (Moreover, strongly competitive randomized algorithms ($\mathsf{PARTITION}$ [21] and $\mathsf{EQUITABLE}$ [1]) appear to be too complex to be implemented in hardware.) On the other hand, Young [26] proposed loose competitiveness. In particular, Young [27] showed that if an algorithm $\mathsf{A}_k$ $k/(k-h+1)$-competes with $\mathsf{OPT}_h$, then for most choices of $k$,

- the total cost of $\mathsf{A}_k$ on sequence $R$ is insignificant, or
- $\mathsf{A}_k$ $c$-competes with $\mathsf{OPT}_k$ on sequence $R$ for a constant $c$.

We note that ratio $c$ depends on what retrieval cost is considered insignificant and the criterion of "most choices of $k$".

**Inherent miss rates.** The derivations of the lower bounds of competitiveness involve request sequences with extremely low miss rates. For example, in the Raghavan and Snir's proof [22] of the $k$-competitiveness lower bound for $\mathsf{RAND}_k$, a request sequence with inherent miss rate $\beta < 1/mk$ is required to make $\mathsf{RAND}_k$ miss with a factor of $k(1-(1-1/k)^m)$ over $\mathsf{OPT}_k$. Moreover, Fiat et al.'s construction [11] of the $H_k$-competitiveness lower bound for any randomized algorithms produces sequences whose inherent miss rate $\beta$ is at most $1/k$. In addition, in the proof of the $k$-competitiveness lower bound for deterministic algorithms, Goemans [12] uses a request sequence with inherent miss rate below $1/k$.

These lower bounds say nothing about request sequences with high (or even moderate) miss rates. In this paper, we present a new approach for competitive analysis that uses the inherent miss rate as a parameter of the analysis. Consequently, despite the apparent meeting of upper and lower bounds in previous analyses, we can obtain better bounds for request sequences with moderate and high miss rates.

# 3   Preliminaries

This section lays the framework for analyzing the RAND replacement algorithm. We introduce notation to describe the behavior of cache replacement algorithms, and we define precisely the notions of "cache hit" and "cache miss." Our framework loosely corresponds to the model presented by Coffman and Denning [7, pages 243-246]. We model a two-level memory system composed of a *(primary) memory* and a *cache*. The memory is a set of *(memory) locations*, where each location is a natural number $r \in \mathbb{N}$. The *cache state* $T \in \mathbb{N}^k$ of a size-$k$ cache is a $k$-tuple of locations, where $T[s] = r$ if memory location $r$ is stored in *slot s* of the cache. The special location 0 of memory is never referenced. Instead, we use 0 to denote an empty cache slot. The cache has additional *control state* $Q$ in order to make decisions about which locations it stores at any given time.

When a $k$-slot cache is required to serve a *(memory) request* $r \in \mathbb{N} - \{0\}$, a *replacement algorithm* $\mathsf{A}_k$ changes its existing cache state $T$ and control state $Q$ to a new cache state $T'$ and control state $Q'$. Specifically, the replacement algorithm $\mathsf{A}_k$ chooses a *replacement slot* $\mathsf{A}_k(T, Q, r)$ such that

$$T'[s] = \begin{cases} r & \text{if } \mathsf{A}_k(T, Q, r) = s, \\ T[s] & \text{otherwise.} \end{cases}$$

Moreover, we require that if there exists a slot $s$ such that $T[s] = r$, then $\mathsf{A}_k(T, Q, r) = s$. Thus, the replacement slot is the only slot whose contents may change. If the contents do not change, that is, if $r = T'[s] = T[s]$, then the request is a *cache hit*. Otherwise, if $r = T'[s] \neq T[s]$, the request is a *cache miss*.

We now define precisely the number of hits (or misses) that a replacement algorithm $\mathsf{A}_k$ incurs on a sequence $R = \langle r_1, r_2, \ldots, r_n \rangle$ of $n$ requests. Let $T_1 = (0, 0, \ldots, 0)$ be the $k$-tuple representing the empty initial cache state, and let $Q_1$ be the initial control state. In order to service request $r_i$ for $i = 1, 2, \ldots, n$, the cache algorithm $\mathsf{A}_k$ inductively changes cache state $T_i$ and control state $Q_i$ to cache state $T_{i+1}$ and control state $Q_{i+1}$. Since $\mathsf{A}_k$ might be a randomized replacement algorithm, define $\mathrm{hit}(\mathsf{A}_k, r_i)$ to be the event that request $r_i$ is a hit, and overload the notation to define the indicator random variable

$$\mathrm{hit}(\mathsf{A}_k, r_i) = \begin{cases} 1 & \text{if } r_i \text{ is a hit,} \\ 0 & \text{if } r_i \text{ is a miss.} \end{cases}$$

Let $\mathrm{hit}(\mathsf{A}_k, R)$ be the total number of hits incurred by $A_k$ over the entire sequence $R$, whence $\mathrm{hit}(\mathsf{A}_k, R) = \sum_{i=1}^{n} \mathrm{hit}(\mathsf{A}_k, r_i)$. Likewise, for misses define $\mathrm{miss}(\mathsf{A}_k, r_i) = 1 - \mathrm{hit}(\mathsf{A}_k, r_i)$ for $i = 1, 2, \ldots, n$, and $\mathrm{miss}(\mathsf{A}_k, R) = n - \mathrm{hit}(\mathsf{A}_k, R)$.

The focus of this paper is the analysis of RAND, a simple, randomized replacement algorithm. RAND is "memoryless," meaning that its control state $Q$ never changes. Suppose $\mathsf{RAND}_k$ is running on a cache of size $k$ with a cache state $T \in \mathbb{N}^k$. For a request $r \in \mathbb{N} - \{0\}$ that causes a miss ($r \notin T$), the algorithm selects a slot to be replaced uniformly at random. That is, for $s = 1, 2, \ldots, k$, we have

$$\Pr\left\{\mathsf{RAND}_k(T, Q, r) = s\right\} = 1/k.$$

We shall compare $\mathsf{RAND}$ with $\mathsf{OPT}$, the optimal, offline replacement algorithm [2] that achieves the minimum-possible number of misses on any given request sequence $R = \langle r_1, r_2, \ldots, r_n \rangle$. For each request $r_i$ that causes a miss, the $\mathsf{OPT}$ algorithm omnisciently replaces the best possible slot to minimize misses. Specifically, let $f_i(r)$ be the *forward distance* of a sequence $R$ defined by

$$f_i(r) = \begin{cases} d & \text{if } r_{i+d} \text{ is the first occurrence of } r \text{ in } \langle r_{i+1}, r_{i+2}, \ldots, r_n \rangle, \\ \infty & \text{if } r \text{ does not appear in } \langle r_{i+1}, r_{i+2}, \ldots, r_n \rangle. \end{cases}$$

For a cache miss $r_i \notin T_i$, the replacement algorithm $\mathsf{OPT}_h$ chooses the location in the cache whose forward distance is largest. That is, it chooses $s = \mathsf{OPT}_h(T_i, Q_i, r_i)$ if $f_i(T_i[s]) = \max_{1 \leq j \leq h} f_i(T_i[j])$, where ties are broken arbitrarily.

Belady [2] showed that for any request sequence $R$, the $\mathsf{OPT}$ algorithm minimizes the total number of misses.

# 4   The Adversary's Strategy

Before presenting our analytical results in Sect. 5, we first develop a framework for describing and analyzing the oblivious adversary. We define formally the notion of the adversary's "strategy," and prove a theorem that shows that specifying a strategy is equivalent to specifying a request sequence. The power of the oblivious adversary lies in the selection of a request sequence $R = \langle r_1, r_2, \ldots, r_n \rangle$, which is then served by the optimal algorithm. As we shall see, however, the actual request locations in the adversary's strategy do not matter. What is important is the time (if ever) that a location is subsequently accessed. Thus, we shall adopt a representation for the adversary's strategy in which the adversary directly specifies for each time step which cache slot to use and whether the cache hits or misses.

In order to formalize the notion of a strategy, we first define some terminology. Cache behavior can be described by two sequences. A *slot sequence* $S = \langle s_1, s_2, \ldots, s_n \rangle$ is a sequence of positive integers such that at time $i = 1, \ldots, n$, a request is brought into slot $s_i$. We define $\text{slots}(S) = \{s_1, s_2, \ldots, s_n\}$ to be the set of slots actually referenced in the sequence. Since the adversary gains no advantage by omitting reference to a slot, we assume that $\text{slots}(S) = \{1, \ldots, h\}$, where $h = |\text{slots}(S)|$. An *outcome sequence* $Z = \langle z_1, z_2, \ldots, z_n \rangle$ is a sequence of 0's and 1's such that, for $i = 1, \ldots, n$, the cache hits at time $i$ if and only if $z_i = 1$.

We shall often wish to refer to the last time that a particular slot was used. In particular, we let $\text{prev}(S, i)$ be $p$ if $s_p = s_i$ and $s_i$ does not appear in $\langle s_{p+1}, \ldots, s_{i-1}\rangle$. In other words, $s_p$ is the last occurrence of slot $s_i$ in $\langle s_1, \ldots, s_{i-1}\rangle$. If slot $s_i$ does not appear in $\langle s_1, \ldots, s_{i-1}\rangle$, we let $\text{prev}(S, i) = \infty$. We can now define the notion of a strategy formally.

**Definition 1.** *A **strategy** is a pair $(S, Z)$, where $S$ is a slot sequence and $Z$ is a hit sequence of the same length.*

As discussed in Sect. 3, given any request sequence $R$, the algorithm OPT determines the outcome and the slot to use at each time $i = 1, \ldots, n$. The following theorem shows that a request sequence can also be deduced from a slot sequence and an outcome sequence. Thus, designing an adversarial strategy is essentially equivalent to designing an adversarial request sequence.

**Theorem 2.** *For each strategy $(S, Z)$, a request sequence $R = \langle r_1, \ldots, r_n\rangle$ exists such that*

1. *request $r_i$ is a hit if and only if outcome $z_i = 1$, and*
2. *running $\text{OPT}_{|slots(S)|}$ on request sequence $R$ produces the slot sequence $S$.*

*Proof.* Let $S = \langle s_1, \ldots, s_n\rangle$, $Z = \langle z_1, \ldots, z_n\rangle$, and $h = |\text{slots}(S)|$. We shall show that a request sequence $R = \langle r_1, \ldots, r_n\rangle$ satisfying both conditions exists. We construct request sequence $R$ by the inductive definition:

$$r_i = \begin{cases} i & \text{if } z_i = 0, \\ r_{\text{prev}(S,i)} & \text{if } z_i = 1. \end{cases} \tag{1}$$

The request sequence $R$ is well defined, because the definition of $\text{prev}(S, i)$ depends on $\langle r_1, r_2, \ldots, r_{i-1}\rangle$ only.

We first show that Condition 1 holds. We observe that if $z_i = 0$, then $i$ does not appear in $\langle r_1, \ldots, r_{i-1}\rangle$, and thus $r_i$ is a miss. If $z_i = 1$, then $r_i = r_{\text{prev}(S,i)}$ is a hit, because slot $s_i$ is not used between time $\text{prev}(S, i)$ and time $i$.

We next show that Condition 2 holds. We show that $s_i$ is selected by $\text{OPT}_h$ at any time $i = 1, 2, \ldots, n$.

- If $z_i = 1$, then by Condition 1, $r_i$ is a hit. In this case, $r_i = r_{\text{prev}(S,i)}$, and thus $\text{OPT}_h$ must select $s_{\text{prev}(S,i)}$. But, by the definition of prev, $s_{\text{prev}(S,i)} = s_i$, and therefore $s_i$ is selected.
- If $z_i = 0$, then we shall show that $\text{OPT}_h$ chooses slot $s_i$ to replace. Recall that $s = \text{OPT}_h(T_i, Q_i, r_i)$ if $f_i(T_i[s]) = \max_{1 \leq j \leq k} f_i(T_i[j])$, where the $T_i$ are cache states and the $Q_i$ are control states (both defined in Sect. 3). If we can show that $f_i(T_i[s_i]) = \infty$, that is, that location $T_i[s_i]$ does not appear in $\langle r_{i+1}, \ldots, r_n\rangle$, then $\text{OPT}_h$ is free to choose $s = s_i$.
  First, if $T_i[s_i] = 0$ (the slot content is invalid), then by definition of (1), $r_i \neq 0$ for all $i$. Therefore, $T_i[s_i]$ does not appear in $\langle r_{i+1}, \ldots, r_n\rangle$.
  Otherwise, if $T_i[s_i] \neq 0$, we show that $T_i[s_i] \neq r_j$ for $j = i + 1, \ldots, n$:
  - If $z_j = 0$, then $r_j = j \neq T_i[s_i]$, because $T_i[s_i] = r_{\text{prev}(S,i)} < i < j$.

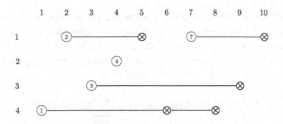

**Fig. 4.** A diagram of the strategy $(S, Z)$, where $S = \langle 4, 1, 3, 2, 1, 4, 1, 4, 3, 1 \rangle$ and $Z = \langle 0, 0, 0, 0, 1, 1, 0, 1, 1, 1 \rangle$. Time runs from left to right, and slot number from top to bottom. Cache hits are represented by $\otimes$; cache misses are represented by $\bigcirc$. The request sequence $\text{req}(S, Z) = \langle 1, 2, 3, 4, 2, 1, 7, 1, 3, 7 \rangle$ for the strategy is illustrated for a miss by the value in the corresponding circle and for a hit by the value in the miss circle at the start of the chain.

- If $z_j = 1$, there are two cases:
    • If $s_j \neq s_i$, then $r_j \neq T_i[s_i]$, because each location stays in one cache slot only.
    • If $s_j = s_i$, then $\text{prev}(S, j) \geq i$. But $T_i[s_i] = r_{\text{prev}(S,i)} < i$, and thus $r_j \neq T_i[s_i]$.
  Since $r_j \neq T_i[s_i]$ for $j = i + 1, \ldots, n$, location $T_i[s_i]$ does not appear in $\langle r_{i+1}, \ldots, r_n \rangle$. $\qquad\square$

We define the **request sequence** of a strategy $(S, Z)$, denoted $\text{req}(S, Z)$, to be the request sequence $R$ provided by (1) of Theorem 2. An example of a strategy for a 4-slot cache is depicted in Fig. 4.

## 5   Analysis of RAND

In this section, we derive a new lower bound on the expected number of hits of RAND on a request sequence. Specifically, we show that for any request sequence $R$ with inherent hit rate $\alpha$ by $\text{OPT}_h$, the expected hit rate of $\text{RAND}_k$ is at least $\alpha e^{-(h-1)/(k-1)\alpha}$. In this extended abstract, the proofs have been omitted.

We first outline our plan of proving the lower bound. Any request sequence $R$ has a corresponding optimal strategy $(S, Z)$ by the off-line algorithm $\text{OPT}_h$. According to the outcome sequence $Z$, every request in $R$ is either an inherent hit or an inherent miss. We can assume that the on-line algorithm $\text{RAND}_k$ cannot hit on any inherent misses, because an adversary can, and should, request never-seen-before locations at the inherent misses. On the other hand, $\text{RAND}_k$, as a randomized algorithm, should have some chance of hitting on the inherent hits. Our goal is to establish a lower bound for the sum of these probabilities.

Our first step is to derive a bound on the expected number of hits by RAND on the inherent hits of a single slot. That is, each inherent hit at time $i = 1, \ldots, n$, is served by a slot $s_i \in \text{slots}(S)$. We focus on one of these slots. We shall later derive bounds for the whole strategy based on these single-slot results.

**Lemma 3.** *Let $(S, Z)$ be an optimal strategy on a request sequence $R$ with $U$ inherent hits and $V$ inherent misses. Consider any slot $s \in slots(S)$ having $u$ inherent hits and $v$ inherent misses. Let $t_1, \ldots, t_u$ be the times at which the $u$ inherent hits of slot $s$ occur. Then, there exist nonnegative integers $m_1, m_2, \ldots, m_u$ satisfying $\sum_{i=1}^{u} m_i \leq U + V - u - v$, such that*

$$\sum_{i=1}^{u} \Pr\{hit(\mathsf{RAND}_k, r_{t_i})\} \geq \sum_{i=1}^{u} (1 - 1/k)^{m_i}. \tag{2}$$

We next present a technical lemma providing a lower bound for the right-hand side of (2). We show that an expression of the form $\sum_{i=1}^{u} \gamma^{m_i}$, with a constraint on the $\sum m_i$, is minimized when the $m_i$'s are evenly distributed.

**Lemma 4.** *Let $m_1, m_2, \ldots, m_u$ be nonnegative real numbers satisfying $\sum_{i=1}^{u} m_i \leq M$ for some nonnegative real number $M$. Then, for any real number $\gamma \in (0, 1)$, we have $\sum_{i=1}^{u} \gamma^{m_i} \geq u\gamma^{M/u}$.*

Equipped with Lemmas 3 and 4 on the expected hit rate of $\mathsf{RAND}_k$ for a single slot, we can now consider all the slots of a strategy together. We can do so by summing up $h$ instances of (2), with the constraints that the sum of inherent hits for all the slots equals to the total inherent hits for the entire strategy, and likewise for inherent misses. The following lemma formalizes this argument.

**Lemma 5.** *Let $R$ be a request sequence. Let $(S, Z)$ be the optimal off-line algorithm $\mathsf{OPT}_h$'s strategy on $R$. Let $u_s = |\{t \in \{1, \ldots, n\} \mid s_t = s, z_t = 1\}|$ be the number of inherent hits and $v_s = |\{t \in \{1, \ldots, n\} \mid s_t = s, z_t = 0\}|$ be the number of inherent misses for each slot $s \in slots(S)$. Let $U = \sum_{s=1}^{h} u_s$ be the total number of inherent hits and $V = \sum_{s=1}^{h} v_s$ be the total number of inherent misses. Then, we have*

$$E[hit(\mathsf{RAND}_k, R)] \geq \sum_{s=1}^{h} u_s (1 - 1/k)^{(U+V-u_s-v_s)/u_s}. \tag{3}$$

We now derive a lower bound for the right-hand side of (3) under the constraints $\sum_{s=1}^{h} u_s = U$ and $\sum_{s=1}^{h} v_s = V$.

**Lemma 6.** *Let $h \geq 1$ be an integer and $\gamma \in (0, 1)$ be a real number, For any real numbers $u_1, u_2, \ldots, u_h$ satisfying $\sum_{s=1}^{h} u_s = U$, and real numbers $v_1, v_2, \ldots, v_h$ satisfying $\sum_{s=1}^{h} v_s = V$, we have*

$$\sum_{s=1}^{h} u_s \gamma^{(U+V-u_s-v_s)/u_s} \geq U\gamma^{(h-1)(U+V)/U}. \tag{4}$$

Finally, armed with Lemmas 5 and 6, we are ready to prove our main theorem, which gives a lower bound for the expected hit rate of $\mathsf{RAND}_k$ on the entire request sequence.

**Theorem 7.** *Let $h \geq 1$ and $k \geq 2$ be integers. Let $\alpha \in [0, 1]$ be a real number. For any request sequence $R$ of length $n$ such that $hit(\mathsf{OPT}_h, R)/n \geq \alpha$, we have*

$$E[hit(\mathsf{RAND}_k, R)]/n \geq \alpha e^{-(h-1)/(k-1)\alpha}. \tag{5}$$

# 6    Conclusions

The contributions of this paper are, first, a new framework for describing the oblivious adversary strategy (Sect. 4) and, secondly, a competitive analysis conditioned on the inherent hit rate of a request sequence (Sect. 5). The analysis we have developed gives better numerical miss-rate bounds than all previously known results for sequences with inherent miss rates larger than 10%. Our ratio is the first competitive bound of an on-line algorithm that does not deteriorate with increasing cache size. This result answers the question posed by Young [25] that whether "we can effectively show constant competitiveness (independent of cache size) for any on-line paging strategy." In addition, we note that this is the first result to remain valid when the on-line cache is smaller than the oblivious adversary's off-line cache. We predict that the competitive ratio derived in Sect. 5 can be further improved. In the proof of Theorem 7, we assumed cautiously that RAND always misses on the inherent hits. When the inherent miss rate is low, however, RAND has a reasonably low probability of missing the inherent hits. A proper utilization of this information might lead to a stronger bound of the expected total number of hits. We are currently pursuing this line of research.

Finally, we are hopeful that the techniques presented in this thesis can be applied to analyses of other on-line algorithms and be generalized to other on-line computational models, such as $k$-servers [19,17,18,20,13,9] and metrical task systems [6].

# References

[1]  D. Achlioptas, M. Chrobak, and J. Noga. Competitive analysis of randomized paging algorithms. In *Annual European Symposium on Algorithms*, 1996.

[2]  L. A. Belady. A study of replacement algorithms for virtual storage computers. *IBM Systems Journal*, 5(2):78–101, 1966.

[3]  S. Ben-David and A. Borodin. A new measure for the study of on-line algorithms. *Algorithmica*, 11:73–91, 1994.

[4]  Allan Borodin and Ran El-Yaniv. *Online Computation and Competitive Analysis*. Cambridge University Press, 1998.

[5]  Allan Borodin, Sandy Irani, Prabhakar Raghavan, and Baruch Schieber. Competitive paging with locality of reference. *Journal of Computer and System Sciences*, 50(2):244–258, April 1995.

[6]  Allan Borodin, Nathan Linial, and Michael E. Saks. An optimal on-line algorithm for metrical task system. *Journal of the ACM*, 39(4):745–763, October 1992.

[7]  Edward G. Coffman, Jr and Peter J. Denning. *Operating Systems Theory*. Prentice Hall, 1973.

[8]  E. Dichterman. Randomized paging algorithms and measures for their performance. Technical Report 692, Israel Institute of Technology, Haifa, Israel, October 1991.

[9]  A. Fiat, Y. Rabani, and Y. Ravid. Competitive $k$-server algorithms. In *31st Annual Symposium on Foundations of Computer Science*, pages 454–463, 1990.

[10]  Amos Fiat and Anna R. Karlin. Randomized and multipointer paging with locality of reference. In *Proceedings of the Twenty-Seventh Annual ACM Symposium on the Theory of Computing*, pages 626–634, Las Vegas, Nevada, 29 May–1 June 1995.

[11] Amos Fiat, Richard M. Karp, Michael Luby, Lyle A. McGeoch, Daniel D. Sleator, and Neal E. Young. Competitive paging algorithms. *Journal of Algorithms*, 12(4):685–699, December 1991.

[12] Michel X. Goemans. Advanced algorithms lecture notes. September 1994.

[13] E. F. Grove. The harmonic online K-server algorithm is competitive. In Lyle A. McGeoch and Daniel D. Sleator, editors, *On-line Algorithms*, volume 7 of *DIMACS Series in Discrete Mathematics and Theoretical Computer Science*, pages 65–77. AMS/ACM, February 1991.

[14] Sandy Irani, Anna R. Karlin, and Steven Phillips. Strongly competitive algorithms for paging with locality of reference. *SIAM Journal on Computing*, 25(3):477–497, June 1996.

[15] Anna R. Karlin, Mark S. Manasse, Larry Rudolph, and Daniel Dominic Sleator. Competitive snoopy caching. *Algorithmica*, 3:77–119, 1988.

[16] Elias Koutsoupias and Christos H. Papadimitriou. Beyond competitive analysis. In *35th Annual Symposium on Foundations of Computer Science*, pages 394–400, Santa Fe, New Mexico, 20–22 November 1994. IEEE.

[17] Elias Koutsoupias and Christos H. Papadimitriou. On the $k$-server conjecture. *Journal of the ACM*, 42(5):971–983, September 1995.

[18] Elias Koutsoupias and Christos H. Papadimitriou. The 2-evader problem. *Information Processing Letters*, 57(5):249–252, 11 March 1996.

[19] Mark S. Manasse, Lyle A. McGeoch, and Daniel D. Sleator. Competitive algorithms for on-line problems. In *Proceedings of the Twentieth Annual ACM Symposium on Theory of Computing*, pages 322–333, Chicago, Illinois, 2–4 May 1988.

[20] Lyle A. McGeoch. *Algorithms for Two Graph Problems: Computing Maximum-Genus Imbeddings and the Two-Server Problem*. PhD thesis, Carnegie Mellon University, Pittsburgh, 1987.

[21] Lyle A. McGeoch and Daniel D. Sleator. A strongly competitive randomized paging algorithm. *Algorithmica*, 6:816–825, 1991.

[22] Prabhakar Raghavan and Marc Snir. Memory versus randomization in on-line algorithms. *IBM Journal of Research and Development*, 38(6):683–707, November 1994.

[23] Daniel D. Sleator and Robert E. Tarjan. Amortized efficiency of list update and paging rules. *Communications of the ACM*, 28(2):202–208, February 1985.

[24] Eric Torng. A unified analysis of paging and caching. In *36th Annual Symposium on Foundations of Computer Science*, pages 194–203, Milwaukee, Wisconsin, 23–25 October 1995. IEEE.

[25] Neal E. Young. On-line caching as cache size varies. In *Proceedings of the Second Annual ACM-SIAM Symposium on Discrete Algorithms*, pages 241–250, San Francisco, California, 28–30 January 1991.

[26] Neal E. Young. The $k$-server dual and loose competitiveness for paging. *Algorithmica*, 11(6):525–541, June 1994.

[27] Neal E. Young. On-line file caching. In *Proceedings of the 9th Annual ACM-SIAM Symposium on Discrete Algorithms (SODA-98)*, pages 82–86, New York, January 25–27 1998. ACM Press.

# Online Routing in Convex Subdivisions*

Prosenjit Bose[1], Andrej Brodnik[2], Svante Carlsson[3], Erik D. Demaine[4],
Rudolf Fleischer[4], Alejandro López-Ortiz[5], Pat Morin[1], and J. Ian Munro[4]

[1] School of Computer Science, Carleton University,
1125 Colonel By Dr., Ottawa, Ontario, Canada, K1S 5B6,
{jit,morin}@scs.carleton.ca
[2] IMFM, University of Ljubljana,
Jadranska 11, SI-1111 Ljubljana, Slovenia
Andrej.Brodnik@IMFM.Uni-Lj.SI
[3] University of Karlskona/Ronneby,
371 41 KARLSKRONA, Sweden,
svante.carlsson@sm.luth.se
[4] Department of Computer Science, University of Waterloo,
Waterloo, Ontario, Canada, N2L 3G1,
{eddemain,rudolf,imunro}@uwaterloo.ca
[5] Faculty of Computer Science, University of New Brunswick,
Fredericton, New Brunswick, Canada, E3B 4A1,
alopez-o@unb.ca

**Abstract.** We consider online routing algorithms for finding paths between the vertices of plane graphs. We show (1) there exists a routing algorithm for arbitrary triangulations that has no memory and uses no randomization, (2) no equivalent result is possible for convex subdivisions, (3) there is no competitive online routing algorithm under the Euclidean distance metric in arbitrary triangulations, and (4) there is no competitive online routing algorithm under the link distance metric even when the input graph is restricted to be a Delaunay, greedy, or minimum-weight triangulation.

## 1  Introduction

Path finding, or routing, is central to a number of fields including geographic information systems, urban planning, robotics, and communication networks. In many cases, knowledge about the environment in which routing takes place is not available beforehand, and the vehicle/robot/packet must learn this information through exploration. Algorithms for routing in these types of environments are referred to as *online* [2] routing algorithms.

In this paper we consider online routing in the following abstract setting [3]: The environment is a plane graph, $G$ (i.e., the planar embedding of $G$) with

---

* This research was partly funded by the Natural Sciences and Engineering Research Council of Canada.

D.T. Lee and S.-H. Teng (Eds.): ISAAC 2000, LNCS 1969, pp. 47–59, 2000.

$n$ vertices. The source $s$ and destination $t$ are vertices of $G$, and a packet can only travel on edges of $G$. Initially, a packet only knows the coordinates of $s$, $t$, and $N(s)$, where $N(v)$ denotes the set of vertices adjacent to a node $v$. When a packet visits a node $v$, it learns the coordinates of $N(v)$.

Bose and Morin [3] classify routing algorithms based on their use of memory and/or randomization. A deterministic routing algorithm is *memoryless* or *oblivious* if, given a packet currently at vertex $v$ and destined for node $t$, the algorithm decides where to forward the packet based only on the coordinates of $v$, $t$ and $N(v)$. A randomized algorithm is oblivious if it decides where to move a packet based only on the coordinates of $v$, $t$, $N(v)$, and the output of a random oracle. An algorithm $\mathcal{A}$ is *defeated* by a graph $G$ if there exists a pair of vertices $s, t \in G$ such that a packet stored at $s$ will never reach $t$ when being routed using $\mathcal{A}$. Otherwise, we say that $\mathcal{A}$ *works* for $G$.

Let $\mathcal{A}(G, s, t)$ denote the length of the walk taken by routing algorithm $\mathcal{A}$ when travelling from vertex $s$ to vertex $t$ of $G$, and let $SP(G, s, t)$ denote the length of the shortest path between $s$ and $t$. We say that $\mathcal{A}$ is *c-competitive* for a class of graphs $\mathcal{G}$ if

$$\frac{\mathcal{A}(G, s, t)}{SP(G, s, t)} \leq c$$

for all graphs $G \in \mathcal{G}$ and all $s, t \in G$, $s \neq t$. We say that $\mathcal{A}$ is simply *competitive* if $\mathcal{A}$ is $c$-competitive for some constant $c$.

Recently, several papers have dealt with online routing and related problems in geometric settings. Kalyanasundaram and Pruhs [7] give a 16-competitive algorithm to *explore* any unknown plane graph, i.e., visit all of its nodes. This online exploration problem makes the same assumptions as those made here, but the goal of the problem is to visit all vertices of $G$, not just $t$. This difference leads to inherently different solutions.

Kranakis *et al.* [8] give a deterministic oblivious routing algorithm that works for any Delaunay triangulation, and give a deterministic non-oblivious algorithm that works for any connected plane graph.

Bose and Morin [3] also study online routing in geometric settings, particularly triangulations. They give a randomized oblivious routing algorithm that works for any triangulation, and ask whether there is a deterministic oblivious routing algorithm for all triangulations. They also give a competitive non-oblivious routing algorithm for Delaunay triangulations.

Cucka et al. [5] experimentally evaluate the performance of routing algorithms very similar to those described by Kranakis *et al.* [8] and Bose and Morin [3]. When considering the Euclidean distance travelled during point-to-point routing, their results show that the GREEDY routing algorithm [3] performs better than the COMPASS routing algorithm [3,8] on random graphs, but does not do as well on Delaunay triangulations of random point sets.[1] However, when one considers not the Euclidean distance, but the number of edges traversed (link

---

[1] Cucka *et al.* call these algorithms P-DFS and D-DFS, respectively.

distance), then the COMPASS routing algorithm is slightly more efficient for both random graphs and Delaunay triangulations.

In this paper we present a number of new fundamental theoretical results that help further the understanding of online routing in plane graphs.

1. We give a deterministic oblivious routing algorithm for all triangulations, solving the open problem posed by Bose and Morin [3].
2. We prove that no deterministic oblivious routing algorithm works for all convex subdivisions, showing some limitations of deterministic oblivious routing algorithms.
3. We prove that the randomized oblivious routing algorithm RANDOM-COMPASS described by Bose and Morin [3] works for any convex subdivision.
4. We show that, under the Euclidean metric, no routing algorithm exists that is competitive for all triangulations, and under the link distance metric, no routing algorithm exists that is competitive for all Delaunay, greedy, or minimum-weight triangulations.

The remainder of the paper is organized as follows: In Section 2 we give our deterministic oblivious algorithm for routing in triangulations. Section 3 presents our results for routing in convex subdivisions. Section 4 describes our impossibility results for competitive algorithms. Finally, Section 5 summarizes and concludes with open problems.

## 2   Oblivious Routing in Triangulations

A *triangulation* $T$ is a plane graph for which every face is a triangle, except the outer face, which is the complement of a convex polygon. In this section we describe a deterministic oblivious routing algorithm that works for all triangulations.

We use the notation $\angle a, b, c$ to denote the angle formed by $a$ $b$ and $c$ as measured in the counterclockwise direction. Let $cw(v)$ be the vertex in $N(v)$ which minimizes the angle $\angle cw(v), v, t$ and let $ccw(v)$ be the vertex in $N(v)$ which minimizes the angle $\angle t, v, ccw(v)$. If $v$ has a neighbour $w$ on the line segment $(v, t)$, then $cw(v) = ccw(v) = w$. In particular, the vertex $t$ is contained in the wedge $cw(v), v, ccw(v)$. Refer to Fig. 1 for an illustration.

The GREEDY-COMPASS algorithm always moves to the vertex among $\{cw(v), ccw(v)\}$ that minimizes the distance to $t$. If the two distances are equal, or if $cw(v) = ccw(v)$, then GREEDY-COMPASS chooses one of $\{cw(v), ccw(v)\}$ arbitrarily.

**Theorem 1** *Algorithm* GREEDY-COMPASS *works for any triangulation.*

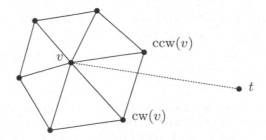

**Fig. 1.** Definition of cw($v$) and ccw($v$).

*Proof.* Suppose, by way of contradiction that a triangulation $T$ and a pair of vertices $s$ and $t$ exist such that GREEDY-COMPASS does not find a path from $s$ to $t$.

In this case there must be a cycle of vertices $C = \langle v_0, \ldots, v_{k-1} \rangle$ of $T$ such that GREEDY-COMPASS moves from $v_i$ to $v_{i+1}$ for all $0 \le i \le k$, i.e., GREEDY-COMPASS gets trapped cycling through the vertices of $C$ (see also Lemma 1 of [3]).[2] Furthermore, it follows from Lemma 2 of [3] that the destination $t$ is contained in the interior of $C$.

**Claim 1** *All vertices of $C$ must lie on the boundary of a disk $D$ centered at $t$.*

*Proof (Proof (of claim)).* Suppose, by way of contradiction, that there is no such disk $D$. Then let $D$ be the disk centered at $t$ and having the furthest vertex of $C$ from $t$ on its boundary. Consider a vertex $v_i$ in the interior of $D$ such that $v_{i+1}$ is on the boundary of $D$. (Refer to Fig. 2.) Assume, w.l.o.g., that $v_{i+1} = \text{ccw}(v_i)$. Then it must be that $\text{cw}(v_i)$ is not in the interior of $D$, otherwise GREEDY-COMPASS would not have moved to $v_{i+1}$. But then the edge $(\text{cw}(v_i), \text{ccw}(v_i))$ cuts $D$ into two regions, $R_1$ containing $v_i$ and $R_2$ containing $t$. Since $C$ passes through both $R_1$ and $R_2$ and is contained in $D$ then it must be that $C$ enters region $R_1$ at $\text{cw}(v_i)$ and leaves $R_1$ at $v_{i+1} = \text{ccw}(v_i)$. However, this cannot happen because both $\text{cw}(\text{cw}(v_i))$ and $\text{ccw}(\text{cw}(v_i))$ are contained in the halfspace bounded by the supporting line of $(\text{cw}(v_i), \text{ccw}(v_i))$ and containing $t$, and are therefore not contained in $R_1$.

Thus, we have established that all vertices of $C$ are on the boundary of $D$. However, since $C$ contains $t$ in its interior and the triangulation $T$ is connected, it must be that for some vertex $v_j$ of $C$, $\text{cw}(v_j)$ or $\text{ccw}(v_j)$ is in the interior of $D$. Suppose that it is $\text{cw}(v_j)$. But then we have a contradiction, since the GREEDY-COMPASS algorithm would have gone to $\text{cw}(v_j)$ rather than $v_{j+1}$.

---

[2] Here, and in the remainder of this proof, all subscripts are taken mod $k$.

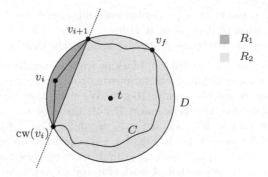

**Fig. 2.** The proof of Theorem 1.

## 3    Oblivious Routing in Convex Subdivisions

A *convex subdivision* is an embedded plane graph such that each face of the graph is a convex polygon, except the outer face which is the complement of a convex polygon. Triangulations are a special case of convex subdivisions in which each face is a triangle; thus it is natural to ask whether the GREEDY-COMPASS algorithm can be generalized to convex subdivisions. In this section, we show that there is no deterministic oblivious routing algorithm for convex subdivisions. However, there is a randomized oblivious routing algorithm that uses only one random bit per step.

### 3.1    Deterministic Algorithms

**Theorem 2** *Every deterministic oblivious routing algorithm is defeated by some convex subdivision.*

*Proof.* We exhibit a finite collection of convex subdivisions such that any deterministic oblivious routing algorithm is defeated by at least one of them.

There are 17 vertices that are common to all of our subdivisions. The destination vertex $t$ is located at the origin. The other 16 vertices $V = \{v_0, \ldots, v_{15}\}$ are the vertices of a regular 16-gon centered at the origin and listed in counterclockwise order.[3] In all our subdivisions, the even-numbered vertices $v_0, v_2, \ldots, v_{14}$ have degree 2. The degree of the other vertices varies. All of our subdivisions contain the edges of the regular 16-gon.

Assume, by way of contradiction, that there exists a routing algorithm $\mathcal{A}$ that works for any convex subdivision. Since the even-numbered vertices in our subdivisions always have the same two neighbours in all subdivisions, $\mathcal{A}$ always

---

[3] In the remainder of this proof, all subscripts are implicitly taken mod 16.

makes the same decision at a particular even-numbered vertex. Thus, it makes sense to ask what $\mathcal{A}$ does when it visits an even-numbered vertex, without knowing anything else about the particular subdivision that $\mathcal{A}$ is routing on.

For each vertex $v_i \in V$, we color $v_i$ black or white depending on the action of $\mathcal{A}$ upon visiting $v_i$, specifically, black for moving counterclockwise and white for moving clockwise around the regular 16-gon. We claim that all even-numbered vertices in $V$ must have the same color. If not, then there exists two vertices $v_i$ and $v_{i+2}$ such that $v_i$ is black and $v_{i+2}$ is white. Then, if we take $s = v_i$ in the convex subdivision shown in Fig. 3.a, the algorithm becomes trapped on one of the edges $(v_i, v_{i+1})$ or $(v_{i+1}, v_{i+2})$ and never reaches the destination $t$, contradicting the assumption that $\mathcal{A}$ works for any convex subdivision.

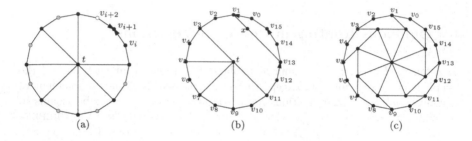

**Fig. 3.** The proof of Theorem 2.

Therefore, assume w.l.o.g. that all even-numbered vertices of $V$ are black, and consider the convex subdivision shown in Fig. 3.b. From this figure it is clear that, if we take $s = v_1$, $\mathcal{A}$ cannot visit $x$ after $v_1$, since then it gets trapped among the vertices $\{v_{12}, v_{13}, v_{14}, v_{15}, v_0, v_1, x\}$ and never reaches $t$.

Note that we can rotate Fig. 3.b by integral multiples of $\pi/4$ while leaving the vertex labels in place and make similar arguments for $v_3$, $v_5$, $v_7$, $v_9$, $v_{11}$, $v_{13}$ and $v_{15}$. However, this implies that $\mathcal{A}$ is defeated by the convex subdivision shown in Fig. 3.c since if it begins at any vertex of the regular 16-gon, it never enters the interior of the 16-gon. We conclude that no oblivious online routing algorithm works for all convex subdivisions.

We note that, although our proof uses subdivisions in which some of the faces are not strictly convex (i.e., have vertices with interior angle $\pi$), it is possible to modify the proof to use only strictly convex subdivisions, but doing so leads to more cluttered diagrams.

## 3.2   Randomized Algorithms

Bose and Morin [3] describe the RANDOM-COMPASS algorithm and show that
it works for any triangulation. For a packet stored at node $v$, the RANDOM-
COMPASS algorithm selects a vertex from $\{\mathrm{cw}(v), \mathrm{ccw}(v)\}$ uniformly at random
and moves to it. In this section we show that RANDOM-COMPASS works for any
convex subdivision.

Although it is well known that a random walk on any graph $G$ will eventually
visit all vertices of $G$, the RANDOM-COMPASS algorithm has two advantages over
a random walk. The first advantage is that the RANDOM-COMPASS algorithm is
more efficient in its use of randomization than a random walk. It requires only
one random bit per step, whereas a random walk requires $\log k$ random bits for
a vertex of degree $k$. The second advantage is that the RANDOM-COMPASS algorithm makes use of geometry to guide it, and the result is that RANDOM-COMPASS
generally arrives at $t$ much more quickly than a random walk. Nevertheless, it
can be helpful to think of RANDOM-COMPASS as a random walk on a directed
graph in which every node has out-degree 1 or 2 except for $t$ which is a sink.

Before we can make statements about which graphs defeat RANDOM-COMPASS,
we must define what it means for a graph to defeat a randomized algorithm. We
say that a graph $G$ defeats a (randomized) routing algorithm if there exists a
pair of vertices $s$ and $t$ of $G$ such that a packet originating at $s$ with destination
$t$ has probability 0 of reaching $t$ in any finite number of steps. Note that, for
oblivious algorithms, proving that a graph does not defeat an algorithm implies
that the algorithm will reach its destination with probability 1.

**Theorem 3** *Algorithm* RANDOM-COMPASS *works for any convex subdivision.*

*Proof.* Assume, by way of contradiction, that there is a convex subdivision $G$
with two vertices $s$ and $t$ such that the probability of reaching $s$ from $t$ using
RANDOM-COMPASS is 0. Then there is a subgraph $H$ of $G$ containing $s$, but not
containing $t$, such that for all vertices $v \in H$, $\mathrm{cw}(v) \in H$ and $\mathrm{ccw}(v) \in H$.

The vertex $t$ is contained in some face $f$ of $H$. We claim that this face must
be convex. For the sake of contradiction, assume otherwise. Then there is a reflex
vertex $v$ on the boundary of $f$ such that the line segment $(t, v)$ does not intersect
any edge of $H$. However, this cannot happen, since $\mathrm{ccw}(v)$ and $\mathrm{cw}(v)$ are in $H$,
and hence $v$ would not be reflex.

Since $G$ is connected, it must be that for some vertex $u$ on the boundary
of $f$, $\mathrm{cw}(u)$ or $\mathrm{ccw}(u)$ is contained in the interior of $f$. But this vertex in the
interior of $f$ is also in $H$, contradicting the fact that $f$ is a convex face of $H$. We
conclude that there is no convex subdivision that defeats RANDOM-COMPASS.

# 4    Competitive Routing Algorithms

If we are willing to accept more sophisticated routing algorithms that make use of memory, then it is sometimes possible to find competitive routing algorithms. Bose and Morin [3] give a competitive algorithm for Delaunay triangulations under the Euclidean distance metric. Two questions arise from this: (1) Can this result be generalized to arbitrary triangulations? and (2) Can this result be duplicated for the link distance metric? In this section we show that the answer to both these questions is negative.

## 4.1    Euclidean Distance

In this section we show that, under the Euclidean metric, no deterministic routing algorithm is $o(\sqrt{n})$-competitive for all triangulations. Our proof is a modification of that used by Papadimitriou and Yannakakis [9] to show that no online algorithm for finding a destination point among $n$ axis-oriented rectangular obstacles in the plane is $o(\sqrt{n})$-competitive.

**Theorem 4** *Under the Euclidean distance metric, no deterministic routing algorithm is $o(\sqrt{n})$ competitive for all triangulations.*

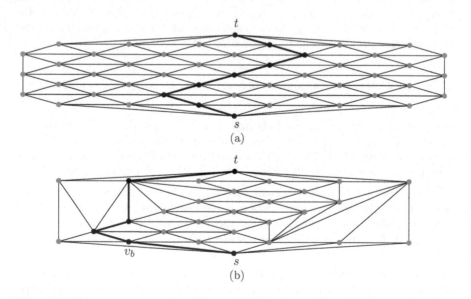

**Fig. 4.** (a) The triangulation $T$ with the path found by $\mathcal{A}$ indicated. (b) The resulting triangulation $T'$ with the "almost-vertical" path shown in bold.

*Proof.* Consider an $n \times n$ hexagonal lattice with the following modifications. The lattice has had its $x$-coordinates scaled so that each edge is of length $\Theta(n)$. The lattice also has two additional vertices, $s$ and $t$, centered horizontally, at one unit below the bottom row and one unit above the top row, respectively. Finally, all vertices of the lattice and $s$ and $t$ have been completed to a triangulation $T$. See Fig. 4.a for an illustration.

Let $\mathcal{A}$ be any deterministic routing algorithm and observe the actions of $\mathcal{A}$ as it routes from $s$ to $t$. In particular, consider the first $n + 1$ steps taken by $\mathcal{A}$ as it routes from $s$ to $t$. Then $\mathcal{A}$ visits at most $n + 1$ vertices of $T$, and these vertices induce a subgraph $T_{\mathrm{vis}}$ consisting of all vertices visited by $\mathcal{A}$ and all edges adjacent to these vertices.

For any vertex $v$ of $T$ not equal to $s$ or $t$, define the *x-span* of $v$ as the interval between the rightmost and leftmost $x$-coordinate of $N(v)$. The length of any $x$-span is $\Theta(n)$, and the width of the original triangulation $T$ is $\Theta(n^2)$. This implies that there is some vertex $v_b$ on the bottom row of $T$ whose $x$-coordinate is at most $n\sqrt{n}$ from the $x$-coordinate of $s$ and is contained in $O(\sqrt{n})$ $x$-spans of the vertices visited in the first $n + 1$ steps of $\mathcal{A}$.

We now create the triangulation $T'$ that contains all vertices and edges of $T_{\mathrm{vis}}$. Additionally, $T'$ contains the set of edges forming an "almost vertical" path from $v_b$ to the top row of $T'$. This almost vertical path is a path that is vertical wherever possible, but uses minimal detours to avoid edges of $T_{\mathrm{vis}}$. Since only $O(\sqrt{n})$ detours are required, the length of this path is $O(n\sqrt{n})$. Finally, we complete $T'$ to a triangulation in some arbitrary way that does not increase the degrees of vertices on the first $n + 1$ steps of $\mathcal{A}$. See Fig. 4.b for an example.

Now, since $\mathcal{A}$ is deterministic, the first $n + 1$ steps taken by $\mathcal{A}$ on $T'$ will be the same as the first $n + 1$ steps taken by $\mathcal{A}$ on $T$, and will therefore travel a distance of $\Theta(n^2)$. However, there is a path in $T'$ from $s$ to $t$ that first visits $v_b$ (at a cost of $O(n\sqrt{n})$), then uses the "almost-vertical" path to the top row of $T'$ (at a cost of $O(n\sqrt{n})$) and then travels directly to $t$ (at a cost of $O(n\sqrt{n})$). Thus, the total cost of this path, and hence the shortest path, from $s$ to $t$ is $O(n\sqrt{n})$.

We conclude that $\mathcal{A}$ is not $o(\sqrt{n})$-competitive for $T'$. Since the choice of $\mathcal{A}$ is arbitary, and $T'$ contains $O(n)$ vertices, this implies that no deterministic routing algorithm is $o(\sqrt{n})$ competitive for all triangulations with $n$ vertices.

## 4.2   Link Distance

The link distance metric simply measures the number of edges traversed by a routing algorithm. For many networking applications, this metric is more meaningful than Euclidean distance. In this section we show that competitive algorithms under the link distance metric are harder to come by than under the Euclidean distance metric. Throughout this section we assume that the reader is familiar with the definitions of Delaunay, greedy and minimum-weight triangulations (*cf.* Preparata and Shamos [10]).

We obtain this result by constructing a "bad" family of point sets as follows. Let $C_i$ be the set of $\sqrt{n}$ points $\{(i\sqrt{n}, 1), (i\sqrt{n}, 2), \ldots, (i\sqrt{n}, \sqrt{n})\}$. We call $C_i$ the *ith column*. Let $D_i = \{(i\sqrt{n}, 1), (i\sqrt{n}, \sqrt{n})\}$, and define a family of point sets $S = \bigcup_{j=1}^{\infty}\{S_{j^2}\}$ where $S_n = \{S_{n,1}, \ldots, S_{n,\sqrt{n}}\}$ and

$$S_{n,i} = \bigcup_{j=1}^{i-1} C_j \cup D_i \cup \bigcup_{j=i+1}^{\sqrt{n}} C_j \cup \{(\sqrt{n}/2, 0), (\sqrt{n}/2, \sqrt{n}+1)\} \qquad (1)$$

Two members of the set $S_{49}$ are shown in Fig. 5.

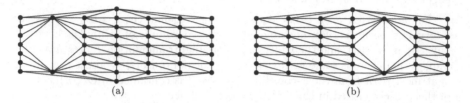

(a)                                           (b)

**Fig. 5.** The point sets (a) $S_{49,2}$ and (b) $S_{49,5}$ along with their Delaunay triangulations.

**Theorem 5** *Under the link distance metric, no routing algorithm is $o(\sqrt{n})$-competitive for all Delaunay triangulations.*

*Proof.* We use the notation $DT(S_{n,i})$ to denote the Delaunay triangulation of $S_{n,i}$. Although the Delaunay triangulation of $S_{n,i}$ is not unique, we will assume $DT(S_{n,i})$ is triangulated as in Fig. 5. Note that, in $DT(S_{n,i})$, the shortest path between the topmost vertex $s$ and bottom-most vertex $t$ is of length 3, independent of $n$ and $i$. Furthermore, any path from $s$ to $t$ whose length is less than $\sqrt{n}$ must visit vertices from one of the columns $C_{i-1}$, $C_i$, or $C_{i+1}$.

The rest of the proof is based on the following observation: If we choose an element $i$ uniformly at random from $\{1, \ldots, \sqrt{n}\}$, then the probability that a routing algorithm $\mathcal{A}$ has visited a vertex of $C_{i-1}$, $C_i$, or $C_{i+1}$ after $k$ steps is at most $3k/\sqrt{n}$. Letting $k = \sqrt{n}/6$, we see that the probability that $\mathcal{A}$ visits a vertex of $C_{i-1}$, $C_i$, or $C_{i+1}$ after $\sqrt{n}/6$ steps is at most $1/2$.

Letting $d_i$ denote the (expected, in the case of randomized algorithms) number of steps when routing from $s$ to $t$ in $S_{n,i}$ using routing algorithm $\mathcal{A}$, we have

$$\frac{1}{\sqrt{n}} \cdot \sum_{i=1}^{\sqrt{n}} d_i \geq \sqrt{n}/12 . \qquad (2)$$

Since, for any $S_{n,i}$, the shortest path from $s$ to $t$ is 3 there must be some $i$ for which the competitive ratio of $\mathcal{A}$ for $S_{n,i}$ is at least $\sqrt{n}/36 \in \Omega(\sqrt{n})$.

**Theorem 6** *Under the link distance metric, no routing algorithm is $o(\sqrt{n})$-competitive for all greedy triangulations.*

*Proof.* This follows immediately from the observation that for any $S_{n,i}$, a Delaunay triangulation of $S_{n,i}$ is also a greedy triangulation of $S_{n,i}$.

**Theorem 7** *Under the link distance metric, no routing algorithm is $o(\sqrt{n})$-competitive for all minimum-weight triangulations.*

*Proof.* We claim that for members of $S$, any greedy triangulation is also a minimum-weight triangulation. To prove this, we use a result on minimum-weight triangulations due to Aichholzer *et al.* [1]. Let $K_{n,i}$ be the complete graph on $S_{n,i}$. Then an edge $e$ of $K_{n,i}$ is said to be a *light edge* if every edge of $K_{n,i}$ that crosses $e$ is not shorter than $e$. Aichholzer *et al.* prove that if the set of light edges contains the edges of a triangulation then that triangulation is a minimum-weight triangulation.

There are only 5 different types of edges in the greedy triangulation of $S_{n,i}$: (1) vertical edges within a column, (2) horizonal edges between adjacent columns, (3) diagonal edges between adjacent columns, (4) edges used to triangulate column $i$, and (5) edges used to join $s$ and $t$ to the rest of the graph. It is straightforward to verify that all of these types of edges are indeed light edges.

## 5 Conclusions

We have presented a number of results concerning online routing in plane graphs. Table 1 summarizes what is currently known about online routing in plane graphs. An arrow in a reference indicates that the result is implied by the more general result pointed to by the arrow. An F indicates that the result is trivial and/or folklore.

**Table 1.** A summary of known results for online routing in plane graphs.

| Class of graphs | Deterministic oblivious | | Randomized oblivious[4] | | Euclidean competitive | | Link competitive | |
|---|---|---|---|---|---|---|---|---|
| DT | Yes | [3,8, ↓] | Yes | [←] | Yes | [3] | No | [here] |
| GT/MWT | Yes | [↓] | Yes | [↓] | Yes | [4] | No | [here] |
| Triangulations | Yes | [here] | Yes | [3, ←] | No | [here] | No | [↑] |
| Conv. Subdv. | No | [here] | Yes | [here] | No | [↑] | No | [↑] |
| Plane graphs | No | [F] | No | [F] | No | [F] | No | [F] |

---

[4] In this column, we consider only algorithms that use a constant number of random bits per step. Otherwise, it is well known that a random walk on any graph $G$ will eventually visit all vertices of $G$.

We have also implemented a simulation of the GREEDY-COMPASS algorithm as well as the algorithms described by Bose and Morin [3] and compared them under the Euclidean distance metric. These results will be presented in the full version of the paper. Here we only summarize our main observations.

For Delaunay triangulations of random point sets, we found that the performance of GREEDY-COMPASS is comparable to that of the COMPASS and GREEDY algorithms [3,5,8]. For triangulations obtained by performing Graham's scan [6] on random point sets, the GREEDY-COMPASS algorithm does significantly better than the COMPASS or GREEDY algorithms.

We also implemented a variant of GREEDY-COMPASS that we call GREEDY-COMPASS-2 that, when located at a vertex $v$, moves to the vertex $u \in \{cw(v), ccw(v)\}$ that minimizes $d(v, u) + d(u, t)$, where $d(a, b)$ denotes the Euclidean distance between $a$ and $b$. Although there are triangulations that defeat GREEDY-COMPASS-2, it worked for all our test triangulations, and in fact seems to be twice as efficient as GREEDY-COMPASS in terms of the Euclidean distance travelled.

We note that currently, under the link distance metric, there are no competitive routing algorithms for any interesting class of geometric graphs (meshes do not count). The reason for this seems to be that the properties used in defining many geometric graphs make use of properties of Euclidean space, and link distance in these graphs is often independent of these properties. We consider it an open problem to find competitive algorithms, under the link distance metric, for an interesting and naturally occuring class of geometric graphs.

**Acknowledgements.** This work was initiated at Schloss Dagstuhl Seminar on Data Structures, held in Wadern, Germany, February–March 2000, and co-organized by Susanne Albers, Ian Munro, and Peter Widmayer. The authors would also like to thank Lars Jacobsen for helpful discussions.

# References

1. O. Aichholzer, F. Aurenhammer, S.-W. Cheng, N. Katoh, G. Rote, M. Taschwer, and Y.-F. Xu. Triangulations intersect nicely. *Discrete and Computational Geometry*, 16(4):339–359, 1996.
2. A. Borodin and R. El-Yaniv. *Online Computation and Competitive Analysis*. Cambridge University Press, 1998.
3. P. Bose and P. Morin. Online routing in triangulations. In *Proceedings of the Tenth International Symposium on Algorithms and Computation (ISAAC'99)*, volume 1741 of *Springer LNCS*, pages 113–122, 1999.
4. P. Bose and P. Morin. Competitive routing algorithms for greedy and minimum-weight triangulations. Manuscript, 2000.
5. P. Cucka, N. S. Netanyahu, and A. Rosenfeld. Learning in navigation: Goal finding in graphs. *International Journal of Pattern Recognition and Artificial Intelligence*, 10(5):429–446, 1996.
6. R. L. Graham. An efficient algorithm for determining the convex hull of a finite planar set. *Information Processing Letters*, 1:132–133, 1972.

7.  B. Kalyanasundaram and K. R. Pruhs. Constructing competitive tours from local information. *Theoretical Computer Science*, 130:125–138, 1994.
8.  E. Kranakis, H. Singh, and J. Urrutia. Compass routing on geometric networks. In *Proceedings of the 11th Canadian Conference on Computational Geometry (CCCG'99)*, 1999.
9.  C. H. Papadimitriou and M. Yannakakis. Shortest paths without a map. *Theoretical Computer Science*, 84:127–150, 1991.
10. F. P. Preparata and M. I. Shamos. *Computational Geometry.* Springer-Verlag, New York, 1985.

# A Simple Linear-Time Approximation Algorithm for Multi-processor Job Scheduling on Four Processors*

Jingui Huang, Jianer Chen**, and Songqiao Chen

College of Information Engineering, Central-South University,
ChangSha, Hunan 410083, P. R. China
hjg@hunnu.edu.cn, {jianer,csq}@mail.csut.edu.cn

**Abstract.** Multiprocessor job scheduling problem has become increasingly interesting, for both theoretical study and practical applications. Theoretical study of the problem has made significant progress recently, which, however, seems not to imply practical algorithms for the problem, yet. Practical algorithms have been developed only for systems with three processors and the techniques seem difficult to extend to systems with more than three processors. This paper offers new observations and introduces new techniques for the multiprocessor job scheduling problem on systems with four processors. A very simple and practical linear time approximation algorithm of ratio bounded by 1.5 is developed for the multi-processor job scheduling problem $P_4|fix|C_{\max}$, which significantly improves previous results. Our techniques are also useful for multiprocessor job scheduling problems on systems with more than four processors.

## 1 Introduction

One of the assumption made in classical scheduling theory is that a job is always executed by one processor at a time. With the advances in parallel algorithms, this assumption may no longer be valid for job systems. For example, in semiconductor circuit design workforce planning, a design project is to be processed by a group of people. The project contains $n$ jobs, and each job is handled by a specific subgroup of people working simultaneously on the job. Note that a person may belong to several different subgroups but he can work for at most one subgroup at a time. Now the question is how we can schedule the jobs so that the project can be finished as early as possible. Other applications include (i) the berth allocation problem [18] where a large vessel may occupy more than one berth for loading and unloading, (ii) diagnosable microprocessor systems [17] where a job must be performed on parallel processors in order to detect faults, (iii) manufacturing, where a job may need machines, tools, and people simultaneously (this gives an example for a system in which processors may have

---

* This work is supported by the China National Natural Science Foundation for Distinguished Young Scholars and by the Changjiang Scholar Reward Project.
** Corresponding author.

D.T. Lee and S.-H. Teng (Eds.): ISAAC 2000, LNCS 1969, pp. 60–71, 2000.
© Springer-Verlag Berlin Heidelberg 2000

different types), and (iv) scheduling a sequence of meetings where each meeting requires a certain group of people [10]. In the scheduling literature [14], this kind of problems are called *multiprocessor job scheduling* problems.

Formally, each instance for the multiprocessor job scheduling problem on a $k$-processor system $(P_1, P_2, \ldots, P_k)$ consists of a set of jobs $J = \{j_1, j_2, \ldots, j_n\}$, where each job $j_i$ is given by a pair $(Q_i, t_i)$ with $Q_i$ a subset of the processors in the $k$-processor system and $t_i$ the execution time, to specify that the job $j_i$ requires the set $Q_i$ of processors with running time $t_i$. Therefore, the job $j_i$ is a multiprocessor job that requires the simultaneous execution of a set of processors instead of a single processor. Of course, no processor can be assigned to participate in the executions of more than one job at any moment. The goal is to construct a scheduling for these multiprocessor jobs so that the $k$-processor system finishes the execution of all the jobs in the minimum amount of time. Preemption is not allowed in the scheduling. This multiprocessor job scheduling problem is denoted as $P_k|fix|C_{\max}$ in the literature [14].

Feasibility and approximability of the $P_k|fix|C_{\max}$ problem have been studied by many researchers. The $P_2|fix|C_{\max}$ problem is a generalized version of the classical job scheduling problem on a 2-processor system [11], thus it is NP-hard. Chen and Lee [7] developed a fully polynomial time approximation scheme for the $P_2|fix|C_{\max}$ problem. Hoogeveen et al. [15] showed that the $P_3|fix|C_{\max}$ problem is NP-hard in the strong sense thus it does not have a fully polynomial time approximation scheme unless P = NP (see also [3,4]). Blazewicz et al. [3] developed a polynomial time approximation algorithm of ratio 4/3 for the problem $P_3|fix|C_{\max}$, which was improved later by Dell'Olmo et al. [9], who gave a polynomial time approximation algorithm of ratio 5/4 for the same problem. Both algorithms are based on the study of a special type of schedulings called *normal schedulings*. Goemans [12] further improved the results by giving a polynomial time approximation algorithm of ratio 7/6 for the $P_3|fix|C_{\max}$ problem. More recently, Amoura et al. [1] developed a polynomial time approximation scheme for the problem $P_k|fix|C_{\max}$ for every fixed integer $k$. Polynomial time approximation schemes for a more generalized version of the $P_k|fix|C_{\max}$ problem have also been developed recently [8,16].

The polynomial time approximation schemes [1,8,16] for multiprocessor job scheduling problems are of great theoretical significance. However, the current versions of the algorithms seem not practically useful yet, because of the very high degree of the polynomials [1,8], or the huge constant coefficient [16] in the time complexity of the algorithms. Chen and Miranda [8] have asked for practically efficient approximation algorithms for the multiprocessor job scheduling problem for systems with small number of processors. For the $P_3|fix|C_{\max}$ problem, Goemans' approximation algorithm [12] runs in linear time and has approximation ratio 7/6, which seems very acceptable practically. On the other hand, no similar results have been developed for the $P_k|fix|C_{\max}$ problem with $k \geq 4$. In particular, the techniques developed for the $P_3|fix|C_{\max}$ problem, including the analysis of normal scheduling [3,9] and the method of splitting 1-processor jobs [12], seem difficult to be generalized to systems of more than 3 processors. Currently, the best practical algorithm for the $P_k|fix|C_{\max}$ problem is due to Chen and Lee [7], which runs in linear time and has approximation ratio $k/2$ for $k \geq 3$.

The current paper is a respondence to the call by [8]. We focus on the $P_4|fix|C_{\max}$ problem. We offer several new observations and introduce several new techniques. First, we derive two lower bounds for the makespan of an optimal scheduling for a job set, one is based on 3-processor jobs and a careful pairing of 2-processor jobs, and the other is based on the total processing time of each processor. The lower bounds are simple but very effective in the analysis of our approximation algorithms. Secondly, we carefully pair the 2-processor jobs and make a partial scheduling of 3-processor jobs and 2-processor jobs. We observe that in these partial schedulings, most processor idle times are within a small region, thus the 1-processor jobs can be inserted in this region to effectively fill the gaps. Our derived lower bounds also help us to effectively handle large gaps. Combining all these, we derive an approximation algorithm of ratio 1.5 for the $P_4|fix|C_{\max}$ problem, which significantly improves the best previous ratio 2 for practical algorithms for the problem.

The paper is organized as follows. Section 2 derives two lower bounds for the makespan of optimal schedulings for the $P_4|fix|C_{\max}$ problem. Section 3 discusses partial schedulings for 3-processor jobs and 2-processor jobs. The approximation algorithm and its analysis are given in section 4. We conclude in section 5 and propose several problems for future research.

## 2   Two Simple Lower Bounds

Suppose that the system has four processors $P_1$, $P_2$, $P_3$, and $P_4$. An instance of the $P_4|fix|C_{\max}$ problem is a set of jobs: $J = \{j_1, j_2, \ldots, j_n\}$, where each job $j_i$ is described by a pair $j_i = (Q_i, t_i)$, $Q_i$ is a subset of $\{P_1, P_2, P_3, P_4\}$ indicating the processor set required to execute the job $j_i$, and $t_i$ is the parallel processing time of the job $j_i$ executed on the processor set $Q_i$. The processor set $Q_i$ is called the *processing mode* (or simply *mode*) of the job $j_i$. To make the job $j_i$ meaningful, the mode $Q_i$ must be a nonempty set.

A scheduling $S$ of the job set $J$ is an assignment of each job $j_i$ in $J$ with a starting time to be executed on the processor set $Q_i$ in the 4-processor system such that no processor is used for execution of more than one job at any moment. The *makespan* of the scheduling $S$ is the latest finish time of a job in $J$ under the scheduling $S$, denoted by $S(J)$. An *optimal scheduling* of the job set $J$ is a scheduling whose makespan is the minimum over all schedulings of $J$. The makespan of an optimal scheduling is denoted by $Opt(J)$. An *approximation algorithm* $A$ of the $P_4|fix|C_{\max}$ problem is an algorithm that for each given instance $J$ of the $P_4|fix|C_{\max}$ problem constructs a scheduling for $J$. We say that the *approximation ratio* of the algorithm $A$ is (bounded by) $r$ if for any instance $J$, the scheduling $S$ constructed by the algorithm $A$ satisfies $S(J)/Opt(J) \leq r$.

We consider approximation algorithms for the $P_4|fix|C_{\max}$ problem. Since we can always schedule jobs of mode $\{P_1, P_2, P_3, P_4\}$ before other jobs without increasing the approximation ratio of an algorithm for the $P_4|fix|C_{\max}$ problem, we can assume, without loss of generality, that an instance of $P_4|fix|C_{\max}$ contains no jobs requiring all four processors in the system. Thus, there are at most $2^4 - 2 = 14$ processing modes for jobs in an instance of the $P_4|fix|C_{\max}$ problem (note that the mode corresponding to the empty set is also excluded). A job is a *1-processor job* if its mode contains a single processor. Similarly, we define *2-processor jobs* and *3-processor jobs*.

Group the jobs in $J$, according to their processing modes into 14 subsets of jobs:

$$J_1, J_2, J_3, J_4, J_{12}, J_{13}, J_{14}, J_{23}, J_{24}, J_{34}, J_{123}, J_{124}, J_{134}, J_{234}$$

here for simplicity, we have used indices instead of processor subsets to indicate the processing modes. For example, $J_{124}$ is the subset of jobs whose mode is $\{P_1, P_2, P_4\}$. For each index label $I$, let $t_I$ be the total processing time of the jobs in the subset $J_I$. For example, $t_{124}$ is the sum of the processing times of the jobs of mode $\{P_1, P_2, P_4\}$ in $J$.

We first derive two lower bounds for the value $Opt(J)$. Let

$$T_1 = t_1 + t_{12} + t_{13} + t_{14} + t_{123} + t_{124} + t_{134}$$
$$T_2 = t_2 + t_{12} + t_{23} + t_{24} + t_{123} + t_{124} + t_{234}$$
$$T_3 = t_3 + t_{13} + t_{23} + t_{34} + t_{123} + t_{134} + t_{234}$$
$$T_4 = t_4 + t_{14} + t_{24} + t_{34} + t_{124} + t_{134} + t_{234}$$

That is, $T_i$ is the total processing time of processor $P_i$ required by all the jobs in the instance $J$.

Since even without any idle time, each processor $P_i$ must spend processing time $T_i$ on the job set $J$, we derive the first lower bound on $Opt(J)$:

$$Opt(J) \geq \max\{T_1, T_2, T_3, T_4\}$$

We say that two modes $Q_1$ and $Q_2$ are *consistent* if a job of mode $Q_1$ and a job of mode $Q_2$ can be executed in parallel (i.e., $Q_1 \cap Q_2 = \emptyset$). For example, the mode $\{P_1, P_2\}$ and mode $\{P_3, P_4\}$ are consistent, and the mode $\{P_1, P_3, P_4\}$ and mode $\{P_2\}$ are consistent.

Partition the 2-processor job subsets and the 3-processor job subsets in $J$ into seven groups:

$$\{J_{123}\}, \{J_{124}\}, \{J_{134}\}, \{J_{234}\}, \{J_{12}, J_{34}\}, \{J_{13}, J_{24}\}, \{J_{14}, J_{23}\} \tag{1}$$

where each group consists of either a single subset of 3-processor jobs of the same mode, or two subsets of 2-processor jobs whose modes are consistent.

**Lemma 1.** *Let* $T_= = t_{123} + t_{124} + t_{134} + t_{234} + T_{\max}^{12,34} + T_{\max}^{13,24} + T_{\max}^{14,23}$, *where* $T_{\max}^{12,34} = \max\{t_{12}, t_{34}\}$, $T_{\max}^{13,24} = \max\{t_{13}, t_{24}\}$, *and* $T_{\max}^{14,23} = \max\{t_{14}, t_{23}\}$. *Then* $Opt(J) \geq T_=$.

*Proof.* Pick any two jobs $j$ and $j'$ in two different groups in (1). It is easy to see that the modes of the jobs $j$ and $j'$ are not consistent so one of them cannot start until the other finishes. Thus, for a group of 3-processor jobs, say $J_{123}$, the system takes at least time $t_{123}$ to process the jobs in the group, during which no jobs in other groups can be processed. Similarly, for a group of 2-processor jobs, say $\{J_{12}, J_{34}\}$, the system takes at least time $T_{\max}^{12,34} = \max\{t_{12}, t_{34}\}$ to process the jobs in the group, during which no jobs in other groups can be processed. Therefore, the makespan of any scheduling for the job set $J$ is at least as large as

$$T_= = t_{123} + t_{124} + t_{134} + t_{234} + T_{\max}^{12,34} + T_{\max}^{13,24} + T_{\max}^{14,23}$$

as claimed by the lemma.    □

According to the above discussion, we have the following lower bound for the makespan of an optimal scheduling for the job set $J$.

**Corollary 1.** *Let* $B_0 = \max\{T_=, T_1, T_2, T_3, T_4\}$. *Then* $Opt(J) \geq B_0$.

## 3   Partial Scheduling of 2- and 3-Processor Jobs

In this section, we consider partial schedulings that assigns only 2-processor jobs and 3-processor jobs in the job set $J$ to the system. A scheduling of the whole job set $J$ will be obtained by properly inserting 1-processor jobs in the job set $J$ into a partial scheduling.

Without loss of generality, we can assume $t_{12} \geq t_{34}$ and $t_{14} \leq t_{23}$. In fact, if $t_{12} < t_{34}$, then we exchange the index pair $\{1, 2\}$ and the index pair $\{3, 4\}$. Under the condition $t_{12} \geq t_{34}$, if $t_{14} > t_{23}$, then we can further swap the indices 1 and 2, and swap the indices 4 and 3. Note that swapping the indices 1 with 2 and the indices 4 with 3 does not affect the relation $t_{12} \geq t_{34}$.

We schedule the 2-processor jobs and 3-processor jobs based on the job groups given in (1) in terms of their processing modes. There are two possible situations, depending on the relation between $t_{13}$ and $t_{24}$. We illustrate our schedulings for these two situations in Figure 1.

The makespan of each of the schedulings in Figure 1 is

$$T_= = t_{123} + t_{124} + t_{134} + t_{234} + T_{\max}^{12,34} + T_{\max}^{14,23} + T_{\max}^{13,24}$$

where $T_{\max}^{12,34} = \max\{t_{12}, t_{34}\}$, $T_{\max}^{14,23} = \max\{t_{14}, t_{23}\}$, $T_{\max}^{13,24} = \max\{t_{13}, t_{24}\}$, By Lemma 1, $Opt(J) \geq T_=$. Note that the ordering of the groups in the scheduling can be permuted arbitrarily without increasing the makespan. Moreover, for each 2-processor job group of two consistent modes (e.g., the group $\{J_{12}, J_{34}\}$), the smaller job subset of one mode (e.g., $J_{34}$) can be scheduled to either have the same starting time, or have the same finishing time as the larger job subset of the other mode (e.g., $J_{12}$).

Fix a scheduling $S$ of 2-processor jobs and 3-processor jobs in Figure 1. Under the scheduling, each group of jobs in (1) may introduce a "gap" for certain processors in the system. For example, the 3-processor job group $\{J_{123}\}$ introduces

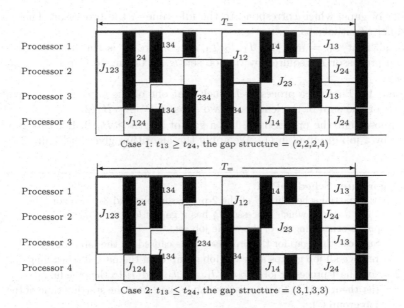

Case 1: $t_{13} \geq t_{24}$, the gap structure = (2,2,2,4)

Case 2: $t_{13} \leq t_{24}$, the gap structure = (3,1,3,3)

**Fig. 1.** Scheduling 2- and 3-processor jobs (assuming $t_{12} \geq t_{34}$ and $t_{14} \leq t_{23}$)

a gap of length $t_{123}$ for processor $P_4$, while the 2-processor job group $\{J_{12}, J_{34}\}$, when $t_{12} > t_{34}$, introduces a gap of length $t_{12} - t_{34}$ for processors $P_3$ and $P_4$. We say that the scheduling $S$ has gap structure $(g_1, g_2, g_3, g_4)$ if under the scheduling $S$, the processor $P_i$ has $g_i$ gaps, for $1 \leq i \leq 4$. The two schedulings in Figure 1 can be distinguished by their gap structures: the first scheduling has gap structure $(2, 2, 2, 4)$, and the second scheduling has gap structure $(3, 1, 3, 3)$. Note that two gaps in a scheduling may be "merged" so they look like a single continuous gap. In this case, however, we still regard them as two gaps.

## 4   An Approximation Algorithm for $P_4|fix|C_{\max}$

We are ready to present our main algorithm. Given a job set $J$, we first group the jobs in $J$ according to their modes, as given in (1). Then we construct a partial scheduling $S$ for the 2-processor job groups and the 3-processor job groups, which takes one of the configurations given in Figure 1 (precisely which configuration is taken depends on the relation of the processing times $t_{13}$ and $t_{24}$). The makespan of this partial scheduling $S$ is $T_=$, which is not larger than $Opt(J)$, according to Lemma 1.

Now consider the 1-processor job subsets $J_1$, $J_2$, $J_3$, and $J_4$ of processing times $t_1$, $t_2$, $t_3$, and $t_4$, respectively. We discuss how we insert the 1-processor job subsets into the partial scheduling $S$ to make a scheduling for the whole job set $J$. Recall that under the partial scheduling $S$, each processor has a certain number of gaps, which correspond to the idle time of the processor. There are two different situations.

Recall that $B_0 = \max\{T_=, T_1, T_2, T_3, T_4\}$, where $T_i$ is the total processing time on processor $P_i$ required by the job set $J$. According to Corollary 1, $B_0 \leq Opt(J)$.

**Case 1.** There is a processor $P_i$ such that one of the gaps of $P_i$ has length $\geq B_0/2$, or the sum of the lengths of two gaps of $P_i$ is $\geq B_0/2$.

Suppose that the processor $P_i$ has a gap of length $\geq B_0/2$. Let this gap be caused by a job group $G$ in (1). We apply the algorithm given in Figure 2.

---

**Algorithm. ScheduleP4-I**

Input: a partial scheduling $S$ of the 2-processor jobs and 3-processor jobs
      in $J$ under which processor $P_i$ has a gap of length $\geq B_0/2$
Output: a scheduling $S_0$ of the whole job set $J$

1. Suppose that gap for the processor $P_i$ is caused by the job group $G$, remove all job groups after the job group $G$ in the partial scheduling $S$;
2. add the 1-processor job subsets $J_1$, $J_2$, $J_3$, and $J_4$ to the scheduling (let them start at their earliest possible time after the starting time of the job group $G$);
3. add back the job groups removed in step 1 (in exactly the same way as they were in the partial scheduling $S$).

---

**Fig. 2.** Scheduling $S_0$ when processor $P_i$ has a large gap

The algorithm **SchedulP4-I** produces a scheduling $S_0$ of the whole job set $J$. We show that in this subcase, the makespan of the constructed scheduling $S_0$ is bounded by $1.5B_0$.

Since the gap of the processor $P_i$ has length at least $B_0/2$ and the gap is caused by the job group $G$, the length of the job group $G$ is $\geq B_0/2$. The makespan of the partial scheduling $S$ is $T_=$, as shown in Figure 1. Suppose after removing all job groups after the job group $G$ in $S$, the remaining scheduling has makespan $T'$, then the part removed from the scheduling $S$ has length exactly $T_= - T'$ since no two jobs from two different job groups can be processed in parallel. Now adding the 1-processor job subsets $J_1$, $J_2$, $J_3$, and $J_4$ results in a new scheduling $S''$. We claim that the makespan $T''$ of the scheduling $S''$ is bounded by $T' + B_0/2$. In fact, suppose $T'' > T' + B_0/2$, then the latest finished job in the scheduling $S''$ must be a 1-processor job subset $J_j$. Suppose that the job subset $J_j$ has mode $\{P_j\}$. Then under the scheduling $S''$, the processor $P_j$ keeps busy since the job group $G$ starts until the job subset $J_j$ finishes (this is because by the algorithm, the job subset $J_j$ starts at its earliest possible time after the starting time of the job group $G$). The processor $P_j$ spends at least $B_0/2$ time units from the beginning to the end of the job group $G$ since the length of the job group $G$ is $\geq B_0/2$. After this, the processor $P_j$ needs to spend more than another $B_0/2$ time units to finish the job subset $J_j$ since $T'' > T' + B_0/2$.

Therefore, the total processing time of the processor $P_j$ is larger than $B_0$. This contradicts the definition of $B_0$, in which we have let $B_0 \geq T_j$ (recall that $T_j$ is the total processing time of the processor $P_j$).

Thus, after adding the 1-processor job subsets, the resulting scheduling $S''$ has makespan $T''$ bounded by $T' + B_0/2$. Finally, when we add back the job groups removed from the partial scheduling $S$ in step 1, we get a scheduling $S_0$ of the whole job set $J$, whose makespan is bounded by $T'' + (T_= - T')$, which is in term bounded by $T_= + B_0/2 \leq 1.5B_0$ (here we have used the fact $T_= \leq B_0$).

The subcase in which the processor $P_i$ has two gaps such that the sum of the lengths of the two gaps is $\geq B_0/2$ can be handled in a similar manner. Suppose the gaps are due to two job groups $G_1$ and $G_2$. We first permute the job groups in the partial scheduling $S$ so that the two job groups $G_1$ and $G_2$ are adjacent under the scheduling and the two gaps of the processor $P_i$ are "merged" into a larger continuous gap. Then we apply an algorithm similar to **ScheduleP4-I** to insert the 1-processor job subsets between the job groups $G_1$ and $G_2$. The detailed algorithm is given in Figure 3.

---

**Algorithm. ScheduleP4-II**

Input: a partial scheduling $S$ of the 2-processor jobs and 3-processor jobs
in $J$ under which processor $P_i$ has two gaps such that the sum of the
lengths of the gaps is $\geq B_0/2$

Output: a scheduling $S_0$ of the whole job set $J$

1.  Suppose that the two gaps of the processor $P_i$ are caused by the job
    groups $G_1$ and $G_2$;
2.  permute the job groups in $S$ so that the job groups $G_1$ and $G_2$
    become adjacent and the two gaps of $P_i$ are merged into a larger
    continuous gap (let $G_2$ start right after $G_1$ finishes);
3.  remove all job groups after the job group $G_2$ in the partial scheduling;
4.  remove the job group $G_2$ from the scheduling;
5.  add the 1-processor job subsets $J_1$, $J_2$, $J_3$, and $J_4$ to the scheduling
    (let them start at their earliest possible time after the starting
    time of the job group $G_1$);
6.  add back the job group $G_2$;
7.  add back the job groups removed in step 3.

---

**Fig. 3.** Scheduling $S_0$ when two gaps of processor $P_i$ make a large gap

The proof that the makespan of the scheduling $S_0$ constructed by the algorithm **ScheduleP4-II** is bounded by $1.5B_0$ is very similar to the proof for the case when the processor $P_i$ has a single gap of length $\geq B_0/2$. For completeness, we give a quick outline as follows.

First of all, the sum of the lengths of the two job groups $G_1$ and $G_2$ is larger than or equal to $B_0/2$. Suppose that the makespan of the scheduling $S'$ obtained in step 3 is $T'$ (thus, the part removed in step 3 has length $T_= - T'$), then the scheduling $S''$ obtained in step 6 has makespan bounded by $T' + B_0/2$ (otherwise a processor $P_j$ would have processing time larger than $B_0$). This derives that the scheduling obtained in step 7 has a makespan bounded by $T_= + B_0/2 \le 1.5B_0$.

Therefore, in case 1, we can always construct a scheduling $S_0$ for the job set $J$ whose makespan is bounded by $1.5B_0$.

**Case 2.** Under the partial scheduling $S$, no processor has either a gap of length larger than or equal to $B_0/2$ or two gaps such that the sum of lengths of them is larger than or equal to $B_0/2$.

We first explain our basic idea in dealing with this case. Look at Figure 1. We first observe that in each scheduling, all processors finish at the same time. Therefore, in order to keep the makespan small, we only need to reduce the amount of idle time, i.e., the gaps, for the processors. By the assumption of the case, the gaps for each processor are small. Therefore, we try to "fill" as many gaps as we can so that at least one processor has at most two gaps. Since the sum of the lengths of any two gaps of any processor is less than $B_0/2$, the processor with at most two gaps left shows that before the makespan of the scheduling, the processor has less than $B_0/2$ idle time units. From this, we can easily derive that the makespan of the scheduling is bounded by $1.5B_0$.

Look at the two situations given in Figure 1. The situations have gap structures $(2, 2, 2, 4)$, and $(3, 1, 3, 3)$, respectively. There is a very nice property between the job groups $\{J_{14}, J_{23}\}$ and $\{J_{13}, J_{24}\}$: in the $(3, 1, 3, 3)$ structure, each of the processors with 3 gaps has at least one gap caused by these two job groups, and the processor with 1 gap has its gap not in these two job groups, while in the $(2, 2, 2, 4)$ structure, the processor with 4 gaps has two gaps caused by these two job groups and the two gaps are merged into a larger continuous gap. This nice property allows us to insert the 1-processor jobs between these two job groups without increasing much makespan.

The algorithm for this case is given in Figure 4.

---

**Algorithm. ScheduleP4-III**
Input: a partial scheduling $S$ of the 2-processor jobs and 3-processor jobs
         in $J$ under which no processor has two gaps such that the sum of
         the lengths of the gaps is $\ge B_0/2$
Output: a scheduling $S_0$ of the whole job set $J$
1.   remove the job group $\{J_{13}, J_{24}\}$ from the partial scheduling in Figure 1;
2.   add the 1-processor job subsets $J_1$, $J_2$, $J_3$, and $J_4$ to the scheduling
       (let them start at their earliest possible time after the starting time
       of the job group $\{J_{14}, J_{23}\}$);
3.   add back the job group $\{J_{13}, J_{24}\}$.

---

**Fig. 4.** Scheduling $S_0$ when gaps of all processors are small

Let the scheduling for the whole job set $J$ constructed by the algorithm **ScheduleP4-III** be $S_0$. If the makespan of $S_0$ is equal to the makespan $T_=$ of the partial scheduling $S$, then by Lemma 1, $S_0$ is an optimal scheduling for the job set $J$.

On the other hand, if the makespan of $S_0$ is larger than $T_=$, then at least one of the gaps between the job groups $\{J_{14}, J_{23}\}$ and $\{J_{13}, J_{24}\}$ is filled by the 1-processor job subsets.

If the filled gap belongs to a processor $P_i$ that has at most 3 gaps in the partial scheduling $S$, then after filling one of its gaps, the processor $P_i$ has at most 2 gaps left. By the assumption in this case, the sum of the lengths of the gaps left is less than $B_0/2$. That is, the total idle time of processor $P_i$ before the makespan is less than $B_0/2$ (note that by our construction, all processors finish at the same time). Since the total processing time of the processor $P_i$ is bounded by $B_0$, we conclude that the makespan of the scheduling $S_0$ is less than $1.5B_0$.

If the filled gap belongs to the processor $P_i$ that has 4 gaps in the partial scheduling $S$, then the filled gap must be the larger gap obtained by merging two gaps in the job groups $\{J_{14}, J_{23}\}$ and $\{J_{13}, J_{24}\}$. Thus, with this gap filled, the processor $P_i$ has two gaps left such that the sum of the lengths of these two gaps is less than $B_0/2$. This again derives that the idle time of the processor $P_i$ before the makespan of $S_0$ is less than $B_0/2$, and the makespan of the scheduling $S_0$ is less than $1.5B_0$.

We summarize all these discussions in the main algorithm given in Figure 5, and conclude with our main theorem.

**Theorem 1.** *The algorithm* **Schedule-P4** *runs in linear time and constructs a scheduling $S_0$ for the input job set $J$ with makespan bounded by $1.5 \cdot Opt(J)$.*

*Proof.* According to the above discussion, the makespan of the scheduling $S_0$ is bounded by $1.5B_0$, which is at most $1.5 \cdot Opt(J)$ according to Corollary 1.     □

---

**Algorithm. Schedule-P4**
Input: an instance $J$ for the $P_4|fix|C_{\max}$ problem
Output: a scheduling $S_0$ for $J$
1.  group the jobs in $J$ by their processing modes, as in (1);
2.  construct the partial scheduling $S$ for 2-processor jobs and
    3-processor jobs, as shown in Figure 1;
3.  **if** a processor $P_i$ has a gap of length $\geq B_0/2$ under $S$
    **then** call **ScheduleP4-I** to construct a scheduling $S_0$ for $J$; **stop**;
4.  **if** a processor $P_i$ has two gaps such that the sum of the lengths of
        the two gaps is $\geq B_0/2$ under the partial scheduling $S$
    **then** call **ScheduleP4-II** to construct a scheduling $S_0$ for $J$; **stop**;
5.  call **ScheduleP4-III** to construct a scheduling $S_0$ for $J$.

---

**Fig. 5.** Approximation algorithm for the $P_4|fix|C_{\max}$ problem

# 5   Final Remarks and Future Work

Multiprocessor job scheduling problem has become increasingly interesting, both in practical applications and in theoretical studies. Much progress has been made in recent years. In particular, polynomial time approximation schemes for variations of multiprocessor job scheduling problems have been derived [1,8,16], which are of great significance from a theoretical point of view. On the other hand, practical algorithms for the problem have not been as successful. Practical algorithms with good approximation ratio are only developed for systems with at most three processors [7,9,12]. The current paper gives new observations, introduces new techniques, and extends the research in this direction to systems with four processors. Our techniques are also applicable to systems with more than four processors. For example, for the $P_5|fix|C_{max}$ problem, we can have a linear time algorithm with approximation ratio bounded by 2, improving the best previous ratio 2.5 for the problem [7]. Further and more subtle applications of our techniques are currently under investigation.

We propose a few open problems for future work in this research area.

The technique of grouping jobs according to their processing modes then scheduling the jobs based on job groups is known as *normal scheduling* [9]. For the problem $P_3|fix|C_{max}$, Dell'Olmo et al. [9] show that the best normal scheduling of a job set $J$ has makespan bounded by $1.25 \cdot Opt(J)$, and proved that this bound is tight. According to this definition, Theorem 1 claims that for any instance $J$ for the problem $P_4|fix|C_{max}$, there is a normal scheduling whose makespan is bounded by $1.5 \cdot Opt(J)$. Is 1.5 a tight bound for normal schedulings for the problem $P_4|fix|C_{max}$, or the bound 1.5 can be further improved?

For each fixed $k$, there is a (practical) approximation algorithm for the $P_k|fix|C_{max}$ problem whose approximation ratio is bounded by a constant [7]. However, this constant depends on the number $k$ of processors in the system. Can we develop practical algorithms of approximation raio bounded by a constant $c$ for the $P_k|fix|C_{max}$ problem for all $k$ such that the constant $c$ is independent of $k$? Note that for the classical scheduling problems, such algorithms exist (for example, Graham's listing scheduling algorithm [13]) with very satisfying approximation ratio [14].

A generalized version of the $P_4|fix|C_{max}$ problem is the $P_4|set|C_{max}$ problem, in which each job may have several alternative processing modes [7]. Based on normal schedulings of approximation ratio 2 for the $P_4|fix|C_{max}$ problem, Chen and Lee [7] have developed an approximation algorithm of ratio $2 + \epsilon$ for any $\epsilon > 0$ for the $P_4|set|C_{max}$ problem. Is it possible to extend the results in the current paper to an improved algorithm for the $P_4|set|C_{max}$ problem?

# References

1. A. K. AMOURA, E. BAMPIS, C. KENYON, AND Y. MANOUSSAKIS, Scheduling independent multiprocessor tasks, *Proc. 5th Ann. European Symposium on Algorithms, Lecture Notes in Computer Science 1284*, (1997), pp. 1-12.

2. L. BIANCO, J. BLAZEWICZ, P. DELL'OLMO, AND M. DROZDOWSKI, Scheduling multiprocessor tasks on a dynamic configuration of dedicated processors, *Annals of Operations Research 58*, (1995), pp. 493-517.

3. J. BLAZEWICZ, P. DELL'OLMO, M. DROZDOWSKI, AND M. SPERANZA, Scheduling multiprocessor tasks on the three dedicated processors, *Information Processing Letters 41*, (1992), pp. 275-280.

4. J. BLAZEWICZ, P. DELL'OLMO, M. DROZDOWSKI, AND M. SPERANZA, Corrigendum to "Scheduling multiprocessor tasks on the three dedicated processors, *Information Processing Letters 41*, (1992), pp. 275-280." *Information Processing Letters 49*, (1994), pp. 269-270.

5. J. BLAZEWICZ, M. DROZDOWSKI, AND J. WEGLARZ, Scheduling multiprocessor tasks to minimize scheduling length, *IEEE Transactions on Computers 35*, (1986), pp. 389-393.

6. J. BLAZEWICZ, W. DROZDOWSKI, AND J. WEGLARZ, Scheduling multiprocessor tasks – a survey, *International Journal of Microcomputer Applications 13*, (1994), pp. 89-97.

7. J. CHEN AND C.-Y. LEE, General multiprocessor tasks scheduling, *Naval Research Logistics 46*, (1999), pp. 59-74.

8. J. CHEN AND A. MIRANDA, A polynomial time approximation scheme for general multiprocessor job scheduling, *Proc. 31st Annual ACM Symposium on Theory of Computing* (STOC'99), (1999), pp. 418-427. Final version to appear in *SIAM J. Comput.*

9. P. DELL'OLMO, M. G. SPERANZA, ZS. TUZA, Efficiency and effectiveness of normal schedules on three dedicated processors, *Discrete Mathematics 164*, (1997), pp. 67-79.

10. G. DOBSON AND U. KARMARKAR, Simultaneous resource scheduling to minimize weighted flow times, *Operations Research 37*, (1989), pp. 592-600.

11. M. R. GAREY AND D. S. JOHNSON, *Computers and Intractability: A Guide to the Theory of NP-Completeness*, Freeman, San Francisco, 1979.

12. M. X. GOEMANS, An approximation algorithm for scheduling on three dedicated machines, *Discrete Applied Mathematics 61*, (1995), pp. 49-59.

13. R. L. GRAHAM, Bounds for certain multiprocessing anomalies, *Bell System Technical Journal 45*, (1966), pp. 1563-1581.

14. L. A. HALL, Approximation algorithms for scheduling, in D. S. HOCHBAUM, ed., *Approximation algorithms for NP-hard problems*, PWS Publishing Company, 1997, pp. 1-45.

15. J. A. HOOGEVEEN, S. L. VAN DE VELDE, AND B. VELTMAN, Complexity of scheduling multiprocessor tasks with prespecified processor allocations, *Discrete Applied Mathematics 55*, (1994), pp. 259-272.

16. K. JANSEN AND L. PORKOLAB, General multiprocessor task scheduling: approximate solutions in linear time, *Lecture Notes in Computer Science 1663* (WADS'99), (1999), pp. 110-121.

17. H. KRAWCZYK AND M. KUBALE, An approximation algorithm for diagnostic test scheduling in multicomputer systems, *IEEE Transactions on Computers 34*, (1985), pp. 869-872.

18. C.-Y. LEE AND X. CAI, Scheduling multiprocessor tasks without prespecified processor allocations, *IIE Transactions*, to appear.

19. C.-Y. LEE, L. LEI, AND M. PINEDO, Current trends in deterministic scheduling, *Annals of Operations Research 70*, (1997), pp. 1-42.

# Classification of Various Neighborhood Operations for the Nurse Scheduling Problem
## (Extended Abstract)

Takayuki Osogami[1] and Hiroshi Imai[2]

[1] IBM Tokyo Research Laboratory, Kanagawa 242-8502, Japan
osogami@jp.ibm.com
[2] Department of Information Science, University of Tokyo, Tokyo 113-0033, Japan
imai@is.s.u-tokyo.ac.jp

**Abstract.** Since the nurse scheduling problem (NSP) is a problem of finding a feasible solution, the solution space must include infeasible solutions to solve it using a local search algorithm. However, the solution space consisting of all the solutions is so large that the search requires much CPU time. In the NSP, some constraints have higher priority. Thus, we can define the solution space to be the set of solutions satisfying some of the important constraints, which are called the elementary constraints. The connectivity of the solution space is also important for the performance. However, the connectivity is not obvious when the solution space consists only of solutions satisfying the elementary constraints and is composed of small neighborhoods. This paper gives theoretical support for using 4-opt-type neighborhood operations by discussing the connectivity of its solution space and the size of the neighborhood. Another interesting point in our model is a special case of the NSP corresponds to the bipartite transportation problem, and our result also applies to it.

## 1 Introduction

We are interested in solving the nurse scheduling problem (NSP) using a local search algorithm. Its performance varies with the neighborhood operations, and we have to carefully specify them. Especially, the connectivity of the solution space and the size of the neighborhood are important. This paper classifies various neighborhood operations for the NSP according to the connectivity of their solution spaces. From the analysis, we obtain useful guidelines for the design of a local search algorithm for the NSP.

### 1.1 The Nurse Scheduling Problem

The shifts of nurses in a hospital consist of a day shift, a night shift, and a late night shift. The director of nursing must solve the NSP [4][8] to plan a schedule once a month. This schedule is an assignment of the three shifts, days off, and other time such as vacation and training days (we will denote them by

D.T. Lee and S.-H. Teng (Eds.): ISAAC 2000, LNCS 1969, pp. 72–83, 2000.

the working time assignment (WTA)) for each nurse. Here, many constraints must be satisfied. To execute the daily work without problems, the number and the combination of nurses for each WTA must be considered. To maintain the physical and mental condition of the nurses, the sequence of WTAs, the number of each WTA in a period, and the requirements of each nurse must be considered. There also exist special constraints that cannot be considered within the scope of a single day or a single nurse.

Observe that other real world problems such as the scheduling of the call takers in call centers have similar constraints, and these problems can also be modeled as the NSP. From a theoretical point of view, the NSP is NP-hard [7], and the construction of good algorithms for it is important.

## 1.2  Why Our Results Are Interesting/Important?

*Searching Only Solutions Satisfying Some Important Constraints.* The local search algorithm starts at an initial solution and iteratively moves to a solution among the neighborhood solutions until a certain condition is satisfied. The solution space is defined to be the set of candidate solutions from which the local search algorithm finds the final solution. Since the NSP is a problem of finding a feasible solution, the solution space must include infeasible solutions. However, the solution space with all the solutions is too large to be searched efficiently. On the other hand, local search algorithms guarantee nothing about the quality of the final solution. Thus, it is important to know which candidate solutions the solution space should include. In the NSP, some constraints have higher priority. Therefore, we can define the solution space to be the set of solutions that satisfy some of the important constraints so that the size of the solution space (i.e., the number of the solutions in the solution space) is reduced and the local search algorithm can efficiently search the restricted solution space; the final solution is at least guaranteed to satisfy these constraints. We don't require that solutions in the solution space should satisfy all the important constraints. If this were strictly required, the initial solution might not be constructed efficiently, or the definition of an appropriate neighborhood might be difficult.

*The Connectivity of the Solution Space and the Size of the Neighborhood.* If the initial solution is located in a subspace (i.e., a set of solutions connected to each other but disconnected from the others) in which no satisfactory solution is located, some local search algorithms such as the simulated annealing algorithm never find a satisfactory solution. On the other hand, in the other local search algorithms such as the multi-start local search algorithm, the connectivity is not so important. However, it is always important to know whether the solution space is connected or not when we design a local search algorithm. For instance, if we know that the solution space is disconnected, we should not adopt the simulated annealing algorithm but use the multi-start local search algorithm.

However, there has been little research on the connectivity of the solution space. Van Laarhoven, et al. [5] have shown that any solution can be transformed to an optimal solution by a type of $k$-opt neighborhood operations in the job shop scheduling problem. Dell'Amico and Trubian [2] have shown that some solutions cannot be transformed to any optimal solution by another type of $k$-opt neighborhood operations in the same problem. In general, if we use larger neighborhoods, the solution space is more likely to be connected. However, searching a larger neighborhood requires more CPU time, and, thus, using large neighborhoods connecting the solution space is sometimes worse than using small neighborhoods not connecting it [6]. Therefore, small neighborhoods connecting the solution space are most preferable.

*Importance of Our Results.* Considering the above discussion, we should choose some constraints from the important ones to include only solutions satisfying such constraints into the solution space, so that the size of the solution space is reduced. We call such constraints the elementary constraints. Here, we must note that an initial solution that satisfies the elementary constraints should be constructed efficiently, and the solution space should be connected and composed of relatively small neighborhoods. This paper tackles these problems, classifying various neighborhood operations for the NSP according to the connectivity of their solution space and find out which neighborhood operations should be used in the local search algorithm for the NSP.

## 1.3    Elementary Constraints for the NSP

Typically, important constraints include the following: The requirements of individual nurses must be satisfied (requirements such as "nurse $n_i$ must be assigned to a WTA $s_j$ on day $d_k$" and "nurse $n_i$ must not be assigned to a WTA $s_j$ on day $d_k$"); the number of nurses for the night shift and the late night shift on each day must be more than a certain number; among all the nurses assigned to a particular WTA, specified skills and experience must be included; the number of days off for each nurse during a certain period must be fixed; the interval between days off must not be more than a certain length; some sequences of WTAs must be avoided (e.g., a night shift must not be followed by a late night shift).

In this paper, we define elementary constraints for the NSP to be the following two constraints: The number of nurses for the night shift and the late night shift on each day must be fixed; the number of days off for each nurse must be fixed. [7] also discusses the case when only the lower bounds for the number of nurses on each shift and the number of days off for each nurse are given as elementary constraints. This paper shows how to construct an initial solution satisfying the elementary constraints efficiently and proves the connectivity of the solution space composed of relatively small neighborhoods.

## 1.4    Neighborhood Operations for the NSP

A straightforward definition of a neighborhood operation for the NSP is the exchange of the WTAs in two arbitrary cells (i.e. intersections of rows (nurses) and columns (days)), which we call 2-opt. We consider other neighborhood operations, the restricted 2-opt (r2-opt), the constrained 2-opt (c2-opt), and the constrained r2-opt (cr2-opt). The r2-opt consists of two types of operations: One is the exchange of the WTAs in two arbitrary cells in the same day or the same column, which is called vertical 2-opt, and the other is the exchange of the WTAs in two arbitrary cells in the same nurse or the same row, which is called horizontal 2-opt. Note that a 2-opt operation and a r2-opt operation may produce a solution that does not satisfy the elementary constraints even if the initial solution does. Next, we define the c2-opt (and the cr2-opt respectively) to be the set of 2-opt (and r2-opt) operations that do not produce a solution that violates the elementary constraints. $rk$-opt, $ck$-opt, and $crk$-opt are defined in a similar way, where a $k$-opt operation is an arbitrary exchange of WTAs among up to $k$ cells. We formally define them in Section 2.

### 1.5 Framework of This Paper

The rest of the paper is organized as follows: Section 2 presents a model of the NSP, shows an efficient construction method for an initial solution, formally defines various neighborhood operations, and introduces the class of neighborhood operations. Using this class, we obtain relationships among various neighborhood operations: cr2-opt, c2-opt, cr3-opt, and c3-opt belong to the same class, while cr4-opt belongs to the different class whose solution space is connected (Theorem 2), and r2-opt and 2-opt belongs to the class whose solution space is connected (Proposition 1). Section 3 proves the connectivity of the solution space when the solution space is composed of cr4-opt neighborhoods, which is our main result, and discusses it. Section 4 proves Theorem 2 and Proposition 1 and presents useful guidelines for the design of local search algorithms for the NSP. Full details and omitted proofs are included in [7].

## 2 Preliminaries

This section first introduces a model of the NSP and shows an efficient construction method for a solution satisfying the elementary constraints. Then, we define various neighborhood operations and the class of neighborhood operations.

### 2.1 The Elementary NSP

In this paper, we consider an elementary model of the NSP, which we call the elementary NSP (ENSP).

**Definition 1 (ENSP).** *Let $m$ be the number of nurses, $n$ be the number of days in a scheduling period, $k$ be the number of different WTAs, and $l_i$ be the total number of the WTA $i$ to be assigned to the nurses in the period for each $i$ $(1 \leq i \leq k)$ in which $\sum_{i=1}^{k} l_i = mn$. The ENSP is defined to be the problem of finding the optimal assignment of the WTAs to $m \times n$ cells so that each cell has exactly one WTA, where the quality of the solution can be arbitrarily determined from the assignment.*

Note that $k$-opt operations and their variants do not change the total number of each WTA in a solution.

In a typical NSP, the set of WTAs $W$ can be divided into three mutually disjoint subsets $W_h$, $W_v$, and $W_a$. $W_h$ is the set of WTAs whose numbers per nurse or row are fixed, $W_v$ is the set of WTAs whose numbers per day or column are fixed, and $W_a$ is the set of WTAs that have no such constraint on numbers. For example, a night shift and a late night shift are in $W_v$, a day off is in $W_h$, and a day shift is in $W_a$.

*Construction of a Solution Satisfying the Elementary Constraints for the ENSP.* Now, we show that an initial solution satisfying the elementary constraints of the ENSP can be obtained, if any exists, by solving a max-flow problem. Consider a network that has one sink vertex, source vertices corresponding to rows or columns, and other vertices corresponding to cells. Each vertex corresponding to a cell is connected to the sink vertex by an edge with capacity one. There are $s + t$ source vertices, where $s$ and $t$ are the number of rows and columns respectively. Each source vertex represents the supply of WTAs on each day or for each nurse, and the amount of the supply represents the number of the WTAs on the day or for the nurse. For instance, if the number of night shifts on a day is three and that of late night shifts on that day is two, then the supply of the vertex corresponding to that day is five. We draw an edge between a source vertex corresponding to a row (and column respectively) and a vertex corresponding to a cell if the cell is in the row (and column). The capacity of each edge is one. Now, we have obtained a network corresponding to the ENSP with the elementary constraints.

From a solution of the max-flow problem of this network, an initial solution meeting the elementary constraints is obtained. The existence of a flow from a source vertex corresponding to a row (and a column respectively) to a vertex $v$ means a WTA in $W_h$ (and $W_v$) is assigned to the cell corresponding to $v$. When $W_h$ (or $W_v$ respectively) has more than one kind of WTAs, each WTA in it can be arbitrarily assigned so that the number of the WTA in the row (or the column) satisfies the elementary constraints. Here, we can use a standard algorithm for the max-flow problem [1], which runs in $O(|E||V|^2)$ time, where $|E|$ is the number of edges and $|V|$ is the number of vertices. In our network, $|E| = O(st)$ and $|V| = O(s + t)$. Thus, an initial solution can be obtained in $O(st(s + t)^2)$ time, if any solution exists.

## 2.2    Neighborhood Operations

The $k$-opt is defined to be the set of operations that exchange WTAs among up to $k$ cells. A $k$-opt operation consists of a set of cyclic exchange operations; a cyclic exchange is the exchange of WTAs among $k'$ shifts, $s_1$, $s_2$, ..., $s_{k'}$, where $s_i$ moves to the cell in which $s_{i+1}$ ($s_1$ if $i = k'$) was originally located. If each $s_i$ moves to the same column or the same row as that of the original cell, then $k$-opt is called r$k$-opt. If the solution space is restricted to the set of solutions that satisfy the elementary constraints, then $k$-opt and r$k$-opt are called c$k$-opt and cr$k$-opt respectively. We also define the constrained cyclic exchange, which is a set of cyclic exchange operations that never produce a solution that violates the elementary constraints unless the initial solution does. We do not use the cyclic exchange but the constrained cyclic exchange only. Therefore, for simplicity, we denote the constrained cyclic exchange as the cyclic exchange (CE).

**Definition 2 (CE).** *A cyclic exchange (CE) operation is the exchange of WTAs, $s_1$, $s_2$, ..., $s_k$, among $k$ cells with the following conditions: If $s_i$ is in $W_h$, then $s_{i+1}$ ($s_1$ if $i = k$) must be located in the same row as $s_i$; if $s_i$ is in $W_v$, then $s_{i+1}$ ($s_1$ if $i = k$) must be located in the same column as $s_i$; $s_i$ moves to the cell in which $s_{i+1}$ ($s_1$ if $i = k$) was originally located. We represent the CE operation as $(s_1, s_2, ..., s_k)$.*

We classify neighborhood operations so that the neighborhood operations in the same class can simulate each other. We say that a set of neighborhood operations $A$ can simulate another set of neighborhood operations $B$ when $A$ can perform all the operations $B$ can do. Here, the number of operations can be different. We define a graph where vertices correspond to all solutions in the solution space and two vertices are connected by an edge when the corresponding solutions can be transformed each other by an operation in the neighborhood operations. The class represents the connectivity of the solution space. In the two solution spaces of two neighborhood operations that belong to the same class, the connectivity of any two solutions is the same. Some local search algorithms do not allow moves to a worse solution in terms of the objective function, but, in this paper, we do not use such an objective function; that is, we assume that any transition is possible if it is allowed using the defined neighborhood operations.

$k$-OPT (R$k$-OPT, C$k$-OPT, or CR$k$-OPT respectively) means the class $k$-opt (r$k$-opt, c$k$-opt, or cr$k$-opt) belongs to. For instance, 2-OPT = 3-OPT means that 2-opt and 3-opt belong to the same class. We use a $k$-opt operation, an r$k$-opt operation, a c$k$-opt operation, or a cr$k$-opt operation to mean each operation of the $k$-opt, the r$k$-opt, the c$k$-opt, or the cr$k$-opt respectively. The connected class (CC) represents the class of neighborhood operations whose solution space is connected.

## 3   CR4-OPT = CC

In this section, we prove the connectivity of the solution space of the ENSP with the elementary constraints when it is composed of cr4-opt neighborhoods and discuss a special case of the result. We first prove that the CE (i.e., a set of CE operations) can transform an arbitrary solution of the ENSP meeting the elementary constraints into another arbitrary solution. Then, we prove that the cr4-opt can simulate an arbitrary CE operation. More detailed proofs are in [7].

### 3.1   Main Theorem

**Lemma 1.** *The solution space of the ENSP with the elementary constraints is connected when it is composed of the CE neighborhoods.*

*Proof.* Let $T_0$ and $T_1$ be two arbitrary solutions of the ENSP meeting the elementary constraints. To transform $T_0$ to $T_1$ by the CE, first find a cell $c_0$ whose WTA $s_0^{(0)}$ in $T_0$ and whose WTA $s_0^{(1)}$ in $T_1$ are different. Next, find a cell $c_1$ whose WTA $s_1^{(0)}$ in $T_0$ is different from $s_0^{(0)}$ and whose WTA $s_1^{(1)}$ in $T_1$ is the same as $s_0^{(0)}$. Here, if $s_0^{(0)}$ is in $W_h$ (or $W_v$ respectively), then at least one such $s_1^{(1)}$ is found in the same row (or column) as the cell $c_0$; let $c_1$ be such a cell and let $s_1^{(0)}$ and $s_1^{(1)}$ be the WTAs in the cell $c_1$ of $T_0$ and $T_1$ respectively. Then, move $s_0^{(0)}$ from $c_0$ to $c_1$ in $T_0$. Then, find a cell $c_2$ whose WTA $s_2^{(0)}$ in $T_0$ is different from $s_1^{(0)}$ and whose WTA $s_2^{(1)}$ in $T_1$ is the same as $s_1^{(0)}$ from the same row (or column respectively) if $s_1^{(}0)$ is in $W_h$ (or in $W_v$); here, the first cell $c_0$ has no WTA in $T_0$ and this cell can always be a candidate for the next cell if the current WTA, in this case $s_2^{(0)}$, is the same as $s_0^{(1)}$. Repeat this procedure until one WTA is moved to the first cell $c_0$. Now, one CE operation was applied to $T_0$. If $T_0$ has become equivalent to $T_1$, the transformation is completed. Otherwise, apply the above procedure again. Each CE operation makes at least two cells that previously had different WTAs between $T_0$ and $T_1$ have the same WTA and never changes the WTAs in cells that have the same WTAs between $T_0$ and $T_1$.

Each CE operation in the procedure in the proof of the lemma can be applied independently without violating the elementary constraints. Therefore, we only need to show that the cr4-opt can simulate an arbitrary CE operation.

**Lemma 2.** *The cr2-opt can simulate a CE operation if the cycle contains at least one WTA in $W_a$.*

*Proof.* Let $s_a$ be one of the WTAs in $W_a$ in the cycle. Let the cycle be $(s_1, s_2, ..., s_{k-1}, s_a)$, where $k$ is the length of the cycle. This CE operation is simulated by a 2-opt operation that swaps $s_{k-1}$ and $s_a$ and a CE operation $(c_1, c_2, ..., s_{k-2}, s_a)$ with length $k-1$. If $s_{k-1}$ is in $W_h$ or $W_v$, because of the definition of the CE the swap of $s_{k-1}$ and $s_a$ is a cr2-opt operation. We need to prove that the cr2-opt can simulate the swap of $s_{k-1}$ and $s_a$ even when $s_{k-1}$ is in $W_a$ and the cell of $s_{k-1}$ is in neither the same row nor the same column as $s_a$. Let $(i_1, j_1)$ be the location of $s_a$ (i.e., the row and the column of $s_a$ are $i_1$ and $j_1$ respectively), $(i_2, j_2)$ be the location of $s_{k-1}$, and $s_t$ be the WTA at the location $(i_2, j_1)$. The following procedure swaps $s_a$ and $s_{k-1}$ using cr2-opt operations: If $s_t$ is in $W_h$, first swap $s_{k-1}$ and $s_t$, $s_a$ and $s_{k-1}$, and finally $s_a$ and $s_t$. Otherwise, first swap $s_a$ and $s_t$, $s_a$ and $s_{k-1}$, and finally $s_{k-1}$ and $s_t$. Note that $s_t$ moves back to its original location. Thus, a CE operation with length $k$ that contains at least one WTA in $W_a$ can be simulated by cr2-opt operations and a CE operation with length $k-1$ that also contains the WTA in $W_a$.

Now, we define the alternate cyclic exchange (ACE) and prove that an arbitrary CE operation in which the cycle does not contain any WTAs in $W_a$ can be simulated by the cr2-opt and the ACE.

**Definition 3 (ACE).** *The alternate cyclic exchange (ACE) is a set of CE operations of the form $(s_1, s_2, ..., s_{2k})$ where $s_i$ is in $W_h$ if $i$ is odd, $s_i$ is in $W_v$ if $i$ is even, and the cycle does not contain any WTAs in $W_a$.*

**Lemma 3.** *An arbitrary CE operation in which the cycle does not contain any WTAs in $W_a$ can be simulated by the cr2-opt and the ACE.*

*Proof.* Suppose that the cycle has two successive WTAs in $W_h$. Without loss of generality, the cycle is represented as $(h_1, h_2, s_1, ..., s_{k-1}, s_{k-2})$, where $h_1$ and $h_2$ are in $W_h$, $s_i$ is an arbitrary WTA for each $i$, and $k$ is the length of the cycle. A CE operation $(h_1, h_2, s_1, ..., s_{k-1}, s_{k-2})$ can be simulated by swapping $h_1$ and $h_2$ and executing a CE operation $(h_2, s_1, ..., s_{k-2})$. Note that the length of the cycle is $k - 1$. If the cycle has two successive WTAs in $W_v$, the CE operation can be simulated in a similar way. Using these procedures recursively as long as the cycle has two successive WTAs in $W_h$ or $W_v$, we can simulate the original CE operation by cr2-opt and ACE operations.

Lemmas 2 and 3 are useful and also used in the proof of Theorem 2 in Section 4. Now, we define the elementary alternate cyclic exchange (EACE) and prove that an arbitrary ACE operation can be simulated by the cr2-opt and the EACE.

**Definition 4 (EACE).** *The elementary alternate cyclic exchange (EACE) is a set of ACE operations where no two WTAs in $W_h$ are in the same row and no two WTAs in $W_v$ are in the same column.*

**Lemma 4.** *An arbitrary ACE operation can be simulated by the cr2-opt and the EACE.*

*Proof.* Suppose the cycle has two WTAs $v_i$ and $v_j$ in $W_v$ that are located in the same column. An ACE operation $(h_1, v_1, ..., h_i, v_i, h_{i+1}, v_{i+1}, ..., h_j, v_j, h_{j+1}, ..., h_k, v_k)$, where the length of the cycle is $2k$, can be simulated by swapping $v_i$ and $v_j$ and executing two ACE operations $(h_1, v_1, ..., h_i, v_j, h_{j+1}, ..., h_k, v_k)$ and $(h_{i+1}, v_{i+1}, ..., h_j, v_i)$. Note that $v_i$ and $v_{i+1}$ $(1 \leq i \leq k-1)$ or $v_k$ and $v_1$ cannot be located in the same column. Therefore, the length of each cycle is at least four; because the total length of the two cycles is $2k$, the length of each cycle is at most $2k - 4$. If the cycle has two WTAs that are located in the same row, the ACE operation can be simulated in a similar way. Using these procedures recursively as long as the cycle has two WTAs in $W_v$ (or in $W_h$ respectively) that are located in the same column (or the same row), a CE operation can be simulated by cr2-opt and EACE operations.

Now, we prove that the cr4-opt can simulate an arbitrary EACE operation. This is our main lemma and plays an important role in the proof of the theorem. So far, we only needed the cr2-opt as well as the EACE for simulating an arbitrary CE operation. However, the cr2-opt cannot simulate the EACE, and we need the cr4-opt for simulating it.

**Lemma 5.** *An arbitrary EACE operation can be simulated by the cr4-opt.*

*Proof.* Let an EACE operation be $(h_1, v_1, h_2, v_2, ..., h_k, v_k)$, where $h_i$ is in $W_h$ and $v_i$ is in $W_v$ for each $i$, and the length of the cycle is $2k$. Let $(r_i, c_i)$ be the location of $h_i$ for each $i$. Then, the location of $v_i$ is $(r_i, c_{i+1})$ for each $i$ $(1 \leq i < k)$ and $(r_k, c_1)$ for $i = k$. We prove the lemma by induction on $k$.

(i) When $k \leq 2$, the CE is the cr4-opt by definition.

(ii) Suppose the cr4-opt can simulate an EACE operation whose length is less than $2k$. Find a cell whose WTA is in $W_v$ or $W_a$ from the cells that are located in $\{(r_i, c_j)|(1 \leq i, j \leq k) \land j \neq i \land j \neq i + 1 \land (i \neq k \lor j \neq 1)\}$. If any exists, let $(r_i, c_j)$ be the location of the cell and denote the WTA assigned to the cell as $V$. If $2 \leq i + 1 < j \leq k$, a CE operation $(h_1, v_1, h_2, v_2, ..., h_k, v_k)$ is simulated by executing two CE operations $(h_1, v_1, h_2, ..., v_{i-1}, h_i, V, h_j, v_j, ..., h_k, v_k)$ and $(h_i, v_i, h_{i+1}, v_{i+1}, ..., h_{j-1}, v_{j-1})$ and swapping $V$ and $v_{j-1}$. The length of the first cycle is $2(k + i - j + 1) < 2k$ and that of the second one is $2(j - i) < 2k$. If $1 \leq j < i \leq k$, a CE operation $(h_1, v_1, h_2, v_2, ..., h_k, v_k)$ is simulated by executing two CE operations $(h_{j+1}, v_{j+1}, ..., h_{i-1}, v_{i-1}, h_i, V)$ and $(h_1, v_1, h_2, ..., v_{j-1}, h_j, v_j, h_i, v_i, ..., h_k, v_k)$ and swapping $V$ and $v_j$. The length of the first cycle is $2(i - j) < 2k$ and that of the second one is $2(k + j - i + 1) < 2k$. Thus, the cr4-opt can simulate both CE operations because of the assumption of the inductive step. Even if the WTA at $(r_i, c_j)$ is in $W_h$, the CE operation can be simulated by two CE operations with shorter lengths and a cr2-opt operation in a similar way because of the symmetry of rows and columns.

Using Lemmas 1–5, we can now derive Theorem 1.

**Theorem 1.** *CR4-OPT = CC.*

The proof of Lemma 5 suggests that not all of the possible cr4-opt operations are required to show the connectivity of the solution space. We further discuss this in Subsection 4.2.

## 3.2    A Special Case of the ENSP: A Flow in a Bipartite Network

Here, we consider a special case of the ENSP with the elementary constraints, where there are only two kinds of WTAs "0" in $W_h$ and "1" in $W_v$. Since the number of 0's in a row is fixed, the number of 1's is also fixed. A solution corresponds to a 0-1 $s \times t$-matrix $M(\mathbf{r}, \mathbf{c})$ with row sums $\mathbf{r}$ and column sums $\mathbf{c}$, where $\mathbf{r} = (r_1, r_2, ..., r_s) \in \mathbf{N}^s$ and $\mathbf{c} = (c_1, c_2, ..., c_t) \in \mathbf{N}^t$.

Consider a bipartite graph where a set of nodes corresponds to rows and the other set of nodes corresponds to columns. That is, the number of nodes in one set corresponding to rows is $s$, and that in the other set corresponding to columns is $t$. Now, consider a integral flow transportation problem where the network is the complete bipartite graph with capacity of each edge one and the demand vector of one set of nodes is $-\mathbf{r}$ and that of the other is $\mathbf{c}$. By solving a max-flow problem for this network, a feasible solution is obtained if any exists. A 0-1 $s \times t$-matrix $M(\mathbf{r}, \mathbf{c})$ corresponds to a feasible solution of this transportation problem. Thus, using Theorem 1, the following corollaries are derived:

**Corollary 1.** *Let $M(\mathbf{r}, \mathbf{c})$ be 0-1 $s \times t$-matrices with row sums $\mathbf{r}$ and column sums $\mathbf{c}$, where $\mathbf{r} = (r_1, r_2, ..., r_s) \in \mathbf{N}^s$ and $\mathbf{c} = (c_1, c_2, ..., c_t) \in \mathbf{N}^t$. If we let vertices correspond to the matrices in $M(\mathbf{r}, \mathbf{c})$ and draw an edge between two vertices if one matrix is transformed to the other by choosing a pair of rows and a pair of columns and modifying these intersecting four entries according to $\begin{smallmatrix} + & - \\ - & + \end{smallmatrix}$ or $\begin{smallmatrix} - & + \\ + & - \end{smallmatrix}$. (the modification adds or subtracts one from each of the four entries as indicated), then the graph is connected.*

**Corollary 2.** *The solution space consisting of the feasible solutions of a transportation problem is connected when it is composed of the neighborhoods defined by the following operation: First select a pair of edges, denote them as $(s_1, t_1)$ and $(s_2, t_2)$ where $s_i$ and $t_i$, respectively, is a head and a tail of the edge for each $i$, decrease the flow of the two edges $(s_1, t_1)$ and $(s_2, t_2)$ by one each, and finally increase the flow of two edges $(s_1, t_2)$ and $(s_2, t_1)$ by one each.*

Note that the connectivity of the non-negative integer $s \times t$-matrices $M(\mathbf{r}, \mathbf{c})$ is discussed in [3]. This corresponds to the transportation problem where there are no capacity constraints on each edge, that is, $x$ can be any non-negative integer vector.

# 4   Relationships among Various Neighborhood Operations

This section shows the relationships among various neighborhood operations for the ENSP, discusses the results obtained in this research, and derives some useful guidelines for designing local search algorithms for the NSP.

## 4.1   Results

First, we prove that cr2-opt, c2-opt, cr3-opt, and c3-opt belong to the same class, and the class is different from that of cr4-opt, i.e., the solution space is not connected when it is composed of any of the above four neighborhoods. Then, we prove that the solution space is connected when it is composed of either r2-opt neighborhoods or 2-opt neighborhoods.

**Theorem 2.** *CR2-OPT = C2-OPT = CR3-OPT = C3-OPT $\subset$ CR4-OPT.*

*Proof.* Since, by definition, CR2-OPT $\subseteq$ CR3-OPT $\subseteq$ C3-OPT and CR2-OPT $\subseteq$ C2-OPT $\subseteq$ C3-OPT, we only need to prove (i) CR2-OPT = C3-OPT and (ii) CR2-OPT $\subset$ CR4-OPT.

(i) CR2-OPT = C3-OPT: It is sufficient to show that the cr2-opt can simulate an arbitrary CE operation with length three. If the cycle contains a WTA in $W_a$, the CE can be simulated by the cr2-opt because of Lemma 2. If all the WTAs in the cycle are in $W_h$ or $W_v$, the cycle must contain at least two WTAs both of which are in $W_h$ or in $W_v$ and these two WTAs must be adjoining, since the length of the cycle is three. Therefore, the cr2-opt can simulate an arbitrary CE operation because of Lemma 3.

(ii) CR2-OPT $\subset$ CR4-OPT: It is sufficient to give a transition that cr4-opt operations can perform but cr2-opt operations cannot, and the transition from $\begin{pmatrix} v' & h' \\ h' & v' \end{pmatrix}$ to $\begin{pmatrix} h' & v' \\ v' & h' \end{pmatrix}$, where $v'$ is in $W_v$ and $h'$ is in $W_h$, is one. Note that the cr2-opt cannot swap $h'$ and $v'$ without violating the elementary constraints.

Theorem 1 states that the cr4-opt is sufficient for the connectivity of the solution space and Theorem 2 states that some cr4-opt operations not in the cr2-opt are necessary for it. Next, we state that the solution space is connected when it is composed of either of r2-opt neighborhoods or 2-opt neighborhoods. Now, the solution space includes solutions that do not satisfy the elementary constraints as well.

**Proposition 1.** *R2-OPT = 2-OPT = CC.*

The detailed proof is in [7], but the outline is as follows: First, R2-OPT = 2-OPT is proved by showing any two WTAs can be swapped by at most three r2-opt operations without changing the locations of the other WTAs. Next, 2-OPT = CC is proved by showing that the 2-opt can transform an arbitrary solution of the ENSP to another arbitrary solution.

## 4.2   Discussion

It is easily seen from the procedures in the proof of Theorem 1 that we need only a subset of the cr4-opt for the solution space to be connected. These are the cr2-opt and the cr4-opt operations that transform $\begin{pmatrix} v_0 & h_0 \\ h_1 & v_1 \end{pmatrix}$ to $\begin{pmatrix} h_1 & v_0 \\ v_1 & h_0 \end{pmatrix}$, where $h_i$ is in $W_h$ and $v_i$ is in $W_v$ for each $i$. We denote a set of neighborhood operations in the cr4-opt that cannot be simulated by the cr2-opt as cr4-opt\cr2-opt.

In practice, the size of the neighborhood is expected to decrease if the neighborhood is restricted to cr2-opt and cr4-opt\cr2-opt instead of cr4-opt. In a typical instance, the number of nurses is 20, the length of the scheduling period is 30 days, and the numbers of days off for each nurse, night shifts on each day, and late night shifts on each day are 9, 3, and 2 respectively. In this instance, the size of a 2-opt neighborhood $|N(\text{2-opt})|$ is 121,500, and that of a cr2-opt neighborhood $|N(\text{cr2-opt})|$ is 3,960 [7]. $|N(\text{2-opt})|$ and $|N(\text{cr2-opt})|$ are independent of the solution, but the size of a r2-opt neighborhood and that of a cr4-opt\cr2-opt neighborhood depend on the solution. Thus, we evaluate them by computational experiments. 10,000 solutions are randomly generated and the size is measured for each neighborhood. The solutions satisfy the elementary constraints when the size of cr4-opt\cr2-opt neighborhoods is evaluated but do not necessarily satisfy them when that of r2-opt neighborhoods is evaluated. We summarize the results in Table 1.

When both cr2-opt and cr4-opt\cr2-opt are used, the solution space is connected, and the size of the neighborhood is about half of that of r2-opt neighborhood.

The number of solutions in the solution space composed of r2-opt neighborhoods is also larger than that composed of cr4-opt\cr2-opt neighborhoods. These fasts imply that the performance of local search algorithms with cr4-opt\cr2-opt is higher than that with r2-opt.

**Table 1.** Size of various neighborhoods in 10,000 randomly generated solutions.

|      | 2-opt   | r2-opt | cr2-opt | cr4-opt\cr2-opt |
|------|---------|--------|---------|-----------------|
| min. | 121,500 | 9,702  | 3,960   | 1037            |
| ave. | 121,500 | 9,895  | 3,960   | 1101            |
| max. | 121,500 | 10,027 | 3,960   | 1167            |

### 4.3 Conclusion

We defined the elementary constraints for the NSP to be (i) the number of night shifts and late night shifts on each day must be fixed and (ii) the number of days off for each nurse in a fixed period must be fixed. Including only solutions satisfying the elementary constraints in the solution space reduces the size of the solution space, which enables efficient search by local search algorithms. It had not been obvious, however, whether a feasible solution, which is used as an initial solution, can be constructed efficiently and whether an appropriate neighborhood can be defined. In this paper, we first showed that an initial solution satisfying the elementary constraints can be constructed efficiently. Then, we proved that the solution space is connected when it is composed of cr4-opt neighborhoods, while it is disconnected when composed of smaller neighborhoods such as cr2-opt, c2-opt, cr3-opt, and c3-opt. From these analyses, we conclude that the cr4-opt, or a subset of it, is the best candidate for neighborhood operations of the local search algorithm for the NSP.

## References

1. Ahuja, R., Magnanti, T., Orlin, J.: *Network Flows: Theory, Algorithms, and Applications.* Prentice-Hall, Inc., New Jersey (1993)
2. Dell'Amico, M., Trubian, M.: Applying Tabu Search to the Job-shop Scheduling Problem. Annals of Operations Research, **41** (1993) 231–252
3. Diaconis, P., Sturmfels, B.: Algebraic Algorithms for Sampling from Conditional Distributions. Annals of Statistics, **26** (1998) 363–397
4. Ikegami, A., Niwa, A.: An Efficient Approach to Nurse Scheduling —Implementation for a 2-Shift Case—. Journal of the Operations Research Society of Japan, **41** (1998) 572–588 (Japanese)
5. van Laarhoven, P., Aarts, E., Lenstra, J.: Job Shop Scheduling by Simulated Annealing. Operations Research, **40** (1992) 113–125
6. Nowicki, E., Smutnicki, C.: A Fast Taboo Search Algorithm for the Job Shop Problem. Management Science, **42** (1996) 797–813
7. Osogami, T., Imai, H.: Classification of Various Neighborhood Operations for the Nurse Scheduling Problem. IBM TRL Research Report, RT0373 (2000)
8. Smith-Daniels, V., Schweikhert, S., Smith-Daniels, D.: Capacity Management in Health Care Services: Review and Future Research Directions. Decision Sciences, **19** (1988) 889–919

# Optimal Bid Sequences for Multiple-Object Auctions with Unequal Budgets

Yuyu Chen[1], Ming-Yang Kao[2], and Hsueh-I. Lu[3]

[1] Department of Computer Science, Yale University, New Haven, CT 06520, USA
(chen-yuyu@cs.yale.edu). Research supported in part by NSF grant CCR-9531028.
[2] Department of Computer Science, Yale University, New Haven, CT 06520, USA
(kao-ming-yang@cs.yale.edu). Research supported in part by NSF grants
CCR-9531028 and CCR-9988376.
[3] Institute of Information Science, Academia Sinica, Taipei 115, Taiwan, R.O.C.
(hil@iis.sinica.edu.tw). Research supported in part by NSC grant
NSC-89-2213-E-001-034.

**Abstract.** In a multiple-object auction, every bidder tries to win as many objects as possible with a bidding algorithm. This paper studies *position-randomized auctions*, which form a special class of multiple-object auctions where a bidding algorithm consists of an initial bid sequence and an algorithm for randomly permuting the sequence. We are especially concerned with situations where some bidders know the bidding algorithms of others. For the case of only two bidders, we give an optimal bidding algorithm for the disadvantaged bidder. Our result generalizes previous work by allowing the bidders to have unequal budgets. One might naturally anticipate that the optimal expected numbers of objects won by the bidders would be proportional to their budgets. Surprisingly, this is not true. Our new algorithm runs in optimal $O(n)$ time in a straightforward manner. The case with more than two bidders is open.

## 1 Introduction

Economists have long recognized the usefulness of auction as a means of price determination without intermediary market makers. As a result, there already exists an enormous Economics literature on auction theory and practice (see, e.g., [17,18,20,12,16,27]). Relatively recently, computer scientists have become aware of the potential efficiency of auction as a general method of resource allocation [7]. For instance, Gagliano, Fraser, and Schaefer [11] applied auction techniques to allocating decentralized network resources. Bertsekas [2] designed an auction-type algorithm for the classical maximum flow problem.

With the advent of the Word Wide Web, Internet-based auction is rapidly becoming an essential buying and selling medium for both individuals and organizations. It is projected that most of the future Internet auctions will necessarily be conducted by software agents instead of human bidders and auctioneers [21,13,22,28]. Consequently, there is an increasing need for highly efficient and

D.T. Lee and S.-H. Teng (Eds.): ISAAC 2000, LNCS 1969, pp. 84–95, 2000.

sophisticated auction mechanisms and bidding algorithms. To meet this need, Computer Science is witnessing heightened research efforts on such mechanisms and algorithms. Among the several basic research themes that have emerged from these efforts, the following three are particularly relevant to this paper.

The first theme is multiple-object auction [8,1,9,19,15,23], where each bidder may bid on several objects simultaneously instead of one at a time. The second theme is the informational security of auction. For instance, Cachin [6] and Stajano and Anderson [26] were concerned with the privacy of bidders. Sako [24] discussed how to hide information about losing bids. The third theme is the computational complexity of auction [10,9,19,15,23]. For example, Sandholm and Suri [25] and Akcoglu, Aspnes, DasGupta, and Kao [1] proposed general frameworks for tackling the computational hardness of the winner determination problem for combinatorial auction, which is a special form of multiple-object auction.

Along these three themes, Kao, Qi, and Tan [14] considered the *position-randomized* multiple-object auction model specified as follows:

M1 There are $m$ bidders competing for $n$ objects, where $m \geq 2$ and $n \geq 1$. Each bidder has a positive budget and aims to win as many objects as possible.

M2 Each bidder submits to the auction (1) an initial sequence of $n$ bids whose total may not exceed the bidder's budget and (2) a randomized algorithm for permuting the bids. Each bid must be positive or zero. The final bid sequence that a bidder actually uses in the auction is obtained by permuting her initial bid sequence with her bid-permuting algorithm. The $i$-th bid of each final sequence is for the $i$-th object. If an object has $m'$ highest bids, then each of these $m'$ bidders wins this object with probability $\frac{1}{m'}$.

M3 Before submitting their initial bid sequences and bid-permuting algorithms, all bidders know $n$, $m$, and the budget of each bidder. Furthermore, some bidders may also know the initial bid sequences and bid-permuting algorithms of others, but not the final bid sequences.

The assumption M3 addresses the extreme case about informational security where electronically transmitted information about bids may be legitimately or illegitimately revealed against the wishes of their bidders. To enforce this assumption, the model can be implemented in an Internet auction as follows. Before the auction starts, each bidder submits her initial bid sequence and bid-permuting algorithm to the trusted auctioneer. After the auction stops accepting any new bid, the auctioneer will execute the bid-permuting algorithm publicly. In such an implementation, while a bidder's initial bid sequence and bid-permuting algorithm may be leaked to others, her final bid sequence is not known to anyone including herself and the auctioneer, until the auction commences.

Kao et al. [14] also considered an assumption M3' alternative to M3. Under M3', each bidder may submit any bidding algorithm which generates a final bid sequence without necessarily specifying an initial bid sequence. Therefore, less information may be revealed under M3' than under M3; in other words, M3' is a weaker security assumption. Moreover, it is not even clear that under M3', a bidder's optimal probability distribution of all possible bids can be computed in finite time. For these two reasons, this paper does not use M3'.

Under the above model, Kao et al. [14] gave optimal bidding algorithms for the case where (1) all bidders have equal budget, (2) every bid must have a positive dollar amount, and (3) the number of bidders is two or is an integral divisor of the number of objects. In this paper, we resolve only the case of two bidders where the *adversary* bidder $\mathcal{A}$ knows the *disadvantaged* bidder $\mathcal{D}$'s initial bid sequence and bid-permuting algorithm, but not vice versa. We give a new optimal bidding algorithm for $\mathcal{D}$ which improves upon the previous results with two generalizations: (1) the bidders may have unequal budgets, and (2) bids with zero dollar amounts are allowed. These two seemingly minor relaxations make the design and analysis of the new algorithm considerably more difficult than those of the previous algorithms [14]. For one thing, one might naturally anticipate that the optimal expected numbers of objects won by $\mathcal{A}$ and $\mathcal{D}$ would be proportional to their budgets. Surprisingly, this is not true (Corollary 1). Our new algorithm runs in optimal $O(n)$ time in a straightforward manner. The case with more than two bidders is open.

To outline the organization of the rest of the paper, we give some technical definitions first. The bid set of a bidder refers to the multiset formed by the bids in her initial bid sequence. For convenience, we refer to an initial sequence and its corresponding bid set interchangeably. Let $B_{\mathcal{A}}$ (respectively, $B_{\mathcal{D}}$) be the bid set of $\mathcal{A}$ (respectively, $\mathcal{D}$). Let $\pi_{\mathcal{A}}$ (respectively, $\pi_{\mathcal{D}}$) be the bid-permuting algorithm of $\mathcal{A}$ (respectively, $\mathcal{D}$). $\mathcal{A}$ may know $\pi_{\mathcal{D}}$ and $B_{\mathcal{D}}$, while $\mathcal{D}$ does not know $\pi_{\mathcal{A}}$ and $B_{\mathcal{A}}$. We assume that $\mathcal{A}$ is *oblivious* in the sense that $\mathcal{A}$ does not know in advance the outcome of permuting $B_{\mathcal{D}}$ with $\pi_{\mathcal{D}}$. Note that bidding against a non-oblivious adversary is trivial.

Let $w(\pi_{\mathcal{A}}, \pi_{\mathcal{D}}, B_{\mathcal{A}}, B_{\mathcal{D}})$ be the expected number of objects that $\mathcal{A}$ wins. Since an auction in our model is a zero-sum game over the objects, the expected number of objects that $\mathcal{D}$ wins is exactly $n - w(\pi_{\mathcal{A}}, \pi_{\mathcal{D}}, B_{\mathcal{A}}, B_{\mathcal{D}})$. Let $w^*(\pi_{\mathcal{D}}, B_{\mathcal{D}})$ be the maximum of $w(\pi_{\mathcal{A}}, \pi_{\mathcal{D}}, B_{\mathcal{A}}, B_{\mathcal{D}})$ over all $\pi_{\mathcal{A}}$ and $B_{\mathcal{A}}$. We give a bidding algorithm $(\pi_{\mathcal{D}}^*, B_{\mathcal{D}}^*)$ which is optimal for $\mathcal{D}$, i.e.,

$$w^*(\pi_{\mathcal{D}}^*, B_{\mathcal{D}}^*) = \min_{\pi_{\mathcal{D}}, B_{\mathcal{D}}} w^*(\pi_{\mathcal{D}}, B_{\mathcal{D}}). \tag{1}$$

Note that the game has an infinite pure strategy space, so it is not immediately clear that von Neumann's min-max theorem is applicable [3,4,5].

It has been shown [14] that without loss of generality, (1) $\mathcal{D}$ always uses the *uniform* bid-permuting algorithm $\pi_{\text{unif}}$ which permutes a sequence $x_1, \ldots, x_n$ with equal probability for every permutation of the indices $1, \ldots, n$ and (2) thus, $\mathcal{A}$ uses the *identity* bid-permuting algorithm $\pi_{\text{id}}$ which leaves a sequence unchanged (see Fact 1). Therefore, our main task is to design an initial bid sequence for $\mathcal{D}$. A sequence $x_1, x_2, \ldots, x_\ell$ of bids is *proportional* if $\frac{x_i}{x_j} = \frac{i}{j}$ holds for all $1 \le i, j \le \ell$. A bid is *unbeatable* if it is greater than the budget of $\mathcal{A}$. In this paper, we give a $B_{\mathcal{D}}^*$ that consists of (i) a sequence of zero bids, (ii) a sequence of proportional bids, and (iii) a sequence of unbeatable bids. The length of each sequence, which could be zero, depends on the ratio $R$ of the budget of $\mathcal{A}$ over that of $\mathcal{D}$.

Section 2 details $B_{\mathcal{D}}^*$. Section 3 proves its optimality for $\mathcal{D}$ by showing that Equation (1) holds. Section 4 concludes the paper with open problems.

## 2    The Bidding Algorithm of the Disadvantaged Bidder

This section gives an optimal bidding algorithm $(\pi_{\mathcal{D}}^*, B_{\mathcal{D}}^*)$ for $\mathcal{D}$. All sets in this paper are multisets. Let $|X|$ be the number of elements in $X$ counting multiplicity. Let $X^d = \bigcup_{i=1}^{d} X$, for each positive integer $d$. Let $X^0 = \emptyset$. Let $\mathrm{sum}(X) = \sum_{x \in X} x$. Let $\beta$ be the budget of $\mathcal{D}$. Hence, the budget of $\mathcal{A}$ is $\beta R$.

We discuss the case $\frac{1}{n} \leq R < n$ first. Let $\Psi = \{0\}^{\ell_0} \cup \left\{ \frac{\beta}{n-\ell_0} \right\}^{n-\ell_0}$, where

$$
\ell_0 = \begin{cases} n & R < \frac{1}{n}; \\ \left\lceil \frac{n-1}{n} \right\rceil & R = \frac{1}{n}; \\ 0 & R > n. \end{cases}
$$

One can easily verify that $(\pi_{\mathrm{unif}}, \Psi)$ is an optimal bidding algorithm for $\mathcal{D}$, where $w^*(\pi_{\mathrm{unif}}, \Psi)$ equals $\min \left\{ \frac{1}{2}, \frac{1}{n} \right\}$ for $R = \frac{1}{n}$ and equals $n - \ell_0$ for $R < \frac{1}{n}$ or $R > n$.

Hence, the rest of the paper assumes $\frac{1}{n} < R \leq n$. In §2.1, we give a bid set $\Psi$ for $\mathcal{D}$. In §2.2, we prove an upper bound on the number of objects that $\mathcal{A}$ can win against $\Psi$. In §3, we prove a matching lower bound, thereby proving the optimality of $\Psi$.

### 2.1    An Optimal Bid Set for the Disadvantaged Bidder

The next fact simplifies our analysis.

**Fact 1 (See [14])**

1. *If $B_{\mathcal{A}} \cap B_{\mathcal{D}} = \emptyset$, then we have $w(\pi_{\mathcal{A}}, \pi_{\mathrm{unif}}, B_{\mathcal{A}}, B_{\mathcal{D}}) = w(\pi_{\mathrm{id}}, \pi_{\mathrm{unif}}, B_{\mathcal{A}}, B_{\mathcal{D}}) \leq w(\pi_{\mathrm{unif}}, \pi_{\mathcal{D}}, B_{\mathcal{A}}, B_{\mathcal{D}})$ for any bid-permuting algorithms $\pi_{\mathcal{A}}$ and $\pi_{\mathcal{D}}$.*
2. *If $\pi_{\mathcal{D}} = \pi_{\mathrm{unif}}$, then $\mathcal{A}$ has an optimal bidding algorithm with $B_{\mathcal{A}} \cap B_{\mathcal{D}} = \emptyset$.*

By Fact 1, the rest of the paper may assume $\pi_{\mathcal{D}} = \pi_{\mathrm{unif}}$ without loss of generality. Thus, let $\pi_{\mathcal{D}}^* = \pi_{\mathrm{unif}}$. Moreover, as long as $B_{\mathcal{A}}$ and $B_{\mathcal{D}}$ are disjoint, we may assume $\pi_{\mathcal{A}} = \pi_{\mathrm{id}}$.

For any positive real numbers $x$ and $y$, define $\phi(x, y) = y \cdot \left( \left\lceil \frac{x}{y} \right\rceil - 1 \right)$, which is the largest integral multiple of $y$ that is less than $x$. Let $\phi(x) = \phi(x, 1)$. Clearly, $\phi(x) = \frac{1}{y} \cdot \phi(xy, y)$. Define

$$
\Psi = \begin{cases} \{0\}^{\ell_1} \cup \left\{ \frac{\beta}{n-\ell_1} \right\}^{n-\ell_1} & \text{if } \frac{1}{n} < R \leq \frac{2}{n+1}; \\ \left\{ \frac{2i}{\ell_2(\ell_2+1)} \cdot \beta \mid i = 1, 2, \ldots, \ell_2 \right\} \cup \{0\}^{n-\ell_2} & \text{if } \frac{2}{n+1} < R \leq n, \end{cases}
$$

where $\ell_1 = \phi\left(2n - \frac{2}{R} + 1\right)$ and $\ell_2 = \min\left\{n, \left\lfloor \frac{n}{R} \right\rfloor\right\}$. Note that $\frac{1}{n} < R \leq \frac{2}{n+1}$ implies $0 < n - \frac{1}{R} < \ell_1 < n$. Also, $\frac{2}{n+1} < R \leq n$ implies $1 \leq \ell_2 \leq n$. Therefore, $\Psi$ is well defined. Clearly, $\mathrm{sum}(\Psi) = \beta$.

## 2.2   An Upper Bound on $\mathcal{A}$'s Winning

For each $\ell = 1, 2, \ldots, n$, let $R_\ell = \phi\left(R, \frac{2}{\ell(\ell+1)}\right)$ and $f(\ell) = n - \ell + \frac{\ell(\ell+1)R_\ell}{2n}$. Define

$$\text{equil}(n, R) = \begin{cases} \frac{\ell_1}{n} & \text{if } \frac{1}{n} < R \le \frac{2}{n+1}; \\ f(\ell_2) & \text{if } \frac{2}{n+1} < R \le n. \end{cases}$$

The next lemma provides an upper bound for $w^*(\pi_{\text{unif}}, \Psi)$.

**Lemma 1.** $w^*(\pi_{\text{unif}}, \Psi) \le \text{equil}(n, R)$.

*Proof.* Case 1: $\frac{1}{n} < R \le \frac{2}{n+1}$. By $\ell_1 > n - \frac{1}{R}$, we know $\frac{\beta}{n-\ell_1} > \beta R$. Since $\Psi$ contains $n - \ell_1$ unbeatable bids, the lemma is proved.

Case 2: $\frac{2}{n+1} < R \le n$. Let $\Psi'$ consist of the nonzero bids in $\Psi$. It suffices to show that $\mathcal{A}$ wins no more than $\frac{\ell_2(\ell_2+1)R_{\ell_2}}{2n}$ bids in $\Psi'$ on average. By Fact 1(2), $\mathcal{A}$ has an optimal algorithm $(\pi_{\text{id}}, B_\mathcal{A})$ with $B_\mathcal{A} \cap \Psi' = \emptyset$. Clearly, for each bid $x \in B_\mathcal{A}$, if $i$ is the largest index with $\frac{2i\beta}{\ell_2(\ell_2+1)} < x$, then $x$ wins $\frac{i}{n}$ bids in $\Psi'$ on average. Hence, the unit price for $\mathcal{A}$ to win a bid in $\Psi'$ is greater than $\frac{2n\beta}{\ell_2(\ell_2+1)}$. By $\pi_\mathcal{D} = \pi_{\text{unif}}$ and $B_\mathcal{A} \cap \Psi' = \emptyset$, the expected number of bids in $\Psi'$ that $B_\mathcal{A}$ wins is an integral multiple of $\frac{1}{n}$. Since the budget of $\mathcal{A}$ is $\beta R$, the expected number of bids in $\Psi'$ that $\mathcal{A}$ wins is at most $\phi\left(\frac{\ell_2(\ell_2+1)\beta R}{2n\beta}, \frac{1}{n}\right) = \frac{1}{n} \cdot \phi\left(\frac{\ell_2(\ell_2+1)R}{2}\right) = \frac{\ell_2(\ell_2+1)}{2n} \cdot \phi\left(R, \frac{2}{\ell_2(\ell_2+1)}\right) = \frac{\ell_2(\ell_2+1)R_{\ell_2}}{2n}$. $\square$

## 3   The Optimality of the Bid Set $\Psi$

The main result of this section is Theorem 1, which shows the optimality of $\Psi$ by proving

$$w^*(\pi_{\text{unif}}, \Psi) = \min_{\pi_\mathcal{D}, B_\mathcal{D}} w^*(\pi_\mathcal{D}, B_\mathcal{D}). \tag{2}$$

Suppose $B_\mathcal{D} = \{\beta_1, \beta_2, \ldots, \beta_n\}$, where $\beta_1 \le \beta_2 \le \cdots \le \beta_n$. Without loss of generality, we may assume $\text{sum}(B_\mathcal{D}) = \beta$. Let $B_\ell = \bigcup_{i=1}^{\ell}\{\beta_{n-\ell+i}\}$ and $t_\ell = \text{sum}(B_\ell)$ for each $\ell = 1, 2, \ldots, n$. For technical reason, define $\beta_0 = 0$.

### 3.1   Technical Lemmas

For each $\ell = 1, 2, \ldots, n$, an $\ell$-set is a multiset over $\{0, 1, \ldots, \ell\}$. For any $\ell$-set $I$, let $\text{bsum}(I, \ell) = \sum_{i \in I} \beta_{n-\ell+i}$. An $\ell$-set $I$ satisfies *Property P* if the following conditions hold:

P1. $|I| \le n$.
P2. $\text{sum}(I) \ge \frac{R_\ell \ell(\ell+1)}{2}$.
P3. $\text{bsum}(I, \ell) + (n - |I|)\beta_{n-\ell} < \beta R$.

For any positive real number $q$, an $\ell$-set $I$ is an $(\ell, q)$-*set* if $\text{sum}(I) \ge \frac{q\ell(\ell+1)}{2}$ and $\text{bsum}(I, \ell) \le q t_\ell$. Clearly, the union of an $(\ell, q_1)$-set and an $(\ell, q_2)$-set is an $(\ell, q_1 + q_2)$-set.

**Lemma 2.** *If there is an $\ell$-set set that satisfies Property P, then $w^*(\pi_{\text{unif}}, B_{\mathcal{D}}) \geq f(\ell)$.*

*Proof.* Let $I$ be the $\ell$-set that satisfies Property P. By Property P1, the $n$-element set $X = \{\beta_{n-\ell}\}^{n-|I|} \cup \{\beta_{n-\ell+i} \mid i \in I\}$ is well defined. By Property P3, $\text{sum}(X) = \text{bsum}(I, \ell) + (n - |I|)\beta_{n-\ell} < \beta R$. Therefore, there exists a positive number $\delta$ such that $B_{\mathcal{A}} = \bigcup_{x \in X}\{x + \delta\}$ satisfies $\text{sum}(B_{\mathcal{A}}) \leq \beta R$ and $B_{\mathcal{A}} \cap B_{\mathcal{D}} = \emptyset$. Since each bid in $B_{\mathcal{A}}$ is greater than $\beta_{n-\ell}$, $\mathcal{A}$ wins all $n - \ell$ bids in $B_{\mathcal{D}} - B_{\ell}$. By Property P2, the expected number of bids in $B_{\ell}$ that $\mathcal{A}$ wins with $B_{\mathcal{A}}$ is at least $\frac{\text{sum}(I)}{n} \geq \frac{R_{\ell}\ell(\ell+1)}{2n}$. Thus, $w^*(\pi_{\text{unif}}, B_{\mathcal{D}}) \geq n - \ell + \frac{R_{\ell}\ell(\ell+1)}{2n} = f(\ell)$. □

Roughly speaking, an $(\ell, q)$-set specifies a good bid set for $\mathcal{A}$ that spends the budget effectively. For example, if $I$ is an $(n, R_n)$-set with $|I| \leq n$, then, by $\beta_0 = 0$ and $R_n < R$, one can easily verify that $I$ satisfies Property P. The next lemma is crucial in designing cost-effective bid sets.

**Lemma 3.** *For each $\ell = 1, 2, \ldots, n$, the following statements hold.*

1. *For each integer $d \geq 0$, there is an $\left(\ell, \frac{2d}{\ell}\right)$-set $I_1(\ell, d)$ with $|I_1(\ell, d)| = 2d$.*

2. *For each integer $h$ with $0 \leq h \leq \frac{\ell+1}{2}$, there is an $\left(\ell, 1 - \frac{2h}{\ell(\ell+1)}\right)$-set $I_2(\ell, h)$ with $\ell - 1 \leq |I_2(\ell, h)| \leq \ell$.*

3. *For each integer $k \geq 1$ and each $h = 0, 1, \ldots, \ell$, there is an $\left(\ell, k + \frac{2h}{\ell(\ell+1)}\right)$-set $I_3(\ell, k, h)$ with $k\ell + \left\lfloor\frac{2h}{\ell+1}\right\rfloor \leq |I_3(\ell, k, h)| \leq k\ell + \left\lceil\frac{2h}{\ell+1}\right\rceil$.*

4. *For each integer $d \geq 1$ and each $h = 0, 1, \ldots, \ell$, there is an $\left(\ell, \frac{2d}{\ell} + \frac{2h}{\ell(\ell+1)}\right)$-set $I_4(\ell, d, h)$ with $|I_4(\ell, d, h)| \leq 2d + 2$.*

5. *If $\ell \leq n - 1$, then for each integer $d \geq 0$, there is an $\ell$-set $I_5(\ell, d)$ with $|I_5(\ell, d)| = 2d$, $\text{sum}(I_5(\ell, d)) \geq \ell d$, and $\text{bsum}(I_5(\ell, d), \ell) \leq \frac{2dt_{\ell+1}}{\ell+1}$.*

*Proof.* Let $L = \{1, 2, \ldots, \ell\}$. For each $i = 0, 1, \ldots, \ell$, let $x_i = \beta_{n-\ell+i}$. Define $y(i) = \frac{2it_{\ell}}{\ell(\ell+1)}$, for any integer $i$. Let $i_0 = \arg\max_{i \in L} x_i - y(i)$. Clearly, $x_i - x_{i_0} \leq y(i - i_0)$ holds for each $i \in L$. By $\sum_{i \in L} x_i - y(i) = 0$, we know $x_{i_0} \geq y(i_0)$. Let

$$i_1 = \arg\min_{i \in L} x_i + x_{\ell-i+1};$$

$$i_2 = \arg\max_{i \in L} x_i + x_{\ell-i+1};$$

$$i_3 = \arg\max_{i \in L-\{\ell\}} x_i + x_{\ell-i}.$$

Statement 1. Clearly, the inequality $x_{i_1} + x_{\ell-i_1+1} \leq x_j + x_{\ell-j+1}$ holds for each $j \in L$. By averaging this inequality over all $\ell$ values of $j$, we have $x_{i_1} + x_{\ell+1-i_1} \leq \frac{2t_{\ell}}{\ell}$. One can easily verify that the statement holds with $I_1(\ell, d) = \{i_1, \ell - i_1 + 1\}^d$.

Statement 2. If $h = 0$ (respectively, $h = \frac{\ell+1}{2}$), then one can easily verify that the statement holds with $I_2(\ell, h) = L$ (respectively, $I_2(\ell, h) = I_1\left(\ell, \frac{\ell-1}{2}\right)$). If $i_0 = h$, then $x_h \geq y(h)$, and thus the statement holds with $I_2(\ell, h) = L - \{h\}$. If $i_0 > h$, then $i_0 - h \in L$, and thus the statement holds with $I_2(\ell, h) = L \cup \{i_0 - h\} - \{i_0\}$.

It remains to prove the statement for the case $1 \leq i_0 < h < \frac{\ell+1}{2}$. Clearly, $i_0 \notin \{\ell - h, \ell + 1 - h\}$ and $\{\ell - h, \ell + 1 - h, i_0 - 2h + \ell, i_0 - 2h + \ell + 1\} \subseteq L$. If $x_{\ell-h} \geq y(\ell - h)$, then the statement holds with $I_2(\ell, h) = L \cup \{i_0 - 2h + \ell\} - \{i_0, \ell - h\}$. If $x_{\ell+1-h} \geq y(\ell + 1 - h)$, then the statement holds with $I_2(\ell, h) = L \cup \{i_0 - 2h + \ell + 1\} - \{i_0, \ell + 1 - h\}$. Now we assume $x_{\ell-h} < y(\ell - h)$ and $x_{\ell+1-h} < y(\ell + 1 - h)$. If $\ell$ is even, then clearly $i_2 \neq \ell + 1 - i_2$. One can verify that the statement holds with $I_2(\ell, h) = L \cup \{\ell + 1 - h\} - \{i_2, \ell + 1 - i_2\}$. If $\ell$ is odd, then clearly $i_3 \neq \ell - i_3$. If $x_{i_3} + x_{\ell-i_3} \geq x_\ell$, then let $J = \{i_3, \ell - i_3\}$; otherwise, let $J = \{\ell\}$. Clearly, $\text{bsum}(J, \ell) \geq \frac{2t_\ell}{\ell+1}$ and $\text{sum}(J) = \ell$. One can verify that the statement holds with $I_2(\ell, h) = L \cup \{\ell - h\} - J$.

Statement 3. If $h = 0$, then the statement holds with $I_3(\ell, k, h) = L^k$. If $\frac{\ell+1}{2} \leq h \leq \ell$, then the statement holds with $I_3(\ell, k, h) = L^{k-1} \cup I_2(\ell, \ell - h)$. If $x_h \leq y(h)$, then the statement holds with $I_3(\ell, k, h) = L^k \cup \{h\}$. It remains to consider the case that both $1 \leq h \leq \frac{\ell}{2}$ and $x_h > y(h)$ hold. If $i_0 + 2h - \ell - 1 \in L$ and $i_0 \neq h$, then, by $x_h > y(h)$, the statement holds with $I_3(\ell, k, h) = L^k \cup I_1(\ell, 1) \cup \{i_0 + 2h - \ell - 1\} - \{i_0, h\}$. When either $i_0 + 2h - \ell - 1 \notin L$ or $i_0 = h$ holds, we show $i_0 + h \in L$, which implies that the statement holds with $I_3(\ell, k, h) = L^k \cup \{i_0 + h\} - \{i_0\}$. If $i_0 = h$, then $i_0 + h \in L$ holds trivially. If $i_0 \neq h$, then, by $2h \leq \ell$, we know $i_0 + 2h - \ell - 1 < i_0$. By $i_0 \in L$ and $i_0 + 2h - \ell - 1 \notin L$, we have $i_0 + 2h \leq \ell + 1$, and thus $i_0 + h \in L$.

Statement 4. If there is an $i_4 \in \{0, 1, \ldots, h\}$ such that $x_{i_4} + x_{h-i_4} \leq y(h)$, then the statement holds with $I_4(\ell, d, h) = I_1(\ell, d) \cup \{i_4, h - i_4\}$. If there is an $i_5 \in \{1, \ldots, \ell - h\}$ such that $x_{h+i_5} + x_{\ell+1-i_5} \leq y(\ell + 1 + h)$, then, by $d \geq 1$, the statement holds with $I_4(\ell, d, h) = I_1(\ell, d - 1) \cup \{h + i_5, \ell + 1 - i_5\}$. If no such $i_4$ or $i_5$ exists, then we have $2t_\ell = \sum_{0 \leq i \leq h}(x_i + x_{h-i}) + \sum_{1 \leq i \leq \ell - h}(x_{h+i} + x_{\ell+1-i}) > (h + 1)y(h) + (\ell - h)y(\ell + h + 1) = 2t_\ell$, a contradiction.

Statement 5. By $\ell + 1 \leq n$ and Statement 1, there is an $\left(\ell + 1, \frac{2d}{\ell+1}\right)$-set $I_1(\ell + 1, d)$ with $|I_1(\ell + 1, d)| = 2d$. We show that the statement holds with $I_5(\ell, d) = \{j - 1 \mid j \in I_1(\ell + 1, d)\}$. By the proof for Statement 1, $I_1(\ell + 1, d)$ is an $(\ell + 1)$-set not containing 0. Thus $I_5(\ell, d)$ is an $\ell$-set. Clearly, $|I_5(\ell, d)| = |I_1(\ell + 1, d)| = 2d$, $\text{sum}(I_5(\ell, d)) = \text{sum}(I_1(\ell + 1, d)) - 2d \geq (\ell + 2)d - 2d = \ell d$, and $\text{bsum}(I_5(\ell, d), \ell) = \text{bsum}(I_1(\ell + 1, d), \ell + 1) \leq \frac{2dt_{\ell+1}}{\ell+1}$. $\square$

For each $\ell = 1, 2, \ldots, n$, let $\delta_\ell = (R - R_\ell)\frac{\ell(\ell+1)}{2}$. Clearly, $0 < \delta_\ell \leq 1$ and

$$R = R_\ell + \frac{2\delta_\ell}{\ell(\ell+1)}. \tag{3}$$

By $R_\ell = \phi\left(R, \frac{2}{\ell(\ell+1)}\right)$, we know that $R_\ell$ is an integral multiple of $\frac{2}{\ell(\ell+1)}$. Let $k_\ell = \lfloor R_\ell \rfloor$, $d_\ell = \lfloor (R_\ell - k_\ell)\frac{\ell}{2} \rfloor$, $d'_\ell = \lfloor (R_\ell - k_\ell)\frac{\ell+1}{2} \rfloor$, $h_\ell = \left(R_\ell - k_\ell - \frac{2d_\ell}{\ell}\right)\frac{\ell(\ell+1)}{2}$, and $h'_\ell = \left(R_\ell - k_\ell - \frac{2d'_\ell}{\ell}\right)\frac{\ell(\ell+1)}{2}$. Since $R_\ell$ is an integral multiple of $\frac{2}{\ell(\ell+1)}$, we know that $k_\ell$, $d_\ell$, $d'_\ell$, $h_\ell$, and $h'_\ell$ are integers with $k_\ell = \lfloor R_\ell \rfloor$, $0 \leq d_\ell < \frac{\ell}{2}$, $0 \leq d'_\ell < \frac{\ell+1}{2}$, $0 \leq h_\ell < \ell + 1$, $0 \leq h'_\ell < \ell$, and

$$R_\ell = k_\ell + \frac{2d_\ell}{\ell} + \frac{2h_\ell}{\ell(\ell+1)} \tag{4}$$

$$= k_\ell + \frac{2d'_\ell}{\ell+1} + \frac{2h'_\ell}{\ell(\ell+1)}. \tag{5}$$

One can easily verify that either $d'_\ell = d_\ell$ or $d'_\ell = d_\ell + 1$ holds. Moreover, if $d'_\ell = d_\ell$, then $h'_\ell = d_\ell + h_\ell$. If $d'_\ell = d_\ell + 1$, then $h'_\ell = d_\ell + h_\ell - \ell < \frac{\ell}{2}$.

**Lemma 4.** *For each $\ell = 1, 2, \ldots, n - 1$, we have*

1. $k_{\ell+1} = k_\ell$ and
2. $d_{\ell+1} = d'_\ell$.

*Proof.* Statement 1. Assume for a contradiction that $k_i < k_j$ holds for some $1 \leq i \neq j \leq n$. By $k_j \leq R_j < R$, we know $k_i \leq k_j - 1 \leq \lceil R \rceil - 2$. It suffices to show $\lceil R \rceil - k_i \leq 1$ as follows. If $i$ is even, then, by $d_i < \frac{i}{2}$, we know $d_i \leq \frac{i-2}{2}$. By Equations (3) and (4), $\delta_i \leq 1$, and $h_i < i + 1$, we have $\lceil R \rceil - k_i = \left\lceil \frac{2d_i}{i} + \frac{2(h_i + \delta_i)}{i(i+1)} \right\rceil \leq \left\lceil \frac{i-2}{i} + \frac{2(i+1)}{i(i+1)} \right\rceil = 1$. If $i$ is odd, then, by $d'_i < \frac{i+1}{2}$, we know $d'_i \leq \frac{i-1}{2}$. By Equations (3) and (5), $\delta_i \leq 1$, and $h'_i < i$, we have $\lceil R \rceil - k_i = \left\lceil \frac{2d'_i}{i+1} + \frac{2(h'_i + \delta_i)}{i(i+1)} \right\rceil \leq \left\lceil \frac{i-1}{i+1} + \frac{2i}{i(i+1)} \right\rceil = 1$.

Statement 2. By Equations (3), (4), and (5) and Statement 1, we have $\frac{2d_{\ell+1}}{\ell+1} + \frac{2h_{\ell+1} + \delta_{\ell+1}}{(\ell+1)(\ell+2)} = \frac{2d'_\ell}{\ell+1} + \frac{2(h'_\ell + \delta_\ell)}{\ell(\ell+1)}$. Therefore, $d_{\ell+1} + \frac{h_{\ell+1} + \delta_{\ell+1}}{\ell+2} = d'_\ell + \frac{h'_\ell + \delta_\ell}{\ell}$. By $h'_\ell < \ell$, $h_{\ell+1} < \ell + 2$, and $0 < \delta_\ell, \delta_{\ell+1} \leq 1$, we have $|d_{\ell+1} - d'_\ell| < 1$, and thus $d_{\ell+1} = d'_\ell$. □

## 3.2 Matching Lower Bounds on $\mathcal{A}$'s Winning

Lemmas 5, 6, and 7 analyze the cases (1) $\frac{1}{n} < R \leq \frac{2}{n+1}$, (2) $\frac{2}{n+1} < R \leq 1$, and (3) $1 < R \leq n$, respectively. By Lemma 4(1), the rest of the section omits the subscript of $k_\ell$.

**Lemma 5.** *If $\frac{1}{n} < R \leq \frac{2}{n+1}$, then $w^*(\pi_{\text{unif}}, B_{\mathcal{D}}) \geq \frac{\ell_1}{n}$.*

*Proof.* Let $\ell$ be the number of bids in $B_{\mathcal{D}}$ that are less than $\beta R$. If $\ell \geq \ell_1$, then the expected number of bids that $\mathcal{A}$ wins with $B_{\mathcal{A}} = \{0\}^{n-1} \cup \{\beta R\}$ is at least $\frac{\ell}{n}$, ensuring $w^*(\pi_{\text{unif}}, B_{\mathcal{D}}) \geq \frac{\ell_1}{n}$. The rest of the proof assumes $\ell < \ell_1$. By $(n-\ell)\beta R \leq \sum_{j=\ell+1}^n \beta_j$, we have $\sum_{j=1}^\ell \beta_j \leq \beta R \left(\ell - n + \frac{1}{R}\right)$. By $(n-\ell)\beta R \leq \beta$, we have $\ell \geq n - \frac{1}{R}$. By $\ell_1 < 2n - \frac{2}{R} + 1$, we know $2\ell + 1 > \ell_1$, which implies $2\ell \geq \ell_1$. Let $i^* = \arg\min_{0 \leq i \leq 2\ell - \ell_1} \beta_{\ell-i} + \beta_{\ell_1 - \ell + i}$. Let $X = \{0\}^{n-2} \cup \{\beta_{\ell-i^*}, \beta_{\ell_1 - \ell + i^*}\}$. Clearly, $\text{sum}(X) \leq \frac{2\sum_{j=\ell_1-\ell}^\ell \beta_j}{2\ell - \ell_1 + 1} < \frac{\sum_{j=1}^\ell \beta_j}{\ell - n + R^{-1}} \leq \beta R$. Let $B_{\mathcal{A}} = \bigcup_{x \in X} \{x + \delta\}$, where $\delta$ is a number such that $0 < \delta \leq \frac{\beta R - \text{sum}(X)}{n}$ and $B_{\mathcal{A}} \cap B_{\mathcal{D}} = \emptyset$. Since $\text{sum}(B_{\mathcal{A}}) \leq \beta R$, $|B_{\mathcal{A}}| = n$, and the expected number of bids that $\mathcal{A}$ wins with $B_{\mathcal{A}}$ is at least $\frac{\ell_1}{n}$, the lemma is proved. □

**Lemma 6.** *If $\frac{2}{n+1} < R \leq 1$, then $w^*(\pi_{\text{unif}}, B_{\mathcal{D}}) \geq f(\ell_2)$.*

*Proof.* By $\frac{2}{n+1} < R \leq 1$, we know $\ell_2 = n \geq 2$ and $f(\ell_2) = \frac{(n+1)R_n}{2}$. By Lemma 2 and $\beta_0 = 0$, it suffices to show an $(n, R_n)$-set with at most $n$ elements. If $R_n = \frac{2}{n+1}$, then, by $n \geq 2$, $\{i^*, n - i^*\}$ is a required $(n, R_n)$-set, where $i^* = \arg\min_{1 \leq i \leq n} \beta_i + \beta_{n-i}$. The rest of the proof assumes $R_n > \frac{2}{n+1}$. Since $R_n$ is an integral multiple of $\frac{2}{n(n+1)}$, we know $R_n \geq \frac{2}{n}$. By $R_n < R \leq 1$ and Equation (4), we know $R_n = \frac{2d_n}{n} + \frac{2h_n}{n(n+1)}$, where $d_n \geq 1$ and $0 \leq h_n \leq n$. By Lemma 3(4), we know that $I_4(n, d_n, h_n)$ is an $(n, R_n)$-set with $|I_4(n, d_n, h_n)| \leq 2d_n + 2$. It remains to consider the case $2d_n + 2 > n$. By $d_n < \frac{n}{2}$, we have $d_n = \frac{n-1}{2}$, and thus $R_n = \frac{n-1}{n} + \frac{2h_n}{n(n+1)}$. By $R_n < 1$, we know $h_n < \frac{n+1}{2}$. It follows that $R_n = 1 - \frac{2h}{n(n+1)}$, where $0 < h = \frac{n+1}{2} - h_n \leq \frac{n+1}{2}$. By Lemma 3(2), $I_2(n, h)$ is an $(n, R_n)$-set with $|I_2(n, h)| \leq n$. □

**Lemma 7.** *If $1 < R \leq n$, then $w^*(\pi_{\text{unif}}, B_{\mathcal{D}}) \geq f(\ell_2)$.*

*Proof.* For notational brevity, the proof omits the subscript of $\ell_2$. By $1 < R \leq n$, we know $\ell = \lfloor \frac{n}{R} \rfloor$, $1 \leq \ell \leq n - 1$, $k \geq 1$, and $R\ell \leq n < R(\ell + 1)$. We first show $f(\ell) \leq f(\ell + 1)$ as follows. Let $\Delta = f(\ell) - f(\ell + 1)$. Clearly, $\Delta = 1 + \frac{1}{n}\left(\left\lceil \frac{R\ell(\ell+1)}{2} \right\rceil - \left\lceil \frac{R(\ell+1)(\ell+2)}{2} \right\rceil\right)$, and thus $\Delta$ is an integral multiple of $\frac{1}{n}$. Therefore, it suffices to show $\Delta < 1 + \frac{R}{2n}(\ell(\ell+1) - (\ell+1)(\ell+2)) + \frac{1}{n} = 1 - \frac{R(\ell+1)}{n} + \frac{1}{n} < \frac{1}{n}$.

By $f(\ell) \leq f(\ell + 1)$ and Lemma 2, it suffices to show an $\ell$-set or an $(\ell+1)$-set that satisfies Property P for each of the following cases.

Case 1: $R\ell \leq n \leq \lfloor \ell R_\ell \rfloor + k$. Let $I = I_1(\ell, d_\ell) \cup I_3(\ell, k, h_\ell)$. By Equation (4) and Lemmas 3(1) and 3(3), we know that $I$ is an $(\ell, R_\ell)$-set with $\lfloor \ell R_\ell \rfloor \leq |I| \leq \lceil \ell R_\ell \rceil \leq \lceil R\ell \rceil \leq n$, proving Property P1. Being an $(\ell, R_\ell)$-set, $I$ satisfies Property P2 and $\text{bsum}(I, \ell) \leq R_\ell t_\ell$. By $|I| \geq \lfloor \ell R_\ell \rfloor \geq n - k$, $k \leq R_\ell < R$, and $\beta_{n-\ell} + t_\ell \leq \beta$, we know $(n - |I|)\beta_{n-\ell} + \text{bsum}(I, \ell) \leq k\beta_{n-\ell} + R_\ell t_\ell < R(t_\ell + \beta_{n-\ell}) \leq \beta R$. Therefore, $I$ satisfies Property P3.

Case 2: $\lfloor \ell R_\ell \rfloor + k + 1 \leq n \leq k(\ell+1) + 2d'_\ell + \lfloor \frac{2h'_\ell}{\ell+1} \rfloor$. Let $I = I_5(\ell, d'_\ell) \cup I_3(\ell, k, h'_\ell)$. By Equation (5), $k \geq 1$, and $2d'_\ell < \ell + 1$, we have $\lfloor \ell R_\ell \rfloor + k = k\ell + \lfloor \frac{2d'_\ell + 2h'_\ell}{\ell+1} \rfloor + k \geq k\ell + \lfloor \frac{2d'_\ell + 2h'_\ell + \ell + 1}{\ell+1} \rfloor \geq k\ell + 2d'_\ell + \lfloor \frac{2h'_\ell}{\ell+1} \rfloor$. By Lemmas 3(3) and 3(5), we have $n - k \leq k\ell + 2d'_\ell + \lfloor \frac{2h'_\ell}{\ell+1} \rfloor \leq |I| \leq k\ell + 2d'_\ell + \lceil \frac{2h'_\ell}{\ell+1} \rceil \leq \lfloor \ell R_\ell \rfloor + k + 1 \leq n$, proving Property P1. By Lemmas 3(3) and 3(5) and Equation (5), we have $\text{sum}(I) \geq \ell d'_\ell + \left(k + \frac{2h'_\ell}{\ell(\ell+1)}\right)\frac{\ell(\ell+1)}{2} = \frac{\ell(\ell+1)}{2}R_\ell$, proving Property P2. By $|I| \geq n - k$, $\beta_{n-\ell} + t_\ell = t_{\ell+1} \leq \beta$, and Equation (5), we know $(n - |I|)\beta_{n-\ell} + \text{bsum}(I, \ell) \leq k\beta_{n-\ell} + \frac{2d'_\ell}{\ell+1}t_{\ell+1} + \left(k + \frac{2h'_\ell}{\ell(\ell+1)}\right)t_\ell \leq R_\ell\beta < \beta R$, proving Property P3.

Case 3: $k(\ell+1) + 2d'_\ell + \lfloor \frac{2h'_\ell}{\ell+1} \rfloor + 1 \leq n < R(\ell+1)$. By $n < R(\ell+1)$, we have $n \leq \lceil R(\ell+1) \rceil - 1$. By $\ell + 1 \leq n$ and Equations (3) and (5), we have $\lceil R(\ell+1) \rceil = k(\ell+1) + 2d'_\ell + \lceil \frac{2(h'_\ell + \delta_\ell)}{\ell} \rceil$. By $k(\ell+1) + 2d'_\ell + \lfloor \frac{2h'_\ell}{\ell+1} \rfloor + 1 \leq n \leq \lceil R(\ell+1) \rceil - 1$, we have $\lfloor \frac{2h'_\ell}{\ell+1} \rfloor + 2 \leq \lceil \frac{2(h'_\ell + \delta_\ell)}{\ell} \rceil$. It follows from $h'_\ell + \delta_\ell \leq \ell$ and

$h'_\ell \geq 0$ that $\left\lfloor \frac{2h'_\ell}{\ell+1} \right\rfloor = 0$ and $\left\lceil \frac{2(h'_\ell + \delta_\ell)}{\ell} \right\rceil = 2$. By $k(\ell+1) + 2d'_\ell + \left\lfloor \frac{2h'_\ell}{\ell+1} \right\rfloor + 1 \leq n \leq k(\ell+1) + 2d'_\ell + \left\lceil \frac{2(h'_\ell+\delta_\ell)}{\ell+1} \right\rceil - 1$, we know $n = k(\ell+1) + 2d'_\ell + 1$. By Lemma 4(2) and Equations (3), (4), and (5), we have $\left\lceil \frac{2(h_{\ell+1}+\delta_{\ell+1})}{\ell+2} \right\rceil = R(\ell + 1) - (k(\ell+1) + 2d_{\ell+1}) = R(\ell+1) - (k(\ell+1) + 2d'_\ell) = \left\lceil \frac{2(h'_\ell+\delta_\ell)}{\ell} \right\rceil = 2$. Therefore $1 < \frac{2(h_{\ell+1}+\delta_{\ell+1})}{\ell+2} \leq 2$. By $0 < \delta_{\ell+1} \leq 1$ and $\ell \geq 1$, we have $0 < \frac{2h_{\ell+1}}{\ell+2} < 2$, and thus $\left\lfloor \frac{2h_{\ell+1}}{\ell+2} \right\rfloor \leq 1 \leq \left\lceil \frac{2h_{\ell+1}}{\ell+2} \right\rceil$. It follows from $n = k(\ell+1) + 2d'_\ell + 1$, Equation (4), and Lemma 4(2) that $\lfloor R_{\ell+1}(\ell+1) \rfloor \leq n \leq \lceil R_{\ell+1}(\ell+1) \rceil$. We prove the statement for the following two sub-cases.

Case 3(a): $n = \lceil R_{\ell+1}(\ell+1) \rceil$. Let $I = I_1(\ell+1, d_{\ell+1}) \cup I_3(\ell+1, k, h_{\ell+1})$. By Equation (4), Lemmas 3(1) and 3(3), we know that $I$ is an $(\ell+1, R_{\ell+1})$-set with $\lfloor (\ell+1)R_{\ell+1} \rfloor \leq |I| \leq \lceil (\ell+1)R_{\ell+1} \rceil = n$, satisfying Property P1. Being an $(\ell+1, R_{\ell+1})$-set, $I$ satisfies Property P2 and $\text{bsum}(I, \ell+1) \leq R_{\ell+1}t_{\ell+1}$. By $|I| \geq \lfloor (\ell+1)R_{\ell+1} \rfloor \geq n-1 \geq n-k$, $k \leq R_{\ell+1} < R$, and $\beta_{n-\ell-1} + t_{\ell+1} \leq \beta$, we know $\text{bsum}(I, \ell+1) + (n-|I|)\beta_{n-\ell-1} \leq R_{\ell+1}t_{\ell+1} + k\beta_{n-\ell-1} < R(t_{\ell+1} + \beta_{n-\ell-1}) \leq \beta R$, satisfying Property P3.

Case 3(b): $n = \lfloor R_{\ell+1}(\ell+1) \rfloor$. Let $J_1 = I_3(\ell, k, 0) \cup I_5(\ell, d'_\ell) \cup \{h'_\ell\}$. Let $J_2 = I_3(\ell, k, 0) \cup I_5(\ell, d'_\ell + 1) - \{h'_\ell\}$. By the proof of Lemma 3(3), we know $h'_\ell \in \{1, 2, \ldots, \ell\} \subseteq I_3(\ell, k, 0)$. Therefore, $|J_1| = |J_2| = k\ell + 2d'_\ell + 1 = n - k$. By $\left\lfloor \frac{2h'_\ell}{\ell+1} \right\rfloor = 0$, we know $\ell - h'_\ell \geq h'_\ell$. By $\ell - h'_\ell \geq h'_\ell$ and Lemmas 3(1) and 3(3), one can verify that each of $J_1$ and $J_2$ satisfies Properties P1 and P2. It remains to show that either $J_1$ or $J_2$ satisfies Property P3 as follows. If $\beta_{n-\ell+h'_\ell} < \frac{2(h'_\ell+\delta_\ell)\beta}{\ell(\ell+1)}$, then, by $t_{\ell+1} = \beta_{n-\ell} + t_\ell \leq \beta$ and Equations (3) and (5), we know $\text{bsum}(J_1, \ell) + (n-|J_1|)\beta_{n-\ell} < \frac{2d'_\ell}{\ell+1}t_{\ell+1} + kt_\ell + \frac{2(h'_\ell+\delta_\ell)\beta}{\ell(\ell+1)} + k\beta_{n-\ell} \leq \beta R$. Thus $J_1$ satisfies Property P3. Now we assume $\beta_{n-\ell+h'_\ell} \geq \frac{2(h'_\ell+\delta_\ell)\beta}{\ell(\ell+1)}$. By $\left\lceil \frac{2(h'_\ell+\delta_\ell)}{\ell} \right\rceil = 2$, we know $h'_\ell + \delta_\ell > \frac{\ell}{2}$, and thus $\ell - (h'_\ell+\delta_\ell) < h'_\ell + \delta_\ell$. It follows from $t_\ell \leq t_{\ell+1} \leq \beta$ and Equations (3) and (5) that $\text{bsum}(J_2, \ell) + (n-|J_2|)\beta_{n-\ell} < kt_\ell + \frac{2(d'_\ell+1)t_{\ell+1}}{\ell+1} - \frac{2(h'_\ell+\delta_\ell)\beta}{\ell(\ell+1)} + k\beta_{n-\ell} \leq \left( k + \frac{2d'_\ell}{\ell+1} + \frac{2(h'_\ell+\delta_\ell)}{\ell(\ell+1)} \right)\beta = \beta R$. Thus $J_2$ satisfies Property P3. □

**Theorem 1.** *$(\pi_{\text{unif}}, \Psi)$ is an optimal bidding algorithm for $\mathcal{D}$. Furthermore, $w^*(\pi_{\text{unif}}, \Psi) = \text{equil}(n, R)$.*

*Proof.* Clearly, $w^*(\pi_{\text{unif}}, \Psi) \geq \min_{\pi_{\mathcal{D}}, B_{\mathcal{D}}} w^*(\pi_{\mathcal{D}}, B_{\mathcal{D}})$ holds trivially. By Lemmas 1, 5, 6, and 7, we know that $w^*(\pi_{\text{unif}}, \Psi) \leq \text{equil}(n, R) \leq w^*(\pi_{\text{unif}}, B_{\mathcal{D}})$ holds for any bid set $B_{\mathcal{D}}$ of $\mathcal{D}$. Therefore, we have Equation (2), and thus the equality $w^*(\pi_{\text{unif}}, \Psi) = \text{equil}(n, R)$. □

It follows from Theorem 1 that the optimal expected winning of $\mathcal{A}$ (respectively, $\mathcal{D}$) is $\text{equil}(n, R)$ (respectively, $n - \text{equil}(n, R)$). We define $\mathcal{A}$'s *effective winning ratio* $E_{\mathcal{A}}(n, R)$ to be $\frac{\text{equil}(n,R)}{\frac{nR}{R+1}}$. Similarly, $\mathcal{D}$'s *effective winning ratio* $E_{\mathcal{D}}(n, R)$ is $\frac{n - \text{equil}(n,R)}{\frac{n}{R+1}}$.

Note that $\frac{R}{R+1}$ (respectively, $\frac{1}{R+1}$) is the fraction of $\mathcal{A}$'s (respectively, $\mathcal{D}'s$) budget in the total budget of $\mathcal{A}$ and $\mathcal{D}$. One might intuitively expect that $\mathcal{A}$ (respectively, $\mathcal{D}$) would win $\frac{nR}{R+1}$ (respectively, $\frac{n}{R+1}$) objects optimally on average. In other words, $E_{\mathcal{A}}(n, R) = E_{\mathcal{D}}(n, R) = 1$. Surprisingly, these equalities are not true, as shown in the next corollary.

**Corollary 1.** *1. If $R \geq 1$, then we have $\lim_{n\to\infty} E_{\mathcal{A}}(n, R) = \frac{(2R-1)(R+1)}{2R^2}$ and $\lim_{n\to\infty} E_{\mathcal{D}}(n, R) = \frac{R+1}{2R}$.*
*2. If $R \leq 1$, then we have $\lim_{n\to\infty} E_{\mathcal{A}}(n, R) = \frac{R+1}{2}$ and $\lim_{n\to\infty} E_{\mathcal{D}}(n, R) = \frac{(2-R)(R+1)}{2}$.*

*Proof.* Straightforward. $\square$

*Remark.* The formulas in Corollary 1 are symmetric in the sense that those in Statement 1 can be obtained from Statement 2 by replacing $R$ with $\frac{1}{R}$.

## 4  Open Problems

This paper solves the case with two bidders. The case with more than two bidders remains open. Another research direction is auction with *collusion*. Note that our model is equivalent to auction with colluding groups where the bidders all have equal budgets, and those in the same group pool their money. For example, if the budgets of two money-pooling bidders are $100 and $100, then either of them can make a bid of $150. If pooling is not allowed, then neither can make a bid of $150. It would be of interest to optimally or approximately achieve game-theoretic equilibria for auctions with non-pooling collusion.

## References

1. K. AKCOGLU, J. ASPNES, B. DASGUPTA, AND M. Y. KAO, *Opportunity-cost algorithms for combinatorial auctions*, 2000. Submitted for conference publication.
2. D. P. BERTSEKAS, *An auction algorithm for the max-flow problem*, Journal of Optimization Theory and Applications, 87 (1995), pp. 69–101.
3. D. BLACKWELL, *An analog of the minimax theorem for vector payoffs*, Pacific Journal of Mathematics, 6 (1956), pp. 1–8.
4. D. BLACKWELL AND M. A. GIRSHICK, *Theory of Games and Statistical Decisions*, Wiley, New York, NY, 1954.
5. A. BORODIN AND R. EL-YANIV, *Online Computation and Competitive Analysis*, Cambridge University Press, Cambridge, United Kingdom, 1998.
6. C. CACHIN, *Efficient private bidding and auctions with an oblivious third party*, in Proceedings of the 6th ACM Conference on Computer and Communications Security, 1999, pp. 120–127.
7. S. H. CLEARWATER, ed., *Market-Based Control, a Paradigm for Distributed Resource Allocation*, World Scientific, River Ridge, NJ, 1996.
8. C. DEMARTINI, A. M. KWASNICA, J. O. LEDYARD, AND D. PORTER, *A new and improved design for multiple-object iterative auctions*, Tech. Rep. SSWP 1054, California Institute of Technology, 1999.

9. Y. FUJISHIMA, K. LEYTON-BROWN, AND Y. SHOHAM, *Taming the computational complexity of combinatorial auctions: Optimal and approximate approaches*, the 16th International Joint Conference on Artificial Intelligence, 1999, pp. 548–553.

10. Y. FUJISHIMA, D. MCADAMS, AND Y. SHOHAM, *Speeding up ascending-bid auctions*, 16th International Joint Conf. on Artificial Intelligence, 1999, pp. 554–563.

11. R. A. GAGLIANO, M. D. FRASER, AND M. E. SCHAEFER, *Auction allocation of computing resources*, Communications of the ACM, 38 (1995), pp. 88–99.

12. K. HENDRICKS AND H. J. PAARSH, *A survey of recent empirical work concerning auctions*, Canadian Journal of Economics, 28 (1995), pp. 403–426.

13. M. N. HUHNS AND J. M. VIDAL, *Agents on the Web: Online auctions*, IEEE Internet Computing, 3 (1999), pp. 103–105.

14. M. Y. KAO, J. F. QI, AND L. TAN, *Optimal bidding algorithms against cheating in multiple object auctions*, SIAM Journal on Computing, 28 (1999), pp. 955–969.

15. D. LEHMANN, L. I. O'CALLAGHAN, AND Y. SHOHAM, *Truth revelation in rapid approximately efficient combinatorial auctions*, in Proceedings of the 1st ACM Conference on Electronic Commerce, SIGecom, ACM Press, 1999, pp. 96–102.

16. J. MCMILLAN AND R. P. MCAFEE, *Auctions and bidding*, Journal of Economic Literature, 25 (1987), pp. 699–738.

17. P. R. MILGROM AND R. J. WEBER, *A theory of auctions and competitive bidding*, Econometrica, 50 (1982), pp. 1089–1122.

18. R. B. MYERSON, *Optimal auction design*, Mathematics of Operations Research, 6 (1981), pp. 58–73.

19. D. C. PARKES AND L. H. UNGAR, *Iterative combinatorial auctions: Theory and practice*, the 18th National Conference on Artificial Intelligence, 2000. To appear.

20. C. PITCHIK AND A. SCHOTTER, *Perfect equilibria in budget-constrained sequential auctions: an experimental study*, RAND J. of Economics, 19 (1988), pp. 363–388.

21. C. PREIST, *Commodity trading using an agent-based iterated double auction*, 3rd International Conference on Autonomous Agents, 1999, pp. 131–138.

22. J. A. RODRMGUEZ-AGUILAR, F. J. MARTMN, P. NORIEGA, P. GARCIA, AND C. SIERRA, *Towards a test-bed for trading agents in electronic auction markets*, AI Communications, 11 (1998), pp. 5–19.

23. M. H. ROTHKOPF, A. PEKEČ, AND R. M. HARSTAD, *Computationally manageable combinatorial auctions*, Management Science, 44 (1998), pp. 1131–1147.

24. K. SAKO, *An auction protocol which hides bids of losers*, in LNCS 1751: 3rd International Workshop on Practice and Theory in Public Key Cryptography, H. Imai and Y. Zheng, eds., Springer-Verlag, New York, NY, 2000, pp. 422–432.

25. T. SANDHOLM AND S. SURI, *Improved algorithms for optimal winner determination in combinatorial auctions and generalizations*, in Proceedings of the 18th National Conference on Artificial Intelligence, 2000, pp. 90–97.

26. F. STAJANO AND R. J. ANDERSON, *The cocaine auction protocol: On the power of anonymous broadcast*, in LNCS 1768: the 3rd International Workshop on Information Hiding, A. Pfitzmann, ed., Springer-Verlag, New York, NY, 1999.

27. R. WILSON, *Strategic analysis of auctions*, in Handbook of Game Theory with Economic Applications, R. J. Aumann and S. Hart, eds., vol. 1, Elsevier Science, New York, NY, 1992, pp. 227–279.

28. P. R. WURMAN, M. P. WELLMAN, AND W. E. WALSH, *The Michigan Internet AcutionBot: A configurable auction server for human and software agents*, 2nd International Conference on Autonomous Agents, 1998, pp. 301–308.

# Coping with Delays and Time-Outs in Binary Search Procedures*

Ferdinando Cicalese and Ugo Vaccaro

Dipartimento di Informatica ed Applicazioni, University of Salerno,
84081 Baronissi (SA), Italy
{cicalese,uv}@dia.unisa.it,
WWW home page: http://www.dia.unisa.it/{~cicalese,~uv}

**Abstract.** How many questions are necessary to guess an unknown number $x$ in the set $S = \{1, 2, \ldots, n\}$, by using only comparison questions, that is questions of the type "Is $x \le a$?", when answers are received with a constant delay $d$, and up to a constant number $c$ of the answers can be lost, i.e. can be not received at all? We exactly solve this problem for all integers $d \ge 0$ and $c = 1$. We also briefly discuss the analogy between the above problem and that of broadcasting over a fully connected network with link latency.

## 1 Introduction

Search problems are among the most important and studied issues in Computer Science [16]. The basic problem of locating an unknown object in a finite set has been thoroughly investigated and many deep connections between this seemingly simple problem and several areas of mathematics have been found, e.g., Information Theory [14,21], Extremal Set Theory [15], Poset Theory [17,18], to mention just a few. We refer the reader to the excellent monograph [1] and to the recent surveys [12,13] for the main results and literature on the topic.

In almost all the work in the area, it is assumed that the information obtained by the execution of a test (question) is immediately available after the question has been made. However, there are several situations in which the time when the question is asked and the time when the corresponding answer becomes available are decoupled. This may be due to several reasons: the elaboration of the answer to the query may be time-consuming, or queries and answers are transmitted via slow channels, etc. It is, therefore, quite surprising that only very recently a rigourous analysis of search procedures in the presence of "delayed answers" has been started [4].

It is worth to remark that the awareness of the necessity to cope with "delayed information" is recently arising also in other areas of Computer Science [3, 6]. The relevance of our result to one of these areas will be also briefly discussed in this paper. In particular, the scenario we have in mind is related to that of [6]:

---

* This work was partially supported by an ENEA grant and by Progetto Cofinanziato: "Allocazioni di Risorse su Reti di Calcolatori"

D.T. Lee and S.-H. Teng (Eds.): ISAAC 2000, LNCS 1969, pp. 96–107, 2000.

questions are delivered on links of a network with transmission latency, so that the answer to a question (if received) is available only after a certain number of time instants; moreover, we assume that *time-outs* are possible, that is, the answer, if not received within the allowable time-bound, is to be considered lost. This should take into account the effect of realistic management of message delivery in computer networks, in which there are mechanisms to prevent messages from remaining in the network too long [7].

**Our Results.** We give an exact analysis (i.e., matching upper and lower bounds) to the problem described in the abstract. More precisely, we find the exact cardinality of a maximal search space successfully searchable with $t$ questions, under the hypothesis that there is a delay of $d$ time units between questions and corresponding answers, and up to *one* answer can be lost. Our result is a fault-tolerant extension of the main result of [4] (when faults correspond to loss of answers).

We would like to point out that the problem of coping with loss of answers in the classical setting (i.e., no delay between questions and answers exists) is completely trivial, and there is no better strategy than repeating the unanswered questions. In our scenario, this simple technique to overcome the effect of losses would result in a slow-down factor of $cd$. Our analysis shows that with a careful choice of questions, one can do much better.

In the final part of this paper we discuss in which sense "delayed search strategies" [4] and broadcast of messages in networks with link latency [6], can be considered isomorphic problems.

**Related Work.** We have already mentioned that our results are a fault-tolerant extension of [4]. We would like to stress that in recent years the research concerning the introduction of fault-tolerance in classical search procedures has been flourishing (see [2,5,8,9,10,19,20,22,23] and references therein quoted).

## 2    The Problem

The problem of searching with delays and cancellations can be formulated as a game between two players, a questioner $Q$ and a responder $R$ : They first agree on three non-negative integers $d, c$ and $n$ so that they fix the search space $S = \{1, 2, \ldots, n\}$. Then player $R$ chooses a number $x$ in $S$. Player $Q$ has to find out $x$ by only using comparison questions, that is questions in the form "Is $x \leq a$?", for some $a \in S$. At any time $i$, for $i = 1, 2, \ldots$, a question must be formulated, so by the $i^{th}$ question we mean the question formulated at time $i$. The answer to the $i^{th}$ question is delivered to $Q$ only after the time $i + d$ and before time $i + d + 1$. Thus, unless $Q$ has already finished questioning, at any time during the game there are $d$ questions pending with respect to the answers given by $R$, so far. Moreover, during the whole game, $R$ can choose not to answer to up to $c$ questions. We also say that up to $c$ questions can be cancelled. We are interested in the minimum number $q$ of questions that $Q$ has to ask in order to be always able to correctly guess the secret number $x$, (in that case we shall also say that $Q$ wins the $(n, d, c)$-game with $q$ questions). We recall here that if the total number of questions asked by $Q$ is $t$, then the game actually ends at time $t + d + 1$.

As a matter of fact, our results are given in terms of a problem that is dual to the above formulated one. Henceforth we shall denote with $A_d^{(c)}(t)$, the largest integer $n$ such that $Q$ wins the $(n, d, c)$-game with $t$ questions. For all $t \geq 0$ and $d \geq 0$, we shall give an exact evaluation of $A_d^{(c)}(t)$, when $c = 1$.

## 3   The Main Result

**Definition 1.** *For any integer $t, d \geq 0$, let*

$$B_d^{(1)}(t) = \begin{cases} \lfloor \frac{t}{2} \rfloor + 1 & \text{if } t \leq d + 1 \\ B_d^{(1)}(t-1) + B_d^{(1)}(t-d-1) & \text{if } t \geq d + 2. \end{cases} \tag{1}$$

We shall prove that for all integers $t \geq 0$, $d \geq 0$ and for $c = 1$, we have

$$A_d^{(1)}(t) = B_d^{(1)}(t).$$

We shall need some preliminary results. In particular, Definition 2 and Theorem 1 were given in [4].

**Definition 2.** *Let*

$$B_d^{(0)}(t) = \begin{cases} 1 & \text{if } t \leq 0 \\ B_d^{(0)}(t-1) + B_d^{(0)}(t-d-1) & \text{if } t > 0. \end{cases}$$

*Remark 1.* Note that by definition for $0 \leq t \leq d + 1$ we have $B_d^{(0)}(t) = t + 1$.

**Theorem 1.** *[4] For all $d \geq 0$ and $t \geq 0$,*

$$A_d^{(0)}(t) = B_d^{(0)}(t).$$

We immediately have the following easy lemma.

**Lemma 1.** *For all integers $d \geq 0$ and $t \geq 0$*

$$B_d^{(1)}(t) \leq B_d^{(0)}(t-1).$$

*Proof.* For $0 \leq t \leq d + 1$, we have

$$B_d^{(1)}(t) = \lfloor \frac{t}{2} \rfloor + 1 \leq t = B_d^{(0)}(t-1).$$

Let $t > d + 1$ and $B_d^{(1)}(i) \leq B_d^{(0)}(i-1)$ for all $i < t$. Then

$$B_d^{(1)}(t) = B_d^{(1)}(t-1) + B_d^{(1)}(t-d-1) \leq B_d^{(0)}(t-2) + B_d^{(0)}(t-d-2) = B_d^{(0)}(t-1).$$

The following two lemmas will be the key technical tools for the Main Result.

**Lemma 2.** *For all integers $d \geq 0$ and $t \geq 0$ we have*

$$B_d^{(1)}(t) \leq B_d^{(0)}(t+1) - B_d^{(1)}(t+1).$$

*Proof.* We argue by induction on $t$.

*Induction Base.* By Remark 1 and Definition 1 we immediately get

$$B_d^{(0)}(t+1) - B_d^{(1)}(t+1) = (t+2) - \lfloor \frac{t+1}{2} \rfloor - 1 \geq \lfloor \frac{t+2}{2} \rfloor$$
$$= \lfloor \frac{t}{2} \rfloor + 1 = B_d^{(1)}(t),$$

for all $t = 0, 1, \ldots, d$.
For $t = d + 1$ we have

$$B_d^{(0)}(t+1) - B_d^{(1)}(t+1) = B_d^{(0)}(d+2) - B_d^{(1)}(d+2)$$
$$= B_d^{(0)}(d+1) + B_d^{(0)}(1) - B_d^{(1)}(d+1) - B_d^{(1)}(1)$$
$$= B_d^{(0)}(d+1) + 2 - B_d^{(1)}(d+1) - 1 \geq 1 + B_d^{(1)}(d)$$
$$\geq B_d^{(1)}(d+1) = B_d^{(1)}(t).$$

*Induction Step.* Now suppose that the claim is true for all $t \leq i$ and $i \geq d+1$. We shall prove that it also holds for $t = i + 1$. Indeed

$$B_d^{(0)}(t+1) - B_d^{(1)}(t+1) = B_d^{(0)}(i+2) - B_d^{(1)}(i+2) =$$
$$= B_d^{(0)}(i+1) - B_d^{(1)}(i+1)$$
$$+ B_d^{(0)}(i+1-d) - B_d^{(1)}(i+1-d)$$
$$\text{(by definition, and rearranging terms)}$$
$$\geq B_d^{(1)}(i) + B_d^{(1)}(i-d)$$
$$\text{(by inductive hypothesis)}$$
$$= B_d^{(1)}(i+1) = B_d^{(1)}(t),$$

which concludes the proof.

**Lemma 3.** *For all integers $d \geq 0$, $t \geq d+2$, and $j = 1, 2, \ldots, \lfloor \frac{d}{2} \rfloor$, we have*

$$B_d^{(1)}(t-j) + B_d^{(1)}(t-(d-j)) \leq B_d^{(1)}(t) + B_d^{(1)}(t-d).$$

*Proof.* Omitted in this extended abstract.

## 3.1  The Upper Bound

**Theorem 2.** *For all integers $t \geq 0$ and $d \geq 0$,*

$$A_d^{(1)}(t) \leq B_d^{(1)}(t).$$

*Proof.* We argue by induction on $t$.

*Induction Base.* $0 \leq t \leq d+1$. In this case the whole questioning is non-adaptive. Recall that $B_d^{(1)}(t) = \lfloor \frac{t}{2} \rfloor + 1$. We shall show that no strategy using $t$ questions can exist to search for an unknown number in a set of cardinality $B_d^{(1)}(t) + 1$, hence $A_d^{(1)}(t) \leq B_d^{(1)}(t)$. By contradiction, suppose that there exists a strategy with $t$ questions to search in the set $S = \{1, 2, \ldots B_d^{(1)}(t) + 1\}$. As a matter of fact, there must exist at least one $i$ such that the question "Is $x \leq i$?" has been asked at most once. Suppose that the answer to this very question is cancelled. Then the questioner can not guess whether the secret number is $i$ or $i+1$. Hence the strategy is not winning, hence, a fortiori, $A_d^{(1)}(t) \leq B_d^{(1)}(t)$, as desired.

*Inductive Hypothesis.* $A_d^{(1)}(i) \leq B_d^{(1)}(i)$, for all $i < t$.

*Induction Step.* Assume that there exists a strategy to win the $(A_d^{(1)}(t), d, c)$-game with $t$ questions.

Let "is $x \leq q_1$?" be the first question in this strategy. Suppose that there exist $j$ queries among the pending ones, asking "is $x \leq a_i$?", with $a_i \geq q_1$, for $i = 1, \ldots, j$. Let $J$ denote this set of questions. Assume, now, that the first answer is to the effect that $x \leq q_1$ (i.e., a positive answer is received). Of course the answers to the questions in $J$ are not informative since they will be obviously positive, since $x \leq q_1 \leq a_i$, for all $i = 1, \ldots, j$.

It turns out that only $t - 1 - j$ of the remaining questions (including the pending ones and the ones still to be asked) can be useful to find the secret number. Thus the set $\{1, 2, \ldots, q_1\}$ is not larger than the largest set which allows a successful searching strategy with $t - 1 - j$ questions, i.e., $q_1 \leq A_d^{(1)}(t - 1 - j)$.

Accordingly, suppose now that the answer to the first question is "no". Then, by hypothesis, only $j$ of the pending queries are useful, that is, exactly those in the set $J$. Hence the set $\{q_1 + 1, \ldots, A_d^{(1)}(t)\}$ is not larger than the largest set which allows a successful searching strategy with $t - 1 - d + j$ questions, i.e, $A_d^{(1)}(t) - q_1 \leq A_d^{(1)}(t - 1 - d + j)$.

Finally, since the answer to the first question may also be cancelled, we have $A_d^{(1)}(t) \leq A_d^{(0)}(t - 1)$. Therefore

$$A_d^{(1)}(t) \leq \min \left\{ \max_{0 \leq j \leq \lfloor \frac{d}{2} \rfloor} \{A_d^{(1)}(t - 1 - j) + A_d^{(1)}(t - 1 - d + j)\}, A_d^{(0)}(t - 1) \right\}$$

$$\leq \min \left\{ \max_{0 \leq j \leq \lfloor \frac{d}{2} \rfloor} \{B_d^{(1)}(t - 1 - j) + B_d^{(1)}(t - 1 - d + j)\}, B_d^{(0)}(t - 1) \right\}$$

(by inductive hypothesis)

$$= \min \left\{ B_d^{(1)}(t-1) + B_d^{(1)}(t-1-d), B_d^{(0)}(t-1) \right\}$$

(by Lemma 3)

$$= \min \left\{ B_d^{(1)}(t), B_d^{(0)}(t-1) \right\} = B_d^{(1)}(t).$$

## 3.2 The Lower Bound

We shall give an algorithm for successfully searching in a space of cardinality $B_d^{(1)}(t)$, with $t$ questions.

**Lemma 4.** *For all integers $d \geq 0$, $t \geq 0$ we have*

$$A_d^{(1)}(t) \geq B_d^{(1)}(t).$$

*Proof.* We shall show that $t$ questions suffice to search successfully in the set $S = \{1, 2, \ldots, B_d^{(1)}(t)\}$.

For $t \leq d+1$ our strategy trivially asks twice for any number $1, 2, \ldots, \lfloor \frac{t}{2} \rfloor$. Since there is at most one cancellation, we are sure to receive at least one answer for any question "Is $x \leq i$?" with $1 \leq i \leq \lfloor \frac{t}{2} \rfloor$, that is we can safely find an unknown number in the set $S$ (recall that $B_d^{(1)}(t) = \lfloor \frac{t}{2} \rfloor + 1$).

For $t \geq d+2$ our strategy asks the first $d+1$ questions, respectively, at points $B_d^{(1)}(t-1), B_d^{(1)}(t-2), \ldots, B_d^{(1)}(t-d-1)$.

- If the answer to the first question is "no", then the unknown number belongs to the set $\{B_d^{(1)}(t-1) + 1, B_d^{(1)}(t-1) + 2, \ldots, B_d^{(1)}(t)\}$ which is of size $B_d^{(1)}(t) - B_d^{(1)}(t-1) = B_d^{(1)}(t-d-1)$. Then, an inductive argument shows that the remaining $t - d - 1$ questions suffice to complete successfully the search.
- If the answer to the first question is "yes" then ask the $d + 2^{nd}$ question at point $B_d^{(1)}(t-d-2)$. Thus we are in the same situation as we were before the answer. In fact, we are now to search in an interval of size $B_d^{(1)}(t-1)$ with $t - 1$ questions. Again the desired result follows by induction.
- If the answer to the first question get cancelled, then our strategy asks the $d + 2^{nd}$ question at point $B_d^{(1)}(t-2) + B_d^{(0)}(t-d-2)$. In other words we start to search the set $\{B_d^{(1)}(t-2) + 1, \ldots, B_d^{(1)}(t)\}$ by using the strategy for a set of cardinality $B_d^{(0)}(t-d-1)$ with no cancellation. This accounts for the case in which the second answer is "no". If this is the case, then the unknown number is indeed in the set $\{B_d^{(1)}(t-2) + 1, B_d^{(1)}(t-2) + 2, \ldots, B_d^{(1)}(t)\}$, of size $B_d^{(1)}(t-d-1) + B_d^{(1)}(t-d-2) \leq B_d^{(0)}(t-d-1)$ (by Lemma 2), and we have the desired result by Theorem 1.

  Conversely suppose that the second answer is "yes". Then there are $t - d - 2$ questions left and we know that the secret number belongs to the set $\{1, 2, \ldots, B_d^{(1)}(t-2)\}$. Remember that there are $d - 1$ useful pending questions at points $B_d^{(1)}(t-3), \ldots, B_d^{(1)}(t-d-1)$, and the $d^{th}$ pending question is a useless one at point $B_d^{(0)}(t-d-2)+B_d^{(1)}(t-2)$. Our strategy consists in continuing to ask questions at points $B_d^{(0)}(t-d-3), B_d^{(0)}(t-d-4), \ldots$ until a "no" answer is received. If the "no" answer is given to one of the pending questions, say the one asked at point $B_d^{(1)}(t-2-i)$ (for some $i \in \{1, 2, \ldots, d-1\}$) then the secret number belongs to the set $\{B_d^{(1)}(t-2-i)+1, \ldots, B_d^{(1)}(t-2-i+1)\}$ of size $B_d^{(1)}(t-d-2-i)$ which can be searched successfully with the remaining $t-d-3-i$ questions, since no more cancellations are allowed and $B_d^{(1)}(t-d-2-i) \le B_d^{(0)}(t-d-3-i)$. If the secret number belongs to the set $\{1, 2, \ldots, B_d^{(1)}(t-d-1)\}$, that is the "no" answer is not given to any of the first $d$ pending queries, then by $B_d^{(1)}(t-d-1) \le B_d^{(0)}(t-d-2)$ the remaining questions allow to search successfully in a set of cardinality $B_d^{(0)}(t-d-2)$ (with no cancellation) and a fortiori we must succeed with the remaining search space of size $B_d^{(1)}(t-d-1)$.

## 4 Extensions

In this section we discuss an alternative formulation of the recurrence (1), which could shed some light on a possible generalization of our result to the case of an arbitrary (fixed) number of cancellations.

**Definition 3.** *For all non-negative integers $d, t$ and $c$ we define*

$$\tilde{B}_d^{(c)}(t) = \begin{cases} 1 & \text{for } t \le 0 \\ \sum_{i=1}^{t+1} G_i^{(c)}(t, d) & \text{otherwise,} \end{cases} \quad (2)$$

*where, for all $i = 1, 2, \ldots, t+1$,*

$$G_i^{(c)}(t, d) = \min_{0 \le j \le \min\{i-1, c\}} \left\{ \tilde{B}_d^{(c-j)}(t-d-i+j) - \sum_{k=1}^{j} G_{i-k}^{(c)}(t, d) \right\} \quad (3)$$

*and*

$$G_i^{(c)}(t, d) = 0 \qquad \text{for } i \le 0.$$

It turns out that for $c = 0, 1$, and for all $d \ge 0$ and $t \ge 0$, we have [1]

$$B_d^{(c)}(t) = \tilde{B}_d^{(c)}(t).$$

We conjecture that under the hypothesis $c \le d$, we have in general

$$\tilde{B}_d^{(c)}(t) = A_d^{(c)}(t).$$

In this extended abstract we shall limit ourselves to sketch the sufficiency of conditions (2)-(3) for the existence of a searching strategy to win the $(\tilde{B}_d^{(c)}(t), d, c)$-game with $t$ questions. This is more formally stated in the following lemma.

---

[1] We shall omit the proof of this result in this extended abstract.

**Lemma 5.** *For all integers $d \geq 0$, $0 \leq c \leq d$ and $t \geq 0$, we have $\tilde{B}_d^{(c)}(t) \leq A_d^{(c)}(t)$.*

*Sketch of the Proof.* We shall outline a winning searching strategy for the $(\tilde{B}_d^{(c)}(t), d, c)$-game, with $t$ questions. Due to the space limit, the technical details will be omitted in this extended abstract, and we shall limit ourselves to describe the main ideas. The argument will be by induction on $t$.

For $i = 1, 2, \ldots$, let us identify the question "Is $x \leq q_i$?" with the integer $q_i$. We also say that $Q$ asks the $i^{th}$ question at $q_i$.

For $1 \leq i \leq d+1$, we set

$$q_i = \tilde{B}_d^{(c)}(t) - \sum_{j=1}^{i} G_j^{(c)}(t, d).$$

If $t \leq d+1$ we have

$$G_i^{(c)}(t, d) = \begin{cases} 1 & \text{for } i = (c+1)j, \ j = 0, 1, \ldots, \lfloor \frac{t}{c+1} \rfloor, \\ 0 & \text{otherwise.} \end{cases}$$

Hence the strategy asks $c + 1$ times the question "Is $x \leq i$?" for all $i \in \{1, 2, \ldots, \lfloor \frac{t}{c+1} \rfloor\}$, so to be able to search successfully in the set $\{1, 2, \ldots, \lfloor \frac{t}{c+1} \rfloor + 1\}$. It is not hard to see that, in fact, in this case our strategy is optimal, in the sense that $\tilde{B}_d^{(c)}(t) = \lfloor \frac{t}{c+1} \rfloor + 1 = A_d^{(c)}(t)$.

If $t > d+1$. Then, when the first answer is received, the strategy proceeds as follows:

1. if the answer is "yes" then our strategy asks the $d + 2^{nd}$ question at point $q_{d+2} = q_{d+1} - G_{d+2}^{(c)}(t, d)$. Then we are in the same situation as before and the correctness of our strategy follows by induction;

2. if the answer is "no" then the set of possible solution reduces to $S' = \{q_1 + 1, \ldots, \tilde{B}_d^{(c)}(t)\}$, and by $|S'| = G_1^{(c)}(t, d) = \tilde{B}_d^{(c)}(t - d - 1)$, we can complete the search with the remaining $t - d - 1$ questions, by inductive hypothesis.

3. Finally, suppose that the first answer is not delivered. Then there are again three possible cases, according to the answer given to the second question. Indeed if the second answer is "no" then the set of possible solutions will become $S'' = \{q_2 + 1, \ldots, \tilde{B}_d^{(c)}(t)\}$. We have $|S''| = G_1^{(c)}(t, d) + G_2^{(c)}(t, d) \leq \tilde{B}_d^{(c-1)}(t - d - 1)$, by the definition of $G_2^{(c)}(t, d)$. Thus, by induction, we can complete the search in the set $S''$ with the remaining $t - d - 1$ questions, provided that we start to ask the $t - d - 2$ question accordingly, i.e., in $S''$. Indeed this is exactly what our strategy does. If, on the contrary, the second answer is "yes", then, the $d + 2^{nd}$ question (the last one, asked in $S''$) becomes useless. However, and in analogy with what we have said in point 1. and 2. above, the pending questions allow to complete the search if the following $i - 1$ answers are "yes" and, next, a "no" answer is received, that is,

the reservoir of possible solutions reduces the interval $I_i = \{q_{i+1}+1, \ldots, q_i\}$, for some $i = 2, 3, \ldots, d$. Indeed, by definition, we have $|I_i| = G_{i+1}^{(c)}(t, d) \leq \tilde{B}_d^{(c)}(t - d - (i + 1)) \leq \tilde{B}_d^{(c-1)}(t - 1 - d - (i + 1))$, hence, a fortiori, the original pending questions are effective to the present situation, now that up to $c - 1$ of the remaining questions can be lost. Then our strategy asks the $d + 3^{(rd)}$ question in order to cover the set $\{1, 2, \ldots, q_{d+1}\}$, with the remaining $t - d - 2$ questions. This is, in fact attainable, by $\tilde{B}_d^{(c)}(t - d - 1) \leq \tilde{B}_d^{(c-1)}(t - d - 2)$. Finally, if the second answer is lost, then we can recurse on the above reasoning, to prove that the search can be completed correctly.

## 4.1   Broadcast with Latency vs. Search with Delay

In this section we analyze the connection between the problem of searching with delay and the important problem of broadcasting in the fully connected network with link latency [6]. Indeed the following lemma shows in which sense the problems considered in [6] and [4] are isomorphic. We believe that this analogy between search procedures and broadcasting algorithms may be a useful tool in both fields.

**Lemma 6.** *Let $\mathcal{N}$ be a fully connected network of size $n$ with link latency $d$. Then, there exists a protocol to complete a broadcast in the network $\mathcal{N}$ within $t$ time units* if and only if *there exists a searching algorithm to win the $(n, d, 0)$-game with $t - d$ questions.*

*Proof.* We shall only discuss the direction *Broadcast $\Rightarrow$ Search*. The converse is completely symmetric.

Let $T$ be a broadcast tree [2] attaining the protocol in the hypothesis. Skipping the trivialities we are assuming that, at any time, if there exists a node that can broadcast to an uniformed node, it actually does. Otherwise we can change the protocol (in order to satisfy this hypothesis) without increasing the overall completion time of the protocol.

We can transform $T$ into a search tree $S$ representing an algorithm to win the $(n, d, 0)$-game, with $t - d$ questions. As a matter of fact any node $z$ of $S$ corresponds to a sequence of up to $d + 1$ questions: the first one is the question which is to be answered next and the remaining ones are the pending queries which have been already formulated. More precisely the sequence of questions associated to a node in $S$, has generally length $d + 1$. Let $q = t - d$ be the overall number of questions to be asked, hence the height of the search tree $S$ is $q$. Then for each $i = 0, 1, 2, \ldots, d - 1$, and any node in $S$ at level $q - i$, the associated sequence of questions has length $i$, since there are exactly $i$ more questions to

---

[2] By a broadcast tree, we mean here the tree obtained by stating a father-son relation between any node $\nu$ sending the message and any uninformed node $\nu'$ receiving the message for the first time by $\nu$. In case the node $\nu'$ receives the message for the first time from more than one node, the father is arbitrarily chosen among the sending nodes.

be asked all of which have been already formulated. Moreover, let the node $y$ be a *left* (resp. *right*) child of a node $z$ and let $[y_1, \ldots, y_{d+1}]$ be the questions in the node $y$ and $[z_1, \ldots, z_{d+1}]$ the questions associated to $z$. Then $y_i = z_{i+1}$, for each $i = 1, 2, \ldots, d$. This account for the fact that after one answer the pending $d$ questions are kept unaltered, and only the last pending query can be chosen.

Our transformation goes as follows (see also Figure 1 for a pictorial representation of the case $d = 2, t = 7, n = 9$ [3]):

Label the node in $T$ by means of a DFS, with edges oriented from the root to the leaves.

Associate to any link incident to the node labelled $i$, the question "Is $x \leq i$?".

Take the first $d + 1$ link stemming from the root of $T$ in order of increasing broadcasting time and put the corresponding questions $[q_1, \ldots, q_{d+1}]$ into the root $r_S$ of the tree S.

Recursively, for any node $\nu$ in $S$ define the two children of $\nu$, respectively, the left child $\nu_\ell$ and the right child $\nu_r$, as the new set of questions after the answer "yes" or "no" to the first question in $\nu$.

Let "Is $x \leq a$?" be the first question in $\nu$.

If the answer is "yes" then the new question to put in $\nu_\ell$ is the one corresponding to the first edge (in order of broadcasting time) stemming in $T$ from the node $a$. If no such edge exists then $\nu_\ell$ is a leaf in $S$ corresponding to the solution $x = a$.

If the answer is "no" then the new question to put in $\nu_r$ is the one corresponding to the first link (not already considered in increasing broadcasting time) stemming from the father of $a$ in $T$. If no such link exists then $\nu_r$ is a leaf in $S$ corresponding to the solution $x = b$, where $b$ is the father of $a$ in $T$.

# 5   Conclusions and Open Problems

We have investigated the problem of searching for an unknown number by using only comparison questions when the answers are received with a fixed delay $d$ and up to $c$ of them can be lost. For any $d \geq 0$, $t \geq 0$ and $c = 1$, we exactly evaluated $A_d^{(c)}(t)$, the size of the largest set for which $t$ questions are necessary and sufficient to complete successfully the search. For the general case $c \geq 1$ we provided a lower bound on $A_d^{(c)}(t)$. Our results leave space for further investigation. For instance, it would be interesting to prove that our lower bound on $A_d^{(c)}(t)$ is tight also for $c \geq 2$.

We also discussed the correspondence between the problem of searching with delay and that of broadcasting over a fully connected network with link latency. We believe that a better understanding of the correspondence between search problems and broadcasting problems may be a useful tool in both fields.

---

[3] Numbers near the edges and nodes of the Broadcast tree represent time of, respectively, sending and receiving information. Numbers inside the nodes are the labels assigned by the DFS.

106     F. Cicalese and U. Vaccaro

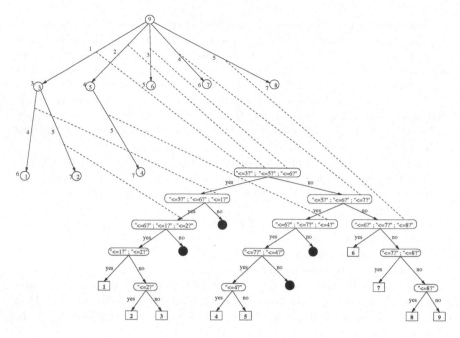

**Fig. 1.** Broadcast Protocol ≡ Searching Strategy

**Acknowledgement.** We thank Matteo Sereno for the useful discussions.

# References

1. M. Aigner, *Combinatorial Search*, Wiley–Teubner, New York–Stuttgart, 1988.
2. M. Aigner, Searching with lies, *J. Combinatorial Theory Ser. A*, **74** (1995) 43-56.
3. S. Albers, M. Charikar, M. Mitzenmacher, *Delayed Information and Action in On-line Algorithms*, in Proc. of $39^{th}$ FOCS, 1998, pp. 71-81.
4. A. Ambainis, S. A. Bloch, D. L. Schweizer, *Delayed Binary Search, or Playing Twenty Questions with a Procrastinator*, in Proc. of $10^{th}$ AMC SIAM SODA (1999), pp. 844-845.
5. J. A. Aslam and A. Dhagat, *Searching in the presence of linearly bounded errors*, In: Proceedings of the 23rd ACM STOC (1991), pp. 486-493.
6. A. Bar-Noy, S. Kipnis, *Designing Broadcast Algorithms in the Postal Model for Message-Passing Systems*, Mathematical System Theory, vol **27** (1994), pp. 431-452.
7. D. Bertsekas, R. Gallager, *Data Networks*, $2^{nd}$ edition, Perentice Hall (1992).
8. F. Cicalese, D. Mundici, *Optimal binary search with two unreliable tests and minimum adaptiveness*, In: Proc. European Symposium on Algorithms, ESA '99, J. Nesetril, Ed., Lecture Notes in Computer Science 1643 (1999), pp. 257-266.
9. F. Cicalese and U. Vaccaro, *Optimal strategies against a liar*, Theoretical Computer Science, **230** (1999), pp. 167-193.

10. A. Dhagat, P. Gacs, and P. Winkler, *On Playing "Twenty Question" with a liar*, In: Proc. 3rd ACM-SIAM SODA (1992), pp. 16-22.
11. M. Golin, A. Schuster, *Optimal Point-to-Point Broadcast Algorithms via Lopsided Trees*, Discrete Applied Mathematics, vol **93** (1999), pp. 233-263.
12. R. Hassin, M. Henig, *Monotonicity and efficient computation of optimal dichotomous search*, Discrete Applied Mathematics, **46** (1993), pp. 221-234.
13. K. Hinderer, M. Stieglitz, *On polychotomous search problems*, European Journal of Operational Research, **73** (1994), pp. 279-294.
14. D. A. Huffman, *A Method for the construction of Minimum Redundancy Codes*, Proceedings of IRE, **40** (1952), pp. 1098-1101.
15. G. Katona, *Combinatorial Search Problems*, in: A Survey of Combinatorial Theory, North-Holland (1966), pp. 285-308.
16. D. Knuth, *Searching and Sorting*, The Art of Computer Programming, vol. **3**, Massachusetts: Addison-Wesley (1998).
17. N. Linial, M. Sacks, *Every Poset has a central Element*, J. Combinatorial Theory A, **40** (1985), pp. 195-210.
18. N. Linial, M. Sacks, *Searching Ordered Structures*, Journal of Algorithms, **6** (1985), pp. 86-103.
19. A. Pelc, *Solution of Ulam's problem on searching with a lie*, J. Combinatorial Theory Ser. A, **44** (1987), pp. 129-142.
20. A. Pelc, *Detecting errors in searching games*, J. Combinatorial Theory Ser. A, **51** (1989), pp. 43-54.
21. C. Picard, *Theory of Questionnaires*, Gauthier-Villars (1965), Paris.
22. R. L. Rivest, A. R. Meyer, D. J. Kleitman, K. Winklmann, J. Spencer, *Coping with errors in binary search procedures*, J. Computer and System Sciences, **20** (1980), pp. 396-404.
23. J. Spencer, *Ulam's searching game with a fixed number of lies*, Theoretical Computer Science, **95** (1992), pp. 307-321.
24. S.M. Ulam, *Adventures of a Mathematician*, Scribner's, New York (1976).

# Some Formal Analysis of Rocchio's Similarity-Based Relevance Feedback Algorithm

Zhixiang Chen[1] and Binhai Zhu[2]

[1] Department of Computer Science, University of Texas-Pan American
Edinburg, TX 78539, USA. Email: chen@cs.panam.edu
[2] Department of Computer Science, Montana State University
Bozeman, MT 59717, USA. Email: bhz@cs.montana.edu

**Abstract.** Rocchio's similarity-based Relevance feedback algorithm, one of the most important query reformation methods in information retrieval, is essentially an adaptive supervised learning algorithm from examples. In spite of its popularity in various applications there is little rigorous analysis of its learning complexity in literature. In this paper we show that in the Boolean vector space model, if the initial query vector is $\mathbf{0}$, then for any of the four typical similarities (inner product, dice coefficient, cosine coefficient, and Jaccard coefficient), Rocchio's similarity-based relevance feedback algorithm makes at least $n$ mistakes when used to search for a collection of documents represented by a monotone disjunction of at most $k$ relevant features (or terms) over the $n$-dimensional Boolean vector space $\{0,1\}^n$. When an arbitrary initial query vector in $\{0,1\}^n$ is used, it makes at least $(n+k-3)/2$ mistakes to search for the same collection of documents. The linear lower bounds are independent of the choices of the threshold and coefficients that the algorithm may use in updating its query vector and making its classification.

## 1 Introduction

Research on relevance feedback in information retrieval has a long history [1,6,5, 11,7,13]. It is regarded as the most popular query reformation strategy [1]. The central idea of relevance feedback is to improve search performance for a particular query by modifying the query step by step, based on the user's judgments of the relevance or irrelevance of some of the documents retrieved. In the vector space model [13,15], both documents and queries are represented as vectors in a discretized vector space. In this case, relevance feedback is essentially an adaptive supervised learning algorithm: A query vector and a similarity measure are used to classify documents as relevant and irrelevant; the user's judgments of the relevance or irrelevance of some of the classified documents are used as examples for updating the query vector as a linear combination of the initial query vector and the examples judged by the user. Especially, when the inner product similarity is used, relevance feedback is just a Perceptron-like learning algorithm [9]. It is known [7] that there is an optimal way for updating the query vector if the sets of relevant and irrelevant documents are known. Practically it

D.T. Lee and S.-H. Teng (Eds.): ISAAC 2000, LNCS 1969, pp. 108–119, 2000.

is impossible to derive the optimal query vector, because the full sets of the relevant and irrelevant documents are not available.

There are many different variants of relevance feedback in information retrieval. However, in this paper we only study Rocchio's similarity-based relevance feedback algorithm [7,5,13]. In spite of its popularity in various applications, there is little rigorous analysis of its complexity as a learning algorithm in literature. This is the main motivation for us to investigate the learning complexity of Rocchio's similarity-based relevance feedback algorithm. The main contribution of our work in this paper is that linear lower bounds on classification mistakes are proved for the algorithm when any of the four typical similarities (inner product, dice coefficient, cosine coefficient, and Jaccard coefficient) listed in [13] is used. Technically, our work in this paper is enlightened by the work in [8] on lower bounds of the Perceptron algorithm. Precisely, we borrow the method developed in [8] for constructing an example sequence with pairwise constant inner products. We extend the method to cope with other similarity measures besides inner product. We also design a new method for selecting trial sequences and prove in a uniform way our lower bounds for Rocchio's similarity-based relevance feedback algorithm.

It should be pointed out that the lower bounds established in this paper for Rocchio's similarity-based relevance feedback algorithm is based on the following worst case considerations: The user acts as an adversary to the algorithm; the algorithm is required to precisely search for the collection of all documents relevant to the given search query; and the algorithm is allowed to receive one document example judged by the user as relevance or irrelevant at each step [1]. In practical applications, in contrast to the above worst case considerations, the user in general may not act as an adversary to the algorithm; the algorithm is usually required to search for a short list of top ranked documents relevant to the given search query; and at each step of the similarity-based relevance algorithm, the user may judge a few documents as relevance feedback to the algorithm. Hence, our lower bounds proved in this paper for Rocchio's similarity-based relevance feedback algorithm *may not affect* the algorithm's effective applicability to the real-world problems despite of their theoretical significance. The formal analysis of the algorithm helps us understand the nature of the algorithm well so that we may find new strategy to improve its effectiveness or design new algorithms for information retrieval.

It should also be pointed out that when considered as an adaptive supervised learning algorithm, Rocchio's similarity-based relevance feedback algorithm [7, 5,13] is a generalization of the Rosenblatt's Perceptron algorithm [12], a well-known and extensively studied algorithm in fields such as Artificial Intelligence, Machine Learning, and Neural Networks. More precisely, the Rosenblatt's Perceptron algorithm is the version of Rocchio's similarity-based relevance feedback algorithm with the inner product similarity. In this sense our work in this paper extends the lower bound results obtained in [8] for the Perceptron algorithm (or

---

[1] This last restriction is not critical to the proof of the lower bounds, but it would make the analysis easier.

in general the linear additive on-line learning algorithm). We refer the readers to the work of [14,9] for discussions of the Perceptron-like learning nature of the similarity-based relevance feedback algorithm. It was stated in [9] that the most important future direction for research in information retrieval is likely to be machine learning techniques which can combine empirical learning with the use of knowledge bases.

## 2   Rocchio's Similarity-Based Relevance Feedback Algorithm

Let $R$ be the set of all real values, and let $R^+$ be the set of all non-negative real values. Let $n$ be a positive integer. In the Boolean vector space model in information retrieval [13,15], a collection of $n$ features or terms $T_1, T_2, \ldots, T_n$ are used to represent documents and queries. Each document $\mathbf{d}$ is represented as a vector $v_{\mathbf{d}} = (d_1, d_2, \ldots, d_n)$ such that for any $i$, $1 \leq i \leq n$, the $i$-th component of $v_{\mathbf{d}}$ is one if the $i$-th feature $T_i$ appears in $\mathbf{d}$ or zero otherwise. Each query $\mathbf{q}$ is represented by a vector $v_{\mathbf{q}} = (q_1, q_2, \ldots, q_n)$ such that for any $i$, $1 \leq i \leq n$, the $i$-th component of $v_{\mathbf{q}} \in R$ is a real value used to determine the relevance (or weight) of the $i$-th feature $T_i$. Because of the unique vector representations of documents and queries, for convenience we simply use $\mathbf{d}$ and $\mathbf{q}$ to stand for their vector representations $v_{\mathbf{d}}$ and $v_{\mathbf{q}}$, respectively.

A similarity in general is a function $m$ from $R^n \times R^n$ to $R^+$. A similarity $m$ is used to determine the *relevance closeness* of documents to the search query and to rank documents according to such closeness. In the Boolean vector space model of information retrieval [13,15,1], to retrieve relevant documents for a given query vector $\mathbf{q}$ with respect to a similarity measure $m$, the system searches for all the documents $\mathbf{d}$, classifies those with similarity values $m(\mathbf{q}, \mathbf{d})$ higher than an explicit or implicit threshold as relevant, and returns to the user a short list of relevant documents with highest similarity values. This information retrieval process is in fact determined by a linear classifier, as defined later in this section, which is composed of a query vector $\mathbf{q}$, a similarity $m$, and a real-valued threshold $\psi$.

Unfortunately, in the real-world information retrieval applications, usually an ideal query vector cannot be generated due to many factors such as the limited knowledge of the users about the whole document collection. A typical example is the real-world problem of web search. In such a case, the user may use a few keywords to express what documents are wanted. However, it is nontrivial for both the user and a web search engine to *precisely* define the collection of documents wanted as a query vector composed of a set of keywords. The alternative solution to the query formation problem is, as stated in [13], to conduct searches iteratively, first operating with a tentative query formation (i.e., an initial query vector), and then improving formations for subsequent searches based on evaluations of the previously retrieved materials. This type of methods for automatically generating improved query formation is called relevance feedback, and one particular and well-known example is Rocchio's similarity-based relevance feedback [7,5,13].

Rocchio's similarity-based relevance feedback algorithm works in a step by step adaptive refinement fashion as follows. Starting at an initial query vector $\mathbf{q}_1$, the algorithm searches for all the documents $\mathbf{d}$ such that $\mathbf{d}$ is *very close* to $\mathbf{q}_1$ according to the similarity $m$, ranks them by $m(\mathbf{q}, \mathbf{d})$, and finally presents a short list of the top ranked documents to the user. The user examines the returned list of documents and judges some of the documents as relevant or irrelevant. At step $t \geq 1$, assume that the list of documents the user judged is $\mathbf{x}_1, \ldots, \mathbf{x}_{t-1}$. Then, the algorithm updates its query vector as $\mathbf{q}_t = \alpha_{t_0} \mathbf{q}_1 + \sum_{j=1}^{t-1} \alpha_{t_j} \mathbf{x}_j$, where the coefficients $\alpha_{t_j} \in R$ for $j = 0, 1, \ldots, t-1$. At step $t+1$, the algorithm uses the updated query vector $\mathbf{q}_t$ and the similarity $m$ to search for relevant documents, ranks the documents according to $m$, and presents the top ranked documents to the user. In practice, a threshold $\theta$ is explicitly (or implicitly) used to select the highly ranked documents. Practically, the coefficients $\alpha_{t_j}$ may be fixed as $1, -1$ or $0.5$ [1,13]. The following four typical similarities were listed in [13]: For any $\mathbf{q}, \mathbf{x} \in R^n$,

$$inner\ product : m_1(\mathbf{q}, \mathbf{x}) = \sum_{i=1}^{n} q_i x_i,$$

$$dice\ coefficient : m_2(\mathbf{q}, \mathbf{x}) = \frac{2m_1(\mathbf{q}, \mathbf{x})}{m_1(\mathbf{q}, \mathbf{q}) + m_1(\mathbf{x}, \mathbf{x})},$$

$$cosine\ coefficient : m_3(\mathbf{q}, \mathbf{x}) = \frac{m_1(\mathbf{q}, \mathbf{x})}{\sqrt{m_1(\mathbf{q}, \mathbf{q})}\sqrt{m_1(\mathbf{x}, \mathbf{x})}},$$

$$Jaccard\ coefficient : m_4(\mathbf{q}, \mathbf{x}) = \frac{m_1(\mathbf{q}, \mathbf{x})}{m_1(\mathbf{q}, \mathbf{q}) + m_1(\mathbf{x}, \mathbf{x}) - m_1(\mathbf{q}, \mathbf{x})}.$$

To make the above definitions valid for arbitrary $\mathbf{q}$ and $\mathbf{x}$, we define that the similarity between two zero vectors is zero, i.e., $m_i(\mathbf{0}, \mathbf{0}) = 0$, for $1 \leq i \leq 4$.

We given the necessary formal definitions in the following.

**Definition 2.1.** *A* linear classifier *over the n-dimensional Boolean vector space* $\{0, 1\}^n$ *is a triple* $(\mathbf{q}, \psi, m)$, *where* $\mathbf{q} \in R^n$ *is a query vector,* $\psi \in R$ *is a threshold, and m from* $R^n \times R^n$ *to* $R^+$ *is a similarity. The linear classifier* $(\mathbf{q}, \psi, m)$ *classifies any documents* $\mathbf{d} \in \{0, 1\}^n$ *as relevant if* $m(\mathbf{q}, \mathbf{d}) \geq \psi$ *or irrelevant otherwise.*

**Definition 2.2.** *An* adaptive supervised learning algorithm *A for learning a target linear classifier* $(\mathbf{q}, \psi, m)$ *over the n-dimensional Boolean vector space* $\{0, 1\}^n$ *from examples is a game played between the algorithm A and the user in a step by step fashion, where the query vector* $\mathbf{q}$ *and the threshold* $\psi$ *are unknown to the algorithm A, but the similarity m is. At any step* $t \geq 1$, *A gives a linear classifier* $(\mathbf{q}_t, \psi_t, m)$ *as a hypothesis to the target classifier to the user, where* $\mathbf{q}_t \in R^n$ *and* $\psi_t \in R$. *If the hypothesis is equivalent to the target, then the user says "yes" to conclude the learning process. Otherwise, the user presents an example* $\mathbf{x_t} \in \{0, 1\}^n$ *such that the target classifier and the hypothesis classifier differ at* $\mathbf{x_t}$. *In this case, we say that the algorithm A makes a mistake. At step*

$t + 1$, *the algorithm $A$ constructs a new hypothetical classifier $(\mathbf{q}_{t+1}, \psi_{t+1}, m)$
to the user based on the received examples $\mathbf{x_1}, \ldots, \mathbf{x_t}$. The learning complexity
(or the mistake bound) of the algorithm $A$ is in the worst case the maximum
number of examples that it may receive from the user in order to learn some
linear classifier.*

**Definition 2.3.** *Rocchio's similarity-based relevance feedback algorithm is an
adaptive supervised learning algorithm for learning any linear classifier $(\mathbf{q}, \psi, m)$
over the n-dimensional Boolean vector space $\{0, 1\}^n$ from examples. Let $\mathbf{q}_1$ be the
initial query vector. At any step $t \geq 1$, the algorithm presents a linear classifier
$(\mathbf{q}_t, \psi_t, m)$ as its hypothesis to the target classifier to the user, where $\psi_t \in R$
is the threshold, and the query vector $\mathbf{q}_t$ is modified as follows. Assume that
at the beginning of step $t$ the algorithm has received a sequence of examples
$\mathbf{x_1}, \ldots, \mathbf{x_{t-1}}$, then the algorithm uses the following modified query vector $\mathbf{q}_t$ for
its next classification:*

$$\mathbf{q}_t = \alpha_{t_0} \mathbf{q}_1 + \sum_{j=1}^{t-1} \alpha_{t_j} \mathbf{x}_j, \qquad (1)$$

*where $\alpha_{t_j} \in R$, for $j = 0, \ldots, t-1$, are called additive updating factors.*

We will use the sets of documents represented by monotone disjunctions of
relevant features to study the mistake bounds of Rocchio's algorithm. The efficient learnability of monotone disjunctions of relevant features (or attributes)
has been extensively studied in machine learning (for example, [10]). Although
very simple in format, monotone disjunctions are very common ways of expressing search queries, especially in the case of web search. All existing popular
search engines support disjunctions of keywords as search query formations. For
any $k$ with $1 \leq k \leq n$, linear classifiers can be defined to precisely classify a
monotone disjunction of at most $k$ relevant features

$$x_{i_1} \vee \cdots \vee x_{i_s}, \ 1 \leq s \leq k. \qquad (2)$$

i.e., to precisely classify whether any given document satisfies the monotone
disjunction of (2) or not.

## 3    Technical Lemmas

The technique used in [8] to prove linear lower bounds for the Perceptron algorithm (or, in general, linear additive on-line learning algorithms) is the con-
struction of an example sequence $B = ((\mathbf{z'}_1, \mathbf{z''}_1), \ldots, (\mathbf{z'}_l, \mathbf{z''}_l))$ with pairwise
constant inner products such that for any given initial query vector (or weight
vector as used in [8]) and any linear classifier with the inner product similarity,
if the initial query vector and the linear classifier differ on the sequence $B$, then
the Perceptron algorithm makes one mistake at one of the two examples in every
pair of $B$. In the words, each pair of the sequence $B$ *preserves* the classification
difference of the linear classifier and the initial query vector for the Perceptron

algorithm when the examples in $B$ are used to update the query vector. It was shown in [8] that row vectors of Hadamard matrices can be used to construct the required example sequence $B$. We will borrow the above technique from [8] to prove linear lower bounds for Rocchio's similarity-based relevance feedback algorithm. However, one must note that when a similarity measure (for example, the Jaccard coefficient similarity) other than the inner product similarity is used, the pairs of the sequence $B$ as used in [8] *may not still preserve* the classification difference of the target linear classifier and the initial query vector. The rotation invariant concept [8] is in general not applicable to learning algorithms with a non-zero initial query vector, nor applicable to non-rotation variants of the linear additive learning algorithms. Therefore, we need to design new methods for constructing example sequences that are applicable to Rocchio's similarity-based relevance feedback algorithm with arbitrary initial query vector and any of the four similarities defined in section 2.

In the following we extend Definition 7 given in [8] to deal with any similarity measure.

**Definition 3.1.** *Let the sequence* $B = ((\mathbf{z}'_1, \mathbf{z}''_1), \ldots, (\mathbf{z}'_l, \mathbf{z}''_l))$, *where* $\mathbf{z}'_t$ *and* $\mathbf{z}''_t$ *are in* $\{0,1\}^n$ *for all* $t$. *Let* $\mathbf{q}_1 \in R^n$ *be a query vector,* $m$ *a similarity, and* $(\mathbf{u}, \psi, m)$ *a linear classifier. Define* $\mathbf{q}_t = \alpha_{t_0} \mathbf{q}_1 + \sum_{j=1}^{t-1} \alpha_{t_j} \mathbf{x}_j$, *for* $t = 1, \ldots, l$, *where* $\mathbf{x}_j \in \{\mathbf{z}'_j, \mathbf{z}''_j\}$ *and* $\alpha_{t_j} \in R$. *We say that the query vector* $\mathbf{q}_t$ *and the linear classifier* $(\mathbf{u}, \psi, m)$ *differ on the sequence* $B$ *with respect to* $m$ *if either*

$$m(\mathbf{q}_t, \mathbf{z}'_t) \le m(\mathbf{q}_t, \mathbf{z}''_t) \text{ and } m(\mathbf{u}, \mathbf{z}'_t) > \psi > m(\mathbf{u}, \mathbf{z}''_t), \text{ or}$$
$$m(\mathbf{q}_t, \mathbf{z}'_t) \ge m(\mathbf{q}_t, \mathbf{z}''_t) \text{ and } m(\mathbf{u}, \mathbf{z}'_t) < \psi < m(\mathbf{u}, \mathbf{z}''_t).$$

In the following we give a weaker version of Lemma 8 in [8] in which only the initial query vector (or weight vector in their term) is required to differ from the target linear classifier on the example sequence, whereas we require that all the query vectors (the initial one and the updated ones) differ from the target linear classifier. We do not use the pairwise constant inner product property, because we may not have such a property for other similarity measure. The proof is similar to that of Lemma 7 in [8].

**Lemma 3.2.** *Let* $m$ *from* $R^n \times R^n$ *to* $R^+$ *be a similarity and let* $\mathbf{q}_1 \in R^n$ *be the initial query vector. Let the sequence* $B = ((\mathbf{z}'_1, \mathbf{z}''_1), \ldots, (\mathbf{z}'_l, \mathbf{z}''_l))$, *where* $\mathbf{z}'_t$ *and* $\mathbf{z}''_t$ *are in* $\{0,1\}^n$ *for all* $t$. *For any linear classifier* $(\mathbf{u}, \psi, m)$ *over the domain* $\{0,1\}^n$, *if* $\mathbf{q}_t$, *which is as defined in Definition 3.3, and* $(\mathbf{u}, \psi, m)$ *differ on* $B$ *with respect to* $m$ *for* $t = 1, \ldots, l$, *then Rocchio's similarity relevance feedback algorithm makes at least* $l$ *mistakes for learning the linear classifier* $(\mathbf{u}, \psi, m)$.

**Definition 3.3.** *Let* $\mathbf{I}_n$ *be the identity matrix of order* $n$. *A Hadamard matrix* $\mathbf{H}_n$ *of order* $n$ *is an* $n \times n$ *matrix with elements in* $\{-1, 1\}$, *such that*

$$\mathbf{H}_n^T \mathbf{H}_n = \mathbf{H}_n \mathbf{H}_n^T = n\mathbf{I}_n. \tag{3}$$

$\mathbf{H}_n$ *is normalized if the first row and the first column consist of ones only.*

The above (2) implies that any two distinct rows (or columns) of an $\mathbf{H}_n$ are orthogonal. Normalized Hadamard matrices can be constructed as follows. Let

$H_1 = (1)$. For any $n = 2^d$ with $d \geq 0$, define

$$H_{2n} = \begin{pmatrix} H_n & H_n \\ H_n & -H_n \end{pmatrix}. \tag{4}$$

The following property follows from (3) and (4).

**Proposition 3.4.** *For $n = 2^d$ with $d > 0$, let $h_t$ be the $t$-th row of the normalized Hadamard matrix $H_n$ for $t = 1, \ldots, n$, we have*

$$m_1(h_i, h_t) = 0, \quad \text{for } 1 \leq i < t \leq n, \tag{5}$$
$$m_1(h_i, h_i) = n, \quad \text{for } 1 \leq i \leq n, \tag{6}$$
$$\sum_{j=1}^{n} h_{1j} = n, \quad \text{and } \sum_{j=1}^{n} h_{ij} = 0 \text{ for } 1 < i \leq n. \tag{7}$$

**Definition 3.5.** *Let $n = 2^d + k - 1$ for some positive integers $d$ and $k$. For $t = 1, \ldots, 2^d$, let $\mathbf{h}_t$ be the $t$-th row of the normalized Hadamard matrix $H_{2^d}$. We define $B_H$ to be the sequence $((\mathbf{z}_1', \mathbf{z}_1''), \ldots, (\mathbf{z}_{2^d}', \mathbf{z}_{2^d}''))$, where*

$$\mathbf{z}_t' = ((h_{t,1} + 1)/2, \ldots, (h_{t,2^d} + 1)/2, 0, \ldots, 0),$$
$$\mathbf{z}_t'' = ((-h_{t,1} + 1)/2, \ldots, (-h_{t,2^d} + 1)/2, 0, \ldots, 0)$$

**Proposition 3.6.** *Let $n = 2^d + k - 1$ for some positive integers $d$ and $k$ and let $B_H = ((\mathbf{z}_1', \mathbf{z}_1''), \ldots, (\mathbf{z}_{2^d}', \mathbf{z}_{2^d}''))$ be the sequence as defined in Definition 3.5. For any $i$ and $j$ with $1 \leq i, j \leq 2^d$, we have*

(a)  $m_1(\mathbf{z}_1', \mathbf{z}_1') = 2^d; \ m_1(\mathbf{z}_1'', \mathbf{z}_1'') = 0;$
     $m_1(\mathbf{z}_i', \mathbf{z}_i') = m_1(\mathbf{z}_i'', \mathbf{z}_i'') = 2^{d-1}, \ if \ 1 < i \leq 2^d.$

(b)  $m_1(\mathbf{z}_1', \mathbf{z}_j') = m_1(\mathbf{z}_1', \mathbf{z}_j'') = 2^{d-1};$
     $m_1(\mathbf{z}_1'', \mathbf{z}_j') = m_1(\mathbf{z}_1'', \mathbf{z}_j'') = 0, \ if \ 1 < j \leq 2^d.$

(c)  $m_1(\mathbf{z}_i', \mathbf{z}_j') = m_1(\mathbf{z}_i', \mathbf{z}_j'') = m_1(\mathbf{z}_i'', \mathbf{z}_j') = m_1(\mathbf{z}_i'', \mathbf{z}_j'') = 2^{d-2},$
     $if \ 1 < i < j \leq 2^d.$

We now introduce a new method for constructing example sequences that are applicable to Rocchio's similarity-based relevance feedback algorithm with any of the four similarities and an arbitrary initial query vector. We expand a Hadamard matrix by adding rows and columns with zeroes, and exchange rows and columns of the expanded matrix according to the initial query vector. The new method is given in the proof of Proposition 3.7.

**Proposition 3.7.** *Given any $n = 2^d + k - 1$ with positive integers $d$ and $k$, for any query vector $\mathbf{q} \in \{0, 1\}^n$, there is a sequence $D(\mathbf{q}) = ((\mathbf{v}_1', \mathbf{v}_1''), \ldots, (\mathbf{v}_{2^{d-1}}', \mathbf{v}_{2^{d-1}}''))$ such that $\mathbf{v}_t'$ and $\mathbf{v}_t''$ are in $\{0, 1\}^n$ for $t = 1, \ldots, 2^{d-1}$, and the sequence satisfies all the three properties given in Proposition 3.6 with each occurrence of*

$2^d$ replaced by $2^{d-1}$ and each occurrence of $\mathbf{z}$ replaced by $\mathbf{v}$, respectively. Furthermore, we have $m_1(\mathbf{q}, \mathbf{v'}_1) = 0$ if $\mathbf{q}$ has at least $2^{d-1}$ zero components or $m_1(\mathbf{q}, \mathbf{v'}_1) = 2^{d-1}$ otherwise; and

$$m_1(\mathbf{q}, \mathbf{v'}_i) = 0, \ for \ i \neq 1;$$
$$m_1(\mathbf{q}, \mathbf{v''}_i) = 0, \ for \ all \ i.$$

**Proof.** Given any vector $\mathbf{q} = (q_1, \ldots, q_n) \in \{0,1\}^n$ with $n = 2^d + k - 1$ for positive integers $d$ and $k$, we have

$$2^{d-1} = \frac{n - k + 1}{2} \leq \frac{n}{2}.$$

This means that we can choose $2^{d-1}$ components of $\mathbf{q}$, denoted by $q_{i_1}, \ldots, q_{i_{2^{d-1}}}$, such that they are either all one or all zero. Define the $n \times n$ matrix $C_n$ as follows.

$$C_n = \begin{pmatrix} H_{2^{d-1}} & \mathbf{0}_{2^{d-1} \times (n - 2^{d-1})} \\ \mathbf{0}_{(n-2^{d-1}) \times 2^{d-1}} & \mathbf{0}_{(n-2^{d-1}) \times (n-2^{d-1})} \end{pmatrix},$$

where $H_{2^{d-1}}$ is the $2^{d-1} \times 2^{d-1}$ Hadamard matrix. We move the first $2^{d-1}$ rows of $C_n$ to the rows $i_1, \ldots, i_{2^{d-1}}$, respectively. This process can be achieved through a sequence of exchanges of two rows. In other words, there is an $n \times n$ transformation matrix $A$ such that $AC_n$ does the work and $AA^T = n\mathbf{I}_n$. We now move the first $2^{d-1}$ columns of $AC_n$ to the columns $i_1, \ldots, i_{2^{d-1}}$, respectively. Similarly, this process can be achieved through a sequence of exchanges of two columns. Moreover, $AC_nA^T$ does the work. Now, for any $j$ with $1 \leq j \leq 2^{d-1}$, let $\mathbf{d}_{i_j} = (x_1, \ldots, x_n)$ denote the $i_j$-th row of $AC_nA^T$. Then, for $1 \leq s \leq 2^{d-1}$, the $i_s$-th component of $\mathbf{d}_{i_j}$ denoted by $x_{i_s}$ is in fact the $s$-th component of the $j$-th row of the Hadamard matrix $H_{2^{d-1}}$. In other words, $\mathbf{d}_{i_j}$ has all zero components except these $2^{d-1}$ components $x_{i_s}$ forming a subvector that is the same as the $j$-th row of $H_{2^{d-1}}$. We finally construct $\mathbf{v'}_j$ from $\mathbf{d}_{i_j}$ by changing all its $-1$ components to zero and keeping all its other components. We also construct $\mathbf{v''}_j$ from $\mathbf{d}_{i_j}$ by changing all its $-1$ components to one and all its one components to zero, and keeping all the other components. Hence, Proposition 3.7 follows from Proposition 3.4 in a manner similar to Proposition 3.6. □

In the following two lemmas we show that the sequence $B_H$ enables the query vector $\mathbf{q}_t$ to preserve the $m_1$ similarity for for any pair of $\mathbf{z'}_t$ and $\mathbf{z''}_t$ in $B_H$ when the zero initial query vector is used, and the sequence $D(\mathbf{q}_1)$ enables the query vector $\mathbf{q}_t$ to preserve the $m_1$ similarity for any pair of $\mathbf{v'}_t$ and $\mathbf{v''}_t$ in $D(\mathbf{q}_1)$ when the arbitrary initial query vector $\mathbf{q}_1$ is used.

**Lemma 3.8.** For $n = 2^d + k - 1$ with positive integers $k$ and $d$, let $B_H$ be the sequence defined in Definition 3.5. Let $\mathbf{q}_t = \alpha_{t_0} \mathbf{q}_1 + \sum_{j=1}^{t-1} \alpha_{t_j} \mathbf{x}_j$ for $t = 1, \ldots, 2^d$, where the initial query vector $\mathbf{q}_1 = \mathbf{0}$, $\alpha_{t_j} \in R$, and $\mathbf{x}_j \in \{\mathbf{z'}_j, \mathbf{z''}_j\}$. Then, $m_1(\mathbf{q}_t, \mathbf{z'}_t) = m_1(\mathbf{q}_t, \mathbf{z''}_t)$ for $1 \leq t \leq 2^d$.

**Proof Sketch.** By Proposition 3.6 (b) and (c). □

**Lemma 3.9.** Let $n = 2^d + k - 1$ with positive integers $k$ and $d$. Given any initial query vector $\mathbf{q}_1 \in \{0,1\}^n$, let $D(\mathbf{q}_1)$ be the sequence given in Proposition

3.7, and $\mathbf{q}_t = \alpha_{t_0}\mathbf{q}_1 + \sum_{j=1}^{t-1}\alpha_{t_j}\mathbf{x}_j$ for $t = 1,\ldots,2^{d-1}$, where $\alpha_{t_j} \in R$ and $\mathbf{x}_j \in \{\mathbf{v}'_j, \mathbf{v}''_j\}$. Then, $m_1(\mathbf{q}_t, \mathbf{v}'_t) = m_1(\mathbf{q}_t, \mathbf{v}''_t)$ for $2 \leq t \leq 2^{d-1}$. Moreover, $m_1(\mathbf{q}_1, \mathbf{v}'_1) = m_1(\mathbf{q}_1, \mathbf{v}''_1)$ if $\mathbf{q}_1$ has at least $2^{d-1}$ zero components.

**Proof Sketch.** By Propositions 3.6 and 3.7. □

The following lemma allows us to choose examples in some subdomain to against a learning algorithm.

**Lemma 3.10.** *Given $n > k-1 \geq 0$, there is an adversary strategy that forces any adaptive supervised learning algorithm to make at least $k - 1$ mistakes for learning the class of disjunctions of at most $k-1$ variables from $\{x_{i_1},\ldots,x_{i_{k-1}}\}$ over the Boolean vector space $\{0,1\}^n$. Moreover, the adversary chooses examples in the vector space with nonzero values only for variables in $\{x_{i_1},\ldots,x_{i_{k-1}}\}$.*

**Proof.** For any given adaptive supervised learning algorithm, at any step $t$ for $1 \leq t \leq k-1$, the adversary uses the example $\mathbf{x}_t$ to against the learning algorithm as follows, where $\mathbf{x}_t$ has all zero components except that its $i_t$-th components is one: If the learning algorithm classifies $\mathbf{x}_t$ as relevant, then the adversary classifies it as irrelevant, otherwise the adversary classifies it as relevant. □

## 4    Linear Lower Bounds

Throughout this section, we let $n = 2^d + k - 1$ with two positive integers $d$ and $k$, and let $\mathbf{u}$ be the vector in $\{0,1\}^n$ such that its first component is one, its last $k - 1$ components have at most $k - 1$ ones (however, these one components are not specified at this point), and all other components are zero. Given any query vector $\mathbf{q}_1 \in \{0,1\}^n$, let $q_{i_1},\ldots,q_{i_{2^{d-1}}}$ be its $2^{d-1}$ components such that they are either all zero or all one. Define $\mathbf{u}(\mathbf{q}_1)$ to be the vector in $\{0,1\}^n$ such that its $i_1$-th component is one, its $i_j$-th components are all zero for $j = 2,\ldots,2^{d-1}$, and among the remaining $n-2^{d-1}$ components there are at most $k-1$ one components (again, setting which of these components to be one is not determined at this point). Note that both $\mathbf{u}$ and $\mathbf{u}(\mathbf{q}_1)$ define respectively a monotone disjunction of at most $k$ relevant features. We use $E(\mathbf{u})$ and $E(\mathbf{u}(\mathbf{q}_1))$ to denote the monotone disjunctions represented by $\mathbf{u}$ and $\mathbf{u}(\mathbf{q}_1)$, respectively.

**Lemma 4.1.** *Let $B_H = ((\mathbf{z}'_1, \mathbf{z}''_1),\ldots,(\mathbf{z}'_{2^d}, \mathbf{z}''_{2^d}))$ be the example sequence defined in Definition 3.5. For any similarity $m_i$, $1 \leq i \leq 4$, there is a $\psi \in R$ such that the query vector $\mathbf{q}_t = \alpha_{t_0}\mathbf{q}_1 + \sum_{j=1}^{t-1}\alpha_{t_j}\mathbf{x}_j$ and the linear classifier $(\mathbf{u}, \psi, m_i)$ differ on $B_H$ with respect to $m_i$ for $t = 1,\ldots,2^d$, where $\alpha_{t_j}$ are arbitrary values in $R$, and $\mathbf{x}_j \in \{\mathbf{z}'_j, \mathbf{z}''_j\}$.*

**Proof Sketch.** As noted section 2, $(\mathbf{u}, 1/2, m_1)$, $(\mathbf{u}, 2/(k + n), m_2)$, $(\mathbf{u}, 1/\sqrt{kn}, m_3)$, and $(\mathbf{u}, 1/(k + n - 1), m_4)$ are respectively linear classifiers for the monotone disjunction $E(\mathbf{u})$ of at most $k$ relevant features. It follows from Definition 3.5 that the first component of $\mathbf{z}'_t$ is one, the first of $\mathbf{z}''_t$ is zero, and the last $k$ components of each of both $\mathbf{z}'_t$ and $\mathbf{z}''_t$ are all zero for $1 \leq t \leq 2^d$. Hence, for any $1 \leq t \leq 2^d$, we have by Proposition 3.6

$$m_1(\mathbf{u}, \mathbf{z}'_t) = 1 > \frac{1}{2}, \tag{8}$$

$$m_2(\mathbf{u}, \mathbf{z}'_t) = \frac{2m_1(\mathbf{u}, \mathbf{z}'_t)}{m_1(\mathbf{u}, \mathbf{u}) + m_1(\mathbf{z}'_t, \mathbf{z}'_t)} \geq \frac{2}{k + 2^{d-1}} > \frac{2}{k+n}, \tag{9}$$

$$m_3(\mathbf{u}, \mathbf{z}'_t) = \frac{m_1(\mathbf{u}, \mathbf{z}'_t)}{\sqrt{m_1(\mathbf{u}, \mathbf{u})}\sqrt{m_1(\mathbf{z}'_t, \mathbf{z}'_t)}} \geq \frac{1}{\sqrt{k2^{d-1}}} > \frac{2}{kn}, \tag{10}$$

$$m_4(\mathbf{u}, \mathbf{z}'_t) = \frac{m_1(\mathbf{u}, \mathbf{z}'_t)}{m_1(\mathbf{u}, \mathbf{u}) + m_1(\mathbf{z}'_t, \mathbf{z}'_t) - m_1(\mathbf{u}, \mathbf{z}'_t)} \geq \frac{1}{k + 2^{d-1} - 1}$$

$$> \frac{1}{k+n-1}, \quad and \tag{11}$$

$$m_i(\mathbf{u}, \mathbf{z}''_t) = 0, \quad for \ 1 \leq i \leq 4. \tag{12}$$

By Lemma 3.8 and the above (8) and (12), for any $1 \leq t \leq 2^d$, $\mathbf{q}_t$ and the linear classifier $(\mathbf{u}, 1/2, m_1)$ differ on the sequence $B_H$ with respect to $m_1$.

For the similarity $m_2$, for any $t \geq 2$ we have by Proposition 3.6 and Lemma 3.8

$$m_2(\mathbf{q}_t, \mathbf{z}'_t) = \frac{2m_1(\mathbf{q}_t, \mathbf{z}'_t)}{m_1(\mathbf{q}_t, \mathbf{q}_t) + m_1(\mathbf{z}'_t, \mathbf{z}'_t)} = \frac{2m_1(\mathbf{q}_t, \mathbf{z}'_t)}{m_1(\mathbf{q}_t, \mathbf{q}_t) + 2^{d-1}},$$

$$m_2(\mathbf{q}_t, \mathbf{z}''_t) = \frac{2m_1(\mathbf{q}_t, \mathbf{z}''_t)}{m_1(\mathbf{q}_t, \mathbf{q}_t) + m_1(\mathbf{z}''_t, \mathbf{z}''_t)} = \frac{2m_1(\mathbf{q}_t, \mathbf{z}'_t)}{m_1(\mathbf{q}_t, \mathbf{q}_t) + 2^{d-1}} = m_2(\mathbf{q}_t, \mathbf{z}'_t),$$

For $t = 1$, we have $m_1(\mathbf{q}_1, \mathbf{z}'_1) = m_1(\mathbf{0}, \mathbf{z}'_1) = 0$, hence $m_2(\mathbf{q}_1, \mathbf{z}'_1) = 0$. Because $\mathbf{z}''_1 = \mathbf{q}_1 = \mathbf{0}$, we also have $m_2(\mathbf{q}_1, \mathbf{z}''_1) = 0$ according to the definition. Thus, for $1 \leq t \leq 2^d$, we have $m_2(\mathbf{q}_t, \mathbf{z}'_t) = m_2(\mathbf{q}_t, \mathbf{z}''_t)$, hence by (9) and (12) the query vector $\mathbf{q}_t$ and the linear classifier $(\mathbf{u}, 2/(k+n), m_2)$ differ on the sequence $B_H$ with respect to $m_2$.

The cases for $m_3$ and $m_4$ can be coped with similarly. □

**Lemma 4.2.** *Given any initial query vector* $\mathbf{q}_1 \in \{0,1\}^n$, *let*

$$D(\mathbf{q}_1) = ((\mathbf{v}'_1, \mathbf{v}''_1), \ldots, (\mathbf{v}'_{2^{d-1}}, \mathbf{v}''_{2^{d-1}}))$$

*be the example sequence defined in Proposition 3.7. For any similarity* $m_i$, $1 \leq i \leq 4$, *there is a* $\psi \in R$ *such that the query vector* $\mathbf{q}_t = \alpha_{t_0}\mathbf{q}_1 + \sum_{j=1}^{t-1} \alpha_{t_j}\mathbf{x}_j$ *and the linear classifier* $(\mathbf{u}, \psi, m_i)$ *differ on* $D(\mathbf{q}_1)$ *with respect to* $m_i$ *for* $t = 2, \ldots, 2^{d-1}$, *where* $\alpha_{t_j}$ *are arbitrary values in* $R$, *and* $\mathbf{x}_j \in \{\mathbf{v}'_j, \mathbf{v}''_j\}$. *Moreover, if* $\mathbf{q}_1$ *has at least* $2^{d-1}$ *zero components, then* $\mathbf{q}_1$ *and* $(\mathbf{u}, \psi, m_i)$ *differ with respect to* $m_i$, *too.*

**Proof.** The proof is the same as what we just did for Lemma 4.1, but we need to replace $\mathbf{u}$ by $\mathbf{u}(\mathbf{q}_1)$, $\mathbf{z}$ by $\mathbf{v}$, and $2^d$ by $2^{d-1}$. We also need to use Proposition 3.7 and Lemma 3.9 to complete our proof. □

We now prove the following main results in this paper.

**Theorem 4.3.** *Let* $n = 2^d + k - 1$ *for some positive integers* $d$ *and* $k$. *For any given similarity* $m_i$ *with* $i \in \{1, 2, 3, 4\}$, *Rocchio's similarity-based relevance feedback algorithm makes at least* $n$ *mistakes for learning the class of monotone disjunctions of at most* $k$ *relevant features over the Boolean vector space* $\{0,1\}^n$, *when the initial query vector* $\mathbf{q}_1 = \mathbf{0}$ *and the similarity* $m_i$ *are used.*

**Proof Sketch.** By Lemmas 3.2, 3.10 and 4.1. □

**Theorem 4.4.** *Let $n = 2^d + k - 1$ for some positive integers $d$ and $k$. For any given similarity $m_i$ with $i \in \{1, 2, 3, 4\}$, Rocchio's similarity-based relevance feedback algorithm makes at least $(n + k - 3)/2$ mistakes for learning the class of monotone disjunctions of at most $k$ relevant features over the Boolean vector space $\{0, 1\}^n$, when an arbitrary initial query vector $q_1 \in \{0, 1\}^n$ and the similarity $m_i$ are used. Moreover, if the initial query vector $q_1$ has at least $2^{d-1}$ zero components, then the algorithm makes at least $(n + k - 1)/2$ mistakes.*

**Proof Sketch.** By Lemmas 3.2, 3.10 and 4.2. □

# 5 Concluding Remarks

Rocchio's similarity-based relevance feedback algorithm is one of the most query reformation method in information retrieval and has been used in various applications. It is essentially an adaptive supervised learning algorithm from examples. However, there is little rigorous analysis of its learning complexity. In this paper we prove linear lower bounds for Rocchio's similarity-based relevance feedback algorithm when any of the four typical similarities listed in [13] is used. Because the linear lower bounds are proved with the worst case analysis, they may not affect the algorithm's effective applicability to the real-world problems. The lower bounds help us understand the nature of the algorithm well so that we may find new strategies to improve the effectiveness of Rocchio's algorithm or design new algorithms for information retrieval.

The lower bound in Theorem 4.4 holds for an arbitrary initial query vector $q_1 \in \{0, 1\}^n$. Choosing a zero-one initial query vector is a very common practice in applications. For example, in web search an initial zero-one query vector may be constructed with the query words submitted by the user. When the initial query vector $q_1$ is chosen from $R^n$, we can prove the same lower bound with the similar but tedious approach for the similarities $m_1, m_2$, and $m_3$. But we do not know whether the same lower bound still holds for $m_4$.

**Acknowledgment.** In early 1997, Dr. Stanley Sclaroff asked the first author whether the relevance feedback algorithm can be used to help the user search for the desired world wide web documents with about *two dozens of examples* judged by the user. At the time, his research group implemented ImageRover [17,16], an image search engine from the user's relevance feedback, while the author and his colleagues started to build intelligent search tools (such as Yarrow [2], WebSail [4] and FEATURES[3] ) with the help of information retrieval and machine learning techniques. Dr. Sclaroff's question together with the authors' own research on building intelligent web search tools inspired the work in this paper. The authors would also acknowledge that the example sequence selection method developed in [8] for proving linear lower bounds for the Perceptron algorithm is the key to the breakthrough of our proofs. Without knowing the method it would take longer for the authors to finish the work in this paper.

# References

1. R. Baeza-Yates and B. Riberiro-Neto. *Modern Information Retrieval*. Addison-Wesley, 1999.
2. Z. Chen and X. Meng. Yarrow: A real-time client site meta search learner. In *Proceedings of the AAAI 2000 Workshop on Artificial Intelligence for Web Search*, pages 12–17, Austin, July 2000.
3. Z. Chen, X. Meng, R.H. Fowler, and B. Zhu. FEATURES: Real-time adaptive feature learning and document learning. Technical Report CS-00-23, Dept. od Computer Science, University of Texas-Pan American, May 26, 2000, 2000.
4. Z. Chen, X. Meng, B. Zhu, and R. Fowler. Websail: From on-line learning to web search. In *Proceedings of the 2000 International Conference on Web Information Systems Engineering*, pages 192–199, Hong Kong, June 2000.
5. E. Ide. Interactive search strategies and dynamic file organization in information retrieval. In G. Salton, editor, *The Smart System - Experiments in Automatic Document Processing*, pages 373–393, Englewood Cliffs, NJ, 1971. Prentice-Hall Inc.
6. E. Ide. New experiments in relevance feedback. In G. Salton, editor, *The Smart System - Experiments in Automatic Document Processing*, pages 337–354, Englewood Cliffs, NJ, 1971. Prentice-Hall Inc.
7. Jr. J.J. Rocchio. Relevance feedback in information retrieval. In G. Salton, editor, *The Smart Retrieval System - Experiments in Automatic Document Processing*, pages 313–323, Englewood Cliffs, NJ, 1971. Prentice-Hall, Inc.
8. J. Kivinen, M.K. Warmuth, and P. Auer. The perceptron algorithm vs. winnow: linear vs. logarithmic mistake bounds when few input variables are relevant. *Artificial Intelligence*, pages 325–343, 1997.
9. D. Lewis. Learning in intelligent information retrieval. In *Proceedings of the Eighth International Workshop on Machine Learning*, pages 235–239, 1991.
10. N. Littlestone. Learning quickly when irrelevant attributes abound: A new linear-threshold algorithm. *Machine Learning*, 2:285–318, 1988.
11. V.V. Raghavan and S.K.M. Wong. A critical analysis of the vector space model for information retrieval. *Journal of the American Society for Information Science*, 37(5):279–287, 1986.
12. F. Rosenblatt. The perceptron: A probabilistic model for information storage and organization in the brain. *Psychological Review*, 65(6):386–407, 1958.
13. G. Salton. *Automatic Text Processing: The Transformation, Analysis, and Retrieval of Information by Computer*. Addison-Wesley, 1989.
14. G. Salton and C. Buckley. Improving retrieval performance by relevance feedback. *Journal of the American Society for Information Science*, 41(4):288–297, 1990.
15. G. Salton, A. Wong, and C.S. Yang. A vector space model for automatic indexing. *Comm. of ACM*, 18(11):613–620, 1975.
16. S. Sclaroff, L. Taycher, and M. La Cascia. Imagerover: A content-based image browser for the world wide web. In *Proceedings of the IEEE Worshop on Content-based Access of Image and Video Libraries*, 1997.
17. L. Taycher, M. La Cascia, and S. Sclaroff. Image digestion and relevance feedback in the imagerover www search engines. In *Proceedings of the International Conference on Visual Information*, pages 85–92, 1997.

# Reasoning with
# Ordered Binary Decision Diagrams*

Takashi Horiyama[1] and Toshihide Ibaraki[2]

[1] Graduate School of Information Science,
Nara Institute of Science and Technology,
Nara, 630-0101 Japan. horiyama@is.aist-nara.ac.jp

[2] Graduate School of Informatics, Kyoto University,
Kyoto, 606-8501 Japan. ibaraki@i.kyoto-u.ac.jp

**Abstract.** We consider problems of reasoning with a knowledge-base, which is represented by an ordered binary decision diagram (OBDD), for two special cases of general and Horn knowledge-bases. Our main results say that both finding a model of a knowledge-base and deducing from a knowledge-base can be done in linear time for general case, but that abduction is NP-complete even if the knowledge-base is restricted to be Horn. Then, we consider the abduction when its assumption set consists of all propositional literals (i.e., an answer for a given query is allowed to include any positive literals), and show that it can be done in polynomial time if the knowledge-base is Horn, while it remains NP-complete for the general case. Some other solvable cases are also discussed.

## 1 Introduction

Logical formulae are the traditional means of representing knowledge-bases in artificial intelligence [13]. However, it is known that deduction from a knowledge-base that consists of a set of propositional clauses is co-NP-complete and abduction is $\sum_2^P$-complete [6]. By restricting the type of propositional clauses, however, such operations may be performed efficiently. For example, it is common to consider Horn clauses, and deduction from a knowledge-base consisting of a set of Horn clauses can be done in linear time [5]. Abduction from a set of Horn clauses can also be done in linear time if the assumption set is restricted to be the set of all propositional literals (i.e., an answer for a given query is allowed to include any positive literals). Nevertheless, abduction from a Horn knowledge-base is still NP-complete [14] if the assumption set has no restriction.

Recently, an alternative way of representing a knowledge-base has been proposed; i.e. it uses a subset of its models called characteristic models (see e.g., [8, 9]). Deduction from a knowledge-base in this model-based approach can be performed in linear time, and abduction is also performed in polynomial time [8].

* This research was partially supported by the Scientific Grant-in-Aid from Ministry of Education, Science, Sports and Culture of Japan.

D.T. Lee and S.-H. Teng (Eds.): ISAAC 2000, LNCS 1969, pp. 120–131, 2000.
© Springer-Verlag Berlin Heidelberg 2000

In addition to these favorable time complexity, empirical evaluation is also performed in the practical sense [9].

In this paper, we consider yet another method of knowledge representation, i.e., the use of ordered binary decision diagrams (OBDDs) [1,3]. An OBDD is a directed acyclic graph representing a Boolean function, and can be considered as a variant of a decision tree. By restricting the order of variable appearances and by sharing isomorphic subgraphs, OBDDs have the following useful properties:

1. When an ordering of variables is specified, an OBDD has the unique reduced canonical form for each Boolean function.
2. Many Boolean functions appearing in practice can be compactly represented.
3. When an OBDD is given, satisfiability and tautology of the represented function can be easily checked in constant time.
4. There are efficient algorithms for many other Boolean operations on OBDDs.

As a result of these properties, OBDDs are widely used for various practical applications, especially in computer-aided design and verification of digital systems (see e.g., [4,16]).

The manipulation of knowledge-bases by OBDDs (e.g., deduction and abduction) was first discussed by Madre and Coudert [12], and then basic theoretical questions were examined by the authors [7]. For example, it was shown that, in some cases, an OBDD-based representation requires exponentially smaller space than the other two; i.e., formula-based and model-based representations. On the other hand, there are also cases in which each of the other two requires exponentially smaller space than that of an OBDD. Although deduction and abduction are important operations for reasoning [14], their computational complexity on the OBDD-based representations was still open.

In this paper, we consider the complexity of reasoning with general and Horn knowledge-bases of OBDDs. We first consider the problem of finding a model of a given OBDD. Although it is obvious that a model can be found in polynomial time for any OBDD, we show that the least model can be output in polynomial time if the given OBDD represents a Horn knowledge-base. As to the deduction with OBDDs, Madre and Coudert discussed the case in which both knowledge and query are given in OBDD-based representations [12]. It is also natural to assume that the query is given in CNF, because formula-based queries are easier to understand. We show that deduction in this case can be done in polynomial time, though a naive algorithm may require exponential time in the input size.

We then discuss abduction with OBDDs. Although enumerating all possible outputs (i.e., explanations for a given query) may require exponential time [12], it was unknown whether or not generating only one explanation can be done in polynomial time. Unfortunately, this problem is shown to be NP-complete even if knowledge-bases are restricted to be Horn. However, by introducing some constraints on assumption set, we show that abduction from Horn OBDDs can be done in polynomial time. The first case of such constraints is that the assumption set contains all propositional literals. The second case is that the number of variables that are not in the assumption set is bounded by a constant. We further show that these two cases remain polynomial time even if there are variables which are constrained to be in the explanation.

The rest of this paper is organized as follows. The next section introduces definitions and basic concepts. The problems of reasoning with general OBDDs and Horn OBDDs are discussed in Sections 3 and 4, respectively.

## 2    Preliminaries

### 2.1    Notations and Basic Concepts

We consider a Boolean function $f : \{0,1\}^n \to \{0,1\}$. An *assignment* is a vector $a \in \{0,1\}^n$, whose $i$-th coordinate is denoted by $a_i$. A *model of* $f$ is a satisfying assignment $a$ of $f$, i.e. $f(a) = 1$, and the *theory* $\Sigma(f)$ *representing* $f$ is the set of all models of $f$. Given $a, b \in \{0,1\}^n$, we denote by $a \leq b$ the usual bitwise ordering; $a_i \leq b_i$ for all $i = 1, 2, \ldots, n$, where $0 < 1$. A model $a$ is *minimal* in $\Sigma$ if no $b \in \Sigma$ satisfies $b < a$. Given a subset $E \subseteq \{1, 2, \ldots, n\}$, $\chi^E$ denotes the characteristic vector of $E$; the $i$-th coordinate $\chi_i^E$ equals 1 if $i \in E$ and 0 if $i \notin E$.

Let $x_1, x_2, \ldots, x_n$ be the $n$ variables of $f$, where each $x_i$ corresponds to the $i$-th coordinate and evaluates to either 0 or 1. Negation of a variable $x_i$ is denoted by $\overline{x}_i$. Variables and their negations are called *literals*. A *clause* is a disjunction of some literals, and a conjunction of clauses is called a *conjunctive normal form* (CNF). We say that $f$ *is represented by a CNF* $\varphi$, if $f(a) = \varphi(a)$ holds for all $a \in \{0,1\}^n$. Any Boolean function can be represented by some CNF, which may not be unique. The *size* of a CNF $\varphi$, denoted by $|CNF(\varphi)|$, is the number of literals in $\varphi$.

We sometimes do not make a distinction among a function $f$, its theory $\Sigma(f)$, and a CNF $\varphi$ that represents $f$, unless confusion arises. We define a *restriction* of $f$ by replacing a variable $x_i$ by a constant $a_i \in \{0,1\}$, and denote it by $f|_{x_i=a_i}$. Namely, $f|_{x_i=a_i}(x_1, \ldots, x_n) = f(x_1, \ldots, x_{i-1}, a_i, x_{i+1}, \ldots, x_n)$ holds. A *smoothing* of $f$, denoted by $\exists_{x_i} f$, is defined as $f|_{x_i=0} \vee f|_{x_i=1}$. Restriction and smoothing may be applied to many variables. Given a set of variables $S \subseteq \{x_1, x_2, \ldots, x_n\}$, $\exists_S f$ denotes the smoothing of $f$ to all variables in $S$. We also define $f \leq g$ (resp., $f < g$) by $\Sigma(f) \subseteq \Sigma(g)$ (resp., $\Sigma(f) \subset \Sigma(g)$).

Denote the bitwise AND operation of assignments $a$ and $b$ by $a \wedge_{bit} b$. For example, if $a = (0011)$ and $b = (0101)$, then $a \wedge_{bit} b = (0001)$. A theory $\Sigma$ is *Horn* if $\Sigma$ is closed under operation $\wedge_{bit}$; i.e., $a, b \in \Sigma$ implies $a \wedge_{bit} b \in \Sigma$. Any Horn theory $\Sigma$ has the *least* (i.e., *unique minimal*) model $a = \bigwedge_{bit \ b \in \Sigma} b$. We also use the operation $\wedge_{bit}$ as a set operation; $\Sigma(f) \wedge_{bit} \Sigma(g) = \{a \mid a = b \wedge_{bit} c$ holds for some $b \in \Sigma(f)$ and $c \in \Sigma(g)\}$. We often denotes $\Sigma(f) \wedge_{bit} \Sigma(g)$ by $f \wedge_{bit} g$, for convenience. Note that the two functions $f \wedge g$ and $f \wedge_{bit} g$ are different.

A Boolean function $f$ is *Horn* if $\Sigma(f)$ is Horn; equivalently if $f \wedge_{bit} f = f$ holds (as sets of models). A clause is *Horn* if the number of positive literals in it is at most one, and a CNF is *Horn* if it contains only Horn clauses. It is known that a theory $\Sigma$ is Horn if and only if $\Sigma$ can be represented by some Horn CNF.

Given two Boolean functions $f$ (called a *background theory*) and $\alpha$ (called a *query*), *deduction* is the problem of deciding whether $f \models \alpha$ (i.e., $f \wedge \overline{\alpha} \equiv 0$) holds or not. *Abduction* is the problem of generating an explanation for a given query. Given a Boolean functions $f$ on $n$ variables $X = \{x_1, x_2, \ldots, x_n\}$, a set $A \subseteq X$ (called an *assumption set*) and a positive literal $x_q \in X$ (called a *query letter*), an *explanation* for $(f, A, x_q)$ is a set $E \subseteq A$ such that

(i)  $f \wedge E$ is consistent  (i.e., $f \wedge E \not\equiv 0$)  and
(ii) $f \wedge E \models x_q$  (i.e., $f \wedge E \wedge \overline{x}_q \equiv 0$),

where $f \wedge E$ denotes $f \wedge (\wedge_{x_i \in E} x_i)$. By combining (i) and (ii), we can replace (i) by the following restriction:

(i')  $f \wedge E \wedge x_q \not\equiv 0$.

We may omit some elements of the triple $(f, A, x_q)$ unless confusion arises. Since the set $E = \{x_q\}$ always satisfies restriction (ii), an explanation that contains $x_q$ is called *trivial*. We focus on how to compute a *non-trivial explanation* efficiently. An explanation is *minimal* if none of whose subsets is an explanation.

## 2.2  Ordered Binary Decision Diagrams

An *ordered binary decision diagram* (OBDD) is a directed acyclic graph that represents a Boolean function. It has two sink nodes 0 and 1, called the *0-node* and the *1-node*, respectively (which are together called the *constant nodes*). Other nodes are called *variable nodes*, and each variable node $v$ is labeled by one of the variables $x_1, x_2, \ldots, x_n$. Let $var(v)$ denote the label of node $v$. Each variable node has exactly two outgoing edges, called a *0-edge* and a *1-edge*, respectively. One of the variable nodes becomes the unique source node, which is called the *root node*. Let $X = \{x_1, x_2, \ldots, x_n\}$ denote the set of $n$ variables. A *variable ordering* is a total ordering $(x_{\pi(n)}, x_{\pi(n-1)}, \ldots, x_{\pi(1)})$, associated with each OBDD, where $\pi$ is a permutation $\{1, 2, \ldots, n\} \rightarrow \{1, 2, \ldots, n\}$. The *level*[1] of a variable $x_{\pi(i)}$, denoted by $level(x_{\pi(i)})$, is defined to be $i$. Similarly, the level of a node $v$, denoted by $level(v)$, is defined by its label; if node $v$ has label $x_{\pi(i)}$, $level(v)$ is defined to be $i$. That is, the root node is in level $n$ and has label $x_{\pi(n)}$, the nodes in level $n - 1$ have label $x_{\pi(n-1)}$ and so on. The level of the constant nodes is defined to be 0. On every path from the root node to a constant node in an OBDD, each variable appears at most once in the decreasing order of their levels. Thus each edge from a node $v$ points to a node $u$ satisfying $level(u) \leq level(v) - 1$.

Every node $v$ of an OBDD also represents a Boolean function $f_v$, defined by the subgraph consisting of those nodes and edges reachable from $v$. If a node $v$ is a constant node, $f_v$ equals to its label. If a node $v$ is a variable node, $f_v$ is defined as $\overline{var(v)} \, f_{0\text{-}succ(v)} \vee var(v) \, f_{1\text{-}succ(v)}$ by Shannon's expansion, where $0\text{-}succ(v)$ and $1\text{-}succ(v)$, respectively, denote the nodes pointed by the 0-edge and the 1-edge of node $v$. The function $f$ represented by an OBDD is the one represented by

---

[1] This definition of level may be different from its common use.

the root node. Given an assignment $a$, the value $f(a)$ is determined by following the path from the root node to a constant node by selecting $a_{var(v)}$-edge at each variable node $v$. The value $f(a)$ is given by the label of the final constant node reachable in this manner.

When two nodes $u$ and $v$ in an OBDD represent the same function, and their levels are the same, they are called *equivalent*. A node whose 0-edge and 1-edge both point to the same node is called *redundant*. An OBDD is called *dense* if every variable node $v$ satisfy $level(0\text{-}succ(v)) = level(1\text{-}succ(v)) = level(v) - 1$ (i.e., all paths from the root node to constant nodes visit $n + 1$ nodes). A dense OBDD which has no mutually equivalent nodes is *quasi-reduced*. An OBDD which has no mutually equivalent nodes and no redundant nodes is *reduced*. Any quasi-reduced OBDD can be transformed into a reduced OBDD by removing all redundant nodes. In the following, we assume that all OBDDs are reduced, unless otherwise stated. The *size* of an OBDD of $f$, denoted by $|OBDD(f)|$, is the number of nodes in the OBDD. Given a function $f$ and a variable ordering, its reduced OBDD is unique and has the minimum size among all OBDDs with the same variable ordering. The sizes of OBDDs that represent a given Boolean function may vary according to the variable orderings [3].

Given an OBDD that represents $f$, the OBDDs of $f|_{x_i=0}$ and $f|_{x_i=1}$ can be obtained in $O(|OBDD(f)|)$ time [2]. The size of an OBDD does not increase by a restriction. Given two OBDDs representing $f$ and $g$, fundamental logic operators, e.g., $f \wedge g$, $f \vee g$, $f \oplus g$ and $f \rightarrow g$, can be applied in $O(|OBDD(f)| \cdot |OBDD(g)|)$ time, and property $f \leq g$ can be also checked in $O(|OBDD(f)| \cdot |OBDD(g)|)$ time [3]. Negation of a function can be done in constant time by introducing attributed edges (e.g., output inverters) [11]. Given an OBDD of $f$ and a set $S \subset X$ satisfying $\forall x_i \in S \; \forall x_j \in (X - S) \; level(x_j) > level(x_i)$, the smoothing $\exists_S f$ can be applied in $O(|OBDD(f)|)$ time, and the size of the resulting OBDD is $O(|OBDD(f)|)$ [15]. Note that a smoothing to an arbitrary variable is applied in $O(|OBDD(f)|^2)$ time.

## 3    Reasoning with General OBDDs

In this section, we consider the complexity of reasoning with general knowledge-bases, which are represented by OBDDs. In particular, we consider the problems of finding a model of a knowledge-base and deducing from a knowledge-base. Then, we consider the problem of finding an abductive explanation. We assume, without loss of generality, that the variable ordering of a given OBDD is always $(x_n, x_{n-1}, \ldots, x_1)$.

### 3.1    Finding a Model and Deduction with OBDDs

We first consider finding a model of a knowledge-base. By definition, paths from the root node to the 1-node of a given OBDD correspond to the models of the theory represented by the OBDD. Thus, we can obtain one of the models in $O(n)$ time by starting from the root node. By putting higher priority to 0-edges (if both 0-edge and 1-edge lead to the 1-node) at all levels, the output gives one of the minimal models. Moreover, it is the least model if a given theory is Horn, since any Horn theory has the unique minimal model, which is the least model.

**Theorem 3.1** *Given an OBDD of a theory $\Sigma(f)$, a minimal model can be obtained in $O(n)$ time by FIND-MODEL. Moreover, FIND-MODEL outputs the least model if $\Sigma(f)$ is Horn.*

Now, we discuss deduction with OBDDs. Madre and Coudert gave the following appealing result, assuming that both background theory $\Sigma(f)$ and query $\alpha$ are given as OBDDs.

**Lemma 3.1** [12] *Given OBDDs of a theory $\Sigma(f)$ and a query $\alpha$ which have the same variable ordering, whether $\Sigma(f) \models \alpha$ holds or not can be decided in $O(|OBDD(f)| \cdot |OBDD(\alpha)|)$ time.*

Here we consider the case in which a query $\alpha$ is given as a CNF formula. We may apply Lemma 3.1 after constructing the OBDD of $\alpha$ from its CNF formula. However, this naive algorithm is intractable even when knowledge-bases are restricted to be Horn. This is because there exists a Horn theory for which the size of CNF is linear in the number of variables, while the size of the smallest OBDD is exponential [7]. We however show that deduction can be done in linear time without explicitly constructing the OBDD of $\alpha$.

**Theorem 3.2** *Given an OBDD of a theory $\Sigma(f)$ and a CNF formula $\alpha$, whether $\Sigma(f) \models \alpha$ holds or not can be decided in $O(|OBDD(f)| \cdot |CNF(\alpha)|)$ time.*

**Proof:** We assume that $\alpha$ is given by a conjunction of $m$ clauses $C_1, C_2, \ldots, C_m$. By definition, the property $\Sigma(f) \models \alpha$ holds if and only if $\Sigma(f) \models C_i$ holds for all $i \in \{1, 2, \ldots, m\}$. Since each $C_i$ is a disjunction of $|CNF(C_i)|$ literals, we can construct the OBDD of $C_i$, whose size is $|CNF(C_i)| + 2$. By Lemma 3.1, $\Sigma(f) \models C_i$ is checked in $O(|OBDD(f)| \cdot |CNF(C_i)|)$ time. Therefore, the check for $\Sigma(f) \models \alpha$ can be done in $O(\sum_{i=1}^{m} |OBDD(f)| \cdot |CNF(C_i)|) = O(|OBDD(f)| \cdot |CNF(\alpha)|)$ time. $\qquad\square$

Therefore, OBDD-based representations can be used in place of traditional knowledge-base systems, even if queries are given in CNF formulae. A strong point of this approach is that once the OBDD of a knowledge-base is constructed, any query $\alpha$ can be answered in linear time, even if the knowledge is not Horn. This contrasts with the CNF-based and model-based approaches, in which the Horness is assumed.

## 3.2   Abduction with General OBDDs

We consider the computational cost of abduction from the OBDD of a general theory. It is known that enumerating all possible explanations may require exponential time (since there may be exponentially many explanations). The following theorem says that finding only one explanation is intractable.

**Theorem 3.3** *Given an OBDD of a theory $\Sigma(f)$ on $n$ variables $X = \{x_1, x_2, \ldots, x_n\}$, an assumption set $A \subseteq X$, and a query letter $x_q \in X$, deciding whether $x_q$ has a non-trivial explanation is NP-complete.*

**Proof:** The problem is in NP, since we can guess a set $E \subseteq A$ and check whether $E$ is an explanation for $x_q$ as follows in polynomial time. The consistency of $f \wedge E$ can be checked by testing the equivalent condition $f \wedge E \not\equiv 0$, where the OBDD of $f \wedge E$ can be constructed in $O(n \cdot |OBDD(f)|)$ time since the size of the OBDD of $\bigwedge_{x_j \in E} x_j$ is $O(n)$. Also deduction $f \wedge E \models x_q$ can be checked in polynomial time by Theorem 3.2 from the OBDD of $f \wedge E$.

The proof of the NP-hardness is based on a reduction from the problem of testing the non-tautology of DNF formulae (NON-TAUTOLOGY). Given a DNF formula $\varphi = \bigvee_{i=1}^{m} T_i$ on $n$ variables $x_1, x_2, \ldots, x_n$, where $T_i = \left( \bigwedge_{j \in P(i)} x_j \right) \wedge \left( \bigwedge_{k \in N(i)} \overline{x}_k \right)$ and $P(i) \cap N(i) = \emptyset$ for $i = 1, 2, \ldots, m$, we construct an OBDD of theory $\Sigma(f_A)$ on $2n + m + 1$ variables $y_1, y_2, \ldots, y_{2n+m+1}$ with variable ordering $(y_{2n+m+1}, y_{2n+m}, \ldots, y_1)$; $f_A$ is defined as follows:

$$f_A = \overline{y}_{2n+m+1} g_A \vee y_{2n+m+1} h_A, \tag{1}$$

$$\text{where} \quad g_A = \bigvee_{i=1}^{m} \left( \left( \bigwedge_{j=i+1}^{m} y_{2n+j} \right) \wedge \overline{y}_{2n+i} \wedge g_i \right),$$

$$g_i = \left( \bigwedge_{j \in P(i)} \overline{y}_{2j-1} y_{2j} \right) \wedge \left( \bigwedge_{j \in N(i)} y_{2j-1} \overline{y}_{2j} \right)$$

$$\wedge \left( \bigwedge_{j \in \{1,2,\ldots,n\} - P(i) - N(i)} y_{2j-1} y_{2j} \right), \tag{2}$$

$$h_A = \left( \bigwedge_{i=1}^{n} \left( \overline{y}_{2i-1} y_{2i} \vee y_{2i-1} \overline{y}_{2i} \right) \right) \wedge \left( \bigwedge_{j=1}^{m} \overline{y}_{2n+j} \right).$$

We can easily observe that $f_A$ is represented by an OBDD of polynomial size. Thus, all we have to do is to prove that there exists a non-trivial explanation for $(f_A, \{y_1, y_2, \ldots, y_{2n}\}, y_{2n+m+1})$ if and only if $\varphi \equiv 1$ does not hold.

We first prove the only-if-part. By assumption, there exist a set $E$ ($\subseteq \{y_1, y_2, \ldots, y_{2n}\}$) satisfying (ii) $f_A \wedge E \wedge \overline{y}_{2n+m+1} \equiv 0$ and (i') $f_A \wedge E \wedge y_{2n+m+1} \not\equiv 0$. Since (1) implies

$$f_A \wedge E \wedge y_{2n+m+1}$$
$$= h_A \wedge y_{2n+m+1} \wedge E$$
$$= \left( \bigwedge_{i=1}^{n} \left( \overline{y}_{2i-1} y_{2i} \vee y_{2i-1} \overline{y}_{2i} \right) \right) \wedge \left( \bigwedge_{j=1}^{m} \overline{y}_{2n+j} \right) \wedge y_{2n+m+1} \wedge E,$$

$E$ does not contain both $y_{2i-1}$ and $y_{2i}$ at the same time for any $i = 1, 2, \ldots, n$. Otherwise (i.e., if there exists some $i$ such that $E$ contains both $y_{2i-1}$ and $y_{2i}$), property $(\overline{y}_{2i-1}y_{2i} \vee y_{2i-1}\overline{y}_{2i}) \wedge E \equiv 0$ holds, which contradict with property (i'). Here, we can construct an assignment $a \in \{0,1\}^n$ satisfying

$$a_i = \begin{cases} 1 & (\text{if } y_{2i} \in E) \\ 0 & (\text{if } y_{2i-1} \in E). \end{cases} \tag{3}$$

Equality (1) also implies

$$f_A \wedge E \wedge \overline{y}_{2n+m+1}$$
$$= g_A \wedge \overline{y}_{2n+m+1} \wedge E$$
$$= \bigvee_{i=1}^{m} \left( \left( \bigwedge_{j=i+1}^{m} y_{2n+j} \right) \wedge \overline{y}_{2n+i} \wedge g_i \wedge \overline{y}_{2n+m+1} \wedge E \right).$$

From property (ii), we have

$$\left( \bigwedge_{j=i+1}^{m} y_{2n+j} \right) \wedge \overline{y}_{2n+i} \wedge \overline{y}_{2n+m+1} \wedge g_i \wedge E \equiv 0 \tag{4}$$

for all $i = 1, 2, \ldots, m$. Since $g_i \wedge E$ does not depend on variables $y_{2n+1}, y_{2n+2}, \ldots,$ $y_{2n+m+1}$, (4) implies $g_i \wedge E \equiv 0$. Namely, from (2), there exists $j \in P(i)$ satisfying $y_{2j-1} \in E$ or there exists $j \in N(i)$ satisfying $y_{2j} \in E$ for $i = 1, 2, \ldots, m$. Since $E$ has a corresponding assignment $a$ by (3), there exists $j \in P(i)$ satisfying $a_j = 0$ or there exists $j \in N(i)$ satisfying $a_j = 1$ for every $i$. Namely, there exists an assignment $a$ which does not satisfy any term $T_i$ in $\varphi$.

The if-part can be proved by a similar argument to the case of the only-if-part. We show that every assignment $a \in \{0,1\}^n$ satisfies $\varphi$ under the assumption that $y_{2n+m+1}$ has no non-trivial explanation.    □

Similarly to the case of abduction from general CNFs, abduction from OBDDs is also intractable. We emphasize the difference, at this point, that abduction from general OBDDs is NP-complete, while abduction from general CNFs is $\sum_2^P$-complete [6].

In many cases, polynomial time algorithms can be obtained by introducing additional constraints. We consider here the case in which the assumption set is the set of all propositional literals. The following corollary, however, gives a negative result even under such condition.

**Corollary 3.1** *Given an OBDD of a theory $\Sigma(f)$ on $n$ variables $X = \{x_1, x_2, \ldots, x_n\}$, an assumption set $A = X$, and a query letter $x_q \in X$, deciding whether $x_q$ has a non-trivial explanation is NP-complete.*

## 4    Reasoning with Horn OBDDs

In this section, we consider the complexity of reasoning with OBDDs of Horn theories. Since finding a model and deducing from a theory can be done in linear time, for an OBDD of a general theory, we only consider the problem of finding an abductive explanation from a Horn OBDD.

### 4.1    Abduction with Horn OBDDs

By restricting to a Horn knowledge-base, the computational cost for abduction may be reduced. For example, in the case of CNFs, it becomes NP-complete from $\sum_2^P$-complete [14]. In the model-based case, the linear time abduction is accomplished by making use of the Horness. However, the following theorem says that abduction is intractable even for Horn OBDDs.

**Theorem 4.1**  *Given an OBDD of a Horn theory $\Sigma(f)$ on $n$ variables $X = \{x_1, x_2, \ldots, x_n\}$, an assumption set $A \subseteq X$, and a query letter $x_q \in X$, deciding whether $x_q$ has a non-trivial explanation is NP-complete.*

**Outline of the proof:**  This theorem is proved in a similar way to Theorem 3.3. The problem is obviously in NP. The NP-hardness is proved by a reduction from NON-TAUTOLOGY by constructing a Horn OBDD that plays the role of $\Sigma(f_A)$ in the proof of Theorem 3.3.                                                                    □

Now, we consider the special case in which the assumption set $A$ consists of all propositional literals. Although abduction under such condition is still NP-complete for a general OBDD, it can be done in quadratic time for a Horn OBDD.

A non-trivial explanation $E$ ($\subseteq X - \{x_q\}$) satisfies (i') in the definition of abduction, if and only if there exists a model $a$ of $\Sigma(f)$ that satisfies $a_q = 1$ and $a_i = 1$ for all $x_i \in E$. This constraint can be rewritten as

$$(\text{I}) \; \exists \, a_{[q]} \in \Sigma(f|_{x_q=1}) \; \text{ s.t. } a_{[q]} \geq \chi^E,$$

where $a_{[q]}$ denotes the vector composed by all the components of $a$ but $a_q$. Similarly, $E$ satisfies (ii) if and only if

$$(\text{II}) \; \forall \, b_{[q]} \in \Sigma(f|_{x_q=0}) \; \; b_{[q]} \not\geq \chi^E.$$

We may find an explanation by checking, for each subset $E$ of $X - \{x_q\}$, whether both (I) and (II) are satisfied or not. Although there may be exponentially many $E$'s, this naive algorithm gives a key to our algorithm.

**Theorem 4.2**  *Given an OBDD of a Horn theory $\Sigma(f)$ on $n$ variables $X = \{x_1, x_2, \ldots x_n\}$, an assumption set $A = X$, and a query letter $x_q$, a non-trivial explanation for $\Sigma(f)$ can be obtained in $O(|OBDD(f)|^2)$ time, if there is any.*

**Proof:**  Consider two sets $E$, $E'$ ($\subseteq X - \{x_q\}$) satisfying $\chi^{E'} \leq \chi^E$ and

(I') $\exists a_{[q]} \in \Sigma(f|_{x_q=1})$ s.t. $a_{[q]} = \chi^E$.

If $E'$ is an explanation, $E$ is also an explanation. Conversely, if $E$ is not an explanation, neither is $E'$. Thus, we consider a subset $E$ that satisfies both (I') and (II).

Consider a model $a_{[q]}$ of $\Sigma(f|_{x_q=1})$ and a model $b_{[q]}$ of $\Sigma(f|_{x_q=0})$ satisfying $a_{[q]} \leq b_{[q]}$. Since $a = (a_{[q]}, 1)$ and $b = (b_{[q]}, 0)$ are the models of $\Sigma(f)$, where the last component corresponds to $x_q$, $a \wedge_{bit} b = (a_{[q]}, 0)$ is also a model. Namely, if $E$ satisfies (I') and $\exists b_{[q]} \in \Sigma(f|_{x_q=0})$ $b_{[q]} \geq \chi^E$, then we have $\exists c_{[q]} \in \Sigma(f|_{x_q=0})$ $c_{[q]} = \chi^E$. Thus, if $E$ satisfies (I') and

(II') $\forall b_{[q]} \in \Sigma(f|_{x_q=0})$ $b_{[q]} \neq \chi^E$,

then $E$ satisfies both (I') and (II). Conversely, if $E$ satisfies (I') and (II), it is clear that $E$ satisfies (I') and (II'). Therefore, $E$ is a non-trivial explanation if and only if $\chi^E$ is a model of $f^* = f|_{x_q=1} \wedge \overline{f|_{x_q=0}}$.

As noted in subsection 2.2, an OBDD representing $f|_{x_q=0}$ (resp., $f|_{x_q=1}$) can be obtained in $O(|OBDD(f)|)$ time from the OBDD of $f$. The size does not increase by restrictions $f|_{x_q=0}$ or $f|_{x_q=1}$. Negation can be done in constant time. Since the OBDD of $g \wedge h$ can be obtained from the OBDDs of $g$ and $h$ in $O(|OBDD(g)| \cdot |OBDD(h)|)$ time, the OBDD of $f^*$ can be obtained in $O(|OBDD(f)|^2)$ time. If $f^* \equiv 0$, there is no non-trivial explanation. Otherwise, we obtain the characteristic vector of an explanation by applying Algorithm FIND-MODEL to the OBDD of $f^*$. □

Once a non-trivial explanation is obtained, a minimal non-trivial explanation can be found in a manner similar to the model-based abduction; eliminate unnecessary propositional literals in turn while maintaining the condition (II).

**Corollary 4.1** *Given an OBDD of a Horn theory $\Sigma(f)$ on $n$ variables $X = \{x_1, x_2, \dots x_n\}$, an assumption set $A = X$, and a query letter $x_q$, a minimal non-trivial explanation for $\Sigma(f)$ can be obtained in $O(|OBDD(f)|^2)$ time, if there is any.*

## 4.2    Polynomial Time Abduction with Horn OBDDs

Theorem 4.2 gives a special case in which a non-trivial explanation for Horn abduction can be obtained in polynomial time. In this subsection, we derive more refined analysis of computation time after introducing two constraints on explanations $E$. This reveals a more general case in which explanations can be obtained in polynomial time.

(1) We may specify an additional set $S$ ($\subseteq A$) which must be included in $E$.

(2) We may consider an assumption set $A$, which is a subset of the set of all propositional literals $X$.

Recall that Theorem 4.1 states the intractability of considering arbitrary assumption sets $A$ in (2).

**Theorem 4.3** *Let $G$ be an OBDD of a Horn theory $\Sigma(f)$ on $n$ variables $X = \{x_1, x_2, \ldots x_n\}$, $A$ ($\subseteq X$) be an assumption set, $x_q$ be a query letter, and $S$ be a subset of $A$. Let $T_1 = \{x_i \mid x_i \in (X - A - \{x_q\})$ and $\exists x_j \in A$ s.t. $level(x_j) < level(x_i)\}$. Then, a non-trivial explanation for $(f, A, x_q)$ which contains $S$ can be obtained in $O(|OBDD(f)|^{2^{|T_1|+1}})$ time, if there is any.*

**Proof:** A set $E$ satisfying $S \subseteq E \subseteq A$ is an explanation for $(f, A, x_q)$ if and only if $E - S$ is an explanation for $(f|_{x_i=1 \ (\forall x_i \in S)}, A - S, x_q)$. We can construct the OBDD of $f_1 = f|_{x_i=1 \ (\forall x_i \in S)}$ in $O(|OBDD(f)|)$ time, and its size is $O(|OBDD(f)|)$.

Now, $E$ is an explanation for $(f_1, A-S, x_q)$ if and only if $E$ is an explanation for $(\exists_{X-A-\{x_q\}} f_1, A - S, x_q)$. We apply smoothing operations to the variables in $T_1$ and $T_2 = (X - A - \{x_q\}) - T_1$. If $T_2 \neq \emptyset$, we first apply a smoothing operation to the variables in $T_2$, and obtain the OBDD of $f_2 = \exists_{T_2} f_1$. The smoothing operation is applied at once, since the variables in $T_2$ constitute the bottom part of the OBDD. The resulting OBDD is obtained in $O(|OBDD(f)|)$ time, and its size is still $O(|OBDD(f)|)$. We then apply smoothing operations to all variables in $T_1$ in turn (i.e., the smoothing operations are applied $|T_1|$ times). The OBDD of $f_3 = \exists_{T_1} f_2$ is obtained in $O(|OBDD(f_1)|^{2^{|T_1|}})$ time, and its size is $O(|OBDD(f_1)|^{2^{|T_1|}})$.

If a function $g$ is Horn, $g|_{x_i=0}$, $g|_{x_i=1}$ and $\exists_{x_i} g$ are also Horn. This implies that $f_1$, $f_2$ and $f_3$ are Horn. Thus, we can apply Theorem 4.2. □

Note that Theorem 4.2 is the special case of Theorem 4.3 with $S = T_1 = T_2 = \emptyset$. It also says that, if $|T_1|$ is bounded by a constant, an explanation can be obtained in polynomial time. The idea in Theorem 4.3 can be also applied to abduction from Horn CNFs. We, however, emphasize the difference that $|T_2|$ can take any size (i.e., it can be $O(n)$) for the OBDD case, while both $|T_1|$ and $|T_2|$ (and also $|X - A - \{x_q\}|$) have to be bounded by a constant for the CNF case.

In contrast with Corollary 4.1, a minimal non-trivial explanation which contains the specified variables in $S$ may not be obtained in quadratic time. This is because no minimal non-trivial explanation derived from the obtained explanation may contain all of the specified variables.

## 5   Conclusion

In this paper, we considered the problems of reasoning with general and Horn knowledge-bases, which are represented by OBDDs. We showed that finding a model of a knowledge-base and deducing from a knowledge-base can both be done in linear time for general case. However, it turned out that abduction is NP-complete even if the knowledge-base restricted to be Horn. Then, by introducing some constraints on a assumption set, it was shown that abduction from Horn OBDDs can be done in polynomial time. The first constraint was that the assumption set $A$ contains all propositional literals. This constraint was then relaxed to that there exist a constant number of variables which are not in $A$ and appear in higher levels than some variable in $A$. It was also pointed out that a set of variables can be given as a constraint that they should be included in the explanation.

OBDDs are dominatingly used in the field of computer-aided design and verification of digital systems. This is because many Boolean functions which we encounter in practice can be compactly represented, and many operations on OBDDs can be efficiently performed. To make the knowledge-base of OBDDs more practice, developing a practical algorithm for abduction should be addressed in the further work.

# References

1. S.B. Akers, "Binary Decision Diagrams," *IEEE Trans. Comput.*, C-27, no.6, pp.509–516, 1978.
2. K.S. Brace, R.L. Rundell, and R.E. Bryant, "Efficient Implementation of a BDD Package," *Proc. of 27th ACM/IEEE DAC*, pp.40–45, 1990.
3. R.E. Bryant, "Graph-Based Algorithms for Boolean Function Manipulation," *IEEE Trans. Comput.*, C-35, no.8, pp.677–691, 1986.
4. O. Coudert, "Doing Two-Level Logic Minimization 100 Times Faster," *Proc. of 6th ACM/SIAM SODA*, pp.112-118, 1995.
5. W.F. Dowling and J.H. Gallier, "Linear Time Algorithms for Testing the Satisfiability of Horn Formula," *J. Logic Programm.*, 3, pp.267–284, 1984.
6. T. Eiter and G. Gottlob, "The Complexity of Logic-Based Abduction," Journal of the ACM, 42(1), pp.3–42, 1995.
7. T. Horiyama and T. Ibaraki, "Ordered Binary Decision Diagrams as Knowledge-Bases," *Proc. of 10th ISAAC*, LNCS 1741, pp.83–92, 1999.
8. H.A. Kautz, M.J. Kearns, and B. Selman, "Reasoning with Characteristic Models," *Proc. of AAAI-93*, pp.34–39, 1993.
9. H.A. Kautz, M.J. Kearns, and B. Selman, "Horn Approximations of Empirical Data," *Artificial Intelligence*, 74, pp.129–245, 1995.
10. H.A. Kautz and B. Selman, "An Empirical Evaluation of Knowledge Compilation by Theory Approximation," *in Proc. AAAI-94*, 1994, pp.155–161.
11. J.C. Madre and J.P. Billion, "Proving Circuit Correctness using Formal Comparison Between Expected and Extracted Behaviour," *Proc. of 25th ACM/IEEE DAC*, pp.205–210, 1988.
12. J.C. Madre and O. Coudert, "A Logically Complete Reasoning Maintenance System Based on a Logical Constraint Solver," *Proc. of IJCAI-91*, pp.294–299, 1991.
13. J. McCarthy and P.J. Hayes, "Some Philosophical Problems from the Standpoint of Artificial Intelligence," *in Machine Intelligence 4*, 1969.
14. B. Selman and H.J. Levesque, "Abductive and Default Reasoning: A Computational Core," *Proc. of AAAI-90*, pp.343–348, 1990.
15. F. Somenzi, CUDD: CU Decision Diagram Package, University of Colorado at Boulder http://vlsi.colorado.edu/, 1998.
16. N. Takahashi, N. Ishiura, and S. Yajima, "Fault Simulation for Multiple Faults Using BDD Representation of Fault Sets," *in Proc. IEEE/ACM ICCAD-91*, pp.550–553, 1991.

# On Approximating Minimum Vertex Cover
# for Graphs with Perfect Matching

Jianer Chen* and Iyad A. Kanj

Department of Computer Science, Texas A&M University,
College Station, Texas 77843-3112, USA
{chen,iakanj}@cs.tamu.edu

**Abstract.** It has been a challenging open problem whether there is a polynomial time approximation algorithm for the VERTEX COVER problem whose approximation ratio is bounded by a constant less than 2. In this paper, we study the VERTEX COVER problem on graphs with perfect matching (shortly, VC-PM). We show that if the VC-PM problem has a polynomial time approximation algorithm with approximation ratio bounded by a constant less than 2, then so does the VERTEX COVER problem on general graphs. Approximation algorithms for VC-PM are developed, which induce improvements over previously known algorithms on sparse graphs. For example, for graphs of average degree 5, the approximation ratio of our algorithm is 1.414, compared with the previously best ratio 1.615 by Halldórsson and Radhakrishnan.

## 1 Introduction

Approximation algorithms for NP-hard optimization problems have been a very active research area in recent years. In particular, the study of approximability for certain famous NP-hard optimization problems has achieved great success. For example, now it is known that the polynomial time approximability for the MAXIMUM SATISFIABILITY problem is exactly 8/7, based on the lower bound derived by Håstad [12] and the algorithm developed by Karloff and Zwick [15].

On the other hand, some other famous NP-hard optimization problems still resist stubbornly improvements. A well-known example is the VERTEX COVER problem. A very simple approximation algorithm based on maximal matchings gives an approximation ratio 2 for the VERTEX COVER problem. However, despite long time efforts, no significant progress has been made on this ratio bound. It has become an outstanding open problem whether there is a polynomial time approximation algorithm for the VERTEX COVER problem whose approximation ratio is bounded by a constant less than 2. On the other hand, the best lower bound for the ratio is 7/6 [12].

Considerable efforts have been made on trying to improve the upper bound on the approximability for the VERTEX COVER problem. Hochbaum [13] presented

---

* Corresponding author. This work was supported in part by the USA National Science Foundation under the Grant CCR-9613805.

D.T. Lee and S.-H. Teng (Eds.): ISAAC 2000, LNCS 1969, pp. 132–143, 2000.

an algorithm of approximation ratio $2 - 2/\Delta$ for graphs of degree bounded by $\Delta$. Monien and Speckenmeyer [17] improved this bound to $2 - (\log \log n)/(2 \log n)$. The same bound was also achieved independently by Bar-Yehuda and Even [1], whose result is also applicable to the weighted vertex cover problem. However, no significant progress has been made on this bound for the last one and a half decades. For the VERTEX COVER problem on sparse graphs, Berman and Fujito [2] presented an approximation algorithm for graphs of degree bounded by 3, whose approximation ratio is bounded by $7/6 + \epsilon$. Halldórsson [9] developed an algorithm of ratio $2 - \log d/d(1 + \epsilon)$ for graphs of degree bounded by $d$, which is further improved very recently by Halperin who derived an algorithm of ratio $2 - O(\log \log d / \log d)$ [11]. On graphs of average degree $\bar{d}$, Hochbaum [13] has studied the approximation algorithms for the INDEPENDENT SET problem. Halldórsson and Radhakrishnan [10] improved Hochbaum's algorithm. Under the assumption that a minimum vertex cover of the input graph contains at least half of the vertices in the graph, Halldórsson and Radhakrishnan's algorithm implies an algorithm of approximation ratio $2 - 5/(2\bar{d} + 3)$ for the VERTEX COVER problem on graphs of average degree $\bar{d}$.

For general graphs, no polynomial time approximation algorithms have been developed for the VERTEX COVER problem whose approximation ratios are bounded by a constant less than 2. Hochbaum has once conjectured that no such approximation algorithm exists [13]. Motivated by these facts, we study in the current paper the VERTEX COVER problem on graphs with perfect matching (or shortly, the VC-PM problem). The VERTEX COVER problem and graph matching are closely related. In fact, the maximum matching problem is the dual problem of the minimum vertex cover problem when they are given in their integer linear programming forms [3]. We first show that unless P = NP, the VC-PM problem cannot be approximated in polynomial time to a ratio less than $13/12 - \epsilon$ for any constant $\epsilon > 0$. We then show that if the VC-PM problem has a polynomial time approximation algorithm with approximation ratio bounded by a constant less than 2, then so does the VERTEX COVER problem on general graphs. Approximation algorithms for the VC-PM problem are then investigated, with its close relation to the MAX-2SAT problem. A polynomial time approximation algorithm is developed for the VC-PM problem, which induces improvements over previous algorithms for the VERTEX COVER problem on sparse graphs. For example, for graphs of average degree 5, the approximation ratio of our algorithm is 1.414, compared with the previously best ratio 1.615 by Halldórsson and Radhakrishnan [10].

## 2   On In-Approximability of VC-PM

We briefly review the related terminologies and notations used in this paper. Let $G = (V, E)$ be a graph. A *vertex cover* $C$ for $G$ is a set of vertices in $G$ such that every edge in $E$ has at least one endpoint in $C$. An *independent set* $I$ in $G$ is a set of vertices in $G$ such that no two vertices in $I$ are adjacent. It is easy to see that a set $C \subseteq V$ is a vertex cover for $G$ if and only if the complement set

$V - C$ is an independent set in $G$. The VERTEX COVER problem is to construct for a given graph a vertex cover of the minimum number of vertices, and the INDEPENDENT SET problem is to construct for a given graph an independent set of the maximum number of vertices. Both VERTEX COVER and INDEPENDENT SET are well-known NP-hard problems [7].

A *matching* $M$ in a graph $G = (V, E)$ is a set of edges in $G$ such that no two edges in $M$ share a common endpoint. A vertex is *matched* if it is an endpoint of an edge in $M$, and is *unmatched* otherwise. A matching $M$ in $G$ is *maximal* if no edge can be added to $M$ to make a larger matching. A matching $M$ is *maximum* if no matching in $G$ is larger than $M$. The MAXIMUM MATCHING problem is to construct for a given graph a maximum matching. A graph $G$ of $n$ vertices has a *perfect matching* if $G$ has a matching of $n/2$ edges. Given a matching $M$ in a graph $G$, an *augmenting path* in $G$ (with respect to $M$) is a simple path $\{u_0, u_1, \ldots, u_{2k+1}\}$ of odd length such that $u_0$ and $u_{2k+1}$ are unmatched, and the edges $[u_{2i-1}, u_{2i}]$, $i = 1, \ldots, k$, are in the matching $M$. It is well-known that a matching $M$ is maximum if and only if there is no augmenting path in $G$ with respect to $M$ [3]. The MAXIMUM MATCHING problem can be solved in time $O(m\sqrt{n})$ [16]. In particular, it can be tested in time $O(m\sqrt{n})$ whether a graph has a perfect matching.

The current paper will concentrate on the VERTEX COVER problem on graphs with perfect matching. Formally, the VC-PM problem is, for each graph $G$ with perfect matching, to construct a minimum vertex cover for $G$. It is not difficult to prove, via a standard reduction from the 4-SATISFIABILITY problem, that the VC-PM problem is NP-hard.

Let $G = (V, E)$ be a graph. For a subset $V' \subseteq V$ of vertices in $G$, denote by $G(V')$ the subgraph induced by $V'$. That is, the vertex set of the subgraph $G(V')$ is $V'$, and an edge $e$ in $G$ is in $G(V')$ if and only if both endpoints of $e$ are in $V'$. We also denote by $Opt(G)$ the size of the minimum vertex cover for the graph $G$. The importance of the following proposition, due to Nemhauser and Trotter [18], to the approximation of the VERTEX COVER problem was first observed by Hochbaum [13].

**Proposition 1 (NT-Theorem).** *Given a graph $G$, there is an $O(m\sqrt{n})$ time algorithm that partitions the vertex set of $G$ into three subsets $I_0$, $C_0$, and $V_0$ such that*

(1) $Opt(G(V_0)) \geq |V_0|/2$; *and*

(2) *for any vertex cover $C$ of $G(V_0)$, $C \cup C_0$ is a vertex cover of $G$ satisfying*

$$\frac{|C \cup C_0|}{Opt(G)} \leq \frac{|C|}{Opt(G(V_0))}$$

According to NT-Theorem, the approximation ratio on vertex cover for the graph $G(V_0)$ implies an equally good approximation ratio on vertex cover for the original graph $G$. Thus, we only need to concentrate on approximating vertex cover for the graph $G(V_0)$, for which the minimum vertex cover has a lower bound $|V_0|/2$.

**Theorem 1.** *Unless* $P = NP$, *the* VC-PM *problem has no polynomial time approximation algorithm with ratio* $13/12 - \epsilon$ *for any constant* $\epsilon > 0$.

*Proof.* Suppose the contrary that there is a polynomial time approximation algorithm $A_{pm}$ of ratio $r = 13/12 - \epsilon$ for the VC-PM problem, where $\epsilon > 0$ is a constant. We show that this would imply a polynomial time approximation algorithm of ratio $7/6 - \delta$ for the VERTEX COVER problem on general graphs for some constant $\delta > 0$, which, in consequence, would imply $P = NP$ [12].

Let $G$ be a graph with $n$ vertices. By NT-Theorem, we can assume that $Opt(G) \geq n/2$. Construct a maximal matching $M$ for $G$. Let $I$ be the set of the unmatched vertices. Then $I$ is an independent set in $G$. Let $s = |I|$. Since $Opt(G) \geq n/2$, we have $s \leq n/2$. Introduce a new clique $Q$ of $s$ vertices. Pair the vertices in $Q$ and the vertices in $I$ arbitrarily, and connect each pair by an edge. Let the resulting graph be $G_+$. The graph $G_+$ has $n + s$ vertices, and has a perfect matching. Moreover, it is easy to verify that

$$Opt(G) + s - 1 \leq Opt(G_+) \leq Opt(G) + s \qquad (1)$$

Now apply the approximation algorithm $A_{pm}$ on the graph $G_+$, we get a vertex cover $C_+$ for the graph $G_+$. By our assumption, $|C_+|/Opt(G_+) \leq r$. Remove all vertices in $C_+ \cap Q$ from $C_+$, we get a vertex cover $C$ for the graph $G$. Since $C_+$ contains at least $s - 1$ vertices and at most $s$ vertices in $Q$, we have

$$|C| + s - 1 \leq |C_+| \leq |C| + s \qquad (2)$$

Using these relations, we can show (a detailed proof can be found in [4]):

$$\frac{|C|}{Opt(G)} \leq 1 + 2(r - 1) + \frac{2}{Opt(G_+)} + \frac{4(r - 1 + (1/Opt(G_+)))}{n - 2}$$

Since $r \leq 13/12 - \epsilon$, we have $1 + 2(r - 1) \leq 7/6 - \epsilon'$ for some constant $\epsilon' > 0$. Now for $n$ sufficiently large, and observing that $Opt(G_+) \geq n/2 + s - 1$, we conclude that $|C|/Opt(G) \leq 7/6 - \delta$ for some constant $\delta > 0$. This, according to Håstad [12], would imply $P = NP$. $\qquad \square$

## 3    Vertex Cover and VC-PM

In this section, we study the relation between approximating VC-PM and approximating VERTEX COVER on general graphs. We show that in order to overcome the bound 2 approximability barrier of VERTEX COVER for general graphs, it suffices to overcome this barrier for VC-PM.

**Theorem 2.** *If the* VC-PM *problem has a polynomial time approximation ratio* $r \leq 2$, *then the* VERTEX COVER *problem on general graphs has a polynomial time approximation ratio* $(r + 2)/2$.

In particular, if the VC-PM problem has a polynomial time approximation ratio $r < 2$ for a constant $r$, then the VERTEX COVER problem on general graphs has a polynomial time approximation ratio $(r + 2)/2 < 2$.

Since the VC-PM problem is NP-hard, any polynomial time approximation ratio $r$ for VC-PM must be strictly larger than 1 (unless P = NP). Thus, the polynomial time approximation ratio for the VERTEX COVER problem on general graphs deduced from Theorem 2 must be strictly larger than 1.5. In the following, we derive a more precise relationship between the approximabilities of VC-PM and VERTEX COVER, which will also be used when we consider approximating the VERTEX COVER problem on everywhere sparse graphs.

Let $M$ be a maximum matching in a graph $G$. For each matched vertex $u$ in $M$, we will denote by $u'$ the partner of $u$ in $M$ (i.e., $[u, u'] \in M$). Note that the set $I_M$ of unmatched vertices is an independent set in $G$.

**Definition 1.** Let $M$ be a maximum matching in a triangle-free graph $G$, and let $I_M$ be the set of the unmatched vertices. Define the following sets.

- $I'_M$ is the subset of unmatched vertices $w$ in $I_M$ such that there are two edges $[u, u']$ and $[v, v']$ in $M$ and $(w, u, u', v', v, w)$ is a 5-cycle.
- $I''_M = I_M - I'_M$.
- $\Gamma(I'_M)$ is the set of matched vertices $u$ such that a vertex $w$ in $I'_M$ and two edges $[u, u']$ and $[v, v']$ in $M$ make a 5-cycle $(w, u, u', v', v, w)$.
- $N(I''_M)$ is the set of matched vertices $u$ such that $[z, u]$ is an edge in $G$ for some $z \in I''_M$.
- $\Gamma'(I'_M) = \{u' \mid [u, u'] \in M \text{ and } u \in \Gamma(I'_M)\}$.
- $N'(I''_M) = \{u' \mid [u, u'] \in M \text{ and } u \in N(I''_M)\}$.

See Figure 1 for illustration, where thicker lines are edges in the matching $M$.

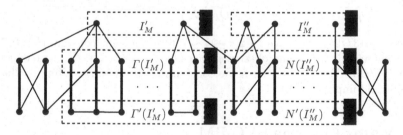

**Fig. 1.** Illustartion of the sets $I'$, $I''$, $\Gamma(I')$, $\Gamma'(I')$, $N(I'')$, and $N'(I'')$

We first list a number of properties for these sets. Note that since the matching $M$ is maximum, there is no augmenting path in the graph $G$.

**Fact 1.** The six sets $I'_M$, $I''_M$, $\Gamma(I'_M)$, $\Gamma'(I'_M)$, $N(I''_M)$, and $N'(I''_M)$ are mutually disjoint.

**Fact 2.** Let $w_1 \in I'_M$ with a 5-cycle $C_1 = (w_1, u_1, u'_1, v'_1, v_1, w_1)$ and $w_2 \in I'_M$ with a 5-cycle $C_2 = (w_2, u_2, u'_2, v'_2, v_2, w_2)$. If $w_1 \neq w_2$ then the 5-cycles $C_1$ and $C_2$ are disjoint.

**Fact 3.** $2|I'_M| \leq |\Gamma(I'_M)| = |\Gamma'(I'_M)|$, and $|N(I''_M)| = |N'(I''_M)|$.

**Fact 4.** The sets $I''_M$, $\Gamma(I'_M)$, and $N'(I''_M)$ are all independent sets in $G$.

**Fact 5.** The set $I''_M \cup N'(I''_M) \cup \Gamma(I'_M)$ is an independent set in $G$.

**Theorem 3.** *If the* VC-PM *problem has a polynomial time approximation algorithm of ratio $r$, then the* VERTEX COVER *problem on general graphs has a polynomial time approximation algorithm with ratio* $\max\{1.5, (2r+2)/3\}$.

*Proof.* Let $A_{pm}$ be an approximation algorithm with ratio $r$ for VC-PM.

We first assume that the input graph $G$ of $n$ vertices is triangle-free and satisfies $Opt(G) \geq n/2$. Consider the algorithm **VC-Apx** given in Figure 2.

---

**Algorithm. VC-Apx.**

Input: a triangle-free graph $G = (V, E)$ with $|V| = n$ and $Opt(G) \geq n/2$.

Output: a vertex cover for the graph $G$.

1. construct a maximum matching $M$ in $G$, let $V_M$ be the set of matched vertices;
2. construct the sets $I'_M$, $I''_M$, $\Gamma(I'_M)$, $\Gamma'(I'_M)$, $N(I''_M)$, and $N'(I''_M)$ defined in Definition 1;
3. $c = (2 - r)/3 + |I'_M|/n$;
4. **if** $(|I'_M| + |I''_M| + |N'(I''_M)| + |\Gamma(I'_M)|) \geq cn$
   **then return** $C_1 = V - (I''_M \cup N'(I''_M) \cup \Gamma(I'_M))$
   **else** let $S$ be the set of minimum cardinality among $I''_M$ and $N(I''_M)$;
   apply the algorithm $A_{pm}$ to the graph $G(V_M)$ and
   let $C$ be the vertex cover returned by $A_{pm}$;
   **return** $C_2 = C \cup S \cup I'_M$.

---

**Fig. 2.** The algorithm **VC-Apx**

We analyze the approximation ratio for the algorithm **VC-Apx**.

If $(|I'_M| + |I''_M| + |N'(I''_M)| + |\Gamma(I'_M)|) \geq cn$, then the set $C_1 = V - (I''_M \cup N'(I''_M) \cup \Gamma(I'_M))$ is returned. By Fact 5, the set $(I''_M \cup N'(I''_M) \cup \Gamma(I'_M))$ is an independent set in $G$ so the set $C_1$ is a vertex cover for $G$. Moreover, from $(|I'_M| + |I''_M| + |N'(I''_M)| + |\Gamma(I'_M)|) \geq cn$, we have $|I''_M| + |N'(I''_M)| + |\Gamma(I'_M)| \geq cn - |I'_M|$, hence $|C_1| \leq n - (cn - |I'_M|)$. Therefore (note $Opt(G) \geq n/2$):

$$\frac{|C_1|}{Opt(G)} \leq \frac{n - (cn - |I'_M|)}{n/2} = 2 - 2c + \frac{2|I'_M|}{n} = \frac{2r + 2}{3}$$

In case $|I'_M| + |I''_M| + |N'(I''_M)| + |\Gamma(I'_M)| < cn$, by the definitions, the vertices in $I''_M$ are only adjacent to vertices in the set $N(I''_M)$. Thus, the set $S$, which is either $I''_M$ or $N(I''_M)$, will cover all the edges incident on vertices in $I''_M$. Since $C$ is a vertex cover for the induced graph $G(V_M)$, the set $C_2 = C \cup S \cup I'_M$ is a vertex cover for the original graph $G$. Now

$$|I'_M| + |I''_M| + |N'(I''_M)| + |\Gamma(I'_M)| \geq 3|I'_M| + |I''_M| + |N(I''_M)|$$
$$\geq 3|I'_M| + 2\min\{|I''_M|, |N(I''_M)|\} = 3|I'_M| + 2|S|$$

The first inequality has used the relations $|\Gamma(I'_M)| \geq 2|I'_M|$ and $|N'(I''_M)| = |N(I''_M)|$ in Fact 3. Thus, $3|I'_M| + 2|S| < cn$ and $|S| < (cn - 3|I'_M|)/2$. This gives

$$|C_2| = |C \cup S \cup I'_M| \leq |C| + |S| + |I'_M| \leq |C| + \frac{cn - 3|I'_M|}{2} + |I'_M| = |C| + \frac{cn - |I'_M|}{2}$$

By our assumption, $|C|/Opt(G(V_M)) \leq r$. We also have $Opt(G) \geq Opt(G(V_M))$ and $Opt(G) \geq n/2$. We finally derive the ratio

$$\frac{|C_2|}{Opt(G)} \leq \frac{|C|}{Opt(G)} + \frac{cn - |I'_M|}{2Opt(G)} \leq \frac{|C|}{Opt(G(V_M))} + \frac{cn - |I'_M|}{n}$$

$$\leq r + c - \frac{|I'_M|}{n} = \frac{2r + 2}{3}$$

This proves that the algorithm **VC-Apx** on a triangle-free graph $G$ with $Opt(G) \geq n/2$ returns a vertex cover $C$ for $G$ satisfying $|C|/Opt(G) \leq (2r+2)/3$.

Now we consider a general graph $G' = (V', E')$. We first remove all disjoint triangles from the graph $G'$ (in an arbitrary order). Let the resulting graph be $G$ and let $V_\Delta$ be the set of vertices of the removed triangles. Then, $G$ is the triangle-free subgraph induced by the vertex set $V = V' - V_\Delta$. Now apply NT-Theorem to the graph $G$ and let $I_0$, $C_0$, and $V_0$ be the three vertex sets given in NT-Theorem. Then the induced subgraph $G(V_0)$ is triangle-free and satisfies $Opt(G(V_0)) \geq |V_0|/2$. Thus, we can apply the algorithm **VC-Apx** to the graph $G(V_0)$. Let $C$ be the vertex cover returned by the algorithm **VC-Apx** on the graph $G(V_0)$. By the discussion above, we have $|C|/Opt(V_0) \leq (2r+2)/3$. According to NT-Theorem, $C_1 = C \cup C_0$ is a vertex cover for the graph $G$ satisfying $|C_1|/Opt(G) \leq (2r+2)/3$.

Obviously, $C_2 = C_1 \cup V_\Delta$ is a vertex cover of the original graph $G'$. According to the Local-Ratio Theorem by Bar-Yehuda and Even [1], we have

$$\frac{|C_2|}{Opt(G')} \leq \max\left\{\frac{|V_\Delta|}{Opt(G(V_\Delta))}, \frac{|C_1|}{Opt(G)}\right\} \leq \max\left\{\frac{|V_\Delta|}{Opt(G(V_\Delta))}, \frac{2r + 2}{3}\right\}$$

The theorem follows from $|V_\Delta|/Opt(G(V_\Delta)) \leq 1.5$, because every vertex cover of $G(V_\Delta)$ contains at least two vertices from each triangle in $G(V_\Delta)$. $\square$

We remark that it is possible to extend the method of Theorem 3 to first consider graphs that have neither triangles nor 5-cycles. However, when we work on general graphs, we need to apply the Local-Ratio Theorem of Bar-Yehuda and Even to eliminate all 5-cycles. This makes the resulting algorithm have approximation ratio at least $5/3 > 1.66$.

## 4    On Approximating VC-PM

In this section, we study approximation algorithms for the VC-PM problem. Recall that an instance of the MAX-2SAT problem is a set $F$ of clauses in which each clause is a disjunction of at most two literals, and we are looking for an assignment $\sigma$ to the variables in $F$ that satisfies the largest number of clauses in $F$. For an assignment $\sigma$ to $F$, we denote by $|\sigma|$ the number of clauses satisfied by $\sigma$. Let $Opt(F)$ be the largest $|\sigma|$ among all assignments $\sigma$ to $F$.

Let $G = (V, E)$ be an instance of the VC-PM problem, i.e., $G$ is a graph with a perfect matching $M$. Define an instance $F_G$ of the MAX-2SAT problem as follows:

$$F_G = \bigcup_{[u,v] \in M} \{(x_u \vee x_v), (\bar{x}_u \vee \bar{x}_v)\} \cup \bigcup_{[u,v] \in E-M} \{(x_u \vee x_v)\}$$

The set $F_G$ consists of $m + n/2$ clauses on Boolean variable set $X_G = \{x_u \mid u \in V\}$.

**Lemma 1.** *Suppose that the graph $G$ has $n$ vertices and $m$ edges. Then from any assignment $\sigma$ to the clause set $F_G$, a vertex cover $C_\sigma$ of at most $m+n-|\sigma|$ vertices for the graph $G$ can be constructed in linear time.*

*Proof.* Suppose $|\sigma| = d$. We first modify the assignment $\sigma$ as follows. If we have both $\sigma(x_u) = \text{FALSE}$ and $\sigma(x_v) = \text{FALSE}$ for an edge $[u, v] \in E$, then we modify $\sigma$ by setting $\sigma(x_u) = \text{TRUE}$, where $u$ is arbitrarily picked from the two endpoints of the edge $[u, v]$.

We claim that this change does not decrease the value $|\sigma|$. In fact, there is only one clause $(\bar{x}_u \vee \bar{x}_w)$ in $F_G$ that contains the literal $\bar{x}_u$, where $[u, w]$ is an edge in the matching $M$. Therefore, converting from $\sigma(x_u) = \text{FALSE}$ to $\sigma(x_u) = \text{TRUE}$ can make at most one satisfied clause become unsatisfied. On the other hand, the unsatisfied clause $(x_u \vee x_v)$ becomes satisfied after this change. Therefore, the value $|\sigma|$ is not decreased.

Let $\sigma'$ be the modified assignment, then $|\sigma'| \geq |\sigma|$, and for each edge $[u, v] \in E$, $\sigma'$ assigns at least one of the variables $x_u$ and $x_v$ the value TRUE.

Now we let $C_\sigma$ be a set of vertices in $G$ as follows: a vertex $u$ is in $C_\sigma$ if and only if $\sigma'(x_u) = \text{TRUE}$. Since for each edge $[u, v] \in E$, we have either $\sigma'(x_u) = \text{TRUE}$ or $\sigma'(x_v) = \text{TRUE}$ (or both), the set $C_\sigma$ is a vertex cover for the graph $G$. By the construction of the assignment $\sigma'$, the $m$ clauses of the form $(x_u \vee x_v)$ in $F_G$ are all satisfied by $\sigma'$. Therefore, exactly $|\sigma'| - m$ clauses of the form $(\bar{x}_u \vee \bar{x}_v)$ in $F_G$ are satisfied by $\sigma'$. Since these $|\sigma'| - m$ clauses correspond to $|\sigma'| - m$ disjoint edges in the matching $M$, we conclude that the assignment $\sigma'$ has assigned exactly $|\sigma'| - m$ Boolean variables in $X_G$ the value FALSE. In consequence, exactly $|\sigma'| - m$ vertices in $G$ are not in $C_\sigma$ and the vertex cover $C_\sigma$ contains exactly $n - (|\sigma'| - m) = m + n - |\sigma'|$ vertices. The lemma follows since $|\sigma'| \geq |\sigma|$.    $\square$

In fact, an optimal assignment to the clause set $F_G$ corresponds to a minimum vertex cover for the graph $G$, as shown in the following theorem.

**Theorem 4.** *Suppose that the graph $G$ has $n$ vertices and $m$ edges. Then*

$$Opt(F_G) = m + n - Opt(G)$$

*Proof.* Let $\sigma$ be an assignment to the clause set $F_G$. By Lemma 1, there is a vertex cover $C_\sigma$ for the graph $G$ that contains at most $m+n-|\sigma|$ vertices. Thus, $m+n-|\sigma| \geq Opt(G)$, which gives $|\sigma| \leq m+n-Opt(G)$. This shows that an optimal assignment satisfies at most $m+n-Opt(G)$ clauses in $F_G$. Thus, to prove the theorem, it suffices to show that there is an assignment to $F_G$ that satisfies $m+n-Opt(G)$ clauses.

Let $C$ be a minimum vertex cover for the graph $G$. Since $C$ contains at least one endpoint of each edge in the matching $M$, the edges in $M$ can be classified into two sets $M_1$ and $M_2$ such that each edge in $M_1$ has exactly one endpoint in $C$ and each edge in $M_2$ has both endpoints in $C$. Thus, $|C| = |M_1| + 2|M_2|$. Define an assignment $\sigma_C$ for $F_G$ such that $\sigma_C(x_u) = \text{TRUE}$ if and only if $u \in C$. Then $\sigma_C$ satisfies all $m$ clauses of the form $(x_u \vee x_v)$ in $F_G$. For each edge $[u,v]$ in $M_1$, $\sigma_C$ satisfies both corresponding clauses $(x_u \vee x_v)$ and $(\bar{x}_u \vee \bar{x}_v)$, while for each edge $[u,v]$ in $M_2$, $\sigma_C$ satisfies exactly one of the corresponding clauses $(x_u \vee x_v)$ and $(\bar{x}_u \vee \bar{x}_v)$ (i.e., the clause $(x_u \vee x_v)$). In conclusion, there are exactly $|M_2|$ clauses in $F_G$ that are not satisfied by the assignment $\sigma_C$. Since the clause set $F_G$ totally contains $m + n/2$ clauses, the number of clauses satisfied by the assignment $\sigma_C$ is (note $n/2 = |M| = |M_1| + |M_2|$)

$$m + n/2 - |M_2| = m + n - (n/2 + |M_2|) = m + n - (|M_1| + 2|M_2|)$$
$$= m + n - |C| = m + n - Opt(G)$$

Thus, there is an assignment that satisfies $m + n - Opt(G)$ clauses in $F_G$. This completes the proof of the theorem.    □

Note that the combination of Lemma 1 and Theorem 4 gives a polynomial time reduction from the VC-PM problem to the MAX-2SAT problem. Since the VC-PM problem is NP-hard, this presents a new proof for the NP-hardness of the MAX-2SAT problem, which seems simpler than the previous proof [8].

Lemma 1 also suggests an approximation algorithm for the VC-PM problem via approximation of the MAX-2SAT problem, as given in Figure 3.

---

**Algorithm. VCPM-Apx.**
Input: a graph $G = (V, E)$ with perfect matching.
Output: a vertex cover for the graph $G$.
1. construct a perfect matching $M$ in $G$;
2. let $F_G$ be the set of clauses constructed from the graph $G$;
3. construct an assignment $\sigma$ to $F_G$;
4. let $C_\sigma$ be the vertex cover constructed from $\sigma$ as in Lemma 1;
5. return $C_\sigma$

---

**Fig. 3.** An approximation algorithm for VC-PM

The approximation ratio of the algorithm **VCPM-Apx** depends on the quality of the assignment $\sigma$ constructed in Step 3 for the clause set $F_G$. The relation is given in the following theorem.

**Theorem 5.** *If the assignment $\sigma$ in Step 3 of the algorithm* **VCPM-Apx** *satisfies $Opt(F_G)/|\sigma| \leq r$, then the vertex cover $C_\sigma$ returned by the algorithm* **VCPM-Apx** *satisfies $|C_\sigma|/Opt(G) < 1 + (r-1)(2m+n)/(rn)$.*

*Proof.* According to Lemma 1, the vertex cover $C_\sigma$ constructed by the algorithm **VCPM-Apx** contains at most $m + n - |\sigma| \leq m + n - Opt(F_G)/r$ vertices in the graph $G$. Combining this with Theorem 4, and noting that $Opt(F_G) \leq m + n/2$:

$$\frac{|C_\sigma|}{Opt(G)} \leq \frac{m + n - Opt(F_G)/r}{m + n - Opt(F_G)} = \frac{r(m+n) - Opt(F_G)}{r(m + n - Opt(F_G))}$$

$$= 1 + \frac{(r-1)Opt(F_G)}{r(m + n - Opt(F_G))} \leq 1 + \frac{(r-1)(m + n/2)}{r(m + n - (m + n/2))}$$

$$= 1 + \frac{(r-1)(2m+n)}{rn}$$

This proves the theorem. $\qquad\square$

Based on currently the best algorithm for the MAX-2SAT problem, we obtain:

**Corollary 1.** *There is a polynomial time approximation algorithm of ratio $1 + 0.069(2m + n)/n$ for the* VC-PM *problem on graphs of $n$ vertices and $m$ edges.*

Corollary 1 gives the best approximation algorithm for the VC-PM problem on sparse graphs. More specifically, for a graph $G$ of $n$ vertices and $m$ edges, we define the *average degree* $\bar{d}$ of $G$ to be $\bar{d} = 2m/n$. Based on a greedy strategy, Halldórsson and Radhakrishnan [10] proposed an approximation algorithm of ratio $(2\bar{d}+3)/5$ for the INDEPENDENT SET problem on graphs of average degree $\bar{d}$. This result, plus the assumption that a minimum vertex cover for the graph $G$ contains at least half of the vertices in $G$, gives us a polynomial time approximation algorithm of ratio $(4\bar{d}+1)/(2\bar{d}+3)$ for the VERTEX COVER problem on graphs of average degree $\bar{d}$. This is also currently the best result for the VC-PM problem on graphs of average degree $\bar{d}$.

According to Corollary 1, our algorithm **VCPM-Apx** improves the above approximation ratio by Halldórsson and Radhakrishnan on the VC-PM problem when the average degree $\bar{d}$ is not larger than 10. The approximation ratios of our algorithm and Halldórsson and Radhakrishnan's are compared as follows:

| Avg-degree | 2 | 3 | 4 | 5 | 6 | 7 | 8 | 9 | 10 |
|---|---|---|---|---|---|---|---|---|---|
| VCPM-Apx | 1.207 | 1.276 | 1.345 | 1.414 | 1.483 | 1.552 | 1.621 | 1.690 | 1.759 |
| H&R [10] | 1.286 | 1.444 | 1.545 | 1.615 | 1.666 | 1.706 | 1.737 | 1.762 | 1.783 |

**Fig. 4.** The approximation ratios of **VCPM-Apx** and the algorithm in [10]

Strictly speaking, neither of Halldórsson and Radhakrishnan's algorithm and the algorithm **VCPM-Apx** is applicable directly to general graphs of average degree $\bar{d}$. Halldórsson and Radhakrishnan's algorithm requires that the minimum vertex cover of the input graph contain at least half of the vertices in the graph, while our algorithm requires that the input graph have a perfect matching. Note that the condition in Halldórsson and Radhakrishnan's algorithm, namely that the minimum vertex cover should contain at least half of the vertices in the input graph, can be obtained by first applying NT-Theorem to the input graph. Unfortunately, applying NT-Theorem does not preserve the average degree of a graph.

A graph class for which both Halldórsson and Radhakrishnan's algorithm and the algorithms we developed in this paper are applicable is the class of everywhere sparse graphs introduced by Clementi and Trevisan [5]. We say that a graph $G$ is *everywhere $k$-sparse* if for any subset $V'$ of vertices in $G$, the number of edges in the induced subgraph $G(V')$ is bounded by $k|V'|$. Note that a graph of degree bounded by $d$ is an everywhere $(d/2)$-sparse graph, and an everywhere $k$-sparse graph has average degree bounded by $2k$. According to Clementi and Trevisan [5], unless P = NP, for each fixed $\epsilon > 0$, there is a constant $k$ such that there is no polynomial time approximation algorithm of ratio $7/6 - \epsilon$ for the VERTEX COVER problem on everywhere $k$-sparse graphs.

**Theorem 6.** *Halldórsson and Radhakrishnan's algorithm has approximation ratio $(8k + 1)/(4k + 3)$ for the VERTEX COVER problem on everywhere $k$-sparse graphs.*

Combining the algorithms **VC-Apx** and **VCPM-Apx** developed in the current paper, we have the following theorem.

**Theorem 7.** *There is a polynomial time approximation algorithm whose ratio is bounded by $\max\{1.5, (0.276k + 4.138)/3\}$ for the VERTEX COVER problem on everywhere $k$-sparse graphs.*

*Proof.* Consider Theorem 3 and the algorithm **VC-Apx** given in Figure 2. First of all, as we proved in Theorem 6, NT-Theorem preserves everywhere $k$-sparseness. Thus, we can assume that the input graph $G$ of $n$ vertices and $m$ edges, which is everywhere $k$-sparse, satisfies $Opt(G) \geq n/2$.

The subgraph $G(V_M)$ induced by the vertices in the maximum matching $M$ in the algorithm **VC-Apx** is still everywhere $k$-sparse. Since the graph $G(V_M)$ has a perfect matching, we can use the algorithm **VCPM-Apx** in Figure 3 to construct a vertex cover $C_2$ for $G(V_M)$. According to Corollary 1, and noticing that $m \leq kn$, we get,

$$r = \frac{|C_2|}{Opt(G(V_M))} \leq 1 + \frac{0.069(2m + n)}{n} \leq 1.069 + 0.138k$$

Now the theorem follows directly from Theorem 3.    □

For certain values of $k$, the approximation ratio in Theorem 7 is better than the one in Theorem 6 derived from Halldórsson and Radhakrishnan's algorithm [10]. For example, for $k = 2.5$, 3, and 3.5, Theorem 6 gives ratios 1.615, 1.667, and 1.705, respectively, while Theorem 7 gives ratios 1.609, 1.655, and 1.701, respectively.

# References

1. Bar-Yehuda, R. and Even, S.: A local-ratio theorem for approximating the weighted vertex cover problem. Annals of Discrete Mathematics **25** (1985) 27-46
2. Berman, P. and Fujito, T.: On approximation properties of the independent set problem for low degree graphs. Theory Comput. Systems **32** (1999) 115-132
3. Chen, J.: Introduction to Tractability and Approximability of Optimization problems Lecture Notes, Department of Computer Science, Texas A&M University (2000)
4. Chen, J. and Kanj, I. A.: On approximating minimum vertex cover for graphs with perfect matching, Tech. Report, Department of Computer Science, Texas A&M University (2000)
5. Clementi, A. and Trevisan, L.: Improved non-approximability results for minimum vertex cover with density constraints. Theoretical Computer Science **225** (1999) 113-128
6. Feige, U., and Goemans, M.: Approximating the value of two prover proof system, with applications to MAX-2SAT and MAX-DCUT. Proc. 3rd Israel Symp. on Theory of Computing and Systems (1995) 182-189
7. Garey, M. and Johnson, D.: Computers and Intractability: A Guide to the Theory of NP-completeness. Freeman, San Francisco, (1979)
8. Garey, M., Johnson, D., and Stockmeyer, L. J.: Some simplified NP-complete graph problems, Theoretical Computer Science **1** (1976) 237-267
9. Halldórsson, M.: Approximating discrete collections via local improvements. Proc. 6th Ann ACM-SIAM Symp. on Discrete Algorithms (1995) 160-169
10. Halldórsson, M. and Radhakrishnan, J.: Greed is good: approximating independent sets in sparse and bounded-degree graphs. Algorithmica **18** (1997) 145-163
11. Halperin, E.: Improved approximation algorithms for the vertex cover problem in graphs and hypergraphs. Proc. 11th Ann ACM-SIAM Symp. on Discrete Algorithms (2000) 329-337
12. Håstad, J.: Some optimal inapproximability results. Proc. 28th Annual ACM Symposium on Theory of Computing (1997) 1-10
13. Hochbaum, D.: Efficient bounds for the stable set, vertex cover and set packing problems. Discrete Applied Mathematics **6**. (1983) 243-254
14. Hochbaum, D.: Approximating covering and packing problems: set cover, vertex cover, independent set, and related problems In: Hochbaum, D. (ed.): Approximation Algorithms for NP-hard Problems. PWS Publishing Company, Boston (1997) 94-143
15. Karloff, H. and Zwick, U.: A 7/8-approximation algorithm for MAX-SAT? Proc. 38th IEEE Symposium on the Foundation of Computer Science (1997) 406-415
16. Micali, S. and Vazirani, V.: An $O(\sqrt{|V|} \cdot |E|)$ algorithm for finding maximum matching in general graphs, Proc. 21st IEEE Symposium on the Foundation of Computer Science (1980) 17-27
17. Monien, B. and Speckenmeyer, E.: Ramsey numbers and an approximation algorithm for the vertex cover problem. Acta Informatica **22** (1985) 115-123
18. Nemhauser, G. L. and Trotter, L. E.: Vertex packing: structural properties and algorithms. Mathematical Programming **8** (1975) 232-248

# A 2-Approximation Algorithm for Path Coloring on Trees of Rings

Xiaotie Deng[1], Guojun Li[2], Wenan Zang[3], and Yi Zhou[1]

[1] City University of Hong Kong, Hong Kong SAR, P. R. China
[2] Shandong University, Jinan 250100, P. R. China
[3] The University of Hong Kong, Hong Kong SAR, P. R. China

**Abstract.** A tree of rings is an undirected graph obtained from a tree by replacing each node of the tree with a cycle and then contracting the edges of the tree so that two cycles corresponding to the two end-nodes of any edge have precisely one node in common. Given a set of paths on a tree of rings, the routing problem is to color the paths with the smallest number of colors so that any two paths sharing an edge are assigned different colors. We present a 2-approximation algorithm in this paper.

## 1 Introduction

Various types of coloring problems on graphs or multigraphs have been very active research areas, partially because of diversified application backgrounds, optical networks [1,2,5], for example. Such types of problems often become combinatorial in nature, and require sophisticated analysis with graph theory techniques.

In this paper, we consider the coloring problem for paths connecting source-sink pairs for trees of rings. The general problem for various types of network architectures has been throughly discussed in Raghavan and Upfal [5]. It is observed to be very difficult to find good solutions for general graphs. With evidence from the work of Aggarwal et al. [1], they commented that this problem may be considerably harder than integer multicommodity flow problems, for which there have been significant progress [3,4]. For trees of rings, there is a nice idea that results in 3-approximation algorithm [5]. It can be shown with an elegant proof based on an intuition to use ideas from algorithms for the trees and for the circular arc graphs in a nontrivial way (we notice that it cannot be obtained simply by combining coloring algorithms for trees and for circular arc graphs.) Even though there are many different optical networks, the network architecture of a tree of rings can often be found in local-area networks (LANs): there is a main ring, with several sub-rings dangling from it, sub-subrings from the subrings, and so on, as observed in [5].

In Section 2, we introduce the necessary notations and the main ideas. In Section 3, we present our algorithm. We proceed cycles one by one in a depth first search order on the underlying tree. While processing one cycle, we color all paths that share some edges with the cycle. Their colors will not be changed

D.T. Lee and S.-H. Teng (Eds.): ISAAC 2000, LNCS 1969, pp. 144–155, 2000.
© Springer-Verlag Berlin Heidelberg 2000

when we process other cycles later. While processing one cycle, we start with a greedy algorithm, but later combine it with ways to readjust the choices of paths in the same color group. In Section 4, we will show that the number of different colors used by the algorithm is no more than $2\omega$ where $\omega$ is the maximum number of paths each pair of which intersect with each other. Obviously, $\omega$ is a lower bound for the problem. It follows that the approximation ratio of the algorithm is no more than 2.

## 2    Preliminaries

The tree of rings is a network constructed as follows: Start from a tree $T = (V^1, E^1)$ with an embedding on the plane. For each node $i \in V^1$, construct a cycle $C_i$ such that the edge sets of $C_i$s are disjoint. Let $E^2 = \cup_{i \in V^1} E(C_i)$. Let $\{e_{ij} : j \in N(i)\}$ be the set of edges incident to $i$, in the clockwise order of their embedding on the plane. For each edge $e_{ij}$, let $\{v_{ij} : j \in N(i)\}$ be a subset of nodes of $C_i$ such that they follow the clockwise order on the cycle $C_i$ (not necessarily consecutively). Moreover, we allow that some or all of $v_{ij}$s be the same node of $C_i$. Then we contract edges of the tree so that two cycles correspoinding to two end-nodes of any edge share exactly one point. That is, we make node $v_{ij}$ the same as node $v_{ji}$. With this in mind, we define $V^2 = \cup_{i \in V^1} V(C_i)$. We call the graph $G = (V^2, E^2)$ created this way a tree of rings. We shall call $T$ the *underlying tree* of $G$, call $G$ a *derived tree of rings* from $T$, and call the node of $G$ corresponding to any edge of $T$ an *enode*.

Let $\mathcal{P}$ be a set of paths in $G$ which corresponds to an arbitrary set of communication requests. Our objective is to assign a color (i.e. wavelength) to each path in $\mathcal{P}$ so that no paths sharing an edge receive the same color and that the total number of colors used is minimized. Since this problem is $NP$-hard, there is no polynomial time algorithm for solving it exactly unless $NP = P$. The purpose of this paper is to present a 2-approximation algorithm for this problem.

Let $w_{opt}$ denote the minimum possible number of colors required to color $\mathcal{P}$ and let $\omega$ denote the maximum number of pairwise intersecting paths, where two paths are called *intersecting* if they have some edges in common. Clearly, $w_{opt} \geq \omega$, in other words, $\omega$ is a lower bound for $w_{opt}$. We point out that an upper bound $w_{opt} \leq 2\omega$ will follow from the algorithm described in this paper.

To proceed with our algorithm, we fix a depth-first search order of the vertices of $T$ (the underlying tree of $G$). E.g., start from a node as the root, follow an edge out of it and do a depth-first search according to the clockwise orders of the edges at their corresponding nodes. We process the cycles in $G$ one by one in this depth-first search order. We call processing of a cycle a stage. At a stage for processing $C$, we color all the paths that have not yet colored and contain some edges of $C$. When we finish the stage for processing $C$, all the paths of $\mathcal{P}$ containing an edge on cycle $C$ are colored (some of them may have been colored before we process $C$). Their colors will not change after the stage is completed.

Then, we proceed to process the next cycle in the depth-first search order, and so on, until all cycles of $G$ are processed.

We introduce some notions before presenting the algorithm. $G$ is embedded on the plane according to the embedding of $T$ on the plane. Thus, each cycle of $G$ is associated with the clockwise direction. Suppose $C$ is the cycle being processed, let us call $C$ the *current* cycle. For each node $x$ of $C$, let $x^-$ and $x^+$ denote the predecessor and successor of $x$ on $C$ in the clockwise direction, respectively. For each path $q$ that intersects $C$, the common segment of $q$ and $C$ corresponds to a path from some node $x$ to $y$ along $C$ in the clockwise direction; we call $x$ the *L-node* of $q$ on $C$ and $y$ the *R-node*, and denote them by $q_L$ and $q_R$, respectively. Throughout this paper, we reserve the symbol $u$ for the unique enode contained in the current cycle $C$ and one of its preceeding cycles. The only exception is when $C$ is the first cycle in the depth-first search order. Then we make $u$ to be the starting node, which can be an arbitrarily fixed vertex on $C$. For any node $x$ of $C$ and any path collection $\mathcal{Z}$ in $G$, let $\mathcal{Z}^x$ denote the paths in $\mathcal{Z}$ that contain edge $x^-x$ or edge $xx^+$. We also partition $\mathcal{Z}^x$ into three sets:

- $\mathcal{Z}_L^x = \{q \in \mathcal{Z}^x : q_L = x\}$;
- $\mathcal{Z}_R^x = \{q \in \mathcal{Z}^x : q_R = x\}$;
- $\mathcal{Z}_M^x = \mathcal{Z}^x - (\mathcal{Z}_L^x \cup \mathcal{Z}_R^x)$.

Intuititvely $\mathcal{Z}_L^x$ contains paths in $\mathcal{Z}^x$ that its portion in the current cycle $C$ has $x$ at the left end; $\mathcal{Z}_R^x$ has $x$ at the right end; and $\mathcal{Z}_M^x$ has $x$ as a node in the middle.

Let $\mathcal{Q}$ denote the set of all the paths in $\mathcal{P}$ containing some edges in $C$; some of $\mathcal{Q}$ may have already been colored. Recall that while processing the current cycle $C$, we need to color all uncolored paths in $\mathcal{Q}$. For those colored paths, it is clear that no three in $\mathcal{Q}^u$ can have the same color. A colored path $p$ in $\mathcal{Q}^u$ is called *matched* if there exists another colored path $q$ in $\mathcal{Q}^u$ such that $p$ and $q$ have the same color. For each matched pair $p$ and $q$, let us cut $p$ and $q$ at $u$ and denote the sections of them having edges in $C$ by $p(C)$ and $q(C)$, respectively. The path obtained by concatenating $p(C)$ and $q(C)$ at $u$ is called a *pseudo-path*. Notice that a pseudo-path may not be a simple path since it may have the same node as its two endnodes and it may contain a node twice. However, this only occurs only at intermediate steps during a stage and will not affect the path set $\mathcal{P}$ under our consideration. In a stage for processing a cycle $C$, we shall discard all matched paths, and, instead, take pseudo-paths into consideration. Let $\bar{\mathcal{Q}}_L^u$ (resp. $\bar{\mathcal{Q}}_R^u$) be the set of all the unmatched paths in $\mathcal{Q}_L^u$ (resp. $\mathcal{Q}_R^u$), and let $\bar{\mathcal{Q}}^u$ be the set of all pseudo-paths. Set $\bar{\mathcal{Q}}_M^u = \mathcal{Q}_M^u \cup \bar{\mathcal{Q}}^u$ and $\mathcal{A} = \bar{\mathcal{Q}}_L^u \cup \bar{\mathcal{Q}}_M^u$.

## 3  Algorithm during a Stage for Processing a Cycle $C$

At each stage, the algorithm is composed of two phases. In the first phase, along $C$ in the clockwise direction, we use $m = |\mathcal{A}|$ colors to construct sets of paths, $A_i$'s, $1 \leq i \leq m$, from $\mathcal{Q}$, such that each $A_i$ contains a set of paths with no edge in common. In the second phase, along $C$ in the counterclockwise direction, we apply a greedy algorithm to partition the rest of paths of $\mathcal{Q}$ into sets of paths, $B_j$'s, $1 \leq j \leq t$, such that each $B_j$ $(1 \leq j \leq t)$ contains a set of paths with no edge in common. We shall prove in the next section that $m + t$ is no more than $2\omega$ where $\omega$ is the maximum number of pairwise intersecting paths.

Recall that $\mathcal{A}$ contains all the paths that contains edge $uu^+$: $\mathcal{A} = \bar{\mathcal{Q}}_L^u \cup \bar{\mathcal{Q}}_M^u$. Let $\mathcal{A} = \{p^{1,0}, p^{2,0}, \ldots, p^{m,0}\}$. Set $\mathcal{B} = \mathcal{Q} - \mathcal{A}$.

## Algorithm (Phase I)

Step 0. For $i = 1, 2, \ldots m$, set $A_i = \{p^{i,0}\}$, $j_i = 0$. Initially, $p^{i,j_i}$ is unmarked for each $i : 1 \leq i \leq m$.

Step 1. If some $p^{i,j_i}$, $1 \leq i \leq m$, is unmarked, go to Step 2. Else, go to Step 6.

Step 2. Let $w_i = p_R^{i,j_i}$. Let $w^*$ be the first node from $u$ along the current cycle $C$ (in the clockwise direction) among all $w_i$, $i : 1 \leq i \leq m$ such that $p^{i,j_i}$ is unmarked. Denote by $K$ the set of indices of unmarked $p^{i,j_i}$ $(1 \leq i \leq m)$ with R-nodes at $w^*$: $K = \{i \mid w_i = w^*$ and $p^{i,j_i}$ is unmarked$\}$. Recall that $\mathcal{B}_L^{w^*}$ contains paths in $\mathcal{B}$ with $w^*$ as left endnodes of their portions in the current cycle $C$. We define a set $available(\mathcal{B}_L^{w^*})$ such that an uncolored path is in $\mathcal{B}_L^{w^*}$ if it is disjoint from all paths in $A_i$ for some $i \in K$. Let $p$ be the path in $available(\mathcal{B}_L^{w^*})$ such that $p_R$ is the first reached when we move from $u$ along $C$ in the clockwise direction. Thus $r = p_R$ is well defined if $available(\mathcal{B}_L^{w^*})$ is not empty. Let $r = w^*$ otherwise. Denote by $\mathcal{N}$ the subset of paths of $(\cup_{i=1}^m A_i) \cap \mathcal{Q}_L^{w^*}$, such that a path $q$ is in $\mathcal{N}$ if $q_R$ is not on the segment of $C$ from $u$ to $r^-$ (in the clockwise direction) and $q_R$ is reached before $p_L^{i,0}$ for some $i \in K$ when moving from $u$ along $C$ in the clockwise direction.

Step 3. If $\mathcal{N} = \emptyset$, go to Step 4. Else, order paths in $\mathcal{N}$ according to their R-nodes in the counter-clockwise direction from $u$, breaking ties arbitrarily. (Note: their L-nodes are the same $(w^*)$.) We construct a subset $\mathcal{M}$ such that $\{p_R : p \in \mathcal{M}\} = \cup_{p \in \mathcal{N}}\{p_R\}$. That is, if two or more paths in $\mathcal{N}$ share the same $R$-node, only one of them is chosen in $\mathcal{M}$. We order the paths in $\mathcal{M}$ $p^{k_1,l_1}, p^{k_2,l_2}, \ldots, p^{k_n,l_n}$ according to their $R$-nodes from $u$ along $C$ in the counterclockwise direction. That is, $p_R^{k_i,l_i}$ is reached before $p_R^{k_{i+1},l_{i+1}}$ for $i = 1, 2, \ldots, n - 1$, when moving from $u$ along $C$ in the counterclockwise direction.

Do Step 3.1 and 3.2 for $h = 1, 2, \cdots, n$:

Step 3.1. Set $v = p_R^{k_h,l_h}$ and set

$$I = \{i \mid A_i \text{ has no path containing } vv^+ \text{ and } 1 \leq i \leq m\},$$

$$Y' = \{p^{i,i'} \in A_i \mid p_L^{i,i'} = w^*, p_R^{i,i'} = v, i \in I\},$$

$$Y'' = \mathcal{B}_L^{w^*} \cap \mathcal{B}_R^v,$$

$$Y = Y' \cup Y'',$$

$$Z = \{p^{i,l-1} \mid p^{i,l} \in Y'\} \cup \{p^{i,j_i} \mid i \in K \cap I\}.$$

Construct a bipartite graph $B$ consisting of two parts of nodes, $Y$ and $Z$, such that $pq$ is an edge of $B$ iff paths $p \in Y$ and $q \in Z$ are edge disjoint. Find a maximum matching $M'$ in $B$.

Step 3.2.  If $|M'| > |Y'|$, go to Step 1 after the following operations: For each edge $pq \in M'$ with $p \in Y$ and $q \in Z \cap A_i$ for some $i$, set $A_i = A_i \cup \{p\}$, and set $A_j = A_j - \{p\}$ if $p \in A_j$. For each $i : 1 \le i \le m$, revise the superscripts of paths in $A_i$, such that $j_i = |A_i|$ and $A_i = \{p^{i,0}, p^{i,1}, \cdots, p^{i,j_i}\}$ where $p^{i,l}$'s $(1 \le l \le j_i)$ are ordered according to their $L$-nodes from $u$ along $C$ (in the clockwise direction). Set $\mathcal{B} = \mathcal{Q} - \cup_{i=1}^{m} A_i$.

Step 4.  If there exists an uncolored path in $\mathcal{B}$ that is disjoint from each path in some $A_i$, $i \in K$, let $p$ be such an uncolored path such that, among all such paths, $p_L$ is the first reached from $w^*$ (in the counterclockwise direction along $C$); and breaking tie by choosing one with $p_R$ the last reached from $w^*$ (in the clockwise direction along $C$); go to Step 5. Else, mark all the paths $p^{i,j_i}$ for $i \in K$ and go to Step 1.

Step 5.  Set $j_i = j_i + 1$, $p^{i,j_i} = p$, $A_i = A_i \cup \{p^{i,j_i}\}$, $\mathcal{B} = \mathcal{B} - \{p^{i,j_i}\}$, and $w_i = p^{i,j_i}$. Go to Step 1.

Step 6.  Return $A_1, A_2, \ldots, A_m$, stop.

Note that at the end of algorithm (phase I), all paths containing $uu^+$ have been colored. It remains to color paths in $\mathcal{B}$. Let us proceed to the second phase of our algorithm.

**Algorithm (Phase II)**

Step 0.  Set $t = 0$.

Step 1.  If $(\mathcal{B} = \emptyset)$ go to Step 4. Let $t = t + 1$. Let $f^{t,0}$ be a path in $\mathcal{B}$ such that $f_R^{t,0}$ is the first reached from $u$ (in the counterclockwise direction along $C$); breaking tie arbitrarily. Set $B_t = \{f^{t,0}\}$ and $j = 0$.

Step 2.  If there exists a path in $\mathcal{B} - (\cup_{i=1}^{t} B_i)$ that is disjoint from all paths in $B_t$, then choose such a path $f$ that $f_R$ is as the first reached from $f_L^{t,j}$ (in the counterclockwise direction along $C$); go to Step 3. Else, go to Step 1.

Step 3.  Set $j = j + 1$, $f^{t,j} = f$, and $B_t = B_t \cup \{f^{t,j}\}$, go to Step 2.

Step 4.  Return $B_1, B_2, \ldots, B_t$, stop.

We process cycles in $G$ one by one in the increasing depth-first search order. While processing each cycle, we carry out the two phases presented above. After processing each cycle except the first one, we assign color to the newly generated classes as follows. Suppose $C$ is the cycle which has just been processed with output $A_i$'s and $B_j$'s (returned by the two-phase algorithm), and suppose $D_l$'s are the color classes generated before processing $C$. We merge a set in $A_i$'s, $B_j$'s and a set in $D_l$'s as long as they have a path in common or the latter contains two paths which correspond to a pseudo-path in the former, repeat the process until no such two sets exist. In the remaining $A_i$'s, $B_j$'s and $D_l$'s, we arbitrarily merge a set in $A_i$'s, $B_j$'s and a set in $D_l$'s until no such two sets exist. The resulting sets are the color classes we get after processing $C$, and the color assigned to a path $p \in \mathcal{Q}$ corresponds to the color class to which $p$ belongs. We can thus define pseudo-paths accordingly and proceed to process the cycle succeeding $C$. The structure of $G$ (a tree of rings), the search order, and the use of pseudo-paths guarantee that we shall never get stuck in merging sets.

# 4    Analysis of the Algorithm

Notice that finding a maximum matching on a bipartite graph in Step 3.1 is polynomially solvable. It is not hard to see that our algorithm runs in polynomial time. We focus on analyzing its approximation ratio.

**Theorem.** *For any tree of rings $G$ and any set $\mathcal{P}$ of paths in $G$, the algorithm uses no more than $2\omega$ colors, where $\omega$ is the maximum number of pairwise intersecting paths in $\mathcal{P}$.*

For convenience, let us introduce some new notions. Suppose that, at some moment in the algorithm, $p$ and $q$ be two paths in the same $A_i$ such that, moving along $C$ in the clockwise direction from $u$, we reach $p_R$ before we reach $q_L$ (we allow for the degenerated case $p_R = q_L$.) We call $q$ a successor of $p$, or $p$ a predecessor of $q$ at that moment. Observe that if a path $p$ is added to some $A_i$ ($1 \leq i \leq m$), it will remain in $\cup_{j=1}^{m} A_j$. However, it can be moved from some $A_i$ to another $A_j$. This may cause the predecessor-successor relation to change.

We prove the theorem by contradiction. Assume the contrary: there must exist a cycle $C$ such that the number of $A_i$'s and $B_j$'s output by the algorithm is great than $2\omega$, in other words, $(m + t) > 2\omega$. Recall that according to our algorithm in phase I, $m$ equals the number of all paths passing the edge $uu^+$. It follows that $m \leq \omega$. Moreover, there is a path $f \in \mathcal{Q} - [(\cup_{i=1}^{m} A_i) \cup (\cup_{j=1}^{2\omega-m} B_j)]$. We denote $f_R$ by $v$ hereafter. Then our algorithm (Phase II) guarantees the existence of a path $f^{j,j'} \in B_j$, for $j = 1, 2, \cdots, 2\omega - m$, such that

- $f$ has a common edge with each $f^{j,j'}$. (We may choose $j'$ such that $j'$ is the minimum index such that $f$ intersects $f^{j,j'}$);
- move from $u$ in clockwise direction along $C$, we reach $v$ no later than any $f_R^{j,j'}$ (for otherwise, $f$ would have been chosen in $A_j$ instead of $f^{j,j'}$ in the algorithm since $f$ shares no common edge with $f^{j,j''}$ for any $j'' < j'$);
- though $v$ is the right endnode of the common segment of $f$ and $C$, $v$ is not an endnode of path $f$ in $G$.

To see that this last statement is true, first $vv^-$ is an edge of $f$. Second, each of $2\omega - m$ paths $f^{j,j'}$ shares an edge with $f$. Since no path in $\mathcal{B}$ contains $uu^+$, they would have contain $vv^-$ to have an common edge with $f$ if $v$ is an endnode of $f$. This would imply that $\omega \geq 2\omega - m + 1 \geq \omega + 1$, a contradiction.

We denote by $F$ the set of these $2\omega - m$ paths, i.e., $F = \{f^{j,j'} \mid j = 1, 2, \ldots, 2\omega - m\}$. Clearly, some two paths in $F$ are not intersecting (otherwise, since they all intersect with $f$, it follows that $\omega \geq |F| + 1 = 2\omega - m + 1 \geq \omega + 1$, a contradiction). We should then have $v \neq u$. Otherwise, all paths in $F$ would pass the edge $uu^-$, implying that all paths in $F$ are pairwise intersecting, a contradiction.

Let $F' = (F \cap \mathcal{Q}_R^v) \cup \{f\}$. Notice that $F' \cap \mathcal{Q}^u = \emptyset$. Let $F''$ be the set of paths in $F'$ with their $L$-node farthest away from $u$ (in the clockwise direction along $C$.) Denote by $w$ their common $L$-node.

Let $A_i$ be the final output of phase $I$, $1 \leq i \leq m$. Define

$$I = \{i \mid A_i \cap (\mathcal{Q}_L^v \cup \mathcal{Q}_M^v) = \emptyset, i = 1, 2, \ldots, m\}.$$

In other words, if $i \in I$, then $A_i$ has no path that contains $vv^+$. Then the algorithm (phase I) guarantees that,

• for each $i \in I$, there is a path $p^{i,i'}$ in $A_i$ such that $p^{i,i'}$ intersects with all paths in $F''$.

Recall that for each $p \in F''$, $p_R = v$ and $p_L = w$. Let $i^*$ be the largest index $j$ such that $p_R^{i,j}$ is reached before $v^+$ when moving from $u$ along $C$ in the clockwise direction. Since each path in $A_i$ with $i \in I$ does not contain $vv^+$ by definition, $p_L^{i,i^*+1}$ would be a node in the segment from $v^+$ to $u$ of $C$ in the clockwise direction. Therefore, no path $p^{i,j}$ with $j > i^*$ intersects $p$. If $p^{i,i^*}$ does not intersect with some $p \in F''$, nor does any path $p^{i,j}$ with $j < i^*$. Therefore, $p$ could be chosen to be included in $A_i$ by Phase I of our algorithm, a contradiction.

For each $i \in I$, we take $i'$ as the minimum index $j$ such that $p^{i,j} \in A_i$ intersects with all paths in $F''$. We denote by $X = \{p^{i,i'} : i \in I\}$. We have the following claim.

(1) For any $p^{i,i'} \in X$, $w$ cannot be reached before $p_L^{i,i'}$ when moving from $u$ along $C$ in the clockwise direction.

Assume the contrary: there is a path $p^{k,k'} \in X$ such that $w$ is reached before $p_L^{k,k'}$ when moving from $u$ along $C$ in the clockwise direction. Note that $p^{k,k'-1}$ is the predesessor of $p^{k,k'}$ in $A_k$ (at the end of Phase I of our algorithm and afterward). By the definiton of $X$, $p^{k,k'-1}$ is disjoint from some path $q$ in $F''$ (otherwise, we should put $p^{k,k'-1}$ into $X$ instead of $p^{k,k'}$). Then $p^{k,k'}$ cannot be the first successor of $p^{k,k'-1}$. Otherwise $q$ would have been chosen into some $A_i$ in Step 3.

*Note: A path $p^{i,j}$ in $A_i$ except the last one (the one with the largest index $j$) has a successor, that may change from time to time in phase I of our algorithm. We call a successor of $p^{i,j}$ its first successor if it is the successor of $p^{i,j}$ at the first time when $p^{i,j}$ has any successor. Similarly, we call a predecessor of $p^{i,j}$ its first predecessor if it is the predecessor of $p^{i,j}$ at the time $p^{i,j}$ is first chosen in Step 3 to be added into some $A_l$ (not necessarily $A_i$ since it may be swaped in later.) Each path in $\cup_{i=1}^m A_i$ has at most one first predecessor and at most one first successor. However, it can be the first successor (or the first predecessor) of several other paths in $\cup_{i=1}^m A_i$.*

Let $p'$ be the first successor of $p^{k,k'-1}$. Then the algorithm (phase I) ensures that, moving from $u$ along $C$ in the clockwise direction, $w$ is not reached before $p'_L$, and $p'_R$ is not reached before $v$. Otherwise, $q$ would have be chosen into some $A_i$ in Step 3.

Consider the $w^*$ at the point $p'$ becomes the first successor of $p^{k,k'-1}$. Moving from $u$ along $C$ in the clockwise direction, $w^*$ must not be reached before $p_R^{k,k'-1}$. Otherwise, if $p'$ is swapped, as a path in $Y'$, into the $A_i$ which contains $p^{k,k'-1}$ at the moment, $p'_L$ must be $w^*$ since all paths of $Y'$ have the property; if $p'$ is chosen from $\mathcal{B}$, then $i \in K$ would not hold for the $A_i$ that contains $p^{k,k'-1}$ at the moment, a contradiction. As Phase I of our algorithm proceeds, $w^*$ would move in the clockwise direction along $C$. Therefore, $p^{k,k'-1}$ will not be a member of any $Y'$ after $p'$ becomes its first successor. That is, $p^{k,k'-1}$ will be a permanent member of $A_k$ from this point on. The only possibility to make $p^{k,k'}$ a successor of $p^{k,k'-1}$ is for $p^{k,k'}$ to be swapped into $A_k$ from some $A_i$ to replace $p'$. But this would require that $p'_R = p_R^{k,k'}$ and $p'_L = p_L^{k,k'}$. Recall that moving from $u$ along $C$ in the clockwise direction, $w$ is not reached before $p'_L$. Therefore $w$ is not reached before $p_L^{k,k'}$, contradcting our assumption. Claim (1) must hold.

(2) Some two paths in $X$ do not intersect with each other.

Assume that, to the contrary, all paths in $X$ are pairwise intersecting. Then, paths in $X \cup F'$ are pairwise intersecting. Since for each $k \in \{1, 2, \ldots, m\} - I$, there is a path of $A_k$ that passes through $vv^+$. Then, all paths in $((\cup\{A_k \mid k \notin I\}) \cap (Q_L^v \cup Q_M^v)) \cup (F - (F' \backslash \{f\}))$ are pairwise intersecting. It then follows that

$$2\omega \geq |X \cup F'| + |[(\cup\{A_k \mid k \notin I\}) \cap (Q_L^v \cup Q_M^v)] \cup (F - (F' \backslash \{f\}))|$$
$$= |X| + |F'| + (m - |I|) + |F| - |F' \backslash \{f\}| = |F| + m + 1$$
$$= 2\omega - m + m + 1 = 2\omega + 1,$$

a contradiction. Claim (2) is proved.

From Claim (1) and (2), for any two paths $p$ and $q$ in $X$ that do not intersect with each other, $w$ must be $L$-node of one path and $R$-node of another. Set $V = X_L^w$ and $W = X_R^w$. From Claim (0), $X \neq \emptyset$. From Claim (2), some two paths in $X$ do not intersect with each other. Therefore, neither $V$ nor $W$ is empty. We shall show that

(3) $p_R^{i,i'} = v$ for all $p^{i,i'} \in V$.

We prove the claim by contradiction. Assume there is a path $p^{k,k'} \in V$ such that $p_R^{k,k'} \neq v$. As no path in $A_k$ contains $vv^+$ and $p_L^{k,k'} = w$, $p_R^{k,k'}$ is reached before $v$ from $u$ along $C$ in the clockwise direction. Let $p'$ be the first predecessor of $p^{k,k'}$. Similar to the discussion in the proof of Claim 1, at the time when $p'$ becomes the first predecessor of $p^{k,k'}$, $w^*$ (at that moment) is not reached before $p'_R$ from $u$ along $C$ in the clockwise direction. Phase I of our algorithm ensures that the first successor of $p'$ has the same $R$-node (and $L$-node) as $p^{k,k'}$ does. Therefore $p'$ intersects with all paths in $F''$. Otherwise the path in $F''$ which is disjoint from $p'$ has priority over the first successor of $p'$. It follows that $p'_R$ must be $w$. For $p^{k,k'-1}$, the predecessor of $p^{k,k'}$ at the end of the algorithm (phase I), by the definition of $X$, $p^{k,k'-1}$ is disjoint from a path $q \in F''$ (otherwise, $p^{k,k'-1}$ would be put into $X$ instead of $p^{k,k'}$). Recall that $p'$ intersects with all paths in $F''$. It follows that $p^{k,k'-1} \neq p$.

After $p'$ becomes the first predecessor of $p^{k,k'}$, $p'$ will not be in $Y'$ since all paths in $Y'$ have $w^*$ as their common $L$-node. Therefore, in sequence, Step 3.2 of our algorithm has to move $p^{k,k'}$ into some $A_i$ to which $p^{k,k'-1}$ belongs. Notice that all paths in $Y$ of our algorithm have the same $L$-node and the same $R$-node. It follows that the first successor of $p^{k,k'-1}$ has the same $L$-node and $R$-node as $p^{k,k'}$ does, a contradiction to the fact that $q$ has priority over the first successor of $p^{k,k'-1}$. Claim (3) is proved.

We denote by $W_1$ a set of all paths in $W$ each of which is disjoint from a path in $V$. Claim (2) ensures that $W_1 \neq \emptyset$.

(4) At the end of the algorithm, each path $p^{i_1,i_1'} \in W_1$ has a successor $p^{i_1,i_1'+1}$ with $L$-node $w$ and with $R$-node $v$.

Assume the contrary: at the end of the algorithm there is $p^{k_1,k_1'} \in W_1$ such that either $p^{k_1,k_1'}$ is a marked path in $A_{k_1}$ or $p^{k_1,k_1'}$ has a successor $p^{k_1,k_1'+1}$ either with $L$-node on the right of $w$ or with $R$-node on the left of $v$ since $A_{k_1}$ contains no path passing $vv^+$. By the definition of $W_1$, there is $p^{k_0,k_0'+1} \in V$ that is disjoint from $p^{k_1,k_1'}$. For $p^{k_0,k_0'}$, the predecessor of $p^{k_0,k_0'+1}$, at the end of the algorithm, the definition of $X$ implies that $p^{k_0,k_0'}$ is disjoint from a path $q$ in $F''$ (otherwise, $p^{k_0,k_0'}$ would have been put into $X$ instead of $p^{k_0,k_0'+1}$.) Now that at the end of algorithm, $p^{k_1,k_1'}$ has no successor with $L$-node at $w$ and with $R$-node at $v$, then either $p^{k_1,k_1'}$ is marked or $p^{k_1,k_1'}$ has the first successor either with $L$-node on the right of $w$ or with $R$-node on the left of $v$. So at the moment before $p^{k_1,k_1'}$ is marked or the first successor of $p^{k_1,k_1'}$ is added, $p^{k_0,k_0'+1}$ has been added into some $A_i$ (otherwise, $p^{k_0,k_0'+1}$ would have priority over the first successor of $p^{k_1,k_1'}$ and thus the successor of $p^{k_1,k_1'}$ would have $L$-node at $w$ and $R$-node at $v$.) At this time point, let $p'$ be a predecessor of $p^{k_0,k_0'+1}$. Then $p'$ is intersecting with all paths of $F''$ (otherwise, Step 3.2 would have found a successor of $p^{k,k'}$ with $L$-node at $w$ and with $R$-node at $v$ since there was an augmentation path: $q, p', p^{k_0,k_0'+1}, p^{k_1,k_1'}$, where $q \in F''$ is disjoint from $p'$). Recall that $p^{k_0,k_0'}$ is disjoint from a path in $F''$. It follows that $p^{k_0,k_0'} \neq p'$. Notice that at the moment before $p^{k_1,k_1'}$ is marked or the first successor of $p^{k_1,k_1'}$ is added, $w^*$ must not be reached before $p_R^{k_1,k_1'}$ when moving from $u$ along $C$ in the clockwise direction. Therefore, $p'$ will not be a member of any $Y'$ after that time.

The only possibility to make $p^{k_0,k_0'+1}$ a successor of $p^{k_0,k_0'}$ is for $p^{k_0,k_0'+1}$ to be swapped into $A_k$ from some $A_i$ to replace some other path. Notice that $A_{k_1}$ contains no path passing $vv^+$. At the point just before the first successor of $p^{k_1,k_1'}$

is considered, the bipartite graph $B = (Y, Z)$ must be constructed in Step 3.1, where $Y$ contains all paths with $L$-node at $w$ and $R$-node at $v$. But then the augmentation path: $q, p^{k_0,k'_0}, p^{k_0,k'_0+1}, p^{k_1,k'_1}$ in $B$ ensures that $p^{k_1,k'_1}$ would have successor with $L$-node at $w$ and with $R$-node at $v$ at the end of the algorithm, a contradiction. The Claim (4) is proved.

At the end of the algorithm, we denote by $V_1$ the set of all successors of paths in $W_1$, and write $\bar{W}_1 = W - W_1$. Keeping in mind that $|V_1| = |W_1|$ and each path in $\bar{W}_1$ is intersecting with all paths in $F' \cup V$, we see that $\bar{W}_1 \neq \emptyset$, and some two paths in $V_1$ and $\bar{W}_1$, respectively, are not intersecting. Otherwise, $2\omega \geq |\bar{W}_1 \cup V_1 \cup F'| + |[(\cup\{A_i \mid i \notin I\}) \cap (Q^v_L \cup Q^v_M)] \cup (F - (F' \backslash \{f\}))| = |X| + |F'| + (m - |X|) + |F| - |F'| + 1 = |F| + m + 1$, a contradiction. Let $W_2$ be a set of all paths in $\bar{W}_1$ each of which is disjoint from a path in $V_1$. Then it follows that $W_2 \neq \emptyset$.

Suppose at the end of the algorithm, we have nonempty sets of paths:
$$V_0, V_1, V_2, \ldots, V_k;$$
$$W_0, W_1, W_2, \ldots, W_k;$$
$$\bar{W}_0, \bar{W}_1, \bar{W}_2, \ldots, \bar{W}_k$$
where $V = V_0$, and, $W_0$ is a set of the predecessors of the paths of $V_0$, $\bar{W}_0 = W, \bar{W}_1 = \bar{W}_0 - W_1, \bar{W}_2 = \bar{W}_1 - W_2, \ldots, \bar{W}_k = \bar{W}_{k-1} - W_k$, which have the following properties:

(i) each path in $V_i$ is a successor of a path in $W_i$ with $L$-node at $w$ and with $R$-node at $v$ for $1 \leq i \leq k$;

(ii) each path in $W_i$ is disjoint from a path in $V_{i-1}$, and intersecting with all paths in $\cup_{j=0}^{i-2} V_j$ for $1 \leq i \leq k$;

(iii) each path in $\bar{W}_i$ is intersecting with all paths in $\cup_{j=0}^{i-1} V_j$ for $1 \leq i \leq k$;

(iv) some two paths in $V_i$ and $\bar{W}_i$, respectively, are not intersecting for $1 \leq i \leq k$.

Let $W_{k+1}$ be a set of paths in $\bar{W}_k$ each of which is disjoint from a path in $V_k$. Then property (iv) implies that $W_{k+1} \neq \emptyset$.

(5) At the end of the algorithm, each path $p^{i_{k+1},i'_{k+1}} \in W_{k+1}$ has a successor $p^{i_{k+1},i'_{k+1}+1}$ with $L$-node at $w$ and with $R$-node at $v$.

Assume the contrary: at the end of the algorithm there is $p^{i_{k+1},i'_{k+1}} \in W_{k+1}$ such that $p^{i_{k+1},i'_{k+1}}$ has no successor with $L$-node at $w$ and with $R$-node at $v$. By the definition of $W_{k+1}$, $p^{i_{k+1},i'_{k+1}}$ is disjoint from a path $p^{i_k,i'_k+1} \in V_k$. For $p^{i_k,i'_k} \in W_k$, a predecessor of $p^{i_k,i'_k+1}$ at the end of the algorithm, the property (ii) implies that $p^{i_k,i'_k}$ is disjoint from a path $p^{i_{k-1},i'_{k-1}+1} \in V_{k-1}$. Repeating similarly, $p^{i_1,i_1'} \in W_1$, a predecessor of $p^{i_1,i_1'+1}$ at the end of algorithm, is disjoint from a path $p^{i_0,i_0'+1} \in V$. Finaly, $p^{i_0,i_0'} \in W_0$, a predecessor of $p^{i_0,i_0'+1}$ at the end of algorithm, is disjoint from a path $q \in F''$ (otherwise, $p^{i_0,i_0'}$ would have been put into $X$ insted of $p^{i_0,i_0'+1}$.)

Now that $A_{i_{k+1}}$ contains no path passing $vv^+$ and $p^{i_{k+1},i_{k+1}'}$ has no successor with $L$-node at $w$ and with $R$-node at $v$ at the end of algorithm, then at the moment before $p^{i_{k+1},i_{k+1}'}$ is marked or whose first successor is added, $p^{i_k,i_k'+1}$ must have been added into some $A_i$ (otherwise, $p^{i_k,i_k'+1}$ would have priority over $p^{i_{k+1},i_{k+1}'+1}$.)

At the moment before $p^{i_{k+1},i_{k+1}'}$ becomes marked or its first successor is added, let $p'$ be a predecessor of $p^{i_k,i_k'+1}$. Then $p'$ intersects with all paths of $F''$ (otherwise, the augmentation path $q, p', p^{i_k,i_k'+1}, p^{i_{k+1},i_{k+1}'}$ implies that $p^{i_{k+1},i_{k+1}'}$ would have a successor with $L$-node at $w$ and with $R$-node at $v$ at the end of algorithm.) Furthermore, $p' \neq p^{i_k,i_k'}$ (otherwise, the augmentation path

$$q, p^{i_0,i_0'}, p^{i_0,i_0'+1}, p^{i_1,i_1'}, \ldots, p^{i_{k-1},i_{k-1}'+1}, p^{i_k,i_k'}, p^{i_k,i_k'+1}, p^{i_{k+1},i_{k+1}'}$$

implies that $p^{i_{k+1},i_{k+1}'}$ would have a successor with $L$-node at $w$ and with $R$-node at $v$ at the end of algorithm.)

Similar to the proof of Claim (4), the only possibility to make $p^{i_k,i_k'+1}$ a successor of $p^{i_k,i_k'}$ is for $p^{i_k,i_k'+1}$ to be swaped into $A_{i_k}$ from some $A_j$ to replace some other path in $A_{i_k}$. Notice that $A_{i_{k+1}}$ contains no path passing $vv^+$.

At this moment right after the algorithm moves $p^{i_k,i_k'+1}$ into some $A_j$ to which $p^{i_k,i_k'}$ belongs, the path $p^{i_{k-1},i_{k-1}'+1} \in V_{k-1}$ must have been put into some $A_j$ (otherwise, the augmentation path

$$p^{i_{k-1},i_{k-1}'+1}, p^{i_k,i_k'}, p^{i_k,i_k'+1}, p^{i_{k+1},i_{k+1}'}$$

implies that $p^{i_{k+1},i_{k+1}'}$ would have a successor with $L$-node at $w$ and with $R$-node at $v$ at the end of algorithm.)

Let $p''$ be a predecessor of $p^{i_{k-1},i_{k-1}'+1}$ at the moment right after $p^{i_k,i_k'+1}$ is moved into some $A_j$ to which $p^{i_k,i_k'}$ belongs. Then $p''$ is intersecting with all paths of $F''$ (otherwise, the augmentation path

$$q, p'', p^{i_{k-1},i_{k-1}'+1}, p^{i_k,i_k'}, p^{i_k,i_k'+1}, p^{i_{k+1},i_{k+1}'},$$

where $q \in F''$ is disjoint from $p''$, implies that $p^{i_{k+1},i_{k+1}'}$ would have a successor with $L$-node at $w$ and with $R$-node at $v$ at the end of algorithm.)

Similar to the discussion above, we see that $p'' \neq p^{i_{k-1},i_{k-1}'}$, and $p^{i_{k-1},i_{k-1}'+1}$ must be moved into some $A_j$ to which $p^{i_{k-1},i_{k-1}'}$ belongs. At the moment right after both $p^{i_{k-1},i_{k-1}'+1}$ is moved into some $A_j$ to which $p^{i_{k-1},i_{k-1}'}$ belongs and $p^{i_k,i_k'+1}$ is moved into some $A_j$ to which $p^{i_k,i_k'}$ belongs, the path $p^{i_{k-2},i_{k-2}'+1} \in V_{k-2}$ must have been put into some $A_j$ (otherwise, the augmentation path $p^{i_{k-2},i_{k-2}'+1}, p^{i_{k-1},i_{k-1}'}, p^{i_{k-1},i_{k-1}'+1}, p^{i_k,i_k'}, p^{i_k,i_k'+1}, p^{i_{k+1},i_{k+1}'}$ implies that $p^{i_{k+1},i_{k+1}'}$ would have a successor with $L$-node at $w$ and with $R$-node at $v$ at the end of algorithm.)

Repeating similarly, $p^{i_{k-l}, i'_{k-l}+1}$ must be moved into some $A_i$ to which $p^{i_{k-l}, i'_{k-l}}$ belongs for $l = 0, 1 \ldots, k$. At the moment right after $p^{i_{k-l}, i'_{k-l}+1}$ is moved into some $A_j$ to which $p^{i_{k-l}, i'_{k-l}}$ belongs (for all $i = 0, 1, \ldots, k$), we have the augmentation path

$q, p^{i_0, i'_0}, p^{i_0, i'_0+1}, p^{i_1, i'_1}, p^{i_1, i'_1+1}, \ldots, p^{i_{k-1}, i'_{k-1}}, p^{i_{k-1}, i'_{k-1}+1}, p^{i_k, i'_k}, p^{i_k, i'_k+1},$
$p^{i_{k+1}, i'_{k+1}}.$

This fact implies that $p^{i_{k+1}, i'_{k+1}}$ would have a successor with $L$-node at $w$ and with $R$-node at $v$ at the end of algorithm, a final contradiction. Claim (5) is proved.

Let $V_{k+1}$ be the set of successors of paths in $W_{k+1}$, and, $\bar{W}_{k+1} = \bar{W}_k - W_{k+1}$. Then $\bar{W}_{k+1} \neq \emptyset$.

Since otherwise, it follows from $V_{k+1} = W_{k+1} = \bar{W}_k$ that
$2\omega \geq |V_0 \cup V_1 \cup \ldots \cup V_k \cup V_{k+1} \cup F'| + |[(\cup\{A_i \mid i \notin i\}) \cap (\mathcal{Q}^v_L \cup \mathcal{Q}^v_M)]$
$\cup (F - F' \backslash \{f\})|$
$= |X| + |F'| + (m - |X|) + |F| - |F'| + 1 = |F| + m + 1$
$= 2\omega - m + m + 1 = 2\omega + 1,$
a contradiction.

Repeating the procedure, we get infinite sequences of nonempty sets of paths:
$$V_0, V_1, V_2, \ldots$$
$$W_0, W_1, W_2, \ldots$$
$$\bar{W}_0, \bar{W}_1, \bar{W}_2, \ldots$$
satisfying the properties $(i)$–$(iv)$, contradicting the finiteness of $|\mathcal{P}|$. The proof of the theorem is completed. $\square$

**Acknowledgement.** Xiaotie Deng would like to acknowledge the support of an RGC CERG grant and an SRG grant of City University of Hong Kong. Guojun Li would like to thank the NNSFC for a research grant. Wenan Zang would like to thank the support of an RGC grant of Hong Kong.

# References

1. A. Aggarwal, A. Bar-Noy, D. Coppersmith, R. Ramaswami, B. Schieber, and M. Sudan. Efficient Routing in Optical Networks. *Journal of the ACM*, Vol. 46, No.6, pp.973-1001, November 1996.
2. N.K. Cheung, K. Nosu, and G. Winzer (eds.) Special issue on Dense WDM networks, *IEEE J. Selected Areas in Communication*: Vol. 8, August, 1990.
3. Leighton, T., F. Makedon, S. Plotkin, C. Stein, I. Tardos, and S. Tragoudas. 1991. Fast approximation algorithms for multicommodity flow problems. In Proceedings of Annual ACM Symposium on Theory of Computing, p. 101-110.
4. Plotkin, S. A., D. B. Shmoys and E. Tardos. Fast approximation algorithms for fractional packing and covering problems. *Mathematics of Operations Research* Vol. 20, pp. 257-301, 1995.
5. P. Raghavan and E. Upfal, Efficient routing in all-optical networks, STOC 94-5/94 Montreal, Quebec, Canada

# An Approximate Algorithm for the Weighted Hamiltonian Path Completion Problem on a Tree

Q. S. Wu[1], C. L. Lu[2], and R. C. T. Lee[3]

[1] Dept. of Computer Science, National Tsing Hua University, Hsinchu, Taiwan 300, R.O.C. Email: solomon@cs.nthu.edu.tw
[2] National Center for High-Performance Computing, P.O. Box 19-136, Hsinchu, Taiwan 300, R.O.C. Email: cllu@nchc.gov.tw
[3] National Chi-Nan University, Puli, Nantou Hsien, Taiwan 545, R.O.C. Email: rctlee@ncnu.edu.tw

**Abstract.** Given a graph, the Hamiltonian path completion problem is to find an augmenting edge set such that the augmented graph has a Hamiltonian path. In this paper, we show that the Hamiltonian path completion problem will unlikely have any constant ratio approximation algorithm unless NP = P. This problem remains hard to approximate even when the given subgraph is a tree. Moreover, if the edge weights are restricted to be either 1 or 2, the Hamiltonian path completion problem on a tree is still NP-hard. Then it is shown that this problem will unlikely have any fully polynomial-time approximation scheme (FPTAS) unless NP=P. When the given tree is a $k$-tree, we give an approximation algorithm with performance ratio 1.5.

## 1 Introduction

Given a graph $G$, a Hamiltonian path is a simple path on $G$ which traverses each vertex exactly once. Finding a Hamiltonian path is often required in problems involving routing and the periodic updating of data structures. In the past, the Hamiltonian path completion problem was defined on unweighted graphs. For a given unweighted graph $G = (V, E_0)$, the Hamiltonian path completion problem is to find an augmenting edge set $E_2$ such that $G' = (V, E_0 \cup E_2)$ has a Hamiltonian path. Such an edge set $E_2$ is called an *augment*. It was shown that to find an edge set $E_2$ with minimum cardinality is an NP-complete problem [9]. If the given graph $G$ is a tree [10,12,14], a forest [18], an interval graph [1], a circular-arc graph [7], a bipartite permutation graph [19] or a block graph [19,20, 22], it was shown that there exist polynomial-time algorithms for this problem by computing the *path covering number*, which is the minimum number of vertex-disjoint paths covering all vertices. In general, for a complete bipartite graph $K_{1,n}$, the path covering number is $n - 1$, and at least $n - 2$ edges must be added to make it have a Hamiltonian path. In other words, for $K_{1,n}$ to have a Hamiltonian path, any optimal augment must have exactly $n - 2$ edges [6]. For

D.T. Lee and S.-H. Teng (Eds.): ISAAC 2000, LNCS 1969, pp. 156–167, 2000.

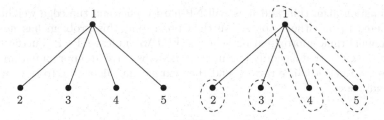

**Fig. 1.** A bipartite graph $K_{1,4}$ which can be covered by 3 paths.

example, in Figure 1, the graph can be covered by three paths $\{(4, 1, 5), (2), (3)\}$, and two edges, say (2,3) and (3,4), may be added to make the original graph have a Hamiltonian path.

In this paper, we shall discuss the weighted Hamiltonian path completion problem, whose formal definition is given below.

*Problem 1 (Weighted Hamiltonian Path Completion Problem).* Given a complete graph $G = (V, E)$ with edge costs $w : E \to R^+$, and an edge subset $E_0 \subseteq E$, find an augment $E_2 \subseteq E$ such that $G' = (V, E_0 \cup E_2)$ has a Hamiltonian path and $\sum_{e \in E_2} w(e)$ is minimized.

For example, in Figure 2, given $E_0 = \{(1, 2), (3, 4), (5, 6)\}$ and the weight of each edge assigned as in the table aside, the optimal augment is $E_2 = \{(1, 7), (2, 5), (3, 6)\}$ with cost 10.

However, this problem is hard to solve if $E_0$ is arbitrary. Throughout this paper, we shall assume that $E_0$ constitutes a tree. The formal definition of the problem is given as below.

*Problem 2 (Weighted Hamiltonian Path Completion Problem on a Tree).* Given a complete graph $G = (V, E)$ with edge costs $w : E \to R^+$, and an edge subset $E_0$ constituting a spanning tree on $G$, find an augment $E_2 \subseteq E$ such that $G' = (V, E_0 \cup E_2)$ has a Hamiltonian path and the cost $\sum_{e \in E_2} w(e)$ is minimized.

In this paper, we shall first show that the weighted Hamiltonian path completion problem on a tree (HPCT) will unlikely have any constant ratio ap-

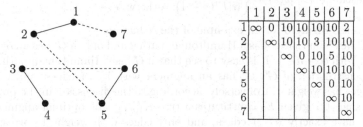

|   | 1 | 2 | 3 | 4 | 5 | 6 | 7 |
|---|---|---|---|---|---|---|---|
| 1 | $\infty$ | 0 | 10 | 10 | 10 | 10 | 2 |
| 2 |   | $\infty$ | 10 | 10 | 3 | 10 | 10 |
| 3 |   |   | $\infty$ | 0 | 10 | 5 | 10 |
| 4 |   |   |   | $\infty$ | 10 | 10 | 10 |
| 5 |   |   |   |   | $\infty$ | 0 | 10 |
| 6 |   |   |   |   |   | $\infty$ | 10 |
| 7 |   |   |   |   |   |   | $\infty$ |

**Fig. 2.** An example for the weighted Hamiltonian path completion problem, where the given edge set $E_0$ is represented by solid lines and augment $E_2$ by dashed lines.

proximation algorithm and it is still NP-hard even when the edge weights are restricted to be either 1 or 2. We then prove that this problem has no fully polynomial-time approximation scheme (FPTAS) unless NP=P. Furthermore, when the given tree has only one internal node, we give an approximation algorithm with performance ratio $\frac{3}{2}$ and then extend this algorithm to trees with $k$ internal nodes.

## 2    Non-approximability of HPCT

To prove that HPCT is hard to approximate, we adopt a technique which is similar to the one applied to prove that the traveling salesperson problem will unlikely have any $\alpha$-approximate algorithm as in [17]. In our proof, we shall reduce the Hamiltonian path problem, which is a well-known NP-complete problem [9], to the weighted Hamiltonian path completion problem. Let us define the problem first.

*Problem 3 (Hamiltonian Path Problem).* Given $G = (V, E)$, where $|V| = n$, determine whether there exists a path $(v_1, v_2, v_3, \cdots, v_n)$ such that $(v_i, v_{i+1})$ in $E$, for all $i = 1, 2, \cdots, n - 1$.

An approximation algorithm $\mathcal{A}$ is said to be $\alpha$-*approximate* if for any problem instance, the cost of the approximate solution obtained by $\mathcal{A}$ is bounded by $\alpha$ times the cost of the optimal solution. We then have the following theorem.

**Theorem 1.** *For any $\alpha > 1$, if there exists an $\alpha$-approximate algorithm for HPCT, then NP = P.*

*Proof.* Suppose there exists an approximation algorithm $\mathcal{A}$ of HPCT that will find an approximation solution of ratio $\alpha$ in polynomial time. We then reduce HP (Hamiltonian Path problem) to HPCT as follows. Given an instance of HP, say $G = (V, E)$ with $V = \{v_1, v_2, \cdots, v_n\}$, we construct an instance of HPCT, say $G' = (V', E')$ and $E_0$, as follows.

- $V' = V \cup \{v_0, v_{n+1}\}$.
- $E' = \{(v_i, v_j) \mid 0 \le i \le n+1, 0 \le j \le n+1 \text{ and } i \ne j\}$.
- $E_0 = \{(v_0, v_i) \mid 1 \le i \le n+1\}$.
- For each $e \in E'$, $w(e) = \begin{cases} 1, & \text{if } e \in E, \\ \alpha|E|(n-1), & \text{otherwise.} \end{cases}$

Let us see Figure 3 for an example of the reduction.

First, we claim that $G$ has a Hamiltonian path if and only if $G'$ has an optimal augment with cost $n-1$. It is easy to see that if $G$ has a Hamiltonian path, then by the construction of $G'$, $G'$ has an augment with $n-1$ edges, and each of these edges has weight 1. Conversely, according to the discussion in the previous section, since the given $E_0$ constitutes a tree $K_{1,n+1}$, any optimal augment for $G'$ must have exactly $n-1$ edges, and only edges with weight 1 corresponds to an edge in $G$. Therefore, $G$ has a Hamiltonian path if and only if $G'$ has an optimal augment with cost $n-1$.

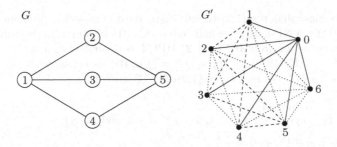

**Fig. 3.** Reduction from $G$ in the Hamiltonian path problem to $G'$ in HPCT. In $G'$, the dashed edges have weight 1 and other edges have weight $24\alpha$.

Second, we claim that if there is an optimal augment for $G'$ with cost $n-1$, $\mathcal{A}$ cannot generate a solution containing any edge with weight $\alpha|E|(n-1)$. If the approximate solution contains any such edge, the cost of the augment would be at least $\alpha|E|(n-1)$. Since $\frac{\alpha|E|(n-1)}{n-1} = \alpha|E| > \alpha$, this violates the assumption that $\mathcal{A}$ is an $\alpha$-approximate algorithm.

Thus, if $G$ has a Hamiltonian path, then the optimal augment for $G'$ has cost $n-1$, and thus $\mathcal{A}$ will generate an augment with cost less than or equal to $|E|$, since it will only contain edges with weight 1. Conversely, if $\mathcal{A}$ generates an augment with cost less than or equal to $|E|$, then we know this augment does not contain any edge with cost $\alpha|E|(n-1)$. In other words, all the edges in this augment are contained in $E$. Since such a subset in $E$ constitutes a Hamiltonian path, it lead to the conclusion that the graph $G$ has a Hamiltonian path.

By the above discussion, $G$ has a Hamiltonian path if and only if $\mathcal{A}$ generates an augment with cost less than $|E|$ for $G'$. Hence we can use $\mathcal{A}$ to solve the Hamiltonian path problem in polynomial time, by examining the cost of the solution returned by $\mathcal{A}$. Thus, if HPCT has an $\alpha$-approximate algorithm, then NP=P. $\qquad\qquad\qquad\qquad\qquad\qquad\qquad\qquad\qquad\qquad\qquad\qquad\qquad\qquad\square$

## 3  NP-Hardness of (1,2)-HPCT

In this section, we shall discuss the (1,2)-HPCT problem, which is the HPCT problem whose edge weights are restricted to be either 1 or 2.

*Problem 4 ((1,2)-Hamiltonian Path Completion Problem on a Tree).* Given a complete graph $G = (V, E)$ with edge costs $w : E \to \{1, 2\}$, and an edge subset $E_0$ constituting a spanning tree on $G$, find an augment $E_2 \subseteq E$ such that $G' = (V, E_0 \cup E_2)$ has a Hamiltonian path and the cost $\sum_{e \in E_2} w(e)$ is minimized.

**Theorem 2.** *The (1,2)-Hamiltonian path completion problem on a tree is NP-hard.*

*Proof.* To show that the (1,2)-Hamiltonian path completion problem on a tree ((1,2)-HPCT) is NP-hard, we shall reduce the Hamiltonian path problem (HP) to it. The reduction from HP to (1,2)-HPCT is described as follows.

For $G = (V, E)$ with $V = \{v_1, v_2, \cdots, v_n\}$ in HP, we construct a corresponding instance $G' = (V', E')$ and $E_0$ in (1,2)-HPCT, such that

- $V' = V \cup \{v_0, v_{n+1}\}$.
- $E' = \{(v_i, v_j) \mid 0 \le i \le n+1, 0 \le j \le n+1 \text{ and } i \ne j\}$.
- For each $e \in E', w(e) = \begin{cases} 1, & \text{if } e \in E, \\ 2, & \text{otherwise.} \end{cases}$
- $E_0 = \{(v_0, v_i) \mid 1 \le i \le n+1\}$.

Now we are going to show that $G$ has a Hamiltonian path if and only if $G'$ has an augment of cost $n - 1$. Let $(v_1, v_2, \cdots, v_n)$ be a Hamiltonian path in $G$. According to our construction, $\{(v_1, v_2), (v_2, v_3), \cdots, (v_{n-1}, v_n)\}$ forms an augment for $E_0$ in $G'$, which yields a Hamiltonian path $(v_{n+1}, v_0, v_1, v_2, \cdots, v_n)$. For all $i = 1, 2, \cdots, n - 1$, we have $w((v_i, v_{i+1})) = 1$ in $G'$ since $(v_i, v_{i+1}) \in E$. Therefore, the cost of this augment is $n - 1$.

On the contrary, suppose $E_0$ has an augment $E_2$ of cost $n - 1$. Since $E_0$ consists of a root vertex and $n + 1$ leaves, at least $n - 1$ edges must be added to make it Hamiltonian. Therefore, each of these $n - 1$ edges must have weight exactly equal to 1 and $E_2 \subseteq E$.

Let $P \subseteq E_0 \cup E_2$ be a Hamiltonian path in $G'' = (V', E_0 \cup E_2)$. Since $V'$ has $n + 2$ vertices, $|P| = n + 1$. Because the path is Hamiltonian, the vertex $v_{n+1}$ must be covered by the path. Since $w((v_i, v_{n+1})) = 2$ for all $1 \le i \le n$, $P$ must pass through $v_0$ to visit $v_{n+1}$ and then stop. In other words, if we delete $v_0$ and $v_{n+1}$ from $P$, we can obtain a path $P'$ which visits all vertices in $\{v_1, v_2, \cdots, v_n\}$. Such a path $P' \subseteq E_2$ is a Hamiltonian path for $G$. Hence $G$ has a Hamiltonian path, since $E_2 \subseteq E$.

Therefore, (1,2)-HPCT has an augment of cost $n - 1$ if and only if $G$ has a Hamiltonian path. Figure 4 illustrates such a reduction.     $\square$

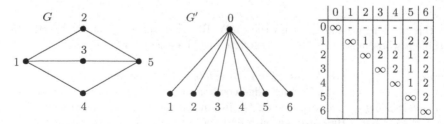

**Fig. 4.** A Hamiltonian path $(2, 1, 3, 5, 4)$ in $G$ corresponds to an augment $\{(2, 1), (1, 3), (3, 5), (5, 4)\}$ with weight $= 4$. (The dash in the above table indicates that the edge is in the given edge set $E_0$ and will cause no cost to the augment, no matter it is equal to 1 or 2.)

## 4    (1,2)-HPCT Will Unlikely Have Any FPTAS

A *polynomial-time approximation scheme* (PTAS) is a family of algorithms, which for any rational value $r > 1$, there is a corresponding approximation algorithm whose solution is within ratio $r$, and the time complexity of this approximation algorithm is polynomial in the size of its input. When the running time of a PTAS is polynomial both in the size of the input and in $1/(r-1)$, the scheme is called a *fully polynomial-time approximation scheme* (FPTAS) [3]. Some problems, like maximum independent set problem on planar graphs and Euclidean traveling salesperson problem are found to have PTASs [2,4], while 0-1 knapsack problem admits an FPTAS [11]. On the contrary, some problems, such as maximum 3-satisfiability problem, maximum leaves spanning tree problem, superstring problem, and traveling salesperson problem with distances one and two, are proved by a reduction from the MAX SNP-complete class that they unlikely have any PTAS unless NP=P [5,8,15,16]. In this section, we shall use a simple method to show that (1,2)-HPCT will unlikely have any FPTAS unless NP=P.

**Theorem 3.** *If (1,2)-HPCT has an FPTAS, then NP=P.*

*Proof.* Suppose (1,2)-HPCT has an FPTAS. That is, for any $\epsilon > 0$, there exists a $(1+\epsilon)$-approximate algorithm for the (1,2)-HPCT problem such that its time complexity is polynomial in the size of the input and $\frac{1}{\epsilon}$. Then let us consider any problem instance with $G = (V, E)$.

Since (1,2)-HPCT has an FPTAS, we may choose $\epsilon = \frac{1}{2|E|}$. Then the fact that the performance ratio is less than or equal to $1 + \epsilon$ implies that

$$\frac{w_{apx}}{w_{opt}} \leq 1 + \frac{1}{2|E|} \Rightarrow w_{apx} \leq w_{opt} + \frac{w_{opt}}{2|E|} \Rightarrow w_{apx} - w_{opt} \leq \frac{w_{opt}}{2|E|}.$$

Notice that the optimal augment $E^*$ will not contain all edges in $E$, i.e., $|E^*| < |E|$. Since the weight on each edge is either 1 or 2, we have

$$\frac{w_{opt}}{2|E|} = \frac{w(E^*)}{2|E|} \leq \frac{2|E^*|}{2|E|} < 1.$$

Therefore, $w_{apx} - w_{opt} < 1$. This inequality and the fact that the weight on each edge is greater than or equal to 1 guarantee that $w_{apx} - w_{opt} = 0$. That is, our approximation algorithm will generate an optimal solution with time complexity which is polynomial in both $|E|$ and $\frac{1}{\epsilon} = 2|E|$ (i.e., polynomial in the size of the input). The (1,2)-HPCT problem, which is shown to be NP-hard in Section 3, can be solved in polynomial time. This implies NP=P.    $\square$

## 5    A 1.5-Approximate Algorithm for (1,2)-Hamiltonian Path Completion Problem on 1-Star

A *1-star* is a tree with only one internal node. Since it is a bipartite graph, we shall use the notation $K_{1,n}$ to denote a 1-star with $n$ leaf nodes. In this section, we shall give a 1.5-approximate algorithm for the (1,2)-Hamiltonian path completion problem on a 1-star.

Suppose $G = (V, E)$, where $V = \{v_0, v_1, v_2, \cdots, v_n\}$ and $v_0$ is the root of the given tree. Our approximation algorithm will first find a minimum-weight maximal matching [13] on $V' = V \backslash \{v_0\}$, and then add edges to concatenate these matching pairs. For example, in Figure 5, the matching may find $\{(v_1, v_2), (v_3, v_4)\}$, then in the second step $(v_4, v_5)$ is added to form a Hamiltonian path. The formal description of our algorithm is as follows.

---

**Algorithm 1**
1. **if** $n \leq 2$, **then** return $E_2 = \emptyset$;
2. Perform a minimum-weight maximal matching algorithm on $V'$;
   Suppose the matching is $\{(v_{i_1}, v_{j_1}), (v_{i_2}, v_{j_2}), \cdots, (v_{i_{\lfloor \frac{n}{2} \rfloor}}, v_{j_{\lfloor \frac{n}{2} \rfloor}})\}$.
3. Concatenate these edges serially by adding $(v_{j_2}, v_{i_3}), \cdots, (v_{j_{\lfloor \frac{n}{2} \rfloor - 1}}, v_{i_{\lfloor \frac{n}{2} \rfloor}})$;
4. Return $E_2 = \left( \bigcup_{k=1}^{\lfloor \frac{n}{2} \rfloor} \{(v_{i_k}, v_{j_k})\} \right) \cup \left( \bigcup_{k=2}^{\lceil \frac{n}{2} \rceil - 1} \{(v_{j_k}, v_{i_{k+1}})\} \right)$;

---

**Lemma 1.** *If the optimal augment $E_2^*$ contains $k$ edges with weight 1, then our algorithm finds at least $\frac{k}{2}$ of edges with weight 1 in the solution.*

*Proof.* It can be seen that for $K_{1,n}$, any optimal augment $E_2^*$ always has exactly $n - 2$ edges. Moreover, in $G' = (V, E_0 \cup E_2^*)$, there exist two edges $(v_0, v_s)$ and $(v_0, v_t)$ in $E_0$ such that they together with these $n - 2$ edges in $E_2^*$ will constitute a Hamiltonian path, as illustrated in Figure 6.

By deleting the vertex $v_0$ from the path, we obtain two vertex-disjoint paths to cover $V' = \{v_1, v_2, \cdots, v_n\}$. (Please note that a single vertex is also regarded as a degenerated path here.) Connect these two paths with "head to head" and "tail to tail" by adding the two corresponding edges, we obtain a cycle $C$. Obviously $E_2^* \subset C$. Without lost of generality, let us label this cycle as $\{(v_1, v_2), (v_2, v_3), \cdots, (v_{n-1}, v_n), (v_n, v_1)\}$, where $(v_s, v_t)$ and $(v_n, v_1)$ are the two added edges. Let $MM$ be the minimum-weight maximal matching obtained in our algorithm.

Case 1. If $n$ is even, then each maximal matching has $\frac{n}{2}$ edges since the given graph is complete. It can be seen that $M_1 = \{(v_1, v_2), (v_3, v_4), \cdots, (v_{n-1}, v_n)\}$ is a maximal matching and $M_2 = \{(v_2, v_3), (v_4, v_5), \cdots, (v_n, v_1)\}$ is also a maximal

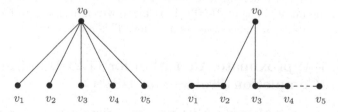

**Fig. 5.** Finding the minimum-weight maximal matching on a 1-star.

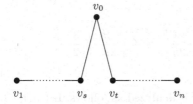

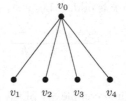

**Fig. 6.** A Hamiltonian path in $G' = (V, E_0 \cup E_2^*)$.

**Fig. 7.** An example showing that ratio 1.5 is tight.

matching. Suppose $MM$ contains $k_1$ edges with weight 1. Then both $M_1$ and $M_2$ contain at most $k_1$ edges with weight 1; otherwise, $MM$ cannot be minimum. Thus, $C = M_1 \cup M_2$ contains at most $2k_1$ edges with weight 1. If $k_1 < \frac{k}{2}$, then $2k_1 < k$ and $C$ contains fewer than $k$ edges with weight 1. This contradicts with the assumption that the subset $E_2^*$ of $C$ already has $k$ edges with weight 1.

Case 2. If $n$ is odd, then each maximal matching has $\frac{n-1}{2}$ edges. It can be seen that $M_1 = \{(v_1, v_2), (v_3, v_4), \cdots, (v_{n-2}, v_{n-1})\}$ is a maximal matching and $M_2 = \{(v_2, v_3), (v_4, v_5), \cdots, (v_{n-1}, v_n)\}$ is a maximal matching, too. Suppose $MM$ contains $k_1$ edges with weight 1. Then with similar reasoning, both $M_1$ and $M_2$ will have less than or equal to $k_1$ edges with weight 1. Again, $k_1 < \frac{k}{2}$ implies that the path $\{(v_1, v_2), (v_2, v_3), (v_3, v_4), \cdots, (v_{n-1}, v_n)\}$ contains fewer than $k$ edges with weight 1. This also causes a contradiction because its subset $E_2^*$ already contains $k$ edges with weight 1.

In either case, our algorithm finds at least $\frac{k}{2}$ edges with weight 1 in the minimum-weight maximal-matching $MM$.                                                    □

**Theorem 4.** *The performance ratio of Algorithm 1 is $\frac{3}{2}$.*

*Proof.* The augment $E_2$ obtained by our algorithm contains $\lfloor \frac{n}{2} \rfloor + \lceil \frac{n}{2} \rceil - 2 = n - 2$ edges, just the same as the optimal augment. Suppose the optimal solution $E_2^*$ contains $k$ edges with weight 1, and $h$ edges with weight 2 (i.e., $k + h = n - 2$). According to Lemma 1, our approximation algorithm which performs minimum-weight maximal-matching to get a partial result will choose at least $\frac{k}{2}$ edges with weight 1. Even in the worst case that all the other edges added later are with weight 2, the performance ratio of our approximate solution will be

$$\frac{\frac{k}{2} + 2(\frac{k}{2} + h)}{k + 2h} = \frac{\frac{3k}{2} + 2h}{k + 2h} \leq \frac{3}{2}.$$

**Remarks.** Precisely, by Lemma 1, the above formula should be written as

$$\frac{\lceil \frac{k}{2} \rceil + 2(k + h - \lceil \frac{k}{2} \rceil)}{k + 2h}.$$

When $k$ is odd, it becomes

$$\frac{\frac{k+1}{2} + 2(k + h - \frac{k+1}{2})}{k + 2h} = \frac{\frac{3k-1}{2} + 2h}{k + 2h} < \frac{\frac{3k}{2} + 2h}{k + 2h} \le \frac{3}{2}.$$

□

The time complexity of the Algorithm 1 is analyzed as follows. Let $n + 1$ be the number of vertices in $G$. The minimum-weight maximal matching in Step 2 takes $O(n^3)$ time [13]. Step 3 will take $O(n)$ time to connect the edges one by one. Therefore, we obtain a 1.5-approximate algorithm to solve the (1,2)-Hamiltonian path completion problem on 1-star that runs in $O(n^3)$ time.

To show that the analysis for the performance ratio of this algorithm is tight, let us see the example in Figure 7, where the edge weights are

$$w(e) = \begin{cases} 1, & \text{if } e \in \{(v_1, v_2), (v_1, v_3)\}, \\ 2, & \text{otherwise.} \end{cases}$$

Our approximation algorithm will find a minimum-weight maximal matching first, say $\{(v_1, v_2), (v_3, v_4)\}$ and adopts this as the approximate solution. Its cost will be 3. However, the optimal augment is $\{(v_1, v_2), (v_1, v_3)\}$, whose cost is 2. The performance ratio then is $\frac{3}{2} = 1.5$.

## 6  A 1.5-Approximate Algorithm for (1,2)-Hamiltonian Path Completion Problem on $k$-Star

A tree with $k$ internal nodes is called a $k$-star. In this section, we are going to show that the approximation algorithm developed in the previous section can be extended to obtain similar results on $k$-stars. Let us introduce some notation first.

**Definition 1.** *Suppose $G = (V, E)$ is a weighted graph with weight function $w(e)$ defined on all edges $e$ in $E$ and let $P = (u_1, \cdots, u_k)$ be a path in $G$. Then the new graph $G' = (V', E')$ obtained from $G$ by shrinking $P$ into a single node is define to be*

- $V' = V \setminus \{u_2, u_3, \cdots, u_k\}$.
- $E' = E \setminus \bigcup_{v \in V, u \in \{u_2, u_3, \cdots, u_k\}} \{(u, v)\}$.
- $w'(e) = \begin{cases} \min\{d(u_1, v), d(u_k, v)\}, & \text{if } e = (u_1, v) \text{ for some } v \in V', \\ w(e), & \text{otherwise.} \end{cases}$

Let $G_{\{P\}}$ denote the graph obtained from G by shrinking the path $P$. For two *vertex-disjoint* paths $P_1$ and $P_2$, the result of shrinking will be the same no matter $P_1$ is shrunk first or $P_2$ is shrunk first, because the `min` operation satisfies the associative law. That is $(G_{\{P_1\}})_{\{P_2\}} = (G_{\{P_2\}})_{\{P_1\}}$. Therefore, it is sound to simply write it as $G_{\{P_1, P_2\}}$.

Informally speaking, our approximation algorithm will first find a minimum-weight maximal-matching on the shrunk graph $G_{\{P_1, P_2, \cdots, P_i\}}$, and then map these matching edges back to $G$. By our construction of $G_{\{P_1,P_2,\cdots,P_i\}}$, each edge in $G_{\{P_1,P_2,\cdots,P_i\}}$ corresponds to an edge in $G$, and each vertex in $G_{\{P_1,P_2,\cdots,P_i\}}$ corresponds to either a single vertex or a path in $G$. Therefore, each edge in $G_{\{P_1,P_2,\cdots,P_i\}}$ will be mapped to a path (containing one or more edges) in $G$. These paths are then concatenated serially to form a Hamiltonian path.

To formally analyze the performance ratio of our approximation algorithm, let us try to introduce some lemmas. In $G$, we call the edges in the given subset $E_0$ the $e_0$-edges, and edges in $E \setminus E_0$ with weight 1 the $e_1$-edges, and edges in $E \setminus E_0$ with weight 2 the $e_2$-edges.

**Observation 1** *Suppose $H$ is a Hamiltonian path in $G$, $E_0$ is a $k$-star and $H \cap E_0$ are vertex-disjoint paths $P_1, P_2, \cdots, P_i$. If we focus on edges in $H$, it can be observed that during the process of shrinking $P_1, P_2, \cdots, P_i$, only $e_0$-edges will be deleted, and some $e_2$-edges may be turned to $e_1$-edges. Therefore, $H_{\{P_1,P_2,\cdots,P_i\}}$ contains at least $n_1$ edges with weight 1 if $H$ contains $n_1$ such edges.*

**Lemma 2.** *If a Hamiltonian path $H$ in graph $G$ contains $n_1$ $e_1$-edges, then a minimum-weight maximal-matching on $G$ contains at least $\frac{n_1}{2}$ $e_1$-edges.*

*Proof.* The proof is similar to that of Lemma 1. $\qquad\qquad\qquad\square$

**Theorem 5.** *If a Hamiltonian path $H$ contains $n_1$ $e_1$-edges and $H \cap E_0$ consists of some vertex-disjoint paths $P_1, P_2, \cdots, P_i$, then a minimum-weight maximal-matching on $G_{\{P_1,P_2,\cdots,P_i\}}$ contains at least $\frac{n_1}{2}$ $e_1$-edges.*

*Proof.* By Observation 1 and Lemma 2. $\qquad\qquad\qquad\qquad\qquad\square$

Informally speaking, we shall map these matching edges in $G_{\{P_1,P_2,\cdots,P_i\}}$ to $G$. For each edge $e = (x, u)$ in $G_{\{P_1,P_2,\cdots,P_i\}}$, let $u$ and $v$ be the terminals of path $P_j$, for $1 \leq j \leq i$. Then we map the $e$ to $e'$ in $G$ as follows.

$$e' = \begin{cases} (x, u), & \text{if } d(x, u) \text{ on G is equal to } d(x, u) \text{ on } G_{\{P_1,P_2,\cdots,P_i\}}, \\ (x, v), & \text{otherwise.} \end{cases}$$

Therefore, if $H$ contains $n_0$ $e_0$-edges, $n_1$ $e_1$-edges, $n_2$ $e_2$-edges, then this result will also contain the same $n_0$ $e_0$-edges, and at least $\frac{n_1}{2}$ edges with weight 1. As we have seen in the previous section, the cost will be less than or equal to $\frac{n_1}{2} + 2 \times (n_1 + n_2 - \frac{n_1}{2}) = \frac{3}{2}n_1 + 2n_2$. Therefore, the performance ratio is $\frac{\frac{3}{2}n_1 + 2n_2}{n_1 + 2n_2} \leq \frac{3}{2}$.

Now we have a natural question: How does our approximation algorithm know what paths in $E_0$ must be chosen to shrink? If we could choose the ones exactly as an optimal path $H^*$ contains, then the cost of the solution obtained by our approximation algorithm is guaranteed to be within $\frac{3}{2}$ times the one of the optimal solution. However, we do not know what edges may be contained in $H^*$ and what may not. If we have to try each possibility, since there are $O(n)$ $e_0$-edges, trying all the $O(2^n)$ combinations will lead to an exponential algorithm. Fortunately, we have the following lemma.

**Lemma 3.** *If H is a Hamiltonian path in G and $E_0$ is a k-star, then H contains at most $2k$ $e_0$-edges.*

*Proof.* All $e_0$-edges must be incident to the $k$ internal nodes. However, in a path, at most two edges are incident to each internal node, so at most $2k$ $e_0$-edges are contained in this path. $\qquad\qquad\square$

Hence, we only have to test all combinations that contain 0 $e_0$-edges, 1 $e_0$-edges, 2 $e_0$-edges, $\cdots$, $2k$ $e_0$-edges. For each combination, we apply the shrink operation and find an approximate solution on it. The minimum one of these solutions will be chosen as our final approximate solution to be reported. Therefore, let us state our algorithm formally below.

---

**Algorithm 2**
1. $W \leftarrow \infty, AUG \leftarrow \emptyset$.
2. **for** all subsets of $E_0$ with no more than $2k$ edges **do**
2.1.  **if** the subset has 3 or more edges incident to the same vertex **then**
        /* Do nothing. */
2.2.  **else**
        Suppose the subset consists of vertex-disjoint paths $P_1, P_2, \cdots, P_i$.
2.2.1.  Shrink paths $P_1, P_2, \cdots, P_i$ to obtain $G_{\{P_1, P_2, \cdots, P_i\}}$;
2.2.2.  Find a minimum-weight maximal-matching $MM$ on $G_{\{P_1, P_2, \cdots, P_i\}}$;
2.2.3.  Map these matching edges to paths in $G$;
        /* Let $MM$ be mapped to $MM'$. */
2.2.4.  Add edges (denoted by $S$) to concatenate these paths serially to form a Hamiltonian path;
2.2.5.  **if** the cost of $S \cup MM'$ is smaller than $W$ **then**
        $W \leftarrow w(S \cup MM'), AUG \leftarrow S \cup MM'$;
3. Report $AUG$ as the solution and stop;

---

There are $O(n^{2k})$ iterations in Step 2 of Algorithm 2, and each iteration takes $O(n^3)$ time as we have seen in the previous section. Hence, we obtain a 1.5-approximate algorithm to solve the (1,2)-Hamiltonian path completion problem on $k$-stars that runs in $O(n^{2k+3})$ time.

# 7    Conclusion

Some version of Hamiltonian completion problems finds the augment to make the given graph having a Hamiltonian circuit instead of a Hamiltonian path. It can be checked that our results can be applied to obtain the same results on Hamiltonian cycle completion problems.

In [21], an approximation algorithm for (1,2)-HPCT with performance ratio 2 was proposed for general trees. For this problem, whether there exists a PTAS or an approximation algorithm with performance ratio less than 2 as we derived for $k$-stars is still unknown.

# References

1. S. R. Arikati and C. Pandu Rangan. Linear algorithm for optimal path cover problem on interval graphs. *Inf. Process. Lett.*, 35(3):149–153, 1990.
2. S. Arora. Polynomial time approximation schemes for euclidean traveling salesman and other geometric problems. In *Proc. 37th Annual IEEE Symposium on Foundations of Computer Science*, pages 2–11. IEEE Computer Society, 1996.
3. G. Ausiello, P. Crescenzi, G. Gambosi, V. Kann, A. Marchetti-Spaccamela, and M. Protasi. *Complexity and Approximation.* Springer-Verlag, Berlin Heidelberg, 1999.
4. B. S. Baker. Approximation algorithms for NP-complete problems on planar graphs. *Journal of the ACM*, 41(1):153–180, 1994.
5. A. Blum, M. Li, J. Tromp, and M. Yannakakis. Linear approximation of shortest superstrings. *Journal of the ACM*, 41(4):630–647, 1994.
6. F. T. Boesch, S. Chen, and J. A. M. McHugh. On covering the points of a graph with point disjoint paths. In *Lecture Notes in Mathematics*, volume 46, pages 201–212. Springer, Berlin, 1974.
7. M. A. Bonuccelli and D. P. Bovet. Minimum node disjoint path covering for circular-arc graphs. *Inf. Process. Lett.*, 8:159–161, 1979.
8. G. Galbiati, F. Maffioli, and A. Morzenti. A short note on the approximability of the maximum leaves spanning tree problem. *Inf. Process. Lett.*, 52:45–49, 1994.
9. M. Garey and D. Johnson. *Computers and Intractability: A Guide to the Theory of NP-Completeness.* Freeman, San Francisco, CA, 1979.
10. S. E. Goodman, S. T. Hedetniemi, and P. J. Slater. Advances on the Hamiltonian completion problem. *Journal of the ACM*, 22(3):352–360, 1975.
11. O. H. Ibarra and C. E. Kim. Fast approximation algorithms for the knapsack and sum of subset problems. *Journal of the ACM*, 22(4):463–468, 1975.
12. S. Kundu. A linear algorithm for the Hamiltonian completion number of a tree. *Inf. Process. Lett.*, 5:55–57, 1976.
13. E. L. Lawler. *Combinatorial Optimization: Networks and Matroids*, chapter 6. Holt, Rinehart and Winston, New York, 1976.
14. J. Misra and R. E. Tarjan. Optimal chain partitions of trees. *Inf. Process. Lett.*, 4:24–26, 1975.
15. C. H. Papadimitriou and M. Yannakakis. Optimization, approximation, and complexity classes. *J. Comput. Syst. Sci.*, 43:425–440, 1991.
16. C. H. Papadimitriou and M. Yannakakis. The traveling salesman problem with distances one and two. *Mathematics of Operations Research*, 18:1–11, 1993.
17. S. Sahni and T. Gonzalez. *P*-complete approximation problems. *Journal of the ACM*, 23(3):555–565, 1976.
18. Z. Skupien. Path partitions of vertices and Hamiltonicity of graphs. In *Proc. 2nd Czechoslovakian Symp. on Graph Theory*, pages 481–491, Prague, 1974.
19. R. Srikant, R. Sundaram, K. S. Singh, and C. P. Rangan. Optimal path cover problem on block graphs and bipartite permutation graphs. *Theoretical Computer Science*, 115(2):351–357, 1993.
20. P.-K. Wong. Optimal path cover problem on block graphs. *Theoretical Computer Science*, 225(1–2):163–169, 1999.
21. Q. S. Wu. *On the Complexity and Approximability of Some Hamiltonian Path Problems.* PhD Thesis, National Tsing Hua University, Taiwan, 2000.
22. J. H. Yan and G. J. Chang. The path-partition problem in block graphs. *Inf. Process. Lett.*, 52:317–322, 1994.

# Finding Independent Spanning Trees
# in Partial $k$-Trees

Xiao Zhou and Takao Nishizeki

Graduate School of Information Sciences, Tohoku University
Aoba-yama 05, Sendai 980-8579, JAPAN zhou@ecei.tohoku.ac.jp
nishi@ecei.tohoku.ac.jp

**Abstract.** Spanning trees rooted at a vertex $r$ of a graph $G$ are independent if, for each vertex $v$ in $G$, all the paths connecting $v$ and $r$ in the trees are pairwise internally disjoint. In this paper we give a linear-time algorithm to find the maximum number of independent spanning trees rooted at any given vertex $r$ in partial $k$-trees $G$, that is, graphs $G$ with tree-width bounded by a constant $k$.

## 1  Introduction

Two paths connecting a pair of vertices in a graph $G = (V, E)$ are said to be *internally disjoint* if they have no common vertices and no common edges except for their end vertices. Two spanning trees rooted at the same vertex, say $r$, in $G$ are *independent* if for each vertex $v \in V$ the two paths from $v$ to $r$, each of which is in each tree, are internally disjoint. The graph in Figure 1(a) has two independent spanning trees $T_1$ and $T_2$ rooted at $r$ depicted in Figures 1(b) and (c). Spanning trees $T_1, T_2, \cdots, T_\alpha$, $\alpha \geq 2$, rooted at the same vertex $r$ in a graph are *independent* if the spanning trees are pairwise independent. For a given vertex $r$ of $G$, the *independent spanning trees problem* is to find the maximum number of independent spanning trees of $G$ rooted at $r$. Since the graph $G$ in Figure 1(a) has no three independent spanning trees rooted at $r$, $\{T_1, T_2\}$ in Figures 1(b) and (c) is a solution of the problem for $G$. A graph $G$ is called an *$\alpha$-channel graph rooted at vertex $r$* if there are $\alpha$ independent spanning trees rooted at $r$ of $G$. If $G$ is an $\alpha$-channel graph rooted at every vertex, $G$ is called an *$\alpha$-channel* graph. Independent spanning trees of a graph play an important role in fault-tolerant broadcasting in a computer network, because they provide a compact representation of reliable routings in the network modeled by the graph [1,8,12].

For any biconnected graph $G$ and for any vertex $r$ of $G$, Itai and Rodeh [8] gave a linear-time algorithm for finding two independent spanning trees rooted at $r$ in $G$, and hence any biconnected graph is 2-channel. Cheriyan and Maheshwari [5] showed how to find three independent spanning trees rooted at some vertex $r$ in any 3-connected graph $G = (V, E)$ in $O(|V||E|)$ time. Zehavi and Itai [13] showed also that any 3-connected graph $G$ is 3-channel. There is a conjecture that any $\alpha$-connected graph has $\alpha$ independent spanning trees rooted at an

D.T. Lee and S.-H. Teng (Eds.): ISAAC 2000, LNCS 1969, pp. 168–179, 2000.

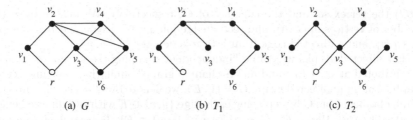

(a) $G$                (b) $T_1$                (c) $T_2$

**Fig. 1.** Independent spanning trees $T_1$ and $T_2$ of graph $G$.

arbitrary vertex $r$, that is, any $\alpha$-connected graph is $\alpha$-channel [10,13]. Recently Huck has proved that for any $\alpha$-connected planar graph with $\alpha = 4$ or $\alpha = 5$ (i.e. for any planar graph since any $\alpha$-connected graph with $\alpha \geq 6$ is nonplanar) there are $\alpha$ independent spanning trees rooted at any vertex [6,7]. Miura *et al.* [11] gave a linear-time algorithm to find four independent spanning trees rooted at any vertex in 4-connected planar graphs. However, for arbitrary $\alpha$-connected graph with $\alpha \geq 4$, the conjecture is still open. Iwasaki *et al.* [9] gave a linear-time algorithm to find four independent spanning trees rooted at any vertex $r$ in chordal rings. Obokata *et al.* [12] showed that if $G_1$ is an $n_1$-channel graph and $G_2$ is an $n_2$-channel graph, then the product graph of $G_1$ and $G_2$ is an $(n_1 + n_2)$-channel graph. Thus an efficient algorithm for the independent spanning trees problem has been known only for planar graphs, chordal rings, or the classes of graphs with small connectivity.

Partial $k$-trees are the same as graphs of tree-width bounded by a constant $k$. The class of partial $k$-trees includes trees ($k = 1$), series-parallel graphs ($k = 2$), Halin graphs ($k = 3$), and $k$-terminal recursive graphs. Most of computer networks are modeled by partial $k$-trees with very small $k$. Therefore, it is desired to design an efficient algorithm for the independent spanning trees problem on partial $k$-trees. However, no efficient algorithm has been known for the independent spanning trees problem; many problems can be solved efficiently for partial $k$-trees, but it is rather difficult to find an efficient algorithm for edge-type problems such as the edge-coloring problem and the edge-disjoint paths problem.

In this paper we give a linear-time algorithm to solve the independent spanning trees problem for partial $k$-trees $G$; the algorithm finds the maximum number of independent spanning trees rooted at any given vertex $r$ in $G$. Our idea is to formulate the independent spanning trees problem on $G$ as a new type of the edge-coloring problem of a directed graph obtained from $G$ by replacing each edge by a pair of oppositely directed edges. We extend techniques developed for the edge-coloring problem [2] and the edge-disjoint paths problem [14], and apply them to the new problem.

## 2   Terminology and Definitions

In this section we present some definitions and easy observations. Let $G = (V, E)$ denote a graph with vertex set $V$ and edge set $E$. We often denote by $V(G)$ and

$E(G)$ the vertex set and the edge set of $G$, respectively. We denote by $n$ the number of vertices in $G$. An undirected edge joining vertices $u$ and $v$ is denoted by $\{u, v\}$, and a directed edge from $u$ to $v$ is denoted by $(u, v)$.

For directed graphs we define "independent spanning trees," an "$\alpha$-channel graph rooted at vertex $r$" and an "$\alpha$-channel graph" similarly as for undirected graphs. For an undirected graph $G = (V, E)$, we denote by $\vec{G} = (V, \vec{E})$ a directed graph obtained from $G$ by replacing each edge $\{u, v\} \in E$ with two directed edges $(u, v)$ and $(v, u)$. Hence $\vec{E} = \{(u, v), (v, u) \mid \{u, v\} \in E\}$. Independent spanning trees in an undirected graph $G$ are not always pairwise edge-disjoint; an edge in $G$ may be contained in two of the trees, but in such a case the two paths pass through the edge in the opposite directions. On the other hand, independent spanning trees in a directed graph $\vec{G}$ are pairwise edge-disjoint. Thus we have the following lemma.

**Lemma 1.** *Let $G$ be an undirected graph, let $r$ be a vertex in $G$, and let $\alpha$ be a positive integer. Then $G$ is $\alpha$-channel rooted at $r$ if and only if $\vec{G}$ is $\alpha$-channel rooted at $r$.*

By Lemma 1 it suffices to solve the independent spanning trees problem for directed graphs $\vec{G}$.

A $k$-tree is defined recursively as follows [2]:

(a) A complete graph with $k$ vertices is a $k$-tree.
(b) If $G = (V, E)$ is a $k$-tree and $k$ vertices $v_1, v_2, \cdots, v_k$ induce a complete subgraph of $G$, then $G' = (V \cup \{w\}, E \cup \{\{v_i, w\} \mid 1 \leq i \leq k\})$ is a $k$-tree, where $w$ is a new vertex not contained in $G$.
(c) All $k$-trees can be formed with rules (a) and (b).

A graph is called a *partial $k$-tree* if it is a subgraph of a $k$-tree. Thus the number of edges in a partial $k$-tree $G$ is at most $kn$. In this paper we assume that $k$ is a fixed constant.

A *tree-decomposition* of a graph $G = (V, E)$ is a binary tree $T_{\text{dec}} = (V_{T_{\text{dec}}}, E_{T_{\text{dec}}})$ whose node set $V_{T_{\text{dec}}}$ is a family of subsets of $V$ satisfying the following properties [2]:

(A1) $\bigcup_{X \in V_{T_{\text{dec}}}} X = V$;
(A2) for each edge $\{u, v\} \in E$, there is a leaf $X \in V_{T_{\text{dec}}}$ such that $u, v \in X$;
(A3) if node $X_p$ lies on the path in $T_{\text{dec}}$ from node $X_s$ to $X_t$, then $X_s \cap X_t \subseteq X_p$;
(A4) each internal node $X_i$ has exactly two children, the left child $X_l$ and the right child $X_r$, such that either $X_i = X_l$ or $X_i = X_r$; and
(A5) the number of nodes in $T_{\text{dec}}$ is $O(n)$.

Figure 2(a) illustrates a tree-decomposition $T_{\text{dec}}$ of the partial 3-tree in Figure 1(a). The *width of a tree-decomposition* $T_{\text{dec}}$, denoted by $width(T_{\text{dec}})$, is $\max_{X \in V_{T_{\text{dec}}}} |X| - 1$. The *treewidth of a graph* $G$ is the minimum width of a tree-decomposition of $G$, taken over all possible tree-decompositions of $G$. It is known that every graph $G$ with treewidth $\leq k$ is a partial $k$-tree, and conversely

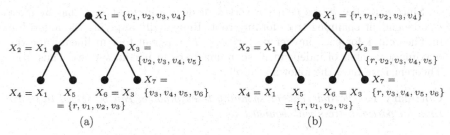

**Fig. 2.** (a) Tree-decomposition $T_{\mathrm{dec}}$ of the partial 3-tree in Figure 1(a), and (b) tree-decomposition $T_{\mathrm{dec}}(r)$.

every partial $k$-tree $G$ has a tree-decomposition $T_{\mathrm{dec}}$ with width $\leq k$. Bodlaender has given a linear-time algorithm to find a tree-decomposition of a partial $k$-tree $G$ with width $\leq k$ for fixed $k$ [3].

By Property (A2) of the tree-decomposition, for each edge $e = \{u, v\} \in E$, we can choose an arbitrary leaf $X_i$ of $T_{\mathrm{dec}}$ such that $u, v \in X_i$, and denote it by $rep(e)$. We define a vertex-set $V_i \subseteq V$ and an edge-set $E_i \subseteq E$ for each node $X_i$ of $T_{\mathrm{dec}}$, as follows. If $X_i$ is a leaf of $T_{\mathrm{dec}}$, then let $V_i = X_i$ and $E_i = \{e \in E | rep(e) = X_i\}$. If $X_i$ is an internal node of $T$ having two children $X_l$ and $X_r$, then let $V_i = V_l \cup V_r$ and $E_i = E_l \cup E_r$. Note that the two edge-sets $E_l$ and $E_r$ are disjoint. Thus node $X_i$ of $T_{\mathrm{dec}}$ corresponds to a subgraph $G_i = (V_i, E_i)$ of $G$. $G_i$ is a union of two edge-disjoint subgraphs $G_l$ and $G_r$, which share common vertices only in $X_i$ because of Property (A3).

For a vertex $r$ in $G$, we denote by $T_{\mathrm{dec}}(r) = (V_{T_{\mathrm{dec}}(r)}, E_{T_{\mathrm{dec}}})$ a tree obtained from $T_{\mathrm{dec}} = (V_{T_{\mathrm{dec}}}, E_{T_{\mathrm{dec}}})$ by adding vertex $r$ to each node $X_i \in V_{T_{\mathrm{dec}}}$, and hence $V_{T_{\mathrm{dec}}(r)} = \{X_i \cup \{r\} \mid X_i \in V_{T_{\mathrm{dec}}}\}$. Clearly $T_{\mathrm{dec}}(r)$ is a tree-decomposition of $G$ and $width(T_{\mathrm{dec}}(r)) \leq width(T_{\mathrm{dec}}) + 1$. Figure 2(b) illustrates $T_{\mathrm{dec}}(r)$ for the tree-decomposition $T_{\mathrm{dec}}$ in Figure 2(a). It should be noted that all nodes of $T_{\mathrm{dec}}(r)$ including the root node $X_1$ contain $r$. This fact is crucial in our algorithm.

## 3    A Linear-Time Algorithm

In this section we give a linear-time algorithm to solve the independent spanning trees problem for partial $k$-trees. Although our algorithm only decides whether $\vec{G}$ is $\alpha$-channel rooted at a given root $r \in V$ for a positive integer $\alpha$, it can be easily modified so that it actually finds $\alpha$ independent spanning trees rooted at $r$.

The main result of this paper is the following theorem.

**Theorem 1.** *Let $G$ be a partial $k$-tree with bounded $k$, let $r$ be a vertex in $G$, and let $\alpha$ be a positive integer. Then one can determine in linear time whether $G$ is $\alpha$-channel rooted at $r$.*

Since a partial $k$-tree $G$ has a vertex of degree at most $k$, $G$ has at most $k$ independent spanning trees for any root. Repeatedly applying the algorithm in Theorem 1 for each integer $\alpha$, $1 \le \alpha \le k$, one can find in linear time the maximum number of independent spanning trees in partial $k$-trees. Thus from Theorem 1 we have the following corollary.

**Corollary 1.** *The independent spanning trees problem can be solved in linear time for partial $k$-trees with bounded $k$.*

In the remainder of this section we will give a proof of Theorem 1. Clearly $G$ is not $\alpha$-channel rooted at $r$ if $\alpha > k$. Therefore one may assume that $\alpha \le k$ and hence $\alpha = O(1)$. Our idea is to formulate the independent spanning trees problem as a new type of an edge-coloring problem, and then to solve the coloring problem using a dynamic programming algorithm with a table of constant size. We use the fact that when doing dynamic programming upward in a tree-decomposition only certain informations of the partial solutions must be kept. These informations concern basically the connectivity among the vertices in a node.

For a positive integer $\alpha$ and an integer $\beta$ ($= 0$ or $1$), we denote by $[\beta, \alpha]$ the set of integers $\beta, \beta + 1, \cdots, \alpha$. For a set $X \subseteq V$, we denote by $\mathcal{F}(X)$ the set of all $\alpha$-tuples $(S_1, S_2, \cdots, S_\alpha)$ such that $S_c \subseteq X \times X$ for each $c \in [1, \alpha]$. Clearly, if $x = |X|$, then $|\mathcal{F}(X)| = 2^{\alpha x^2}$.

Let $f$ be a mapping $\vec{E} \to [0, \alpha]$ of a directed graph $\vec{G} = (V, \vec{E})$, and hence $f$ is an (edge-)coloring of $\vec{G}$ with $\alpha + 1$ colors. For each $c \in [0, \alpha]$, we denote by $\vec{G}(f, c) = (V, \vec{E}_c)$ the so-called color class for $c$, that is, $\vec{E}_c = \{e \in \vec{E} | f(e) = c\}$. If $c \ne 0$, then $\vec{G}(f, c)$ represents the $c$th tree in a set of $\alpha$ independent spanning trees. On the other hand, $\vec{G}(f, 0)$ represents a subgraph of $\vec{G}$ induced by the edges used by none of the $\alpha$ trees. Figure 3(a) depicts a coloring of $\vec{G}$ with $\alpha + 1 = 3$ colors, representing the two independent spanning trees $T_1$ and $T_2$ in Figure 1.

Let $X_i$ be a node of $T_{\mathrm{dec}}(r)$, and let $f$ be a coloring of the subgraph $\vec{G}_i$ of $\vec{G}$. Then $\vec{G}_i(f, c)$, $c \in [1, \alpha]$, represent $\alpha$ spanning forests of $\vec{G}_i$, which have been obtained by the bottom-up computation from leaves to node $X_i$. Each forest $\vec{G}_i(f, c)$ of $\vec{G}_i$ must be completed to a spanning tree in $\vec{G}$ by adding some paths each of which connects two vertices in $X_i$ and passes through only edges in $\vec{E} - \vec{E}_i$. (In Figure 4(a) the edges of $\vec{G}_i(f, c)$ are drawn by solid lines, and the edges in $\vec{E} - \vec{E}_i$ added to it are drawn by dotted lines.) These paths for a forest $\vec{G}_i(f, c)$ is represented by a set $S_c \subseteq X_i \times X_i$ of directed edges, and the paths for the $\alpha$ forests are represented by an $\alpha$-tuple $\mathbf{S}_i = (S_1, S_2, \cdots, S_\alpha) \in \mathcal{F}(X_i)$. For each $c \in [1, \alpha]$, we denote by $\vec{G}_i(f, c) + S_c$ the graph obtained from $\vec{G}_i(f, c)$ by adding to it all elements in $S_c$ as directed edges. (See Figure 4(b).) Then $f$ is called a *feasible coloring of $\vec{G}_i$ for $\mathbf{S}_i$* if $\vec{G}_i(f, 1) + S_1$, $\vec{G}_i(f, 2) + S_2$, $\cdots$, $\vec{G}_i(f, \alpha) + S_\alpha$ are $\alpha$ independent spanning trees rooted at $r$ of the directed graph $\vec{G}_i + X_i \times X_i$. Figure 3(a) depicts a feasible coloring of $\vec{G} = \vec{G}_1$ for $\mathbf{S}_1 = (\emptyset, \emptyset)$, where $G$ is the partial 3-tree in Figure 1(a), $\alpha = 2$, and $X_1 = \{r, v_1, v_2, v_3.v_4\}$ is the root of $T_{\mathrm{dec}}(r)$ in Figure 2(b). Figure 3(b) depicts a feasible coloring of

$\vec{G}_2$ for $\mathbf{S}_2 = (S_{21}, S_{22})$, where $X_2 = X_1$ is the left child of root $X_1$ in $T_{\mathrm{dec}}(r)$, $S_{21} = \{(v_4, v_2)\}$, $S_{22} = \{(v_2, v_3)\}$, and all edges in $\mathbf{S}_2$ are drawn by dotted lines. Figure 3(c) depicts a feasible coloring of $\vec{G}_3$ for $\mathbf{S}_3 = (S_{31}, S_{32})$, where $X_3$ is the right child of root $X_1$ in $T_{\mathrm{dec}}(r)$, $S_{31} = \{(v_2, r), (v_3, v_2)\}$ and $S_{32} = \{(v_3, r), (v_4, v_3)\}$. Clearly the following lemma holds.

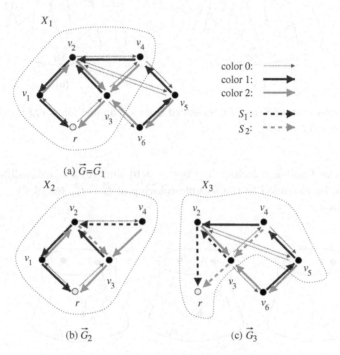

**Fig. 3.** Colorings of $\vec{G}_1$, $\vec{G}_2$ and $\vec{G}_3$.

**Lemma 2.** $\vec{G}$ is $\alpha$-channel rooted at $r$ if and only if $\vec{G}$ has a feasible coloring $f^* : \vec{E} \to [0, \alpha]$ for $(\emptyset, \emptyset, \cdots, \emptyset) \in \mathcal{F}(X_1)$, where $X_1$ is the root node of $T_{\mathrm{dec}}(r)$.

Thus the remaining problem is how to determine whether $\vec{G}$ has a feasible coloring $f : E \to [0, \alpha]$ for $(\emptyset, \emptyset, \cdots, \emptyset) \in \mathcal{F}(X_1)$.

We say that a feasible coloring $f$ of $\vec{G}_i$ for $\mathbf{S}_i = (S_1, S_2, \cdots, S_\alpha) \in \mathcal{F}(X_i)$ is *extensible* if there is a feasible coloring $f^*$ of $\vec{G} = \vec{G}_1$ for $(\emptyset, \emptyset, \cdots, \emptyset) \in \mathcal{F}(X_1)$ such that

(B1) the restriction of $f^*$ to $\vec{E}_i$ is $f$, that is, $f^* \mid \vec{E}_i = f$, and

(B2) for each element $S_c \in \mathbf{S}_i$, $(v, w) \in S_c$ if and only if there is a directed path from $v$ to $w$ in the graph $\vec{G}(f^*, c) - \vec{E}_i$, which is obtained from $\vec{G}(f^*, c)$ by deleting all the edges in $\vec{E}_i$.

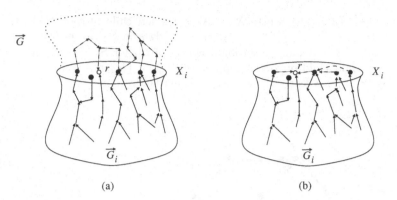

**Fig. 4.** (a) A spanning tree of $\vec{G}$ extended from a spanning forest $\vec{G}_i(f,c)$ of $\vec{G}_i$, and (b) a graph $\vec{G}_i(f,c) + S_c$.

Both of the feasible colorings in Figures 3(b) and (c) are extensible because either can be extended to the feasible coloring of $\vec{G} = \vec{G}_1$ for $(\emptyset, \emptyset) \in \mathcal{F}(X_1)$ in Figure 3(a).

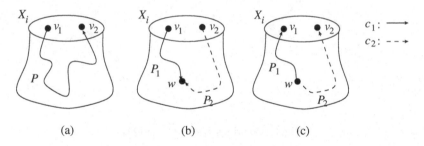

**Fig. 5.** Illustration of $\mathcal{C}(X_i)$.

Since $\vec{G}_i$ has an exponential number of extensible colorings, we shall consider another compact representation of the equivalence classes of extensible colorings, called a "color vector" on $X_i$.

For a set $X \subseteq V$, let

$$\mathcal{H}(X) = \{\{(v_1, c_1), (v_2, c_2)\} | v_1, v_2 \in X, v_1 \neq v_2, c_1, c_2 \in [1, \alpha], c_1 \neq c_2\}.$$

If $x = |X|$, then $|\mathcal{H}(X)| \leq x^2 \alpha^2$.

We call $\mathcal{C}(X_i) = (\mathbf{S}_i, \mathbf{D}_i, \mathbf{J}_i, \mathbf{B}_i)$ a *color vector on* $X_i$ if $\mathbf{S}_i, \mathbf{D}_i \in \mathcal{F}(X_i)$ and $\mathbf{J}_i, \mathbf{B}_i \subseteq \mathcal{H}(X_i)$. Let $\mathbf{S}_i = (S_1, S_2, \cdots, S_\alpha)$, and let $\mathbf{D}_i = (D_1, D_2, \cdots, D_\alpha)$. We say that a color vector $\mathcal{C}(X_i)$ on $X_i$ is *active* if $\vec{G}_i$ has a feasible coloring $f$ for $\mathbf{S}_i$ such that

(C1) for each element $D_c \in \mathbf{D}_i$, $(v_1, v_2) \in D_c$ if and only if $\vec{G}_i(f, c)$ has a path $P$ going from $v_1$ to $v_2$ without passing through any vertex in $X_i - \{v_1, v_2\}$ (see Figure 5(a));

(C2) $\{(v_1, c_1), (v_2, c_2)\} \in \mathbf{J}_i$ if and only if, for some vertex $w$ in $V_i - X_i$, $\vec{G}_i(f, c_1)$ has a path $P_1$ going from $v_1$ to $w$ without passing through any vertex in $X_i - \{v_1, w\}$, and $\vec{G}_i(f, c_2)$ has a path $P_2$ going from $v_2$ to $w$ without passing through any vertex in $X_i - \{v_2, w\}$ (see Figure 5(b)); and

(C3) $\{(v_1, c_1), (v_2, c_2)\} \in \mathbf{B}_i$ if and only if, for some vertex $w$ in $V_i - X_i$, $\vec{G}_i(f, c_1)$ has a path $P_1$ going from $w$ to $v_1$ without passing through any vertex in $X_i - \{w, v_1\}$, and $\vec{G}_i(f, c_2)$ has a path $P_2$ going from $w$ to $v_2$ without passing through any vertex in $X_i - \{w, v_2\}$ (see Figure 5(c)).

Each $D_c$ in $\mathbf{D}_i$ represents the descendance relation among the vertices in $X_i$ induced by the forest $\vec{G}_i(f, c)$. $\mathbf{J}_i$ represents which paths in $\vec{G}_i(f, c)$ of different colors $c$ join at a vertex. $\mathbf{B}_i$ represents which paths of different colors branch at a vertex. The coloring of $\vec{G}_1$ depicted in Figure 3(a) has an active color vector $\mathcal{C}(X_1) = (\mathbf{S}_1, \mathbf{D}_1, \mathbf{J}_1, \mathbf{B}_1)$ such that

$$
\begin{aligned}
\mathbf{S}_1 &= (\emptyset, \emptyset), \\
\mathbf{D}_1 &= (D_{11}, D_{12}), \\
D_{11} &= \{(v_1, r), (v_2, v_1), (v_3, v_2), (v_4, v_2)\}, \\
D_{12} &= \{(v_3, r), (v_1, v_2), (v_2, v_3), (v_4, v_3)\}, \\
\mathbf{J}_1 &= \emptyset, \text{ and} \\
\mathbf{B}_1 &= \{\{(v_4, 1), (v_3, 2)\}\}.
\end{aligned}
$$

Note that $\vec{G}_1(f, 1)$ has a path $P_1 = v_5 v_4$, $\vec{G}_1(f, 2)$ has a path $P_2 = v_5 v_6 v_3$, and hence they branch at $v_5$. On the other hand, the coloring of $\vec{G}_2$ in Figure 3(b) has an active color vector $\mathcal{C}(X_2) = (\mathbf{S}_2, \mathbf{D}_2, \mathbf{J}_2, \mathbf{B}_2)$ such that

$$
\begin{aligned}
\mathbf{S}_2 &= (S_{21}, S_{22}), \\
S_{21} &= \{(v_4, v_2)\}, \\
S_{22} &= \{(v_2, v_3)\}, \\
\mathbf{D}_2 &= (D_{21}, D_{22}), \\
D_{21} &= \{(v_1, r), (v_2, v_1), (v_3, v_2)\}, \\
D_{22} &= \{(v_3, r), (v_1, v_2), (v_4, v_3)\}, \\
\mathbf{J}_2 &= \emptyset, \text{ and} \\
\mathbf{B}_2 &= \emptyset.
\end{aligned}
$$

The coloring of $\vec{G}_3$ in Figure 3(c) has an active color vector $\mathcal{C}(X_3) = (\mathbf{S}_3, \mathbf{D}_3, \mathbf{J}_3, \mathbf{B}_3)$ such that

$$
\begin{aligned}
\mathbf{S}_3 &= (S_{31}, S_{32}), \\
S_{31} &= \{(v_2, r), (v_3, v_2)\}, \\
S_{32} &= \{(v_3, r), (v_4, v_3)\}, \\
\mathbf{D}_3 &= (D_{31}, D_{32}), \\
D_{31} &= \{(v_4, v_2), (v_5, v_4)\}, \\
D_{32} &= \{(v_2, v_3)\},
\end{aligned}
$$

$$\mathbf{J}_3 = \emptyset, \text{ and}$$
$$\mathbf{B}_3 = \{\{(v_4, 1), (v_3, 2)\}\}.$$

Then we have the following lemma.

**Lemma 3.** *Let $X_i$ be a node of $T_{\text{dec}}(r)$, and let two feasible colorings $f$ and $g$ of $\vec{G}_i$ have the same active color vector $\mathcal{C}(X_i) = (\mathbf{S}_i, \mathbf{D}_i, \mathbf{J}_i, \mathbf{B}_i)$. Then $f$ is extensible if and only if $g$ is extensible.*

Thus a color vector on $X_i$ characterizes an equivalence class of extensible colorings of $\vec{G}_i$. Since $\alpha \leq k$ and $|X_i| \leq k + 2$, we have $|\mathcal{F}(X_i)| \leq 2^{k(k+2)^2}$ and $|\mathcal{H}(X_i)| \leq k^2(k+2)^2$. Hence the number of color vectors is at most

$$2^{2k(k+2)^2} 2^{2k^2(k+2)^2} = O(1).$$

The main step of our algorithm is to compute a table of all active color vectors on each node of $T_{\text{dec}}(r)$ from leaves to the root $X_1$ of $T_{\text{dec}}(r)$ by means of dynamic programming. From the table on $X_1$ one can easily check whether $\vec{G}$ has $\alpha$ independent spanning tree rooted at $r$, as follows.

**Lemma 4.** *$\vec{G}$ has $\alpha$ independent spanning tree rooted at $r$ if and only if the table on the root $X_1$ has at least one active color vector $\mathcal{C}(X_1) = (\mathbf{S}_1, \mathbf{D}_1, \mathbf{J}_1, \mathbf{B}_1)$ such that $\mathbf{S}_1 = (\emptyset, \emptyset, \cdots, \emptyset) \in \mathcal{F}(X_1)$.*

We first compute the table of all active color vectors on each leaf $X_i$ of $T_{\text{dec}}(r)$ as follows:

(1) enumerate all mappings (colorings): $\vec{E}_i \to [0, \alpha]$; and

(2) compute all active color vectors on $X_i$ from the colorings of $\vec{G}_i = (V, \vec{E}_i)$.

Since $\alpha \leq k$, $|V_i| = |X_i| \leq k + 2$ and $|\vec{E}_i| \leq (k + 2)^2$ for leaf $X_i$, the number of distinct colorings $f : \vec{E}_i \to [0, \alpha]$ is at most $(k + 1)^{(k+2)^2}$. For each coloring $f$ of $\vec{G}_i$ and each color vector $\mathcal{C}(X_i) = (\mathbf{S}_i, \mathbf{D}_i, \mathbf{J}_i, \mathbf{B}_i)$, one can determine in $O(1)$ time whether $f$ is a feasible coloring of $\vec{G}_i$ for $\mathbf{S}_i$ and $f$ has such a color vector $\mathcal{C}(X_i)$. Therefore, steps (1) and (2) can be done for a leaf in $O(1)$ time. Since $T_{\text{dec}}(r)$ has $O(n)$ leaves, the tables on all leaves can be computed in time $O(n)$.

We next compute all active color vectors on each internal node $X_i$ of $T_{\text{dec}}(r)$ from all active color vectors of its children $X_l$ and $X_r$. We first introduce some notions. For sets $D_l \subseteq X_l \times X_l$ and $D_r \subseteq X_r \times X_r$, we define $\text{Union}(D_l, D_r, X_i)$ as follows:

$\text{Union}(D_l, D_r, X_i)$

$\quad = \{(v, w) \in X_i \times X_i |$ the directed graph $(X_l \cup X_r, D_l \cup D_r)$ has a
$\quad\quad$ path going from $v$ to $w$ without passing through any vertex in
$\quad\quad X_i - \{v, w\}\}$.

For an $\alpha$-tuple $\mathbf{D}_r = (D_{r1}, D_{r2}, \cdots, D_{r\alpha}) \in \mathcal{F}(X_r)$ and a set $\mathbf{J}_r \subseteq \mathcal{H}(X_r)$, we define $\mathrm{Join}(\mathbf{D}_r, \mathbf{J}_r, X_i)$ as follows:

$\mathrm{Join}(\mathbf{D}_r, \mathbf{J}_r, X_i)$
$\quad = \{\{(v_1, c_1), (v_2, c_2)\} \in \mathcal{H}(X_i)|$
$\qquad$ for some $\{(u_1, c_1), (u_2, c_2)\} \in \mathbf{J}_r$, the directed graph $(X_r, D_{rc_1})$
$\qquad$ has a path going from $v_1$ to $u_1$ without passing through any vertex
$\qquad$ in $X_i - \{v_1, u_1\}$, and the directed graph $(X_r, D_{rc_2})$ has a path
$\qquad$ going from $v_2$ to $u_2$ without passing through any vertex in $X_i -$
$\qquad$ $\{v_2, u_2\}\}$.

For an $\alpha$-tuple $\mathbf{D}_r = (D_{r1}, D_{r2}, \cdots, D_{r\alpha}) \in \mathcal{F}(X_r)$ and a set $\mathbf{B}_r \subseteq \mathcal{H}(X_r)$, we define $\mathrm{Branch}(\mathbf{D}_r, \mathbf{B}_r, X_i)$ as follows:

$\mathrm{Branch}(\mathbf{D}_r, \mathbf{B}_r, X_i)$
$\quad = \{\{(v_1, c_1), (v_2, c_2)\} \in \mathcal{H}(X_i)|$
$\qquad$ for some $\{(u_1, c_1), (u_2, c_2)\} \in \mathbf{B}_r$, the directed graph $(X_r, D_{rc_1})$
$\qquad$ has a path going from $u_1$ to $v_1$ without passing through any vertex
$\qquad$ in $X_i - \{u_1, v_1\}$, and the directed graph $(X_r, D_{rc_2})$ has a path
$\qquad$ going from $u_2$ to $v_2$ without passing through any vertex in $X_i -$
$\qquad$ $\{u_2, v_2\}\}$.

For a set $X \subseteq V$, an $\alpha$-tuple $\mathbf{D} = (D_1, D_2, \cdots, D_\alpha) \in \mathcal{F}(X)$ and a set $\mathbf{J} \subseteq \mathcal{H}(X)$, we define $\mathrm{Total\text{-}Join}(\mathbf{D}, \mathbf{J}, X)$ as follows:

$\mathrm{Total\text{-}Join}(\mathbf{D}, \mathbf{J}, X)$
$\quad = \{\{(v_1, c_1), (v_2, c_2)\} \in \mathcal{H}(X)|$
$\qquad$ for some $\{(u_1, c_1), (u_2, c_2)\} \in \mathbf{J}$, the directed graph $(X, D_{c_1})$ has
$\qquad$ a path going from $v_1$ to $u_1$, and the directed graph $(X, D_{c_2})$ has
$\qquad$ a path going from $v_2$ to $u_2\}$.

For a set $X \subseteq V$, an $\alpha$-tuple $\mathbf{D} = (D_1, D_2, \cdots, D_\alpha) \in \mathcal{F}(X)$ and a set $\mathbf{B} \subseteq \mathcal{H}(X)$, we define $\mathrm{Total\text{-}Branch}(\mathbf{D}, \mathbf{B}, X)$ as follows:

$\mathrm{Total\text{-}Branch}(\mathbf{D}, \mathbf{B}, X)$
$\quad = \{\{(v_1, c_1), (v_2, c_2)\} \in \mathcal{H}(X)|$
$\qquad$ for some $\{(u_1, c_1), (u_2, c_2)\} \in \mathbf{B}$, the directed graph $(X, D_{c_1})$ has
$\qquad$ a path going from $u_1$ to $v_1$, and the directed graph $(X, D_{c_2})$ has
$\qquad$ a path going from $u_2$ to $v_2\}$.

For two $\alpha$-tuples $\mathbf{D} = (D_1, D_2, \cdots, D_\alpha)$ and $\mathbf{D}' = (D'_1, D'_2, \cdots, D'_\alpha)$ in $\mathcal{F}(X)$, we denote by $\mathbf{D} \cup \mathbf{D}'$ the new $\alpha$-tuple $(D_1 \cup D'_1, D_2 \cup D'_2, \cdots, D_\alpha \cup D'_\alpha)$.

By Property (A4) of a tree-decomposition one may assume without loss of generality that $X_i = X_l$. Note that $V_i = V_l \cup V_r$, $E_i = E_l \cup E_r$ and $E_l \cap E_r = \emptyset$. Then we have the following lemma, whose proof is omitted in this extended abstract due to the page limitation.

**Lemma 5.** *Let an internal node $X_i$ of $T_{\text{dec}}(r)$ have two children $X_l$ and $X_r$, let $X_i = X_l$, let $\mathbf{S}_i = (S_1, S_2, \cdots, S_\alpha)$, and let $\mathbf{D}_i = (D_1, D_2, \cdots, D_\alpha)$. Then a color vector $\mathcal{C}(X_i) = (\mathbf{S}_i, \mathbf{D}_i, \mathbf{J}_i, \mathbf{B}_i)$ on $X_i$ is active if and only if there are two active color vectors $\mathcal{C}(X_l) = (\mathbf{S}_l, \mathbf{D}_l, \mathbf{J}_l, \mathbf{B}_l)$ on $X_l$ and $\mathcal{C}(X_r) = (\mathbf{S}_r, \mathbf{D}_r, \mathbf{J}_r, \mathbf{B}_r)$ on $X_r$ such that*

(a) $D_c = \text{Union}(D_{lc}, D_{rc}, X_i)$ *for each* $c \in [1, \alpha]$,
(b) $S_c = S_{lc} - D_c$ *for each* $c \in [1, \alpha]$,
(c) $\text{Union}(S_{lc} \cup D_{lc}, \emptyset, X_i) \supseteq S_{rc}$ *for each* $c \in [1, \alpha]$,
(d) $\mathbf{J}_i = \mathbf{J}_l \cup \text{Join}(\mathbf{D}_r, \mathbf{J}_r, X_i)$,
(e) $\mathbf{B}_i = \mathbf{B}_l \cup \text{Branch}(\mathbf{D}_r, \mathbf{B}_r, X_i)$, *and*
(f) $\text{Total-Join}(\mathbf{D}_l \cup \mathbf{D}_r \cup \mathbf{S}_i, \mathbf{J}_l \cup \mathbf{J}_r, X_l \cup X_r) \cap \text{Total-Branch}(\mathbf{D}_l \cup \mathbf{D}_r \cup \mathbf{S}_i, \mathbf{B}_l \cup \mathbf{B}_r, X_l \cup X_r) = \emptyset$. *(Otherwise, paths in trees are not internally disjoint.)*

Using Lemma 5, we compute all *active* color vectors $\mathcal{C}(X_i)$ on $X_i$ from all pairs of active color vectors $\mathcal{C}(X_l)$ on $X_l$ and $\mathcal{C}(X_r)$ on $X_r$, as follows. We first consider all color vectors $\mathcal{C}(X_i)$ on $X_i$. There are at most $2^{2\alpha(k+2)^2} 2^{2\alpha^2(k+2)^2} = O(1)$ color vectors $\mathcal{C}(X_i)$ on $X_i$. For each $\mathcal{C}(X_i)$ of them, we then determine whether $\mathcal{C}(X_i)$ is active or not by examining whether there are active color vectors $\mathcal{C}(X_l)$ and $\mathcal{C}(X_r)$ satisfying Conditions (a)–(f) in Lemma 5. Since $|\mathbf{J}_i| = O(1)$, $|\mathbf{B}_i| = O(1)$, $|D_{lc}| = O(1)$ and $|D_{rc}| = O(1)$ for each $c \in [1, \alpha]$, one can check Conditions (a)–(f) in $O(1)$ time for each pair of color vectors $\mathcal{C}(X_l)$ on $X_l$ and $\mathcal{C}(X_r)$ on $X_r$. The number of pairs of such color vectors is at most $2^{4\alpha(k+2)^2} 2^{4\alpha^2(k+2)^2} = O(1)$. Thus one can compute all active color vectors on $X_i$ in $O(1)$ time. Since $T_{\text{dec}}(r)$ has $O(n)$ internal nodes, one can compute the tables for all internal nodes in $O(n)$ time.

This completes a proof of Theorem 1.

# 4    Conclusion

In the paper we have given a linear-time algorithm to solve the independent spanning trees problem for partial $k$-trees. One can immediately obtain a parallel algorithm to solve the problem for partial $k$-trees, slightly modifying the sequential algorithm as follows. For a given tree-decomposition of a partial $k$-tree $G$ with width at most $k$, one can obtain a new tree-decomposition $T_{\text{dec}}$ of $G$ with height $O(\log n)$ and width at most $3k + 2$ in $O(\log n)$ parallel time using $O(n)$ operations on the EREW PRAM [4]. Since each leaf $X_i$ of $T_{\text{dec}}(r)$ has at most $3k + 4$ vertices, the graph $\vec{G}_i = (V_i, \vec{E}_i)$ satisfies $|\vec{E}_i| \leq (3k + 4)^2 = O(1)$. Therefore the tables of all active color vectors on each leaf of $T_{\text{dec}}(r)$ can be computed in $O(1)$ parallel time using $O(1)$ operations on the CREW PRAM. Since the number of all leaves of $T_{\text{dec}}(r)$ is $O(n)$, the tables of all active color vectors on all leaves of $T_{\text{dec}}(r)$ can be computed in $O(1)$ parallel time using $O(n)$ operations on the CREW PRAM. For each internal node $X_i$ of $T_{\text{dec}}(r)$, the number of all active color vectors is at most $2^{2\alpha(3k+4)} 2^{2\alpha^2(3k+4)^2} = O(1)$. Therefore the table of all active color vectors on each internal node can be computed from those of $X_i$'s two children in $O(1)$ parallel time using $O(1)$ operations on the CREW PRAM. Since the number of all internal nodes of $T_{\mathrm{dec}}(r)$ is $O(n)$ and the height of $T_{\mathrm{dec}}(r)$ is $O(\log n)$, one can compute the table on the root in $O(\log n)$ parallel time using $O(n)$ operations on the CREW PRAM. Thus the parallel algorithm runs in $O(\log n)$ parallel time using $O(n)$ operations on the common CRCW PRAM.

**Acknowledgment.** We thank Md. Salim Zabir for his helpful discussions on the early results on this paper.

# References

1. F. Bao and Y. Igarashi. Reliable broadcasting in product networks with byzantine faults. In *Proceedings of the 26th Ann. Int. Symp. Fault-Tolerant Computing (FTCS'96)*, pp. 262–271, 1996.
2. H. L. Bodlaender. Polynomial algorithms for graph isomorphism and chromatic index on partial $k$-trees. *Journal of Algorithms*, 11(4):631–643, 1990.
3. H. L. Bodlaender. A linear time algorithm for finding tree-decompositions of small treewidth. *SIAM Journal on Computing*, 25:1305–1317, 1996.
4. H. L. Bodlaender and T. Hagerup. Parallel algorithms with optimal speedup for bounded treewidth. In *Proc. of the 22nd International Colloquium on Automata, Languages and Programming, LNCS*, 944, pp. 268–279, 1995.
5. J. Cheriyan and S.N. Maheshwari. Finding nonseparating induced cycles and independent spanning trees in 3-connected graphs. *J. of Algorithms*, 9:507–537, 1988.
6. A. Huck. Independent trees in graphs. *Graphs & Combin.*, 10:29–45, 1994.
7. A. Huck. Independent trees in graphs. *Manuscript, Institut für Mathematik, Universität Hannover*, 1996.
8. A. Itai and M. Rodeh. The multi-tree approach to reliability in distributed networks. *Inform. and Comput.*, 79:43–59, 1988.
9. Y. Iwasaki, Y. Kajiwara, K. Obokata, and Y. Igarashi. Independent spanning trees of chordal rings. *Information Processing Letters*, 69:155–160, 1999.
10. S. Khuller and B. Schieber. Routing through a generalized switchbox. *Information Processing Letters*, 42:321–323, 1992.
11. K. Miura, D. Takahashi, S. Nakano, and T. Nishizeki. A linear-time algorithm to find four independent spanning trees in four-connected planar graphs. *International Journal of Foundations of Computer Science*, 10:195–210, 1999.
12. K. Obokata, Y. Iwasaki, F. Bao, and Y. Igarashi. Independent spanning trees of product graphs. In *Proc. of the 22nd International Workshop on Graph-Throretic Concepts in Computer Science, LNCS*, 1197, pp. 338–351, 1996.
13. A. Zehavi and A. Itai. Three tree-paths. *J. Graph Theory*, 13:175–188, 1989.
14. X. Zhou, S. Tamura, and T. Nishizeki. Finding edge-disjoint paths in partial $k$-trees. *Algorithmica*, 26:3–30, 2000.

# On Efficient Fixed Parameter Algorithms for
## Weighted Vertex Cover

Rolf Niedermeier[1]* and Peter Rossmanith[2]

[1] Wilhelm-Schickard-Institut für Informatik, Universität Tübingen, Sand 13, D-72076
Tübingen, Fed. Rep. of Germany, `niedermr@informatik.uni-tuebingen.de`
[2] Institut für Informatik, Technische Universität München, Arcisstr. 21,
D-80290 München, Fed. Rep. of Germany, `rossmani@in.tum.de`

**Abstract.** We investigate the fixed parameter complexity of one of the
most popular problems in combinatorial optimization, Weighted Ver-
tex Cover. Given a graph $G = (V, E)$, a weight function $\omega : V \to \mathbf{R}^+$,
and $k \in \mathbf{R}^+$, Weighted Vertex Cover (WVC for short) asks for a
subset $C$ of vertices in $V$ of weight at most $k$ such that every edge of $G$
has at least one endpoint in $C$. WVC and its variants have all been
shown to be *NP*-complete. We show that, when restricting the range
of $\omega$ to positive integers, the so-called Integer-WVC can be solved as
fast as unweighted Vertex Cover. Our main result is that if the range
of $\omega$ is restricted to positive reals $\geq 1$, then so-called Real-WVC can
be solved in time $O(1.3954^k + k|V|)$. If we modify the problem in such a
way that $k$ is not the weight of the vertex cover we are looking for, but
the number of vertices in a minimum weight vertex cover, then the same
running time can be obtained. If the weights are arbitrary (referred to by
General-WVC), however, the problem is not fixed parameter tractable
unless $P = NP$.

## 1 Introduction

An interesting and challenging open problem in computational complexity theory
is related to the polynomial time approximability of (Weighted) Vertex Cover [3,9,20,27]: A great number of researchers believe that there is no polynomial
time approximation algorithm achieving an approximation factor strictly smaller
than $2 - \epsilon$, for a positive constant $\epsilon$, unless $P = NP$. Currently, the best known
lower bound for this factor is 1.1666 [18]. According to Crescenzi and Kann [10],
(Weighted) Vertex Cover is the most popular problem in combinatorial
optimization. This motivates the search for *exact* algorithms providing a vertex
cover of *optimal* weight. This paper deals with efficient exact "fixed parameter" algorithms for Weighted Vertex Cover problems, which have provable
performance bounds.

A set $C \subseteq V$ is called a *vertex cover* of a graph $G = (V, E)$ if every edge
in $E$ has at least one endpoint in $C$. The Weighted Vertex Cover problem

---

* Work performed within the "PEAL" project (Parameterized complexity and Exact
ALgorithms), supported by the Deutsche Forschungsgemeinschaft (NI-369/1-1).

D.T. Lee and S.-H. Teng (Eds.): ISAAC 2000, LNCS 1969, pp. 180–191, 2000.

(WVC for short) is: given a graph $G = (V, E)$, a weight function $\omega : V \to \mathbf{R}^+$, and $k \in \mathbf{R}^+$, find a vertex cover $C$ with total weight $\leq k$. In the special case that all vertices have weight 1, one speaks of UNWEIGHTED VERTEX COVER (UVC for short). Even when restricted to planar graphs with maximum vertex degree 3, UVC is $NP$-complete [16]. There are linear time algorithms giving approximation factor 2 for the unweighted case [16] as well as for the weighted case [6]. Both results can be improved to an approximation factor that is asymptotically better: $2 - \log \log |V| / 2 \log |V|$ [7,21]. Until now, no further improvements of these bounds have been obtained.

The parameterized complexity [12] of UVC recently has received considerable interest [4,8,12,14,23,29]. Here, for a given $k$, the question is to find a vertex cover of at most $k$ vertices or to report "no" if no vertex cover of size $\leq k$ exists. In many applications, it makes sense to assume that $k$ is small compared to the total number of vertices $n := |V|$. Hence, exact algorithms with running time exponential *only* in the *parameter* $k$ are considered to be valuable [12,14]. The currently best known result in this direction is an $O(1.271^k + kn)$ algorithm for UVC [8]. In this paper, we study the more general and so far unexplored question concerning the parameterized complexity of WVC. More precisely, for a given $k$, the problem now is to find a vertex cover of weight at most $k$. Herein, we consider three natural variants of WVC:

1. INTEGER-WVC, where the weights are arbitrary positive integers.
2. REAL-WVC, where the weights are real numbers $\geq 1$.
3. GENERAL-WVC, where the weights are positive real numbers.

Whereas all three versions are clearly $NP$-complete, it turns out that their parameterized complexity differs significantly: While INTEGER-WVC and REAL-WVC are *fixed parameter tractable*, GENERAL-WVC is *not* fixed parameter tractable unless $P = NP$.

Our results are as follows. INTEGER-WVC can be solved as fast as UVC, which currently has running time $O(1.271^k + kn)$ [8]. Our main result is that REAL-WVC can be solved in time $O(1.3954^k + kn)$. As an important corollary, this implies that if we modify the problem in such a way that $k$ is *not the weight* of the vertex cover we are looking for, but *the number of vertices* in a minimum weight vertex cover, then the same running time can be obtained. This enables a direct comparison with the unweighted case, where we also count the number of vertices in the vertex cover. Conversely, one easily sees that GENERAL-WVC is fixed parameter intractable unless $P = NP$. Hence, there is little hope to find an $O(f(k)n^{O(1)})$ time algorithm for GENERAL-WVC, where $f$ may be a function growing arbitrarily fast in the parameter $k$.

Due to lack of space we omit some details and proofs.

## 2    Preliminaries and Basic Notation

We assume familiarity with the basic notions and concepts of algorithms, complexity, and graph theory. If $x$ is a vertex in a graph, then by $N(x)$ we denote the set of its neighbors. A graph is called regular if all vertices in the graph have the same degree, that is, the same number of neighbors. The whole paper only works with *simple* graphs, i.e., there are no double edges between two vertices.

The (parameterized) problem GENERAL-WVC we study is defined as follows:
**Given:** A graph $G = (V, E)$, a weight function $\omega : V \to \mathbf{R}^+$, and $k \in \mathbf{R}^+$.
**Question:** Does there exist a vertex cover of weight at most $k$?

Our algorithms are based on two key techniques of parameterized complexity [12]: *reduction to problem kernel* (see Section 3) and *bounded search tree* (see Section 5). The former deals with reducing the size of the search space and the latter with a clever search through the search space. Both will be explained in detail in later sections. To estimate the size of bounded search trees (and, thus, the complexity of the algorithm), we make use of *recurrence relations*. As a rule, we use linear recurrences with constant coefficients for which there exist several well-known techniques for solving them [4,23]. If the algorithm solves a problem of size $k$ and calls itself recursively for problems of sizes $k - d_1, \ldots, k - d_r$, then $(d_1, \ldots, d_r)$ is called the *branching vector* of this recursion. It corresponds to the recurrence

$$t_k = t_{k-d_1} + \cdots + t_{k-d_r}. \tag{1}$$

The characteristic polynomial of this recurrence is

$$z^d = z^{d-d_1} + \cdots + z^{d-d_r}, \tag{2}$$

where $d = \max\{d_1, \ldots, d_r\}$. If $\alpha$ is a root of (2) with maximum absolute value, then $t_k$ is bounded by $|\alpha|^k$ up to a polynomial factor. We call $|\alpha|$ the *branching number* that corresponds to the branching vector $(d_1, \ldots, d_r)$. Moreover, if $\alpha$ is a single root, then $t_k = O(\alpha^k)$. All branching numbers that will occur in this paper are single roots.

Finally, without going into details, let us briefly say a few words about *parameterized complexity theory* [12] (also refer to the survey articles [2,13,14]). Parameterized complexity, as chiefly developed by Downey and Fellows, is one of the latest approaches to attack problems that are *NP*–complete. The basic observation is that for many hard problems the seemingly inherent combinatorial explosion can be restricted to a "small part" of the input, the *parameter*. For instance, the UNWEIGHTED VERTEX COVER problem can be solved by an algorithm with running time $O(kn + 1.271^k)$ [8], where the parameter $k$ is a bound on the maximum size of the vertex cover set we are looking for and $n$ is the number of vertices in the given graph. The fundamental assumption is $k \ll n$. As can easily be seen, this yields an efficient, practical algorithm for small values of $k$. A problem is called *fixed parameter tractable* if it can be solved in time $f(k)n^{O(1)}$ for an arbitrary function $f$ which depends only on $k$. The corresponding complexity class is called *FPT*.[1]

---

[1] As a rule, $k$ is defined to be a positive integer, but it can also be generalized to the positive reals. (Usually, $k$ is given explicitly as part of the input, but for some problems it is implicit in the encoding of the input.)

## 3   Reduction to Problem Kernel

Suppose we are given a graph $G$ and want to find a vertex cover of weight $k$. By means of *reduction to problem kernel*—a kind of a preprocessing step—we can reduce the original instance to a "smaller one," $(G', k')$, where $G'$ is a subgraph of $G$ and $k' \leq k$. It holds that $G$ has a vertex cover of weight $k$ iff $G'$ has a vertex cover of weight $k'$. Assuming positive vertex weights $\geq 1$, a simple standard reduction to problem kernel by Buss works based on the following [12]: Each vertex with degree greater than $k$ has to be in the vertex cover set, since, otherwise, not all edges can be covered. From this it is easy to obtain that $G$ can be replaced with $G'$ such that $G'$ consists of at most $k^2$ edges and at most $k^2 + k$ vertices and $k'$ is obtained from $k$ by reducing by the weight of the high-degree vertices added to the cover, *if there is in fact a vertex cover of size $k$ for $G$*. If $G'$ has more than $k^2 + k$ vertices, it follows that the original problem has no solution and we can stop.

Chen *et. al.* [8] noted that using a well-known theorem of Nemhauser and Trotter [22] (also see, e.g., [7,27]), one can even obtain a problem kernel with a number of vertices linear in $k$. They used the linear size of the problem kernel to improve the exponential term in the running time of their algorithm and also to get rid of a factor of $k$. The resulting algorithm has running time $O(1.271^k k + kn)$. By a new technique, however, the whole factor $k^2$ can be discarded and the improvement in the exponential term can also be easily achieved without a linear size problem kernel [24]. Therefore, the problem kernel size requires no special attention in this paper, where reduction to problem kernel is assumed as a preprocessing for the bounded search tree algorithms for INTEGER- and REAL-WVC in Sections 4 and 5.

## 4   INTEGER– and GENERAL–WEIGHTED VERTEX COVER

In this section, we show that INTEGER-WVC can be solved as fast as UVC and that GENERAL-WVC is not fixed parameter tractable unless $P = NP$. To see the latter, it suffices to make the following simple observation: GENERAL-WVC is $NP$-complete for any fixed $k > 0$. For example, there is a straightforward reduction from the $NP$-complete, unweighted VERTEX COVER to General-WVC with $k = 1$. However, this implies that there cannot be a time $f(k)n^{O(1)}$ or even $n^{O(k)}$ algorithm for GENERAL-WVC unless $P = NP$. This is true because otherwise we would obtain a polynomial time algorithm for an $NP$-complete problem.

In the remaining section, we show that we can reduce INTEGER-WVC to UVC via a simple parameterized many-one reduction (see [12] for any details) that does not change the value of the parameter. To prove the following theorem, we may safely assume that the maximum vertex weight is bounded by $k$ (the according preprocessing needs only polynomial time).

**Theorem 1.** INTEGER–WVC *can be solved as fast as* UVC *up to an additive term polynomial in $k$.*

*Proof.* An instance of INTEGER–WVC is transformed into an instance of UVC as follows: Replace each vertex $i$ of weight $u$ with a cluster $i'$ consisting of $u$ vertices. We do not add intra-cluster edges to the graph. Furthermore, if $\{i, j\}$ is an edge in the original graph, then we connect every vertex of cluster $i'$ to every vertex of cluster $j'$. Now, it is easy to see that both graphs (the instance for INTEGER-WVC and the new instance for UVC) have minimum vertex covers of same weight/size. Here, it is important to observe that the following is true for the constructed instance for UVC: Either all vertices of a cluster are in a minimum vertex cover or none of them is. Assume that one vertex of cluster $i$ is not in the cover but the remaining are. Then all vertices in all neighboring clusters have to be included and, hence, it makes no sense to include the remaining vertices of cluster $i$ in the vertex cover.

Let $t(k, n)$ be the time needed to solve UVC. The running time of the algorithm on the "cluster instance" is clearly bounded by $t(k, wn) \leq t(k, kn)$, where $w \leq k$ is the maximum vertex weight in the given graph. Because of reduction to problem kernel, a bigger graph with same parameter needs only an *additive* polynomial time preprocessing.                                           □

Chen *et al.* [8] state that INTEGER-WVC can be solved in time $O(1.271^k k + kn)$ (which can be improved to $O(1.271^k + kn)$ [24]). As a consequence, Theorem 1 implies that INTEGER-WVC can be solved in the same time.

## 5    REAL–WEIGHTED VERTEX COVER

In this section, we prove our main result. We study the case of weights that are real numbers $\geq 1$ and we prove that REAL-WVC can be solved in time $O(1.3954^k + kn)$. We proceed as follows. First, we observe that if a graph has maximum vertex degree two, then there is an easy dynamic programming solution. After that, we study in detail three main cases (in the given order): the case when there is a vertex of degree one in the graph, when there is a triangle (i.e., a clique of size 3) in the graph, and when there is no triangle in the graph. Note that the existence of weights makes the reasoning quite different from bounded search tree algorithms for UVC. The overall structure of our algorithm is as follows. The subsequent instructions are executed in a loop until all edges of the graph are covered or $k = 0$, which means that no cover could be found.

1. If there is no vertex with degree $> 2$, then solve REAL-WVC in polynomial time by dynamic programming (see Subsection 5.1).
2. Execute the lowest numbered, applicable step of the following.
   a) If there is a vertex $x$ of degree at least 4, then branch into the two cases of either bringing itself or all its neighbors into the vertex cover. (The corresponding branching vector is at least $(1, 4)$, implying branching number 1.3803 or better.)
   b) If there is a degree-1 vertex, then proceed as described in Subsection 5.2. (The corresponding branching vector is at least $(1, 4)$, implying branching number 1.3803 or better.)

c) If there is triangle in the graph, then proceed as described in Subsection 5.3. (The corresponding branching vector is at least $(3, 4, 3)$, implying branching number 1.3954 or better.)

d) If there is no triangle in the graph, then proceed as described in Subsection 5.4. (The corresponding branching vector is at least $(3, 4, 3)$, implying branching number 1.3954 or better.)

Finally, let us only mention in passing that the clever trick of so-called "folding degree-2 vertices," as described by Chen et al. [8] for UVC, does not apply to weighted Vertex Cover problems. Subsequently, we prove our main theorem, following the outline given above.

**Theorem 2.** REAL–WVC *can be solved in time* $O(1.3954^k + kn)$.

Because of step 2.(a) above, in order to prove Theorem 2 we only have to deal with graphs with maximum vertex degree 3.

## 5.1    Graphs with Maximum Vertex Degree 2

Clearly, graphs with maximum vertex degree 2 are either paths or cycles. We can find an optimal vertex cover for them in polynomial time by dynamic programming: Assume that we have a path or cycle of $n$ vertices, numbered consecutively from $n$ to 1. Say we start with vertex $n$. Then this vertex is in the vertex cover or it is not. If it is not, then its neighbor has to be in the vertex cover. This can easily be reflected by a simple system of recurrences: Let $D_n$ denote the minimum weight cover containing vertex $n$ and let $N_n$ denote the minimum weight cover not containing vertex $n$, both referring to a path or a cycle of $n$ vertices. One easily verifies that the following recurrences hold:

$$\begin{aligned}
N_1 &= 0, \\
D_1 &= w_1, \\
N_n &= D_{n-1}, \\
D_n &= w_n + \min\{D_{n-1}, N_{n-1}\},
\end{aligned}$$

where $w_i$ is the weight of vertex $i$. This can easily be solved in linear time, using dynamic programming. Moreover, it is easy to extend this in order to explicitly give a vertex cover set of minimum weight, which is $\min\{D_n, N_n\}$.

## 5.2    Degree One Vertices

In this subsection, we assume that there is at least one vertex that has degree 1. Let $x$ be such a vertex and let $a$ be its only neighbor. In addition, let $w$ be the weight of $x$ and let $w'$ be the weight of $a$. If $w \geq w'$, then it is optimal to include $a$ in the vertex cover. In the following, we handle the more complicated case that $w < w'$.

*Case 1: a has degree 2.* Then a path starts at $x$ that proceeds over vertices with degree 2 and ends in a vertex $y$ that has degree 1 or 3. If $y$ has degree 1, then we can find an optimal cover for this graph component by dynamic programming as described in Subsection 5.1. Otherwise we branch on $y$, bringing either $y$ or its three neighbors into the vertex cover. This gives branching vector $(1, 3)$. If we put $y$ into the vertex cover, we create a new graph component that includes $x$ and $a$ and has only vertices with degree at most 2. We can again apply dynamic programming (Subsection 5.1) and we get a branching vector at least $(2, 3)$ for the whole subgraph.

*Case 2: a has degree 3 and has at least one neighbor with degree 3.* Let $y$ be $a$'s degree-3 neighbor. We branch on $y$. If $y$ is in the cover, then $a$ will have degree 2 and Case 1 applies. The $(1, 3)$ branching vector thus can be improved to $(1 + 2, 1 + 3, 3) = (3, 4, 3)$.

*Case 3: a has degree 3 and has two neighbors with degree 2.* Let $y$ and $b$ be $a$'s degree-2 neighbors. We branch on $x$. If $x$ is in the cover, then $a$ is not and $a$'s other neighbors $y$ and $b$ are in the cover. This gives branching vector $(1, 3)$, which is not yet good enough. Hence, by considering several more subcases, we do a more complicated branching.

Let $z$ be $y$'s other neighbor and assume that $y$ has weight $u$, $z$ has weight $v$, and $u \geq v$. Then we can branch on $a$ and get branching vector $(2, 3)$; note that if $a$ is in the cover, then it is optimal to also include $z$ (instead of $y$).

Assume next that the weight $w'$ of $a$ is at least 2: Then, branching on $a$, we have branching vector $(2, 3)$. Let $w$ be the weight of $x$. We can assume in the following that $w' < w + v$ and $u < v$.

Let us return to the branch on $x$: If $x$ is in the cover, so are $y$ and $b$. We can now assume that $z$ is *not* in the cover. Otherwise, we could replace $x$ and $y$ with $a$, which is better and is already covered by the branch that does not include $x$. Then all neighbors of $z$ are in the cover, too, and among them must be some vertex other than $x$, $y$, or $b$. If not, change the roles of $y$ and $b$. In this way, we get branching vector of at least $(1, 4)$ (unless the component has only 6 vertices and, thus, can be handled in constant time).

*Case 4: Remaining cases.* What remains to be considered are the case when $a$ has degree 3 and all its neighbors have degree 1, and when $a$ has degree 3 and two of its neighbors have degree 1 and one has degree 2. The first case is easily handled in constant time, because we then have a graph component of constant size. For to the second subcase, basically the same strategy as in Case 1 can be applied, because the second degree 1 neighbor of $a$ (besides $x$) only makes necessary a slight, obvious modification to what is done in Case 1.

## 5.3   Triangles

In this subsection, we assume that the degree of all vertices is between 2 and 3 and that there is at least one triangle, consisting of the vertices $a$, $b$, and $c$, with weights $w$, $u$, and $v$. We distinguish between three cases.

*Case 1: Only one of a, b, c has degree 3.* We assume that $c$ has degree 3 and $a$, $b$ have degree 2. Then it is optimal to put $a$ into the vertex cover if $w \leq u$ and $b$ otherwise. No branching of the recursion occurs.

*Case 2: Two of a, b, c have degree 3.* We assume that $b$ and $c$ have degree 3 and $a$ has degree 2. Then we branch according to $b$, which directly gives branching vector $(1, 3)$. If we bring $b$ into the cover, then the degree of $a$ becomes 1 and the degree of its neighbor $c$ becomes 2. Hence, we have a $(2, 3)$-subbranch (see Case 1 in Subsection 5.2) and altogether get branching vector $(1 + 2, 1 + 3, 3) = (3, 4, 3)$.

*Case 3: a, b, c have degree 3.* We branch according to $a$, where $a$ has minimum weight among $a$, $b$, $c$. If $a$ is not in the cover, all its neighbors, and, particularly, $b$ and $c$ are in the cover. Then, however, $b$'s and $c$'s other neighbors are, without loss of generality, *not* in the cover, since it would be equally good to include $a$ instead of $b$ or $c$. Hence, all neighbors of $a$ and one neighbor of $b$'s and $c$'s neighbors different from $a$ are in the cover (otherwise $N(a) \cup N(b) \cup N(c)$ were a small component, easily solvable), and that makes at least 4. The branching vector, then, is at least $(1, 4)$.

## 5.4 No Triangles

First, note that the only possible case for the graph being regular could be that the graph is 3-regular, that is, each vertex has exactly three neighbors. Branching once on an arbitrary vertex, however, this situation can never occur again, since afterwards, vertices with degree one or two must always exist. Clearly, this "one-time-branch" plays no role for the asymptotic complexity of our algorithm. (This technique was introduced by Robson [28].) Hence, in the following we may assume that the graph has no triangles, it is not regular, and all vertices have degree 2 and 3. Furthermore, there are no vertices whose weight is 2 or more. Before we come to the actual case distinction, we verify the correctness of the last assumption: Assume that there is a weight $\geq 2$ vertex $x$. If $x$ has degree 3, then simply branch on $x$, yielding branching vector $(2, 3)$ or better. If $x$ has degree 2 and at least one degree-3 neighbor $y$, then branch on $y$, resulting in a branching vector of at least $(1, 4)$. Finally, if $x$ has two degree-2 neighbors $y$ and $z$, whose weight is without loss of generality no bigger than the weight of $x$, then branch on $y$. In the case of bringing $y$ into the vertex cover, $x$ becomes a degree-1 vertex and its weight is bigger than the weight of $z$ so, without further branching, we know it is optimal to additionally include $z$ into the vertex cover. Hence, we obtain the branching vector $(1 + 1, 3) = (2, 3)$ or better.

*Case 1: There is a degree-2 vertex that has a degree-2 vertex as its neighbor.* Let $x$ and $y$ be degree-3 vertices that are connected by a path consisting of at least two degree-2 vertices. If $x = y$ then branching on $x$ gives easily a branching vector of at least $(2, 3)$, since including $x$ splits off a path. If $x$ and $y$ are neighbors, then we branch according to $x$: If $x$ is in the cover, then the resulting graph corresponds to Case 1 of Subsection 5.2 with branching vector $(2, 3)$. Together with $x$, the branching vector becomes $(3, 4)$. If $x$ is not in the cover, its three neighbors are. Altogether, we get the branching vector $(3, 4, 3)$.

If $x$ and $y$ are not neighbors and $x \neq y$, then we either bring $x$ and $y$ or $x \cup N(y)$ or $N(x)$ into the cover. We claim a branching vector $(3, 4, 3)$ or better. The vector's third component is trivial. If $x$ and $y$ are in the cover, then the path between $x$ and $y$ becomes an isolated component and can be handled by dynamic programming as described in Subsection 5.1. At least one more vertex comes into the cover, and so the first component of the branching vector becomes 3. Since $x$ and $y$ are not neighbors, $x$ and the neighbors of $y$ are 4 vertices with minimum weight 4, justifying the second component of the branching vector.

*Case 2: Every degree-2 vertex has only degree-3 vertices as neighbors and vice versa.* Let $x$, $y$, and $z$ be degree-3 vertices such that $z$ is connected to $x$ and, resp. to $y$, by a degree-2 vertex. We make three branches: $N(x)$, $\{x\} \cup N(y)$, and $\{x, y, z\}$. Then, the branching vector is $(3, 4, 3)$. The branches cover all possibilities because it is optimal to put $z$ into the cover if it already contains $x$ and $y$, since then, $z$ has two neighbors with degree 1 and the weight of $z$ is less than 2.

*Case 3: The first two cases do not apply.* This case is slightly more complicated. First, we make a simple observation: The situation is not hard, if a degree-3 vertex $x$ has a neighbor $a$ that is a degree-2 vertex such that the weight of $a$ is no smaller than the weight of $x$. If $y$ is $a$'s other neighbor, then we can branch as $N(y)$ and $\{x, y\}$, because if $y$ is in the cover then it is optimal to include $x$, too. This yields a branching vector $(3, 2)$. In the following, we can therefore assume that the weight of a degree-3 vertex is bigger than the weights of all those neighbors that are degree-2 vertices.

Now we can find a degree-3 vertex $x$ that has a neighbor $a$ that is a degree-2 vertex, where $a$ has a neighbor $z$ that is a degree-3 vertex. Furthermore, $z$ has a neighbor $y$ that is again a degree-3 vertex, because, otherwise, this situation would already have been handled by Cases 2 and 1: If the first two cases do not apply, then there must be two neighboring degree 3 vertices. Now look at all vertices that are reachable from these two via a path that consists only of degree 3 vertices. This set contains some $z$ that has, of course, itself degree 3 and has one neighbor that has degree 2 (otherwise, there would be a connected regular component, which is not the case, since we assumed that the graph is connected and not 3-regular). Obviously, $z$ also has a neighbor with degree 3 that we call $y$. (It must exist: Just follow the path one step backwards.) Call $z$'s degree-2 neighbor $a$. Call $a$'s other neighbor $x$. Observe that $x$ has degree 3 since otherwise Case 1 would apply.

Now that we have seen that we can find $x$, $a$, $z$, and $y$, let $b$ be the third neighbor of $z$. If $b$ has degree 2, then let $c$ be $b$'s other neighbor. We branch into $N(y)$, $N(z)$, and $\{y, z, x, c\}$. This is correct; since if $z$ is in an optimal cover, it cannot be optimal to include $a$ or $b$, because the weights of $a$ and $b$ each are smaller than the weight of $z$, and, therefore, we can safely include $x$ and $c$. The branching vector is $(3, 3, 4)$ unless $x$ and $c$ are identical. If, however, $x$ and $c$

are identical, then we branch on $y$: Let us first consider an easy special case, namely $y \in N(x)$. Then, however, bringing $y$ into the cover, we get an isolated component of a cycle of 4 vertices. Hence, we get at least two more vertices into the cover without further branching. In total, we get the branching vector $(1+2,3)$ for this special case. Now, assume that $y \notin N(x)$. Then we branch into $\{y, x\}$, $\{y\} \cup N(x)$, and $N(y)$. In the first branch, however, we get an isolated component consisting of vertices $a$, $b$, and $z$. Hence, we can determine in constant time which of them (at least one) has to be added to the vertex cover. In total, we get branching vector $(3, 4, 3)$.

If $b$ has degree 3, then we branch into $N(b)$, $\{b\} \cup N(y)$, and $\{b, y, a\}$, resulting in a branching vector $(3, 4, 3)$. If $b$ and $y$ are in the cover, then we can also include $a$ because the weight of $a$ is smaller than the weight of $z$.

### 5.5  An Application to Minimum Weight Vertex Covers with a Bound on the Number of Vertices

So far, we always studied the case that the parameter $k$ bounds the weight of the vertex cover we are searching for. It may be even more natural, however, to look for a minimum weight vertex cover with at most $k$ vertices. This is addressed in the following theorem, which we obtain as a corollary to Theorem 2.

**Theorem 3.** *Given a graph* $G = (V, E)$, *a weight function* $\omega : V \to [1, \infty)$, *and* $k \in \mathbf{N}$, *is there a vertex cover of minimum weight that consists of at most* $k$ *vertices? This problem can be solved as fast as Real-WVC, i.e., in time* $O(1.3954^k + kn)$.

*Proof.* (Sketch) We reduce the stated problem to REAL-WVC as follows: Given the graph $G = (V, E)$. Let $w := \sum_{v \in V} \omega(v)$. Then consider the following new weight function: If the original weight of vertex $v$ was $\omega(v)$, then it is assigned the new weight $1 + \omega(v)/w$. It is not hard to see that the original graph has a vertex cover of minimum weight that consists of at most $k$ vertices iff the graph with modified weights has a vertex cover of weight at most $k + 1$. This implies the result.  □

## 6  Conclusion and Open Questions

In this paper, we contributed to the search for exact solutions for $NP$-hard problems, a field of increasing importance [1,2,5,8,13,14,11,15,17,19,25,26,28]. More precisely, here we continued and extended the research on the fixed parameter complexity of unweighted VERTEX COVER [4,8,12,14,23,29] to weighted cases. In this way, we generalize and improve known exact algorithms for one of the most important problems in combinatorial optimization [10].

With regard to future work, it is of particular interest to improve the exponential base for REAL-WVC. Moreover, it remains to give efficient implementations of our algorithms and to evaluate and tune them experimentally. Finally, note that it seems possible to apply a dynamic programming technique of Robson [28] in order to improve our exponential terms (search tree size) somewhat. This requires, however, exponential space, whereas our focus in this paper was to develop efficient fixed parameter algorithms using polynomial space.

**Acknowledgement.** We are greatful to an anonymous referee for her/his insightful remarks.

# References

1. J. Alber, H. L. Bodlaender, H. Fernau, and R. Niedermeier. Fixed parameter algorithms for Planar Dominating Set and related problems. In *Proceedings of the 7th Scandinavian Workshop on Algorithm Theory*, number 1851 in Lecture Notes in Computer Science, pages 97–110, Bergen, Norway, July 2000. Springer-Verlag.

2. J. Alber, J. Gramm, and R. Niedermeier. Faster exact solutions for hard problems: a parameterized point of view. Accepted for *Theoretical Computer Science*, August 2000.

3. G. Ausiello, P. Crescenzi, G. Gambosi, V. Kann, A. Marchetti-Spaccamela, and M. Protasi. *Complexity and Approximation—Combinatorial Optimization Problems and their Approximability Properties*. Springer-Verlag, 1999.

4. R. Balasubramanian, M. R. Fellows, and V. Raman. An improved fixed parameter algorithm for vertex cover. *Information Processing Letters*, 65(3):163–168, 1998.

5. N. Bansal and V. Raman. Upper bounds for MaxSat: Further improved. In *Proceedings of the 10th International Symposium on Algorithms and Computation*, number 1741 in Lecture Notes in Computer Science, pages 247–258, Chennai, India, Dec. 1999. Springer-Verlag.

6. R. Bar-Yehuda and S. Even. A linear-time approximation algorithm for the Weighted Vertex Cover problem. *Journal of Algorithms*, 2:198–203, 1981.

7. R. Bar-Yehuda and S. Even. A local-ratio theorem for approximating the weighted vertex cover problem. *Annals of Disc. Math.*, 25:27–46, 1985.

8. J. Chen, I. Kanj, and W. Jia. Vertex cover: Further observations and further improvements. In *Proceedings of the 25th International Workshop on Graph-Theoretic Concepts in Computer Science*, number 1665 in Lecture Notes in Computer Science, pages 313–324, Ascona, Switzerland, June 1999. Springer-Verlag.

9. P. Crescenzi and V. Kann. A compendium of NP optimization problems. Available at http://www.nada.kth.se/theory/problemlist.html, Aug. 1998.

10. P. Crescenzi and V. Kann. How to find the best approximation results—a follow-up to Garey and Johnson. *ACM SIGACT News*, 29(4):90–97, 1998.

11. E. Dantsin, A. Goerdt, E. A. Hirsch, and U. Schöning. Deterministic algorithms for $k$-SAT based on covering codes and local search. In *Proceedings of the 27th International Conference on Automata, Languages, and Programming*, Lecture Notes in Computer Science. Springer-Verlag, July 2000.

12. R. G. Downey and M. R. Fellows. *Parameterized Complexity*. Springer-Verlag, 1999.

13. R. G. Downey and M. R. Fellows. Parameterized complexity after (almost) ten years: Review and open questions. In *Combinatorics, Computation & Logic, DMTCS'99 and CATS'99*, Australian Computer Science Communcations, Volume 21 Number 3, pages 1–33. Springer-Verlag Singapore, 1999.

14. R. G. Downey, M. R. Fellows, and U. Stege. Parameterized complexity: A framework for systematically confronting computational intractability. *DIMACS Series in Discrete Mathematics and Theoretical Computer Science*, 49:49–99, 1999.

15. H. Fernau and R. Niedermeier. An efficient exact algorithm for Constraint Bipartite Vertex Cover. In *Proceedings of the 24th Conference on Mathematical Foundations of Computer Science*, number 1672 in Lecture Notes in Computer Science, pages 387–397, Szklarska Poreba, Poland, Sept. 1999. Springer-Verlag.

16. M. Garey and D. Johnson. *Computers and Intractability: A Guide to the Theory of NP-completeness*. Freeman, San Francisco, 1979.

17. J. Gramm, E. A. Hirsch, R. Niedermeier, and P. Rossmanith. New worst-case upper bounds for MAX-2-SAT with application to MAX-CUT. Invited for submission to a special issue of *Discrete Applied Mathematics*. Preliminary version available as ECCC Technical Report R00-037, Trier, Fed. Rep. of Germany, May 2000.

18. J. Håstad. Some optimal inapproximability results. In *Proceedings of the 29th ACM Symposium on Theory of Computing*, pages 1–10, 1997.

19. E. A. Hirsch. New worst-case upper bounds for SAT. *Journal of Automated Reasoning*, 24(4):397–420, 2000.

20. D. S. Hochbaum, editor. *Approximation algorithms for NP-hard problems*. Boston, MA: PWS Publishing Company, 1997.

21. B. Monien and E. Speckenmeyer. Ramsey numbers and an approximation algorithm for the vertex cover problem. *Acta Informatica*, 22:115–123, 1985.

22. G. L. Nemhauser and L. E. Trotter, Jr. Vertex packings: Structural properties and algorithms. *Mathematical Programming*, 8:232–248, 1975.

23. R. Niedermeier and P. Rossmanith. Upper bounds for Vertex Cover further improved. In C. Meinel and S. Tison, editors, *Proceedings of the 16th Symposium on Theoretical Aspects of Computer Science*, number 1563 in Lecture Notes in Computer Science, pages 561–570. 1999, Springer-Verlag.

24. R. Niedermeier and P. Rossmanith. A general method to speed up fixed-parameter-tractable algorithms. *Information Processing Letters*, 73:125–129, 2000.

25. R. Niedermeier and P. Rossmanith. New upper bounds for maximum satisfiability. *Journal of Algorithms*, 36:63–88, 2000.

26. R. Niedermeier and P. Rossmanith. An efficient fixed parameter algorithm for 3-Hitting Set. To appear in *Journal of Discrete Algorithms*, 2000.

27. V. T. Paschos. A survey of approximately optimal solutions to some covering and packing problems. *ACM Computing Surveys*, 29(2):171–209, June 1997.

28. J. M. Robson. Algorithms for maximum independent sets. *Journal of Algorithms*, 7:425–440, 1986.

29. U. Stege and M. Fellows. An improved fixed-parameter-tractable algorithm for vertex cover. Technical Report 318, Department of Computer Science, ETH Zürich, April 1999.

# Constructive Linear Time Algorithms for Small Cutwidth and Carving-Width*

Dimitrios M. Thilikos[1,**], Maria J. Serna[1], and Hans L. Bodlaender[2]

[1] Departament de Llenguatges i Sistemes Informàtics, Universitat Politècnica de Catalunya, Campus Nord – Mòdul C5, c/Jordi Girona Salgado, 1-3. E-08034, Barcelona, Spain
{mjserna,sedthilk}@lsi.upc.es
[2] Department of Computer Science, Utrecht University, P.O. Box 80.089, 3508 TB Utrecht, The Netherlands
hansb@cs.uu.nl

**Abstract.** Consider the following problem: For any constant $k$ and any input graph $G$, check whether there exists a tree $T$ with internal vertices of degree 3 and a bijection $\chi$ mapping the vertices of $G$ to the leaves of $T$ such that for any edge of $T$, the number of edges of $G$ whose endpoints have preimages in different components of $T - e$, is bounded by $k$. This problem is known as the MINIMUM ROUTING TREE CONGESTION problem and is relevant to the design of minimum congestion telephone networks. If, in the above definition, we consider lines instead of trees with internal vertices of degree 3 and bijections mapping the vertices of $G$ to *all* the vertices of $T$, we have the well known MINIMUM CUT LINEAR ARRANGEMENT problem. Recent results of the Graph Minor series of Robertson and Seymour imply (non-constructively) that *both* these problems are fixed parameter tractable. In this paper we give a *constructive proof* of this fact. Moreover, the algorithms of our proof are optimal and able to output the corresponding pair $(T, \chi)$ in case of an affirmative answer.

## 1 Introduction

Linear layouts provide the framework for the definition of several graph theoretic parameters with a wide range of applications. The cutwidth of a layout is the maximum number of edges connecting vertices on opposite sides of any of the "gaps" between successive vertices in the linear layout. The cutwidth of a graph is the minimum cutwidth over all possible layouts of $G$. Deciding whether, for a given $G$ and an integer $k$, cutwidth$(G) \leq k$, is an NP-complete problem known in the bibliography as the MINIMUM CUT LINEAR ARRANGEMENT (see [12]). Cutwidth has been extensively examined (see [7,10,11,14,16,17,21]). It is closely

---

* Supported by the EU project ALCOM-FT (IST-99-14186).
** The research of the first author was supported by the Ministry of Education and Culture of Spain, Grant number MEC-DGES SB98 0K148809.

D.T. Lee and S.-H. Teng (Eds.): ISAAC 2000, LNCS 1969, pp. 192–203, 2000.

related with other graph theoretic parameters like pathwidth, bandwidth, modified bandwidth (see [15,7,16,14,8]), and it is approximable (see [9]) within a factor of $O(\log n \log \log n)$ in polynomial time (where $n$ is the number of vertices of the input graph). Finally, while it remains NP-complete even for planar graphs with maximum degree 3 (see [17]), it is polynomially computable for trees (see [21]).

Our results concern the fixed parameter tractability of cutwidth. Recall that a graph $H$ is said to be immersed to $G$ if a graph isomorphic to $H$ can be obtained from a subgraph of $G$ after lifting pairs of adjacent edges (i.e. removing two adjacent edges $\{a,b\}, \{b,c\}$ and adding the edge $\{a,c\}$). The main motivation of our research were the results of Robertson and Seymour in their Graph Minors series where, among others, they prove that any set of graphs contains a finite number of immersion minimal elements (see [18]). As a consequence, we have that for any class $C$ of graphs the set of graphs *not* in $C$ contains a *finite* set (we call it immersion obstruction set of $C$) of immersion minimal elements. Therefore, we have the following characterization for any immersion closed class $C$: a graph $G$ is in $C$ iff none of the graphs in the immersion obstruction set of $C$ is immersed in $G$. Combining this observation with the fact that, for any fixed $H$, there exists a polynomial time algorithm deciding: given $G$ as input, whether $H$ is immersed in $G$ (see [19,10]), we imply the existence of a polynomial time recognition algorithm for any immersion-closed graph class. Unfortunately, the result of Robertson and Seymour is *non-constructive* in the sense that it does not provide any method of constructing the corresponding obstruction set. Therefore, it only guaranties the *existence* of a polynomial time algorithm and does not provide a way to construct it. However, it provides a strong motivation towards identifying the corresponding algorithms for a wide range of graph classes and parameters. So far, it appears that the most popular class (see [10, 11]) that is immersion-closed, is the class of graphs with cutwidth bounded by a fixed constant. A direct consequence is that, for any fixed $k$, there exists a polynomial time algorithm checking whether a graph has cutwidth at most $k$. The first algorithm checking whether cutwidth$\leq k$ was given by Makedon and Sudborough in [16] where a $O(n^{k-1})$ dynamic programming algorithm is described. This time complexity has been considerably improved by Fellows and Langston in [11] where, among others, they prove that for any fixed $k$, a $O(n^3)$ algorithm can be constructed checking whether a graph has cutwidth at most $k$. Furthermore, a technique introduced in [10] (see also [3]) further reduced the bound to $O(n^2)$, while in [1] it is given a general method to construct a linear time algorithm that decides whether a given graph has cutwidth at most $k$, for $k$ constant. However the methodology in [1] gives only a decision algorithm: it does not give any way to construct, in the case of a positive answer, the corresponding vertex ordering. In this paper, we give an explicit description, for any $k \geq 1$, of a linear time algorithm that checks whether an input graph $G$ has cutwidth$\leq k$ and, if this is the case, it further *outputs* a vertex ordering of $G$ of minimum cutwidth.

The second immersion-closed class we examine in this paper is the class of graphs with carving-width bounded by a fixed constant. Carving-width was defined by Seymour and Thomas in [20] and is related with the design of multi-commodity flow trees. Its definition is a "tree fashion" extension of cutwidth. In particular, let $G$ be a graph where the existence of an edge in $G$ represents a communication demand (i.e. telephone calls) between its endpoints. A *call routing tree* (or a *carving*) of a graph $G$ is a tree $T$ with internal vertices of degree 3 whose leaves correspond to the vertices of $G$. We say that $T$ has *congestion* $\leq k$ if, for any edge $e$ of $T$, the communication demands that need to be routed through $e$ or, more explicitly, the number of edges of $G$ that share endpoints corresponding to different connected components of $T - e$, is bounded by $k$ (we denote as $T - e$ the graph obtained from $T$ after the removal of $e$). The *carving-width* of a graph $G$ is the minimum $k$ for which there exists a call routing tree $T$ with congestion bounded by $k$. In [20], Seymour and Thomas proved that computing the carving-width of a graph is NP-complete. Moreover, in the same paper, they give a $O(n^4)$ algorithm computing the carving-with of any planar graph $G$. Finally, the problem of designing call routing trees of minimum congestion has been studied in [13] where a polynomial time algorithm is given, computing a call routing tree $T$ whose congestion is within a $O(\log n)$ factor from the optimal. It is easy to check that the class of graphs with carving-width bounded by $k$ is immersion-closed for any $k$. Therefore, the results of Robertson and Seymour in [18,19,10] guaranties the existence, for any $k$, of a polynomial time algorithm deciding whether an input graph $G$ has carving-width at most $k$. However, as in the case of cutwidth, an optimal constructive algorithm was missing. In this paper, we provide a linear time algorithm that checks whether an input graph $G$ has carving-width$\leq k$ and, if this is the case, outputs a call routing tree of minimum congestion.

A consequence of our algorithms is that, for any $k$, there exists an algorithm able to determine the immersion obstruction set for the class of the graphs with cutwidth (carving-width) at most $k$. We mention that optimal constructive results exist so far only for minor closed parameters such as treewidth and pathwidth [2,4], agile graph searching parameters [6], linear-width [6], and branch-width [5]. Besides the fact that that our techniques are motivated by those used for the aforementioned minor closed parameters, in our knowledge, our results are the first concerning immersion-closed parameters and we believe that our approach is applicable to other parameters as well (e.g. MODIFIED CUTWIDTH, 2-D GRID LOAD FACTOR, or BINARY GRID LOAD FACTOR– see [10]).

## 2    Definitions and Preliminary Results

All the graphs of this paper are finite, undirected, and without loops or multiple edges (our results can be straightforwardly generalized in the case where the last restriction is altered). We will denote as $V(G)$ ($E(G)$) the vertex (edge) set of a graph $G$. A linear (one-dimensional) layout of the vertices of $G$ is a bijection, mapping $V(G)$ to the integers in $\{1, \ldots, n\}$. We will denote such a layout as a sequence $[v_1, \ldots, v_n]$.

We proceed with a number of definitions and notations, dealing with finite sequences (i.e., ordered sets) of a given finite set $\mathcal{O}$ where $\mathcal{O}$ can be a set of numbers, sequences of numbers, vertices, or vertex sets. Let $\omega$ be a sequence of elements from $\mathcal{O}$. We use the notation $[\omega_1, \ldots, \omega_r]$ to represent $\omega$ and we define $\omega[i, j]$ as the subsequence $[\omega_i, \ldots, \omega_j]$ of $\omega$ (in case $j < i$, the result is the empty subsequence $[\ ]$). We also denote as $\omega(i)$ the element of $\omega$ indexed by $i$.

Given a set $S$ containing elements of $\mathcal{O}$, we denote as $\omega[S]$ the subsequence of $\omega$ that contains only the elements of $\omega$ that are in $S$. Given two sequences $\omega^1, \omega^2$, defined on $\mathcal{O}$, where $\omega^i = [\omega_1^i, \ldots, \omega_{r_i}^i], i = 1, 2$ we define the *concatenation* of $\omega_1$ and $\omega_2$ as $\omega^1 \oplus \omega^2 = [\omega_1^1, \ldots, \omega_{r_1}^1, \omega_1^2, \ldots, \omega_{r_2}^2]$. Unless mentioned otherwise, we will always consider that the first element of a sequence $\omega$ is indexed by 1, i.e. $\omega = \omega[1, |\omega|]$.

Let $G$ be a graph and $S \subseteq V(G)$. We call the graph $(S, E(G) \cap \{\{x, y\} \mid x, y \in S\})$ *subgraph of $G$ induced by $S$* and we denote it by $G[S]$. For any $e \in E(G)$, we set $G - e = (V(G), E(G) - \{e\})$ and we denote by $E_G(S)$ the set of edges of $G$ that have an endpoint in $S$; we also set $E_G(v) = E_G(\{v\})$. If $E \subseteq E(G)$ then we denote as $V(E)$ the set of all the endpoints of the edges in $E$ i.e. we set $V(E) = \cup_{e \in E} e$. The neighborhood of a vertex $v$ in graph $G$ is the set of vertices in $G$ that are adjacent, in $G$, with $v$ and we denote it as $N_G(v)$, i.e. $N_G(v) = V(E_G(v)) - \{v\}$. If $l$ is a sequence of vertices, we denote the set of its vertices as $V(l)$. If $x \in V(l)$ then we set $l - x = l[V(l) - \{x\}]$. If $l$ is a sequences of all the vertices of $G$ without repetitions, then we will call it *vertex ordering of $G$*. Given a tree $T$, we will denote as $A(T)$ the set of leaves of $T$, i.e. the vertices of $T$ that have degree 1. Finally, whenever we deal with a function $\varphi : A \to B$ we will use the notation $\varphi(S)$ to denote the set $\{\varphi(\alpha) \mid \alpha \in S\}$ for any $S \subseteq A$.

## 2.1  Treewidth

A *tree decomposition* of a graph $G$ is a pair $(X, U)$ where $U$ is a tree whose vertices we will call *nodes* and $X = (\{X_i \mid i \in V(U)\})$ is a collection of subsets of $V(G)$ such that

(i) $\bigcup_{i \in V(U)} X_i = V(G)$,

(ii) for each edge $\{v, w\} \in E(G)$, there is an $i \in V(I)$ such that $v, w \in X_i$,

(iii) for each $v \in V(G)$ the set of nodes $\{i \mid v \in X_i\}$ forms a subtree of $U$.

The *width* of a tree decomposition $(\{X_i \mid i \in V(U)\}, U)$ equals $\max_{i \in V(U)} \{|X_i| - 1\}$. The *treewidth* of $G$ is the minimum width over all its tree decompositions.

A *rooted* tree decomposition is a triple $D = (X, U, r)$ in which $U$ is a tree rooted on $r$ and $(X, U)$ is a tree decomposition. Let $D = (X, U, r)$ be a rooted tree decomposition of a graph $G$. For each node $i$ of $T$, let $U_i$ be the subtree of $U$, rooted at node $i$. We set $V_i = \cup_{v \in V(U_i)} X_v$ and let $G_i = G[V_i]$. Notice that if $r$ is the root of $U$, then $G_r = G$. We call $G_i$ the subgraph of $G$ *rooted* at $i$. We finally set, for any $i \in V(U)$, $D_i = (X^i, U_i)$ where $X^i = \{X_v \mid v \in V(U_i)\}$. Observe that for each node $i \in V(U)$, $D_i$ is a tree decomposition of $G_i$.

Let $D = (X, U, r)$ be a rooted tree decomposition of a graph $G$ where $X = \{X_i \mid i \in V(U)\}$. $D$ is called a *nice* tree decomposition if (i) Every node of $U$ has at most two children, (ii) if a node $i$ has two children $j, h$ then $X_i = X_j = X_h$, (iii) if a node $i$ has one child, then either $|X_i| = |X_j| + 1$ and $X_j \subset X_i$ or $|X_i| = |X_j| - 1$ and $X_i \subset X_j$. Notice that a nice tree decomposition is always a rooted tree decomposition. For the following, see e.g. [4].

**Lemma 1.** *For any constant $k \geq 1$, given a tree decomposition of a graph $G$ of width $\leq k$ and $O(|V(G)|)$ nodes, there exists an algorithm that, in $O(|V(G)|)$ time, constructs a nice tree decomposition of $G$ of width $\leq k$ and with at most $4|V(G)|$ nodes.*

We now observe that a nice tree decomposition $(\{X_i \mid i \in V(U)\}, U)$ contains nodes of the following four possible types. A node $i \in V(U)$ is called *"start"* if $i \in A(U)$, *"join"* if $i$ has two children, *"forget"* if $i$ has one child $j$ and $|X_i| < |X_j|$, *"introduce"* if $i$ has one child $j$ and $|X_i| > |X_j|$. We may also assume that if $i$ is a *start* node then $|X_i| = 2$: the effect of *start* nodes with $|X_i| > 2$ can be obtained by using a *start* node with a set containing 2 vertices, and then $|X_i| - 2$ *introduce* nodes, which add all the other vertices.

## 2.2 Pathwidth

A *path decomposition* of a graph $G$ is defined as a tree decomposition with the difference that the tree $U$ is a line. For simplicity, we will denote a path decomposition as a sequence $X = [X_1, \ldots, X_r]$ of subsets of $V(G)$. The *width of* $X$ equals $\max_{1 \leq i \leq r}\{|X_i| - 1\}$ and the *pathwidth* of a graph $G$ is the minimum width over all path decompositions of $G$. We say that a path decomposition $X = [X_1, \ldots, X_r]$ is *nice* if $|X_1| = 1$ and $\forall_{2 \leq i \leq |X|} |(X_i - X_{i-1}) \cup (X_{i-1} - X_i)| = 1$. The following lemma follows directly from the definitions.

**Lemma 2.** *For some constant $k$, given a path decomposition of a graph $G$ that has width at most $k$ and $O(|V(G)|)$ nodes, one can find a nice path decomposition of $G$ that has width at most $k$ and at most $2|V(G)|$ nodes in $O(|V(G)|)$ time.*

Let $i$ be a node of a nice path decomposition $X$ such that $i \geq 1$. We say that $i$ is an *introduce* (*forget*) node if $|X_i - X_{i-1}| = 1$ ($|X_{i-1} - X_i| = 1$). It is easy to observe that any node $i \geq 2$ of a nice path decomposition is either an *introduce* or a *forget* node. We call the first node of $X$, *start* node.

Finally, for $i = 1, \ldots, r$, we define $V_i = \cup_{1 \leq j \leq i} X_j$ and $G_i = G[V_i]$.

## 2.3 Cutwidth

The cutwidth of a graph $G$ is defined as follows. Let $l = [v_1, \ldots, v_n]$ an ordering of $V(G)$ ($n = |V(G)|$). For $i = 1, \ldots, n-1$, we define $\delta_{l,G}(i) = E_G(l[1, i]) \cap E_G(l[i + 1, n])$ (i.e. $\delta_{l,G}(i)$ is the set of edges of $G$ that have one endpoint in $l[1, i]$ and one in $l[i + 1, n]$). The cutwidth of an ordering $l$ of $V(G)$ is $\max_{1 \leq i \leq n-1}\{|\delta_{l,G}(i)|\}$. The cutwidth of a graph is the minimum cutwidth over all the orderings of $V(G)$. It is easy to see the following (see also [16]).

**Lemma 3.** *For any graph $G$, cutwidth$(G) \geq$ pathwidth$(G)$.*

If $l = [v_1, \ldots, v_n]$ is a vertex ordering of a graph $G$, we set $\mathbf{Q}_{G,l} = [[0], [|\delta_{l,G}(1)|], \ldots, [|\delta_{l,G}(n-1)|], [0]]$. We also assume that the indices of the elements of $\mathbf{Q}_{G,l}$ start from 0 and finish on $n$, i.e. $\mathbf{Q}_{G,l} = \mathbf{Q}_{G,l}[0, n]$.

## 2.4   Carving-Width

A *carving* of a graph $G$ is a pair $c = (T, \chi)$ where $T$ is a tree with internal vertices of degree 3 and $|V(G)|$ leaves and $\chi : A(T) \rightarrow V(G)$ is a bijection mapping the leaves of $T$ to the vertices of $G$. Given a carving $c$, of a graph $G$, we define the function $b_{G,c}$ such that, for any edge $e$ in $E(T)$, $\delta_{G,c}(e) = E_G(V_1) \cap E_G(V_2)$ and $b_{G,c}(e) = [|\delta_{G,c}(e)|]$ where $V_i = \chi(A(T) \cap A(T_i)), i = 1, 2$ and $T_i, i = 1, 2$ are the connected components of $T - e$. Notice that the images of $b_{G,c}$ are sequences of only one integer. The width of a carving $c = (T, \chi)$ of $G$ is defined as $\max\{\max(b_{G,c}(e)) \mid e \in E(T)\}$ (i.e. the maximum number appearing in the sequences corresponding to the edges of $T$). The carving-width of a graph is the minimum width over all of its carvings.

**Lemma 4.** *For any graph $G$, treewidth$(G) \leq 3 \cdot$ carving-width$(G)$.*

## 2.5   Sequences of Integers

We denote as $\mathcal{S}$ the set of all the sequences of non-negative integers. For any sequence $A = [a_1, \ldots, a_{|A|}] \in \mathcal{S}$ and any integer $t \geq 0$ we set $A + t = [a_1 + t, \ldots, a_{|A|} + t]$. If $A = [a_1, \ldots, a_{|A|}] \in \mathcal{S}$, we define $\tau(A)$ as the sequence obtained after iterating the following operations, until none is possible any more.

(i) If for some $i, 1 \leq i \leq |A| - 1$ $a_i = a_{i+1}$, then set $A \leftarrow A(1, i) \oplus A(i+2, |A|)$.

(ii) If the sequence contains two indices $i$ and $j$ such that $j - i > 1$ and $\forall_{i<k<j}\ a_i \leq a_k \leq a_j$ or $\forall_{i<k<j}\ a_i \geq a_k \geq a_j$, then set $A \leftarrow A(1, i) \oplus A(j, |A|)$.

We call a sequence $A \in \mathcal{S}$ *typical* if $\tau(A) = A$. The following result has been proved in [2] (Lemma 3.5).

**Lemma 5.** *The number of different typical sequences consisting of integers in $\{0, 1, \ldots, L\}$ is at most $\frac{8}{3}2^{2L}$.*

For any $A \in \mathcal{S}$ we define $\theta(A)$ in the same way as $\tau(A)$ with the difference that only operation (i) is considered. If now $A$ is a typical sequence, we define the set of extensions of $A$ as $\mathcal{E}(A) = \{\tilde{A} \in \mathcal{S} \mid \theta(\tilde{A}) = A\}$.

Let $A = [a_1, \ldots, a_{r_1}]$ and $B = [b_1, \ldots, b_{r_2}]$ be two sequences in $\mathcal{S}$. We say that $A \leq B$ if $r_1 = r_2$ and $\forall_{1 \leq i \leq r_1}\ a_i \leq b_i$. In general, we say that $A \prec B$ if there exist extensions $\tilde{A} \in \mathcal{E}(A), \tilde{B} \in \mathcal{E}(B)$ such that $|\tilde{A}| = |\tilde{B}|$ and $\tilde{A} \leq \tilde{B}$.

Suppose now that $\mathbf{A} = [A_1, \ldots, A_r]$ and $\mathbf{B} = [B_1, \ldots, B_r]$ are two sequences of typical sequences with the same length. We say that $\mathbf{A} \prec \mathbf{B}$ if $\forall_{1 \leq i \leq r}\ A_i \prec B_i$. For any integer $t$ we set $\mathbf{A} + t = [A_1 + t, \ldots, A_{|\mathbf{A}|} + t]$ and $\max(\mathbf{A}) = \max_{1 \leq i \leq |\mathbf{A}|}\{\max(A_i)\}$. Finally, for any sequence of sequences $\mathbf{A}$ we set $\tau(\mathbf{A}) = \tau(\mathbf{A}(1) \oplus \cdots \oplus \mathbf{A}(|\mathbf{A}|))$.

Let $A, B \in \mathcal{S}$ where $A = [a_1, \ldots, a_r], B = [b_1, \ldots, b_r]$. We define $A + B = [a_1 + b_1, \ldots, a_r + b_r]$ and we say that $A \sim B$ iff $\forall_{1 \leq i < r} \; a_i \neq a_{i+1} \Leftrightarrow b_i = b_{i+1}$ (and, therefore, $b_i \neq b_{i+1} \Leftrightarrow a_i = a_{i+1}$).

The *interleaving* $A \otimes B$ of two typical sequences $A$ and $B$ is the following set of typical sequences: $A \otimes B = \{\tau(\tilde{A} + \tilde{B}) \mid \tilde{A} \in \mathcal{E}(A), \tilde{B} \in \mathcal{E}(B) \text{ and, } \tilde{A} \sim \tilde{B}\}$.

## 3   Characteristics and Overview of the Algorithms

In this section, we will describe the general structure of both of our algorithms along with their basic mathematical concepts. A key tool in both cases already used in the bibliography for other parameters like pathwidth and treewidth in [2], linear-width in [6], and branchwidth in [5], is the notion of *characteristics*. In a few words, a characteristic serves as a mathematical tool that filters the data of the main structure of a parameter to its essential part, that is, the part able to reproduce it with respect to a node $i$ of the path (tree) decomposition. Moreover, as we will see, the information encoded by a characteristic depends on the width of this decomposition and, therefore, it is constant for graphs with bounded pathwidth or treewidth.

Our algorithms roughly work as follows. Given a path (tree) decomposition of the input graph $G$, we transform it in a nice path (tree) decomposition as it is indicated in Lemma 2 (1). We correspond to any of the subgraphs $G_i$ a set of characteristics that "represent" the vertex orderings (carvings) of $G_i$ that have cutwidth (width) $\leq k$. Our algorithms are based on a bottom up procedure that is able to compute a set of characteristics of $G_i$ using the information of the set of characteristics corresponding to $G_{i-1}$ in the case of cutwidth and to the children of $i$ in the case of carving-width. The procedure starts from the first node of the path decomposition in the case of cutwidth and from the leaf nodes of the tree decomposition in the case of carving-width. In the rest of this section we will specify these characteristics for the cases of cutwidth and carving-width and we will demonstrate the main theorems supporting their use in our algorithms.

### 3.1   Characteristic of a Vertex Ordering of a Graph

Let $G$ be a graph with $n$ vertices and let $l = [v_1, \ldots, v_n]$ be a vertex ordering of $G$. For simplicity, we denote $\mathbf{Q}_{G,l} = \mathbf{R}$. Given a set $S \subseteq V(G)$, the *S-characteristic* $C_S(G, l)$ of the vertex ordering $l$ of $G$ is a pair $(\lambda, \mathbf{A})$ defined as follows:

1. $\lambda \leftarrow l[S]$. Assume the notations $l = [v_1, \ldots, v_n]$ and $\lambda = [v_{i_1}, v_{i_2}, \ldots, v_{i_\rho}]$.
2. $\mathbf{A} \leftarrow [\tau(\mathbf{R}[0, i_1 - 1]), \tau(\mathbf{R}[i_1, i_2 - 1]), \ldots, \tau(\mathbf{R}[i_{\rho-1}, i_\rho - 1]), \tau(\mathbf{R}[i_\rho, |l|])]$.

Given two $S$-characteristics $(\lambda^i, \mathbf{A}^i), i = 1, 2$ of two different orderings of $V(G)$ we say that $(\lambda^1, \mathbf{A}^1) \prec (\lambda^2, \mathbf{A}^2)$ when $\lambda^1 = \lambda^2$ and $\mathbf{A}^1 \prec \mathbf{A}^2$.

### 3.2   Characteristic of a Carving of a Graph

Let $c = (T, \chi)$ be a carving of $G$. Let also $S \subseteq V(G)$. We define the *S-characteristic* $C_S(G, c)$ of the carving $c$ of $G$ as the pair $(\gamma, \beta)$ defined as follows:

1. Let $T_{\text{trunk}} = T[(V(T) - A(T)) \cup \chi^{-1}(S)]$, i.e. $T_{\text{trunk}}$ is the tree obtained from $T$ after removing all the leaves that do not map through $\chi$ to vertices in $S$.

2. While $A' = A(T_{\text{trunk}}) - A(T) \neq \emptyset$, set $T_{\text{trunk}} = T_{\text{trunk}}[V(T_{\text{trunk}}) - A']$, (i.e. remove leaves of $T_{\text{trunk}}$ that are not leaves of $T$ as long as such leaves exist.)

3. Replace any maximal path with all internal vertices of degree 2 $(t_1, \ldots, t_\rho)$ of $T_{\text{trunk}}$ with an edge $e$ and set $\beta(e) = \tau(\{b_{G,c}(\{t_1, t_2\}) \oplus \cdots \oplus b_{G,c}(\{t_{\rho-1}, t_\rho\})\})$.

4. Let $\gamma = (Y, \theta)$ where $Y$ is the resulting tree and $\theta$ is the restriction of $\chi$ to the leaves of $Y$.

Notice that if $(\gamma, \beta)$ is an $S$-characteristic of some carving of $G$, then $\gamma$ is a carving of $G[S]$. Given two $S$-characteristics $(\gamma_i, \beta_i), i = 1, 2$ of two carvings of $V(G)$ where $\gamma_i = (Y_i, \theta_i), i = 1, 2$, we say that $\gamma_1 \equiv_\phi \gamma_2$ if $\phi : V(Y_1) \to V(Y_2)$ is an isomorphic bijection between $Y_1$ and $Y_2$ whose restriction on $A(Y_1)$ and $A(Y_2)$ is the bijection $\theta_1 \circ \theta_2^{-1} : A(Y_1) \to A(Y_2)$. Suppose that $\gamma_1 \equiv_\phi \gamma_2$. We define $\beta_1 \otimes_\phi \beta_2 = \{\beta \mid \forall_{\{t,t'\} \in E(Y_1)} \beta(\{t,t'\}) \in \beta_1(\{t,t'\}) \otimes \beta_2(\{\phi(t), \phi(t')\})\}$. We also say that $(\gamma_1, \beta_1) \prec_\phi (\gamma_2, \beta_2)$ when, for any $\{t, t'\} \in E(Y_1)$, $\beta_1(\{t, t'\}) \prec \beta_2(\phi(\{t, t'\}))$. Finally, $(\gamma_1, \beta_1) \prec (\gamma_2, \beta_2)$ if there exist a bijection $\phi$ such that $(\gamma_1, \beta_1) \prec_\phi (\gamma_2, \beta_2)$.

## 3.3  Analysis of the Algorithms

Using now Lemma 5 and Lemma 4 and working in a similar way as in the proof of Lemma 3.1 in [2], we can prove the following lemma.

**Lemma 6.** *Let $X = [X_1, \ldots, X_r]$ be a nice path decomposition of $G$ with width at most $w$. Let $i, 1 \leq i \leq r$ be some node in $X$. The number of different $X_i$-characteristics of all possible vertex orderings of $G_i$ with cutwidth at most $k$ (all possible carvings of $G_i$ with carving-width at most $k$), is bounded by a function depending only on $k$ and $w$.*

A set $FS(i)$ of $X_i$-characteristics of vertex orderings (carvings) of a graph $G_i$ with cutwidth (carving-width) at most $k$ is called a *full set of characteristics of vertex orderings (carvings)* for $G_i$ if for each vertex ordering (carving) $\mu$ of $G_i$ with cutwidth (width) at most $k$, there is a vertex ordering (carving) $\mu'$ of $G_i$ such that $C_{X_i}(G_i, \mu') \prec C_{X_i}(G_i, \mu)$ and $C_{X_i}(G_i, \mu') \in FS(i)$, i.e. the $X_i$-characteristic of $\mu'$ is in $FS(i)$.

The following lemma can be derived directly from the definitions.

**Lemma 7.** *A full set of characteristics of vertex orderings (carvings) for $G_i$ is non-empty if and only if the cutwidth (carving-width) of $G_i$ is at most $k$. If some full set of characteristics of vertex orderings (carvings) for $G_i$ is non-empty, then any full set of characteristics of vertex orderings (carvings) for $G_i$ is non-empty.*

An important consequence of Lemma 7 is that the cutwidth (carving-width) of $G$ is at most $k$, if and only if any full set of characteristics of vertex orderings (carvings) for $G_r = G$ is non-empty.

In what follows, it remains to show how to compute a full set of characteristics of vertex orderings (carvings) at a node $i$ in $O(1)$ time, when a full set of characteristic of vertex orderings (carvings) for $G_{i-1}$ (for the children of $i$) is given. This will be demonstrated in the next two sections (section 4 for cutwidth and section 5 for carving-width) and will make it possible, given any pair of integers constants $k, w$, to construct an algorithm that given a graph and a nice path (tree) decomposition of $G$ of width at most $w$, to decide whether $G$ has cutwidth (carving-width) at most $k$.

# 4   Basic Subroutines for Cutwidth

We first give a full set of characteristics for the starting node of $X = [X_1, \ldots, r]$. Clearly, $G_1$ consists only of the unique vertex in $\{x\} = X_1$ and a full set of characteristics is $\{[x], [[0], [0]]\}$.

We will now consider the case where $X_i$ is an *introduce* node. The following procedure will appear useful.

**Procedure** $\mathsf{Ins}(G', u, S, \lambda, \mathbf{A}, j, m)$.
*Input:* A graph $G'$, a vertex $u \in V(G')$, a set $S \subseteq V(G') - \{u\}$, a $S$-characteristic $(\lambda, \mathbf{A})$ of some vertex ordering $l$ of $G = G'[V(G) - \{u\}]$, an integer $j, 0 \le j \le |\lambda|$, and an integer $m, 1 \le m \le |\mathbf{A}(j)|$.
*Output:* An $(S \cup \{u\})$-characteristic $(\lambda', \mathbf{A}')$ of some vertex ordering $l' = l[1, \ldots, j'] \oplus [u] \oplus l[j' + 1, \ldots, |l|]$ of $G'$ where $0 \le j' \le |l|$.
**1:** If $\lambda = [u_1, \ldots, u_\rho]$, then let $[u_{j_1}, \ldots, u_{j_\sigma}] = \lambda[N_G(u)]$.
**2:** (insertion of $u$) Set $\lambda' = \lambda[1, j] \oplus [u] \oplus \lambda[j + 1, \rho]$
    and $\mathbf{A}' = \mathbf{A}[0, j - 1] \oplus [\mathbf{A}(j)[1, m]] \oplus [\mathbf{A}(j)[m, |\mathbf{A}(j)|]] \oplus \mathbf{A}[j + 1, \rho]$.
**3:** (insertion of edges in $E_G(u)$) For $h = 1, \ldots, \sigma$, apply:
    **(i)** If $j_h \ge j$ then set $\mathbf{A}' \leftarrow \mathbf{A}'[0, j_h - 1] \oplus (\mathbf{A}'[j_h, j] + 1) \oplus \mathbf{A}'[j + 1, \rho + 1]$.
    **(ii)** If $j_h \ge j + 1$ then set $\mathbf{A}' \leftarrow \mathbf{A}'[0, j] \oplus (\mathbf{A}'[j + 1, j_h] + 1) \oplus \mathbf{A}'[j_h + 1, \rho + 1]$.
**4:** Output $(\lambda', \mathbf{A}')$.
We now give an algorithm that, for $i = 2, \ldots, |X|$, computes a full set of characteristics $FS(i)$ for $G_i$, given a full set of characteristics $FS(i - 1)$ for $G_{i-1}$.

**Algorithm** Introduce-Node
*Input:* A full set of characteristics $FS(i - 1)$ of vertex orderings for $G_{i-1}$.
*Output:* A full set of characteristics $FS(i)$ of vertex orderings for $G_i$.
**1:** Initialize $FS(i) = \emptyset$ and set $\rho = |X_{i-1}|$ and $\{u\} = X_i - X_{i-1}$.
**2:** For any $X_{i-1}$-characteristic $(\lambda, \mathbf{A}) \in FS(i - 1)$ apply step **3**.
**3:** For any $j = 0, \ldots, \rho$, apply step **4**.
**4:** for any $m = 1, \ldots, |\mathbf{A}(j)|$, apply step **5**.
**5:** Let $(\lambda', \mathbf{A}') = \mathsf{Ins}(G_i, u, X_{i-1}, \lambda, \mathbf{A}, j, m)$ and if $\max(\mathbf{A}') \le k$, then set $FS(i) \leftarrow FS(i) \cup \{(\lambda', \mathbf{A}')\}$.
**5:** Output $FS(i)$.

We will now consider the case where $X_i$ is a *forget* node. Given a full set of characteristics $FS(i - 1)$ for $X_{i-1}$, the following algorithm computes a full set of characteristics $FS(i)$ for $X_i$.

**Algorithm** Forget-Node
*Input:* A full set of characteristics $FS(i - 1)$ of vertex orderings for $G_{i-1}$.
*Output:* A full set of characteristics $FS(i)$ of vertex orderings for $G_i$.
**1:** Initialize $FS(i) = \emptyset$.
**2:** For any $(\lambda, \mathbf{A}) \in FS(i - 1)$ apply step **3**.

**3:** Apply the following 4 steps:
  (i) If $\lambda = [u_1, \ldots, u_\rho]$ then let $\{u_j\} = X_{i-1} - X_i$ and $[u_{j_1}, \ldots, u_{j_\sigma}] = \lambda[N_{G_i}(u_j)]$.
  (ii) $\lambda \leftarrow \lambda(1, j-1) \oplus l(j+1, \rho)$.
  (iii) $\mathbf{A} \leftarrow \mathbf{A}[0, j-2] \oplus [\tau(\mathbf{A}(j-1) \oplus \mathbf{A}(j))] \oplus \mathbf{A}[j+1, \rho]$.
  (iv) $FS(i) \leftarrow FS(i) \cup \{(\lambda, \mathbf{A})\}$.
**4:** Output $FS(i)$.

## 5   Basic Subroutines for Carving-Width

If $X_p$ is a *start* then, clearly, $V(G_p) = X_p = \{x, x'\}$ and
$FS(p) = \{((((\{t, t'\}, \{\{t, t'\}\}), \{(t, x), (t', x')\}), \{(\{t, t'\}, [|E(G[\{x, x'\}])|])\})\}$.

We will now consider the case where $X_p$ is an *introduce* node. Let $q$ be the unique child of $p$ in $U$. The following procedure will appear useful.

**Procedure** $\mathsf{Ins}(G', u, S, \gamma, \beta, e, m)$.
*Input:* A graph $G'$, a vertex $u \in V(G')$, a set $S \subseteq V(G') - \{u\}$, a $S$-characteristic $(\gamma, \beta)$ of some carving $c$ of $G = G'[V(G) - \{u\}]$ where $\gamma = (Y, \theta)$, an edge $e = \{t_{\text{left}}, t_{\text{right}}\} \in E(Y)$, and an integer $m, 1 \leq m \leq |\beta(e)|$.
*Output:* An $(S \cup \{u\})$-characteristic $(\gamma', \beta')$ $(\gamma' = (Y', \theta'))$ of some carving $c'$ of $G'$.
**1:** Let $\{t_1, \ldots, t_\sigma\} = \theta^{-1}(N_G(u))$.
**2:** (insertion of $u$) Set
$$Y' = (V(Y) \cup \{t_{\text{mid}}, t_{\text{new}}\}, E(Y)-$$
$$\{\{t_{\text{left}}, t_{\text{right}}\}\} \cup \{\{t_{\text{left}}, t_{\text{mid}}\}, \{t_{\text{right}}, t_{\text{mid}}\}, \{t_{\text{mid}}, t_{\text{new}}\}\}),$$
$$\theta' = \theta \cup \{(t_{\text{new}}, u)\}, \text{ and}$$
$$\beta' = \beta - \{(e, \beta(e))\}$$
$$\cup \{(\{t_{\text{left}}, t_{\text{mid}}\}, \beta(e)[1, m]), (\{t_{\text{right}}, t_{\text{mid}}\}, \beta(e)[m, |\beta(e)|]), (\{t_{\text{mid}}, t_{\text{new}}\}, [0])\}.$$
**3:** (insertion of edges in $E_G(u)$) For $h = 1, \ldots, \sigma$ and for any edge $f$ in the (unique) path of $Y'$ connecting $t_h$ and $t_{\text{new}}$ set $\beta'(f) \leftarrow \beta'(f) + 1$.
**4:** Output $(\gamma', \beta')$ (where $\gamma' = (Y', \theta')$).

We now give an algorithm that, if $X_p$ is an *introduce* node, computes a full set of characteristics $FS(p)$ for $G_p$, given a full set of characteristics $FS(q)$ for $G_q$ where $q$ is the (unique) child of $p$ in $U$.

**Algorithm** Introduce-Node
*Input:* A full set of characteristics $FS(q)$ of carvings for $G_q$.
*Output:* A full set of characteristics $FS(p)$ of carvings for $G_p$.
**1:** Initialize $FS(p) = \emptyset$ and set $\rho = |X_q|$ and $\{u\} = X_p - X_q$.
**2:** For any $X_q$-characteristic $(\gamma, \beta) \in FS(q)$ where $\gamma = (Y, \theta)$ apply step **3**.
**3:** For any edge $e \in E(Y)$ apply step **4**.
**4:** for any $m = 1, \ldots, |\beta(e)|$, apply step **5**.
**5:** Let $(\beta', \gamma') = \mathsf{Ins}(G_i, u, X_{i-1}, \beta, \gamma, e, m)$ where $\beta' = (Y', \theta')$ and
  if $\max\{\max(\beta'(e)) \mid e \in E(Y')\} \leq k$, then set $FS(p) \leftarrow FS(p) \cup \{(\beta', \gamma')\}$.
**6:** Output $FS(p)$.
  is

We will now consider the case where $X_p$ is a *forget* node and $q$ is the (unique) child of $p$ in $U$. Given a full set of characteristics $FS(q)$ for $X_q$, the following algorithm computes a full set of characteristics $FS(p)$ for $X_p$.

**Algorithm** Forget-Node
*Input:* A full set of characteristics of carvings $FS(q)$ for $G_q$.

*Output:* A full set of characteristics of carvings $FS(p)$ for $G_p$.
**1:** Initialize $FS(p) = \emptyset$.
**2:** For any $(\gamma, \beta) \in FS(q)$ where $\gamma = (Y, \theta)$ apply step **3**.
**3:** Apply the following 5 steps:
   (i) Let $\{t_1, \ldots, t_\sigma\} = \theta^{-1}(N_G(u))$. Let $t_{\text{del}} = \theta^{-1}(u)$, let $t_{\text{mid}}$ be the unique neighbor of $t_{\text{del}}$ in $Y$ and let $t_{\text{del}}, t_{\text{left}}, t_{\text{right}}$ be the neighbors of $t_{\text{mid}}$ in $Y$.
   (ii) Let $Y' = (V(Y) - \{t_{\text{del}}, t_{\text{mid}}\}, E(Y) - \{\{t_{\text{mid}}, t_{\text{del}}\}, \{t_{\text{mid}}, t_{\text{left}}\}, \{t_{\text{mid}}, t_{\text{right}}\}\} \cup \{\{t_{\text{left}}, t_{\text{right}}\}\})$,
   (iii) Let $\theta' = \theta - \{(t_{\text{del}}, u)\}$,
   (iv) Let $\beta' = \beta - \{(\{t_{\text{mid}}, t_{\text{new}}\} \; \beta(\{t_{\text{mid}}, t_{\text{new}}\})), (\{t_{\text{mid}}, t_{\text{left}}\}, \beta(\{t_{\text{mid}}, t_{\text{left}}\})),$
$(\{t_{\text{ned}}, t_{\text{right}}\}, \beta(\{t_{\text{mid}}, t_{\text{right}}\}))\} \cup \{(\{t_{\text{left}}, t_{\text{right}}\}, \tau(\beta(\{t_{\text{left}}, t_{\text{mid}}\}) \oplus \beta(\{t_{\text{mid}}, t_{\text{left}}\})))\}$
   (v) $FS(p) \leftarrow FS(p) \cup \{(\gamma', \beta')\}$.
**4:** Output $FS(p)$.

We will now consider the case where $X_p$ is a *join* node and $q_i, i = 1, 2$ are the two children of $p$ in $U$. We observe that $V(G_{q_1}) \cap V(G_{q_2}) = X_p$, $G_{q_1} \cup G_{q_2} = G_p$ and we may assume that $E(G_{q_1}) \cap E(G_{q_2}) = \emptyset$. Given a full set of characteristics $FS(q_1)$ for $X_{q_1}$ and a full set of characteristics $F_{q_2}$ for $X_{q_2}$, the following algorithm computes a full set of characteristics $FS(p)$ for $X_p$.

**Algorithm Join-Node**
*Input:* A full set of characteristics $FS(q_1)$ of carvings for $G_{q_1}$ and a full set of characteristics $FS(q_2)$ of carvings for $G_{q_2}$.
*Output:* A full set of characteristics $FS(p)$ of carvings for $G_p$.
**1:** Initialize $FS(p) = \emptyset$.
**2:** For any pair of $X_{q_i}$-characteristics $(\gamma_i, \beta_i) \in FS(q_i), i = 1, 2$, apply step (**3**).
**3:** For any isomorphic bijection $\phi : Y_1 \to Y_2$ where $\gamma_1 \equiv_\phi \gamma_2$ apply step (**4**).
**4:** For any $\beta' \in \beta_1 \otimes_\phi \beta_2$ apply step (**5**),
**5:** If $\max\{\max(\beta'(e)) \mid e \in E(Y_1)\} \leq k$, set $FS(p) \leftarrow FS(p) \cup \{(\gamma_1, \beta')\}$.
**6:** Output $FS(p)$.

# 6    Conclusions

Notice that, because of Lemma 6, both versions of the algorithms Introduce-node and Forget-node run in $O(1)$ time when $k$ and $w$ are fixed. The details of how to transform the decision algorithms to constructive are direct consequences of the machinery in the proofs of correctness of the given algorithms. We resume the results of sections 3–5 in the following.

**Theorem 1.** *For all $k, w \geq 1$ there exists an algorithm that, given a graph $G$ and a $m$-node path (tree) decomposition $X$ of $G$ with width at most $w$, computes whether the cutwidth (carving-width) of $G$ is at most $k$ and, if so, constructs a vertex ordering (carving) of $G$ with cutwidth (width) at most $k$ and that uses $O(V(G) + m)$ time.*

Lemmata 3, 4, Theorem 1, and the results in [2] and [4], yield our main result:

**Theorem 2.** *For all $k$, there exists an algorithm, that given a graph $G$, computes whether the cutwidth (carving-width) of $G$ is at most $k$, and if so, constructs a vertex ordering (carving) of $G$ with minimum cutwidth (width) in $O(|V(G)|)$ time.*

# References

1. K. R. Abrahamson and M. R. Fellows. Finite automata, bounded treewidth and well-quasiordering. In N. Robertson and P. Seymour, editors, *Proceedings of the AMS Summer Workshop on Graph Minors, Graph Structure Theory, Contemporary Mathematics vol. 147*, pages 539–564. American Mathematical Society, 1993.
2. H. Bodlaender and T. Kloks. Efficient and constructive algorithms for the pathwidth and treewidth of graphs. *J. Algorithms*, 21:358–402, 1996.
3. H. L. Bodlaender. Improved self-reduction algorithms for graphs with bounded treewidth. *Disc. Appl. Math.*, 54:101–115, 1994.
4. H. L. Bodlaender. A linear time algorithm for finding tree-decompositions of small treewidth. *SIAM Journal on Computing*, 25:1305–1317, 1996.
5. H. L. Bodlaender and D. M. Thilikos. Constructive linear time algorithms for branchwidth. In P. Degano, R. Gorrieri, and A. Marchetti-Spaccamela, editors, *Proceedings 24th International Colloquium on Automata, Languages, and Programming, ICALP'97*, pages 627–637. Springer-Verlag, Lecture Notes in Computer Science, Vol. 1256, 1997.
6. H. L. Bodlaender and D. M. Thilikos. Computing small search numbers in linear time. Technical Report Technical Report No. UU-CS-1998-05, Dept. of Computer Science, Utrecht University, 1998.
7. F. R. K. Chung. On the cutwidth and topological bandwidth of a tree. *SIAM J. Alg. Disc. Meth.*, 6:268–277, 1985.
8. F. R. K. Chung and P. D. Seymour. Graphs with small bandwidth and cutwidth. *Disc. Math.*, 75:113–119, 1989.
9. G. Even, J. Naor, S. Rao, and B. Schieber. Divide-and-conquer approximation algorithms via spreading metrics. In *Proc. 36th Symp. on Foundations of Computer Science (FOCS)*, pages 62–71, 1995.
10. M. R. Fellows and M. A. Langston. On well-partial-order theory and its application to combinatorial problems of VLSI design. *SIAM J. Disc. Meth.*, 5:117–126, 1992.
11. M. R. Fellows and M. A. Langston. On search, decision and the efficiency of polynomial-time algorithms. *J. Comp. Syst. Sc.*, 49:769–779, 1994.
12. M. R. Garey and D. S. Johnson. *Computers and Intractability, A Guide to the Theory of NP-Completeness*. W.H. Freeman and Company, New York, 1979.
13. S. Khuller, B. Raghavachari, and N. Young. Designing multi-commodity flow trees. *Inform. Proc. Letters*, 50:49–55, 1994.
14. E. Korach and N. Solel. Tree-width, path-width and cutwidth. *Disc. Appl. Math.*, 43:97–101, 1993.
15. F. S. Makedon, C. H. Papadimitriou, and I. H. Sudborough. Topological bandwidth. *SIAM J. Alg. Disc. Meth.*, 6:418–444, 1985.
16. F. S. Makedon and I. H. Sudborough. On minimizing width in linear layouts. *Disc. Appl. Math.*, 23:243–265, 1989.
17. B. Monien and I. H. Sudborough. Min cut is NP-complete for edge weighted trees. *Theor. Comp. Sc.*, 58:209–229, 1988.
18. N. Robertson and P. D. Seymour. Graph minors. XXIII. the Nash-Williams immersion conjecture. To appear.
19. N. Robertson and P. D. Seymour. Graph minors. XIII. The disjoint paths problem. *J. Comb. Theory Series B*, 63:65–110, 1995.
20. P. D. Seymour and R. Thomas. Call routing and the ratcatcher. *Combinatorica*, 14(2):217–241, 1994.
21. M. Yannakakis. A polynomial algorithm for the min-cut linear arrangement of trees. *J. ACM*, 32:950–988, 1985.

# Approximation Algorithms for the Maximum Power Consumption Problem on Combinatorial Circuits

Takao Asano[1], Magnús M. Halldórsson[2], Kazuo Iwama[3], and Takeshi Matsuda[4]

[1] Department of Information and System Engineering,
Chuo University, Bunkyo-ku, Tokyo 112-8551, Japan,
asano@ise.chuo-u.ac.jp
[2] Science Institute, University of Iceland, Reykjavik, Iceland,
mmh@hi.is
[3,4] School of Informatics, Kyoto University, Kyoto 606-8501, Japan,
{iwama,matsuda}@kuis.kyoto-u.ac.jp

**Abstract.** The maximum power consumption problem on combinatorial circuits is the problem of estimating the maximum power consumption of a given combinatorial circuit. It is easy to see that this problem for general circuits is hard to approximate within a factor of $m^{1-\epsilon}$, where $m$ is the number of gates in an input circuit and $\epsilon$ is any positive (small) constant. In this paper, we consider restricted circuits, namely, those consisting of only one level of AND/OR gates. Then the problem becomes a kind of MAX 2SAT where each variable takes one of four values, $f$, $t$, $d$ and $u$. This problem is NP-hard and the main objective of this paper is to give approximation algorithms. We consider two cases, the case that positive and negative appearances of each variable are well balanced and the general case. For the first case, we achieve an approximation ratio of $\frac{2(3k-\ell)}{\alpha(3k+\ell)}$ where $\alpha = 0.87856$ and $\frac{k}{\ell}$ is the maximum ratio of the number of positive appearances over the number of negative appearances of each variable. For the general case, we obtain an approximation ratio of 1.7. Both results involve deep, systematic analyses.

## 1   Introduction

Estimating maximum power consumption for CMOS logic circuits is important in designing low power circuits, although it is quite difficult since the amount of power consumed by the circuits depend on many factors such as input signals, circuit topologies, clock frequencies, delays in switching times, etc. Several approaches have been proposed to cope with these difficulties [1,2,5]. For example, Devadas, Keutzer and White [1] transformed this problem into a MAX

---

[1,3] Supported in part by Grant in Aid for Scientific Research of the Ministry of Education, Science, Sports and Culture of Japan.
[2] A part of this work was done while this author was staying in School of Informatics, Kyoto University.

D.T. Lee and S.-H. Teng (Eds.): ISAAC 2000, LNCS 1969, pp. 204–215, 2000.

SAT and used a branch-and-bound algorithm to solve it. They also showed some experimental results.

In this paper we view this problem as a simple combinatorial problem. It is assumed that power consumption occurs only in gates, that is, a unit power is consumed at a gate when its output changes from true to false or vice versa. Other kinds of power consumption, due to propagation delays, hazardous signals, wire links etc., are not considered. It should be noted that these secondary forms of power consumption are much less than the primary power consumption at logic gates, especially in CMOS circuits. Thus our problem is to obtain, for a given combinatorial circuit $X$, a pair of true/false input vectors $A_1$ and $A_2$ such that the input change from $A_1$ to $A_2$ causes the maximum number of output-changing gates.

Unfortunately, this problem is still hard. Let $m$ be the total number of gates in the given circuit. Then the problem is hard to approximate within a factor of $m^{1-\epsilon}$ for any small constant $\epsilon > 0$ [4]. For this reason, we focus our attention on restricted circuits consisting of only one level of AND/OR gates (Fig. 1) in this paper. Note that gates of the second level or higher can consume power only when the first-level gates do so. Also, the number of first-level gates can be as many as a half of all gates if the circuit is tree-like. Thus, the gap between the restricted and the general problems is smaller than it may appear.

It turns out that our problem can be formulated as a kind of MAX 2SAT problem by introducing four logic values $f$, $t$, $d$ and $u$ and it is NP-hard [4]. Thus, the objective of this paper is to give approximation algorithms and our main results include (i) a $\frac{2(3k-\ell)}{\alpha(3k+\ell)}$-approximation algorithm for "balanced" instances where $\alpha = 0.87856$, $k_i$ ($\ell_i$) is the number of total appearances of literal $x_i$ ($\bar{x}_i$, the negation of $x_i$) and $\frac{k}{\ell} = \max_{i=1}^{n}\{\frac{k_i}{\ell_i}\}$ (we can assume $k_i \geq \ell_i$), and (ii) a 1.7-approximation algorithm for general instances. Our analysis is described in a systematic way, and may be useful for obtaining further improvements.

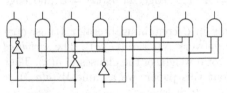

**Fig. 1.** A circuit consisting of only one level of AND gates

**Table 1.** Value of a clause $c = (x_i, x_{i'})$

| $x_i$ | $x_{i'}$ | | | |
|---|---|---|---|---|
| | $f$ | $t$ | $d$ | $u$ |
| $f$ | 0 | 0 | 0 | 0 |
| $t$ | 0 | 0 | 1 | 1 |
| $d$ | 0 | 1 | 1 | 0 |
| $u$ | 0 | 1 | 0 | 1 |

## 2 Problem Formulation

Suppose that we are given a one-level circuit $X$ as shown in Fig. 1. Then our task is to find a pair $A_1$ and $A_2$ of true/false input vectors for $X$ such that changing from $A_1$ to $A_2$ causes output-value changes of as many AND gates as possible. We do not count the value changes of NOT gates following practice. Also, we can assume that there are no OR gates, since they can transformed into AND gates using De Morgan's theorem. One can see that the pair of input vectors can be combined into a single input vector by using four values, $f$, $t$, $d$ and $u$. Here $f$ ($t$, $d$ and $u$, respectively) corresponds to the input change from false to false (true to true, true to false and false to true, respectively).

The problem now is a constraint satisfaction problem, a variation of MAX 2SAT. An instance of the problem is defined by $(\mathcal{C}, w)$, where $\mathcal{C}$ is a set of clauses such that each clause $c \in \mathcal{C}$ is a form of unordered pair $(x_i, x_{i'})$ with a positive weight $w(c)$. Let $X = \{x_1, \ldots, x_n\}$ be the set of variables in the clauses of $\mathcal{C}$. A *literal* is a variable $x \in X$ or its negation $\bar{x}$. For simplicity, we assume $x_{n+i} = \bar{x}_i$ ($x_i = \bar{x}_{n+i}$). Thus, $\bar{X} = \{\bar{x} \mid x \in X\} = \{x_{n+1}, \ldots, x_{2n}\}$ and $X \cup \bar{X} = \{x_1, \ldots, x_{2n}\}$. Each literal can take a value in $\{f, t, d, u\}$. If $x_i = f$, then $\bar{x}_i = t$ (and if $x_i = t$ then $\bar{x}_i = f$). Similarly, if $x_i = d$ then $\bar{x}_i = u$ (and if $x_i = u$ then $\bar{x}_i = d$).

A clause $c = (x_i, x_{i'})$ is satisfied if $x_i = t$ and $x_{i'} \in \{d, u\}$ (or symmetrically, $x_{i'} = t$ and $x_i \in \{d, u\}$) or if $x_i = x_{i'}$ and $x_{i'} \in \{d, u\}$. Otherwise, the clause $(x_i, x_{i'})$ is not satisfied.

Table 1 shows the value of a clause $(x_i, x_{i'})$ where 1 represents that $(x_i, x_{i'})$ is satisfied or the gate where input is $(x_i, x_{i'})$ consumes power. For example, if $x_i = t$ (true to true) and $x_{i'} = d$ (true to false), then its output should be $d$ (true to false). Thus, a clause $c = (x_i, x_{i'})$ is a function $c = c(\boldsymbol{x})$ on $(f, t, d, u)$-assignment $\boldsymbol{x}$. The *value* $F_{\mathcal{C}}(\boldsymbol{x}) = \sum_{c \in \mathcal{C}} w(c)c(\boldsymbol{x})$ is the sum of the weights of the clauses in $\mathcal{C}$ satisfied by $\boldsymbol{x}$. The maximum power consumption problem is to find an optimal $(f, t, d, u)$-assignment, i.e., an $(f, t, d, u)$-assignment of maximum value.

## 2.1    Notation

An instance $(\mathcal{C}, w)$ of the maximum power consumption problem is a network $N(\mathcal{C}) = (G, w)$ with vertex set $V(G) = X \cup \bar{X}$, edge set $E(G) = \mathcal{C}$ and edge weight function $w$ (Fig. 2(a)).

We denote by $\delta(x)$ the set of clauses in $\mathcal{C}$ containing literal $x$ (thus, $\delta(x)$ is the set of edges incident to $x$ in the network $N(\mathcal{C}) = (G, w)$). The *weighted degree* of $x$, denoted by $W(\delta(x))$, is the total weight of the clauses in $\delta(x)$. That is, $W(\delta(x)) = \sum_{e \in \delta(x)} w(e)$. Throughout this paper, we assume $W(\delta(x_i)) \geq W(\delta(x_{i+n}))$ for literals $x_i, x_{i+n} = \bar{x}_i$ ($i = 1, 2, \ldots, n$).

For an $(f, t, d, u)$-assignment $\boldsymbol{x}$ to $N(\mathcal{C})$, we introduce the following definitions. Let $X_a$ denote the set of variables assigned the value $a$ in $\boldsymbol{x}$, for each of the values $a = f, t, d, u$,

$$X_a = X_a(\boldsymbol{x}) = \{x_i \in X \cup \bar{X} \mid x_i = a\} \quad (a = f, t, d, u).$$

Let $E_{ab}$ denote the set of clauses where one variable is assigned $a$ in $\boldsymbol{x}$ and the other assigned $b$,

$$E_{ab} = E_{ab}(\boldsymbol{x}) = \{(x_i, x_{i'}) \in \mathcal{C} \mid x_i = a, x_{i'} = b\}, \qquad (a, b = f, t, d, u),$$

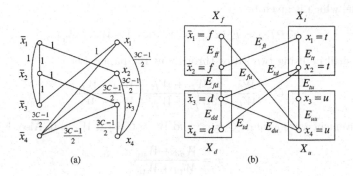

**Fig. 2.** (a) Network $N(\mathcal{C}) = (G, w)$ for an instance $(\mathcal{C}, w)$ with $\mathcal{C} = \mathcal{C}_1 \cup \mathcal{C}_2 \cup \mathcal{C}_3$ such that $\mathcal{C}_1 = \{(\bar{x}_1, \bar{x}_2), (\bar{x}_2, \bar{x}_3), (\bar{x}_3, \bar{x}_1)\}$, $\mathcal{C}_2 = \{(\bar{x}_1, x_2), (\bar{x}_2, x_3), (\bar{x}_3, x_1)\}$, $\mathcal{C}_3 = \{(x_1, \bar{x}_4), (x_2, \bar{x}_4), (x_3, \bar{x}_4), (x_1, x_4), (x_2, x_4), (x_3, x_4)\}$ and $w(e) = 1$ for $e \in \mathcal{C}_1 \cup \mathcal{C}_2$, $w(e) = \frac{3C-1}{2}$ for $e \in \mathcal{C}_3$. (b) Clauses $E_{ab}(\boldsymbol{x}) = \{(x_i, x_{i'}) \in \mathcal{C} \mid x_i = a, x_{i'} = b\}$ $(a, b = f, t, d, u)(E_{ab}(\boldsymbol{x})$ is denoted by $E_{ab}$).

and let $W_{ab}$ denote the sum of the weights of those clauses

$$W_{ab} = W_{ab}(\boldsymbol{x}) = \sum_{e \in E_{ab}(\boldsymbol{x})} w(e) \qquad (a, b = f, t, d, u).$$

Let $\boldsymbol{x}^*$ denote the optimal $(f, t, d, u)$-assignment to $N(\mathcal{C})$ and let $OPT$ denote its value. We shall use the notation $W_{ab}$ primarily for the the optimal assignment $\boldsymbol{x}^*$, Thus, we shall drop the indicator for improved readability, e.g. $W_{ud} = W_{ud}(\boldsymbol{x}^*)$ etc. Note that $E_{ab} = E_{ba}$ and $W_{ab} = W_{ba}$.

Define $W_a$ as the sum over all vertices assigned $a$ in $\boldsymbol{x}^*$ of the weights of the incident clauses.

$$W_a = W_a(\boldsymbol{x}^*) = \sum_{x \in X_a(\boldsymbol{x}^*)} W(\delta(x)) = \sum_{x \in X_a(\boldsymbol{x}^*)} \sum_{e \in \delta(x)} w(e) \qquad (a = f, t, d, u).$$

This differs from the sum of weights of clauses with at least one variable assigned $a$, in that if both variables are assigned $a$, the clause is counted twice. In particular,

$$W_t = 2W_{tt} + W_{tf} + W_{td} + W_{tu},$$

and

$$W_f = 2W_{ff} + W_{ft} + W_{fd} + W_{fu},$$

As defined in Table 1, we have

$$OPT = F_{\mathcal{C}}(\boldsymbol{x}^*) = W_{td} + W_{tu} + W_{dd} + W_{uu}. \tag{1}$$

If no $f$ (and thus no $t$) is used in an $(f, t, d, u)$-assignment $\boldsymbol{x}$, we call it a $(d, u)$-assignment. Let $\boldsymbol{x}^*_{du}$ denote an optimal $(d, u)$-assignment, and let $OPT_{du}$ denote its value, which is given by

$$OPT_{du} = F_C(\boldsymbol{x}_{du}^*) = W_{dd}(\boldsymbol{x}_{du}^*) + W_{uu}(\boldsymbol{x}_{du}^*).$$

We shall be using two ratios throughout the paper. Let

$$C = \frac{W_t}{W_f} = \frac{2W_{tt} + W_{ft} + W_{td} + W_{tu}}{2W_{ff} + W_{ft} + W_{fd} + W_{fu}}. \tag{2}$$

For convenience, we assume $C = \infty$ and $W_t = CW_f$ if $W_f = 0$. Also, let

$$r = \frac{W_{dd} + W_{uu}}{W_{td} + W_{tu}}. \tag{3}$$

Let $W = \sum_{e \in E(G)} w(e)$ denote the total sum of the clause weights. That is,

$$W = W_{tt} + W_{ff} + W_{dd} + W_{uu} + W_{tf} + W_{tu} + W_{td} + W_{fu} + W_{fd} + W_{ud}. \tag{4}$$

Let $\alpha = 0.87856$ be the (inverse) ratio obtained by Goemans and Williamson [3] on MAX 2SAT.

## 3    Bounds on Balanced Instances

In this section, we will give bounds on balanced intances where $\frac{k}{\ell}$, the maximum ratio of the number of positive appearances over the number of negative appearances of each variable, is small. These bounds leads to a $\frac{2(3k-\ell)}{\alpha(3k+\ell)}$-approximation algorithm for balanced instances.

From the optimal $(f, t, d, u)$-assignment $\boldsymbol{x}^*$, we can obtain $(d, u)$-assignments $\boldsymbol{x}_{du}^{t \to d}$ and $\boldsymbol{x}_{du}^{t \to u}$ as follows. $\boldsymbol{x}_{du}^{t \to d}$ is obtained by re-assigning $d$ to each literal assigned $t$ (and thus, re-assigning $u$ to each literal assigned $f$). Similarly, $\boldsymbol{x}_{du}^{t \to u}$ is obtained by re-assigning $u$ to each literal assigned $t$ (and thus, re-assigning $d$ to each literal assigned $f$). Then clearly

$$F_C(\boldsymbol{x}_{du}^{t \to d}) = W_{fu} + W_{ff} + W_{td} + W_{tt} + W_{dd} + W_{uu},$$
$$F_C(\boldsymbol{x}_{du}^{t \to u}) = W_{fd} + W_{ff} + W_{tu} + W_{tt} + W_{dd} + W_{uu}.$$

Thus, we can bound the value of the optimal $(d, u)$-assignment by

$$OPT_{du} \geq \frac{F_C(\boldsymbol{x}_{du}^{t \to d}) + F_C(\boldsymbol{x}_{du}^{t \to u})}{2}$$

$$= W_{ff} + W_{tt} + W_{dd} + W_{uu} + \frac{W_{fd} + W_{fu} + W_{td} + W_{tu}}{2}$$

$$\geq \frac{W_{td} + W_{tu}}{2} + W_{dd} + W_{du} + \frac{W_f - W_{ft}}{2}$$

by the definition of $W_f$. By (1), this implies

$$0 \leq OPT - OPT_{du} \leq \frac{W_{td} + W_{tu}}{2} - \frac{W_f - W_{ft}}{2}. \tag{5}$$

On the other hand, fixing every literal assigned $u$ or $d$ in the optimal $(f, t, d, u)$-assignment $\boldsymbol{x}^*$, and randomly assigning $u$ or $d$ with equal probability $(1/2)$ to the other remaining literals (assigned $f$ or $t$ in $\boldsymbol{x}^*$), we obtain a random $(d, u)$-assignment $\boldsymbol{x}_{du}^r$. The expected value $F_C(\boldsymbol{x}_{du}^r)$ of $\boldsymbol{x}_{du}^r$ is

$$W_{dd} + W_{uu} + \frac{W_{ff} + W_{ft} + W_{tt} + W_{fd} + W_{fu} + W_{td} + W_{tu}}{2}$$

$$\geq W_{dd} + W_{uu} + \frac{W_{td} + W_{tu}}{2} + \frac{W_f - W_{ff}}{2}.$$

Thus, there exists a $(d, u)$-assignment $\boldsymbol{x}_{du}$ with value at least $F_C(\boldsymbol{x}_{du}^r)$, and $OPT - OPT_{du}$ is at most $\frac{W_{td} + W_{tu}}{2} - \frac{W_f - W_{ff}}{2}$.

Combined, we have that

$$OPT - OPT_{du} \leq \frac{W_{td} + W_{tu} - W_f + \min\{W_{ft}, W_{ff}\}}{2} \tag{6}$$

Now we are ready to obtain the following theorem, which plays a central role in the analysis of our algorithms later.

**Theorem 1.** *Let $\boldsymbol{x}^*$, $OPT$, $OPT_{du}$, $C$, and $r$ be as previously defined. Then $C \geq 1$ and*

$$\frac{OPT_{du}}{OPT} \geq 1 - \frac{3(C - 1)}{2(1 + r)(3C - 1)} \geq \frac{3C + 1}{2(3C - 1)}. \tag{7}$$

*Furthermore, there are infinitely many instances attaining $\frac{OPT_{du}}{OPT} = \frac{3C+1}{2(3C-1)}$.*

**Proof.** By (5), $W_f \leq W_{td} + W_{tu} + W_{ft} \leq W_t$, thus $C \geq 1$.

Now, observe that

$$W_f = \frac{2}{3C - 1}W_t + \frac{C - 1}{3C - 1}W_f$$

$$\geq \frac{2}{3C - 1}(W_{tu} + W_{td} + W_{ft}) + \frac{C - 1}{3C - 1}(2W_{ff} + W_{ft})$$

$$= \frac{2}{3C - 1}(W_{tu} + W_{td}) + \frac{(C + 1)W_{ft} + 2(C - 1)W_{ff}}{3C - 1}$$

$$\geq \frac{2}{3C - 1}(W_{tu} + W_{td}) + \min\{W_{ft}, W_{ff}\}.$$

Thus, using (1), (6) and (3),

$$OPT - OPT_{du} \leq \frac{1}{2}(W_{td} + W_{tu})(1 - \frac{2}{3C - 1})$$

$$= \frac{1}{2}(W_{td} + W_{tu})\frac{3C - 3}{3C - 1} = \frac{1}{2}\left(\frac{OPT}{1 + r}\right)\frac{3C - 3}{3C - 1}.$$

We now have that

$$\frac{OPT_{du}}{OPT} = 1 - \frac{OPT - OPT_{du}}{OPT} \geq 1 - \frac{1}{1 + r} \cdot \frac{3C - 3}{2(3C - 1)}. \tag{8}$$

The right hand side of (8) is increasing with $r \geq 0$, with minimum at $r = 0$. Hence, (7) follows, as desired.

Consider an instance $(\mathcal{C}, w)$ with $\mathcal{C} = \mathcal{C}_1 \cup \mathcal{C}_2 \cup \mathcal{C}_3$ such that

$$\mathcal{C}_1 = \{(\bar{x}_i, \bar{x}_{i+1}) \mid i = 1, 2, ..., n - 2\} \cup \{(\bar{x}_{n-1}, \bar{x}_1)\},$$
$$\mathcal{C}_2 = \{(\bar{x}_i, x_{i+1}) \mid i = 1, 2, ..., n - 2\} \cup \{(\bar{x}_{n-1}, x_1)\},$$
$$\mathcal{C}_3 = \{(x_i, \bar{x}_n) \mid i = 1, 2, ..., n - 1\} \cup \{(x_i, x_n) \mid i = 1, 2, ..., n - 1\},$$

$$w(e) = \begin{cases} 1 & \text{if } e \in \mathcal{C}_1 \cup \mathcal{C}_2 \\ \frac{3C-1}{2} & \text{if } e \in \mathcal{C}_3 \end{cases}$$

(Fig. 2(a) where $n = 4$). It is easy to observe that $\boldsymbol{x}$ with $x_i = t$ ($\bar{x}_i = f$) ($i = 1, 2, ..., n - 1$), $x_n = u$ ($\bar{x}_n = d$) is an optimal $(f, t, d, u)$-assignment with value $OPT = (3C-1)(n-1)$ and that $\boldsymbol{x}$ with $x_i = u$ ($\bar{x}_i = d$) ($i = 1, 2, ..., n$) is an optimal $(d, u)$-assignment with value $OPT_{du} = \frac{(3C-1)(n-1)}{2} + n - 1 = \frac{(3C+1)(n-1)}{2}$. Thus, $\frac{OPT_{du}}{OPT} = \frac{3C+1}{2(3C-1)}$. □

**Corollary 1.** *Let $\mathcal{C}$ be an instance of the (unweighted) maximum power consumption problem and let $k_i$ ($\ell_i$) be the number of total appearences of literal $x_i$ ($\bar{x}_i$, the negation of $x_i$) in $\mathcal{C}$. We can assume, without loss of generality, $k_i \geq \ell_i$. Let $\frac{k}{\ell} = \max_{i=1}^{n}\{\frac{k_i}{\ell_i}\}$. Then $\frac{OPT_{du}}{OPT} \geq \frac{3k+\ell}{2(3k-\ell)}$.*

**Proof.** Since $\frac{|\delta(x)|}{|\delta(\bar{x})|} \leq \frac{k}{\ell}$ for any literal $x \in X = \{x_1...., x_n\}$ ($|\delta(x)| = W(\delta(x))$), we have

$$C = \frac{W_t}{W_f} = \frac{\sum_{x \in X_t(\boldsymbol{x}^*)} |\delta(x)|}{\sum_{x \in X_f(\boldsymbol{x}^*)} |\delta(x)|} = \frac{\sum_{x \in X_t(\boldsymbol{x}^*)} |\delta(x)|}{\sum_{x \in X_t(\boldsymbol{x}^*)} |\delta(\bar{x})|} \leq \frac{k}{\ell}$$

by (2) and

$$\frac{OPT_{du}}{OPT} \geq \frac{3C+1}{2(3C-1)} \geq \frac{3k+\ell}{2(3k-\ell)}$$

(note that $\frac{3C+1}{2(3C-1)} = \frac{1}{2} + \frac{1}{3C-1}$ is decreasing with $C \geq 1$). □

Theorem 1 and Corollary 1 suggest that an algorithm for finding optimal $(d, u)$-assignments can be used as an approximation algorithm for finding optimal $(f, t, d, u)$-assignments. For example, if $k_i = \ell_i$ for each $i = 1, 2, ..., n$, then $k = \ell$ and an optimal $(d, u)$-assignment is an optimal $(f, t, d, u)$-assignment by Corollary 1. However, the problem of finding an optimal $(d, u)$-assignment is also difficult and approximation algorithms are known [4].

One algorithm uses a random $(d, u)$-assignment $\boldsymbol{x}^r$ which assigns independently $d$ or $u$ to each variable with probability $1/2$. Since a clause $c = (x_i, x_{i'})$ is satisfied if and only if $x_i = x_{i'} = d$ or $x_i = x_{i'} = u$, the clause $c = (x_i, x_{i'})$ is satisfied with probability $c(\boldsymbol{x}^r) = 1/2$. Thus, the expected value is $F_{\mathcal{C}}(\boldsymbol{x}^r) = \sum_{c \in \mathcal{C}} w(c)c(\boldsymbol{x}^r) = \sum_{c \in \mathcal{C}} w(c)/2 = \frac{W}{2}$. This random assignment can be derandomized using the method of conditional probability [6].

Another algorithm uses semidefinite programming approach which was proposed for MAX 2SAT by Goemans-Williamson [3]. This algorithm obtains a $(d, u)$-assignment $\boldsymbol{x}_{du}$ with value at least $\alpha OPT_{du}$, where $\alpha = 0.87856$.

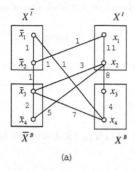 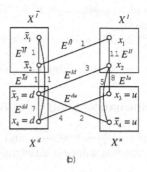

(a)                          (b)

**Fig. 3.** (a) Example of an instance $(\mathcal{C}, w)$ with $C_\theta = 6$. (b) Example of an assignment of $\{d, u\}$ to literals in $X^B \cup \bar{X}^B$ ($E^{\bar{I}u} = E^{uu} = \emptyset$).

## 4 Algorithm for General Instances

For a given instance $(\mathcal{C}, w)$, consider a threshold $C_\theta \geq 1$ (which will be fixed later). A variable $x_i$ is called an *imbalanced variable* (for short, IB-variable) if

$$W(\delta(x_i)) \geq C_\theta W(\delta(\bar{x}_i)) \tag{9}$$

(we assume $W(\delta(x_i)) \geq W(\delta(x_{i+n}))$ for $i = 1, 2, ..., n$, as described before). Let $X^I$ be the set of IB-variables and $X^{\bar{I}} = \bar{X}^I$ be the set of negations of IB-variables. Note that $X^I \subseteq X = \{x_1, ..., x_n\}$ and $X^{\bar{I}} \subseteq \bar{X} = \{x_{n+1}, ..., x_{2n}\}$. Let $X^B = X - X^I$ ($\bar{X}^B = \bar{X} - X^{\bar{I}}$). Let $(\mathcal{C}^B, w^B)$ the subinstance obtained from $(\mathcal{C}, w)$, where $\mathcal{C}^B$ is the set of clauses in $\mathcal{C}$ consisting of both literals in $X^B \cup \bar{X}^B$ and $w^B(e) = w(e)$ for $e \in \mathcal{C}^B$ (Fig. 3). Now we are ready to present our algorithm.

**Algorithm A** for a general instance $(\mathcal{C}, w)$
1. Given a threshold $C_\theta$, compute $X^I$, $X^{\bar{I}}$, $X^B = X - X^I$ and $\bar{X}^B = \bar{X} - X^{\bar{I}}$.
2. For each $x \in X^B$, set $x := u$ with probability $1/2$ and $x := d$ with probability $1/2$. Let $\boldsymbol{x}^{BR}$ be the resulting assignment. Note that $\boldsymbol{x}^{BR}$ is a random $(d, u)$-assignment for $(\mathcal{C}^B, w^B)$. Let $\boldsymbol{x}^{Br}$ be a $(d, u)$-assignment for $(\mathcal{C}^B, w^B)$ with value at least the expected value of $\boldsymbol{x}^{BR}$ obtained by derandomization.
3. For each $x \in X^I$ ($\bar{x} \in X^{\bar{I}}$), set $x := t$ ($\bar{x} := f$) with probability $\frac{1}{3} - \lambda$, $x := d$ ($\bar{x} := u$) with probability $\frac{1}{3} + \frac{\lambda}{2}$, and $x := u$ ($\bar{x} := d$) with probability $\frac{1}{3} + \frac{\lambda}{2}$ ($\lambda$ is a parameter with $-\frac{2}{3} \leq \lambda \leq \frac{1}{3}$ and will be fixed later). Let $\boldsymbol{x}^{IR}$ be the resulting assignment. Let $\boldsymbol{x}^{Ir}$ be an $(f, t, d, u)$-assignment with value at least the expected value of $\boldsymbol{x}^{IR}$ obtained by derandomization.
4. Set $x := d$ for each $x \in X^I$ ($\bar{x} := u$ for $\bar{x} \in X^{\bar{I}}$) and let $\boldsymbol{x}^{Id}$ be the resulting assignment. Similarly, set $x := u$ for each $x \in X^I$ ($\bar{x} := d$ for $\bar{x} \in X^{\bar{I}}$) and let $\boldsymbol{x}^{Iu}$ be the resulting assignment.
5. Find a random $(d, u)$-assignment $\boldsymbol{x}^R$ for $(\mathcal{C}, w)$ by setting $x := u$ with probability $1/2$ and $x := d$ with probability $1/2$. Let $\boldsymbol{x}^r$ be a $(d, u)$-assignment with value at least the expected value of $\boldsymbol{x}^R$ obtained by derandomization.

6. Find a $(d, u)$-assignment $x^s$ for $(C, w)$ based on the semidefinite programming relaxation.
7. Let $x^{ar}$ be the assignment for $(C, w)$ obtained by combining $x^{Ia}$ and $x^{Br}$ $(a = r, d, u)$.
8. Choose $x^A$ with maximum value among $x^{rr}$, $x^{dr}$, $x^{ur}$, $x^r$, and $x^s$.

## 4.1  Performance Analysis of Algorithm A

Since $F_C(x^r) = \frac{W}{2} = \frac{\sum_{e \in C} w(e)}{2}$ and $F_C(x^s) \geq \alpha OPT_{du}$ as described before, our algorithm yields a solution satisfying

$$F_C(x^A) \geq \max\{\frac{W}{2}, \alpha OPT_{du}\}, \tag{10}$$

where $\alpha = 0.87856$.

In this section we will give another lower bound on $F_C(x^A)$ in Theorem 2 and, using these bounds, we show that Algorithm A described above yields a 1.7-approximation.

**Theorem 2.** Let $C$ and $r$ be as defined in (2) and (3) and let $C_\theta$ satisfy $C > C_\theta > 1$. Then

$$F_C(x^A) \geq \frac{1}{2}W + \frac{2(C_\theta - 1)}{16 + 3(C_\theta - 1)^2}\left(\frac{C - C_\theta}{C}\right)\frac{OPT}{1 + r}. \tag{11}$$

Before giving a proof of this theorem, we prove our main result, namely that Algorithm A is a 1.7-approximation algorithm, using Theorems 1 and 2 and (10). In order to use (11), we need to bound $C$ and $1 + r$, which we do in terms of parameters representing the size of the optimal solution and the quality of our solution.

Let $\delta$ be such that

$$OPT = (1 - \frac{\delta}{2})W. \tag{12}$$

This gives $0 \leq \delta \leq 1$ and that by (4)

$$\frac{W_f}{2} \leq W_{ff} + W_{ft} + W_{fd} + W_{fu} \leq W - OPT = \frac{\delta}{2}W.$$

Thus,

$$OPT = (1 + r)(W_{td} + W_{tu}) \leq (1 + r)W_t = (1 + r)CW_f \leq \delta(1 + r)CW. \tag{13}$$

Combining (12) and (13),

$$1 - \frac{\delta}{2} \leq \delta(1 + r)C. \tag{14}$$

Assume, for the sake of a contradiction, that

$$OPT = (2 - \epsilon)F_C(x^A) \tag{15}$$

for some $\epsilon > 0$. Namely, the performance ratio of our algorithm is $2 - \epsilon$. By (10), $\delta \le \epsilon$ (but it can be expected to be less). Using (10), (15), and Theorem 1, we have

$$\frac{1}{2-\epsilon} \ge \frac{\alpha OPT_{ud}}{OPT} \ge \alpha \left(1 - \frac{3(C-1)}{2(1+r)(3C-1)}\right). \tag{16}$$

This gives

$$1 \le 1 + r \le \frac{3(C-1)}{2(3C-1)(1 - \frac{1}{\alpha(2-\epsilon)})} \tag{17}$$

since $r \ge 0$ and $\alpha - \frac{1}{2-\epsilon} > 0$.

If $C \ne \infty$, then by (14) and (17),

$$\frac{1 - \frac{\delta}{2}}{\delta C} \le 1 + r \le \frac{3(C-1)}{2(3C-1)(1 - \frac{1}{\alpha(2-\epsilon)})}. \tag{18}$$

Let $C_{\epsilon,\delta}$ be the value attaining equality in

$$\frac{C(3C-3)}{3C-1} \ge \frac{2(1 - \delta/2)(1 - 1/\alpha(2-\epsilon))}{\delta}. \tag{19}$$

Then, $C \ge C_{\epsilon,\delta}$, since $C \ge 1$, and $C(3C-3)/(3C-1) = C - \frac{2C}{3C-1}$ is increasing with $C$. If $C = \infty$ (i.e., $W_f = 0$), then, by (17), we have $1 + r < \frac{1}{2(1 - \frac{1}{\alpha(2-\epsilon)})}$. Then the inequality $\frac{2(3C-1)(1 - \frac{1}{\alpha(2-\epsilon)})}{3(C-1)} \le \frac{1}{1+r}$ from (18) holds also when $C = \infty$. By (11), we have

$$F_C(\boldsymbol{x}^A) \ge \frac{1}{2}W + \frac{4(C_\theta - 1)}{3(16 + 3(C_\theta - 1)^2)} \frac{(C - C_\theta)(3C - 1)(1 - \frac{1}{\alpha(2-\epsilon)})}{C(C-1)} OPT.$$

Furthermore, $\frac{(C-C_\theta)(3C-1)}{C(C-1)} = 3 - \frac{C_\theta}{C} - \frac{2(C_\theta - 1)}{C-1}$ is increasing with $C \ge C_{\epsilon,\delta}$. Thus, we have

$$F_C(\boldsymbol{x}^A) \ge \left[\frac{1}{2-\delta} + \frac{4(C_\theta - 1)}{3(16 + 3(C_\theta - 1)^2)} \frac{(C_{\epsilon,\delta} - C_\theta)(3C_{\epsilon,\delta} - 1)(1 - \frac{1}{\alpha(2-\epsilon)})}{C_{\epsilon,\delta}(C_{\epsilon,\delta} - 1)}\right] OPT. \tag{20}$$

The performance ratio of Algorithm A is then at most the ratio of $OPT/F_C(\boldsymbol{x}^A)$ given by (20). This is a ratio $\rho = \rho(\epsilon, \delta, C_\theta)$ that is parameterized by $\epsilon$, $\delta$, and $C_\theta$, where $C_\theta$ must satisfy $C_\theta \le C_{\epsilon,\delta}$.

We set $\epsilon = 0.3$. Thus, $\delta \le 0.3$. For $\delta$ in the range $[0.14, 0.3]$, we set $C_\theta = 2.1$. $C_{\epsilon,\delta}$ is monotone decreasing with $\delta$, with a minimum of $2.65 \ge C_\theta$ when $\delta = 0.3$. In the given range, the ratio $\rho$ is also monotone decreasing with $\delta$, with maximum of $1.69978$ at $\delta = 0.14$.

When $\delta < 0.14$, we set $C_\theta = 2.6$. In the given range, the performance ratio is monotone increasing with $\delta$, with maximum of $1.69903$ when $\delta = 0.14$. Thus, in either case, the performance ratio is less than $1.7$. This contradicts the assumption of (15).

Thus, if we choose the better solution of two solutions $\boldsymbol{x}_1^A$ and $\boldsymbol{x}_2^A$ which are obtained by setting $C_\theta := 2.1$ and $C_\theta := 2.6$ in Algorithm A respectively, then the performance ratio of our algorithm is less than $1.7$.

## 4.2  Proof of Theorem 2

Below we will give an outline of our proof of Theorem 2. For this, we first estimate the expected value of $(\boldsymbol{x}^{IR}, \boldsymbol{x}^{Br})$ (which is a random assignment obtained by combining $\boldsymbol{x}^{IR}$ and $\boldsymbol{x}^{Br}$). For $\boldsymbol{x}^{Br}$, let

$$X^d = \{x \in X^B \cup \bar{X}^B \mid x = d\}, \quad X^u = \{x \in X^B \cup \bar{X}^B \mid x = u\}. \tag{21}$$

Thus, $X^d$ $(X^u)$ is the set of literals in $X^B \cup \bar{X}^B$ assigned $d$ $(u)$ in the assignment $\boldsymbol{x}^{Br}$. We use here superscript as $X^a$ to distinguish $X^a$ from $X_a$ in Section 2. Let

$$E^{ab} = \{(x_i, x_{i'}) \in \mathcal{C} \mid x_i \in X^a, x_{i'} \in X^b\}, \quad W^{ab} = \sum_{e \in E^{ab}} w(e) \quad (a, b = I, \bar{I}, d, u),$$

$$W^a = \sum_{x \in X^a} W(\delta(x)) = \sum_{x \in X^a} \sum_{e \in \delta(x)} w(e) \quad (a = I, \bar{I}, d, u).$$

Thus, $W^{ab} = W^{ba}$, $W^I = 2W^{II} + W^{I\bar{I}} + W^{Id} + W^{Iu}$, $W^{\bar{I}} = 2W^{\bar{I}\bar{I}} + W^{I\bar{I}} + W^{\bar{I}d} + W^{\bar{I}u}$, and $W = W^{II} + W^{I\bar{I}} + W^{Id} + W^{Iu} + W^{\bar{I}\bar{I}} + W^{\bar{I}d} + W^{\bar{I}u} + W^{dd} + W^{du} + W^{uu}$. Let $C^{\bar{I}} = \frac{W^I}{W^{\bar{I}}}$. We assume $C^{\bar{I}} = \infty$ and $C^{\bar{I}} W^{\bar{I}} = W^I$ if $W^{\bar{I}} = 0$ as $C$ in (2). Then $C^{\bar{I}} \geq C_\theta \geq 1$, since $C^{\bar{I}} = \frac{\sum_{x \in X^I} W(\delta(x))}{\sum_{\bar{x} \in X^{\bar{I}}} W(\delta(\bar{x}))}$.

To estimate the expected value of $(\boldsymbol{x}^{IR}, \boldsymbol{x}^{Br})$, we consider the probability $Pr((x_i, x_{i'}) = 1)$ that a clause $(x_i, x_{i'}) \in \mathcal{C} - \mathcal{C}^B$ is satisfied by $(\boldsymbol{x}^{IR}, \boldsymbol{x}^{Br})$. Since $(x_i, x_{i'}) \in \mathcal{C} - \mathcal{C}^B$ is satisfied if and only if it is in $E^{Id} \cup E^{Iu}$, we have:

$$Pr((x_i, x_{i'}) = 1) = \begin{cases} \frac{2}{3} - \frac{3\lambda^2}{2} & \text{if } x_i \in X^I, \ x_{i'} \in X^I \\[4pt] \frac{4}{9} + \frac{\lambda}{3} - \frac{\lambda^2}{2} & \text{if } x_i \in X^I, \ x_{i'} \in X^{\bar{I}} \\[4pt] \frac{2}{9} + \frac{2\lambda}{3} + \frac{\lambda^2}{2} & \text{if } x_i \in X^{\bar{I}}, \ x_{i'} \in X^{\bar{I}} \\[4pt] \frac{2}{3} - \frac{\lambda}{2} & \text{if } x_i \in X^I, \ x_{i'} \in X^u \cup X^d \\[4pt] \frac{1}{3} + \frac{\lambda}{2} & \text{if } x_i \in X^{\bar{I}}, \ x_{i'} \in X^u \cup X^d. \end{cases} \tag{22}$$

Thus, the value of $\boldsymbol{x}^{rr}$ obtained by the derandomization from $(\boldsymbol{x}^{IR}, \boldsymbol{x}^{Br})$ is at least $G(\lambda) \equiv (\frac{2}{3} - \frac{3\lambda^2}{2})W^{II} + (\frac{4}{9} + \frac{\lambda}{3} - \frac{\lambda^2}{2})W^{I\bar{I}} + (\frac{2}{9} + \frac{2\lambda}{3} + \frac{\lambda^2}{2})W^{\bar{I}\bar{I}} + (\frac{2}{3} - \frac{\lambda}{2})(W^{Id} + W^{Iu}) + (\frac{1}{3} + \frac{\lambda}{2})(W^{\bar{I}d} + W^{\bar{I}u}) + W^{dd} + W^{uu} = \frac{2}{3}(W^{Id} + W^{Iu}) + \frac{2}{3}W^{II} + \frac{4}{9}W^{I\bar{I}} + \frac{2}{9}W^{\bar{I}\bar{I}} + \frac{1}{3}(W^{\bar{I}d} + W^{\bar{I}u}) + W^{dd} + W^{uu} - \frac{1}{2}(3W^{II} + W^{I\bar{I}} - W^{\bar{I}\bar{I}})(\lambda - \lambda_0)^2 + \frac{1}{2}(3W^{II} + W^{I\bar{I}} - W^{\bar{I}\bar{I}})\lambda_0^2$, where $\lambda_0 \equiv \frac{1}{3} - \nu$ and $\nu \equiv \frac{(C^{\bar{I}} - 1)W^{\bar{I}}}{2(3W^{II} + W^{I\bar{I}} - W^{\bar{I}\bar{I}})}$. From now on we assume that in Algorithm A we set

$$\lambda := \begin{cases} \lambda_0 & \text{if } 0 \leq \nu \leq 1 \\ -\frac{2}{3} & \text{if } \nu \geq 1 \text{ or } \nu < 0 \end{cases} \tag{23}$$

so that $G(\lambda)$ is maximized. Thus, the value of $\boldsymbol{x}^{rr}$ is at least $G(\lambda_0)$ if $0 \leq \nu \leq 1$ and at least $G(-\frac{2}{3})$ otherwise. By routine calculations we have $F(\boldsymbol{x}^A) \geq$

$F(\boldsymbol{x}^{rr}) \geq \frac{1}{2}W + h_1$ if $\nu \geq 0$, where $h_1 \equiv \frac{\nu_1}{4}(C^{\bar{I}} - 1)W^{\bar{I}}$ and $\nu_1 \equiv \min\{|\nu|, 1\}$, and $F(\boldsymbol{x}^A) \geq F(\boldsymbol{x}^{rr}) \geq \frac{1}{2}W + \frac{1}{2}(C^{\bar{I}} - 1)W^{\bar{I}} \geq \frac{1}{2}W + h_1$ if $\nu < 0$.

Similarly, the better value of $\boldsymbol{x}^{dr}$, $\boldsymbol{x}^{ur}$ is at least $\frac{W^{\bar{I}d}+W^{\bar{I}u}}{2} + W^{II} + W^{\bar{I}\bar{I}} + \frac{W^{Id}+W^{Iu}}{2}+W^{dd}+W^{uu}$ and $F_{\mathcal{C}}(\boldsymbol{x}^A) \geq \frac{1}{2}W + h_2$ with $h_2 \equiv \left(\frac{1}{12\nu}C^{\bar{I}} - \left(\frac{2}{3} + \frac{1}{12\nu}\right)\right) W^{\bar{I}}$. Thus, if $\nu > 0$ then $F_{\mathcal{C}}(\boldsymbol{x}^A) \geq \frac{1}{2}W + \max\{h_1, h_2\}$. Since $h_1$ is increasing with $\nu > 0$ and $h_2$ is decreasing with $\nu > 0$, we have $h_1 = h_2$ with $\nu_0 \equiv \frac{-4+\sqrt{16+3(C^{\bar{I}}-1)^2}}{3(C^{\bar{I}}-1)} < \frac{1}{\sqrt{3}}$. Thus,

$$\max\{h_1, h_2\} = (\eta(\nu)C^{\bar{I}} - \xi(\nu))W^{\bar{I}} \geq (\eta(\nu_0)C^{\bar{I}} - \xi(\nu_0))W^{\bar{I}}$$

for

$$\eta(\nu) \equiv \begin{cases} \dfrac{\nu_1(C^{\bar{I}}-1)}{4(C^{\bar{I}}-C_\theta)} & \text{if } \nu \geq \nu_0 \\[2ex] \dfrac{1}{C^{\bar{I}}-C_\theta}\left(\dfrac{C^{\bar{I}}}{12\nu} - \left(\dfrac{2}{3} + \dfrac{1}{12\nu}\right)\right) & \text{if } 0 < \nu < \nu_0, \end{cases}$$

$$\xi(\nu) \equiv \eta(\nu)C_\theta,$$

and

$$\eta(\nu) \geq \eta(\nu_0) \quad \text{for any } \nu > 0.$$

Furthermore, $\eta(\nu_0) = \frac{\nu_0(C^{\bar{I}}-1)}{4(C^{\bar{I}}-C_\theta)} = \frac{-4+\sqrt{16+3(C^{\bar{I}}-1)^2}}{12(C^{\bar{I}}-C_\theta)}$ and $(C^{\bar{I}} - C_\theta)^2\eta'(\nu_0)$ is increasing with $C^{\bar{I}}$ and takes value $0$ at $C^{\bar{I}} = C_0^{\bar{I}} \equiv C_\theta - 1 + \frac{16(C_\theta-1)+3(C_\theta-1)^3}{16-3(C_\theta-1)^2}$, where $\eta'(\nu_0)$ is the derivative of $\eta(\nu_0)$ with respect to $C^{\bar{I}}$. Thus, $\eta(\nu_0)$ takes the minimum $\frac{2(C_\theta-1)}{16+3(C_\theta-1)^2}$ at $C^{\bar{I}} = C_0^{\bar{I}}$ and $F_{\mathcal{C}}(\boldsymbol{x}^A) \geq \frac{1}{2}W + \frac{2(C_\theta-1)}{16+3(C_\theta-1)^2}(C^{\bar{I}}-C_\theta)W^{\bar{I}}$.

By further arguments similar to the above one we can obtain a bound on $W^I$ with $C^I$ and Theorem 2.

# References

1. Devadas S., Keutzer K., and White J.: Estimation of power dissipation in CMOS combinatorial circuits using boolean function manipulation. *IEEE Transactions on Computer-Aided-Design* **11** (1992) 373–383.
2. Ding C., Tsui C., and M. Pedram: Power estimation using tagged probabilistic simulation. *IEEE Transactions on Computer-Aided-Design* **17** (1998) 1099–1107.
3. Goemans M.X., and Williamson D.P.: Improved approximation algorithms for maximum cut and satisfiability problems using semidefinite programming. *Journal of the ACM* **42** (1995) 1115–1145.
4. Matsuda T., Iwama K., and Halldórsson M.: The approximability of MAX power consumption problem of logic circuits. Technical Report of Information Processing Society of Japan, **2000-AL-72-2** (2000) 9–16.
5. Monterio J., Devadas S., Ghosh A., Keutzer K., and White J.: Estimation of average switching activity in combinatorial logic circuit using symbolic simulation. *IEEE Transactions on Computer-Aided-Design* **16** (1997) 121–127.
6. Motwani R., and Raghavan P.: *Randomized Algorithms*. Cambridge University Press, 1995.

# A Simple and Quick Approximation Algorithm for Traveling Salesman Problem in the Plane

Norihiro Kubo[1], Katsuhiro Muramoto[2], and Shinichi Shimozono[3]*

[1] Graduate School of Computer Science and Systems Enginieering,
Kyushu Inst. of Tech., Iizuka, Japan 820–8502
kubo@daisy.ai.kyutech.ac.jp
[2] FAD, Iwashita Engineering Inc., Nakahara Shinmachi 2–3, Tobata-ku, Kitakyushu,
Japan 804-0003
[3] Dept. of Artificial Intelligence, Kyushu Inst. of Tech., Iizuka, Japan 820–8502
sin@ai.kyutech.ac.jp

**Abstract.** We present a quite simple, fast and practical algorithm to find a short cyclic tour that visits a set of points distributed on the plane. The algorithm runs in $O(n \log n)$ time with $O(n)$ space, and is simple enough to easily implement on resource restricted machines. It constructs a tour essentially by axis-sorts of the points and takes a kind of the 'fixed dissection strategy,' though it neither tries to find best tours in subregions nor optimizes the order among subregions. As well as the worst-case approximation ratio of produced tours, we show that the algorithm is a 'probabilistic' constant-ratio approximation algorithm for uniform random distributions. We made computational comparisons of our algorithm, Karp's partitioning algorithm, Lin–Kernighan local search, Arora's randomized PTAS, etc. The results indicate that in running time our algorithm overwhelms existing ones, and the average approximation ratio is better or competitive.

## 1 Introduction

Traveling salesman problem (TSP) asks, given a set of points with the distances among them, to find a tour that visits every point exactly once then return to the origin with the minimum total sum of the transfer distances. This is one of the most classic and well-known combinatorial optimization problems and has gathered a huge amount of both theoretical and practical interest (e.g. [11]). It is known that TSP is NP-hard [9] and in general hard to approximate in polynomial time unless P=NP [16]. The natural subproblem $\Delta$-TSP (or metric TSP) whose instance provides the distance satisfying the triangle inequality is also intractable and APX-complete, though it is approximable within a constant ratio in polynomial time [2,5,11]. These have led us to develop algorithms that are efficient and answers always nearly optimal solutions.

---

* This research is partially supported by Grants-in-Aid for Encouragement of Young Scientists, Japan Society for the Promotion of Science, No. 12780286.

D.T. Lee and S.-H. Teng (Eds.): ISAAC 2000, LNCS 1969, pp. 216–227, 2000.
© Springer-Verlag Berlin Heidelberg 2000

Our target problem, traveling salesman problem in the plane (or 2-dimensional Euclidean TSP), is a special case of $\Delta$-TSP and is known to still remain NP-hard [6,13]. An instance is a set of points in 2-dimensional Euclidean space with the Euclid norm distances between them. It formalizes a number of practical problems, such as to find a shortest routing for geographic cities, to plan a robot motion in automated assemblies of printed circuit boards, etc. Although the problem is solvable as $\Delta$-TSP, algorithms that benefit by the positions of points have been extensively studied.

In [10] Karp presented a recursive-partitioning algorithm for TSP in the plane that utilizes positions of the points in its divide-and-conquer manner. It runs in $O(n \log n + n \cdot c^t)$ time with $n$ points, where $t$ is the maximum number of points in a subregion for which the algorithm stops partitioning, and $c^t$ with $c > 2$ is time to find a optimum tour for a subregion. This algorithm produces tours whose absolute worst-case deviation of the length from the optimum is proportional to $\sqrt{n}$. Furthermore, for sets of points with uniform and random distribution, it works as a polynomial-time "probabilistic" $(1 + \epsilon)$-approximation scheme, where $\epsilon$ is the worst-case relative error depending on $t$. Also the probabilistic run-time analysis of a simplified algorithm for the same random distribution was provided. These were generalized in [7] as a fixed dissection strategy for $d$-dimensional TSP with Lebesgue measure. For uniform and random inputs, it runs in subquadratic time probabilistically and produces a tour whose length is asymptotically proportional to the optimum.

Very recently Arora [1] devised a *Polynomial-Time Approximation Scheme* (PTAS) for TSP in $d$-dimensional Euclidean space. It achieves for every fixed $\epsilon > 0$ a worst-case approximation ratio $1 + \epsilon$ in polynomial-time with the number of points, while it depends exponentially upon $\epsilon$. From our point of view, this algorithm deals with the worst-case instances of Karp's partitioning algorithm by perturbing and enumerating both the boundaries and the visiting orders of subregions. Although this algorithm and its randomized version seem to be difficult to implement as a practical and fast algorithm, the result has settled an open problem whether TSP in the plane has a PTAS.

In this paper, we present a quite simple, fast and practical algorithm for TSP in the plane. In the literature, the primary request to algorithms for TSP has been to achieve a better approximation ratio of their outputs. It is reasonable since the problem originates in strongly cost-dependent requests, such as optimization in CAD and trip planning. However, nowadays, there is a considerable amount of requests for an algorithm that runs very quickly even for quite large inputs, with achieving an acceptable approximation ratio guarantee. For example, Just-In-Time production (lean production) systems adopted by modern manufacturers relay on small-lot productions dealing with a variety kinds of products. Determining a short tour for hundreds or thousands of points in nearly-zero lead-in time is requested for various automated assembly processes.

Our algorithm *divide-and-sort* runs in $O(n \log n)$ time with $n$ points and achieves a constant approximation ratio for uniform random inputs with probability

1. The key idea is to find a tour essentially only by the axis-sorts of the points. The algorithm divides the bounding box of all the points by $2k$ right-aligned wide rectangles and one tall left-aligned rectangle, where the number $k$ is proportional to the square root of both $n$ and the aspect ratio of the bounding box. Then it makes paths in the rectangles according to the axis-sorts, and connect them together in a fixed order to form a comb-shaped cyclic tour, like the fixed dissection algorithm by Halton and Terada [7].

The running time of divide-and-sort is outstanding among other subquadratic-time partitioning algorithms. Existing partitioning algorithms search for optimum tours in $O(n)$ subregions of the bounding box. To keep the approximation performance good, the number of points in those subregions should not not be small, and thus hidden constant factors in running time tend to be large. Also, it must be noted that the worst-case running time of the fixed dissection algorithm by Halton and Terada is exponential with the number of points. From another point of view, our divide-and-sort gives a practical implementation of the fixed dissection algorithms to achieve both good approximation ratio and $O(n \log n)$ worst-case running time.

The rest of this paper is organized as follows. We introduce and review some notions and definitions briefly, and then describe our algorithm. Next we show that the worst-case approximation ratio of divide-and-sort, and prove that it is a 'probabilistic' constant-ratio approximation algorithm for nontrivial and uniform random Poisson instances. This suggests that the algorithm performs well in practical usage in spite of its worst case approximation ratio.

We confirm these analysis by observing computational experiments. Firstly we measure the best constant factor to determine the partition number $k$. Next we examine the results on running time and relative performance ratio of tours by divide-and-sort and well-known approximation algorithms. The results indicate that divide-and-sort has no competitors in running time, and for randomly generated inputs it produces rather better tours than other quadratic or subquadratic time algorithms. Furthermore, we have executed computational experiments for TSP instances whose optimum are known. Competitor algorithms in these experiments include Karp's partitioning algorithm, Lin–Kernighan [12] and 2-Opt local search, and Arora's random PTAS. To our knowledge, this is the first computational experiments that evaluates an implementation of Arora's PTAS.

## 2    Notions and Definitions

First of all, we assume that TSP instances dealt with throughout this paper are all discretized with some appropriate granularity and thus points in the plane are supplied as pairs of nonnegative integers. Note that, without any changes in the following discussions, we can apply our algorithm and obtain the same result to the non-discretized TSP in the plane. Let $c = (c_x, c_y)$ and $c' = (c'_x, c'_y)$ be points in $\mathbf{Z}^{+2}$.

We denote by $d_E(c, c')$ the Euclid distance between $c$ and $c'$,

$$d_E(c, c') = \sqrt{(c_x - c'_x)^2 + (c_y - c'_y)^2} \,.$$

Let $C$ be a set of points in $\mathbf{Z}^{+2}$. The *bounding box of* $C$ is the smallest rectangle that contains all the cities in $C$ and has the sides parallel to the axes.

By assuming some standard encoding on a finite alphabet $\Sigma$, a *minimization problem* $\Pi$ is defined by three polynomial-time functions specifying the following: (i) an *instance* $x \in \Sigma^*$ of $\Pi$, (ii) a *solution* $s \in \Sigma^*$ of $x$, and (iii) the nonnegative integer *measure* $m_\Pi(x, s)$ of $s$ with respect to $x$.

Let $\Pi$ be a minimization problem, $x$ an instance of $\Pi$ and $s$ a solution of $x$. The *performance ratio of* $s$ *with respect to* $x$ is the ratio $\frac{m_\Pi(x,s)}{Opt(x)}$ of the measure $m_\Pi(x, s)$ to the measure of an optimum solution $Opt_\Pi(x)$ of $x$. Let $\alpha$ be a rational number greater than one. An algorithm $A$ for $\Pi$ is a *polynomial-time $\alpha$-approximation algorithm* (or achieves the performance ratio $\alpha$) for $\Pi$ if, for any instance $x \in \Pi$, (i) $A$ produces a solution $A(x)$ of $x$ in polynomial time with respect to $|x|$, and (ii) the performance ratio of $A(x)$ is at most $\alpha$.

With these notions, the traveling salesman problem in the plane is defined as follows:

**Definition 1. Traveling Salesman Problem in the Plane**
*Instance: A set $C = \{c_1, \ldots, c_n\}$ of points in $\mathbf{Z}^{+2}$.*
*Solution: A tour $\pi$ of $C$, that is, a permutation $\pi = \langle \pi(1), \ldots, \pi(n) \rangle$ of integers $1, \ldots, n$.*
*Cost (Measure): The total sum of the distances in the tour $\pi$,*

$$\sum_{i=1}^{n-1} d_E(c_{\pi(i)}, c_{\pi(i+1)}) + d_E(c_{\pi(n)}, c_{\pi(1)}) \,.$$

Here, due to the naturalness, we extended the measure function as a mapping to real numbers, and defined the cost of a tour by the sum of Euclidean distances. To cling to the discrete computation model, we can replace this cost by the sum of the Manhattan transfer length ($L_1$ distance). Again, note that this does not make any difference in the following discussions.

## 3 Algorithm Divide-and-Sort

Let $C$ be a set of points in $\mathbf{Z}^{+2}$, and let $l_H$ and $l_V$ be the lengths of the horizontal and vertical sides of the bounding box of $C$, respectively. For the convenience, without loss of generality, we assume that the bounding box is a wide rectangle, i.e. satisfying $l_H \geq l_V$.

For a positive integer $k > 0$, we define a partition of the bounding box of $C$ tiled with the following mutually disjoint rectangles:

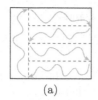
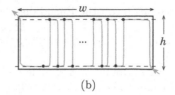

(a)                                              (b)

**Fig. 1.** (a) The $(2k+1)$-partition and an abstracted tour of a bounding box with $k = 2$. (b) The worst case distribution and its subtour in a wide rectangle.

(i) One tall, left aligned rectangle of the size width $\frac{1}{2k} \cdot l_V$ by height $l_V$, and
(ii) $2k$ wide, right-aligned congruent rectangles of $l_H - \frac{1}{2k} l_V$ by $\frac{1}{2k} \cdot l_V$.

We say this partition a $(2k+1)$-*partition* of the bounding box of $C$, and $k$ the *partition number*. By ordering points with respect to their coordinates, we can find in each rectangle a path visiting all points contained in the rectangle along its longer side. By connecting up these paths into one cyclic tour, we obtain a tour of the points in $C$ as shown in Fig. 1 (a).

The idea given above can be formalized as the following algorithm that produces a tour for a set $C$ of points.

**Algorithm divide-and-sort:**

Input: A set $C = \{c_1, \ldots, c_n\}$ of points in $\mathbf{Z}^{+2}$.
Output: A tour $T$ of $C$, a permutation of integers $1, \ldots, n$.
1. Sort two sequences of integers from 1 to $n$ as $L_x = (x_1, \ldots, x_n)$ and $L_y = (y_1, \ldots, y_n)$ that give the sorted points $c_{x_1}, \ldots, c_{x_n}$ and $c_{y_1}, \ldots, c_{y_n}$ according to $x$ and $y$ coordinates, respectively.
2. Specify the bounding box and the rectangles for the $(2k+1)$-partition.
3. Count the number of points contained in each rectangle, and compute the table of indices for the left-most points of wide rectangles in the final tour. This table will be referred and updated to make a complete tour.
4. Construct the paths in the rectangles along their longer sides, and patch them into a cyclic tour. This can be carried out by scanning $L_x$ once for the wide rectangles and $L_y$ once for the tall rectangle, with looking up and modifying the table to place points at the appropriate positions in the output tour.

This algorithm runs in $O(n \log n)$ time, which is dominated by two sorts of the lists in Step 1. The space resource required by this algorithm is $O(n)$, including the lists of points and work space for sorting.

Compared to the recursive-partitioning algorithm by Karp [10], divide-and-sort has given up searching for a "better partitioning." The result is always a comb-shaped tour in the bounding box. In return, divide-and-sort can be implemented with only a few arrays of integers for the sorted lists, although the Karp's algorithm requires $O(n \log n)$ space. The partition scheme is similar to that of the fixed dissection algorithm by Halton and Terada [7], but it requires a huge constant factor, and in the worst case exponential time, to find the best subtours in small regions.

## 4    The Worst-Case Analysis of Approximate Tours

In this section, we show a worst-case analysis for the divide-and-sort algorithm which gives an absolute upper bound of the tour as well as an approximation ratio obtained by the algorithm. With this analysis, we derive the optimal value of the partition number $k$ which reduces the worst-case upper bound.

Let $k$ be the partition number (a positive integer no less than one), and let $l_H$ and $l_V$ be the lengths of the horizontal side and the vertical side of the bounding box of $C$, respectively. Let $R_i$ for each $1 \leq i \leq 2k$ be a horizontal rectangle of width $w = l_H - \frac{1}{2k}l_V$ and height $h = \frac{1}{2k}l_V$, and let $R_{2k+1}$ be the vertical rectangle of width $w' = h = \frac{1}{2k}l_V$ and height $l_V$. The number of points in the $i$th rectangle $R_i$ is denoted by $N_i$.

Clearly, the worst case for a wide rectangle of a partition is (see Fig. 1 (b) ) that (i) the points are distributed on nearly the upper and the lower horizontal sides of $R_i$, and (ii) the points sorted by the horizontal axis are placed on the top and the bottom alternatively. The length of a path in $R_i$ is at most $h(N_i+1)+w$, and the length of a path in the vertical rectangle $R_{2k+1}$ is at most $w'(N_{2k+1}+1)+l_V$. In all the $2k + 1$ rectangles, we have totally $n$ points. Since we have assumed $l_H \geq l_V$, the length $W_C$ of a possible longest tour produced by divide-and-sort is

$$W_C \leq \sum_{i=1}^{2k} \{h(N_i + 1) + w\} + w'(N_{2k+1} + 1) + l_V \leq \frac{1}{2k}l_V \cdot n + 2(k+1) \cdot l_H .$$

**Lemma 1.** *The algorithm divide-and-sort produces a tour whose length is at most $n \cdot l_V/2k + 2(k + 1) \cdot l_H$ with a partition number $k \geq 1$ for an instance in the bounding box of width $l_H$ by height $l_V$.*

Next, we consider that before running the algorithm we choose a partition number $k$ that reduces the tour length on-line. If, fortunately, sample instances which would be likely occur are available, then this parameter can be determined with the help of computational results. Here, we continue our worst-case analysis by choosing $k = \left\lceil \frac{1}{2}\sqrt{l_V/l_H} \cdot \sqrt{n} \right\rceil$ derived by differentiating the upper bound in Lemma 1. Then the absolute upper bound of length of tours is

$$W_C \leq l_H \left( \frac{3}{2}\sqrt{\frac{l_V}{l_H} \cdot n} + 4 \right) .$$

Now let $Opt(C)$ be the length of an optimal tour for $C$. Since $\sqrt{l_H \cdot l_V} \leq l_H$ and $2 \cdot l_H \leq Opt(C)$ hold, the worst-case performance ratio of divide-and-sort is

$$W_C / Opt(C) \leq \frac{3}{4}\sqrt{n} + 2.$$

**Lemma 2.** *The algorithm divide-and-sort produces a tour whose length is at most $\frac{3}{4}\sqrt{n} + 2$ times the optimum.*

## 5    Asymptotic Probabilistic Analysis of Approximation

The ratio given in the previous section is quite wrong. However, in practice, we can expect more good behavior to our algorithm.

Assume that $l_V/l_H$ is bounded or grows slowly than $n$, i.e. if $l_H$ grows then $l_V$ also grows. It is sufficiently reasonable since the height of bounding box of nontrivial instances would (possibly slowly but) grow with the number of points. With this assumption, for sufficiently large $n$ there exists a small constant $c > 0$ such that

$$W_C \leq \left(\frac{3}{2} + c\right) \sqrt{l_V l_H \cdot n}.$$

Now, as in the literature, we consider that the unit system is normalized as $l_H \cdot l_V = 1$. (Or we may temporary take the definition that an instance is a set of points in $[0,1)^2 \subseteq \mathbf{R}^2$.) We make an asymptotic probabilistic analysis of our algorithm by a theorem due to Beardwood, Halton and Hammersley [4], along the lines in [10].

Suppose that a random distribution of points in a bounding box $X$ on the plane is modeled by a two-dimensional Poisson distribution $\Pi_n(X)$. It is determined by the following assumption: (i) the number of cities in disjoint subregions are distributed independently of each other; (ii) the expected number of cities in a region $Y$ within $X$ is $n\mathcal{A}(Y)$, where $\mathcal{A}(Y)$ is the area of $Y$; and (iii) as $\mathcal{A}(Y)$ tends to zero, the probability of more than one point occurring in $Y$ tends to zero faster than $\mathcal{A}(Y)$. From these assumptions it follows that

$$\Pr(Y \text{ contains exactly } m \text{ points}) = e^{-\lambda}\lambda^m/m!,$$

where $\lambda = n\mathcal{A}(Y)$.

Assuming that the points are distributed according to $\Pi_n(X)$, let $T_n^*(X)$ be the random variable denoting the length of an optimum tour for $X$. Then it is known by [4] that there exists a positive constant $\beta$ independent of $X$ such that, for every $\epsilon > 0$,

$$\left| \lim_{n \to \infty} \frac{T_n^*(X)}{\sqrt{n}} - \beta \right| \leq \epsilon$$

with probability 1.

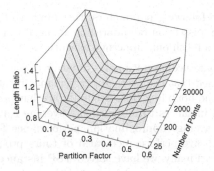

**Fig. 2.** Computational estimation of the factor for the partition number.

We conclude the above discussion as that the divide-and-sort is a polynomial-time "probabilistic" constant-ratio approximation algorithm.

**Theorem 1.** *For sufficiently large, nontrivial and random Poisson inputs, there exists a constant $\alpha > \frac{3}{2}$ such that the algorithm divide-and-sort produces with probability 1 a tour whose length is less than $\alpha$ times the optimum.*

## 6   Computational Results

In this section, we present computational results of our divide-and-sort and compared well-known algorithms. We have implemented all algorithms by C++ with Standard Template Library (STL) on UNIX. Sort procedures in the algorithms are carried out by the quick sort provided in STL and thus its worst-case processing time is $O(n^2)$. Although we have carefully implemented all algorithms, there may be left much space for optimization to obtain better programs.

The competitor algorithms are the following. (i) Karp's partitioning algorithm [10] terminating its partitioning at 3 or less points (referred as **Karp 3**), and at 8 or less (at least 5) points (**Karp 8**): This is a typical $O(n \log n)$ worst-case running time algorithm, and behave like a fixed-dissection algorithm. Since the number 8 of points is still small, we applied a simple enumeration of possible $(n-1)!/2$ permutations to find shortest tours in subregions, though there is $O(n^2 2^n)$ time DP procedures [3,8]. (ii) Nearest Neighbor greedy algorithm [15] starting from a randomly chosen point (**N Neighbor**): This runs in $O(n^2)$ time, and represents greedy algorithms whose performance ratio is proportional to $\log n$. (iii) Double minimum spanning tree algorithm (**D Spantree**): It achieves a constant performance ratio 2, and is a replacement of Christofides' $\frac{3}{2}$-approximation algorithm [5]. (iv) Lin–Kernighan local search algorithm featuring both 2-Opt and 3-Opt (**L–K**) [12], and (v) 2-Opt local search (**2-opt**): Lin–Kernighan local search is referred as a champion heuristic [14], and 2-Opt can be regarded as its simplified version. (vi) Arora's randomized PTAS (**Arora**) [1]: Arora's randomized PTAS is executed with the following parameters: the number of portals is 3, and the number of crosses on dissection boundaries is at most 1. These values are quite small, but selected to finish our numerous executions.

Firstly, we have made a computational estimation of the factor for the partition number, and confirmed that the average performance ratio does not depend on the aspect ratio of the bounding box. Secondly, we have executed test runs for randomly generated instances to measure the average running time. Then, we have examined the average approximation performance for the same random instances, by the relative performance ratio of tours produced by divide-and-sort and competitors. Finally, we have solved TSP instances from TSPLIB [17], whose optimal tours are known, and inspected the real performance ratio.

## A Constant Factor of Partition Number for Random Instances

We show the computational experiments for finding the optimal value of the partition number. Here we define the partition number by $k = \left\lceil t \cdot \sqrt{l_V/l_H} \cdot \sqrt{n} \right\rceil$ with the *partition factor* $t$. For each sample pair of the factor $t$ and the number of points, we have generated 100 random instances in a square bounding box $\frac{l_V}{l_H} = 1$. Then we have computed the average of ratios $l(t,x)/l^*(x)$ for those instances, where $l(t,x)$ and $l^*(x)$ are the lengths of the tours produced for an instance $x$ with the partition factors $t$ and 0.5 (value from the theoretical analysis), respectively. We can see that in Fig. 2 the partition factor around 0.29 is the best for randomly generated instances.

We tested the same experiments with various aspect ratios of bounding boxes, from 1 : 1 to 1 : 16. However, no notable difference could be observed in the optimal partition factors. Therefore, in the following experiments, we have fixed the partition factor to $\frac{1}{3.4} \sim 0.294$.

## Running Time

We have compared running time of our divide-and-sort and other algorithms for random instances. Test runs were executed on Sun SPARC Ultra-1/170 workstation. Instances were generated as sets of points distributed randomly in a square bounding box whose sides grow proportionally to the square root of the number of points.

As in Table 1 and Fig. 3, divide-and-sort is stably fast for instances from quite small ones to very huge ones. The running time of Karp 8 is wriggling since it strongly depends on the size of the regions at which best tours should be searched for.

## Approximation Performance

We compared the approximation performance of divide-and-sort and other algorithms for random instances. To avoid the intractability to find optimal tours for large instances, we measured the average ratio of 'performance ratio' of each competitor algorithm to that of our divide-and-sort, by simply computing the ratio of the length produced by a competitor to that of divide-and-sort. We have tested on the same 100 instances used in the measurment of the running time.

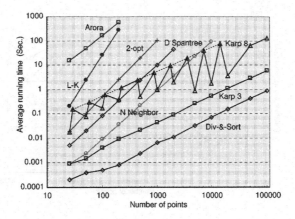

**Fig. 3.** Average running time of algorithms for 100 random instances.

**Table 1.** Average running time (in seconds) of algorithms for 100 random instances consisting of each number of points. The numbers 113, 225, 1793 and 14337 are specially chosen for **Karp 8** to yield all final subregions containning 8 points.

| Points | Div-&-Sort | Karp 3 | Karp 8 | N Neighbor | D Spantree | L–K | 2-opt | Arora |
|--------|-----------|--------|--------|-----------|-----------|-----|-------|-------|
| 100 | 0.0005 | 0.0040 | 0.170 | 0.0091 | 0.0858 | 26.2 | 0.508 | 165 |
| *113* | | | *0.604* | | | | | |
| 200 | 0.0008 | 0.0091 | 0.376 | 0.0378 | 0.363 | 293 | 2.50 | 586 |
| *225* | | | *1.21* | | | | | |
| 1000 | 0.0066 | 0.0444 | 1.00 | 0.909 | 10.27 | | 102 | |
| *1793* | | | *9.72* | | | | | |
| 2000 | 0.0115 | 0.0903 | 1.96 | 3.68 | 43.9 | | | |
| 10000 | 0.0694 | 0.533 | 1.80 | 92.9 | | | | |
| *14337* | | | *77.8* | | | | | |
| 100000 | 0.879 | 6.00 | 130 | | | | | |

The relative performance ratio of **Karp 3** and **Karp 8** indicate that fixed dissection algorithms output good tours when subregions for which exact solutions are searched for could be large. The result is shown in Fig. 4. Here the random heuristics Lin–Kernighan, 2-Opt and Arora's PTAS are executed only once for each instance. Even though, these three algorithms have produced good tours as they are expected. Note that, among low-order running time algorithms, divide-and-sort is producing better or comparable tours.

**Approximation Ratio for Solved TSP**

In the following we present computational results for instances from TS-PLIB [17] whose optimum are known. Thus these are real performance ratios

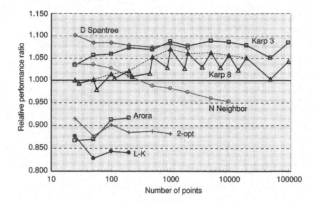

**Fig. 4.** Relative performance ratio of tours produced by algorithms to those produced by divide-and-sort.

achieved by tested algorithms. For some instances, such as kroA100 and pr1002, our divide-and-sort produces tours whose length is longer than or nearly $\frac{3}{2}$ times the optimum. In such case, it is observed that known best tours are very different from comblike shape.

**Table 2.** Performance ratios for TSPLIB instances whose shortest tour is known. Lin–Kernighan and 2-Opt were executed only once (i.e. with the unique initial solution) for each instance, while Arora's randomized PTAS was tried 50 random executions for each instance.

| Name | Points | Div-&-Sort | Karp 8 | N Neighbor | D Spantree | L–K | 2-opt | Arora |
|------|--------|-----------|--------|-----------|-----------|------|-------|-------|
| eli101 | 101 | 1.17 | 1.11 | 1.29 | 1.29 | 1.05 | 1.13 | 1.12 |
| kroA100 | 100 | 1.38 | 1.24 | 1.26 | 1.28 | 1.04 | 1.05 | 1.11 |
| lin105 | 105 | 1.36 | 1.49 | 1.27 | 1.03 | 1.14 | 1.12 | 1.10 |
| pr1002 | 1002 | 1.54 | 1.42 | 1.22 | 1.33 | 1.06 | 1.09 | 1.24 |
| st70 | 70 | 1.23 | 1.30 | 1.19 | 1.29 | 1.04 | 1.08 | 1.10 |

## 7    Concluding Remarks

We have designed divide-and-sort as a simple and quick algorithm that find a short tour essentially by axis sorts of given points. It has been shown in computational experiments that the algorithm divide-and-sort runs very fast, and can cope with huge size of instances. Also, in spite of its worst-case performance ratio, it seems that divide-and-sort produces good approximate tours.

These advantages can be easily obtained by a straightforward implementation. Of course, divide-and-sort constructs only comb-shaped tours, and thus there are instances for which divide-and-sort fails to find nearly-optimal tours. However, divide-and-sort rarely produces unacceptable tours, especially compared with other fast algorithms. Furthermore, it is quite interesting that even with such a simple strategy we can find good tours in usual. We believe that our divide-and-sort supplies a practical solution or a basic idea to achieve sufficient results in factory automations, rapid prototyping and development, and other area where the time-cost trade off plays important roles.

# References

1. S. Arora, Polynomial time approximation schemes for Euclidean traveling salesman and other geometric problems, *J. ACM* 45 (5), 753–782, 1998.
2. G. Ausiello, P. Crescenzi, G. Gambosi, V. Kann, A. Marchetti-Spaccamela, M. Protasi, *Complexity and Approximation*, Springer, 1999.
3. R. E. Bellman, Dynamic programming treatment of the traveling salesman problem, *J. ACM* 9, 61–63, 1962.
4. J. Beardwood, J. H. Halton, J. M. Hammersley, The shortest path through many points, In *Proc. Cambridge Philosophical Society* 55, 299–327, 1959.
5. N. Christofides, Worst-case analysis of a new heuristic for the traveling salesman problem, Report 388, Graduate School of Industrial Administration, Carnegie-Mellon University, Pittsburgh, PA., 1976.
6. M. R. Garey, R. L. Graham, D. S. Johnson, Some NP-complete geometric problems, In *Proc. the Eighth ACM Symposium on Theory of Computing*, 10–22, 1976.
7. J. H. Halton, R. Terada, A fast algorithm for the Euclidean traveling salesman problem, optimal with probability one, *SIAM J. Comput.* 11, 28–46, 1982.
8. M. Held, R. M. Karp, A dynamic programming approach to sequencing problems, SIAM J. 10, 196–210, 1962.
9. R. M. Karp, Reducibility among combinatorial problems, *Complexity of Computer Computations*, Plenum Press, 85–103, 1972.
10. R. M. Karp, Probabilistic analysis of partitioning algorithms for the traveling-salesman problem in the plane, *Math. Oper. Res.* 2, 209–224, 1977.
11. E. L. Lawler, J. K. Lenstra, A. H. G. Rinnooy Kan, D.B. Shmoys, *The Traveling Salesman Problem*, Wiley, 1992.
12. S. Lin, B. W. Kernighan, An effective heuristic algorithm for the traveling-salesman problem, *Oper. Res.* 21, 498–516, 1973.
13. C. H. Papadimitriou, Euclidean TSP is NP-complete, *Theoret. Comput. Sci.* 4, 237–244, 1977.
14. C. H. Papadimitriou, The complexity of the Lin–Kernighan heuristic for the traveling salesman problem, *SIAM J. Copmut.* 21, 450–465, 1992.
15. D. J. Rozenkrantz, R. E. Stearns, P. M. Lewis II, An analysis of several heuristics for the traveling salesman problem, *SIAM J. Comput.* 6 (3), 563–581, 1977.
16. S. Sahni, T. Gonzales, P-complete approximation problems, *J. ACM* 23, 555–565, 1976.
17. TSPLIB, Traveling salesman problem library, http://www.iwr.uni-heidelberg.de/iwr/comopt /software/TSPLIB95/

# Simple Algorithms for a Weighted Interval Selection Problem

Thomas Erlebach[1] and Frits C.R. Spieksma[2]

[1] Computer Engineering and Networks Laboratory, ETH Zürich, CH-8092 Zürich, Switzerland,
erlebach@tik.ee.ethz.ch
[2] Department of Mathematics, Maastricht University, P.O. Box 616, NL-6200 MD Maastricht,
The Netherlands, spieksma@math.unimaas.nl

**Abstract.** Given a set of jobs, each consisting of a number of weighted intervals on the real line, and a number $m$ of machines, we study the problem of selecting a maximum weight subset of the intervals such that at most one interval is selected from each job and, for any point $p$ on the real line, at most $m$ intervals containing $p$ are selected. This problem has applications in molecular biology, caching, PCB assembly, and scheduling. We give a parameterized algorithm GREEDY$_\alpha$ and show that there are values of the parameter $\alpha$ so that GREEDY$_\alpha$ produces a $\frac{1}{2}$-approximation in the case of unit weights, a $\frac{1}{8}$-approximation in the case of arbitrary weights, and a $(3 - 2\sqrt{2})$-approximation in the case where the weights of all intervals corresponding to the same job are equal. Algorithm GREEDY$_\alpha$ belongs to the class of "myopic" algorithms, which are deterministic algorithms that process the given intervals in order of non-decreasing right endpoints and can either reject or select each interval (rejections are irrevocable). We use competitive analysis to show that GREEDY$_\alpha$ is an optimal myopic algorithm in the case of unit weights and in the case of equal weights per job, and is close to optimal in the case of arbitrary weights.

## 1 Introduction

We study a *weighted job interval selection problem*, called WJISP. The input consists of jobs, each of which is given by a set of intervals on the real line, and a number $m$ of available machines. (We use "WJISP$_m$" instead of "WJISP" if we want to make an explicit reference to the number $m$ of machines.) Each interval $i$ has a positive weight $w(i)$. A feasible solution is a subset of the given intervals such that (1) at most one interval is selected from each job, and (2) for any point $p$ on the real line, at most $m$ intervals overlapping $p$ are selected. The goal is to find a feasible solution that maximizes the sum of the weights of the selected intervals. We let $n$ denote the total number of intervals in the input. We assume that a sorted list of all interval endpoints is available; such a list can be constructed in time $O(n \log n)$.

The requirement that any point on the real line is overlapped by at most $m$ selected intervals is equivalent to the requirement that the selected intervals can be partitioned into $m$ subsets such that the intervals in each subset are pairwise disjoint. In some applications this partition (in addition to specifying the selected intervals) is required as output. However, the subproblem of computing such a partition given the selected

D.T. Lee and S.-H. Teng (Eds.): ISAAC 2000, LNCS 1969, pp. 228–240, 2000.
© Springer-Verlag Berlin Heidelberg 2000

intervals can be solved efficiently by coloring the corresponding interval graph. In fact, $n$ intervals can be colored in time $O(n)$ if the sorted list of interval endpoints is given. We concentrate on the problem of selecting the intervals and assume that, if required, an appropriate coloring procedure is employed to compute the partitioning.

WJISP$_m$ has applications in diverse areas. Problems in printed circuit board assembly (see [7], [12]), in molecular biology ([5]) and in time-constrained scheduling on identical machines ([3,4]) each give rise to instances that can be modelled as (special cases of) instances of WJISP (see [8] for details).

Motivated by these applications we distinguish a number of variants of WJISP that concern the weights of the intervals:

- the *unweighted case* (called JISP) where each interval has the same weight $w$,
- *WJISP with equal weights per job* refers to instances of WJISP in which intervals that belong to the same job have the same weight, but intervals that belong to different jobs can have different weights, and finally
- *WJISP with arbitrary weights.*

We consider a class of simple deterministic algorithms for WJISP, and we investigate so-called *worst-case ratios* (or approximation ratios) that can be obtained using algorithms from this class. Using standard terminology (see e.g. [11], [1]) we say that an algorithm for WJISP achieves (approximation) ratio $\rho$ if it always outputs a feasible solution whose weight is at least as large as $\rho$ times the weight of an optimal solution. We exhibit an algorithm from this class that achieves a ratio that equals the best possible ratio for algorithms within this class in the unweighted case and in the case with equal weights per job. In case of arbitrary weights, the algorithm achieves a ratio close to the best possible ratio.

## 1.1 Known Results

Theoretical work on WJISP has largely been confined to ratios for polynomial time algorithms. The unweighted version of WJISP$_1$, called JISP$_1$, is studied in [12]. It is shown that JISP$_1$ is MAX SNP-hard even if every job contains only two intervals and all intervals have the same length. Furthermore, it is shown that the value of the natural LP relaxation of JISP$_1$ is at most twice the value of an integral optimum, and a simple greedy algorithm that achieves approximation ratio $\frac{1}{2}$ is presented.

Several authors have considered a machine scheduling problem with hard deadlines that is closely related to WJISP. In that application, a job consists of all (infinitely many) time intervals of the required length between its release time and its deadline. Bar-Noy et al. [3] give algorithms for $m$ identical machines with ratio $1 - 1/(1 + 1/m)^m$ in the unweighted case (using a greedy algorithm) and in the case with arbitrary weights (using linear programming), and an algorithm with ratio $1/3$ for unrelated machines. They also present a combinatorial algorithm ADMISSION with running-time $O(mn^2 \log n)$, where $n$ is the number of jobs, that achieves approximation ratio $3 - 2\sqrt{2}$ for jobs with arbitrary weights on unrelated machines. Berman and DasGupta [4] present a combinatorial two-phase algorithm with ratio $1/2$ for unrelated machines and arbitrary weights and with ratio $1 - 1/(1 + 1/m)^m$ for $m$ identical machines, thus matching the LP-based bounds of [3]. Bar-Noy et al. [2] use the so-called *local ratio technique* to obtain a combinatorial two-phase algorithm with approximation ratio $1/2$ for unrelated machines and arbitrary weights as well. The results of [3,4,2] also apply to WJISP$_m$.

The on-line variant of this machine scheduling problem is studied in [9] and [10] in the single-machine case. The weight of a job is equal to its length and the algorithms receive the jobs in order of non-decreasing release times. Preemption is not allowed. In [9], a deterministic algorithm with ratio $1/2$ if all jobs have the same length and a randomized algorithm with expected ratio $\Omega(1/\log c)$ if the ratio of the longest to the shortest job length is $c$ are presented. In [10], better bounds are derived for the case that the slack of a job is at least proportional to its length.

## 1.2    Our Results

A natural class of algorithms to consider for WJISP instances is the class of *single-pass* algorithms. Very generally stated, single-pass algorithms are algorithms in which a feasible solution is obtained by iteratively making a decision concerning an item or an object. The first-fit decreasing algorithm for the bin packing problem and the nearest neighbor algorithm for the traveling salesman problem are prime examples of single-pass algorithms. This kind of algorithms can be useful since they need little computing time and/or little information (i.e., they can be applied in an on-line setting). In our context, we call an algorithm a single-pass algorithm when given some sequence of the intervals, each interval is (iteratively) either rejected or accepted (selected) without considering the intervals that will be processed later. Rejections are permanent, but an accepted interval can be rejected (preempted) at a later time. At any time, the set of currently selected intervals must be a feasible solution. After the last interval is presented, the set of currently selected intervals is taken as the solution computed by the algorithm.

When considering a specific single-pass algorithm for WJISP, it is crucial to specify the mechanism that determines the sequence in which the intervals will be processed. We investigate the special class of deterministic single-pass algorithms that process the intervals in order of non-decreasing right endpoints. We call these algorithms *myopic algorithms*. These algorithms seem to be the simplest algorithms for which constant approximation ratios can be achieved.

Analyzing myopic algorithms for WJISP can be seen as studying an on-line problem. Thus, we can use competitive analysis to prove lower bounds on the best approximation ratio that can be achieved by any myopic algorithm. In applications where the intervals correspond to time periods, an on-line scenario in which the algorithm receives the intervals in order of non-decreasing right endpoints may appear unnatural. For instances where all intervals have the same length, however, the order of the left endpoints and the order of the right endpoints coincide. So the concept of myopic algorithms applies to the "real" on-line problem for such instances. For the machine scheduling problem discussed in Sect. 1.1, "the special case of all jobs having the same length under the arbitrary delay model is of great interest" (quoted from [9]).

Table 1 describes our results. In Sect. 2, we give an algorithm called GREEDY$_\alpha$ that can be implemented to run in $O(n^2 \min(m, \log n))$ time. GREEDY$_\alpha$ achieves the ratios described in Table 1; each of these ratios is tight. In Sect. 3, we prove that no myopic algorithm achieves better ratios than the ones described in Table 1 under "Lower Bound".

**Table 1.** The results

| Variant of WJISP | Ratio of GREEDY$_\alpha$ | Lower Bound |
|---|---|---|
| JISP | $\frac{1}{2}\ \forall m \geq 1$ | $\frac{1}{2}\ \forall m \geq 1$ |
| WJISP with equal weights per job | $3 - 2\sqrt{2} \approx 0.172\ \forall m \geq 1$ | $3 - 2\sqrt{2} \approx 0.172\quad m = 1$ |
| WJISP with arbitrary weights | $\frac{1}{8}\ \forall m \geq 1$ | $\approx \frac{1}{7.103} \approx 0.141\quad m = 1$ |

(Notice that these "lower bounds" do actually mean that any myopic algorithm achieves an approximation ratio smaller than the given values; nevertheless, we refer to these bounds as "lower bounds", because this term is commonly used for negative results.) We emphasize that our lower bounds for myopic algorithms apply only to deterministic algorithms, not to randomized algorithms.

## 2   Algorithm GREEDY$_\alpha$

We propose a myopic algorithm called GREEDY$_\alpha$, shown in Fig. 1, as an approximation algorithm for WJISP. It has a parameter $\alpha$ that can take (meaningful) values in the range $[0, 1]$. GREEDY$_\alpha$ considers the intervals in order of non-decreasing right endpoints. It maintains a set $S$ of currently selected intervals. When it processes an interval $i$, it computes a set $C_i \subseteq S$ such that $i$ could be selected after preempting the intervals in $C_i$ and such that $C_i$ has minimum weight among all such sets. $C_i$ is called the *cheapest conflict set* for $i$. The algorithm selects $i$ only if $w(C_i) \leq \alpha w(i)$, i.e., if the total weight of selected intervals increases by at least $(1 - \alpha)w(i)$ if $i$ is selected and the intervals from $C_i$ are preempted. The algorithm can be seen as a parameterized variant of the general double-the-gain paradigm. We can prove the following result:

**Theorem 1.** *For JISP$_m$, GREEDY$_\alpha$ achieves approximation ratio $\frac{1}{2}$ for any $\alpha$ in the range $[0, 1)$. For WJISP$_m$ with equal weights per job, GREEDY$_\alpha$ achieves approximation ratio $\frac{\alpha(1-\alpha)}{1+\alpha}$. For WJISP$_m$ with arbitrary weights, GREEDY$_\alpha$ achieves approximation ratio $\frac{\alpha(1-\alpha)}{2}$. These results are tight.*

*Proof.* Let $A$ be the set of intervals returned by GREEDY$_\alpha$, and let $T$ be the set of intervals that were selected by GREEDY$_\alpha$ at least at some time during the execution. If all intervals have the same weight, GREEDY$_\alpha$ never preempts a selected interval (provided that $0 \leq \alpha < 1$), so we have $A = T$ in case of JISP$_m$. In general, we have

$$w(A) \geq (1 - \alpha)w(T),\tag{1}$$

because GREEDY$_\alpha$ selects a new interval $i$ only if the total weight of selected intervals increases by at least $(1 - \alpha)w(i)$.

Let $OPT$ be an optimal solution. We charge the weight of the intervals in $OPT$ to intervals in $T$ and then prove a bound on the total weight charged to every single interval

---

**Algorithm GREEDY$_\alpha$**

$S = \emptyset$; { set of currently accepted intervals }
**for** all intervals, in order of non-decreasing right endpoints **do**
    $i = $ current interval;
    $C_i = $ minimum-weight subset of $S$ such that $(S \setminus C_i) \cup \{i\}$ is feasible;
    **if** $w(C_i) \leq \alpha w(i)$ **then**
        $S = (S \setminus C_i) \cup \{i\}$;
    **fi**;
**od**;
**return** S;

---

**Fig. 1.** Algorithm GREEDY$_\alpha$

in $T$. In this way, we can bound $w(OPT)$ in terms of $w(T)$ and, using (1), in terms of $w(A)$. The details of the charging depend on the variant of WJISP.

Consider an interval $i \in OPT$. If $i \in T$, we charge $w(i)$ to $i$. If $i \in OPT \setminus T$, consider the time when GREEDY$_\alpha$ processed interval $i$. Let $C_i$ denote the minimum-weight set of intervals whose removal from $S$ would have allowed to accept $i$. Let $C_i'$ be the subset of $C_i$ that contains all intervals that do not belong to the same job as $i$. If $S$ contains an interval from the same job as $i$, denote that interval by $i'$ and note that $C_i' = C_i \setminus \{i'\}$; otherwise, we let $i'$ be an imaginary interval with zero weight (just to simplify the formulas) and observe that $C_i' = C_i$.

Let $Q_i$ denote the set of all intervals in $S$ that intersect $i$ and that do not belong to the same job as $i$. As $S$ is feasible, $Q_i$ can be partitioned into $m$ sets $Q_{i1}, \ldots, Q_{im}$ of intervals such that the intervals in each set $Q_{i\ell}$ are pairwise disjoint. Note that

$$w(i') + w(Q_{i\ell}) > \alpha w(i) \text{ for } 1 \leq \ell \leq m, \tag{2}$$

because of the definition of $C_i$ and because GREEDY$_\alpha$ did not accept $i$.

First, consider the case of JISP$_m$. All intervals have the same weight. We charge $w(i)$ to the interval in $S$ that belongs to the same job, if such an interval exists; otherwise, we charge $\frac{1}{m} w(i)$ to an arbitrary interval from each of the sets $Q_{i\ell}$ (note that all the sets $Q_{i\ell}$ must be non-empty in this case). As every interval $j$ receives charge at most $w(j)$ from intervals of the same job and charge at most $m \cdot \frac{1}{m} w(j)$ from intervals overlapping the right endpoint of $j$, we have that $w(OPT) \leq 2w(T) = 2w(A)$.

Now consider WJISP$_m$ with arbitrary weights. We charge $\min\{w(i), \frac{1}{\alpha} w(i')\}$ to $i'$. If the remaining weight $w(i) - \min\{w(i), \frac{1}{\alpha} w(i')\}$ is positive, we divide it into $m$ equal parts and distribute each part among the intervals in one set $Q_{i\ell}$, where the charge one interval in $Q_{i\ell}$ receives is proportional to the weight of that interval. More precisely, interval $j \in Q_{i\ell}$ is charged

$$\frac{w(i) - \min\{w(i), \frac{1}{\alpha} w(i')\}}{m} \cdot \frac{w(j)}{w(Q_{i\ell})} .$$

We can deduce from (2) that every interval $j \in Q_i$ is charged by $i$ for at most $\frac{1}{\alpha m} w(j)$ in this way. Altogether, every interval $j \in T$ can receive charge at most $\frac{2}{\alpha} w(j)$ (charge

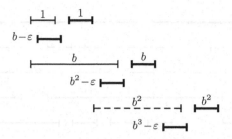

**Fig. 2.** Worst-case example for GREEDY$_\alpha$

at most $\frac{1}{\alpha}w(j)$ from an interval belonging to the same job and charge at most $\frac{1}{\alpha}w(j)$ from intervals in $OPT$ that overlap the right endpoint of $j$), implying that $w(OPT) \leq \frac{2}{\alpha}w(T) \leq \frac{2}{\alpha(1-\alpha)}w(A)$.

Finally, consider WJISP$_m$ with equal weights per job. If there was an interval $i'$ in $S$ belonging to the same job as $i$ at the time when GREEDY$_\alpha$ processed $i$, charge $w(i)$ to $i'$. Otherwise, distribute the weight of $i$ among the intervals in $Q_i$ in the same way as above. It is easy to see that every interval $j \in T$ is charged at most $w(j)$ by intervals from the same job and at most $\frac{1}{\alpha}w(j)$ by other intervals. Therefore, we get $w(OPT) \leq (1 + \frac{1}{\alpha})w(T) \leq \frac{1+\alpha}{\alpha(1-\alpha)}w(A)$.

The analysis of the approximation ratio of GREEDY$_\alpha$ is tight for all three cases. For example, consider the instance of WJISP$_1$ with equal weights per job shown in Fig. 2. Intervals in the same row belong to the same job, and the labels correspond to the weights of the intervals, where $b = \frac{1}{\alpha}$ and $\varepsilon$ is a very small positive value. Every group of three intervals is called a *phase*; the shown example consists of 3 phases. In an example with $k$ phases, GREEDY$_\alpha$ will output a single interval of weight $b^{k-1}$ (shown dashed in Fig. 2), while the optimal solution contains $2k$ intervals (shown bold in Fig. 2) of total weight $\sum_{i=0}^{k-1}(b^i + b^{i+1} - \varepsilon) = (1 + b)\frac{b^k - 1}{b - 1} - k\varepsilon$. Simple calculations show that the approximation ratio of GREEDY$_\alpha$ tends to $\frac{\alpha(1-\alpha)}{1+\alpha}$ as $\varepsilon \to 0$ and $k \to \infty$.

Worst-case instances for WJISP with arbitrary weights can be constructed in a similar way. Furthermore, these constructions can be adapted to WJISP$_m$ for $m > 1$ by including $m$ copies of every interval (putting each copy in a different job). □

By optimizing the choice of $\alpha$, we obtain the following corollary of Theorem 1.

**Corollary 1.** *For WJISP$_m$ with equal weights per job, GREEDY$_\alpha$ achieves approximation ratio $3 - 2\sqrt{2} \approx 0.172$ for $\alpha = \sqrt{2} - 1 \approx 0.414$. For WJISP$_m$ with arbitrary weights, GREEDY$_\alpha$ achieves approximation ratio $\frac{1}{8}$ for $\alpha = \frac{1}{2}$.*

The running time of GREEDY$_\alpha$ depends on how efficient the cheapest conflict set $C_i$ can be determined. We use dynamic programming to show that this can be done in $O(\min(n \log n, nm))$ time, yielding a time complexity of $O(n^2 \min(\log n, m))$ for GREEDY$_\alpha$.

First, we explain the dynamic programming approach for determining $C_i$ in time $O(nm)$. We use the notation from the proof of Theorem 1. It suffices to show how $C_i'$ is

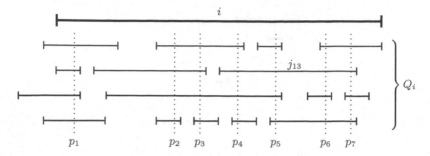

**Fig. 3.** Current interval $i$ and intersecting intervals in $S$

```
C(0) = 0;
for h = 1 to r do C(h) = ∞; od;
for ℓ = 1 to s do
    if first(jₑ) is not undefined then
        for h = first(jₑ) to last(jₑ) do
            C(h) = min{C(h), C(first(jₑ) − 1) + w(jₑ)};
        od;
    fi;
od;
```

**Fig. 4.** Dynamic programming algorithm

computed. See Fig. 3. For every interval $j \in Q_i$, consider a point $p$ just before the right endpoint of $j$. If $p$ is contained in $m$ intervals of $Q_i$, at least one of these intervals must be in $C'_i$. Let $p_1, \ldots, p_r$ be all such points (i.e., points just before the right endpoint of an interval in $Q_i$) that are contained in $m$ intervals of $Q_i$. $C'_i$ is a minimum-weight subset of $Q_i$ such that every point $p_h$, $1 \leq h \leq r$, is covered. (A set of intervals *covers* a point if the point is contained in at least one interval of that set.)

Let $j_1, j_2, \ldots, j_s$ denote the intervals in $Q_i$ in order of non-decreasing right endpoints. For every interval $j_\ell \in Q_i$, let $first(j_\ell)$ and $last(j_\ell)$ be the smallest resp. largest index of a point $p_h$ that is contained in $j_\ell$. (If $j_\ell$ does not contain any point $p_h$, $first(j_\ell)$ and $last(j_\ell)$ are undefined.) In Fig. 3, we have $first(j_{13}) = 4$ and $last(j_{13}) = 7$, for example. The points $p_1, \ldots, p_r$, the intervals $j_1, \ldots, j_s$, and the tables $first$ and $last$ can all be constructed in time $O(n)$. Then we use the dynamic programming procedure shown in Fig. 4 to compute values $C(h)$, $1 \leq h \leq r$.

*Claim.* After $\ell$ iterations of the outer for-loop, it holds for $1 \leq h \leq r$ that $C(h)$ is the weight of a minimum-weight subset of $\{j_1, \ldots, j_\ell\}$ that covers $p_1, \ldots, p_h$ (or $\infty$ if no such subset exists).

This claim can be proved easily by induction. It implies that $C(r) = w(C'_i)$ at the end of the execution of the procedure, and additional bookkeeping will allow to construct $C'_i$ at no extra cost. The running-time of the procedure in Fig. 4 is $O(rm) = O(nm)$, because the body of the inner for-loop is executed exactly $rm$ times. (For each of the $r$ points $p_h$, the body of the inner for-loop is executed only for the $m$ intervals containing $p_h$.)

In order to get an implementation that runs in $O(n \log n)$ time, we observe that the costs $C(h)$, $0 \le h \le r$, are always non-decreasing. This implies that one does not have to enumerate over $h = first(j_\ell)$ up to $h = last(j_\ell)$, but instead can find the "breakpoint value" for $h$ (say $h^*$) such that $C(h)$ remains unchanged for $h < h^*$ and is updated to $C(first(j_\ell) - 1) + w(j_\ell)$ for all $h^* \le h \le last(j_\ell)$. We use a balanced search tree $T$ that stores elements of the form $(h, C(h))$, sorted by $h$ (and thus also by $C(h)$) in non-decreasing order. If $T$ contains $(h_1, C(h_1))$ and $(h_2, C(h_2))$ but no pair $(h', C(h'))$ with $h_1 < h' < h_2$, this means that $C(h) = C(h_1)$ for $h_1 \le h < h_2$. In each iteration, we use $T$ to determine $h^*$ in time $O(\log n)$, insert $(h^*, C(h^*))$ into $T$, and remove invalid pairs $(h, C(h))$ from $T$. See [8] for details.

$Q_i$ constitutes an $m$-colorable interval graph, and $Q_i \setminus C_i'$ is a maximum-weight $(m - 1)$-colorable subgraph of $Q_i$. So we have the following corollary:

**Corollary 2.** *A maximum weight $k$-colorable subgraph in a $k + 1$ colorable interval graph can be obtained in $O(n \min(\log n, k))$ time.*

This is a speedup compared to the $O(kS(n))$ algorithm for the general case of the maximum weight $k$-colorable subgraph problem in interval graphs ([6]) (where $S(n)$ is the running time for finding a shortest path in graphs with $O(n)$ edges).

## 3    Competitive Lower Bounds

We are interested in the best approximation ratio that can be achieved by any myopic algorithm for WJISP, and we use competitive analysis to answer this question. We phrase our arguments in terms of an adversary who constructs worst-case instances for a myopic algorithm incrementally, depending on previous decisions made by the algorithm. Thus, we present the construction of worst-case examples for myopic algorithms as a game played by the adversary and the algorithm.

**Theorem 2.** *No myopic algorithm for JISP$_m$ can achieve an approximation ratio better than $\frac{1}{2}$. No myopic algorithm for WJISP$_1$ with equal weights per job can achieve an approximation ratio better than $3 - 2\sqrt{2} \approx 1/5.828 \approx 0.172$. No myopic algorithm for WJISP$_1$ with arbitrary weights can achieve an approximation ratio better than $1/7.103 \approx 0.141$.*

*Proof.* We restrict ourselves here to proving only the first two claims of the theorem. The proof of the third claim uses a similar approach as the proof of the second claim, but is more complicated. Details can be found in [8].

Consider the following construction for JISP$_m$. Initially, the adversary presents a set $Q$ of $2m$ intervals with the same right endpoint $p$. Let $S$ be the set of at most $m$ intervals that are selected by the algorithm at this time. Let $S'$ be a subset of $Q$ that contains all intervals in $S$ and that has cardinality $m$. For every interval in $S'$, the adversary presents an interval that belongs to the same job and that is to the right of $p$. The optimal solution contains $2m$ intervals, while the algorithm accepts at most $m$ intervals. This proves the first claim of the theorem. All intervals in this construction can have equal length.

Now consider WJISP$_1$ with equal weights per job. When the adversary presents an interval $i$ to the algorithm, we say that the adversary *plays* $i$. We can assume that the adversary knows exactly for which values of $w(i)$ the algorithm would accept $i$ and for which values of $w(i)$ the algorithm would reject $i$. Assume that the algorithm has currently selected a single interval $c$ and that the adversary is about to present an interval $i$ that intersects $c$. Let $A(i)$ be the set of all possible weights $w(i)$ for which the algorithm would accept $i$, and let $R(i)$ be the set of all possible weights $w(i)$ for which the algorithm would reject $i$. We can assume without loss of generality that $A(i) \neq \emptyset$, $R(i) \neq \emptyset$, and that $\sup R(i)$ is finite; otherwise, the approximation ratio of the algorithm would be unbounded. We would like to define $la(i)$ ("lightest accept") as the smallest value of $w(i)$ for which the algorithm would accept $i$ and $hr(i)$ ("heaviest reject") as the largest value of $w(i)$ for which the algorithm would reject $i$. More formally, these values are defined as follows, where $\delta_i > 0$ is a parameter that depends on $i$. If $\min A(i)$ exists, let $la(i) = \min A(i)$. Otherwise, let $la(i)$ be an arbitrary value in $A(i)$ such that $|la(i) - \inf A(i)| < \delta_i$. If $\max R(i)$ exists, let $hr(i) = \max R(i)$. Otherwise, let $hr(i)$ be an arbitrary value in $R(i)$ such that $|hr(i) - \sup R(i)| < \delta_i$. As $\sup R(i) \geq \inf A(i)$, we get

$$la(i) \leq hr(i) + 2\delta_i. \tag{3}$$

At any time of the game, the following conditions will hold: exactly one interval $c$ of weight $w(c)$ is currently selected by the algorithm; among the intervals that were presented to the algorithm before $c$, there is a subset $P \neq \emptyset$ of independent intervals with total weight $w(P) > 0$ such that no interval in $P$ belongs to the same job as $c$; the rightmost right endpoint of an interval in $P$ is to the left of the right endpoint of $c$. We use $x := w(P)/w(c)$ as an indicator for the *progress* made by the adversary so far; note that the ratio of the weight of an optimal solution to the weight of the solution of the algorithm is at least $x$ at all times (equivalently, the approximation ratio of the algorithm is no better than $1/x$).

Let $\varepsilon > 0$ be a small positive constant. We require $\varepsilon < 1/37$. The adversary tries to show that the approximation ratio of the algorithm is no better than $(1+40\varepsilon)/(3+2\sqrt{2})$. As we can choose $\varepsilon$ arbitrarily small and as $1/(3 + 2\sqrt{2}) = 3 - 2\sqrt{2}$, this implies the second claim of the theorem. The main part of the game consists of a number of steps. We will ensure that in every step either $x$ increases by the factor $1/(1 - \varepsilon)$ (we say that *the adversary has made progress* when this happens) or the game ends in favor of the adversary (i.e., the ratio of the algorithm is $(1 + 40\varepsilon)/(3+2\sqrt{2})$ or worse). The strategy used by the adversary in every step is sketched in Fig. 5. Here, $b$ is implicitly understood to be an interval belonging to the same job as $c$ and to the right of all previously presented intervals. At the beginning of the step, $a$ is understood to be an interval that belongs to a new job and that intersects $c$, but no interval presented before $c$. Finally, $a'$ is an interval that belongs to a new job and that intersects $a$, $b$ and $c$, but no interval presented before $c$. See Fig. 6 for a sketch of $a$, $b$, $c$ and $a'$.

Initially, the adversary presents an interval $i_0$ of weight $w(i_0) = 1$. The algorithm must accept this interval. Then the adversary presents an interval $i_1$ of weight $w(i_1) = 6$ that belongs to a new job, that intersects $i_0$, and whose right endpoint is to the right of the right endpoint of $i_0$. The algorithm must accept $i_1$ and preempt $i_0$; otherwise, its approximation ratio would be no better than $1/6$. We let $c = i_1$ and $P = \{i_0\}$,

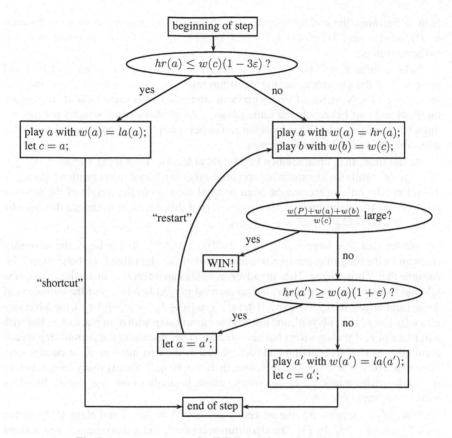

**Fig. 5.** Adversary strategy for WJISP$_1$ with equal weights per job

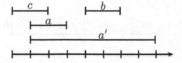

**Fig. 6.** Intervals played in a step without restart and shortcut. At the beginning of the step, only $c$ is accepted by the algorithm; during the step, the algorithm rejects $a$, accepts or rejects $b$, and accepts $a'$; at the end of the step, only $a'$ is accepted by the algorithm

thus getting $x = w(P)/w(c) = 1/6$. This completes the initialization of the game; the remainder of the game consists of steps that are carried out as sketched in Fig. 5.

We explain one step of the game in detail. Let $a$ be an interval of a new job that intersects $c$, but no earlier interval. For the definition of $hr(a)$ and $la(a)$, let $\delta_a = \varepsilon w(c)$. If $hr(a) \leq w(c) - 3\delta_a = w(c)(1 - 3\varepsilon)$, set $w(a) = la(a)$. Note that $la(a) \leq w(c) - \delta_a$ by (3). The adversary plays $a$; the algorithm accepts $a$ and preempts $c$.

Now $a$ becomes the current interval, and the adversary has made progress because $w(P)/w(a) \geq w(P)/(w(c) - \delta_a) = w(P)/w(c) \cdot 1/(1 - \varepsilon)$. The adversary proceeds to the next step.

Now assume that $hr(a) > w(c) - 3\delta_a$. The adversary sets $w(a) = hr(a)$ and presents $a$ to the algorithm, and the algorithm rejects $a$. Let $\alpha = w(a)/w(c)$, and note that $\alpha \geq 1 - 3\varepsilon$. Next, the adversary plays an interval $b$ that is to the right of all previous intervals and that belongs to the same job as $c$. As we have equal weights per job, we must have $w(b) = w(c)$. The algorithm can either accept $b$ (and preempt $c$) or not; this does not affect the adversary's strategy.

At this time, an optimal solution has weight at least $w(P) + w(a) + w(b) = w(P) + (1+\alpha)w(c)$, while the algorithm has accepted only the interval ($b$ or $c$) with weight $w(c)$. Therefore, the ratio of the weight of an optimal solution to the weight of the solution produced by the algorithm is at least $x + 1 + \alpha$ at this time. Let us denote this ratio by $\beta$, i.e., $\beta = \frac{w(P)+w(a)+w(b)}{w(c)} \geq x + 1 + \alpha$.

We say that $\beta$ is large if $\beta \geq (3 + 2\sqrt{2})/(1 + 40\varepsilon)$. If $\beta$ is large, the adversary stops and wins the game: the approximation ratio of the algorithm is no better than $1/\beta$. Assume that $\beta$ is not large. Then the adversary plays an interval $a'$ that belongs to a new job and that intersects $a$, $b$ and $c$, but no interval played before $c$. For the definition of $hr(a')$ and $la(a')$, let $\delta_{a'} = \varepsilon w(a)$. If $hr(a') \geq w(a) + \delta_{a'} = w(a)(1+\varepsilon)$, the adversary sets $w(a') = hr(a')$, plays $a'$, and restarts the current step with $a'$ in place of $a$ (and with $b$ in place of $c$, if the algorithm has accepted $b$). Here, restarting the current step means continuing as if $a'$ instead of $a$ had been played as the first interval of the current step. Note that $w(a') \geq w(a)(1+\varepsilon)$; therefore, there can be only finitely many restarts before the approximation ratio of the algorithm (which is smaller than $w(c)/w(a)$) becomes worse than, say, $1/6$.

If $hr(a') < w(a) + \delta_{a'}$, the adversary sets $w(a') = la(a')$ and plays $a'$. Note that $la(a') \leq w(a) + 3\delta_{a'}$ by (3). The algorithm accepts $a'$, and $a'$ becomes the new current interval. Observe that $P \cup \{a, b\}$ is a set of independent intervals. The progress of the adversary is now

$$\frac{w(P) + w(a) + w(b)}{w(a')} \geq \frac{w(P) + w(a) + w(b)}{w(a) + 3\delta_{a'}} = \frac{\frac{x}{\alpha} + 1 + \frac{1}{\alpha}}{1 + 3\varepsilon}.$$

If $\frac{\frac{x}{\alpha}+1+\frac{1}{\alpha}}{1+3\varepsilon} \geq \frac{x}{1-\varepsilon}$, the adversary has made progress, and the next step begins with current interval $a'$. Assume that the adversary has not made progress. Then we must have $\frac{\frac{x}{\alpha}+1+\frac{1}{\alpha}}{1+3\varepsilon} < \frac{x}{1-\varepsilon}$. This implies

$$\frac{1}{\alpha} < \frac{x\frac{1+3\varepsilon}{1-\varepsilon} - 1}{x + 1}. \tag{4}$$

If $x\frac{1+3\varepsilon}{1-\varepsilon} - 1 \leq 0$, this cannot happen. Therefore, we must have

$$x > \frac{1 - \varepsilon}{1 + 3\varepsilon}. \tag{5}$$

We obtain from (4) that $\alpha > (x+1)/(x\frac{1+3\varepsilon}{1-\varepsilon} - 1)$. Therefore,

$$\beta \geq x + 1 + \alpha \geq x + 1 + \frac{x+1}{x\frac{1+3\varepsilon}{1-\varepsilon} - 1} = \frac{x^2 + x}{x - \frac{1-\varepsilon}{1+3\varepsilon}}.$$

We claim that $(x^2 + x)/(x - \frac{1-\varepsilon}{1+3\varepsilon})$ is large, implying that the adversary has actually won the game already before presenting $a'$.

First, consider the case that $x \leq 1.1$. As $\varepsilon \leq 1/37$, we have $\frac{1-\varepsilon}{1+3\varepsilon} = 1 - \frac{4}{1/\varepsilon+3} \geq 0.9$. Therefore, we get $x - \frac{1-\varepsilon}{1+3\varepsilon} \leq 1.1 - 0.9 = 0.2$ and, by (5), $x^2 + x \geq 0.9^2 + 0.9 = 1.71$. This implies that $\beta \geq 1.71/0.2 = 8.55$. Obviously, $\beta$ is large.

Now consider the case that $x > 1.1$. We get: $x - \frac{1-\varepsilon}{1+3\varepsilon} \leq x - 1 + 4\varepsilon = (x-1)(1 + 40\varepsilon) - 40\varepsilon x + 44\varepsilon \leq (x-1)(1 + 40\varepsilon)$. Therefore, we obtain

$$\frac{x^2 + x}{x - \frac{1-\varepsilon}{1+3\varepsilon}} \geq \frac{x^2 + x}{x - 1} \cdot \frac{1}{1 + 40\varepsilon}.$$

Is is easy to show that the function $f(x) = \frac{x^2+x}{x-1}$, where $x$ is in the range $[1.1, \infty)$, is minimized for $x = 1 + \sqrt{2}$ with $f(1 + \sqrt{2}) = 3 + 2\sqrt{2}$. Therefore, $\beta$ is large, and the adversary won the game already before $a'$ was played.  $\square$

# References

1. G. Ausiello, P. Crescenzi, G. Gambosi, V. Kann, A. Marchetti-Spaccamela, and M. Protasi. *Complexity and Approximation. Combinatorial Optimization Problems and their Approximability Properties.* Springer, Berlin, 1999.
2. A. Bar-Noy, R. Bar-Yehuda, A. Freund, J. S. Naor, and B. Schieber. A unified approach to approximating resource allocation and scheduling. In *Proceedings of the 32nd Annual ACM Symposium on Theory of Computing STOC'00*, pages 735–744, 2000.
3. A. Bar-Noy, S. Guha, J. S. Naor, and B. Schieber. Approximating the throughput of multiple machines under real-time scheduling. In *Proceedings of the 31st Annual ACM Symposium on Theory of Computing STOC'99*, pages 622–631, 1999.
4. P. Berman and B. DasGupta. Improvements in throughput maximization for real-time scheduling. In *Proceedings of the 32nd Annual ACM Symposium on Theory of Computing STOC'00*, pages 680–687, 2000.
5. P. Berman, Z. Zhang, J. Bouck, and W. Miller. Aligning two fragmented sequences. Manuscript, 1999.
6. M. C. Carlisle and E. L. Lloyd. On the $k$-coloring of intervals. *Discrete Appl. Math.*, 59:225–235, 1995.
7. Y. Crama, O. Flippo, J. van de Klundert, and F. Spieksma. The assembly of printed circuit boards: a case with multiple machines and multiple board types. *European Journal of Operational Research*, 98:457–472, 1997.
8. T. Erlebach and F. Spieksma. Simple algorithms for a weighted interval scheduling problem. Technical Report M00-01, Department of Mathematics, Maastricht University, April 2000. http://www.tik.ee.ethz.ch/~erlebach/Report-M00-01.ps.gz.
9. S. A. Goldman, J. Parwatikar, and S. Suri. Online scheduling with hard deadlines. *Journal of Algorithms*, 34(2):370–389, 2000.

10. M. H. Goldwasser. Patience is a virtue: The effect of slack on competitiveness for admission control. In *Proceedings of the 10th Annual ACM–SIAM Symposium on Discrete Algorithms SODA'99*, pages 396–405, 1999.
11. D. Hochbaum. *Approximation algorithms for NP-hard problems*. PWS Publishing Company, Boston, 1997.
12. F. Spieksma. On the approximability of an interval scheduling problem. *Journal of Scheduling*, 2:215–227, 1999.

# Efficient Minus and Signed Domination in Graphs*

Chin Lung Lu[1], Sheng-Lung Peng[2], and Chuan Yi Tang[3]

[1] National Center for High-Performance Computing, P.O. Box 19-136, Hsinchu, Taiwan 300, R.O.C. Email: cllu@nchc.gov.tw
[2] Department of Computer Science and Information Engineering, National Dong Hwa University, Hualien, Taiwan, R.O.C. Email: lung@csie.ndhu.edu.tw
[3] Department of Computer Science, National Tsing Hua University, Hsinchu, Taiwan 300, R.O.C. Email: cytang@cs.nthu.edu.tw

**Abstract.** We show that the efficient minus (resp., signed) domination problem is NP-complete for chordal graphs, chordal bipartite graphs, planar bipartite graphs and planar graphs of maximum degree 4 (resp., for chordal graphs). Based on the forcing property on blocks of vertices and automata theory, we provide a uniform approach to show that in a special class of interval graphs, every graph (resp., every graph with no vertex of odd degree) has an efficient minus (resp., signed) dominating function. Besides, we show that the efficient minus domination problem is equivalent to the efficient domination problem on trees.

## 1 Introduction

Let $G = (V, E)$ be a finite, undirected and simple graph. For a vertex $v \in V$, let $N(v) = \{u \in V | (u, v) \in E\}$. The *closed neighborhood* of $v$ is $N[v] = \{v\} \cup N(v)$. Let $f : V \to Y$ be a function which assigns to each $v \in V$ a value in $Y$. For simplicity, we let $f(S) = \sum_{u \in S} f(u)$ for any set $S \subseteq V$. We call $f(V)$ the *weight* of $f$. The function $f$ is called an *efficient $Y$-dominating function* if $f(N[v]) = 1$ for all $v \in V$ and $Y$ is called the *weight set* of $f$. In particular, $f$ is called an *efficient* (resp., *efficient minus* and *efficient signed*) *dominating function* if the weight set $Y$ is $\{0, 1\}$ (resp., $\{-1, 0, 1\}$ and $\{-1, 1\}$). In [1], Bange *et al.* showed that if $f_1$ and $f_2$ are any two efficient $Y$-dominating functions of $G$, then $f_1(V) = f_2(V)$. That is, all the efficient $Y$-dominating functions of $G$ have the same weight. Hence, the *efficient $Y$-domination problem* is the problem of finding an efficient $Y$-dominating function of $G$. The efficient minus and signed domination problems have applications in sociology, electronics, etc [7,8,9,14,15]. Note that not every graph has an efficient (minus, signed) dominating function. By the definition, an efficient (signed) dominating function is also an efficient minus dominating function, but the converse is not true.

There is an extensive number of papers concerning the algorithmic complexity of the efficient domination problem in several graph classes [2,4,5,6,10,17,18,

---

* Supported partly by the National Science Council of the Republic of China under grant NSC 89-2213-E-259-010.

D.T. Lee and S.-H. Teng (Eds.): ISAAC 2000, LNCS 1969, pp. 241–253, 2000.

19,20]. The most frequently used algorithmic technique for solving the efficient domination problems is dynamic programming based on the *forcing property* on vertices, i.e., the value 1 assigned to a vertex $v$ forces the other vertices in $N[v]$ to be assigned the value 0. However, for the efficient minus and signed domination problems, this forcing property does not work because of the "neutralization" of values $-1$ and 1. Hence, the techniques used for the efficient domination problem cannot be applied to these two problems. To date, the only known result is that the efficient signed domination problem is NP-complete on general graphs [1].

In this paper, we show that the efficient minus domination problem is NP-complete on chordal graphs, chordal bipartite graphs, planar bipartite graphs and planar graphs of maximum degree 4; the efficient signed domination problem is NP-complete on chordal graphs. We find that a special class of interval graphs, which we call chain interval graphs, can be represented as a sequence of blocks, where a *block* is a set of vertices in which all vertices have the same closed neighborhood. According to clique and block structures, the chain interval graphs can be described by a formal language $\mathcal{L}$. By applying the forcing property on blocks, we create a finite state automaton which exactly accepts $\mathcal{L}$. As a result, every chain interval graph has an efficient minus dominating function. Similarly, we show that every chain interval graph with no vertex of odd degree has an efficient signed dominating function. In addition, we give linear-time algorithms to find them. For trees, we show that the efficient minus domination problem coincides with the efficient domination problem. According to [2], we can hence find an efficient minus dominating function of a tree in linear time.

## 2    NP-Completeness Results

A graph is *chordal* if every cycle of length greater than 3 has a *chord*, i.e., an edge between two non-consecutive vertices of the cycle [13]. *Chordal bipartite graphs* are bipartite graphs in which every cycle of length greater than 4 has a chord [13].

**Efficient Domination (*ED*)**
**Instance:** A graph $G = (V, E)$.
**Question:** Does $G$ have an efficient dominating function?
**Efficient Minus Domination (*EMD*)**
**Instance:** A graph $G = (V, E)$.
**Question:** Does $G$ have an efficient minus dominating function?

It is known that *ED* is NP-complete even when restricted to chordal graphs [20], chordal bipartite graphs [18], planar bipartite graphs [18] and planar graphs of maximum degree 3 [10].

**Theorem 1.** *EMD is NP-complete for chordal graphs, chordal bipartite graphs, planar bipartite graphs and planar graphs of maximum degree 4.*

*Proof.* It is not difficult to see that *EMD* on chordal graphs (chordal bipartite graphs, planar bipartite graphs and planar graphs of maximum degree 4) is in

NP. Hence, we only show that this problem can be reduced from *ED* on the same graphs in polynomial time.

Given a graph $G = (V_G, E_G)$, we construct the graph $H = (V_H, E_H)$ by adding a path of length 3, say $v$—$v_1$—$v_2$—$v_3$, to each vertex $v$ of $G$. That is, $V_H = V_G \cup (\bigcup_{v \in V_G} \{v_1, v_2, v_3\})$ and $E_H = E_G \cup (\bigcup_{v \in V_G} \{(v, v_1), (v_1, v_2), (v_2, v_3)\})$. Then, $H$ is a chordal graph (resp., chordal bipartite graph, planar bipartite graph and planar graph of maximum degree 4) if $G$ is a chordal graph (resp., chordal bipartite graph, planar bipartite graph and planar graph of maximum degree 3). The construction of $H$ can be done in polynomial time.

Now, we show that $G$ has an efficient dominating function $f$ if and only if $H$ has an efficient minus dominating function $g$. First, suppose that $G$ has an efficient dominating function $f$. Note that for each $v \in V_G$, there are four corresponding vertices $v, v_1, v_2$ and $v_3$ in $V_H$. Define a function $g : V_H \to \{-1, 0, 1\}$ of $H$ as follows. Let $g(v) = f(v)$ for each $v \in V_G$. Furthermore, if $g(v) = 0$, then let $g(v_1) = 0, g(v_2) = 1$ and $g(v_3) = 0$; otherwise, let $g(v_1) = g(v_2) = 0$ and $g(v_3) = 1$. It can be verified that $g(N[v]) = g(N[v_1]) = g(N[v_2]) = g(N[v_3]) = 1$. Hence, $g$ is an efficient minus dominating function of $H$.

Conversely, suppose that $H$ has an efficient minus dominating function $g$. We then claim that $g(v) \geq 0, g(v_1) = 0, g(v_2) \geq 0$ and $g(v_3) \geq 0$ for each $v \in V_G$. If $g(v_3) = -1$, then $g(N[v_3]) \leq 0$, which contradicts the fact that $g(N[v_3]) = 1$. If $g(v_2) = -1$, then $g(N[v_3]) \leq 0$, a contradiction again. If $g(v_1) = -1$, then $g(N[v_2]) = 1$ implies that $g(v_2) = g(v_3) = 1$, which leads to $g(N[v_3]) = 2$, a contradiction. If $g(v_1) = 1$, then $g(N[v_2]) = 1$ implies that $g(v_2) = g(v_3) = 0$, which leads to $g(N[v_3]) = 0$, a contradiction. If $g(v) = -1$, then $g(N[v_1]) = 1$ and $g(N[v_2]) = 1$ imply that $g(v_1) = g(v_2) = 1$ and $g(v_3) = -1$, which contradicts the fact that $g(v_3) \geq 0$. Define a function $f : V_G \to \{0, 1\}$ of $G$ by letting $f(v) = g(v)$ for every $v \in V_G$. It is not hard to see that $f$ is an efficient dominating function of $G$ since $f(N[v]) = 1$ for all $v$ in $V_G$.  □

### One-in-three 3SAT

**Instance:** A set $U$ of $n$ boolean variables and a collection $\mathcal{C}$ of $m$ clauses over $U$ such that each clause has exactly three literals.

**Question:** Is there a truth assignment $t : U \to \{true, false\}$ for $\mathcal{C}$ such that each clause in $\mathcal{C}$ has exactly one true literal?

### Efficient Signed Domination (*ESD*)

**Instance:** A graph $G = (V, E)$.

**Question:** Does $G$ have an efficient signed dominating function?

Next, we will show that one-in-three 3SAT, which is known to be NP-complete [11], is reducible to *ESD* on chordal graphs in polynomial time.

**Theorem 2.** *ESD is NP-complete for chordal graphs.*

*Proof.* It is not hard to see that *ESD* on chordal graphs is in NP. We now show that one-in-three 3SAT is polynomially reducible to this problem. Let $U = \{u_1, u_2, \ldots, u_n\}$ and $\mathcal{C} = \{C_1, C_2, \ldots, C_m\}$ be an arbitrary instance of one-in-three 3SAT, where each clause $C_j, 1 \leq j \leq m$, contains three literals $l_{j,1}, l_{j,2}$ and $l_{j,3}$. We assume that no clause contains both a literal and its negation because

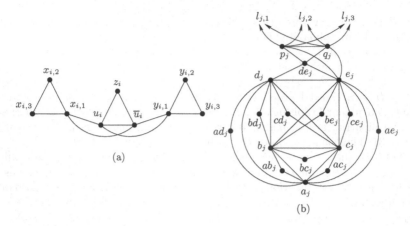

**Fig. 1.** (a) The subgraph $G_{u_i}$. (b) The subgraph $G_{C_j}$.

this clause is always true and can be omitted. Let $U' = \{u_i, \overline{u}_i | 1 \le i \le n\}$. We construct a chordal graph $G = (V, E)$ as follows.

(1) For each variable $u_i$, $1 \le i \le n$, we construct the subgraph $G_{u_i}$ of $G$ as shown in Figure 1 (a).
(2) For each clause $C_j$, $1 \le j \le m$, we construct the subgraph $G_{C_j}$ of $G$ as shown in Figure 1 (b), where each $G_{C_j}$ is connected to the three vertices corresponding to the three literals in clause $C_j$.
(3) We add all possible edges in $G_{U'}$ such that $G_{U'}$ forms a complete graph, *i.e.*, any two vertices of $U'$ are adjacent in $G$.

Note that $l_{j,1}, l_{j,2}, l_{j,3} \in U'$. Since the subgraphs $G_{u_i}$, $1 \le i \le n$, and $G_{C_j}$, $1 \le j \le m$, are all chordal and the subgraph $G_{U'}$ is complete, $G$ is a chordal graph and can be constructed in polynomial time.

Let $f : V \to \{-1, 1\}$ be an efficient signed dominating function of $G$. Clearly, for a vertex $v$ of degree $2k$, where $k$ is a positive integer, $f$ must assign $k + 1$ vertices of $N[v]$ values of 1 and $k$ vertices of $N[v]$ values of $-1$. Consider each subgraph $G_{C_j}$, $1 \le j \le m$. Suppose that $f(a_j) = -1$. Then, $f(ab_j) = f(b_j) = f(ac_j) = f(c_j) = f(ad_j) = f(d_j) = f(ae_j) = f(e_j) = 1$ (since $ab_j, ac_j, ad_j$ and $ae_j$ are vertices of degree 2) and hence $f(N[a_j]) = 8 - 1 > 1$, a contradiction. Therefore, $f(a_j) = 1$ and similarly, $f(b_j) = f(c_j) = 1$. Suppose that $f(d_j) = -1$. Then, $f(ad_j) = f(bd_j) = f(cd_j) = 1$ and $f(d_j) + f(de_j) + f(e_j) \ge -3$. As a result, $f(N[d_j]) \ge 6 - 3 > 1$, a contradiction. Hence, $f(d_j) = 1$ and similarly, $f(e_j) = 1$. For each vertex $v$ of degree 2 in $G(C_j)$, $f(v) = -1$ since $f(a_j) = f(b_j) = f(c_j) = f(d_j) = f(e_j) = 1$. Note that $f(N[d_j]) = 1$ implies that $f(de_j) = -1$ and then $f(N[e_j]) = 1$ implies that $f(p_j) + f(q_j) = 0$. Consider each $G_{u_i}$, $1 \le i \le n$. Since $N[y_{i,1}] = N[y_{i,2}] \cup \{u_i, \overline{u}_i\}$ and $f(N[y_{i,1}]) = f(N[y_{i,2}]) = 1$, $f(u_i) + f(\overline{u}_i) = 0$ and hence $f(z_i) = 1$. Note that $u_i$ (resp., $\overline{u}_i$) is adjacent to $p_j$ if and only if $u_i$ (resp., $\overline{u}_i$) is adjacent to $q_j$, and for each $1 \le i' \le n$ with $i' \ne i$, both $u_{i'}$ and $\overline{u}_{i'}$ are adjacent to $u_i$ (resp., $\overline{u}_i$). Hence, $f(N[u_i]) = 1 + f(x_{i,1}) + f(y_{i,1}) = 1$, which means that $f(x_{i,1}) + f(y_{i,1}) = 0$. Moreover, $f(y_{i,1}) + f(y_{i,2}) + f(y_{i,3}) = 1$ and $f(x_{i,1}) + f(x_{i,2}) + f(x_{i,3}) = 1$ since $f(N[y_{i,2}]) = 1$ and $f(N[x_{i,2}]) = 1$, resp.

Now, we show that $\mathcal{C}$ has a satisfying truth assignment if and only if $G$ has an efficient signed dominating function. First, suppose that $f$ is an efficient signed dominating function of $G$. Since $f(p_j) + f(q_j) = 0$, $f(de_j) = -1$ and $f(e_j) = 1$, $f(N[p_j]) = 1$ implies that there is exactly one of $l_{j,1}, l_{j,2}$ and $l_{j,3}$ whose function value is $-1$. Let $t : U \rightarrow \{true, false\}$ be defined by $t(u_i) = true$ if and only if $f(u_i) = -1$. Since $f(u_i) + f(\overline{u}_i) = 0$, $t(u_i)$ is $true$ if and only if $t(\overline{u}_i)$ is $false$. Hence, $t$ is a one-in-three satisfying truth assignment for $\mathcal{C}$.

Conversely, suppose that $\mathcal{C}$ has a satisfying truth assignment. Then, we can identify an efficient signed dominating function $f$ of $G$ according to the mention above. In particular, $f(u_i) = -1$ if $u_i$ is assigned $true$; otherwise, $f(u_i) = 1$.   $\square$

## 3   Interval Graphs

A graph $G = (V, E)$ is an *interval graph* if there exists a one-to-one correspondence between $V$ and a family $F$ of intervals such that two vertices in $V$ are adjacent if and only if their corresponding intervals overlap [3,13]. $S \subseteq V$ is a *clique* if $S$ induces a complete subgraph of $G$. A clique is *maximal* if there is no clique properly containing it as a subset. Gilmore and Hoffman [12] showed that for an interval graph $G$, its maximal cliques can be linearly ordered such that for every vertex $v$ of $G$, the maximal cliques containing $v$ occur consecutively. We use $G = (C_1, C_2, \ldots, C_s)$ to denote the interval graph $G$ with $s$ linearly ordered maximal cliques and call it the *clique structure* of $G$ (see Figure 2 (c)).

The efficient domination problem on interval graphs can be solved in linear time using dynamic programming, which based on the forcing property on vertices. However, this technique seems not be applied for both the efficient minus and signed domination problems on interval graphs because the forcing property on vertices does not work due to the "neutralization" of values $-1$ and $1$.

A *chain interval graph* $G = (C_1, C_2, \ldots, C_s)$ is an interval graph in which $C_{i-1} \cap C_i \cap C_{i+1} = \varnothing$ for any $1 < i < s$. By the definition, any clique $C_i$ of $G$, $1 \leq i \leq s$, can be partitioned into three subsets $B_{i,l} = C_{i-1} \cap C_i$, $B_{i,r} = C_i \cap C_{i+1}$ and $B_{i,m} = C_i \setminus (B_{i,l} \cup B_{i,r})$, where $C_0 = C_{s+1} = \varnothing$. We call these subsets *blocks* and say that $C_i$ *contains* blocks $B_{i,l}, B_{i,m}$ and $B_{i,r}$. Note that block $B_{i,m}$ might be empty. Let $bn(C_i)$ be the number of non-empty blocks of $C_i$.

*Remark 1.* If $s \geq 2$, then both $C_1$ and $C_s$ contain exactly two blocks.

*Remark 2.* For any two consecutive cliques $C_i$ and $C_{i+1}$ of $G$, $B_{i,r} = B_{i+1,l}$. For a vertex $v \in B_{i,r}$, $N[v] = C_i \cup C_{i+1} = C_i \cup (C_{i+1} \setminus B_{i+1,l})$.

*Remark 3.* Let $C_i$ be a clique with $bn(C_i) = 3$. For a vertex $v \in B_{i,m}$, $N[v] = C_i = B_{i,l} \cup B_{i,m} \cup B_{i,r}$.

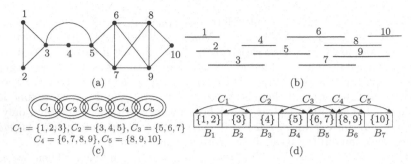

**Fig. 2.** (a) A chain interval graph $G$. (b) An interval representation of $G$. (c) The clique structure of $G$. (d) The block structure of $G$.

Based on the clique structure of $G$, we can represent $G$ by linearly ordered blocks $B_1, B_2, \ldots, B_t$, $t \geq s$, such that each clique contains either consecutive two or three blocks. We call this representation the *block structure* of $G$ and denote it by $G = (B_1, B_2, \ldots, B_t)$ (see Figure 2 (d)). Note that $B_1, B_2, \ldots, B_t$ is a partition of $V$. We define the *block-number string* $bs(G)$ of $G$ to be the string $bn(C_1)\, bn(C_2) \cdots bn(C_s)$. For example, the block-number string of $G$ shown in Figure 2 is 23222. For convenience, if $G$ contains only one clique, we define $bs(G) = 2$. Let $\mathcal{L}$ be the language consisting of the block-number strings of all chain interval graphs. Then, we have the following lemma.

**Lemma 1.** $\mathcal{L}$ *is a regular language and its regular expression is* $2 + 2(2+3)^*2$.

### 3.1  The Efficient Minus Domination Problem

Let $f$ be an efficient minus dominating $(EMD)$ function of $G = (B_1, B_2, \cdots, B_t)$. We call $f$ a *simple EMD function* of $G$ if $f(B_i) \in \{-1, 0, 1\}$ for all $B_i$, $1 \leq i \leq t$. A clique $C_i$, $1 \leq i \leq s$, is $P$ type if $bn(C_i) = 2$ and $Q$ type if $bn(C_i) = 3$. The clique $C_i$ is called a $P_{(a,b)}$ clique if $C_i$ is $P$ type, $f(B_{i,l}) = a$ and $f(B_{i,r}) = b$, and a $Q_{(a,b,c)}$ clique if $C_i$ is $Q$ type, $f(B_{i,l}) = a, f(B_{i,m}) = b$ and $f(B_{i,r}) = c$. According to Remarks 2 and 3, resp., we have the following two lemmas.

**Lemma 2.** *Let $f$ be an $EMD$ function of $G$ and let $C_i$ and $C_{i+1}$ be two consecutive cliques of $G$. Then, $f(C_i) + f(C_{i+1} \setminus B_{i+1,l}) = 1$.*

**Lemma 3.** *Let $f$ be an $EMD$ function of $G$ and $C_i$ be a $Q$ type clique. Then, $f(B_{i,l}) + f(B_{i,m}) + f(B_{i,r}) = 1$.*

**Lemma 4.** *Let $f$ be a simple $EMD$ function of $G$. If $s \geq 2$, then $C_1$ and $C_s$ are either a $P_{(0,1)}$ or $P_{(1,0)}$ clique.*

*Proof.* Let $v \in B_{1,l}$. Clearly, $N[v] = C_1 = B_{1,l} \cup B_{1,r}$. $f(N[v]) = 1$ implies that either (1) $f(B_{1,l}) = 0$ and $f(B_{1,r}) = 1$, or (2) $f(B_{1,l}) = 1$ and $f(B_{1,r}) = 0$. That is, $C_1$ is either a $P_{(0,1)}$ or $P_{(1,0)}$ clique. Similarly, $C_s$ is either a $P_{(0,1)}$ or $P_{(1,0)}$ clique. $\qquad \square$

**Lemma 5.** *Let $f$ be a simple EMD function of $G$ and $1 < i < s$. If clique $C_i$ is $Q$ type, then $C_i$ is either a $Q_{(0,0,1)}, Q_{(0,1,0)}, Q_{(1,0,0)}$ or $Q_{(1,-1,1)}$ clique.*

*Proof.* By Lemma 3, we have $f(B_{i,l}) + f(B_{i,m}) + f(B_{i,r}) = 1$. We claim that $f(B_{i,r}) \neq -1$ and $f(B_{i,l}) \neq -1$. Suppose that $f(B_{i,r}) = -1$. Then, $f(B_{i,l}) + f(B_{i,m}) = 2$. If $C_{i+1}$ is $Q$ type, then by Lemma 2, $f(B_{i,l}) + f(B_{i,m}) + f(B_{i,r}) + f(B_{i+1,m}) + f(B_{i+1,r}) = 1$. As a result, $f(B_{i+1,l}) + f(B_{i+1,m}) + f(B_{i+1,r}) = -1$, which contradicts Lemma 3. That is, $C_{i+1}$ is $P$ type. By Lemma 2, we have $f(B_{i+1,r}) = 0$ and hence $C_{i+1}$ is a $P_{(-1,0)}$ clique. According to Lemma 4, $i + 1 < s$. If $C_{i+2}$ is $P$ type, then since $f(B_{i+2,r}) \in \{-1, 0, 1\}$, $f(B_{i+1,l}) + f(B_{i+1,r}) + f(B_{i+2,r}) \leq 0$, a contradiction to Lemma 2. If $C_{i+2}$ is $Q$ type, then $f(B_{i+1,l}) + f(B_{i+1,r}) + f(B_{i+2,m}) + f(B_{i+2,r}) = 1$ by Lemma 2. As a result, $f(B_{i+2,l}) + f(B_{i+2,m}) + f(B_{i+2,r}) = 2$, which contradicts Lemma 3. Therefore, $f(B_{i,r}) \neq -1$. Similarly, we have $f(B_{i,l}) \neq -1$.

By the above discussion, $f(B_{i,l}), f(B_{i,r}) \in \{0, 1\}$, $f(B_{i,m}) \in \{-1, 0, 1\}$ and $f(B_{i,l}) + f(B_{i,m}) + f(B_{i,r}) = 1$. We have the following two cases.

Case 1: $f(B_{i,r}) = 0$. Either $f(B_{i,l}) = 0$ and $f(B_{i,m}) = 1$, or $f(B_{i,l}) = 1$ and $f(B_{i,m}) = 0$. That is, $C_i$ is a $Q_{(0,1,0)}$ or $Q_{(1,0,0)}$ clique.

Case 2: $f(B_{i,r}) = 1$. Either $f(B_{i,l}) = 0$ and $f(B_{i,m}) = 0$, or $f(B_{i,l}) = 1$ and $f(B_{i,m}) = -1$. That is, $C_i$ is a $Q_{(0,0,1)}$ or $Q_{(1,-1,1)}$ clique. $\qquad \square$

Similar to Lemma 5, we have the following lemma.

**Lemma 6.** *Let $f$ be a simple EMD function of $G$ and $1 < i < s$. If clique $C_i$ is $P$ type, then $C_i$ is either a $P_{(0,0)}, P_{(0,1)}$ or $P_{(1,0)}$ clique.*

**Lemma 7.** *Let $f$ be a simple EMD function of $G$ and $1 \leq i < s$.*

(1) *If $C_i$ is a $P_{(0,0)}$ clique, then $C_{i+1}$ is either a $P_{(0,1)}$, $Q_{(0,0,1)}$ or $Q_{(0,1,0)}$ clique.*
(2) *If $C_i$ is a $P_{(0,1)}$ clique, then $C_{i+1}$ is either a $P_{(1,0)}$, $Q_{(1,0,0)}$ or $Q_{(1,-1,1)}$ clique.*
(3) *If $C_i$ is a $P_{(1,0)}$ clique, then $C_{i+1}$ is a $P_{(0,0)}$ clique.*
(4) *If $C_i$ is a $Q_{(0,0,1)}$ clique, then $C_{i+1}$ is either a $P_{(1,0)}$, $Q_{(1,0,0)}$ or $Q_{(1,-1,1)}$ clique.*
(5) *If $C_i$ is a $Q_{(0,1,0)}$ clique, then $C_{i+1}$ is a $P_{(0,0)}$ clique.*
(6) *If $C_i$ is a $Q_{(1,0,0)}$ clique, then $C_{i+1}$ is a $P_{(0,0)}$ clique.*
(7) *If $C_i$ is a $Q_{(1,-1,1)}$ clique, then $C_{i+1}$ is either a $P_{(1,0)}$, $Q_{(1,0,0)}$ or $Q_{(1,-1,1)}$ clique.*

*Proof.* Due to the limitation of space, we only show the Statement (1).

(1) Let $C_i$ be a $P_{(0,0)}$ clique. If $C_{i+1}$ is $P$ type, then by Lemma 2, $f(B_{i,l}) + f(B_{i,r}) + f(B_{i+1,r}) = 1$ and hence $f(B_{i+1,r}) = 1$, i.e., $C_{i+1}$ is a $P_{(0,1)}$ clique. If

$C_{i+1}$ is $Q$ type, then $f(B_{i,l}) + f(B_{i,r}) + f(B_{i+1,m}) + f(B_{i+1,r}) = 1$ and hence $f(B_{i+1,m}) + f(B_{i+1,r}) = 1$. According to Lemma 5, $C_{i+1}$ may be a $Q_{(0,0,1)}$ or $Q_{(0,1,0)}$ clique.

□

According to Lemmas 4 and 7, we can create a directed graph $H = (V_H, E_H)$, where $V_H = \{P_{(0,0)}, P_{(0,1)}, P_{(1,0)}, Q_{(0,0,1)}, Q_{(0,1,0)}, Q_{(1,0,0)}, Q_{(1,-1,1)}\}$ and $E_H = \{\overrightarrow{uv} \mid u, v \in V$ and $u, v$ satisfy one of the conditions of Lemma 7$\}$. We add a $start$ node in $H$ such that there are two edges from $start$ node to $P_{(0,1)}$ and $P_{(1,0)}$. For each edge $\overrightarrow{uv}$, if $v \in \{P_{(0,0)}, P_{(0,1)}, P_{(1,0)}\}$, then we label $\overrightarrow{uv}$ with 2; otherwise, we label $\overrightarrow{uv}$ with 3. By letting $P_{(0,1)}$ and $P_{(1,0)}$ be two termination nodes, $H$ becomes a nondeterministic finite state automaton and we denote it as $\mathcal{M}$ (see Figure 3). In $\mathcal{M}$, each path $p$ from $start$ node to a termination node specifies a string $str(p)$ by concatenating the characters that label the edges of $p$. Clearly, $str(p)$ is a string accepted by $\mathcal{M}$. Furthermore, $\mathcal{M}$ can be reduced into a deterministic finite state automaton $\mathcal{M}''$ with the minimum states (see Figure 4) using a standard transformation [16].

According to $\mathcal{M}''$, it is not hard to see that the accepted language of $\mathcal{M}''$ is $2 + 2(2 + 3)^*2$. Hence, we have the following lemma.

**Lemma 8.** *The accepted language of $\mathcal{M}$ is $2 + 2(2 + 3)^*2$.*

According to Lemmas 1 and 8, $\mathcal{L}$ is accepted by $\mathcal{M}$. That is, for any chain interval graph $G$, we can find a path $p = (start, n_1, n_2, \ldots, n_r)$ from $start$ node to a termination node $n_r$ in $\mathcal{M}$ such that $str(p)$ is equal to $bs(G)$. The existence of path $p$ implies that $G$ affirmatively admits a simple $EMD$ function $f$ defined as follows. Let $f(B_{i,l}) = a$ and $f(B_{i,r}) = b$ if $n_i = P_{(a,b)}$, and let $f(B_{i,l}) = a$, $f(B_{i,m}) = b$ and $f(B_{i,r}) = c$ if $n_i = Q_{(a,b,c)}$. Furthermore, for each block $B_j$ of $G$, we first randomly choose one vertex $u$ of $B_j$ and let $f(u) = f(B_j)$. Then, for each vertex $v \in B_i \setminus \{u\}$, we let $f(v) = 0$. It is not hard to see that $f$ is a simple $EMD$ function of $G$. For example, considering the graph $G$ as shown in Figure 2, we have $p = (start, P_{(0,1)}, Q_{(1,-1,1)}, P_{(1,0,)}, P_{(0,0)}, P_{(0,1)})$. Then, we find a simple $EMD$ function $f$ of $G$ by letting $f(B_1) = 0, f(B_2) = 1, f(B_3) = -1, f(B_4) =$

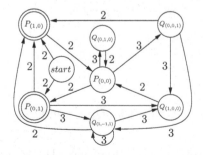

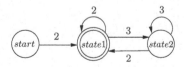

**Fig. 3.** The nondeterministic finite state automaton $\mathcal{M}$.

**Fig. 4.** The refined deterministic finite state automaton $\mathcal{M}''$.

$1, f(B_5) = 0, f(B_6) = 0, f(B_7) = 1, f(1) = f(2) = f(6) = f(7) = f(8) = f(9) = 0, f(3) = f(5) = f(10) = 1$ and $f(4) = -1$. Since a simple $EMD$ function is an efficient minus dominating function, we have the following theorem.

**Theorem 3.** *Every chain interval graph has an efficient minus dominating function.*

The remaining work is to efficiently find a path $p$ of $G$ in $\mathcal{M}$ such that $str(p) = bs(G)$. First, according to the clique structure $G = (C_1, C_2, \ldots C_s)$ and $\mathcal{M}$, we construct a directed acyclic graph $DAG(G)$ with $s$ layers as follow. For simplicity, we use $V_i$ to denote the set of nodes in layer $i$ and $E_i$ to denote the set of the directed edges $\overrightarrow{uv}$ with $u \in V_i$ and $v \in V_{i+1}$.

1. $V_1 = \{P_{(0,1)}, P_{(1,0)}\}$.
2. Suppose that $V_i = \{u_1, u_2, \ldots, u_k\}$ for $1 \le i < s - 1$. Then $E_i = \bigcup_{1 \le j \le k} \{\overrightarrow{u_j v} | \overrightarrow{u_j v}$ is an edge of $\mathcal{M}$ with label $bn(C_{i+1})\}$ and $V_{i+1} = \{v | \overrightarrow{uv} \in E_i\}$.
3. $E_{s-1} = \{\overrightarrow{uv} | u \in V_{s-1}, v \in \{P_{(0,1)}, P_{(1,0)}\}$ and $\overrightarrow{uv}$ is an edge of $\mathcal{M}\}$ and $V_s = \{v | \overrightarrow{uv} \in E_s\}$.

For example, considering the graph $G$ of Figure 2, the $DAG(G)$ is illustrated in Figure 5. After constructing $DAG(G)$, $p$ can be easily found by starting a node in layer $s$ and backtracking to node in layer 1. Since $s = O(|V|)$ and $|V_i| \le 7$ for all $i$, $1 \le i \le s$, the construction of $DAG(G)$ and the finding of $p$ can be done in $O(|V|)$ time. Hence, we have the following theorem.

**Theorem 4.** *The efficient minus domination problem can be solved in linear time on chain interval graphs.*

### 3.2   The Efficient Signed Domination Problem

*Remark 4.* Any graph with a vertex of odd degree has no efficient signed dominating function.

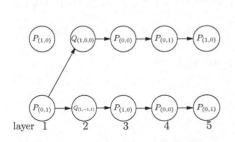

layer   1      2      3      4      5

**Fig. 5.** $DAG(G)$.

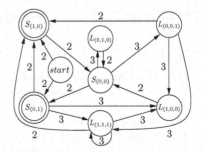

**Fig. 6.** The finite state automaton $\mathcal{N}$.

By Remark 4, the graphs such as trees, cubic graphs and $k$-regular graphs, where $k$ is odd, have no efficient signed dominating function. Therefore, the efficient signed domination problem is only considered on the graphs with no vertex of odd degree. In the following, we assume that $G$ is a connected chain interval graph with no vertex of odd degree. We still make use of the forcing property on blocks to deal with the efficient signed domination problem. However, we consider the size of a block instead of the function value of a block. For a vertex set $W$, we define $odd(W) = 1$ if $|W|$ is odd; otherwise, $odd(W) = 0$.

*Remark 5.* For every vertex $v$ of $G$, $odd(N[v]) = 1$.

Let $B_1, B_2, \ldots, B_t$ be the block structure of $G$ and $os(G)$ be the string $odd(B_1)\, odd(B_2) \cdots odd(B_t)$. A clique $C_i$ of $G$ is called an $S_{(a,b)}$ clique if $bn(C_i) = 2$, $odd(B_{i,l}) = a$ and $odd(B_{i,r}) = b$, and an $L_{(a,b,c)}$ clique if $bn(C_i) = 3$, $odd(B_{i,l}) = a$, $odd(B_{i,m}) = b$ and $odd(B_{i,r}) = c$. By Remarks 2, 3 and 5, we have the following lemmas.

**Lemma 9.** *Let $bn(C_i) = 3$. Then, $odd(B_{i,l} \cup B_{i,m} \cup B_{i,r}) = 1$.*

**Lemma 10.** *Let $C_i$ and $C_{i+1}$ be two consecutive cliques of $G$. Then, $odd(C_i \cup (C_{i+1} \setminus B_{i+1,l})) = 1$.*

**Lemma 11.** *If $s \geq 2$, then $C_1$ and $C_s$ are either an $S_{(0,1)}$ or $S_{(1,0)}$ clique.*

By Lemmas 9, 10 and 11, we have the following lemmas. Due to the limitation of space, we omit their details.

**Lemma 12.** *For each clique $C_i$, $1 < i < s$, if $bn(C_i) = 3$, then $C_i$ is either an $L_{(0,0,1)}, L_{(0,1,0)}, L_{(1,0,0)}$ or $L_{(1,1,1)}$ clique.*

**Lemma 13.** *For each clique $C_i$, $1 < i < s$, if $bn(C_i) = 2$, then $C_i$ is either an $S_{(0,0)}, S_{(0,1)}$ or $S_{(1,0)}$ clique.*

**Lemma 14.** *Let $1 \leq i < s$.*

(1) *If $C_i$ is an $S_{(0,0)}$ clique, then $C_{i+1}$ is either an $S_{(0,1)}, L_{(0,0,1)}$ or $L_{(0,1,0)}$ clique.*

(2) *If $C_i$ is an $S_{(0,1)}$ clique, then $C_{i+1}$ is either an $S_{(1,0)}, L_{(1,0,0)}$ or $L_{(1,1,1)}$ clique.*

(3) *If $C_i$ is an $S_{(1,0)}$ clique, then $C_{i+1}$ is an $S_{(0,0)}$ clique.*

(4) *If $C_i$ is an $L_{(0,0,1)}$ clique, then $C_{i+1}$ is either an $S_{(1,0)}, L_{(1,0,0)}$ or $L_{(1,1,1)}$ clique.*

(5) *If $C_i$ is an $L_{(0,1,0)}$ clique, then $C_{i+1}$ is an $S_{(0,0)}$ clique.*

(6) *If $C_i$ is an $L_{(1,0,0)}$ clique, then $C_{i+1}$ is an $S_{(0,0)}$ clique.*

(7) *If $C_i$ is an $L_{(1,1,1)}$ clique, then $C_{i+1}$ is either an $S_{(1,0)}, L_{(1,0,0)}$ or $L_{(1,1,1)}$ clique.*

By Lemmas 11 and 14, we can create a nondeterministic finite state automaton $\mathcal{N}$ as shown in Figure 6, where $S_{(0,1)}$ and $S_{(1,0)}$ are termination nodes. It is interesting that $\mathcal{N}$ is equivalent to $\mathcal{M}$. Moreover, each $S_{(a,b)}$ node of $\mathcal{N}$ corresponds to a $P_{(a,b)}$ node of $\mathcal{M}$ and each $L_{(a,b,c)}$ node corresponds to a $Q_{(a,b,c)}$ node except $L_{(1,1,1)}$ corresponds to $Q_{(1,-1,1)}$. As discussed in the previous subsection, there is a simple $EMD$ function $f$ for $G = (B_1, B_2, \ldots, B_t)$. It is not hard to see that for each block $B_i$ of $G$, if $f(B_i) = 0$, then the size of $B_i$ must be even; otherwise, the size of $B_i$ must be odd. This fact implies that $f$ can be easily modified into an efficient signed dominating function of $G$ as follows.

- If $f(B_i) = 0$, then $|B_i| = 2k$ and hence we assign $+1$ to $k$ vertices in $B_i$ and $-1$ to the remaining $k$ vertices.
- If $f(B_i) = 1$, then $|B_i| = 2k + 1$ and hence we assign $+1$ to $k + 1$ vertices in $B_i$ and $-1$ to the remaining $k$ vertices.
- If $f(B_i) = -1$, then $|B_i| = 2k + 1$ and hence we assign $-1$ to $k + 1$ vertices in $B_i$ and $+1$ to the remaining $k$ vertices.

That is, every chain interval graph $G$ with no vertex of odd degree has an efficient signed dominating function, which can be found just according to $os(G)$. Because, from $\mathcal{N}$ and $\mathcal{M}$, we can find that the number of the consecutive ones in $os(G)$ is $2k + 1$ and the function values of the corresponding blocks are $+1, -1, +1, -1, \ldots, +1$ (totally $2k + 1$ values). Hence, we can easily determine the function value of each block in $G$ just from $os(G)$ and then assign the value of each vertex in this block using the above method. Considering the graph $G$ of Figure 2 for an example, we have $os(G) = 0111001$. Then, we can find an efficient signed dominating function $f$ of $G$ such that $f(B_1) = 0$, $f(B_2) = 1$, $f(B_3) = -1$, $f(B_4) = f(B_5) = 0$ and $f(B_6) = 1$. Hence, we have $f(1) = 1, f(2) = -1, f(3) = 1, f(4) = -1, f(5) = 1, f(6) = 1, f(7) = -1, f(8) = 1, f(9) = -1$ and $f(10) = 1$.

**Theorem 5.** *For every chain interval graph $G$ with no vertex of odd degree, $G$ has an efficient signed dominating function $f$. Furthermore, $f$ can be found in linear time.*

## 4    Trees

According to Remark 4, trees have no efficient signed dominating function since they contain leaves. In [2], Bange *et al.* have proposed a linear-time algorithm for solving the efficient domination problem on trees. In the following, we will show the efficient minus domination problem is equivalent to the efficient domination problem on trees.

Suppose that $f$ is an efficient minus dominating function of a tree $T$ and there is a node $u$ in $T$ with $f(u) = -1$. Then, we consider $T$ as a rooted tree with root $u$. For each node $v$ in $T$, let $\mathcal{P}(v)$ be the parent of $v$ and $\mathcal{C}(v)$ be the set of all children of $v$. Clearly, $f(N[v]) = f(v) + f(\mathcal{P}(v)) + f(\mathcal{C}(v)) = 1$. Note that if $v$ is a leaf of $T$, then $f(v) \geq 0$; otherwise we have $f(N[v]) \leq 0$, a contradiction. Since $u$ is the root and $f(u) = -1$, we have $f(\mathcal{C}(u)) = 2$, which means that there are at least two children of $u$, say $x_1$ and $y_1$, with $f(x_1) = f(y_1) = 1$ and $f(\mathcal{C}(x_1)) = f(\mathcal{C}(y_1)) = 1$. Then, $f(\mathcal{C}(x_1)) = 1$ implies that there is at least a child of $x_1$, say $x_2$, with $f(x_2) = 1$ and $f(\mathcal{C}(x_2)) = -1$; $f(\mathcal{C}(x_2)) = -1$ implies that there is at least a child of $x_2$, say $x_3$, with $f(x_3) = -1$ and $f(\mathcal{C}(x_3)) = 1$; $f(\mathcal{C}(x_3)) = 1$ implies that there is at least a child of $x_3$, say $x_4$, with $f(x_4) = f(x_1)$ and $f(\mathcal{C}(x_4)) = f(\mathcal{C}(x_1))$. In this way, since $T$ is finite, we will finally see that there is at least a leaf $x_l$ of $T$ whose $(f(x_l), f(\mathcal{C}(x_l)))$ is either $(1,1), (1,-1)$ or $(-1,1)$. Since $x_l$ is a leaf and $\mathcal{C}(x_l) = \varnothing$, however, $(f(x_l), f(\mathcal{C}(x_l)))$ is either $(0,0)$ or $(1,0)$, which leads to a contradiction. Hence, $f(v) \geq 0$ for all $v \in T$. Therefore, we have the following theorem.

**Theorem 6.** *The efficient minus domination problem equals the efficient domination problem on trees.*

# References

1. D.W. Bange, A.E. Barkauskas, L.H. Host, and P.J. Slater, Generalized domination and efficient domination in graphs, *Discrete Mathematics*, **159** (1996) 1–11.
2. D.W. Bange, A. Barkauskas, and P.J. Slater, Efficient dominating sets in graphs, in: R.D. Ringeisen and F.S. Roberts, eds., *Application of Discrete Mathematics*, (SIAM, Philadelphia, PA, 1988) 189–199.
3. A. Brandstädt, V.B. Le, and J.P. Spinrad, *Graph Classes—A Survey*, SIAM Monographs on Discrete Mathematics and Applications, Philadelphia, 1999.
4. G.J. Chang, C. Pandu Rangan, and S.R. Coorg, Weighted independent perfect domination on cocomparability graphs, *Discrete Applied Mathematics*, **63** (1995) 215–222.
5. M.S. Chang, Weighted domination of cocomparability graphs, *Discrete Applied Mathematics*, **80** (1997) 135–148.
6. M.S. Chang and Y.C. Liu, Polynomial algorithm for the weighted perfect domination problems on chordal graphs and split graphs, *Information Processing Letters*, **48** (1993) 205–210.
7. P. Damaschke, Minus domination in small-degree graphs, in: *Proceedings of the 24th International Workshop on Graph-Theoretic Concepts in Computer Science*, Lecture Notes in Computer Science, **1517** (1998) 17–25.
8. J. Dunbar, W. Goddar, S. Hedetniemi, A. McRae, and M.A. Henning, The algorithmic complexity of minus domination in graphs, *Discrete Applied Mathematics*, **68** (1996) 73–84.
9. J. Dunbar, S.T. Hedetniemi, M.A. Henning, and P.J. Slater, Signed domination in graphs, in: Y. Alari and A. Schwenk, eds., *Proc. 7th International Conference on the Theory and Applications of Graphs*, (Wiley, New York, 1995) 311–321.
10. M.R. Fellows and M.N. Hoover, Perfect domination, *Australasian Journal of Combinatorics*, **3** (1991) 141–150.
11. M.R. Garey and D.S. Johnson, *Computers and Intractability—A Guide to the Theory of NP-Completeness*, San Francisco, Freeman, 1979.
12. P.C. Gilmore and A.J. Hoffman, A characterization of comparability graphs and of interval graphs, *Canadian Journal of Mathematics*, **16** (1964) 539–548.
13. M.C. Golumbic, *Algorithmic Graph Theory and Perfect Graphs*, Academic Press, New York, 1980.

14. J.H. Hattingh, M.A. Henning, and P.J. Slater, The algorithmic complexity of signed domination in graphs, *Australasian Journal of Combinatorics*, **12** (1995) 101–112.
15. T.W. Haynes, S.T. Hedetniemi, and P.J. Slater, *Fundamentals of Domination in Graphs*, Marcel Dekker, New York, 1998.
16. J.E. Hopcroft and J.D. Ullman, *Introduction to Automata Theory, Languages, and Computation*, Addison-Wesley, Reading, MA, 1979.
17. Y.D. Liang, C.L. Lu, and C.Y. Tang, Efficient domination on permutation graphs and trapezoid graphs, in: T. Jiang and D.T. Lee, eds., *Proc. 3rd Annual International Computing and Combinatorics Conference (COCOON'97)*, Lecture Notes in Computer Science, **1276** (Springer-Verlag, 1997) 232–241.
18. C.L. Lu, *On the Study of Weighted Efficient Domination*, PhD Thesis, Department of Computer Science, National Tsing Hua University, Taiwan, 1998.
19. C.C. Yen, *Algorithmic Aspects of Perfect Domination*, PhD Thesis, Department of Computer Science, National Tsing Hua University, Taiwan, 1992.
20. C.C. Yen and R.C.T. Lee, The weighted perfect domination problem and its variants, *Discrete Applied Mathematics*, **66** (1996) 147–160.

# Convex Grid Drawings of Four-Connected Plane Graphs

## (Extended Abstract)

Kazuyuki Miura[1], Shin-ichi Nakano[2], and Takao Nishizeki[3]

[1] Nishizeki Lab. Graduate School of Information Sciences
Tohoku University, Aoba-yama 05, Sendai, 980-8579, Japan.
miura@nishizeki.ecei.tohoku.ac.jp
[2] Department of Computer Science, Faculty of Engineering
Gunma University, 1-5-1 Tenjin-cho, Kiryu, Gunma 376-8515, Japan
nakano@cs.gunma-u.ac.jp
[3] Graduate School of Information Sciences
Tohoku University, Aoba-yama 05, Sendai, 980-8579, Japan.
nishi@ecei.tohoku.ac.jp

**Abstract.** A convex grid drawing of a plane graph $G$ is a drawing of $G$ on the plane so that all vertices of $G$ are put on grid points, all edges are drawn as straight-line segments between their endpoints without any edge-intersection, and every face boundary is a convex polygon. In this paper we give a linear-time algorithm for finding a convex grid drawing of any 4-connected plane graph $G$ with four or more vertices on the outer face boundary. The algorithm yields a drawing in an integer grid such that $W + H \leq n - 1$ if $G$ has $n$ vertices, where $W$ is the width and $H$ is the height of the grid. Thus the area $W \times H$ of the grid is at most $\lceil (n-1)/2 \rceil \cdot \lfloor (n-1)/2 \rfloor$. Our bounds on the grid sizes are optimal in the sense that there exist an infinite number of 4-connected plane graphs whose convex drawings need grids such that $W + H = n - 1$ and $W \times H = \lceil (n-1)/2 \rceil \cdot \lfloor (n-1)/2 \rfloor$.

## 1 Introduction

Recently automatic aesthetic drawing of graphs created intense interest due to their broad applications. As a consequence, many drawing methods appeared [BETT99,CK97,CN98,CON85,CP95,CYN84,Fa48,FPP90,He97,Ka96,Sc90], [Tu63]. In this paper, we deal with the "convex grid drawing" of a plane graph. Throughout the paper we denote by $n$ the number of vertices of a graph $G$. The $W \times H$ *integer grid* consists of $W + 1$ vertical grid lines and $H + 1$ horizontal grid lines, and has a rectangular contour. $W$ and $H$ are called the *width* and *height* of the integer grid, respectively.

The most typical drawing of a plane graph $G$ is *the straight line drawing* in which all vertices of $G$ are drawn as points and all edges are drawn as straight line segments without any edge-intersection. A straight line drawing of $G$ is called a *grid drawing* of $G$ if the vertices of $G$ are put on grid points of integer

D.T. Lee and S.-H. Teng (Eds.): ISAAC 2000, LNCS 1969, pp. 254–265, 2000.

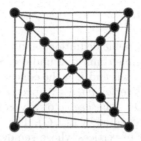

**Fig. 1.** Nested quadrangles attaining our bounds.

coordinates. Every plane graph has a grid drawing on an $(n - 2) \times (n - 2)$ grid [BETT99,CP95,FPP90,Sc90]. A straight line drawing of a plane graph $G$ is often aesthetically pretty if every face boundary is drawn as a convex polygon [CON85,Tu63]. Such a drawing is called a *convex drawing* of $G$. Not every plane graph has a convex drawing, but every 3-connected plane graph has a convex drawing [Tu63], and such a grid drawing can be found in linear time [CON85, CYN84]. A convex drawing is called a *convex grid drawing* if it is a grid drawing. Every 3-connected plane graph has a convex grid drawing on an $(n-2) \times (n-2)$ grid, and such a grid drawing can be found in linear time [CK97,ST92]. The size of an integer grid required by a convex grid drawing would be smaller than $(n - 2) \times (n - 2)$ for 4-connected plane graphs, but it has not been known how small the grid size is.

In this paper we give an answer to this problem. That is, we give an algorithm which finds in linear time a convex grid drawing of any given 4-connected plane graph $G$ on an integer grid such that $W + H \leq n-1$ if $G$ has four or more vertices on the outer face boundary. Since $W+H \leq n-1$, $W \times H \leq \lceil (n-1)/2 \rceil \cdot \lfloor (n-1)/2 \rfloor$. The outer face boundary of $G$ is always drawn as a rectangle as illustrated in Figs. 1 and 5(d). The assumption that a given plane graph has four or more vertices on the outer face boundary does not lose much generality, because any 4-connected plane graph has at least three vertices on the outer face boundary. Our bounds on $W + H$ and $W \times H$ are optimal in the sense that there exist an infinite number of 4-connected plane graphs, for example the nested quadrangles depicted in Fig. 1, which need grids such that $W + H = n - 1$ and $W \times H = \lceil (n - 1)/2 \rceil \cdot \lfloor (n - 1)/2 \rfloor$. Thus the area of an integer grid can be reduced to $1/4$ and the contour length to half for 4-connected plane graphs than those for 3-connected plane graphs. It should be noted that any 4-connected plane graph $G$ with four or more vertices on the outer face boundary has a grid drawing on a rectangular grid with $W + H \leq n$ [He97] and on an almost square grid with $W = \lceil (n - 1)/2 \rceil$ and $H = \lceil (n - 1)/2 \rceil$ [MNN99], but the the drawing is not always convex.

## 2    Preliminaries

In this section we introduce some definitions and a lemma.

Let $G = (V, E)$ be a simple connected undirected graph having no multiple edge or loop. $V$ is the vertex set, and $E$ is the edge set of $G$. Let $x(v)$ and $y(v)$ be the $x$- and $y$-coordinates of vertex $v \in V$, respectively. An edge joining vertices $u$ and $v$ is denoted by $(u, v)$. The *degree* of a vertex $v$ in $G$ is the number of neighbors of $v$ in $G$, and is denoted by $d(v, G)$. The *connectivity* $\kappa(G)$ of a graph $G$ is the minimum number of vertices whose removal results in a disconnected graph or a single-vertex graph $K_1$. A graph $G$ is *$k$-connected* if $\kappa(G) \geq k$.

A graph is *planar* if it can be embedded in the plane so that no two edges intersect geometrically except at a vertex to which they are both incident. A *plane graph* is a planar graph with a fixed embedding. A plane graph divides the plane into connected regions called *faces*. We denote the boundary of a face by a clockwise sequence of the vertices on the boundary. We call the boundary of the outer face of a plane graph $G$ *the contour* of $G$, and denote it by $C_o(G)$.

The "4-canonical decomposition" of a plane graph $G$ [NRN97] playing a crucial role in our algorithm is a generalization of two well-known concepts: the "canonical ordering," which is used to find a convex grid drawing of a 3-connected plane graph [Ka96]; and the "4-canonical ordering," which is used to find a "visibility representation" and a grid drawing of a 4-connected plane graph [He97,KH97,MNN99]. A 4-canonical decomposition $\Pi = (U_1, U_2, \cdots, U_{12})$ is illustrated in Fig. 2 for a 4-connected plane graph. Let $m$ be a natural number, and let $\Pi = (U_1, U_2, \cdots, U_m)$ be a partition of set $V$ to $m$ subsets $U_1, U_2, \cdots, U_m$ of $V$ where $U_1 \bigcup U_2 \bigcup \cdots \bigcup U_m = V$ and $U_i \bigcap U_j = \phi$ for any $i$ and $j$, $i \neq j$. Let $G_k$, $1 \leq k \leq m$, be the plane subgraph of $G$ induced by the vertices in $U_1 \bigcup U_2 \bigcup \cdots \bigcup U_k$, and let $\overline{G_k}$ be the plane subgraph of $G$ induced by the vertices in $U_{k+1} \bigcup U_{k+2} \bigcup \cdots \bigcup U_m$. Thus $G = G_m = \overline{G_0}$. We say that $\Pi$ is a *4-canonical decomposition* of $G$ if the following three conditions are satisfied:

(co1) $U_1$ consists of the two ends of an edge on $C_o(G)$, and $U_m$ consists of the two ends of another edge   on $C_o(G)$;

(co2) for each $k$, $2 \leq k \leq m - 1$, both $G_k$ and $\overline{G_{k-1}}$ are biconnected (in Fig. 3 $G_k$ is darkly shaded, and    $\overline{G_{k-1}}$ is lightly shaded); and

(co3) for each $k$, $2 \leq k \leq m - 1$, one of the following three conditions holds (the vertices in $U_k$ are drawn    by black circles in Fig. 3):

(a) $U_k$ is a singleton set of a vertex $u$ on $C_o(G_k)$ such that $d(u, G_k) \geq 2$ and $d(u, \overline{G_{k-1}}) \geq 2$ (see Fig. 3(a)).

(b) $U_k$ is a set of two or more consecutive vertices on $C_o(G_k)$ such that $d(u, G_k) = 2$ and $d(u, \overline{G_{k-1}}) \geq 3$ for each vertex $u \in U_k$ (see Fig. 3(b)).

(c) $U_k$ is a set of two or more consecutive vertices on $C_o(G_k)$ such that $d(u, G_k) \geq 3$ and $d(u, \overline{G_{k-1}}) = 2$ for each vertex $u \in U_k$ (see Fig. 3(c)).

Although the definition of a 4-canonical decomposition above is slightly different from that in [NRN97], they are effectively equivalent to each other. The following lemma is known.

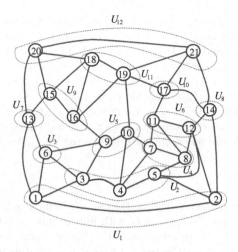

**Fig. 2.** A 4-canonical decomposition of a 4-connected plane graph having $n = 21$ vertices.

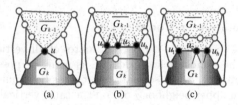

**Fig. 3.** Illustration for the three conditions (a)–(c) of (co3).

**Lemma 1.** [NRN97] Let $G$ be a 4-connected plane graph having at least four vertices on $C_o(G)$. Then $G$ has a 4-canonical decomposition $\Pi$, and $\Pi$ can be found in linear time.

By the condition (co3), one may assume that for each $k$, $1 \le k \le m$, the vertices in $U_k$ consecutively appear clockwise on $C_o(G_k)$. However, the clockwise order on $C_o(G_1)$ is not well-defined since $G_1 = K_2$. So we assume that the two vertices in $U_1$ consecutively appear counterclockwise on $C_o(G)$ as illustrated in Fig. 2. We number all vertices of $G$ by $1, 2, \cdots, n$ so that they appear in $U_1, U_2, \cdots, U_m$ in this order, and call each vertex in $G$ by the number $i, 1 \le i \le n$. Thus one can define an order $<$ among the vertices in $G$.

In the remainder of this section, we define some terms which are used in our algorithm. The *lower neighbor* of $u$ is the neighbors of $u$ which are smaller than $u$. The *upper neighbor* of $u$ is the neighbors of $u$ which are larger than $u$. Every upper neighbor $v$ of any vertex $u$ satisfies $y(v) \ge y(u)$ in our drawing. The number of lower neighbors of $u$ is denoted by $d_{low}(u, G)$, and the number of upper neighbors of $u$ is denoted by $d_{up}(u, G)$. Every vertex $u$ except vertex 1 satisfies

$d_{low}(u, G) \geq 1$, and every vertex $u$ except vertex $n$ satisfies $d_{up}(u, G) \geq 1$. Let $2 \leq k \leq m - 1$ and $U_k = \{u_1, u_2, \cdots, u_h\}$. If $U_k$ satisfies the condition (co3)(a), then $h = 1$ and $d_{low}(u_1), d_{up}(u_1) \geq 2$. If $U_k$ satisfies condition (co3)(b), then $d_{low}(u_i) = 1$ for each $u_i$, $1 \leq i \leq h - 1$, $d_{low}(u_h) = 2$, $d_{up}(u_i) \geq 3$ for each $u_i$, $1 \leq i \leq h - 1$, and $d_{up}(u_h) \geq 2$. If $U_k$ satisfies condition (co3)(c), then $d_{low}(u_1) \geq 2$, $d_{low}(u_i) \geq 3$ for each $u_i$, $2 \leq i \leq h$, $d_{up}(u_1) = 2$, and $d_{up}(u_i) = 1$ for each $u_i$, $2 \leq i \leq h$. We denote by $w_m(u)$ the largest neighbor of $u$, $1 \leq u \leq n - 1$. The *in-degree* of a vertex $u$ in a directed graph $D$ is denoted by $d_{in}(u, D)$, while the *out-degree* of $u$ is denoted by $d_{out}(u, D)$.

## 3    Algorithm

In this section, we present our algorithm which finds a convex grid drawing of any given 4-connected plane graph $G$ with four or more vertices on the contour $C_o(G)$. Our algorithm determines only the integer coordinates of the vertices $1, 2, \cdots, n$ of $G$ effectively in this order. One can immediately find a (straight line) grid drawing of $G$ from the coordinates. We first determine the $x$-coordinates of all vertices, and then determine the $y$-coordinates.

### 3.1    How to Compute $x$-Coordinates

We first show how to compute the $x$-coordinates of all vertices. Our algorithm puts vertices on the same vertical grid line as many as possible to reduce the width $W$ of the drawing. Suppose that vertex $i$ has been put on a grid point. If possible, we put an upper neighbor $j$ of $i$ on the same vertical grid line as $i$, that is, we determine $x(j) = x(i)$ and hence $y(j) > y(i)$ of course, as illustrated in Fig. 4. We wish to choose as $j$ the largest neighbor $w_m(i)$ of $i$ (this is crucial for making every face boundary a convex polygon). However, it is impossible for a case where $w_m(i)$ has been already put on the same vertical grid line as a vertex $i'(< i)$, which was put on a grid point before $i$, that is, $w_m(i') = w_m(i)$. Thus, if there exist upper neighbors of $i$ which have not been put on the same vertical grid line as any vertex $i'(< i)$, then we put the largest one $j$ among them on the same vertical grid line as $i$. If there dose not exist such an upper neighbor of $i$, then we do not put any vertex $(> i)$ on the same vertical grid line as $i$. In this way, the following **procedure** Construct-$F$ constructs a directed forest $F = (V, E_F)$. All vertices in each component of $F$ have the same $x$-coordinate; if there is a directed edge $(i, j)$ in $F$, then $x(j) = x(i)$ and $y(j) > y(i)$.

**Procedure Construct-$F$**
**begin**  $\{F = (V, E_F)\}$
1    $E_F := \phi$ ; {the initial forest $F = (V, \phi)$ consists of isolated vertices}
2    **for** $i := 1$ **to** $n$ **do**
        **if** vertex $i$ has upper neighbors $j$ such that $d_{in}(j, F) = 0$ **then**
3            let $j$ be the largest one among them, and add a directed edge $(i, j)$
            to the directed graph $F$, that is, $E_F := E_F \bigcup \{(i, j)\}$;
    **end.**

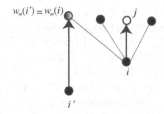

**Fig. 4.** Selection of an $i$'s upper neighbor $j$ above $i$.

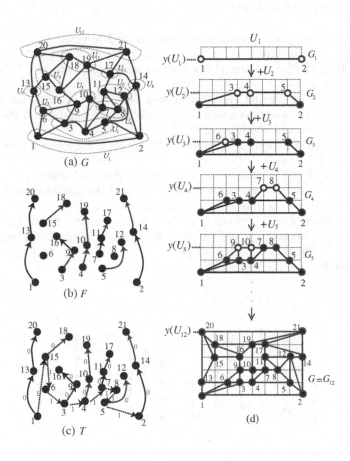

**Fig. 5.** Illustration of our algorithm.

Since $d_{in}(i, F), d_{out}(i, F) \leq 1$ for each vertex $i$, $1 \leq i \leq n$, $F$ is a forest and each component of $F$ is a directed path. Clearly $d_{in}(1, F) = d_{in}(2, F) = 0$ and $d_{out}(n - 1, F) = d_{out}(n, F) = 0$. Fig. 5(b) illustrates the directed forest $F$ of the graph $G$ in Fig. 5(a). Both the path $1, 13, 20$ going clockwise on $C_o(G)$ from 1 to $n - 1 = 20$ and the path $2, 14, 21$ going counterclockwise on $C_o(G)$ from 2 to $n = 21$ are directed paths in $F$, and hence these two paths are put on vertical grid lines as shown in the bottom figure of Fig. 5(d). Each of the other paths in $F$ is put on a vertical grid line, too.

We then show how to arrange the paths in $F$ from left to right. That is, we determine a total order among all starting vertices of paths in $F$. For this purpose, using the following **procedure** Total-Order, we find a directed path $P$ going from vertex 1 to vertex 2 passing through all starting vertices of $F$. In Fig. 5(c), the directed path $P$ is drawn by dotted lines.

**Procedure Total-Order**
**begin**
1     let $P$ be the path directly going from vertex 1 to vertex 2;
2    **for** $i := 3$ **to** $n$ **do**
      **if** $d_{in}(i, F) = 0$ **then** $\{i$ is a starting vertex of a path in $F\}$
      **begin**
3          let $j$ be the first lower neighbor of $i$ in the $i$'s adjacency list in which the $i$'s neighbors appear counterclockwise around $i$, and the first element of which is $w_m(i)$;
4          let $j'$ be the starting vertex of the path in $F$ containing vertex $j$; $\{2 \neq j' < i\}$
5          let $k$ be the successor of $j'$ in path $P$; {the path starting from vertex $k$ in $F$ has been put next to the right of the path starting from vertex $j'$ as illustrated in Fig. 6(a)}
6          insert $i$ in $P$ between $j'$ and $k$; {the path starting from $i$ in $F$ is put between the path starting from $j'$ and the path starting from $k$ as illustrated in Fig. 6(b)}
      **end**
  **end**.

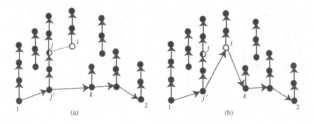

**Fig. 6.** Illustration of Total-Order.

We construct a weighted tree $T$ rooted at vertex 1 by adding the path $P$ to the forest $F$; every edge of $F$ has weight 0, and every edge of $P$ has weight 1 in $T$. (See Fig. 5(c).) Then the $x$-coordinate $x(i)$ of each vertex $i$, $1 \leq i \leq n$, is the length of the path from root 1 to $i$ in $T$. Thus $x(1) = 0$, and the width $W = x(2)$ of our drawing is equal to the number of paths in $F$ except one starting from vertex 1, i.e., the number of vertices of in-degree 0 in $F$ except vertex 1. Thus one may regard that a vertex of in-degree 0 in $F$ except vertex 1 increases $W$ by one.

## 3.2  How to Compute $y$-Coordinates

We now show how to compute $y$-coordinates. For each $k$, $1 \leq k \leq m$, $y$-coordinates of all vertices in $U_k = \{u_1, u_2, \cdots, u_h\}$ are determined as the same integer, which is denoted by $y(U_k)$. Thus the path $u_1, u_2, \cdots, u_h$ on $C_o(G_k)$ is drawn as a horizontal line segment connecting points $(x(u_1), y(U_k))$ and $(x(u_h), y(U_k))$. (See Fig. 5(d).) Furthermore, we determine the $y$-coordinates $y(U_1), y(U_2), \cdots, y(U_m)$ in this order. Thus $H = y(U_m)$.

We first determine the $y$-coordinate $y(U_1)$ of $U_1 = \{1, 2\}$ as $y(U_k) = 0$. Thus we draw $G_1 = K_2$ as a horizontal line segment connecting points $(x(1), 0)$ and $(x(2), 0)$, as illustrated in the top figure of Fig. 5(d).

Suppose that $y(U_1), y(U_2), \cdots, y(U_{k-1})$, $k \geq 2$, have already been determined, that is, $G_{k-1}$ has already been drawn, and we are now going to determine $y(U_k)$ and obtain a drawing of $G_k$ by adding the vertices in $U_k$ to the drawing of $G_{k-1}$. Let $C_o(G_{k-1}) = w_1, w_2, \cdots, w_t$, where $w_1 = 1$ and $w_t = 2$. Let $C_o(G_k) = w_1, w_2, \cdots, w_l, u_1, u_2, \cdots, u_h, w_r, \cdots, w_t$, where $1 \leq l < r \leq t$. Let $y_{max}$ be the maximum value of $y$-coordinates of vertices $w_l, w_{l+1}, \cdots, w_r$; all these vertices were on $C_o(G_{k-1})$, but all these vertices except $w_l$ and $w_r$ are not on $C_o(G_k)$. (See Fig. 7.) Clearly we must determine $y(U_k) \geq y_{max}$ to obtain a plane drawing of $G_k$. Our algorithm determines $y(U_k)$ to be either $y_{max}$ or $y_{max} + 1$ so that the height $H$ of the drawing becomes as small as possible. There are the following six cases.

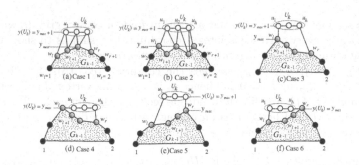

**Fig. 7.** Illustration for the six cases.

**Case 1:** $y_{max} > y(w_l), y(w_r)$. (See Fig. 7(a).)

In this case, if we determined $y(U_k) = y_{max}$, then $G_k$ could not be a plane drawing. Therefore we determine $y(U_k) = y_{max} + 1$.

**Case 2:** $y_{max} = y(w_l) = y(w_r)$. (See Fig. 7(b).)

In this case, if we determined $y(U_k) = y_{max}$, then $G_k$ might not be a plane drawing. Therefore we determine $y(U_k) = y_{max} + 1$.

**Case 3:** $y_{max} = y(w_l) > y(w_r)$, and $F$ has a directed edge $(w_l, u_1)$, that is, $x(w_l) = x(u_1)$. (See Fig. 7(c).)

In this case, if we determined $y(U_k) = y_{max}$, then vertices $w_l$ and $u_1$ would overlap each other. Therefore we determine $y(U_k) = y_{max} + 1$.

**Case 4:** $y_{max} = y(w_l) > y(w_r)$, and $F$ does not have a directed edge $(w_l, u_1)$, that is, $x(w_l) < x(u_1)$. (See Fig. 7(d).)

In this case, we determine $y(U_k) = y_{max}$.

**Case 5:** $y_{max} = y(w_r) > y(w_l)$, and $F$ has a directed edge $(w_r, u_h)$, that is, $x(w_r) = x(u_h)$. (See Fig. 7(e).)

In this case, if we determined $y(U_k) = y_{max}$, then vertices $w_r$ and $u_h$ would overlap each other. Therefore we determine $y(U_k) = y_{max} + 1$.

**Case 6:** $y_{max} = y(w_r) > y(w_l)$, and $F$ does not have a directed edge $(w_r, u_h)$, that is, $x(u_h) < x(w_r)$. (See Fig. 7(f).)

In this case, we determine $y(U_k) = y_{max}$.

We then have the following theorem.

**Theorem 1.** Our algorithm takes linear time.

*Proof.* By Lemma 1, a 4-canonical decomposition can be found in linear time. Clearly the forest $F$ and the rooted tree $T$ can be found in linear time, and the $x$-coordinates of vertices can be found from $T$ in linear time. Furthermore, the $y$-coordinates can be found in linear time as above. Thus our algorithm runs in linear time. □

## 4    Proof for Convex Grid Drawing

In this section, we prove that our algorithm finds a convex grid drawing of $G$. Since clearly every vertex has integer coordinates, it suffices to show that the drawing obtained by our algorithm is a convex drawing.

If $U_k = \{u_1, u_2, \cdots, u_h\}$ satisfies the condition (co3)(b), then for each $i$, $2 \le i \le h - 1$, $d_{in}(u_i, F) = 0$ and hence $u_i$ is a starting vertex of a directed path of $F$. Similarly, if $U_k$ satisfies the condition (co3)(c), then for each $i$, $2 \le i \le h-1$, $d_{out}(u_i, F) = 0$ and hence $u_i$ is an ending vertex of a directed path of $F$. We thus have the following lemma.

**Lemma 2.** Let $2 \le k \le m$, let $U_k = \{u_1, u_2, \cdots, u_h\}$, and let $C_o(G_k) = w_1, w_2, \cdots, w_l, u_1, u_2, \cdots, u_h, w_r, \cdots, w_t$, where $w_1 = 1$, $w_t = 2$, and $1 \le l < r \le t$. Then $x(w_l) \le x(u_1) < x(u_2) < \cdots < x(u_h) \le w_r$.

Since $y(U_k)$ is equal to either $y_{max}$ or $y_{max} + 1$, the following lemma clearly holds.

**Lemma 3.** If vertices $u$ and $v$ are adjacent and $u < v$, then $y(u) \leq y(v)$.

Our algorithm finds the drawing of $G_1, G_2, \cdots, G_m (= G)$ in this order, as illustrated in Fig. 5(d). Thus, assuming that the drawing of $G_{k-1}$, $k \geq 2$, is convex, we shall show that the drawing of $G_k$ is convex. However, it is difficult to show that the drawing of $G_k$ is convex for the case where either $k = m$ or $U_k$, $2 \leq k \leq m - 1$, satisfies the condition (co3)(c). Therefore, subdividing all such sets $U_k$, we obtain another partition of $V$ as follows. Let $\Pi = (U_1, U_2, \cdots, U_m)$ be a 4-canonical decomposition of $G$. For each $U_k$ such that either $k = m$ or $U_k$ satisfies the condition (co3)(c), let $U_k = \{u_1, u_2, \cdots, u_{l_k}\}$ and replace $U_k$ in $\Pi$ with singleton sets $\{u_1\}, \{u_2\}, \cdots, \{u_{l_k}\}$. We call the resulting partition $\Pi' = (U_1, U_2^1, U_2^2, \cdots, U_2^{l_2}, U_3^1, U_3^2, \cdots, U_3^{l_3}, \cdots, U_m^1, U_m^2)$ of $V$ a *refined decomposition* of $G$. If either $k = m$ or $U_k$ satisfies the condition (co3)(c), then $U_k = U_k^1 \bigcup U_k^2 \bigcup \cdots \bigcup U_k^{l_k}$, $l_k = |U_k|$ and $|U_k^i| = 1$ for each $i$, $1 \leq i \leq l_k$. Otherwise, $l_k = 1$ and $U_k = U_k^1$.

For each $k$, $2 \leq k \leq m$, and for each $i$, $1 \leq i \leq l_k$, we denote by $G_k^i$ the plane subgraph of $G$ induced by the vertices in $U_1 \bigcup U_2 \bigcup \cdots \bigcup U_{k-1} \bigcup U_k^1 \bigcup U_k^2 \bigcup \cdots \bigcup U_k^i$. Moreover, for each $k$, $2 \leq k \leq m$, and for each $i$, $0 \leq i \leq l_k - 1$, we denote by $\overline{G_k^i}$ the plane subgraph of $G$ induced by the vertices in $U_k^{i+1} \bigcup U_k^{i+2} \bigcup \cdots \bigcup U_k^{l_k} \bigcup U_{k+1} \bigcup \cdots \bigcup U_m$. For notational convenience, let $G_k^0 = G_{k-1}$ and $\overline{G_k^{l_k}} = \overline{G_k}$.

Let $k \geq 2$ and $U_k^i = \{u_1, u_2, \cdots, u_h\}$. By the definition of a refined decomposition, vertices $u_1, u_2, \cdots, u_h$ consecutively appear clockwise on $C_o(G_k^i)$ in this order. Let $C_o(G_k^{i-1}) = w_1, w_2, \cdots, w_t$, where $w_1 = 1$ and $w_t = 2$. Let $C_o(G_k^i) = w_1, w_2, \cdots, w_l, u_1, u_2, \cdots, u_h, w_r, \cdots, w_t$, where $1 \leq l < r \leq t$. We call $w_l$ the *left leg* of $U_k^i$, and $w_r$ the *right leg* of $U_k^i$. By the definition of a 4-canonical decomposition and a refined decomposition, the left leg of $U_k^i$ is different from the right leg of $U_k^i$.

We now have the following lemma for the drawing of $G_k^i$.

**Lemma 4.** For each $k$, $2 \leq k \leq m$, and each $i$, $0 \leq i \leq l_k$, the following (i)–(iii) hold:

(i) the path going clockwise on $C_o(G_k^{i-1})$ from vertex $w_1 = 1$ to vertex $w_t = 2$ is "x-monotone," that is, $x(w_1) \leq x(w_2) \leq \cdots \leq x(w_t)$ (such a path is drawn by thick solid lines in Fig. 8);

(ii) the path going clockwise on $C_o(G_k^{i-1})$ from $w_l$ to $w_r$ is "quasi-convex," that is, there is no vertex $w_p$ such that $l < p < r$ and $y(w_{p-1}) < y(w_p) > y(w_{p+1})$ (all vertices in such a path are drawn by gray circles in Fig. 8), and $w_l, w_{l+1}, \cdots, w_r, w_l$ is a convex polygon in particular if $U_k$ satisfies the condition (co3)(b) (as illustrated in Fig. 8(a)); and

(iii) if a vertex $v$ on $C_o(G_k^{i-1})$ is an inner vertex of $G$, that is, $v$ is not on $C_o(G)$, and the interior angle of the polygon $C_o(G_k^{i-1})$ at vertex $v$ is less than $180°$, then $v$ has at least one neighbor in $\overline{G_k^{i-1}}$ (the edges joining $v$ and such neighbors are drawn by thin dotted line in Fig. 8).

*Proof.* Investigating the algorithm in detail and using Lemmas 2 and 3, one can prove the lemma. The detail is omitted in this extended abstract due to the page limitation. □

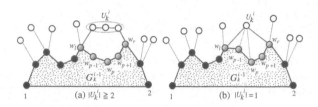

**Fig. 8.** Illustration for Lemma 5.

Using Lemma 4, one can prove that our algorithm obtains a convex grid drawing. Note that all inner face boundaries newly formed in $G_k^i$ are convex polygons as illustrated in Fig. 8 (all such faces are not shaded in Fig. 8).

## 5   Grid Size

In this section, we prove the following theorem.

**Theorem 2.** Our algorithm finds a convex grid drawing of $G$ on a grid such that $W + H \leq n - 1$.

*Proof.* Due to the page limitation, we outline a proof in this extended abstract. We denote the height of the drawing of $G_k^i$ by $H(G_k^i)$. We say that a vertex $u_j \in U_k^i$, $3 \leq u_j \leq n$, is *increasing* if $d_{in}(u_j, F) = 0$ and $H(G_k^i) = H(G_k^{i-1}) + 1$, that is, $u_j$ increases $W + H$ by two. We say that a vertex $u_j \in U_k^i$ is *preserving* if $d_{in}(u_j, F) \neq 0$ and $H(G_k^i) = H(G_k^{i-1})$, that is, $u_j$ preserves $W + H$. In particular, we say that vertex 1 is preserving, since the graph consisting of only vertex 1 can be drawn on a $0 \times 0$ grid with $W + H = 0$. Vertex 2 is neither increasing nor preserving, since $G_1$ can be drawn on a $1 \times 0$ grid with $W + H = 1$ and hence vertex 2 increases $W + H$ by one. Let $I$ be the set of all increasing vertices in $G$, and let $P$ be the set of all preserving vertices in $G$. Then each of the vertices in $V - P - I$ increases $W + H$ by one. Therefore $W + H = 2|I| + (n - |I| - |P|) = n + |I| - |P|$. Investigating the method for deciding $x$- and $y$-coordinates of vertices in detail, one can prove that for each increasing vertex $v$ there is at least one preserving vertex (other than vertex 1) around $v$ and all these preserving vertices are distinct from each other. For example, if $u_1$ is increasing in Case 1 illustrated in Fig. 7(a), then $u_2$ is preserving. (The detail is omitted in this extended abstract.) Thus we have $|P| \geq |I| + 1$, and hence $W + H \leq n - 1$. □

# References

[BETT99]  G. Di Battista, P. Eades, R. Tamassia and I.G. Tollis, *Graph Drawing*, Prentice Hall, NJ (1999).

[CK97]  M. Chrobak and G. Kant, *Convex grid drawings of 3-connected planar graphs*, International Journal of Computational Geometry and Applications, 7, 211-223 (1997).

[CN98]  M. Chrobak and S. Nakano, *Minimum-width grid drawings of plane graphs*, Computational Geometry: Theory and Applications, 10, 29-54 (1998).

[CON85]  N. Chiba, K. Onoguchi and T. Nishizeki, *Drawing planar graphs nicely*, Acta Inform., 22, 187-201 (1985).

[CP95]  M. Chrobak and T. Payne, *A linear-time algorithm for drawing planar graphs on a grid*, Information Processing Letters, 54, 241-246 (1995).

[CYN84]  N. Chiba, T. Yamanouchi and T. Nishizeki, *Linear algorithms for convex drawings of planar graphs*, in Progress in Graph Theory, J.A. Bondy and U.S.R. Murty (eds.), Academic Press, 153-173 (1984).

[Fa48]  I. Fáry, *On straight lines representation of plane graphs*, Acta. Sci. Math. Szeged, 11, 229-233 (1948).

[FPP90]  H. de Fraysseix, J. Pach and R. Pollack, *How to draw a planar graph on a grid*, Combinatorica, 10, 41-51 (1990).

[He97]  X. He, *Grid embedding of 4-connected plane graphs*, Discrete & Computational Geometry, 17, 339-358 (1997).

[Ka96]  G. Kant, *Drawing planar graphs using the canonical ordering*, Algorithmica, 16, 4-32 (1996).

[KH97]  G. Kant and X. He, *Regular edge labeling of 4-connected plane graphs and its applications in graph drawing problems*, Theoretical Computer Science, 172, 175-193 (1997).

[MNN99]  K. Miura, S. Nakano and T. Nishizeki, *Grid drawings of four-connected plane graphs*, Proc. Graph Drawing'99 (GD'99), LNCS 1731, 145-154 (1999).

[NRN97]  S. Nakano, M. Saidur  Rahman and T. Nishizeki, *A linear time algorithm for four partitioning four-connected planar graphs*, Information Processing Letters, 62, 315-322 (1997).

[Sc90]  W. Schnyder, *Embedding planar graphs in the grid*, Proc. 1st Annual ACM-SIAM Symp. on Discrete Algorithms, San Francisco, 138-147 (1990).

[ST92]  W. Schnyder and W. Trotter, *Convex drawings of planar graphs*, Abstracts of the AMS, 13, 5, 92T-05-135 (1992).

[Tu63]  W.T. Tutte, *How to draw a graph*, Proc. London Math. Soc., 13, 743-768 (1963).

# An Algorithm for Finding Three Dimensional Symmetry in Series Parallel Digraphs *

Seok-Hee Hong and Peter Eades

Basser Department of Computer Science, University of Sydney, Australia.
{shhong, peter}@staff.cs.usyd.edu.au

**Abstract.** Symmetry is one of the most important aesthetic criteria which clearly reveals the structure of the graph. However, previous work on symmetric graph drawing has focused on two dimensions. In this paper, we extend symmetric graph drawing into three dimensions. Symmetry in three dimensions is much richer than that of two dimensions. We present a linear time algorithm for finding maximum number of three dimensional symmetries in series parallel digraphs.

## 1 Introduction

Symmetry is a much admired property in Graph Drawings. It clearly reveals the structure and the properties of a graph visually. Symmetric graph drawing has been investigated by a number of authors (see [11,12,13]).

However, previous work on symmetric graph drawing has focused on two dimensions. The problem of determining whether a given graph can be drawn symmetrically is NP-complete in general [13]. Heuristics for symmetric drawings of general graphs have been suggested [3,6]. For restricted classes of planar graphs, there are polynomial time algorithms: Manning presents algorithms for constructing symmetric drawings of trees, outerplanar graphs [11,12,13]; Hong gives algorithms for finding maximum number of symmetries in series parallel digraphs and planar graphs [7,8]. Recently, Hong and Eades present an algorithm to find maximum number of three dimensional symmetries in trees [9].

In this paper, we extend three dimensional symmetric drawing into series parallel digraphs. Series parallel digraphs are one of the most common types of graphs: they appear in flow diagrams, dependency charts, and in PERT networks. Algorithms for drawing series parallel digraphs in two and three dimensions have appeared in [2,4,7]. Note that the previous symmetric drawing algorithm is in two dimensions and three dimensional drawing algorithm is to minimize the footprints [7].

Symmetry in three dimensions is much richer than symmetry in two dimensions. Note that in two dimensions, a series parallel digraph can have at most 4

---

* This research has been supported by a Postdoctoral Fellowship from the Korean Science and Engineering Foundation and a grant from the Australian Research Council. Animated drawings are available from S. Hong; http://www.cs.usyd.edu.au/~shhong/research4.htm.

D.T. Lee and S.-H. Teng (Eds.): ISAAC 2000, LNCS 1969, pp. 266–277, 2000.

symmetries, two axial symmetries and two rotational symmetries as in Figure 1 (a). However, the maximal symmetric drawing of the same series parallel digraph in three dimensions can show up to $4k$ symmetries as in Figure 1 (b) (here $k$ = 4). Further, it is possible to construct a series parallel digraph which has no symmetric drawing in two dimensions as in Figure 1 (c), but has a symmetric drawing in three dimensions which shows 6 symmetries as in Figure 1 (d).

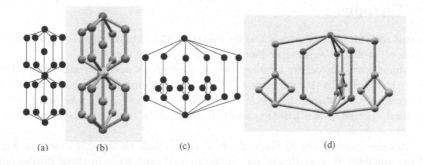

(a)     (b)     (c)         (d)

**Fig. 1.** *Symmetric drawings of series parallel digraphs in two and three dimensions.*

This paper is organized as follows. In the next section, we define series parallel digraphs. Three dimensional symmetry in series parallel digraphs are analyzed in Section 3. Section 4 presents an algorithm for finding maximum number of three dimensional symmetries in series parallel digraphs. Section 5 concludes.

## 2 Series Parallel Digraphs

First we define series parallel digraphs and then review some basic notions for series parallel digraphs.

A digraph consisting of two vertices $u$ and $v$ joined by a single edge is a series parallel digraph, and if $G_1, G_2, \ldots, G_k$ are series parallel digraphs, then so are the digraphs constructed by each of the following operations:

- *series* composition: identify the sink of $G_i$ with the source of $G_{i+1}$, for $1 \leq i < k$.
- *parallel* composition: identify all the sources of $G_i$ for $1 \leq i \leq k$, and identify all the sinks of $G_i$ for $1 \leq i \leq k$.

A *component* of $G$ is one of the subgraphs $G_1, G_2, \ldots, G_k$. A series parallel digraph can be represented as the *Canonical Decomposition Tree* (CDT), such as in Figure 3 (a). Leaf nodes in the CDT represent edges in the series parallel digraph, and internal nodes are labeled $S$ or $P$ to represent series or parallel compositions. The CDT was used to find two dimensional symmetries in series parallel digraphs [7], and it is useful for finding three dimensional symmetries.

However, we need an additional data structure to find the full three dimensional symmetries. It will be defined in Section 4.

The CDT can be computed from the binary decomposition tree in linear time using the algorithm of Valdes *et al.* [15] followed by a simple depth first search restructuring operation.

## 3    Three Dimensional Symmetry in Series Parallel Digraphs

In this section, first we review the symmetry model in two and three dimensions. Then we present a symmetry model for series parallel digraphs.

Models for symmetric drawings in two dimensions were introduced by Manning [11,12,13], Lin [10] and Hong [7,8]. In two dimensions, there are two kinds of symmetry, *rotational symmetry* and *reflectional (or axial) symmetry*. A rotational symmetry is a rotation about a *point* and a reflectional symmetry is a reflection by an *axis*.

However, symmetry in three dimensions is much richer and more complex than symmetry in two dimensions. The types of symmetry in three dimensions can be roughly divided into two cases, *direct symmetry* and *indirect (or opposite) symmetry*. These are further refined as *rotation, reflection, inversion* and *rotary reflection (or rotary inversion)* [14]. The difference from two dimensions is that a rotational symmetry in three dimensions is a rotation about an *axis*. Also a reflectional symmetry in three dimensions is a reflection in a *plane*. Inversion (or central inversion) is a reflection in a point. Rotary reflection (inversion) is a rotation followed by a reflection (inversion). The combinations rotation-reflection and rotation-inversion amount to the same.

A *finite rotation group* in three dimensions is one of following three types. A *cyclic group ($C_n$)*, a *dihedral group ($D_n$)* and the rotation group of one of the *Platonic solids* [14]. The *full symmetry group* of a finite object in three dimensions is more complex than the rotation group. The complete list of all possible symmetry groups in three dimensions can be found in  [14]

However, the full symmetry groups of series parallel digraphs are quite simple. This is because the set which is composed of the source and the sink should be fixed by all symmetries. The basic idea of constructing a symmetric drawing of series parallel digraphs in three dimensions is to place the source and the sink on a rotation axis. Suppose that a series parallel digraph $G$ is a parallel composition of $G_1, G_2, \ldots, G_k$. Then we place each $G_i$ on a reflection plane which containing the rotation axis. The three dimensional symmetry of series parallel digraphs can be classified as follows.

1. rotation axes.
   a) a $k$-fold principal rotation axis (*vertical rotation axis*).
   b) $k$ 2-fold secondary rotation axes (*horizontal rotation axes*).
2. reflection planes.
   a) $k$ reflection planes, each of which contain the principal rotation axis (*vertical planes*).

   b) a reflection plane which is perpendicular to the principal rotation axis
   (*horizontal plane*).
3. inversion.
   a) central inversion.
   b) $k - 1$ rotary inversions.

An axis of a $k$-fold rotation is called a $k$-fold axis and $k$-fold rotation is a
rotation of $2\pi/k$ degrees (The largest possible value of $k$ is chosen to label the
axis). Note that a vertical rotation is a direction-preserving symmetry that fixes
the source and fixes the sink. A horizontal reflection is a direction-reversing symmetry that swaps the source and the sink. An inversion also reverses directions,
and swaps the source and the sink.

Figure 2 shows types of three dimensional symmetry in series parallel digraphs. In this Figure, edges are directed upward, and arrowheads are omitted.
Figure 2 (a) displays vertical rotations and Figure 2 (b) displays a horizontal
reflection. Figure 2 (c) displays an inversion and Figure 2 (d) displays the maximum $4k$ symmetries (here $k = 4$).

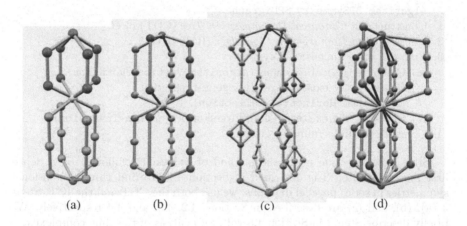

(a)          (b)          (c)          (d)

**Fig. 2.** *Types of three dimensional symmetry in series parallel digraphs.*

Before giving an algorithm to find three dimensional symmetries in series
parallel digraphs, first we explain the relationship between the three dimensional symmetries in series parallel digraphs. These are described in the following
lemma.

**Lemma 1.** *Suppose that $G$ is a series parallel digraph.*

1. *If $G$ has $k$-fold vertical rotations, then it also has $k$ vertical reflection planes.*
2. *If $G$ has $k$-fold vertical rotations and a horizontal reflection, then it also has
   $k$ horizontal rotations.*

*3. If G has k-fold vertical rotations and an inversion, then it also has k − 1 rotary inversions.*

*Proof.* Omitted.[1]

Based on this lemma, now we can compute the maximum size full symmetry group of series parallel digraphs by computing the maximum $k$-fold vertical rotations and testing whether there exist a horizontal reflection and an inversion. In the next section, we present an algorithm for finding these three symmetries.

## 4    Symmetry Finding Algorithm

In this section we present an algorithm for finding maximum number of three dimensional symmetry in series parallel digraphs. Based on the analysis of three dimensional symmetries in series parallel digraphs described in the previous section, the overall algorithm can be divided into four steps. Let $G$ be a series parallel digraph.

> **Algorithm 3DSymmetry_SPDigraph**
> 1. Construct the *Canonical Decomposition Tree* (CDT) of $G$.
> 2. Construct the *Isomorphism Class Tree* (ICT) of $G$.
> 3. Find the three dimensional symmetry.
>    a) Compute vertical rotations (**Algorithm Vertical_Rotation**).
>    b) Check for the existence of a horizontal reflection
>       (**Algorithm Horizontal_Reflection**).
>    c) Check for the existence of an inversion (**Algorithm Inversion**).
> 4. Compute the full symmetry group.

Step 1 can be done using the method of Valdes [15] followed by a depth first search [7]. Step 2 is described in Section 4.1. To find three dimensional symmetries in series parallel digraphs, we use both the CDT and the ICT. Steps 3 (a), (b), and (c) are described in Sections 4.2, 4.3, and 4.4 respectively. We briefly describe Step 4 in Section 4.5 with an analysis of the time complexity.

### 4.1    The Isomorphism Class Tree

In this section, we define the *Isomorphism Class Tree (ICT)* and then present an algorithm to construct the ICT. The ICT of a series parallel digraph $G$ represents the isomorphism classes (that is, equivalence classes under isomorphism) of components of $G$, and the size of each class. The ICT plays very important role in computing the maximum size symmetry group of series parallel digraphs. The ICT for series parallel digraphs plays a similar role to the ICT for finding three dimensional symmetries in trees [9]. However, we define the structure of the ICT for series parallel digraphs in a slightly different way.

---

[1] In this extended abstract, proofs are omitted.

In the ICT, each node represents an isomorphism class of components. Each node $v$ in the ICT keeps the integer $n_v$ representing the size of the isomorphism class.

We use the ICT to compute the $k$-fold vertical rotation of a series parallel digraph, which is the most important symmetry to maximize the three dimensional symmetry group. We construct the ICT from the CDT. In the CDT, each internal node $v$ is labeled as $P$ or $S$. If $v$ is labeled as $P$ in the CDT, then we divide its children into isomorphism classes and then assign a new node to represent each isomorphism class in the ICT. If it is labeled as $S$ in the CDT, then we keep the same structure. Figure 3 (a) shows an example of the CDT and Figure 3 (b) shows an example of the ICT.

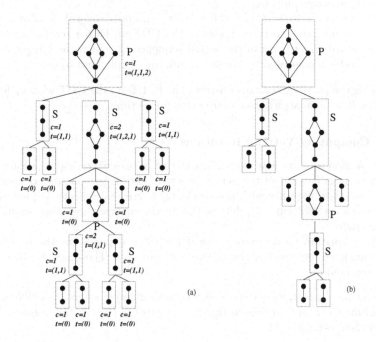

**Fig. 3.** *The Canonical Decomposition Tree (CDT) and the Isomorphism Class Tree (ICT).*

To construct the ICT, we need to divide the children of a $P$ node of the CDT into isomorphism classes and compute the size of each class. To do this, we label each node of the CDT in such a way that nodes corresponding to isomorphic components receive the same label. The method is an adaptation of a tree isomorphism algorithm [1].

The labeling algorithm assigns labels to the nodes on the same level, starting from the lowest level and towards to the root. Each node $v$ receives two labels:

an integer $code(v)$ and a list $tuple(v)$ of integers. The values of $code(v)$ define the isomorphism class of the components at the same level as $v$. Figure 3 (a) shows an example of the labeling.

**Algorithm CDT_labeling**
1. Initialize the tuples for each leaf $v$ of the CDT: $tuple(v) = (0)$.
2. Repeat for each level $i$, from the lowest level to the root level:
   a) For each internal node $v$ of the CDT at level $i$,
      $tuple(v) = (code(u_1), code(u_2), ..., code(u_k))$,
      where $u_1, u_2, \ldots, u_k$ are the children of $v$, from left to right.
   b) If $v$ is a $P$ node, then sort $tuple(v)$.
   c) Let $Q$ be the sequence of tuples for the nodes of the CDT on level $i$. Sort $Q$ lexicographically.
   d) For each node $v$ of the CDT at level $i$, compute $code(v)$ as follows. Assign the integer 1 to those nodes of the CDT on level $i$ represented by the first distinct tuple of the sorted sequence $Q$, assign the integer 2 to the nodes represented by the second distinct tuple, and so on.

Using the labeling, we can construct the ICT from the CDT with $n_v$ for each $v$ in the ICT. The algorithm clearly takes linear time.

## 4.2   Computing Vertical Rotations

In this section we show how to compute the set of sizes of vertical rotation groups. The maximum element of this set is the size of the largest possible vertical rotation group, and together with the checks for horizontal reflections (Section 4.3) and inversions (Section 4.4), defines the maximum size three dimensional symmetry group.

The algorithm to compute vertical rotations depends on the components which are fixed (setwise) by the vertical rotation axis. These are classified in the following Lemma.

**Lemma 2.** *Suppose that $G$ is a series parallel digraph, where the children of the root in the CDT of $G$ represent the components $G_1, G_2, \ldots, G_k$. Suppose that $\alpha$ is a vertical rotation of $G$.*

*1. If $G$ is a series composition, then $\alpha$ fixes each one of $G_1, G_2, \ldots, G_k$.*
*2. If $G$ is a parallel composition, then $\alpha$ fixes at most one of $G_1, G_2, \ldots, G_k$.*

Suppose that a component $G_j$ belongs to an isomorphism class $I_i$ and $v$ represents $I_i$ in the ICT. We define $L_v$ as the set of sizes of all possible vertical rotation groups of $G_j$. The aim of this section is to compute $L_r$, where $r$ is the root of the ICT; in fact we show how to compute $L_v$ for every node $v$ of the ICT. If $v$ is a leaf then $L_v = \{\infty\}$. Let $v$ be an internal node of the ICT and $u_1, u_2, \ldots, u_k$ be the children of $v$ in the ICT. Then the computation of $L_v$ can be divided into two cases, when $v$ is a $P$ node and when $v$ is an $S$ node. Using Lemma 2 one can derive the following theorem, which forms the basis of the algorithm to follow.

**Theorem 1.** *Suppose that $G$ is a series parallel digraph, $r$ is the root node of the ICT of $G$, and $u_1, u_2, \ldots, u_k$ are the children of $r$ in the ICT. Suppose that $n_i$ is the number of components in the isomorphism class represented by $u_i$. If $G$ has a $g$-fold vertical rotation and $r_i$ be the remainder when $n_i$ is divided by $g$, then $g$ satisfies the following condition.*

1. *If $r$ is an $S$ node, then $L_v = L_1 \cap L_2 \cap \ldots \cap L_k$.*
2. *If $r$ is a $P$ node, then at most one of the $r_i$ is 1 and $g \in L_i$.*

Now we consider the two cases, where $v$ is an $S$ node and where $v$ is a $P$ node.

The simpler case is where $v$ is an $S$ node. Using part 1 of Theorem 1 and representing $L_v$ and each $L_i$ as bit arrays, one can define an **Algorithm ComputeLvSeries** which computes $L_v$ as the bitwise AND of all the $L_i$. This takes time proportional to the minimum of the maximum elements over all the $L_i$. Since each element is a positive integer, this is $O(\min_i \mid L_i \mid)$. Note that summing over all $S$ nodes gives linear time.

Now suppose that $v$ is a $P$ node, the components $G_1, G_2, \ldots, G_m$ of $v$ are divided into isomorphism classes $I_1, I_2, \ldots, I_k$, and each $u_i$ in the ICT represents each $I_i$. We can construct a symmetric drawing by placing the source and the sink on the vertical rotation axis and then placing each component $G_i$ around the axis. We can place at most one child component $G_i$ on the vertical rotation axis. Thus the computation of $L_v$ can be divided into two cases: no fixed component, or one fixed component on the vertical rotation axis. Let $g$ be the size of a vertical rotation group.

The first case, with no fixed component, is relatively simple: $g$ must divide each of $n_1, n_2, \ldots, n_k$, and thus we insert every divisor of $gcd(n_1, n_2, \ldots, n_k)$ into the list $L_v$. There are less than $\min(n_1, n_2, \ldots, n_k)$ divisors of $gcd(n_1, n_2, \ldots, n_k)$, and so this case takes linear time.

The second case, with one fixed component, is more complex. We need to compute the intersection of two rotation groups, one of the fixed component $G_i$ and the other formed by the remaining components except $G_i$, that is $G_1, G_2, \ldots, G_{i-1}, G_{i+1}, \ldots, G_m$. To compute all possible vertical rotation groups, we need to compute all intersections by taking a component from each isomorphism class as the fixed component. Therefore, for each $i$, first compute $g_i = gcd(n_1, n_2, \ldots, n_i - 1, \ldots, n_k)$. Then for each $u_i$, we compute $g = gcd(g_i, e)$, where $e \in L_i$. We insert every divisor of $g$ into the list $L_v$.

Again we represent $L_v$ as a bit array. If the component $G_j$ in $I_i$ has a rotation group of size $k$, then $L_i[k] = 1$ and $L_i[k] = 0$ otherwise. Note that if $L_i[k] = 1$, then $L_i[j] = 1$ for all divisors $j$ of $k$. We also represent the set of divisors of $g_i$ as an array $GG_i$ using the same representation. That is, for each divisor $j$ of $g_i$, $GG_i[j] = 1$. Then to compute the intersection of $g_i$ and $L_i$, take the bitwise AND of $L_i$ and $GG_i$.

To achieve a linear time complexity, we further divide into the following two subcases.

(i) For some $p$, $n_p = 1$. In this case, for $i \neq p$, $g_i = 1$ and $gcd(g_i, e) = 1$, for each $e \in L_i$; thus we only need to compute for the single case $i = p$.

(ii) For all $p$, $n_p > 1$. In this case, $gcd(n_1, n_2, \ldots, n_i - 1, \ldots, n_k) \leq \min(n_1, n_2, \ldots, n_i - 1, \ldots, n_k)$.

We are now ready to state Algorithm ComputeLvParallel.

Algorithm ComputeLvParallel
(i) if ($n_p = 1$ for some $p$) then
    a) $g = gcd(n_1, n_2, \ldots, n_{p-1}, n_{p+1}, \ldots, n_k)$.
    b) $GG$ = the set of divisors of $g$.
    c) Add $GG \cap L_p$ to $L_v$.
(ii) else for $g = min(n_i)$ down to 1
    a) Compute $r_i$ = remainder of $n_i$ divided by $g$ for each $i$.
    b) If $r_i = 0$ for each $i$, then add $g$ to $L_v$.
    c) If $r_p = 1$, $r_i = 0$ for each $i \neq p$, and $g \in L_p$, then add $g$ to $L_v$.

Note that, at each node $v$, part (i) of Algorithm ComputeLvParallel takes time proportional to $g$; this is linear. Part (ii) takes time $O(k \min_i(n_i))$. Summing over all $P$ nodes, the algorithm takes linear time overall.

An algorithm for computing $L_v$ for each node $v$ in the ICT and $k$-fold vertical rotations can be described as follows.

Algorithm Vertical_Rotation
1. For each leaf $v$ in the ICT, assign $\infty$ to $L_v$.
2. Repeat for each internal node $v$ on the level $i$, from the lowest level to the root level:
    if $v$ is a $P$ node
    then ComputeLvParallel.
    else ComputeLvSeries.
3. Return the maximum element of $L_r$, where $r$ is the root.

From the remarks above, Algorithm Vertical_Rotation runs in linear time.

### 4.3    Detecting a Horizontal Reflection

In this section, we describe an algorithm to test whether there is a horizontal reflection in series parallel digraphs.

We use the CDT to find horizontal reflections. However, a horizontal reflection is direction-reversing, and detection requires a "reversing operation". Thus we need three steps: (a) reversing the CDT, (b) label the CDT and (c) find a horizontal reflection recursively.

The reversing step effectively reverses the order of the children of $S$ nodes of the half of the CDT. In fact, this reversing step marks $S$ nodes in the half of the CDT as "reversed". We omit this algorithm.

The labeling step for a horizontal reflection is very similar to Algorithm CDT_labeling. The only difference is that if an $S$ node is marked as "reversed" during the reversing step, then we reverse the order of the children of the $S$ node when we make a tuple. We omit this labeling step.

Now we give an algorithm to find horizontal reflections. As with vertical rotations, fixed components of a horizontal reflection play an important role.

**Lemma 3.** *Suppose that $G$ is a series parallel digraph, where the children of the root in the CDT of $G$ represent the components $G_1, G_2, \ldots, G_k$. Suppose that $\alpha$ is a horizontal reflection of $G$.*

1. *If $G$ is a parallel composition, then $\alpha$ fixes each one of $G_1, G_2, \ldots, G_k$.*
2. *If $G$ is a series composition and $k$ is even, then $\alpha$ has no fixed component.*
3. *If $G$ is a series composition and $k$ is odd, then $\alpha$ fixes $G_{(k+1)/2}$ and has no other fixed component.*

This Lemma leads to the following theorem, which is the basis for our algorithm for finding horizontal reflections.

**Theorem 2.** *Suppose that $G$ is a series parallel digraph.*

1. *If $G$ is a parallel composition of $G_1, G_2, \ldots, G_k$, then $G$ has a horizontal reflection if and only if all of $G_1, G_2, \ldots, G_k$ have horizontal reflections.*
2. *Suppose that $G$ is a series composition of $G_1, G_2, \ldots, G_k$. Let $r$ be the root node of the CDT of $G$.*

    a) *If $tuple(r)$ is a not a palindrome, then $G$ has no horizontal reflection.*

    b) *If $tuple(r)$ is a palindrome and has even length, then $G$ has a horizontal reflection.*

    c) *If $tuple(r)$ is a palindrome but has odd length, then $G$ has a horizontal reflection if and only if the component of the "middle" node of the palindrome has a horizontal reflection.*

The overall algorithm to find horizontal reflections can be described recursively as follows.

```
Algorithm Horizontal_Reflection(u)
If u is a P node
then
```

a) if **Horizontal_Reflection**$(v)$ for every child $v$ of $u$,
   then return($true$)
   else return($false$).

else /* $u$ is an $S$ node */

a) If $tuple(u)$ is a not a palindrome then return($false$).

b) If $tuple(u)$ is a palindrome and has even length then return($true$).

c) If $tuple(u)$ is a palindrome but has odd length
   then return(**Horizontal_Reflection**$(v)$), where $v$ is the "middle" node of the palindrome.

It is clear that **Algorithm Horizontal_Reflection** runs in linear time.

## 4.4    Detecting an Inversion

An inversion, like a horizontal reflection, is direction-reversing, and we need a similar "reversing operation". This is followed by the labeling step, and finally a step to find an inversion. We omit details of inversion detection, and merely state the central theorem.

**Theorem 3.** *Suppose that $G$ is a series parallel digraph.*

1. *Suppose that $G$ is a parallel composition of $G_1, G_2, \ldots, G_k$; suppose that the corresponding nodes of the CDT are $v_1, v_2, \ldots v_k$. Form pairs $(v_i, v_j)$, $1 \le i < j \le k$, such that $tuple_R(v_i)$ is the reverse of $tuple_R(v_j)$. Continue this pairing until no further pairs can be formed.*

   a) *If there is more than one component that cannot be paired, then $G$ has no inversion.*

   b) *If all of $G_1, G_2, \ldots, G_k$ are paired, then $G$ has an inversion.*

   c) *If one component is not paired, then $G$ has an inversion if and only if the unpaired component has an inversion.*

2. *Suppose that $G$ is a series composition of $G_1, G_2, \ldots, G_k$. Let $r$ be the root node of the CDT of $G$.*

   a) *If $tuple(r)$ is a not a palindrome, then $G$ has no inversion.*

   b) *If $tuple(r)$ is a palindrome and has even length, then $G$ has an inversion.*

   c) *If $tuple(r)$ is a palindrome but has odd length, then $G$ has an inversion if and only if the component of the "middle" node of the palindrome has an inversion.*

An algorithm, called `Algorithm Inversion`, can be deduced from Theorem 3. We omit details.

## 4.5    Computing the Full Symmetry Group

Computing the full symmetry group is trivial using Lemma 1. Let $G$ be a series parallel digraph. If $G$ has only $k$-fold vertical rotations, then the size of the full symmetry group is $2k$. If $G$ has $k$-fold vertical rotations and a horizontal reflection, then the size of the full symmetry group is $3k + 1$. If $G$ has $k$-fold vertical rotations and an inversion, then the size of the full symmetry group is $3k - 1$. If $G$ has $k$-fold vertical rotations, a horizontal reflection and an inversion, then the full symmetry group has the maximum size of $4k$.

The time complexity of the overall algorithm is described in the following theorem.

**Theorem 4.** *The time complexity of* `Algorithm 3DSymmetry_SPDigraph` *is linear.*

# 5    Conclusion

In this paper, we extend symmetric graph drawing into three dimensions. We present a linear time algorithm for finding maximum number of three dimensional symmetry in series parallel digraphs. This algorithm can be easily extended to the symmetric drawing algorithm for series parallel digraphs in three dimensions. As further research, we would like to draw planar graphs symmetrically in three dimensions.

# References

1. A. Aho, J. Hopcroft and J. Ullman, *The Design and Analysis of Computer Algorithms*, Addison-Wesley, 1974.
2. P. Bertolazzi, R.F. Cohen, G. D. Battista, R. Tamassia and I. G. Tollis, How to Draw a Series Parallel Digraph, *International Journal of Computational Geometry and Applications*, 4 (4), pp 385-402, 1994.
3. H. Carr and W. Kocay, An Algorithm for Drawing a Graph Symmetrically, *Bulletin of the ICA*, Vol. 27, pp. 19-25, 1999.
4. R.F. Cohen, G. D. Battista, R. Tamassia and I. G. Tollis, Dynamic Graph Drawing:Trees, Series Parallel Digraphs, and Planar st-Digraphs, *SIAM Journal on Computing*, 24 (5), pp 970-1001, 1995.
5. P. Eades and X. Lin, Spring Algorithms and Symmetry, *Computing and Combinatorics*, Springer Lecture Notes in Computer Science 1276, (Ed. Jiang and Lee), pp. 202-211.
6. H. Braysseix, An Heuristic for Graph Symmetry Detection, *Graph Drawing'99*, Lecture Notes in Computer Science 1731, (Ed. J. Kratochvil), pp. 276-285, Springer Verlag, 1999.
7. S. Hong, P. Eades, A. Quigley and S. Lee, Drawing Algorithms for Series Parallel Digraphs in Two and Three Dimensions, In S. Whitesides, editor, Graph Drawing (Proc. GD'98), vol. 1547 of Lecture Notes in Computer Science, pp. 198-209, Springer Verlag, 1998.
8. S. Hong, P. Eades and S. Lee, An Algorithm for Finding Geometric Automorphisms in Planar Graphs, *Algorithms and Computation*, (Proc. of ISAAC98), Lecture Notes in Computer Science 1533, (Ed. Chwa and Ibarra), pp. 277-286, Springer Verlag, 1998.
9. S. Hong and P. Eades, An Algorithms for Finding Three Dimensional Symmetry in Trees, to appear Graph Drawing (Proc. GD'2000), Lecture Notes in Computer Science, Springer Verlag, 2000.
10. X. Lin, Analysis of Algorithms for Drawing Graphs, *Ph.D. Thesis, University of Queensland*, 1992.
11. J. Manning and M. J. Atallah, Fast Detection and Display of Symmetry in Trees, *Congressus Numerantium*, 64, pp. 159-169, 1988.
12. J. Manning and M. J. Atallah, Fast Detection and Display of Symmetry in Outerplanar Graphs, *Discrete Applied Mathematics*, 39, pp. 13-35, 1992.
13. J. Manning, Geometric Symmetry in Graphs, *Ph.D. Thesis, Purdue Univ.*, 1990.
14. G. E. Martin, *Transformation Geometry, an Introduction to Symmetry*, Springer, New York, 1982.
15. J. Valdes, R. Tarjan and E. Lawler, The Recognition of Series Parallel Digraphs, *SIAM Journal on Computing* 11(2), pp. 298-313, 1982.

# Undecidability Results for Monoids with Linear-Time Decidable Word Problems

Masashi Katsura[1], Yuji Kobayashi[2], and Friedrich Otto[3]

[1] Department of Mathematics, Kyoto-Sangyo University, Kyoto 603, Japan
katura@ksuvx0.kyoto-su.ac.jp
[2] Department of Information Science, Toho University, Funabashi 274, Japan
kobayasi@is.sci.toho-u.ac.jp
[3] Fachbereich Mathematik/Informatik, Universität Kassel, 34109 Kassel, Germany
otto@theory.informatik.uni-kassel.de

**Abstract.** Using a particularly adopted simulation of Turing machines by finite string-rewriting systems we show that all strong Markov properties are undecidable for the class $C_{\text{lin}}$ of finitely presented monoids with linear-time decidable word problems. Expanding on this construction it is then shown that also many other properties are undecidable for $C_{\text{lin}}$, among them the property of having a context-free (or a regular) cross-section, the existence of a finite convergent presentation, and the homological and homotopical finiteness conditions left- and right-$\mathsf{FP}_n$ ($n \geq 3$), left- and right-$\mathsf{FP}_\infty$, $\mathsf{FDT}$ and $\mathsf{FHT}$.

## 1 Introduction

A finitely presented monoid $M$ is given through a finite alphabet $\Sigma$, that is, a finite set of generators, and a finite string-rewriting system $R$ on $\Sigma$, that is, a finite set of defining relations. Although $M$ is defined through a finite set of data, many algebraic properties of $M$ are undecidable in general. In fact, Markov established a large class of properties of monoids, nowadays known as *Markov properties*, and proved that, if $P$ is such a property, then it is undecidable in general whether a given finitely presented monoid has property $P$ [11]. In his proof Markov uses a finitely presented monoid with an undecidable word problem at a central point. It follows that his undecidability result only applies to classes of monoids containing monoids with undecidable word problems.

Sattler-Klein [16] improved upon this result by showing that some Markov properties remain undecidable even for the class $C_{\text{poly}}$ of finitely presented monoids with word problems decidable in polynomial time. Actually, for each recursively enumerable language $L$, she constructs a family $\{M_w \mid w \in \Gamma^*\}$ of finitely presented monoids satisfying the following properties: each monoid $M_w$ has word problem decidable in polynomial time, and $M_w$ is trivial if $w \in L$, on the other hand, $M_w$ is infinite, non-commutative, non-free etc. if $w \notin L$. Thus, these properties are undecidable for the class $C_{\text{poly}}$.

Later Sattler-Klein's construction has been extended to show that also the homotopical finiteness condition $\mathsf{FDT}$ [13] and the homological finiteness condi-

D.T. Lee and S.-H. Teng (Eds.): ISAAC 2000, LNCS 1969, pp. 278–289, 2000.

tions left- and right-FP$_n$ ($n \geq 3$) and left- and right-FP$_\infty$ are undecidable for $C_{\text{poly}}$ [4].

Here we improve upon these results. Our improvements are threefolds. First of all our undecidability results hold for the class $C_{\text{lin}}$ of finitely presented monoids with linear-time decidable word problems, thus pushing the time bound from polynomial to linear time. Secondly we present a systematic way to carry over Markov's proof of undecidability to this class of monoids, therewith showing that each Markov property (in some strong sense) is undecidable for the class $C_{\text{lin}}$. Thirdly our construction is technically less involved than that of Sattler-Klein. In particular, the extention to proving the undecidability of the above-mentioned homotopical and homological finiteness conditions is less complicated. Finally, we can use our construction to also show that the property of having a context-free (or a regular) cross-section is undecidable for the class $C_{\text{lin}}$.

This paper is structured as follows. After recalling some basic definitions on monoid presentations in Section 2, we introduce the notion of strong Markov property and state our main undecidability results in Section 3. In Section 4 we present a technical result on which all our proofs are based. In the following section we apply this result to show the undecidability of strong Markov properties for the class $C_{\text{lin}}$. In Section 6 we prove that the existence of certain cross-sections is undecidable for $C_{\text{lin}}$, and in Section 7 we present the corresponding result for the aforementioned finiteness conditions. We conclude with some additional observations in Section 8. Because of the page limit no formal proofs will be given in the paper. They will appear elsewhere.

## 2  Preliminaries

Here we fix some notation on rewriting systems and monoid presentations. For more information we refer to the monograph by Book and Otto [3].

Let $\Sigma$ be a (finite) alphabet. Then $\Sigma^*$ denotes the free monoid generated by $\Sigma$, and 1 denotes the empty string. For a string $x \in \Sigma^*$, $|x|$ denotes the length of $w$. A *string-rewriting system* $S$ is a set of pairs of strings from $\Sigma^*$. An element of $S$ is usually written as $\ell \to r$, and it is called a *rewrite rule*. By dom($S$) we mean the set $\{\ell \in \Sigma^* \mid \exists r \in \Sigma^* : (\ell \to r) \in S\}$ of all left-hand sides of rules of $S$. The system $S$ is called *left-regular* if dom($S$) is a regular language.

The *reduction relation* $\to_S^*$ induced by $S$ is the reflexive and transitive closure of the relation $\to_S := \{(x\ell y, xry) \mid x, y \in \Sigma^*, (\ell \to r) \in S\}$. The reflexive, symmetric and transitive closure $\leftrightarrow_S^*$ of $\to_S$ is the *Thue congruence* generated by $S$. The monoid $M(\Sigma; S)$ given through the presentation $(\Sigma; S)$ is the quotient $\Sigma^*/\leftrightarrow_S^*$. A monoid $M$ is said to be *finitely presented*, if it admits a finite presentation of this form.

The *word problem* for the presentation $(\Sigma; S)$ is the following decision problem: Given two strings $u, v \in \Sigma^*$, decide whether $u \leftrightarrow_S^* v$ holds! It is well-known that there exist finite presentations for which the word problem is undecidable. In fact, the decidability as well as the complexity of the word problem are invariants of finite presentations [1]. Thus, we can speak of the complexity of the word problem for a monoid. In this paper we will be concerned with those finitely presented monoids for which the word problem is decidable in linear time, that is, given $u$ and $v$ the question of whether or not $u \leftrightarrow_S^* v$ holds can be answered by a deterministic multi-tape Turing machine in time $c \cdot (|u| + |v|)$ for some constant c. By $C_{\mathrm{lin}}$ we denote the class consisting of all these monoids.

A rewriting system $S$ is *noetherian (terminating)* if there is no infinite sequence of the form $x_1 \to_S x_2 \to_S \cdots$. It is *confluent* if, for all $x, y, z \in \Sigma^*$, $x \to_S^* y$ and $x \to_S^* z$ imply that $y \to_S^* w$ and $z \to_S^* w$ hold for some $w \in \Sigma^*$. The system $S$ is called *convergent* if it is both noetherian and confluent. A string $w$ is *irreducible* (with respect to $S$) if no rule of $S$ is applicable to it. If $S$ is convergent, then each string $x \in \Sigma^*$ has a unique irreducible descendant $\hat{x}$, which is called the *normal form* of $x$. For $x, y \in \Sigma^*$, we have $x \leftrightarrow_S^* y$ if and only if $\hat{x} = \hat{y}$, which shows that the word problem for a finite convergent system $S$ is decidable. Thus, in this situation the set IRR($S$) of strings that are irreducible mod $S$ is a *cross-section* for the monoid $M(\Sigma; S)$.

It is well-known that a noetherian system $S$ is confluent if and only if all its critical pairs are resolvable. Here a pair $(z_1, z_2)$ of strings is a critical pair of $S$, if there are rules $u_1 \to v_1, u_2 \to v_2 \in S$ such that

(i) $u_1 = xu_2y$, $z_1 = v_1$, and $z_2 = xv_2y$, or
(ii) $u_1x = yu_2$, $z_1 = v_1x$, and $z_2 = yv_2$ for some $x, y \in \Sigma^*$ satisfying $|x| < |u_2|$.

A critical pair $(z_1, z_2)$ is *resolvable* if $z_1$ and $z_2$ have a common descendant mod $S$.

If $S$ has an unresolvable critical pair $(p, q)$, then we can simply add the rule $(\hat{p} \to \hat{q})$ or $(\hat{q} \to \hat{p})$ to $S$ in order to resolve this critical pair, where $\hat{p}$ $(\hat{q})$ is an irreducible descendant of $p$ $(q)$. Of course, it must be ensured that the extended system is still noetherian. For this a well-ordering $\geq$ on $\Sigma^*$ is used that is compatible with $S$, that is, $u > v$ holds for each rule $u \to v$ of $S$. Unfortunately each new rule may lead to new unresolvable critical pairs, and hence, this process may not terminate. In this case it will enumerate an infinite system $S^\infty$ that is *equivalent* to $S$, that is, $S$ and $S^\infty$ generate the same Thue congruence on $\Sigma^*$, and that is convergent and compatible with the given well-ordering. This procedure, which is the basic form of the well-known Knuth-Bendix completion procedure [6,8], will in fact terminate if and only if there exists a finite system that has these properties.

## 3   The Undecidability Results

Here we introduce the strong Markov properties and some other properties and state our main undecidability results. The proof outlines will be given in the subsequent sections.

If $P$ is a property of monoids, then $P(M)$ will denote the fact that the monoid $M$ does have this property. A property $P$ of monoids is called *invariant* if $P(M)$ implies that $P(M')$ holds for each monoid $M'$ isomorphic to $M$. An invariant property $P$ is called a *strong Markov property* if there exist monoids $M_1$ and $M_2$ in $C_{\mathrm{lin}}$ such that

(i) $M_1$ has property $P$, but
(ii) $M_2$ cannot be embedded in any monoid in $C_{\text{lin}}$ with property $P$, that is, no monoid in $C_{\text{lin}}$ containing a submonoid isomorphic to $M_2$ has property $P$.

It is easily seen that left-cancellativity is a strong Markov property, and so it follows that cancellativity, the property of being a group, freeness, triviality etc. are all strong Markov properties. Further, the property of satisfying some fixed nontrivial (quasi-)identities is a strong Markov property, which implies that commutativity, idempotency, nilpotency, finiteness etc. are strong Markov properties. Finally, the property of not having an element (or a subset) with a certain local property is a strong Markov property. Examples are the negations of the property of having a nontrivial idempotent or of the property of containing a nontrivial subgroup.

Our first undecidablity result concerns the strong Markov properties.

**Theorem 1.** *Any strong Markov property is undecidable for the class $C_{\text{lin}}$.*

A subset $C \subseteq \Sigma^*$ is called a *cross-section* for the monoid $M(\Sigma; S)$ if $C$ contains exactly one element of each congruence class mod $S$. In Section 6 we will derive the following result.

**Theorem 2.** *For the class $C_{\text{lin}}$ the following properties are undecidable:*
*(1.) the existence of a context-free cross-section;*
*(2.) the existence of a regular cross-section;*
*(3.) the existence of a left-regular convergent presentation;*
*(4.) the existence of a finite convergent presentation.*

It should be pointed out that it is not known whether or not these properties are (strong) Markov properties. Actually the same is true for the finiteness conditions discussed below.

Let $M = M(\Sigma; S)$. Then by $F$ we denote the integral monoid ring $\mathbb{Z}\Sigma^*$ of the free monoid $\Sigma^*$, and $A := \mathbb{Z}M$ is the integral monoid ring of $M$.

An abelian group $C$ is called a *left $A$-module*, if there exists a *left action* of $A$ on $C$, it is called a *right $A$-module*, if there is a *right action* of $A$ on $C$, and it is an *$A$-bimodule*, if there is a left action and a right action of $A$ on $C$ that are compatible. Observe that the ring $\mathbb{Z}$ itself is an $A$-bimodule via the trivial actions from the left and from the right. A sequence $C_1 \xrightarrow{\alpha} C_2 \xrightarrow{\beta} C_3$ of $A$-module homomorphisms is called *exact at* $C_2$ if $\text{im}(\alpha) = \text{ker}(\beta)$ holds. Further a sequence $C_1 \xrightarrow{\alpha_1} C_2 \xrightarrow{\alpha_2} \cdots \xrightarrow{\alpha_n} C_{n+1}$ is called *exact*, if it is exact at $C_i$ for all $i = 2, \ldots, n$.

The monoid $M$ is said to be *left-FP$_k$* (*right-FP$_k$*) for some integer $k \geq 1$, if there exists an exact sequence of finitely generated free left $A$-modules (right $A$-modules) of the form $C_k \xrightarrow{\delta_k} C_{k-1} \xrightarrow{\delta_{k-1}} \ldots \xrightarrow{\delta_2} C_1 \xrightarrow{\delta_1} C_0 \xrightarrow{\delta_0} \mathbb{Z} \longrightarrow 0$. It is *left-FP$_\infty$* (*right-FP$_\infty$*) if it is left-FP$_k$ (right-FP$_k$) for all $k \geq 1$. It is known that a monoid is left- and right-FP$_\infty$ if it admits a finite convergent presentation [2, 10,18].

With the monoid presentation $(\Sigma; S)$ an infinite graph $\Gamma(\Sigma; S)$ can be associated that depicts the single-step reduction relation $\to_S$ on $\Sigma^*$. By $P(\Gamma(\Sigma; S))$ we denote the set of all paths in this graph, and $P^{(2)}(\Gamma(\Sigma; S))$ is the set of all pairs of parallel paths. Here two paths $p, q \in P(\Gamma(\Sigma; S))$ are called *parallel* if they have the same initial vertex and the same terminal vertex. Squier [17] studied certain subsets of $P^{(2)}(\Gamma(\Sigma; S))$ that he called *homotopy relations*. For each $B \subseteq P^{(2)}(\Gamma(\Sigma; S))$ there is a uniquely determined smallest homotopy relation $\sim_B$ that contains $B$. Now $(\Sigma; S)$ is said to be of *finite derivation type*, FDT for short, if there exists a finite set $B$ such that $\sim_B$ is all of $P^{(2)}(\Gamma(\Sigma; S))$. Squier proved that this property is actually an invariant of finitely presented monoids, and that each monoid with a finite convergent presentation has the property FDT [17]. In fact, he proved that the set of critical pairs of a convergent system together with the corresponding resolutions yields a homotopy base for $P^{(2)}(\Gamma(\Sigma; S))$.

Finally Pride associated an $A$-bimodule $\Pi$ with the monoid presentation $(\Sigma; S)$ [14], and he introduced the notion of *finite homology type* (FHT) for $(\Sigma; S)$, which means that $\Pi$ is finitely generated as an $A$-bimodule. Again this is an invariant of finitely presented monoids [19]. In fact, $\Pi$ is embedded in the free $A$-bimodule $A \cdot S \cdot A$ generated by $S$ [5], and a homotopy base $B \subseteq P^{(2)}(\Gamma(\Sigma; S))$ yields a set $\partial_2(B)$ of generators for the $A$-bimodule $\Pi$ [9].

In Section 7 we will establish the following undecidability results.

**Theorem 3.** *For the class $C_{\text{lin}}$ the properties left-$FP_n$ for all $n \geq 3$ and left-$FP_\infty$, the properties right-$FP_n$ for all $n \geq 3$ and right-$FP_\infty$, and the properties FDT and FHT are undecidable in general.*

## 4    Rewriting Systems Simulating Turing Machines

Here we present the main construction on which the proofs of all the undecidability results above will be based.

Let $L$ be a recursively enumerable language over $\Gamma$, and let $\mathbf{TM} = (\Gamma_b, Q, q_0, q_k, \delta)$ be a deterministic single-tape Turing machine accepting $L$. Here $\Gamma_b = \Gamma \cup \{b\}$ is the tape alphabet, where $b \notin \Gamma$ is the blank symbol, $Q = \{q_0, q_1, \ldots, q_k\}$ is the set of states, $q_0$ is the initial state, $q_k$ is the halting state, and $\delta : Q' \times \Gamma_b \to Q \times \Gamma_b \times \{\lambda, \rho\}$ is the transition function, where $\lambda$ and $\rho$ are the symbols for the left and right moves of $\mathbf{TM}$'s head, respectively, and $Q' = Q \smallsetminus \{q_k\}$.

A string $xqy$, where $x, y \in \Gamma_b^*$ and $q \in Q$, is a *configuration* of $\mathbf{TM}$. By $\vdash$ we denote the single-step computation relation on the set of configurations that is defined as follows:

(i) $xqay \vdash xa'q'y$ if $\delta(q, a) = (q', a', \rho)$ for $a, a' \in \Gamma_b$, $x, y \in \Gamma_b^*$, and $q, q' \in Q$,

(ii) $xcqay \vdash xq'ca'y$ if $\delta(q, a) = (q', a', \lambda)$ for $a, a', c \in \Gamma_b$, $x, y \in \Gamma_b^*$, and $q, q' \in Q$, and

(iii) $xq \vdash uq'v$ if $xqb \vdash uq'v$ by (i) or (ii).

As we can assume without loss of generality that the head of $\mathbf{TM}$ never moves to the left of its initial position, the above relation suffices to completely describe the behaviour of **TM**. Given a string $w \in \Gamma^*$ as input, **TM** will halt in state $q_k$ after a finite number of steps if $w$ belongs to $L$, but **TM** will not halt and run forever if $w \notin L$. Thus, $L = \{w \in \Gamma^* \mid q_0 w \vdash^* x q_k y$ for some $x, y \in \Gamma_b^*\}$, where $\vdash^*$ denotes the reflexive transitive closure of $\vdash$.

Now we construct a string-rewriting system $R_w$ that simulates the computation of **TM** on input $w$. Let $\Xi = \Gamma_b \cup Q \cup \{H, E, A, \overline{A}, B, \overline{B}, O\}$, where $H, E, A, \overline{A}, B, \overline{B}, O$ are new letters, and let $w \in \Gamma^*$. In the following $a, a'$ and $c$ are any letters from $\Gamma_b$, $q$ and $q'$ are any states from $Q$, and for a set $X$ of strings, $X \to O$ denotes the collection of rules $x \to O$ for all $x \in X$. The system $R_w$ consists of the following rules :

**0** : $HAq_0 w \overline{B} E \to O$,
**1a** : $a\overline{A} \to \overline{A}a$,
**1b** : $H\overline{A} \to HA$,
**1c** : $Aa \to aA$,
**1a'** : $\overline{B}a \to a\overline{B}$,
**1b'** : $\overline{B}EE \to BbE$,
**1c'** : $aB \to Ba$,
**2a** : $AqBa \to \overline{A}a'q'\overline{B}$   if $\delta(q, a) = (q', a', \rho)$,
**2b** : $cAqBa \to \overline{A}q'ca'\overline{B}$   if $\delta(q, a) = (q', a', \lambda)$,
**3a** : $aAq_k B \to Aq_k B$ , $Aq_k Ba \to Aq_k B$,
**3b** : $HAq_k BE \to HE$,
**3c** : $HEE \to HE$,
**4a** : $O\sigma \to O, \sigma O \to O$   for all $\sigma \in \Xi$,
**4b** : $\{A, \overline{A}, B, \overline{B}\}^2 \smallsetminus \{\overline{A}, B\}\{A, \overline{B}\} \to O$,
**4c** : $\{qBAq', qq', \overline{B}q, q\overline{A}, qAq', qBq'\} \to O$,
**4d** : $\{AE, HB\} \to O$,
**4e** : $\sigma H \to O$   for all $\sigma \in \Xi$,
**4e'** : $E\sigma \to O$   for all $\sigma \in \Xi \smallsetminus \{E\}$.

By $T_w$ we denote the monoid $M(\Xi; R_w)$ presented by $(\Xi; R_w)$. If $w \notin L$, then for each $t \geq 1$ there exists a configuration $xqy$ such that $q_0 w \vdash^t xqy$. Let $\mathbf{0}_t$ denote the rule $\mathbf{0}_t : HxAqy'\overline{B}E \to O$, where $y' \in y \cdot b^*$ is determined by the equality $|xy'| = |w| + t$. Finally, let $\overline{R}_w = R_w \cup \{\mathbf{0}_t \mid t \geq 1\}$. The rule **0** can be seen as the rule $\mathbf{0}_0$.

For each $t \geq 0$ the rule $\mathbf{0}_t$ overlaps with the rule **1b'**:

$$O \leftarrow_{(\mathbf{4a})} OE \leftarrow_{(\mathbf{0}_t)} HxAqy'\overline{B}EE \to_{(\mathbf{1b'})} HxAqy'BbE \to^*_{(\mathbf{1c'})} HxAqBy'bE.$$

Now assume that $y' = ay_1$ and that $\delta(q, a) = (q', a', \rho)$. Then we have the following sequence of reductions:

$$HxAqBy'bE \quad = \quad HxAqBay_1 bE \quad \to_{(\mathbf{2a})} \quad Hx\overline{A}a'q'\overline{B}y_1 bE$$
$$\to^*_{(\mathbf{1a}),(\mathbf{1a'})} H\overline{A}xa'q'y_1 b\overline{B}E \to^*_{(\mathbf{1b}),(\mathbf{1c})} Hxa'Aq'y_1 b\overline{B}E.$$

It is easily seen that $Hxa'Aq'y_1 b\overline{B}E \to O$ is just the rule $\mathbf{0}_{t+1}$, that is, if **TM** does not halt on input $w$, then the completion procedure will add all the rules $\mathbf{0}_t$ $(t \geq 1)$ to $R_w$. In fact, $R_w$ and $\overline{R}_w$ have the following properties.

**Lemma 1.** *(1.) The system $R_w$ is noetherian.*

*(2.) There is only a single critical pair of $R_w$ that is not resolvable, and this is the pair resulting from overlapping the rules $\mathbf{0}$ and $\mathbf{1b}$'.*

*(3.) If $w \notin L$, then $\overline{R}_w$ is a convergent system that is equivalent to $R_w$.*

Based on this technical lemma the following properties of the monoid $T_w$ can be established.

**Theorem 4.** *(1) If $w$ is in $L$, then $HE = O$ in $T_w$.*

*(2) If $w$ is not in $L$, then $HE \neq O$ in $T_w$, and the word problem for $T_w$ is decidable in linear time.*

**Proof outline.** (1.) If $w \in L$, then $q_0 w \vdash^t x q_k y$ for some $t > 0$. Hence, we have $HxAq_k y' \overline{B}E \leftrightarrow^*_{R_w} O$ for some string $y' \in y \cdot b^*$, and so

$$O \leftrightarrow^*_{R_w} HxAq_k y' \overline{B}EE \to_{(1b')} HxAq_k y' BbE \to^*_{(1c')} HxAq_k By' bE$$
$$\to^*_{(3a)} HAq_k BE \to_{(3b)} HE.$$

(2.) If $w \notin L$, then $\overline{R}_w$ is convergent and equivalent to $R_w$. As $O$ and $HE$ are both irreducible mod $\overline{R}_w$, we see that $HE \neq O$ in $T_w$. Concerning the word problem it can be shown that the normal form $\hat{u} \in \mathrm{IRR}(\overline{R}_w)$ of a string $u \in \varXi^*$ can be computed in linear time. However, as the reduction sequence $u \to^*_{\overline{R}_w} \hat{u}$ is not linearly bounded in length, $\hat{u}$ cannot simply be determined by applying the rules of $\overline{R}_w$. A more sophisticated algorithm must be used instead.    □

## 5    Undecidability of Strong Markov Properties

Let $(\varSigma; R)$ be a finite presentation, and let $M = M(\varSigma; R)$. Further, let $\alpha, \beta, \gamma$ be new letters, and let $x, y \in \varSigma^*$. Over $\varSigma' = \varSigma \cup \{\alpha, \beta, \gamma\}$ we consider the system $S = \{\alpha x \beta \to 1, \alpha y \beta \to \gamma\} \cup \{\sigma \gamma \to \gamma, \gamma \sigma \to \gamma \mid \sigma \in \varSigma'\}$.

We define the monoid $\varPhi_{x,y}(M)$ through $\varPhi_{x,y}(M) = M(\varSigma'; R \cup S)$. Then this monoid is determined by the given presentation $(\varSigma; R)$ and the strings $x$ and $y$. Let $\phi : M \to \varPhi_{x,y}(M)$ be the morphism that is induced by the inclusion $\varSigma \hookrightarrow \varSigma'$.

**Lemma 2.** *(1.) If $x = y$ in $M$, then $\varPhi_{x,y}(M)$ is the trivial monoid.*

*(2.) If $x \neq y$ in $M$, then $\phi$ is injective. Moreover, if the word problem for $M$ is decidable in linear time, then so is the word problem for $\varPhi_{x,y}(M)$.*

**Proof.** If $x = y$ in $M$, then $\gamma = 1$ in $\varPhi_{x,y}(M)$, and hence, $\sigma = \sigma \gamma = \gamma = 1$ for each $\sigma \in \varSigma'$. Hence, $\varPhi_{x,y}(M)$ is trivial. Now assume that $x \neq y$ in $M$, and let $\overline{R}$ be a convergent system equivalent to $R$. Let $\hat{x}$ and $\hat{y}$ be the normal forms of $x$ and $y$ with respect to $\overline{R}$, respectively. By our assumption $\hat{x} \neq \hat{y}$. Let $\overline{S} = \{\alpha \hat{x} \beta \to 1, \alpha \hat{y} \beta \to \gamma, \sigma \gamma \to \gamma, \gamma \sigma \to \gamma \mid \sigma \in \varSigma'\}$. Then $\overline{R} \cup \overline{S}$ is a convergent system that is equivalent to $R \cup S$. It is easily seen that strings over $\varSigma$ that are irreducible with respect to $\overline{R}$ are also irreducible with respect to $\overline{R} \cup \overline{S}$. This implies that $\phi$ is injective. Finally, it follows that the word problem for $\varPhi_{x,y}(M)$ is decidable in linear time, if the word problem for $M$ is.    □

To prove the undecidability of strong Markov properties we combine the construction in Section 4 with the construction above. For a monoid $M = M(\varSigma; R)$

and a string $w \in \Gamma^*$ we define the monoid $\Psi_w(M) := \Phi_{HE,O}(M \times T_w)$, where $M \times T_w$ denotes the direct product of $M$ and the monoid $T_w$ of the previous section, that is, the monoid $\Psi_w(M)$ is defined over the alphabet $\Sigma' \cup \Xi$ by the system $R \cup R_w \cup C \cup S$, where $C = \{\eta\zeta \to \zeta\eta \mid \eta \in \Sigma, \zeta \in \Xi\}$ and
$$S = \{\alpha HE\beta \to 1, \alpha O\beta \to \gamma, \sigma\gamma \to \gamma, \gamma\sigma \to \gamma \mid \sigma \in \Sigma' \cup \Xi\}.$$
By Theorem 4 and Lemma 2 we have the following result.

**Corollary 1.** *(1.) If $w$ is in $L$, then $\Psi_w(M)$ is the trivial monoid.*
*(2.) If $w$ is not in $L$, then $\Psi_w(M)$ contains $M$ as a submonoid.*
*(3.) If the word problem for $M$ is decidable in linear time, then so is the word problem for $\Psi_w(M)$.*

Based on Corollary 1, the proof of Theorem 1 is now standard. Let $P$ be a strong Markov property, let $M_1$ be a monoid in $C_{\mathrm{lin}}$ having property $P$, and $M_2$ be a monoid in $C_{\mathrm{lin}}$ that is not embeddable in any monoid in $C_{\mathrm{lin}}$ that has property $P$. We choose a recursively enumerable language $L$ that is nonrecursive. Let $M_w := M_1 \times \Psi_w(M_2)$. Then the word problem for $M_w$ is decidable in linear time by Corollary 1. Moreover, $M_w$ is isomorphic to $M_1$ if $w \in L$, and it contains $M_2$ as a submonoid, otherwise. Thus, $M_w$ has property $P$ if and only if $w$ belongs to $L$. As $L$ is nonrecursive, this completes the proof of Theorem 1.

# 6 Cross-Sections

Here we will show that the existence of context-free cross-sections is undecidable for the class $C_{\mathrm{lin}}$.

Let $\Pi = \{a, b, c, \gamma\}$ and $R_K := \{ba \to ab, bc \to aca, cc \to \gamma\} \cup \{x\gamma \to \gamma, \gamma x \to \gamma \mid x \in \Pi\}$. By $K$ we denote the monoid $M(\Pi; R_K)$. It is shown in [12] that $K$ has the convergent presentation $(\Pi; R_K^\infty)$, where $R_K^\infty := R_K \cup \{a^n ca^n c \to \gamma \mid n \geq 1\}$, and that $K$ does not have a context-free cross-section. Here we will need the following additional properties of $K$.

**Lemma 3.** *(1.) The word problem for $K$ is decidable in linear time.*
*(2.) Let $C \subseteq \Pi^*$ be a context-free language. If $C$ contains a cross-section for $K$, then the set $C \cap [\gamma]_{R_K}$ is infinite.*

Part (1.) is easy, as the normal form of a string $w \in \Pi^*$ with respect to the system $R_K^\infty$ can be computed in linear time. Part (2.) is shown in the proof of [12] Proposition 6.3.

Let $N_w = M(\Delta; S_w)$ denote the monoid $\Phi_{HE,O}(T_w)$, that is, $N_w$ is obtained from the monoid $T_w$ of Section 4 by the embedding presented in Section 5. The word problem for $N_w$ is decidable in linear time, $N_w$ is the trivial monoid if $w \in L$, and if $w \notin L$, then $T_w$ is embedded in $N_w$ by the identity mapping.

Without loss of generality we can assume that $\Pi \cap \Delta = \{\gamma\}$. We define the monoid $K_w$ as the zero-direct product of $K$ and $N_w$, that is, $K_w$ is given through the finite presentation $(\Pi \cup \Delta; R_{K,w})$, where $R_{K,w} := R_K \cup S_w \cup \{\sigma\tau \to \tau\sigma \mid \tau \in \Pi \setminus \{\gamma\}, \sigma \in \Delta \setminus \{\gamma\}\}$. From the properties of $N_w$ and the fact that the letter $\gamma$ serves as a zero for $K$ as well as for $N_w$ the following facts about $K_w$ can be derived.

**Lemma 4.** *(a) If $w \in L$, then $K_w$ is the trivial monoid.*
*(b) If $w \notin L$, then $K$ is embedded in $K_w$ by the identity mapping on $\Pi^*$.*

In fact, if $w \notin L$, then the infinite system

$$R^\infty_{K,w} := R^\infty_K \cup S^\infty_w \cup \{\sigma\tau \to \tau\sigma \mid \tau \in \Pi \smallsetminus \{\gamma\}, \sigma \in \Delta \smallsetminus \{\gamma\}\}$$

is a convergent system that is equivalent to $R_{K,w}$. Here $S^\infty_w$ denotes the infinite system on $\Delta$ that is equivalent to the system

$$S_w = R_w \cup \{\alpha H E \beta \to 1, \alpha O \beta \to \gamma\} \cup \{\sigma\gamma \to \gamma, \gamma\sigma \to \gamma \mid \sigma \in \Delta\}.$$

Now let $\varphi_1$ and $\varphi_2$ denote the projections from $(\Pi \cup \Delta)^*$ onto $\Pi^*$ and $\Delta^*$, respectively. If $w \in L$, then by Lemma 4(a) $K_w$ is the trivial monoid, and hence, the word problem for $K_w$ is decidable in linear time, and the set $\{1\}$ is a (context-free) cross-section for $K_w$. To solve the word problem for $K_w$ efficiently in the case that $w \notin L$, the following technical results are important. They are easily derived using the system $R^\infty_{K,w}$.

**Lemma 5.** *Suppose that $w \notin L$, and let $x \in (\Pi \cup \Delta)^*$. Then the following three statements hold:*

*(1.)* $x \leftrightarrow^*_{R_{K,w}} \varphi_1(x)\varphi_2(x)$.
*(2.)* $x \leftrightarrow^*_{R_{K,w}} \gamma$ iff $\varphi_1(x) \leftrightarrow^*_{R_K} \gamma$ or $\varphi_2(x) \leftrightarrow^*_{S_w} \gamma$.
*(3.)* *If $x \leftrightarrow^*_{R_{K,w}} y$ for some $y \in \Pi^*$ such that $y \leftrightarrow^*_{R_K} \gamma$, then $\varphi_2(x) \leftrightarrow^*_{S_w} 1$.*

Based on this lemma the following result can be established.

**Lemma 6.** *The word problem for $K_w$ is decidable in linear time.*

We have already noted that the set $\{1\}$ is a cross-section for the monoid $K_w$ if $w \in L$. For $w \notin L$ we have the following contrasting result.

**Lemma 7.** *If $w \notin L$, then $K_w$ does not have a context-free cross-section.*

**Proof.** Assume that $w \notin L$, but that $C \subseteq (\Pi \cup \Delta)^*$ is a context-free cross-section for $K_w$. Hence, there exists a unique element $z \in C$ such that $z \leftrightarrow^*_{R_{K,w}} \gamma$. For each string $x \in \Pi^*$ satisfying $x \leftrightarrow^*_{R_K} \gamma$, we have $x \leftrightarrow^*_{R_{K,w}} \gamma$, as $K$ is embedded in $K_w$ by the identity mapping on $\Delta^*$. Hence, there exists some $y \in C \smallsetminus \{z\}$ such that $x \leftrightarrow^*_{R_{K,w}} y$. From Lemma 5(3.) it follows that $\varphi_2(y) \leftrightarrow^*_{S_w} 1$ and that $\varphi_1(y) \leftrightarrow^*_{R_K} x$. Thus, the context-free language $C_1 := \varphi_1(C \smallsetminus \{z\}) \cup \{\gamma\}$ contains a cross-section for $K$. By Lemma 3 this implies that $C_1 \cap [\gamma]_{R_K}$ is infinite. Hence, there exists some element $v \in C \smallsetminus \{z\}$ such that $\varphi_1(v) \leftrightarrow^*_{R_K} \gamma$, and so we have

$$v \leftrightarrow^*_{R_{K,w}} \varphi_1(v)\varphi_2(v) \leftrightarrow^*_{R_{K,w}} \gamma \leftrightarrow^*_{R_{K,w}} z.$$

This, however, contradicts the assumption that $C$ is a cross-section for $K_w$. $\square$

By combining the technical results above we obtain the following undecidability result.

**Theorem 5.** *Let $P$ be an invariant property of finitely presented monoids that satisfies the following two conditions:*

*(1) The trivial monoid has property P.*
*(2) Any finitely presented monoid having property P has a context-free cross-section.*
*Then the property P is undecidable in general for the class $C_{\text{lin}}$.*

**Proof.** Let the language $L$ underlying the construction of the monoid $N_w$ be nonrecursive. Given a string $w$, the presentation $(\Pi \cup \Delta; R_{K,w})$ of the monoid $K_w$ can be constructed effectively. By Lemma 6 the word problem for $K_w$ is decidable in linear time.

If $w \in L$, then $K_w$ is the trivial monoid (Lemma 4(a)), and hence, $K_w$ has property $P$. If, however, $w \notin L$, then $K_w$ does not have a context-free cross-section (Lemma 7), and hence, it does not have property $P$. Thus, $w \in L$ iff $K_w$ has property $P$. Hence, it is undecidable whether or not $K_w$ has property $P$. $\square$

As the existence of a finite or a left-regular convergent presentation for a monoid $M$ implies that $M$ has a regular cross-section, this yields Theorem 2.

# 7   Finiteness Conditions

Finally we turn to the undecidability of the various homological and homotopical finiteness conditions.

Let $\Sigma = \{a', b', c', d', f', g'\}$, let $R = \{a'b'c' \to a'c', d'a' \to f'a'b', g'f' \to 1\}$, and let $M := M(\Sigma; R)$. The system $R$ is noetherian, but not confluent. It is equivalent to the infinite convergent system $R^\infty := R \cup \{a'b'^n c' \to a'c' \mid n \geq 2\}$. The monoid $M$ has the following properties.

**Proposition 1.** [7]
*$M$ belongs to the class $C_{\text{lin}}$, it is right-$\text{FP}_\infty$, but it is not left-$\text{FP}_3$.*

Pride and Wang [15] have observed that Squier's example monoid $S_1$ is left-$\text{FP}_\infty$, but not right-$\text{FP}_3$. Here we use the monoid $M$, as it is easier than $S_1$.

As in the previous section $N_w = M(\Delta; S_w)$ denotes the monoid $\Phi_{HE,O}(T_w)$. Without loss of generality we can assume that $\Delta$ and $\Sigma$ are disjoint alphabets. Further, let $\delta_1, \delta_2$ be two additional new symbols, and let $\Omega := \Sigma \cup \Delta \cup \{\delta_1, \delta_2\}$. We define a monoid $E_w$ as an extension of the free product $M * N_w$ by taking $E_w := M(\Omega; R \cup S_w \cup \{\delta_1 O \delta_2 \to O, \delta_1 \delta_2 b' \to \delta_1 \delta_2\})$.

**Lemma 8.** *If $w \in L$, then the word problem for $E_w$ is decidable in linear time, and $E_w$ has a finite convergent presentation.*

For the remaining part of this section we assume that $w$ does not belong to $L$. Obviouly, $E_w$ has the infinite presentation $(\Omega; S^\infty)$, where $S^\infty := R^\infty \cup S_w^\infty \cup \{\delta_1 O \delta_2 \to O, \delta_1 \delta_2 b' \to \delta_1 \delta_2\}$. As $\Sigma$ and $\Delta$ are disjoint, and as $\delta_1$ and $\delta_2$ are two new symbols, it is easily seen that the system $S^\infty$ is convergent. Using the rules of $S^\infty$ each string can be reduced to its normal form. However, as the subsystem $S_w^\infty$ contains some commutation rules, this strategy may lead to an algorithm of quadratic time complexity. Nevertheless we have the following result which is based on a different strategy for computing normal forms with respect to $S^\infty$.

**Lemma 9.** *The normal form* $\hat{u} \in \mathrm{IRR}(S^\infty)$ *of a string* $u \in \Omega^+$ *can be computed in linear time, and thus, the word problem for* $E_w$ *is decidable in linear time.*

Further, following the arguments used in [4] it can be shown that the monoid $E_w$ is not left-$\mathsf{FP}_3$, if $w \notin L$. From this result and from Lemmata 8 and 9 we obtain the following undecidability result.

**Theorem 6.** *Let* $P$ *be an invariant property of finitely presented monoids that satisfies the following two conditions:*

*(1) Each monoid with a finite convergent presentation has property* $P$.
*(2) For each finitely presented monoid* $N$, *if* $N$ *has property* $P$, *then* $N$ *is left-*$\mathsf{FP}_3$.

*Then the property* $P$ *is undecidable in general for the class* $C_{\mathrm{lin}}$.

As the properties left-$\mathsf{FP}_n$ ($n \geq 3$), left-$\mathsf{FP}_\infty$, FDT, and FHT all satisfy the conditions of the above theorem, it follows that they are undecidable for the class $C_{\mathrm{lin}}$. The undecidability of the properties right-$\mathsf{FP}_n$ ($n \geq 3$) and right-$\mathsf{FP}_\infty$ follows by a symmetric argument.

# 8    Concluding Remarks

The simulation of a Turing machine presented in Section 4 and the embedding considered at the beginning of Section 5 form the technical tools for all our proofs of undecidability. Using these tools we have shown in a uniform way that all strong Markov properties as well as certain additional properties are undecidable for the class $C_{\mathrm{lin}}$. In fact, our tools easily yield further undecidability results. For a function $f$ satisfying $f(n) \geq n$ for all $n \in \mathbb{N}$, let $C_f$ denote the class of all finitely presented monoids the word problems of which can be solved in time $O(f)$.

**Theorem 7.** *Let* $C_f$ *and* $C_g$ *be classes of finitely presented monoids such that* $C_g$ *properly contains* $C_f$. *Then it is undecidable in general whether a given finitely presented monoid from* $C_g$ *belongs to* $C_f$.

Finally we remark that in our construction the zero element plays an essential role. So there does not seem to be an easy way to carry our construction over to derive similar undecidability results for groups with linear-time decidable word problems.

**Acknowledgement.** Part of this work was performed while the second author was visiting at the Fachbereich Mathematik/Informatik, Universität Kassel, supported by the Deutsche Forschungsgemeinschaft. He gratefully acknowledges this support and the hospitality of the university.

# References

1. J. Avenhaus and K. Madlener. Subrekursive Komplexität bei Gruppen : I. Gruppen mit vorgeschriebener Komplexität. *Acta Inform.*, 9:87–104, 1977.
2. D.J. Anick. On the homology of associative algebra. *Trans. Amer. Math. Soc.*, 296:641–659, 1987.
3. R.V. Book and F. Otto. *String-Rewriting Systems*. Springer-Verlag, New York, 1993.
4. R. Cremanns and F. Otto. FP$_\infty$ *is undecidable for finitely presented monoids with word problems decidable in polynomial time*. Mathematische Schriften Kassel 11/98, Universität Kassel, September 1998.
5. V.S. Guba and M. Sapir. Diagram groups. *Memoirs Amer. Math. Soc.*, 130:1–117, 1997.
6. D. Knuth and P. Bendix. Simple word problems in universal algebras. In J. Leech, editor, *Computational Problems in Abstract Algebra*, pages 263–297. Pergamon Press, New York, 1970.
7. M. Katsura, Y. Kobayashi, and F. Otto. *Undecidable properties of monoids with word problems solvable in linear time – II. Cross-sections and homological and homotopical finiteness conditions*. Mathematische Schriften Kassel, Universität Kassel, 2000. In preparation.
8. D. Kapur and P. Narendran. The Knuth-Bendix completion procedure and Thue systems. *SIAM J. Comput.*, 14:1052–1072, 1985.
9. Y. Kobayashi and F. Otto. *On homotopical and homological finiteness conditions for finitely presented monoids*. Mathematische Schriften Kassel 1/00, Universität Kassel, January 2000.
10. Y. Kobayashi. Complete rewriting systems and homology of monoid algebras. *J. Pure Applied Algebra*, 65:263–275, 1990.
11. A. Markov. Impossibility of algorithms for recognizing some properties of associative systems. *Doklady Adakemii Nauk SSSR*, 77:953–956, 1951.
12. F. Otto, M. Katsura, and Y. Kobayashi. Infinite convergent string-rewriting systems and cross-sections for finitely presented monoids. *J. Symb. Comput.*, 26:621–648, 1998.
13. F. Otto and A. Sattler-Klein. The property FDT is undecidable for finitely presented monoids that have polynomial-time decidable word problems. *Intern. J. Algebra Comput.*, 10:285–307, 2000.
14. S.J. Pride. Low-dimensional homotopy theory for monoids. *Intern. J. Algebra Comput.*, 5:631–649, 1995.
15. S.J. Pride and J. Wang. Rewriting systems, finiteness conditions, and associated functions. In J.C. Birget, S. Margolis, J. Meakin, and M. Sapir, editors, *Algorithmic Problems in Groups and Semigroups*, pages 195–216. Birkhäuser, Boston, 2000.
16. A. Sattler-Klein. New undecidability results for finitely presented monoids. In H. Comon, editor, *Rewriting Techniques and Applications*, Lecture Notes in Computer Science 1232, pages 68–82. Springer-Verlag, Berlin, 1997.
17. C.C. Squier, F. Otto, and Y. Kobayashi. A finiteness condition for rewriting systems. *Theoret. Comput. Sci.*, 131:271–294, 1994.
18. C.C. Squier. Word problems and a homological finiteness condition for monoids. *J. Pure Applied Algebra*, 49:201–217, 1987.
19. X. Wang and S.J. Pride. *Second order Dehn functions of groups and monoids*. Preprint, 1998.

# Secret Key Exchange Using Random Deals of Cards on Hierarchical Structures

Reina Yoshikawa, Shimin Guo, Kazuhiro Motegi, and Yoshihide Igarashi[1]

Department of Computer Science, Gunma University, Kiryu, Japan 376-8515
igarashi@comp.cs.gunma-u.ac.jp

**Abstract.** We propose the problem of how to transmit an information-theoretically secure bit using random deals of cards among players in hierarchical groups and a computationally unlimited eavesdropper. A player in the highest group wants to send players in lower groups a secret bit which is secure from the eavesdropper and some other players. We formalize this problem and design protocols for constructing secret key exchange spanning trees on hierarchical groups. For each protocol we give sufficient conditions to successfully construct a secret key exchange spanning tree for the hand sizes of the players and the eavesdropper.

**key words:** card games, hierarchical groups, information-theoretically secure, key exchange graphs, secret bit transmission

## 1 Introduction

Suppose that there are $n$ players and a passive eavesdropper, Eve, whose computational power is unlimited. The $n$ players are partitioned into hierarchical groups, $G_1, \cdots, G_h$, where $G_1 = \{P_{1,1}, \cdots, P_{1,k_1}\}, \cdots, G_h = \{P_{h,1}, \cdots, P_{h,k_h}\}$ and $|G_i| \geq 1$ for each $1 \leq i \leq h$ ($|G_i|$ is the cardinality of $G_i$). For each pair of $i$ and $j$ ($i \neq j$), $G_i \bigcap G_j = \phi$, and $\bigcup_{i=1}^{h} G_i$ is the set of $n$ players ($n = \sum_{i=1}^{h} k_i$). $G_i$ is higher than $G_j$ in the hierarchy if $i < j$. Using random deals of cards we want to construct a spanning tree with node set $\bigcup_{i=1}^{h} G_i$ satisfying the following three conditions, where a node denotes a player:

(1) A pair of nodes directly connected by an edge of the spanning tree has a secret key exchange.
(2) For each $1 \leq j \leq h$, the subgraph of the spanning tree consisting of the nodes in $\bigcup_{i=1}^{j} G_i$ and their incident edges is a spanning tree of the nodes of $\bigcup_{i=1}^{j} G_i$.
(3) If a pair of nodes are connected by an edge of the spanning tree, then both the nodes are in the same group, or one of them is in $G_i$ and the other is in $G_{i+1}$ for some $i$ ($1 \leq i \leq h-1$).

Once such a spanning tree is constructed, bit secret communication is possible between a pair of nodes directly connected by an edge of the spanning tree. We want to send a secret bit from a player in the highest group to a player through

D.T. Lee and S.-H. Teng (Eds.): ISAAC 2000, LNCS 1969, pp. 290–301, 2000.

a path in hierarchical order, where players in higher groups are assumed to be more trustworthy than players in lower groups. The problem was coming from such an organization, where a secret message from a member of the highest group is sent to members in lower groups. This is a motivation of studying the problem. If player $P_{i,j}$ wants to send a secret bit $r$ to its neighbor player $P_{i',j'}$ along an edge $(P_{i,j}, P_{i',j'})$, $P_{i,j}$ computes the *exclusive-or* $r \oplus r'$ and sends it to $P_{i',j'}$, where $r'$ is a secret one-bit key between $P_{i,j}$ and $P_{i'j'}$. Then $P_{i',j'}$ obtains $r$ by computing $r \oplus r' \oplus r' = r$. Applying this type of transmission at each node on a path in the spanning tree, the player at the root can send a secret bit to any node of the tree. This bit transmission is information-theoretically secure not only from Eve but also any node not in the path of the bit transmission. When the number of the hierarchical groups is just 1, the problem is the same as the secret key exchange using a random deal of cards studied in [1][2][3][4].

## 2    Preliminary

In this section we briefly review the secret bit transmission using a random deal of cards for the players in a non-hierarchical group. Suppose that there are $n$ players and a passive eavesdropper, Eve. Let each player $P_i$ hold $c_i$ cards and Eve hold $e$ cards. We call, $\xi = (c_1, \cdots, c_n; e)$ the signature of the deal. A player $P_i$ is said to be feasible (1) if $c_i > 1$, or (2) if $c_i = 1$, $e = 0$, and $c_j > 1$ for all $j \neq i$. To construct a spanning tree of $n$ nodes (players) we start a graph with $n$ isolated nodes (players). Fischer and Wright [2] proposed a protocol called the smallest feasible player (SFP) key set protocol as described below:

(1) Let $P$ be the feasible player holding the smallest hand. (Ties are broken in favor of the lower-numbered player.) If no player is feasible, then $P$ is the lowest-numbered player holding a non-empty hand.
(2) $P$ chooses a random card $x$ in her hand and a random card $y$ not in her hand, and proposes $K = \{x, y\}$ as a key set by asking, "Does any player hold a card in $K$ ?"
(3) If another player $Q$ holds $y$, she accepts $K$ by announcing that she holds a card in $K$. The cards $x$ and $y$ are discarded, and nodes $P$ and $Q$ are connected by an edge. Whichever player of $P$ and $Q$ holds fewer cards exposes the remaining cards in her hand, which are discarded, and drops out of the protocol. The remaining players go back to step (1). (Ties are broken in favor of the lower-numbered player.)
(4) If none of the players holds $y$ (i.e., Eve holds $y$), then $K$ is rejected. In this case, $x$ and $y$ are discarded, and the players go back to step (1).

In step (3) of the SFP key set protocol, a key set $K = \{x, y\}$ is opaque to Eve and the players other than $P$ and $Q$ (i.e., it is likely equal for Eve and the players other than $P$ and $Q$ that $P$ holds $x$ and $Q$ holds $y$ or that $P$ holds $y$ and $Q$ holds $x$). In step (3) the following rule is used to obtain a one-bit secret key $r'$ between $P$ and $Q$: $r' = 1$ if $x > y$; $r' = 0$, otherwise. The execution of the protocol continues until either there are not enough cards left to complete steps (1) and (2), or until only one or no player is left. The first case is where the protocol fails, and the second case is where the protocol is successful to construct a spanning tree of the players. If we are allowed to choose any feasible player (e.g., the largest feasible player, or a player randomly chosen from feasible players) in step (1) above, we call such a protocol the feasible player (FP) key set protocol. The SFP key set protocol is a kind of FP key set protocol. A spanning tree where any pair of nodes directly connected by an edge can share a one-bit secret key is called a secret key exchange spanning tree.

**Theorem 1.** (*Fischer and Wright [2]* ) *Let $\xi = (c_1, \cdots, c_n; e)$ be the signature of the deal. Let $c_i \geq 1$ for $1 \leq i \leq n$, and $max\{c_i | 1 \leq i \leq n\} + min\{c_i | 1 \leq i \leq n\} \geq n + e$. Then the SFP key set protocol performs successfully the construction of a secret key exchange spanning tree with $n$ nodes.*

The condition $c_i \geq 1$ for $1 \leq i \leq n$ and $max\{c_i | 1 \leq i \leq n\} + min\{c_i | 1 \leq i \leq n\} \geq n + e$ provides a sufficient condition for the SFP key set protocol to be successful on the signature. This condition provides also a sufficient condition for any FP key set protocol to be successful on the signature. As shown in [3][6], it is not a necessary condition. For example, a signature $\xi = (3, 3, 2, 1; 1)$ has $max\{c_i | 1 \leq i \leq 4\} + min\{c_i | 1 \leq i \leq 4\} = 4 < 4 + 1 = 5$, but the SFP key set protocol always succeeds on the signature. Note that the largest feasible player key set protocol may not succeed on this signature. The hands of the players and Eve may proceed in the order of $(3, 3.2, 1; 1)$, $(2, 0, 2, 1; 1)$, $(1, 0, 0, 1; 1)$, $(0, 0, 0, 1; 0)$, and then the protocols stops unsuccessfully. A necessary and sufficient condition for the SFP key set protocol to be successful on a signature was recently given by Mizuki, *et al.* [6]. However, the description of the necessary and sufficient condition is not simple, and its proof complicated [6]. For another example, a signature $\xi = (3, 3, 3, 3, 3, 3, 3, 3; 0)$ has $max\{c_i | 1 \leq i \leq 8\} + min\{c_i | 1 \leq i \leq 8\} = 6 < 8 + 0 = 8$. However, any FP key set protocol always succeeds on signature $\xi = (3, 3, 3, 3, 3, 3, 3, 3, ; 0)$. Fisher and Wright [2] showed that the SFP key set protocol is optimal among all FP key set protocols. That is, if a FP key set protocol is always successful on a signature $\xi$, then the SFP key set protocol is also always successful on the same signature $\xi$. All logarithms in this paper are to the base 2.

## 3    Hierarchical Groups with Two Levels

In this section we give a protocol called *2-level protocol* for constructing a secret key exchange spanning tree satisfying the conditions listed in Section 1 on hierarchical groups with two levels. Suppose that $n$ players are divided into two non-empty hierarchical groups $G_1$ and $G_2$. Let $\{P_{1,1}, \cdots, P_{1,k_1}\}$ be the set of the players in $G_1$ and $\{P_{2,1}, \cdots, P_{2,k_2}\}$ be the set of the players in $G_2$, where $k_1 \geq 1$ and $k_2 \geq 1$. The current size of $P_{i,j}$'s hand is denoted by $c_{i,j}$ for each pair of $i$ and $j$ ($1 \leq i \leq 2$, $1 \leq j \leq k_i$), and the current size of Eve's hand is denoted by $e$. At each stage of this protocol only a suitable player in $G_1$ can propose a key set of two cards. We define feasible players only in $G_1$. A player $P_{1,j}$ is said to be *feasible* if (1) $c_{1,j} > 1$, or (2) $c_{1,j} = 1$, $e = 0$, for every other player $P_{1,t}$ $(j \neq t)$ in $G_1$, $c_{1,t} \neq 1$, and all players in $G_2$ have already dropped out of the protocol. We use the lexicographical order of the indices of the players. That is, $(i, j) < (i', j')$ if and only if $i < i'$, or $i = i'$ and $j < j'$. The signature of the deal to the players in the hierarchical groups and Eve is denoted by $\xi = (c_{1,1}, \cdots, c_{1,k_1}; c_{2,1}, \cdots, c_{2,k_2}; e)$. Initially every node (player) in $G_1 \cup G_2$ is not connected with any other node (player).

**2-Level Protocol**:

(1) If there is no player with a non-empty hand in $G_1$ and if a spanning tree of the players in $G_1 \cup G_2$ has not been completed, then the protocol stops and fails. If a spanning tree of the players in $G_1 \cup G_2$ has been completed, then the protocol stops successfully. Let $P_{1,j}$ be the *feasible* player holding the smallest hand in $G_1$. (Ties are broken in favor of the lower-ordered player.) If no player in $G_1$ is *feasible*, then the lowest-ordered player holding a non-empty hand, say $P_{1,j}$, is chosen.

(2) For $P_{1,j}$ chosen in (1), $P_{1,j}$ chooses a random card $x$ in her hand and a random card $y$ not in her hand, and proposes $K = \{x, y\}$ as a key set by asking, "Does any player hold a card in $K$ ?" If no player other than $P_{1,j}$ has a non-empty hand, then $P_{1,j}$ discards her hand and all the remaining players go back to step (1).

(3) If another player in $G_1$, say $P_{1,s}$, holds $y$, then $P_{1,s}$ accepts $K$ by announcing that she holds a card in $K$. Then the cards, $x$ and $y$, are discarded, and nodes $P_{1,j}$ and $P_{1,s}$ are connected by an edge. Whichever players $P_{1,j}$ and $P_{1,s}$ holds fewer cards exposes the remaining cards in her hand, which are discarded, and drops out of the protocol. (Ties are broken in favor of the lower-ordered player who remains in the protocol.) Then all the remaining players go back to step (1). If a player in $G_2$, say $P_{2,s}$, holds $y$, then $P_{2,s}$ accepts $K$ by announcing that she holds a card in $K$, the cards $x$ and $y$ are discarded, nodes $P_{1,j}$ and $P_{2,s}$ are connected by an edge, and then $P_{2,s}$ exposes the remaining cards in her hand, which are discarded, and drops out of the protocol. Then all the remaining players go back to step (1).

(4) If none of the players holds $y$ (i.e., Eve holds $y$), then $x$ and $y$ are discarded and all the remaining players go back to step (1).

Note that *2-level protocol* never constructs a spanning tree with an edge directly connecting two nodes in $G_2$, although such a spanning tree may satisfy the conditions listed in Section 1. By modifying *2-level protocol* we can obtain a protocol that constructs spanning trees of the players in $G_1 \cup G_2$ possibly containing such edges.

The next theorem (Theorem 2) is weaker than Theorem 3.

**Theorem 2.** *Let* $\xi = (c_{1,1}, \cdots, c_{1,k_1}; c_{2,1}, \cdots, c_{2,k_2}; e)$ *be the signature of a deal on hierarchical groups, $G_1$ and $G_2$, where $k_1 \geq 1$ and $k_2 \geq 1$. If the following two inequalities hold, then 2-level protocol performs successfully to construct a secret key exchange spanning tree satisfying the conditions listed in Section 1.*

(1) $max\{c_{1,j}|1 \leq j \leq k_1\} \geq k_1 + k_2 + e - 1$
(2) $min\{c_{i,j}|1 \leq i \leq 2, 1 \leq j \leq k_i\} \geq 1$

*Proof.* In any connected component constructed by *2-level protocol* at any stage, there is exactly one player in the connected component who has not yet dropped out of the protocol. Hence, there is no chance of making a cycle in the construction. Since no player in $G_2$ can be connected with any other player in $G_2$ by *2-level protocol*, there is no chance of constructing a spanning tree that does not satisfy the conditions listed in Section 1.

Suppose that conditions (1) and (2) in the theorem are satisfied for signature $\xi$. Let $G_1 = \{P_{1,1}, \cdots, P_{1,k_1}\}$ and $G_2 = \{P_{2,1}, \cdots, P_{2,k_2}\}$. The proof is an induction on $k_1 + k_2 + e$.

**Basis**: Suppose that $k_1 = k_2 = 1$ and $e = 0$. In this case $P_{1,1}$ proposes $K = \{x, y\}$ in step (1), $P_{2,1}$ accepts $K$ in step 3, and then nodes $P_{1,1}$ and $P_{2,1}$ are connected by an edge. Hence, the assertion of the theorem holds in this case.

**Induction Step**: Suppose that for the case where $2 \leq k_1 + k_2 + e \leq r$, the assertion of the theorem holds. Let $k_1 + k_2 + e = r + 1$. Since condition (2) in the theorem is satisfied, a player in $G_1$, say $P_{1,j}$, initially proposes $K = \{x, y\}$, where $x$ is in $P_{1,j}$'s hand and $y$ is not in $P_{1,j}$'s hand. It is sufficient to consider the following three cases.

**Case 1**: A player in $G_1$, say $P_{1,s}$ accepts $K = \{x, y\}$ in step (3).

The cards $x$ and $y$ are discarded, and nodes $P_{1,j}$ and $P_{1,s}$ are connected by an edge. Then exactly one of $P_{1,j}$ and $P_{1,s}$ is dropped out of the protocol. The value $max\{c_{1,j}|1 \leq j \leq k_1\}$ just after the step (3) is equal to or less than the corresponding value just before the step (3) by at most 1. The construction of a spanning tree from the stage just after the step (3) is equivalent to the construction of a spanning tree in the case where the number of players in $G_1$ is $k_1 - 1$, the maximum hand size of the players in $G_1$ is equal to or less than the initial maximum hand size by at most 1, and the other conditions are the same as the corresponding ones at the initial stage of execution. Hence, the conditions in the theorem are also satisfied just after the step (3) if we ignore the player who dropped out of the protocol. Therefore, from the induction hypothesis we can successfully construct a secret key exchange spanning tree satisfying the conditions listed in Section 1.

**Case 2**: A player in $G_2$ accepts $K = \{x, y\}$ in step (3).

The proof is almost the same as the proof in Case 1 above.

**Case 3**: No player accepts $K = \{x, y\}$ (i.e., Eve holds $y$) in step (3):

Since cards $x$ and $y$ are discarded, Eve's hand is reduced by 1 and the maximum hand size of the players in $G_1$ is reduced by at most 1. Thus, for the updated hands the conditions in the theorem are also satisfied just after the step (3). Hence, from the induction hypothesis we can successfully construct a secret key exchange spanning tree satisfying the conditions listed in Section 1.

□

The conditions (1) and (2) in Theorem 2 are sufficient but not necessary conditions. For example, a signature $\xi = (3, 3, 3, 3, 3, 3; 1; 0)$ has $max\{c_{1,i}|1 \leq$

$i \leq k_1\} = 3 < k_1 + k_2 + e - 1 = 6 + 1 + 0 - 1 = 6$, but *2-level protocol* always succeeds on the signature. It does not seem to be easy to give an elegant necessary and sufficient condition on signatures to successfully construct a secret key exchange spanning tree satisfying the conditions listed in Section 1. We will give sufficient conditions in Theorem 3 which are stronger than the conditions in Theorem 2. For the proof of Theorem 3 we prepare the definition of a component value and three lemmas.

For simplicity we return to the problem of constructing a spanning tree of non-hierarchical $n$ players without Eve for a while. Let $P_1, \cdots, P_n$ be $n$ players and let $c_i$ be the hand size of $P_i$ ($1 \leq i \leq n$). Consider a process of joining connected components of players by a key set protocol. We define inductively the component value $comp(C)$ of each connected component $C$. Initially, each player is a connected component consisting of herself. The component value of a set consisting of a single player is 0. Suppose that two connected components $C_1$ and $C_2$ are combined by connecting a node in $C_1$ and a node in $C_2$ by an edge at a stage of the execution of a key set protocol. Let $C$ be the combined component (i.e., $C = C_1 \cup C_2$). Then $comp(C)$ is defined to be $min\{comp(C_1), comp(C_2)\}+1$.

**Lemma 1.** *Let $C$ be a connected component at a stage of execution by a FP key set protocol. If $comp(C) = k$ then $|C| \geq 2^k$.*

*Proof.* From the definition of a component value, $|C| = 1$ if and only if $comp(C) = 0$. Assume that for $comp(C) \leq k$, $|C| \geq 2^k$. Let $comp(C_1) = k_1 \leq k$ and $comp(C_2) = k_2 \leq k$. Suppose that two connected components $C_1$ and $C_2$ are combined at a stage of the execution by a FP key set protocol. From the induction hypothesis $|C_1 \cup C_2| \geq 2^{k_1} + 2^{k_2} \geq 2^{min\{k_1,k_2\}+1} = 2^{comp(C)}$. □

**Lemma 2.** *For any connected component $C$ at a stage of execution by a FP key set protocol on $n$ players, $comp(C) \leq \lfloor \log n \rfloor$.*

*Proof.* From Lemma 1, $n \geq |C| \geq 2^{comp(C)}$. Since $comp(C)$ is an integer, $comp(C) \leq \lfloor \log n \rfloor$. □

**Lemma 3.** *Let $\xi = (c_1, \cdots, c_n; 0)$ be the initial signature of $n$ players $P_1, \cdots, P_n$. Let $C$ be a connected component at a stage of execution by a FP key set protocol, and let $c_m = min\{c_i | P_i \in C\}$. Let $P$ be the only player in $C$ who has not yet dropped out so far. Then $P$ holds at least $c_m - comp(C)$ cards in her hand at that stage.*

*Proof.* The proof is an induction on the number of steps in the execution by a FP key set protocol. Since $comp(P_i) = 0$ for each $1 \leq i \leq n$, the assertion of the lemma initially holds. Suppose that the assertion of the lemma holds until a stage of the execution. Let a pair of connected components $C_1$ and $C_2$ be combined immediately after the stage, and let $C = C_1 \cup C_2$. Let $P_a$ in $C_1$ and $P_b$ in $C_2$ be the players who remain so far in the protocol. From the induction hypothesis, $P_a$ holds at least $c_{m_1} - comp(C_1)$ cards and $P_b$ holds at least $c_{m_2} - comp(C_2)$ cards, where $c_{m_1} = min\{c_i | P_i \in C_1\}$ and $c_{m_2} = min\{c_i | P_i \in C_2\}$. Then $P$ holds at least $max\{c_{m_1} - comp(C_1), c_{m_2} - comp(C_2)\} - 1$ cards just after combining $C_1$ and $C_2$. Without loss of generality we may assume that $comp(C_1) \leq comp(C_2)$. Then $comp(C) = comp(C_1) + 1$ and $max\{c_{m_1} - comp(C_1), c_{m_2} - comp(C_2)\} - 1 \geq c_{m_1} - comp(C_1) - 1 \geq c_m - comp(C)$. Thus $P$ holds at least $c_m - comp(C)$ cards just after combining $C_1$ and $C_2$.                                                    $\square$

**Theorem 3.** *Let $\xi = (c_{1,1}, \cdots, c_{1,k_1}; c_{2,1}, \cdots, c_{2,k_2}; e)$ be the signature of a deal on hierarchical groups, $G_1$ and $G_2$, where $k_1 \geq 1$ and $k_2 \geq 1$. If the following two conditions are satisfied, then 2-level protocol performs successfully to construct a secret key exchange spanning tree satisfying the conditions listed in Section 1.*

*(1) For an appropriate $k_0$, there are at least $k_1 - k_0$ players in $G_1$ such that each of them holds initially at least $\lfloor \log(k_1 - k_0) \rfloor + k_0 + k_2 + e$ cards.*

*(2) $min\{c_{i,j} | 1 \leq i \leq 2, 1 \leq j \leq k_i\} \geq 1$.*

*Proof.* Suppose that for the signature the two conditions in the theorem are satisfied. We partition $G_1$ into two groups, $G_{1,1}$ and $G_{1,2}$, where $G_{1,1}$ consists of the players in $G_1$ who hold initially at least $\lfloor \log(k_1 - k_0) \rfloor + k_0 + k_2 + e$ cards and $G_{1,2}$ consists of other players in $G_1$.

We imagine that each player in $G_{1,1}$ holds two sets of cards, one set with at least $\lfloor \log(k_1 - k_0) \rfloor$ cards and the other set with $k_0 + k_2 + e$ cards. This partition is just imaginary. This imaginary partition of the cards is used to clearly describe the proof. In fact we cannot specify in advance which cards are in the first set or in the second set for each player in $G_{1,1}$. When a player $P$ in $G_{1,1}$ proposes a key set $K = \{x, y\}$, if another player in $G_{1,1}$ holds $y$ then we imagine that $x$ belongs to the first set of $P$'s hand, and otherwise (i.e., a player in $G_{1,2} \cup G_2$ or Eve holds $y$) we imagine that $x$ belongs to the second set of $P$'s hand. For each player in $G_{1,1}$ the number of cards in the first set of the player is enough to combine all players in $G_{1,1}$, since from Lemma 2 and Lemma 3 any player in $G_{1,1}$ who remains in the execution of the protocol holds a non-empty hand at any stage before the completion of the construction of a spanning tree. The number of cards in the second set of each player in $G_{1,1}$ is also enough to combine all players in $G_{1,2} \cup G_2$ and to discard Eve'cards. There may exist a case where a player in $G_{1,2}$ proposes a key set $K = \{x, y\}$. In this case, if a player in $G_{1,1}$ holds $y$ then we imagine that $y$ belongs to the second set of the player in $G_{1,1}$, and the situation is the same as the case where a player in $G_{1,1}$ proposes the key set. If a player in $G_{1,2}$ proposes a key set $K = \{x, y\}$ and a player in $G_{1,2} \cup G_2$ or Eve holds $y$, the situation becomes even easier, since the number of players in $G_{1,2} \cup G_2$ who remain, or the size of Eve's hand is reduced by one. Hence, the conditions (1) and (2) in the theorem are sufficient for the protocol to construct a secret key exchange spanning tree satisfying the conditions listed in Section 1.                                                    $\square$

Note that if $k_2 = 0$ (i.e, the problem on non-hierarchical structures), then conditions (1) and (2) in Theorem 3 are not sufficient conditions to construct a secret key exchange spanning tree. For example, for $\xi = (2, 2, 2, 2, 2, 2; 0; 0)$

*2-level protocol* does not succeed on constructing a spanning tree. For this example, the signature of their hands may proceed in the order of (2,2,2,2,2,2;0;0), (1,0,2,2,2,2;0;0), (1,0,1,0,2,2;0;0), (1,0,1,0,1;0;0), (0,0,0,0,1;0;0). Then the protocol stops unsuccessfully since there are no cards left in the hands of the first player who still remains, and the first four players and the last two players cannot be connected. For $k_2 = 0$, if we replace $\lfloor \log(k_1 - k_0) \rfloor + k_0 + e$ by $\lceil \log(k_1 - k_0) \rceil + k_0 + e$ in condition (1) of Theorem 3, then the two conditions are sufficient conditions to construct a secret key exchange spanning tree. If we choose $k_0 = k_1 - 1$ then the two conditions in Theorem 3 are the same as the two conditions in Theorem 2. Hence, the conditions in Theorem 3 are stronger than the conditions in Theorem 2. However, the conditions in Theorem 3 are still not necessary conditions. For example, $\xi = (3, 3, 3, 2, 2; 1; 0)$ does not satisfy condition (1) in Theorem 3, but *2-level protocol* always performs successfully on the signature. Note that the choice of the smallest feasible player in step (1) of *2-level protocol* does not have an effect on the proof of Theorem 3. That is, the conditions in Theorem 3 are still sufficient conditions to construct a secret key exchange spanning tree even if we choose an arbitrary feasible player in $G_1$ in step (1) of *2-level protocol* instead of choosing the feasible player with the smallest hand.

## 4    Hierarchical Groups with Three Levels

We first show that any single deal does not guarantee the construction of a legitimate spanning tree by any FP key set protocol on hierarchical groups with three levels. Let $G_1 = \{P_{1,1}, \cdots, P_{1,k_1}\}$, $G_2 = \{P_{2,1}, \cdots, P_{2,k_2}\}$ and $G_3 = \{P_{3,1}, \cdots, P_{3,k_3}\}$ be the groups of players at level 1, level 2 and level 3, respectively, where $k_1 \geq 1$, $k_2 \geq 1$ and $k_3 \geq 1$.

**Theorem 4.** *Let $\xi = (c_{1,1}, \cdots, c_{1,k_1}; c_{2,1}, \cdots, c_{2,k_2}; c_{3,1}, \cdots, c_{3,k_3}; e)$ be the signature of a deal, where $k_1 \geq 1$, $k_2 \geq 1$ and $k_3 \geq 1$. Any FP key set protocol does not guarantee the construction of a secret key exchange spanning tree satisfying the conditions listed in Section 1.*

*Proof.* Let us consider the case where we are allowed to use only a single deal. If a player in $G_1$ proposes a key set $K = \{x, y\}$ and there exists at least one player with a non-empty hand in $G_3$, then the probability that a player in $G_3$ holds $y$ is not zero. Similarly, if a player in $G_3$ proposes a key set $K = \{x, y\}$ and there exists at least one player with a non-empty hand in $G_1$, then the probability that a player in $G_1$ holds $y$ is not zero. In any of these two cases, the players discards the cards $x$ and $y$. Since a direct connection between a player in $G_1$ is not allowed with a a player in $G_3$, these operations do not make any contribution to connect players by edges. Hence, players in $G_2$ must be employed to directly connect players if there are any players with non-empty hands who still remain in $G_1$ and in $G_3$.

When a player in $G_2$ proposes a key set $K = \{x, y\}$, the probability that a player in $G_1$ holds $y$ is not zero if there exists at least one player with a non-empty hand in $G_1$. Hence, there is a possible case where no pairs of players in

$G_2$ and players in $G_3$ are directly connected to each other before the hands of all players in $G_1$ become empty. Suppose that we have such a case. If the hands of all players in $G_2$ become empty before the hands of all players in $G_1$ become empty, then any player in $G_3$ cannot be connected with a player in $G_2$. If the hands of all players in $G_1$ become empty before the hands of all players in $G_2$ become empty then the players in $G_1$ cannot be connected to each other. Therefore, the probability that any FP key set protocol fails to construct a secret key exchange spanning tree satisfying the conditions listed in Section 1 is not zero.     □

As shown in Theorem 4, we need at least two deals to complete the construction of a secret key exchange spanning tree satisfying the conditions listed in Section 1. We give a protocol using two deals. We first construct a spanning tree of the players in $G_1 \cup G_2$ using a single deal, and then use a new deal to extend the spanning tree of the players in $G_1 \cup G_2$ to a complete spanning tree of the players in $G_1 \cup G_2 \cup G_3$. Using the second deal, players of $G_3$ propose key sets to connect a player of $G_3$ with a player of $G_2$ and to connect players in $G_3$ with each other.

A feasible player in $G_3$ in *3-level protocol* can be defined similarly to a feasible player in *2-level protocol*. That is, a player in $G_3$ is said to be feasible if (1) she holds at least two cards in her hand, or (2) she holds just one card in her hand, the number of cards in the hand of any other player in $G_3$ is not one, all players in $G_2$ have already dropped out of the protocol, and Eve holds no card.

**3-Level Protocol:**

(1) For the first deal to the players in $G_1 \cup G_2$ and Eve, apply *2-level protocol*. If the execution by *2-level protocol* is successful, then go to step (2) with a new deal distributed to the players in $G_2 \cup G_3$ and Eve, otherwise the execution of the protocol stops and fails.

(2) If there is no player with a non-empty hand in $G_3$, and if a spanning tree of the players in $G_1 \cup G_2 \cup G_3$ has not been completed, then the protocol stops and fails. If a spanning tree of the players in $G_1 \cup G_2 \cup G_3$ has been completed, then the protocol stops successfully. Let $P$ be the feasible player in $G_3$ holding the smallest hand. (Ties are broken in favor of the lower-ordered player.) If no player is feasible, then $P$ is the lowest-ordered player in $G_3$ holding a non-empty hand.

(3) For $P$ chosen in step (2), $P$ chooses a random card $x$ in her hand and a random card $y$ not in her hand, and proposes $K = \{x, y\}$ as a key set by asking, "Does any player hold a card in $K$ ?" If there are no cards not in the hand of $P$, then we use a dummy card $y$.

(4) If another player $Q$ in $G_3$ holds $y$, then she accepts $K$ by announcing that she holds a card in $K$, otherwise go to step (5). The cards $x$ and $y$ are discarded, and $P$ and $Q$ are connected by an edge. Whichever player of $P$ and $Q$ holds fewer cards exposes the remaining cards in her hand, which are discarded, and drops out of the protocol. All the remaining players go back to step (2).

(5) If a player $Q$ in $G_2$ holds $y$, then she accepts $K$ by announcing that she holds a card in $K$, otherwise go to step (6). The cards $x$ and $y$ are discarded, $P$ and $Q$ are connected by an edge, and all players in $G_2$ expose all cards in their hands, which are discarded. All players in $G_2$ drop out of the protocol, and all the remaining players go back to step (2).

(6) If none of the players holds $y$ (i.e., Eve holds $y$ or $y$ is a dummy card), then $K$ is rejected, the cards $x$ and $y$ are discarded, and go back to step (2).

**Theorem 5.** *Suppose that a spanning tree of the players in $G_1 \cup G_2$ has been constructed by 2-level protocol in step (1) of 3-level protocol. Let the signature of a new deal to the players in $G_2 \cup G_3$ and Eve be $\xi = (c_{2,1}, \cdots, c_{2,k_2}; c_{3,1}, \cdots, c_{3,k_3}; e)$. Then 3-level protocol completes the construction of a secret key exchange spanning tree satisfying the conditions listed in Section 1 if the following three conditions are satisfied.*

*(1) For an appropriate $k_0$, there are at least $k_3 - k_0$ players in $G_3$, each of them holding initially at least $\lfloor \log(k_3 - k_0) \rfloor + k_0 + 1 + e$ cards.*

*(2) $max\{c_{2,j} | 1 \le j \le k_2\} \ge 1$.*

*(3) $min\{c_{3,j} | 1 \le j \le k_3\} \ge 1$.*

*Proof.* Suppose that a spanning tree of the players in $G_1 \cup G_2$ has been constructed by *2-level protocol* in step (1) of *3-level protocol*. Suppose that the signature of a new deal to the players in $G_2 \cup G_3$ and Eve satisfies the three conditions in the theorem. Since only players in $G_3$ propose key sets and just one player in $G_2$ might be directly connected with a player in $G_3$, for $G_2$ a single card in any of the hands of the players in $G_2$ is sufficient. Other cards in the hands of the players in $G_2$ are redundant. Hence, concerning the hands of the players in $G_2$, the second condition in the theorem is sufficient. The execution of completing the construction of a spanning tree from step (2) of *3-level protocol* is analogous to the execution of constructing a spanning tree on signature $\xi' = (c_{3,1}, \cdots, c_{3,k_3}; 1; e)$ by *2-level protocol*. Hence, from Theorem 3 the conditions in the theorem are sufficient to complete a secret key exchange spanning tree of the players satisfying the conditions listed in Section 1.    □

As in Theorem 3, the conditions in Theorem 5 are still sufficient to construct a secret key exchange spanning tree even if we choose an arbitrary feasible player in $G_3$ in step (2) of *3-level protocol* instead of choosing the feasible player with the smallest hand.

## 5    Hierarchical Groups with More Than Three Levels

In this section, we suggest a protocol, called *4-level protocol*, on hierarchical groups with 4 levels. We can then generalize the protocol for hierarchical groups with any number of levels. A player in $G_3$ in *4-level protocol* is said to be feasible if (1) she holds at least two cards in her hand, or (2) she holds just one card in her hand, the number of cards in the hand of any other player in $G_3$ is not one, all players in $G_2$ and $G_4$ have already dropped out of the protocol, and Eve holds no cards.

**4-Level Protocol:**

(1) For the first deal to the players in $G_1 \cup G_2$ and Eve, apply *2-level protocol*. If the execution by *2-level protocol* is successful, then go to step (2) with a new deal distributed to the players in $G_2 \cup G_3 \cup G_4$ and Eve, and otherwise the execution of the protocol stops and fails.

(2) If there is no player with a non-empty hand in $G_3$, and if a spanning tree of the whole players has not been completed, then the protocol stops and fails. If a spanning tree of the whole players has been completed, then the protocol stops successfully. Let $P$ be the feasible player in $G_3$ holding the smallest hand. (Ties are broken in favor of the lower-ordered player.) If no player is feasible, then $P$ is the lowest-ordered player in $G_3$ holding a non-empty hand.

(3) For $P$ chosen in step (2), $P$ chooses a random card $x$ in her hand and a random card $y$ not in her hand, proposes $K = \{x, y\}$ as a key set by asking, "Does any player hold a card in $K$ ?" If there are no cards not in the hand of $P$, then we use a dummy card, $y$.

(4) If another player $Q$ in $G_3$ holds $y$, then she accepts $K$ by announcing that she holds a card in $K$, otherwise go to step (5). The cards $x$ and $y$ are discarded, and $P$ and $Q$ are connected by an edge. Whichever player of $P$ and $Q$ holds fewer cards exposes the remaining cards in her hand, which are discarded, and drops out of the protocol. All the remaining players go back to step (2).

(5) If a player $Q$ in $G_2$ holds $y$, then she accepts $K$ by announcing that she holds a card in $K$, otherwise go to step (6). The cards $x$ and $y$ are discarded, $P$ and $Q$ are connected by an edge, and all players in $G_2$ expose all cards in their hands, which are discarded. All players in $G_2$ drop out of the protocol, and all the remaining players go back to step (2).

(6) If a player $Q$ in $G_4$ holds $y$, then she accepts $K$ by announcing that she holds a card in $K$, otherwise go to step (7). The cards $x$ and $y$ are discarded, and $P$ and $Q$ are connected by an edge. $Q$ exposes the remaining cards in her hand, which are discarded, and drops out of the protocol. All the remaining players go back to step (2).

(7) If none of the players holds $y$ (i.e., Eve holds $y$ or $y$ is a dummy card), then $K$ is rejected, the cards $x$ and $y$ are discarded, and go back to step (2).

The next theorem can be proved similarly to Theorem 5.

**Theorem 6.** *Suppose that a spanning tree of the players in $G_1 \cup G_2$ has been constructed by 2-level protocol in step (1) of 4-level protocol. Let*
$\xi = (c_{2,1}, \cdots, c_{2,k_2}; c_{3,1}, \cdots, c_{3,k_3}; c_{4,1}, \cdots, c_{4,k_4}; e)$ *be the signature of a new deal to the players in $G_2 \cup G_3 \cup G_4$ and Eve. Then 4-level protocol completes the construction of a secret key exchange spanning tree satisfying the conditions listed in Section 1 if the following three conditions are satisfied.*

(1) *For an appropriate $k_0$, there are at least $k_3 - k_0$ players in $G_3$, each of them holding initially at least $\lfloor \log(k_3 - k_0) \rfloor + k_0 + k_4 + e + 1$ cards.*

(2) $max\{c_{2,j} | 1 \le j \le k_2\} \ge 1$.

(3) $min\{c_{i,j} | 3 \le i \le 4, 1 \le j \le k_i\} \ge 1$.

The conditions in Theorem 6 are still sufficient conditions to construct a secret key exchange spanning tree even if we choose an arbitrary feasible player in $G_3$ in step (2) of *4-level protocol* instead of choosing the SFP.

By applying repeatedly the techniques used in *4-level protocol* (or *3-level protocol*) we can design a protocol to construct a secret key exchange spanning tree of the players in hierarchical groups, $\bigcup_{i=1}^{h} G_i$, for any $h$ greater than 4. The protocol needs $\lceil h/2 \rceil$ deals, the first deal to $G_1 \cup G_2$, the second deal to $G_2 \cup G_3 \cup G_4$, the third deal to $G_4 \cup G_5 \cup G_6$, and so on. There are a number of variations of the protocols given in this paper, but we omit them here.

# 6    Concluding Remarks

For any of *2-level protocol*, *3-level protocol* and *4-level protocol*, the conditions given in this paper are not necessary conditions. We are interested in giving elegant, necessary and sufficient conditions for each of these protocols to construct a secret key exchange spanning tree. We are also interested in designing an efficient protocol to construct a well shaped spanning tree satisfying the conditions listed in Section 1. If we want to send an information-theoretically secure $k$-bits message in a similar way, we should prepare $k$ secret key exchange spanning trees. In this paper we have only considered a linearly ordered hierarchy of groups. The problem of secret bit transmission on different types of hierarchical structures would be also interesting.

# References

1. M.J.Fischer, M.S.Paterson and C.Rackoff, "Secret bit transmission using a random deal of cards", *DIMACS Series in Discrete Mathematics and Theoretical Computer Science*, AMS, vol.2, pp.173–181, 1991.
2. M.J.Fischer and R.N.Wright, "Multiparty secret key exchange using a random deal of cards", *Advances in Cryptology–CRYPTO'91*, Lecture Notes in Computer Science, Springer, vol.576, pp.141–155, 1992.
3. M.J.Fischer and R.N.Wright, "An application of game-theoretic techniques to cryptography", *DIMACS Series in Discrete Mathematics and Theoretical Computer Science*, AMS, vol.13, pp.99–118, 1993.
4. M.J.Fischer and R.N.Wright, "An efficient protocol for unconditional secure secret key exchange", *Proc. 4th Annual Symposium on Discrete Algorithms*, pp.475–483, 1993.
5. M.J.Fischer and R.N.Wright, "Bounds on secret key exchange using random deal of cards", *J. Cryptology*, vol.9, pp.71–99, 1996.
6. T.Mizuki, H.Shizuya, and T.Nishizeki, "Dealing necessary and sufficient numbers of cards for sharing a one-bit secret key", *Advances in Cryptology–EUROCRYPT'99*, Lecture Notes in Computer Science, Springer, vol.1592, pp.389–401, 1999.

# Derandomizing Arthur-Merlin Games under Uniform Assumptions

Chi-Jen Lu

Institute of Information Science
Academia Sinica
Taipei, Taiwan, R.O.C.
cjlu@iis.sinica.edu.tw

**Abstract.** We study how the nondeterminism versus determinism problem and the time versus space problem are related to the problem of derandomization. In particular, we show two ways of derandomizing the complexity class **AM** under uniform assumptions, which was only known previously under non-uniform assumptions [13,14]. First, we prove that either **AM** = **NP** or it appears to any nondeterministic polynomial time adversary that **NP** is contained in deterministic subexponential time infinitely often. This implies that to any nondeterministic polynomial time adversary, the graph non-isomorphism problem appears to have subexponential-size proofs infinitely often, the first nontrivial derandomization of this problem without any assumption. Next, we show that either all **BPP** = **P**, **AM** = **NP**, and **PH** ⊆ ⊕**P** hold, or for any $t(n) = 2^{\Omega(n)}$, **DTIME**$(t(n))$ ⊆ **DSPACE**$(t^\epsilon(n))$ infinitely often for any constant $\epsilon > 0$. Similar tradeoffs also hold for a whole range of parameters. This improves previous results [17,5] and seems to be the first example of an interesting condition that implies three derandomiztion results at once.

## 1 Introduction

During the last two decades, people have started to realize the power of randomness as a computational resource. There are several important problems for which randomized algorithms are much simpler or much more efficient than the currently known deterministic ones. However, from a complexity theoretical point of view, whether or not randomness can be completely removed remains unknown. An important open problem in complexity theory is the **P** versus **BPP** problem, asking whether or not any language with a randomized polynomial time algorithm can be decided in deterministic polynomial time.

A general framework of derandomizing **BPP** was initiated by Blum and Micali [4] and Yao [21], who introduced the concept of trading hardness for randomness. The idea is that if we have some hard-to-compute functions, then we can use them to construct pseudo-random generators suitable for derandomization purposes. Nisan and Wigderson [5] weakened the hardness assumption and derived a whole range of tradeoffs between hardness and randomness, and

D.T. Lee and S.-H. Teng (Eds.): ISAAC 2000, LNCS 1969, pp. 302–312, 2000.

their methodology formed the basis of a series of later work [3,9,10,18,13,14,7,8, 11]. Since then, the assumption for derandomizing **BPP** has been relaxed from average case hardness to worst case hardness, culminating in the result of Impagliazzo and Wigderson [9], stating that **P** = **BPP** if **E** requires exponential-size circuits. Sudan, Trevisan, and Vadhan [18] are able to achieve optimal conversion from average case hardness to worst case hardness for a whole range of parameters.

The derandomization of other randomized complexity classes, most noticeably the class **AM**, has just started to receive attention [13,14]. **AM** can be seen as a randomized version of **NP**. There are problems not known to be in **NP** which can be easily shown to be in **AM**. The most interesting one is the graph non-isomorphism problem, denoted as GNISO, that determines whether or not two given graphs are non-isomorphic. GNISO is in **coNP**, as for any two isomorphic graphs, there is a short proof certifying that: the isomorphism between the two graphs. On the other hand, it is not known whether or not GNISO in **NP**. That is, given any two non-isomorphic graphs, is there always a short proof certifying that?

Klivans and van Melkebeek [13] observed that the argument of Nisan and Wigderson [5] relativizes, and showed that **AM** = **NP** if **NE** ∩ **coNE** requires exponential-size circuits with SAT-oracle gates. Miltersen and Vinodchandran [14], improving on [13], showed that **AM** = **NP** if **NE** ∩ **coNE** requires exponential size SV-nondeterministic circuits[1]. Note that the assumptions are in non-uniform settings: lower bounds of uniform classes in non-uniform models. This gives connection between the problem of derandomizing **AM** and the problem of uniformity versus non-uniformity. In this paper, we will show how to derandomize **AM** under assumptions in uniform settings, and how the problem of derandomization is related to other interesting complexity problems.

First, we study how the problem of derandomizing **AM** is related to the problem of nondeterminism versus determinism. Just as previous derandomization results in the uniform settings [10,11], we need to deal with the notion of simulations that may not be correct but appear correct to computationally bounded adversaries. To formalize this idea, Kabanets [11] introduced the notion of *refuters*. A refuter is a Turing machine $R$ with $R(1^n) \in \{0,1\}^n$ which tries to generate a hard instance for every input length. We say that a problem appears to some refuters to have some simulation if for any such refuter $R$, the simulation on the input $R(1^n)$ is correct for almost every $n$. We will consider nondeterministic ones called **FNP** refuters, which run in nondeterministic polynomial times with each nondeterministic branch either producing a string or being marked with *reject*.

Our first result is inspired by that of Kabanets [11] on derandomizing **RP** under some uniform assumption. We show that **AM** = **NP** unless it appears to **FNP** refuters that **NP** is contained in deterministic sub-exponential time

---

[1] Please refer to [14] for the definition of SV-nondeterministic circuits. We just note that SV-nondeterministic circuits of size $2^{O(1)}$ correspond to the non-uniform version of **NE** ∩ **coNE**.

infinitely often. From this we show that it appears to **FNP** refuters that the class **coNP∩AM** is contained in nondeterministic subexponential time infinitely often. As the graph non-isomorphism problem is in **coNP ∩ AM**, we have the first nontrivial simulation of this problem in nondeterministic subexponential time without using any unproven assumption. A more careful analysis gives a more efficient simulation.

Next, we study how the problem of time versus space is related to the derandomization of three complexity classes **BPP**, **AM**, and **PH** [2]. Hopcroft, Paul, and Valiant [6] showed the first nontrivial simulation of deterministic time by deterministic space: **DTIME**$(t(n)) \subseteq$ **DSPACE**$(t(n)/\log t(n))$, for any $t(n)$ at least linear. Sipser [17] was the first to discover the surprising connection between the time versus space problem and derandomization. His result was based on an assumption on the existence of some explicit dispersers, which was later proved by Saks, Srinivasan, and Zhou [16]. So Sipser's result now can be stated as follows. Either for any $t(n) = n^{\Omega(1)}$ every problem in **DTIME**$(t(n))$ can be simulated in **DSPACE**$(t^\epsilon(n))$ for infinitely many inputs, for some constant $\epsilon \in (0,1)$, or **RP** = **P**. It can be shown that the statement holds for **BPP** in place of **RP**, by using optimal extractors [20] (instead of dispersers) to reduce the error probability of **BPP**, and using the idea that hitting sets suffices for derandomizing **BPP** [1,2].

Nisan and Wigderson [5] used a completely different approach to derive a comparable result to Sipser's. Their idea is that either some particular language cannot be computed by small circuits, which implies derandomization of **BPP**, or the small circuit for that language enables the simulation of deterministic time by smaller deterministic space. We can immediately improve their result just by using progress developed afterwards [9,18]. Moreover, we observe that the argument works for the setting of oracle circuits too, and we can have simultaneous derandomization of three complexity classes. We show that either for any $t(n) = 2^{\Omega(n)}$, **DTIME**$(t(n)) \subseteq$ **DSPACE**$(t^\epsilon(n))$ for infinitely many $n$, for any constant $\epsilon > 0$, or all **BPP** = **P**, **AM** = **NP**, and **PH** $\subseteq \oplus$**P** hold[3]. That is, either we have a much better simulation of time by space than that of [6], or we have complete derandomizations of three complexity classes. Either way we are happy. We tend to believe that **DTIME**$(t(n))$ is contained in **DSPACE**$(t^\epsilon(n))$ (for infinitely many $n$) for any constant $\epsilon > 0$, instead of seeing this as an evidence for all three complete derandomizations. Similar tradeoffs can be derived towards the other end of the spectrum (time could be simulated more efficiently by space, or less efficient derandomization could be achieved), which may have more meaning on derandomization.

---

[2] The class **PH** is related to derandomization by Toda's result [19] that **PH** $\subseteq$ **BP** · $\oplus$**P**.

[3] The statement still holds if the phrase "for infinitely many $n$" is switched from the first part to the second part of the statement. That is, either **DTIME**$(t(n)) \subseteq$ **DSPACE**$(t^\epsilon(n))$ or the three derandomization hold for infinitely many $n$. Similar switchings can be done for results proved throughout the paper.

Notice several differences between our result and Sipser's. Our result is only weaker in the aspect that the function $t(n)$ needs to be at least exponential, instead of at least polynomial. Our result is stronger in the following aspects. First, Sipser's simulation of time by space only works for infinitely many inputs, while our simulation works for all inputs of length $n$ for infinitely many $n$. Secondly, Sipser could simulate $\mathbf{DTIME}(t(n))$ by $\mathbf{DSPACE}(t^\epsilon(n))$ for some constant $\epsilon \in (0,1)$, while we can do it for any constant $\epsilon > 0$. Thirdly, if the simulation of time by space would fail, we could have derandomizations for three classes, instead of just one. Finally, Sipser only got the tradeoff at one point of the spectrum and his method does not appear to work for other settings, while we can derive a whole spectrum of tradeoffs.

Our two results are based on the methods of [11] and [5] respectively. The performance bottleneck of each method invloves a procedure of enumerating and evaluating ordinary Boolean circuits of certain size. In this paper we consider oracle circuits with SAT or $\oplus$SAT gates instead, in order to derandomize the complexity classes $\mathbf{BP} \cdot \mathbf{NP}$ and $\mathbf{BP} \cdot \oplus \mathbf{P}$. Enumerating both kinds of circuits takes about the same complexity. On the other hand, evaluating an oracle circuit seems much more costly, and a brute-force way takes time exponentially or space linearly in terms of the circuit size. This is not a problem for us since after all we are going through all such circuits, and it takes that time or space anyway. So the overall time or space does not blow up, from the complexity-theoretical point of view.

We give definitions and describe previous results in Section 2. We prove in Section 3 the relation between nondeterminism versus determinism and the derandomization of $\mathbf{AM}$. In Section 4, we prove the relation between time versus space and the derandomization of $\mathbf{BPP}$, $\mathbf{AM}$, and $\mathbf{PH}$.

## 2   Preliminaries

For notational convenience, we will use $\log m$ to denote $\lceil \log_2 m \rceil$ throughout the paper. Also, let $\text{poly}(n)$ denote $n^{O(1)}$ and let $\exp(n)$ denote $2^{n^{O(1)}}$. For a function $f : \{0,1\}^* \to \{0,1\}$ and a positive integer $n$, let $f_n : \{0,1\}^n \to \{0,1\}$ denote the restriction of $f$ on inputs of length exactly $n$. Similarly, for a set $S \subseteq \{0,1\}^*$ and a positive integer $n$, let $S_n$ denote the restriction of $S$ to strings of length exactly $n$, i.e. $S_n = S \cap \{0,1\}^n$. We assume standard textbook [15] definitions of complexity classes, such as $\mathbf{P}$, $\mathbf{NP}$, $\mathbf{coNP}$, $\mathbf{BPP}$, $\mathbf{PH}$, $\mathbf{E}$, and $\mathbf{coNE}$. We give the definition of $\mathbf{AM}$, which basically says that $\mathbf{AM} = \mathbf{BP} \cdot \mathbf{NP}$.

**Definition 1.** *A language $L$ is in $\mathbf{AM}$ if there exist a relation $M \in \mathbf{NP}$ and a polynomial $m = \text{poly}(n)$, such that for any $x \in \{0,1\}^n$,*

$$x \in L \quad \Rightarrow P_{y \in \{0,1\}^m}[M(x,y) = 1] \geq \tfrac{3}{4}, \text{ and}$$
$$x \notin L \quad \Rightarrow P_{y \in \{0,1\}^m}[M(x,y) = 1] < \tfrac{1}{4}.$$

We will also deal with complexity classes related to so-called parity time.

**Definition 2.** *Let* $\oplus\mathbf{TIME}(t(n))$ *denote the class of Boolean functions* $L$ *with a nondeterministic Turing machine running in time* $t(n)$, *such that* $x \in L$ *if and only if* $M$ *on input* $x$ *has an odd number of accepting paths.* $\oplus\mathbf{P}$ *is the class* $\oplus\mathbf{TIME}(\mathrm{poly}(n))$.

We need the following complexity classes corresponding to quasi-polynomial time and sub-exponential time.

**Definition 3.** *Let* $\mathbf{QP}$ *denote the complexity class* $\mathbf{DTIME}(2^{\mathrm{poly}(\log n)})$ *and let* $\mathbf{SUBEXP}$ *denote* $\cap_{\epsilon>0}\mathbf{DTIME}(2^{n^{\epsilon}})$. *Let* $\mathbf{NQP} = \mathbf{NTIME}(2^{\mathrm{poly}(\log n)})$ *and* $\mathbf{NSUBEXP} = \cap_{\epsilon>0}\mathbf{NTIME}(2^{n^{\epsilon}})$. *Let* $\oplus\mathbf{QP} = \oplus\mathbf{TIME}(2^{\mathrm{poly}(\log n)})$ *and* $\oplus\mathbf{SUBEXP} = \cap_{\epsilon>0}\oplus\mathbf{TIME}(2^{n^{\epsilon}})$.

We also need non-uniform complexity classes defined by circuits with oracle gates.

**Definition 4.** *For a language* $A$, *let* $\mathbf{SIZE}^A(s(n))$ *denote the class of Boolean functions computable by circuits of size* $s(n)$ *with* AND/OR/NOT *gates together with oracle gates to* $A$. *For a Boolean function* $f_n$, *we abuse the notation to let* $\mathbf{SIZE}^A(f_n)$ *denote the size of the smallest such circuits computing* $f_n$. *If no oracle gate is allowed, we write* $\mathbf{SIZE}(s(n))$ *and* $\mathbf{SIZE}(f_n)$ *respectively.*

We need the notion of simulations that only succeed infinitely often.

**Definition 5.** *For a complexity class* $\mathcal{C}$, *let* io-$\mathcal{C}$ *denote the class of Boolean functions* $f$ *for which there is a Boolean function* $f' \in \mathcal{C}$ *such that* $f_n = f'_n$ *for infinitely many* $n$.

A nondeterministic procedure is said to produce some desired objects if each nondeterministic branch of the procedure either produces a desired object or is marked with *reject*. The concept of refuters was introduced by Kabanets [11], and we consider a slight generalization to nondeterministic ones. A nondeterministic refuter is a nondeterministic Turing machine such that on input $1^n$, each nondeterministic branch either produces a string in $\{0,1\}^n$ or is marked with *reject*. We say that two functions $f_n$ and $f'_n$ are *distinguishable* by a nondeterministic refuter $R$ if every string $y$ produced by $R(1^n)$ in a branch witnesses $f_n(y) \neq f'_n(y)$. We will consider **FNP** refuters, refuters running in nondeterministic polynomial time.

**Definition 6.** *Let* $\mathcal{C}$ *be a complexity class. Let* $[\mathrm{pseudo_{FNP}}]$-$\mathcal{C}$ *denote the class of Boolean functions* $f$ *for which there is a Boolean function* $f' \in \mathcal{C}$ *such that any* **FNP** *refuter must fail to distinguish* $f_n$ *and* $f'_n$ *for all but finitely many* $n$. *Let* $[\mathrm{io\text{-}pseudo_{FNP}}]$-$\mathcal{C}$ *denote the class of Boolean functions* $f$ *for which there is a Boolean function* $f' \in \mathcal{C}$ *such that any* **FNP** *refuter must fail to distinguish* $f_n$ *and* $f'_n$ *for infinitely many* $n$.

An important primitive for derandomization is the explicit construction of so-called pseudo-random sets (or pseudo-random generators). A pseudo-random set is a small sample space that looks random to some class of computationally-bounded statistical tests.

**Definition 7.** *We say that a set $G \subseteq \{0,1\}^*$ is a pseudo-random set that fools a complexity class $\mathcal{C}$ if for any $C \in \mathcal{C}$ and for every $m$,*

$$|P_{x \in \{0,1\}^m}[C_m(x) = 1] - P_{y \in G_m}[C_m(y) = 1]| \leq \frac{1}{m}.$$

Klivans and Melkebeek [13] oberved that previous constructions of pseudo-random set ([5,3,9]) relativize, so the following two theorems easily follow.

**Theorem 1.** *[13] Let $A$ be any language and suppose $f$ is a Boolean function with $\mathbf{SIZE}^A(f_\ell) = 2^{\Omega(\ell)}$. There is a procedure running in deterministic time $2^{O(\ell)}$ that transforms the truth table of $f_\ell$ into a pseudo-random set that fools $\mathbf{SIZE}^A(2^{\Omega(\ell)})$.*

**Theorem 2.** *[13] Let $A$ be any language and suppose $f$ is a Boolean function with $\mathbf{SIZE}^A(f_\ell) \geq m(\ell)$. There is a procedure running in deterministic time $2^{O(\ell)}$ that transforms the truth table of $f_\ell$ into a pseudo-random set that fools $\mathbf{SIZE}^A((m(\ell^\epsilon))^\epsilon)$ for some positive constant $\epsilon < 1$.*

To derandomize various randomized complexity classes, we need various pseudo-random sets that fool classes of circuits with corresponding oracle gates. The following is a well known fact.

**Lemma 1.** *If a pseudo-random set that fools $\mathbf{SIZE}(n)$ can be produced in deterministic time $t(n)$, then $\mathbf{BPP} \subseteq \mathbf{DTIME}(\mathrm{poly}(t(\mathrm{poly}(n))))$.*

It is also known that we can derandomize the class $\mathbf{BP} \cdot \oplus\mathbf{P}$ with a pseudo-random set that fools $\mathbf{SIZE}^{\oplus\mathrm{SAT}}(n)$. Since Toda's theorem [19] says that $\mathbf{PH} \subseteq \mathbf{BP} \cdot \oplus\mathbf{P}$, we have the following.

**Lemma 2.** *If a pseudo-random set that fools $\mathbf{SIZE}^{\oplus\mathrm{SAT}}(n)$ can be produced in deterministic time $t(n)$, then $\mathbf{PH} \subseteq \oplus\mathbf{TIME}(\mathrm{poly}(t(\mathrm{poly}(n))))$.*

A similar statement holds for $\mathbf{AM} = \mathbf{BP} \cdot \mathbf{NP}$. In fact, a slightly weaker condition suffices for derandomizing $\mathbf{AM}$: we only need to produce a pseudo-random set nondeterministically. The following seems to be a known fact, but we show the proof for completeness.

**Lemma 3.** *If a pseudo-random set that fools $\mathbf{SIZE}^{\mathrm{SAT}}(n)$ can be produced in nondeterministic time $t(n)$, then $\mathbf{AM} \subseteq \mathbf{NTIME}(\mathrm{poly}(t(\mathrm{poly}(n))))$.*

**Proof:** Let $L$ be a language in $\mathbf{AM}$. Then there exists a relation $M$ in $\mathbf{P}$ and a polynomial $m = \mathrm{poly}(n)$ such that for any $x \in \{0,1\}^n$,

$$x \in L \quad \Rightarrow P_{y \in \{0,1\}^m}[\exists z \in \{0,1\}^m \ M(x,y,z) = 1] \geq \tfrac{3}{4}, \text{ and}$$
$$x \notin L \quad \Rightarrow P_{y \in \{0,1\}^m}[\exists z \in \{0,1\}^m \ M(x,y,z) = 1] < \tfrac{1}{4}.$$

For any fixed $x$, the predicate

$$\exists z \in \{0,1\}^m M(x,y,z) = 1$$

on $y$ is in $\mathbf{SIZE}^{\mathrm{SAT}}(m^c)$ for some constant $c$. We use the nondeterministic procedure, running in time $t(m^c) = t(\mathrm{poly}(n))$, to produce a pseudo-random set $G = \{g_1, g_2, \ldots, g_{|G|}\}$ that fools $\mathbf{SIZE}^{\mathrm{SAT}}(m^c)$. Then,

$$x \in L \quad \text{iff} \quad P_{y \in G}[\exists z \in \{0,1\}^m \ M(x,y,z) = 1] \geq \frac{1}{2}.$$

So to compute $L$, we guess $|G|$ strings $z_1, z_2, \ldots, z_{|G|}$ from $\{0,1\}^m$, and accept $x$ iff $M(x, g_i, z_i) = 1$ for most $i$. As $|G| \leq t(\mathrm{poly}(n))$, this procedure runs in nondeterministic time $\mathrm{poly}(t(\mathrm{poly}(n)))$. $\qquad\square$

Note that For $t(n) = \mathrm{poly}(n)$ the lemma says that if a pseudo-random set that fools $\mathbf{SIZE}^{\mathrm{SAT}}(n)$ can be produced in nondeterministic polynomial time, then $\mathbf{AM} = \mathbf{NP}$.

## 3   Nondeterminism vs. Determinism

**Theorem 3.** *Either* $\mathbf{NP} \subseteq \bigcap_{\epsilon > 0} [\text{io-pseudo}_{\mathbf{FNP}}]\text{-}\mathbf{DTIME}(2^{n^\epsilon})$ *or* $\mathbf{AM} = \mathbf{NP}$.

**Proof:** The idea of the proof is the following. We attempt to simulate $\mathbf{NP}$ by using easy functions as potential witnesses. If this would succeed, we could have an efficient deterministic simulation of $\mathbf{NP}$. Otherwise we would have a way to find hard functions for constructing pseudo-random sets.

Suppose $A$ is a language in $\mathbf{NP}$ but not in $[\text{io-pseudo}_{\mathbf{FNP}}]\text{-}\mathbf{DTIME}(2^{n^\epsilon})$ for some constant $\epsilon \in (0,1)$. As $A \in \mathbf{NP}$, there exists a relation $M \in \mathbf{P}$ and a polynomial $m = \mathrm{poly}(n)$, such that for any $x \in \{0,1\}^n$,

$$x \in A \quad \text{iff} \quad \exists y \in \{0,1\}^m \ \text{s.t.} \ M(x,y) = 1.$$

Let $S_m^\delta$ denote the set of truth tables of all $\log m$-variable Boolean functions in $\mathbf{SIZE}^{\mathrm{SAT}}(m^\delta)$. Consider the procedure $D_M^\delta$ that for $x \in \{0,1\}^n$,

$$\text{accepts } x \quad \text{iff} \quad \exists y \in S_m^\delta \ \text{s.t.} \ M(x,y) = 1.$$

$S_m^\delta$ contains at most $2^{m^{2\delta}}$ truth tables as there are at most this number of circuits in $\mathbf{SIZE}^{\mathrm{SAT}}(m^\delta)$. As a SAT gate in a circuit of size $m^\delta$ can be evaluated in deterministic time $2^{O(m^\delta)}$, each truth table in $S_m^\delta$ can be generated in deterministic time $2^{O(m^\delta)}$. So $D_M^\delta$ is in $\mathbf{DTIME}(2^{m^{c\delta}})$, for some constant $c$, and thus in $\mathbf{DTIME}(2^{n^\epsilon})$, by choosing the constant $\delta$ so that $m^{c\delta} \leq n^\epsilon$.

From the assumption that $A \notin [\text{io-pseudo}_{\mathbf{FNP}}]\text{-}\mathbf{DTIME}(2^{n^\epsilon})$, there is a nondeterministic polynomial time refuter $R$ such that for almost every $n$, every string produced in a branch of $R(1^n)$ is misclassified by $D_M^\delta$. A string $x$ is misclassified only when $M(x,y) = 0$ for all $y \in S_m^\delta$ but $M(x,y) = 1$ for some $y \in \{0,1\}^m \setminus S_m^\delta$. Let $\ell = \log m$. This gives us a nondeterministic polynomial time procedure for producing the truth table of an $\ell$-variable Boolean function outside of $\mathbf{SIZE}^{\mathrm{SAT}}(2^{\delta\ell})$, for almost every $\ell$:

– Use $R$ to nondeterministically produce a misclassified input $x$.

– Guess $y$ of length $2^\ell$ and produce it if $M(x,y) = 1$, for a misclassified $x$.

Having obtained a hard function, Theorem 1 gives us a way to produce in time $2^{O(\ell)}$ a pseudo-random set that fools $\mathbf{SIZE}^{\mathrm{SAT}}(2^{\Omega(\ell)})$.

As the desired pseudo-random set can be produced in nondeterministic polynomial time, from Lemma 3 we have $\mathbf{AM} = \mathbf{NP}$. □

**Theorem 4.** $\mathbf{coNP} \cap \mathbf{AM} \subseteq \bigcap_{\epsilon>0} [\text{io-pseudo}_{\mathbf{FNP}}]\text{-}\mathbf{NTIME}(2^{n^\epsilon})$.

**Proof:** Note that $\bigcap_{\epsilon>0} [\text{io-pseudo}'_{\mathbf{FNP}}]\text{-}\mathbf{DTIME}(2^{n^\epsilon})$ is closed under complementation. Then Theorem 3 implies that

$$\text{either } \mathbf{coNP} \subseteq \bigcap_{\epsilon>0} [\text{io-pseudo}_{\mathbf{FNP}}]\text{-}\mathbf{DTIME}(2^{n^\epsilon})$$
$$\text{or } \quad \mathbf{AM} = \mathbf{NP} \subseteq \bigcap_{\epsilon>0} [\text{io-pseudo}_{\mathbf{FNP}}]\text{-}\mathbf{NTIME}(2^{n^\epsilon}).$$

So $\mathbf{coNP} \cap \mathbf{AM} \subseteq \bigcap_{\epsilon>0} [\text{io-pseudo}_{\mathbf{FNP}}]\text{-}\mathbf{NTIME}(2^{n^\epsilon})$. □

As the graph non-isomorphism problem is in $\mathbf{coNP} \cap \mathbf{AM}$, we have the following immediately.

**Corollary 1.** $\mathrm{GNISO} \in \bigcap_{\epsilon>0} [\text{io-pseudo}_{\mathbf{FNP}}]\text{-}\mathbf{NTIME}(2^{n^\epsilon})$.

Next we show a more general tradeoff. For a function $t(n)$, let $\hat{t}(n)$ denote its inverse function (i.e. $t(\hat{t}(n)) = n$).

**Theorem 5.** For any $t(n) = \Omega(n)$, either $\mathbf{NP} \subseteq [\text{io-pseudo}_{\mathbf{FNP}}]\text{-}\mathbf{DTIME}(t(n))$ or $\mathbf{AM} \subseteq \mathbf{NTIME}(\exp(\log \hat{t}(\exp(n))))$.

**Proof:** The proof is very similar to that for Theorem 3, but we use Theorem 2 instead of Theorem 1. Suppose $A$ is a language in $\mathbf{NP}$ but not in $[\text{io-pseudo}_{\mathbf{FNP}}]\text{-}\mathbf{DTIME}(t(n))$. As $A \in \mathbf{NP}$, there exists a relation $M \in \mathbf{P}$ and a polynomial $m = \mathrm{poly}(n)$, such that for any $x \in \{0,1\}^n$,

$$x \in A \quad \text{iff} \quad \exists y \in \{0,1\}^m \text{ s.t. } M(x,y) = 1.$$

Let $T_m$ denote the set of truth tables of all $\log m$-variable Boolean functions in $\mathbf{SIZE}^{\mathrm{SAT}}(\log^{2/3} t(n))$. Consider the procedure $D_M$ that

$$\text{accepts } x \in \{0,1\}^n \quad \text{iff} \quad \exists y \in T_m \text{ s.t. } M(x,y) = 1.$$

Clearly $D_M$ is in $\mathbf{DTIME}(t(n))$.

From the assumption that $A \notin [\text{io-pseudo}_{\mathbf{FNP}}]\text{-}\mathbf{DTIME}(t(n))$, there is a nondeterministic $\mathrm{poly}(n)$ time refuter $R$ such that for almost every $n$, every string produced in a branch of $R(1^n)$ is misclassified by $D_M$. A string $x$ is misclassified only when $M(x,y) = 0$ for all $y \in T_m$ but $M(x,y) = 1$ for some $y \in \{0,1\}^m \setminus T_m$. We then have a nondeterministic $\mathrm{poly}(n)$ time procedure for producing the truth table of a $\log m$-variable Boolean function outside of $\mathbf{SIZE}^{\mathrm{SAT}}(\log^{2/3} t(n))$ for almost every $m$: guess $y \in \{0,1\}^m$ and verify whether or not $M(x,y) = 1$ for a misclassified $x$. From Theorem 2, we can produce in time $\mathrm{poly}(n)$ a pseudo-random set that fools $\mathbf{SIZE}^{\mathrm{SAT}}(\log^\epsilon t(2^{\log^\epsilon n}))$, for some constant $\epsilon$. Then from Lemma 3, we have $\mathbf{AM} = \mathbf{NTIME}(\exp(\log \hat{t}(\exp(n))))$. □

By choosing $t(n) = 2^{2^{\log^{o(1)} n}}$ in the above theorem, we have the following better simulation of GNISO.

**Corollary 2.** $\mathrm{GNISO} \in [\text{io-pseudo}_{\mathbf{FNP}}]\text{-}\mathbf{NTIME}(2^{2^{\log^{o(1)} n}})$.

## 4    Time vs. Space

**Theorem 6.** *Either* $\mathbf{DTIME}(t(n)) \subseteq \bigcap_{\epsilon>0}$ io-$\mathbf{DSPACE}(t^\epsilon(n))$ *for any function* $t(n) = 2^{\Omega(n)}$, *or all* $\mathbf{BPP} = \mathbf{P}$, $\mathbf{AM} = \mathbf{NP}$, *and* $\mathbf{PH} \subseteq \oplus\mathbf{P}$ *hold.*

**Proof:** The proof follows closely that of Nisan and Wigderson [5]. Let $L$ denote the language containing exactly those quadruple $\langle M, x, t, d \rangle$ such that $M$'s action on input $x$ at time $t$ is $d$, where $d$ encodes information such as the state, the location of heads, *etc.* Clearly $L \in \mathbf{DTIME}(2^{O(n)})$. Suppose both $\mathbf{SIZE}^{\mathrm{SAT}}(L)$ and $\mathbf{SIZE}^{\oplus\mathrm{SAT}}(L)$ are $2^{\Omega(n)}$. Then from Theorem 1, Lemma 1, Lemma 3, and Lemma 2, we have $\mathbf{BPP} = \mathbf{P}$, $\mathbf{AM} = \mathbf{NP}$, and $\mathbf{PH} \subseteq \oplus\mathbf{P}$.

Otherwise, $L \in$ io-$\mathbf{SIZE}^A(2^{\epsilon n})$ for any arbitrary constant $\epsilon > 0$, for some language $A \in \{\mathrm{SAT}, \oplus\mathrm{SAT}\}$. From this we will show that $\mathbf{DTIME}(t(n)) \subseteq \bigcap_{\epsilon>0}$ io-$\mathbf{DSPACE}(t^\epsilon(n))$. This is similar to results of Karp and Lipton [12] that translate non-uniform upper bounds to uniform ones.

Fix any function $t(n) = 2^{\Omega(n)}$ and any Turing machine $M$ which runs in deterministic time $t(n)$. To determine whether $M$ accepts input $x$ of length $n$, we check whether $\langle M, x, t(n), d_0 \rangle$ is in $L$ for some accepting action $d_0$. Let $m$ denote the length of $\langle M, x, t(n), d_0 \rangle$. Then $m = O(1) + n + \log t(n) + O(1) \leq c \log t(n)$ for some constant $c$. Fix an arbitrary constant $\epsilon > 0$. Consider the following procedure attempting to determine whether $M$ accepts $x$:

- Enumerate all circuits in $\mathbf{SIZE}^A(2^{\epsilon m})$, trying to find one that is correct for $L_m$.
- Output yes iff a correct circuit is found and it accepts $\langle M, x, t(n), d_0 \rangle$ for some accepting action $d_0$.

As observed by [5], checking whether a circuit is a correct one is easy, since it only needs to be consistent between consecutive accesses to the same cell, for every input. The description of a circuit needs only $O(2^{\epsilon m})$ space to record, so does the evaluation of a circuit on an input, and the checking of a circuit being a correct one. As the space can be reused when we check the next circuit, the total amount of space needed is just $O(2^{\epsilon m}) = O(t^{\epsilon c}(n))$. Whenever $L_m$ is computable by a circuit in $\mathbf{SIZE}^A(2^{\epsilon m})$, the above procedure correctly decides all inputs $x$ of length $n$.

As the argument above holds for any constant $\epsilon > 0$, the language accepted by $M$ is in $\bigcap_{\epsilon>0}$ io-$\mathbf{DSPACE}(t^{c\epsilon}(n)) = \bigcap_{\epsilon>0}$ io-$\mathbf{DSPACE}(t^\epsilon(n))$.    □

By using Theorem 2 in place of Theorem 1, we can derive similar tradeoffs for a whole range of parameters. For example, we have the following two theorems.

**Theorem 7.** *Either* $\mathbf{DTIME}(t(n)) \subseteq \bigcap_{\epsilon>0}$ io-$\mathbf{DSPACE}(2^{\log^\epsilon t(n)})$ *for any function* $t(n) = 2^{\Omega(n)}$, *or all* $\mathbf{BPP} \subseteq \mathbf{QP}$, $\mathbf{AM} \subseteq \mathbf{NQP}$, *and* $\mathbf{PH} \subseteq \oplus\mathbf{QP}$ *hold.*

**Theorem 8.** *Either* $\mathbf{DTIME}(t(n)) \subseteq$ io-$\mathbf{DSPACE}(\mathrm{poly}(\log t(n)))$ *for any function* $t(n) = 2^{\Omega(n)}$, *or all* $\mathbf{BPP} \subseteq \mathbf{SUBEXP}$, $\mathbf{AM} \subseteq \mathbf{NSUBEXP}$, *and* $\mathbf{PH} \subseteq \oplus\mathbf{SUBEXP}$ *hold.*

# References

1. A.E. Andreev, A.E.F. Clement, and J.D.P. Rolim, Hitting sets derandomize BPP, *Proceedings of the 23rd International Colloquium on Automata, Languages, and Programming*, pages 357–368, 1996.
2. H. Buhrman, L. Fortnow, One-sided versus two-sided randomness, *Proceedings of the 16th Symposium on Theoretical Aspects of Computer Science*, pages 100–109, 1999.
3. L. Babai, L. Fortnow, N. Nisan, and A. Wigderson, BPP has subexponential time simulations unless EXPTIME has publishable proofs, *Computational Complexity*, 3(4), pp 307–318, 1993.
4. M. Blum and S. Micali, How to generate cryptographically strong sequences of pseudo-rnadom bits, *SIAM Journal on Computing*, 13, pages 850–864, 1984.
5. N. Nisan and A. Wigderson, Hardness vs. randomness, *Journal of Computer and System Sciences*, 49, pages 149–167, 1994.
6. J. Hopcroft, W. Paul, and L. Valiant, On time versus space, *Journal of ACM*, 24, pages 332–337, 1977.
7. R. Impagliazzo, R. Shaltiel, and A. Wigderson, Near optimal conversion of hardness into pseudo-randomness, *Proceedings of the 40th Annual IEEE Symposium on the Foundations of Computer Science*, pages 181–190, 1999.
8. R. Impagliazzo, R. Shaltiel, and A. Wigderson, Extractors and pseudo-random generators with optimal seed length, *Proceedings of the 32th Annual ACM Symposium on Theory of Computing*, pages 1–10, 2000.
9. R. Impagliazzo and A. Wigderson, P=BPP if E requires exponential circuits: derandomizing the XOR lemma, *Proceedings of the 29th Annual ACM Symposium on Theory of Computing*, pages 220–229, 1997.
10. R. Impagliazzo and A. Wigderson, Randomness vs. time: de-randomization under a uniform assumption, *Proceedings of the 39th Annual IEEE Symposium on the Foundations of Computer Science*, pages 734–743, 1998.
11. V. Kabanets, Easiness assumptions and hardness tests: trading time for zero error, In *Proceedings of the 15th Annual IEEE Conference on Computational Complexity*, 2000.
12. R.M. Karp and R. Lipton, Turing machines that take advices, *L'Ensignment Mathematique*, 28, pages 191–209, 1982.
13. A. Klivans and D. van Melkebeek, Graph nonisomorphism has subexponential size proofs unless the polynomial-time hierarchy collapses, *Proceedings of the 31th Annual ACM Symposium on Theory of Computing*, pages 659 667, 1999.
14. P. B. Miltersen and N.V. Vinodchandran, Derandomizing Arthur-Merlin games using hitting sets, *Proceedings of the 40th Annual IEEE Symposium on the Foundations of Computer Science*, 1999.
15. C. Papadimitriou, *Computational Complexity*, Addison-Wesley, 1994.
16. M. Saks, A. Srinivasan, and S. Zhou, Explicit OR-dispersers with polylogarithmic degree, *Journal of ACM*, 41(1), pages 123–154, 1998.
17. M. Sipser, Expanders, randomness, or time vs. space, *Journal of Computer and System Sciences*, 36, pages 379–383, 1988.
18. M. Sudan, L. Trevisan, and S. Vadhan, Pseudorandom generators without the XOR lemma, *Proceedings of the 31st Annual ACM Symposium on Theory of Computing*, pages 537–546, 1999.
19. S. Toda, PP is as hard as the polynomial-time hierarchy, *SIAM Journal on Computing*, 20(5), pages 865–877, 1991.

20. L. Trevisan, Construction of near-optimal extractors using pseudo-random generators, *Proceedings of the 31st Annual ACM Symposium on Theory of Computing*, pages 141–148, 1999.
21. A. Yao, Theory and applications of trapdoor functions, *Proceedings of the 23rd Annual IEEE Symposium on the Foundations of Computer Science*, pages 80–91, 1982.

# A Near Optimal Algorithm for Vertex Connectivity Augmentation

Bill Jackson[1*] and Tibor Jordán[2**]

[1] Department of Mathematical and Computing Sciences, Goldsmiths College,
London SE14 6NW, England.
e-mail: b.jackson@gold.ac.uk
[2] Department of Operations Research, Eötvös University, 1053 Budapest, Hungary.
e-mail: jordan@cs.elte.hu

**Abstract.** Given an undirected graph $G$ and a positive integer $k$, the $k$-vertex-connectivity augmentation problem is to find a smallest set $F$ of new edges for which $G + F$ is $k$-vertex-connected. Polynomial algorithms for this problem are known only for $k \leq 4$ and a major open question in graph connectivity is whether this problem is solvable in polynomial time in general. For arbitrary $k$, a previous result of Jordán [14] gives a polynomial algorithm which adds an augmenting set $F$ of size at most $k - 3$ more than the optimum, provided $G$ is $(k - 1)$-vertex-connected. In this paper we develop a polynomial algorithm which makes an $l$-connected graph $G$ $k$-vertex-connected by adding an augmenting set of size at most $((k - l)(k - 1) + 4)/2$ more than (a new lower bound for) the optimum. This extends the main results of [14,15]. We partly follow and generalize the approach of [14] and we adapt the splitting off method (which worked well on edge-connectivity augmentation problems) to vertex-connectivity. A key point in our proofs, which may also find applications elsewhere, is a new tripartite submodular inequality for the sizes of neighbour-sets in a graph.

## 1 Introduction

An undirected graph $G = (V, E)$ is called *k-vertex-connected* if $|V| \geq k + 1$ and the deletion of any $k - 1$ or fewer vertices leaves a connected graph. Given a graph $G = (V, E)$ and a positive integer $k$, the $k$-vertex-connectivity augmentation problem is to find a smallest set $F$ of new edges for which $G' = (V, E \cup F)$ is $k$-connected. This problem (and a number of versions with different connectivity requirements and/or edge weights) is an important and well-studied optimization problem in network design, see [8].

* This research was carried out while the first named author was visiting the Department of Operations Research, Eötvös University, Budapest, supported by an Erdős visiting professorship from the Alfréd Rényi Mathematical Institute of the Hungarian Academy of Sciences.
** Supported by the Hungarian Scientific Research Fund no. T029772, T030059 and FKFP grant no. 0607/1999.

D.T. Lee and S.-H. Teng (Eds.): ISAAC 2000, LNCS 1969, pp. 313–325, 2000.

The complexity of the vertex-connectivity augmentation problem is one of the most challenging open questions of this area. It is open even if the graph $G$ to be augmented is $(k-1)$-vertex-connected. Polynomial algorithms are known for small values of $k$. The cases $k = 2, 3, 4$ have been settled by Eswaran and Tarjan [4], Watanabe and Nakamura [20] and Hsu [10], respectively. For general $k$ – but assuming that $G$ is $(k-1)$-connected – Jordán [14] developed a polynomial algorithm which finds a feasible augmenting set but may add more edges than the optimum. There is an additive 'approximation gap', which depends only on $k$: the algorithm adds at most $k-3$ edges more than necessary. (The gap was reduced to $\lceil (k-1)/2 \rceil$ in [15].)

Our goal is to extend this result to arbitrary graphs by relaxing the $(k-1)$-connectivity hypothesis on $G$ and developing a polynomial algorithm with a similar additive 'approximation gap', depending on $k$ (and the vertex-connectivity $l$ of the input graph) only. The bound we get is at most $((k-l)(k-1)+4)/2$. When $l = k-1$ this gives a linear gap, almost matching the result of [15].

Note that the approach of increasing the connectivity one by one up to the target $k$ does not work if we want to guarantee an overall approximation gap which depends on $k$ only, even if we are allowed to add a certain number (depending on $k$) of surplus edges at every iteration. Consider the following $(k-2)$-connected graph on $3p + p(k-2) + k - 1$ vertices ($k \geq 3, p \geq 2$ is even). Take a complete graph $K_{k-1+p(k-2)}$ and let the sets $A, B$ ($|A| = k-1, |B| = p(k-2)$) bipartition its vertices. Then add a set $X$ of $2p$ vertices, each with neighbour set $A$, and add a set $Y$ of $p$ vertices, each with $k-2$ neighbours from $B$, such that these neighbour sets are pairwise disjoint. This graph can be made $k$-connected by adding $2p$ edges, whereas making this graph $k$-connected in two steps will lead to $O(p)$ surplus edges.

We follow some of the ideas of the approach of [14], which used, among others, the splitting off method. We further develop this method for $k$-vertex-connectivity. We also need a new fact about local separators and their meshing properties. This new observations extends a result of Cheriyan and Thurimella [3]. Our proofs also use a new tripartite submodular inequality for the sizes of the neighbour-sets in a graph. This may have applications in other vertex-connectivity problems.

We remark that the other three basic augmentation problems (where one wants to make $G$ $k$-edge-connected or wants to make a digraph $k$-edge- or $k$-vertex-connected) have been shown to be polynomially solvable. These results are due to Watanabe and Nakamura [19], Frank [5], and Frank and Jordán [7], respectively. Different versions of the $k$-vertex-connectivity augmentation problem have also been investigated. To mention some results, Ishii et al. [12] augmented vertex- and edge-connectivities simultaneously, while Hsu and Kao [11] increased the connectivity maintaining bipartiteness. For more results on connectivity augmentation see the survey by Frank [6] and Nagamochi [18]. In the rest of the introduction we introduce some definitions and our new lower bounds for the size of an augmenting set which makes $G$ $k$-vertex-connected. We also state our main results.

In what follows we deal with undirected graphs and $k$-connected refers to $k$-vertex-connected. Let $G = (V, E)$ be a graph with $|V| \geq k + 1$. For $X \subseteq V$ let $N(X)$ denote the set of *neighbours* of $X$, that is, $N(X) = \{v \in V - X : uv \in E$ for some $u \in X\}$. Let $n(X)$ denote $|N(X)|$. We use $X^*$ to denote $V - X - N(X)$. We call $X$ a *fragment* if $X, X^* \neq \emptyset$. Let $a_k(G)$ denote the size of a smallest augmenting set of $G$ with respect to $k$. It is easy to see that every set of new edges $F$ which makes $G$ $k$-connected must contain at least $k - n(X)$ edges from $X$ to $X^*$ for every fragment $X$. A family $\{X_1, ..., X_p\}$ of fragments is called *half-disjoint* if every (new) edge connects $X_i$ to $X_i^*$ for at most two members of the family. Let $t'(G) = \max\{\sum_{i=1}^{p} k - n(X_i) : X_1, ..., X_p$ is a half-disjoint family of fragments in $V\}$. We also introduce $t(G) = \max\{\sum_{i=1}^{r} k - n(X_i) : X_1, ..., X_r$ are pairwise disjoint fragments$\}$. Clearly, pairwise disjoint fragments form a half-disjoint family. Thus $t'(G) \geq t(G)$. By summing up these 'deficiencies' over the members of a half-disjoint family we obtain a useful lower bound. (In the corresponding edge-connectivity augmentation problem a similar lower bound, based on families of pairwise disjoint 'deficient sets', was sufficient to characterize the optimum value.)

$$a_k(G) \geq \lceil t'(G)/2 \rceil. \tag{1}$$

Another lower bound for $a_k(G)$ comes from 'shredders'. For $K \subset V$ let $b(K, G)$ denote the number of components in $G - K$. Let $b(G) = \max\{b(K, G) : K \subset V, |K| = k - 1\}$. Sometimes we call a set $K \subset V$ with $|K| = k - 1$ and $b(K, G) = q$ a *q-shredder*. Since $G - K$ has to be connected in the augmented graph, we have the following lower bound.

$$a_k(G) \geq b(G) - 1. \tag{2}$$

These lower bounds extend the two natural lower bounds used e.g. in [4,9, 14]. Although these bounds suffice to characterize $a_k(G)$ for $k \leq 3$, there are examples showing that $a_k(G)$ can be strictly larger than the maximum of these lower bounds, consider for example the complete bipartite graph $K_{3,3}$ with target $k = 4$. On the other hand our main result shows that these bounds get very close to the optimum in question. Let

$$f(k, l) = \frac{(k - l)(k - 1) + 4}{2}.$$

**Theorem 1.** *If $G$ is $l$-connected then $a_k(G) \leq \max\{b(G) - 1, \lceil t'(G)/2 \rceil + f(k, l)\}$.*

The proof of this theorem, given in the subsequent sections, easily leads to a polynomial algorithm which finds an augmenting set of size at most $f(k, l)$ more than the optimum.

**Theorem 2.** *There is a polynomial algorithm which finds an augmenting set for an $l$-connected graph $G$ of size at most $a_k(G) + f(k, l)$.*

The proof techniques given in this paper for general $l$, yield a gap of $k-1$ for the special case when $l = k-1$. Since this is weaker than the results obtained in [14,15], we shall concentrate on obtaining bounds for the case when $l \leq k-2$. Some of the proofs will be omitted from this extended abstract.

## 2   Preliminaries

In this section first we introduce new notation and then present some preliminary results. The tripartite submodular inequality in Proposition 2 and the results about local separators below are new and will play an important role in our proofs.

For two disjoint sets of vertices $X, Y$ in a graph $H = (V, E)$ we denote the number of edges from $X$ to $Y$ by $d_H(X, Y)$ (or simply $d(X, Y)$). If we count edges from $X$ to $Y$ taken from a subset $A \subseteq E$ then we write $d_A(X, Y)$. We use $d(X) = d(X, V - X)$ to denote the *degree* of $X$. For a single vertex $v$ we write $d(v)$. Let $X, Y \subseteq V$ be given. We call $X$ and $Y$ *independent* if $X \subseteq N(Y)$ or $Y^* \subseteq N(X)$ or $X^* \subseteq N(Y)$ or $Y \subseteq N(X)$ holds. Notice that, if $X$ and $Y$ are independent fragments, then no edge can connect both $X$ to $X^*$ and $Y$ to $Y^*$.

### 2.1   Submodular Inequalities

Each of the following three inequalitites can be verified easily by counting the contribution of every vertex to the two sides. Inequality (3) is well-known and appears e.g. in [14]. Inequality (4) is similar.

**Proposition 1.** *In a graph $H = (V, E)$ every pair $X, Y \subseteq V$ satisfies*

$$n(X) + n(Y) \geq n(X \cap Y) + n(X \cup Y) + |(N(X) \cap N(Y)) - N(X \cap Y)|$$
$$+ |(N(X) \cap Y)) - N(X \cap Y)| + |(N(Y) \cap X)) - N(X \cap Y)| (3)$$

$$n(X) + n(Y) \geq n(X \cap Y^*) + n(Y \cap X^*). \tag{4}$$

The following new inequality is crucial in the proof of one of our main lemmas. It may be applicable in other vertex-connectivity problems as well.

**Proposition 2.** *In a graph $H = (V, E)$ every triple $X, Y, Z \subseteq V$ satisfies*

$$n(X) + n(Y) + n(Z) \geq n(X \cap Y \cap Z) + n(X \cap Y^* \cap Z^*) + n(X^* \cap Y^* \cap Z) +$$
$$n(X^* \cap Y \cap Z^*) - |N(X) \cap N(Y) \cap N(Z)|. \tag{5}$$

The following result is an easy consequence of a theorem of Mader [16]. It was used in [14] in the special case when $G$ is $(k-1)$-connected.

**Theorem 3.** *[14][16] Let $F$ be a minimal augmenting set of $G = (V, E)$ with respect to $k$ and let $B$ be the set of those vertices of $G$ which have degree at least $k+1$ in $G + F$. Then $F$ induces a forest on $B$.*   □

## 2.2 Local Separators

For two vertices $u, v \in V$ a $uv$-cut is a set $K \subseteq V - \{u, v\}$ for which there is no $uv$-path in $G - K$. A set $S \subset V$ is a *local separator* if there exist $u, v \in V - S$ such that $S$ is an inclusionwise minimal $uv$-cut. We also say $S$ is a *local uv-separator* and we call the components of $G - S$ containing $u$ and $v$ *essential components* of $S$ (with respect to the pair $u, v$). Note that $S$ may be a local separator with respect to several pairs of vertices and hence it may have more than two essential components. Clearly, $N(C) = S$ for every essential component $C$ of $S$. If $S$ is a local $uv$-separator and $T$ is a local $xy$-separator then we say $T$ *meshes* $S$ if $T$ intersects the two essential components of $S$ containing $u$ and $v$, respectively. The following lemma extends [3, Lemma 4.3(1)].

**Lemma 1.** *If $T$ meshes $S$ then $S$ intersects every essential component of $T$ (and hence $S$ meshes $T$).*  □

## 3 Properties of Extensions of $G$

In the so-called 'splitting off method' one extends the input graph $G$ by a new vertex $s$ and a set of appropriately chosen edges incident to $s$ and then obtains an optimal augmenting set by splitting off pairs of edges incident to $s$. This approach was initiated by Cai and Sun [1] for the $k$-edge-connectivity augmentation problem and further developed and generalized by Frank [5], see also [18] for more efficient algorithms. In this section we adapt this method to vertex-connectivity and prove several basic properties of the extended graph as well as the splittable pairs.

Given the input graph $G = (V, E)$, an *extension* $G + s = (V + s, E + F)$ of $G$ is obtained by adding a new vertex $s$ and a set $F$ of new edges from $s$ to $V$. In $G + s$ we define $\bar{d}(X) = n_G(X) + d(s, X)$ for every $X \subseteq V$. We say that $G + s$ is $(k, s)$-*connected* if

$$\bar{d}(X) \geq k \text{ for every fragment } X \subset V, \tag{6}$$

and that it is a *critical extension* (with respect to $k$) if $F$ is an inclusionwise minimal set with respect to (6). The minimality of $F$ implies that every edge $su$ in a critical extension is $(k, s)$-*critical*, that is, deleting $su$ from $G + s$ destroys (6). An edge $su$ is $(k, s)$-critical (or simply *critical*) if and only if there exists a fragment $X$ in $V$ with $u \in X$ and $\bar{d}(X) = k$. A fragment $X$ with $d(s, X) \geq 1$ and $\bar{d}(X) = k$ is called *tight*. A fragment $X$ with $d(s, X) \geq 2$ and $\bar{d}(X) \leq k + 1$ is called *dangerous*. Observe that if $G$ is $l$-connected then for every $v \in V$ we have $d(s, v) \leq k - l$ in any critical extension of $G$.

Since the function $d(s, X)$ is modular on the subsets of $V$ in $G + s$, Propositions 1 and 2 yield the following inequalities.

**Proposition 3.** *In a graph $G + s$ every pair $X, Y \subseteq V$ satisfies*

$$\bar{d}(X) + \bar{d}(Y) \geq \bar{d}(X \cap Y) + \bar{d}(X \cup Y) + |(N(X) \cap N(Y)) - N(X \cap Y)|$$
$$+ |(N(X) \cap Y) - N(X \cap Y)| + |(N(Y) \cap X) - N(X \cap Y)|, \tag{7}$$

$$\bar{d}(X) + \bar{d}(Y) \geq \bar{d}(X \cap Y^*) + \bar{d}(Y \cap X^*) + d(s, X - Y^*) + d(s, Y - X^*). \quad (8)$$

**Proposition 4.** *In a graph $G + s$ every triple $X, Y, Z \subseteq V$ satisfies*

$$\bar{d}(X) + \bar{d}(Y) + \bar{d}(Z) \geq \bar{d}(X \cap Y \cap Z) + \bar{d}(X \cap Y^* \cap Z^*) + \bar{d}(X^* \cap Y^* \cap Z) +$$
$$\bar{d}(X^* \cap Y \cap Z^*) - |N(X) \cap N(Y) \cap N(Z)| + 2d(s, X \cap Y \cap Z). \quad (9)$$

It follows from (6) that we can construct an augmenting set for $G$ by adding edges between the vertices in $N(s)$ for any critical extension $G + s$ of $G$. We can use this fact to obtain good bounds on $a_k(G)$.

**Lemma 2.** *Let $A$ be a minimal augmenting set of $G$ for which every edge in $A$ connects two vertices of $N(s)$ in $G + s$. Then $|A| \leq d(s) - 1$.*

*Proof.* Let $B = \{v \in N(s) : d_{G+A}(v) \geq k + 1\}$ and let $C = N(s) - B$. We have $d_A(x) \leq d(s, x)$ for each $x \in C$ and, by Theorem 3, $B$ induces a forest in $A$. Let $e_A(B)$ and $e_A(C)$ denote the number of those edges of $A$ which connect two vertices of $B$ and of $C$, respectively. The previous observations imply the following inequality.

$$|A| = e_A(C) + d_A(B, C) + e_A(B) \leq \sum_{x \in C} d_A(x) + |B| - 1 \leq$$
$$\leq (d(s) - |B|) + |B| - 1 = d(s) - 1.$$

This proves the lemma.    □

**Lemma 3.** $\lceil d(s)/2 \rceil \leq \lceil t'(G)/2 \rceil \leq a_k(G) \leq d(s) - 1$.

*Proof.* The last two inequalities follow immediately from (1) and Lemma 2. To verify the first inequality we proceed as follows. Let $\mathcal{X} = \{X_1, ..., X_m\}$ be a family of tight sets such that $N(s) \subseteq \cup_{i=1}^m X_i$ and such that $m$ is minimum and $\sum_{i=1}^m |X_i|$ is minimum. Such a family exists since the edges incident to $s$ in $G + s$ are critical. We claim that for every $1 \leq i < j \leq m$ either $X_i$ and $X_j$ are independent or $X_i \cap X_j = \emptyset$.

To see this, suppose that $X_i \cap X_j \neq \emptyset$. Then by the minimality of $m$ the set $X_i \cup X_j$ cannot be tight. Thus (7) implies that $X_i^* \cap X_j^* = \emptyset$. Hence either $X_i$ and $X_j$ are independent or $X_i \cap X_j^*$ and $X_j \cap X_i^*$ are both non-empty. In the former case we are done. In the latter case we apply (8) to $X_i$ and $X_j$ and conclude that $X_i \cap X_j^*$ and $X_j \cap X_i^*$ are both tight and all the edges from $s$ to $X_i \cup X_j$ enter $(X_i \cap X_j^*) \cup (X_j \cap X_i^*)$. Thus we could replace $X_i$ and $X_j$ in $\mathcal{X}$ by two strictly smaller sets $X_i \cap X_j^*$ and $X_j \cap X_i^*$, contradicting the choice of $\mathcal{X}$. This proves the claim.

To finish the proof of the lemma observe that $\sum_{i=1}^m k - n(X_i) = \sum_{i=1}^m d(s, X_i) \geq d(s)$. In other words, the sum of 'deficiencies' of $\mathcal{X}$ is at least $d(s)$. Furthermore, our claim implies that $\mathcal{X}$ is a half-disjoint family of fragments. (Otherwise we must have, without loss of generality, $X_1, X_2, X_3 \in \mathcal{X}$ such that there exists an edge $uv$ connecting $X_i$ to $X_i^*$ for $1 \leq i \leq 3$. This implies that $X_1, X_2, X_3$ are pairwise non-independent. The above claim now shows that $X_1 \cap X_2 = X_1 \cap X_3 = X_2 \cap X_3 = \emptyset$. This contradicts the choice of $uv$.) Hence $d(s) \leq t'(G)$ follows.    □

It follows from the next two lemmas that, if $d(s)$ is large enough compared to $l$ and $k$, then $d(s)$ is equal to $t(G)$.

**Lemma 4.** *Suppose $d(s) \geq 2f(k,l)$ and let $X, Y \subset V$ be intersecting sets. Then*
*(a) if $X$ and $Y$ are tight then $X \cup Y$ is tight,*
*(b) if $X$ is tight and $Y$ is dangerous then $X \cup Y$ is dangerous,*
*(c) if $X$ and $Y$ are dangerous and $d(s, X - Y) \neq 0$ then $X^* \cap Y^* \neq \emptyset$.* □

**Lemma 5.** *If $d(s) \geq 2f(k,l)$ then $d(s) = t(G)$.* □

*Splitting off* two edges $su, sv$ in $G+s$ means deleting $su, sv$ and adding a new edge $uv$. Such a split is *admissible* if the graph obtained by the splitting also satisfies (6). Notice that if $G+s$ has no edges incident to $s$ then (6) is equivalent to the $k$-connectivity of $G$. Hence it would be desirable to know, when $d(s)$ is even, that there is a sequence of admissible splittings which isolates $s$. In this case (using the fact that $d(s) \leq 2a_k(G)$ by Lemma 3), the resulting graph on $V$ would be an *optimal* augmentation of $G$ with respect to $k$. This approach works for the $k$-edge-connectivity augmentation problem [5] but does not always work in the vertex connectivity case. The reason is that such 'complete splittings' do not necessarily exist. On the other hand, we shall prove results which are 'close enough' to yield a near optimal algorithm for $k$-connectivity augmentation using the splitting off method.

Non-admissible pairs $sx, sy$ can be characterized by tight and dangerous 'certificates' as follows. The proof of the following simple lemma is omitted.

**Lemma 6.** *The pair $sx, sy$ is not admissible for splitting in $G + s$ with respect to $k$ if and only if one of the following holds:*
*(a) there exists a tight set $T$ with $x \in T$, $y \in N(T)$,*
*(b) there exists a tight set $U$ with $y \in U$, $x \in N(U)$,*
*(c) there exists a dangerous set $W$ with $x, y \in W$.* □

## 4   The Main Lemmas

In this section we prove the two main lemmas we need to settle Theorems 1 and 2. Let $G$ be an $l$-connected graph that we wish to make $k$-connected and let $G + s$ be a critical extension of $G$ with respect to $k$.

**Lemma 7.** *Suppose $d(s) \geq 2f(k,l)$. If there is no admissible split at $s$ then either $d(s) = b(G)$, or $l = k - 1$ and $|V(G)| \leq 2k - 2$.*

*Proof.* If $\ell = k - 1$ then the lemma follows from [15, Theorem 1.3b]. Henceforth we will assume that $l \leq k - 2$.

Let $X_0$ be a maximal tight set in $G + s$ chosen such that $d(s, X_0)$ is as large as possible. Choose a family of maximal tight sets $\mathcal{T} = \{X_1, ..., X_m\}$ such that $X_i \cap N(X_0) \neq \emptyset$, $1 \leq i \leq m$, and such that $(\cup_{i=1}^{m} X_i) \cap N(s)$ is as large as possible and $m$ is as small as possible. Note that $X_i \cap X_j = \emptyset$ for $0 \leq i < j \leq m$ by Lemma 4(a). Thus we have $d(s, \cup_{i=0}^m X_i) = d(s, X_0) + d(s, \cup_{i=1}^m X_i)$.

Since each $X_i \in \mathcal{T}$ contains a neighbour of $X_0$ and $X_0$ is tight, we have $m \leq n(X_0) = k - d(s, X_0)$. Since each $X_i \in \mathcal{T}$ is tight and $G$ is $l$-connected, we have $d(s, X_i) \leq d(s, X_0) \leq k - l$. So

$$d(s, \cup_{i=0}^m X_i) \leq d(s, X_0) + d(s, X_0)(k - d(s, X_0)) \tag{10}$$

Choose $x_0 \in N(s) \cap X_0$. Since there is no admissible split of $s x_0$, by Lemma 6 and by the choice of $\mathcal{T}$ there exists a family of maximal dangerous sets $\mathcal{W} = \{W_1, ..., W_r\}$ such that $x_0 \in W_i$ for all $1 \leq i \leq r$ and $R := N(s) - \cup_{i=0}^m X_i \subseteq \cup_{j=1}^r W_i$. Let us assume that $\mathcal{W}$ is chosen so that $r$ is as small as possible. By Lemma 4(b), $X_0 \subseteq W_i$ for all $1 \leq i \leq r$. Since $d(s, W_i - X_0) \leq k+1-l-d(s, X_0)$, we can use (10) and the fact that $d(s) \geq 2f(k, l)$ to deduce that $r \geq 2$. For $W_i, W_j \in \mathcal{W}$ we have $W_i^* \cap W_j^* \neq \emptyset$ by Lemma 4(c) and hence applying (7) we obtain

$$k + 1 + k + 1 \geq \bar{d}(W_i) + \bar{d}(W_j) \geq \bar{d}(W_i \cap W_j) + \bar{d}(W_i \cup W_j) \geq k + k + 2. \tag{11}$$

Thus $W_i \cap W_j$ is tight, since $W_i \cup W_j$ is not dangerous by the maximality of $W_i$. Hence $W_i \cap W_j \subseteq X_0$, since $x_0 \in W_i \cap W_j$. Furthermore, since we have equality in (11), we can use (7) to deduce that $W_j \cap N(W_i) \subseteq N(W_i \cap W_j)$ and $N(W_i) \cap N(W_j) \subseteq N(W_i \cap W_j)$. So $W_j \cap N(W_i) \subseteq X_0 \cup N(X_0)$ and $W_i \cap N(W_j) \subseteq X_0 \cup N(X_0)$. Hence $N(s) \cap W_i \cap N(W_j) \subseteq \cup_{i=0}^m X_i$. So by the choice of $\mathcal{W}$, $R \cap W_i \cap W_j^* \neq \emptyset$ and $R \cap W_j \cap W_i^* \neq \emptyset$ follows.

By (8) we get $2k+2 = \bar{d}(W_i) + \bar{d}(W_j) \geq \bar{d}(W_i \cap W_j^*) + \bar{d}(W_j \cap W_i^*) + 2 \geq 2k+2$, and so we have equality throughout. Thus all edges from $s$ to $W_i$, other than the single edge $s x_0$, end in $W_i \cap W_j^*$. So $R \cap W_j \cap W_i^* = (R \cap W_j) - x_0$. Since $d(s, (W_i \cup W_j) - X_0) \leq k + 2 - l - d(s, X_0)$, we can use (10) and the fact that $d(s) \geq 2f(k, l)$ to deduce that $r \geq 3$. Thus $\emptyset \neq (R \cap W_j) - x_0 \subseteq W_j \cap W_i^* \cap W_k^*$ holds for every triple. Applying (9), and using $d(s, W_i \cap W_j \cap W_h) \geq 1$, we get

$$3k + 3 \geq \bar{d}(W_i) + \bar{d}(W_j) + \bar{d}(W_h) \geq \bar{d}(W_i \cap W_j \cap W_h) + \bar{d}(W_i \cap W_j^* \cap W_h^*) +$$
$$+ \bar{d}(W_j \cap W_i^* \cap W_h^*) + \bar{d}(W_h \cap W_i^* \cap W_j^*) - |N(W_i) \cap N(W_j) \cap N(W_h)|$$
$$+ 2 \geq 4k - |N(W_i) \cap N(W_j) \cap N(W_h)| + 2 \geq 3k + 3. \tag{12}$$

For $S = N(W_i) \cap N(W_j) \cap N(W_h)$ we have $|S| = k-1$ by (12). Hence $N(W_i \cap W_j \cap W_h) = S$. Also $W_i \cap W_j^* \cap W_h^*$ is tight and $d(s, W_i \cap W_j \cap W_h) = 1$. Since $n(W_i) = k - 1$ and $W_i$ is dangerous, $d(s, W_i) = 2$ follows. Thus $d(s, W_i \cap W_j^* \cap W_h^*) = 1$ and we have $r+1$ components $X_0 = C_0, C_1, ..., C_r$ in $G - S$, where $C_i = W_i - X_0$ for $1 \leq i \leq r$.

Also, by Lemma 4(b), $X_0 \subseteq W_i$ for all $i$, so $\cap_{i=1}^r W_i = X_0$ and $d(s, X_0) = 1$. If $\{x_0\} \cup R = N(s)$ then we are done. Hence suppose $\{x_0\} \cup R \neq N(s)$. Choose $X_i \in \mathcal{T}$. Since $X_i \cap N(X_0) \neq \emptyset$, we have $X_i \cap S \neq \emptyset$. Since $X_i \cap R = \emptyset$, $N(X_i) \cap C_i \neq \emptyset$ for $0 \leq i \leq r$. Since $r = |R| \geq d(s) - d(s, \cup_{i=0}^m X_i) \geq k - 1$ by (10) and the facts that $d(s, X_0) = 1$, $l \leq k - 2$, and $d(s) \geq 2f(k, l)$, this yields $\bar{d}(X_i) \geq r + 1 + 1 \geq k + 1$. This contradicts the fact that $X_i$ is tight (using $d(s, X_i) \geq 1$). □

When $l = k - 1$, Lemma 7 implies that if $d(s) \geq 2k - 1$ and there is no admissible split then $d(s) = b(G)$. Putting $G = K_{k-1,k-1}$ we see that this bound on $d(s)$ is tight. It remains an open problem to determine the best possible bound on $d(s)$ for arbitrary $l$.

Let $K$ be a shredder of $G$. A component $C$ of $G - K$ is called a *leaf component* of $K$ (in $G + s$) if $d(s, C) = 1$ holds. Note that $d(s, C') \geq 1$ for each component $C'$ of $G - K$ by (6). If $d(s) \leq 2b(G) - 2$ then every $b(G)$-shredder $K$ has at least two leaf components, $K$ is a local separator, and every leaf component of $K$ is an essential component of $K$ in $G$. The next claim is also easy to verify by (6).

**Lemma 8.** *Let $K$ be a shredder in $G$ and let $C_1, C_2$ be leaf components of $K$ in $G + s$. Then there exist $k - 1$ vertex-disjoint paths in $G$ from every vertex of $C_1$ to every vertex of $C_2$.* ☐

**Lemma 9.** *Let $K$ be a shredder in $G$ with at least $2k - l + 1$ leaf components in $G + s$ and $Y \subseteq V$ such that $Y$ is either tight or dangerous in $G + s$. Then $Y \cap K = \emptyset$. Furthermore $d(s, K) = 0$ in $G + s$.* ☐

**Lemma 10.** *If $d(s) \leq 2b(G) - 2f(k, l)$ then $a_k(G) = b(G) - 1$.*

*Proof.* Since $2b(G) \geq d(s) + 2f(k, l) \geq b(G) + 2f(k, l)$, we have $d(s) \geq b(G) \geq 2f(k, l)$. Furthermore, every $b(G)$-shredder of $G$ has at least $2f(k, l)$ leaves.

Let us choose a $b(G)$-shredder $K$ with the maximum number $\omega$ of leaves. Suppose $d(s) = b(G)$. Then all components of $G - K$ are leaf components. Let $F$ be the edge set of a tree $T$ on the vertices of $N(s)$. We shall show that $G + F$ is $k$-connected. If not, then we can partition $V$ into three sets $\{X, Y, Z\}$ such that $|Z| = k - 1$ and no edge of $G + F$ joins $X$ to $Y$. Since each pair of vertices of $N(s)$ are joined by $k$ vertex-disjoint paths in $G + F$, $(k - 1)$ paths in $G$ by Lemma 8 and one path in $T$, either $X$ or $Y$ is disjoint from $N(s)$. Assuming $X \cap N(s) = \emptyset$, we have $\bar{d}(X) = n(X) \leq k - 1$, contradicting the fact that $G + s$ satisfies (6). Hence $G + F$ is a $k$-connected augmentation of $G$ with $b(G) - 1$ edges.

Hence we may assume that $d(s) > b(G)$. Choose a leaf component $C_u$ of $K$, where $\{u\} = N(s) \cap V(C_u)$ and a non-leaf component $C_w$ of $K$, where $w \in N(s) \cap V(C_w)$. By Lemma 4, 6 and 9 it can be shown that the pair $su, sw$ is an admissible split in $G + s$.

Splitting $su, sw$ we obtain $G' + s$ where $d_{G'+s}(s) = d_{G+s}(s) - 2$. Adding the edge $uw$ to $G$ we obtain $G'$. If $b(G') = b(G) - 1$ then, using the fact that $G' + s$ is a critical extension of $G'$, we apply induction and we are done. Hence $b(G') = b(G)$ and so $G$ has a $b(G)$-shredder $K'$ such that $u, w$ belong to the same component $C'$ of $G - K'$. (Note that $\{u, w\} \cap K' = \emptyset$ by Lemma 9.) In this case we can prove (we omit the details) that $K$ and $K'$ are meshing local separators. However, by Lemma 1 this is impossible since $K$ and $K'$ have at least $2f(k, l) \geq k$ essential components. This contradiction completes the proof of Lemma 10. ☐

# 5   The Algorithm

In this section we give an algorithmic proof of Theorem 1 when $l \leq k - 2$ which will also verify Theorem 2 in this case. (We refer the reader to [15] for the case when $l = k - 1$.) Let our $l$-connected input graph be $G = (V, E)$ and let the target connectivity value be $k \geq l + 2$. We shall construct an augmenting set $F$ which satisfies the conclusions of both Theorems 1 and 2.

First we build a critical extension $G + s$ of $G$ with respect to $k$. Then we apply the following three steps. In the first step we iteratively split off pairs of edges from $s$ in the current graph (which we will always denote by $G^* + s$). In the second or third step we terminate by adding an augmenting set.

STEP 1: While $d_{G^*+s}(s) \geq \max\{2b(G^*) - 2f(k, l), 2f(k, l) + 2\}$ holds we split off pairs $su, sv$ of edges in $G^* + s$. (Thus we delete $su, sv$ from $G^* + s$ and add the edge $uv$ to $G^*$.) Such pairs exist by Lemma 7 and the fact that the inequality $d_{G^*+s}(s) \geq b(G^*)$ must be strict in this case. Then we continue with either STEP 2 or STEP 3.

STEP 2: If $d_{G^*+s}(s) \leq 2f(k, l) + 1$ then we pick a minimal augmenting set $F''$ on $N_{G^*+s}(s)$. The output augmenting set $F$ is the union of $F''$ and the set $F'$ of edges that have been added to $G$ in previous iterations via splittings in STEP 1.

STEP 3: In the remaining case, we have $d_{G^*+s}(s) \leq 2b(G^*) - 2f(k, l) - 1$. By Lemma 10 there exists an augmenting set $F''$ of size $b(G^*) - 1$. The output augmenting set $F$ is the union of $F''$ and the set $F'$ of edges that have been added to $G$ in previous iterations via splittings in STEP 1.

To see that the size of the output is as required, suppose first that we terminate in STEP 2. If $d_{G^*+s}(s) \leq 2f(k, l) - 1$ before termination then no edges have been added via splittings in STEP 1 so $G = G^*$ and $F = F''$. By Lemmas 2 and 3 and by (1) we have $|F| \leq d(s) - 1 \leq \lceil t'(G)/2 \rceil + (2f(k, l) - 3)/2 \leq a_k(G) + (2f(k, l) - 3)/2$. Otherwise $d_{G^*+s}(s) \geq 2f(k, l)$. Then $d_{G^*+s}(s) = t(G^*)$ by Lemma 5. Also, every split edge added in STEP 1 reduced $t(G)$ by two so $t(G) - t(G^*) = 2|F'|$. Therefore, by Lemma 2,

$$|F| = |F'| + |F''| \leq (t(G) - t(G^*))/2 + (d_{G^*+s}(s) - 1) < t(G)/2 + f(k, l).$$

Hence $|F| \leq a_k(G) + f(k, l)$ by (1).

Now suppose we terminate in STEP 3. If no split edges have been added so far then $|F| = b(G) - 1 = a_k(G)$ by (2). Otherwise $d_{G^*+s}(s) \geq 2b(G^*) - 2f(k, l) - 2$. Since $2b(G^*) - 2f(k, l) - 1 \geq d_{G^*+s}(s) \geq b(G^*)$, it follows that $d_{G^*+s}(s) \geq 2f(k, l)$ and hence $d_{G^*+s}(s) = t(G^*)$ by Lemma 5. Thus $|F| = |F'| + |F''| \leq (t(G) - t(G^*))/2 + (b(G^*) - 1)$. Since $b(G^*) \leq (d_{G^*+s}(s) + f(k, l) + 2)/2$, this gives $|F| \leq t(G)/2 + f(k, l)$ and hence $|F| \leq a_k(G) + f(k, l)$ by (1).

This proves Theorem 1.

## 5.1   Running Time

In this subsection we sketch how our algorithmic proofs yield a polynomial algorithm and prove Theorem 2. Let $G = (V, E)$ and $k \geq 2$ be given. Let $n := |V|$ and $m := |E|$. Our first observation is that we can work with a sparse subgraph $G'$ of $G$ which can be found in linear time. In detail, [2] and [17] showed that $G = (V, E)$ has a spanning subgraph $G' = (V, E')$ with $|E'| \leq k(n-1)$ satisfying $\kappa_{G'}(u, v) \geq \min\{k, \kappa_G(u, v)\}$ for each pair $u, v \in V$. (Here $\kappa_H(u, v)$ denotes the maximum number of openly disjoint paths from $u$ to $v$ in graph $H$.) Such a subgraph can be found in linear time [17]. The following lemma implies that, for a set $F$ of edges, $G' + F$ is $k$-connected if and only if $G + F$ is $k$-connected. It also shows that the parameters we work with are the same in $G$ and $G'$.

**Lemma 11.** $X \subset V$ is a fragment in $G'$ with $n_{G'}(X) =: p \leq k - 1$ if and only if $X$ is a fragment in $G$ with $n_G(X) = p$. A set $S \subset V$ with $|S| = k - 1$ is a $q$-shredder in $G'$ if and only if $S$ is a $q$-shredder in $G$. Furthermore, $b(G') = b(G)$, $t(G') = t(G)$ and $t'(G') = t'(G)$.    □

In what follows we assume that we have executed this preprocessing step in linear time and hence $m = O(kn)$. Note also that $d(s) = O(kn)$ in any extension $G + s$ of $G$ we work with in the algorithm.

There are four basic operations in our algorithm: (i) determine whether an edge $su$ is critical in an extension $G + s$ of $G$, (ii) decide whether splitting off a pair $su, sv$ preserves (6) in $G + s$, (iii) determine whether an edge $uv$ is critical with respect to $k$-connectivity in a $k$-connected supergraph of $G$, (iv) decide whether $d(s) < 2b(G) - 2f(k, l)$ and if yes, find all $b(G)$-shredders.

Steps (i), (ii), (iii) can be implemented in time $O(k^2 n)$ in our sparse graph, using network flow techniques. To execute operation (iv) we can use Claim 9 to show that if $d(s) < 2b(G) - 2f(k, l)$ then every $b(G)$-shredder $K$ can be obtained as $K = N(X)$ for a maximal tight set $X$ with $d(s, X) = 1$. For a given $u \in N(s)$ a maximal tight set $X$ with $N(s) \cap X = \{u\}$ can be found by a maximum flow computation. Thus (iv) needs time $O(k^2 n^3)$.

To compute the overall time bound let us consider the three steps of our algorihtm. We start with creating a critical extension of $G$. This takes $O(k^2 n^2)$ time. In STEP 1 we first compare $d(s)$ and $b(G^*)$ and either split off an admissible pair or go to one of the terminal steps. Finding an admissible splitting takes at most $n^2$ attempts and can be done in $O(k^2 n^3)$ time. We repeat STEP 1 at most $O(kn)$ times and hence we have the bound $O(k^3 n^4)$ for this step. In STEP 2 we greedily delete edges from a $k$-connected supergraph of $G$. We have to check $O(k^4)$ edges for deletion, which gives $O(k^6 n)$ for this step. STEP 3 adds $b(G^*) - 1 = O(n)$ edges in rounds. In each round we pick a $b(G^*)$-shredder $K$ with the maximum number of leaves and then add an appropriately chosen edge to $G^*$. To find $K$ we need $O(k^2 n^3)$ time. Thus our bound for STEP 3 is $O(k^2 n^4)$. Hence the overall runnig time of our algorithm is $O(k^3 n^4)$.

## 6    Remarks

Recently T. Ishii and H. Nagamochi [13] have independently proved a slightly weaker form of Theorem 2 in which the approximation gap is larger but still of order $(k - l)k$.

## References

1. G.R. Cai and Y.G. Sun, The minimum augmentation of any graph to a k-edge-connected graph, Networks 19 (1989) 151-172.
2. J. Cheriyan, M.Y. Kao, and R. Thurimella, Scan-first search and sparse certificates: An improved parallel algorithm for $k$-vertex connectivity, SIAM J. Comput. 22 (1993), 157-174.
3. J.Cheriyan and R.Thurimella, Fast algorithms for $k$-shredders and $k$-node connectivity augmentation, Journal of Algorithms 33 (1999), 15–50.
4. K.P. Eswaran and R.E. Tarjan, Augmentation problems, SIAM J. Computing, Vol. 5, No. 4, 653-665, 1976.
5. A. Frank, Augmenting graphs to meet edge-connectivity requirements, SIAM J. Discrete Mathematics, Vol.5, No 1., 22-53, 1992.
6. A. Frank, Connectivity augmentation problems in network design, Mathematical Programming: State of the Art (J.R. Birge, K.G. Murty eds.), 34-63, 1994.
7. A. Frank and T. Jordán, Minimal edge-coverings of pairs of sets, J. Combinatorial Theory, Ser. B. 65, 73-110 (1995).
8. M. Grötschel, C.L. Monma and M. Stoer, Design of survivable networks, in: Handbook in Operations Research and Management Science Vol. 7, Network Models (M.O. Ball, T.L. Magnanti, C.L. Monma and G.L. Nemhauser, eds.) North-Holland, Amsterdam, 617-672, 1994.
9. T-S. Hsu, On four-connecting a triconnected graph, Journal of Algorithms 35, 202-234, 2000.
10. T-S. Hsu, Undirected vertex-connectivity structure and smallest four-vertex-connectivity augmentation, Algorithms and computation (Proc. 6th ISAAC '95), Springer Lecture Notes in Computer Science 1004, 274-283, 1995.
11. T-S. Hsu and M-Y. Kao, Optimal augmentation for bipartite componentwise biconnectivity in linear time, Algorithms and Computation (Proc. ISAAC '96), Springer Lecture Notes in Computer Science 1178, 213-222, 1996.
12. T. Ishii and H. Nagamochi and T. Ibaraki, Augmenting edge and vertex connectivities simultaneously, Algorithms and computation (Proc. ISAAC '97), Springer Lecture Notes in Computer Science 1350, 102-111, 1997.
13. T. Ishii and H. Nagamochi, On the minimum augmentation of an $l$-connected graph to a $k$-connected graph, Proc. SWAT 2000 (M.M. Halldórsson ed.) Springer LNCS 1851, pp. 286-299, 2000.
14. T. Jordán, On the optimal vertex-connectivity augmentation, J. Combinatorial Theory, Ser. B. 63, 8-20,1995.
15. T. Jordán, A note on the vertex-connectivity augmentation problem, J. Combinatorial Theory, Ser. B. 71, 294-301, 1997.
16. W.Mader, Ecken vom Grad $n$ in minimalen $n$-fach zusammenhängenden Graphen, Archive der Mathematik 23 (1972), 219–224.
17. H. Nagamochi and T. Ibaraki, A linear-time algorithm for finding a sparse $k$-connected spanning subgraph of a $k$-connected graph, Algorithmica 7 (1992), 538-596.

18. H. Nagamochi, Recent development of graph connectivity augmentation algorithms, IEICE Trans. Inf. and Syst., vol E83-D, no.3, March 2000.
19. T. Watanabe and A. Nakamura, Edge-connectivity augmentation problems, Computer and System Siences, Vol 35, No. 1, 96-144, 1987.
20. T. Watanabe and A. Nakamura, A minimum 3-connectivity augmentation of a graph, J. Computer and System Sciences, Vol. 46, No.1, 91-128, 1993.

# Simultaneous Augmentation of Two Graphs to an $\ell$-Edge-Connected Graph and a Biconnected Graph

Toshimasa Ishii and Hiroshi Nagamochi

Department of Information and Computer Sciences,
Toyohashi University of Technology, Aichi 441-8580, Japan.
{ishii,naga}@ics.tut.ac.jp

**Abstract.** Given two undirected multigraphs $G = (V, E)$ and $H = (V, K)$, and two nonnegative integers $\ell$ and $k$, we consider the problem of augmenting $G$ and $H$ by a smallest edge set $F$ to obtain an $\ell$-edge-connected multigraph $G + F = (V, E \cup F)$ and a $k$-vertex-connected multigraph $H + F = (V, K \cup F)$. The problem includes several augmentation problems that require to increase the edge- and vertex-connectivities simultaneously. In this paper, we show that the problem with $\ell \geq 2$ and $k = 2$ can be solved by adding at most one edge over the optimum in $O(n^4)$ time for two arbitrary multigraphs $G$ and $H$, where $n = |V|$. In particular, we show that if $\ell$ is even, then the problem can be solved optimally.

## 1 Introduction

The problem of augmenting a graph by adding the smallest number of new edges to meet edge-connectivity or vertex-connectivity requirements has been extensively studied as an important subject in the network design problem, the data security problem, the graph drawing problem and others, and many efficient algorithms have been developed so far.

In a communication network where both link and node failures can occur, it seems natural to consider the network design problem that handles both the edge- and vertex-connectivities. Hsu and Kao [3] first treated the problem of augmenting the edge- and vertex-connectivities simultaneously, and presented a liner time algorithm for the problem of augmenting a graph $G = (V, E)$ with two specified vertex sets $X, Y \subseteq V$ by adding a minimum number of edges such that two vertices in $X$ (resp., in $Y$) are 2-edge-connected (resp., 2-vertex-connected). Afterwards, Ishii et al. considered the problem of augmenting a multigraph $G = (V, E)$ with two integers $\ell$ and $k$ by adding the minimum number of edges such that $G$ becomes $\ell$-edge-connected and $k$-vertex-connected. They showed polynomial time algorithms for $k = 2$ [5] and for a fixed $\ell$ and $k = 3$ [6,8], and they also gave a polynomial time approximation algorithm which produces a solution whose size is at most $\max\{\ell + 1, 2k - 4\}$ over the optimum [4] for general $\ell$ and $k$. Recently, by extending the result of the edge-connectivity augmentation, Jordán [9] proved that for two integers $\ell, k \geq 2$, two given multigraphs

D.T. Lee and S.-H. Teng (Eds.): ISAAC 2000, LNCS 1969, pp. 326–337, 2000.

$G = (V, E)$ and $H = (V, K)$ with the same vertex set $V$ can be augmented in polynomial time to an $\ell$-edge-connected graph $G + F$ and a $k$-edge-connected graph $H + F$, respectively by adding a new edge set $F$ whose size is at most one over the optimal.

In this paper, aiming to obtain a common generalization of two augmentation problems by [3] and [5] from the context observed by Jordán [9], we consider the following augmentation problem. Given two undirected multigraphs $G = (V, E)$ and $H = (V, K)$ and two nonnegative integers $\ell$ and $k$, augment $G$ and $H$ by adding a smallest edge set $F$ such that $G + F = (V, E \cup F)$ is $\ell$-edge-connected and $H + F = (V, K \cup F)$ is $k$-vertex-connected, respectively. (In fact, to include the Hsu and Kao's problem, we need to further specify subsets $X$ in $G$ and $Y$ in $H$ to be 2-edge and 2-vertex-connected, respectively.) We call this problem *the simultaneous edge-connectivity and vertex-connectivity augmentation problem*, denoted by SEVAP$(\ell, k)$.

In this paper, we consider problem SEVAP$(\ell, 2)$ for two arbitrary multigraphs $G$ and $H$ and an integer $\ell \geq 2$, and present an $O(|V|^4)$ time algorithm that outputs a solution whose size is at most one over the optimal. Observe that if $G = H$, then the problem becomes the one studied by [5]. After introducing a lower bound on the number of edges that is necessary to make given multigraphs $G$ and $H$ $\ell$-edge-connected and 2-vertex-connected, respectively, we show that the lower bound suffices for an even $\ell \geq 2$ but the lower bound plus one edge suffices for an odd $\ell \geq 3$ (there is an example whose optimal value attains the lower bound plus one). This property is different from the problem in [5]. We also observe that computing the lower bound is a polymatroid intersection problem (see Section 2.2 for details). However, we do not need to apply a general polymatroid intersection algorithm. By using the recent result on a submodular function [12], we can show that such problem can be converted into a network flow problem and admits a simple and efficient algorithm.

In Section 2, after introducing basic definitions, we derive some lower bounds on the optimal value to SEVAP$(\ell, k)$ and some graph transformations for preserving the edge- or vertex-connectivity of a given graph. In Section 3, we outline our algorithm, called SEV-AUG2, that makes two given multigraphs $G$ and $H$ $\ell$-edge-connected and 2-vertex-connected, respectively, by adding a new edge set whose size is equal to the lower bound plus at most one. The algorithm consists of four major steps. In Section 4, we state some concluding remarks.

## 2   Preliminaries

### 2.1   Definitions

Let $G = (V, E)$ stand for an undirected multigraph with a set $V$ of vertices and a set $E$ of edges. We denote the number of vertices by $n$, and the number of pairs of adjacent vertices by $m$. For a multigraph $G = (V, E)$, an edge with end vertices $u$ and $v$ is denoted by $(u, v)$. Given a multigraph $G = (V, E)$, its vertex set $V$ and edge set $E$ may be denoted by $V(G)$ and $E(G)$, respectively. A singleton set $\{x\}$ may be simply written as $x$, and " $\subset$ " implies proper inclusion while " $\subseteq$ " means " $\subset$ " or " $=$ ". A subset $X$ *intersects* another subset $Y$ if none of subsets $X \cap Y$, $X - Y$ and $Y - X$ is empty. A family $\mathcal{X}$ of subsets $X_1, \ldots, X_p$ is called *laminar* if no two subsets in $\mathcal{X}$ intersect each other (possibly $X_i \subseteq X_j$ for some $X_i, X_j \in \mathcal{X}$). A *partition* $X_1, \ldots, X_t$ of the vertex set $V$ means a family of nonempty disjoint subsets of $V$ whose union is $V$, and a *subpartition* of $V$ means a partition of a subset $V'$ of $V$.

For a subset $V' \subseteq V$ (resp., $E' \subseteq E$) in $G$, $G[V']$ (resp., $G[E']$) denotes the subgraph induced by $V'$ (resp., $G[E'] = (V, E')$). For $V' \subset V$ (resp., $E' \subseteq E$), we denote subgraph $G[V - V']$ (resp., $G[E - E']$) also by $G - V'$ (resp., $G - E'$). For $E' \subset E$, we denote $V(G[E'])$ by $V[E']$. For an edge set $F$ with $F \cap E = \emptyset$, we denote the augmented multigraph $G = (V, E \cup F)$ by $G + F$. For two disjoint subsets of vertices $X$, $Y \subset V$, we denote by $E_G(X, Y)$ the set of edges connecting a vertex in $X$ and a vertex in $Y$, and denote $c_G(X, Y) = |E_G(X, Y)|$. In particular, $E_G(u, v)$ is the set of multiple edges with end vertices $u$ and $v$ and $c_G(u, v) = |E_G(u, v)|$ denotes its multiplicity.

A *cut* is defined to be a subset $X$ of $V$ with $\emptyset \neq X \neq V$, and the *size* of a cut $X$ is defined by $c_G(X, V - X)$, which may also be written as $c_G(X)$. In particular, $c_G(v)$ for $v \in V$ denotes the *degree* of $v$. A cut with the minimum size is called a *minimum cut*, and its size, denoted by $\lambda(G)$, is called the *edge-connectivity* of $G$. The *local edge-connectivity* $\lambda_G(x, y)$ for two vertices $x, y \in V$ is defined to be the minimum size of a cut $X$ in $G$ that separates $x$ and $y$ (i.e., $|\{x, y\} \cap X| = 1$), or equivalently the maximum number of edge-disjoint paths between $x$ and $y$ by Menger's theorem.

For a subset $X$ of $V$, a vertex $v \in V - X$ is called a *neighbor* of $X$ if it is adjacent to some vertex $u \in X$, and the set of all neighbors of $X$ is denoted by $\Gamma_G(X)$. A maximal connected subgraph $G'$ in a multigraph $G$ is called a *component* of $G$, and the number of components in $G$ is denoted by $p(G)$.

A *disconnecting set* of $G$ is defined as a cut $S$ of $V$ such that $p(G - S) > p(G)$ holds and no $S' \subset S$ has this property. In particular, $v$ is called a *cut vertex* if $v$ is a disconnecting set in $G$. Let $\hat{G}$ denote the simple graph obtained from $G$ by replacing multiple edges in $E_G(u, v)$ by a single edge $(u, v)$ for all $u, v \in V$. A component $G'$ of $G$ with $|V(G')| \geq 3$ always has a disconnecting set unless $\hat{G}'$ is a complete graph. If $G$ is connected and contains a disconnecting set, then a disconnecting set of the minimum size is called a *minimum disconnecting set*, whose size is equal to $\kappa(G)$; we define $\kappa(G) = 0$ if $G$ is not connected, and $\kappa(G) = n - 1$ if $G$ is a complete graph. A cut $T \subset V$ is called *tight* if $\Gamma_G(T)$ is a minimum disconnecting set in $G$. A tight set $D$ is called *minimal* if no proper subset $D'$ of $D$ is tight (hence, the induced subgraph $G[D]$ is connected). We denote a family of all minimal tight sets in $G$ by $\mathcal{D}(G)$, and denote the maximum number of pairwise disjoint minimal tight sets by $t(G)$. For a vertex set $S$ in $G$, we call the components in $G - S$ *the $S$-components*, and denote the family of all $S$-components by $\mathcal{C}(G - S)$. Note that the vertex set $S$ is a disconnecting set in a connected multigraph $G$ if and only if $|\mathcal{C}(G - S)| \geq 2$. Clearly, for a minimum disconnecting set $S$, every $S$-component is tight, and the union of two or more (but not all) $S$-components is also tight. We denote $b(G) = \max\{p(G - S)|S$ is a minimum disconnecting set in $G\}$. We call a disconnecting set $S$ a *shredder* if $|\mathcal{C}(G - S)| \geq 3$.

**Lemma 1.** [4] *If $\kappa(G) = 2$, then any two minimal tight sets $X$ and $Y$ in $G$ are pairwise disjoint.*  □

## 2.2  Lower Bounds and Main Theorem

For two multigraphs $G = (V, E)$ and $H = (V, K)$ and a fixed integer $\ell \geq 2$, let $opt(G, H)$ denote the optimal value of SEVAP($\ell, 2$) in $G$ and $H$, i.e., the minimum size $|F|$ of a set $F$ of new edges to obtain an $\ell$-edge-connected graph $G + F$ and a 2-vertex-connected graph $H + F$. In this section, we derive two types of lower bounds, $\alpha(G, H)$ and $\beta(G, H)$, on $opt(G, H)$.

(a) Let $X \subset V$ be a cut in $G$ and $H$. To make $G$ $\ell$-edge-connected it is necessary to add at least $\max\{\ell - c_G(X), 0\}$ edges between $X$ and $V - X$. To make $H$ 2-vertex-connected it is necessary to add at least $\max\{2 - |\Gamma_H(X)|, 0\}$ edges between $X$ and $V - X - \Gamma_H(X)$ if $V - X - \Gamma_H(X) \neq \emptyset$. Given a subpartition $\mathcal{X} = \{X_1, \ldots, X_{p_1}, X_{p_1+1}, \ldots, X_{p_2}\}$ of $V$, where $V - X_i - \Gamma_H(X_i) \neq \emptyset$ holds for $i = p_1 + 1, \ldots, p_2$, we sum up "deficiencies" $\max\{\ell - c_G(X_i), 0\}$, $i = 1, \ldots, p_1$, and $\max\{2 - |\Gamma_H(X_i)|, 0\}$, $i = p_1 + 1, \ldots, p_2$. Let

$$\alpha(G, H) = \max_{\text{all subpartitions } \mathcal{X}} \left\{ \sum_{i=1}^{p_1}(\ell - c_G(X_i)) + \sum_{i=p_1+1}^{p_2} (2 - |\Gamma_H(X_i)|) \right\}, \quad (1)$$

where the maximum is taken over all subpartitions $\mathcal{X} = \{X_1, \ldots, X_{p_1}, X_{p_1+1}, \ldots, X_{p_2}\}$ of $V$ with $V - X_i - \Gamma_H(X_i) \neq \emptyset$, $i = p_1 + 1, \ldots, p_2$. As adding one edge to $G$ contributes to the deficiency of at most two cuts in $\mathcal{X}$, we need at least $\lceil \alpha(G, H)/2 \rceil$ new edges to make $G$ and $H$ $\ell$-edge-connected and 2-vertex-connected, respectively. To compute $\alpha(G, H)$, we add a new vertex $s$ together with a set $F_1$ of edges between $s$ and $V$ such that the resulting graph $G_1 = (V \cup \{s\}, E \cup F_1)$ and $H_1 = (V \cup \{s\}, K \cup F_1)$ satisfy

$$c_{G_1}(X) \geq \ell \quad \text{for all nonempty } X \subset V, \quad (2)$$

$$|\Gamma_H(X)| + |\Gamma_{H_1}(s) \cap X| \geq 2 \quad \text{for all } X \subset V \text{ with } V - X - \Gamma_H(X) \neq \emptyset$$
$$\text{and } |X| \geq 2, \quad (3)$$

$$|\Gamma_H(x)| + c_{H_1}(s, x) \geq 2 \quad \text{for all vertices } x \in V,$$

where the size $|F_1|$ is minimized. In other words, we compute a $|V|$-dimensional vector $t$ with nonnegative integer entries $\{t(v) \mid v \in V\}$ which satisfies

$$c_G(X) + \sum_{v \in X} t(v) \geq \ell \quad \text{for all nonempty } X \subset V, \quad (4)$$

$$|\Gamma_H(X)| + \sum_{v \in X} \min\{1, t(v)\} \geq 2 \quad \text{for all } X \subset V \text{ with } V - X - \Gamma_H(X) \neq \emptyset$$

$$\text{and } |X| \geq 2, \tag{5}$$

$$|\Gamma_H(x)| + t(x) \geq 2 \quad \text{for all vertices } x \in V,$$

where $\sum_{v \in V} t(v)$ is minimized. Since both vector sets described by (4) and (5), respectively are represented by polymatroids, finding a vector $t$ with the minimum $\sum_{v \in V} t(v)$ is formulated as a polymatroid intersection problem. However, by using the result that the vector set described by (4) has a simple structure represented by a laminar family [12], we can show that a minimum vector $t$ and a subpartition of $V$ that attains $\alpha(G, H)$ can be found in $O(mn + n^2 \log n)$ time by applying the minimum flow maximum cut theorem [1] in an auxiliary network (the further detail is omitted).

(b) We now consider another case in which different type of new edges become necessary. For a vertex $v^* \in V$, let $T_1, \ldots, T_q$ denote all the components in $H - v^*$, where $q = p(H - v^*)$. To make $H$ 2-vertex-connected, a new edge set $F$ must be added to $H$ so that all $T_i$ form a single connected component in $(H + F) - v^*$. For this, it is necessary to add at least $p(H - v^*) - 1$ edges to connect all components in $H - v^*$. Moreover, if $\ell > c_G(v^*)$ holds, then it is necessary to add at least $\ell - c_G(v^*)$ edges in order to make $G$ $\ell$-edge-connected. In the above discussion, none of augmented edges for connecting components in $H - v^*$ is incident to $v^*$, and all augmented edges for making the degree of $v^*$ at least $\ell$ are incident to $v^*$; hence there is no edge that belongs to both types of augmented edges. Therefore, it is necessary to add at least $p(H - v^*) - 1 + \max\{\ell - c_G(v^*), 0\}$ edges for $v^* \in V$. Define

$$\beta(G, H) = \max_{\text{all vertices } v \in V} \left\{ p(H - v) - 1 + \max\{\ell - c_G(v), 0\} \right\}. \tag{6}$$

Thus at least $\beta(G, H)$ new edges are necessary to make $G$ and $H$ $\ell$-edge-connected and 2-vertex-connected, respectively.

The next lemma combines the above two lower bounds.

**Lemma 2. (Lower Bound)** *For two given multigraphs $G$ and $H$ with $V(G) = V(H)$, let*

$$\gamma(G, H) = \max\{\lceil \alpha(G, H)/2 \rceil, \beta(G, H)\}.$$

*Then $\gamma(G, H) \leq opt(G, H)$ holds, where $opt(G, H)$ denotes the minimum number of edges augmented to make $G$ and $H$ $\ell$-edge-connected and 2-vertex-connected, respectively.* □

Based on this, we shall prove the next result in this paper.

**Theorem 1.** *Let $G = (V, E)$ and $H = (V, K)$ be two arbitrary multigraphs. Then, for any integer $\ell \geq 2$, if $\ell$ is even (resp., $\ell$ is odd), then $\gamma(G, H) = opt(G, H)$ (resp., $\gamma(G, H) \leq opt(G, H) \leq \gamma(G, H) + 1$) holds and a feasible solution $F$ of $\text{SEVAP}(\ell, 2)$ with $|F| = \gamma(G, H)$ (resp., $\gamma(G, H) \leq |F| \leq \gamma(G, H) + 1$) can be found in $O(n^4)$ time, where $n$ is the number of vertices in $G$ and $H$.* □

In fact, there is an example of $\mathrm{SEVAP}(\ell, 2)$ such that the optimal value is $\gamma(G, H) + 1$; $G = (V = \{u_1, u_2, u_3, u_4\}, \{(u_1, u_2), (u_2, u_3), (u_3, u_4), (u_4, u_1)\})$, $H = (V, \{(u_1, u_3), (u_2, u_4)\})$ and $\ell = 3$. In this example, we have $\gamma(G, H) = 2$, but we see that any set $F'$ of two edges cannot attain a 3-edge-connected multigraph $G + F'$ or a 2-vertex-connected multigraph $H + F'$. (Clearly set $F'$ of three edges $(u_1, u_2), (u_2, u_3), (u_3, u_4)$ is a solution to the example.)

In the rest of this section, we review and derive some graph transformations for preserving the edge- or vertex-connectivity of a given graph, which will be a basis of constructing an algorithmic proof of Theorem 1.

## 2.3  Preserving Edge-Connectivity

Given a multigraph $G = (V, E)$ and two vertices $u, v \in V$ with $(u, v) \in E$, we construct a multigraph $G' = (V, E')$ by deleting one edge $(u, v)$ from $E_G(u, v)$, and adding a new edge to $E_G(u, w)$ with $w \in V - v$. We say that $G'$ is obtained from $G$ by *shifting* $(u, v)$ to $(u, w)$.

Let $G' = (V \cup \{s\}, E)$ have a designated vertex $s \notin V$ and satisfy

$$c_{G'}(X) \geq \ell \text{ for all cuts } X \subset V. \tag{7}$$

For an edge $e = (s, v)$ with $v \in V$, if there is a cut $X' \subset V$ satisfying $c_{G'-e}(X') < \ell$, then there is a cut $X_v \subset V$ with $c_{G'}(X_v) = \ell$ and $v \in X_v$ such that all cuts $X'' \subset X_v$ with $v \in X''$ satisfies $c_{G'}(X'') > \ell$. It is easy to see that such cut $X_v$ is unique for each $v \in V$. We call such $X_v$ $\lambda$-*critical* with respect to $v \in \Gamma_{G'}(s)$.

**Theorem 2.** [4,7] *Let* $G' = (V \cup \{s\}, E)$ *be a multigraph with a designated vertex* $s \notin V$ *satisfying* (7). *Let* $X$ *be a* $\lambda$-*critical cut* $X_v$ *with respect to a vertex* $v \in \Gamma_{G'}(s)$ *with* $|X_v| \geq 2$ *if any,* $X = V$ *otherwise. Then for any* $v' \in X \subset V$, *the shifted multigraph* $G' - (s, v) + (s, v')$ *also satisfies* (7).  □

Similarly, we obtain the following theorem.

**Lemma 3.** *Let* $G' = (V \cup \{s\}, E)$ *be a multigraph with a designated vertex* $s \notin V$ *and* $|V| \geq 3$ *satisfying* (7). *Assume that* $G'$ *has an edge* $e = (u, v) \in E$ *with* $u, v \in V$ *and* $c_{G'}(v) > \ell$ *holds. Then there is a vertex* $v' \in V - \{u, v\}$ *such that the shifted multigraph* $G' - (u, v) + (u, v')$ *also satisfies* (7).  ⊔

Given a multigraph $G' = (V \cup \{s\}, E)$, a designated vertex $s \notin V$, vertices $u, v \in \Gamma_{G'}(s)$ (possibly $u = v$) and a nonnegative integer $\delta \leq \min\{c_{G'}(s, u), c_{G'}(s, v)\}$, we construct multigraph $G'' = (V \cup \{s\}, E')$ by deleting $\delta$ edges from $E_{G'}(s, u)$ and $E_{G'}(s, v)$, respectively, and adding new $\delta$ edges to $E_{G'}(u, v)$. We say that $G''$ is obtained from $G'$ by *splitting* $\delta$ pairs of edges $(s, u)$ and $(s, v)$. Conversely, we say that $G''$ is obtained from $G'$ by *hooking up* an edge $(u, v)$, if we construct $G''$ by replacing $(u, v)$ with two edges $(s, u)$ and $(s, v)$ in $G'$. A sequence of splittings is *complete* if the resulting multigraph $G''$ does not have any neighbor of $s$.

Let $G' = (V \cup \{s\}, E)$ have a designated vertex $s \notin V$ and satisfy (7). A pair $\{(s, u), (s, v)\}$ of two edges in $E_{G'}(s)$ is called $\lambda$-*splittable*, if the multigraph $G''$

resulting from splitting edges $(s, u)$ and $(s, v)$ also satisfies (7). The following theorem is proven by Lovász [10].

**Theorem 3.** [2,10] *Let* $G' = (V \cup \{s\}, E)$ *be a multigraph with a designated vertex* $s \notin V$ *with even* $c_{G'}(s)$, *and* $\ell \geq 2$ *be an integer such that* $G'$ *satisfies* (7). *Then for each* $u \in \Gamma_{G'}(s)$ *there is a vertex* $v \in \Gamma_{G'}(s)$ *such that* $\{(s, u), (s, v)\}$ *is* $\lambda$-*splittable.* □

By repeating the splitting operation in this theorem, we see that, if $c_{G'}(s)$ is even, there always exists a complete splitting at $s$ such that the resulting multigraph $G''$ satisfies $\lambda_{G''-s}(X) \geq \ell$ for every cut $X \subset V$. It is shown in [11] that such a complete splitting at $s$ can be computed in $O((m + n \log n)n \log n)$ time.

We call a cut $X \subset V$ *dangerous* if $c_{G'}(X) \leq \ell + 1$ holds. Note that $\{(s, u), (s, v)\}$ is not $\lambda$-splittable if and only if there is a dangerous cut $X \subset V$ with $\{u, v\} \subseteq X$. The following lemma is given in [4, Lemma 2.3.1].

**Lemma 4.** [4,7] *Let* $G' = (V \cup \{s\}, E)$ *be a multigraph with a designated vertex* $s \notin V$, *and* $\ell \geq 2$ *be an integer such that* $G'$ *satisfies* (7). *Let* $u \in \Gamma_{G'}(s)$ *and* $N \subseteq \Gamma_{G'}(s) - u$ *denote a set of all vertices* $x \in \Gamma_{G'}(s)$ *such that* $\{(s, u), (s, x)\}$ *is not* $\lambda$-*splittable. If* $c_{G'}(s, N) \geq 3$ *holds, then for every edge* $(s, y)$ *with* $y \in \Gamma_{G'}(s) - N$ *and every set* $\{x_1, x_2\} \subseteq N$ *of two vertices, at least one of* $\{(s, y), (s, x_1)\}$ *and* $\{(s, y), (s, x_2)\}$ *is* $\lambda$-*splittable.* □

We show a new property of edge-splittings while preserving the $\ell$-edge-connectivity (the proof is omitted).

**Lemma 5.** *Let* $G' = (V \cup \{s\}, E)$ *be a multigraph with a designated vertex* $s \notin V$, *and* $\ell \geq 2$ *be an integer such that* $G'$ *satisfies* (7). *Assume that* $G'$ *has neighbors* $u_1, u_2, v_1, v_2$ *of* $s$ *(only* $v_1 = v_2$ *can hold). If* $\{(s, u_1), (s, u_2)\}$ *is* $\lambda$-*splittable and* $\{(s, u_i), (s, v_j)\}$ *is not* $\lambda$-*splittable for all pairs* $\{i, j\}$, $1 \leq i \leq 2$, $1 \leq j \leq 2$, *then* $\ell$ *is odd,* $c_{G'}(s) = |\Gamma_{G'}(s)| = 4$ *holds and a partition* $A_1 \cup A_2 \cup A_3 \cup A_4$ *of* $V$ *satisfies the followings.*

(i) $c_{G'}(A_i) = \ell$ *for* $i = 1, 2, 3, 4$.
(ii) $c_{G'}(A_1, A_3) = c_{G'}(A_2, A_4) = 0$.
(iii) $|A_i \cap \Gamma_{G'}(s)| = 1$ *for* $i = 1, 2, 3, 4$.
(iv) $c_{G'}(A_1, A_2) = c_{G'}(A_2, A_3) = c_{G'}(A_3, A_4) = c_{G'}(A_4, A_1) = (\ell - 1)/2$.
(v) $\lambda((G' - s) + \{(a_1, a_2), (a_1, a_3), (a_3, a_4)\}) \geq \ell$ *and* $\lambda((G' - s) + \{(a_1, a_2), (a_2, a_3), (a_3, a_4)\}) \geq \ell$ *where* $\{a_i\} = A_i \cap \Gamma_{G'}(s)$ *for* $i = 1, 2, 3, 4$. □

## 2.4 Preserving Vertex-Connectivity

Let $G' = (V \cup \{s\}, E)$ denote a multigraph with $s \notin V$ and $|V| \geq 3$, and let $G = G' - s$ satisfy

$$|\Gamma_G(X)| + |\Gamma_{G'}(s) \cap X| \geq 2 \text{ for all nonempty } X \subset V \text{ with } |X| \geq 2$$
$$\text{and } V - X - \Gamma_G(X) \neq \emptyset \tag{8}$$
$$|\Gamma_G(x)| + c_{G'}(s, x) \geq 2 \text{ for all vertices } x \in V.$$

A pair $\{(s,u),(s,v)\}$ of two edges in $E_{G'}(s)$ is called $\kappa$-splittable, if the multi-graph $G''$ resulting from splitting edges $(s,u)$ and $(s,v)$ preserves (8). Then the following lemma holds (the proof is omitted).

**Lemma 6.** *Let* $G' = (V \cup \{s\}, E)$ *be a multigraph with a designated vertex* $s \notin V$ *satisfying (8) and* $\kappa(G) = 0$, *where* $G = G' - s$. *Then* $\{(s,u),(s,v)\}$ *is* $\kappa$-*splittable for any pair of two edges* $(s,u)$ *and* $(s,v)$ *such that* $u$ *and* $v$ *are contained in distinct components in* $G$. □

We further observe the following theorem (the proof is omitted).

**Theorem 4.** *Let* $G' = (V \cup \{s\}, E)$ *be a multigraph with a designated vertex* $s \notin V$ *satisfying (8) and* $\kappa(G) = 1$, *where* $G = G' - s$. *Let* $v^* \in V$ *be a shredder in* $G$. *If* $G$ *has a cut* $T_1 \in \mathcal{C}(G - v^*)$ *with* $c_{G'}(s, T_1) \geq 2$, *then* $\{(s,u),(s,v)\}$ *is* $\kappa$-*splittable for any pair* $\{u,v\}$ *such that* $u \in \Gamma_{G'}(s) \cap T_1$ *and* $v \in \Gamma_{G'}(s) \cap (V - T_1)$. □

## 2.5   Preserving Edge- and Vertex-Connectivity Simultaneously

Consider two graphs $G' = (V \cup \{s\}, E \cup F)$ and $H' = (V \cup \{s\}, K \cup F)$ with $F = E_{G'}(s) = E_{H'}(s)$ such that $G'$ satisfies (7) for an integer $\ell \geq 2$ and $H'$ satisfies (8). Here we give conditions that admit a splitting of two edges in $F$ which is $\lambda$-splittable in $G'$ and $\kappa$-splittable in $H'$. The following lemmas follow from Theorems 2 – 4 and Lemmas 3 – 6 (the proofs are omitted).

**Lemma 7.** *Let* $G' = (V \cup \{s\}, E \cup F)$ *and* $H' = (V \cup \{s\}, K \cup F)$ *be two graphs with* $F = E_{G'}(s) = E_{H'}(s)$ *and* $\ell$ *be an integer with* $\ell \geq 2$ *such that* $G'$ *satisfies* (7) *and* $H'$ *satisfies (8). Assume that* $\kappa(H' - s) = 0$ *holds. If there is no pair of two edges in* $F$ *which is* $\lambda$-*splittable in* $G'$ *and* $\kappa$-*splittable in* $H'$ *and decreases the number of components in* $H' - s$, *then* $|F| = 4$ *holds and there is a set* $F'$ *of new edges with* $|F'| = 3$ *such that* $\lambda((G' - s) + F') \geq \ell$ *and* $\kappa((H' - s) + F') \geq 2$. □

**Lemma 8.** *Let* $G' = (V \cup \{s\}, E \cup F)$ *and* $H' = (V \cup \{s\}, K \cup F)$ *be two graphs with* $F = E_{G'}(s) = E_{H'}(s)$ *and* $\ell$ *be an integer with* $\ell \geq 2$ *such that* $G'$ *satisfies* (7), $H'$ *satisfies (8) and we have* $\kappa(H' - s) = 1$, $b(H' - s) \geq 3$ *and* $b(H' - s) - 1 \geq \lceil t(H' - s)/2 \rceil$. *Assume that* $H' - s$ *has a* $v^*$-*component* $T_1 \in \mathcal{C}((H' - s) - v^*)$ *with* $c_{H'}(s, T_1) \geq 2$ *for a vertex* $v^* \in V$ *with* $b(H' - s) = p((H' - s) - v^*)$. *If there is no pair of two edges in* $F$ *which is* $\lambda$-*splittable in* $G'$ *and* $\kappa$-*splittable in* $H'$ *decreasing the number of cut vertices* $v \in V$ *with* $b(H' - s) = p((H' - s) - v)$, *then one of the following properties* (i) *and* (ii) *holds:*
(i) $|F| = 4$ *holds and there is a set* $F'$ *of new edges with* $|F'| = 3$ *such that* $\lambda((G' - s) + F') \geq \ell$ *and* $\kappa((H' - s) + F') \geq 2$.
(ii) $H' - s$ *has exactly one cut vertex* $v^* \in V$ *with* $b(H' - s) = p((H' - s) - v^*)$, *and* $G' - s$ *has a dangerous cut* $X \subset V$ *with* $\Gamma_{G'}(s) \cap (V - v^*) \subseteq X$. □

**Lemma 9.** *Let $G' = (V \cup \{s\}, E \cup F)$ and $H' = (V \cup \{s\}, K \cup F)$ be two graphs with $F = E_{G'}(s) = E_{H'}(s)$ and $\ell$ be an integer with $\ell \geq 2$ such that $G'$ satisfies (7) and $H'$ satisfies (8). Assume that $\kappa(H' - s) = 1$ and $b(H' - s) \leq \lceil t(H' - s)/2 \rceil$ hold. If there is no pair of two edges in $F$ which is $\lambda$-splittable in $G'$ and is $\kappa$-splittable in $H'$ decreasing $t(H' - s)$ or decreasing the number of cut vertices in $H' - s$, then one of the following properties (i) and (ii) holds:*
*(i) $|F| = 4$ holds and there is a set $F'$ of new edges with $|F'| = 3$ such that $\lambda((G' - s) + F') \geq \ell$ and $\kappa((H' - s) + F') \geq 2$.*
*(ii) $G' - s$ has a dangerous cut $Z \subset V$ with $(V - v^*) \cap \Gamma_{G'}(s) \subseteq Z$ for a shredder $v^*$ in $H' - s$. There is a sequence of edge-splittings at $s$ so that $G''$ satisfies (7), $H''$ satisfies (8) and we have $|\Gamma_{G''}(s)| = |\Gamma_{H''}(s)| \leq 2n$, where $G''$ and $H''$ denote the resulting graphs from $G'$ and $H'$, respectively.* □

## 3   Algorithm for SEVAP($\ell, 2$)

In this section, given two arbitrary graphs $G$ and $H$ with $V(G) = V(H)$ and an integer $\ell \geq 2$, we present a polynomial time algorithm, called SEV-AUG2, for finding a nearly optimal solution to SEVAP($\ell, 2$) whose size is at most $\gamma(G, H) + 1$. The algorithm SEV-AUG2 consists of four major steps. In the first step, we compute a smallest edge set $F_1$ satisfying (2) and (3), and then we try to split edges in $F_1$ while keeping condition (2) and (3). Note that after splitting all edges incident to $s$ $G$ and $H$ receive $|F_1|/2 = \alpha(G, H)/2$ edges (if $|F_1|$ is even), which is a lower bound on the optimal value. In the second and third steps, we increase the vertex-connectivity of $H$ from zero to one and from one to two, respectively, by splitting edges incident to $s$ or by shifting some split edges (where some pair of edges for splitting may be rechosen). In each step, we also give some properties to verify its correctness. The proof sketches for some of these properties will be given in the subsequent sections.

**Algorithm SEV-AUG2**

**Input:** Two undirected multigraphs $G = (V, E)$ and $H = (V, K)$ with $|V| \geq 3$, and an integer $\ell \geq 2$.
**Output:** A set of new edges $F$ with $|F| \leq opt(G, H) + 1$ such that $G^* = G + F$ and $H^* = H + F$ satisfies $\lambda(G^*) \geq \ell$ and $\kappa(H^*) \geq 2$.
**Step I (Addition of vertex $s$ and associated edges):** Add a new vertex $s$ together with a set $F_1$ of edges between $s$ and $V$ such that the resulting graph $G_1 = (V \cup \{s\}, E \cup F_1)$ and $H_1 = (V \cup \{s\}, K \cup F_1)$ satisfies (2) and (3), where $|F_1|$ is *minimum* subject to (2) and (3).

*Property 1.* The above set of edges $F_1$ satisfies $|F_1| = \alpha(G, H)$. □

If $|F_1|$ is odd, then add one edge $\hat{e} = (s, w)$ to $F_1$ for a vertex $w$ arbitrarily chosen from $V$, denoting the resulting graphs again by $G_1$ and $H_1$, respectively. After setting $F^* := \emptyset$, $F_2 := F_1$, $G_2 := G_1$, $H_2 := H_1$, $\overline{G_2} := G_1 - s$ and $\overline{H_2} := H_1 - s$, we go to Step II.

**Step II (Edge-splitting for 1-Vertex-Connectivity in $H$):** While $\kappa(\overline{H_2}) = 0$, repeat the following procedure (if $\kappa(\overline{H_2}) = 1$ holds, then go to Step III).
**(1)** If there is a pair $\{e_1 = (s, u), e_2 = (s, v)\} \subseteq F_2$ which is $\lambda$-splittable in $G_2$ and $\kappa$-splittable in $H_2$ and $u$ and $v$ are contained in two distinct components in $\overline{H_2}$, then after setting $F^* := F^* + (u, v)$, $F_2 := F_2 - \{e_1, e_2\}$, $G_2 := G_2 - \{e_1, e_2\} + \{(u, v)\}$, $H_2 := H_2 - \{e_1, e_2\} + \{(u, v)\}$, $\overline{G_2} := G_2 - s$ and $\overline{H_2} := H_2 - s$, go to Step II.
**(2)** Otherwise Lemma 7 implies that $|F_2| = 4$ holds and there is a set $F'$ of new edges such that $|F'| = 3$, $\lambda(\overline{G_2} + F') \geq \ell$ and $\kappa(\overline{H_2} + F') \geq 2$ hold. Halt after outputting $F^* \cup F'$ as a solution whose size is the optimum plus at most one (note $|F^*| + |F'| = \lceil \alpha(G, H)/2 \rceil + 1$).
**Step III (Edge-splitting for 2-Vertex-Connectivity in $H$):** While $\kappa(\overline{H_2}) = 1$, repeat the following procedure (A) or (B); if the condition $b(\overline{H_2}) - 1 \geq \lceil t(\overline{H_2})/2 \rceil$ holds, then procedure (A) else procedure (B) (if $\kappa(\overline{H_2}) \geq 2$, then go to Step IV).

**Procedure (A)**

**(Case-1)** There is a cut vertex $v^*$ in $\overline{H_2}$ satisfying $p(\overline{H_2} - v^*) = b(\overline{H_2})$ such that $\overline{H_2}$ has a cut $T_1 \in \mathcal{C}(\overline{H_2} - v^*)$ with $c_{H_2}(s, T_1) \geq 2$, and such that $\overline{G_2}$ has no dangerous cut $Z$ with $\Gamma_{G_2}(s) \cap (V - v^*) \subseteq Z$.
**(1)** If there is a pair $\{e_1 = (s, u), e_2 = (s, v)\} \subseteq F_2$ which is $\lambda$-splittable in $G_2$ and is $\kappa$-splittable in $H_2$ and decreasing the number of cut vertices $x \in V$ with $p(\overline{H_2} - x) = b(\overline{H_2})$ at least by one, then after setting $F^* := F^* + (u, v)$, $F_2 := F_2 - \{e_1, e_2\}$, $G_2 := G_2 - \{e_1, e_2\} + \{(u, v)\}$, $H_2 := H_2 - \{e_1, e_2\} + \{(u, v)\}$, $\overline{G_2} := G_2 - s$ and $\overline{H_2} := H_2 - s$, go to Step III.
**(2)** Otherwise Lemma 8 implies that there is a set $F_2'$ of new edges such that $|F_2'| = \lceil \alpha(G, H)/2 \rceil + 1$, $\lambda(G + F_2') \geq \ell$ and $\kappa(H + F_2') \geq 2$ hold. Halt after outputting $F_2'$ as a solution whose size is the optimum plus at most one.
**(Case-2)** $\overline{H_2}$ has exactly one cut vertex $v^*$ satisfying $p(\overline{H_2} - v^*) = b(\overline{H_2})$. Every cut $T \in \mathcal{C}(\overline{H_2} - v^*)$ satisfies $c_{H_2}(s, T) = 1$ or $\overline{G_2}$ has a dangerous cut $Z \subset V$ with $(V - v^*) \cap \Gamma_{G_2}(s) \subseteq Z$.
**(1)** If $(a)$ there is a split edge $e \in F^*$ with $v^* \notin V[e]$ and $p(\overline{H_2} - v^*) = p((\overline{H_2} - e) - v^*)$ or $(b)$ $|(F^* \cup F_2) \cap E_{G_2}(v^*)| > \ell - c_G(v^*) > 0$ holds, then we can obtain $G_2'$ and $H_2'$ satisfying the conditions of Case-1 by hooking up at most one split edge in $F^*$ and shifting at most one edge in $F^* \cup F_2$. Hence we go to Case-1.
**(2)** Otherwise we execute a complete splitting at $s$ so that the resulting graph $G_2^* = (V, E \cup F_2^*)$ (ignoring the isolated vertex $s$) satisfies $\lambda(G_2^*) \geq \ell$. Then any split edge $e \in F_2^*$ with $V[e] \subseteq V - v^*$ satisfies $p((H_2^* - e) - v^*) = p(H_2^* - v^*) + 1$ and we have $|E_{G_2^*}(v^*) \cap F_2^*| = \max\{\ell - c_G(v^*), 0\}$, where $H_2^* = (V, K \cup F_2^*)$. Let $\mathcal{C}(H_2^* - v^*) = \{T_1, T_2, \ldots, T_b\}$, where $b = p(H_2^* - v^*)$. Then $\kappa(H_2^* + F_3^*) \geq 2$ holds for $F_3^* = \{(x_i, x_{i+1}) \mid i = 1, \ldots, b-1\}$, where $x_i$ is a vertex in $T_i \cap \Gamma_{H_2}(s)$. Note that $|F_2^*| + |F_3^*| = |F_2^*| + p(H_2^* - v^*) - 1 = p(H - v^*) - 1 + \max\{\ell - c_G(v^*), 0\} \leq \beta(G, H)$ implies that $F_2^* \cup F_3^*$ is an optimal solution since $\beta(G, H)$ is a lower bound on the optimal value. Halt after outputting $F_2^* \cup F_3^*$.

*Property* 2. Each two iterations of procedure (A) decrease $b(\overline{H_2})$ at least by one, and does not increase $c_{G_2}(s) = c_{H_2}(s)$. $\qquad\square$

## Procedure (B)

(**Case-3**) $\overline{H_2}$ has a shredder $v^* \in V$ such that $\overline{G_2}$ has a dangerous cut $Z \subset V$ with $(V - v^*) \cap \Gamma_{G_2}(s) \subseteq Z$. By executing a sequence of edge-splittings at $s$ according to Lemma 9, we obtain $G_2'$ and $H_2'$ such that $c_{G_2'}(s) = c_{H_2'}(s) \le 2n$. After setting $F^* := E(G_2' - s) - E(= E(H_2' - s) - K)$, $F_2 := E_{G_2'}(s)(= E_{H_2'}(s))$, $G_2 := G_2'$, $H_2 := H_2'$, $\overline{G_2} := G_2 - s$ and $\overline{H_2} := H_2 - s$, go to Step III.

(**Case-4**) Case-3 does not hold.

(**1**) If there is a pair $\{e_1 = (s, u), e_2 = (s, v)\}$ of two edges incident to $s$ such that $\{e_1, e_2\}$ is $\lambda$-splittable in $G_2$ and $\kappa$-splittable in $H_2$ and decreases $t(\overline{H_2})$ or the number of cut vertices in $\overline{H_2}$, then after setting $F^* := F^* + (u, v)$, $F_2 := F_2 - \{e_1, e_2\}$, $G_2 := G_2 - \{e_1, e_2\} + \{(u, v)\}$, $H_2 := H_2 - \{e_1, e_2\} + \{(u, v)\}$, $\overline{G_2} := G_2 - s$ and $\overline{H_2} := H_2 - s$, go to Step III.

(**2**) Otherwise Lemma 9 implies that there is a set $F_2'$ of new edges with $|F_2'| = \lceil \alpha(G, H)/2 \rceil + 1$, $\lambda(G + F_2') \ge \ell$ and $\kappa(H + F_2') \ge 2$. Halt after outputting $F_2'$ as a solution whose size is the optimum plus at most one.

*Property* 3. Each iteration of the procedure Case-4 decreases $t(\overline{G'})$ or the number of cut vertices in $\overline{H_2}$ and $c_{G_2}(s) = c_{H_2}(s)$ at least by one, respectively. Each iteration of the procedure Case-3 decreases $c_{G_2}(s) = c_{H_2}(s)$ at least by one, and moreover, after each iteration of Case-3, the number of edges incident to $s$ is at most $2n$. $\qquad\square$

**Step IV (Edge Splitting for the $\ell$-Edge-Connectivity):** We have $\kappa(\overline{H_2}) \ge 2$ and $G_2$ satisfies (2). Then find a complete edge-splitting at $s$ in $G_2$ according to Theorem 3 to obtain $G_3 = (V, E \cup F^* \cup F_3)$ (ignoring the isolated vertex $s$) with $\lambda(G_3) \ge \ell$. Note that $|F^* \cup F_3| = \lceil \alpha(G, H)/2 \rceil$ holds and $H_3 = (V, K \cup F^* \cup F_3)$ is 2-vertex-connected. Output $F^* \cup F_3$ as an optimal solution. $\qquad\square$

**Remarks:** All the cases that the algorithm SEV-AUG2 outputs a solution $F$ with $|F| = \gamma(G, H) + 1$ follow from Lemma 5 which holds only for an odd integer $\ell \ge 2$. Hence we see that SEV-AUG2 outputs an optimal solution for an even integer $\ell$. $\qquad\square$

**Remarks:** It takes $O(n^3)$ time to find a pair of two edges incident to $s$ which is $\lambda$-splittable in $G_2$ and $\kappa$-splittable in $H_2$ in Steps II and III of the algorithm SEV-AUG2. This depends on the computation of dangerous cuts containing some vertex in $G_2$, a $\lambda$-critical cut with respect to some vertex in $G_2$ (the details are omitted). $\qquad\square$

# 4  Concluding Remarks

In this paper, we considered the problem of augmenting two given multigraphs $G$ and $H$ with $V(G) = V(H)$ to an $\ell$-edge-connected graph and a 2-vertex-connected graph, respectively, by adding the smallest number of new edges. First we gave a lower bound $\gamma(G, H)$ on the optimal value of the problem, and gave a polynomial time algorithm which outputs a solution $F$ with $|F| = \gamma(G, H)$ if $\ell$ is even or $|F| \leq \gamma(G, H) + 1$ if $\ell$ is odd. In fact, for an odd integer $\ell$, there is an example that the problem cannot be solved by adding $\gamma(G, H)$ edges. However, it is open to obtain a complete characterization of the case where the optimal value is equal to $\gamma(G, H) + 1$.

# References

1. R. K. Ahuja, T. L. Magnanti and J. B. Orlin, Network Flows: Theory, Algorithms, and Applications, Prentice-Hall, Englewood Cliffs, NJ, 1993.

2. A. Frank, *Augmenting graphs to meet edge-connectivity requirements*, SIAM J. Discrete Math., Vol.5, 1992, pp. 25–53.

3. T. Hsu and M. -Y. Kao, *Optimal bi-level augmentation for selectively enhancing graph connectivity with applications*, Lecture Notes in Comput. Sci., 1090, Springer-Verlag, 2nd International Symp. on Computing and Combinatorics, Computing and Combinatorics (Proc. COCOON '96), 1996, pp. 169–178.

4. T. Ishii, *Studies on multigraph connectivity augmentation problems*, PhD thesis, Dept. of Applied Mathematics and Physics, Kyoto University, Kyoto, Japan, 2000.

5. T. Ishii, H. Nagamochi and T. Ibaraki, *Augmenting edge-connectivity and vertex-connectivity simultaneously*, Lecture Notes in Comput. Sci., 1350, Springer-Verlag, Algorithms and Computation (Proc. ISAAC '97), 1997, pp. 102–111.

6. T. Ishii, H. Nagamochi and T. Ibaraki, *k-edge and 3-vertex connectivity augmentation in an arbitrary multigraph*, Lecture Notes in Comput. Sci., 1533, Springer-Verlag, Algorithms and Computation (Proc. ISAAC '98), 1998, pp. 159–168.

7. T. Ishii, H. Nagamochi and T. Ibaraki, *Augmenting a (k − 1)-vertex-connected multigraph to an $\ell$-edge-connected and k-vertex-connected multigraph*, Lecture Notes in Comput. Sci., 1643, Springer-Verlag, Algorithms (Proc. ESA '99), 1999, pp. 414–425.

8. T. Ishii, H. Nagamochi and T. Ibaraki, *Optimal augmentation of a 2-vertex-connected multigraph to a k-edge-connected and 3-vertex-connected multigraph*, J. Combinatorial Optimization, Vol.4, 2000, pp. 35–77.

9. T. Jordán, *Edge-splitting problems with demands*, Lecture Notes in Comput. Sci., 1610, Springer-Verlag, Integer Programming and Combinatorial Optimization (IPCO '99), 1999, pp. 273–288.

10. L. Lovász, Combinatorial Problems and Exercises, North-Holland, 1979.

11. H. Nagamochi and T. Ibaraki, *Deterministic $\tilde{O}(nm)$ time edge-splitting in undirected graphs*, J. Combinatorial Optimization, Vol.1, 1997, pp. 5–46.

12. H. Nagamochi and T. Ibaraki, *Polyhedral structure of submodular and posi-modular systems*, Lecture Notes in Comput. Sci., 1533, Springer-Verlag, Algorithms and Computation (Proc. ISAAC '98), 1998, pp. 169–178 (to appear in Discrete Applied Mathematics).

# Location Problems Based on Node-Connectivity and Edge-Connectivity between Nodes and Node-Subsets

Hiro Ito[1], Motoyasu Ito[2],
Yuichiro Itatsu[1], Hideyuki Uehara[1], and Mitsuo Yokoyama[1]

[1] Department of Information and Computer Sciences, Toyohashi University of
Technology, Toyohashi, 441-8580, Japan,
{ito@,itatsu@yilab.,uehara@,yokoyama@}tutics.tut.ac.jp.
[2] Semiconductor & Integrated Circuits Group, Hitachi, Ltd.,
ito@ss.iij4u.or.jp.

**Abstract.** Let $G = (V, E)$ be an undirected multi-graph where $V$ and
$E$ are a set of nodes and a set of edges, respectively. Let $k$ and $l$ be fixed nonnegative integers. This paper considers location problems of finding a minimum size of node-subset $S \subseteq V$ such that node-connectivity
between $S$ and $x$ is greater than or equal to $k$ and edge-connectivity
between $S$ and $x$ is greater than or equal to $l$ for every $x \in V$. This problem has important applications for multi-media network control and
design. For a problem of considering only edge-connectivity, i.e., $k = 0$,
an $O(L(|V|, |E|, l)) = O(|E| + |V|^2 + |V|\min\{|E|, l|V|\}\min\{l, |V|\})$
time algorithm was already known, where $L(|V|, |E|, l)$ is a time to find
all $h$-edge-connected components for $h = 1, 2, \ldots, l$. This paper presents
an $O(L(|V|, |E|, l))$ time algorithm for $0 \leq k \leq 2$ and $l \geq 0$. It also
shows that if $k \geq 3$, the problem is NP-hard even for $l = 0$. Moreover, it
shows that if the size of $S$ is regarded as a parameter, the parameterized
problem for $k = 3$ and $l \leq 1$ is FPT (fixed parameter tractable).

## 1 Introduction

Problems for selecting the best location for facilities in a given network for
satisfying a certain property are called location problems[9]. Many studies have
been done for the problems, however, most of these studies treated problems
having objective functions which are measured by sum or the maximum value
of distances between a facility and a node. Recently, some papers treated the
location problems with objective functions measured by edge-connectivity, or
flow-amount and they presented polynomial time algorithms[2,7,8,11,12].

Considering connectivity or flow-amount is very important for applications
to multimedia network control and design. In a multimedia network, some nodes
of the network may have functions of offering several types of services for users.
A user in a node $x$ can use a service $i$ by connecting node $x$ to one of the
nodes that offers the service $i$ in the network. The possible flow-amount and
connectivity between a node and nodes that offers a service directly affects the
maximum data amount of the service which can be used by users in the node and
robustness of the service for network failures. Thus, the service provider must

D.T. Lee and S.-H. Teng (Eds.): ISAAC 2000, LNCS 1969, pp. 338–349, 2000.

determine the best location of nodes that offers the service with consideration about flow-amount and connectivity.

Tamura, et al.[11,12] examined a problem for a given undirected graph, edge capacities, and real numbers $d(x)$, $x \in V$, for finding the minimum size node-subset for locating sources, such that the possible *flow-amount* between the sources and each node $x$ is greater than or equal to $d(x)$. It presented an $O(n^2 \cdot s(n, m))$ time algorithm for the problem, where $n$ and $m$ are the number of nodes and edges, respectively and $s(n, m)$ is the time required to solve the maximum flow problem. For this problem, Ito, et al.[8] presented an $O(np \cdot s(n, m))$ time algorithm, where $p$ is the number of different values of $d(v)$. Recently, Arata, et al.[2] improved the algorithm of Tamura, et al. and attained $O(n \cdot s(n, m))$ running time.

Reference [7] considered a problem for a given undirected graph and an integer $l$, for finding the minimum size node-subset for locating sources, such that the *edge-connectivity* between the sources and each node is greater than or equal to $l$. Although it is well-known that the edge-connectivity between a pair of nodes is equal to the maximum flow-amount between them, hence this problem can be regarded as a special case of the problem treated in References [2,8,11, 12], the paper proposed a faster algorithm for solving this problem. The algorithm runs in $O(L(n, m, l))$ time, where $L(n, m, l)$ is the time required for finding all $h$-edge-connected components for $h = 1, 2, \ldots l$. It was shown that $L(n, m, l) = O(m + n^2 + n \min\{m, ln\} \min\{l, n\})$ by [10].

In this paper, location problems considering node-connectivity and edge-connectivity simultaneously are treated. That is, for a given graph $G$ and fixed integers $k, l \geq 0$, it requires the minimum size node-subset $S \subseteq V$ such that node-connectivity between $S$ and $x$ is greater than or equal to $k$ and edge-connectivity between $S$ and $x$ is greater than or equal to $l$ for every $x \in V$. We call it $(k, l)$-connectivity location problem, or $(k, l)$-CONLOC for short. Although edge-connectivity can be regarded as a special case of maximum flow-amount, node-connectivity can not be expressed by using maximum flow-amount in undirected graphs. Thus this problem is not a subproblem of the problem treated in References [2,8,11,12].

This paper introduces a dual solution of $(k, l)$-CONLOC. By using the primal-dual property, an $O(L(n, m, l))$ time algorithm for $(k, l)$-CONLOC with $k \leq 2$ and an arbitrary $l$ is presented. It finds all optimal solutions in the same time. Moreover, it is shown that $(k, 0)$-CONLOC is NP-hard if $k \geq 3$. Furthermore, it is also shown that if the size of $S$ is regarded as a parameter, the parameterized version for $k = 3$ and $l \leq 1$ has an $O(3^{|S|}n + m)$ time algorithm, i.e., it is FPT (fixed parameter tractable)[3].

The contents of the paper are as follows. Section **2** is for some definitions. A dual solution $(k, l)$-isolated-set and a lower bound are introduced in **3**. In the section, necessary and sufficient conditions for $(2, 0)$- and $(3, 0)$- CONLOC are also shown. By using them, $O(L(n, m, l))$ time algorithm for $(k, l)$-CONLOC with $k \leq 2$ and an arbitrary $l$ is presented in **4**. Results on NP-hardness and FPT are shown in **5**. Conclusion and remaining works are in **6**.

## 2    Definitions

Let $G = (V, E)$ be an undirected multi-graph, where $V$ is a node set and $E$ is an edge set. It may have multiple edges but no self-loop. Denote $n = |V|$ and $m = |E|$. Unless confusion arises, an edge may be denoted by $(x, y)$, where $x, y \in V$ are the end points of the edge. For $x \in V$, $N(x)$ denotes a set of adjacent nodes to $x$, i.e., $N(x) = \{y \in V \mid (x, y) \in E\}$. For a graph $G = (V, E)$ and a node subset $X \subseteq V$, a graph $(X, \{(x, y) \in E \mid x, y \in X\})$ is called an *induced subgraph* of $G$ by $X$.

For a pair of node-subsets $X, Y \subseteq V$, $E(X, Y)$ denotes an edge set $\{(x, y) \in E \mid x \in X, y \in Y\}$. $E(X, V - X)$ is called an *edge-cut* and may be written as $E(X)$ also. For nodes $x, y \in V$, if there is a path which contains $x$ and $y$, then $x$ and $y$ are *connected*. For node-subsets $X, Y \subseteq V$, if there exists no edge-cut $E(W)$ such that $X \subseteq W$, $Y \subseteq V - W$, and $|E(W)| < l$, then we say that $X$ and $Y$ are *l-edge-connected*. The maximum number $l$ such as $X$ and $Y$ are $l$-edge-connected is called *edge-connectivity* between $X$ and $Y$ and is denoted by $\lambda(X, Y)$. Note that if $X \cap Y \neq \emptyset$, $\lambda(X, Y) = \infty$.

If three node-subsets $W, X, Y \subset V$ satisfy that $X \neq \emptyset$, $Y \neq \emptyset$, $W \cap X = W \cap Y = X \cap Y = \emptyset$, $W \cup X \cup Y = V$, and $E(X, Y) = \emptyset$, then $W$ is called a *node-cut*. Further for $X' \subseteq X$ and $Y' \subseteq Y$, we say that $W$ *separates* $X'$ and $Y'$. If a singleton set $\{w\}$ is a node-cut, $w$ is called a *cut-node*. For node-subsets $X, Y \subseteq V$, if there exists no node-cut $W$ such that $|W| < k$ and $W$ separates $X$ and $Y$, then we say that $X$ and $Y$ are *k-node-connected*. The minimum number $k$ such as $X$ and $Y$ are $k$-node-connected is called *node-connectivity* between $X$ and $Y$ and is denoted by $\kappa(X, Y)$. Note that if $X \cap Y \neq \emptyset$ or $E(X, Y) \neq \emptyset$, then $\kappa(X, Y) = \infty$. A singleton set $\{x\}$ may be written as $x$ for notational simplicity. If $\lambda(x, y) \geq l$ (respectively, $\kappa(x, y) \geq k$) for all $x, y \in V$, then the graph is $l$-edge-connected (respectively, $k$-node-connected).

This paper considers the following problem.

$(k, l)$**-connectivity location problem** ($(k, l)$**-CONLOC**)
>   *Input:* $G = (V, E)$,
>   *Output:* $S \subseteq V$,
>   *Objective function:* $|S| \rightarrow \min.$,
>   *Constraint:* $\kappa(S, x) \geq k$ and $\lambda(S, x) \geq l$ for all $x \in V$.

Moreover, the parameterized problem is also considered.

$(k, l)$**-CONLOC (parameterized problem)**
>   *Input:* $G = (V, E)$,
>   *Output:* $S \subseteq V$,
>   *Parameter:* an integer $p$,
>   *Constraint:* $|S| = p$, and $\kappa(S, x) \geq k$ and $\lambda(S, x) \geq l$ for all $x \in V$.

A problem instance of a parameterized problem is expressed as $(x, p) \in \Sigma^* \times \Sigma^*$ where $p$ is called a parameter. If a parameterized problem has an algorithm whose running time is at most $f(p)|x|^c$, where $f$ is an arbitrary function and

$c$ is a constant (independent of $p$), it is called *FPT (fixed parameter tractable)*. Downey and Fellow[3] defined detailed classes in NP-complete by using the idea of parameterized problems: $FPT$, $W[1]$, $W[2]$, ..., $W[SAT]$, $W[P]$. Moreover, they conjectured that each class is a proper subset of the following class. By using their classification, we can say that FPT is the most tractable class in NP-complete problems. For details of them, please see the reference [3].

**$l$-edge- ($k$-node-) connected components and their structure tree**

For treating edge or node connectivity, $k$-node- or $l$-edge- connected components and their structure trees, which are traditional ideas, are very useful. Please see [1], [6], and [10] for 2-node, 3-node, and $l$-edge -connected components, respectively. 3-node-connected components are of three types: *bonds* of the form $(\{x, y\}, \{(x, y), (x, y), (x, y), ...\})$ (edges are at least three), cycles, and 3-node-connected graphs. For $h \geq 1$,

$$\mathcal{C}(h) := \{C \mid C \text{ is an } h\text{-edge-connected component of } G\}.$$

$\mathcal{C}(h)$ for all $h = 1, \ldots, l$ can be constructed in $O(m + n^2 + n \min\{m, \, ln\} \min\{l, \, n\})$ time[10]. "2-node-connected components and the structure tree" and "3-node-connected components and the structure tree" can be obtained in linear time[1, 6]. Let $D$ and $D'$ be 2-node-connected components or 3-node-connected components. If they have at least one common node, then $D$ and $D'$ are *adjacent*. In this paper, a node set of a $k$-node-connected component (respectively, $l$-edge-connected component) may be also called $k$-node-connected component (respectively, $l$-edge-connected component) unless confusion arises.

## 3 A Lower Bound and Some Conditions

First, we present an idea of $(k, l)$-isolated-set, which is a dual solution of $S$ of $(k, l)$-CONLOC. By using the idea, a lower bound of $|S|$ cam be obtained (Theorem 1). It will be show in the next section that the maximum of the dual solution is equal to the minimum of the primal solution if $k \leq 2$ by presenting an algorithm for finding them.

For an $W \subseteq V$ of a graph $G = (V, E)$, the *boundary* of $W$ is defined as

$$B(W) := \{x \in W \mid E(x, \, V - W) \neq \emptyset\}.$$

Let $\{X_1, X_2, \ldots, X_p\}$ be a set of node-subsets such that $X_i \cap X_j = \emptyset$ for $i \neq j$. If "$X_i - B(X_i) \neq \emptyset$ and $B(X_i) < k$" or "$E(X_i) < l$" for each $i \in \{1, \, 2, \, \ldots, \, p\}$, then $\{X_1, X_2, \ldots, X_p\}$ is called a $(k, l)$-*isolated-set*.

**Theorem 1.** *If $S$ is a feasible solution of $(k, l)$-CONLOC, the following inequality holds:*

$$|S| \geq \max\{p \mid \text{ there exists a } (k, l)\text{-isolated-set } \{X_1, \, X_2, \, \ldots, \, X_p\}\}.$$

*Proof:* Assume that $X_i \cap S = \emptyset$ for an $X_i$. $X_i$ satisfies "$X_i - B(X_i) \neq \emptyset$ and $B(X_i) < k$" or "$E(X_i) < l$." If the first case is occured, $\kappa(x, S) < k$ for $x \in X_i - B(X_i)$. If the second case is occured, $\lambda(x, S) < l$ for $x \in X_i$. Thus, $X_i \cap S \neq \emptyset$ for all $X_i$. Moreover, any $X_i$ and $X_j$ are disjoint if $i \neq j$. Therefore, the inequality holds. $\square$

The inequality of Theorem 1 presents a lower bound of $|S|$. From this theorem, we can regard a $(k, l)$-isolated-set is a dual solution of $(k, l)$-CONLOC. The inequality will be used for assuring the optimality of our algorithm for $(2, l)$-CONLOC presented in **4**, i.e., the algorithm finds a primal-dual solution.

From Theorem 1, we can use an approach of finding a maximum $(k, l)$-isolated-set. However, the number of such $X_i$s is exponentially large. We should select some node-subsets necessary to check. For this porpuse, necessary and sufficient conditions for $(0, l)$-CONLOC, $(2, 0)$-CONLOC, and $(3, 0)$-CONLOC, respectively are presented as follows. Before showing them, some notations are introduced.

Here, $l \geq 1$ is an integer and $k = 1, 2, 3$. For an $h$-node-connected component $D$ ($h \leq k$), if $|B(D)| < k$ and $B - B(D) \neq \emptyset$, then $D$ is called a $(k, 0)$-*leaf-component*. For a $C \in \bigcup_{h=1}^{l} \mathcal{C}(h)$, if $|E(C)| < l$, then $C$ is called a $(0, l)$-*leaf-component*. Denote a set of $(0, l)$-leaf-components by $\Gamma_l$ and denote a set of $(k, 0)$-leaf-components by $\Delta_k$.

The next theorem was presented by the authors[7]. (In the original paper, the word "$(0, l)$-leaf-component" is not used, the word is presented in this paper.)

**Theorem A** *For a graph $G = (V, E)$ and a node-subset $S \subseteq V$, $\lambda(S, x) \geq l$ for all $x \in V$ if and only if $C \cap S \neq \emptyset$ for all $(0, l)$-leaf-components $C$.*

This paper also presents the following two conditions.

**Theorem 2.** *Let $G = (V, E)$ be a graph and let $S$ be a subset of $V$. $\kappa(S, x) \geq 2$ for all $x \in V$ if and only if $D \cap S \neq \emptyset$ for all $(2, 0)$-leaf-components $D$.*

**Theorem 3.** *Let $G = (V, E)$ be a graph and let $S$ be a subset of $V$. $\kappa(S, x) \geq 3$ for all $x \in V$ if and only if the following (1) and (2) hold:*

*(1) $D \cap S \neq \emptyset$ for all $(3, 0)$-leaf-components $D$.*
*(2) If there is a node $x$ such that $|N(x)| < 3$, then $(\{x\} \cup N(x)) \cap S \neq \emptyset$.*

For proving Theorems 2 and 3, the following lemma is used.

**Lemma 1.** *For a graph $G = (V, E)$, a node subset $Y \subseteq V$, and an integer $k \in \{1, 2, 3\}$, if $Y - B(Y) \neq \emptyset$ and $|B(Y)| < k$, then the following (1) or (2) holds:*

*(1) There is a $(k, 0)$-leaf-component $D \subseteq Y$ such that $D - B(D) \neq \emptyset$.*
*(2) There is a node $x$ such that $|N(x)| < k$.*

*Proof:* In this proof, we consider only node-connectivity. Thus it is sufficient to treat simple graphs. For multigraphs, the following discussions can be applied by regarding each set of parallel edges as an edge. If $Y$ includes a connected component $D$, then $D$ satisfies the condition (1). Hence we assume that $Y$ doesn't include any connected component in the following part of this proof.

$\langle 1 \rangle$ **Case "$|B(Y)| = 0$":**
  $Y$ includes at least one connected component $D$, then it contradicts to the assumption.

$\langle 2 \rangle$ **Case "$|B(Y)| = 1$":**
  $B(Y)$ is a cut-node of $G$. Thus there exists at least one 2-node-connected component in $Y$. Relations of adjacency between 2-node-connected components can be represented by a structure tree $T^2$, hence, $Y$ includes at least one $(2,0)$-leaf-component $D$. $D$ satisfies the condition of (1).

$\langle 3 \rangle$ **Case "$|B(Y)| = 2$":**
  $B(Y)$ is a node-cut consists of two nodes. There are two cases: $\langle 2.1 \rangle$ each node of $B(Y)$ is a node of a boundary of a 2-node-connected component and $\langle 2.2 \rangle$ otherwise.

  $\langle 2.1 \rangle$ **Case "each node of $B(Y)$ is a node of a boundary of a 2-node-connected component":**
     There are three cases (i), (ii), and (iii) as follows:
     (i) **$Y$ is a 2-node-connected component:**
        In this case, from $Y - B(Y) \neq \emptyset$, $D = Y$ satisfies the condition (1).
     (ii) **There are at least two 2-node-connected components in $Y$ and an induced subgraph of $G$ by $Y$ is connected:**
        In this case, if there is a $(2,0)$-leaf-component in $Y$, then the statement can be proved by using the same discussion used in Case $\langle 2 \rangle$. Hence, we assume that there is no $(2,0)$-leaf-component in $Y$. Thus, for each 2-node-connected component $D$ in $Y$, $|B(D)| = 2$. If there are at least two 2-node-connected components such that each of them includes only one edge and they are adjacent each other (i.e., there is a common boundary node $x$), then $x$ is a node satisfying the condition (2). Otherwise, there exists at least one 2-node-connected component $D$ in $Y$ such that $D$ includes at least two edges. $D$ satisfies the condition (1).
     (iii) **Otherwise, i.e., there are at least two 2-node-connected components in $Y$ and an induced subgraph of $G$ by $Y$ is disconnected:**
        By using the same discussion used in Cases $\langle 1 \rangle$ or $\langle 2 \rangle$, there is a $(2,0)$-leaf-component $D$ in $Y$. $D$ satisfies the condition (1).

  $\langle 2.2 \rangle$ **Otherwise, i.e., at least one node in $B(Y)$ is not contained in a boundary of 2-node-connected components:**
     In this case, the both node in $B(Y)$ are not contained in boundaries of 2-node-connected components. If there is a 2-node-connected component contained in $Y$, then there must be a $(2,0)$-leaf-component in $Y$ and the statement can be proved similarly to Cases $\langle 1 \rangle$ or $\langle 2 \rangle$. Thus, we assume

that there is no 2-node-connected component included in $Y$. Hence, there is a 2-node-connected component $D$ such that $Y \subset D$. Each node in $B(Y)$ is included in a boundary of 3-node-connected components. There are the following two cases:

(i) $B(Y) \subset C_p$ **for a cycle-type 3-node-connected component** $C_p$:
If there is no 3-node-connected component that is adjacent to $C_p$ in $Y$, then there is a node $x$ in $C_p - B(C_p)$ such that the degree of $x$ is equal to two (the condition (2) is satisfied). Otherwise, there is a $(3,0)$-leaf-component $D$ in $Y$. Clearly $|B(D)| = 2$. A $(3,0)$-leaf-component never be a bond-graph, thus, $D - B(D) \neq \emptyset$.

(ii) **Otherwise:**
There is a $(3,0)$-leaf-component $D$ in $Y$. $D$ satisfies the condition (1). □

*Proof of Theorems 2 and 3*: The necessity is clear. The sufficiency is guaranteed by Lemma 1. □

# 4  An Algorithm for $(k, l)$-CONLOC with $k \leq 2$

In this section, we present an algorithm for $(2, l)$-CONLOC. From Theorem 1, we can use an approach of finding a maximum $(2, l)$-isolated-set. For this purpose, it is important to find minimal elements of $\Gamma_l \cup \Delta_2$.

Let $\Gamma(2, l)$ be a set of $C \in \Gamma_l$ such that $Y$ is not a proper subset of $C$ for all $Y \in \Gamma_l \cap \Delta_2$. Let $\Delta(2, l)$ be a set of $D \in \Delta_2$ such that $Y$ is not a proper subset of $D$ for all $Y \in \Gamma_l \cap \Delta_2$. There may be a common element of $\Gamma(2, l)$ and $\Delta(2, l)$, hence, we define that $\Gamma'(2, l) := \Gamma(2, l) - \Delta(2, l)$.

In $\Gamma(2, l)$, any two elements are disjoint. However, in $\Delta(2, l)$, there may be $D, D' \in \Delta(2, l)$ such that $B(D) = B(D')(= \{z\})$. Denote a set of nodes $z$ such that $B(D) = \{z\}$ for at least two $D \in \Delta(2, l)$ by $Z$. $\Delta'(2, l) := \{D \in \Delta(2, l) \mid z \notin Z \ (B(D) = \{z\})\}$. We express as follows:

$$\Gamma'(2, l) = \{C_1, \ldots, C_c\}, \ \Delta'(2, l) = \{D_1, \ldots, D_d\}, \ Z = \{z_1, \ldots, z_h\}.$$

Now, by using $\Gamma'(2, l)$, $\Delta'(2, l)$, and $Z$, we construct a $(2, l)$-isolated-set $\{X_1, X_2, \ldots, X_p\}$ that achieves the maximum $p(= c + d + h)$ as follows.

$$X_i = C_i, \text{ for } i = 1, 2, \ldots, c,$$
$$X_i = D_{i-c}, \text{ for } i = c+1, c+2, \ldots, c+d,$$
$$X_i = \bigcup \{D \in \Delta(2, l) \mid B(D) = \{z_{i-c-d}\}\}, \text{ for } i = c+d+1, \ldots, c+d+h. \text{ (1)}$$

**Lemma 2.** $\{X_1, X_2, \ldots, X_p\}$ of (1) is a $(2, l)$-isolated-set.

We will use the next lemma presented in Reference [7].

**Lemma B**    *For a graph $G = (V, E)$ and a node-subset $W \subseteq V$, if $E(W) < l$, then there is a $(0, l)$-leaf-component $C$ contained in $W$.*

*Proof of Lemma 2:* "$X_i - B(X_i) \neq \emptyset$ and $B(X_i) < 2$" or "$E(X_i) < l$" for each $1 \leq i \leq c+d+h$ is clear from the definition. Then we prove that $X_i$ and $X_j$ are disjoint for $1 \leq i < j \leq c+d+h$. If $1 \leq i < j \leq c$ or $c+1 \leq i < j \leq c+d+h$, then $X_i$ and $X_j$ are clearly disjoint. Thus it remains that $1 \leq i \leq c < j \leq c + d + h$. Assume that there are $X_i$ and $X_j$ such that $1 \leq i \leq c < j \leq c + d + h$ and $X_i \cap X_j \neq \emptyset$. From the definition of $\Gamma(2, l)$ and $\Delta(2, l)$, $X_i$ is not a subset of $X_j$ and $X_j$ is not a subset of $X_i$. Hence, $X_i - X_j \neq \emptyset$ and $X_j - X_i \neq \emptyset$. Let $B(X_j) = \{z\}$.

- Assume that $z \notin X_i \cap X_j$. $|E(X_i \cap X_j)| \leq |E(X_i)| < k$, hence from Lemma B, there is a $(2, l)$-leaf-component $C \subseteq X_i \cap X_j \subset X_i$, i.e., $X_i \notin \Gamma(2, l)$. It is a contradiction.
- Assume that $z \in X_i \cap X_j$. $|E(X_j - X_i)| \leq |E(X_i)| < k$, hence from Lemma B, there is a $(2, l)$-leaf-component $C \subseteq X_j - X_i \subset X_j$, i.e., $X_j \notin \Delta(2, l)$. It is a contradiction. $\square$

From Theorem 1 and Lemma 2, $|S| \geq c + d + h$ if $S$ is a feasible solution of $(2, l)$-CONLOC. Moreover, we show that a feasible solution $S$ achieving the lower bound can be constructed from the $(2, l)$-isolated-set of (1) by using the following algorithm.

**Procedure** $(2, l)$-FIND
**begin**
$S = \emptyset$.
For each $X_i$ $(i = 1, 2, \ldots, c+d)$, select an arbitrary $x \in X_i$ and $S := S \cup \{x\}$.
For each $X_i$ $(i = c+d+1, c+d+2, \ldots, c+d+h)$, $S := S \cup \{z_{i-c-d}\}$.
**end.**

**Lemma 3.** *An $S$ constructed by $(k, l)$-FIND is a feasible solution of $(2, l)$-CONLOC.*

*Proof:* Assume that $S$ is not feasible. From Theorems A and 2, there is a $C \in \Gamma_l$ such that $S \cap C = \emptyset$ or there is a $D \in \Delta_k$ such that $S \cap D = \emptyset$. From the minimality of $\Gamma(2, l)$ and $\Delta(2, l)$, there must be a $C \in \Gamma(2, l)$ such that $S \cap C = \emptyset$ or a $D \in \Delta(2, l)$ such that $S \cap D = \emptyset$.

(1) Assume that there is a $C \in \Gamma(2, l)$ such that $S \cap C = \emptyset$. If $C \in \Gamma'(2, l)$, then $C$ is equal to an $X_i$, $i = 1, 2, \ldots, c$, hence a node is selected from $C$ to be in $S$. If $C \notin \Gamma'(2, l)$, i.e., $C \in \Delta(2, l)$, thus this case is considered in (2).
(2) Assume that there is a $D \in \Delta(2, l)$ such that $S \cap D = \emptyset$. If $D \in \Delta'(2, l)$, then $D$ is equal to an $X_i$, $i = c + 1, c + 2, \ldots, c + d$, hence a node is selected from $D$ to be in $S$. If $D \notin \Delta'(2, l)$, then $z \in B(D)$ is in $Z$, thus $D \cap S \neq \emptyset$. $\square$

Lemmas 2 and 3 means that maximum value of the dual solution $p$ is equal to the minimum value of the primal solution $|S|$. Therefore, we establish the next.

**Theorem 4.** $(k, l)$-*CONLOC can be solved in* $O(L(n, m, l))$ *time if* $k \leq 2$, *where* $L(n, m, l)$ *is the time required for finding all* $h$-*edge-connected components for* $h = 1, 2, \ldots l$.

*Proof:* If $k \leq 1$ and $l \geq 1$, the problem is equivalent to $(0, l)$-CONLOC and can be solved in $O(L(n, m, l))$ time[7]. For $k = 2$, $S$ constructed by procedure $(2, l)$-FIND is an optimal solution from Theorem 1 and Lemmas 2 and 3. Finding all $h$-edge-connected components for $h = 1, 2, \ldots l$ requires $O(L(n, m, l))$ time. All 2-node-connected components can be found in linear-time[1]. Other parts of the algorithm uses $O(n + m)$ time. Therefore, it requires $O(L(n, m, l))$ time. □

From Theorem 4 and Reference [10], the following corollary can be directly obtained.

**Corollary 1.** $(k, l)$-*CONLOC can be solved in* $O(m + n^2 + n \min\{m, kn\} \min\{k, k + n\})$ *time if* $k \leq 2$. *Moreover, it can be solved in linear time if* $k \leq 2$ *and* $l \leq 3$.

From the discussions of this section, a more interesting property can be shown.

**Corollary 2.** $S = \{x_1, x_2, \ldots, x_p\}$ *is an optimal solution if and only if* $x_i \in C_i(= X_i)$ *for* $1 \leq i \leq c$, $x_i \in D_{i-c}(= X_i)$ *for* $c + 1 \leq i \leq c + d$, *and* $x_i = z_{i-c-d}$ *for* $c + d + 1 \leq i \leq c + d + h$.

*Proof:* If $S$ is feasible, a node must be selected from each $X_i$. Hence, if a $z_i$, $1 \leq i \leq h$ is not selected, there is at least one $D \in \Delta(2, l)$ such that $D \cap S = \emptyset$. It is a contradiction. □

From Corollary 2, we can obtain all optimal solutions in the same time by out putting $\Gamma'(2, l)$, $\Delta'(2, l)$, and $Z$. This property is very convenient for real network design because other restrictions, for example, flow-amount, distance, and cost, can be taken into account for determining the best location from the many candidates of solution.

## 5    NP-Hardness of $(k,0)$-CONLOC with $k \geq 3$

**Theorem 5.** $(k, l)$-*CONLOC is NP-hard for each* $k \geq 3$ *and* $l \geq 0$. *Furthermore, (3,0)-CONLOC (parameterized problem) can be solved in* $O(3^p n + m)$ *time, i.e., it is FPT.*

*Proof:* First, we will prove the NP-hardness of (3,0)-CONLOC. For other $k$ and $l$, the proof is easily extended. We reduce the vertex cover problem (VC)[4], which is a well-known NP-hard problem, to (3,0)-CONLOC.

**Vertex cover problem (VC)**
 *Input:* $G = (V, E)$, *Output:* $U \subseteq V$, *Objective function:* $|U| \to$ min .,
 *Constraint:* $\{x, y\} \cap U \neq \emptyset$ for all $(x, y) \in E$.

 Let $G_0 = (V_0, E_0)$ be an instance of VC. We construct an instance $G = (V, E)$ of (3,0)-CONLOC as follows. An example is shown in Figure 1.

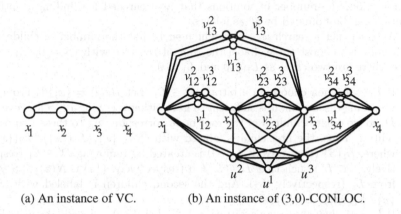

(a) An instance of VC.          (b) An instance of (3,0)-CONLOC.

**Fig. 1.** An example of reductions from VC to (3,0)-CONLOC.

$$V = V_0 \cup V' \cup V'',$$
$$V' = \{u^1,\ u^2,\ u^3\},\ V'' = \{v_{ij}^1,\ v_{ij}^2,\ v_{ij}^3 \mid (x_i,\ x_j) \in E_0\},$$
$$E = E' \cup E'' \cup E''',$$
$$E' = \{(x_i,\ v_{ij}^1),\ (x_i,\ v_{ij}^2),\ (x_i,\ v_{ij}^3),\ (x_j,\ v_{ij}^1),\ (x_j,\ v_{ij}^2),\ (x_j,\ v_{ij}^3),$$
$$(v_{ij}^1,\ v_{ij}^2),\ (v_{ij}^2,\ v_{ij}^3),\ (v_{ij}^3,\ v_{ij}^1) \mid (x_i,\ x_j) \in E_0\},$$
$$E'' = \{(x_i,\ u^1),\ (x_i,\ u^2),\ (x_i,\ u^3) \mid x_i \in V_0\},$$
$$E''' = \{(u^1,\ u^2),\ (u^2,\ u^3),\ (u^3,\ u^1)\},$$

$G$ is 2-node-connected. There are $|E_0| + 1$ 3-node-connected components and each 3-node-connected component is denoted by $D_{ij}$ or $D_0$, where, $D_{ij}$ consists of $\{x_i,\ x_j,\ v_{ij}^1,\ v_{ij}^2,\ v_{ij}^3\}$ and $D_0$ consists of $V_0 \cup \{u^1,\ u^2,\ u^3\}$.
 The equivalence of the two instances $G_0$ and $G$ is clear. (Note that it is sufficient to search a solution $S$ such that $S \subseteq V_0$ for solving $G$.) Thus, (3, 0)-CONLOC is NP-hard.

 Next, we will show an $O(3^p n + m)$ time algorithm for solving (3,0)-CONLOC (parameterized problem). (Note that (3,0)-CONLOC is equal to (3,1)-CON-LOC.) First, make a list $L_1$ of (3, 0)-leaf-components and a list $L_2$ of nodes

$z$ such that $|N(z)| < 3$. If $S$ is a feasible solution, a node $x \in D \in L_1$ must be chosen for a member of $S$. Moreover, for obtaining an optimal solution, it is sufficient to choose $x$ from $B(D)$. Because if there is a node $x \in (D - B(D)) \cap S$ for a $D \in L_1$ and a feasible solution $S$, $S' = (S - \{x\}) \cup \{y\}$ $(y \in B(D))$ is also a feasible solution. Thus, it is sufficient to select a node from two candidates (nodes in $B(D)$) for each $D \in L_1$ and to select a node from three candidates ($z$ and the two adjacent nodes) from each $z \in L_2$. Hence, by using a simple enumeration, the number of solutions that are searched for finding a optimal solution can be bounded by $3^p$ as follows.

We construct a search tree of height $p$ such that the number of children of each node is at most three. Label the root of the tree with $(S = \emptyset, L_1, L_2)$. Here, there are two cases as $L_1 \neq \emptyset$ and $L_1 = \emptyset$.

(1) If $L_1 \neq \emptyset$, then choose an arbitrary $D \in L_1$. Let $B(D) = \{x, y\}$. From the preceding discussion, it is sufficient to have either $x \in S$ or $y \in S$ for covering $D$, so we create children of the root node corresponding to these two possibilities. Thus, the first child is labeled with $(S = \{x\}, L_1(\{x\}), L_2(\{x\}))$, where, $L_1(S)$ (respectively, $L_2(S)$) is created by removing $D' \in L_1$ (respectively, $z \in L_2$) such that $D' \cap S \neq \emptyset$ (respectively, $(\{z\} \cup N(z)) \cap S \neq \emptyset$) from $L_1$ (respectively, $L_2$). And the second children is labeled with $(S = \{y\}, L_1(\{y\}), L_2(\{y\}))$.

(2) If $L_1 = \emptyset$, then choose an arbitrary $z \in L_2$. Let $N(z) = \{x, y\}$. We must have $x \in S$, $y \in S$, or $z \in S$, so we create three children of the root. The first, the second, and the third children are labeled with $(S = \{x\}, L_1(\{x\}), L_2(\{x\}))$, $(S = \{y\}, L_1(\{y\}), L_2(\{y\}))$, and $(S = \{z\}, L_1(\{z\}), L_2(\{z\}))$, respectively.

$S$ represents a halfway of a feasible solution, and two lists represent what remains to cover. In general, for a node (of the tree) labeled with $(S, L_1(S), L_2(S))$. We choose $D \in L_1(S)$ or $z \in L_2(S)$ and create two or three children labeled, respectively, $(S \cup \{x\}, L_1(S \cup \{x\}), L_2(S \cup \{x\}))$, $(S \cup \{y\}, L_1(S \cup \{y\}), L_2(S \cup \{y\}))$, or $(S \cup \{z\}, L_1(S \cup \{z\}), L_2(S \cup \{z\}))$. If we create a node at height at most $p$ in the tree that is labeled with $(S, \emptyset, \emptyset)$, then we can obtain a feasible solution from $S$. (Note that if $|S| = p$, then $S$ is a feasible solution. If $|S| < p$, it is enough to add arbitrary $p - |S|$ nodes to $S$.) There is no need to explore the tree beyond height $p$.

The number of nodes of the tree is at most $3^{p+1}$. The procedure executed in each node of the tree is $O(n)$. Then the computation time is $O(3^p n + m)$. □

## 6    Conclusion and Remaining Works

This paper treats location problems of finding a minimum size node-subset $S$ such that $\kappa(S, x) \geq k$ and $\lambda(S, x) \geq l$ for all $x \in V$, called $(k, l)$-CONLOC. First, it shows dual solutions of $(k, l)$-CONLOC, called $(k, l)$-isolated-set. By using the primal-dual property, $O(L(n, m, l))$ time algorithm for solving $(k, l)$-CONLOC with $0 \leq k \leq 2$ and $l \geq 0$ is obtained. The algorithm finds all optimal solutions in the same time. Moreover, it shows that it is NP-hard for each $k \geq 3$ and $l \geq 0$, and the parameterized problem is FPT if $k = 3$ and $l \leq 1$ ($|S|$ is the parameter) by showing an $O(3^{|S|}n + m)$ time algorithm.

The remaining problems are as follows. In a viewpoint of whether NP-hard or P, $(k, l)$-CONLOC have been made clear completely. However, if the parameterized problem is considered, "$k = 3$ and $l \geq 2$" and "$k \geq 4$" are remaining. If $k$ is fixed, they may be FPT. Especially, the case of "$k = 3$ and $l \geq 2$" seems to be solved by mixing Theorems A and 3.

In this paper, only undirected graphs are treated, however, directed graphs are also important. In Reference [5] similar problems based on directed graphs are defined and it is shown that the problem can be solved in polynomial time if $k \leq 1$ and $l \leq 3$. If $k \geq 3$, the problem is obviously NP-hard from the results of this paper. For $k = 2$ or $l \geq 4$, it remains for the future works.

**Acknowledgments.** We would like to express our appreciation to Professor Nagamochi Hiroshi of Toyohashi University of Technology for his valuable comments.

# References

1. Aho, A. V., Hopcroft, J. E., and Ullman, J. D., *The Design and Analysis of Computer Algorithms*, Addison-Wesley (1974).
2. Arata, K., Iwata, S., Makino, K., and Fujishige, S., Locating sources to meet flow demands in undirected networks, manuscript (2000).
3. Downey, R. G. and Fellows, M. R., *Parameterized Complexity*, Springer (1997).
4. Garey, M. R. and Johnson, D. S., *Computers and Intractability: a Guide to the Theory of NP-Completeness*, Freeman (1979).
5. Honami, S., Ito, H., Uehara, H., and Yokoyama, M., An algorithm for finding a node-subset having high connectivity from other nodes, *IPSJ SIG Notes*, AL-66, **99**, 8, pp. 9–16 (1999). (in Japanese)
6. Hopcroft, J. E. and Tarjan, R. E., Dividing a graph into triconnected components, *SIAM J. Comput.*, **2**, pp. 135–158 (1973).
7. Ito, H. and Yokoyama, M., Edge connectivity between nodes and node-subsets, *Networks*, **31**, pp. 157–164 (1998).
8. Ito, H., Uehara H., and Yokoyama, M., A faster and flexible algorithm for a location problem on undirected flow networks, *IEICE Trans.*, **E83-A**, 4, pp. 704–712 (2000).
9. Labbe, M., Peeters, D., and Thisse, J.-F., Location on networks, In M. O. Ball et al. (eds.), *Handbooks in OR & MS*, **8**, North-Holland, pp. 551–624 (1995).
10. Nagamochi, H. and Watanabe, T., Computing $k$-edge-connected components in multigraphs, IEICE Trans., **E76-A**, pp. 513–517 (1993).
11. Tamura, H., Sengoku, M., Shinoda, S., and Abe, T., Location problems on undirected flow networks, *IEICE Trans.*, **E73**, pp. 1989–1993 (1990).
12. Tamura, H., Sugawara, H., Sengoku, M., and Shinoda, S., Plural cover problem on undirected flow networks, *IEICE Trans. A*, **J81-A**, pp. 863–869 (1998). (in Japanese)

# An Intuitive and Effective New Representation for Interconnection Network Structures*

Jianer Chen[1]**, Lihua Liu[1], Weijia Jia[2], and Songqiao Chen[1]

[1] College of Information Engineering, Central-South University,
ChangSha, Hunan 410083, P. R. China
[2] Department of Computer Science, City University of Hong Kong,
Hong Kong SAR, P. R. China

**Abstract.** Based on the classical voltage graph theory, we develop a new representation scheme for interconnection network structures. We show that all popular interconnection networks have very simple and intuitive representations under the new scheme. The new representation scheme offers powerful tools for the study of network routing and network emulation. As examples, we present simple constructions for optimal network emulations from cube-connected cycles networks to butterfly networks, and from butterfly networks to hypercube networks.

## 1 Introduction

Many interconnection network topologies have been proposed in the study of parallel computers [14]. An important theoretic interest is to study the relations between different interconnection networks, and to compare the capability and performance of the network structures. A popular technique to investigate and compare the relations and capability of different network structures is *network emulation*, which studies methods of embedding one network $G$ (the guest network) into another network $H$ (the host network). Embedding the network $G$ into the network $H$ shows that the computation of $G$ can be effectively emulated by $H$. This, in particular, yields a canonical translation of any programs written for the network $G$ into the onces suitable for the network $H$.

A general difficulty in network emulations is that the underlying networks are very large. Thus, the network structures are not intuitive and cannot be easily realized. Most constructions of network emulations are based on networks' formal definitions and on case by case combination analysis [14]. In general the analysis is very model-oriented and cannot be applied to other network structures. New techniques based on algebraic methods have been proposed [1,2].

In this paper, we respond to the approach suggested in [1,2], and propose a new approach that is a combination of algebraic methods and combinatorial methods. We develop a new representation scheme for interconnection network structures based on the classical voltage graph theory [8]. We demonstrate

---

* This work is supported by the China National Natural Science Foundation for Distinguished Young Scholars and by the Changjiang Scholar Reward Project.
** Corresponding author. Email: `jianer@mail.csut.edu.cn` or `chen@cs.tamu.edu`.

D.T. Lee and S.-H. Teng (Eds.): ISAAC 2000, LNCS 1969, pp. 350–361, 2000.

that the voltage graph theory is a powerful tool for representing well-known interconnection networks and for implementing optimal network emulation algorithms. In particular, we show that most popular interconnection network structures, such as the hypercube networks, the butterfly networks, and the cube-connected cycles networks, have very neat and simple structures under the new representation scheme. Moreover, our new representation scheme makes certain optimal network emulations become very intuitive and simple. We demonstrate optimal network emulations from the cube-connected cycles networks to the butterfly networks and from the butterfly networks to the hypercube networks based on our new representations and new techniques.

We briefly review the fundamentals of voltage graph theory. Let $G$ be an undirected graph and let $A$ be a finite group. For each edge $[u, v]$ in $G$, we pick a direction, say from $u$ to $v$, and assign a group element $a_{[u,v]}$ in $A$ to $[u, v]$ (so in the direction from $v$ to $u$, the group element assigned to the edge is the inverse of $a_{[u,v]}$ in $A$). Call this assignment a *voltage assignment* $\Psi$. The triple $(G, A, \Psi)$ is called a *voltage graph*, the group $A$ is called the *voltage group*, and the graph $G$ is called the *base graph*.

Given a voltage graph $(G, A, \Psi)$, where $G = (V, E)$, the *derived graph* of $(G, A, \Psi)$, denoted $G^{\Psi}$, has vertex set $V \times A$. A vertex of $G^{\Psi}$ will be given as $v_a$, where $v \in V$ and $a \in A$. An edge $[u, v]$ in $G$ assigned with voltage $b$ in the direction from $u$ to $v$ corresponds to $|A|$ edges in the derived graph $G^{\Psi}$ of form $[u_a, v_{a*b}]$, for each $a \in A$, where $*$ is the group operator for the group $A$.

In the current paper, the voltage group $A$ is always a $k$-dimensional binary vector space $Z_2^k$ under the bitwise addition operation mod 2 (i.e., $0*0 = 1*1 = 0$, and $0 * 1 = 1 * 0 = 1$). Since $\alpha = \alpha^{-1}$ for every element $\alpha$ in $Z_2^k$, the voltage assignment to each edge does not depend on the direction of the edge.

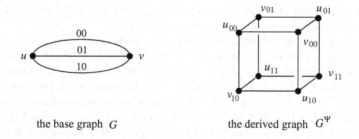

the base graph $G$        the derived graph $G^{\Psi}$

**Fig. 1.** A simple voltage graph and its derived graph

Figure 1 shows an example. Here the base graph $G$ has two vertices $u$ and $v$ connected by three multiple edges. The voltage group is the 2-dimensional binary vector space $Z_2^2$ consisting of four elements $\{00, 01, 10, 11\}$. The voltage assignment $\Psi$ is shown on the edges of the base graph $G$. Since the base graph $G$ has 2 vertices and 3 edges, and the voltage group $A$ has 4 elements, the derived graph $G^{\Psi}$ has $2 \times 4 = 8$ vertices and $3 \times 4 = 12$ edges. As shown in Figure 1, the derived graph $G^{\Psi}$ is actually the 3-dimensional hypercube.

## 2    Interconnection Networks by Voltage Graphs

A number of interconnection network topologies have been suggested in the literature. We review a few popular ones here.

An *n-dimensional hypercube network* $H_n$ is a graph of $2^n$ vertices. Each vertex is labeled by a different binary string of length $n$. A vertex $\alpha$ in $H_n$ is adjacent to those vertices whose label has exactly one bit different from $\alpha$. Two vertices $\alpha$ and $\beta$ in $H_n$ differing only by the $i$th bit (the bit positions are numbered from right to left) are said to be *bit-i adjacent*, and the edge $[\alpha, \beta]$ is called a *bit-i edge*. For recent research on hypercube networks, the reader is referred to [12] (see also [10,15]). Figure 2(A) shows a 3-dimensional hypercube network $H_3$.

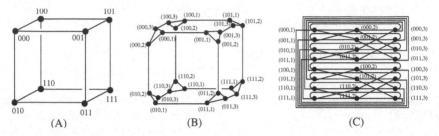

**Fig. 2.** (A) Hypercube $H_3$; (B) Cube-connected cycles $CCC_3$; (C) Butterfly $F_3$

An *n-dimensional cube-connected cycles network* $CCC_n$ is a graph of $n2^n$ vertices. Each vertex is labeled by a pair $(\alpha, k)$, where $\alpha$ is a binary string of length $n$ and $k$ is an integer satisfying $1 \leq k \leq n$. Each vertex $(\alpha, k)$ in $CCC_n$ is adjacent to three vertices $(\alpha, k - 1)$, $(\alpha, k + 1)$, and $(\alpha', k)$, where $\alpha$ and $\alpha'$ differ by only the $k$th bit, and we have let $0 = n$ and $n + 1 = 1$. Some recent work on cube-connected cycles networks is reported in [7,11]. Figure 2(B) shows a 3-dimensional cube-connected cycles network $CCC_3$.

An *n-dimensional butterfly network* $F_n$ is a graph of $n2^n$ vertices. Each vertex is labeled by a pair $(\alpha, k)$, where $\alpha$ is a binary string of length $n$ and $k$ is an integer satisfying $1 \leq k \leq n$. Each vertex $(\alpha, k)$ in $F_n$ is adjacent to four vertices $(\alpha, k - 1)$, $(\alpha, k + 1)$, $(\alpha', k - 1)$, and $(\alpha'', k + 1)$, where $\alpha'$ is the binary string that differs from $\alpha$ by the $(k - 1)$st bit, while $\alpha''$ is the binary string that differs from $\alpha$ by the $k$th bit. Here we have let $0 = n$ and $n + 1 = 1$. See [3,4,5] for some recent development in butterfly networks. Figure 2(C) shows a 3-dimensional butterfly network $F_3$.

We present a few voltage graphs whose derived graphs are the hypercube networks, the butterfly networks, and the cube-connected cycles networks, respectively.

**Definition 1.** A *dipole* $D_n$ *of n edges* is a graph with two vertices $u$ and $v$ connected by $n$ multiple edges. Define the voltage graph $(D_n, Z_2^{n-1}, \Psi_h)$, where the voltage assignment $\Psi_h$ assigns one edge of $D_n$ with $0^{n-1}$, and each of the other $n - 1$ edges of $D_n$ with a different element of form $0^{n-i-2}10^i$ in $Z_2^{n-1}$, for $0 \leq i \leq n - 2$. Figure 3(A) gives an illustration for $n = 4$.

Define the *parity function* $p(\cdot)$ as follows: for a binary string $\alpha$, $p(\alpha) = 0$ if the number of 1's in $\alpha$ is even, and $p(\alpha) = 1$ otherwise. Let $\bar{p}$ be the negation of $p$, i.e., for any binary string $\alpha$, $\bar{p}(\alpha) = p(\alpha) + 1 \bmod 2$. For two binary strings $\alpha$ and $\beta$, let $\alpha \cdot \beta$ be the concatenation of $\alpha$ and $\beta$.

**Theorem 1.** *The derived graph of the voltage graph $(D_n, Z_2^{n-1}, \Psi_h)$ is the $n$-dimensional hypercube network $H_n$.*

Intuitively, each edge in the base graph $D_n$ corresponds to an $i$, $1 \leq i \leq n$, and represents the set of all bit-$i$ edges in the hypercube $H_n$, and the vertices $u$ and $v$ in $D_n$ represent the bi-partition of the vertices in $H_n$ in terms of the parity value of their labels (compare Figure 1 and Figure 2(A) for illustration).

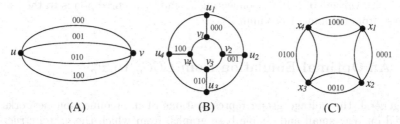

(A)                    (B)                    (C)

**Fig. 3.** Voltage graphs for (A) hypercube $H_4$; (B) cube-connected cycles $CCC_4$ (unlabeled edges assigned "000"); (C) butterfly $F_4$ (unlabeled edges assigned "0000")

Now we consider the voltage graph representations for the butterfly networks and for the cube-connected cycles networks.

**Definition 2.** A *circular ladder* $CL_n$ consists of two $n$-cycles: $\{u_1, \ldots, u_n\}$ and $\{v_1, \ldots, v_n\}$ plus $n$ "rung-edges" $[u_i, v_i]$, $i = 1, \ldots, n$. Define the voltage graph $(CL_n, Z_2^{n-1}, \Psi_c)$ such that the edge $[u_1, v_1]$ is assigned by $0^{n-1}$, the edge $[u_i, v_i]$ is assigned by $0^{n-i}10^{i-2}$, for $2 \leq i \leq n$, and all other edges are assigned $0^{n-1}$. See Figure 3(B) for illustration.

**Definition 3.** A *cobblestone circle* $CC_n$ consists of $n$ vertices $x_1, \ldots, x_n$ such that the vertices $x_i$ and $x_{i+1}$ are connected by two multiple edges, for $i = 1, \ldots, n$ (we have taken $x_{n+1} = x_1$). A voltage graph $(CC_n, Z_2^n, \Psi_b)$ is defined such that for $i = 1, \ldots, n$, one of the edges connecting $x_i$ and $x_{i+1}$ is assigned $0^{n-i}10^{i-1}$, and the other edge connecting $x_i$ and $x_{i+1}$ is assigned $0^n$. See Figure 3(C) for illustration.

**Theorem 2.** *The derived graph of the voltage graph $(CL_n, Z_2^{n-1}, \Psi_c)$ is the $n$-dimensional cube-connected cycles network $CCC_n$, and the derived graph of the voltage graph $(CC_n, Z_2^n, \Psi_b)$ is the $n$-dimensional butterfly network $F_n$.*

We give an intuitive explanation on Theorem 2. It is known that the $n$-dimensional cube-connected cycles network $CCC_n$ can be obtained from the $n$-dimensional hypercube network $H_n$ by replacing each vertex in $H_n$ by a cycle of $n$ vertices. This construction is also reflected in the voltage graph constructions $(D_n, Z_2^{n-1}, \Psi_h)$ for $H_n$ and $(CL_n, Z_2^{n-1}, \Psi_c)$ for $CCC_n$: the vertices $u$ and $v$ in $D_n$ are replaced by the $n$-cycles $\{u_1, \ldots, u_n\}$ and $\{v_1, \ldots, v_n\}$ in $CL_n$, respectively. Note that the edges on these cycles are assigned "zero" voltage $0^{n-1}$ thus the cycles remain cycles in the derived graph, corresponding to the cycles in $CCC_n$ replacing the vertices in $H_n$. Also the $n$ rung-edges in $CL_n$ in $(CL_n, Z_2^{n-1}, \Psi_c)$ have the same voltage assignments as the $n$ edges in $D_n$ in $(D_n, Z_2^{n-1}, \Psi_h)$ so they correspond to "dimension edges" in $CCC_n$.

In the voltage graph $(CC_n, Z_2^n, \Psi_b)$, each vertex $x_i$ in $CC_n$ corresponds to a column of $2^n$ vertices $(\beta, i)$, where $\beta \in Z_2^n$, in the butterfly network $F_n$, and the edge with voltage $0^{n-i}10^{i-1}$ connecting $x_i$ and $x_{i+1}$ corresponds to the "shuffle edges" from column $i$ to column $i+1$.

## 3   An Optimal Emulation from $CCC_n$ to $F_n$

In general, the voltage graph representations of interconnection networks are based on very small and simple base graphs, from which the graph structures of the corresponding large networks can be easily realized and analyzed. This provides us with a powerful technique in network emulation constructions. In this section, we use this technique to construct an optimal emulation from the cube-connected cycles network $CCC_n$ to the butterfly network $F_n$.

According to Theorem 2, each vertex in the $n$-dimensional cube-connected cycles network $CCC_n$ can be written as either $(u_i)_\alpha$ or $(v_i)_\alpha$, where $1 \le i \le n$ and $\alpha \in Z_2^{n-1}$, and each vertex in the $n$-dimensional butterfly network $F_n$ can be written as $(x_i)_\beta$, where $1 \le i \le n$ and $\beta \in Z_2^n$. Consider the following mapping $\mathcal{M}$ from $CCC_n$ to $F_n$: for $1 \le i \le n$ and $\alpha \in Z_2^{n-1}$,

$$\mathcal{M}((u_i)_\alpha) = (x_i)_{\alpha \cdot p(\alpha)} \quad \text{and} \quad \mathcal{M}((v_i)_\alpha) = (x_{i+1})_{\alpha \cdot \bar{p}(\alpha)}$$

We first show that the mapping $\mathcal{M}$ maps different vertices in $CCC_n$ to different vertices in $F_n$. Note that a $u$-vertex $(u_i)_\alpha$ in $CCC_n$ is mapped to the vertex $(x_i)_{\alpha \cdot p(\alpha)}$ in $F_n$ whose subscript $\alpha \cdot p(\alpha)$ is an element in $Z_2^n$ containing an even number of 1's, while a $v$-vertex $(v_i)_\alpha$ in $CCC_n$ is mapped to the vertex $(x_{i+1})_{\alpha \cdot \bar{p}(\alpha)}$ in $F_n$ whose subscript $\alpha \cdot \bar{p}(\alpha)$ is an element in $Z_2^n$ containing an odd number of 1's. Thus, no $u$-vertex and $v$-vertex in $CCC_n$ will be mapped by $\mathcal{M}$ to the same vertex in $F_n$.

Two $u$-vertices $(u_i)_\alpha$ and $(u_j)_\beta$ in $CCC_n$ are mapped by $\mathcal{M}$ to the vertices $(x_i)_{\alpha \cdot p(\alpha)}$ and $(x_j)_{\beta \cdot p(\beta)}$, which are two different vertices in $F_n$ in case either $i \ne j$ or $\alpha \ne \beta$ (or both). Similarly, two different $v$-vertices in $CCC_n$ are mapped to two different vertices in $F_n$. Summarizing all these, we conclude that no two vertices in $CCC_n$ are mapped by $\mathcal{M}$ to the same vertex in $F_n$.

Now we show that the mapping $\mathcal{M}$ also preserves the adjacency relation. Each of the edges in $CCC_n$ is in one of the following forms:

$$[(u_i)_\alpha, (u_{i+1})_\alpha], \quad [(v_i)_\alpha, (v_{i+1})_\alpha], \qquad \text{for } 1 \leq i \leq n \text{ and } \alpha \in Z_2^{n-1}$$
$$\text{where we have taken } n+1 = 1$$
$$[(u_1)_\alpha, (v_1)_\alpha], \qquad \text{for } \alpha \in Z_2^{n-1}$$
$$[(u_i)_\alpha, (v_i)_{\alpha*\delta_{i-1}}], \qquad \text{for } 2 \leq i \leq n \text{ and } \alpha \in Z_2^{n-1} \text{ where } \delta_{i-1} = 0^{n-i}10^{i-2}$$

For the edge of form $[(u_i)_\alpha, (u_{i+1})_\alpha]$, vertices $(u_i)_\alpha$ and $(u_{i+1})_\alpha$ in $CCC_n$ are mapped by $\mathcal{M}$ to vertices $(x_i)_{\alpha \cdot p(\alpha)}$ and $(x_{i+1})_{\alpha \cdot p(\alpha)}$ in $F_n$, which are adjacent in $F_n$ because in the voltage graph $(CC_n, Z_2^n, \Psi_b)$ for $F_n$ there is an edge with voltage $0^n$ from $x_i$ to $x_{i+1}$. Similarly, the endpoints of the edge $[(v_i)_\alpha, (v_{i+1})_\alpha]$ in $CCC_n$ are mapped by $\mathcal{M}$ to adjacent vertices in $F_n$. Moreover, the two endpoints of the edge of form $[(u_1)_\alpha, (v_1)_\alpha]$ in $CCC_n$ are mapped by $\mathcal{M}$ to two adjacent vertices $(x_1)_{\alpha \cdot p(\alpha)}$ and $(x_2)_{\alpha \cdot \bar{p}(\alpha)}$ because in the voltage graph $(CC_n, Z_2^n, \Psi_b)$ for $F_n$ there is an edge from $x_1$ to $x_2$ with voltage $0^{n-1}1$.

Finally, consider the edges of form $[(u_i)_\alpha, (v_i)_{\alpha*\delta_{i-1}}]$, where $2 \leq i \leq n$ and $\delta_{i-1} = 0^{n-i}10^{i-2}$. The two endpoints of this edge are mapped by $\mathcal{M}$ to the vertices $(x_i)_{\alpha \cdot p(\alpha)}$ and $(x_{i+1})_{(\alpha*\delta_{i-1}) \cdot \bar{p}(\alpha*\delta_{i-1})}$. Note that $p(\alpha) = \bar{p}(\alpha * \delta_{i-1})$, and $\delta_{i-1}$ has a 1 at the $(i-1)$st position. Thus, the two strings $\alpha \cdot p(\alpha)$ and $(\alpha * \delta_{i-1}) \cdot \bar{p}(\alpha * \delta_{i-1})$ differ only by the $i$th bit. Therefore, the vertices $(x_i)_{\alpha \cdot p(\alpha)}$ and $(x_{i+1})_{(\alpha*\delta_{i-1}) \cdot \bar{p}(\alpha*\delta_{i-1})}$ are adjacent in $F_n$ because in the voltage graph $(CC_n, Z_2^n, \Psi_b)$ for $F_n$ there is an edge from $x_i$ to $x_{i+1}$ with voltage $0^{n-i}10^{i-1}$.

This completes the proof that adjacent vertices in $CCC_n$ are mapped by $\mathcal{M}$ to adjacent vertices in $F_n$. The following theorem concludes the above discussion:

**Theorem 3.** *The $n$-dimensional cube-connected cycles network $CCC_n$ is a subgraph of the $n$-dimensional butterfly network $F_n$.*

Note that the $n$-dimensional cube-connected cycles network $CCC_n$ and the $n$-dimensional butterfly network $F_n$ have the same number $n2^n$ of vertices. Thus, Theorem 3 presents an optimal emulation of the cube-connected cycles network by the butterfly network. We should point out that this proof is very simple and intuitive based on the voltage graph representations. The construction would be much more complicated if combinatorial methods are used instead. In fact, this is the major result of the paper by Feldman and Unger [6] based on combinatorial methods. Moreover, note that the voltage graph representations and the regular representations of the networks $CCC_n$ and $F_n$ can be easily converted, so the emulation in Theorem 3 can be easily and very efficiently implemented: each processor $P$ in the $n$-dimensional butterfly network $F_n$ can determine directly which processor $P'$ in the $n$-dimensional cube-connected cycles network $CCC_n$ is being simulated, and which of the neighbors of $P$ in $F_n$ are simulating the processors in $CCC_n$ that are the neighbors of the processor $P'$.

# 4   Voltage Graph Representations for Hypercube Networks

In this section, we show that the hypercube networks have a very flexible representation in terms of voltage graphs, which induces a powerful technique in the study of the structures of hypercube and related networks.

**Definition 4.** Let $n$ and $m$ be two integers such that $0 < n \leq m$. An $(n, m)$ *multi-edge hypercube* $Q_{n,m}$ is an $m$-regular graph that is the $n$-dimensional hypercube $H_n$ with multiple edges allowed to connect adjacent vertices in $H_n$, such that for each index $i$, $1 \leq i \leq n$, all pairs of bit-$i$ adjacent vertices are connected by the same number of multiple edges.

There is exactly one $(1, m)$ multi-edge hypercube, which is the dipole of $m$ edges, and exactly one $(n, n)$ multi-edge hypercube, which is the standard $n$-dimensional hypercube $H_n$. For general integers $n$ and $m$, there can be more than one different $(n, m)$ multi-edge hypercubes. Figure 4(B) gives a $(3, 11)$ multi-edge hypercube $Q_{3,11}$, where each pair of bit-1 adjacent vertices are connected by 3 multiple edges, each pair of bit-2 adjacent vertices are connected by 5 multiple edges, and each pair of bit-3 adjacent vertices are connected by 3 multiple edges.

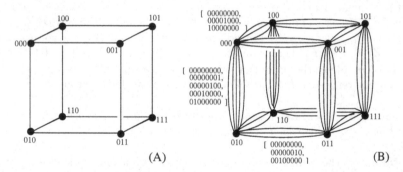

**Fig. 4.** (A) a regular 3-dimensional hypercube $H_3$; (B) a $(3, 11)$ multi-edge hypercube $Q_{3,11}$ with a normal voltage assignment

**Definition 5.** Let $(Q_{n,m}, Z_2^{m-n}, \Psi)$ be a voltage graph, where $Q_{n,m}$ is an $(n, m)$ multi-edge hypercube. The assignment $\Psi$ is *normal* if it satisfies the conditions:

1. For each pair of adjacent vertices $v$ and $u$ in $Q_{n,m}$, exactly one edge connecting $v$ and $u$ is assigned $0^{m-n}$;
2. For each vertex $v$ in $Q_{n,m}$, $m - n$ edges incident to $v$ are assigned the $m - n$ different voltages $0^{m-n-i}10^{i-1}$, $i = 1, 2, \ldots, m - n$, respectively (the other $n$ edges incident to $v$ are assigned $0^{m-n}$ according to condition 1).
3. For two pairs of bit-$i$ adjacent vertices $\{u_1, u_2\}$ and $\{v_1, v_2\}$, the set of voltages assigned to the multiple edges connecting $u_1$ and $u_2$ should be equal to the set of voltages assigned to the multiple edges connecting $v_1$ and $v_2$.

Figure 4(B) gives a normal voltage assignment on the $(3, 11)$ multi-edge hypercube $Q_{3,11}$. The 3 multiple edges connecting a pair of bit-1 adjacent vertices are assigned elements 00000000, 00000010, and 00100000 in $Z_2^8$, respectively, the 5 multiple edges connecting a pair of bit-2 adjacent vertices are assigned elements 00000000, 00000001, 00000100, 00010000, and 01000000 in $Z_2^8$, respectively, and the 3 multiple edges connecting a pair of bit-3 adjacent vertices are assigned elements 00000000, 00001000, and 10000000, respectively,

**Theorem 4.** Let $(Q_{n,m}, Z_2^{m-n}, \Psi)$ be a voltage graph where $Q_{n,m}$ is an $(n, m)$ multi-edge hypercube and $\Psi$ is a normal assignment on $Q_{n,m}$. Then the derived graph $Q_{n,m}^{\Psi}$ is the $m$-dimensional hypercube network $H_m$.

*Proof.* Denote by $\delta_{n,i}$ the string $0^{n-i}10^{i-1}$ in $Z_2^n$. We define a function $p_{\Psi}$ from $Z_2^{m-n}$ to $Z_2^n$, which generalizes the parity function $p(\cdot)$ defined in Section 2. Let $\omega \in Z_2^{m-n}$ such that the $h_1$st, $h_2$nd, ..., $h_r$th bits of $\omega$ are 1 and all other bits of $\omega$ are 0. Then $\omega$ can be written as $\omega = \delta_{m-n,h_1} * \delta_{m-n,h_2} * \cdots * \delta_{m-n,h_r}$.[1] Note that each $\delta_{m-n,h_i}$ is an element the normal assignment $\Psi$ assigns to an edge in the $(n, m)$ multi-edge hypercube $Q_{n,m}$. Suppose that for $1 \le i \le r$, the element $\delta_{m-n,h_i}$ is assigned by $\Psi$ to a bit-$g_i$ edge in $Q_{n,m}$. Then we define

$$p_{\Psi}(\omega) = \delta_{n,g_1} * \delta_{n,g_2} * \cdots * \delta_{n,g_r}$$

As an example, consider the voltage graph given in Figure 4(B), where $n = 3$, $m = 11$, and the assignment $\Psi$ is a normal assignment to $Q_{3,11}$. Let $\omega = 01101011 \in Z_2^8$. Then we have $\omega = \delta_{8,1} * \delta_{8,2} * \delta_{8,4} * \delta_{8,6} * \delta_{8,7}$. Now in the voltage graph in Figure 4(B), the elements $\delta_{8,1}$, $\delta_{8,2}$, $\delta_{8,4}$, $\delta_{8,6}$, and $\delta_{8,7}$ are assigned to a bit-2 edge, a bit-1 edge, a bit-3 edge, a bit-1 edge, and a bit-2 edge, respectively. Thus, by our definition we have

$$p_{\Psi}(\omega) = \delta_{3,2} * \delta_{3,1} * \delta_{3,3} * \delta_{3,1} * \delta_{3,2} = 010 * 001 * 100 * 001 * 010 = 100$$

Now we are ready to define a mapping $\mathcal{M}$ from the derived graph $Q_{n,m}^{\Psi}$ of the voltage graph $(Q_{n,m}, Z_2^{m-n}, \Psi)$ to the $m$-dimensional hypercube network $H_m$. Recall that "." is the concatenation operation of binary strings. Each vertex of the derived graph $Q_{n,m}^{\Psi}$ is of the form $\alpha_{\omega}$, where $\alpha \in Z_2^n$ is a vertex in the base graph $Q_{n,m}$ and $\omega$ is an element in the voltage group $Z_2^{m-n}$. Our mapping is given by

$$\mathcal{M}(\alpha_{\omega}) = (\alpha * p_{\Psi}(\omega)) \cdot \omega$$

Note that by the definitions of the operations "*" and ".", $\mathcal{M}(\alpha_{\omega})$ is a binary string of length $m$, thus a vertex in the $m$-dimensional hypercube network $H_m$.

We first show that the mapping $\mathcal{M}$ maps different vertices in $Q_{n,m}^{\Psi}$ to different vertices in $H_m$. Suppose $\mathcal{M}$ maps two vertices $\alpha_{\omega}$ and $\alpha'_{\omega'}$ in $Q_{n,m}^{\Psi}$ to the same vertex in $H_m$. By the definition, we have $(\alpha * p_{\Psi}(\omega)) \cdot \omega = (\alpha' * p_{\Psi}(\omega')) \cdot \omega'$. Since both $\omega$ and $\omega'$ are in $Z_2^{m-n}$, and they are the postfix of the same binary string

---

[1] For simplicity and without any confusion, we will use "*" for the bitwise addition operation mod 2 over the group $Z_2^k$ for any $k$.

of length $m$, we must have $\omega = \omega'$. This gives $(\alpha * p_\Psi(\omega)) = (\alpha' * p_\Psi(\omega))$, which implies immediately $\alpha = \alpha'$. Thus $\alpha_\omega$ and $\alpha'_{\omega'}$ are the same vertex in $Q_{n,m}^\Psi$.

Now we show that the mapping $\mathcal{M}$ also preserves adjacency. By the definition, each edge in the derived graph $Q_{n,m}^\Psi$ must be of the form $[\alpha_\omega, (\alpha * \delta_{n,i})_\omega]$ or $[\alpha_\omega, (\alpha * \delta_{n,i})_{\omega * \delta_{m-n,j}}]$, where $\omega \in Z_2^{m-n}$ and $\delta_{m-n,j}$ is the voltage assigned by $\Psi$ to a bit-$i$ edge in $Q_{n,m}$.

For an edge of the form $[\alpha_\omega, (\alpha * \delta_{n,i})_\omega]$ in $Q_{n,m}^\Psi$, the mapping $\mathcal{M}$ maps the two endpoints $\alpha_\omega$ and $(\alpha * \delta_{n,i})_\omega$ to the two vertices $(\alpha * p_\Psi(\omega)) \cdot \omega$ and $((\alpha * \delta_{n,i}) * p_\Psi(\omega)) \cdot \omega$ in $H_m$, respectively. Since $\alpha$ and $\alpha * \delta_{n,i}$ only differ by the $i$th bit, the two vertices $(\alpha * p_\Psi(\omega)) \cdot \omega$ and $((\alpha * \delta_{n,i}) * p_\Psi(\omega)) \cdot \omega$ only differ by the $(m - n + i)$th bit. Thus, they are two adjacent vertices in $H_m$.

For an edge of the form $[\alpha_\omega, (\alpha * \delta_{n,i})_{\omega * \delta_{m-n,j}}]$, the mapping $\mathcal{M}$ maps the two endpoints $\alpha_\omega$ and $(\alpha * \delta_{n,i})_{\omega * \delta_{m-n,j}}$ to the two vertices $(\alpha * p_\Psi(\omega)) \cdot \omega$ and $((\alpha * \delta_{n,i}) * p_\Psi(\omega * \delta_{m-n,j})) \cdot (\omega * \delta_{m-n,j})$ in $H_m$, respectively. Since $\delta_{m-n,j}$ is the voltage assigned by $\Psi$ to a bit-$i$ edge in $Q_{n,m}$, and $\omega * \delta_{m-n,j}$ differs from $\omega$ only by the $j$th bit, by the definition of $p_\Psi$, $p_\Psi(\omega * \delta_{m-n,j})$ and $p_\Psi(\omega)$ differ only by the $i$th bit. So $\alpha * p_\Psi(\omega) = (\alpha * \delta_{n,i}) * p_\Psi(\omega * \delta_{m-n,j})$ and the vertices $(\alpha * p_\Psi(\omega)) \cdot \omega$ and $((\alpha * \delta_{n,i}) * p_\Psi(\omega * \delta_{m-n,j})) \cdot (\omega * \delta_{m-n,j})$ only differ by the $j$th bit, thus are adjacent in $H_m$.

This proves that the mapping $\mathcal{M}$ maps adjacent vertices in $Q_{n,m}^\Psi$ to adjacent vertices in $H_m$. Since the derived graph $Q_{n,m}^\Psi$ has $2^n \times 2^{m-n} = 2^m$ vertices and $m2^{n-1} \times 2^{m-n} = m2^{m-1}$ edges, which are the same as those for the hypercube $H_m$, we conclude that $Q_{n,m}^\Psi$ is isomorphic to $H_m$.    □

Theorem 4 seems very powerful and flexible. For each given dimension $m$, there are many ways to pick an $n$ and construct an $(n, m)$ multi-edge hypercube. For each $(n, m)$ multi-edge hypercube $Q_{n,m}$, there are many ways to construct a normal voltage assignment on $Q_{n,m}$. This provides great flexibility for us to characterize different properties of the hypercube $H_m$. For example, if the base graph is a dipole $Q_{1,m} = D_m$, then the voltage graph representation for $H_m$ emphasizes the bipartiteness of $H_m$, while when $n > 1$, the base graph $Q_{n,m}$ provides more detailed structural properties for $H_m$. In particular, when $n = m$, the base graph $Q_{m,m}$ is the hypercube $H_m$ itself. For each base graph characterization, a normal voltage assignment can provide further properties for $H_m$. We will give an example of applications of Theorem 4 in the next section.

# 5    An Optimal Emulation from Butterfly to Hypercube

In this section, we give another example to show the power of our new representations for interconnection network structures. This example gives an optimal emulation from the butterfly networks to the hypercube networks. The construction is motivated by the following observations.

**Definition 6.** A voltage graph $(G_1, A_1, \Psi_1)$ is a *subgraph* of a voltage graph $(G_2, A_2, \Psi_2)$ if (1) $G_1$ is a subgraph of $G_2$; (2) $A_1$ is a subgroup of $A_2$; and (3) the voltage assigned by $\Psi_1$ to an edge in $G_1$ is equal to the voltage assigned by $\Psi_2$ to the corresponding edge in $G_2$.

**Theorem 5.** *If a voltage graph* $(G_1, A_1, \Psi_1)$ *is a subgraph of a voltage graph* $(G_2, A_2, \Psi_2)$, *then the derived graph* $G_1^{\Psi_1}$ *of* $(G_1, A_1, \Psi_1)$ *is a subgraph of the derived graph* $G_2^{\Psi_2}$ *of* $(G_2, A_2, \Psi_2)$.

By Theorem 5, in order to prove that the butterfly network is a subgraph of the hypercube network, it suffices to construct a voltage graph $F$ for the butterfly network and a voltage graph $H$ for the hypercube network, and prove that $F$ is a subgraph of $H$.

We will use the voltage graph $(CC_n, Z_2^n, \Psi_b)$ given in Definition 3 for the butterfly network (see Theorem 2), and construct a voltage graph based on the multi-edge hypercubes for the hypercube network which contains $(CC_n, Z_2^n, \Psi_b)$ as a subgraph.

**Theorem 6.** *If* $n$ *is a power of* 2, $n = 2^q$, *then the* $n$-*dimensional butterfly network* $F_n$ *is a subgraph of the* $(n + q)$-*dimensional hypercube network* $H_{n+q}$.

*Proof.* Consider the $q$-dimensional hypercube $H_q$. It is well known [14] that $H_q$ contains a Hamiltonian circuit of length $2^q = n$:

$$C: \ e_1 = [v_1, v_2], e_2 = [v_2, v_3], \cdots, e_{n-1} = [v_{n-1}, v_n], e_n = [v_n, v_1]$$

Based on the Hamiltonian circuit $C$ we define an $(q, n+q)$ multi-edge hypercube $Q_{q,n+q}^C$ as follows: for each $i$, $1 \leq i \leq q$, if there are $h_i$ bit-$i$ edges in $C$, then the number of multiple edges connecting a pair of bit-$i$ adjacent vertices in $Q_{q,n+q}^C$ is $h_i + 1$. Now construct a voltage graph $(Q_{q,n+q}^C, Z_2^n, \Psi)$ such that, for $1 \leq j \leq n$, if edge $e_j$ in $C$ is a bit-$i$ edge in $H_q$, then a bit-$i$ edge in $Q_{q,n+q}^C$ is assigned by $\Psi$ the value $\delta_{n,j}$. Moreover, for each pair of bit-$i$ adjacent vertices, there is an edge connecting them assigned with voltage $0^n$.

As an example, look at Figure 4, where $q = 3$ and $n = 8$. Figure 4(A) is the 3-dimensional hypercube $H_3$ with a Hamiltonian circuit:

$$C: e_1 = [000, 010], e_2 = [010, 011], e_3 = [011, 001], e_4 = [001, 101],$$
$$e_5 = [101, 111], e_6 = [111, 110], e_7 = [110, 100], e_8 = [100, 000]$$

where $e_2$ and $e_6$ are bit-1 edges, $e_1$, $e_3$, $e_5$, and $e_7$ are bit-2 edges, and $e_4$ and $e_8$ are bit-3 edges. Thus, the resulting $(3, 11)$ multi-edge hypercube $Q_{3,11}^C$ has 3 multiple edges for each bit-1 adjacent vertices, 5 multiple edges for each bit-2 adjacent vertices, and 3 multiple edges for each bit-3 adjacent vertices, which is as given in Figure 4(B). As for the voltage graph $(Q_{3,11}^C, Z_2^8, \Psi)$, the base graph $Q_{3,11}^C$ has two bit-1 edges assigned with voltages $\delta_{8,2}$ and $\delta_{8,6}$, respectively, four bit-2 edges assigned with voltages $\delta_{8,1}$, $\delta_{8,3}$, $\delta_{8,5}$, and $\delta_{8,7}$, respectively, and two bit-3 edges assigned with voltages $\delta_{8,4}$ and $\delta_{8,8}$, respectively.

It is easy to verify that the assignment $\Psi$ in the voltage graph $(Q_{q,n+q}^C, Z_2^n, \Psi)$ is a normal assignment. Thus, by Theorem 4, the derived graph $(Q_{q,n+q}^C)^\Psi$ is the $(n + q)$-dimensional hypercube network $H_{n+q}$. Moreover, the voltage graph $(Q_{q,n+q}^C, Z_2^n, \Psi)$ contains the voltage graph $(CC_n, Z_2^n, \Psi_b)$ in Definition 3 as a subgraph: for each $1 \leq i \leq n$, in the multiple edges connecting the vertices $v_i$ and $v_{i+1}$, which corresponds to the edge $e_i$ in $C$, there are two multiple edges, one with voltage $0^n$ and the other with voltage $\delta_{n,i}$. Here we have taken $n+1 = 1$. These multiple edges constitute exactly the voltage graph $(CC_n, Z_2^n, \Psi_b)$.

Now the theorem follows directly from Theorem 5.    $\square$

The condition in Theorem 6 that $n$ is a power of 2 is not necessary. Theorem 6 can be further strengthened as follows.

**Theorem 7.** *For any even number $n$, the $n$-dimensional butterfly network $F_n$ is a subgraph of the $(n+q)$-dimensional hypercube network $H_{n+q}$, where $q = \lceil \log n \rceil$.*

Theorems 6 and 7 are the best possible results since the butterfly network $F_n$ has $n2^n$ vertices and $2^{n+q-1} < n2^n \leq 2^{n+q}$. Thus, $H_{n+q}$ is the smallest hypercube that may possibly contain $F_n$ as a subgraph. Moreover, for an odd number $n$, the butterfly network $F_n$ contains a cycle of length $n$, while no hypercube network may contain any cycle of odd length [16]. Thus, in this case, the butterfly network $F_n$ cannot be a subgraph of any hypercube network. The theorems also show the effectiveness and simplicity of our new techniques. Previous combinatorical proofs for these results take more than ten pages [9].

## 6    Conclusion

We have proposed an intuitive and effective new representation scheme for interconnection network structures. We have shown by examples the power of this new method in the constructions of representations and emulations of popular interconnection networks. These examples are not accidental phenomena. In fact, as shown in [13], most proposed interconnection networks are Cayley graphs (see also [1]). In the viewpoint of voltage graph theory, every Cayley graph is a derived graph of a voltage graph with a single vertex (i.e., a "bouquet"). The representation scheme based on voltage graph theory has advanced the approach of Cayley graphs significantly for the study of interconnection network structures. First, the new scheme allows certain asymmetry in the network structures so certain non-Cayley graph networks such as the FFT network [14] can still be represented concisely by our new scheme. More importantly, the new scheme provides great flexibility for the level of details in representations of interconnection network structures. Take the hypercube network as an example, the dipole representation characterizes the bipartiteness of the network while the multi-edge hypercube representation indicates a butterfly structure in the network. The flexibility for different levels of details in a parallel system is extremely important in the design of parallel algorithms: most parallel algorithms partition the system processors into groups, and let each group of processors perform similar operations. Our new scheme seems to fit in this environment very well.

We have also obtained other results based on our new scheme. For example, we have obtained optimal emulations from the FFT networks and the cube-connected cycles networks to the hypercube networks; from the shuffle-exchange networks to the deBruijn networks; we have constructed optimal Hamiltonian decompositions of the hypercube networks, and optimal network layout for the hypercube networks and the star networks. All these show that our new scheme has great potential in the study of interconnection network structures.

# References

1. S. B. AKERS AND B. KRISHNAMURTHY,   A group-theoretic model for symmetric interconnection networks, *IEEE Transactions on Computers* **38**, (1989), pp. 555-566.
2. F. ANNEXSTEIN, M. BAUMSLAG, AND A. L. ROSENBERG,   Group action graphs and parallel architectures, *SIAM Journal on Computing* **19**, (1990), pp. 544-569.
3. A. AVIOR, T. CALAMONERI, S. EVEN, A. LITMAN, AND A. L. ROSENBERG,   A tight layout of the butterfly network, *Theory of Computing Systems* **31**, (1998), pp. 475-488.
4. S. N. BHATT, F. R. K. CHUNG, J.-W. HONG, F. T. LEIGHTON, B. OBRENIC, A. L. ROSENBERG, AND E. J. SCHWABE,   Optimal emulations by butterfly-like networks, *Journal of ACM* **43**, (1996), pp. 293-330.
5. J-C. BERMOND, E. DARROT, O. DELMAS, AND S. PERENNES,   Hamilton cycle decomposition of the butterfly network, *Parallel Processing Letters* **8**, (1998), pp. 371-385.
6. R. FELDMAN AND W. UNGER,   The cube-connected cycles network is a subgraph of the butterfly network, *Parallel Processing Letters* **2**, (1992), pp. 13-19.
7. A. GERMA, M.-C. HEYDEMANN, AND D. SOTTEAU,   Cycles in the cube-connected cycles graph, *Discrete Applied Mathematics* **83**, (1998), pp. 135-155.
8. J. L. GROSS,   Voltage graphs, *Discrete Mathematics* **9**, (1974), pp. 239-246.
9. D. S. GREENBERG, L. S. HEATH, AND A. L. ROSENBERG,   Optimal embeddings of butterfly-like graphs in the hypercube, *Mathematical Systems Theory* **23**, (1990), pp. 61-77.
10. Q.-P. GU AND S. PENG,   Unicast in hypercubes with large number of faulty nodes, *IEEE Transactions on Parallel and Distributed Systems* **10**, (1999), pp. 964-975.
11. R. KLASING,   Improved compressions of cube-connected cycles networks, *IEEE Transactions on Parallel and Distributed Systems* **9**, (1998), pp. 803-812.
12. S. LAKSHMIVARAHAN AND S. K. DHALL,   Ring, torus and hypercube architectures/algorithms for parallel computing, *Parallel Computing* **25**, (1999), pp. 1877-1906.
13. S. LAKSHMIVARAHAN, J.-S. JWO, AND S. K. DHALL,   Symmetry in interconnection networks based on Cayley graphs of permutation groups: a survey, *Parallel Computing* **19**, (1993), pp. 361-407.
14. F. T. LEIGHTON,   *Introduction to Parallel Algorithms and Architectures: Arrays, Trees, Hypercubes*, Morgan Kaufmann, 1992.
15. Y.-R. LEU AND S.-Y. KUO,   Distributed fault-tolerant ring embedding and reconfiguration in hypercubes, *IEEE Transactions on Computers* **48**, (1999), pp. 81-88.
16. Y. SAAD AND M. H. SCHULTZ,   Topological properties of hypercubes, *IEEE Transactions on Computers* **37**, (1988), pp. 867-872.

# Randomized Leader Election Protocols in Radio Networks with no Collision Detection *

Koji Nakano[1] and Stephan Olariu[2]

[1] Department of Electrical and Computer Engineering, Nagoya Institute of
Technology, Showa-ku, Nagoya 466-8555, Japan
[2] Department of Computer Science, Old Dominion University, Norfolk, VA 23529,
USA

**Abstract.** The main contribution of this work is to propose energy-efficient randomized leader election protocols for single-hop, single-channel radio networks (RN) that do not have collision detection (CD) capabilities. We first presents a leader election protocol for the case the number $n$ of stations is known beforehand. The protocol runs in $O(\log f)$ time slots with no station being awake for more than $O(\log \log f + \frac{\log f}{\log n})$ time slots with probability at least $1 - \frac{1}{f}$ for any $f \geq 1$. We then present three leader election protocols for the case where $n$ is not known beforehand. The first protocol terminates, with probability exceeding $1 - \frac{1}{f}$, in $O((\log n)^2 + (\log f)^2)$ time slots, with no station being awake for more than $O(\log n + \log f)$ time slots. Clearly, this first protocol terminates in $O((\log n)^2)$ expected time slots. Our second protocol reduces the expected termination time to $O(\log n)$ time slots. This second protocol terminates, with probability exceeding $1 - \frac{1}{f}$ in $O(f^{\frac{3}{5}} \log n)$ time slots. Finally, by combining these two protocols, we obtain a third leader election protocol that terminates in $O(\log n)$ expected time slots. This latter protocol terminates, with with probability exceeding $1 - \frac{1}{f}$, in $O(\min((\log n)^2 + (\log f)^2, f^{\frac{3}{5}} \log n))$ time slots, with no station being awake for more than $O(\log n + \log f)$ time slots.

## 1 Introduction

A radio network (RN, for short) is a distributed system with no central arbiter, consisting of $n$ radio transceivers, henceforth referred to as *stations*. We assume that the stations are identical and cannot be distinguished by serial or manufacturing number. As customary, time is assumed to be slotted and all the stations have a local clock that keeps synchronous time, perhaps by interfacing with a GPS system. The stations are assumed to have the computing power of a usual laptop computer; in particular, they all run the same protocol and can generate random bits that provide local data on which the stations may perform computations.

* Work supported in part by ONR grant N00014-91-1-0526 and by Grant-in-Aid for Encouragement of Young Scientists (12780213) from Ministry of Education, Science, Sports, and Culture of Japan.

D.T. Lee and S.-H. Teng (Eds.): ISAAC 2000, LNCS 1969, pp. 362–373, 2000.

We assume that the stations run on batteries and, therefore, saving battery power is exceedingly important, as recharging batteries may not be possible while on mission. It is well known that a station expends power while its transceiver is active that is, while transmitting or receiving a packet [1,2,3,9,10,11]. Consequently, we are interested in developing protocols that allow stations to power their transceiver off (i.e. go to sleep) to the largest extent possible. Accordingly, we judge the goodness of a protocol by the following two yardsticks:

– the overall number of time slots required by the protocol to terminate, and
– for each individual station the total number of time slots when it has to be awake in order to transmit/receive packets.

The goals of optimizing these parameters are, of course, conflicting. It is relatively straightforward to minimize overall completion time at the expense of energy consumption. Similarly, one can minimize energy consumption at the expense of completion time [11,12,13]. The challenge is to strike a sensible balance between the two, by designing protocols that take a small number of time slots to terminate while being, at the same time, as energy-efficient as possible.

We employ the commonly-accepted assumption that when two or more stations are transmitting on a channel in the same time slot, the corresponding packets *collide* and are lost. In terms of their collision detection capabilities, the RNs come in two flavors. In the RN with *collision detection* (CD) the status of the channel is:

**NULL:** if no station transmitted on the channel in the current time slot,
**SINGLE:** if one station transmitted on the channel in the current time slot,
**COLLISION:** if two or more stations transmitted in the current time slot.

In the RN with no collision detection (no-CD) the status of a radio channel is:

**NOISE:** if either no station transmitted or two or more stations transmitted in the current time slot, and
**SINGLE:** if one station transmitted in the current time slot.

In other words, the RN with no-CD cannot distinguish between no transmissions on the channel and the result of two or more stations transmitting at the same time.

The *leader election* problem asks to designate one of the stations as *leader*. In other words, after performing the leader election protocol, exactly one station learns that it was elected leader, while the remaining stations learn the identity of the leader elected. The leader election problem is fundamental, for many protocols rely directly or indirectly on the presence of a leader in a network [7, 14]. Further, once a leader is available, the RN with CD can be simulated by the RN with no-CD with a constant factor slowdown [4].

It is customary to address the leader election problem on the RN in two different scenarios:

**known** $n$: Every station knows in advance the number $n$ of stations;
**unknown** $n$: The number $n$ of stations is not known beforehand.

It is intuitively clear that the task of leader election for known $n$ is the easiest.

Several randomized protocols for single-channel RNs have been presented in the literature. Metcalfe and Boggs [5] presented a simple leader election protocol for the RN with no-CD for known $n$ that is guaranteed to terminate in $O(1)$ expected rounds. For unknown $n$, several protocols have been proposed for the RN with CD and no-CD. Willard [14] showed that the leader election on the RN with CD can be solved in $\log \log n + o(\log \log n)$ expected time slots. Later, Nakano and Olariu [7] presented two leader election protocols for the RN with CD that terminate in $O(\log n)$ time slots with probability at least $1 - \frac{1}{n}$ and in $O(\log \log n)$ time slots with probability at least $1 - \frac{1}{\log n}$. Recently, Nakano and Olariu [8] improved the protocol of [7] showing that the leader election on the RN with CD can be performed in $\log \log n + 2.78 \log f + o(\log \log n + \log f)$ time slots with probability at least $1 - \frac{1}{f}$ for every $f \geq 1$. Hayashi et al. [4] proposed a leader election protocol for the RN with no-CD that terminates in $O((\log n)^2)$ time slots with probability at least $1 - \frac{1}{n}$.

The main contribution of this work is to propose energy-efficient randomized leader election protocols for single-hop, single-channel radio networks that do not have collision detection capabilities. Consider an arbitrary parameter $f \geq 1$. We begin by showing that a leader can be elected among $n$ identical stations, with probability exceeding $1 - \frac{1}{f}$, in $O(\log f)$ time slots, with no station being awake for more than $O(\log \log f + \frac{\log f}{\log n})$ time slots, provided that the number $n$ of stations is known beforehand.

Turning to the more realistic case where $n$ is not known beforehand, we first discuss a leader election protocol that terminates, with probability exceeding $1 - \frac{1}{f}$, in $O((\log n)^2 + (\log f)^2)$ time slots, with no station being awake for more than $O(\log n + \log f)$ time slots. This first protocol terminates in $O((\log n)^2)$ expected time slots. Next, we propose a second protocol that reduces the expected termination time to $O(\log n)$ time slots. This second protocol terminates, with probability exceeding $1 - \frac{1}{f}$ in $O(f^{\frac{3}{5}} \log n)$ time slots. Finally, by combining the two protocols above, we obtain a third protocol that terminates in $O(\log n)$ expected time slots. This latter protocol terminates, with with probability exceeding $1 - \frac{1}{f}$, in $O(\min((\log n)^2 + (\log f)^2, f^{\frac{3}{5}} \log n))$ time slots, with no station being awake for more than $O(\log n + \log f)$ time slots.

## 2    Deterministic Leader Election on RNs with IDs

This section is devoted to proposing a simple deterministic leader election protocol for RNs in which every station has a unique ID. This protocol is a key ingredient in our energy-efficient leader election protocols.

Assume that each of the $n$, $(n \leq m)$, stations of the RN has a unique ID in the range $[1, m]$ and let $S_i$, $(1 \leq i \leq m)$, denote the station with ID $i$. Note that $S_i$ may not exist for some $i$. We are interested in choosing the station with minimum ID as leader. The following simple protocol performs this task in $m$ time slots. In time slot $i$, $(1 \leq i \leq m)$, station $S_i$ announces its existence by transmitting on the channel. If the status of the channel is SINGLE then $i$ is the minimum ID and every station terminates the protocol. Clearly, this protocol requires every station to monitor the channel in all the $m$ time slots, and hence, is not energy-efficient. We can reduce the number of awake time slots

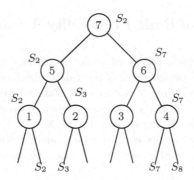

**Fig. 1.** *Illustrating the protocol for finding station with minimum ID.*

per station by using a binary tree with $m$ leaves as illustrated in Figure 1. The leaves corresponds to the stations. The internal nodes of the binary tree are numbered as indicated in Figure 1. The idea is to traverse the internal nodes in increasing order, identifying for each of them the station with minimum ID in the subtree rooted at that node. The details are spelled out as follows.

---

Protocol **Election-with-ID**
**for** $i \leftarrow 1$ **to** $m - 1$ **do**
 the minimum ID station in the left subtree of node $i$ sends on the channel;
 the minimum ID station in the right subtree of node $i$ monitors the channel;
 **if** the status of the channel is SINGLE **then**
  the station with minimum ID in the left subtree becomes
  the station with minimum ID in the subtree rooted at node $i$;
 **else**
  the station with minimum ID in the right subtree becomes
  the station with minimum ID in the subtree rooted at node $i$;
**endfor**
the station with minimum ID in the tree is declared the leader.

---

The reader should have no difficulty to confirm that when the protocol **Election-with-ID** terminates the station with minimum ID is elected the leader. Since the tree has exactly $m - 1$ internal nodes, protocol **Election-with-ID** always terminates in $m - 1$ time slots and each station is awake for at most a number of time slots equal to the height of the binary tree. Thus, we have proved the following result.

**Lemma 1.** *Assume that each of the n stations of a single-hop, single-channel radio network has a unique ID in the range* $[1, m]$, $(n \leq m)$. *A leader can be elected among these n-stations in* $m - 1$ *time slots, with no station being awake for more than* $\log m$ *time slots.*

## 3    A Refresher of Basic Probability Theory

This section offers a quick review of basic probability theory results that are useful for analyzing the performance of our randomized leader election protocols. For a more detailed discussion of background material we refer the reader to [6].

Throughout, $\Pr[A]$ will denote the probability of event $A$. For a random variable $X$, $E[X]$ denotes the expected value of $X$. Let $X$ be a random variable denoting the number of successes in $n$ independent Bernoulli trials with parameters $p$ and $1 - p$. It is well known that $X$ has a *binomial distribution* and that for every $r$, $(0 \leq r \leq n)$,

$$\Pr[X = r] = \binom{n}{r} p^r (1 - p)^{n-r}.$$

Further, the expected value of $X$ is given by

$$E[X] = \sum_{r=0}^{n} r \cdot \Pr[X = r] = np.$$

To analyze the tail of the binomial distribution, we shall make use of the following estimate, commonly referred to as *Chernoff bound*:

$$\Pr[X > (1 + \delta)E[X]] < \left( \frac{e^\delta}{(1 + \delta)^{(1+\delta)}} \right)^{E[X]}. \tag{1}$$

For later reference, we state the following result.

**Lemma 2.** *Let X be a random variable taking on a value smaller than or equal to* $T(F)$ *with probability at most* $F$, $(0 \leq F \leq 1)$, *where T is a non-decreasing function. Then,* $E[X] \leq \int_0^1 T(F)dF$.

## 4    Randomized Leader Election for Known $n$

The main goal of this section is to provide leader election protocols for radio networks where the number $n$ of stations in known beforehand. The protocol discussed in Subsection 4.1 is energy-inefficient. In Subsection 4.2 we show how it can be made energy-efficient.

## 4.1   An Energy-Inefficient Protocol

Let $P = \langle p_1, p_2, p_3, \ldots \rangle$ be a sequence of probabilities and suppose that in time slot $i$ each of the $n$ stations of the RN is transmitting on the channel with probability $p_i$. If the status of the channel is SINGLE, the unique station that has transmitted becomes the leader. Otherwise, in time slot $i + 1$ every station transmits with probability $p_{i+1}$. This is repeated until either the sequence $P$ is exhausted or the status of the channel is SINGLE. The details are spelled out in the following protocol.

---

Protocol Election($P$)
for $i \leftarrow 1$ to $|P|$ do
    each station transmits on the channel with probability $p_i$
    and every station monitors the channel;
    if the status of the channel is SINGLE then
        the station that has transmitted becomes the leader
        and the protocol terminates
endfor

---

Since correctness is easy to see, we now turn to evaluating the number of time slots it takes protocol Election($P$) to terminate. Let $X$ be the random variable denoting the number of stations that transmit in the $i$-th time slot. Then, the status of the channel is SINGLE with probability

$$\Pr[X = 1] = \binom{n}{1} p_i (1 - p_i)^{n-1}$$

To maximize the probability $\Pr[X = 1]$, we choose $p_i = \frac{1}{n}$ and so

$$\Pr[X = 1] = \left(1 - \frac{1}{n}\right)^{n-1} > \frac{1}{e}.$$

Therefore, if every station knows $n$, we choose $P = \langle \frac{1}{n}, \frac{1}{n}, \frac{1}{n}, \ldots \rangle$. Thus, each iteration of the for loop of Election($P = \langle \frac{1}{n}, \frac{1}{n}, \frac{1}{n}, \ldots \rangle$) succeeds in electing a leader with probability at least $\frac{1}{e}$. Suppose that the first $t$, $(t \geq 0)$, iterations of the for loop fail to elect a leader. Since each such trial is independent, the probability of this occurring is at most $(1 - \frac{1}{e})^t \leq e^{-\frac{t}{e}}$. It follows that with probability exceeding $1 - e^{-\frac{t}{e}}$ the protocol elects a leader in at most $t$ time slots. For $f$ satisfying $f = e^{\frac{t}{e}}$, the protocol terminates, with probability exceeding $1 - \frac{1}{f}$, in $e \ln f$ time slots. By Lemma 2, the expected number of time slots taken by the protocol to terminate is bounded by $\int_0^1 e \ln \frac{1}{F} dF = e$. Thus, we have the following result.

**Lemma 3.** *Protocol* Election($\langle \frac{1}{n}, \frac{1}{n}, \frac{1}{n}, \ldots \rangle$) *terminates in at most $e$ expected time slots. Also, for every $f \geq 1$, the protocol terminates, with probability exceeding $1 - \frac{1}{f}$, in $O(\log f)$ time slots.*

## 4.2    An Energy-Efficient Protocol

Note that protocol Election is energy-inefficient since with probability exceeding $1 - \frac{1}{f}$, each station has to be awake for $O(\log f)$ time slots to monitor
the channel. The main goal of this subsection is to reduce the awake time to
$O(\log \log f + \frac{\log f}{\log n})$ time slots.

The idea is simple: in every time slot only the transmitting stations monitor
the channel. The others don't. However, if a station never monitors the channel,
it cannot know whether or not a leader was elected. The new protocol identifies *candidates* to becoming the leader and selects one of them using protocol
Election-with-ID discussed in Section 2. Let $Q = \langle p_1, p_2, \ldots p_{|Q|} \rangle$ be a finite
sequence of probabilities, where $|Q|$ denotes the number of elements in $Q$.

---

Protocol EPS$(Q)$
**if** $|Q| = 1$ **then** perform Election$(Q)$;
**else**
    **for** $i \leftarrow 1$ to $|Q|$ **do**
        every non-candidate station transmits on the channel with probability $p_i$;
        (Note: only the transmitting stations monitor the channel)
        **if** the status of the channel is SINGLE **then**
            the unique station that has transmitted becomes a *candidate* with ID $i$
    **endfor**
    use protocol Election-with-ID to elect a leader from the candidates;
    the leader transmits on the channel to announce its identity and
    every station monitors the channel to learn the identity of the leader;    $(\star)$

---

Note that since only the candidates are awake to run protocol Election-with-ID,
the non-candidates are not aware of the election of the leader, if any. Thus, the
last transmission in $(\star)$ is necessary to ensure the correctness of the protocol.

If $|Q| = 1$, protocol EPS$(Q)$ runs in one time slot. Otherwise, the **for** loop
takes $|Q|$ time slots, and by Lemma 1, Election-with-ID terminates in $|Q| -$
1 time slots. Also, as discussed, one final time slot $(\star)$ is necessary for non-
candidate stations to learn the identity of the leader, if any. Thus, for $|Q| \geq 2$, this
protocol always takes $2|Q|$ time slots. Notice that, by Lemma 1, each candidate is
awake for at most $\log |Q|$ time slots to participate in protocol Election-with-ID.

Given an infinite sequence $P = \langle p_1, p_2, p_3, \ldots \rangle$ of probabilities, partition $P$
into subsequences $P_1, P_2, \ldots$ such that $P_i = \langle p_{2^{i-1}}, p_{2^{i-1}+2}, \ldots, p_{2^i-1} \rangle$ for every
$i, (i \geq 1)$. Thus, $P_1 = \langle p_1 \rangle$, $P_2 = \langle p_2, p_3 \rangle$ $P_3 = \langle p_4, p_5, p_6, p_7 \rangle$, ..., and clearly,
$|P_i| = 2^{i-1}$. The following protocol uses EPS as a building-block.

---

Protocol Election-PS$(P)$
**for** $i \leftarrow 1$ to $+\infty$ **do**
    perform EPS$(P_i)$;
    **if** a leader was elected **then** the protocol terminates
**endfor**

---

Since $n$ is known, the best is to execute `Election-PS`$(\langle \frac{1}{n}, \frac{1}{n}, \frac{1}{n}, \dots, \rangle)$. Instead of evaluating the performance of `Election-PS`$(\langle \frac{1}{n}, \frac{1}{n}, \frac{1}{n}, \dots \rangle)$, we will discuss the relation between `Election`$(P)$ and `Election-PS`$(P)$ for an arbitrary sequence $P = \langle p_1, p_2, p_3, \dots \rangle$ of probabilities. We then evaluate the performance of `Election-PS`$(\langle \frac{1}{n}, \frac{1}{n}, \frac{1}{n}, \dots \rangle)$.

It is clear that for every $T \geq 1$, the following two events have the same probability:

**Event1**$(T)$ `Election`$(P)$ elects a leader when the stations transmit with probability $p_T$ in the $T$-th trial, and

**Event2**$(T)$ `Election-PS`$(P)$ elects the first candidate when the stations transmit with probability $p_T$ in the $T$-th trial.

Actually, each of the two events occurs if

- for $1 \leq t \leq T - 1$ when the stations transmit with probability $p_t$ the status of the channel is NOISE, and
- the status of the channel is SINGLE when the stations transmit with probability $p_T$.

Observe that if Event1$(T)$ occurs, then `Election`$(P)$ terminates in $T$ time slots. If Event2$(T)$ occurs, the number of time slots taken by `Election`$(P)$ to terminate can be evaluated as follows. Let $s$ be the integer satisfying

$$2^0 + 2^1 + \cdots + 2^{s-1} < T \leq 2^0 + 2^1 + \cdots + 2^s.$$

In this case, `EPS`$(P_1)$, `EPS`$(P_2)$, ..., `EPS`$(P_{s-1})$ fail to elect a leader, while `EPS`$(P_s)$ succeeds in finding a leader. Now, `Election-PS`$(P)$ takes at most

$$1 + (2^2 + \cdots + 2^{s+1}) < 4T$$

time slots, because `Election-PS`$(P_s)$ terminates in $2|P_s| = 2^{s+1}$ time slots for $s \geq 2$ and `Election-PS`$(P_1)$ takes one time slot. Therefore, if `Election`$(P)$ elects a leader in $g(n, f)$ time slots with probability $1 - \frac{1}{f}$ then `Election-PS`$(P)$ elects a leader in at most $4g(n, f)$ time slots with the same probability. Thus, we have the following result.

**Lemma 4.** *If protocol `Election`$(P)$ terminates with probability at least $1 - \frac{1}{f}$ in $g(n, f)$ time slots with probability $1 - \frac{1}{f}$ for any $f \geq 1$, then `Election-PS`$(P)$ terminates, with probability at least $1 - \frac{1}{f}$ in $4g(n, f)$ time slots with probability $1 - \frac{1}{f}$.*

We now turn to the task of evaluating the maximum number of awake time slots over all stations. Suppose that `Election-PS`$(P)$ calls `EPS`$(P_1)$, `EPS`$(P_2)$, ..., `EPS`$(P_{s+1})$, and `EPS`$(P_{s+1})$ succeeds in electing a leader. Further, let $T' = 2^0 + 2^1 + \cdots + 2^s + 2^{s+1}$ be the number of trials involved in `Election-PS`$(P)$. In other words, a station transmits with probability $p_i$, $(1 \leq i \leq T')$, in the $i$-th trial of `Election-PS`$(P)$. Clearly, every station monitors the channel in one time slot for each $\texttt{EPS}(P_i)$, $(1 \leq i \leq s+1)$, to check the existence of the leader. Also, the candidates transmit/monitor the channel at most $s$ times to find the candidate with minimum ID in $\texttt{EPS}(P_{s+1})$. Note that, by assumption, no candidate has been identified in $\texttt{EPS}(P_1)$, $\texttt{EPS}(P_2)$, ..., $\texttt{EPS}(P_s)$. Thus, for these two tasks, every station transmits/monitors the channel for at most $2(s+1) = O(\log T')$ time slots.

Next, we will evaluate the number of awake time slots for $T'$ trials, in each of which the stations transmit/monitor with probability $p_i$, $(1 \leq i \leq T')$. Let $\text{SUM}_i(P)$ denote the prefix sum $p_1 + p_2 + \cdots + p_i$ of $P$. For a particular station, let $X$ be the random variable denoting the number of awake time slots in these $T'$ trials. Clearly, $E[X] = \text{SUM}_{T'}(P) = p_1 + p_2 + \cdots + p_{T'}$ and from the Chernoff bound (1), for every $\delta > 0$, we have

$$\Pr[X > (1+\delta)\text{SUM}_{T'}(P)] < \left( \frac{e^{\delta}}{(1+\delta)^{(1+\delta)}} \right)^{\text{SUM}_{T'}(P)} < \left( \frac{e}{1+\delta} \right)^{(1+\delta)\text{SUM}_{T'}(P)}.$$

Let $\alpha$ be a function satisfying

$$\left( \frac{ex}{\alpha(x)} \right)^{\alpha(x)} = \frac{1}{nf}. \tag{2}$$

By choosing $\delta$ to satisfy $(1+\delta)\text{SUM}_{T'}(P) = \alpha(\text{SUM}_{T'}(P))$, we have

$$\Pr[X > \alpha(\text{SUM}_{T'}(P))] < \left( \frac{e\text{SUM}_{T'}(P)}{\alpha(\text{SUM}_{T'}(P))} \right)^{\alpha(\text{SUM}_{T'}(P))} \leq \frac{1}{nf}.$$

It follows that with probability at most $\frac{1}{nf}$, a particular station is awake for more than $\alpha(\text{SUM}_{T'}(P))$ time slots in the first $T'$ trials. Hence, with probability at least $1 - \frac{1}{f}$, none of the $n$ stations is awake for more than $\alpha(\text{SUM}_{T'}(P))$ time slots in the first $T'$ trials. Thus, if $\texttt{Election-PS}(P)$ finds a candidate in $T'$ time slots with probability $1 - \frac{1}{f}$, then with probability at least $1 - \frac{1}{f}$ no station is awake for more than $O(\alpha(\text{SUM}_{T'}(P)))$ time slots.

Recall that every station must be awake for $O(\log T')$ time slots to find the minimum ID candidate and to detect the existence of the leader. To summarize our discussion, we state the following result.

**Lemma 5.** *If* $\texttt{Election-PS}(P)$ *terminates, with probability* $1 - \frac{1}{f}$ *for any* $f \geq 1$, *in* $T'$ *time slots, then with probability* $1 - \frac{1}{f}$ *no station is awake for more than* $O(\log T' + \alpha(\text{SUM}_{T'}(P)))$ *time slots, where* $\alpha$ *is a function satisfying* (2).

Let us now evaluate the number of awake time slots for $\texttt{Election-PS}(P)$ with $P = \langle \frac{1}{n}, \frac{1}{n}, \frac{1}{n}, \ldots \rangle$. By Lemmas 3 and 4 protocol $\texttt{Election-PS}(P)$ terminates, with probability $1 - \frac{1}{f}$, in $O(\log f)$ time slots. Hence, we apply $T' = O(\log f)$ to Lemma 5. Since $\text{SUM}_{O(\log f)}(P) = O(\frac{\log f}{n})$ and and $\alpha(\text{SUM}_{O(\log f)}(P)) = O(\frac{\log nf}{\log n}) = O(\frac{\log f}{\log n} + 1)$, no station is awake for more than

$$O(\log T' + \alpha(\text{SUM}_{T'}(P))) = O(\log \log f + \frac{\log f}{\log n})$$

time slots. Thus, we have proved the following result.

**Theorem 1.** *Protocol* Election-PS$(\langle\frac{1}{n},\frac{1}{n},\frac{1}{n},\ldots\rangle)$ *takes* $O(1)$ *expected time slots, as well as* $O(\log f)$ *time slots with no station being awake for more than* $O(\log\log f + \frac{\log f}{\log n})$ *time slots with probability at least* $1 - \frac{1}{f}$ *for any* $f \geq 1$.

## 5    Randomized Leader Election for Unknown $n$

The purpose of this section is to discuss three randomized leader election protocols for the $n$-station RN under the assumption that the number $n$ of stations is not know beforehand.

### 5.1    Electing a Leader in $O((\log n)^2 + (\log f)^2)$ Time Slots

Let $U_i$ $(1 \geq 1)$ be the sequence of probabilities

$$U_i = \langle\frac{1}{2^1}, \frac{1}{2^2}, \ldots, \frac{1}{2^i}\rangle$$

We have the following lemma.

**Lemma 6.** *Protocol* Election$(U_i)$ *succeeds in electing a leader with probability at least* $\frac{3}{5}$ *whenever* $i \geq \log n > 2$.

Due to the page limitation, we omit the proof.

Let $U = U_1 \cdot U_2 \cdot U_3 \cdots = \langle\frac{1}{2},\frac{1}{2},\frac{1}{4},\frac{1}{2},\frac{1}{4},\frac{1}{8},\ldots\rangle$ be the infinite sequence of probabilities, where "$\cdot$" denotes the concatenation of sequences. We are going to evaluate the performance Election-PS$(U)$. From Lemma 4, it is sufficient to evaluate the performance Election$(U)$ instead. Let $s$ be an integer satisfying $2^{s-1} < n \leq 2^s$. Suppose that Election$(U_1 \cdot U_2 \cdots U_{s+t-1})$ for some $t \geq 1$ is executed. Essentially, this contains the execution of Election$(U_s)$, Election$(U_{s+1})$, ..., Election$(U_{s+t-1})$, each of them succeeds in electing a leader with probability at least $\frac{3}{5}$ from Lemma 6. Thus, Election$(U_1 \cdot U_2 \cdots U_{s+t-1})$ fails in electing a leader with probability at most $(\frac{2}{5})^t$. Since $U_1 \cdot U_2 \cdots U_{s+1+t}$ contains $1 + 2 + \cdots + (s+t-1) = O((s+t)^2)$ trials, Election$(U)$ elects a leader in $O((s+t)^2) = O((\log n)^2 + t^2)$ time slots with probability at least $1 - (\frac{2}{5})^t$. Let $f = (\frac{5}{2})^t$. Then, Election$(U)$ elects a leader in $O((\log n)^2 + (\log f)^2)$ with probability $1 - \frac{1}{f}$.

Next, we will evaluate the awake time slots of Election-PS$(U)$. For this purpose, let $T' = O((\log n)^2 + (\log f)^2)$ and apply Lemma 5 to Election-PS$(U)$. Since SUM$_{T'}(U) = O(\log n + \log f)$, we have $\alpha(\text{SUM}_{T'}(U)) = O(\log n + \log f)$. Thus, we have the following lemma.

**Lemma 7.** *Protocol* Election-PS$(U)$ *elects a leader in* $O((\log n)^2 + (\log f)^2)$ *time slots with no station is being awake for more than* $O(\log n + \log f)$ *with probability at least* $1 - \frac{1}{f}$ *for any* $f \geq 1$.

Lemmas 2 and 7 combined, this protocol runs in $\int_0^1 O((\log n)^2 + (\log\frac{1}{F})^2)dF = O(\log^2 n)$ expected time slots

## 5.2   Electing a Leader in $O(\log n)$ Expected Time Slots

Let $V = U_{2^0} \cdot U_{2^1} \cdot U_{2^2} \cdot U_{2^3} \cdots$ be the infinite sequence of probabilities. We are going to show that Election$(V)$ elects a leader in $O(\log n)$ expected time slots. It follows that, Election-PS$(V)$ elects a leader in $O(\log n)$ expected time slots from Lemma 4.

Again, let $s$ be an integer satisfying $2^{s-1} < n \leq 2^s$. Further, let $J$ be the minimum integer satisfying $2^J \geq s$. Clearly, $2^J = O(\log n)$. Essentially, Election$(V)$ involves Election$(U_{2^0})$, Election$(U_{2^1})$, Election$(U_{2^{J-1}})$ before executing Election$(U_{2^J})$. Thus, it has spent $2^0 + 2^1 + \cdots + 2^J = 2^J - 1$ time slots before executing Election$(U_{2^J})$. After that, Election$(U_{2^J})$, Election$(U_{2^{J+1}})$, ..., are executed, and each of them has ability of electing a leader with probability at least $\frac{3}{5}$ from Lemma 6. Thus, Election$(U_{2^{J+k}})$ ($k \geq 0$) is executed if all of the execution of Election$(U_{2^0})$, Election$(U_{2^1})$, Election$(U_{2^{J+k-1}})$ fails electing a leader, and this probability is at most $(\frac{2}{5})^k$. Therefore, the expected number of time slots that Election$(V)$ runs is at most

$$2^J - 1 + \sum_{k=0}^{\infty} |U_{2^{J+k}}|(\frac{2}{5})^k = O(\log n) + 2^J \sum_{k=0}^{\infty} (\frac{4}{5})^k = O(\log n).$$

Therefore, we have,

**Lemma 8.** *Protocol* Election-PS$(V)$ *elects a leader in* $O(\log n)$ *expected time slots.*

However, with probability $\frac{1}{f}$, Election-PS$(V)$ runs in $O(f^{\frac{3}{5}} \log n)$ time slots. This can be proved as follows: Since Election$(U_{2^{J+k}})$ for $k \geq 0$, elects a leader with probability $\frac{3}{5}$, $K = \frac{\log f}{\log \frac{5}{3}}$ calls Election$(U_{2^J})$, Election$(U_{2^{J+1}})$, ..., Election$(U_{2^{J+K}})$ finds a leader with probability at least $1 - (\frac{3}{5})^K = 1 - \frac{1}{f}$. This $K$ calls takes $2^0 + 2^1 + \cdots + 2^{J+K} - 1 = O(f^{\frac{3}{5}} \log n)$ time slots.

## 5.3   Combining Randomized Leader Election Protocols

Let $U$ and $V$ be the sequences of probabilities defined in the previous subsections and $u_i$ and $v_i$ be the $i$-th probabilities in $U = \langle u_1, u_2, \ldots \rangle$ and $V = \langle v_1, v_2, \ldots, \rangle$, respectively. Let $W$ be the combined sequence of $U$ and $V$ such that $W = \langle u_1, v_1, u_2, v_2, u_3, v_3, \ldots \rangle$. In this subsection, we will evaluate the performance of Election-PS$(W)$.

Let $U' = \langle u_1, 0, u_2, 0 \ldots \rangle$ and $V' = \langle 0, v_1, 0, v_2, \ldots \rangle$. Clearly, Election-PS$(U')$ and Election-PS$(V')$ run, with probability at least $1 - \frac{1}{f}$, in $O((\log n)^2 + (\log f)^2)$ and $O(f^{\frac{3}{5}} \log n)$ time slots, respectively. Thus, Election-PS$(W)$ runs in $O(\min((\log n)^2 + (\log f)^2, f^{\frac{3}{5}} \log n))$ time slots.

Next we will evaluate the awake time slots. For this purpose, let $T' = O((\log n)^2 + (\log f)^2)$ and apply Lemma 5 for Election-PS$(W)$ as follows:

$$\begin{aligned} \text{SUM}_{T'}(W) &< \text{SUM}_{T'}(U) + \text{SUM}_{T'}(V) \\ &= O(\log n + \log f) + O(\log \log n + \log \log f) \\ &= O(\log n + \log f). \end{aligned}$$

Thus, from Lemma 5, Election-PS($W$) runs with stations being awake for at most $O(\log(\min((\log n)^2 + (\log f)^2, f^{\frac{3}{5}}\log n)) + \alpha(\text{SUM}_{T'}(W)) = O(\log n + \log f)$ time slots with probability at least $1 - \frac{1}{f}$. Therefore, we have,

**Theorem 2.** *Protocol* Election-PS($W$) *elects a leader in* $O(\log n)$ *expected time slots, as well as* $O(\min((\log n)^2 + (\log f)^2, f^{\frac{3}{5}}\log n))$ *time slots with no station being awake for more than* $O(\log n + \log f)$ *time slots with probability at least* $1 - \frac{1}{f}$ *for any* $f \geq 1$.

# References

1. K. Feher, *Wireless Digital Communications*, Prentice-Hall, Upper Saddle River, NJ, 1995.
2. W. C. Fifer and F. J. Bruno, Low cost packet radio, *Proceedings of the IEEE*, 75, (1987), 33–42.
3. E. P. Harris and K. W. Warren, Low power technologies: a system perspective, *Proc. 3-rd International Workshop on Multimedia Communications*, Princeton, 1996.
4. T. Hayashi, K. Nakano, and S. Olariu, Randomized initialization protocols for Packet Radio Networks, *Proc. 13th International Parallel Processing Symposium*, (1999), 544–548.
5. R. M. Metcalfe and D. R. Boggs, Ethernet: distributed packet switching for local computer networks, *Communications of the ACM*, 19, (1976), 395–404.
6. R. Motwani and P. Raghavan, *Randomized Algorithms*, Cambridge University Press, 1995.
7. K. Nakano and S. Olariu, Randomized $O(\log \log n)$-round leader election protocols in Packet Radio Networks, *Proc. of International Symposium on Algorithms and Computation*, (LNCS 1533), 209–218, 1998.
8. K. Nakano and S. Olariu, Randomized Leader Election Protocols for Ad-hoc Networks to appear in *Proc. of SCIROCCO* (2000).
9. R. A. Powers, Batteries for low-power electronics, *Proceedings of the IEEE*, 83, (1995), 687–693.
10. A. K. Salkintzis and C. Chamzas, An in-band power-saving protocol for mobile data networks, *IEEE Transactions on Communications*, COM-46, (1998), 1194–1205.
11. K. Sivalingam, M. B. Srivastava, and P. Agrawal, Low power link and access protocols for wireless multimedia networks, *Proc. IEEE Vehicular Technology Conference VTC'97*, Phoenix, AZ, May, 1997.
12. M. Stemm, P. Gauthier, and D. Harada, Reducing power consumption on network interfaces in hand-held devices, *Proc. 3-rd International Workshop on Multimedia Communications*, Princeton, 1996.
13. J. E. Wieselthier, G. D. Nguyen, and A. Ephemerides, Multicasting in energy-limited ad-hoc wireless networks, *Proc. MILCOM'98*, 1998.
14. D. E. Willard, Log-logarithmic selection resolution protocols in a multiple access channel, *SIAM Journal on Computing*, 15, (1986), 468–477.

# Deterministic Broadcasting Time with Partial Knowledge of the Network

Gianluca De Marco[1] and Andrzej Pelc[2]

[1] Dipartimento di Informatica e Applicazioni, Università di Salerno, 84081 Baronissi
(SA), Italy. E-mail: demarco@dia.unisa.it
This research was done during the stay of Gianluca De Marco at the Université du
Québec à Hull.
[2] Département d'Informatique, Université du Québec à Hull, Hull, Québec J8X 3X7,
Canada. E-mail: pelc@uqah.uquebec.ca
Andrzej Pelc was supported in part by NSERC grant OGP 0008136.

**Abstract.** We consider the time of deterministic broadcasting in networks whose nodes have limited knowledge of network topology. Each node $v$ knows only the part of the network within *knowledge radius* $r$ from it, i.e., it knows the graph induced by all nodes at distance at most $r$ from $v$. Apart from that, each node knows only the maximum degree $\Delta$ of the network and the number $n$ of nodes. One node of the network, called the *source*, has a message which has to reach all other nodes. We adopt the widely studied communication model called the *one-way* model in which, in every round, each node can communicate with at most one neighbor, and in each pair of nodes communicating in a given round, one can only send a message while the other can only receive it. This is the weakest of all store-and-forward models for point-to-point networks, and hence our algorithms work for other models as well in at most the same time.

We show tradeoffs between knowledge radius and time of deterministic broadcasting, when knowledge radius is small, i.e., when nodes are only aware of their close vicinity. While for knowledge radius 0, minimum broadcasting time is $\Theta(e)$, where $e$ is the number of edges in the network, broadcasting can be usually completed faster for positive knowledge radius. Our main results concern knowledge radii 1 and 2. We develop fast broadcasting algorithms and analyze their execution time. We also prove lower bounds on broadcasting time, showing that our algorithms are close to optimal, for a given knowledge radius. For knowledge radius 1 we develop a broadcasting algorithm working in time $O(\min(n, D^2\Delta))$, where $n$ is the number of nodes, $D$ is the diameter of the network, and $\Delta$ is the maximum degree. We show that for bounded maximum degree $\Delta$ this algorithm is asymptotically optimal. For knowledge radius 2 we show how to broadcast in time $O(D\Delta \log n))$ and prove a lower bound $\Omega(D\Delta)$ on broadcasting time, when $D\Delta \in O(n)$. This lower bound is valid for any constant knowledge radius. For knowledge radius $\log^* n + 3$ we show how to broadcast in time $O(D\Delta)$. Finally, for any knowledge radius $r$, we show a broadcasting algorithm working in time $O(D^2\Delta/r)$.

D.T. Lee and S.-H. Teng (Eds.): ISAAC 2000, LNCS 1969, pp. 374–385, 2000.
© Springer-Verlag Berlin Heidelberg 2000

# 1    Introduction

## 1.1    The Problem

Broadcasting is one of the fundamental tasks in network communication. One node of the network, called the *source*, has a message which has to reach all other nodes. In *synchronous* communication, messages are sent in *rounds* controled by a global clock. In this case the number of rounds used by a broadcasting algorithm, called its *execution time*, is an important measure of performance. Broadcasting time has been extensively studied in many communication models (cf. surveys [11,15]) and fast broadcasting algorithms have been developed.

If network communication is to be performed in a distributed way, i.e., message scheduling has to be decided locally by nodes of the network, without the intervention of a central monitor, the efficiency of the communication process is influenced by the amount of knowledge concerning the network, a priori available to nodes. It is often the case that nodes know their close vicinity (for example they know their neighbors) but do not know the topology of remote parts of the network.

The aim of this paper is to study the impact of the amount of local information available to nodes on the time of broadcasting. Each node $v$ knows only the part of the network within *knowledge radius* $r$ from it, i.e., it knows the graph induced by all nodes at distance at most $r$ from $v$. Apart from that, each node knows only the maximum degree $\Delta$ of the network and the total number $n$ of nodes. We concentrate on the case when knowledge radius is small, i.e., when nodes are only aware of their close vicinity. We develop fast broadcasting algorithms and analyze their execution time. We also prove lower bounds on broadcasting time, showing that our algorithms are close to optimal, for a given knowledge radius.

## 1.2    Related Work

Network communication with partial knowledge of the network has been studied by many researchers. This topic has been extensively investigated, e.g., in the context of radio networks. In [4] broadcasting time was studied under assumption that nodes of a radio network know a priori their neighborhood. In [5] an even more restrictive assumption has been adopted, namely that every node knows only its own label (knowledge radius zero in our terminology). In [7] a restricted class of radio networks was considered and partial knowledge available to nodes concerned the range of their transmitters.

In [13] time of broadcasting and of two other communication tasks was studied in point-to-point networks assuming that each node knows only its own degree. However, the communication model was different from the one assumed in this paper: every node could simultaneously receive messages from all of its neighbors.

In [3] broadcasting was studied assuming a given knowledge radius, as we do in this paper. However the adopted efficiency measure was different: the authors studied the number of messages used by a broadcasting algorithm, and not its execution time, as we do.

A topic related to communication in an unknown network is that of graph exploration [1,19]: a robot has to traverse all edges of an unknown graph in order to draw a map of it. In this context the complexity measure is the number of edge traversals which is proportional to execution time, as only one edge can be traversed at a time.

In the above papers communication algorithms were deterministic. If randomization is allowed, very efficient broadcasting is possible without knowing the topology of the network, cf., e.g., [4,10]. In fact, in [4] the differences of broadcasting time in radio networks between the deterministic and the randomized scenarios were the main topic of investigation.

Among numerous other graph problems whose distributed solutions with local knowledge available to nodes have been studied, we mention graph coloring [18], and label assignment [12].

## 1.3   The Model and Terminology

The communication network is modeled by a simple undirected connected graph with a distinguished node called the *source*. $n$ denotes the number of nodes, $e$ denotes the number of edges, $\Delta$ denotes the maximum degree, and $D$ the diameter. All nodes have distinct labels which are integers between 1 and $n$, but our algorithms and arguments are easy to modify when labels are in the range 1 to $M$, where $M \in O(n)$.

Communication is deterministic and proceeds in synchronous rounds controled by a global clock. Only nodes that already got the source message can transmit, hence broadcasting can be viewed as a wake-up process. We adopt the widely used *one-way* model, also called the *1-port half-duplex model* [11]. In every round, each node can communicate with at most one neighbor, and in each pair of nodes communicating in a given round, one can only send an (arbitrary) message, while the other can only receive it. This model has been used, e.g., in [9,14,17]. It has the advantage of being the weakest of all store-and-forward models for point-to-point networks (cf. [11]), and hence our algorithms work also for other models (allowing more freedom in sending and/or receiving), in at most the same time.

For a natural number $r$ we say that $r$ is the *knowledge radius* of the network if every node $v$ knows the graph induced by all nodes at distance at most $r$ from $v$. Apart from that partial topological information, each node knows only the maximum degree $\Delta$ of the network and the number $n$ of nodes. For example, if knowledge radius is 1, each node knows its own label, labels of all neighbors, knows which of its adjacent edges joins it with which neighbor, and knows which neighbors are adjacent between them. The latter assumption is where our definition of knowledge radius differs from that in [3], where knowledge radius $r$ meant that a node $v$ knows the graph induced by all nodes at distance at most $r$ from $v$ *with the exception of* adjacencies between nodes at distance exactly $r$ from $v$. However all our results hold for this weaker definition as well. In fact, we show that our lower bounds are valid even under the stronger notion and we construct the algorithms using only the weaker version from [3], thus obtaining all results under both definitions of knowledge radius.

## 1.4  Overview of Results

We show tradeoffs between knowledge radius and time of deterministic broadcasting, when knowledge radius is small, i.e., when nodes are only aware of their close vicinity. While for knowledge radius 0, minimum broadcasting time is $\Theta(e)$, where $e$ is the number of edges in the network, broadcasting can be usually completed faster for positive knowledge radius. Our main results concern knowledge radii 1 and 2. For knowledge radius 1 we develop a broadcasting algorithm working in time $O(\min(n, D^2\Delta))$, and we show that for bounded maximum degree $\Delta$ this algorithm is asymptotically optimal. For knowledge radius 2 we show how to broadcast in time $O(D\Delta \log n))$ and prove a lower bound $\Omega(D\Delta)$ on broadcasting time, when $D\Delta \in O(n)$. This lower bound is valid for any constant knowledge radius. For knowledge radius $\log^* n + 3$ we show how to broadcast in time $O(D\Delta)$. Finally, for any knowledge radius $r$, we show a broadcasting algorithm working in time $O(D^2\Delta/r)$.

## 2  Preliminary Results: Knowledge Radius 0

For knowledge radius 0 tight bounds on broadcasting time can be established: the minimum broadcasting time in this case is $\Theta(e)$, where $e$ is the number of edges in the network.

We first make the following observation (cf.[13]).

**Proposition 1.** *In every broadcasting algorithm with knowledge radius 0 the source message must traverse every edge at least once.*

The following result establishes a natural lower bound on broadcasting time. Its proof is based on that of Theorem 4.6 from [12].

**Theorem 1.** *Every broadcasting algorithm with knowledge radius 0 requires time at least $e$ for networks with $e$ edges.*

In the classic depth first search algorithm a token (the source message) visits all nodes and traverses every edge twice. In this algorithm only one message is sent in each round and hence the specifications of the one-way model are respected. This is a broadcasting algorithm working in $2e$ rounds and hence its execution time has optimal order of magnitude. In view of Theorem 1, we have the following result.

**Theorem 2.** *The minimum broadcasting time with knowledge radius 0 is $\Theta(e)$, where $e$ is the number of edges in the network.*

# 3   Knowledge Radius 1

In order to present our first algorithm we need the notion of a layer of a network. For a natural number $k$, the $k$th *layer* of network $G$ is the set of nodes at distance $k$ from the source. The idea of Algorithm Conquest-and-Feedback is to inform nodes of the network layer by layer. After the $(k-1)$th layer is informed (*conquered*) every node of this layer transmits to any other node of this layer information about its neighborhood. This information travels through a partial tree constructed on nodes of the previous layers and consumes most of the total execution time of the algorithm. As soon as this information is exchanged among nodes of the $(k-1)$th layer (*feedback*), they proceed to relay the source message to nodes of layer $k$. The knowledge of all adjacencies between nodes from layer $k-1$ and nodes from layer $k$ enables transmitting the source message without collisions.

We now present a detailed description of the algorithm.

**Algorithm Conquest-and-Feedback**

All rounds are divided into consecutive *segments* of length $\Delta$. Rounds in each segment are numbered 1 to $\Delta$. The set of segments is in turn partioned into *phases*. We preserve the invariant that after the $k$th phase all nodes of the $k$th layer know the source message.

The first phase consists of the first segment (i.e., it lasts $\Delta$ rounds). In consecutive rounds of this segment the source informs all of its neighbors, in increasing order of their labels. (If the degree of the source is smaller than $\Delta$, the remaining rounds of the segment are idle.)

Any phase $k$, for $k > 1$, consists of $2k - 1$ segments (i.e., it lasts $\Delta(2k - 1)$ rounds). Suppose by induction that after phase $k-1$ all nodes of layer $k-1$ have the source message. Moreover suppose that a tree spanning all nodes of layers $j < k$ is distributedly maintained: every node $v$ of layer $j$ remembers from which node $P(v)$ of layer $j - 1$ it received the source message for the first time, and remembers the round number $r(v) \le \Delta$ in a segment in which this happened.

We now describe phase $k$ of the algorithm. Its first $2(k - 1)$ segments are devoted to exchanging information about neighborhood among nodes of layer $k - 1$ (feedback). Every such node transmits a message containing its own label and labels of all its neighbors. During the first $k - 1$ segments messages travel toward the source: one segment is devoted to get the message one step closer to the source. More precisely, a node $v$ of layer $j < k - 1$ which got feedback messages in a given segment transmits their concatenation to $P(v)$ in round $r(v)$ of the next segment. The definitions of $r(v)$ and $P(v)$ guarantee that collisions are avoided. After these $k - 1$ segments the source gets all feedback messages. From the previous phase the source knows all labels of nodes in layer $k - 2$. Since neighbors of a node in layer $k - 1$ can only belong to one of the layers $k - 2$, $k - 1$ or $k$, the source can deduce from information available to it the entire bipartite graph $B_k$ whose node sets are layers $k - 1$ and $k$ and edges are all graph edges between these layers. The next $k - 1$ segments are devoted to broadcasting the message describing graph $B_k$ to all nodes of layer $k - 1$. Every node of layer $j < k - 1$ which already got this message relays it to nodes of layer $j + 1$ during the next segment, using precisely the same schedule as it used to broadcast the source message in phase $j + 1$. By the inductive assumption collisions are avoided.

Hence after $2(k - 1)$ segments of phase $k$ the graph $B_k$ is known to all nodes of layer $k - 1$. The last segment of the phase is devoted to relaying the source message to all nodes of layer $k$. This is done as follows. Every node $v$ of layer $k - 1$ assigns consecutive *slots* $s = 1, ..., \delta$, $\delta \le \Delta$ to each of its neighbors in layer $k$, in increasing order of their labels. Since $B_k$ is known to all nodes of layer $k - 1$, all slot assignments are also known to all of them. Now transmissions are scheduled as follows. For any node $v$ of layer $k - 1$ and any round $r$ of the last segment, node $v$ looks at its neighbor $w$ in layer $k$ to which it assigned slot $r$. It looks at all neighbors of $w$ in layer $k - 1$ and defines the set $A(w)$ of those among them which assigned slot $r$ to $w$. If the label of $v$ is the smallest among all labels of nodes in $A(w)$, node $v$ transmits the source message to $w$ in round $r$ of the last segment, otherwise $v$ remains silent in this round. This schedule avoids collisions and guarantees that all nodes of layer $k$ get the source message by the end of the $k$th phase. Hence the invariant is preserved, which implies that broadcasting is completed after at most $D$ phases.

Phase 1 lasts $\Delta$ rounds, and each phase $k$, for $k > 1$, lasts $\Delta(2k - 1)$ rounds. Since broadcasting is completed after $D$ phases, its execution time is at most

$$\Delta(1 + \sum_{k=2}^{D}(2k - 1)) \in O(D^2 \Delta).$$

Hence we get.

**Theorem 3.** *Algorithm Conquest-and-Feedback completes broadcasting in any network of diameter $D$ and maximum degree $\Delta$ in time $O(D^2 \Delta)$.*

For large values of $D$ and $\Delta$ the following simple Algorithm Fast-DFS may be more efficient than Algorithm Conquest-and-Feedback. It is a DFS-based algorithm using the idea from [2]. The source message is considered as a token which visits all nodes of the graph. In every round only one message is transmitted, hence collisions are avoided. The token carries the list of previously visited nodes. At each node $v$ the neighborhood of $v$ is compared to this list. If there are yet non visited neighbors, the token passes to the lowest labeled of them. Otherwise the token backtracks to the node from which $v$ was visited for the first time. If there is no such a node, i.e., if $v$ is the source, the process terminates. In this way all nodes are visited, and the token traverses only edges of an implicitly defined DFS tree, rooted at the source, each of these edges exactly twice. Avoiding sending the token on non-tree edges speeds up the process from time $\Theta(e)$ to $\Theta(n)$. Hence we get

**Proposition 2.** *Algorithm Fast-DFS completes broadcasting in any $n$-node network in time $O(n)$.*

Since the diameter $D$ may be unknown to nodes, it is impossible to predict which of the two above algorithms is faster for an unknown network. However, simple interleaving of the two algorithms guarantees broadcasting time of the order of the better of them in each case. Define Algorithm Interleave which, for any network $G$ executes steps of Algorithm Conquest-and-Feedback in even rounds and steps of Algorithm Fast-DFS in odd rounds. Then we have

**Theorem 4.** *Algorithm Interleave completes broadcasting in any n-node network of diameter $D$ and maximum degree $\Delta$ in time $O(min(n, D^2\Delta))$.*

The following lower bound shows that, for constant maximum degree $\Delta$, execution time of Algorithm Interleave is asymptotically optimal.

**Theorem 5.** *Any broadcasting algorithm with knowledge radius 1 requires time $\Omega(min(n, D^2))$ in some constant degree n-node networks of diameter $D$.*

PROOF Fix parameters $n$ and $D < n$. Since $D$ is the diameter of a constant degree network with $n$ nodes, we must have $D \in \Omega(\log n)$. Consider a complete binary tree rooted at the source, of height $h \leq D/3$ and with $k$ leaves $a_1, ..., a_k$, where $k \in \Omega(n/D)$. It has $2k - 1$ nodes. Assume for simplicity that $D$ is even and let $L = D/2 - h$. Thus $L \in \Omega(D)$. Attach disjoint paths of length $L$ (called *threads*) to all leaves. Denote by $b_i$ the other end of the thread attached to $a_i$, and call this thread the $i$th thread. Again assume for simplicity that $2k - 1 + kL = n$, and thus the resulting tree $T$ has $n$ nodes and diameter $D$. (It is easy to modify the construction in the general case.)

Next consider any nodes $u$ and $v$ belonging to distinct threads, respectively $i$th and $j$th, of $T$. Define the graph $T(u, v)$ as follows: remove the part of the $i$th thread between $u$ and $b_i$ (including $b_i$), and the part of the $j$th thread between $v$ and $b_j$ (including $b_j$), and add a new node $w$ joining it to $u$ and to $v$. Arrange the remaining nodes in a constant degree tree attached to the source, so as to create an $n$-node graph of constant degree and diameter $D$.

We now consider the class of graphs consisting of the tree $T$ and of all graphs $T(u, v)$ defined above. We will show that any broadcasting algorithm with knowledge radius 1 which works correctly on this class requires time $\Omega(min(n, D^2))$ in the tree $T$. Fix a broadcasting algorithm $A$.

Since the algorithm must work correctly on $T$, the source message must reach all nodes $b_i$, and consequently it must traverse all threads. For each thread define the *front* as the farthest node from the source in this thread, that knows the source message. Call each move of a front a *unit of progress*. Consider only the second half of each thread, the one farther from the source. Thus $kL/2$ units of progress must be made to traverse those parts of threads.

Consider fronts $u$ and $v$ in second halves of two distinct threads and suppose that these fronts move in the same round $t$. Observe that before this is done, information which $u$ has about its neighborhood must be transmitted to $v$ or vice-versa. Otherwise the local states of $u$ and $v$ in round $t$ are the same when the algorithm is run on $T$ and on $T(u, v)$. However simultaneous transmission from $u$ and $v$ in $T(u, v)$ results in a collision in their common neighbor $w$ and thus the assumptions of the model are violated. Since $u$ and $v$ are in second halves of their respective threads, the distance between them is at least $L$, hence transmission of information from $u$ to $v$ requires at least $L$ rounds after $u$ becomes a front.

Units of progress are *charged* to rounds in which they are made in the following way. If at least two units of progress are made in a round, all of them are charged to this round. We call this the *first way of charge*. If only one unit of progress is made in a round we charge this unit to this round and call it the *second way of charge*.

Partition all rounds into disjoint segments, each consisting of $L$ consecutive rounds. Fix such a segment of rounds, and let $t_1 < ... < t_s$ be rounds of this segment in which at least two units of progress are made. Let $A_{t_i}$, for $i = 1, ..., s$, be the set of thread numbers in which progress is made in round $t_i$. Notice that, for any $i \leq s$, the set $(A_{t_1} \cup \cdots \cup A_{t_{i-1}}) \cap A_{t_i}$ can have at most 1 element. Indeed, if $a, b \in (A_{t_1} \cup \cdots \cup A_{t_{i-1}}) \cap A_{t_i}$, for $a \neq b$, then fronts $u$ in thread $a$ and $v$ in thread $b$ move simultaneously in round $t_i$ but neither information about neighborhood of $u$ could reach $v$ nor information about neighborhood of $v$ could reach $u$ because this information could only be sent less than $L$ rounds before $t_i$.

Since $|(A_{t_1} \cup \cdots \cup A_{t_{i-1}}) \cap A_{t_i}| \leq 1$ for any $i \leq s$, it follows that $|A_{t_1}| + \cdots + |A_{t_s}| \leq k + s \leq k + L$. Hence at most $k + L$ units of progress can be charged to rounds of a segment in the first way. Clearly at most $L$ units of progress can be charged to rounds of a segment in the second way. Hence a total of at most $k+2L$ units of progress can be charged to rounds of each segment. Since $kL/2$ units of progress must be made to traverse second halves of all threads, broadcasting requires at least $kL/(2(k + 2L))$ segments and thus at least $kL^2/(2(k + 2L))$ rounds. If $k \leq L$ we have $kL^2/(2(k + 2L)) \geq kL/6 \in \Omega(n)$, and if $k \geq L$ we have $kL^2/(2(k + 2L)) \geq L^2/6 \in \Omega(D^2)$. Hence we have always the lower bound $\Omega(\min(n, D^2))$ on broadcasting time in the tree $T$. $\square$

## 4   Knowledge Radius 2

In this section we show the existence of a broadcasting algorithm with knowledge radius 2 working in $O(D\Delta \log n)$ rounds for $n$-node networks of diameter $D$ and maximum degree $\Delta$.

Let $v$ be any node of a network $G$. If the degree $d$ of $v$ is strictly less than $\Delta$, add $\Delta - d$ "dummy" edges with one endpoint $v$, using a different new endpoint for each edge. The number of new nodes added this way is less than $n\Delta$. Any node $v$ of $G$ fixes an arbitrary local enumeration $(v, i)|i = 1, ..., \Delta$ of all directed edges starting at $v$. $v$ is called the *beginning* of the edge $(v, i)$ and the other endpoint of this edge is called its *end*. The set $\Omega = \{(v, i)| \; v \in V(G), 1 \leq i \leq \Delta\}$ contains all directed edges of $G$ together with all dummy edges. Notice that $|\Omega| = n\Delta$.

Suppose that node $w$ is the end of edge $(v, i)$. Denote by $\Phi_w$ the set of all edges with end $w$, and by $R(v, i)$ the *reverse* of edge $(v, i)$, i.e., the edge having beginning and end interchanged. Given an arbitrary set $T$ of edges, let

$R(T) = \{R(x) |\ x \in T\}$. Let $[\Omega]_k$ denote the set of all $k$-element subsets of $\Omega$. Any sequence of random members of $[\Omega]_k$ will be called a $k$-list.

**Definition 1.** *Consider an $n$-list $L = (Q_1, \ldots, Q_t)$, and let $I$ be the set of all edges with beginning $v$, for a given node $v$. For any $I' \subseteq I$, an element $Q_i$ of $L$ is said to* isolate an edge $(v, l)$ in $I'$ *if*

$$Q_i \cap (I' \cup R(I) \cup \Phi_w \cup R(\Phi_w)) = \{(v, l)\}, \tag{1}$$

*where $w$ is the end of $(v, l)$.*

We also say that an $n$-list $L$ isolates an edge $(v, l)$ in $I$ when there exists an element $Q_i$ in $L$ such that (1) holds. The following lemma is similar to Lemma 5.2.1 from [8].

**Lemma 1.** *Let $L = (Q_1, \ldots, Q_\Delta)$, be an $n$-list. For every set $I \in [\Omega]_\Delta$ of edges with common beginning $v$ and every $1 \le i \le \Delta$, with probability at least $e^{-5}$ there is an edge $(v, l) \in I$ isolated by $Q_i$ but not by any $Q_k$ for $1 \le k < i$.*

The next two lemmas follow respectively from Lemma 5.2.2 and Lemma 5.2.3 of [8] that are reformulations of results first obtained in [16].

**Lemma 2.** *A $n$-list $Q_1, \ldots, Q_\Delta$ isolates at least $\Delta/e^{-8}$ edges in any set $I \in [\Omega]_\Delta$ of edges with common beginning $v$, with probability at least $1 - e^{-b\Delta}$, where $b > 0$.*

**Lemma 3.** *For $\Delta \ge 2$, a $n$-list $Q_1, \ldots, Q_t$ of length $t \in O(\Delta \log n)$ isolates at least $\Delta/e^{-8}$ edges in any set $I \in [\Omega]_\Delta$ of edges with common beginning $v$.*

Clearly a concatenation of two or more $n$-lists is itself a $n$-list. In the following, a $n$-list defined as a concatenation of $n$-lists $L_1, \ldots, L_m$ will be denoted by $\mathcal{L}_{L_1, \ldots, L_m}$. Notice that, given a set $I$ of edges, a $n$-list $\mathcal{L}_{L_1, \ldots, L_m}$ defines a family $\mathcal{L}(I) = \{I_1, \ldots, I_{m+1}\}$ of sets such that $I_1 = I$ and every $I_j$, for $2 \le j \le m + 1$, is the subset of $I_{j-1}$ obtained by deleting from $I_{j-1}$ all the edges isolated by $L_{j-1}$ in $I_{j-1}$.

**Definition 2.** *Given a $n$-list $\mathcal{L}_{L_1, \ldots, L_m}$ and a set $I$ of edges, an element $Q_i \in [\Omega]_n$ of $\mathcal{L}_{L_1, \ldots, L_m}$ is said to* select $(v, l)$ in $I$ *if $Q_i$ isolates $(v, l)$ in $I_j$, for some $I_j \in \mathcal{L}(I)$.*

The following theorem is a reformulation of Theorem 5.2.4 proved in [8], using Lemma 3.

**Theorem 6.** *For $\Delta \ge 2$ there exists a $n$-list $\mathcal{L}_{L_1, \ldots, L_m}$ of length $O(\Delta \log n)$ which selects all the edges in $I$, for every set $I \in [\Omega]_\Delta$ of edges with common beginning $v$.*

In the following algorithm we assume that all nodes have as input the same $n$-list $\mathcal{L}_{L_1,\ldots,L_m}$ of length $l \in O(\Delta \log n)$ (with the appropriate selection property) whose existence is guaranteed by Theorem 6. This is the only non-constructive ingredient of the algorithm. Given this input, the algorithm is deterministic. If time of local computations is ignored, as it is often the case in distributed algorithms (see, e.g., [18]) all nodes can locally find the same list using a predetermined deterministic exhaustive search, depending only on parameters $n$ and $\Delta$.

## Algorithm Select-and-Transmit

The algorithm works in phases. The first phase lasts $\Delta$ rounds and each of the following phases lasts $l$ rounds, where $l \in O(\Delta \log n)$ is the length of the $n$-list. Each round $r$ of a phase $p \geq 2$ corresponds to the $r$th element $Q_r \in [\Omega]_n$ of $\mathcal{L}_{L_1,\ldots,L_m}$.

- In phase 1 the source sends the message to all of its neighbors.
- In round $r$ of phase $p$, for $p \geq 2$, any node $v$ that got the source message for the first time in the previous phase $p - 1$, sends the message on edge $(v, i)$ if and only if $Q_r$ selects $(v, i)$ in $I$, where $I$ is the set of all edges with beginning $v$. If $(v, i)$ happens to be a dummy edge, $v$ is idle in round $r$.

**Theorem 7.** *Algorithm Select-and-Transmit completes broadcasting in any $n$-node network of diameter $D$ and maximum degree $\Delta$ in time $O(D\Delta \log n)$.*

PROOF First observe that in order to decide if a given edge $(v, i)$ is selected by a set $Q_r$, node $v$ must only know the part of the network at distance at most 2 from it, and hence Algorithm Select-and-Transmit is indeed an algorithm with knowledge radius 2.

Let $I$ be the set of all edges with beginning $v$. Since Theorem 6 guarantees that all elements of $I$ are selected within $l \in O(\Delta \log n)$ rounds, we conclude that at the end of phase $p$, any node $v$ informed in phase $p - 1$, transmits the source message to all of its neighbors. Hence after $D$ phases broadcasting is completed.

It remains to show that all transmissions respect the model specifications, i.e., that collisions are avoided. When node $v$ sends the message on edge $(v, i)$ in round $r$ of a given phase, $Q_r$ selects $(v, i)$ in $I$. By Definition 2, this means that there exists $I_j \in \mathcal{L}(I)$ such that $Q_r$ isolates $(v, i)$ in $I_j$. Hence, if $w$ is the end of $(v, i)$, we have

$$Q_r \cap (I_j \cup R(I) \cup \Phi_w \cup R(\Phi_w)) = \{(v, i)\}.$$

This implies that, apart from all edges in $I \setminus I_j$ that have been already selected in some previous round, any other edge $(v, k) \in I$, for $k \neq i$, is not in $Q_r$. Also, no edge with end $v$ and no other edge with beginning or end $w$ can be in $Q_r$. Therefore none of these edges can be selected by the same set $Q_r$ which selects $(v, i)$. Hence no transmission in round $r$ can collide with the transmission on edge $(v, i)$. □

We now present a lower bound on broadcasting time showing that Algorithm Select-and-Transmit is close to optimal for knowledge radius 2. In fact our lower bound is valid for any constant knowledge radius $r$.

**Theorem 8.** *Assume that $D\Delta \in O(n)$ and let $r$ be a positive integer constant. Any broadcasting algorithm with knowledge radius $r$ requires time $\Omega(D\Delta)$ on some $n$-node tree of maximum degree $\Delta$ and diameter $D$.*

# 5   Larger Knowledge Radius

In this section we show that for larger knowledge radius the time of brodcasting can be significantly improved. Our first algorithm uses knowledge radius $\log^* n + 3$ and completes broadcasting in time $O(D\Delta)$. It has again a non-constructive ingredient, similarly as Algorithm Select-and-Transmit (see the remark after Theorem 6). More specifically, using methods similar to those in Section 4, the following theorem was proved in [6].

A *distributed $k$-edge coloring* of a graph is an assignment of $k$ colors to all edges of the graph, so that incident edges have different colors and every node knows the colors of all of its incident edges.

**Theorem 9.** *If nodes have knowledge radius $\log^* n + 3$ then distributed $O(\Delta)$-edge coloring of an $n$-node graph of maximum degree $\Delta$ can be achieved without any communication among nodes.*

**Algorithm Color-and-Transmit**

All nodes of the network have as input a fixed distributed $k$-coloring of edges, where $k \in O(\Delta)$, guaranteed by Theorem 9 More specifically, every node knows colors of its incident edges. The algorithm works in phases. The first phase lasts $\Delta$ rounds and each of the following phases lasts $k$ rounds. In phase 1 the source sends the message to all of its neighbors. In round $r$ of phase $p$, for $p \geq 2$, any node $v$ that got the source message for the first time in the previous phase $p - 1$, sends the message on its incident edge of color $r$.

By definition of $k$-edge coloring collisions are avoided. After $D$ phases broadcast is completed. Hence we get.

**Theorem 10.** *Algorithm Color-and-Transmit completes broadcasting in any $n$-node network of diameter $D$ and maximum degree $\Delta$ in time $O(D\Delta)$.*

We finally observe that for larger knowledge radius $r$ Algorithm Conquest-and-Feedback, described in Section 3, can be modified in a straightforward way allowing faster broadcasting.

**Proposition 3.** *For any positive integer $r$, there exists a broadcasting algorithm with knowledge radius $r$ which completes broadcasting in any network of diameter $D$ and maximum degree $\Delta$ in time $O(D^2\Delta/r)$.*

# References

1. S. Albers and M. R. Henzinger, Exploring unknown environments, Proc. 29th Symp. on Theory of Computing (1997), 416-425.

2. B. Awerbuch, A new distributed depth-first-search algorithm, Information Processing Letters 20 (1985), 147-150.
3. B. Awerbuch, O. Goldreich, D. Peleg and R. Vainish, A Tradeoff Between Information and Communication in Broadcast Protocols, J. ACM 37, (1990), 238-256.
4. R. Bar-Yehuda, O. Goldreich, and A. Itai, On the time complexity of broadcast in radio networks: An exponential gap between determinism and randomization, Proc. 6th ACM Symp. on Principles of Distr. Comp. (1987), 98 - 108.
5. B.S. Chlebus, L. Gasieniec, A. Gibbons, A. Pelc and W. Rytter, Deterministic broadcasting in unknown radio networks, Proc. 11th Ann. ACM-SIAM Symposium on Discrete Algorithms (SODA'2000), 861-870.
6. G. De Marco and A. Pelc, Fast distributed graph coloring with $O(\Delta)$ colors, manuscript.
7. K. Diks, E. Kranakis, D. Krizanc and A. Pelc, The impact of knowledge on broadcasting time in radio networks, Proc. 7th Annual European Symposium on Algorithms, ESA'99, Prague, Czech Republic, July 1999, LNCS 1643, 41-52.
8. D. Z. Du and F. H. Hwang, Combinatorial group testing and its applications, World Scientific, Singapore, 1993.
9. S. Even and B. Monien, On the number of rounds necessary to disseminate information, Proc. 1st ACM Symp. on Par. Alg. and Arch., June 1989, 318-327.
10. U. Feige, D. Peleg, P. Raghavan and E. Upfal, Randomized broadcast in networks, Random Structures and Algorithms 1 (1990), 447-460.
11. P. Fraigniaud and E. Lazard, Methods and problems of communication in usual networks, Disc. Appl. Math. 53 (1994), 79-133.
12. P. Fraigniaud, A. Pelc, D. Peleg and S. Perennes, Assigning labels in unknown anonymous networks, Proc. 19th ACM Symp. on Principles of Distributed Computing (PODC'2000), July 2000, Portland, Oregon, U.S.A., 101-112.
13. L. Gargano, A. Pelc, S. Perennes and U. Vaccaro, Efficient communication in unknown networks, Proc. 26th International Workshop on Graph-Theoretic Concepts in Computer Science (WG'2000), June 2000, Konstanz, Germany, to appear.
14. L.Gasieniec and A. Pelc, Broadcasting with a bounded fraction of faulty nodes, Journal of Parallel and Distributed Computing 42 (1997), 11-20.
15. S.M. Hedetniemi, S.T. Hedetniemi and A.L. Liestman, A survey of Gossiping and Broadcasting in Communication Networks, Networks 18 (1988), 319-349.
16. J. Komlós and A. G. Greenberg, An asymptotically nonadaptive algorithm for conflict resolution in multiple-access channels, IEEE Trans. on Information Theory, IT-31 n. 2 (1985), 302-306.
17. D.W. Krumme, Fast gossiping for the hypercube, SIAM J. Computing 21 (1992), 365-380.
18. N. Linial, Locality in distributed graph algorithms, SIAM J. Computing 21 (1992), 193-201.
19. P. Panaite and A. Pelc, Exploring unknown undirected graphs, Proc. 9th Ann. ACM-SIAM Symposium on Discrete Algorithms (SODA'98), 316-322.

# Minimizing Makespan in Batch Machine Scheduling *

Chung Keung Poon[1] and Pixing Zhang[2]

[1] Dept. of Computer Science, City University of Hong Kong, China
ckpoon@cs.cityu.edu.hk
[2] Dept. of Computer Science, Fudan University, China
972402@fudan.edu.cn

**Abstract.** We study the scheduling of a set of $n$ jobs, each characterized by a release (arrival) time and a processing time, for a batch processing machine capable of running at most $B$ jobs at a time. We obtain an $O(n \log n)$-time algorithm when $B$ is unbounded. When there are only $m$ distinct release times and the inputs are integers, we obtain an $O(n(BR_{max})^{m-1}(2/m)^{m-3})$-time algorithm where $R_{max}$ is the difference between the maximum and minimum release times. When there are $k$ distinct processing times and $m$ release times, we obtain an $O(k^{k+2}B^{k+1}m^2 \log m)$-time algorithm. We obtain even better algorithms for $m = 2$ and for $k = 1$. These algorithms improve most of the corresponding previous algorithms for the respective special cases and lead to improved approximation schemes for the general problem.

## 1 Introduction

In this paper, we study the problem of job scheduling in a batch processing system. More precisely, we are given a set of jobs $\mathcal{J} = \{J_1, \ldots, J_n\}$ and a *batch machine*. Each job, $J_i$, is associated with a release time $r_i$ which specifies when the job becomes available and a processing time $p_i$ which specifies the minimum time needed to process the job by the machine. The batch machine can process up to $B$ jobs simultaneously. Jobs processed in the same batch have the same start time and completion time. Here, we concentrate on the *burn-in* model in which the processing time of a batch is the largest processing time of any job in the batch. (This model is motivated by the problem of scheduling burn-in operations in the manufacturing of VLSI circuits. For more detail, see Lee et al. [7].) Our goal is to find a schedule for the jobs so that the makespan, $C_{max}$, defined as the completion time of the last job, is minimized. Using the notation of Graham et al. [4], we denote this problem as $1|r_j, B|C_{max}$. Previous algorithms for $1|r_j, B|C_{max}$ deal with various special cases of the problem and are mostly based on dynamic programming (DP). In this paper, we propose several new algorithms which improve most of these algorithms. The improvements are

---

* This research was fully supported by a grant from City U. of Hong Kong (Project No. 7100068).

D.T. Lee and S.-H. Teng (Eds.): ISAAC 2000, LNCS 1969, pp. 386–397, 2000.

achieved by either improving the DP formulation or optimizing the evaluation of the state-space defined by the DP formulation. Below, we give a brief survey on the previous work and state our results for the corresponding cases.

For the unbounded model, the value $B$ is infinite compared with the number of jobs. That is, $B = \infty$, or equivalently, $B \geq n$. This is motivated by those manufacturing processes in which the capacity of the machine is very large (practically infinite) compared with the number of jobs. In this model, Lee and Uzsoy [6] give an $O(n^2)$-time DP-based algorithm. An alternative algorithm with the same time complexity is provided by Brucker et al. [2] indirectly. Here, we derive an $O(n \log n)$-time algorithm by optimizing the algorithm of [6].

For the bounded model (where $B < n$), the general $1|r_j, B|C_{max}$ problem is shown to be strongly NP-hard indirectly by Brucker et al. [2]. It is therefore natural to consider special cases of this problem. Two common special cases are obtained by restricting the number of release times and processing times respectively. In fact, when there is only one release time, the problem becomes the $1|B|C_{max}$ problem (batch machine scheduling for jobs without release times) and can be solved efficiently by the FBLPT rule of Bartholdi [1] and Brucker et al. [2]. When there are two distinct release times, the problem already becomes NP-hard, see Liu and Yu [8]. With the additional assumption that the inputs are integers, Lee and Uzsoy [6] propose an algorithm running in $O(nB^2 P_{sum} P_{max})$ time where $P_{max} = \max_{i=1,...,n}\{p_i\}$ and $P_{sum} = \sum_{i=1}^{n} p_i$ are the maximum and total processing time respectively. Thus their algorithm runs in pseudo-polynomial time. This is improved and generalized by Deng et al [3] to the case when there are $m$ distinct release times. They showed that $O(nm(BP_{max}P_{sum})^{m-1})$ time is sufficient for the problem. Independently, Liu and Yu [8] propose an $O(nB^m(P_{max}P_{sum})^{m-1})$-time algorithm. Here, we design an $O(nR_{max} \log B)$-time algorithm when $m = 2$, and an $O(n(BR_{max})^{m-1}(2/m)^{m-3})$-time algorithm for general $m$ where $R_{max}$ is the difference between the maximum and minimum release times. Moreover, we present a simple $O(n \log n)$ time preprocessing that generates a new input (of no greater size than the original input) in which $R_{max} < P_{sum}$. Thus, our algorithm improves both the algorithms of [3] and [8].

In comparison, the special case with constant number of processing times has received much less attention. The only known previous result is due to Ikura and Gimple [5]. They show that when the jobs have equal processing time, the problem can be solved in $O(n \log n)$ time using their First-Only-Empty (FOE) algorithm. (In fact, it takes only $O(n)$ time when the jobs are pre-sorted in nondecreasing order of release times.) The FOE algorithm is quite unusual among algorithms in this area because it is not DP-based. Unfortunately, little intuition is provided by this algorithm and the proof of its correctness. It is not obvious how to extend their idea to the case where there are $k > 1$ distinct processing times. Here, we developed an alternative algorithm with time complexity $O(Bm \log m)$ for the case where $k = 1$. We then extend the idea to an $O(k^{k+2}B^{k+1}m^2 \log m)$-time algorithm for general $k$. To our knowledge, this is the first algorithm in the literature that deals with the case where $k > 1$.

In the next section, we define some useful notations employed throughout the whole paper. This is followed by our algorithms for the unbounded case, the bounded case with $m$ release times and $k$ processing times in sections 3, 4 and 5 respectively. For simplicity, we only describe the algorithms for computing the minimum makespan instead of the actual schedules. The paper is then concluded by some open problems in section 6.

## 2   Preliminaries

We let $R_1 < \cdots < R_m$ be the $m$ distinct release times and $P_1 > P_2 > \cdots > P_k$ be the $k$ distinct processing times. For convenience, we assume without loss of generality that $R_1 = 0$, and we take $R_{m+1} = \infty$. Therefore, $R_{max} = R_m - R_1 = R_m$. We denote by $\Delta_i$ the time interval $[R_i, R_{i+1})$ and let $|\Delta_i| = R_{i+1} - R_i$ for $i = 1, \ldots, m$. We call a job a $P_l$-job if its processing time is $P_l$; an *unscheduled* job at time $t$ if it has been released at or before time $t$ but not yet scheduled by $t$. We call a batch containing exactly $B$ jobs a *full batch*.

We formally define a schedule for $\mathcal{J}$ as a sequence of ordered pairs $(\mathcal{J}_1, t_1)$, $(\mathcal{J}_2, t_2)$, $\ldots$, $(\mathcal{J}_l, t_l)$ such that $\{\mathcal{J}_1, \mathcal{J}_2, \ldots, \mathcal{J}_l\}$ is a partition of $\mathcal{J}$ and for all $i = 1, \ldots, l$, we have (1) $|\mathcal{J}_i| \leq B$; (2) every job in $\mathcal{J}_i$ is released at or before $t_i$; and (3) the processing time of the batch $\mathcal{J}_i$ is at most $t_{i+1} - t_i$.

## 3   The Unbounded Model

As observed in Proposition 1 of [6], if job $J_i$ is released before $J_j$ and has a smaller processing time than $J_j$, then $J_i$ can be scheduled in the same batch as $J_j$. Therefore, we need only consider the case where jobs that come later have smaller processing times. That is, we assume $r_1 \leq r_2 \leq \cdots \leq r_n$ and $p_1 > p_2 > \cdots > p_n$. Define $f(i)$ as the minimum makespan of a schedule for $J_1, J_2, \ldots, J_i$. The general strategy is to schedule $J_1, \ldots, J_j$, for some $0 \leq j < i$, in the best way and then schedule $J_{j+1}, \ldots, J_i$ in the same batch at time $r_i$ or $f(j)$, whichever comes later. Then a recurrence formula for $f(i)$ (which is essentially the same as that in [6]) is:

$$f(0) = 0 \text{ and } f(i) = \min_{0 \leq j \leq i-1}\{\max\{f(j), r_i\} + p_{j+1}\} \text{ for } i > 0.$$

Our algorithm will compute $f(0), f(1), \ldots, f(n)$ one by one and store the result in an array $f[0..n]$. A straightforward implementation requires $O(i)$ time to compute $f(i)$ and hence $O(n^2)$ time for $f[0..n]$. Instead, we will make use of the work done in computing $f(i-1)$ to speed up the computation of $f(i)$. First, note that $f$ is monotonic non-decreasing, i.e., $f(0) \leq f(1) \leq \cdots \leq f(n)$. Therefore, we can find an index $h_i$ such that $f(h_i) \leq r_i < f(h_i + 1)$. Then $\max\{f(j), r_i\} = r_i$ if $j \leq h_i$ and $\max\{f(j), r_i\} = f(j)$ otherwise. Therefore,

$$f(i) = \min\{r_i + p_{h_i+1}, f(h_i + 1) + p_{h_i+2}, \ldots, f(i-1) + p_i\}.$$

Let $A_i = \{f(j) + p_{j+1} \mid h_i + 1 \leq j \leq i - 1\}$. To obtain $A_{i+1}$ from $A_i$, we compute $h_{i+1}$ (by a binary search for $r_{i+1}$ on $f[0..n]$), delete the elements in $A_i \backslash A_{i+1}$

$(= \{f(j) + p_{j+1} \mid h_i + 1 \le j \le h_{i+1}\})$ and insert the element $f(i) + p_{i+1}$. We store $A_i$ as a heap and keep an array $P$ of pointers so that $P[j]$ points to the element $f(j) + p_{j+1}$ in the heap when it was inserted. Then it is fairly easy to see that our algorithm requires $O(n \log n)$ time in total.

## 4    The Bounded Model with $m$ Release Times

In this section, we assume that the release times and processing times are integers. First we describe a preprocessing step which ensures that $R_{max} < P_{sum}$. Define $P_{sum,i}$ as the sum of processing times for all jobs released at or before time $R_i$, that is $P_{sum,i} = \sum_{(j \text{ s.t. } r_j \le R_i)} p_j$ for $i = 1, \ldots, m - 1$. The following lemma shows that if $P_{sum,i} \le R_{i+1}$ for some $i$, then the original problem can be separated into two sub-problems, one trivial and the other simpler than the original one.

**Lemma 1.** *Let $P_{sum,i}$ be defined as above and let $j$ be the smallest index such that $P_{sum,j} \le R_{j+1}$. Then the jobs released at or before $R_j$ can be finished at or before the next release time $R_{j+1}$.*

Based on Lemma 1, our preprocessing proceeds as follows. Sort the jobs by release times. Compute $P_{sum,i}$ for $i = 1, \ldots, m - 1$. Scan the jobs in non-decreasing order of release times. If $P_{sum,i} \le R_{i+1}$ for some $i$, let $j$ be the smallest such index. Then we finish the jobs arrive at or before $R_j$ by time $R_{j+1}$ according to Lemma 1. Then we are left with the jobs that arrived at or after $R_{j+1}$. We continue the scanning and compare $P_{sum,i} - P_{sum,j}$ with $R_{i+1} - R_{j+1}$ for $i \ge j + 1$. After the preprocessing, we can assume $P_{sum} > R_{max}$ in the remaining problem.

The following lemma (i.e., Lemma 1 of [3]) states that we just need to search for an optimal schedule from those that observe the Full-Batch-Longest-Processing-Time (FBLPT) rule locally in each interval. That is, for jobs scheduled (started but not necessarily finished) within the same interval, those with larger processing time are scheduled first and each batch is a full batch except possibly the last one.

**Lemma 2.** *([3]) For any schedule $\Psi$ with makespan $C_{max}$, there exists a schedule $\Psi'$ with makespan $C'_{max} \le C_{max}$ such that both schedules assign the same set of jobs to each interval and $\Psi'$ schedules the jobs in each interval according to the FBLPT rule.*

By this lemma, it is natural to consider the jobs in non-increasing order of processing time. For convenience, we assume the jobs are indiced such that $p_1 \ge p_2 \ge \cdots \ge p_n$.

### 4.1    Algorithm for $m = 2$

We first describe an algorithm with time complexity $O(nBR_{max})$. Following the idea of [3], we consider a schedule for jobs $J_1, \ldots, J_i$. Suppose it started $n_1$ jobs in interval $\Delta_1$ and completed the last of them at time $t_1$. Then Deng et al. [3] define the state reached by this schedule as the 4-tuple, $(i, b_2, t_1, n_1 \bmod B)$ where $b_2$ is the start time of the first batch in $\Delta_2$. They continue to define $f(i, b, c, s)$ as the minimum makespan of a schedule for $J_1, \ldots, J_i$ that reaches the state $(i, b, c, s)$ and derive a recurrence formula for $f$.

Our first major observation is that the parameter $b_2$ is redundant. If $t_1 \leq R_{max}$, we have $b_2 = 0$; and if $t_1 > R_{max}$, we have $b_2 = t_1 - R_{max}$. Accordingly, we have the following definition.

**Definition 1.** *A schedule for* $J_1, \ldots, J_i$ *is said to reach a state* $(i, c, s)$ *if it schedules* $n_1$ *jobs in* $\Delta_1$ *and completes the last of them at time* $t_1$ *(=0 if* $n_1 = 0$*) such that* $c = n_1 \bmod B$ *and* $s = \min\{t_1, R_{max}\}$*. The makespan of a state* $(i, c, s)$*, denoted as* $f(i, c, s)$*, is defined as the maximum between* $R_{max}$ *and the minimum makespan of a schedule that reaches state* $(i, c, s)$*.*

Compared with that of [3], our definition results in a smaller number of states but slightly more complex recurrence relation for $f$. For the base case, we have:
(1) $f(1, \min\{p_1, R_{max}\}, 1) = \max\{R_{max}, p_1\}$ (when $J_1$ is placed in $\Delta_1$),
(2) $f(1, 0, 0) = R_{max} + p_1$ (when $J_1$ is placed in $\Delta_2$), and
(3) $f(1, c, s) = \infty$ for all other $(c, s)$.
For the recursive case (where $i \geq 2$), consider the two choices for placing $J_i$. Suppose job $J_i$ is scheduled in interval $\Delta_2$. If the number of jobs among $J_1, \ldots, J_{i-1}$ that are scheduled in $\Delta_2$ is not a multiple of $B$, (i.e., $i - 1 \neq s \bmod B$), then the last batch in $\Delta_2$ before inserting $J_i$ is not a full batch (because we apply the FBLPT rule) and its processing time is no less than $p_i$ (by the order we index the jobs). Therefore, adding $J_i$ to this batch will not increase its completion time. On the other hand, if $i - 1 = s \bmod B$, then $J_i$ has to be placed in a new batch. This will increase the makespan by $p_i$. Therefore, the minimum makespan of a schedule that places job $J_i$ in interval $\Delta_2$ and reaches state $(i, c, s)$ is:

$$f_2 = \begin{cases} f(i-1, c, s) & \text{if } i-1 \neq s \bmod B \\ f(i-1, c, s) + p_i & \text{if } i-1 = s \bmod B \end{cases}$$

Now suppose job $J_i$ is scheduled in interval $\Delta_1$. (This is possible only if $J_i$ arrives at time $R_1 = 0$ and there is room in $\Delta_1$.) If $s \neq 1 \bmod B$, then by a similar argument as above, placing $J_i$ in interval $\Delta_1$ does not increase the completion time of the jobs started in $\Delta_1$. If $s = 1 \bmod B$, the completion time will increase by $p_i$. If $c < R_{max}$, the completion time of the jobs in $\Delta_1$ before adding $J_i$ is $c' = c - p_i$. The interesting case is when $c = R_{max}$. The completion time before adding $J_i$ could be any $c'$ such that $c' + p_i \geq R_{max}$. Placing $J_i$ in $\Delta_1$ will then delay the start time of the jobs in $\Delta_2$ by $c' + p_i - R_{max}$. This will in turn increase the makespan by the same amount. Therefore, the minimum makespan of a schedule that places job $J_i$ in interval $\Delta_1$ and reaches state $(i, c, s)$ is:

$$f_1 = \begin{cases} f(i-1, c, s-1) & \text{if } s \neq 1 \\ f(i-1, c-p_i, s-1) & \text{if } s = 1 \text{ and } c < R_{max} \\ \min_{x=0,\ldots,p_i-1}\{f(i-1, R_{max}-p_i+x, s-1)+x\} & \text{if } s = 1 \text{ and } c = R_{max} \end{cases}$$

Finally, $f(i, c, s) = \min\{f_1, f_2\}$ if $J_i$ arrives at time $R_1$, and $f(i, c, s) = f_2$ otherwise.

Our algorithm first computes $f(1, c, s)$ for all possible $(c, s)$'s, then proceeds to $f(2, c, s)$ and so on. The minimum makespan is computed as $\min_{(c,s)}\{f(n, c, s)\}$. Since $1 \leq i \leq n$, $0 \leq s \leq B - 1$ and $0 \leq c \leq R_{max}$, there are $nB(R_{max} + 1)$ states. For those states with $c < R_{max}$ or $s \neq 1$, the time to compute $f(i, c, s)$ is constant. For those with $c = R_{max}$ and $s = 1$, the time is $O(\min\{R_{max}, P_{max}\}) = O(R_{max})$. Since there are only $n$ such states, the total time of the whole algorithm is $O(nBR_{max})$. We can reduce the time complexity to $O(nR_{max} \log B)$ by evaluating only $O(1/B)$-th of the $O(nBR_{max})$ states, each taking $O(\log B)$ time. Due to space limitation, we omit the algorithm here.

## 4.2 Algorithm for General $m$

We first generalize Definition 1 as follows.

**Definition 2.** *A schedule for $J_1, \ldots, J_i$ is said to reach the state $(i, \boldsymbol{C}, \boldsymbol{S})$ if, for $j = 1, \ldots, m - 1$, it started $n_j$ jobs in interval $\Delta_j$ and completed the last of those started in $\Delta_1 \cup \cdots \cup \Delta_j$ at time $t_j$ ($t_j = 0$ if no jobs are started in $\Delta_1 \cup \cdots \cup \Delta_j$) such that $\boldsymbol{C} = (c_1, \ldots, c_{m-1})$ and $\boldsymbol{S} = (s_1, \ldots, s_{m-1})$ where $c_j = \min\{\max\{0, t_j - R_j\}, |\Delta_j|\}$; and $s_j = n_j \bmod B$ for $j = 1, \ldots, m - 1$.*

Note that by definition $0 \leq c_j \leq |\Delta_j|$ even when $t_j < R_j$ or $t_j > R_{j+1}$. The makespan, $f(i, \boldsymbol{C}, \boldsymbol{S})$, of a state $(i, \boldsymbol{C}, \boldsymbol{S})$ is defined analogously as previous subsection. Here, the derivation of a recurrence formula for $f$ is more difficult compared with that in the case $k = 1$. Let $\boldsymbol{C} = (c_1, \ldots, c_{m-1})$, $\boldsymbol{S} = (s_1, \ldots, s_{m-1})$, $\boldsymbol{C}' = (c'_1, \ldots, c'_{m-1})$ and $\boldsymbol{S}' = (s'_1, \ldots, s'_{m-1})$. Consider the value of $f(i, \boldsymbol{C}', \boldsymbol{S}')$. If $J_i$ is placed in some interval $\Delta_l$ where $c'_l = |\Delta_l|$ and $s'_l = 1$, then there may be many possible previous states $(i - 1, \boldsymbol{C}, \boldsymbol{S})$. The problem is even more complicated if $c'_{l+1} = |\Delta_{l+1}|, \ldots, c'_h = |\Delta_h|$ for some $h > l$ as well. It is possible that $c_l, \ldots, c_h$ are less than their respective maximum but $p_i$ is large enough to fill up the remaining time in all the intervals. Our second major observation is that we can evaluate the state-space in a "bottom-up forward" order: Suppose we have computed $f(i-1, \boldsymbol{C}, \boldsymbol{S})$ for all $(\boldsymbol{C}, \boldsymbol{S})$. Then for each state $(i-1, \boldsymbol{C}, \boldsymbol{S})$ and each possible placement of $J_i$, we compute the next state $(i, \boldsymbol{C}', \boldsymbol{S}')$ reached and the makespan $C_{max}$ of the schedule. If $C_{max}$ is less than the current estimate of $f(i, \boldsymbol{C}', \boldsymbol{S}')$, we update $f(i, \boldsymbol{C}', \boldsymbol{S}')$ with the better estimate (i.e., $C_{max}$). When we have done that for all $(\boldsymbol{C}, \boldsymbol{S})$, we would have computed $f(i, \boldsymbol{C}', \boldsymbol{S}')$ for all $(\boldsymbol{C}', \boldsymbol{S}')$. For comparison, our algorithm for the case of $m = 2$ evaluates the state-space in a "bottom-up backward" order. The computation of $(i, \boldsymbol{C}', \boldsymbol{S}')$ and $f(i, \boldsymbol{C}', \boldsymbol{S}')$ from $(i-1, \boldsymbol{C}, \boldsymbol{S})$ and $f(i-1, \boldsymbol{C}, \boldsymbol{S})$ can be done by careful case analysis. Due to space limitation, we omit the details here.

The pseudocode of our algorithm is shown in Figure 1. There are $nB^{m-1}$ $\prod_{i=1}^{m-1}(|\Delta_i| + 1) \leq nB^{m-1}(2R_{max}/(m-1))^{m-1}$ possible states as $\sum_{j=1}^{m-1}(|\Delta_j| + 1) = R_{max} + m - 1 \leq 2R_{max}$. (Note that $R_{max} \geq m - 1$.) Here we just state that for each $l$ and each state $(i - 1, \boldsymbol{C}, \boldsymbol{S})$, it takes $O(m)$ time to compute the new state $(i, \boldsymbol{C}', \boldsymbol{S}')$ when $J_i$ is placed in $\Delta_l$. Therefore, the total time of our algorithm is $O(m^2 n B^{m-1}(2R_{max}/(m-1))^{m-1}) = O(n(BR_{max})^{m-1}(2/m)^{m-3})$.

```
Algorithm CMAXRm
Begin
1   Set f(i, C, S) = ∞ for all (i, C, S)
2   Let r₁ = Rᵢ'
    for l = i' to m do
        compute state (1, C, S) and makespan Cₘₐₓ if J₁ is placed in Δₗ
        if Cₘₐₓ < f(1, C, S) then f(1, C, S) = Cₘₐₓ
3   for i = 2 to n do
        let rᵢ = Rᵢ'
        for l = i' to m do
            for each (i − 1, C, S) s.t. f(i − 1, C, S) < ∞ do
                compute state (i, C', S') and makespan Cₘₐₓ if Jᵢ is placed in Δₗ
                if Cₘₐₓ < f(i, C', S') then f(i, C', S') = Cₘₐₓ
4   return(min₍C,S₎{f(n, C, S)})
End
```

**Fig. 1.** Algorithm $CMAXRm$ for $m$ release times

# 5   Bounded Model with $k$ Processing Times

In this section, the inputs are not necessarily integers.

## 5.1   Algorithm for $k = 1$

For convenience, we let $n_i$ be the number of jobs arrived at time $R_i$ throughout this subsection. Suppose there are $\gamma$ unscheduled jobs at some moment $t \in \Delta_i$ (i.e., $R_i \le t < R_{i+1}$) and the machine is not processing any batch which will complete after $t$. So, the machine is free to start (or not start) a batch at this moment. We say that the machine reaches state $(t, \gamma)$. We formally define the state below.

**Definition 3.** *A schedule is said to reach a state $(t, \gamma)$ if it does not start a batch before time $t$ which completes after $t$, and there are $\gamma$ unscheduled jobs at $t$. A state $(t, \gamma)$ is a reachable state if there exists a schedule that reaches this state.*

If a schedule reaches some state $(t, \gamma)$ where $t \in \Delta_i$, it has basically two choices: start a batch at $t$ or wait until $R_{i+1}$. If it waits, it will arrive at the state $(R_{i+1}, \gamma + n_{i+1})$. If it starts, it will arrive at some state $(t + P_1, \sum_{h=i+1}^{j} n_h)$ where $t + P_1 \in \Delta_j$. It is then natural to define the function $f(t, \gamma)$ as the minimum makespan of a schedule that reaches state $(t, \gamma)$ and derive a recursive formula of the following form:

$$f(t, \gamma) = \min\{f(t + P_1, \gamma \ominus B + \sum_{h=i+1}^{j} n_h), f(R_{i+1}, \gamma + n_{i+1})\}$$

where $\gamma \ominus B = \gamma - B$ if $\gamma \ge B$ and $\gamma \ominus B = 0$ otherwise.

Applying a top-down implementation directly, one obtains a recursive algorithm with high complexity because of many repeated calls to the same subproblems. Using dynamic programming, one computes $f(t, \gamma)$ for all possible $(t, \gamma)$'s in a bottom-up manner. Since $0 \leq \gamma \leq n$ and $t$ must be of the form $R_j + xP_1$ for some index $j$ and integer $x$, there are $O(mn^2)$ states in total. Hence it takes $O(mn^2)$ time, which is still much slower than the FOE algorithm. Our algorithm will evaluate the state-space in a "top-down" order and make use of Lemma 3, 4 and 5 below to cut down the number of states to at most 2 per interval.

**Lemma 3.** *Let $\Psi$ and $\Psi'$ be schedules that reach states $(t, \gamma)$ and $(t', \gamma')$ respectively where $R_i \leq t \leq t' < R_{i+1}$ for some $i$ and $\gamma \leq \gamma'$. Then there exists a schedule that reaches state $(t, \gamma)$ and has makespan no larger than that of $\Psi'$.*

By lemma 3, if $(t, \gamma)$ is a reachable state where $R_i \leq t < R_{i+1}$ for some $i$, then it is unnecessary to consider any other state $(t', \gamma')$ where $t \leq t' < R_{i+1}$ and $\gamma \leq \gamma'$. If an optimal schedule reaches state $(t', \gamma')$, there must be an optimal schedule that reaches state $(t, \gamma)$.

**Lemma 4.** *Let $\Psi$ be a schedule that reaches state $(t, \gamma)$ where $t \in \Delta_i$ and $\gamma > B - 1$. Then there exists a schedule that reaches state $(t + P_1, \gamma - B + \sum_{h=i+1}^{j} n_h)$ where $t + P_1 \in \Delta_j$. Moreover the schedule has makespan no more than that of $\Psi$.*

By lemma 4, we can start a full batch whenever we have $B$ or more unscheduled jobs. Hence we just need to consider those states $(t, \gamma)$ in which $\gamma < B$. We call these states the *basic states*. Combined with lemma 3, there are at most $B$ basic states that need to be considered in each interval.

**Lemma 5.** *Let $(t, \gamma)$ and $(t', \gamma')$ be two reachable states where $R_i \leq t < t' < R_{i+1}$ for some $i$ and $B > \gamma > \gamma'$.*

(a) *Suppose there is a schedule $\Psi$ that reaches state $(t, \gamma)$ and then waits until time $R_{i+1}$. Then there is a schedule $\Phi$ that reaches state $(t', \gamma')$, and has makespan no more than that of $\Psi$.*

(b) *Suppose there is a schedule $\Psi'$ that reaches state $(t', \gamma')$ and then starts a batch at time $t'$. Then there is a schedule $\Phi'$ that reaches state $(t, \gamma)$, and has makespan no more than that of $\Psi'$.*

A corollary of Lemma 5 is that we just need to consider at most two basic states in each interval. Moreover, we need only consider starting a batch from the state $(t, \gamma)$ and waiting from the state $(t', \gamma')$.

Having described Lemma 3, 4 and 5, we are ready to present our algorithm. Initially, the algorithm calls the procedure *Insert* to place the state $(R_1, n_1)$ (or an appropriately derived state) into the appropriate interval. Then it examines the states in each interval, starting from $\Delta_1$. Suppose we have processed intervals $\Delta_1, \ldots, \Delta_{i-1}$ and let the two states in $\Delta_i$ be $(t, \gamma)$ and $(t', \gamma')$ where $R_i \leq t < t' < R_{i+1}$ and $B > \gamma > \gamma'$. Then we will generate the state $(R_{i+1}, \gamma' + n_{i+1})$ (which is reached if the machine reaches state $(t', \gamma')$ and then waits) and the state $(t + P_1, \sum_{h=i+1}^{j} n_h)$ where $R_j \leq t + P_1 < R_{j+1}$ (which is reached if the machine reaches state $(t, \gamma)$ and then starts a batch). We process these states by calling *Insert*. To insert the state $(t, \gamma)$, the procedure *Insert* will check if $\gamma \geq B$. If so, it applies Lemma 4 to reduce $\gamma$ to less than $B$, and increase $t$ accordingly. New jobs may arrive when $t$ increases, therefore $\gamma$ may increase and the process of checking $\gamma \geq B$ and applying Lemma 4 is repeated until a basic state is reached. It then locates the interval to which this basic state belongs, inserts it and removes any unnecessary states in that interval using Lemma 3 and 5. The pseudocode of our algorithm is shown in Figure 2.

Algorithm *CMAXP1*
Begin
1    *Insert*$(R_1, n_1)$
2    for $i = 1$ to $m - 1$ do
    (a)    if $\Delta_i$ does not contain any state then skip to next interval
    (b)    let $(t, \gamma)$ and $(t', \gamma')$ be the 2 states in $\Delta_i$, where $t < t'$ and $B > \gamma > \gamma'$
        { Comment: If there is only 1 state, set $(t, \gamma) = (t', \gamma')$ }
    (c)    { Comment: Start a batch from $(t, \gamma)$ }
        if $\gamma > 0$ then
            compute $j$ such that $t + P_1 \in \Delta_j$;
            if $j > i$ then *Insert*$(t + P_1, \sum_{h=i+1}^{j} n_h)$ else *Insert*$(R_{i+1}, n_{i+1})$
    (d)    { Comment: Delay jobs in $(t', \gamma')$ to $R_{i+1}$ }
        *Insert*$(R_{i+1}, \gamma' + n_{i+1})$
3    compare the 2 states in $\Delta_m$ to obtain the minimum $C_{max}$
End

Procedure *Insert*$(t, \gamma)$
Begin
1    compute $i$ such that $t \in \Delta_i$
2    while $\gamma \geq B$ do
    (a)    compute $j$ such that $t + \lfloor \gamma/B \rfloor P_1 \in \Delta_j$
    (b)    $t = t + \lfloor \gamma/B \rfloor P_1$; $\gamma = \gamma \bmod B + \sum_{h=i+1}^{j} n_h$; $i = j$
3    insert $(t, \gamma)$ into $\Delta_j$
4    if $\Delta_j$ contains more than 1 state then
        compare and remove any unnecessary state if possible
End

**Fig. 2.** Algorithm *CMAXP1* for $k = 1$

In each call to the procedure *Insert*, the while-loop iterates at most $m$ times, and in each iteration it takes $O(\log m)$ to locate the time interval to which $t$ belongs. Therefore the procedure requires $O(m \log m)$ time. Hence the whole algorithm requires $O(m^2 \log m)$. In each time interval, it stores at most 2 states. Therefore, its space complexity is $O(m)$.

Finally, we remark that the time complexity of algorithm *CMAXP1* can be improved to $O(Bm \log m)$ by a slight modification. Due to space limitation, we omit the details here.

## 5.2   The Case for General $k$

We now study the case for general $k$. Let $n_{l,i}$ be the number of $P_l$-jobs arrived at $R_i$. We generalize the definition of *state* and Lemma 3 as follows.

**Definition 4.** *A schedule is said to reach state* $(t, \gamma_1, \ldots \gamma_k)$ *if it does not start a batch before time $t$ which completes after $t$ and there are $\gamma_l$ unscheduled $P_l$-jobs at time $t$, for $l = 1, \ldots, k$.*

**Lemma 6.** *Let $\Psi$ and $\Psi'$ be schedules that reach states $(t, \gamma_1, \ldots, \gamma_k)$ and $(t', \gamma_1', \ldots, \gamma_k')$ respectively where $R_i \leq t \leq t' < R_{i+1}$ for some $i$ and $\gamma_l \leq \gamma_l'$ for $l = 1 \ldots, k$. Then there exists a schedule that reaches state $(t, \gamma_1, \ldots, \gamma_k)$ with makespan no more than that of $\Psi'$.*

Unfortunately, Lemma 4 cannot be generalized in a straightforward manner. In particular, for those $P_l$-jobs where $l > 1$, it is not always true that we can start a full batch of $P_l$-jobs whenever there are at least $B$ unscheduled $P_l$-jobs. Below, we show a generalization of Lemma 4.

**Theorem 1.** *Let $\Psi$ be a schedule that reaches state $(t, \gamma_1, \ldots, \gamma_k)$ where $t \in \Delta_i$ and $\gamma_l > l(B - 1)$ for some $l$. Then there exists a schedule that reaches state $(t + P_l, \gamma_1', \ldots, \gamma_k')$ where $t + P_l \in \Delta_j$, $\gamma_x' = \gamma_x + \sum_{h=i+1}^{j} n_{x,h}$ (for all $x \neq l$) and $\gamma_l' = \gamma_l - B + \sum_{h=i+1}^{j} n_{l,h}$. Moreover, the schedule has makespan no more than that of $\Psi$.*

By Theorem 1, we need only consider states $(t, \gamma_1, \ldots, \gamma_k)$ where $0 \leq \gamma_l \leq l(B-1)$ for $l = 1, \ldots, k$. Again, we call these *basic* states. Combined with Lemma 6, there are at most $\prod_{l=1}^{k}(l(B - 1) + 1) = O(k!B^k) = O((kB)^k)$ relevant basic states in each time interval. For each basic state, there are $k + 1$ choices: wait until next release time or start a batch with processing time $P_l$, $l = 1, \ldots, k$. Once we pick the value of $l$, we schedule the $B$ (or as many as available) largest available jobs with processing time at most $P_l$.

Now, we are ready to describe our algorithm. We first call procedure *Insert* to insert the state $(R_1, n_{1,1}, \ldots, n_{k,1})$ into the appropriate interval. We then process the basic states interval by interval starting from $\Delta_1$. Suppose we have processed all the states in $\Delta_1, \ldots, \Delta_{i-1}$. Then we process the basic states in $\Delta_i$ in non-decreasing order of $t$. For each possible choice of a basic state $(t, \gamma_1, \ldots, \gamma_k)$, we compute the next state $(t', \gamma_1', \ldots, \gamma_k')$ and call procedure *Insert* to place it in the appropriate interval. Similar to the case of $k = 1$, procedure *Insert* here will check for applicability of Theorem 1 and derive the appropriate basic state $(t'', \gamma_1'', \ldots, \gamma_k'')$. Then it inserts $(t'', \gamma_1'', \ldots, \gamma_k'')$ in the interval $\Delta_j$ where $t'' \in \Delta_j$. If another basic state $(\tilde{t}, \gamma_1'', \ldots, \gamma_k'')$ is already present in $\Delta_j$, it keeps the one with a smaller time. By the order we process the states in an interval, the time of a new state must be larger than that of any processed state. Therefore, it is not possible to remove a processed state. Consequently we process at most $\prod_{l=1}^{k}(l(B-1)+1)$ states for each interval.

Algorithm $CMAXPk$
begin
1   $Insert(R_1, n_{1,1}, \ldots, n_{k,1})$
2   for $i = 1$ to $m - 1$ do
   (a)  if $\Delta_i$ does not contain any state then skip to next interval
   (b)  sort the basic states in $\Delta_i$ in non-decreasing order of $t$
       let $t_1 \leq t_2 \leq \cdots \leq t_{sum}$ where $sum$ = number of basic states in $\Delta_i$
   (c)  for $j = 1$ to $sum$ do
         $Insert\ (R_{i+1}, \gamma_1 + n_{1,i+1}, \cdots, \gamma_k + n_{k,i+1})$   { Comment: wait until $R_{i+1}$ }
         for $l = 1$ to $k$ do   {Comment: start a batch of length $P_l$ }
            let $\gamma_1', \cdots, \gamma_k'$ be the number of unscheduled jobs at $t_j + P_l$
            $Insert(t_j + P_l, \gamma_1', \ldots, \gamma_k')$
3   Compare the basic states in $\Delta_m$ to obtain the minimal makespan
end

**Fig. 3.** Algorithm $CMAXPk$ for general $k$

Pseudocode of our algorithm is shown in Figure 3. For each time interval, there are $O((kB)^k)$ different basic states. It takes $O(k^{k+1}B^k \log(kB))$ time to sort the basic states. For each basic state there are at most $k+1$ different choices. Thus there are $O(k^{k+1}B^k)$ calls to procedure $Insert$. In each call to $Insert$, the while-loop iterates at most $O(m)$ times, and in each iteration it takes $O(k+\log m)$ to locate the time interval to which $t$ belongs and update the $\gamma$'s. Therefore procedure $Insert$ requires $O(m(k + \log m))$ time. Hence the whole algorithm requires $O(m(k^{k+1}B^k \log(kB) + k^{k+1}B^k m(k + \log m))) = O(k^{k+2}B^{k+1}m^2 \log m)$ time. Since we have to store all the basic states for each time interval, the space complexity of the above algorithm is $O((kB)^k m)$.

## 6   Conclusion

Our algorithm for $m$ release times leads to a more efficient polynomial time approximation scheme (PTAS) for $1|r_j, B|C_{max}$ using the technique of [3]. An open problem is to design even more efficient PTAS. One way is to improve our algorithm for $m$ release times. Another possible approach is to turn our algorithm for $k$ processing times into a PTAS. Another line of research is to improve the exact algorithms here. Can one combine the techniques in section 4 and 5 to obtain an even better algorithm when there are $m$ release times and $k$ processing times? Are there other interesting special cases? Finally, we believe that the algorithm for the unbounded case is time optimal. Can one prove a matching lower bound?

# References

1. J.J. Bartholdi. unpublished manuscript, 1988.
2. P. Brucker, A. Gladky, H. Hoogeveen, M.Y. Kovalyov, C.N. Potts, T. Tautenhahn, and S.L. van de Velde. Scheduling a batching machine. *Journal of Scheduling*, 1:31–54, 1998.
3. X. Deng, C.K. Poon, and Y. Zhang. Approximation algorithms in batch processing. In *The 8th Annual International Symposium on Algorithms and Computation*, volume 1741 of *Lecture Notes in Computer Science*, pages 153–162, Chennai, India, December 1999. Spring-verlag.
4. R.L. Graham, Lawler, J.K. Lenstra, and A.H.G. Rinnooy Kan. Optimization and approximation in deterministic sequencing and scheduling. *Annals of Discrete Mathematics*, 5:387–326, 1979.
5. Y. Ikura and M. Gimple. Scheduling algorithm for a single batch processing machine. *Operations Research Letters*, 5:61–65, 1986.
6. C.Y. Lee and R. Uzsoy. Minimizing makespan on a single batch processing machine with dynamic job arrivals. Technical report, Department of Industrial and System Engineering, University of Florida, January 1996.
7. C.Y. Lee, R. Uzsoy, and L.A. Martin Vega. Efficient algorithms for scheduling semiconductor burn-in operations. *Operations Research*, 40:764–775, 1992.
8. Z. Liu and W. Yu. Scheduling one batch processor subject to job release dates. To appear, *Discrete Applied Mathematics*.

# Preemptive Parallel Task Scheduling in $O(n) + \text{Poly}(m)$ Time [*]

Klaus Jansen[1] and Lorant Porkolab[2]

[1] Institut für Informatik und praktische Mathematik, Christian Albrechts University of Kiel, Germany, kj@informatik.uni-kiel.de
[2] Department of Computing, Imperial College, London, United Kingdom, porkolab@doc.ic.ac.uk

**Abstract.** We study the problem of scheduling a set of $n$ independent parallel tasks on $m$ processors, where in addition to the processing time there is a size associated with each task indicating that the task can be processed on any subset of processors of the given size. Based on a linear programming formulation, we propose an algorithm for computing a preemptive schedule with minimum makespan, and show that the running time of the algorithm depends polynomially on $m$ and only linearly on $n$. Thus for any fixed $m$, an optimal preemptive schedule can be computed in $O(n)$ time. We also present extensions of this approach to other (more general) scheduling problems with malleable tasks, release times, due dates and maximum lateness minimization.

## 1 Introduction

In classical scheduling theory, each task is processed by only one processor at a time. However recently, due to the rapid development of parallel computer systems, new theoretical approaches have emerged to model scheduling on parallel architectures. One of these is scheduling multiprocessor tasks, see e.g. [1,4,6,8,9, 11,17,23].

In this paper we address a multiprocessor scheduling problem, where a set $\mathcal{T} = \{T_1, \ldots, T_n\}$ of $n$ tasks has to be executed by $m$ processors such that each processor can execute at most one task at a time and a task must be processed simultaneously by several processors. Let $M = \{1, \ldots, m\}$, $N = \{1, \ldots, n\}$, and let $p_j$ denote the processing time of task $T_j$, for every $j \in N$. In the *dedicated* variant of the model, each task requires the simultaneous use of a prespecified set of processors. In the *parallel* variant, which is also called *non-malleable* parallel task scheduling, the multiprocessor architecture is disregarded and there is simply a size $size_j \in M$ associated with each task $T_j$ which indicates that the task can be processed on any subset of processors of the given size. In the *malleable* variant, each task can be executed on an arbitrary (non-empty) subset of processors, and the execution time of the task depends on the number of processors assigned to it.

[*] Supported in part by CEC, Project APPOL, IST-1999-14084.

D.T. Lee and S.-H. Teng (Eds.): ISAAC 2000, LNCS 1969, pp. 398–409, 2000.
© Springer-Verlag Berlin Heidelberg 2000

Depending on the particular application considered, preemptions of tasks may or may not be allowed. In the *non-preemptive* model, a task once started has to be completed without interruption. In the *preemptive* model, each task can be interrupted any time at no cost and restarted later possibly on a different set of processors. The objective of the scheduling problems discussed in this paper is to minimize the makespan, i.e. the maximum completion time $C_{max}$. We will mainly consider the parallel (or non-malleable) version of the problem which has recently been discussed in several papers, see e.g. [4,8,9,14,16,22]. We will focus on those preemptive schedules where migration is allowed, that is task $T_j$ may be assigned to different processor sets of $size_j$ during different execution phases [4,8,9]. Approximation algorithms for preemptive scheduling without migration can be found e.g. in [21].

The dedicated and parallel variants of preemptive scheduling for independent multiprocessor tasks (on a fixed number of processors) are denoted by $P|fix_j, pmtn|C_{max}$ ($Pm|fix_j, pmtn|C_{max}$) and $P|size_j, pmtn|C_{max}$ ($Pm|size_j, pmtn|C_{max}$), respectively. Regarding the complexity, it is known that problem $P|size_j, pmtn|C_{max}$ is NP-hard [8,9], however the question whether it is strongly NP-hard was open [8,9]. Problem $Pm|size_j, pmtn|C_{max}$ (with constant number of processors) can be solved in polynomial time [4] by formulating it as a linear program with $n$ constraints and $O(n^m)$ nonnegative variables and computing an optimal solution by any polynomial-time linear programming algorithm. Even though (for any constant $m$), the running time in this approach is polynomial in $n$, the degree of the polynomial depends linearly on $m$. Therefore it is natural to ask (see also [2]) whether there are more efficient algorithms for $Pm|size_j, pmtn|C_{max}$ (of running time, say for instance, $O(n)$) that compute exact or approximate solutions. This question was answered in an affirmative way for the dedicated variant in [1], where it was shown that $Pm|fix_j, pmtn|C_{max}$ can be solved in linear time.

In this paper we focus on computing (exact) optimal solutions and present a linear time algorithm for $Pm|size_j, pmtn|C_{max}$ providing a significant improvement of the best previously known complexity result and also answering an open question in [2]. In fact, we propose an algorithm for solving the general problem $P|size_j, pmtn|C_{max}$ and show that this algorithm runs in $O(n) + poly(m)$ time, where $poly(.)$ is a univariate polynomial. This gives a strongly polynomial complexity for any $m$ that is polynomially bounded by $n$, and hence also implies that $P|size_j, pmtn|C_{max}$ cannot be strongly NP-hard, unless P=NP. Our approach is based on a linear programming formulation, where the number of variables is exponential in $m$ (and does not depend on $n$) and the number of constraints is polynomial in $m$. We study the dual linear program and show that the corresponding strong separation problem can be solved in polynomial time. This implies along with one of the general results of [12], that a basic optimal solution of the primal can also be computed in polynomial time. Furthermore, we show that the number of preemptions generated by the algorithm is bounded by a polynomial in $m$.

We mention in passing that the non-preemptive variants of the above problems are strongly NP-hard even when $m$ is fixed, in particular this holds for $P3|fix_j|C_{max}$ [13] and $P5|size_j|C_{max}$ [9]. The authors have also studied these problems (along with a generalization to malleable tasks) [14] and proposed an approximation scheme that runs in linear time for any fixed number of processors. The parallel task scheduling problem is also closely related to rectangle packing (see e.g. [16,22]).

## 2  Linear Programming Formulation - First Approach

In this section first we study a linear programming formulation for preemptive parallel task scheduling. This also allows us to introduce those algorithmic tools that will be used in subsequent sections. Extensions of this simple linear programming formulation for more general models will be given in Section 6 and the full version of the paper. As it was mentioned in the introduction, we consider preemptive schedules, where any task is allowed to be executed by different processor sets during different execution phases. For problem $P|size_j, pmtn|C_{max}$ a configuration will be a compatible (or feasible) subset of tasks that can be scheduled simultaneously. Let $F$ be the set of all configurations, and for every $f \in F$, let $x_f$ denote the length (in time) of the configuration $f$ in the schedule. (Clearly, $f \in F$ iff $\sum_{j \in f} size_j \leq m$.) It is easy to check [4] that problem $P|size_j, pmtn|C_{max}$ can be formulated as the following linear program $LP_1$:

$$\text{Min} \sum_{f \in F} x_f$$
$$\text{s.t.} \sum_{f \in F: j \in f} x_f \geq p_j, \quad \forall j \in N, \qquad (1)$$
$$x_f \geq 0, \quad \forall f \in F.$$

Since the number of variables in $LP_1$ is bounded by $n^m$ (i.e. polynomial in $n$ for any fixed $m$), one can conclude that an optimal schedule for $Pm|size_j, pmtn| C_{max}$ can be computed in polynomial time [4] (by applying any polynomial-time linear programming algorithm). However this complexity result can be improved by a more careful analysis based on the dual of $LP_1$,

$$\text{Max} \sum_{j \in N} p_j y_j$$
$$\text{s.t.} \sum_{j: j \in f} y_j \leq 1, \quad \forall f \in F, \qquad (2)$$
$$y_j \geq 0, \quad \forall j \in N.$$

This linear program $DLP_1$ has $n$ non-negative variables and $n^m$ constraints. The separation problem for $DLP_1$ is the following: Given an $n$-vector $y$, decide whether $y$ is a feasible solution of (2), and if not, find an inequality that separates $y$ from the solution set of (2).

**Lemma 1.** *The separation problem for $DLP_1$ can be solved in $poly(m, n)$ time, where $poly(., .)$ is some bivariate polynomial.*

*Proof.* Let $F_{ik}$ denote the set of all subsets of tasks from $\{1, \ldots, k\}$ that can be scheduled simultaneously on machines from $\{1, \ldots, i\}$, and let $F(i, k) =$

$\max\{ \sum_{j:j\in f_{ik}} y_j \; : \; f_{ik} \in F_{ik} \}$. (Clearly, $F = F_{mn}$.) Then the problem of testing the feasibility of a given $n$-vector $y$ for (2) is equivalent to computing $\max\{F(m',n) \; : \; m' = 1,\ldots,m\}$ (assuming w.l.o.g. that $y$ is nonnegative), which can be done by using a dynamic programming procedure based on the following recursions.

$$F(0,k) = F(i,0) = 0, \quad i \in M, \; k = 0,1,\ldots,n,$$
$$F(i,k) = F(i,k-1), \quad i = 1,\ldots,size_k - 1, \; k \in N,$$
$$F(i,k) = \max\{F(i,k-1), F(i - size_k, k-1) + y_k\}, \quad i = size_k,\ldots,m; k \in N.$$

It is easy to check that the required number of operations (in the dynamic programming procedure) is polynomial in $m$ and $n$, and this procedure can also be used to compute (within the same time complexity) a violated inequality when there is any.

Since the constraint matrix of $DLP_1$ consists only 0's and 1's, Theorem (6.6.5) of [12] along with the previous lemma imply that a basic optimal solution of $LP_1$ can be computed in time polynomial in $m$ and $n$. Hence the following result holds.

**Theorem 1.** *Problem $P|size_j, pmtn|C_{max}$ can be solved in $poly(m,n)$ time, where $poly(.,.)$ is a bivariate polynomial.*

This result can be strengthened by using a different linear programming formulation, which will be discussed in subsequent sections. This will allow us to solve problem $P|size_j, pmtn|C_{max}$ in $O(n) + poly(m)$ time, and also to conclude that an optimal solution for $Pm|size_j, pmtn|C_{max}$ can be computed in linear time.

## 3    Linear Programming Formulation - Second Approach

For each $\ell \in M$, let $\mathcal{T}^\ell \subseteq \mathcal{T}$ denote the subset of tasks that have to be processed on $\ell$ processors (also called $\ell$-processor tasks). Furthermore, let $p_1^{(\ell)}, p_2^{(\ell)}, \ldots, p_{n_\ell}^{(\ell)}$ be the processing times of the tasks $T_1^{(\ell)}, T_2^{(\ell)}, \ldots, T_{n_\ell}^{(\ell)}$ in $\mathcal{T}^\ell$. One may assume that $n_\ell \geq \lfloor m/\ell \rfloor$, otherwise some dummy jobs with zero processing times can be included. We will also assume that for each $\ell \in M$,

$$p_1^{(\ell)} \geq p_2^{(\ell)} \geq \ldots \geq p_{\lfloor m/\ell \rfloor - 1}^{(\ell)} \quad \text{and} \quad p_{\lfloor m/\ell \rfloor - 1}^{(\ell)} \geq p_k^{(\ell)}, \; k = \lfloor m/\ell \rfloor,\ldots,n_\ell. \quad (3)$$

Now a configuration $C_i$ is an $m$-vector $(a_{i1},\ldots,a_{im})$ corresponding to an integer partition of $m$ into integers $1,2,\ldots,m$; i.e. $a_{i1} \cdot 1 + a_{i2} \cdot 2 + \ldots + a_{im} \cdot m = m$ where $a_{i\ell} \in \{0,1,\ldots,\lfloor m/\ell \rfloor\}$. For each configuration $C_i$ we use a variable $x_i$ to indicate the length of configuration $C_i$ in the schedule. For each configuration $C_i = (a_{i1},\ldots,a_{im})$ with $K_i = a_{i1} + \ldots + a_{im}$, there are several partitions of $M$ into subsets $U_1,\ldots,U_{K_i}$ such that $a_{i\ell} = |\{j \; : \; |U_j| = \ell, \; j = 1,\ldots,K_i\}|$. Furthermore, for each configuration $C_i$ one can easily compute a partition of the set of processors into subsets such that the number of subsets of cardinality $\ell$ is equal to $a_{i\ell}$, for each $\ell \in M$. One can assign to each preemptive schedule (of $n$

tasks) a sequence $S$ of configurations $C_i$ of lengths $x_i$ such that the makespan of the schedule is $\sum_{C_i \in S} x_i$.

Next we give a set of necessary constraints for the variables $x_i$ and the $\ell$-processor tasks $T^\ell$ in our input. Based on these constraints, we will show later how to generate a feasible schedule for the tasks in $T^\ell$, $\ell \in M$. Let $\ell \in M$ be fixed in the following and let $Y_{\ell k} = \{C_i \in C : a_{i\ell} = k\}$ and $\bar{Y}_{\ell k} = \bigcup_{h=k}^{\lfloor \frac{m}{\ell} \rfloor} Y_{\ell h}$. Clearly, the set $C$ of all configurations of $m$ processors can be partitioned into the sets $Y_{\ell 0}, Y_{\ell 1}, \ldots, Y_{\ell, \lfloor \frac{m}{\ell} \rfloor}$. Consider the following set of constraints.

$$(\ell, 1) \qquad \sum_{C_i \in \bar{Y}_{\ell 1}} x_i \geq p_1^{(\ell)},$$
$$(\ell, 2) \qquad \sum_{C_i \in \bar{Y}_{\ell 1}} x_i + \sum_{C_i \in \bar{Y}_{\ell 2}} x_i \geq p_1^{(\ell)} + p_2^{(\ell)},$$
$$\ldots$$
$$(\ell, \lfloor m/\ell \rfloor - 1) \qquad \sum_{h=1}^{\lfloor m/\ell \rfloor - 1} \sum_{C_i \in \bar{Y}_{\ell h}} x_i \geq \sum_{h=1}^{\lfloor m/\ell \rfloor - 1} p_h^{(\ell)},$$
$$(\ell, \lfloor m/\ell \rfloor) \qquad \sum_{h=1}^{\lfloor m/\ell \rfloor} \sum_{C_i \in \bar{Y}_{\ell h}} x_i \geq \sum_{h=1}^{n_\ell} p_h^{(\ell)}.$$

Notice that the left hand side of each constraint $(\ell, k)$, $k = 1, \ldots, \lfloor m/\ell \rfloor$ can also be written in the form:

$$\sum_{C_i \in Y_{\ell 1}} x_i + \sum_{C_i \in Y_{\ell 2}} 2x_i + \ldots + \sum_{C_i \in Y_{\ell k}} kx_i + \sum_{C_i \in Y_{\ell, k+1}} kx_i + \ldots + \sum_{C_i \in Y_{\ell, \lfloor m/\ell \rfloor}} kx_i.$$

**Lemma 2.** *The constraints* $(\ell, 1), \ldots, (\ell, \lfloor m/\ell \rfloor)$, $\ell = 1, \ldots, m$, *are necessary conditions for each preemptive schedule of* $T$.

*Proof.* Let $PS$ be a preemptive schedule of $T$, and let $C_1, \ldots, C_N$ be a corresponding sequence of configurations with lengths $x_1^*, \ldots, x_N^*$. Furthermore, let us study $k$ tasks $\bar{T}_1, \ldots, \bar{T}_k \in T^\ell$ with largest processing times $p_1^{(\ell)} \geq \ldots \geq p_k^{(\ell)}$. Each task $\bar{T}_j$ is processed in $PS$ for $p_j^{(\ell)}$ time units (probably with some preemptions). Each task $\bar{T}_j$ use exactly $\ell$ processors in parallel at each time step in $PS$. Therefore, the tasks $\bar{T}_1, \ldots, \bar{T}_k$ are processed on at most $k$ groups of $\ell$ processors in $PS$ at each time step. In other words, we do not use more than $k$ groups of $\ell$ processors at each time step. On the other hand, these tasks must fit in the space generated by the configurations. The maximum space for $k$ tasks that use $\ell$ processors produced by the configurations $C_i$ and their lengths $x_i$ is given by $\sum_{C_i \in \bar{Y}_{\ell 1}} x_i^* + \ldots + \sum_{C_i \in \bar{Y}_{\ell k}} x_i^*$. This implies the inequality $(\ell, k)$ for $1 \leq k \leq \lfloor m/\ell \rfloor - 1$. The last inequality $(\ell, \lfloor m/\ell \rfloor)$ means that all $\ell$-processor tasks (or their load) must fit in the space generated by all configurations.

For each $\ell \in M$, let $b_{\ell k} = p_1^{(\ell)} + \ldots + p_k^{(\ell)}$, $k = 1, \ldots, \lfloor m/\ell \rfloor - 1$, and $b_{\ell, \lfloor m/\ell \rfloor} = p_1^{(\ell)} + \ldots + p_{n_\ell}^{(\ell)}$. Then constraint $(\ell, k)$ can be written as $\sum_{h=1}^{\lfloor m/\ell \rfloor} \sum_{C_i \in Y_{\ell h}} \min(h, k) \cdot x_i \geq b_{\ell k}$, or equivalently as $\sum_{C_i \in C} \min(a_{i\ell}, k) \cdot x_i \geq b_{\ell k}$, since for every $C_i \in Y_{\ell h}$, we have $a_{i\ell} = h$. Therefore the complete linear program $LP_2$ (including all of the constraints for each $\ell$ and $k$) has the following form.

$$\text{Min} \sum_{C_i} x_i$$
$$\text{s.t.} \sum_{C_i \in C} \min(a_{i\ell}, k) \cdot x_i \geq b_{\ell k}, \qquad \forall \ell \in M, \ k = 1, \ldots, \lfloor m/\ell \rfloor, \qquad (4)$$
$$x_i \geq 0, \qquad \forall C_i \in C.$$

In Section 5 we will consider the dual of this linear program to compute a basic optimal solution of (4) in polynomial time. But before doing so we show in the next section how an optimal solution of $LP_2$ can be converted into an optimal preemptive schedule of $\mathcal{T}$.

## 4   Generating a Schedule

Assume that we are given an optimal solution $(x_i^*)_{C_i \in \mathcal{C}}$ of $LP_2$ with objective function value $OPT_{LP} = \sum_{C_i} x_i^*$. In what follows, we show how to generate (by using the values $x_i^*$) a preemptive schedule $PS$ with makespan $OPT_{LP}$. Since all of the constraints of the linear program are necessary, the feasible schedule we generate this way is indeed an optimal preemptive schedule for $P|size_j, pmtn|C_{max}$. Let $Y^* = \{C_i \in \mathcal{C} : x_i^* > 0\}$ and $Y_{\ell k}^* = \{C_i \in Y^* : a_{i\ell} = k\}$, $x_{\ell k}^* = \sum_{C_i \in Y_{\ell k}^*} x_i^*$, for each $\ell \in M$, $k = 0, \ldots, \lfloor m/\ell \rfloor$. Furthermore let $L_{\ell k} = \sum_{h=k}^{\lfloor m/\ell \rfloor} x_{\ell h}^*$ denote the space of the $k$-th stripe. Clearly, we can order the configurations according to the sets $Y_{\ell 0}^*, Y_{\ell 1}^*, \ldots, Y_{\ell, \lfloor m/\ell \rfloor}^*$. Using this ordering, we get a staircase pattern indicating processor availability. (See Figure 1 for $\lfloor m/\ell \rfloor = 4$.)

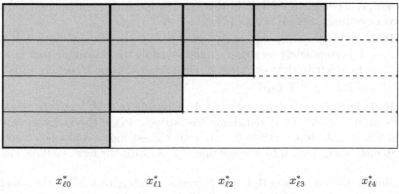

$$x_{\ell 0}^* \qquad x_{\ell 1}^* \qquad x_{\ell 2}^* \qquad x_{\ell 3}^* \qquad x_{\ell 4}^*$$

**Fig. 1.**   Ordering of configurations for $\ell$-processor tasks to form a staircase pattern.

The first region of length $x_{\ell 0}^*$ cannot be used for $\ell$ processor tasks. The second region consists of a stripe of width $\ell$ and length $x_{\ell 1}^*$, the third region consists of two parallel stripes of length $x_{\ell 2}^*$, and so on. The idea is to place the $\ell$-processor tasks into these stripes of width $\ell$. That means that the configurations (or corresponding subsets of size $\ell$) are filled by $\ell$ processor tasks. The main problem is to avoid executing a task parallel in two or more stripes. To this end we use the constraints of (4). Notice, that for the $\ell$-processor tasks the constraints $(\ell, 1)$, $(\ell, 2)$, $\ldots$, $(\ell, \lfloor m/\ell \rfloor)$ can be reformulated by using the (newly introduced) notation $L_{\ell k}$ as follows:

$$
\begin{aligned}
p_1^{(\ell)} &\leq L_{\ell 1}, \\
p_1^{(\ell)} + p_2^{(\ell)} &\leq L_{\ell 1} + L_{\ell 2}, \\
&\cdots \\
p_1^{(\ell)} + \ldots + p_{\lfloor m/\ell \rfloor - 1}^{(\ell)} &\leq L_{\ell 1} + \ldots + L_{\ell, \lfloor m/\ell \rfloor - 1}, \\
p_1^{(\ell)} + \ldots + p_{n_\ell}^{(\ell)} &\leq L_{\ell 1} + \ldots + L_{\ell, \lfloor m/\ell \rfloor}.
\end{aligned}
$$

This system of linear inequalities is related to scheduling with limited machine availability [19,20]. One can transform the subproblem for any fixed $\ell$ into a scheduling problem on $\lfloor m/\ell \rfloor$ parallel processors where each task has to be processed on one machine at each time and processor $i$ is only available during the interval $[OPT_{LP} - L_{\ell i}, OPT_{LP}]$, for each $i = 1, \ldots, \lfloor m/\ell \rfloor$. Given $L_{\ell i}$, $i = 1, \ldots, \lfloor m/\ell \rfloor$, one can compute a schedule for the $\ell$-processor tasks as follows. Assume that the $(\lfloor m/\ell \rfloor - 1)$ largest tasks in $T^\ell$ are ordered by the processing times, i.e. $p_1^{(\ell)} \geq \ldots \geq p_{\lfloor m/\ell \rfloor - 1}^{(\ell)}$ and $p_{\lfloor m/\ell \rfloor - 1}^{(\ell)} \geq p_k^{(\ell)}$, $k = \lfloor m/\ell \rfloor - 1, \ldots, n_\ell$. One can schedule the tasks in this order one by one using the three rules below. Let $A_\ell$ denote the set of available stripes, i.e. initially $A_\ell = \{1, \ldots, \lfloor m/\ell \rfloor\}$.

**Rule 1:** If $p_j^{(\ell)} = L_{\ell k}$ and $k \in A_\ell$, schedule $T_j^{(\ell)}$ on stripe $k$ such that the stripe is completely filled. In this case, stripe $k$ can not be used for other $\ell$-processor tasks. Set $A_\ell = A_\ell \setminus \{k\}$.

**Rule 2:** If $p_j^{(\ell)} < L_{\ell k}$, $p_j^{(\ell)} > L_{\ell k'}$, and $k, k' \in A_\ell$, schedule task $T_j^{(\ell)}$ up to a length $L_{\ell k'}$ completely on stripe $k'$, and schedule the remaining part of length $p_j - L_{\ell k'}$ from left to right on stripe $k$. Then remove stripe $k'$, set $A_\ell = A_\ell \setminus \{k'\}$ and $L_{\ell k} = L_{\ell k} - p_j^{(\ell)} + L_{\ell k'}$.

**Rule 3:** If $p_j^{(\ell)} < L_{\ell k}$ for each $k \in A_\ell$, schedule task $T_j^{(\ell)}$ and the remaining tasks in any order in the remaining free stripes. Place the tasks successively from left to right into a stripe $k \in A_\ell$ with highest index, and when a stripe is completely filled, switch to a free stripe $k' \in A_\ell$ with the next smallest index.

Notice that after using Rule 1 or 2 (and scheduling task $T_j^{(\ell)}$), the remaining stripes form again a staircase pattern and the remaining processing requirements and loads also satisfy the constraints above. On the other hand, we can apply these rules only at most $\lfloor m/\ell \rfloor$ times. This procedure is a simplified variant of the algorithm proposed in [19] for scheduling with limited machine availability. It can be implemented in $O(n_\ell + \lfloor m/\ell \rfloor \log \lfloor m/\ell \rfloor)$ time, and produces at most $\lfloor m/\ell \rfloor - 1$ preemptions.

We apply the above procedure for each $\ell \in M$, one after another. Furthermore, we get for each configuration $C_i \in Y_{\ell k}^*$ a schedule of $\ell$-processor tasks on $k$ stripes where each stripe has width $\ell$. We store the starting and ending times of assigned tasks $T_j^{(\ell)}$ in relation to the length $x_i^*$ of configuration $C_i$. Notice that in order to guarantee the staircase pattern, we have to reorder the configurations after each iteration. But this can be done (at the expense of introducing some additional preemptions) without changing the assignment of previously scheduled tasks to individual configurations. The total running time of this step can be bounded by $O(n + (\log m)^2)$ plus the time $O(n + |Y^*|m)$ to reorder the configurations and compute the schedule for the individual configurations $C_i \in Y^*$. Hence we have shown the following lemma.

**Lemma 3.** *Given an optimal solution $x$ of $LP_2$, one can compute an optimal preemptive schedule of $T$ in $O(n + Qm)$ time, where $Q$ is the number of positive coordinates in $x$.*

Since for any fixed $m$, the number of variables in $LP_2$ is constant, we obtain the following result.

**Corollary 1.** *Problem $Pm|size_j, pmtn|C_{max}$ can be solved in $O(n)$ time.*

The above procedure generates for each $\ell \in M$ at most $\lfloor m/\ell \rfloor$ preemptions. Then due to the repeated reordering of the configurations, there are at most $|Y^*|m$ additional preemptions. Hence we obtain that the total number of preemptions generated by the previous algorithm is bounded by $|Y^*|m + \sum_{\ell=1}^{m} \lfloor m/\ell \rfloor \leq |Y^*|m + m(1 + \ln m)$.

## 5    Solving the Linear Program

In this section we study the problem of computing an optimal solution of $LP_2$ and extend Corollary 1 to $P|size_j, pmtn|C_{max}$ by proving the following result.

**Theorem 2.** *For problem $P|size_j, pmtn|C_{max}$ with $m$ parallel machines and $n$ independent tasks, an optimal schedule with $O(m^2 \log m)$ preemptions can be computed in $O(n) + poly(m)$ time, where $poly(.)$ is a univariate polynomial.*

The number of variables in $LP_2$ is equal to the number $P(m)$ of integer partitions of $m$. Although partitions have been studied by mathematicians for hundreds of years and many interesting results are known, there is no known formula for $P(m)$. However the growth rate of $P(m)$ is known: $P(m) = \Theta(e^{\pi\sqrt{2m/3}}/m)$, which is clearly not polynomial in terms of $m$. On the other hand, the number of constraints is polynomial in $m$ and can be bounded by $\sum_{\ell=1}^{m} \lfloor m/\ell \rfloor \leq m \cdot \sum_{\ell=1}^{m} 1/\ell \leq m(1 + \ln m)$. This implies that an optimal basic feasible solution of $LP_2$ has at most $m(1 + \ln m)$ non-zero components. Hence there are optimal solutions of $LP_2$ for which the number of positive components is bounded by $m(1 + \ln m)$.

To compute an optimal (basic feasible) solution for $LP_2$ we study the dual linear program $DLP_2$, which - in contrast to $LP_2$ - contains a polynomial number of variables and an exponential number of constraints. $DLP_2$ has the following form.

$$\text{Max} \sum_{\ell=1}^{m} \sum_{k=1}^{\lfloor m/\ell \rfloor} b_{\ell k} \cdot y_{\ell k}$$
$$\text{s.t.} \sum_{\ell=1}^{m} \sum_{k=1}^{\lfloor m/\ell \rfloor} \min(k, a_\ell) \cdot y_{\ell k} \leq 1, \qquad \forall C = (a_1, \ldots, a_m) \in \mathcal{C}, \qquad (5)$$
$$y_{\ell k} \geq 0, \qquad \forall \ell \in M, \ k = 1, \ldots, \lfloor m/\ell \rfloor.$$

Let $P \subseteq \mathbb{R}^d$ be the solution set of $DLP_2$, where $d = \sum_{\ell=1}^{m} \lfloor m/\ell \rfloor$. Clearly, $P$ is a polytope. Next we study the separation problem for $DLP_2$: Given a vector $y = (y_{\ell k})_{1 \leq \ell \leq m, 1 \leq k \leq \lfloor m/\ell \rfloor}$, decide whether $y$ is feasible with respect to (5), and if not, find an inequality that separates $y$ from $P$. We will assume without loss of generality that for any given vector $y$, all of the coordinates are nonnegative, since otherwise the separation problem can be trivially solved. Then to decide whether a given vector $y$ is feasible, it suffices to compute the value

$$T = \max\{ \sum_{\ell=1}^{m} \sum_{k=1}^{\lfloor m/\ell \rfloor} \min(k, a_\ell) \cdot y_{\ell k} \; : \; (a_1, \ldots, a_m) \text{ integer partition of } m \}.$$

Clearly, $y$ is feasible iff $T \leq 1$. Now we show how $T$ and a violated inequality when $T > 1$ can be computed in time polynomial in $m$.

**Lemma 4.** *The separation problem for $DLP_2$ requires $O(m^2 \log m)$ time.*

*Proof.* Let $\mathbb{N}_0$ denote the set of nonnegative integers, and for any $i, j \in M$, let $IP(i, j)$ be the set of all integer partitions of $j$ into integers $1, \ldots, i$, i.e.

$$IP(i, j) = \{ (a_1, \ldots, a_i) \in \mathbb{N}_0^i \; : \; j = a_1 \cdot 1 + \ldots + a_i \cdot i \}.$$

Clearly, $\mathcal{C} = IP(m, m)$. Suppose we are given a $d$-dimensional vector $y = (y_{\ell k})_{1 \leq \ell \leq m, 1 \leq k \leq \lfloor m/\ell \rfloor}$. For any $\ell \in M$ and $a \in \{0, 1, \ldots, \lfloor m/\ell \rfloor\}$, let

$$t(\ell, a) = \sum_{k=1}^{\lfloor m/\ell \rfloor} \min(k, a) \cdot y_{\ell k},$$

and for any $(a_1, \ldots, a_i) \in \mathbb{N}_0^i$, $i \in M$, let

$$s(a_1, \ldots, a_i) = \sum_{\ell=1}^{i} t(\ell, a_\ell).$$

Finally, for any $i, j \in M$, let

$$T(i, j) = \max\{ s(a_1, \ldots, a_i) \; : \; (a_1, \ldots, a_i) \in IP(i, j) \}.$$

With this notation $T = T(m, m)$. In order to solve the separation problem for $DLP_2$, first we compute for the given vector $y$ the auxiliary values $t(\ell, a)$ for every $a = 0, 1, \ldots, \lfloor m/\ell \rfloor$, and then use a dynamic programming procedure for computing $T(m, m)$ based on the following recursions.

$$T(i, 0) = T(0, j) = 0, \quad i \in M, \; j = 0, 1, \ldots, m,$$
$$T(i, j) = \max\{T(i - 1, j - hi) + t(i, h) \; : \; h = 0, 1, \ldots, \lfloor j/i \rfloor\}, \quad i \in M, j \in M.$$

Notice, that we can also compute a violated inequality (and the corresponding integer partition $(a_1, \ldots, a_m)$ of $m$ for which $s(a_1, \ldots, a_m) > 1$) when $T > 1$. To do this, we store for each pair $(i, j) \in M \times M$ the number $h(i, j)$ that generates the maximum value $T(i, j)$ in the equality above. Using the numbers $h(i, j)$, one can easily compute the violated inequality when $T > 1$. The overall time required to solve the separation problem can be estimated as follows. The auxiliary values $t(\ell, a)$ can be computed in $O(\sum_{\ell=1}^{m} \lfloor m/i \rfloor) = O(m \ln m)$ time. Furthermore, determining the values $T(\ell, j)$ requires $O(\sum_{i=1}^{m} m \cdot \lfloor m/i \rfloor) = O(m^2 \log m)$ time, and this time complexity also holds for computing a violated inequality when $T > 1$.

By using Theorem (6.6.5) of [12], one can conclude that a basic optimal solution of $LP_2$ can be computed in $poly(m)$ time, where $poly(.)$ is some univariate polynomial. This also implies that we can assume that $Q$ in Lemma 3 is at most $m(1 + \log m)$ and the total number of preemptions generated by the algorithm is bounded by $O(m^2 \log m)$. This finishes the proof of Theorem 2. Notice that the results of Theorems 1 and 2 do not imply that problem $P|size_j, pmtn|C_{max}$ (which is known to be NP-hard [9]) can be solved in polynomial time. (This would require an algorithm with running time polynomial in both $n$, $\log m$, and $\log p_{max}$, where $p_{max}$ is the maximum processing time in the input instance.) However the pseudo-polynomial complexity of Theorem 2 implies interestingly the following strongly polynomial bound without making any restriction on the processing times.

**Corollary 2.** *For any $m$ bounded by a polynomial in $n$, there is a strongly polynomial algorithm that computes an optimal solution for $P|size_j, pmtn|C_{max}$ with $m$ parallel processors and $n$ independent tasks.*

**Corollary 3.** *$P|size_j, pmtn|C_{max}$ is not strongly NP-hard, unless P=NP.*

## 6 Extension - Maximum Lateness Minimization

Consider the parallel multiprocessor task scheduling problem. Suppose that for each task $T_j \in \mathcal{T}$, in addition to the original input parameters $size_j$ and $p_j$ there is also a due date $d_j$ given, and the goal is to find a schedule for which the maximum lateness $L_{max} = \max\{C_j - d_j : j = 1, \ldots, n\}$ is minimized. The results presented in previous sections can be extended to this more general variant of the problem denoted as $P|size_j, pmtn|L_{max}$. However for simplicity, we discuss in this section the extension of the simpler linear programming formulation $LP_1$ given in Section 2, and leave the technical details of the other extensions for the full version of the paper.

We assume w.l.o.g. that the tasks are ordered according to their due dates, i.e. $d_1 \leq \ldots \leq d_n$. As before, a configuration is a compatible subset of tasks that can be scheduled simultaneously. Let $F_\ell$ be the set of all configurations that consists of only tasks from the subset $\{\ell, \ell+1, \ldots, n\}$, i.e. those which will be considered to be executable in the $\ell$-th subinterval $I_\ell$, where $I_1 = [d_0 \equiv 0, d_1 + L_{max}]$ and $I_\ell = [d_{\ell-1} + L_{max}, d_\ell + L_{max}]$ for $\ell = 2, \ldots, n$. For $f \in F_\ell$, let $x_f^{(\ell)}$ denote the length of configuration $f$ in the $\ell$-th subinterval of the schedule. Then $P|size_j, pmtn|L_{max}$

can be formulated as a linear program $LP_3$ with variables $L_{max}, x_f^{(\ell)}$, for each $f \in F_\ell, \ell \in N$, as follows:

$$
\begin{aligned}
\text{Min } & L_{max} \\
\text{s.t. } & \sum_{f \in F_1} x_f^{(1)} \leq d_1 - d_0 + L_{max}, \\
& \sum_{f \in F_\ell} x_f^{(\ell)} \leq d_\ell - d_{\ell-1}, && \forall \ell \in N \setminus \{1\}, \\
& \sum_{\ell=1}^{j} \sum_{f \in F_\ell : j \in f} x_f^{(\ell)} \geq p_j, && \forall j \in N, \\
& x_f^{(\ell)} \geq 0, && \forall f \in F_\ell, \ \ell \in N.
\end{aligned}
\tag{6}
$$

Since the number of variables in $LP_3$ is $O(n^{m+1})$, one can conclude [5] that $Pm|size_j, pmtn|L_{max}$ can be solved in polynomial time for any fixed $m$. The dual linear program $DLP_3$ has the following form:

$$
\begin{aligned}
\text{Max } & \sum_{\ell=1}^{n}(d_{\ell-1} - d_\ell)y_\ell + \sum_{j=1}^{n} p_j z_j \\
\text{s.t. } & y_1 = 1 \\
& \sum_{j \in f} z_j - y_\ell \leq 0, && \forall \ell \in N, \ f \in F_\ell, \\
& y_\ell \geq 0, \ z_j \geq 0, && \forall \ell \in N, \ \forall j \in N.
\end{aligned}
\tag{7}
$$

This linear program has $2n$ variables and $O(n^{m+1})$ constraints. In the separation problem for $DLP_3$, one has to check whether a given vector $(y_1, \ldots, y_n, z_1, \ldots, z_n)$ is feasible for (7). Notice that this can be answered by considering the constraints in (7) for each $\ell \in \{1, \ldots, n\}$ independently. For a given $\ell$, one has to decide whether $\max_{f \in F_\ell} \sum_{j \in F_\ell} z_j \leq y_\ell$, which can be done in time polynomial in $m$ and $n$ similarly as in Lemma 1. Furthermore, one can generalize the argument in Section 3 and use sets of integer partitions for each interval $[0, d_1 + L_{max}]$, $[d_i + L_{max}, d_{i+1} + L_{max}]$, $i = 1, \ldots, n - 1$, to improve the linear programming formulation (6)-(7) and hence provide similar complexity results as those in Section 5.

We mention in closing that the previous formulations can also be modified to handle malleable tasks and/or release times. The extensions will be presented in the full version of the paper. Complexity and approximability questions regarding the closely related problems $P|fix_j, pmtn|C_{max}$, $P|set_j, pmtn|C_{max}$ and their variants are addressed in [15].

## References

1. A.K. Amoura, E. Bampis, C. Kenyon and Y. Manoussakis, Scheduling independent multiprocessor tasks, *Proceedings of the 5th European Symposium on Algorithms* (1997), LNCS 1284, 1-12.
2. A.K. Amoura, E. Bampis, C. Kenyon and Y. Manoussakis, Scheduling independent multiprocessor tasks, manuscript of an extended version of [1], submitted to *Algorithmica*, 1998.
3. L. Bianco, J. Blazewicz, P. Dell Olmo and M. Drozdowski, Scheduling multiprocessor tasks on a dynamic configuration of dedicated processors, *Annals of Operations Research* 58 (1995), 493-517.

4. J. Blazewicz, M. Drabowski and J. Weglarz, Scheduling multiprocessor tasks to minimize schedule length, *IEEE Transactions on Computers*, C-35-5 (1986), 389-393.

5. J. Blazewicz, M. Drozdowski, D. de Werra and J. Weglarz, Deadline scheduling of multiprocessor tasks, *Discrete Applied Mathematics* 65 (1996), 81-96.

6. J. Chen and A. Miranda, A polynomial time approximation scheme for general multiprocessor job scheduling, *Proceedings of the 31st ACM Symposium on the Theory of Computing* (1999), 418-427.

7. M. Drozdowski, On the complexity of multiprocessor task scheduling, *Bulletin of the Polish Academy of Sciences*, 43 (1995), 381-392.

8. M. Drozdowski, Scheduling multiprocessor tasks - an overview, *European Journal on Operations Research*, 94 (1996), 215-230.

9. J. Du and J. Leung, Complexity of scheduling parallel task systems, *SIAM Journal on Discrete Mathematics*, 2 (1989), 473-487.

10. U. Feige and J. Kilian, Zero knowledge and the chromatic number, *Journal of Computer and System Sciences*, 57 (1998), 187-199.

11. A. Feldmann, J. Sgall and S.H. Teng, Dynamic scheduling on parallel machines, *Proceedings of the 32nd IEEE Symposium on Foundations of Computer Science* (1991), 111-120.

12. M. Grötschel, L. Lovász and A. Schrijver, Geometric Algorithms and Combinatorial Optimization, Springer Verlag, Berlin, 1988.

13. J.A. Hoogeveen, S.L. van de Velde and B. Veltman, Complexity of scheduling multiprocessor tasks with prespecified processor allocations, *Discrete Applied Mathematics* 55 (1994), 259-272.

14. K. Jansen and L. Porkolab, Linear-time approximation schemes for scheduling malleable parallel tasks, *Proceedings of the 10th ACM-SIAM Symposium on Discrete Algorithms* (1999), 490-498.

15. K. Jansen and L. Porkolab, Preemptive scheduling on dedicated processors: applications of fractional graph coloring, *Proceedings of the 25th International Symposium on Mathematical Foundations of Computer Science*, MFCS 2000, Springer Verlag.

16. C. Kenyon and E. Remila, Approximate strip packing, *Proceedings of the 37th IEEE Symposium on Foundations of Computer Science* (1996), 31-36.

17. W. Ludwig and P. Tiwari, Scheduling malleable and nonmalleable parallel tasks, *Proceedings of the 5th ACM-SIAM Symposium on Discrete Algorithms* (1994), 167-176.

18. C. Lund and M. Yannakakis, On the hardness of approximating minimization problems, *Journal of ACM*, 41 (1994), 960-981.

19. G. Schmidt, Scheduling on semi-identical processors, *Zeitschrift für Oper. Res.* 28 (1984), 153-162.

20. G. Schmidt, Scheduling with limited machine availability, *International Computer Science Institute Technical Report TR-98-036*, Berkeley, California, October 1998.

21. U. Schwiegelshohn, Preemptive weighted completion time scheduling of parallel jobs, *Proceedings of the 4th European Symposium of Algorithms* (1996), LNCS 1136, 39-51.

22. A. Steinberg, A strip-packing algorithm with absolute performance bound two, *SIAM Journal on Computing* 26 (1997), 401-409.

23. J. Turek, J. Wolf and P. Yu, Approximate algorithms for scheduling parallelizable tasks, *Proceedings of the 4th ACM Symposium on Parallel Algorithms and Architectures* (1992), 323-332.

# Compressed Text Databases
# with Efficient Query Algorithms
# Based on the Compressed Suffix Array

Kunihiko Sadakane

Department of System Information Sciences
Graduate School of Information Sciences
Tohoku University
sada@dais.is.tohoku.ac.jp

**Abstract.** A compressed text database based on the compressed suffix array is proposed. The compressed suffix array of Grossi and Vitter occupies only $O(n)$ bits for a text of length $n$; however it also uses the text itself that occupies $O(n \log |\Sigma|)$ bits for the alphabet $\Sigma$. On the other hand, our data structure does not use the text itself, and supports important operations for text databases: *inverse*, *search* and *decompress*. Our algorithms can find *occ* occurrences of any substring $P$ of the text in $O(|P| \log n + occ \log^\epsilon n)$ time and decompress a part of the text of length $l$ in $O(l + \log^\epsilon n)$ time for any given $1 \geq \epsilon > 0$. Our data structure occupies only $n(\frac{2}{\epsilon}(\frac{3}{2} + H_0 + 2 \log H_0) + 2 + \frac{4 \log^\epsilon n}{\log^\epsilon n - 1}) + o(n) + O(|\Sigma| \log |\Sigma|)$ bits where $H_0 \leq \log |\Sigma|$ is the order-0 entropy of the text. We also show the relationship with the opportunistic data structure of Ferragina and Manzini.

## 1 Introduction

As the cost of disks decreases and the number of machine-readable texts grows, we can use huge amount of disks and store huge amount of text databases in them. Therefore it becomes difficult to find data from the databases and text search techniques become important. Traditional algorithms perform sequential search to find a keyword from a text; however it is not practical for huge databases. We create indices of the text in advance for querying in sublinear time.

In the area of text retrieval, the inverted index [7] is commonly used due to its space requirements and query speed. The inverted index is a kind of *word indices*. It is suitable for English texts, while it is not suitable for Japanese texts or biological sequences because it is difficult to parse them into words. For such texts a kind of *full-text indices* is used, for example suffix arrays [14] and suffix trees [15]. These indices enable finding any substring of a text. However, the size of full-text indices are quite larger than that of word indices. Recent researches are focused on reducing the sizes of full-text indices [13,6,5,10]. The compressed suffix array of Grossi and Vitter [6] reduces the size of the suffix array from $O(n \log n)$ bits to $O(n)$ bits. It is used with succinct representation of suffix trees in $O(n)$ bits. Though they only considered binary alphabets, it can

D.T. Lee and S.-H. Teng (Eds.): ISAAC 2000, LNCS 1969, pp. 410–421, 2000.

be generalized for texts with alphabet size $|\Sigma| > 2$. However, this representation also uses the text itself to obtain a part of the text containing a given pattern. The text occupies $n \log |\Sigma|$ bits. We assume that the base of logarithm is two. Indeed, the data size is always larger than that of the original text size.

Though some algorithms for finding words from a compressed text have been proposed [4,12], the algorithms have to scan the whole compressed text. As a result, their query time is proportional to the size of the compressed text and they are not applicable to huge texts. Though a search index using the suffix array of a compressed text has also been proposed [16], it is difficult to search arbitrary strings because the compression is based on word segmentation of the text. Furthermore, this search index can be also compressed by our algorithm. The opportunistic data structure of Ferragina and Manzini [5] allows to enumerate any pattern $P$ in a compressed text in $(|P| + occ \log^\epsilon n)$ time for any fixed $1 \geq \epsilon > 0$. The compression algorithm is the block sorting [2] based on a permutation of the text defined by the suffix array. It has good compression ratio and fast decompressing speed. Space occupancy of the opportunistic data structure of Ferragina and Manzini is $O(nH_k) + O(\frac{n}{\log n}(\log \log n + |\Sigma| \log |\Sigma|))$ bits where $H_k$ is the order-$k$ entropy of the text. Unfortunately, the second term is often too large in practice.

In this paper we propose algorithms for compressed text databases using the compressed suffix array of Grossi and Vitter. We support three basic operations for text databases, *inverse*, *search* and *decompress*, without using the text itself. Since we do not need the original text, the size of our data structure can become smaller than the text size. The *inverse* returns the inverse of the suffix array. It has many applications, for example the lexicographic order of a suffix in any part of the text can be efficiently computed by using the inverse of the suffix array. This enables efficient proximity search [11], which finds positions of keywords which appear in the neighborhood.

The *search* returns the interval in the suffix array that corresponds to a pattern $P$ from the text of length $n$ in $O(|P| \log n)$ time. The *decompress* returns a substring of length $l$ in the compressed database in $O(l + \log^\epsilon n)$ time. Space occupancy is only $n(\frac{2}{\epsilon}(\frac{3}{2} + H_0 + 2 \log H_0) + 2 + \frac{4 \log^\epsilon n}{\log^\epsilon n - 1}) + o(n) + O(|\Sigma| \log |\Sigma|)$ bits where $H_0$ is the order-0 entropy of the text and $1 \geq \epsilon > 0$ is a fixed constant. Assume that $n < 2^{32}$ and $H_0 = 2$, which is practical for English texts. If we use $\epsilon = 0.8$, $\log^\epsilon n \approx 16$. Then the size of the index is approximately $15n$ bits. On the other hand, the text itself and its suffix array occupies $8n + 32n = 40n$ bits. Therefore our search index reduces the space complexity by 63%.

## 2    Preliminaries

We consider a problem of enumerating all positions of occurrences of a pattern $P[1..m]$ in a text $T[1..n]$. We create in advance a data structure for finding any pattern from $T$ to achieve query time that is sublinear to $n$. In this paper we call a data structure with such a query function *search index*. Examples of search indices are the inverted index [7], the $q$-gram index [9], the suffix array [14] and the suffix tree [15].

## 2.1   Inverted Index

Inverted index [7] is a set of lists of positions in the text $T$. Each list corresponds to a word and consists of positions of all occurrences of the word. The positions of each word are located in a consecutive regions of memory or disk in sorted order of the positions. The pointer to the head of each list is stored in a table. In the implementation of the data structure, we can compress the size of indices by encoding positions not by the original values but by the difference of positions between adjacent occurrences. The size of the inverted index is $O(n)$ bits in practice. Query time is $O(m + occ)$ where $occ$ is the number of occurrences of $P$.

## 2.2   Rank and Select Algorithms

We briefly describe the rank algorithm of Jacobson [8] and the select algorithm [17,18] used in both the compressed suffix arrays [6,5] and in our algorithm. A function $rank(T, i, c)$ returns the number of occurrences of a character $c$ in a prefix of the string $T[1..i]$ of $T[1..n]$. The most basic case is that the alphabet is binary. In this case, the $rank$ function can be implemented easily by using table lookups. We use three levels of tables; each table can be accessed in constant time. In the first table, the numbers of ones in prefixes $T[1..i \log^2 n]$ are stored. In the second table the numbers of ones in substrings $T[1 + i \log^2 n + j \log n..i \log^2 n + (j + 1) \log n]$ are stored. The third table stores values of ranks for all strings of length $\frac{\log n}{2}$. This table has size $\sqrt{n} \cdot \log \frac{\log n}{2} \cdot \frac{\log n}{2}$ bits and it can be accessed in constant time. We use this table two times. Therefore the function $rank$ takes constant time. It is possible to implement $rank$ for non-binary strings in constant time. We call the tables *directory* of the string. Additional space for the directory is $O(n \log \log n / \log n)$ bits.

We also use the inverse of the rank function, *select* function. A function $select(B, i)$ returns the position of $i$-th one in the bit-vector $B[1..n]$. We group positions of $\log n \log \log n$ ones and use different encoding according to their ranges, difference between positions of the first one and the last one. If the range is too large, we encode the positions by fixed-length encodings. Otherwise we encode them by difference between adjacent ones like the inverted index. Additional bits for the directory is $O(n / \log \log n)$ bits.

## 2.3   Compressed Suffix Arrays

Very recently two types of compressed suffix arrays have been proposed [6,5]. The suffix array [14] of a text $T[1..n]$ is an array $SA[1..n]$ of lexicographically sorted indices of all suffixes $T[j..n]$. An equation $SA[i] = j$ means that the suffix $T[j..n]$ is lexicographically the $i$-th smallest suffix in $T$. It can find any substring $P$ of length $m$ from a text of length $n$ in $O(m \log n + occ)$ time where $occ$ is the number of occurrences of $P$. It is further reduced to $O(m + \log n + occ)$ time by using an auxiliary array.

A defect of the suffix array is its size. It occupies $O(n \log n)$ bits. To reduce the size, two types of compressed suffix arrays were proposed. The search index of Grossi and Vitter [6] is an abstract data structure which has size $O(n \log \log n)$ bits and supports an access to the $i$-th element of a suffix array in $O(\log \log n)$ time, whereas in the case of the suffix array it has size $n \log n$ bits and supports constant time access. Thus, it can find positions of $P$ in $O((m \log n + occ) \log \log n)$ time using only the compressed suffix array and the text. This search index is further extended to have $O(n)$ size and support $O(\log^\epsilon n)$ time access for any fixed constant $1 \geq \epsilon > 0$.

The compressed suffix array of Grossi and Vitter [6] is a hierarchical data structure. The $k$-th level stores information on the suffix array of a text of length $n/2^k$ in which a character consists of $2^k$ consecutive characters in $T$. The $l = \lceil \log \log n \rceil$-th level stores a suffix array explicitly. To achieve $O(n)$ size, only the 0-th, the $l' = \lceil \frac{1}{2} \log \log n \rceil$-th level and the $l$-the level are used. Each level occupies $O(n)$ bits; therefore the total of the three levels is also $O(n)$ bits. The $O(\log^\epsilon n)$ access time is achieved by using more levels. Fig. 1 shows an example of the compressed suffix array for a text of length 16. The second level is skipped. Suffixes in the level 0 are divided into two groups: even suffixes and odd suffixes. Even suffixes are represented by the corresponding suffix in the level-1 and odd suffixes are represented by the even suffix in the level-0 using a function $\Psi$. In level-1, a suffix whose index is a multiple of four is represented by the level-3 suffix. The function $\Psi$ is defined by the following formula:

$$SA[\Psi[i]] = SA[i] + 1.$$

The function $\Psi$ is the key of our algorithms.

The element of the hierarchical suffix array $SA_k[i]$ is represented by

$$SA_k[i] = \begin{cases} d \cdot SA_{k+1}[rank(B_k, i, 1)] & (B_k[i] = 1) \\ SA_k[\Psi[i]] & (B_k[i] = 0) \end{cases}$$

where $B_k[i] = 1$ represents that suffix $SA_k[i]$ is also stored in the next level.

## 2.4   The Opportunistic Data Structure

There is another compressed suffix array called *opportunistic data structures*. The search index of Ferragina and Manzini [5] has size at most $O(nH_k) + o(n)$ bits where $H_k$ is the $k$-th order empirical entropy of the text $T$. It can find $P$ in $O(m + occ \log^\epsilon n)$ time for any fixed constant $1 \geq \epsilon > 0$. This search index is based on the block sorting compression algorithm [2]. The block sorting compresses a text after permuting characters by the BW-transformation. After the transformation the string becomes more *compressible* and it can be compressed by a simple algorithm. The transformation is defined by the suffix array $SA[1..n]$ of a text $T[1..n]$. We assume that the last character of the text does not appear in other positions. Then the result of the BW-transformation is a string $W[1..n]$ where $W[i] = T[SA[i] - 1]$, that is, characters in $W$ are arranged in lexicographic order of their following strings. If $SA[i] = 1$, we let $W[i] = T[n]$. Fig. 2 shows an example of the BW-transformation.

To decompress the compressed string, the inverse of the BW-transformation is computed as follows. First, the string $W$ is converted to a string $Y$ in which

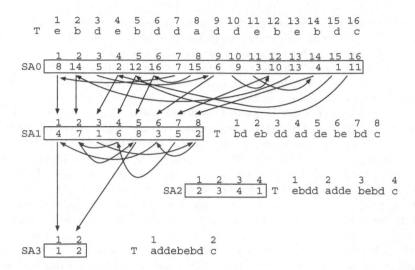

**Fig. 1.** The compressed suffix array

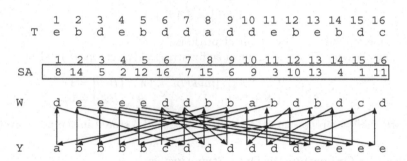

**Fig. 2.** The BW-transformation

characters are arranged alphabetically. Secondly, for each character $c$, $i$-th occurrences of $c$ in $W$ and $Y$ are linked by a pointer. Finally the pointers are traversed to recover the original string $T$. The array $Y$ can be represented by an integer array $C$ whose size is the same as alphabet size. The entry $C[c]$ is the summation of occurrences of characters that are smaller than $c$. Then the pointer from $W[i]$ to $Y[j]$ is calculated by

$$j = LF[i] \equiv C[W[i]] + rank(W, i, W[i]).$$

This implies that

$$SA[LF[i]] = SA[i] - 1.$$

Note that $Y$ corresponds to the *first* characters of suffixes and $W$ corresponds to the *last* characters of cyclic shift of $T$. Hence it is called LF-mapping. It can be calculated in constant time by using the array $C$ and the directory for $W$.

The string $W$ is compressed by using the recency rank [1] or interval rank. The interval rank of an entry $W[i]$ of $W$ is $i - l(i)$, where $l(i)$ is the position of the rightmost occurrence to the left of $i$ of the same characters as $W[i]$, while the recency rank is the number of distinct characters between $W[i]$ and $W[l(i)]$. Therefore the recency rank of a character is at most the interval rank. The ranks are encoded by the $\delta$-code [3]. The $\delta$-code encodes a number $r$ in $1 + \lfloor \log r \rfloor + 2\lfloor \log(1 + \log r) \rfloor$ bits. Therefore compression ratio using recency ranks is better than using interval ranks. The compression ratio is close to the entropy of the string.

From the compressed text we can recover both the text $T$ and its suffix array $SA$. Therefore $W$ can be used as a compressed suffix array. It was shown that by traversing the pointers until $SA[1]$, the suffix array $SA$ is recovered in $O(n)$ time [20]. It is necessary to recover only a small part of $SA$ quickly in the context of pattern matching. We logically mark suffixes $T[j..n]$ ($j = 1 + k\eta$, $\eta = \Theta(\log^2 n)$) and store explicitly the index $j$ in a table using its lexicographical order $i$ ($j = SA[i]$) as the key. The mark is stored in Packet B-tree. It occupies $O(n \log \log n / \log n)$ bits. To achieve $O(\log^\epsilon n)$ access time, some levels of $W$ are used like the compressed suffix array of Grossi and Vitter.

A problem of the search index of Ferragina and Manzini is its practical space occupancy. It stores a table of recency ranks for each piece of $W$ of length $O(\log n)$. The space occupancy becomes $O(\frac{n}{\log n}|\Sigma| \log |\Sigma|)$ bits. Though it is reduced by using heuristics, it will be large for large alphabets.

## 3    Text Databases Using the Compressed Suffix Array

We propose algorithms for compressed text databases using the compressed suffix array of Grossi and Vitter. We support three more operations in addition to the original compressed suffix array:

- *inverse(j)*: return the index $i$ such that $SA[i] = j$.
- *search(P)*: return an interval $[l, r]$ of indices of $SA$ where substrings $T[SA[i]..SA[i] + |P| - 1]$ ($l \leq i \leq r$) matches with the pattern $P$.
- *decompress(s, e)*: return the substring $T[s..e]$.

In text databases these operations are very important. A database returns texts or sentences containing given keywords [21] using the *search* and the *decompress* functions. The *inverse* function is a fundamental function and it has many applications.

The search index of Ferragina and Manzini is a compressed text by the block sorting with directories for fast operations; therefore it can recover both the original text and its suffix array. On the other hand, the compressed suffix array of Grossi and Vitter is used with the text or the Patricia trie. A binary search on the suffix array requires the text for string comparisons. However, we show that the text is not necessary to perform a binary search. We also show that a part of the text can be decompressed using an additional array.

The data structure of our search index is based on the compressed suffix array. They differ in the $\Psi$ function. In the basic case of the compressed suffix array, the values of the $\Psi$ function are stored only for odd suffixes, while ours stores for all suffixes. We also use auxiliary arrays to compute inverse of the suffix array and directories for the select function.

### 3.1   The Inverse of the Suffix Array

We show an $O(\sqrt{\log n})$ time algorithm for the inverse function $i = SA^{-1}[j]$. It is modified to $O(\log^\epsilon n)$ time for any given $1 \geq \epsilon > 0$ by using the same technique as the compressed suffix array [6].

We use three levels of the compressed suffix array: 0, $l' = \lceil \frac{1}{2} \log \log n \rceil$ and $l = \lceil \log \log n \rceil$. In the $l$-th level the suffix array $SA_l$ of size $n/\log n$ is explicitly stored. We also store its inverse $SA_l^{-1}$ explicitly in the $l$-th level. To find $SA^{-1}[i + j\sqrt{\log n} + k\log n]$ becomes as follows. First, we obtain $x_1 = SA_l^{-1}[k]$. This corresponds to $x_2 = SA_{l'}^{-1}[k\sqrt{\log n}]$, which is calculated by $x_2 = select(B_{l'}, x_1)$. Secondly, we obtain $x_3 = SA_{l'}^{-1}[j + k\sqrt{\log n}]$ by $x_3 = (\Psi')^j[x_2]$ because $SA_{l'}[x_3] = j + k\sqrt{\log n} = SA_{l'}[x_2] + j = SA_{l'}[(\Psi')^j[x_2]]$. Thirdly, we obtain $x_4 = SA^{-1}[j\sqrt{\log n} + k\log n]$ by $x_4 = select(B_0, x_3)$. Finally, we obtain $x = SA^{-1}[i + j\sqrt{\log n} + k\log n]$ by $x = (\Psi)^i[x_4]$.

To achieve the $O(\log^\epsilon n)$ time complexity, we use $1/\epsilon$ levels. In each level the $\Psi$ function is used at most $\log^\epsilon n$ times. Thus we have this theorem.

**Theorem 1.** *The inverse of the suffix array* $SA^{-1}[j]$ *can be computed in* $O(\log^\epsilon n)$ *time.*

### 3.2   Searching for Pattern Positions

We propose an algorithm for finding the interval $[l, r]$ in the suffix array that corresponds to suffixes containing a given pattern $P$. Our algorithm runs in $O(|P| \log n)$ time, which is the same as the original suffix array. Our algorithm has two merits. One is that the text itself is not necessary for string comparisons and the other is that in the time complexity a multiplicative factor $\log^\epsilon n$ does not appear even if the compressed suffix array is used.

We search for a pattern $P$ by a binary search on the suffix array $SA[1..n]$. In a classical algorithm $P$ is compared with the suffix $T[SA[m]..n]$. Therefore $O(\log^\epsilon n)$ time is necessary to find $SA[m]$ and the text $T$ is used to obtain the suffix. On the other hand, our algorithm decodes the suffix from the compressed suffix array. We use the following proposition.

**Proposition 1.**

$$T[SA[m] + i] = C^{-1}[\Psi^i[m]]$$

The function $C^{-1}[j]$ is the inverse of the array of cumulative frequencies $C$, that is, it returns the character $T[SA[j]]$.

*Proof.* Assume that $SA[m] = j$. Note that we do not know the exact value of $j$. Since suffixes are lexicographically sorted in the suffix array, The first character $T[j]$ of the suffix $T[j..n]$ becomes $C^{-1}[m]$. To compute the $i$-th character $T[j+i]$, we need the lexicographical position $m'$ such that $SA[m'] = j + i$. By using the relation $SA[\Psi[m]] = SA[m] + 1$, we can calculate $m' = \Psi^i[m]$.    □

The function $C^{-1}$ takes constant time using a bit-vector $D[1..n]$ and the directory for the rank function. We set $D[j] = 1$ if $T[SA[j]] \neq T[SA[j-1]]$. Then $rank(D, j, 1)$ represents the number of distinct characters in $T[SA[1]]$, $T[SA[2]]$, $\ldots, T[SA[j]]$ minus one. The rank can be converted to the character $T[SA[j]]$ by a table of size $|\Sigma| \log |\Sigma|$ bits.

By using the proposition, we can obtain the substring of $T$ used in a string comparison in $O(|P|)$ time, which is the same as using the uncompressed suffix array and the text itself.

### 3.3    Decompressing the Text

We show an algorithm to obtain a substring of length $l$, $T[j..j+l-1]$, from the text of length $n$ in $O(l + \log^\epsilon n)$ time. It can be performed by using the inverse of the suffix array and Proposition 1. We can compute the lexicographical position $i$ of the suffix $T[j..n]$ ($i = SA^{-1}[j]$) in $O(\log^\epsilon n)$ time. After that we can obtain the prefix $T[j..j+l-1]$ of the suffix in $O(l)$ time.

**Theorem 2.** *A substring of length $l$ can be decompressed from the compressed suffix array of a text of length $n$ in $O(l + \log^\epsilon n)$ time.*

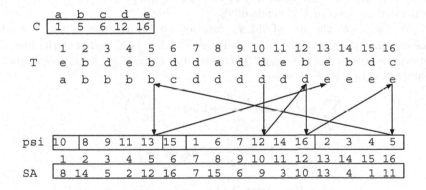

**Fig. 3.** Decompressing the text

Fig. 3 shows an example of decompressing $T[9..13] = $ ddebe. We first calculate the index of the suffix array storing the suffix $T[9..16]$ by using the inverse function $SA^{-1}[9] = 10$. Then we traverse elements of the suffix array by using the $\Psi$ function and decode the characters by using $C^{-1}$. Note that exact values of $SA^{-1}[i]$ are not necessary except for $SA^{-1}[9]$.

We can also create a small suffix array corresponding a part of the text, $T[s..s+l-1]$, by using the inverse function $SA^{-1}[s]$ and traversing the $\Psi$ function.

**Theorem 3.** *The suffix array of a part of the text of length $l$ can be computed from the compressed suffix array in $O(l + \log^\epsilon n)$ time.*

Note that it is necessary to sort positions $j$ of suffixes in order of $SA^{-1}[j]$. However it can be done in linear time using a radix sort.

## 4    The Size of the Search Index

We consider the size of our compressed suffix array. It consists of at most $l + 1$ levels ($l = \lceil \log \log n \rceil$). The $l$-th level is the suffix array $SA_l$ and its inverse $SA_l^{-1}$. The size of each array is $n \log n / \log n = n$ bits.

In the level $k$, we store three components: a bit-vector $B_k$, the function $\Psi_k$, $C_k^{-1}$, and their directories. The bit-vector $B_k$ has length $n/2^k$ representing whether each suffix in level $k$ appears in the next level. We use the directory for the rank function. The number of bits for the vector and the directory is $n/2^k + o(n/2^k)$ bits. We also use the select function for the inverse function. It occupies at most $n/2^k + o(n/2^k)$ bits.

For storing $\Psi_k$, we use the inverted index. In level $k$, consecutive $2^k$ characters in the text $T$ form a new character. Therefore the length of the text becomes $\frac{n}{2^k}$. We call the text as $T_k$ and the corresponding suffix array as $SA_k$. $\Psi_k[i]$ is encoded in a list by the $\delta$-code representing $\Psi_k[i] - \Psi_k[i-1]$ if $T_k[SA_k[i]] = T_k[SA_k[i-1]]$, otherwise encoded by the $\delta$-code of $\Psi_k[i]$.

We represent the size of the $\Psi_k$ function by the entropy of the text. We assume that the probability of a character $c \in \Sigma^{2^k}$ is $p_c$ and that the number of occurrences of $c$ is $n_c = \frac{n}{2^k} p_c$. Then the total number of bits $z_k$ to encode all values of $\Psi$ in level $k$ becomes

$$z_k \le \sum_{c \in \Sigma^{2^k}} n_c \left( 1 + \log \frac{n/2^k}{n_c} + 2 \log \log \frac{n/2^k}{n_c} \right)$$

$$= \frac{n}{2^k} \sum_{c \in \Sigma^{2^k}} p_c \left( 1 + \log \frac{1}{p_c} + 2 \log \log \frac{1}{p_c} \right)$$

$$\le \frac{n}{2^k} (1 + H_{2^k} + 2 \log H_{2^k}) \le \frac{n}{2^k} (1 + 2^k H_0 + 2 \log 2^k H_0)$$

$$= n \left( \frac{2k+1}{2^k} + H_0 + 2 \log H_0 \right) \le n \left( \frac{3}{2} + H_0 + 2 \log H_0 \right)$$

where $H_{2^k}$ is the order-$2^k$ entropy.

The function $C_k^{-1}$ is used to obtain $\Psi_k[i]$. $C_k$ is represented by a bit-vector $D_k[1..n/2^k]$ for each level $k$. The element $D_k[i]$ represents whether $T_k[SA_k[i]] =$

$T_k[SA_k[i-1]]$ or not. In other words, $i$ is the first element in a list encoding the $\Psi_k$ values for a character $c$ if $D_k[i] = 1$ and the rank of $D_k[i]$ is $c$. Therefore we can find the character $c$ using $D_k$ and its directory for the rank function. We also encode positions of ones in $D_k$ and use the directory for the select function to calculate the number of elements $i - select(D_k, rank(D_k, i, 1))$ in the list of $\Psi_k$ corresponding to $c$. The number of required bits is at most $n/2^k + o(n/2^k)$ bits.

We also use a bit-vector $Z_k[1..z_k]$ to store the bit-position of the first element of a list of $\Psi_k$ for each character as is used in the opportunistic data structure. We make the bit-vector $Z_k$ so that $Z_k[i] = 1$ represents that the position $i$ is the first bit representing the first element of the $\Psi_k$ list. Therefore $c$-th 1 in $Z_k$ represents the bit-position for the character $c$. We can compute the bit-position for the character $c$ in constant time using the directory for the select function.

The bit-vectors $B_k$ and $D_k$ and their directories are expressed in $4n/2^k + z_k + o(n)$ bits for the level $k$. We use levels $0$, $\epsilon \log \log n$, $2\epsilon \log \log n, \ldots, \log \log n$. Therefore the total of all levels is less than $4n\frac{\log^\epsilon n}{\log^\epsilon n - 1} + \sum_k z_k + o(n)$ bits. Note that it is not necessary to know exact values of $C^{-1}$ except for level 0. We use an array to convert the rank of a character in the text to the character code. Its size is at most $|\Sigma| \log |\Sigma|$ bits.

We use $1/\epsilon$ levels of the compressed suffix arrays to achieve $O(\log^\epsilon n)$ access time. In the last level $l$, we store two arrays $SA_l$ and $SA_l^{-1}$ explicitly. By adding the above numbers, we have the following theorem:

**Theorem 4.** *The number of bits of the proposed search index for a text of length $n$ is at most $n(\frac{2}{\epsilon}(\frac{3}{2} + H_0 + 2\log H_0) + 2 + \frac{4\log^\epsilon n}{\log^\epsilon n - 1}) + o(n) + O(|\Sigma| \log |\Sigma|)$ bits where $H_0$ is the order-0 entropy of the text and $|\Sigma|$ is the alphabet size.*

Note that we encode $\Psi$ explicitly if it is smaller than encoding $\Psi$ and $C^{-1}$ by the above method.

Our search index stores all $n/2^k$ values of $\Psi_k$ in all levels, while the original compressed suffix array stores $\frac{n}{2^k}\frac{\log^\epsilon n - 1}{\log^\epsilon n}$ values of $\Psi_k$. We also requires additional $n$ bits to store the inverse suffix array $SA^{-1}$ in level $l$ explicitly. However, ours does not require the text itself that occupies $n \log |\Sigma|$ bits.

## 5    Relationship between Two Compressed Suffix Arrays

In this section we show relationship between the compressed suffix array and the opportunistic data structure. Both search indices use pointers between two adjacent suffixes in the suffix array; however they differ in their directions:

$$SA[LF[i]] = SA[i] - 1$$
$$SA[\Psi[i]] = SA[i] + 1.$$

This implies that $LF[\Psi[i]] = i$. Both functions $LF$ and $\Psi$ can be used to decompress the compressed text.

The LF-mapping is encoded by the block sorting compression, while the $\Psi$ function is encoded by the inverted index. Compression ratio of the block sorting is better than the inverted index. However the size of the directory for the rank function highly depends on the alphabet size.

The search indices differ in keyword search time. The compressed suffix array takes $O(|P|\log n)$ time for finding a pattern $P$ if no additional index is used, while the opportunistic data structure takes only $O(|P|)$ time using a technique like the radix sort. Therefore reducing its practical size is important.

Concerning keyword search, we want to perform case-insensitive search. On the other hand, we want to extract the text as it is. We create search indices of a text in which capital letters are converted to the corresponding small letters. We call this conversion *unification*. The modified Burrows-Wheeler transformation [19] allows to decode both the original text before unification and the suffix array of the text after unification. This transformation is also used in the opportunistic data structure. We encode recency ranks of non-unified characters, while directories are computed using unified characters. In the case of using the compressed suffix array, we first create the unified text and then create the index. We have to store flags separately which represents whether each letter is capital or small.

# 6   Concluding Remarks

We have proposed algorithms for text databases using the compressed suffix array. We support keyword search and text decompression. Since our search index does not require the text itself, its size is small even in non-binary alphabet cases. We also support a basic operation which has many applications, inverse of the suffix array. As future works we develop other basic operations which are used to simulate the suffix tree.

**Acknowledgment.** The author would like to thank Prof. Takeshi Tokuyama and anonymous referees for their valuable comments. The author also wish to thank Dr. Giovanni Manzini, who kindly supplied his paper.

# References

1. J. L. Bentley, D. D. Sleator, R. E. Tarjan, and V. K. Wei. A Locally Adaptive Data Compression Scheme. *Communications of the ACM*, 29(4):320–330, April 1986.
2. M. Burrows and D. J. Wheeler. A Block-sorting Lossless Data Compression Algorithms. Technical Report 124, Digital SRC Research Report, 1994.
3. P. Elias. Universal codeword sets and representation of the integers. *IEEE Trans. Inform. Theory*, IT-21(2):194–203, March 1975.
4. M. Farach and T. Thorup. String-matching in Lempel-Ziv Compressed Strings. In *27th ACM Symposium on Theory of Computing*, pages 703–713, 1995.
5. P. Ferragina and G. Manzini. Opportunistic Data Structures with Applications. Technical Report TR00-03, Dipartimento di Informatica, Università di Pisa, March 2000.

6. R. Grossi and J. S. Vitter. Compressed Suffix Arrays and Suffix Trees with Applications to Text Indexing and String Matching. In *32nd ACM Symposium on Theory of Computing*, pages 397–406, 2000. http://www.cs.duke.edu/~jsv/Papers/catalog/node68.html.

7. D. A. Grossman and O. Frieder. *Information Retrieval: Algorithms and Heuristics.* Kluwer Academic Publishers, 1998.

8. G. Jacobson. Space-efficient Static Trees and Graphs. In *30th IEEE Symp. on Foundations of Computer Science*, pages 549–554, 1989.

9. P. Jokinen and E. Ukkonen. Two Algorithms for Approximate String Matching in Static Texts. In A. Tarlecki, editor, *Proceedings of Mathematical Foundations of Computer Science*, LNCS 520, pages 240–248, 1991.

10. J. Kärkkäinen and E. Sutinen. Lempel-Ziv Index for $q$-Grams. *Algorithmica*, 21(1):137–154, 1998.

11. T. Kasai, H. Arimura, R. Fujino, and S. Arikawa. Text data mining based on optimal pattern discovery – towards a scalable data mining system for large text databases –. In *Summer DB Workshop*, SIGDBS-116-20, pages 151–156. IPSJ, July 1998. (in Japanese).

12. T. Kida, Y. Shibata, M. Takeda, A. Shinohara, and S. Arikawa. A Unifying Framework for Compressed Pattern Matching. In *Proc. IEEE String Processing and Information Retrieval Symposium (SPIRE'99)*, pages 89–96, September 1999.

13. S. Kurtz. Reducing the Space Requirement of Suffix Trees. Technical Report 98-03, Technische Fakultät der Universität Bielefeld, Abteilung Informationstechnik, 1998.

14. U. Manber and G. Myers. Suffix arrays: A New Method for On-Line String Searches. *SIAM Journal on Computing*, 22(5):935–948, October 1993.

15. E. M. McCreight. A Space-economical Suffix Tree Construction Algorithm. *Journal of the ACM*, 23(12):262–272, 1976.

16. E. Moura, G. Navarro, and N. Ziviani. Indexing compressed text. In *Proc. of WSP'97*, pages 95–111. Carleton University Press, 1997.

17. J. I. Munro. Tables. In *Proceedings of the 16th Conference on Foundations of Software Technology and Computer Science (FSTTCS '96)*, LNCS 1180, pages 37–42, 1996.

18. J. I. Munro. Personal communication, July 2000.

19. K. Sadakane. A Modified Burrows-Wheeler Transformation for Case-insensitive Search with Application to Suffix Array Compression. In *Proceedings of IEEE Data Compression Conference (DCC'99)*, page 548, 1999. poster session.

20. K. Sadakane and H. Imai. A Cooperative Distributed Text Database Management Method Unifying Search and Compression Based on the Burrows-Wheeler Transformation. In *Advances in Database Technologies*, number 1552 in LNCS, pages 434–445, 1999.

21. K. Sadakane and H. Imai. Text Retrieval by using $k$-word Proximity Search. In *Proceedings of International Symposium on Database Applications in Non-Traditional Environments (DANTE'99)*, pages 23–28. Research Project on Advanced Databases, 1999.

# A Better Lower Bound for Two-Circle Point Labeling

Alexander Wolff[1], Michael Thon[1], and Yinfeng Xu[2]

[1] Institute of Mathematics and Computer Science, Ernst Moritz Arndt University,
Greifswald, Germany. awolff@mail.uni-greifswald.de, mithon42@gmx.de
[2] School of Management, Xi'an Jiaotong University, Xi'an, China. yfxu@xjtu.edu.cn

**Abstract.** Given a set $P$ of $n$ points in the plane, the two-circle point-labeling problem consists of placing $2n$ uniform, non-intersecting, maximum-size open circles such that each point touches exactly two circles.

It is known that it is NP-hard to approximate the label size beyond a factor of $\approx 0.7321$. In this paper we improve the best previously known approximation factor from $\approx 0.51$ to $2/3$. We keep the $O(n \log n)$ time and $O(n)$ space bounds of the previous algorithm.

As in the previous algorithm we label each point within its Voronoi cell. Unlike that algorithm we explicitly compute the Voronoi diagram, label each point *optimally* within its cell, compute the smallest label diameter over all points and finally shrink all labels to this size.

## 1 Introduction

Label placement is one of the key tasks in the process of information visualization. In diagrams, maps, technical or graph drawings, features like points, lines, and polygons must be labeled to convey information. The interest in algorithms that automate this task has increased with the advance in type-setting technology and the amount of information to be visualized. Due to the computational complexity of the label-placement problem, cartographers, graph drawers, and computational geometers have suggested numerous approaches, such as expert systems [AF84,DF89], zero-one integer programming [Zor90], approximation algorithms [FW91,DMM⁺97,WW97,ZP99], simulated annealing [CMS95] and force-driven algorithms [Hir82] to name only a few. An extensive bibliography about label placement can be found at [WS96]. The ACM Computational Geometry Impact Task Force report [C⁺96] denotes label placement as an important research area. Manually labeling a map is a tedious task that is estimated to take 50 % of total map production time [Mor80].

In this paper we deal with a relatively new variant of the general label placement problem, namely the two-label point-labeling problem. It is motivated by maps used for weather forecasts, where each city must be labeled with two labels that contain for example the city's name or logo and its predicted temperature or rainfall probability.

The two-label point-labeling problem is a variant of the one-label problem that allows sliding. Sliding labels can be attached to the point they label anywhere on their boundary. They were first considered by Hirsch [Hir82] who gave

D.T. Lee and S.-H. Teng (Eds.): ISAAC 2000, LNCS 1969, pp. 422–431, 2000.
© Springer-Verlag Berlin Heidelberg 2000

an iterative algorithm that uses repelling forces between labels in order to eventually find a placement without or only few intersecting labels. Van Kreveld et al. gave a polynomial time approximation scheme and a fast factor-2 approximation algorithm for maximizing the number of points that are labeled by axis-parallel sliding rectangular labels of common height [vKSW99]. They also compared several sliding-label models with so-called fixed-position models where only a finite number of label positions per point is considered, usually a small constant like four [FW91,CMS95,WW97]. Sliding rectangular labels have also been considered for labeling rectilinear line segments [KSY99]. Another generalization was investigated in [DMM⁺97,ZQ00], namely arbitrarily oriented sliding labels.

Point labeling with circular labels, though not as relevant for real-world applications as rectangular labels, is a mathematically interesting problem. The one-label case has already been studied extensively [DMM⁺97,SW00,DMM00]. For maximizing the label size, the best approximation factor now is $\frac{1}{3.6}$ [DMM00].

The two- or rather multi-label labeling problem was first considered by Kakoulis and Tollis who presented two heuristics for labeling the nodes and edges of a graph drawing with several rectangles [KT98]. Their aim was to maximize the number of labeled features. The algorithms are based on their earlier work; one is iterative, while the other uses a maximum-cardinality bipartite matching algorithm that matches cliques of pairwise intersecting label positions with the elements of the graph drawing that are to be labeled. They do not give any runtime bounds or approximation factors.

For the problem that we consider in this paper, namely maximizing the size of circular labels, two per point, Zhu and Poon gave the first approximation algorithm [ZP99]. They achieved an approximation factor of $\frac{1}{2}$. Like all following algorithms, their algorithm relies on the fact that there is a region around each input point $p$ such that $p$ can be labeled within this region and this region does not intersect the region of any other input point. The size of the region—in their case a circle centered at $p$—and thus the labels is a constant fraction of an upper bound for the maximum label size.

Recently Qin et al. improved this result [QWXZ00]. They gave an approximation algorithm with a factor of $\frac{1}{1+\cos 18°} \approx 0.5125$. They also state that it is NP-hard to approximate the label size beyond a factor of $\approx 0.7321$. The regions into which they place the labels are the cells of the Voronoi diagram. However, they do not compute the Voronoi diagram explicitly, but use certain properties of its dual, the Delauney triangulation. For estimating the approximation factor of their algorithm they rely on the same upper bound for the maximum label size as Zhu and Poon, namely the minimum (Euclidean) distance of any pair of input points.

In this paper we give an algorithm that also places the labels of each point into its Voronoi cell. However, unlike the previous algorithm we do this optimally and compare the label diameter of our algorithm not to an upper bound but directly to the optimal label diameter. This yields an approximation factor of 2/3, which nearly closes the gap to the non-approximability result stated above.

At the same time we keep the $O(n \log n)$ time and $O(n)$ space bounds of the previous algorithms, where $n$ is the number of points to be labeled.

This paper is organized as follows. In Section 2 we prove that in each cell of the Voronoi diagram of the given point set $P$ there is enough space for a pair of uniform circular labels whose diameter is $2/3$ times the optimal diameter for labeling $P$ with circle pairs. In Section 3 we show how to label points optimally within their Voronoi cells and state our central theorem.

The actual label placement is a special case of a gift wrapping problem, where the gift is a coin (as large as possible) and the wrapping a convex polygonal piece of paper that can only be folded once along a line. Our problem is special in that it specifies a point on the folding line and thus takes away a degree of freedom. For the more general problem, the currently best known algorithm takes $O(m \log m)$ time where $m$ is the number of vertices of the convex polygon [KKSY99]. For our special problem we have a linear-time algorithm, but due to space constraints we can only give an algorithm that uses standard techniques for computing the lower envelope of a set of "well-behaving functions". It runs in $O(m \log m)$ time.

Throughout this paper we consider labels being topologically *open*, and we define the *size* of a solution to be the diameter of the uniform circular labels. A label placement is *optimal* if no two labels intersect and labels have the largest possible size. We will only consider point sets of size $n \geq 2$.

## 2    The Lower Bound

The two-circle point-labeling problem is defined as follows.

**Definition 1 (two-circle point-labeling problem).** *Given a set $P$ of $n$ points in the plane, find a set of $2n$ uniform, non-intersecting, maximum-size open circles such that each point touches exactly two circles.*

Zhu and Poon [ZP99] have suggested the first approximation algorithm for the two-circle point-labeling problem. Their algorithm always finds a solution of at least half the optimal size. The algorithm is very simple; it relies on the fact that $D_2$, the minimum Euclidean distance between any two points of the input point set $P$ is an upper bound for the optimal label size (i.e. diameter), see Figure 1. On the other hand, given two points $p$ and $q$ in $P$, open circles $C_{p,D_2/2}$ and $C_{q,D_2/2}$ with radius $\frac{1}{2}D_2$ centered at $p$ and $q$ do not intersect. Thus if each point is labeled within its circle, no two labels will intersect. Clearly this allows labels of maximum diameter $\frac{1}{2}D_2$, i.e. half the upper bound for the optimal label size.

The difficulty of the problem immediately comes into play when increasing the label diameter $d$ beyond $\frac{1}{2}D_2$, since then the intersection graph of the (open) disks $C_{p,d}$ with radius $d$ centered at points $p$ in $P$ changes abruptly; the maximum degree jumps from 0 to 6.

Recently Qin et al. have given an approximation algorithm that overcomes this difficulty and labels all points with circles slightly larger than the threshold

**Fig. 1.** $D_2$ is an upper bound for the optimal label size.

of $\frac{1}{2}D_2$. Their diameter is $d_{\text{old}} = \frac{1}{1+\cos 18°}D_2 \approx 0.5125\, D_2$. Their algorithm also assigns each point a certain region such that no two regions intersect and each point can be labeled within its region. The regions they use are not circles but the cells of the Voronoi diagram of $P$, a well-known multi-purpose geometrical data structure [Aur91]. Instead of computing the Voronoi diagram explicitly they use the dual of the Voronoi diagram, the Delauney triangulation $\text{DT}(P)$ to apply a packing argument. $\text{DT}(P)$ is a planar geometric graph with vertex set $P$ and edges for each pair of points that can be placed on the boundary of an open disc that does not contain any other points of $P$ [Aur91]. Qin et al. argue that in $\text{DT}(P)$ each point $p$ can have at most six short edges, where an edge $pq$ is short if the Euclidean distance $d(p,q)$ of $p$ and $q$ is shorter than $2d_{\text{old}}$. They show that among the lines that go through these short edges there must be a pair of neighboring lines that forms an angle $\alpha$ of at least 36°. They place the circular labels of $p$ with diameter $d_{\text{old}}$ such that their centers lie on the angular bisector of $\alpha$. Finally they prove that these labels lie completely within the Voronoi cell $\text{Vor}(p)$ of $p$. The Voronoi cell of $p$ is the (convex) set of all points in the plane that are closer to $p$ than to any other input point. Thus the Voronoi cells of two different input points are disjoint and the labels of one input point cannot intersect the labels of any other.

Both the idea of our new algorithm and the proof of its approximation factor are simpler than those of its predecessor. However, in order to keep the $O(n \log n)$ time bound the implementation becomes slightly more involved. Our strategy is as follows. We first show that there is a region $Z_{\text{free}}(p)$ around each input point $p$ that cannot contain any other input point. The size of $Z_{\text{free}}(p)$ only depends on the optimal label diameter. Let $Z_{\text{label}}(p)$ be the Voronoi cell of $p$ that we would get if all points on the boundary of $Z_{\text{free}}(p)$ were input points. We can compute the largest label diameter $d_{\text{lower}}$ such that two disjoint circular labels of $p$ completely fit into $Z_{\text{label}}(p)$. We do not know the orientation of $Z_{\text{label}}(p)$ relative to $p$, but we know that $Z_{\text{label}}(p)$ lies completely in $\text{Vor}(p)$. Thus our algorithm must go the other way round: we label each point optimally within its Voronoi cell, compute the smallest label diameter over all points and finally shrink all labels to this size. Then we know that each label is contained in the Voronoi cell of its point, and that the labels are at least as large as those that would have fit into $Z_{\text{label}}(p)$.

Let $\mathcal{C}_{\text{opt}}$ be a fixed optimal solution of the input point set $P$. $\mathcal{C}_{\text{opt}}$ can be specified by the label size $d_{\text{opt}}$ and an angle $0 \leq \alpha_p < 180°$ for each input point.

The angle $\alpha_p$ specifies the position of a line through $p$ that contains the centers of the labels of $p$ (at a distance $d_{\mathrm{opt}}/2$ from $p$). By convention we measure $\alpha_p$ from the horizontal (oriented to the right) through $p$ to the line (oriented upwards) through the label centers. In the following we assume that $d_{\mathrm{opt}} = 1$; the input point set can always be scaled so that this is true.

**Definition 2.** *Let $C_{m,r}$ be an open disk with radius $r$ centered at a point $m$ and let $H_{pq}$ be the open halfplane that contains $p$ and is bounded by the perpendicular bisector of $p$ and $q$. For each $p \in P$ let the* point-free zone $Z_{\mathrm{free}}(p) = C_{Z_1, \frac{1}{2}\sqrt{3}} \cup C_{Z_2, \frac{1}{2}\sqrt{3}} \cup C_{p,1}$, *where $Z_1$ and $Z_2$ are the centers of the labels $L_1$ and $L_2$ of $p$ in a fixed optimal solution $C_{\mathrm{opt}}$. The* label zone $Z_{\mathrm{label}}(p)$ *is the intersection of all halfplanes $H_{pq}$ with $q$ a point on the boundary of $Z_{\mathrm{free}}(p)$.*

Note that $Z_{\mathrm{free}}(p)$ and $Z_{\mathrm{label}}(p)$ are symmetric to the lines that form angles of $\alpha_p$ and $\alpha_p + 90°$ through $p$. The size of these areas only depends on $d_{\mathrm{opt}}$, their orientation only on $\alpha_p$, see Figure 2.

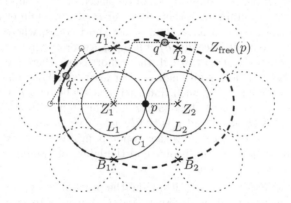

**Fig. 2.** The point-free zone does not contain any input point other than $p$.

**Lemma 1.** *$Z_{\mathrm{free}}(p)$ does not contain any input points except $p$.*

*Proof.* Refer to Figure 2. It indicates that the boundary of $Z_{\mathrm{free}}(p)$ is the locus of all input points that are as close to $p$ as possible. First we will show that the two disks $C_i := C_{Z_i, \frac{1}{2}\sqrt{3}}$ $(i = 1, 2)$ do not contain any input point other than $p$.

Let $T_i$ and $B_i$ be the top- and bottommost points on $C_i$, respectively. The arc that forms the boundary of $Z_{\mathrm{free}}(p)$ between the points $B_1$ and $T_1$ stems from rotating a potential input point $q$ around the label $L_1$ of $p$ in $C_{\mathrm{opt}}$ such that the labels of $q$ both touch $L_1$. This means that the centers of these three labels of diameter 1 form an equilateral triangle whose height $\frac{1}{2}\sqrt{3}$ corresponds to the distance of $q$ and $Z_1$. In other words, if there was a point $q \in P \setminus \{p\}$

with $d(q, Z_1) < \frac{1}{2}\sqrt{3} = \mathrm{radius}(C_1)$, then in $\mathcal{C}_{\mathrm{opt}}$ a label of $q$ would intersect $L_1$, a contradiction to $\mathcal{C}_{\mathrm{opt}}$ being an optimal solution. Due to symmetry the same holds for $C_2$. It remains to show that $C_{p,1}$, the third of the three circles that contributes to $Z_{\mathrm{free}}(p)$, does not contain any input point other than $p$.

Consider the arc that forms the boundary of $Z_{\mathrm{free}}(p)$ between the points $T_1$ and $T_2$. This arc is caused by rotating another potential input point $q'$ around $p$ such that each of the labels of $q'$ touches a label of $p$. Observe that the centers of the four labels of $q'$ and $p$ form a rhombus of edge length 1 when $q'$ moves continously from $T_1$ to $T_2$. Since $q'$ and $p$ are the midpoints of two opposite edges of the rhombus, their distance during this movement remains constant. Clearly the distance of the edge midpoints equals the edge length of the rhombus, i.e. 1, which in turn is the radius of $C_{p,1}$. Thus if $q'$ entered the area $C_{p,1} \setminus (C_1 \cup C_2)$, a label of $q'$ would intersect a label of $p$ in $\mathcal{C}_{\mathrm{opt}}$ —a contradiction.  ⌀

**Lemma 2.** *The Voronoi cell of $p$ contains the label zone $Z_{\mathrm{label}}(p)$ of $p$.*

*Proof.* The Voronoi cell of $p$ can be be written as $\mathrm{Vor}(p) = \bigcap_{v \in P \setminus \{p\}} H_{pv}$. It contains $Z_{\mathrm{label}}(p) = \bigcap_{v' \in \mathrm{boundary}(Z_{\mathrm{free}}(p))} H_{pv'}$ since for all input points $v \neq p$ there is a $v' \in \mathrm{boundary}(Z_{\mathrm{free}}(p))$ such that $H_{pv}$ contains $H_{pv'}$.  ⌀

**Lemma 3.** *For each input point $p$ there are two disjoint circles of diameter $d_{\mathrm{lower}} = \frac{2}{3} d_{\mathrm{opt}}$ that touch $p$ and lie completely within $Z_{\mathrm{label}}(p)$.*

*Proof.* We do not compute the boundary of $Z_{\mathrm{label}}(p)$ explicitly but parameterize the radius $r$ of the labels of $p$ such that we get the largest possible labels that do not touch the constraining halfplanes of $Z_{\mathrm{label}}(p)$.

Our coordinate system is centered at $p$ and uses four units for $d_{\mathrm{opt}}$, see Figure 3. We show that for any point $q$ on the boundary of $Z_{\mathrm{free}}(p)$ the halfplane $H_{pq}$ does not intersect the labels of $p$ whose centers we place at $Z_1(-r, 0)$ and $Z_2(r, 0)$. The interesting case is that $q$ lies on the circle $C_2$ and above the $x$-axis. Let $q'$ be the point in the center of the line segment $\overline{pq}$. Then $q'$ lies on the bold dashed circle with the equation $(x - 1)^2 + y^2 = 3$. We parameterize the $x$-coordinate of $q'$ using the variable $t \in [1, 1 + \sqrt{3}]$. The vector $q' = (t, \sqrt{3 - (t - 1)^2})$ is normal to the boundary $h_{pq}$ of the halfplane $H_{pq}$. Hence the distance of any point $s$ to $h_{pq}$ is given by the normalized scalar product of $(s - q')$ and $q'$, namely $d(s, h_{pq}) = \frac{|(s-q')q'|}{\|q'\|}$. For $s = Z_2(r, 0)$, the center of one of the labels of $p$, we have

$$r = d(Z_2, h_{pq}) = \frac{|rt - 2t - 2|}{\sqrt{2(t + 1)}}.$$

Since the enumerator is always less, and the denominator greater than zero, we get $r = f(t) = \frac{2(t+1)}{t + \sqrt{2(t+1)}}$. The zeros of $f'$ are given by the equation $0 = \sqrt{2(t + 1)} - 1 - \frac{(t+1)}{\sqrt{2(t+1)}}$ which yields a minimum of $r = \frac{4}{3}$ at $t = 1$ for $t \in [1, 1 + \sqrt{3}]$. This value of $r$ corresponds to a label diameter of $\frac{2}{3}$ according to the original scale with $d_{\mathrm{opt}} = 1$. The case for $Z_1(-r, 0)$ is symmetric.  ⌀

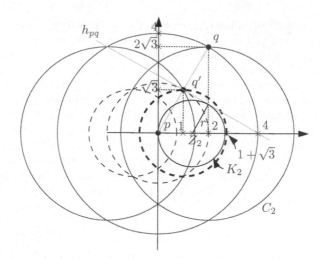

**Fig. 3.** Estimating the size of the label $K_2$ of $p$.

## 3    The Algorithm

In this section we first show how to label a point optimally within its Voronoi cell and then combine this result with the lower bound of the previous section to design a new approximation algorithm for two-circle point-labeling.

**Lemma 4.** *A point $p$ that lies in the interior of a convex polygon $G$ with $m$ vertices $v_1, \ldots, v_m$ can be labeled with two disjoint uniform circles of maximum size in $O(m \log m)$ time and $O(m)$ space.*

*Proof.* Our algorithm works conceptually as follows. We compute a continuous function $f$ that maps an angle $0 \le \alpha < 2\pi$ to the largest radius $r_\alpha$ such that the disk $C_{z_\alpha, r_\alpha}$ touches $p$ and lies completely within $G$, and such that at the same time the disk's center $z_\alpha$, the point $p$ and the horizontal $\overrightarrow{h_p}$ (directed to the right) through $p$ form an angle of size $\alpha$.

Since we want to find an angle that maximizes the common radius of *two* disjoint circular labels of $p$, we have to determine an angle $\alpha$ such that $\min(r_\alpha, r_{\alpha+\pi})$ is maximized. We do this by computing the maximum of the lower envelope of $f$ and $f'$ where $f'(\alpha) = f(\alpha + \pi \mod 2\pi)$. Since $f$ (and thus $f'$, too) consists of at most $2n$ monotonous pieces (see below), the maximum value of the piecewise minimum of $f$ and $f'$ can be computed from a suitable representation of $f$ in linear time. Finally the position of the centers of the maximum size labels of $p$ is given by the angle $\alpha$ that yields the maximum value of $\min(f(\alpha), f'(\alpha))$. The labels' radius is of course $r_\alpha$.

It remains to show how to compute $f$. This can actually be done by a kind of circular sweep around $p$ in $O(m)$ time and space if the vertices of $G$ are given in the order in which they appear on $G$. During the sweep the problem is to find out on the fly which edges do and which do not contribute to $f$.

However, since a runtime of $O(m \log m)$ suffices for the sequel, we can use a much more general approach, namely again the computation of lower envelopes. Let $\ell_i$ be the line that goes through the polygon vertices $v_i$ and $v_{i+1 \bmod m}$ and let $\beta_i$ be the angle that $\ell_i$ (directed upwards) forms with $\overrightarrow{h_p}$, see Figure 4. Let $f_i$ be the function that maps $0 \leq \alpha < 2\pi$ to the radius of the unique circle that touches $\ell_i$ and $p$ and makes the ray from $p$ to its center $c_i(\alpha)$ form an angle of $\alpha$ with $\overrightarrow{h_p}$. $f_i$ has a unique minimum at $\beta_i + \pi/2$ (to which it is symmetric modulo $2\pi$) and a discontinuity at $\beta_i + 3\pi/2$.

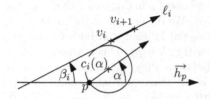
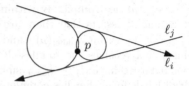

**Fig. 4.** Notation.          **Fig. 5.** There are exactly two circles that touch $\ell_i$, $\ell_j$ and $p$.

Two functions $f_i$ and $f_j$ with $i \neq j$ intersect exactly twice, namely in the angles that correspond to the two circles that touch $\ell_i$, $\ell_j$ and $p$, see Figure 5. (Note that if $\ell_i$ and $\ell_j$ are parallel, $p$ has to lie between them.) The $f_i$ can be represented (and these representations can be computed in constant time each) such that the intersections of $f_i$ and $f_j$ can be computed in constant time for each pair $(i, j)$. Thus we can use the simple devide-and-conquer algorithm described in [AS99][Theorem 2.8] to compute the lower envelope of $f_1, \ldots, f_m$ in $O(m \log m)$ time using $O(m)$ space. The lower envelope of these functions corresponds to $f$, since the minimum over $f_1, \ldots, f_m$ gives us, for each angle $\alpha$, the radius of the largest (open) circle that does not intersect any of the constraining lines $\ell_1, \ldots, \ell_m$ and whose center lies in the desired direction relative to $p$. The discontinuities of the $f_i$ do not matter; they disappear already after the first merge operation of the devide-and-conquer algorithm.          ⌀

**Theorem 1.** *A set $P$ of $n$ points in the plane can be labeled with $2n$ non-intersecting circular labels, two per point, of diameter $2/3$ times the optimal label size in $O(n \log n)$ time using linear space.*

*Proof.* Our algorithm is as follows. First we compute the Voronoi diagram of $P$. This takes $O(n \log n)$ time and linear space [Aur91]. Then for each input point $p$ we use the algorithm described in the proof of Lemma 4 to compute the largest pair of circles that labels $p$ within the Voronoi cell $\mathrm{Vor}(p)$ of $p$. Let $d_p$ be the diameter of these circles. Let $m_p < n$ be the number of edges of $\mathrm{Vor}(p)$. Since the complexity of the Voronoi diagram is linear [Aur91], we have $\sum_{p \in P} m_i =$

$O(n)$. Thus, with Lemma 4, we can place all labels in $O(\sum_{p\in P} m_i \log m_i) = O(\sum_{p\in P} m_i \log n) = O(n \log n)$ time in total, using $O(\sum_{p\in P} m_i) = O(n)$ space. We set $d_{\text{algo}} = \min_{p\in P} d_p$ and go through all input points once more. We scale the labels of each point $p$ by a factor of $\frac{d_{\text{algo}}}{d_p}$ using $p$ as the scaling center. We output these scaled labels, all of which now have diameter $d_{\text{algo}}$. Clearly this algorithm runs in $O(n \log n)$ time and uses linear space.

Its correctness can be seen as follows. Since $\frac{d_{\text{algo}}}{d_p} \leq 1$, the scaled labels lie completely in the original labels. Each of these lies in its label zone which in turn lies in the corresponding Voronoi cell according to Lemma 2. Thus no two of the scaled labels intersect. It remains to show that $d_{\text{algo}} \geq d_{\text{lower}}$.

Lemma 1 guarantees that for each input point $p$ there is an orientation (namely that determined by the centers of the labels of $p$ in $\mathcal{C}_{\text{opt}}$) such that the label zone $Z_{\text{label}}(p)$ lies completely within $\text{Vor}(p)$. We do not know this orientation, but Lemma 3 asserts that there are two disjoint labels for $p$, both of diameter $d_{\text{lower}}$, that lie within $Z_{\text{label}}(p)$—and thus within $\text{Vor}(p)$. This is true even for a point $q$ that receives the smallest labels before scaling, i.e. $d_q = d_{\text{algo}}$. On the other hand we have $d_q \geq d_{\text{lower}}$ since $d_q$ is the maximum label diameter for a pair of labels for $q$ that lies completely within $\text{Vor}(q)$.                          $\wp$

**Acknowledgments.** We are extremely indebted to Tycho Strijk, Utrecht University, for pointing out a mistake in the proof of Lemma 2.

# References

[AF84]     John Ahn and Herbert Freeman. AUTONAP - an expert system for automatic map name placement. In *Proceedings International Symposium on Spatial Data Handling*, pages 544–569, 1984.

[AS99]     Pankaj Agarwal and Micha Sharir. Davenport-Schinzel sequences and their geometric applications. In Jörg-Rüdiger Sack and Jorge Urrutia, editors, *Handbook of Computational Geometry*. Elsevier Science Publishers B.V. North-Holland, Amsterdam, 1999.

[Aur91]    Franz Aurenhammer. Voronoi diagrams: A survey of a fundamental geometric data stru cture. *ACM Comput. Surv.*, 23(3):345–405, September 1991.

[C+96]     Bernard Chazelle et al. Application challenges to computational geometry: CG impact task force report. Technical Report TR-521-96, Princeton University, April 1996. http://www.cs.princeton.edu/~chazelle/taskforce/CGreport.ps.

[CMS95]    Jon Christensen, Joe Marks, and Stuart Shieber. An empirical study of algorithms for point-feature label placement. *ACM Transactions on Graphics*, 14(3):203–232, 1995.

[DF89]     Jeffrey S. Doerschler and Herbert Freeman. An expert system for dense-map name placement. In *Proc. Auto-Carto 9*, pages 215–224, 1989.

[DMM+97]   Srinivas Doddi, Madhav V. Marathe, Andy Mirzaian, Bernard M.E. Moret, and Binhai Zhu. Map labeling and its generalizations. In *Proceedings of the 8th ACM-SIAM Symposium on Discrete Algorithms (SODA'97)*, pages 148–157, New Orleans, LA, 4–7 January 1997.

[DMM00]    Srinivas Doddi, Madhav V. Marathe, and Bernard M.E. Moret. Point labeling with specified positions. In *Proc. 16th Annu. ACM Sympos. Comput. Geom. (SoCG'00)*, pages 182–190, Hongkong, 12–14 June 2000.

[FW91]    Michael Formann and Frank Wagner. A packing problem with applications to lettering of maps. In *Proc. 7th Annu. ACM Sympos. Comput. Geom. (SoCG'91)*, pages 281–288, 1991.

[Hir82]    Stephen A. Hirsch. An algorithm for automatic name placement around point data. *The American Cartographer*, 9(1):5–17, 1982.

[KKSY99]    Sung Kwon-Kim, Chan-Su Shin, and Tae-Cheon Yang. Placing two disks in a convex polygon. Technical Report HKUST-TCSC-99-07, Hong Kong University of Science and Technology, Theoretical Computer Science Center, 1999.

[KSY99]    Sung Kwon Kim, Chan-Su Shin, and Tae-Cheon Yang. Labeling a rectilinear map with sliding labels. Technical Report HKUST-TCSC-1999-06, Hongkong University of Science and Technology, July 1999.

[KT98]    Konstantinos G. Kakoulis and Ioannis G. Tollis. On the multiple label placement problem. In *Proc. 10th Canadian Conf. Computational Geometry (CCCG'98)*, pages 66–67, 1998.

[Mor80]    Joel L. Morrison. Computer technology and cartographic change. In D.R.F. Taylor, editor, *The Computer in Contemporary Cartography*. J. Hopkins Univ. Press, New York, 1980.

[QWXZ00]    Zhongping Qin, Alexander Wolff, Yinfeng Xu, and Binhai Zhu. New algorithms for two-label point labeling. In *Proc. 8th Annu. Europ. Symp. on Algorithms (ESA'00)*, Lecture Notes in Computer Science, Saarbrücken, 5–8 September 2000. Springer-Verlag. to appear.

[SW00]    Tycho Strijk and Alexander Wolff. Labeling points with circles. *International Journal of Computational Geometry and Applications*, 2000. to appear.

[vKSW99]    Marc van Kreveld, Tycho Strijk, and Alexander Wolff. Point labeling with sliding labels. *Computational Geometry: Theory and Applications*, 13:21–47, 1999.

[WS96]    Alexander Wolff and Tycho Strijk. A map labeling bibliography. http://www.math-inf.uni-greifswald.de/map-labeling/bibliography/, 1996.

[WW97]    Frank Wagner and Alexander Wolff. A practical map labeling algorithm. *Computational Geometry: Theory and Applications*, 7:387–404, 1997.

[Zor90]    Steven Zoraster. The solution of large 0-1 integer programming problems encountered in automated cartography. *Operations Research*, 38(5):752–759, 1990.

[ZP99]    Binhai Zhu and Chung Keung Poon. Efficient approximation algorithms for multi-label map labeling. In A. Aggarwal and C. Pandu Rangan, editors, *Proc. 10th Annual International Symposium on Algorithms and Computation (ISAAC'99)*, Lecture Notes in Computer Science 1741, pages 143–152, Chennai, India, 16–18 December 1999. Springer-Verlag.

[ZQ00]    Binhai Zhu and Zhongping Qin. New approximation algorithms for map labeling with sliding labels. Dept. of Computer Science, City University of Hong Kong, 2000.

# Voronoi Diagram of a Circle Set Constructed from Voronoi Diagram of a Point Set

Deok-Soo Kim[1], Donguk Kim[1], and Kokichi Sugihara[2]

[1] Department of Industrial Engineering, Hanyang University
17 Haengdang-Dong, Sungdong-Ku, Seoul, 133-791, Korea
dskim@email.hanyang.ac.kr
donguk@cadcam.hanyang.ac.kr
[2] Department of Mathematical Engineering and Information Physics, Graduate School of
Engineering, University of Tokyo, 7-3-1, Hongo, Bunkyo-ku, Tokyo, 113, Japan
sugihara@simplex.t.u-tokyo.ac.jp

**Abstract.** Presented in this paper is an algorithm to compute the exact Voronoi diagram of circle set from the Voronoi diagram of point set. In particular, the topology aspect of the algorithm is presented here. The circles are located in a two dimensional Euclidean space, the radii of circles are not necessarily equal, and the circles are allowed to intersect. Even though the time complexity is $O(n^2)$, the algorithm turns out to be fast and robust. The algorithm uses the topology of the point set Voronoi diagram as an initial solution, and finds the correct topology of the Voronoi diagram of circle set from its point set counterpart. Hence, the algorithm is as stable as point set Voronoi diagram algorithm.

## 1 Introduction

Suppose that a circle set is given in a two dimensional Euclidean space. The radii of circles are not necessarily equal, and the circles are not necessarily disjoint. Given this circle set, we assign every location in the plane to the closest member in the circle set. As a result, the set of locations assigned to each member in the circle set forms it own region, and the set of regions forms a tessellation, called a Voronoi diagram, of the space.

There are a few researches on this or related problems. Lee and Drysdale first considered Voronoi diagram for a set of non-intersecting circles [6], and suggested an algorithm running in $O(n\log^2 n)$. They also reported another algorithm running in $O(nc^{\sqrt{\log n}})$ [1,2]. Sharir reported an algorithm computing the Voronoi diagram of circle set in $O(n\log^2 n)$, where the circles may intersect [10]. Gavrilova and Rokne reported an algorithm to maintain the data structure valid when circles are dynamically moving [3]. While the above are concerned with the exact Voronoi diagram, Sugihara reported an approximation algorithm for circle set [11]. In his work, each circle in the circle set is approximated by a set of points on the circle, and the Voronoi diagram of all points is computed. Then, the superfluous Voronoi edges and vertices are removed. However, this approach can be used only when a numerically robust and fast algorithm like the one discussed in [12] is available.

D.T. Lee and S.-H. Teng (Eds.): ISAAC 2000, LNCS 1969, pp. 432-443, 2000.

Hamann and Tsai reported another approximation algorithm for calculating generalized Voronoi diagram [4].

Presented in this paper is an algorithm for constructing the Voronoi diagram of circle set correctly, efficiently, and robustly. The main idea of the algorithm is the following. First, we construct a point set Voronoi diagram for the centers of circles as a preprocessing. Second, we use the topological information of this point set Voronoi diagram as a seed and modify it to get the correct topology of the Voronoi diagram of circle set. Third, we obtain the correct geometry of the Voronoi diagram using the topology information and the geometry of the circles. In this particular article, the topology perspective of the algorithm is only presented. The third step, the computation of the geometry, will not be discussed in this paper and will be presented in a separate article [5].

The main advantage of the proposed algorithm is in its robustness. It is as robust as the point set Voronoi diagram algorithm since what the step 2 in our algorithm does is nothing but flipping the existing edges of point set Voronoi diagram. It turns out that the time complexity of our algorithm is $O(n^2)$, but runs quite fast so that the speed is comparable to the speed of ordinary point set Voronoi diagram algorithm. In addition, the algorithm is quite simple to implement.

Illustrated in *Fig. 1a* is two Voronoi diagrams: the one shown with dotted lines is Voronoi diagram of point set $\{\mathbf{p}_i | i = 1, 2, ..., n\}$ where $\mathbf{p}_i$ is the center of circle $\mathbf{c}_i$, and the other with solid curves is the Voronoi diagram of circle set. From the figure, it can be shown that these two Voronoi diagrams are quite similar except some details of their geometries. Especially, the topologies of these two Voronoi diagrams are identical. However, it is not always the case in general. The topology of circle set Voronoi diagram may be different from that of point set Voronoi diagram. For example, if the circle $\mathbf{c}_6$ increases its radius so that *Fig. 1b* results, the resulting topology of circle set Voronoi diagram is different from its counterpart. Roughly speaking, however, the topological change is local, and applying this local change rule recursively can solve the other seemingly complex cases.

## 2  Preliminaries

Let $\mathbf{P} = \{\mathbf{p}_i | i = 1, 2, ..., n\}$ is a set of center points $\mathbf{p}_i$ of circles $\mathbf{c}_i$, and $\mathbf{C} = \{\mathbf{c}_i | i = 1, 2, ..., n\}$ is a set of circles $\mathbf{c}_i = (\mathbf{p}_i, r_i)$ where $r_i$ is the radius of $\mathbf{c}_i$. VD(P) and VD(C) are the Voronoi diagrams for point set $\mathbf{P}$ and circle set $\mathbf{C}$, respectively. $\mathbf{e}_i'$ means that $\mathbf{e}_i$ has been flipped in VD(C). Let $CC_i$ be a circumcircle about three generator circles corresponding to a Voronoi vertex $\mathbf{v}_i$. Let CH(A) be the convex hull of set $\mathbf{A}$. The *edge* and *vertex* will be used in this paper to mean a Voronoi edge and a Voronoi vertex unless otherwise stated.

The boundary edges of a Voronoi region are called *scale edges* of a generator (meaning the scales of a fish $\mathbf{c}$ or $\mathbf{p}$), and the edges emanating from a Voronoi region are called *quill edges* of the generator (meaning the quills of a porcupine $\mathbf{c}$ or $\mathbf{p}$).

In Fig. 2, there are two vertices $\mathbf{v}_1$ and $\mathbf{v}_2$ on an edge $\mathbf{e}_1$. When the edge $\mathbf{e}_1$ is considered, the generator $\mathbf{c}_3$ is called a mating generator of $CC_1$ and denoted as $\mathbf{M}_1$.

In this paper, we make assumptions for the input data: the degrees of vertices of VD(P) as well as VD(C) are three. We also assume that VD(P) is available a priori by

434     D.-S. Kim, D. Kim, and K. Sugihara

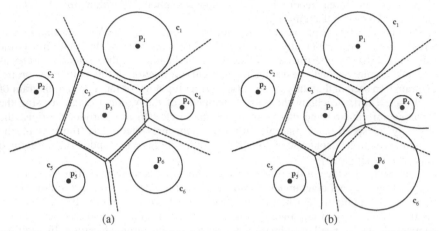

(a)                                    (b)

**Fig. 1.** Point set Voronoi diagrams (dotted line) and circle set Voronoi diagrams (solid line). (a) The topology of point set Voronoi diagram is identical to the topology of circle set Voronoi diagram. (b) The topologies of two Voronoi diagrams are not identical.

a robust code such as [12], and is represented by an efficient data structure such as a winged-edge data structure or a half-edge data structure. For the details of these data structure, the readers are recommended to refer to [7,9]. Note that the code to compute the point set Voronoi diagram in our implementation is actually the one available in [13].

## 3   Topology Update

One of the key parts of the algorithm is how to get the correct topological structure of VD($\mathbf{C}$) from VD($\mathbf{P}$). This part of the algorithm consists of two major steps: the analysis of flipping condition for an edge of VD($\mathbf{P}$), and the execution of the flipping operation to update the topology of the corresponding edge. Note that the execution of flipping operation is simply changing the pointers among five edges and two vertices appropriately

Topology update procedure is based on three cases depending on the condition of an edge: i) two circumcircles exist at the vertices of the edge, ii) only one circumcircle exists, and iii) no circumcircle exists.

### 3.1  Both CC Exist

This case is divided again into three subcases depending on the configuration of the point set and circle set: i) both circumcircles intersect with their mating generators, ii) only one circumcircle intersects with its mating generator, and iii) no circumcircle intersects with the mating generator. In the last case, the edge does not need to be flipped and will not be discussed further since it is obvious.

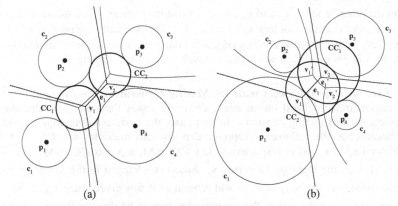

(a)                                                          (b)

**Fig. 2.** Point sets in both figures (a) and (b) are identical, and therefore the point set Voronoi diagrams (shown with dotted lines) are identical as well. However, the corresponding circle set Voronoi diagrams (shown with solid curves) differ.

**Both Circumcircles Intersect with Mating Generators.** Consider *Fig. 2. Fig. 2a* and *2b* have identical point sets, but different circle sets since the radii of the circles are different. The edge $e_1$, shown with dotted lines, has two vertices $v_1$ and $v_2$ in VD(**P**). The vertex $v_1$ has three associated generators $p_1$, $p_2$ and $p_4$, and the vertex $v_2$ has three associated generators $p_3$, $p_4$ and $p_2$. Note that this information is stored in the vertices of VD(**P**). Suppose that an efficient algorithm to compute the circumcircle of three given circles is available. (Note that this is feasible but not easy and will be discussed in another article [5].) Let $CC_1$ be a circumcircle to three circles $c_1$, $c_2$ and $c_4$. From the definition of vertex $v_1$ of VD(**P**), it can be determined that $CC_1$ should be computed from $c_1$, $c_2$ and $c_4$. Similarly, $CC_2$ is a circumcircle to $c_3$, $c_4$ and $c_2$. Note that we call $c_3$ (or $p_3$, depending on the context) a mating generator circle (or point) of $CC_1$.

Shown in *Fig. 2a*, $CC_1 \cap c_3 = \phi$. This means that any point inside or on $CC_1$ is closer to either $c_1$, $c_2$ or $c_4$ than any point on the mating circle $c_3$. Similarly, $CC_2 \cap c_1 = \phi$, and any point inside or on $CC_2$ is closer to either $c_2$, $c_3$ or $c_4$ than $c_1$. Since same property holds for the point set $\{p_1, ..., p_4\}$ of the centers of circles, the topology of VD(**P**) should be identical to the topology of VD(**C**). In this case, therefore, the topology of VD(**P**) can be immediately used as one for VD(**C**) without any modification.

On the other hand, both $CC_1$ and $CC_2$ in *Fig. 2b* intersect with mating circles $c_3$ and $c_1$, respectively. An important property of a Voronoi vertex is that the vertex has three associated generators and these are closest generators to that vertex. The fact that $CC_1$ intersects with the mating circle $c_3$ means that $c_3$ has a point on the circle which is closer to the vertex $v_1$ than any point on the three associated circles $c_1$, $c_2$ and $c_4$. This suggests that the topology of vertex $v_1$, as was given in VD(**P**), cannot exist as a member of vertex set in VD(**C**). Similarly, the vertex $v_2$ cannot be a member of vertex set of VD(**C**), since $CC_2$ also intersects with $c_1$. Therefore, the edge $e_1$ cannot exist in VD(**C**) as the topological structure given in VD(**P**) because both end vertices of the edge should disappear simultaneously.

On the other hand, $c_1$, $c_2$, and $c_3$ define a valid new vertex $v_1'$ as shown in *Fig. 2b*, and $c_1$, $c_4$, and $c_3$ define another valid vertex $v_2'$. Topologically connecting $v_1'$ and $v_2'$ with an edge creates a new Voronoi edge $e_1'$. Therefore, a new edge $e_1'$ should be born while the old edge $e_1$ disappears, and this results in an edge flipping.

**One Circumcircle Intersects with Its Mating Generator.** Even though there are two circumcircles defined on an edge, there are cases that only one circumcircle intersects with its mating generator. In this case, the corresponding edge should not flip because of the following. Suppose that the circumcircles are $CC_1$ and $CC_2$ corresponding to $v_1$ and $v_2$, respectively. Let $CC_1 \cap M_1 \neq \phi$ and $CC_2 \cap M_2 = \phi$. Since $CC_1 \cap M_1 \neq \phi$, the topology of vertex $v_1$ should be changed in the topology update process, while the topology of $v_2$ should remain as it was given since $CC_2 \cap M_2 = \phi$. Because of this small conflict, the current edge cannot be directly flipped. However, this conflict can be resolved by flipping another edge incident to the vertex $v_1$ in a later step so that the topological structure of $v_1$ is valid, while the topology of $v_2$ remains at this moment.

Unlike the Voronoi diagram of point set, the Voronoi diagram of circle set may have pathological degenerate faces which are bounded by only two edges and therefore only two vertices as shown in the figure below. We call this kind face as a *two-edge face*. (See Voronoi region of $p_5$ in *Fig. 3*.) It turns out that the VD(C) may have such a face when one circumcircle intersects with its mating generator.

Consider *Fig. 3*. Suppose the topology territory of $p_1$ is being expanded. Then, the quill edges $e_2$ and $e_4$ are tested for the possibility of flipping. Since both circumcircles at the vertices of the edge do intersect with their mating generators, $e_2$ should be flipped to $e_2'$ to result in *3b*.

By the recursive nature of the algorithm, then, the edges $e_3$ and $e_6$ becomes new elements of the quill edge set, which currently has only $e_4$ as its element, for the generator $c_1$. Therefore, we should now check the validity of edges $e_3$, $e_6$ and $e_4$. Note that $e_3$ has four associated generators $c_1$, $p_5$, $p_4$ and $c_3$ (Note that the points $p_4$ and $p_5$ are considered as circles with radii of zero.).

*3b* shows that there are two valid circumcircle instances, $CC_i'$ and $CC_i''$, to three generators $c_1$, $p_5$ and $c_3$, which are pointed by the data structure of one vertex $v_i$ (a vertex at the right extreme of $e_3$) of $e_3$, and both circumcircle instances do not intersect with the mating generator $p_4$. As was discussed earlier, the edge should not be flipped because both $CC_i'$ and $CC_i''$ do not intersect their mating generators. A possible configuration of generators in this case is shown in *3b*. Suppose that $e_3$ is currently being considered for the possibility of flipping, and $CC_i'$ shown in the figure play a role of circumcircle instance for a vertex $v_i$ of $e_3$. Now, the fact that there is another circumcircle instance $CC_i''$ means that there must be another vertex which corresponds to this circumcircle. Since there are two edges emanating to the left from the vertex $v_i$ of $e_3$, they should meet at this new vertex, which is the required by the existence of $CC_i''$. Therefore, if both $CC_i'$ and $CC_i''$ are both empty, $v_i$ should be a vertex of two-edge face. On the other hand, the circumcircle of the generators $c_3$, $p_5$ and $p_4$, which are also pointed by the other vertex of the same edge $e_3$, intersects with the mating generator circle $c_1$.

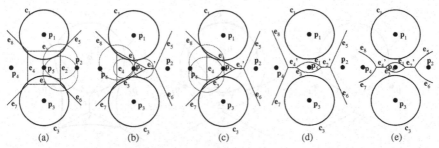

**Fig. 3.** The sequence for generating a two-edge face.

Therefore, we can say that the edge $e_3$ generates a two-edge face with another edge. In this example, it turns out that $p_5$ generates a two-edge face with $e_1$ and $e_3$ after the edge $e_4$ is flipped. *3c* shows that $e_4$ should be flipped because both circumcircles intersect with their mating generators. Illustrated in *Fig. 3d*, as a result, is the valid topology after territory expansion procedure of generator $c_1$ is terminated. The quill edge $e_6$ is not discussed here because it is immaterial for the case discussed in this section. The geometry of Voronoi edges, in addition to the topology, is shown in *Fig. 3e*.

Note that the numbers of vertices and edges of Voronoi diagram in *3e* are same as those in *3a*. This means that the edge flipping operation described here does not change the cardinality of topology.

## 3.2 One CC Exists

Depending on the configuration of the point set and the circle set, it is possible to have only one valid circumcircle. The other circumcircle does not exist for the given configuration, but only inscribing circle may do. In addition, the circumcircle may or may not intersect with its mating generator, and this results in different situations for flipping.

**Circumcircle Intersects with the Mating Generator.** As shown in *Fig. 4b* there is a case that no circumcircle, corresponding to vertex $v_1$, exists to three generators $p_1$, $c_2$, and $p_3$. Note that both dotted circles, associated to vertex $v_1$, in the figure are not valid circumcircles, but circles inscribing $c_2$. The fact that there is no circumcircle to three generator circles means the Voronoi vertex of three generator circles should disappear. In the given case, on the other hand, a circumcircle corresponding to vertex $v_2$ exists and the circumcircle intersects with the mating generator $c_2$. When this phenomenon happens an edge $e_1$ should flip to $e_1{}'$.

**Circumcircle Does Not Intersects with the Mating Generator.** Even though a circumcircle exists, it is possible that the existing circumcircle does not intersect with the mating generator circle. Obviously, the edge should not flip in this case. In the case that shown in *Fig. 5*, $CC_2$ exists but does not intersect with $p_4$, and the topology of the edges as well as vertices remain as they were.

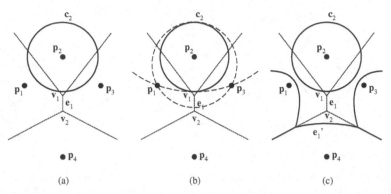

**Fig. 4.** A case that only one circumcircle exists and the existing circumcircle intersects with the mating generator.

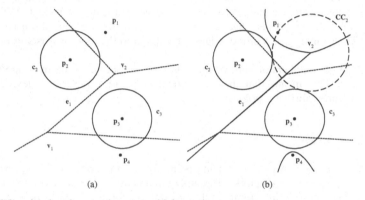

**Fig. 5.** $CC_2$ exists but does not intersect with its mating generator.

### 3.3 No CC Exists

It is even possible that a Voronoi edge of VD(P) does not yield any valid circumcircles. Consider *Fig. 6*. Suppose that two circles $c_1$ and $c_2$ are given, and two points $p_1$ and $p_4$ are located in-between two tangent lines $L_1$ and $L_2$ defined by two circles. Since there are only two vertices, $v_1$ and $v_2$, in the VD(P), the edge $e_1$ is tested for the possibility of flipping. In this case, a valid circumcircle $CC_1$ for $v_1$ does not exist but only inscribing circle does. Same is true for $CC_2$ for $v_2$. Therefore, this is the case that no valid circumcircle is defined for the edge to check for flipping. Hence, the edge does not flip.

What happens in this case is, as indicated in *Fig. 6b* which shows VD(C) with solid curves, is the following. The edge $e_1$ does not flip, and two vertices and two edges are lost (This will be explained later using the concept of convex hull property). Note that this case can be easily handled by including four fictitious generators, as is discussed in later section.

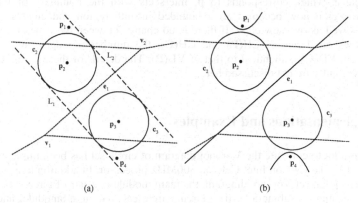

(a)                                    (b)

**Fig. 6.** No circumcircle exists.

## 4  Special Cases Due to Convex Hull

Suppose that we view the topology change from VD(P) to VD(C) as a continual change of the Voronoi diagram as the radius of a center point of a circle, one by one, increases continuously. Then, an edge flipping may occur in the middle of the radius increase since the Voronoi region of a circle becomes larger as the radius of the circle becomes larger.

A flipping operation does not change the cardinality of topology while the generator stays inside of CH(P). Since it is viewed as a continual process, there could be an incident that four generators are circumcircular and one edge disappears. However, it is assumed that this case, which can be handled by extending the proposed algorithm, does not exist in this paper.

As the radius of a generator increases, a number of interesting and tricky problems may occur. The edges and vertices of VD(P) may sometimes disappear, and new edges and vertices, which were not in VD(P), are created when certain conditions are satisfied. Both cases, which have a direct relationship with the convex hulls of both generator sets, are elaborated in this section.

Similarly to a Voronoi diagram of a point set, a Voronoi region of $c_i$ of VD(C) is infinite if and only if $c_i \cap \partial CH(C) \neq \phi$. Due to this observation, a Voronoi region defined by generators interior to CH(C) always defines a bounded region. Since CH(P) and CH(C) may have different generators in their boundaries, there may be changes of bounded and unbounded regions in both Voronoi diagrams. This process involves the changes of the cardinality as well as the structure of the topology of Voronoi diagrams.

Suppose that a point **p** was a vertex of CH(P), and located interior to CH(C). Then, as will be discussed soon, one unbounded region of VD(P) becomes a bounded one in VD(C). This causes changes in the number of vertices and edges, too. The number of edges is increased by one, and so is the number of vertices. Similar phenomenon exists in the opposite case. In other words, when a point **p** was interior to CH(P) and the circle **c**, which corresponds to **p**, intersects with the boundary of CH(**C**), a bounded region now becomes an unbounded infinite region and creates one new vertex as well as one new edge. If there is no change between the generator sets that lie on the boundaries of CH(**P**) and CH(**C**), the number of edges, and therefore vertices, of VD(**C**) is identical to that of VD(**P**). The details of these cases related to the convex hulls are not discussed here.

## 5   Implementations and Examples

The algorithm to compute the Voronoi diagram of circle set has been implemented in Microsoft Visual C++ on Intel Celeron 300MHz processor. In addition to a module to construct a point set Voronoi diagram, the main module consists of three submodules: i) an edge flipping submodule, ii) a circumcircle calculation submodule, and iii) an edge geometry (bisector) calculation submodule (not discussed in this article). Among these, the edge flipping submodule, which consists of testing the topological validity of an edge and execution of flipping, is the main concern of this article.

*Fig. 7* and *Fig. 8* show two examples. In *Fig. 7*, the 3,500 circles generated at random do not intersect each other and have different radii. And In *Fig. 8*, the 800 non-intersecting circles with different radii generated on a spiral. *Fig. 7a* and *8a* show results, and *Fig. 7b* and *8b* show the computation time taken by a number of generator sets with varying cardinality. In the figure, the computation time taken by a code to compute the Voronoi diagram of point sets is denoted by VD(**P**), and the time taken by our code to compute the Voronoi diagram of circle sets is denoted by VD(**C**). The point sets are the centers of circles generated at random, in this example. Note that the time denoted by VD(**C**) does not include the time taken by a preprocessing, which is actually the time denoted by VD(**P**). Therefore, the actual computation time to compute VD(**C**) from a given circle set is the accumulation of both computation times.

Comparing VD(**C**) with VD(**P**), it can be deduced that VD(**C**) is not as big as it might have been expected. Through experiences, there are cases that VD(**C**) is even much smaller than VD(**P**). Also, note that the correlation coefficient shown in the figure suggests that the average running behavior is a strong linear one. We have experimented with many other cases, and all the cases shows similar linear pattern. Based on these experiments we claim that the proposed algorithm is very efficient and robust. Even though the worst-case scenario, which will given $O(n^2)$ time performance, is theoretically possible, it is difficult to expect to face such a case in reality. *Fig. 9* shows that our algorithm works for the cases that the circles intersect each other. *Fig. 9a* shows the result of preprocessing which is the Voronoi diagram of point set, and *9b* shows the Voronoi diagram of circle set.

## 6   Conclusions

Presented in this paper is an algorithm to compute the exact Voronoi diagram of circle set from the Voronoi diagram of point set. In particular, the topology aspect of the

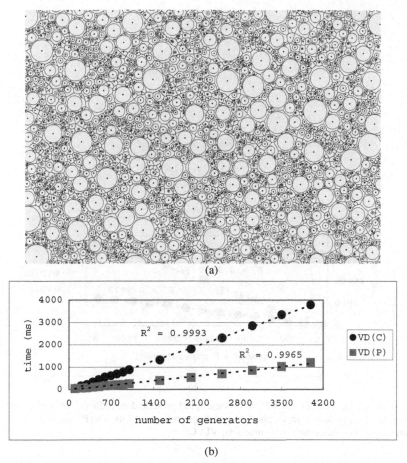

(a)

(b)

**Fig. 7.** (a) Voronoi diagram of 3,500 random circles. (b) The computation time taken to compute the Voronoi diagram of point sets, VD(**P**), and our code to compute the Voronoi diagram of circle sets, VD(**C**).

algorithm is presented here. Even though the time complexity of the proposed algorithm is $O(n^2)$, the algorithm is quite fast, produces exact result, and robust.

The algorithm uses the Voronoi diagram of point set as an initial solution, and finds the correct topology of the Voronoi diagram of circle set from its counterpart of point set. The algorithm chooses each edge of point set Voronoi diagram and tests if it can stay as it is in the Voronoi diagram of circle set.

The main advantage of the proposed algorithm is in its robustness as well as the conceptual simplicity. Since the algorithm is based on the result of point set Voronoi diagram and the flipping operation, when it is necessary, is the only one, the algorithm is as stable as the Voronoi diagram construction algorithm of point set. After the valid topology of circle set Voronoi diagram is obtained, the geometries of the Voronoi edges will have to be computed. This geometry update operation will be presented in a separate article [5].

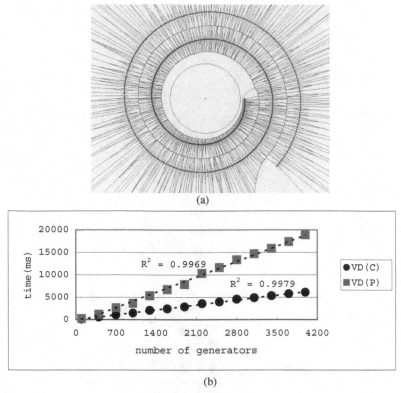

(b)

**Fig. 8.** (a) Voronoi diagram of 800 circles on a spiral with random radii. (b) The computation time taken by a code to compute the Voronoi diagram of point sets, VD(**P**), and our code to compute the Voronoi diagram of circle sets, VD(**C**).

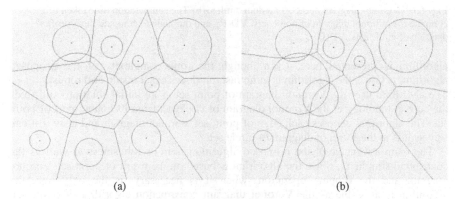

**Fig. 9.** Voronoi diagram of a few random circles, where some circles intersect each other and have different radii. (a) the Voronoi diagram of point set, (b) the Voronoi diagram of circle set

# References

1. Drysdale, R.L.III, and Lee, D.T, Generalized Voronoi diagram in the plane, Proceedings of the 16th Annual Allerton Conference on Communications, Control and Computing, Oct. (1978) 833-842.
2. Drysdale, R.L.III, Generalized Voronoi diagrams and geometric searching, Ph.D. Thesis, Department of Computer Science, Tech. Rep. STAN-CS-79-705, Stanford University, Stanford CA (1979).
3. Gavrilova, M. and Rokne, J., Swap conditions for dynamic Voronoi diagram for circles and line segments, Computer Aided Geometric Design, Vol. 16 (1999) 89-106.
4. Hamann, B. and Tsai, P.-Y., A tessellation algorithm for the representation of trimmed NURBS surfaces with arbitrary trimming curves, Computer-Aided Design, Vol. 28, No. 6/7 (1996) 461-472.
5. Kim, D.-S., Kim, D., and Sugihara, K., Voronoi diagram of a circle set from Voronoi diagram of a point set: II. Geometry, (in preparation)
6. Lee, D.T. and Drysdale, R.L.III, Generalization of Voronoi diagrams in the plane, SIAM J. COMPUT., Vol. 10, No. 1, February (1981) 73-87.
7. Mäntylä, M., An introduction to solid modeling, Computer Science Press (1988).
8. Okabe, A., Boots, B. and Sugihara, K., Spatial Tessellations Concepts and Applications of Voronoi Diagram, John Wiley & Sons (1992).
9. Preparata, F.P. and Shamos, M.I. Computational Geometry An Introduction Springer-Verlag (1985).
10. Sharir, M., Intersction and closest-pair problems for a set of planar discs, SIAM J. COMPUT., Vol. 14, No. 2, May (1985) 448-468.
11. Sugihara, K., Approximation of generalized Voronoi diagrams by ordinary Voronoi diagrams, Graphical Models and Image Processing, Vol. 55, No. 6 (1993) 522-531.
12. Sugihara, K. and Iri, M., Construction of the Voronoi diagram for one million generators in single-precision arithmetic, Proc. IEEE 80 (1992) 1471-1484.
13. Sugihara, K., http://www.simplex.t.u-tokyo.ac.jp/~sugihara/, (2000).

# An Improved Algorithm for Subdivision Traversal without Extra Storage *

Prosenjit Bose and Pat Morin

School of Computer Science, Carleton University
Ottawa, Canada, K1S 5B6
{jit,morin}@scs.carleton.ca

**Abstract.** We describe an algorithm for enumerating all vertices, edges and faces of a planar subdivision stored in any of the usual pointer-based representations, while using only a constant amount of memory beyond that required to store the subdivision. The algorithm is a refinement of a method introduced by de Berg *et al* (1997), that reduces the worst case running time from $O(n^2)$ to $O(n \log n)$. We also give experimental results that show that our modified algorithm runs faster not only in the worst case, but also in many realistic cases.

## 1 Introduction

A planar subdivision $S$ is a partitioning of the plane into a set $V$ of vertices (points), a set $E$ of edges (line segments), and a set $F$ of faces (polygons). Planar subdivisions are frequently used in geographic information systems as a representation for maps. A common operation on subdivisions is that of traversal. Traversing a subdivision involves reporting each vertex, edge and face of $S$ exactly once, so that, e.g., some operation can be applied to each.

The usual method of traversing a subdivision involves a breadth-first or depth-first traversal of the primal (vertices and edges) or dual (faces and edges) graph of $S$. Unfortunately, this requires the use of mark bits on the edges, vertices, or faces of $S$ and a stack or queue. If the data structure used to represent $S$ does not have extra memory allocated to the vertex/edge/face records for these mark bits, then an auxiliary array must be allocated and some form of hashing is required to map vertex/edge/face records to array indices. Even if extra memory is available for mark bits, this approach has the problem that traversal cannot be done simultaneously by more than one thread of execution without some type of locking mechanism.

For these reasons, researchers have investigated methods of traversing subdivisions and other graph-like data structures without the use of mark bits [2, 3,4,5,6]. Generally speaking, these techniques use geometric properties of $S$ to define a spanning tree $T$ of the vertices, edges or faces of $S$ and then apply a well-known tree-traversal technique to traverse $T$ using $O(1)$ additional memory.

---

* This research was funded by the Natural Sciences and Engineering Research Council of Canada.

D.T. Lee and S.-H. Teng (Eds.): ISAAC 2000, LNCS 1969, pp. 444–455, 2000.

The most recent and general result on traversing planar subdivisions is that of de Berg *et al* [2] who show how to traverse any connected subdivision $S$ using only $O(1)$ additional storage. The running time of their algorithm is $O(\sum_{f \in F} |f|^2)$, where $|f|$ denotes the number of edges on the boundary of the face $f$. Unfortunately, in the worst case this results in a running time of $O(n^2)$ for a subdivision with $n$ vertices.

In this paper we show how to modify the algorithm of de Berg *et al* so that it runs in $O(\sum_{f \in F} |f| \log |f|) \subseteq O(n \log n)$ time. The modification we describe is quite simple and does not significantly affect the constants in the running time of the algorithm. The resulting algorithm is also similar enough to the original algorithm that all the extensions described by de Berg *et al* also work for our algorithm, often with an improved running time. We also give experimental results comparing our modified algorithm to the original algorithm as well as a traditional traversal algorithm that uses mark bits and a stack.

The remainder of the paper is organized as follows: Section 2 describes the primitive constant time operations required by our algorithm and defines some notation. Section 3 presents the traversal algorithm. Section 4 discusses our experimental results. Section 5 summarizes and concludes with open problems.

## 2   Notation and Primitive Operations

In this section we describe the constant-time primitives used by our algorithm.

Rather than assume a specific representation of the subdivision $S$ we will only state the primitives used by our algorithm. We assume that the representation of $S$ includes the notions of vertices, edges, and faces and that edges can be directed so that the edges $(u, v)$ and $(v, u)$ are two different entities. Note that, while we assume the *representation* of $S$ has directed edges, we still have to report each (undirected) edge of $S$ exactly once.

For an edge $e = (u, v)$ of $S$, $src(e)$ returns a pointer to $u$, $tgt(e)$ returns a pointer to $v$, and $face\_of(e)$ returns a pointer to the face with $e$ on its boundary and on the left of $e$. The function $succ(e)$ returns a pointer to the next edge on the boundary of $face\_of(e)$ when traversing $e$ in direction $uv$. The function $pred(e)$ returns the next edge on the boundary of $face\_of(e)$ when traversing $e$ in direction $vu$. Finally, $rev(e)$ returns a pointer to the edge $(v, u)$. See Figure 1 for an illustration of these functions.

This functionality is available in or can be simulated by the most commonly used data structures for storing planar subdivisions including the doubly-connected edge list [11,14], the quad edge structure [8], the fully topological network structure [1], the ARC-INFO structure [12], and the DIME file [13].

Our algorithm also requires the use of some geometric operations. Let $dist(a, b)$ be the distance between two points $a$ and $b$. Let $\vec{ab}$ be the direction of the ray originating at $a$ and containing $b$. The angle formed by three points $a$, $b$ and $c$ is denoted by $\angle abc$ and always refers to the smaller of the two angles as measured in the clockwise and counterclockwise directions. When referring specifically to clockwise and counterclockwise angles we will use the notations

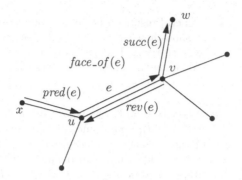

**Fig. 1.** The operations required on subdivisions.

$\overset{\text{cw}}{\angle} abc$ and $\overset{\text{ccw}}{\angle} abc$, respectively. Let $right\_turn(a, b, c)$ be the predicate that is true if and only if $\overset{\text{cw}}{\angle} abc < \pi$. We use the notation $cone(a, b, c)$ to denote the cone with apex $b$, with supporting lines passing through $b$ and $c$, and interior angle $\overset{\text{ccw}}{\angle} abc$. We will assume that $cone(a, b, c)$ contains the bounding ray passing through $a$ and $b$, but not the bounding ray passing through $b$ and $c$. If $a$, $b$, and $c$ are collinear then $cone(a, b, c)$ is a single ray.

Although we use angles, distances and directions that involve square roots and trigonometric functions, this is only to simplify the description of our algorithm. Since these values are always only being compared, it is not necessary to explicity compute them, and it is a simple exercise to implement the algorithm using only algebraic functions.

## 3    The Algorithm

In this section we describe the subdivision traversal algorithm. The algorithm requires only that we are given a pointer to some edge $e_{start}$ of $S$ and a point $p$ contained in the interior of $face\_of(e_{start})$. The point $p$ is not strictly necessary since it can be obtained by using symbolic perturbation to create a point just to the left of the midpoint of $e_{start}$.

The algorithm works by defining a relation between the faces of $S$ that produces a spanning tree of the faces of $S$. The relation is based on a total order on the edges of $S$ that defines a special edge for each face.

### 3.1    The $\preceq_p$ Order and Entry Edges

Next we define the total order $\preceq_p$ on the edges of $S$. For an edge $e$, let $dist(e, p)$ be the radius of the smallest circle $C$, centered at $p$, that intersects $e$, and let $pt(e)$ be the intersection point of $C$ and $e$.

For an edge $e = (u, v)$ such that $pt(e) = x$ and $dist(u, p) \leq dist(v, p)$ we define the *key* of $e$ as the 4-tuple

$$key(e) = \left( dist(e, p), \quad \overrightarrow{px}, \quad \angle puv, \quad \overset{ccw}{\angle} puv \right) . \tag{1}$$

It is not difficult to verify that for any two edges $e_1$ and $e_2$ of $S$, $key(e_1) = key(e_2)$ if and only if $e_1 = e_2$. (This follows from the fact that edges of $S$ intersect only at their endpoints.) The total order $\preceq_p$ is defined by lexicographic comparison of the numeric *key* values using $\leq$. Figure 2 gives examples of how the four values of $key(e)$ are used to compare two edges.

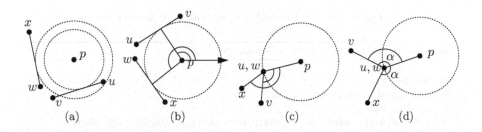

(a)          (b)          (c)          (d)

**Fig. 2.** Cases in which determining that $(u, v) \preceq_p (w, x)$ requires the use of (a) their first key, (b) their second key, (c) their third key, and (d) their fourth key.

For a face $f$ of $S$, we define $entry(f)$ as

$$entry(f) = e \in f : e \preceq_p e' \text{ for all } e' \neq e \in f , \tag{2}$$

i.e., $entry(f)$ is the minimum edge on the boundary of $f$ with respect to the order $\preceq_p$.

### 3.2   Traversing the Face Tree

For a face $f$, let $parent(f)$ be the face $f'$ that has the edge $entry(f)$ on its boundary. de Berg *et al* [2] prove the following lemma.

**Lemma 1 (de Berg et al 1997)** *For any face $f$ that does not contain $p$, $parent(f) \neq f$ and the values of $parent(f)$ define a rooted tree whose vertices correspond to the faces of $S$ and whose root is $face\_of(e_{start})$.*

We call this tree the *face tree* of $S$ with respect to $p$. See Figure 3 for an example.

The traversal algorithm (Algorithm 1) performs a depth-first traversal of the face tree in order to report each vertex, face, and edge of $S$ exactly once. An example of a traversal performed by Algorithm 1 is shown in Figure 3.

**Lemma 2** *Algorithm 1 reports each vertex, edge and face of $S$ exactly once.*

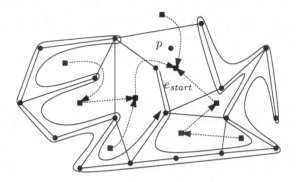

**Fig. 3.** The face tree of $S$ and a traversal of the face tree.

---

**Algorithm 1** Traverses the subdivision $S$

---
1: $e \leftarrow e_{start}$
2: **repeat**
3:     {* report $e$ if necessary *}
4:     Let $(u, v) = e$
5:     **if** $dist(u, p) < dist(v, p)$ or $(dist(u, p) = dist(v, p)$ and $\overrightarrow{up} < \overrightarrow{vp})$ **then**
6:         **report** $e$
7:     **end if**
8:     {* report $v$ if necessary *}
9:     Let $(v, w) = succ(e)$
10:     **if** $p$ is contained in $cone(w, v, u)$ **then**
11:         **report** $v$
12:     **end if**
13:     **if** $e = entry(face\_of(e))$ **then**
14:         {* return to parent of $face\_of(e)$ *}
15:         **report** $face\_of(e)$
16:         $e \leftarrow rev(e)$
17:     **else if** $rev(e) = entry(face\_of(rev(e)))$ **then**
18:         {* descend to child of $face\_of(e)$ *}
19:         $e \leftarrow rev(e)$
20:     **end if**
21:     $e \leftarrow succ(e)$
22: **until** $e = e_{start}$
23: **report** $face\_of(e_{start})$

---

*Proof.* A proof that this algorithm performs a depth-first traversal of the face tree that visits all faces of $S$ is given by de Berg *et al* [2]. This traversal has two important properties.

1. Each face $f$ of $S$ is traversed exactly once.
2. Each (directed) edge $e = (u, v)$ of $S$ is visited exactly once.

That the algorithm reports each face exactly once is clear, since the algorithm reports a face $f$ when returning to the parent of $f$ (line 15), and each face has exactly one parent, except for the face containing $p$, which is treated as a special case (line 23). See Figure 4.a for an illustration.

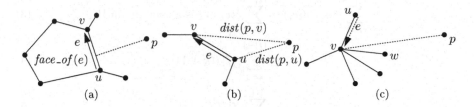

**Fig. 4.** When the edge $e$ is visited in direction , (a) $face\_of(e)$ is reported, (b) $e$ is reported, (c) $v$ is reported.

That each (undirected) edge is reported exactly once follows from the fact that an edge is reported only when it is visited in the direction moving "away-from" $p$ (line 5), and by property (2), each edge is visited exactly once in each direction. See Figure 4.b for an illustration.

That each vertex is reported exactly once follows from the fact that a vertex $v$ is reported only while traversing the unique edge $e$ satisfying the conditions of line 10 (see Figure 4.c) in the direction for which $tgt(e) = v$. Since, by property (2), each edge is traversed exactly once in each direction, $v$ is reported exactly once. See Figure 4.c for an illustration.   □

If we ignore the cost of the tests in lines 13 and 17, then the running time of the algorithm is clearly $O(n)$, since each face is traversed only once. The test $e = entry(f)$ can be implemented in $O(|f|)$ time by walking around $f$ until finding an edge $e' \neq e$ such that $e' \preceq_p e$ or until returning to $e$. Since, by property (2) each edge of $S$ is tested 4 times (twice in each direction), the overall running time of this algorithm is $O(\sum_{f \in F} |f|^2)$, and this is basically the algorithm given by de Berg et al [2].

### 3.3   Testing Entry Edges

In this section we show how to implement the test $e = entry(f)$ so that the running time of Algorithm 1 is $O(\sum_{f \in F} |f| \log |f|)$.

Let $e_0, \ldots, e_{|f|-1}$ be the edges of $f$ in counterclockwise order. Then we say that $e_i$ is a $k$-minimum if $e_i \preceq_p e_j$ for all $i - k \leq j \leq i + k$.[1] We define $minval(e_i)$ as the maximum $k$ for which $e_i$ is a $k$-minimum. The following lemma provides an efficient means of testing whether $e_i = entry(f)$.

---

[1] In this section, subscripts are implicitly taken mod $|f|$.

**Lemma 3** $\sum_{i=0}^{|f|-1} minval(e_i) \leq |f| \cdot (H_{|f|} - 1)$, where $H_x$ is the xth harmonic number, defined as $H_x = \sum_{i=1}^{x} 1/x$.

*Proof.* If $e_i$ is a $k$-minimum, then none of $e_{i-k}, \ldots, e_{i-1}, e_{i+1}, \ldots, e_{i+k}$ is a $k$-minimum. Therefore, at most $\lfloor |f|/(k+1) \rfloor$ edges of $f$ are $k$-minima. Thus,

$$\sum_{i=0}^{|f|-1} minval(e_i) = \sum_{k=1}^{|f|-1} |\{e_i : e_i \text{ is a } k\text{-minimum}\}| \tag{3}$$

$$\leq \sum_{k=1}^{|f|-1} \lfloor |f|/(k+1) \rfloor \tag{4}$$

$$= \sum_{k=1}^{|f|} \lfloor |f|/k \rfloor - |f| \tag{5}$$

$$\leq |f| \cdot (H_{|f|} - 1) \tag{6}$$

$\square$

Harmonic numbers have been studied extensively, and are known to satisfy the inequalies $\ln x \leq H_x \leq \ln x + 1$ (cf. [7, Section 6.3]). Therefore, Lemma 3 suggests that it is more efficient to perform the test $e_i = entry(f)$ by traversing $f$ in the clockwise and counterclockwise directions "in parallel." This leads to Algorithm 2 for testing the condition $e_i = entry(f)$.

---

**Algorithm 2** Tests the condition $e_i = entry(f)$.

---
1: $e^{cw} \leftarrow e^{ccw} \leftarrow e_i$
2: **while** $1 < 2$ **do**
3:     $e^{cw} \leftarrow pred(e^{cw})$
4:     **if** $e^{cw} = e^{ccw}$ **then**
5:         **return** true
6:     **else if** $e^{cw} \preceq_p e_i$ **then**
7:         **return** false
8:     **end if**
9:     $e^{ccw} \leftarrow succ(e^{ccw})$
10:     **if** $e^{cw} = e^{ccw}$ **then**
11:         **return** true
12:     **else if** $e^{ccw} \preceq_p e_i$ **then**
13:         **return** false
14:     **end if**
15: **end while**

---

Clearly Algorithm 2 is correct, since it only returns false after finding an edge $e'$ such that $e' \preceq_p e$ and returns true only after it has compared $e$ to every other edge of $f$. Furthermore, the number of comparisons performed by Algorithm 2 is at most $2 \cdot (minval(e_i) + 1)$. We are now ready to prove our main result.

**Theorem 1** *Algorithm 1 reports all vertices, edges and faces of a connected planar subdivision $S$ with $n$ vertices in $O(n \log n)$ time.*

*Proof.* The correctness of the algorithm was proven in Lemma 2.

Next we note that if we run Algorithm 2 on each edge of a face $f$ then, by Lemma 3, the total number of comparisons performed is at most $2 \cdot |f| \cdot H_{|f|}$. By property (2) each edge of $S$ is tested for being an entry edge at most 4 times (twice in each direction) during the execution of Algorithm 1. Therefore, the total number of comparisons performed during these tests is at most $\sum_{f \in F} 8 \cdot |f| \cdot H_{|f|} \in O(n \log n)$. Since all other operations can be bounded by the number of comparisons performed during these tests, the theorem follows.     □

Any reader familiar with the field of distributed algorithms may notice the similarity between the analysis used in this section and the analysis of the Hirschberg-Sinclair [9] leader election algorithm for the ring. Indeed, there are deep links between the two problems. In the leader election problem, each processor in a ring must determine whether it has the smallest processor ID in the ring. In our problem we must determine if each edge on the boundary of a face is a minimum with respect to the $\preceq_p$ order. In the case of leader election, the challenge comes from the fact that processors can only communicate with their immediate neighbours, while in our problem the difficulty comes from the $O(1)$ memory restriction.

## 4   Experimental Results

In this section we give experimental results on the running times of subdivision traversal algorithms. All tests were implemented in C++ using the LEDA library [10]. Subdivisions were represented using the data type GRAPH<point,int> in which vertex coordinates are represented using double-precision floating point. All numerical values presented in this section are the average of 40 different tests. The test machine was a PC with a Pentium II 350Mhz processor and 128MB of 100Mhz memory running Linux kernel release 2.0.36.

Table 1 compares the running times of three subdivision traversal algorithms on Delaunay triangulations of points uniformly distributed in the unit circle. The DFS algorithm requires the use of mark bits and a stack and does a depth-first search on the vertices (to report vertices and edges) and on the faces (to report faces). The BKOO algorithm is the algorithm described by de Berg *et al* [2] and the BM algorithm is the one described in this paper.

From these results it is clear that, in terms of running time, DFS is far more efficient than the the other two algorithms, being somewhere between 15–20 times faster. This is due simply to the fact that evaluating the geometric predicates required to implement BKOO and BM involves expensive floating-point computations.

However, the reader should note that these tests strongly favour the DFS algorithm for several reasons. The first is that vertices, edges and faces of the

**Table 1.** Running times (in seconds) for DFS, BKOO and BM on subdivisions ranging from $10^4$ to $10^5$ vertices.

| $n/10^4$ | 1 | 2 | 3 | 4 | 5 | 6 | 7 | 8 | 9 | 10 |
|---|---|---|---|---|---|---|---|---|---|---|
| DFS | 0.093 | 0.190 | 0.282 | 0.386 | 0.481 | 0.575 | 0.695 | 0.787 | 0.884 | 0.979 |
| BKOO | 1.531 | 3.050 | 4.563 | 6.098 | 7.701 | 9.234 | 10.769 | 12.143 | 13.857 | 15.392 |
| BM | 1.537 | 3.067 | 4.595 | 6.140 | 7.794 | 9.355 | 10.906 | 12.220 | 14.038 | 15.594 |

LEDA graph type are given integer identifiers which makes it possible to implement mark bits very efficiently through the use of auxilliary arrays, without the use of hashing. The price of this is, of course, an increase in storage cost, even when mark bits are not needed.

The second advantage enjoyed by the DFS algorithm is that the functions for reporting vertices, edges, and faces were implemented as empty stubs. Thus, the running time represents only the overhead incurred by the traversal algorithm. In many cases, this overhead is negligible if the reporting functions are more complicated. Along similar lines, the subdivision being traversed may be stored in external memory. In this case the cost of disk accesses in the subdivision data structure will be the dominant cost, rather than the geometric predicates used by the BKOO and BM algorithms.

Next we compare the BKOO and BM algorithms. Let $S$ be a planar subdivision with $n + \alpha n$ vertices. We obtain a subdivision $S'$ with a *failure rate* of $\alpha$ by deleting $\alpha n$ randomly chosen vertices of $S$. Intuitively, the failure rate $\alpha$ is a measure of how complex the faces of $S'$ are, compared to the faces of $S$. Our test cases for the BKOO and BM algorithms involved generating graphs with $n + \alpha n$ vertices and then deleting $\alpha n$ randomly chosen vertices. Any resulting graph with more than one connected component was discarded.

Figure 5 compares the performance of the BKOO and BM algorithms when the initial graph is the Delaunay triangulation of points randomly distributed in the unit circle. As our theoretical analysis predicts, the performance of the BKOO and BM algorithms is comparable as long as all faces are of constant complexity, but the performance of the BKOO algorithm degrades as the complexity of the faces (failure rate) of the subdivision increases. In contrast, the complexity of the faces seems to have no noticeable effect on the performance of the BM algorithm.

Figures 6 and 7 show similar results for the case of regular quadrangle meshes and triangulations generated by first sorting the points by $x$-coordinate and then using Graham's scan (c.f., [14]) to triangulate the points. Overall, these results suggest that the BM algorithm not only performs better than BKOO in the worst case, but also in many practical cases.

## 5   Conclusions

We have shown how to traverse a connected planar subdivision with $n$ vertices using $O(1)$ additional memory and $O(n \log n)$ time. De Berg *et al* [2] describe

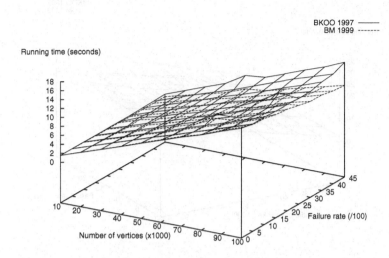

**Fig. 5.** Comparison of BKOO and BM on Delaunay triangulations.

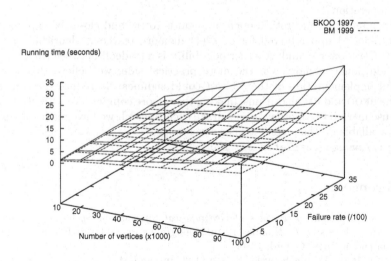

**Fig. 6.** Comparison of BKOO and BM on Meshes.

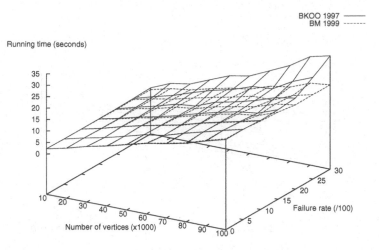

BKOO 1997 ———
BM 1999 -------

**Fig. 7.** Comparison of BKOO and BM on Graham triangulations.

various extensions of their algorithm, including curved subdivisions, window queries, and traversing connected subsets of faces with a common attribute. Our modification of their algorithm results in improved running times for all of these operations.

An interesting theoretical open problem is to try and close the gap between our $O(n \log n)$ upper bound for an $O(1)$ memory traversal algorithm and the trivial $\Omega(n)$ lower bound. Another possibility is a tradeoff between running time and additional memory. On the more practical side, we believe that a more careful implementation of the $\preceq_p$ test could significantly reduce the constants for the BKOO and BM algorithms, making them more competitive with algorithms that use mark bits. In order to encourage such research we have made our source code available on the second author's web page (http://www.scs.carleton.ca/~morin).

## References

1. P. A. Burrough. *Principles of Geographical Information Systems for Land Resources Assessment.* Number 12 in Monographs on Soil and Resources Survey. Clarendon Press, Oxford, 1986.
2. M. de Berg, M. van Kreveld, R. van Oostrum, and M. Overmars. Simple traversal of a subdivision without extra storage. *International Journal of Geographic Information Systems*, 11:359–373, 1997.
3. H. Edelsbrunner, L. J. Guibas, and J. Stolfi. Optimal point location in a monotone subdivision. *SIAM Journal on Computing*, 15:317–340, 1986.

4. C. Gold and S. Cormack. Spatially ordered networks and topographic reconstructions. In *Proceedings of the 2nd International Symposium on Spatial Data Handling*, pages 74–85, 1986.
5. C. M. Gold, T. D. Charters, and J. Ramsden. Automated contour mapping using triangular element data and an interpolant over each irregular triangular domain. *Computer Graphics*, 11(2):170–175, 1977.
6. C. M. Gold and U. Maydell. Triangulation and spatial ordering in computer cartography. In *Proceedings of the Canadian Cartographic Association Annual Meeting*, pages 69–81, 1978.
7. Ronald L. Graham, Donald E. Knuth, and Oren Patashnik. *Concrete Mathematics*. Addison-Wesley, 2nd edition, 1994.
8. L. J. Guibas and J. Stolfi. Primitives for the manipulation of general subdivisions and the computation of Voronoi diagrams. *ACM Transactions on Graphics*, 4:74–123, 1985.
9. D. S. Hirschberg and J. B. Sinclair. Decentralized extrema-finding in circular configurations of processes. *Communications of the ACM*, 23(11):627–628, 1980.
10. Kurt Mehlhorn and Stefan Näher. *LEDA A Platform for Combinatorial and Geometric Computing*. Cambridge University Press, 1999.
11. D. E. Muller and F. P. Preparata. Finding the intersection of two convex polyhedra. *Theoretical Computer Science*, 7(2):217–236, 1978.
12. D. J. Peuquet and D. F. Marble. ARC/INFO: An example of a contemporary geographic information system. In *Introductory Readings in Geographic Information Systems*, pages 90–99. Taylor & Francis, 1990.
13. D. J. Peuquet and D. F. Marble. Technical description of the DIME system. In *Introductory Readings in Geographic Information Systems*, pages 100–111. Taylor & Francis, 1990.
14. Franco P. Preparata and Michael Ian Shamos. *Computational Geometry*. Springer-Verlag, New York, 1985.

# Generalized $H$-Coloring of Graphs

Petter Kristiansen and Jan Arne Telle

Department of Informatics, University of Bergen, N-5020 Bergen, Norway
{petterk, telle}@ii.uib.no

**Abstract.** For fixed simple graph $H$ and subsets of natural numbers $\sigma$ and $\rho$, we introduce $(H, \sigma, \rho)$-colorings as generalizations of $H$-colorings of graphs. An $(H, \sigma, \rho)$-coloring of a graph $G$ can be seen as a mapping $f : V(G) \to V(H)$, such that the neighbors of any $v \in V(G)$ are mapped to the closed neighborhood of $f(v)$, with $\sigma$ constraining the number of neighbors mapped to $f(v)$, and $\rho$ constraining the number of neighbors mapped to each neighbor of $f(v)$. A traditional $H$-coloring is in this sense an $(H, \{0\}, \{0, 1, \ldots\})$-coloring. We initiate the study of how these colorings are related and then focus on the problem of deciding if an input graph $G$ has an $(H, \{0\}, \{1, 2, \ldots\})$-coloring. This $H$-COLORDOMINATION problem is shown to be no easier than the $H$-COVER problem and $\mathcal{NP}$-complete for various infinite classes of graphs.

## 1 Introduction

Let $H$ be a fixed simple graph with $k$ vertices $V(H) = \{h_1, h_2, \ldots, h_k\}$, and let $\sigma$ and $\rho$ be fixed subsets of natural numbers. We define an $(H, \sigma, \rho)$-*coloring* of a graph $G$ to be a partition $V_1, V_2, \ldots, V_k$ of $V(G)$ such that for all $1 \leq i, j \leq k$

$$\forall v \in V_i : |N_G(v) \cap V_j| \in \begin{cases} \sigma & \text{if } i = j \\ \rho & \text{if } h_i h_j \in E(H) \\ \{0\} & \text{otherwise ,} \end{cases}$$

where $N_G(v)$ denotes the (open) neighborhood of $v$ in $G$ and $E(H)$ the edges of $H$. We will also view the partition as given by a function $f : V(G) \to V(H)$, with $f(v) = h_i$ for $v \in V_i$. We refer to the vertices of $H$ as 'colors' and denote $\mathbb{N} = \{0, 1, \ldots\}$, $\mathbb{N}^+ = \{1, 2, \ldots\}$. The well-known $H$-COLORING, also known as $H$-HOMOMORPHISM, problem asks for an assignment of 'colors' to the vertices of an input graph $G$ such that adjacent vertices of $G$ obtain adjacent 'colors'. This corresponds to asking if an input graph $G$ has an $(H, \{0\}, \mathbb{N})$-coloring. Similarly, an $H$-cover of a graph $G$ is a 'local isomorphism' between $G$ and $H$, a degree-preserving mapping of vertices where the set of 'colors' assigned to the neighbors of a vertex 'colored' $h$ is exactly equal to the set of 'colors' adjacent to $h$, and corresponds to an $(H, \{0\}, \{1\})$-coloring. A third example is given by a so-called $H$-partial cover of a graph $G$ which exists if and only if $G$ is the subgraph of a graph having an $H$-cover, and corresponds precisely to the existence of an $(H, \{0\}, \{0, 1\})$-coloring.

D.T. Lee and S.-H. Teng (Eds.): ISAAC 2000, LNCS 1969, pp. 456–466, 2000.

For an arbitrary input graph $G$, the $H$-COLORING problem is known to be solvable in polynomial time whenever the fixed graph $H$ is bipartite, and $\mathcal{NP}$-complete for all other $H$ [5]. For the $H$-COVER problem, i.e. deciding if an input graph $G$ has an $H$-cover, even if a variety of results are known about its complexity, see e.g. [1,9,10,8], it is still unclear what characterizes the class of graphs $H$ that lead to polynomial-time $H$-COVER problems. Recently there has been some interest also in the $H$-PARTIAL COVER problem [9,2,7], deciding if an input graph $G$ has an $H$-partial cover, and again the complexity of the problem seems quite rich and hard to settle up to $\mathcal{P}$ versus $\mathcal{NP}$-complete.

In this paper we view the $H$-COLORING, $H$-COVER, and $H$-PARTIAL COVER problems as instances of a more general problem parameterized not only by $H$, but also by $\sigma, \rho \subseteq \mathbb{N}$. A $(\sigma, \rho)$-set in a graph $G$ [13] is a subset of vertices $S \subseteq V(G)$ such that for any vertex $v \in V(G)$ we have

$$|N(v) \cap S| \in \begin{cases} \sigma \text{ if } v \in S \\ \rho \text{ if } v \notin S \end{cases}.$$

In this sense $H$-colorings arise from independent sets ($\sigma = \{0\}, \rho = \mathbb{N}$), $H$-covers from perfect codes ($\sigma = \{0\}, \rho = \{1\}$), and $H$-partial covers from 2-packings, also called strong stable sets, ($\sigma = \{0\}, \rho = \{0, 1\}$) [3]. See [13] for a list of other vertex subset properties from the literature expressed as $(\sigma, \rho)$-sets.

Asking about the existence of a partitioning of the vertices of a graph $G$ into $k$ $(\sigma, \rho)$-sets corresponds in this setting to asking for a $(K_k, \sigma, \rho)$-coloring, and the complexity of this question has been resolved for most values of $k \in \mathbb{N}$ and $\sigma, \rho \in \{\{0\}, \{0, 1\}, \{1\}, \mathbb{N}, \mathbb{N}^+\}$ [4]. We mention that the minimum value of $k$ such that a graph $G$ has a $(K_k, \{0\}, \mathbb{N})$-coloring is known as the chromatic number of $G$, while the maximum value of $k$ such that $G$ has a $(K_k, \mathbb{N}, \mathbb{N}^+)$-coloring is known as its domatic number, and the maximum value of $k$ such that it has a $(K_k, \mathbb{N}^+, \mathbb{N}^+)$-coloring its total domatic number. See [3] for an in-depth treatment of domination and related subset problems in graphs.

In the next section we initiate the study of $(H, \sigma, \rho)$-colorings of graphs by giving several observations on their interconnectedness. We then focus on the problem of deciding if an input graph $G$ has an $(H, \{0\}, \mathbb{N}^+)$-coloring. Since $(\sigma = \{0\}, \rho = \mathbb{N}^+)$-sets are exactly the independent dominating sets of a graph, we call this the $H$-COLORDOMINATION problem. The complexity of $H$-COLORDOMINATION is related to the $H$-COVER problem, and moreover we show it to be $\mathcal{NP}$-complete for infinite classes of graphs such as $H$ a cycle on at least three vertices, $H$ a star with at least two leaves, or $H$ a path of at least three vertices.

## 2    Observations

We first state, without proof, some general facts about the existence of $(H, \sigma, \rho)$-colorings.

**Fact 1** *The trivial partition of $V(H)$ into singleton sets is an $(H, \{0\}, \{1\})$-coloring of $H$ (in fact it is an $(H, \sigma, \rho)$-coloring as long as $0 \in \sigma, 1 \in \rho$.) At the other extreme, the trivial partition of $V(G)$ into one block is a $(K_1, \sigma, \rho)$-coloring of $G$ as long as $\forall v \in V(G) : |N_G(v)| \in \sigma$ (adding empty blocks as needed, it is in fact an $(H, \sigma, \rho)$-coloring for any $H$, if in addition $0 \in \rho$.)*

**Fact 2** *If $r$ is a positive integer and $H$ is a connected graph, then all blocks of an $(H, \sigma, \{r\})$-coloring $V_1, \ldots, V_{|V(H)|}$ of a graph $G$ must be of the same cardinality, $|V_i| = |V(G)|/|V(H)|$ for $i = 1, \ldots, |V(H)|$.*

To investigate how $(H, \sigma, \rho)$-colorings in $G$ interact with $(H', \sigma', \rho')$-colorings in $H$, we first define, for two non-empty sets of natural numbers, $A$ and $B$

$$A \oplus B \stackrel{\text{def}}{=} \{a + b : a \in A, b \in B\}$$

$$A \otimes B \stackrel{\text{def}}{=} \{b_1 + \cdots + b_a : a \in A, b_i \in B\}$$

$$\forall B : \{0\} \otimes B \stackrel{\text{def}}{=} \{0\} .$$

**Fact 3** $\forall A \in \{\{0\}, \{1\}, \{0, 1\}, \mathbb{N}, \mathbb{N}^+\} : A \otimes A = A$.

Viewed as a relation on graphs $(H, \sigma, \rho)$-coloring exhibits transitive properties for certain values of $\sigma$ and $\rho$. For these values $(H, \sigma, \rho)$-colorability of $G$ and $(H', \sigma, \rho)$-colorability of $H$ will imply $(H', \sigma, \rho)$-colorabiliy of $G$. We first state a more general result.

**Theorem 1.** *If a graph $G$ is $(H, \sigma, \rho)$-colorable, and $H$ is $(H', \sigma', \rho')$-colorable, then $G$ is $(H', \sigma \oplus (\sigma' \otimes \rho), \rho' \otimes \rho)$-colorable.*

*Proof.* Let the functions $f : V(G) \rightarrow V(H)$ and $g : V(H) \rightarrow V(H')$ be the $(H, \sigma, \rho)$-coloring of $G$ and the $(H', \sigma', \rho')$-coloring of $H$, respectively. We show that $f$ composed with $g$ is an $(H', \sigma \oplus (\sigma' \otimes \rho), \rho' \otimes \rho)$-coloring of $G$. For vertices $v', u' \in V(H')$ we let $V'_H = \{w \in V(H) : g(w) = v'\}$ and $U'_H = \{w \in V(H) : g(w) = u'\}$, and let $V'_G = \{v \in V(G) : f(v) \in V'_H\}$ and $U'_G = \{v \in V(G) : f(v) \in U'_H\}$. For any vertex $v \in V(G)$ we want to count the number of neighbors of $v$ mapped to a vertex $u' \in V(H')$, which is $|N_G(v) \cap U'_G|$. We assume without loss of generality that $v \in V'_G$. There are three cases to consider: $v' = u'$, $v'u' \in E(H')$, and $v'u' \notin E(H')$.

If $v' = u'$ then $V'_G = U'_G$, and the number of neighbors of $v$ mapped to $u'$ consists of (i) the number of neighbors of $v$ mapped to $f(v)$ plus (ii) the number of neighbors of $v$ mapped to each vertex in $N_H(f(v)) \cap U'_H$. Since $|N_G(v) \cap \{u \in V(G) : f(u) = f(v)\}| \in \sigma$, we have that (i) is an element-of-$\sigma$. And since $|N_H(f(v)) \cap U'_H| \in \sigma'$, and for any $w \in N_H(f(v))$ we have $|N_G(v) \cap \{u \in V(G) : f(u) = w\}| \in \rho$ so that (ii) is the sum of some element-of-$\sigma'$ terms from $\rho$. This gives $|N_G(v) \cap U'_G| \in \sigma \oplus (\sigma' \otimes \rho)$ for $v' = u'$.

If $v'u' \in E(H')$ the number of neighbors of $v$ mapped to $u'$ consists simply of part (ii) above i.e. the number of neighbors of $v$ mapped to each vertex in

$U'_H$. We now have $|N_H(f(v)) \cap U'_H| \in \rho'$, and for any $w \in N_H(f(v))$ we have $-N_G(v) \cap \{u \in V(G) : f(u) = w\}| \in \rho$. Thus $|N_G(v) \cap U'_G| \in \rho' \otimes \rho$ for $v'u' \in E(H')$.

If $v'u' \notin E(H')$ the number of neighbors of $v$ mapped to $u'$ is 0. $\qquad \square$

The following result which follows from Theorem 1 and Fact 3, shows that $(H, \sigma, \rho)$-coloring is a transitive relation on graphs for certain values of $\sigma$ and $\rho$.

**Corollary 1.** *If $G$ is $(H, \sigma, \rho)$-colorable and $H$ is $(H', \sigma, \rho)$-colorable, with $\sigma = \{0\}$ and $\rho \in \{\{0\}, \{1\}, \{0, 1\}, \mathbb{N}, \mathbb{N}^+\}$, or $\sigma = \rho = \mathbb{N}$, then $G$ is $(H', \sigma, \rho)$-colorable.*

From this it follows that $H$-coloring, $H$-covering, $H$-partial covering and $H$-colordomination are all transitive relations on graphs. In the following we consider how $(H, \sigma, \rho)$-colorings of $G$ interact with $(\sigma', \rho')$-sets in $H$.

**Theorem 2.** *If a graph $G$ has an $(H, \sigma, \rho)$-coloring and $S$ is a $(\sigma', \rho')$-set in $H$, then $S' = \{v \in V(G) : f(v) \in S\}$ is a $(\sigma \oplus (\sigma' \otimes \rho), \rho' \otimes \rho)$-set in $G$.*

*Proof.* For space reasons we only sketch the proof, as it is similar to that of Theorem 1. Here we want to count the number of neighbors of an arbitrary vertex $v \in V(G)$ mapped to a vertex in $S$, which is $|N_G(v) \cap \{u \in V(G) : f(u) \in S\}|$. There are two cases to consider: $v \in S'$ and $v \notin S'$. The argument for the first case is similar to the argument for the case $v' = u'$ in the proof of Theorem 1, and the argument for the second case similar to that of the case $v'u' \in V(H')$. $\qquad \square$

Let us assume that a graph $G$ is $(H, \sigma, \rho)$-colorable. The following result, which follows from Theorem 2 and Fact 3, shows that a $(\sigma, \rho)$-set in $H$ will induce a $(\sigma, \rho)$-set in $G$, for certain values of $\sigma$ and $\rho$.

**Corollary 2.** *If $G$ is $(H, \sigma, \rho)$-colorable, with $\sigma = \{0\}$ and $\rho \in \{\{0\}, \{1\}, \{0, 1\}, \mathbb{N}, \mathbb{N}^+\}$, or $\sigma = \rho = \mathbb{N}$, then a $(\sigma, \rho)$-set in $H$ will induce a $(\sigma, \rho)$-set in $G$.*

We observe that Corollary 2 holds for some of the most common variants of $(\sigma, \rho)$-sets, such as perfect codes, 2-packings, independent sets, and independent dominating sets, as defined in the introduction.

## 3   The Complexity of $H$-COLORDOMINATION

The complexity of deciding if an arbitrary input graph $G$ has an $(H, \sigma, \rho)$-coloring will depend on the three fixed values $H$, $\sigma$, and $\rho$. As mentioned in the introduction, for values of $\sigma$ and $\rho$ that arise from independent sets ($\sigma = \{0\}, \rho = \mathbb{N}$), perfect codes ($\sigma = \{0\}, \rho = \{1\}$), and 2-packings ($\sigma = \{0\}, \rho = \{0, 1\}$) the complexity of the corresponding $(H, \sigma, \rho)$-problems, respectively named $H$-COLORING, $H$-COVER, and $H$-PARTIAL COVER, have been investigated for varying $H$.

Several of the $(\sigma, \rho)$-sets that have been studied in the literature have $\sigma \neq \{0\}$, but here we continue the setting from the already studied $(H, \sigma, \rho)$-colorings and focus on the case $\sigma = \{0\}$. The most natural $(H, \{0\}, \rho)$-problem that to our knowledge has not been studied in general, is maybe the case where $\rho = \mathbb{N}^+$. In this section we therefore initiate the investigation of the complexity of the $(H, \sigma, \rho)$-coloring problem that arises from independent dominating sets ($\sigma = \{0\}, \rho = \mathbb{N}^+$). We call this the $H$-COLORDOMINATION problem.

We show that $H$-COLORDOMINATION is no easier than $H$-COVER, and also present complexity results for $H$-COLORDOMINATION for classes of graphs for which $H$-COVER is in $\mathcal{P}$. We will in the following consider the graphs to be connected, and without loops.

We first mention the following result on cliques $K_k$ which, albeit with different terminology, can be found in [4].

**Theorem 3.** [4] *For every $k \geq 3$ the $K_k$-COLORDOMINATION problem is $\mathcal{NP}$-complete.*

## 3.1    No Easier than $H$-COVER

The *degree partition* of a graph $G$ is the partition of its vertices, $V(G)$, into the minimum number of blocks $B_1, \ldots, B_k$, for which there are constants $r_{ij}$ such that for each $i, j (1 \leq i, j \leq k)$ each vertex in $B_i$ is adjacent to exactly $r_{ij}$ vertices in $B_j$. For a given ordering of degree partition blocks, the $k \times k$ matrix $R, R[i, j] = r_{ij}$, is called the *degree refinement*.

The degree partition and degree refinement are computed in polynomial time by stepwise refinement. We start with the vertices partitioned by their degree values, and arrange the blocks of this partition in descending order, by degree value. We then iteratively refine this partition until any two vertices in the same block have the same number of neighbors in any other given block. When we are done, we will quite naturally have the blocks numbered by lexicographic order, as follows. Assume at the start of an iteration we have blocks ordered $B_1, \ldots, B_{k'}$, and that block $B_i$ is in this iteration split into $C$ and $D$ since vertices from $C$ and $D$ differ in the number of neighbors they have in some of the blocks from the previous iteration. Let $B_j$ be the lowest-numbered such block they differ on, with vertices in $D$ having $d$ neighbors in $B_j$ and vertices in $C$ having $c > d$ neighbors in $B_j$. In the refinement the position of $C$ should then be right before $D$, and they should maintain their order relative to the other blocks. The following result is similar to one from [7], where it was shown that if $G$ has an $H$-partial cover and $G$ and $H$ have the same degree refinement, then $G$ has an $H$-cover.

**Lemma 1.** *If a graph $G$ has an $(H, \{0\}, \mathbb{N}^+)$-coloring, and the graphs $G$ and $H$ have the same degree refinement matrix, then $G$ has an $(H, \{0\}, \{1\})$-coloring, or $H$-cover.*

*Proof.* Assume $G$ has an $(H, \{0\}, \mathbb{N}^+)$-coloring $f : V(G) \to V(H)$, and that $G$ and $H$ have the same degree refinement matrix. Let $b_G(v) = i$ be the index such that vertex $v \in V(G)$ belongs to the $i$th block $B_i(G)$ of the degree refinement of $G$, with blocks ordered lexicographically as explained above. We will show that necessarily we have $b_G(v) = b_H(f(v))$, to prove the lemma.

Since $f$ is an $(H, \{0\}, \mathbb{N}^+)$-coloring, $\forall v \in V(G) : \deg_G(v) \geq \deg_H(f(v))$ holds, because $\rho = \mathbb{N}^+$. This implies that $\forall v \in V(G) : b_G(v) \geq b_H(f(v))$.

For $v \in B_1(G)$, $b_G(v) = 1$, and since $b_G(v) \geq b_H(f(v))$, this implies that $b_H(f(v)) = 1$. Assume a vertex $v \in V(G)$ exists with $b_G(v) > b_H(f(v))$, and let $u$ be an arbitrary vertex from $B_1(G)$. Consider a path $P$ from $u$ to $v$ in $G$. $P$ must contain an edge $u'v' \in E(G)$ such that $b_G(u') = b_H(f(u'))$ and $b_G(v') > b_H(f(v'))$. Since $u'$ and $f(u')$ have the same number of neighbors in blocks with the same index, and neighbor $v'$ of $u'$ has been sent to a block numbered lower, there must exist a neighbor $w'$ of $u'$ that is sent to a block numbered higher, $b_G(w') < b_H(f(w'))$. But this is a contradiction. This implies that $\forall v \in V(G) : b_G(v) = b_H(f(v))$ holds, so $\forall v \in V(G) : \deg_G(v) = \deg_H(f(v))$ also holds. This in turn implies that $f$ is a valid $(H, \{0\}, \{1\})$-coloring, or $H$-cover, of $G$. □

**Theorem 4.** *If $H$-COVER is $\mathcal{NP}$-complete, then $H$-COLORDOMINATION is $\mathcal{NP}$-complete.*

*Proof.* If there is a polynomial-time algorithm for $H$-COLORDOMINATION then Lemma 1 gives us the following polynomial-time algorithm for $H$-COVER: Given a graph $G$, answer YES if $G$ and $H$ have the same degree refinement and $G$ has an $(H, \{0\}, \mathbb{N}^+)$-coloring; otherwise answer NO. □

### 3.2 Cycles

In this section we show the following for the cycles $C_k$:

**Theorem 5.** *For every $k \geq 3$ the $C_k$-COLORDOMINATION problem is $\mathcal{NP}$-complete.*

The result will follow from three lemmata.

**Lemma 2.** *The $(C_k, \{0\}, \mathbb{N}^+)$-coloring problem is $\mathcal{NP}$-complete for all $k = 2i + 1, i \geq 1$.*

*Proof.* We use a reduction from $C_k$-COLORING, $\mathcal{NP}$-complete for all odd $k$ [5]. Given a graph $G$ we construct a graph $G'$ which will have a $(C_k, \{0\}, \mathbb{N}^+)$-coloring if and only if $G$ has a $C_k$-coloring. $G'$ is constructed by replacing the vertices $v \in V(G)$ with a cycle of length $k$, $C_k^{(v)}$, each such cycle with a designated vertex $c_1^{(v)}$, and all edges $uv \in E(G)$ by an edge $c_1^{(u)}c_1^{(v)}$.

The cycles $C_k^{(v)}$ ensure that $G'$ has a $(C_k, \{0\}, \mathbb{N}^+)$-coloring whenever $G$ is $C_k$-cororable. If $G$ has no $C_k$-coloring the subgraph induced by the designated vertices prevents a $(C_k, \{0\}, \mathbb{N}^+)$-coloring of $G'$. □

In the next reduction we use the following problem which was shown to be $\mathcal{NP}$-complete in [12].

[NAESAT] **NOT-ALL-EQUAL SATISFIABILITY**
INSTANCE: A collection $C$ of clauses on a finite set $U$ of variables such that each clause $c \in C$ has $|c| = 3$.
QUESTION: Is there a truth assignment for $U$ such that each clause in $C$ has at least one TRUE literal and one FALSE literal?

**Lemma 3.** *The* $(C_4, \{0\}, \mathbb{N}^+)$-*coloring problem is* $\mathcal{NP}$-*complete.*

*Proof.* The reduction is from NAESAT. Let $U$ be the set of variables and $C$ be the set of clauses. We can assume that all literals, $u$ and $\bar{u}$, occur in some clause, otherwise for each literal that does not occur, we find a clause where the opposite literal occurs, and add a copy of this clause with all literals negated. We construct a bipartite graph $G$ which will have a $(C_k, \{0\}, \mathbb{N}^+)$-coloring if and only if the variables of $U$ can be assigned values TRUE or FALSE, such that all clauses in $C$ have at least one literal that is TRUE and one that is FALSE. For each variable $u$ there is a variable gadget, $P_3^{(u)}$, with literal vertices $v_u$ and $v_{\bar{u}}$ as the endpoints, and a center vertex $v_{u\bar{u}}$. For each clause $c$ there is a vertex $v_c$ with edges to the literal vertices corresponding to the literals occurring in this clause.

Let $T$ be a valid truth assignment for the NAESAT instance, and label the vertices of $C_4$ $A$, $B$, $C$, and $D$, following the cycle. We define a mapping $f :$ $V(G) \rightarrow \{A, B, C, D\}$ giving a $(C_4, \{0\}, \mathbb{N}^+)$-coloring of $G$. Let $f(v_c) = A$, for all $v_c$. And let $f(v_u) = B$ if $T(u) = $ TRUE or $f(v_u) = D$ if $T(u) = $ FALSE, for all literal vertices $v_u$ and $v_{\bar{u}}$. Let $f(u_{u\bar{u}}) = C$, for all variable vertices. Since all clauses have at least one literal set to TRUE and one set to FALSE, $f$ is a $(C_4, \{0\}, \mathbb{N}^+)$-coloring of $G$.

For the other direction of the proof we assume $f$ is a valid $(C_4, \{0\}, \mathbb{N}^+)$-coloring of $G$. A clause vertex $v_c$ is mapped to a vertex of $C_4$, call this vertex $A$. This forces the literal vertices to be mapped to $B$ or $C$, in such a way that if $v_u$ is mapped to $B$, then $v_{\bar{u}}$ is mapped to $C$. The other clause vertices are mapped to either $A$ or $D$, but in both cases the literal vertices are mapped to $B$ or $C$. Since $f$ is a valid $(C_4, \{0\}, \mathbb{N}^+)$-coloring each clause vertex must have at least one neighbor in each of $B$ and $C$. We define a valid truth assignment $T$ for the NAESAT instance by taking $T(u) = $ TRUE if $f(v_u) = B$, and $T(u) = $ FALSE if $f(v_u) = C$.                                                     □

**Lemma 4.** *The* $(C_{2k}, \{0\}, \mathbb{N}^+)$-*coloring problem is* $\mathcal{NP}$-*complete if the* $(C_k, \{0\}, \mathbb{N}^+)$-*coloring problem is* $\mathcal{NP}$-*complete.*

*Proof.* Given a graph $G$ we construct a graph $G'$ which will be $(C_{2k}, \{0\}, \mathbb{N}^+)$-colorable if and only if $G$ is $(C_k, \{0\}, \mathbb{N}^+)$-colorable, by subdividing all the edges of $G$ once.                                                     □

## 3.3   Paths

Let $P_k$ denote a path with $k$ vertices and $k-1$ edges. We first look at the case $k = 2$ and observe that the $(P_2, \{0\}, \mathbb{N}^+)$-coloring problem is easily solvable in polynomial time.

**Observation 1** *A graph $G$ has a $(P_2, \{0\}, \mathbb{N}^+)$-coloring if and only if it is bipartite.*

For $k \geq 3$ the situation is different. We show the following result for paths $P_k$:

**Theorem 6.** *For every $k \geq 3$ the $P_k$-COLORDOMINATION problem is $\mathcal{NP}$-complete.*

The result will follow from four lemmata.

**Lemma 5.** *The $(P_3, \{0\}, \mathbb{N}^+)$-coloring problem is $\mathcal{NP}$-complete.*

*Proof.* The reduction is from NAESAT. Let $U$ be the set of variables and $C$ the set of clauses. We construct a bipartite graph $G$ which will have a $(P_3, \{0\}, \mathbb{N}^+)$-coloring if and only if the variables of $U$ can be assigned values TRUE or FALSE, such that all clauses of $C$ have at least one literal that is TRUE and one that is FALSE. For each variable $u$ there is a variable gadget, $P_3^{(u)}$, with literal vertices $v_u$ and $v_{\bar{u}}$ as the endpoints, and a center vertex $v_{u\bar{u}}$. For each clause $c$ there is a vertex $v_c$ with edges to the literal vertices corresponding to the literals occurring in this clause. In addition to this we add a new clause vertex $v_x$, and a new variable gadget $P_3^{(y)}$. We connect $v_x$ to both $v_u$ and $v_{\bar{u}}$ of one already existing variable $u$, and to $v_y$ of the added variable gadget $P_3^{(y)}$. This augmentation will not affect the satisfiability of the original instance.

Let $T$ be a valid truth assignment for the NAESAT instance, and label the vertices of $P_3$ $A$, $B$, and $C$, with $B$ as the center vertex. We define a mapping $f : V(G) \rightarrow \{A, B, C\}$ giving a $(P_3, \{0\}, \mathbb{N}^+)$-coloring of $G$. Let $f(v_c) = f(v_{u\bar{u}}) = B$, for all $u \in U$ and all $c \in C$. And let $f(v_u) = A$ and $f(v_{\bar{u}}) = C$ if $T(u) =$ TRUE, or $f(v_{\bar{u}}) = A$ and $f(v_u) = C$ if $T(u) =$ FALSE. Since all clauses have at least one literal set to TRUE and one set to FALSE, $f$ is a $(P_3, \{0\}, \mathbb{N}^+)$-coloring.

For the other direction of the proof we assume $f$ is a valid $(P_3, \{0\}, \mathbb{N}^+)$-coloring of $G$. Since $v_y$ has degree one, it must map to either $A$ or $C$. As $G$ is bipartite this forces all clause vertices to be mapped to $B$. Since $f$ is a valid $(P_3, \{0\}, \mathbb{N}^+)$-coloring each clause vertex must have at least one neighbor in each of $A$ and $C$. We define a valid truth assignment $T$ for the NAESAT instance by taking $T(u) =$ TRUE if $f(v_u) = A$, and $T(u) =$ FALSE if $f(v_u) = C$. $\qquad\square$

The same technique can be applied to all paths of odd length.

**Lemma 6.** *The $P_k$-COLORDOMINATION problem is $\mathcal{NP}$-complete for all $k = 2i + 1, i \geq 1$.*

*Proof.* The proof is essentially the same as that of Lemma 5. We modify it to hold for all $k = 2i + 1$ by replacing the variable gadgets with paths of length $k$, and connecting the clause vertices to the literal vertices using paths with $\lfloor k/2 \rfloor$ edges.                                                                            □

For paths of even length we apply a variation of the same technique.

**Lemma 7.** *The $(P_4, \{0\}, \mathbb{N}^+)$-coloring problem is $\mathcal{NP}$-complete.*

*Proof.* The reduction is again from NAESAT. Let $U$ be the set of variables and $C$ the set of clauses. We construct a graph $G$ which will have a $(P_4, \{0\}, \mathbb{N}^+)$-coloring if and only if the variables of $U$ can be assigned values TRUE or FALSE, such that all clauses of $C$ have at least one literal that is TRUE and one that is FALSE. For each variable $u$ there is a variable gadget, $P_5^{(u)}$, with literal vertices $v_u$ and $v_{\bar{u}}$ as the endpoints. For each clause $c$ there is a clause gadget consisting of two components: (i) $P_2^{(c)}$ with a designated vertex $v_c$ as one of its endpoints, and (ii) a vertex $v_{c'}$. For each literal that occurs in a clause $c$ there is an edge between the corresponding literal vertex and the vertex $v_c$, and an edge between the corresponding negated literal vertex (the other end of $P_5^{(u)}$) and $v_{c'}$.

Let $T$ be a valid truth assignment for the NAESAT instance, and label the vertices of $P_4$ in order, $A$, $B$, $C$, and $D$. We define a mapping $f : V(G) \rightarrow \{A, B, C, D\}$ giving a $(P_4, \{0\}, \mathbb{N}^+)$-coloring of $G$. Let the clause gadget $P_2^{(c)}$ map to $A, B$ with $f(v_c) = B$, for all $v_c$. Let $f(v_u) = A$ and $f(v_{\bar{u}}) = C$ if $T(u) = $ TRUE, or let $f(v_{\bar{u}}) = A$ and $f(v_u) = C$ if $T(u) = $ FALSE. Finally let $f(V_{c'}) = B$, for all $v_{c'}$. This enforces a mapping of the remaining vertices of the variable gadgets. The path $P_5^{(u)}$ of the variable gadget is either mapped $A, B, C, D, C$, if $T(u) = $ TRUE, or $C, D, C, B, A$, if $T(u) = $ FALSE. Since all clauses have at least one literal set to TRUE and one set to FALSE, $f$ is a $(P_4, \{0\}, \mathbb{N}^+)$-coloring.

For the other direction of the proof we assume $f$ is a valid $(P_4, \{0\}, \mathbb{N}^+)$-coloring of $G$. Since each clause gadget $P_2^{(c)}$ has one endpoint of degree one, $A, B$ or $C, D$ are the only possible mappings of the clause gadgets. Without loss of generality we may assume that $G$ is connected, in which case the lengths of the varible gadget paths ensure that all clause gadgets will map to the same pair of vertices, say $A, B$. So we must have $f(v_c) = B$. The clause gadgets are paths of length five, and they must be mapped either $A, B, C, D, C$ or $C, D, C, B, A$, so we must have $f(v_{c'}) = B$. We define a valid truth assignment $T$ for the NAESAT instance by taking $T(u) = $ TRUE if $f(v_u) = A$, and $T(u) = $ FALSE if $f(v_u) = C$.                                                                            □

The technique used for $P_4$ can be applied for all paths of even length.

**Lemma 8.** *The $P_k$-COLORDOMINATION problem is $\mathcal{NP}$-complete for all $k = 2i, i \geq 2$.*

*Proof.* The proof is essentially the same as that of Lemma 7. We modify it to hold for all $k = 2i, i \geq 2$ by replacing the variable gadgets with paths of length $2k - 3$.                                                                            □

### 3.4    Stars

Let $S_k$ denote the graph $K_{1,k}$, a star with $k$ leaves. In the reduction below we use the following problem.

[$k$-EC] $k$-**EDGE-COLORING**
INSTANCE: A graph $G = (V, E)$.
QUESTION: Can $E(G)$ be partitioned into $k'$ disjoint sets $E_1, E_2, \ldots, E_{k'}$, with $k' \leq k$, such that, for $1 \leq i \leq k'$, no two edges in $E_i$ share a common endpoint in $G$?

If $G$ is a $k$-regular graph, the question becomes whether each vertex is incident to $k$ distinctly colored edges. This last problem was shown to be $\mathcal{NP}$-complete for $k = 3$ in [6], and for $k \geq 3$ in [11]. We get the following result for the complexity of $S_k$-COLORDOMINATION.

**Theorem 7.** *For all $k \geq 2$ the $S_k$-COLORDOMINATION problem is $\mathcal{NP}$-complete.*

*Proof.* Since $P_3 = S_2$ we use Lemma 5 for this case. For $k \geq 3$ the reduction is from $k$-EC on $k$-regular graphs, defined above. Let $G$ be an instance of $k$-EC, such that $G$ is $k$-regular. We construct a $k$-regular graph $G'$, such that $G'$ has an $(S_k, \{0\}, \mathbb{N}^+)$-coloring if and only if $G$ is $k$-edge-colorable. $G'$ is constructed by replacing vertices and edges by simple gadgets as shown in Figure 1.

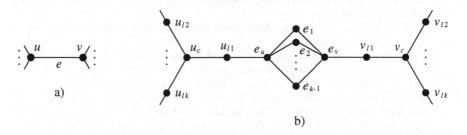

**Fig. 1.** a) An edge in $G$, and b) the corresponding subgraph in $G'$

We let $c$ be the center vertex of the star $S_k$, $l_1, l_2, \ldots, l_k$ the leaves, and assume there exists a mapping $f : V(G') \rightarrow \{c, l_1, l_2, \ldots, l_k\}$ that is a valid $(S_k, \{0\}, \mathbb{N}^+)$-coloring of $G'$. We must have $f(u_c) = c$, since $u_c$ has neigbors of degree two. This implies that $f(u_{li}) = \{l_1, l_2, \ldots, l_k\}, i = 1, 2, \ldots, k$, and that $f(e_u) = c$. This gives $f(e_j) = \{l_1, l_2, \ldots, l_k\} \setminus f(u_{l1}), j = 1, 2, \ldots, k-1$, and $f(e_v) = c$. This enforces $f(v_{l1}) = f(u_{l1})$, and thus $f(v_c) = c$. In $G$ we can color the edge $e = uv$ with the color $f(u_{l1})$. Coloring every edge in the same manner, we can conclude that $G$ is $k$-edge-colorable if $G'$ is $(S_k, \{0\}, \mathbb{N}^+)$-colorable.

For the other direction of the proof we assume $G'$ is $k$-edge-colorable and apply a reversal of the mapping described above.                                  $\square$

# 4   Conclusion

We have introduced a generalization of $H$-colorings of graphs, initiated the study of these colorings, and given some results on the complexity of one class of problems that it gives rise to. We leave as an open problem the question of whether $H$-COLORDOMINATION is $\mathcal{NP}$-complete for all connected $H$ on at least three vertices.

# References

1. James Abello, Michael R. Fellows, and John C. Stillwell. On the complexity and combinatorics of covering finite complexes. *Australasian Journal of Combinatorics*, 4:103–112, 1991.
2. Jiř Fiala, Ton Kloks, and Jan Kratochvíl. Fixed parameter complexity of $\lambda$-labelings. In *Graph-Theoretic Concepts in Computer Science, 25th International Workshop, WG-99, Ascona, Switzerland, June 17–19, Proceedings*, volume 1665 of *Lecture Notes in Computer Science*. Springer-Verlag, 1999.
3. Theresa W. Haynes, Stephen T. Hedetniemi, and Peter J. Slater. *Domination in Graphs*. Marcel Dekker, 1998.
4. Pinar Heggernes and Jan Arne Telle. Partitioning graphs into generalized dominating sets. *Nordic Journal of Computing*, 5:128–142, 1998.
5. Pavol Hell and Jaroslav Nešetřil. On the compexity of H-colouring. *Journal of Combinatorial Theory, Series B*, 48:92–110, 1990.
6. Ian Holyer. The NP-completeness of edge coloring. *SIAM Journal on Computing*, 10:718–720, 1981.
7. Jiř Fiala and Jan Kratochvíl. Generalized channel assignment problem and partial covers of graphs. (Submitted).
8. Jan Kratochvíl, Andrzej Proskurowski, and Jan Arne Telle. Complexity of colored graph covers I. In *Graph-Theoretic Concepts in Computer Science, 23rd International Workshop, WG-97, Berlin, Germany, June 18–20, Proceedings*, volume 1335 of *Lecture Notes in Computer Science*, pages 242–257. Springer-Verlag, 1997.
9. Jan Kratochvíl, Andrzej Proskurowski, and Jan Arne Telle. Covering regular graphs. *Journal of Combinatorial Theory, Series B*, 71(1), 1997.
10. Jan Kratochvíl, Andrzej Proskurowski, and Jan Arne Telle. Complexity of graph covering problems. *Nordic Journal of Computing*, 5:173–195, 1998.
11. D. Leven and Z. Galil. NP-completeness of finding the chromatic index of regular graphs. *Journal of Algorithms*, 4(1):35–44, 1983.
12. Thomas J. Shaefer. The complexity of satisfiability problems. *ACM Symposium on Theory of Computing*, 10:216–226, 1978.
13. Jan Arne Telle and Andrzej Proskurowski. Algorithms for vertex partitioning problems on partial k-trees. *SIAM Journal on Discrete Mathematics*, 10(4):529–550, 1997.

# Finding a Two-Core of a Tree in Linear Time

Biing-Feng Wang and Jyh-Jye Lin

Department of Computer Science, National Tsing Hua University
Hsinchu, Taiwan 30043, Republic of China
bfwang@cs.nthu.edu.tw;g884377@oz.nthu.edu.tw

**Abstract.** Let $T$ be an edge-weighted tree. A $p$-core of $T$ is a set of $p$ mutually disjoint paths in $T$ that minimizes the sum of the distances of all vertices in $T$ from any of the $p$ paths, where $p \geq 1$ is an integer. Let $n$ be the number of vertices in $T$. In this paper, an $O(n)$ time algorithm is proposed for the case $p=2$. Applying our 2-core algorithm as a procedure, we also show that the $p$-core problem can be solved in $O(n^{p-1})$ time for any constant $p \geq 2$.

## 1 Introduction

Many network location problems have been defined and studied in the literature [1-5, 7-9, 10-17]. These location problems usually have important applications in transportation and communication and thus have received much attention from researchers in the fields.

Let $T$ be an edge-weighted tree of $n$ vertices. Let $p \geq 1$ be an integer. A $p$-median of $T$ is a set of $p$ vertices in $T$ that minimizes the sum of the distances of all vertices in $T$ from any of the $p$ vertices. Goldman [3] gave a linear time algorithm for finding a 1-median of a tree. Gavish and Sridhar [2] presented an $O(n\log n)$ time algorithm for finding a 2-median of a tree. Based upon dynamic programming, Tamir [13] solved the general $p$-median problem on a tree in $O(pn^2)$ time. A $p$-center of $T$ is a set of $p$ vertices in $T$ that minimizes the distance to the farthest vertex from any of the $p$ vertices. Linear time algorithms for finding a 1-center and a 2-center of a tree had been proposed by Handler [5]. By developing an elegant tree decomposition scheme to find the $k$th longest path in a tree, Megiddo et al. [7] solved the general $p$-center problem on a tree in $O(n\log^2 n)$ time.

A $p$-core of $T$ is a set of $p$ mutually disjoint paths in $T$ that minimizes the sum of the distances of all vertices in $T$ from any of the $p$ paths [4]. The case $p=1$ of the problem was firstly studied by Slater [12]. A linear time algorithm was proposed by Morgan and Slater [9]. Minieka and Patel [8] studied the problem of finding in a tree a 1-core of a specified length, which is a variant of the 1-core problem. Wang [15] solved the problem in $O(n^2)$ time. Assuming that $T$ is unweighted, Peng and Lo [10] showed that the problem of finding a core of a specified length can be solved in $O(n\log n)$ time.

The 2-core problem was firstly considered by Becker and Perl [1]. They proposed two efficient algorithms for the problem. The first requires $O(n^2)$ time and the second requires $O(dn)$ time, where $d$ is the maximum number of edges of any simple path in

D.T. Lee and S.-H. Teng (Eds.): ISAAC 2000, LNCS 1969, pp. 467–478, 2000.
© Springer-Verlag Berlin Heidelberg 2000

$T$. In the worst-case and average-case, the second algorithm requires $O(n^2)$ time and $O(n\sqrt{n})$ time, respectively. The general $p$-core problem was firstly studied by Hakimi *et al.* [4]. They showed that the problem is *NP*-hard if $p$ is a variable and gave a polynomial-time algorithm for the case $p$ is a constant. Hakimi *et al.* were interested in only the complexity of the $p$-core problem. Thus, their algorithm is simple but not efficient. The time complexity of their algorithm is $O(n^{2p+1})$.

In this paper, an $O(n)$ time algorithm is proposed for finding a 2-core of a tree. Applying our 2-core algorithm as a procedure, we also show that the general $p$-core problem can be solved in $O(n^{p-1})$ time for any constant $p \geq 2$.

The remainder of this paper is organized as follows. In the next section, notation and preliminary results are presented. In Section 3, a linear time algorithm is proposed to solve an optimization problem, which is called the $r$-point core problem. In Section 4, using the algorithm proposed in Section 3 as a key procedure, we solve the 2-core problem in $O(n)$ time. In Section 5, we solve the general $p$-core problem in $O(n^{p-1})$ time. Finally, in Section 6, we conclude this paper with some final remarks.

## 2   Notation and Preliminary Results

Let $T=(V, E)$ be a free tree. Let $n=|V|$. Each edge $e \in E$ has a positive length $w(e)$. If $w(e)=1$ for every $e \in E$ then $T$ is *unweighted*, otherwise $T$ is *weighted*. For any two vertices $u, v \in V$, let $P(u, v)$ be the unique path from $u$ to $v$ and $d(u, v)$ be its length. A path in $T$ is a *v-path*, where $v \in V$, if $v$ is one of its endpoints. For each $v \in V$, let $N(v)$ be the set of vertices in $T$ adjacent to $v$. Consider a given vertex $v \in V$. The are $|N(v)|$ subtrees of $T$ attached to $v$ through the edges incident on $v$. For each $u \in N(v)$, denote by $T_u^v$ the subtree of $T$ attached to $v$ through the edge $(u, v)$, excluding this edge and the vertex $v$.

For a subgraph $X$ of $T$, the vertex set and edge set of $X$ is $V(X)$ and $E(X)$, respectively. For easy description, given a vertex $v \in V$, the subgraph having vertex set $\{v\}$ and edge set $\varnothing$ is simply denoted by $v$. Given two subgraphs $X$ and $Y$ of $T$, we denote by $X \cup Y$ the subgraph having vertex set $V(X) \cup V(Y)$ and edge set $E(X) \cup E(Y)$. For a vertex $v \in V$ and a subgraph $X$ of $T$, the *distance* from $v$ to $X$ is $d(v, X) = \min_{u \in V(X)} d(v, u)$ and $close(v, X)$ is the vertex in $X$ nearest to $v$. For two subgraphs $Y$ and $X$ of $T$, the *distancesum* from $Y$ to $X$ is $D(Y, X) = \sum_{v \in V(Y)} d(v, X)$. If $Y=T$, we simply write $D(X)$ in place of $D(T, X)$. The *distance saving* of a path $P(x, y)$ in $T$ is $\delta(P(x, y))=D(x)-D(P(x, y))$, where $x, y \in V$. For each edge $(u, v) \in E$, let $n_u^v = |V(T_u^v)|$, $s_u^v = D(T_u^v, v)$, $l_u^v$ be a vertex in $T_u^v$ having $\delta(P(v, l_u^v)) = \max_{x \in V(T_u^v)} \delta(P(v, x))$, and $m_u^v = \delta(P(v, l_u^v))$.

A *1-core* of $T$ is a path $A$ in $T$ that minimizes $D(A)$. A *p-core* of $T$ is a set of $p$ mutually disjoint paths $\{A_1, A_2, ..., A_p\}$ in $T$ that minimizes $D(A_1 \cup A_2 \cup ... \cup A_p)$, where $p \geq 2$ is an integer. Our 2-core algorithm in Section 4 needs to solve two variants of the 1-core problem, which are defined as follows. Let $r \in V$ be a given vertex. An *r rooted-*

*1-core* of *T* is an *r*-path *A* in *T* that minimizes $D(A)$. An *r-point core* of *T* is a path *A* in *T* that does not contain *r* and minimizes $D(r \cup A)$.

*Lemma 1* [1, 9]. The values of $n_u^v$, $s_u^v$, $m_u^v$, and $l_u^v$ can be computed in $O(n)$ time for every $(u, v) \in E$.

*Lemma 2* [9]. A 1-core of a tree can be computed in $O(n)$ time.

*Lemma 3* [1]. The value of $D(v)$ can be computed in $O(n)$ time for every $v \in V$.

*Lemma 4* [15]. An *r* rooted-1-core of a tree can be computed in $O(n)$ time.

*Lemma 5.* Let *Y* be a subgraph of *T*. Let $(s, t) \in E$ be an edge such that $s \in V(Y)$ and $V(T_t^s) \cap V(Y) = \varnothing$. Let *x* be a vertex in $T_t^s$. Then, $D(Y \cup P(s, x)) = D(Y) - \delta(P(s, x))$.

*Proof:* Since $V(T_t^s) \cap V(Y) = \varnothing$, $D(Y \cup P(s, x)) = D(T_s^t, Y) + D(T_t^s, P(s, x))$. (See Fig. 1.) Clearly, $D(T_s^t, Y) = D(Y) - D(T_t^s, s)$ and $D(T_t^s, P(s, x)) = D(P(s, x)) - D(T_s^t, s)$. Thus, $D(Y \cup P(s, x)) = D(Y) - D(T_s^t, s) - D(T_s^t, s) + D(P(s, x)) = D(Y) - D(s) + D(P(s, x))$. By definition, $D(s) - D(P(s, x)) = \delta(P(s, x))$. Thus, $D(Y \cup P(s, x)) = D(Y) - \delta(P(s, x))$. Q.E.D.

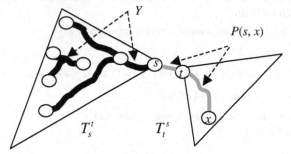

**Fig. 1.** Proof of Lemma 5.

## 3  Finding an *r*-Point Core

Let $r \in V$ be a vertex. For easy description, throughout this section, we assume that *T* is an rooted tree with root *r*. Assuming that *T* is unweighted, Becker and Perl [1] had proposed an $O(n)$ time algorithm for the *r*-point core problem. In this section, we show that an *r*-point core of a weighted tree *T* can be found in $O(n)$ time. Our *p*-point core algorithm is obtained by modifying Becker and Perl's. Therefore, we begin by describing their algorithm.

An edge is a *bisector* of a simple path if it contains the midpoint of the path. In case the midpoint is located at a vertex, both of the two edges connecting the vertex are bisectors.

*Lemma 6* [1]. Let $a$, $b \in V$. Let $(x, y)$ be an edge in $E$ such that $x$ is nearer to $a$ than $y$ and $(x, y)$ is a bisector of $P(a, b)$. We have $D(a \cup b) = D(a) - (s_y^x + n_y^x \times d(a, x)) + D(b) - (s_x^y + n_x^y \times d(b, y))$.

*Lemma 7* [1]. Let $v \in V$ be a vertex such that there is an $r$-point core $A$ of $T$ satisfying $close(r, A) = v$. Let $u_1$ and $u_2$ be the two sons of $v$ maximizing $m_{u_1}^v + m_{u_2}^v$. Then, $P(l_{u_1}^v, l_{u_2}^v)$ is an $r$-point core of $T$ and $D(P(l_{u_1}^v, l_{u_2}^v)) = D(r \cup v) - m_{u_1}^v - m_{u_2}^v$.

Becker and Perl presented the following algorithm for finding an $r$-point core.

**Algorithm 1.** POINT_CORE($T$, $r$)
**Input:** a tree $T = (V, E)$ and a vertex $r \in V$
**Output:** an $r$-point core of $T$
**begin**
1     Orient $T$ into a rooted tree with root $r$
2     **for** each $(u, v) \in E$ **do** compute $n_u^v$, $s_u^v$, $m_u^v$, and $l_u^v$
3     **for** each $v \in V$ **do** compute $D(v)$ and $d(r, v)$
4     $W \leftarrow V - \{r\}$
5     **for** each $v \in W$ **do** $(x_v, y_v) \leftarrow$ a bisector of $P(r, v)$ such that $x_v$ is the parent of $y_v$
6     **for** each $v \in W$ **do**
7         $(u_1, u_2) \leftarrow$ the two sons of $v$ maximizing $m_{u_1}^v + m_{u_2}^v$
8         $A_v \leftarrow P(l_{u_1}^v, l_{u_2}^v)$
9         $D(r \cup v) \leftarrow D(r) - (s_{y_v}^{x_v} + n_{y_v}^{x_v} \times d(r, x_v)) + D(v) - (s_{x_v}^{y_v} + n_{x_v}^{y_v} \times (d(r, v) - d(r, y_v)))$
10        $D(r \cup A_v) \leftarrow D(r \cup v) - (m_{u_1}^v + m_{u_2}^v)$
11    $CORE \leftarrow$ the $A_z$ with $D(r \cup A_z) = \min_{v \in W} D(r \cup A_v)$
12    **return**($CORE$)
**end**

It is not difficult to check that except line 5, all computation in Algorithm 1 requires $O(n)$ time no matter whether or not $T$ is unweighted. Becker and Perl assumed that $T$ is unweighted and implemented Line 5 in linear time by performing a depth-first traversal on $T$ maintaining the path from the root $r$ to the current vertex $v$ in an array $H$ such that $H[i]$ stores the $i$th vertex on $P(r, v)$. While a vertex $v$ is visited during the traversal, $(x_v, y_v)$ is computed in $O(1)$ time as $(H[\lfloor l/2 \rfloor], H[\lfloor l/2 \rfloor + 1])$, where $l = d(r, v)$. We have the following theorem.

*Theorem 1* [1]. An $r$-point core of an unweighted tree can be found in $O(n)$ time.

Line 5 of Algorithm 1 is to compute for every $v \in V - \{r\}$ a bisector of $P(r, v)$. Wang *et al.* [17] showed that the computation has an $\Omega(n \log n)$ lower bound if $T$ is weighted. Thus, Becker and Perl's algorithm requires $\Omega(n \log n)$ time for weighted trees. The lower bound can be achieved as follows. We perform a depth-first traversal on $T$ maintaining two arrays $H$ and $D$ such that $H[i]$ stores the $i$th vertex on $P(r, v)$ and $D[i]$ stores $d(r, H[i])$. During the traversal, a bisector edge of $P(r, v)$ is computed in $O(\log n)$ time by performing a binary search for $l/2$ on $D$, where $l=d(r, v)$.

*Theorem 2.* Finding an $r$-point core of a weighted tree can be done in $O(n\log n)$ time.

In the remainder of this section, we show that finding an $r$-point core of a weighted tree $T$ can be done in $O(n)$ time.

*Lemma 8.* Let $k \in V$ and $P(k, g)$ be a $k$ rooted-1-core of $T$. For any $v \in V$, $\delta(P(c, g)) \geq \delta(P(c, v))$, where $c=close(v, P(k, g))$.
*Proof:* By letting $Y=P(k, c)$, $s=c$, and $x=g$ in Lemma 5, we have $D(P(k, g))=D(P(k, c))- \delta(P(c, g))$. Similarly, by letting $Y=P(k, c)$, $s=c$, and $x=v$ in Lemma 5, we have $D(P(k, v))=D(P(k, c))- \delta(P(c, v))$. Since $P(k, g)$ is an $r$ rooted-1-core, $D(P(k, g)) \leq D(P(k, v))$ and thus $\delta(P(c, g)) \geq \delta(P(c, v))$. Therefore, lemma holds.         Q.E.D.

Recall that $T$ was assumed to be an rooted tree with root $r$. Every $u \in N(r)$ is a son of $r$. For each $u \in N(r)$, we denote by $X_u$ the subtree of $T$ rooted at $u$. Let $A$ be an $r$-point core of $T$. Since $A$ does not contain $r$, there is a vertex $k \in N(r)$ such that $A$ is totally contained in $X_k$. Let $M_k$ be a $k$ rooted-1-core of $X_k$. We have the following lemma.

*Lemma 9.* $V(A) \cap V(M_k) \neq \emptyset$.
*Proof:* We prove this lemma by contradiction. Suppose that $V(A) \cap V(M_k)=\emptyset$. Let $A=P(w, z)$ and $a=close(k, A)$. Let $M_k=P(k, g)$ and $b=close(a, M_k)$. Let $A'=P(g, z)$, which is $P(g, b) \cup P(b, a) \cup P(a, z)$. By using Lemma 5 twice, we have $D(r \cup A) = D(r \cup a) - \delta(P(a, w)) - \delta(P(a, z))$. By using Lemma 5 twice, we have $D(r \cup A') = D(r \cup P(b, a)) - \delta(P(b, g)) - \delta(P(a, z))$. Thus, $D(r \cup A') - D(r \cup A) = D(r \cup P(b, a)) - D(r \cup a) - \delta(P(b, g)) + \delta(P(a, w))$. Since $M_k$ is a $k$ rooted-1-core of $X_k$, by Lemma 8, $\delta(P(b, g)) \geq \delta(P(b, w)) \geq \delta(P(a, w))$. Therefore, $D(r \cup A') - D(r \cup A) \leq D(r \cup P(b, a)) - D(r \cup a)$. Since $V(A) \cap V(M_k)= \emptyset$, we have $a \neq b$. Thus, $r \cup a$ is a proper subgraph of $r \cup P(b, a)$. Therefore, $D(r \cup P(b, a)) < D(r \cup a)$. Consequently, $D(r \cup A') - D(r \cup A) < 0$, which contradicts to the fact that $A$ is an $r$-point core of $T$. Therefore, $V(A) \cap V(M_k) \neq \emptyset$ and the lemma holds.         Q.E.D.

Since $T$ is a tree, using Lemma 9, we can obtain the following lemma easily.

*Lemma 10.* $close(r, A) \in V(M_k)$.

For each $u \in N(r)$, let $M_u$ be a $u$ rooted-1-core of $X_u$. According to Lemma 10, $close(r, A) \in \bigcup_{u \in N(r)} V(M_u)$ for any $r$-point core $A$ of $T$. Therefore, we can modify Algorithm 1 by replacing Line 4 with the following.

4    $W \leftarrow \bigcup_{u \in N(r)} V(M_u)$, where $M_u$ is an $u$ rooted-1-core of $T'_u$

In the following, we show that after the replacement, Algorithm 1 can be implemented in $O(n)$ time no matter whether or not $T$ is unweighted. By Lemma 4, the computation of all $M_u$, where $u \in N(r)$ requires $O(\sum_{u \in N(r)} |V(T_u^r)|) = O(n)$ time. Thus, Line 4 takes $O(n)$ time. Consider a fixed vertex $u \in N(r)$. Since $M_u$ is a path, we can easily compute a bisector of $P(r, v)$ for every $v \in V(M_u)$ in $O(|V(M_u)|)$ time by resorting to a linear time merging algorithm. Thus, Line 5 can be implemented in $O(\sum_{u \in N(r)} |V(M_u)|) = O(n)$ time. All the other computation of Algorithm 1 requires $O(n)$ time. Therefore, we obtain the following theorem.

*Theorem* 3. An $r$-point core of a weighted tree can be computed in $O(n)$ time.

## 4   Finding a Two-Core in Linear Time

For easy description of our 2-core algorithm, we define a $(a, b)$ *rooted-2-core* of $T$, where $a, b \in V$ and $a \neq b$, as a pair of two disjoint paths $(A, B)$ such that $A$ is an $a$-path, $B$ is a $b$-path, and $D(A \cup B)$ is minimized. One of the most critical steps of our 2-core algorithm is to compute a $(a, b)$ rooted-2-core of $T$ for two given vertices $a, b \in V$. The computation is complicated. We describe it first in subsection 4.1. Our 2-core algorithm is then proposed in subsection 4.2.

### 4.1  Finding a $(a, b)$ Rooted-2-Core

We begin by giving some notations. Let $(c_1, c_2, ..., c_d)$ be the sequence of vertices on $P(a, b)$, where $c_1 = a$ and $c_d = b$. For each $i$, $1 \leq i < d$, let $Q_i$ be subtree $T_{c_i}^{c_{i+1}}$ and $U_i$ be the subtree $T_{c_{i+1}}^{c_i}$. Let $S_1, S_2, ..., S_d$ be the subtrees obtained from $T$ by deleting all edges on $P(a, b)$ such that $S_i$, $1 \leq i \leq d$, is the one that contains $c_i$. (See Fig. 2.)

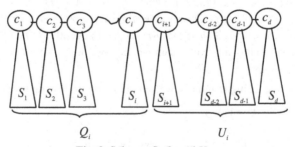

**Fig. 2.** Subtrees $S_i$, $Q_i$, and $U_i$.

*Lemma 11* [1]. There is an integer $k$, $1 \leq k < d$, such that an $a$ rooted-1-core of $Q_k$ and a $b$ rooted-1-core of $U_k$ constitute a $(a, b)$ rooted-2-core of $T$.

According to Lemma 11, we can compute a $(a, b)$ rooted 2-core of $T$ as follows.

**Algorithm 2.** ROOTED_2_CORE($T$, $a$, $b$)
**Input:** a tree $T=(V, E)$ and two vertices $a$, $b \in V$
**Output:** a $(a, b)$ rooted-2-core of $T$
**begin**
1.  **for** each $k$, $1 \leq k < d$, **do**
2.      $A_k \leftarrow$ an $a$ rooted-1-core of $Q_k$
3.      $DA_k \leftarrow D(Q_k, A_k)$
4.  **for** each $k$, $1 \leq k < d$, **do**
5.      $B_k \leftarrow$ a $b$ rooted-1-core of $U_k$
6.      $DB_k \leftarrow D(U_k, B_k)$
7.  $CORE \leftarrow$ the $(A_z, B_z)$ with $(DA_z+DB_z)=\min_{1 \leq k < d}(DA_k+DB_k)$
8.  **return**($CORE$)
**end**

As we will show later, Lines 1-3 of Algorithm 2 requires $O(n)$ time. The computation of Lines 4-6 is the same with that of Lines 1-3 and thus also requires $O(n)$ time. Line 7 requires $O(d)$ time. Therefore, Algorithm 2 performs in $O(n)$ time.

*Theorem 4.* A rooted-2-core of a weighted tree can be computed in $O(n)$ time.

To complete the proof of Theorem 4, in the following, we show that Lines 1-3 of Algorithm 2 can be done in $O(n)$ time. That is, we show that finding an $a$ rooted-1-core $A_k$ for every $Q_k$, $1 \leq k < d$, can be done in $O(n)$ time. First, we describe a procedure to preprocess $T$. In the preprocessing, a vertex $g_i \in V(S_i)$ is computed for each subtree $S_i$, $1 \leq i < d$, such that $P(c_i, g_i)$ is a $c_i$ rooted-1-core of $S_i$. Besides, four auxiliary arrays $L$, $UN$, $UD$, and $GD$ are computed such that $L[i]=d(a, c_i)$, $UN[i]=|V(U_i)|$, $UD[i]=D(U_i, c_i)$, and $GD[i]=D(P(a, g_i))$, where $1 \leq i < d$. The procedure is as follows. (With some efforts, it is not difficult to show that it is correct and requires $O(n)$ time.)

**Procedure** PREPROCESS($T$, ($c_1=a$, $c_2$, ..., $c_d=b$))
**begin**
1.  **for** each $i$, $1 \leq i < d$, **do**
2.      $g_i \leftarrow$ a vertex in $S_i$ such that $P(c_i, g_i)$ is a $c_i$ rooted-1-core of $S_i$
3.  **for** each $i$, $1 \leq i < d$, **do** $L[i] \leftarrow d(a, c_i)$
4.  **for** each $i$, $1 \leq i < d$, **do** $UN[i] \leftarrow n_{c_{i+1}}^{c_i}$          /* by definition, $|V(U_i)| = n_{c_{i+1}}^{c_i}$ */
5.  **for** each $i$, $1 \leq i < d$, **do** $UD[i] \leftarrow s_{c_{i+1}}^{c_i}$          /* by definition, $D(U_i, c_i)= s_{c_{i+1}}^{c_i}$ */
6.  **for** each $i$, $1 \leq i < d$, **do** $\delta(P(c_i, g_i)) \leftarrow D(S_i, c_i)-D(S_i, P(c_i, g_i))$
7.  $D(P(a, c_1)) \leftarrow D(a)$
8.  **for** each $i$, $2 \leq i < d$, **do** $D(P(a, c_i)) \leftarrow D(P(a, c_{i-1}))-d(c_{i-1}, c_i)UN[i-1]$
9.  **for** each $i$, $1 \leq i < d$, **do** $GD[i] \leftarrow D(P(a, c_i)) - \delta(P(c_i, g_i))$ /* by Lemma 5 */
10. **return** ($g_1$, $g_2$, ..., $g_{d-1}$, $L$, $UN$, $UD$, $GD$)
**end**

For easy discussion, in the remainder of this subsection, $k$ is assumed to be a fixed integer between 1 to $d$-1 unless explicitly specified as otherwise. Consider the computation of $A_k$. One of the two endpoints of $A_k$ is $a$. To compute $A_k$, we shall select a vertex among the vertices in $Q_k$ to be the other endpoint. Since for each $i$, $1 \leq i \leq d$, $P(c_i, g_i)$ is a $c_i$ rooted-1-core of $S_i$, we can prove the following lemma, which shows that in order to select a correct vertex to be the other endpoint of $A_k$, in each subtree $S_i$, $1 \leq i \leq k$, we can consider only the vertex $g_i$.

*Lemma 12.* $D(Q_k, P(a, g_i)) = \text{MIN}_{u \in V(S_i)} D(Q_k, P(a,u))$ , $1 \leq i \leq k < d$.

Let $G_i = P(a, g_i)$, $1 \leq i < d$. We call $(G_1, G_2, ..., G_k)$ the *candidate sequence* of $A_k$, since it can be easily concluded from Lemma 12 that the path in the sequence minimizing $D(Q_k, G_i)$ is an $a$ rooted-1-core of $Q_k$.

Since $V(Q_k)$ and $V(U_k)$ is a partition of $V$, we can obtain the following lemma.

*Lemma 13.* $D(Q_k, G_i) = D(G_i) - D(U_k, c_k) - d(c_k, c_i)|V(U_k)|$, $1 \leq i \leq k < d$.

By Lemma 13, we can compute $D(Q_k, G_i) = GD[i] - UD[k] - (L[k]-L[i])UN[k]$ for any two given integers $i$ and $k$, $1 \leq i \leq k < d$, in $O(1)$ time using the auxiliary arrays. Thus, we can determine $A_k$ from its candidate sequence in $O(k)$ time. Consequence, all $A_k$, $k=1$, 2, ..., $d$-1, can be computed in $O(1 + 2 + ... + d$-1$) = O(d^2)$ time, which is $O(n^2)$ time in the worst case. We need more techniques to speedup the computation of $A_k$.

We define the function $f(G_x, G_y)$, for two paths $G_x$ and $G_y$, $1 \leq x < y < d$, to be

$$f(G_x, G_y) = (D(G_x) - D(G_y)) / d(c_x, c_y).$$

Using arrays $L$ and $GD$, the value of $f(G_x, G_y)$ can be easily determined in $O(1)$ time for any two given integers $x$ and $y$, $1 \leq x < y < d$.

*Lemma 14.* For $1 \leq x < y \leq s < d$, to determine whether $D(Q_s, G_x) <, =,$ or $> D(Q_s, G_y)$, respectively, is equivalent to determine whether $f(G_x, G_y) <, =,$ or $> |V(U_s)|$.
*Proof*: By Lemma 13, we have $D(Q_s, G_x) - D(Q_s, G_y) = D(G_x) - D(G_y) - d(c_x, c_y)|V(U_s)|$, from which we can conclude that to determine whether $D(Q_s, G_x) <, =,$ or $> D(Q_s, G_y)$ is equivalent to determine whether $(D(G_x)-D(G_y))/d(c_x, c_y) <, =,$ or $> |V(U_s)|$.    Q.E.D.

Based upon Lemma 14, in the following, two properties are proposed to further recognize in $(G_1, G_2, ..., G_k)$ some paths that we can ignore while computing $A_k$. Due to the page limitation, their proofs are omitted here.

*Property 1.* For $1 \leq x < y < k$, if $f(G_x, G_y) < f(G_y, G_k)$, then $G_y$ cannot be an $a$ rooted-1-core of $Q_k, Q_{k+1}, ..., Q_{d-1}$.

*Property 2.* For $1 \leq x < y \leq k$, if $f(G_x, G_y) > |V(U_k)|$, then $G_x$ cannot be an $a$ rooted-1-core of $Q_k, Q_{k+1}, ..., Q_{d-1}$.

Now, we are ready to present our algorithm for computing all $A_k$, $k=1, 2, ..., d$-1. In our algorithm, we compute the $d$-1 rooted-1-cores one at a time, from $A_1$ to $A_{d-1}$. During the computation, we maintain a sequence of paths $D$. Initially, $D$ is an empty sequence. Before the computation of $A_k$, $D$ is adjusted by adding $G_k$ and removing according to Properties 1 and 2 some paths that we can ignore while computing $A_k$, $A_{k+1}$, ..., and $A_{d-1}$. After the adjustment, we then compute $A_k$ as the $G_i$ in $D$ that minimizes $D(Q_k, G_i)$. The path sequence $D$ is implemented as a *deque* [6]. We denote by $|D|$, *Head*, and *Tail*, respectively, the number of paths, the first path, and the last path in $D$. And, for any path $w$ in $D$, we denote by $w.next$ and $w.last$, respectively, the next and last paths of $w$ in $D$. The adjustment is described as the following procedure.

**Procedure** ADJUST($D$, $k$)
**begin**
1. **while** $|D|{\geq}2$ and ($f(Tail.last, Tail){<}f(Tail, G_k)$) **do**
2.     delete *Tail* from $D$  /* Remove paths according to Property 1 */
3. Add $G_k$ to the tail of $D$
4. **while** $|D|{\geq}2$ and ($f(Head, Head.next){>}UN[k]$) **do**
5.     delete *Head* from $D$  /* Remove paths according to Property 2 */
6. **return**($D$)
**end**

In our algorithm, $d$-1 calls to ADJUST($D$, $k$) are performed, for $k$=1, 2, ..., $d$-1, respectively. Each $G_k$ is added to $D$ only once, while Line 3 of the procedure call ADJUST($D$, $k$) is performed. The addition of each $G_k$ is at the tail of $D$. Thus, at any time all the paths $G_i$ in $D$ are in an increasing order of $i$, which guarantees the validity of the deletion in Lines 1-2 and 4-5. Since each $G_k$ is added to $D$ only once, there are $d$-1 insertion operations involved in the $d$-1 calls. The total number of deletion operations on $D$ involved in the $d$-1 calls is not larger than the number of insertion operations. Therefore, in total, there are $O(d)$ insertion and deletion operations involved in the $d$-1 calls. Each insertion and deletion on a deque takes $O(1)$ time. Thus, the $d$-1 calls to ADJUST($D$, $k$), $k$=1, 2, ..., $d$-1, take $O(d)$ time in total. After calling ADJUST($D$, $k$), we compute $A_k$ as the $G_i$ in $D$ minimizing $D(Q_k, G_i)$. The following lemma is very helpful to the computation, which can be proved, with some efforts, by an induction on $k$.

*Lemma 15.* Let $(G_{i_1}, G_{i_2}, ..., G_{i_r})$ be the path sequence stored in $D$ after calling ADJUST($D$, $k$), $1{\leq}k{<}d$. If $|D|$=1 we have $D$=$(G_k)$; otherwise we have $UN[k]{\geq}$ $f(G_{i_1}, G_{i_2}){\geq}f(G_{i_2}, G_{i_3}){\geq}...{\geq}f(G_{i_{r-1}}, G_{i_r})$.

After calling to ADJUST($D$, $k$), we compute $A_k$ as the path $G_i$ in $D$ minimizing $D(Q_k, G_i)$. In the following, we show that the computation takes $O(1)$ time. Let $(G_{i_1}, G_{i_2}, ..., G_{i_r})$ be the path sequence stored in $D$ after calling to ADJUST($D$, $k$). If $|D|$=1, trivially, we compute $A_k$ as *Head* in $O(1)$ time. Assume $|D|{>}1$. By Lemma 15, we have $UN[k]{\geq}f(G_{i_1}, G_{i_2}){\geq}f(G_{i_2}, G_{i_3}){\geq}...{\geq}f(G_{i_{r-1}}, G_{i_r})$. Combining this and Lemma 14, we conclude that $D(Q_k, G_{i_1}){\leq}D(Q_k, G_{i_2}){\leq}D(Q_k, G_{i_3}){\leq}...{\leq}D(Q_k, G_{i_r})$. Thus, in case $|D|{>}1$, we also compute $A_k$ as *Head* in $O(1)$ time.

We summarize the above discussion in the following algorithm and lemma.

**Algorithm 3.** ROOTED_1_CORES($T$, $C$)
**Input:** a tree $T=(V, E)$ and a path $C=(c_1, c_2, ..., c_d)$ in $T$
**Output:** a $c_1$ rooted-1-core of each $T_{c_k}^{c_{k+1}}$, $1 \leq k < d$
**begin**
1     $(g_1, g_2, ..., g_{d-1}, L, UN, UD, GD) \leftarrow$ PREPROCESS($T$, $C$)
2     $D \leftarrow \varnothing$
3     **for** each $k$, $1 \leq k < d$, **do**
4            $D \leftarrow$ ADJUST($D$, $k$)
5            $A_k \leftarrow$ *Head* of $D$.
6     **return**($A_1, A_2, ..., A_{d-1}$)
**end**

*Lemma 16.* Let $(c_1, c_2, ..., c_d)$ be a path in $T$. In $O(n)$ time, we can find a $c_1$ rooted-1-core for every $T_{c_k}^{c_{k+1}}$, $1 \leq k < d-1$.

### 4.2  Finding a 2-Core

Let $C=(c_1, c_2, ..., c_d)$ be a 1-core of $T$. Let $S_i$, $i=1, 2, ..., d$, be the $d$ subtrees obtained from $T$ by removing all edges in $C$ such that $S_i$ is the one containing $c_i$. Becker and Perl gave the following important property for finding a 2-core.

*Theorem 5* [1]. There exists a 2-core $\{A, B\}$ of $T$ satisfying one of the following:
    (1) $A=C$ and $B$ is a $c_i$-point core for some subtree $S_i$, $2 \leq i \leq d-1$, or
    (2) $(A, B)$ is a $(c_1, c_d)$ rooted-2-core of $T$.

On the basis of Theorem 5, the 2-core problem can be solved as follows.

**Algorithm 4.** TWO_CORE($T$)
**Input:** a tree $T=(V, E)$
**Output:** a two-core of $T$
**begin**
1.    $C=(c_1, c_2, ..., c_d) \leftarrow$ a 1-core of $T$
2.    **for** each $i$, $2 \leq i \leq d-1$, **do**
3.            $R_i \leftarrow$ POINT_CORE($S_i$, $c_i$)
4.    $R \leftarrow$ the $R_z$ with $D(C \cup R_z)=\min_{2 \leq i \leq d-1} D(C \cup R_i)$
5.    $(X, Y) \leftarrow$ ROOTED_2_CORE($T$, $c_1$, $c_d$)
6.    **If** $D(C \cup R) \leq D(X \cup Y)$
7.            **then return** ($\{C, R\}$)
8.            **else return** ($\{X, Y\}$)
**end**

By Lemma 2, Line 1 takes $O(n)$ time. The for-loop in Lines 2-3 takes $O(\sum_{2 \leq i \leq d-1} |V(S_i)|)=O(n)$ time. Lines 4 and 5, respectively, takes $O(d)$ and $O(n)$ time. Lines 6-8 takes $O(1)$ time. Therefore, Algorithm 4 requires $O(n)$ time in total.

*Theorem 6.* A two-core of a weighted tree can be found in $O(n)$ time.

## 5  Finding a $p$-Core of a Tree

*Lemma 17.* There is an edge $(x, y) \in E$ such that a 1-core of $T_x^y$ and a $(p-1)$-core of $T_y^x$ constitute a $p$-core of $T$.

Due to the limitation of pages, the proof of Lemma 17 is omitted here. Based upon Lemma 17, the $p$-core problem can be solved as follows.

**Algorithm 5.** P_CORE($T$, $p$)
**Input:** a tree $T=(V, E)$ and an integer $p \geq 2$
**Output:** a $p$-core of $T$.
**begin**
1  **if** $p=2$ **then return** (TWO_CORE($T$))

2  **for** each $(x, y) \in E$ **do**

3        $A_1^{(x,y)} \leftarrow$ a 1-core of $T_x^y$

4        $\{ A_2^{(x,y)}, A_3^{(x,y)}, ..., A_p^{(x,y)} \} \leftarrow$ P_CORE($T_y^x$, $p$-1)  /* a recursive call */

5  $CORE \leftarrow$ the $\{ A_1^{(x,y)}, A_2^{(x,y)}, ..., A_p^{(x,y)} \}$ that minimizes $D( A_1^{(x,y)} \cup A_2^{(x,y)} \cup ... \cup A_p^{(x,y)} )$
        over all $(x, y) \in E$

6  **return** ($CORE$)

**end**

Let $T(n, p)$ be the running time of P_CORE($T$, $p$). With some efforts, we can obtain
$$T(n, p) = \begin{cases} O(n) & \text{if } p = 2, \\ (n-1) \times (O(n) + T(n, p-1)) + O(n) & \text{otherwise.} \end{cases}$$
By induction, it is easy to show that $T(n)=O(n^{p-1})$. We have the following theorem.

*Theorem 7.* A $p$-core of a weighted tree can be computed in $O(n^{p-1})$ time, where $p \geq 2$ is an integer.

## 6  Concluding Remarks

The definition of the $p$-core problem restricts the $p$ paths selected as a $p$-core are mutually disjoint. In case the restriction is removed the $p$-core problem becomes an easy one. Define an *intersection $p$-core* of $T$ as a set of $p$ paths $\{I_1, I_2, ..., I_p\}$ in $T$ minimizing $D(I_1 \cup I_2 \cup ... \cup I_p)$. Becker and Perl [1] had studied the case $p=2$ of the intersection $p$-core problem and gave an $O(n^2)$ time algorithm. It is easy to show that the problem of finding an intersection $p$-core of $T$ is equivalent to the problem of finding a subtree $S$ of $T$ such that $S$ has at most $2p$ leaves and $S$ minimizes $D(S)$ over all subtrees of $T$ having at most $2p$ leaves. Shioura and Uno [11], and Wang [14] had solved the latter problem in $O(n)$ time. Thus, the intersection $p$-core problem can be solved in $O(n)$ time.

Based upon the well-known divide-and-conquer strategy, a 2-core of a weighted tree can be computed in $O(\log^2 n)$ time using $O(n\log n)$ work on the EREW PRAM [16]. One direction for further studies is to solve the 2-core problem in poly-logarithmic time using $O(n)$ work on the PRAM. Another direction is to find an efficient approximation algorithm for the general $p$-core problem. Hakimi et al.'s proof for the NP-hardness of the general $p$-core problem is under the assumption that $T$ is weighted. Therefore, to study the complexity of the general $p$-core problem on an unweighted tree is also a possible direction for further studies.

# References

1. R. I. Becker and Y. Perl, "Finding the two-core of a tree," *Discrete Applied Mathematics*, vol. 11, no. 2, pp.103-113, 1985.
2. B. Gavih and S. Sridhar, "Computing the 2-median on tree networks in $O(n\lg n)$ time," *Networks*, vol. 26, iss. 4, pp. 305-317, 1995.
3. A.J. Goldman, "Optimal center location in simple networks", *Transportation Science*, vol. 5, pp. 212-221, 1971.
4. S. L. Hakimi, E. F. Schmeichel, and M. Labbe, "On locating path- or tree-shaped facilities on networks," *Networks*, vol. 23, pp. 543-555, 1993.
5. G.Y. Handler and P. Mirchandani, *Location on Networks*, MIT Press, Cambridge, MA, 1979.
6. D.E. Knuth, *The Art of Computer Programming*, vol. 1, Addison-Wesley, Reading, MA, 1968.
7. N. Megiddo, A. Tamir, E. Zemel, and R. Chandrasekaran, "An $O(n\log^2 n)$ time algorithm for the $k$th longest path in a tree with applications to location problems," *SIAM Journal on Computing*, vol. 10, pp. 328-337, 1981.
8. E. Minieka and N.H. Patel, "On finding the core of a tree with a specified length", *Journal of Algorithms*, vol. 4, pp. 345-352, 1983.
9. C.A. Morgan and P.L. Slater, "A linear time algorithm for a core of a tree", *Journal of Algorithms*, vol. 1, pp. 247-258, 1980.
10. S. Peng and W. Lo, "Efficient algorithms for finding a core of a tree with specified length", *Journal of Algorithms*, vol. 15, pp. 143-159, 1996.
11. A. Shioura and T. Uno, "A linear time algorithm for finding a $k$-tree core," *Journal of Algorithms*, vol. 23, pp. 281--290, 1997.
12. P.J. Slater, "Locating central paths in a network", *Transportation Science*, vol. 16, no. 1, pp.1-18, 1982.
13. A. Tamir, "An $O(pn^2)$ time algorithm for the $p$-median and related problems on tree graphs," *Operations Research Letters*, vol. 19, iss. 2, pp. 59-64, 1996.
14. B.-F. Wang, "Finding a $k$-tree core and a $k$-tree center of tree network in parallel", *IEEE Transactions on Parallel and Distributed Systems*, vol. 9, no. 2, pp. 186-191, 1999.
15. B.-F. Wang, "Efficient parallel algorithms for optimally locating a path and a tree of a specified length in a weighted tree network", *Journal of Algorithms*, vol. 34, pp. 90-108, 2000.
16. B.-F. Wang, "Finding a 2-core of a tree in linear time", manuscript.
17. B.-F. Wang, S.-C. Ku, K.-H. Shi, T.-K. Hung, and P.-S. Liu, "Parallel algorithms for the tree bisector problem and applications," in *Proceedings of the 1999 International Conference on Parallel Processing*, 1999, pp. 192-199.

# Unbalanced and Hierarchical Bipartite Matchings with Applications to Labeled Tree Comparison

Ming-Yang Kao[1]*, Tak-Wah Lam[2]**, Wing-Kin Sung[3], and Hing-Fung Ting[2]

[1] Department of Computer Science, Yale University, New Haven, CT06520, USA.
kao-ming-yang@cs.yale.edu
[2] Department of Computer Science and Information Systems, University of Hong Kong, Hong Kong. {twlam, hfting}@csis.hku.hk
[3] E-Business Technology Institute, University of Hong Kong, Hong Kong.
wksung@eti.hku.hk

**Abstract.** This paper is concerned with maximum weight matchings of bipartite graphs. We show how to speed up the existing matching algorithms when the input graphs are node unbalanced or weight unbalanced. Based on these improved matching algorithms, we can solve efficiently a new matching problem called the hierarchical bipartite matching problem, and thus obtain a simple and faster algoirthm for finding the maximum agreement subtree of two labeled trees. The significance of our subtree algorithm lies in the fact that it matches or outperforms all previously known subtree algorithms that were designed for two special cases of labeled trees, namely, *uniformly labeled* trees and *evolutionary* trees.

## 1 Introduction

Let $G$ be a bipartite graph with positive integer weights on its edges. The problem of finding a maximum weight matching of a given $G$ has a rich history. The most efficient known algorithm is due to Gabow and Tarjan [9]; it runs in $O(\sqrt{n}m \log nN)$ time, where $n, m$ and $N$ are the number of nodes, number of edges and the maximum edge weight of $G$, respectively. For some applications where the total edge weight, $W$ is small (say, $W = O(m)$), the algorithm by Kao *et al.* [13], which runs in $O(\sqrt{n}W)$ time, is slightly faster.

In this paper, we introduce techniques for speeding up the existing matching algorithms when $G$ is either *node unbalanced* or *weight unbalanced*. A weighted bipartite graph is node unbalanced if there are much fewer nodes on one side than the other. It is weight unbalanced if its total weight is dominated by the edges incident to a few nodes; we call these nodes *dominating nodes*.

Node-unbalanced bipartite graphs have many practical applications (see e.g., [11]). The node-unbalanced property has already been exploited to improve various graph algorithms. For example, Ahuja *et al.* [1] have used it to improve

---

* Research supported in part by NSF Grant CCR-9531028.
** Research supported in part by Hong Kong RGC Grant HKU-7027/98E.

D.T. Lee and S.-H. Teng (Eds.): ISAAC 2000, LNCS 1969, pp. 479–490, 2000.
© Springer-Verlag Berlin Heidelberg 2000

several bipartite network flow algorithms; they adapted the algorithms in such a way that the running times depend on the number of nodes in the smaller side of the bipartite graphs instead of the total number of nodes. For maximum weight matching, we obtain similar improvement. Specifically, we show that the running time of Gabow and Tarjan's algorithm and that of Kao et al.'s algorithm can be improved to $O(\min\{m + n_s^{2.5} \log n_s N, \sqrt{n_s} m \log n_s N\})$ and $O(\sqrt{n_s} W)$, respectively, where $n_s$ is the number of nodes in the smaller side of the input bipartite graph.

The weight-unbalanced property can be exploited as follows. Let $G$ be a weight-unbalanced bipartite graph, and $G'$ be the subgraph of $G$ with its dominating nodes removed. Since $G'$ has weight much smaller than $G$ does, running Kao et al.'s algorithm to find a maximum weight matching of $G'$ is much faster than running the algorithm for $G$. To take advantage of this fact, we design an efficient method that finds a maximum weight matching of $G$ from that of $G'$. This method enables us to improve substantially the time for directly using Kao et al.'s algorithm.

We apply the enhanced matching algorithms to improve the algorithm for labeled tree comparison, which finds applications in many areas including biology [7,19], linguistics [8,17], and structured text databases [15,16]. A *labeled* tree is a rooted tree with an arbitrary subset of nodes being labeled with symbols. A widely-used measure of the similarity of two labeled trees is the notion of a maximum agreement subtree, which is defined as follows.

A labeled tree $R$ is a *label-preserving homeomorphic* subtree of another labeled tree $T$ if there exists a one-to-one mapping $f$ from the nodes of $R$ to the nodes of $T$ such that for any nodes $u, v, w$ of $R$, (1) $u$ and $f(u)$ have the same label; and (2) $w$ is the least common ancestor of $u$ and $v$ if and only if $f(w)$ is the least common ancestor of $f(u)$ and $f(v)$. Let $T_1$ and $T_2$ be two labeled trees. An *agreement* subtree of $T_1$ and $T_2$ is a labeled tree which is also a label-preserving homeomorphic subtree of the two trees. A *maximum* agreement subtree (MAST) is one that maximizes the number of labeled nodes.

In the literature, many algorithms for computing the maximum agreement subtree have been developed. However, these algorithms focus on the special cases where $T_1$ and $T_2$ are (1) uniformly labeled trees, i.e., trees with all their nodes unlabeled or equivalently, labeled with the same symbol [2,10] or (2) *evolutionary trees*, i.e., leaf-labeled trees with distinct symbols for distinct leaves [3,6,12,13,18]. Instead of solving special cases, this paper gives an algorithm to handle the general case when $T_1$ and $T_2$ are unrestricted labeled trees (i.e., labels are not restricted to leaves and may not be distinct). Our algorithm not only is more general but also uniformly improves or matches the best known algorithms for the two special cases. The core of our algorithm is a novel trade-off technique for solving a new matching problem called the *hierarchical bipartite matching* problem, which is defined as follows.

Let $T$ be a rooted tree. Denote $r$ as the root of $T$. Every node $u$ of $T$ is associated with a positive integer $w(u)$ and a weighted bipartite graph $G_u$. Let $C(u)$ denote the set of children of $u$. We have the following two conditions:

- $w(u) \geq \sum_{v \in C(u)} w(v)$. (For example, $T$ may consist of $\ell$ leaves each associated with a $w$ value 1, and $w(u) = \sum_{v \in C(u)} w(v)$; in this case, $w(r) = \ell$.)

- $G_u = (X_u, Y_u, E_u)$ where $X_u = C(u)$. Each edge of $G_u$ has a positive integer weight, and there is no isolated node. For any node $v \in X_u$, the total weight of all the edges incident to $v$ is at most $w(v)$. Thus, the edges in $G_u$ have a total weight at most $w(u)$.

For any weighted bipartite graph $G$, let MWM($G$) denote a maximum weight matching of $G$. The *hierarchical matching problem* is to compute MWM($G_u$) for all internal nodes $u$ of $T$. Let $d = \max_{u \in T}\{\min\{|X_u|, |Y_u|\}\}$ and $e = \sum_{u \in T} |E_u|$. The problem can be solved by applying directly our technique on node-unbalanced graphs; e.g., it can be solved in $O(\sum_{u \in T} \sqrt{d}|E_u| \log dw(u)) = O(\sqrt{d}e \log w(r))$ time using the enhanced Gabow and Tarjan's algorithm. However, this running time is not desirable because for our application on labeled tree comparison, we often encounter problem instances with $e$ very large; in particular, it is asymptotically greater than $w(r)$. In this paper, we improve the running time to $O(\sqrt{d}w(r) + e)$ by further making use of our technique on weight-unbalanced graphs, and exploiting some special trade-off relationship between the size of bipartite graphs and their total edge weight.

Using our result on hierarchical bipartite matching, we derive a simple and faster algorithm for computing the MAST of any labeled trees $T_1$ and $T_2$. Let $n$ be the total number of nodes in $T_1$ and $T_2$, and $d$ be the maximum degree of $T_1$ and $T_2$. Let $W_{T_1,T_2}$ (or simply $W$ when the context is clear) denote $\sum_{u \in T_1} \sum_{v \in T_2} \delta(u, v)$ where $\delta(u, v) = 1$ if nodes $u$ and $v$ are labeled with the same symbol, and 0 otherwise. Our new MAST algorithm runs in $O(\sqrt{d}W_{T_1,T_2} \log \frac{n}{d})$ time. It is a factor of $\log \frac{n}{d}$ faster than the earlier $O(\sqrt{d}W \log^2 \frac{n}{d})$-time algorithm of ours [14]. This improvement is theoretically significant because it enables the new algorithm to outperform the previously best known algorithm in the following key cases, where the old algorithm under-performs. If $T_1$ and $T_2$ are evolutionary trees then $W \le n$ and the time complexity of our algorithm is $O(\sqrt{d}n \log \frac{n}{d})$, which is better than the $O(\sqrt{d}n \log n)$ bound claimed by Przytycka [18]. Notice that like our old algorithm, the new algorithm matches or outperforms the $O(n^{1.5})$-time algorithm [13] since $\sqrt{d}n \log \frac{n}{d} = O(n^{1.5})$ for any degree $d$. Therefore, the new algorithm now dominates the previous algorithms in every major case that has been discussed in the evolutionary tree literature. If $T_1$ and $T_2$ are uniformly labeled trees then $W \le n^2$ and our algorithm takes $O(\sqrt{d}n^2 \log \frac{n}{d})$ time and it outperforms the $O(n^{2.5} \log n)$-time algorithm of Gupta and Nishimura [10] for any $d$.

The rest of the paper is organized as follows. In Section 2, we detail our techniques of speeding up the existing algorithms for unbalanced graphs. In Section 3, we give an efficient algorithm for solving the hierarchical matching problem. Finally, in Section 4, we describe our algorithm for computing maximum agreement subtrees.

## 2    Maximum Weight Matching of Unbalanced Graphs

Let $G = (X, Y, E)$ be a weighted bipartite graph with no isolated nodes. Let $n = |X| + |Y|$, $n_s = \min\{|X|, |Y|\}$, $m = |E|$, and $N$ be the largest edge weight.

Suppose $n_s = |X| \leq |Y|$, and every edge of $G$ has a positive integer weight. Gabow and Tarjan [9] and Kao *et al.* [13] gave an $O(\sqrt{n}m \log(nN))$-time and an $O(\sqrt{n}W)$-time algorithm for computing MWM($G$), respectively. The following theorem shows that we can speed up the computation of MWM($G$) if $G$ is node-unbalanced.

**Theorem 1.**

1. MWM($G$) can be computed in $O(\sqrt{n_s}m \log(n_s N))$ time.
2. MWM($G$) can be computed in $O(m + n_s^{2.5} \log n_s N)$ time.
3. MWM($G$) can be computed in $O(\sqrt{n_s}W)$ time.

*Proof.* Statement 1. For any node $v$ in $G$, let $\alpha(v)$ be the number of edges incident to $v$. Suppose $Y = \{y_1, y_2 \cdots, y_{kn_s+r}\}$ where $k \geq 1$, $0 \leq r < n_s$, and $\alpha(y_1) \leq \alpha(y_2) \leq \cdots \leq \alpha(y_{kn_s+r})$. We partition $Y$ into $Y_0 = \{y_1, \ldots, y_r\}, Y_1 = \{y_{r+1}, \ldots, y_{r+n_s}\}, \ldots$, and $Y_k = \{y_{r+(k-1)n_s+1}, \ldots, y_{r+kn_s}\}$. Note that other than $Y_0$, every set has $n_s$ nodes.

For any $Y' \subseteq Y$, denote $G(Y')$ as the subgraph of $G$ induced by all the edges incident to $Y'$. Suppose that $M_i$ is a maximum weight matching of $G(Y_0 \cup Y_1 \cup \ldots \cup Y_i)$. Let $Y_{M_i} = \{y \mid (x, y) \in M_i\}$. Note that a maximum weight matching of $G(Y_{M_i} \cup Y_{i+1})$ is also a maximum weight matching of $G(Y_0 \cup Y_1 \cup \ldots \cup Y_{i+1})$. Therefore, we can compute MWM($G$) using the following algorithm.

1. Compute a maximum weight matching $M_0$ of $G(Y_0)$;
2. For $i = 1$ to $k$,
   - let $Y_{M_{i-1}} = \{y \mid (x, y) \in M_{i-1}\}$;
   - compute a maximum weight matching $M_i$ of $G(Y_{M_{i-1}} \cup Y_i)$;
3. Return $M_k$;

The running time is analyzed below. Let $\alpha(G(Y'))$ be the total number of edges in $G(Y')$. For $1 \leq i \leq k$, $\alpha(G(Y_{M_{i-1}})) \leq \alpha(G(Y_i))$, and $\alpha(G(Y_{M_{i-1}} \cup Y_i)) \leq 2\alpha(G(Y_i))$. Using the matching algorithm by Gabow and Tarjan [9], we can compute MWM($G(Y_{M_{i-1}} \cup Y_i)$) in $O(\sqrt{|Y_{M_{i-1}} \cup Y_i|}\alpha(G(Y_i)) \log(|Y_{M_{i-1}} \cup Y_i|N))$ time. Note that $|Y_{M_{i-1}}| \leq n_s$ and $|Y_i| = n_s$. Hence, the whole algorithm uses $O(\sum_{i=1}^{k} \sqrt{n_s}\alpha(G(Y_i)) \log(n_s N)) = O(\sqrt{n_s}m \log(n_s N))$ time.

Statement 2. Since we suppose $|X| \leq |Y|$, any matching of $G$ contains at most $|X| = n_s$ edges. Thus, for every $u \in X$, we can throw away the edges incident to $u$ that are not among the $n_s$ heaviest ones; the remaining $n_s^2$ edges must still contain a maximum weight matching of $G$. Note that we can find these $n_s^2$ edges in $O(m)$ time, and from Statement 1, we can compute MWM($G$) from them in $O(\sqrt{n_s}n_s^2 \log n_s N)$ time. The total time taken is $O(m + n_s^{2.5} \log n_s N)$.

Statement 3. Using technique similar to that we use in proving statement 1, we improve the $O(\sqrt{n}W)$-time matching algorithm by Kao *et al.* [13] so that we can find MWM($G$) in $O(\sqrt{n_s}W)$ time.

Now, we show how to speed up the execution of Kao *et al.*'s algorithm when the input graph $G$ is weight-unbalanced. Theorem 2 below summarizes the core technique; it shows how to compute MWM($G$) efficiently from a maximum weight matching of any of its subgraph constructed by removing some nodes. To get some feeling on how this theorem helps, let us suppose that $G$ has $O(1)$ dominating nodes. Let $G'$ be the subgraph of $G$ with the dominating nodes removed, and let $W'$ be the total edge weight of $G'$. Since $G$ is weight unbalanced, we further suppose $W' = o(W)$. To compute $\text{MWM}(G)$, we can first compute $\text{MWM}(G')$ using the enchanced Kao *et al.*'s algorithm in $O(\sqrt{n_s}W')$ time and then apply Theorem 2 to compute $\text{MWM}(G)$ from $\text{MWM}(G')$ in $O(m \log n_s)$ time. The total running time of this process is $O(m \log n_s + \sqrt{n_s}W') = o(\sqrt{n_s}W)$, which is smaller than the running time of using Kao *et al.*'s algorithm to find $\text{MWM}(G)$ directly.

**Theorem 2.** *Let $H = \{x_1, x_2, \ldots, x_h\}$ be a subset of $h$ nodes of $X$. Let $G - H$ be the subgraph of $G$ constructed by removing the nodes in $H$. Denote by $E'$ the set of edges in $G - H$. Given $\text{MWM}(G - H)$, we can compute $\text{MWM}(G)$ in $O(|E| + (h^2|E'| + h^3) \log n_s)$ time.*

*Proof.* First, we show that using $O(|E|)$ time, we can find a set $\Sigma$ of only $O(\min\{h|E'| + h^2, n_s^2\})$ edges such that $\Sigma$ still contains a maximum weight matching of $G$. In previous discussion, it has already been shown that we can find in $O(|E|)$ time a set of $O(n_s^2)$ edges that contains $\text{MWM}(G)$. Thus, it suffices to find in $O(|E|)$ time another set of $O(h|E'| + h^2)$ edges that contains $\text{MWM}(G)$; $\Sigma$ is just the smaller of these two sets. Let $Y'$ be the subset of nodes of $Y$ that are endpoints of $E'$. For any $x_i \in H$, we select, among the edges incident to $x_i$, a subset of edges $E_i$, which is the union of the following two sets:

- $\{(x_i, y) \mid y \in Y'\}$;
- $\{(x_i, y) \mid (x_i, y)$ is among the $h$ heaviest edges with $y \notin Y'\}$.

Observe that $E' \cup E_1 \cup \cdots \cup E_h$ must contain a maximum weight matching of $G$, and these $|E' \cup E_1 \cup \cdots E_h| = O(h|E'| + h^2)$ edges can be found in $O(|E|)$ time.

Given $\Sigma$, we can assume that $G$ has only $O(\min\{h|E'| + h^2, n_s^2\})$ edges; we simply throw away all the edges that are not in $\Sigma$ nor $\text{MWM}(G - H)$. Making this assumption costs an extra $O(|E|)$ time for finding $\text{MWM}(G)$.

Below, we describe a procedure which, given any bipartite graph $D$ and any node $x$ of $D$, finds $\text{MWM}(D)$ from $\text{MWM}(D - \{x\})$ in $O(m_D \log m_D)$ time, where $m_D$ are the number edges of $D$. Then, starting from $G - H$, we can apply this procedure repeatedly $h$ times to find $\text{MWM}(G)$ from $\text{MWM}(G - H)$. Since $G$ is assumed to have only $O(\min\{h|E'| + h^2, n_s^2\})$ edges, this process takes $O(h[(h|E'| + h^2) \log n_s])$ time. The lemma follows.

Let $M$ and $M_x$ be a maximum weight matching of $D$ and $D - \{x\}$, respectively. Denote by $S$ the set of augmenting paths and cycles formed in $M \cup M_x - M \cap M_x$, and $\sigma$ the augmenting path in $S$ starting from $x$. Note that the augmenting paths and cycles in $S - \{\sigma\}$ cannot improve the matching $M_x$; otherwise, $M_x$ is not a maximum weight matching of $D - \{x\}$. Thus, we can transform $M_x$ to $M$ using $\sigma$. Note that $\sigma$ is indeed a maximum augmenting path starting from $x$, which can be found in $O(m_D \log m_D)$ time [4].

## 3    Hierarchical Bipartite Matching

Let $T$ be a rooted tree as defined in the definition of the hierarchical bipartite matching problem in Section 1. Let $d = \max_{u \in T} \{\min\{|X_u|, |Y_u|\}\}$ and $e = \sum_{u \in T} |E_u|$. In this section, we describe an algorithm for computing $\text{MWM}(G_u)$ for all $u \in T$; it runs in $O(\sqrt{d}w(r) + e)$ time.

Intuitively, our algorithm is based on two observations. First, we observe there is a trade-off among the associated bipartite graphs, namely, there are at most $2w(r)/x$ graphs with its second maximum edge weight greater than $x$. Second, most of the graphs have their total weight dominated by edges incident to a few nodes. For those graphs with large second maximum edge weight, we compute their maximum weight matchings using less 'weight-sensitive' algorithm. As there are not too many of them, the computation is efficient. For the other graphs, we prove that their weights are dominated by the edges incident to a few nodes. Thus, by the technique described in Theorem 2, together with a weight-efficient matching algorithm, we can compute the maximum weight matchings for these graphs efficiently. Details are as follows.

Consider any set $C$ of nodes of $T$. Let $\delta = \min_{u \in C} w(u)$. We say that $C$ has *critical degree h* if for every $u \in C$, $u$ has at most $h$ children with weight greater than or equal to $\delta$. For any internal node $u$, define $\text{SECW}(u) = \text{2nd-}\max\{w(v) \mid v \in C(u)\}$ (i.e., the value of the second largest $w(v)$ among all the children $v$ of $u$). Lemmas 1 and 2 below show the importance of the notions of $\text{SECW}(u)$ and critical degree.

**Lemma 1.** *Let $x$ be any positive number. Let $A$ be the set of nodes $u$ of $T$ with* $\text{SECW}(u) > x$. *Then $|A| < 2w(r)/x$.*

*Proof.* Let $B = \{u \mid u \in A$ and has at most one child in $A\}$. Observe that the forest in $T$ induced by $A$ has at most $2|B|$ nodes, and thus $|A| \le 2|B|$.

For any node $u$, let $\text{SECC}(u)$ denote some child $v$ of $u$ with $w(v) = \text{SECW}(u)$. Note that the subtrees rooted at the nodes in $\{\text{SECC}(u) \mid u \in B\}$ are disjoint, and hence $\sum_{u \in B} \text{SECW}(u) \le w(r)$. Since $B \subseteq A$, every node $u \in B$ has $\text{SECW}(u) > x$. Thus, $\sum_{u \in B} x < \sum_{u \in B} \text{SECW}(u) \le w(r)$. Hence, $|B| < w(r)/x$, and the lemma follows.

**Lemma 2.** *Let $C$ be any set of nodes of $T$. If $C$ has critical degree $h$, then we can compute $\text{MWM}(G_u)$ for all $u \in C$ in $O((\sqrt{d} + h^3 \log d)w(r) + \sum_{u \in C} |E_u|)$ time.*

*Proof.* For every node $u \in C$, let $H(u)$ be the set of $u$'s children that have their weight at least $\delta = \min_{u \in C} w(u)$. Let $L(u)$ be the set of the rest of $u$'s children. Note that $|H(u)| \le h$ because $C$ has critical degree $h$. Since the weight of $G_u - H(u)$ is at most $\sum_{x \in L(u)} w(x)$ and $d \ge \min\{|X_u|, |Y_u|\}$, by Theorem 1, we can compute $\text{MWM}(G_u - H(u))$ in time

$$O(\sqrt{d}\textstyle\sum_{x \in L(u)} w(x) + |E_u|). \tag{1}$$

Since $G_u - H(u)$ has at most $\sum_{x \in L(u)} w(x)$ edges and $|H(u)| \leq h$, by Theorem 2, we can compute MWM$(G_u)$ from MWM$(G_u - H(u))$ in time

$$O(|E_u| + (h^2 \sum_{x \in L(u)} w(x) + h^3) \log d) = O(h^3 \log d \sum_{u \in L(u)} w(x) + |E_u|). \quad (2)$$

From (1) and (2), we can compute MWM$(G_u)$ for all $u \in C$ in time

$$O\left(\sum_{u \in C} \left((\sqrt{d} + h^3 \log d) \sum_{x \in L(u)} w(x) + |E_u|\right)\right).$$

Note that the subtrees rooted at some node in $\bigcup_{u \in C} L(u)$ are disjoint, and hence $\sum_{u \in C} \sum_{x \in L(u)} w(x) \leq w(r)$. The lemma follows.

We are now ready to explain how to compute MWM$(G_u)$ for all nodes $u$ of $T$. We divide all the nodes in $T$ into two sets: $\Phi = \{u \in T \mid \text{SECW}(u) > d^3\}$ and $\Pi = \{u \in T \mid \text{SECW}(u) \leq d^3\}$. Since every node $u \in \Phi$ has $\text{SECW}(u) > d^3$ and $w(u) < w(r)$, by Theorem 1 and Lemma 1, we can find MWM$(G_u)$ for all $x \in \Phi$ using $O(\frac{w(r)}{d^3} \sqrt{d} d^2 \log w(r) + \sum_{u \in \Phi} |E_u|) = O(w(r) \frac{\log w(r)}{\sqrt{d}} + \sum_{u \in \Phi} |E_u|)$ time. Note that $\log w(r)$ may be much larger than $\sqrt{d}$. To improve the time complexity, we first note that by using the technique in Theorem 2, we can compute MWM$(G_u)$ in time depending only on $\text{SECW}(u)$. Then, by making a better estimation of $\text{SECW}(u)$, we show the time complexity can be reduced to $O(w(r) + \sum_{u \in \Phi} |E_u|)$. For $\Pi$, we can handle the nodes $u \in \Pi$ with $w(u) > d^3$ easily. For nodes with $w(u) < d^3$, we apply the algorithm in Lemma 2 to compute MWM$(G_u)$. Basically, we partition the nodes $u$ into a constant number of sets according to the value of $w(u)$ such that every set has critical degree $d^{\frac{1}{7}}$. This will ensure that the total time to compute all the MWM$(G_u)$ is $O(\sqrt{d} w(r) + \sum_{u \in \Pi} |E_u|)$. The following theorem gives the details on handling $\Phi$ and $\Pi$.

**Theorem 3.** *We can compute* MWM$(G_u)$ *for all nodes* $u \in T$ *in* $O(\sqrt{d} w(r) + e)$ *time.*

*Proof.* First, we show that we can compute MWM$(G_u)$ for all $u \in \Phi$ in time $O(w(r) + \sum_{u \in \Phi} |E_u|)$. Observe that for any $u \in \Phi$, $G_u$ has only $O(d^2)$ edges relevant to the computation of MWM$(G_u)$, and they can be found in $O(|E_u|)$ time. Let $|E_u'|$ be this set of edges. Below, we assume that, for every $u \in \Phi$, $G_u$ has only edges in $E_u'$. Making this assumption costs us $O(\sum_{u \in \Phi} |E_u|)$ extra time.

For every $k \geq 1$, define $\Phi_k = \{u \in \Phi \mid 2^{k-1} d^3 < \text{SECW}(u) \leq 2^k d^3\}$. Obviously, the $\Phi_k$'s partition $\Phi$. Below, we show that for any non-empty $\Phi_k$, we can compute MWM$(G_u)$ for all $u \in \Phi_k$ using time $O\left(w(r)k/2^k + \sum_{u \in \Phi_k} |E_u'| \log d\right)$. Then, we can compute MWM$(G_u)$ for all $u \in \Phi$ using time $O(\sum_{k \geq 1} w(r)k/2^k + \sum_{u \in \Phi} |E_u'| \log d) = O(w(r) + \sum_{u \in \Phi} |E_u'| \log d) = O(w(r) + (w(r)/d^3) d^2 \log d) = O(w(r))$.

We give the details of computing MWM$(G_u)$ for all $u \in \Phi_k$. Let $u$ be a node in $\Phi_k$. Let $u'$ be the child of $u$ where $w(u')$ is the largest among all children of $u$. Since $\text{SECW}(u) \leq 2^k d^3$, every edge of $G_u - \{u'\}$ has weight at most $2^k d^3$. By Theorems 1 and 2, and the fact that $d \geq \min\{|X_u|, |Y_u|\}$, we can find MWM$(G_u)$

in $O(\sqrt{d}d^2 \log(d2^k d^3) + |E'_u| \log d)$ time. By Lemma 1, $|\Phi_k| \leq \frac{2w(r)}{2^k d^3}$. Thus, we can compute $\text{MWM}(G_u)$ for all $u \in \Phi_k$ in time

$$O\left(\sum_{u \in \Phi_k} \sqrt{d}d^2 \log(d2^k d^3) + |E'_u| \log d\right)$$
$$= O\left(\frac{w(r)d^{2.5}}{2^k d^3}(k + \log d) + \sum_{u \in \Phi_k} |E'_u| \log d\right)$$
$$= O\left(w(r)k/2^k + \sum_{u \in \Phi_k} |E'_u| \log d\right).$$

Now, we show that we compute $\text{MWM}(G_u)$ for all $u \in \Pi$ in time $O(\sqrt{d}w(r) + \sum_{u \in \Pi} |E_u|$. We partition $\Pi$ as follows. Let $\Pi'$ be the set of nodes in $\Pi$ with weight greater than $d^3$. For any $0 \leq k \leq 20$, define $\Pi_k = \{u \mid u \in \Pi \text{ and } d^{\frac{k}{7}} \leq w(u) < d^{\frac{k+1}{7}}\}$. Obviously, $\Pi = \Pi' \cup \Pi_0 \cup \cdots \Pi_{20}$.

Since $\text{SECW}(u) < d^3$ for all nodes in $\Pi'$, $\Pi'$ has critical degree one. By Lemma 2, we can compute $\text{MWM}(G_u)$ for all nodes in $\Pi'$ using $O(\sqrt{d}w(r) + \sum_{u \in \Pi'} |E_u|)$ time.

Each $\Pi_k$ is handled as follows. For every node $u \in \Pi_k$, $u$ has at most $d^{\frac{1}{7}}$ children with weight greater than $d^{\frac{k}{7}}$; otherwise $w(u) \geq d^{\frac{k+1}{7}}$ and it is not in $\Pi_k$. This implies that $\Pi_k$ has critical degree $d^{\frac{1}{7}}$. By Lemma 2, we can compute $\text{MWM}(G_u)$ for all $u \in \Pi_k$ in $O((\sqrt{d} + d^{\frac{3}{7}} \log d)w(r) + \sum_{u \in \Pi_k} |E_u|) = O(\sqrt{d}w(r) + \sum_{u \in \Pi_k} |E_u|)$ time. Altogether, we can compute $\text{MWM}(G_u)$ for all $u \in \Pi$ using $O(\sqrt{d}w(r) + \sum_{u \in \Pi} |E_u|)$ time.

Finally, the theorem follows because $T = \Phi \cup \Pi$ and $\sum_{u \in T} |E_u| = e$.

## 4  Computing Maximum Agreement Subtrees

In this section, we give an efficient algorithm for computing a maximum agreement subtree of any two labeled trees. The bottleneck of the algorithm is solving an instance of hierarchical bipartite matching problem. By applying the result summarized in Theorem 3, we have the fastest known MAST algorithm. We will first introduce all the necessary concepts and notations for computing MAST. Then, we give the details of our MAST algorithm.

### 4.1  Basic Concepts

For a rooted tree $T$ and any node $u$ of $T$, let $T^u$ denote the subtree of $T$ that is rooted at $u$. For any set $L$ of symbols, the *restricted subtree* of $T$ with respect to $L$, denoted by $T\|L$, is the subtree of $T$ whose nodes are the nodes labeled with $L$ and the least common ancestors of any two nodes labeled with $L$, and whose edges preserve the ancestor-descendant relationship of $T$. Note that $T\|L$ may contain nodes with labels outside $L$. For any labeled tree $\Upsilon$, let $T\|\Upsilon$ denote the restricted subtree of $T$ with respect to the set of symbols used in $\Upsilon$.

A *centroid path decomposition* [3] of a rooted tree $T$ is a partition of its nodes into disjoint paths as follows. For each internal node $u$ in $T$, let $C(u)$ denote the set of children of $u$. Among the children of $u$, one of them is chosen to be the *heavy* child, denoted by hvy$(u)$, if the subtree of $T$ rooted at hvy$(u)$ contains the largest number of nodes; the other children of $u$ are *side* children. We call the edge from $u$ to its heavy child a *heavy* edge. A *centroid path* is a maximal path formed by heavy edges; the *root* centroid path is the centroid path that contains the root of $T$.

Let $\mathcal{D}(T)$ denote the set of the centroid paths of $T$. Note that $\mathcal{D}(T)$ can be constructed in $O(|T|)$ time. For every $P \in \mathcal{D}(T)$, the root of $P$, denoted $r(P)$, refers to the the node on $P$ that is the closest to the root of $T$, and $\mathcal{A}(P)$ denotes the set of the side children of the nodes on $P$. For any node $u$ on $P$, a subtree rooted at some side child of $u$ is called a *sidetree* of $u$, as well as a side tree of $P$. Let SIDE_T$(P)$ be the set of side trees of $P$. Note that, for every $R \in$ SIDE_T$(P)$, $|R| \leq |T^{r(P)}|/2$.

The following lemma, whose proof will be given in the full paper, states two properties about the centroid path decomposition. Recall that $T_1$ and $T_2$ are of degree $d$, and $W_{T_1,T_2} = \sum_{u \in T_1} \sum_{v \in T_2} \delta(u,v)$ where $\delta(u,v) = 1$ if nodes $u$ and $v$ are labeled with the same symbol, and 0 otherwise.

**Lemma 3.**

1. $\sum_{P \in \mathcal{D}(T_1)} W_{T_1^{r(P)},T_2} \leq W_{T_1,T_2} \log n$;

2. $\sum_{P \in \mathcal{D}(T_1)} \sqrt{\min(d,|T_1^{r(P)}|)} W_{T_1^{r(P)},T_2} \leq \sqrt{d} W_{T_1,T_2} \log \frac{n}{d}$.

## 4.2   The MAST Algorithm

Let $T_1$ and $T_2$ be labeled trees of degree $d \geq 2$. Our algorithm is based on the following recurrence, which generalizes the one given in [6] to handle labeled trees.

$$\text{MAST}(T_1^u, T_2^v) = \max \begin{cases} \max\{\text{MAST}(T_1^u, T_2^c) \mid x \in C(v)\}, \\ \max\{\text{MAST}(T_1^c, T_2^v) \mid x \in C(u)\}, \\ |\text{MWM}(G_{uv})| \text{ if } u \text{ and } v \text{ are both unlabeled}, \\ |\text{MWM}(G_{uv})| + 1, \end{cases} \quad (3)$$

where $|\text{MWM}(G_{uv})|$ denotes the size of the matching.

For any node $x \in T_1$ or $T_2$, let $\mathcal{L}(x)$ to be the set of symbols labeled in the sidetrees rooted at $x$. Define INP$(P,Q)$ to be the set of $(u,v) \in P \times Q$ such that $\mathcal{L}(u) \cap \mathcal{L}(v) \neq \emptyset$.

Equation (3) suggests a bottom-up dynamic programming approach to computing MAST. The following lemma generalizes Cole *et al.*'s technique [3] on speeding up the dynamic programming. Consider any centroid path $P \in \mathcal{D}(T_1)$. Define $\mathcal{M}_P$ to be the time to compute MWM$(H_{uv})$ for all node pairs $(u,v) \in$ INP$(P,T_2)$, where $H_{uv}$ is constructed from $G_{uv}$ by removing all the zero-weight edges and all the edges adjacent to the heavy child of $u$ and $v$. Note that the total edge weight of $H_{uv}$ can be significantly smaller than that of $G_{uv}$, yet by Theorem 2, we can recover MWM$(G_{uv})$ from MWM$(H_{uv})$ efficiently.

**Lemma 4.** *Let $r = r(P)$. Suppose for every node $u \in \mathcal{A}(P)$, we are given the values* $\mathrm{MAST}(T_1^u, (T_2\|T_1^u)^v)$ *for all $v \in T_2\|T_1^u$. Then* $\mathrm{MAST}(T_1^r, (T_2\|T_1^r)^v)$ *for all $v \in T_2\|T_1^r$ can be computed in* $O([\tau(T_1^r) - \sum_{u\in\mathcal{A}(P)} \tau(T_1^u) + W_{T_1^r,T_2}] \log d + \mathcal{M}_P)$ *time, where $\tau(R) = W_{R,T_2} \log |(T_2\|R)|$.*

*Proof.* To be given in the full paper.

Note that if $P$ is the root centroid path of $T_1$, then $r(P)$ is also the root of $T$ and $\mathrm{MAST}(T_1^{r(P)}, (T_2\|T_1^{r(P)})) = \mathrm{MAST}(T_1, T_2)$. Lemma 4 suggests that $\mathrm{MAST}(T_1, T_2)$ can be computed in a bottom-up fashion.

Let $\prec$ denote the ordering on $\mathcal{D}(T)$ where $P_1 \prec P_2$ if the root of $P_1$ is a descendant of the root $P_2$.

For every $P \in \mathcal{D}(T_1)$ in increasing order according to $\prec$, let $r$ denote the root of $P$; apply Lemma 4 to find $(T_1^r, (T_2\|T_1^r)^v)$ for every node $v \in T_2\|T_1^r$.

The next lemma states the running time of the above computation.

**Lemma 5.** *We can compute* $\mathrm{MAST}(T_1, T_2)$ *in* $O(W \log n \log d + \sum_{P\in\mathcal{D}(T_1)} \mathcal{M}_P)$, *where $W = W_{T_1,T_2}$.*

*Proof.* To derive the time for computing $\mathrm{MAST}(T_1, T_2)$, we simply sum the time bound stated in Lemma 4 over all centroid paths of $T_1$. Observe that

$$\sum_{P\in\mathcal{D}(T_1)} \left[ \tau(T_1^{r(P)}) - \sum_{u\in\mathcal{A}(P)} \tau(T_1^u) \right] = t(T_1^{r_o}), \text{ where } r_o \text{ is the root of of } T_1$$
$$= W_{T_1,T_2} \log |T_2\|T_1|$$
$$= W_{T_1,T_2} \log |T_2| = W \log n.$$

Therefore, $\mathrm{MAST}(T_1, T_2)$ can be computed in time $O(W \log n \log d + \sum_{P\in\mathcal{D}(T_1)} \mathcal{M}_P + \sum_{P\in\mathcal{D}(T_1)} W_{T_1^{r(P)},T_2})$. By Lemma 3, $\sum_{P\in\mathcal{D}(T_1)} W_{T_1^{r(P)},T_2}) = W \log n$. Thus, Lemma 5 follows.

**Matchings:** In the rest of this section, we show that $\sum_{P\in\mathcal{D}(T_1)} \mathcal{M}_P \leq \sqrt{d}W \log \frac{2n}{d}$. That is, we want to compute efficiently $\mathrm{MWM}(H_{uv})$ for all $(u, v) \in \bigcup_{P\in\mathcal{D}(T_1)} \mathrm{INP}(P, T_2)$. Then, together with Lemma 5 and the fact that $\log d \log n \leq \sqrt{d} \log \frac{2n}{d}$, we conclude the following theorem.

**Theorem 4.** $\mathrm{MAST}(T_1, T_2)$ *can be computed in* $O(\sqrt{d}W_{T_1,T_2} \log \frac{2n}{d})$ *time.*

First of all, let us show that the total number of edges in the graphs $H_{uv}$ for all $(u, v) \in \bigcup_{P\in\mathcal{D}(T_1)} \mathrm{INP}(P, T_2)$, denoted as *toe*, is $O(W \log n)$. For any centroid path $P \in \mathcal{D}(T_1)$, let *toe(P)* be the total number of edges in the graphs $H_{uv}$ for all $(u, v) \in \mathrm{INP}(P, T_2)$. Lemma 6 states that

$$toe(P) = O\left( \sum_{w\in\mathcal{A}(P)} |T_2\|T_1^w| \log \frac{|T_2\|T_1^{r(P)}|}{|T_2\|T_1^w|} \right).$$

Then, we can conclude that *toe* is in the order of

$$\sum_{P\in\mathcal{D}(T_1)} \left[ \sum_{w\in\mathcal{A}(P)} |T_1||T_1^w| \log \frac{|T_2||T_1^{r(P)}|}{\log |T_2||T_1^w|} \right]$$

$$\leq \sum_{P\in\mathcal{D}(T_1)} \left[ \sum_{w\in\mathcal{A}(P)} W_{T_1^w,T_2} \log \frac{|T_2||T_1^{r(P)}|}{\log |T_2||T_1^w|} \right]$$

$$\leq \sum_{P\in\mathcal{D}(T_1)} \left[ W_{T_1^{r(P)},T_2} \log |T_2||T_1^{r(P)}| - \sum_{w\in\mathcal{A}(P)} W_{T_1^w,T_2} \log |T_2||T_1^w| \right]$$

$$= W_{T_1^{r_o},T_2} \log |T_2||T_1^{r_o}|, \text{ where } r_o \text{ is the root of } T_1$$

$$= W_{T_1,T_2} \log |T_2| = W \log n.$$

**Lemma 6.** *For any $P \in \mathcal{D}(T_1)$, $toe(P) = O\left( \sum_{w\in\mathcal{A}(P)} |T_2||T_1^w| \log \frac{|T_2||T_1^{r(P)}|}{|T_2||T_1^w|} \right)$.*

*Proof.* To be given in the full paper.

A bipartite graph is said to be *non-trivial* if both node sets have at least two nodes. Computing MWM($H_{uv}$) for all trivial $H_{uv}$ where $(u,v) \in \bigcup_{P\in\mathcal{D}(T_1)}$ INP $(P,T_2)$, takes only linear time, bounded by $O(toe)$, which is $O(W \log n)$. Thus, we focus on those non-trivial $H_{uv}$'s.

Consider any centroid path $P$ in $\mathcal{D}(T_1)$ and fix a node $u$ of $P$. Define $\mathcal{H}_u$ to be the set of all non-trivial graphs $H_{uv}$ where $(u,v) \in$ INP$(P,T_2)$. Define $\mathcal{M}_u$ to be the time for finding MWM($H_{uv}$) for all the graphs in $\mathcal{H}_u$, and let $toe(u)$ be the number of edges of all the graphs in $\mathcal{H}_u$. Let $S_u$ is the set of sidetrees of $u$ in $T_1$ and $W_{S_u,T_2} = \sum_{r\in S_u} W_{r,T_2}$. We have the following lemma.

**Lemma 7.** $\mathcal{M}_u = O(\sqrt{\min(d,|T_1^u|)} W_{S_u,T_2} + toe(u))$.

*Proof.* To be given in the full paper.

We can then conclude that

$$\sum_{P\in\mathcal{D}(T_1)} \mathcal{M}_P = O\left( \sum_{P\in\mathcal{D}(T_1)} \sum_{u\in P} \mathcal{M}_u \right)$$

$$= O\left( \sum_{P\in\mathcal{D}(T_1)} \sum_{u\in P} (\sqrt{\min(d,|T_1^u|)} W_{S_u,T_2} + toe(u)) \right)$$

$$= O\left( toe + \sum_{P\in\mathcal{D}(T_1)} \sum_{u\in P} \sqrt{\min(d,|T_1^u|)} W_{S_u,T_2} \right)$$

$$= O\left( toe + \sum_{P\in\mathcal{D}(T_1)} \sqrt{\min(d,|T_1^{r(P)}|)} W_{T_1^{r(P)},T_2} \right)$$

By Lemma 3, we can further deduce that the latter is $O(toe + \sqrt{d} W_{T_1,T_2} \log \frac{n}{d})$ $= O(\sqrt{d} W \log \frac{n}{d})$.

# References

1. R. K. Ahuja, J. B. Orlin, C. Stein, and R. E. Tarjan. Improved algorithms for bipartite network flow. *SIAM Journal on Computing*, 23(5):906–933, 1994.
2. M. J. Chung. $O(n^{2.5})$ time algorithms for the subgraph homeomorphism problem on trees. *Journal of Algorithms*, 8:106–112, 1987.
3. R. Cole, M. Farach, R. Hariharan, T. M. Przytycka, and M. Thorup. An $O(n \log n)$ time algorithm for the maximum agreement subtree problem for binary trees. *SIAM Journal on Computing*. To appear.
4. T. H. Cormen, C. L. Leiserson, and R. L. Rivest. *Introduction to Algorithms*. MIT Press, Cambridge, MA, 1991.
5. M. Farach, T. M. Przytycka, and M. Thorup. Computing the agreement of trees with bounded degrees. In *Lecture Notes in Computer Science 979: Proceedings of the 3rd Annual European Symposium on Algorithms*, pages 381–393. 1995.
6. M. Farach and M. Thorup. Sparse dynamic programming for evolutionary-tree comparison. *SIAM Journal on Computing*, 26(1):210–230, 1997.
7. C. R. Finden and A. D. Gordon. Obtaining common pruned trees. *Journal of Classification*, 2:255–276, 1985.
8. J. Friedman. Expressing logical formulas in natural languages. In *Formal methods in the study of language*, pages 113–130. Mathematical Centre, Amsterdam, 1981.
9. H. N. Gabow and R. E. Tarjan. Faster scaling algorithms for network problems. *SIAM Journal on Computing*, 18(5):1013–1036, 1989.
10. A. Gupta and N. Nishimura. Finding largest subtrees and smallest supertrees. *Algorithmica*, 21(2):183–210, 1998.
11. D. Gusfield, C. Martel, and D. Fernández-Baca. Fast algorithms for bipartite network flow. *SIAM Journal on Computing*, 16:237–251, 1987.
12. M. Y. Kao. Tree contractions and evolutionary trees. *SIAM Journal on Computing*, 27(6):1592–1616, 1998.
13. M. Y. Kao, T. W. Lam, W. K. Sung, and H. F. Ting. A decomposition theorem for maximum weight bipartite matchings with applications to evolutionary trees. In *Lecture Notes in Computer Science: Proceedings of the 8th Annual European Symposium on Algorithms*, pages 438–449. 1999.
14. M. Y. Kao, T. W. Lam, W. K. Sung, and H. F. Ting. A faster and unifying algorithm for comparing trees. In *Proceedings of the 11th Symposium on Combinatorial Pattern matching*, 2000. To appear.
15. P. Kilpeläinen and H. Mannila. Grammatical tree matching. In *Lecture Notes in Computer Science 644: Proceedings of the 3rd Annual Symposium on Combinatorial Pattern Matching*, pages 162–174. 1992.
16. H. Mannila and K. J. Räihä. On query languages for the p-string data model. In *Information Modelling and Knowledge Bases*, pages 469–482. 1990.
17. P. Materna, P. Sgall, and Z. Hajicova. Linguistic constructions in transparent intensional logic. *Prague Bulletin on Mathematical Linguistics*, pages 27–32, 1985.
18. T. Przytycka. Sparse dynamic programming for maximum agreement subtree problem. In *Mathematical Hierarchies and Biology*, pages 249–264, 1997.
19. B. Shapiro and K. Zhang. Comparing multiple RNA secondary structures using tree comparisons. *Computer Applications in Bioscience*, pages 309–318, 1990.

# Optimal Beam Penetrations in Two and Three Dimensions*

Danny Z. Chen, Xiaobo (Sharon) Hu[1], and Jinhui Xu[2]

[1] Department of Computer Science and Engineering
University of Notre Dame
Notre Dame, IN 46556, USA
{chen,shu}@cse.nd.edu
[2] Department of Computer Science and Engineering
State University of New York at Buffalo
226 Bell Hall Box 602000
Buffalo, NY, 14260, USA
jxu@cse.nd.edu

**Abstract.** The problem of computing an optimal beam among weighted regions (called the *optimal beam problem*) arises in several applied areas such as radiation therapy, stereotactic brain surgery, medical surgery, geological exploration, manufacturing, and environmental engineering. In this paper, we present computational geometry techniques that enable us to develop efficient algorithms for solving various optimal beam problems among weighted regions in two and three dimensions. In particular, we consider two types of problems: the *covering problems* (seeking an optimal beam to *contain* a specified target region), and the *piercing problems* (seeking an optimal beam of a fixed shape to *pierce* the target region). We investigate several versions of these problems, with a variety of beam shapes and target region shapes in 2-D and 3-D. Our algorithms are based on interesting combinations of computational geometry techniques and optimization methods, and transform the optimal beam problems to solving a collection of instances of certain special non-linear optimization problems. Our approach makes use of interesting geometric observations, such as utilizing some new features of Minkowski sums.

## 1  Introduction

In this paper, we study the following geometric optimization problem (called the *optimal beam problem*): Given an $n$-vertex subdivision $R$ in the 2-D (or 3-D) space, divided into $m$ polygonal (or polyhedral) regions $R_i, i = 1, 2, \ldots, m$, find a beam $B$, whose shape may change depending on the directions, such

---

* The research of the first and third authors was supported in part by NSF under Grants CCR-9623585 and CCR-9988468. The research of the second author was supported in part by NSF under Grants MIP-9701416 and CCR-9988468, and by HP Labs, Bristol, England, under an external research program grant. The majority of the research of the third author was done when the author was a graduate student at the CSE Dept., Univ. of Notre Dame, and supported in part by a fellowship from the Center for Applied Mathematics, and by a summer graduate research fellowship from the Graduate School, Univ. of Notre Dame, Notre Dame, Indiana, USA.

D.T. Lee and S.-H. Teng (Eds.): ISAAC 2000, LNCS 1969, pp. 491–502, 2000.
© Springer-Verlag Berlin Heidelberg 2000

that $B$ originates from outside $R$ and intersects a specified *target region* $T \in \{R_1, R_2, \ldots, R_m\}$, and such that the weighted sum $W(B) = \sum_{B \cap R_i \neq \phi} w_i \times f_i(B)$ is minimized. Here, $w_i$ is a weight factor associated with region $R_i$ and $f_i(B)$ is a function defined on the pair $(R_i, B)$. The weights of $T$ and of the free space $\overline{R}$ outside $R$ are normally set to 0. Such a beam is called an *optimal beam*. A beam is the union of a set of rays with a common "source", and the beam shapes can be, for example, strips and sectors in 2-D, and cylinders, cones, and convex polygonal cylinders in 3-D. We denote the sets of vertices and segments of $R$ by $V$ and $S$, respectively. In this paper, we let function $f_i(B)$ represent the area (resp., volume) of $B \cap R_i$ in 2-D (resp., 3-D). We are mainly interested in two kinds of intersection of $B \cap T$: (a) $B$ contains $T$ (see Figure 1(a)), and (b) $B$ pierces $T$ (see Figure 1(b)). We say that $B$ *covers* $T$ if every point of $T$ intersects $B$, and $B$ *pierces* $T$ if every constituent ray of $B$ intersects $T$. Correspondingly, we consider two types of optimal beam problems: (1) the *covering problems* ($B$ is required to contain $T$; the shape of $B$ may be allowed to change for the containment of $T$), and (2) the *piercing problems* ($B$ is required to pierce $T$; the shape of $B$ is usually fixed).

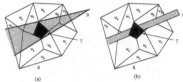

**Fig. 1.** (a) The covering problem. (b) The piercing problem.

The optimal beam problem finds applications in several areas, such as radiation therapy, stereotactic brain surgery, medical surgery, geological exploration, manufacturing, and environmental engineering. In radiation therapy, for example, $R$ may model a portion of a human body, with the regions $R_i$ representing different organs inside $R$ and the target region $T$ representing a tumor. The tumor should be treated by strong radiation, while healthy organs should suffer as less radiation exposure as possible. Due to their own characteristics, different organs may have different degrees of tolerance to radiation, as indicated by their weight factors. Hence, minimizing the total damage to healthy organs is equivalent to finding a beam direction such that the weighted sum of the beam is minimized. Some applications may desire a beam to cover the whole tumor region while allowing the beam shape to change depending on different directions. For a given direction, the beam shape can be determined by the shape of a projection of the tumor with respect to that direction. The piercing problem appears in stereotactic brain surgery and mineral exploration. In stereotactic brain surgery, piercing problems arise in computer/robot-assisted minimally invasive tumor biopsy and draining fluid from cysts, abscesses, and cerebral hemorrhages [11,12]. In mineral exploration, a penetrating beam models a tunnel of a certain shape through a region consisting of various geological structures. Different geological structures may require different costs to penetrate. Therefore, the optimal solution for this problem is a beam direction that incurs the minimum total penetration cost.

A number of results have been obtained on solving the optimal beam and related problems [3,4,5,6,7,8,9,10,13,14,18,19,20,21,22,23,24,30,31]. In radiation therapy (teletherapy), three parameters are considered to be of particular importance: beam fluency distribution (the dose distribution to be delivered to a region of the body), beam energy (the radiation field that produces the dose distribution), and beam directions. Most previous work focuses on optimizing the first two parameters, by assuming that some prespecified beam directions are to be used. But, as discussed in [18], determining optimal beam directions is in practice one of the most difficult problems in radiation treatment optimization. The general beam direction problem is challenging because it may involve multiple beams and may be tangled with other constraints and optimization parameters such as dose distribution and beam energy. The problem considered in this paper is a useful special case of the general beam direction problem.

So far, only a few results on beam direction optimization are known, which can be classified into two classes. The first class [13,18] uses brute-force methods (e.g., try many directions and select the best one among those) or heuristic methods in a discretized beam direction space (e.g., use a function on the points of a grid as an approximation). But, such methods cannot guarantee the optimality of their solutions. The second class [14,26] uses a continuous beam direction space. Schweikard, Adler, and Latombe [26] studied a simplified version of the problem in which the subdivision $R$ consists of three types of regions: (1) the target region $T$, assumed to be a 3-D ball, (2) critical healthy organs, modeled as obstacles (i.e., with a weight factor of $+\infty$), and (3) other normal body structures (with a weight factor of 0). The algorithm in [26] computes a map of all obstacle-avoiding directions for cylinder beams that cover $T$. Recently, Chen *et al.* [14] gave efficient algorithms for finding an optimal penetrating ray among weighted regions in 2-D and 3-D. Note that a ray is a special beam with only a single ray. By making use of some visibility structures, the approach in [14] reduces the ray penetration problem to solving a set of non-linear optimization problems under linear constraints.

In this paper, we extend the study on ray penetrations [14] to beam penetrations. (Clearly, a ray is a very special case of a beam.) We present computational geometry techniques for optimizing a penetrating beam among weighted regions in 2-D and 3-D. Our techniques are based on some interesting mappings, deformations, and arrangements of curves, and utilize certain new features of Minkowski sums. For example, we use the *frame structures* of Minkowski sums which include both the boundary of the Minkowski sums and certain *interior structures*. Our techniques lead to a unified way to partition the continuous beam space into a set of cells, such that the optimization computations for all beams in the same cell have a similar description (i.e., they share the same constraints and objective function). Consequently, an optimal beam problem is reduced to solving a set of instances of a certain special non-linear optimization problem, each on exactly one of the cells in the partitioned beam space. The problem instances on all cells can be efficiently generated in an on-line fashion. We consider various versions of the optimal beam problem, with different shapes of beams and of target regions, and develop efficient geometric algorithms for solving them.

Our results on partitioning the continuous beam space into cells and generating the optimization problem instances are summarized as follows.

- In 2-D, we give $(n \log n + q)$ time algorithms for the piercing problems, and $O(n \log n)$ time algorithms for the covering problems, for a triangulated $R$ of size $O(n)$, where $q$ is an integer between $O(k)$ and $O(n^2)$, and $k$ is the actual total size of the set of partitioned cells ($k$ is upper-bounded by $O(n^2)$). Our algorithms are for the cases in which the beam shape is either a parallel strip or a sector, and the target region $T$ is a polygon or a disk.
- In 3-D, we present $O(N \log N + k_1)$ time algorithms for the covering problems (the beam shape is a cylinder or a cone and $T$ is a ball) and for the piercing problem (the beam shape is a vertical cylinder and $T$ is a simple polyhedron), and an $O(bN \log(bN) + k_2)$ time algorithm for the piercing problem (the beam shape is a $b$-edge vertical convex polygonal cylinder), for a tetrahedralized $R$ of size $O(N)$, where $k_1$ and $k_2$ are respectively the actual total sizes of the sets of resulted cells ($k_1$ is upper-bounded by $O(N^2)$ and $k_2$ is upper-bounded by $O(b^2 N^2)$).

Our algorithms are all deterministic and our analysis is the worst case analysis through out this paper.

We should point out that many versions of the optimal beam problems that we study are motivated by considerations used in practical applications. For example, in radiation therapy, beam shapes of parallel strips and sectors in 2-D and cylinders, cones, and convex polyhedral cylinders in 3-D have been considered (see [18,26,27,29]), and target region shapes of 3-D balls and convex polyhedra have been used to approximate the tumor regions (see [18,26]).

Due to the space limit, we omit from this extended abstract some proofs of lemmas, details of our 2-D covering algorithms, and details of our 3-D algorithms.

## 2    2-D Beam Penetration Algorithms

This section presents a unified approach for handling optimal beam problems in 2-D. This approach enables us to obtain efficient algorithms for several versions of the problems, in which the target region $T$ is either an $m$-vertex convex polygon or a disk, and the beams are either parallel strips or sectors. All our algorithms share the following general steps: (a) Partition the continuous beam space into a set of cells such that the optimization tasks for all beams in the same cell have a similar description (i.e., their objective functions and constraints are the same). (b) Generate the objective function and constraints for every such cell in an on-line fashion, and solve the optimization problem instance on that cell.

In 2-D, since we allow the beam shapes to be a parallel strip or a sector, and the target region $T$ to be a convex polygon[1] or a disk, a covering problem can be classified into one of four types, denoted as CPP, CPS, CDP, and CDS. Here, the first letter C is for "covering", the second letter P (or D) indicates that the target region is a convex polygon (or a disk), and the third letter P (or S) means that the beam shape is a parallel strip (or a sector). Similarly, there are four types of piercing problems, denoted as PPP, PPS, PDP, and PDS.

---

[1] In fact, our solutions hold for $T$ being a simple polygon.

## 2.1  Partitioning the Beam Space

We use a general representation for 2-D beams. Without loss of generality (WLOG), we assume that each beam $B$ originates from a location in the free space $\overline{R}$, called the *beam source* of $B$. $B$ is bounded by two rays, $B_l$ (the left bounding ray) and $B_r$ (the right bounding ray), starting at its source. $B_l$ (resp., $B_r$) intersects a subset of segments of $R$, denoted by $S_{B_l}$ (resp., $S_{B_r}$). We call $S_{B_l}$ and $S_{B_r}$ the *sequences of penetrated segments* of a beam $B$.

Similar to the ray penetration problem in [14], we define a *point order* $\leq_{B_l}$ (resp., $\leq_{B_r}$) for the points on $B_l$ (resp., $B_r$). For any two points $p, q$ on $B_l$, we say $p \leq_{B_l} q$ if a ray starting at $p$ and passing through $q$ is in the same direction as $B_l$. The segments in $S_{B_l}$ (resp., $S_{B_r}$) can be sorted based on the point order of their intersections with $B_l$ (resp., $B_r$), and we assume that $S_{B_l}$ (resp., $S_{B_r}$) is maintained as such a sorted segment sequence. Note that $S_{B_l}$ or $S_{B_r}$ changes only when the beam $B$ is rotated or translated on the plane $P$ such that a segment of $R$ is removed from or added to $S_{B_l}$ or $S_{B_r}$. We say that an *event* occurs if a segment of $R$ is deleted from or inserted to one of $S_{B_l}$ and $S_{B_r}$.

We assume WLOG that each region $R_i$ of $R$ has already been triangulated. Note that for a triangle $\Delta$ of $R$ such that $\Delta \cap B \neq \phi$, either $\Delta \subset B$ or the bounding rays of $B$ cross the boundary $bd(\Delta)$ of $\Delta$ at most four times. In fact, $\Delta \cap B$ is either a triangle, quadrangle, or pentagon, possibly with some vertices of $\Delta \cap B$ being the intersection points of $B_l$ or $B_r$ with $bd(\Delta)$. Consequently, the weighted sum $W(B)$ of $B$ is determined by such triangles, quadrangles, and pentagons inside $B$. If $\Delta \subset B$, then the contribution of $\Delta$ to $W(B)$ is a positive constant (since its vertices are all fixed, the weighted area is a constant). If $\Delta \cap B \neq \phi$ but $\Delta \not\subset B$, then the area of $\Delta \cap B$ depends on the intersection points of $B_l$ or $B_r$ with $bd(\Delta)$; thus the contribution of $\Delta$ to $W(B)$ is a function depending on the positions of $B_l$ and $B_r$ while $B$ is moving. Therefore, $W(B)$ can be described as a function of $B$, whose coefficients are determined by the segments in $S_{B_l} \cup S_{B_r}$, $B_l$ and $B_r$, and the vertices of $R$ inside $B$.

**Lemma 1.** *For any two beams $B$ and $B'$, if their sequences of penetrated segments are the same, i.e., $S_{B_l} = S_{B'_l}$ and $S_{B_r} = S_{B'_r}$, then their objective functions can be similarly described.*

Based on Lemma 1, the continuous beam space can be partitioned into a set of connected components (called *cells*) such that the beams corresponding to the same cell all have the same sequences of penetrated segments. In the special case of $B$ being a ray (i.e., $B_l = B_r$), the union of rays with the same sequence of penetrated segments forms an "hourglass" on the plane $P$ which can be characterized by some visibility structures, as shown in [14]. However, this nice property for rays does not seem to extend to beams in general, since a beam may contain vertices of $R$ in its interior. A key to our solution for the beam problem is to characterize the partitioning of the continuous beam space by an arrangement of some planar curves.

It may be helpful to begin our discussion with the case of a ray. Let $L$ be the line containing a ray and $s = \overline{ab}$ be a segment in $S_L$ on the plane $P$, where $S_L$ denotes the sequence of segments of $R$ intersected by $L$. By the duality transform [25], the set of all lines on $P$ intersecting $s$ is mapped to points in a double cone $DC(s)$ on the dual plane $\overline{P}$. $DC(s)$ is bounded by two lines $a^*$ and

$b^*$ which are the duals of the two endpoints $a$ and $b$ of $s$ respectively, and the two lines $a^*$ and $b^*$ intersect each other at a point $L_{ab}^*$ on $\overline{P}$ that is the dual of the line $L_{ab}$ containing the segment $s = \overline{ab}$ on $P$. Hence for the line $L$, its dual point $L^* \in DC(s)$. This implies that $L^*$ is inside the common intersection of the double cones for all segments in $S_L$. Further, for all lines $L$ on the plane $P$, a partition of their dual points $L^*$ on $\overline{P}$ is the arrangement (see [15,28] for definition) $A(V^*)$, where $V^*$ is the set of the $n$ lines dualized from the set $V$ of the $n$ vertices of $R$; each cell of $A(V^*)$ corresponds to a set of lines $L$ that penetrate the same segment sequence $S_L$ of $R$. Note that $S_L$ changes (i.e., an event occurs) if and only if $L$ is moved to cross a vertex of $R$.

For a beam $B$ that is being translated or rotated, an event occurs if $B_l$ or $B_r$ crosses a vertex of $R$. We let $B_r$ be the *anchor ray* of $B$. To capture all events of $B$ involving $B_r$, we can simply use the arrangement $A(V^*)$ (we denote it as $A_r$), as discussed in the above paragraph (by dualizing the line $L_r$ containing $B_r$ to the point $L_r^*$ on $\overline{P}$). But, to characterize the events of $B$ involving $B_l$, we need to use a different arrangement $A_l$ on $\overline{P}$.

Let $y = mx + p$ and $y = m'x + p'$ be the lines $L_l$ and $L_r$ containing $B_l$ and $B_r$, respectively. We assume that $B_r$ can be completely determined by $B_l$ and by the target region $T$, i.e., $m' = f_T(m,p)$ and $p' = g_T(m,p)$ are some continuous functions on $m$ and $p$ (with respect to $T$). By the duality transform, $L_l$ is mapped to point $L_l^*$ : $(m, -p)$ on $\overline{P}$, and $L_r$ is mapped to point $L_r^*$ : $(f_T(m,p), -g_T(m,p))$.

For a vertex $v = (x_v, y_v)$ of $R$, consider all events of $B$ caused by $L_l$ crossing $v$. Clearly, this involves all possible positions $L_l(v) : y = m_v x + p_v$ of $L_l$ such that $L_l$ contains $v$. For every such line $L_l(v)$, there is a corresponding line $L_r(v)$ : $y = m_v' x + p_v'$, with $m_v' = f_T(m_v, p_v)$ and $p_v' = g_T(m_v, p_v)$. The meaning of the locus of $(m_v', p_v')$ is: Whenever $L_r$ is at a position of $L_r(v) : y = m_v' x + p_v'$, the line $L_l$ for $B_l$ touches vertex $v$. Corresponding to the set of such locus of $(m_v', p_v')$ for $L_r$ ($L_r$ is on $P$), $L_r^*(v)$ : $(f_T(m_v, p_v), -g_T(m_v, p_v))$ is a curve on $\overline{P}$. Let $\Gamma$ be the set of $n$ curves $L_r^*(v_i)$ on $\overline{P}$, for every vertex $v_i$ of $R$. Note that curve $L_r^*(v_i) \in \Gamma$ is the image of a straight line $v_i^* \in V^*$ under the continuous mapping $\Phi = (f_T(m,p), -g_T(m,p))$ (i.e., $L_r^*(v_i)$ is a deformation of $v_i^*$). Let $A(\Gamma)$ be the arrangement of $\Gamma$.

Let $q = L_r^*$ be a point on $\overline{P}$ (i.e., $q$ is the dual of $L_r$). As $q$ moves in $\overline{P}$ (corresponding to $L_r$ as well as $B$ changing on $P$), it may cross the boundaries of $A(V^*)$ or $A(\Gamma)$. When $q$ crosses the boundary of $A(V^*)$ (resp., $A(\Gamma)$), an event of $B$ involving $L_r$ (resp., $L_l$) occurs. Hence, the cells of the overlapping arrangement $A(V^* \cup \Gamma)$ of $A(V^*)$ and $A(\Gamma)$ on $\overline{P}$ capture all events of $B$.

**Lemma 2.** *The 2-D beam space can be partitioned into cells by overlapping arrangements $A(V^*)$ and $A(\Gamma)$ together, such that all beams $B$ in each cell share a similarly described objective function $W(B)$.*

The efficiency of the algorithm for computing the cells of $A(V^* \cup \Gamma)$ depends on the properties of the continuous mapping $\Phi = (f_T(m,p), -g_T(m,p))$. In the next subsection, we shall show that most versions of the problems we study have "nice" mappings, in the sense that any two curves in $V^* \cup \Gamma$ intersect each other only $O(1)$ times. In consequence, $A(V^* \cup \Gamma)$ can be obtained efficiently by using standard arrangement construction algorithms (e.g., [1,2,16,17]).

## 2.2  Beam Space Partitioning for Piercing Problems

We assume that $B_l$ is parameterized as line $L_l : y = mx + p$, and let $\Phi = (f(x,y), g(x,y))$ denote the mapping from $L_l^*$ to $L_r^*$ on $\overline{P}$ after dualizing $L_l$ and $L_r$ on $P$ to $L_l^*$ and $L_r^*$ on $\overline{P}$ (i.e., $\Phi$ maps a line $L_l^*$ to a curve $L_r^*$).

In every 2-D piercing problem, $B_l$ and $B_r$ both intersect the target region $T$. For the PPP and PDP problems, let the beam $B$ be a parallel strip with a fixed width $d$. $B_r$ can be represented by line $L_r : y = mx + p + d\sqrt{1 + m^2}$. After the duality transform, $L_l$ and $L_r$ are mapped to points $L_l^* : (m, -p)$ and $L_r^* : (m, -p - d\sqrt{1 + m^2})$ on $\overline{P}$. Thus the mapping from $L_l^*$ to $L_r^*$ is $\Phi = (f(x,y), g(x,y))$, with $f(x,y) = x$ and $g(x,y) = y - d\sqrt{1 + x^2}$. The following properties are useful to our algorithms for the PPP and PDP problems.

*Property 1.* For a PPP or PDP problem, every curve in $\Gamma \cup V^*$ is $x$-monotone, any two curves in $\Gamma$ intersect each other at most once, and each curve $C_i \in \Gamma$ intersects any line $L_j \in V^*$ at most twice.

Since all curves in $\Gamma \cup V^*$ are algebraic curves with $O(1)$ pairwise intersections, by using the algorithm in [1], the arrangement $A(\Gamma \cup V^*)$ can be computed in $O(n \log n + k)$ time and $O(n + k)$ space. Thus, we have the following lemma.

**Lemma 3.** *For every PPP or PDP problem, the beam space can be partitioned into cells with similar problem descriptions in $O(n \log n + k)$ time and $O(n + k)$ space, where $k$ is the complexity of the set of cells which in worst case is $O(n^2)$.*

For a PDS or PPS problem, we consider the cases in which the beam source $s$ moves along a circle $Cl$ enclosing $R$ (note that this assumption is often valid in radiation therapy applications) or a line $L_s$ outside $R$, and have below properties.

*Property 2.* For a PDS or PPS problem whose beam source $s$ moves along a circle enclosing $R$, the pairwise intersections of any two curves in $V^* \cup \Gamma$ is $\leq 4$.

*Property 3.* The beam space of a PDS or PPS problem whose beam source $s$ moves along a straight line outside $R$ can be partitioned into two half-planes, $\overline{P}_-$ and $\overline{P}_+$, and in each of the two half-planes, any two curves in $V^* \cup \Gamma$ intersect each other at most twice.

**Lemma 4.** *For every PPS or PDS problem with the beam source moving along a circle enclosing $R$ or a straight line outside $R$, the beam space can be partitioned into cells with similar optimization problem descriptions in $O(n \log n + k)$ time and $O(n + k)$ space, where $k$ is the complexity of the set of cells with $k \leq O(n^2)$.*

## 2.3  Generating the Objective Functions and Constraints

In Sections 2.1 and 2.2, the cells of the beam space for a piercing problem are produced by overlapping the two arrangements $A(V^*)$ and $A(\Gamma)$. The constraints for the optimization task on each cell $C$ are defined by the boundary edges of $C$ in the arrangement $A(V^* \cup \Gamma)$, which are available once $A(V^* \cup \Gamma)$ is constructed. Thus our focus is on the generation of the objective functions for the cells.

As shown in the previous sections, coming up with the objective function $W(B)$ for a beam $B$ involves using the two sequences of penetrated segments $S_{B_l}$ and $S_{B_r}$ and the set of triangles $B_\Delta$ intersected by $B$. Computing $W(B)$ for a single cell may certainly take $O(n)$ time, but paying a price of $O(n)$ time on every cell is too costly. To efficiently generate the objective function for each cell, we use an algorithm which reports the objective functions one after another while it traverses on the cells of $A(V^* \cup \Gamma)$. When traversing from a cell $C_1$ to the next cell $C_2$, $S_{B_l}$, $S_{B_r}$, and $B_\Delta$ are dynamically maintained, and the objective function for $C_1$ is updated to obtain the objective function for $C_2$. The algorithm visits the cells of $A(V^* \cup \Gamma)$ in such a way that two consecutively visited cells share a common edge of $A(V^* \cup \Gamma)$. This edge-sharing traversal makes the amortized computational cost on each cell small.

To see why this is true, let us consider the arrangement $A(V^*)$ associated with $B_r$. Assume that each vertex $v \in R$ stores a doubly-linked adjacency list $v_{adj}$ for all segments of $R$ adjacent to $v$, sorted in the angular order around $v$. The segments in $S_{B_r}$ are sorted based on the point order $\leq_{B_r}$. For each $\overline{uv} \in S_{B_r}$, we maintain two pointers to its positions in $u_{adj}$ and $v_{adj}$, respectively.

Suppose that we are to update $S_{B_r}$ while entering the cell $C_2$ from its neighboring $C_1$ by crossing an edge $\overline{ab}$ of $A(V^*)$. Let $v^*$ be the line containing $\overline{ab}$, and $u^*$ and $w^*$ be the other two lines in $A(V^*)$ that generate $a$ and $b$ with $v^*$, respectively. Obviously, $v^*$, $u^*$, and $w^*$ are all dualized respectively from vertices (say) $v$, $u$, and $w$ of $R$. Note that segment $\overline{ab}$ of $A(V^*)$ (on $\overline{P}$) corresponds to a double-cone $DC(\overline{ab})$ on $P$ with vertex $v$ and two bounding lines $a^*$ and $b^*$, where $a^*$ and $b^*$ are the two dual lines of $a$ and $b$ respectively. $DC(\overline{ab})$ contains all possible positions of $B_r$ (on $P$) whose duals are on $\overline{ab}$. By the duality transform, $u$ and $w$ are incident to $a^*$ and $b^*$ respectively. Moving the point $B_r^*$ on $\overline{P}$ in the cell $C_1$ to cross $\overline{ab}$ and enter the cell $C_2$ is equivalent to moving $B_r$ outside $DC(\overline{ab})$ on $P$. Such a movement changes the sequence of segments of $R$ penetrated by $B_r$. Let $v_{B_r}$ be the set of segments in $S_{B_r}$ that are adjacent to $v$. Observe that all segments in $v_{B_r}$ appear consecutively in $S_{B_r}$. Thus $v_{B_r}$ is a consecutive sublist of $v_{adj}$. (Note that this is true only for the vertices of $R$ whose duals contribute an edge to the boundary of $C_1$; for other vertices, say $u$, $u_{B_r}$ need not be consecutive in $S_{B_r}$.) Since $\overline{ab}$ is an edge of $A(V^*)$, there is no vertex of $R$ in the interior of $DC(\overline{ab})$ (otherwise $\overline{ab}$ would be split by the dual lines of such vertices). Hence $B_r^*$ crossing $\overline{ab}$ makes all segments in $v_{adj}$ which are previously not penetrated by $B_r$ become penetrated and all segments in $v_{B_r}$ become no longer penetrated. Therefore, updating $S_{B_r}$ can be easily done by replacing $v_{B_r}$ with $v_{adj} - v_{B_r}$. Since both $v_{adj}$ and $S_{B_r}$ are maintained as doubly-linked lists, this updating can be done in $O(1)$ time per segment in $v_{adj}$. Thus, the total time for updating $S_{B_r}$ is $O(deg(v))$, where $deg(v)$ is the degree of the vertex $v$ in $R$.

For the arrangement $A(\Gamma)$ associated with $B_l$, since $A(\Gamma)$ is mapped from $A(V^*)$ by the continuous mapping $\Phi$, each edge $e$ of $A(\Gamma)$ is mapped from a portion of an edge $e'$ in $A(V^*)$. By maintaining a pointer to $e'$ for each edge $e$ in $A(\Gamma)$, $S_{B_l}$ can be updated in a similar way as $S_{B_r}$.

Our algorithm for the arrangement $A(V^* \cup \Gamma)$ is as follows. First, it traverses the cells of $A(V^* \cup \Gamma)$ such that any two consecutively visited cells share an edge of $A(V^* \cup \Gamma)$. Then, for each crossed edge $e$, we update either $S_{B_r}$ or $S_{B_l}$, depending on which arrangement $e$ appears, and pay a price $O(deg(v))$, where $e$ is on the dual or deformed dual of $v$. Summing over all cells of $A(V^* \cup \Gamma)$, we have the following lemma.

**Lemma 5.** *For each 2-D piercing problem whose mapping $\Phi$ is continuous and whose curves in $V^* \cup \Gamma$ have $O(1)$ pairwise intersections, the sequences $S_{B_l}$ and $S_{B_r}$ can be maintained in altogether $O(n \log n + q)$ time when traversing the cells of $A(\Gamma \cup V^*)$, where $k \leq q \leq O(n^2)$, and $k$ is the size of $A(\Gamma \cup V^*)$.*

**Remark:** In above lemma, $q$ depends on the walk of $A(V^* \cup \Gamma)$. A good traversal which normally leads to a fast solution can be obtained by using the Euler tour on a minimum spanning tree $T$ of the dual graph $G$ of $A(V^* \cup \Gamma)$.

Observe that crossing an edge $e$ of $A(V^* \cup \Gamma)$ also changes the set $B_\Delta$ of triangles intersected by the beam $B$. Let $e$ be the common edge of two neighboring cells $C_i$ and $C_j$ in $A(V^* \cup \Gamma)$. Then the value difference between the numbers of such triangles for the two cells $C_i$ and $C_j$ is bounded by $O(deg(v))$ (since each penetrated segment bounds at most two triangles). For each triangle $\Delta$ that is newly added to $B_\Delta$, we compute the function for the weighted area of $B \cap \Delta$, which can be done in $O(1)$ time, and store this function along with $\Delta$, until $\Delta$ is later deleted from $B_\Delta$. The objective function for the cell of $A(V^* \cup \Gamma)$ that is currently being visited is the summation of such functions over all penetrated triangles. Therefore, the total time used for obtaining the objective function for $C_j$ by updating the (previous) objective function for $C_i$ is at most $O(deg(v))$. Thus we have the following lemma.

**Lemma 6.** *The objective functions $W(B)$ for each 2-D piercing problem we consider can be computed for all cells of $A(V^* \cup \Gamma)$ in $O(n \log n + q)$ time.*

The exact form of $W(B)$ depends on the types of the problems we consider. The objective function for the PPP and PDP problems has the following form: $W(B) = C_0 + \sum_{\Delta_i \in B_\Delta} \frac{c_i y^2 + d_i y + e_i y \sqrt{1+x^2} + f_i x^2 + g_i}{x - h_i}$, where $C_0, c_i, d_i, e_i, f_i$, and $h_i$ are constants depending on the weights of triangles in $B_\Delta$, $S_{B_l}$, and $S_{B_r}$. The objective functions for other piercing problems can be similarly obtained.

**Theorem 1.** *Every 2-D piercing problem we consider can be solved in $O(n \log n + q + \sum_{i=1}^{O(n+k)} T_i)$ time and $O(n+k+S_{max})$ space, where $T_i$ is the time for solving the special non-linear optimization problem instance on cell $C_i$ of $A(V^* \cup \Gamma)$, $S_{max}$ is the maximum space needed for solving each of the special optimization problem instances on all the cells of $A(V^* \cup \Gamma)$, $k$ is the size of $A(V^* \cup \Gamma)$, and $k \leq q \leq O(n^2)$.*

## 3   3-D Beam Penetration Algorithms

In this section, we sketch efficient algorithms for solving several optimal beam penetration problems in 3-D. Our solutions are based on a unified approach for such 3-D problems, and make use of special contact surfaces and some interior structures of *Minkowski sums*.

### 3.1   Partitioning the Beam Space

We assume that $R$ has been tetrahedralized, with $N$ tetrahedra (and thus $O(N)$ edges and vertices). The beam shapes can be a cylinder, cone, or convex polygonal cylinder. We consider four versions of problems in 3-D. The first two are covering problems which seek an optimal penetration for a cylinder beam or a cone beam to cover a ball $T$, denoted as CBC and CBN, respectively. For the CBN problem, we assume that the beam source $s$ moves on a sphere $S_O$ that contains $R$ and has the same center $o$ as $T$. The other two are piercing problems in which the target $T$ is a (possibly unbounded) polyhedral region, and we seek an optimal *vertical* penetration for a cylinder beam or a convex polygonal cylinder beam. We denote these two problems as PVC and PVP, respectively. The following lemma is a key observation to our algorithms.

**Lemma 7.** *For any two beams $B$ and $B'$ in a CBC, CBN, or PVC problem, if they penetrate the same sequence of tetrahedra of $R$ as well as the same sequence of $0, 1$, and $2$-faces in each penetrated tetrahedron, then their objective functions (i.e., sums of weighted volumes) can be similarly described.*

Hence, our objective in solving the CBC, CBN, and PVC problems is to partition their beam space into cells such that the beams in each cell penetrate the same sequence of tetrahedra and the same sequence of $0, 1, 2$-faces in each penetrated tetrahedron.

For a CBC or CBN problem, we use the contact surfaces of the beam with respect to the vertices and segments in $R$ to partition the beam space. The contact surfaces of $B$ and a vertex $v$ (or segment $e$) is the loci of $B$'s source $s$ on $S_O$ while moving $s$ such that the boundary of $B$ remains in contact with (or tangent to) $v$ (or $e$). The contact surfaces form certain curves on $S_O$ and we denote the set of such curves for all vertices and segments of $R$ as $\Gamma$.

For a PVC or PVP problem, we use the Minkowski sum structure. Specifically, we project vertically each vertex and segment of $R$ to a horizontal plane $P$, and compute the Minkowski sums of these projected vertices and segments with the vertical projection of $B$. For the PVP problem, other new features (e.g., the interior structure) of Minkowski sums will also be needed. (An example of the interior structure is shown in Figure 2, where (b) is the frame structure, formed by the contour and the interior structure of the Minkowski sums, of the dashed segment $e$ and the convex polygon in (a).) The boundary curves and the interior structure of all such Minkowski sums together form a set $\Gamma$ of curves on the plane $P$, and the arrangement $A(\Gamma)$ partitions the beam space.

We following lemma holds for the four types of 3-D problems.

**Lemma 8.** *The beam space of a CBC, CBN or PVC problem (or a PVP problem) can be partitioned into a set of cells with similar optimization problem descriptions by computing the arrangement $A(\Gamma)$ on the sphere $S_O$ or plane $P$ (or plane $P$) with a time complexity $O(N \log N + k_1)$ (or $O(bN \log(bN) + k_2)$) and space complexity $O(N + k_1)$ (or $O(bN + k_2)$), where $k_1$ (or $k_2$) is the complexity of the set of cells which in worst case is $O(N^2)$ (or $O(b^2 N^2)$), and $b$ is the number of vertical edges of the beam in a PVP problem.*

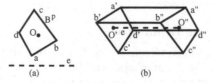

**Fig. 2.** The frame structure of segment $e$ and a convex polygon $B^p$.

## 3.2 Generating Objective Functions and Constraints

To efficiently generate the objective functions for all cells of $A(\Gamma)$, we take a walk on the cells of $A(\Gamma)$, and dynamically maintain the sets of vertices, segments, triangles, and tetrahedra penetrated by beams in each cell. The objective function for the currently visiting cell is obtained from an updating of a previously visited cell. Using an interesting cost-charging scheme, we are able to show that the amortized cost for generating the objective function for each cell is $O(1)$. Thus, we have the following theorem.

**Theorem 2.** *A CBC, CBN, or PVC problem can be solved in $O(N \log N + k_1 + \sum_{i=1}^{O(N+k_1)} T_i)$ time and $O(N + k_1 + S_{max})$ space, and a 3-D PVP problem can be solved in $O(bN \log(bN) + k_2 + \sum_{i=1}^{O(bN+k_2)} T_i)$ time and $O(bN + k_2 + S_{max})$ space, where $T_i$ is the time for solving the special non-linear optimization problem instance on cell $C_i$ and $S_{max}$ is the maximum space for solving one of such problem instance.*

**Acknowledgments.** The authors are very grateful to Dr. Cedric Yu, Department of Radiation Oncology, School of Medicine, University of Maryland at Baltimore, for discussing the problems with us and for providing many useful references. The authors also like to thank Dr. Ovidiu Daescu for some helpful discussions.

## References

1. Amato, N.M., Goodrich, M.T., Ramos, E.A.: Computing the arrangement of curve segments: Divide-and-conquer algorithms via sampling. *Proc. 11th Annual ACM-SIAM Symposium on Discrete Algorithms* (2000) 705–706.
2. Asano, T., Guibas, L.J., Tokuyama, T.: Walking in an arrangement topologically. *Int. J. of Computational Geometry and Applications* 4 (1994) 123–151.
3. Bahr, G.K., Kereiakes, J.G., Horowitz, H., Finney, R., Galvin, J., Goode, K.: The method of linear programming applied to radiation treatment planning. *Radiology* 91 (1968) 686–693.
4. Bortfeld, T., Bürkelbach, J., Boesecke, R., Schlegel, W.: Methods of image reconstruction from projections applied to conformation radiotherapy. *Phys. Med. Biol.* 38 (1993) 291–304.
5. Bortfeld, T., Schlegel, W.: Optimization of beam orientations radiation therapy: Some theoretical considerations. *Phys. Med. Biol.* 35 (1990) 1423–1434.
6. Boyer, A.L., Bortfeld, T.R., Kahler, L., Waldron, T.J.: MLC modulation of x-ray beams in discrete steps. *Proc. 11th Conf. on the Use of Computers in Radiation Therapy* (1994) 178–179.
7. Boyer, A.L., Desobry, G.E., Wells, N.H.: Potential and limitations of invariant kernel conformal therapy. *Med. Phys.* 18 (1991) 703–712.
8. Brahme, A.: Optimization of stationary and moving beam radiation therapy techniques. *Radiother. Oncol.* 12 (1988) 129–140.
9. Brahme, A.: Inverse radiation therapy planning: Principles and possibilities. *Proc. 11th Conf. on the Use of Computers in Radiation Therapy* (1994) 6–7.
10. Brahme, A.: Optimization of radiation therapy. *Int. J. Radiat. Oncol. Biol. Phys.* 28 (1994) 785–787.

11. Bucholz, R.D.: Introduction to the journal of image guided surgery. *Journal of Image Guided Surgery* 1(1) (1995) 1–11.
12. Burckhardt, C.W., Flury, P., Glauser, D.: Stereotactic brain surgery. *IEEE Engineering in Medicine and biology* 14(3) (1995) 314–317.
13. Censor, Y., Altschuler, M.D., Powlis, W.D.: A computational solution of the inverse problem in radiation-therapy treatment planning. *Applied Math. and Computation* **25** (1988) 57–87.
14. Chen, D.Z., Daescu, O., Hu, X.S., Wu, X., Xu, J.: Determining an optimal penetration among weighted regions in two and three dimensions. *Proc. 15th ACM Annual Symposium on Computational Geometry* (1999) 322-331.
15. Edelsbrunner, H.: *Algorithms in Combinatorial Geometry*, Springer-Verlag, New York, 1987.
16. Edelsbrunner, H., Guibas, L.J.: Topologically sweeping an arrangement. *Journal of Computer and System Sciences* **38** (1989) 165–194.
17. Edelsbrunner, H., Guibas, L.J., Pach, J., Pollack, R., Seidel, R., Sharir, M.: Arrangements of curves in the plane: Topology, combinatorics, and algorithms. *Theoretical Computer Science* **92** (1992) 319–336.
18. Gustafsson, A., Lind, B.K., Brahme, A.: A generalized pencil beam algorithm for optimization of radiation therapy. *Med. Phys.* **21** (1994) 343–356.
19. Holmes, T., Mackie, T.R.: A comparison of three inverse treatment planning algorithms. *Phys. Med. Biol.* **39** (1994) 91–106.
20. Legras, J., Legras, B., Lambert, J.P., Aletti, P.: The use of a microcomputer for non-linear optimization of doses in external radiotherapy. *Phys. Med. Biol.* **31** (1986) 1353–1359.
21. Lind, B.K.: Properties of an algorithm for solving the inverse problem in radiation therapy. *Proc. 9th Int. Conf. on the Use of Computers in Radiation Therapy* (1987) 235–239.
22. Lind, B.K., Brahme, A.: Optimization of radiation therapy dose distributions with scanned photon beams. *Inv. Prob.* **16** (1990) 415–426.
23. McDonald, S.C., Rubin, P.: Optimization of external beam radiation therapy. *Int. J. Radiat. Oncol. Biol. Phys.* **2** (1977) 307–317.
24. Powlis, W.D., Altschuler, M.D., Censor, Y., Buhle, E.L.: Semi-automated radiotherapy treatment planning with a mathematical model to satisfy treatment goals. *Int. J. Radiat. Oncol. Biol. Phys.* **16** (1989) 271–276.
25. Preparata, F. P., Shamos, M. I.: *Computational Geometry: An Introduction*, Springer-Verlag, New York, 1985.
26. Schweikard, A., Adler, J.R., Latombe, J.-C.: Motion planning in stereotaxic radiosurgery. *IEEE Trans. on Robotics and Automation* **9** (1993) 764–774.
27. Schweikard, A., Tombropoulos, R., Kavraki, L., Adler, J.R., Latombe, J.-C.: Treatment planning for a radiosurgical system with general kinematics. *Proc. IEEE Int'l Conference on Robotics and Automation* (1994) 1720–1727.
28. Sharir, M., Agarwal, P.K.: *Davenport-Schinzel Sequences and Their Geometric Applications*, Cambridge University Press, 1995.
29. Tombropoulos, R.Z., Adler, J.R., Latombe, J.-C.: CARABEAMER: A treatment planner for a robotic radiosurgical system with general kinematics. *Medical Image Analysis* **3** (1999) 1–28.
30. Webb, S.: Optimization of conformal radiotherapy dose distributions by simulated annealing. *Phys. Med. Biol.* **34** (1989) 1349–1369.
31. Webb, S.: Optimizing the planning of intensity-modulated radiotherapy. *Phys. Med. Biol.* **39** (1994) 2229–2246.

# Searching a Simple Polygon by a $k$-Searcher

Xuehou Tan

Tokai University, Numazu 410-0321, Japan

**Abstract.** The *polygon search problem* is the problem of searching for
a mobile intruder in a simple polygon by the mobile searcher who holds
flashlights and whose visibility is limited to the rays emanating from his
flashlights. The goal is to decide whether there exists a *search schedule* for
the searcher to detect the intruder, no matter how fast he moves, and if
so, generate such a schedule. A searcher is called the $k$-*searcher* if he can
see along $k$ rays emanating from his position, and the $\infty$-*searcher* if he has
a $360^0$ field of vision. We present necessary and sufficient conditions for a
polygon to be searchable by a $k$-searcher (for $k = 1$ or 2), and give $O(n^2)$
time algorithms for testing the k-searchability of simple polygons and
generating a search schedule if it exists. We also show that any polygon
that is searchable by an $\infty$-searcher is searchable by a 2-searcher. Our
results solve a long-standing open problem in computational geometry
and robotics, and confirm a conjecture due to Suzuki and Yamashita.

## 1 Introduction

In recent years, much attention has been devoted to the problem of searching for
a mobile intruder in a polygonal region $P$ by the mobile searcher who holds flashlights and whose visibility is limited to the rays emanating from his flashlights [2,
4,5,8,9,11,12,15,16]. The goal is to decide whether there exists a *search schedule*
for the searcher to detect the intruder, no matter how fast he moves, and if so,
generate such a schedule. This problem, called the *polygon search problem*, was
introduced by Suzuki and Yamashita [11]. Both the searcher and the intruder
are modeled by points that can move continuously in $P$. A searcher is called the
$k$-searcher if he has $k$ flashlights, where $k$ is a positive integer, and can see along
the rays emanating from his flashlights, or the $\infty$-searcher if he has a light bulb
and is of a 360° field of vision. The searcher can rotate a flashlight continuously
with bounded speed to change its direction. A polygon is said *searchable* by a
given searcher if a search schedule exists.

An important motivation of studying the polygon search problem stems from
robotics applications. Suppose that a building security system involes a mobile
robot equipped with cameras or range sensors that can detect a mobile intruder.
A patrolling route should be planned that guarantees that any intruder will
eventually be found, if it exists. The search target need not be adversarial. For
example, it might be another mobile robot, or even a person in a search/rescue
effort. More applications can be envisioned for the problem of searching for
mobile intruders in a polygonal environment [3]. Besides, the polygon search
problem can be considered as a dynamic version of the *watchman route problem*,

D.T. Lee and S.-H. Teng (Eds.): ISAAC 2000, LNCS 1969, pp. 503–514, 2000.

which asks for a shortest route such that each point in the interior of the polygon can be seen from at least one point along the route [1,13,14].

Suzuki and Yamashita gave a simple necessary condition for a polygon to be searchable by a $k$-searcher, which states that no polygon $P$ is 1-searchable ($\infty$-searchable) if there are three points in $P$ such that no point in the Euclidean shortest path between any pair of points is visible (link-2-visible) to the third. But, it is not sufficient. Guibas *et al.* presented a complete algorithm for generating a search schedule, if it exists, for an $\infty$-searcher [5]. However, the time complexity of their algorithm is unknown. It is even suspected that the problem of deciding whether a polygon is searchable lies in $NP$ [5]. Very recently, LaValle *et al.* made a new progress on this problem [8]. They succeeded in developing a search schedule for a 1-searcher, without explicitly giving the characterization of the polygons to be 1-searchable. Due to the limit of their method, it is not an easy work to analyze the performace of their algorithm. Moreover, their method does not immediately imply a solution to the polygon search problem in the case where the searcher holds $k$ flashlights, $k > 1$. In the special case that there are an entrance and an exit on the boundary of the given polygon, which is called the *two-guard problem* or the *corridor search problem*, necessary and sufficient conditions have been found by several groups of researchers [2,6,7,15]. Recently, the problem is solved in the situation where only a door (entrance or exit) on the polygon boundary is given [9]. Since the intruder should be either kept untouched to a given door or evicted through it, the problems with doors become simpler.

Despite of the importance of the problem and a number of attempts to solve it, the problem of characterizing the class of polygons to be searchable by a single searcher has stayed open until now [5,9,10,11]. Suzuki and Yamashita also made a conjecture that any polygon that is searchable by an $\infty$-searcher is searchable by a 2-searcher.

The main contribution of this paper is to characterize the class of the polygons to be $k$-searchable, for $k = 1$ or 2, and show that any polygon that is searchable by an $\infty$-searcher is searchable by a 2-searcher. In addition to the necessary condition given by Suzuki and Yamashita, we establish the other, which states that no polygon $P$ is $k$-searchable if for each vertex $a$, there are two vertices $b$, $c$ such that any search schedule starting at $a$ becomes *trivial* (i.e., the regions have been exploited at two different times are identical) when $b$ or $c$ is cleared. To show that the same conditions are sufficient, we first observe that a successful search schedule should start at a vertex $d$ that demolishes the second condition and thus $d$ can be considered as a *pseudo-door* (the intruder can visit it, but he cannot leave polygon $P$ through it). It is important because we are now able to identify the order of critical visibility events occurred in the search schedule starting at $d$. The concept of *essential cuts*, which is widely used in the solutions to the watchman route and related problems [1,13,14], can be adopted to give these events. Based on the computed events, we can then decompose the search schedule into some instances of two-guard or corridor search problem and rotations of rays of the flashlights dynamically. All of these ideas give a reasonably simple and elegant characterization, although the proof consists of a rather technical case analysis.

# 2  Preliminary

We will first give basic definitions for the polygon search problem, and then review the well-known two-guard problem [2,6,7,15].

## 2.1  Basic Definitions

Let $P$ denote a simple polygon in the plane, i.e., a polygon without selfintersections or holes. For convenience, we assume that the given polygon $P$ is in a general position in the plane. That is, no three vertices of $P$ are collinear, and no three edge extensions have a common point. Two points $x$, $y \in P$ are said to be mutually *visible* if the line segment $\overline{xy}$ connecting them is entirely contained in $P$. For two regions $R$, $Q \subseteq P$, we say that $R$ is *weakly visible* from $Q$ if every point in $R$ is visible from some point in $Q$.

Let $s(t)$ denote the position of a $k$-searcher and $f_1(t)$, ..., $f_k(t)$ the positions of endpoints of his flashlights on the boundary of $P$ at time $t$, respectively. A point $x \in P$ is said to be *detected* (or *illuminated*) at time $t$ if $x$ lies on one of the line segments $\overline{s(t)f_1(t)}$, ..., $\overline{s(t)f_k(t)}$. Any region that might contain the intruder at a time (whose position is unknown to the searcher as he is capable of moving arbitrarily fast) is said to be *contaminated*; otherwise it is said to be *clear*. A *search schedule* of the $k$-searcher for $P$ is a tuple $S =< s, f_1, \cdots, f_k >$ of $k + 1$ continuous functions $s$, $f_1$, ..., $f_k \colon [0,1] \to P$ such that the intruder is located at at least one of $\overline{s(1)f_1(1)}$, ..., $\overline{s(1)f_k(1)}$, no matter how he moves. A schedule of the $\infty$-searcher can be given analogously [11]. Polygon $P$ is said to be $k$-searchable (or $\infty$-searchable) if there exists a search schedule of the $k$-searcher (or $\infty$-searcher) for $P$.

A search schedule is *trivial* if the cleared regions at time $t_1$ degenerate into the line segments $\overline{s(t_1)f_1(t_1)}$, ..., $\overline{s(t_1)f_k(t_1)}$, or are identical to those at time $t_2$, where $0 < t_1, t_2 < 1$.

**Observation 1.** Polygon $P$ is searchable if and only if there is a non-trivial search schedule for $P$.

## 2.2  Two-Guard Walkability of Simple Polygons

Given a simple polygon $P$ with two marked vertices $u$ and $v$, the two-guard problem asks if there is a walk in $P$ such that two guards $l$ and $r$ move along two polygonal chains $L$ and $R$ oriented form $u$ to $v$, one clockwise and the other counterclockwise, in such a way that $l$ and $r$ are always mutually visible. For two points $p, p' \in L$, we say that $p$ *precedes* $p'$ (and $p'$ *succeeds* $p$) if we encounter $p$ before $p'$ when traversing $L$ from $s$ to $t$. We write $p < p'$. The definition for $R$ is symmetric. Let $l(t)$ and $r(t)$ denote the moving functions of two guards $l$ and $r$ on $L$ and $R$, respectively. A *walk* in polygon $P$ can then be formulated as a pair of continuous functions $l : [0,1] \to L$ and $r : [0,1] \to R$, where $l(0) = r(0) = u$, $l(1) = r(1) = v$, and $l(x)$ and $r(x)$ are mutually visible for all $x$. Any line segment $\overline{l(x)r(x)}$ is called a *walk segment*. Also, a *walk in $P$ from a walk segment $\overline{p_0 q_0}$ to the other $\overline{p_1 q_1}$*, where $p_0 < p_1$ and $q_0 < q_1$, has to fulfill the conditions $l(0) = p_0$, $r(0) = q_0$, $l(1) = p_1$ and $r(1) = q_1$.

For a vertex $x$ of a polygonal chain, let $Succ(x)$ denote the vertex of the chain immediately succeeding $x$, and $Pred(x)$ the vertex immediately preceding $x$. A vertex of $P$ is *reflex* if its interior angle is greater than 180°; otherwise, it is *convex*. An important definition for reflex vertices is that of *ray shots*: the backward ray shot from a reflex vertex $r$ of chain $L$ or $R$, denoted by $Backw(r)$, is the first point of $P$ hit by a "bullet" shot at $r$ in the direction from $Succ(r)$ to $r$, and the forward ray shot $Forw(r)$ is the first point hit by the bullet shot at $r$ in the direction from $Pred(r)$ to $r$. We define the orientation of the line segment $\overline{rBackw(r)}$ or $\overline{rForw(r)}$ as from $r$ to $Backw(r)$ or $Forw(r)$ (Fig. 1). A pair of reflex vertices $p \in L$, $q \in R$ is said to form a *deadlock* if $q < Backw(p) \in R$ and $p < Backw(q) \in L$ hold or if $q > Forw(p) \in R$ and $p > Forw(q) \in L$ hold. See Fig. 1.

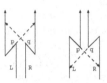

**Fig. 1.** Deadlocks.

**Lemma 1** *[7,6] A simple polygon $P$ is walkable if and only if the chains $L$ and $R$ are mutually weakly visible and no deadlocks occur. Furthermore, it takes $\theta(n)$ time to test the two-walkability of a simple polygon, and $O(n \log n + k)$ time to generate a search schedule where $k$ ($\leq n^2$) is the minimal number of search instructions.*

## 3    Necessary and Sufficient Conditions for 1-Searchable Polygons

A search instruction of a 1-searcher is one of the following elementary actions [11, 15]: (i) Both the searcher $s$ and the endpoint $f_1$ of his flashlight move forward along segments of single edges, (ii) one moves forward but the other moves backward along segments of single edges, and (iii) $s$ or $f_1$ jumps from one point $x$ (it should be a reflex vertex) on the boundary of $P$ to the other point $y$ such that the ray between $s$ and $f_1$ is extended. (For $s$ to jump from $x$ to $y$, it means that the searcher fixes the flashlig and then moves from $x$ to $y$ [11].) See Fig. 2.

Both $s$ and $f_1$ move continuously on the boundary of polygon $P$ for a search instruction (i) or (ii), while $s$ or $f_1$ moves discontinuously on the boundary of $P$ for a search instruction (iii). The first two instructions of a 1-searcher are allowed for two guards, if we regard $s$ and $f_1$ as two guards $l$ and $r$. But, the last one is not. It then follows that any polygon that is walkable by two guards is 1-searchable. However, the converse is not true.

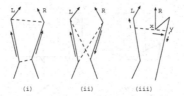

**Fig. 2.** Search instructions of a 1-searcher.

The role of instructions (iii) is to allow the ray of the flashlight to move backwards "jumping over a dent", i.e., make the corner between $x$ and $y$ in Fig. 2 be *recontaminated*. (If a region becomes contaminated for the second or more time, it is referred to as *recontaminated*.) So an instruction (iii) should be followed by an instruction (ii), as shown by dotted arrows in Fig. 2. For simplicity, we refer to a *ray rotation* as an instruction (ii) or (iii) or a set of continuous instructions (ii) and/or (iii). Observe that any ray rotation involving an instruction (iii) is not reversible. As we will see, such irreversible recontaminations are necessary for the polygon search problem. On the contrary, all recontaminations occurred in the execution of a search schedule of two guards (i.e., clearing a wedge in [7]) are reversible.

We will present two necessary conditions for a polygon to be 1-searchable and then show that the same conditions are sufficient. Without loss of generality, we assume that a search schedule of the 1-searcher starts at some point (vertex) $a$ of the boundary of $P$. Let us order the points on the polygon boundary by a counterclockwise scan of the boundary of $P$, starting at $a$. For a complete ordering, we consider the point $a$ as two points $a_l$ and $a_r$ such that $a_l \leq p \leq a_r$, for all points $p$ in the boundary of $P$.

Similar definitions can be given as those in the previous section. For a vertex $x$ of $P$, $Succ(x)$ denotes the vertex succeeding $x$, and $Pred(x)$ the vertex immediately preceding $x$. For a reflex vertex $r$, the backward and forward ray shots $Backw(r)$ and $Forw(r)$ are the first points of $P$ hit by the bullets shot at $r$ in the directions from $Succ(r)$ to $r$ and from $Pred(r)$ to $r$, respectively. Note that all points visible to both $Pred(r)$ and $Backw(r)$ are contained in the interval $[Forw(r), Backw(r)]$, and that if $a$ is not contained in $[Forw(r), Backw(r)]$, then $Forw(r) < Backw(r)$. Analogously, a deadlock between two disjoint chains can be defined. (Since the points on the boundary of $P$ are now ordered from $a_l$ to $a_r$, the inequalities for deadlocks should be accordingly changed.)

Before characterizing the polygons to be 1-searchable, we first give several classes of the polygons which are not 1-searchable. The first example shown in Fig. 3a satisfies the necessary condition given by Suzuki and Yamashita [11] that there are three points $p_1$, $p_2$ and $p_3$ in the polygon such that no point of the shortest path between any pair of points is visible to the third. Although other three examples shown in Fig. 3b-d do not satisfy the above condition, they are not 1-searchable, either. (It is actually shown in [11] that the polygons given in Figs. 3c-d are not 1-searchable. It will be shown by Theorem 1 that the polygon given Fig. 3b is not 1-searchable.) Observe that any search schedule starting at $a$ for the polygon shown in Fig. 3b becomes trivial when the vertex $Succ(v_1)$ or

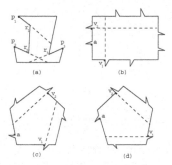

**Fig. 3.** The polygons which are not 1-searchable.

$Pred(v_2)$ is cleared, and for the polygon shown in Fig. 3c (Fig. 3d) has to clear first $Succ(v_2)$ $(Pred(v_1))$ and then $Succ(v_1)$ $(Pred(v_2))$. Our second necessary condition is derived from this observation.

**Theorem 1** *Polygon $P$ is not 1-searchable if one of the following conditions is true.*

*(**A1**) There are three points in polygon $P$ such that no point of the shortest path between any pair of points is visible to the third (Fig. 3a).*

*(**A2**) For any vertex $a$ of polygon $P$, there are two reflex vertices $v_1$ and $v_2$ such that (**A2-a**) $v_1 < Backw(v_1) < v_2$ and $v_1 < Forw(v_2) < v_2$ (Fig. 3b), or (**A2-b**) $v_1 < Backw(v_1) < v_2 < Backw(v_2)$ (Fig. 3c) or $Forw(v_1) < v_1 < Forw(v_2) < v_2$ (Fig. 3d).*

**Proof.** The necessity of the condition **A1** is already proved in [11]. In the following, we show that if the condition **A2** is true, any search schedule starting at a vertex $a$ of the polygon $P$ is trivial. Since the condition **A2-a** or **A2-b** is also true for any point in either edge incident to $a$ (excluding the other endpoint of the edge), it then follows from Observation 1 that polygon $P$ is not 1-searchable.

For the condition **A2-a**, any search schedule starting at $a$ becomes trivial when the vertex $Succ(v_1)$ or $Pred(v_2)$ is cleared. (For a detailed proof, see [7, 15].) Since the vertex $Succ(v_1)$ or $Pred(v_2)$ has to be cleared once, any search schedule starting at $a$ is trivial.

Consider now the condition **A2-b**. Assume without loss of generality that the first alternative of condition **A2-b** applies, that is, $a$ and $v_2$ are to the left of $\overline{v_1 Backw(v_1)}$, and $a$ and $v_1$ are to the left of $\overline{v_2 Backw(v_2)}$. Any search schedule starting at $a$ has to clear first $Succ(v_2)$ and then $Succ(v_1)$ (Fig. 3c); otherwise, it would be trivial. Assume without loss of generality that the region cleared at a time $t_1$ $(0 < t_1 < 1)$ is exactly the one lying to the right of $\overline{v_2 Backw(v_2)}$. Take $v_2$ as the vertex $a'$. Then for $a'$, there are two vertices $v_1'$ and $v_2'$ such that the condition **A2-a** or **A2-b** is true. Again, the search schedule becomes trivial when some adjacent vertices of $v_1'$ and $v_2'$ are cleared or, these adjacent vertices have to be cleared in a specified order. In this way, if the condition **A2-a** is ever met, any search schedule starting at $a$ is trivial. If the condition **A2-b** is repeatedly met, some vertex (say, $Succ(v_2)$) has to be cleared once again at a time $t_2$ ($t_2 > t_1$). It implies that the region cleared at time $t_2$ is exactly the same as that at time $t_1$. Thus, any search schedule starting at $a$ is trivial. It completes the proof. $\square$

**Observation 2.** For any three points $p_1$, $p_2$ and $p_3$ satisfying the condition **A1**, we can find three reflex vertices $r_1$, $r_2$ and $r_3$ such that each $r_i$ ($i = 1, 2$ and 3) blocks the corresponding point $p_i$ from being visible to any point in the shortest path between other two points (Fig. 3a). For short presentation, we also say that such three reflex vertices satisfy the condition **A1**.

Before we proceed to show that the same conditions are sufficient, we introduce an important concept of *essential cuts* or *essential ray shots*, which is widely used in the solutions to the watchman route and related problems [1,13, 14]. Let $a$ be a vertex of $P$. Polygon $P$ is divided into two pieces by either ray shot of a reflex vertex $r$. A ray shot $t$ is a *visibility shot* if it produces a convex angle at $r$ in the piece of $P$ containing $a$, which is denoted by $P(t)$. (In this case, either $r < Backw(r)$ or $r > Forw(r)$ holds. But, both of them cannot hold simultaneously.) Further, shot $t$ is *essential* if $P(t)$ is not contained in any other $P(t')$, where $t'$ is another visibility shot. We call the reflex vertices where essential ray shots are defined the *critical vertices*.

**Theorem 2** *A simple polygon $P$ is 1-searchable if none of the conditions of Theorem 1 applies.*

**Proof.** Let $a$ be a vertex of $P$ that does not satisfy the condition **A2** of Theorem 1. We assume that not the whole polygon $P$ is visible from $a$; otherwise polygon $P$ can be simply cleared. Let $r_1, \cdots, r_m$ be the sequence of critical vertices indexed in a counterclockwise scan of the boundary of $P$, starting at $a$. Let $Ray(r_i)$ denote the other endpoint of the essential shot defined at $r_i$. Observe that any shot $\overline{r_i Ray(r_i)}$ should intersect with $\overline{r_j Ray(r_j)}$, except for the case that $Ray(r_i) < r_i < r_j < Ray(r_j)$; otherwise, the condition **A2-a** or **A2-b** is true or the shot defined at $r_i$ or $r_j$ is not essential, a contradiction.

Let $P(r_i)$ and $P - P(r_i)$ denote the regions which are to the left and right of the line segment $\overline{r_i Ray(r_i)}$, respectively. Our scheme for clearing polygon $P$ is to clear the regions $P(r_i)$ in the order $i = 1, \cdots, m$ and finally $P - P(r_m)$. Let $r_0 = P(r_0) = a$. Assume that the region $P(r_{i-1})$ has been cleared by now. According to whether or not $a$ is contained in $P(r_{i-1})$ and/or $P(r_i)$, we classify the cases of clearing $P(r_i)$ into five categories. In the following, we denote by $R(x, y)$ or $L(x, y)$ the chain from $x$ to $y$ with $x < y$. (Usually, $x = r_{i-1}$ and $y = r_i$ for $R(x, y)$.) If a reflex vertex in a chain blocks one of its adjacent vertices from being visible to any point in the opposite chain, we call it a *blocking* vertex.

*Case 1 The vertex $a$ is contained in both $P(r_{i-1})$ and $P(r_i)$.*

*Case 1.1 $i = 1$.* First, two chains $R(a_l, r_1)$ and $L(Ray(r_1), a_r)$ are mutually weakly visible. Otherwise, there are some other critical vertices before $r_1$ (Fig. 4a) or the condition **A2-a** or **A2-b** is true (Figs. 4b-d), a contradiction. No deadlocks between $R(a_l, r_1)$ and $L(Ray(r_1), a_r)$ occur because of the existence of $r_1$; otherwise, the condition **A2-a** (Fig. 4e) or **A1** (Fig. 4f) would be satisfied. Hence, the region $P(r_1)$ is walkable and also 1-searchable from vertex $a$ to the line segment $\overline{r_1 Ray(r_1)}$.

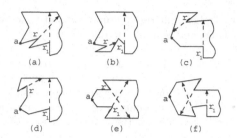

**Fig. 4.** Case 1.1.

*Case 1.2 i > 1.* In this case, the line segment $\overline{r_{i-1}Ray(r_{i-1})}$ intersects with $\overline{r_iRay(r_i)}$. If the chain $R(r_{i-1}, r_i)$ is weakly visible to $L(Ray(r_{i-1}), Ray(r_i))$, the line segment $\overline{r_{i-1}Ray(r_{i-1})}$ can be rotated into $\overline{r_iRay(r_i)}$ as follows. If all points between $r_{i-1}$ and $r_i$ are visible to the intersection point of $\overline{r_{i-1}Ray(r_{i-1})}$ and $\overline{r_iRay(r_i)}$, the ray rotation can be done by fixing the center at the intersection point. Otherwise, let $r^*$ be the first reflex vertex in $R(r_{i-1}, r_i)$ such that the vertex $Pred(r^*)$ is invisible to the intersection point. (It is impossible for $Succ(r^*)$ to be invisible to that point; otherwise, the vertex $r^*$ would be critical.) The line segment $\overline{r_{i-1}Ray(r_{i-1})}$ can then be rotated into $\overline{r^*Forw(r^*)}$ (Fig. 5a). This procedure is repeatedly performed until the ray of the flashlight is rotated into $\overline{r_iRay(r_i)}$.

Consider the situation where $R(r_{i-1}, r_i)$ is not weakly visible to $L(Ray(r_{i-1}), Ray(r_i))$. Let $r$ be the blocking vertex in $R(r_{i-1}, r_i)$ whose ray shot $Forw(r)$ is the maximum among those of the blocking vertices (Fig. 5b). (Again, it is impossible for $r$ to block $Succ(r)$ from being visible to any point in $L(Ray(r_{i-1}), Ray(r_i))$; otherwise, the vertex $r$, instead of $r_{i-1}$, would be critical.) Since $Forw(r) > Ray(r_i)$, the line segment $\overline{rForw(r)}$ intersects with $\overline{r_{i-1}Ray(r_{i-1})}$, but does not intersect with $\overline{r_iRay(r_i)}$. Since the chain $R(r_{i-1}, r)$ is weakly visible to $L(Ray(r_{i-1}), Forw(r))$, the line segment $\overline{r_{i-1}Ray(r_{i-1})}$ is first rotated into $\overline{rForw(r)}$. The current chain $R(r, r_i)$ is weakly visible to $L(Ray(r_i), Forw(r))$. The converse is also true; otherwise, $r$, $r_i$ and the blocking vertex in $L(Ray(r_i), Forw(r))$ would satisfy the condition **A1**. Because of the vertices $r$ and $r_i$, there are no deadlocks between two chains; otherwise, three vertices satisfying the condition **A1** could be found. Hence, the line segment $\overline{rForw(r)}$ can be further moved into $\overline{r_iRay(r_i)}$ by a walk.

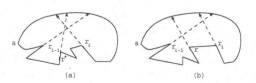

**Fig. 5.** Case 1.2.

*Case 2 The vertex $a$ is contained in $P(r_{i-1})$, but not in $P(r_i)$.*

*Case 2.1* $i = 1$. Assume without loss of generality that there are no vertices in the chain $R(a_l, r_1)$ where visibility shots are defined. (Otherwise, let $v$ be the last of the vertices where visibility shots are defined and $Ray(v)$ the other endpoint of the visibility shot. The region which is to the left of $\overline{vRay(v)}$ can be cleared as done in Case 1.1, and then we consider the vertex $v$ as $a$. A more direct method is to consider the search schedule starting at $v$.) Consider the shortest path between $a$ and $r_1$. All turn points of the path should lie in the chain $L(r_1, a_r)$. Extend all segments of this path until they hit the polygon boundary. Let $a'$ be the other endpoint of the first extended segment (Fig. 6). Since all points preceding $a'$ are visible to $a$, the region lying to the right of $\overline{aa'}$ (its orientation is from $a$ to $a'$) can be first cleared. If $a' > Ray(r_1)$, the region $P(r_1)$ is cleared by rotating the line segment $\overline{aa'}$ into $\overline{r_1Ray(r_1)}$. This can be safely done, as all points between $a'$ and $r_1$ are visible to $r_1$ (which is the intersection point of $\overline{aa'}$ and $\overline{r_1Ray(r_1)}$); otherwise, there would some critical vertices before $r_1$, or the vertex $r_1$ would not be critical. If $a' < Ray(r_1)$, the region $P(r_1)$ can be also cleared by rotating the line segment $\overline{aa'}$ into $\overline{r_1Ray(r_1)}$, along every extended segment of the shortest path between $a$ and $r_1$ (Fig. 6).

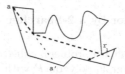

**Fig. 6.** Case 2.1.

*Case 2.2* $i > 1$. In this case, the line segment $\overline{r_{i-1}Ray(r_{i-1})}$ intersects with $\overline{r_iRay(r_i)}$, and $a$ is contained in the chain $L(a_l, Ray(r_i)) \cup L(Ray(r_{i-1}), a_r)$. All vertices in the chain $R(r_{i-1}, r_i)$ are visible to the intersection point of $\overline{r_{i-1}Ray(r_{i-1})}$ and $\overline{r_iRay(r_i)}$; otherwise some of them, instead of $r_{i-1}$ or $r_i$, would be critical. The line segment $\overline{r_{i-1}Ray(r_{i-1})}$ can then be rotated into $\overline{r_iRay(r_i)}$.

*Case 3 The vertex $a$ is not contained in $P(r_{i-1})$, but in $P(r_i)$.* Omitted in this extended abstract.

*Case 4 The vertex $a$ is not contained in $P(r_{i-1})$ nor $P(r_i)$.* Omitted in this extended abstract.

*Case 5 The region $P(r_m)$ is cleared.* First, the final region $P - P(r_m)$ can be symmetrically cleared as the region $P(r_1)$ is cleared in Case 1.1 or Case 2.1. Since the walk in Case 1.1 and the ray rotation in Case 2.1 are reversible, we obtain that the region $P - P(r_m)$ is also 1-searchable from $\overline{r_mRay(r_m)}$ to $a$. Thus, we obtain that the whole polygon $P$ is cleared. $\square$

**Theorem 3** *It takes $O(n^2)$ time to test the 1-searchability of a simple polygon and generate a search schedule if it exists.*

**Proof.** A trivial algorithm takes $O(n^3)$ to test the conditions **A1** and **A2**. The time bound can be reduced to $O(n^2)$. Due to space limit, we omit the detail in this extended abstract.

After it is verified that none of **A1** and **A2** is true, we run the constructive algorithm presented in the proof of Theorem 2 to give a search schedule. Observe that clearing a region $P(r_i)$ requires a ray rotation and a walk. Since a ray rotation is done clockwisely or counterclockwisely, it runs in $O(n)$ time. Since the chains $R(x, y)$ considered for all walks are disjoint, the time taken for all walks is $O(n^2)$ [7]. Hence, the time complexity of our algorithm is $O(n^2)$. $\square$

## 4    Extension to 2-Searchable Polygons

We will extend the results obtained for 1-searchable polygons to those for 2-searchable polygons. The extension is based on a generalization of the notion of visibility to that of link-2-visibility. Similar to the instructions given for 1-searchers, we can define the search instructions of 2-searchers and $\infty$-searchers. See also [11,15] for details.

### 4.1    Searching a Corridor by a 2-Searcher

A generalization of the two-guard problem, called the *corridor search problem* is studied in [2,15]. Given a simple polygon $P$ with two marked vertices $u$ and $v$, which is called a *corridor*, can the $k$-searcher, starting at $u$, force the intruder out of $P$ through $v$ (but not $u$)? Recall that the boundary of $P$ is divided into two chains, $L$ and $R$, with common endpoints $u$ and $v$, and both chains $L$ and $R$ are oriented from $u$ to $v$.

The concept of link-2-visibility is used for solving the corridor search problem [2,15]. Two points $x$, $y \in P$ are said to be mutually *link-2-visible* if there exists another point $z$ such that the line segments $\overline{xz}$ and $\overline{zy}$ are entirely contained in $P$. For two regions $R$, $Q \subseteq P$, we say that $R$ is *weakly link-2-visible* from $Q$ if every point in $R$ is link-2-visible from some point in $Q$.

The ray shots can be also defined with link-2-visibility [15]. For a point $p < Backw(p) \in L$ or a point $p > Forw(p) \in L$, the forward and backward *link-2-ray shot* $Forw^2(p)$, $Backw^2(p)$ can be defined. For details, see [15]. A pair of reflex vertices $p \in L$, $q \in R$ is then said to form a *link-2-deadlock* if $q < Backw^2(p) \in R$ and $p < Backw^2(q) \in L$ hold or if $q > Forw^2(p) \in R$ and $p > Forw^2(q) \in L$ hold.

**Lemma 2** *[15] A corridor is 2-searchable if and only if the chains $L$ and $R$ are mutually weakly link-2-visible and no link-2-deadlocks occur. Furthermore, it takes $O(n \log n)$ time to test the 2-searchability of a corridor, and $O(n \log n + k)$ time to generate a search schedule where $k$ ($\leq n^2$) is the minimal number of search instructions.*

## 4.2   Searching a Simple Polygon by a 2-Searcher

Any search schedule of a 2-searcher should start at some point (vertex) $a$ of the boundary of $P$. We order the points on the boundary of $P$ counterclockwisely, starting at $a$. For the reflex vertices $r$ such that $r < Backw(r)$ or $r > Forw(r)$, we compute their link-2-ray shots $Backw^2(r)$ and $Forw^2(r)$. However, since only a door $a$ is given, the algorithm for computing all link-2-ray shots presented for the corridor search problem [15] cannot be used here. Observe that for a vertex $r$ with $r < Backw(r)$ ($r > Forw(r)$), all points of the interval $[Forw^2(r), Backw^2(r)]$ are link-2-visible to $Succ(r)$ ($Pred(r)$), and that if $a$ is not contained in $[Forw^2(r), Backw^2(r)]$, then $Forw^2(r) < Backw^2(r)$. So we can find the link-2-ray shots $Forw^2(r)$ and $Backw^2(r)$ from the link-2-visible region of the vertex $Succ(r)$ ($Pred(r)$).

The results obtained for 1-searchable polygons can be generalized to those for 2-searchable and $\infty$-searchable polygons as follows.

**Theorem 4** *Polygon $P$ is not $\infty$-searchable if one of the following conditions is true.*

(**B1**) *There are three points in $P$ such that no point of the shortest path between any pair of points is link-2-visible to the third.*

(**B2**) *For any vertex $a$, there are two reflex vertices $v_1$ and $v_2$ such that* (**B2-a**) $v_1 < Backw^2(v_1) < v_2$ *and* $v_1 < Forw^2(v_2) < v_2$, *or* (**B2-b**) $v_1 < Backw^2(v_1) < v_2 < Backw^2(v_2)$ *or* $Forw^2(v_1) < v_1 < Forw^2(v_2) < v_2$.

**Proof.** By an argument similar to the proof of Theorem 1, with a slight modification that $Forw$, $Backw$, visibility and the 1-searcher are replaced by $Forw^2$, $Backw^2$, link-2-visibility and the $\infty$-searcher, respectively. Note that the searchability of any $k$-searcher ($k \geq 2$) cannot be changed in the situation where the condition **B1** or **B2** is satisfied, no matter how many flashlights he holds. □

**Theorem 5** *A simple polygon $P$ is 2-searchable if none of the conditions of Theorem 4 applies.*

**Proof.** Since the algorithm for searching a corridor by a 1-searcher (or two guards) has been generalized to that by a 2-searcher and a ray rotation can be simply generalized to a link-2-ray rotation, the rest of the proof is similar to that of Theorem 2. We omit the detail. □

It follows from Theorems 4 and 5 that any polygon that is searchable by an $\infty$-searcher is searchable by a 2-searcher.

**Theorem 6** *It takes $O(n^2)$ time to test the 2-searchability of a simple polygon and generate a search schedule if it exists.*

**Proof.** By an argument similar to the proof of Theorem 3, with a slight modification that the notions concerning visibility are replaced by those concerning link-2-visibility. □

# References

1. W.P.Chin and S.Ntafos, Shortest watchman routes in simple polygons, *Disc. Comp. Geom.* **6**, (1991) 9-31.
2. D.Crass, I.Suzuki and M.Yamashita, Searching for a mobile intruder in a corridor, *Int. J. Comput. Geom. & Appl.* **5** (1995) 397-412.
3. L.J.Guibas, J.Hershberger, D.Leven, M.Sharir and R.E.Tarjan, Linear-time algorithms for visibility and shortest path problems inside triangulated simple polygons, *Algorithmica*, **2** (1987) 209-233.
4. L.J.Guibas, J.C.Latombe, S.M.Lavalle, D.Lin and R.Motwani, Finding an unpredictable target in a workspace with obstacle, in *Proc. IEEE int. Conf. Robotics and Automation*, 1997.
5. L.J.Guibas, J.C.Latombe, S.M.Lavalle, D.Lin and R.Motwani, Visibility-based pursuit-evasion in a polygonal environment, *Int. J. Comp. Geom. & Appl.* **9**, (1999) 471-493.
6. P.J.Heffernan, An optimal algorithm for the two-guard problem, *Int. J. Comput. Geom. & Appl.* **6** (1996) 15-44.
7. C. Icking and R. Klein, The two guards problem, *Int. J. Comput. Geom. & Appl.* **2** (1992) 257-285.
8. S.M.LaValle, B.Simov and G.Slutzki, An algorithm for searching a polygonal region with a flashligh, *Proc. 16th Annu. ACM Symp. Comput. Geom.*
9. J.H. Lee, S.Y.Shin and K.Y.Chwa, Visibility-based pursuit-evasion in a polygonal room with a door, *Proc. 15th Annu. ACM Symp. Comput. Geom.* (1999) 281-290.
10. T.Shermer, Recent results in art galleries *Proceedings of IEEE* **80** (1992) 1384-1399.
11. I.Suzuki and M.Yamashita, Searching for mobile intruders in a polygonal region, *SIAM J. Comp.* **21** (1992) 863-888.
12. I.Suzuki, M.Yamashita, H.Umemoto and T.Kameda, Bushiness and a tight worst-case upper bound on the search number of a simple polygon, *Inform. Process. Lett.* **66** (1998) 49-52.
13. X.Tan, T.Hirata and Y.Inagaki, An incremental algorithm for constructing shortest watchman routes, *Int. J. Comp. Geom. & Appl.* **3**, (1993) 351-365.
14. X.Tan, T.Hirata and Y.Inagaki, Corrigendum to "An incremental algorithm for constructing shortest watchman routes", *Int. J. Comp. Geom. & Appl.* **3**, (1999) 319-323.
15. X.Tan, An efficient solution to the corridor search problem, Lect. Notes Comput. Sci. **1763** (*Proc. JCDCG'98*) (2000) 317-332.
16. M.Yamashita, H.Umemoto, I.Suzuki and T.Kameda, "Searching for mobile intruders in a polygonal region by a group of mobile searchers. In *Pro. 13th Annu. ACM Symp. Comput. Geom.* (1997) 448-450.

# Characterization of Rooms
# Searchable by Two Guards*

Sang-Min Park[1], Jae-Ha Lee[2], and Kyung-Yong Chwa[1]

[1] Department of Computer Science,
Korea Advanced Institute of Science & Technology, Korea
{smpark,kychwa}@jupiter.kaist.ac.kr
[2] Max-Planck-Institut für Informatik, Germany
lee@mpi-sb.mpg.de

**Abstract.** We consider the problem of searching for mobile intruders in a polygonal region with one door by two guards. Given a simple polygon $\mathcal{P}$ with one door $d$, which is called a room $(\mathcal{P}, d)$, two guards start at $d$ and walk along the boundary of $\mathcal{P}$ to detect a mobile intruder with a laser beam between the two guards. During the walk, two guards are required to be mutually visible all the time and eventually meet at one point. We give the characterization of the class of rooms searchable by two guards, which naturally leads to $O(n \log n)$-time algorithm for testing the searchability of an $n$-sided room.

## 1   Introduction

The polygon search problem is the problem of searching for mobile intruders in a polygonal region by one or more mobile searchers. A searcher and an intruder are represented as points that can move continuously inside a given polygon and the intruder is assumed to be able to move arbitrarily faster than the searcher. A searcher *finds* an intruder if the intruder is within the range of the searcher's vision or sensor at any moment. We have to compute a schedule for the searchers so that all intruders will eventually be detected by one of the searchers regardless of the unpredictable trajectories of the intruders. We say that a polygon is *searchable* by given searchers if there exists such a schedule.

The visibility of a searcher is defined using the number of flashlights. The *k-searcher* has $k$ flashlights whose visibility is limited to $k$ rays emanating from his position, where the directions of the rays can be changed continuously with bounded angular rotation speed. The 1-searcher has one flashlight, so he can see along one ray of light emanating from his position by changing its direction. The searcher having a point light source who can see in all directions simultaneously is called ∞-searcher. *Two guards* are two 1-searchers which move on the polygon boundary continuously aiming their flashlights at each other all the time.

* This work was supported by KOSEF(Korea Science and Engineering Foundation) under grant 98-0102-0701-3.

D.T. Lee and S.-H. Teng (Eds.): ISAAC 2000, LNCS 1969, pp. 515–526, 2000.
© Springer-Verlag Berlin Heidelberg 2000

When a searcher starts to search intruders in a given polygon, it is hard to decide where to start. Many variants of the polygon search problem restrict the starting point of searching. A *room* $(\mathcal{P}, d)$ is an $n$-sided polygon $\mathcal{P}$ with a designated point $d$ on the boundary, called a *door*. A door is the point where a searcher starts to search as well as on which he has to keep his eye in order not to let the intruder escape. For each of the 1-searcher and the $\infty$-searcher, the characterization of the class of searchable rooms and an $O(n^2)$-time algorithm to construct a search schedule are presented [8,9].

A *corridor* is a simple polygon $\mathcal{P}$ with two distinguished vertices, $d$ and $g$, which divide the boundary of $\mathcal{P}$ into two polygonal chains, $L$ and $R$. Icking and Klein [6] introduced *two guards problem* in a corridor, where two guards simultaneously walk along $L$ and $R$ respectively, from $d$ to $g$, in such a way that they are always mutually visible. Actually, the objective of these two guards is to find the intruder or evict it out of the corridor through $g$. Whether the corridor $(\mathcal{P}, d, g)$ is searchable by two guards can be tested in $O(n \log n)$ time and linear space [6], where $n$ is the number of sides of $\mathcal{P}$. Heffernan presented a linear-time test algorithm for a special case of this problem [5]. The related results to corridors have been suggested in literature [2,5,10].

Some previous work considered a simple polygon $\mathcal{P}$, without fixing either the starting or the ending point. Suzuki and Yamashita presented some necessary or sufficient conditions for a polygon to be searchable by various searchers [11]. The problem of motion planning of one or more searchers in a polygon was studied by Guibas *et al.* [4]. Recently, Lavalle *et al.* gave an $O(n^2)$-time algorithm to decide whether the polygon can be cleared by a 1-searcher, and if so, output a search schedule [7]. For two guards, Tseng *et al.* tested if there exists a pair of boundary points $d$ and $g$ that admits a corridor walk from $d$ to $g$ in $O(n \log n)$ time and linear space [12].

In this paper, we consider two guards to search a given room. The search schedule of rooms is distinguished from that of corridors in the following sense. Suppose a room $(\mathcal{P}, d)$ is searchable by two guards and has a search schedule ending at a point $g'$. During the search, two guards may go across $g'$ in a room but they cannot in a corridor $(\mathcal{P}, d, g')$. For examples, the room in Figure 1(b) cannot have a point $g$ such that $(\mathcal{P}, d, g)$ admits a corridor walk, but two guards are able to search this room where the endpoint of the search is $g'$. We give the characterization of the class of rooms that are searchable by two guards. We will also show that to test if a given room is searchable by two guards can be done in $O(n \log n)$ time.

The rest of the paper is organized as follows. The preliminaries including the notation and previous key results on two guards are presented in Section 2. Based on the main theorem by Icking and Klein [6], we will present the sufficient conditions for a room to be unsearchable by two guards in Section 3.1. In Section 3.2, we suggest the necessary and sufficient condition equivalent to the conditions in Section 3.1. Finally, we prove the necessity of the condition suggested in Section 3.2.

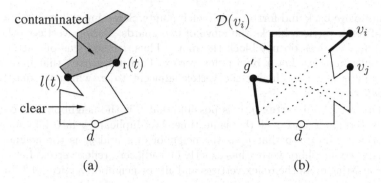

contaminated

$r(t)$

$l(t)$

clear

$d$

(a)

$\mathcal{D}(v_i)$

$v_i$

$g'$

$v_j$

$d$

(b)

**Fig. 1.** (a) clear vs. contaminated (b) the dominated chain

## 2   Preliminaries

### 2.1   Notations

A simple polygon $\mathcal{P}$ with a point $d$ on its boundary is called a *room* $(\mathcal{P}, d)$. We denote by $\partial\mathcal{P}$ the boundary of $\mathcal{P}$. We define an ordering on the points of $\partial\mathcal{P}$ as follows: for points $p, q \in \partial\mathcal{P}, p \prec q$ if $p$ is encountered before $q$ when we traverse $\partial\mathcal{P}$ from $d$ clockwise. We say that '$p$ *precedes* $q$' if $p \prec q$. As the boundary condition, we imagine two points $d_l$ and $d_r$ such that $d_l \preceq p \preceq d_r$ for every point $p \in \partial\mathcal{P}$. Both $d_l$ and $d_r$ are 'aliases' of $d$.

In general, two points inside a polygon are said to be *visible* from each other if the line segment joining them is contained in the polygon. Two guards are defined as two points $l$ and $r$ on $\partial\mathcal{P}$ moving continuously such that the line segment $\overline{lr}$ is at each time fully contained in the polygon, i.e., $l$ and $r$ are always mutually visible. More formally, we define the movement of two guards as follows.

**Definition 1.** *A search schedule on $(\mathcal{P}, d)$ is a pair $(l, r)$ of continuous functions such that:*

$$l : [0, 1] \longrightarrow \partial\mathcal{P}, \qquad r : [0, 1] \longrightarrow \partial\mathcal{P},$$
$$l(0) = r(0) = d, \qquad l(1) \text{ and } r(1) \text{ are on the same edge of } \mathcal{P},$$
$$\text{For every } t \in (0, 1), \ l(t) \prec r(t), \text{ and, } l(t) \text{ and } r(t) \text{ are mutually visible.}$$

The line segment $\overline{l(t)r(t)}$ should sweep all the points in the room. During the search, the room is always divided into two areas: one is below $\overline{l(t)r(t)}$, which is *clear* in the sense that there is no undetected intruder, and the other is above $\overline{l(t)r(t)}$, which is *contaminated* in that there might be an intruder. The clear area should always contain the door $d$ as depicted in Figure 1(a) to ensure that the intruder does not escape through the door.

When two guards search the room, what makes the searching difficult is a *reflex* vertex, which is a vertex with interior angle larger than 180°. Because a point behind the reflex vertex is not visible from another point, two guards should move back and forth to visit such points. Sometimes, it is possible that a set of reflex vertices blocks the move of two guards. Convex vertices other than the reflex vertices do not block the move. Thus, let us focus our attention on the reflex vertices. Let $x$ be a reflex vertex. Then the vertex that may become invisible is not $x$ itself but the vertex adjacent to $x$, which we denote by a *neighbor* vertex of $x$.

For a neighbor vertex $y$, it is possible that $y$ is the neighbor of two distinct reflex vertices $x$ and $z$ at the same time. We duplicate $y$ into imaginary twin vertices $y_x$ and $y_z$ so that $y_x$ is the neighbor of $x$ and $y_z$ is the neighbor of $z$. Thus, every neighbor vertex has exactly one adjacent reflex vertex. Let $S$ be the set consisting of all the reflex vertices and all the neighbor vertices of $P$ including duplicated ones. Then we label the vertices in $S$ as $v_0(\succeq d_l), v_1, v_2, \cdots, v_m(\preceq d_r)$ in clockwise order from $d_l$. Thus, $v_i$ precedes $v_{i+1}$ for $0 \le i \le m - 1$ and $m = O(n)$.

For points $p, q \in \partial P$, the *chain* $C[p, q]$ denotes the connected boundary chain from $p$ to $q$ in clockwise order. Analogously, $C(p, q)$ (respectively, $C(p, q], C[p, q)$) denotes $C[p, q] \setminus \{p, q\}$ (respectively, $C[p, q] \setminus \{p\}, C[p, q] \setminus \{q\}$).

For each neighbor vertex $v_i$, we define the *dominated chain* $\mathcal{D}(v_i)$ as follows. Let $x$ be a neighbor vertex and $y$ be the reflex vertex of $x$. When we shoot the ray from $x$ in the direction of $\overrightarrow{xy}$, let $shot(x)$ be the first hit point on $\partial P$. For a neighbor $v_i$ of the reflex vertex $v_{i+1}$, $\mathcal{D}(v_i)$ is defined as the polygonal chain $C[shot(v_i), v_{i+1}]$. Symmetrically, for a neighbor $v_j$ of the reflex vertex $v_{j-1}$, $\mathcal{D}(v_j)$ is defined as the chain $C[v_{j-1}, shot(v_j)]$; see Figure 1(b). Note that the dominated chain of a neighbor vertex $v_i$ is not always equivalent to the set of points on $\partial P$ visible from $v_i$. Moreover, $\mathcal{D}(v_i)$ is independent of the location of $d$.

Let $\mathcal{N}$ be the set of neighbor vertices of $P$. Then $\mathcal{N}$ is divided into two disjoint sets $\mathcal{N}_{attic}$ and $\mathcal{N}_{cellar}$ as follows.

$$\mathcal{N}_{attic} = \{x | x \in \mathcal{N} \quad \text{such that} \quad d \notin \mathcal{D}(x)\}$$

$$\mathcal{N}_{cellar} = \{x | x \in \mathcal{N} \quad \text{such that} \quad d \in \mathcal{D}(x)\}$$

We call the vertex in $\mathcal{N}_{attic}$ an *attic* and that in $\mathcal{N}_{cellar}$ a *cellar*. Especially, an attic which precedes(succeeds) its adjacent reflex vertex is called an *l-attic*(*r-attic*, respectively). An *l-cellar* and an *r-cellar* are defined analogously. In Figure 1(b), $v_j$ is an *r*-cellar and $v_i$ is an *l*-attic.

Let $\mathcal{ND}$ denote the relation "non-dominating each other" for the vertices of $\mathcal{N}$. Then $\mathcal{ND}(x, y)$ if and only if $x \notin \mathcal{D}(y)$ and $y \notin \mathcal{D}(x)$. A pair of vertices $\langle x, y \rangle$ such that $\mathcal{ND}(x, y)$ is called an *ND-pair*. We call an ND-pair $\langle x, y \rangle$ an *aa-pair* if both $x$ and $y$ are attics, and a *cc-pair* if both are cellars. We say that a point $x$ *has a cc-pair* if $\langle v_i, v_j \rangle$ is a cc-pair and $v_i \prec x \prec v_j$.

Basically, we assume that the polygon is in a general position, meaning that, no three lines extending three edges of $P$ have a point in common, and no three vertices are collinear.

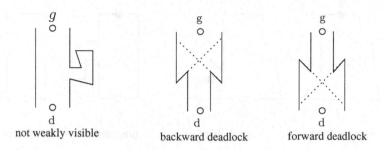

**Fig. 2.** Examples of corridors that cannot have a walk

## 2.2   Revisit of the Corridor Problem

In order to describe our idea, we review the two guards problem in corridors - studied by Icking and Klein [6]. A *corridor* is a simple polygon $\mathcal{P}$ with two distinguished vertices $d$ and $g$, which divide the boundary of $\mathcal{P}$ into two polygonal chains $L(= C[d, g])$ and $R(= C[g, d])$. $L$ is called *weakly visible* from $R$, if for each point $p \in L$ there exists a point $q \in R$ such that $p$ is visible from $q$ [1]. Given a corridor $(\mathcal{P}, d, g)$, two guards simultaneously walk along $L$ and $R$ respectively, from $d$ to $g$, in such a way that they are always mutually visible. A *walk* is defined as a movement of two guards $l$ and $r$ subject to the above constraints. We say that a corridor is *walkable* if it admits a walk. Icking and Klein [6] gave the necessary and sufficient condition for the corridor to admit a walk: (1) $L$ and $R$ are weakly visible from each other, and (2) $(\mathcal{P}, d, g)$ has neither *forward deadlock* nor *backward deadlock*. The typical examples of corridors that cannot have a walk are depicted in Figure 2. In the following theorem, we rewrite the condition (1) and (2) using the terminology defined in Section 2.1.

**Theorem 1.** [6] *A corridor $(\mathcal{P}, d, g)$ is walkable if and only if:*

(a) *There is no attic $x$ such that $\mathcal{D}(x) \subset C(d, g)$ or $\mathcal{D}(x) \subset C(g, d)$, and*
(b) *There is no aa-pair $\langle x, y \rangle$ such that $x$ is in $C(d, y)$ and $y$ is in $C(g, d)$, and*
(c) *There is no cc-pair $\langle x, y \rangle$ such that $x$ is in $C(d, g)$ and $y$ is in $C(g, d)$.*

The condition (a) means the weak visibility of $C(d, g)$ and $C(g, d)$, the condition (b) means the absence of backward deadlocks, and the condition (c) means the absence of forward deadlocks.

In corridors, the location of $g$ is important. As shown in examples of Figure 3, the searchability can change when the location of $g$ changes. However, a room differs from a corridor because the point where the searching ends is not predetermined. Let us define the *final point* $\bar{g}$ as the point where the searching ends in a room. The concept of $\bar{g}$(in rooms) is different from that of $g$(in corridors). In corridors, the left guard $l$(the right guard $r$) cannot go over $g$ to $R(L$, respectively), in other words, $g$ is a dead end. But two guards in a room may pass

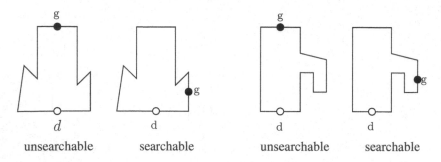

**Fig. 3.** Corridor examples: The searchability depends on the location of $g$.

over $\bar{g}$ as long as $l$ precedes $r$. Thus, in a room the weak-visibility condition of Theorem 1(a) is not valid any more. In Section 3.1, we will explain where the searching ends by applying Theorem 1 to the rooms.

## 3   Characterization

### 3.1   Sufficient Conditions

By adjusting Theorem 1 to a room, we will give the sufficient conditions for rooms to be unsearchable. First, consider Theorem 1(b).

**Lemma 1.** *If a room $(\mathcal{P}, d)$ has an aa-pair, $(\mathcal{P}, d)$ is unsearchable.*

*Proof.* Suppose that there is an aa-pair $\langle v_i, v_j \rangle$ in $(\mathcal{P}, d)$. When two guards clear $v_i$ first, an intruder at $v_j$ can escape through $d$. Symmetrically, when they clear $v_j$ first, an intruder at $v_i$ has a chance to escape. However clearing both $v_i$ and $v_j$ simultaneously is impossible since they are mutually invisible. Thus, $(\mathcal{P}, d)$ is unsearchable.                                                                                  □

Second, we will compute the range of the final point $\bar{g}$. Based on Theorem 1(c), we obtain Lemma 2, which directly leads to Corollary 1.

**Lemma 2.** *Let $l$ and $r$ be two guards that search the room $(\mathcal{P}, d)$. Assume that $(\mathcal{P}, d)$ is searchable. If there is a cc-pair $\langle v_i, v_j \rangle$, then either $l$ should stay in $C[d, v_{i+1}]$ or $r$ should stay in $C[v_{j-1}, d]$ at each moment $t \in [0, 1)$ .*

*Proof.* Suppose that at a moment both $l$ and $r$ went out of $C[d, v_{i+1}]$ and $C[v_{j-1}, d]$, respectively. This means that two guards go beyond the forward deadlock, which is impossible. Thus either $l$ should stay in $C[d, v_{i+1}]$ or $r$ should stay in $C[v_{j-1}, d]$ at each moment.                                                                                  □

**Corollary 1.** *If a room $(\mathcal{P}, d)$ is searchable, $(\mathcal{P}, d)$ has $\bar{g}$ in $C[d, v_{i+1}]$ or $C[v_{j-1}, d]$ for each cc-pair $\langle v_i, v_j \rangle$.*

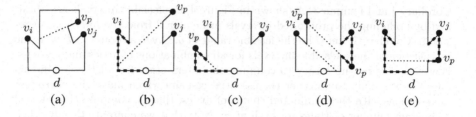

**Fig. 4.** The ranges of $\bar{g}$ constrained by an attic and a cc-pair

Because the two guards can pass over $\bar{g}$, Theorem 1(a) will be applied in a different way.

**Lemma 3.** *Assume that a room $(\mathcal{P}, d)$ is searchable by two guards. Let $\langle v_i, v_j \rangle$ be a cc-pair, $v_p$ be an l-attic and $v_q$ be an r-attic in $(\mathcal{P}, d)$. Then the location of $\bar{g}$ must satisfy the following constraints:*

(a) *$\bar{g}$ cannot lie in $C(v_{p+1}, d)$.*
(b) *$\bar{g}$ cannot lie in $C(d, v_{q-1})$.*
(c) *If $\mathcal{ND}(v_p, v_i)$ or $\mathcal{ND}(v_q, v_i)$, then $\bar{g}$ cannot lie in $C(d, v_{i+1})$.*
(d) *If $\mathcal{ND}(v_p, v_j)$ or $\mathcal{ND}(v_q, v_j)$, then $\bar{g}$ cannot lie in $C(v_{j-1}, d)$.*

*Proof.* **(a)** Suppose $\bar{g}$ lies in $C(v_{p+1}, d)$. When clearing $v_p$, both of two guards should lie in $\mathcal{D}(v_p) \subset C[d, v_{p+1}]$. After clearing $v_p$, the two guards $l$ and $r$ should go to $C(v_{p+1}, d)$ to walk toward the final point. When $l$ passes $v_p$, $r$ should lie inside $\mathcal{D}(v_p)$ to see $l$. To satisfy the condition that $l$ always precedes $r$, $r$ must be on the edge $\overline{v_p, v_{p+1}}$, which means the searching ends there. This contradicts to the assumption that $\bar{g}$ is in $C(v_{p+1}, d)$. Therefore, $\bar{g}$ can not lie in $C(v_{p+1}, d)$.
**(b)** Symmetric to (a).
**(c)** First, assume that $\mathcal{ND}(v_p, v_i)$. Then $v_p$ should be in $C(v_{i+1}, d)$. If $v_p \in C(v_{i+1}, v_{j-1})$, then $\mathcal{D}(v_p) \subset C(v_{i+1}, v_{j-1})$. In order to clear $v_p$, $l$ and $r$ should go up to $C(v_{i+1}, v_{j-1})$. Then two guards violate Lemma 2. Thus they cannot clear $v_p$ regardless of the location of $\bar{g}$. Thus $v_p$ must be in $C[v_{j-1}, d)$. See Figure 4(d). Suppose now that $\bar{g}$ lies in $C(d, v_{i+1})$. Let $\bar{v}_p$ be $shot(v_p)$. Then $\bar{v}_p \succ v_{i+1}$ because $\mathcal{ND}(v_p, v_i)$. After clearing $v_p$, $l$ should move to $\bar{g}$ in $C(d, v_{i+1})$. By Lemma 2, while $l$ moves from $\bar{v}_p$ to $v_{i+1}$, $r$ must stay in $C[v_{j-1}, d]$. However, when $l$ passes $v_{i+1}$ to reach $\bar{g}$, $v_p$ always becomes recontaminated because $v_i$ and $v_p$ are non-dominating each other. Thus, searching cannot be completed inside $C(d, v_{i+1})$.
Second, assume that $\mathcal{ND}(v_q, v_i)$. Then $v_q$ should be in $C(v_{i+1}, d)$. By the statement in (b), $\bar{g}$ cannot lie in $C(d, v_{q-1}) \supset C(d, v_{i+1})$.
**(d)** Symmetric to (c). □

Lemma 3 shows that any combination of an attic and a cc-pair prohibits specific intervals of points from being a final point of searching. Figure 4 shows examples, where the thick dashed lines indicate the range of $\bar{g}$ constrained by

Corollary 1 and Lemma 3. As shown in Figure 4, the feasible intervals are obtained by excluding the prohibited intervals in Lemma 3 from the intervals sugge-
sted in Corollary 1. Let $\mathcal{G}$ be the feasible range of $\bar{g}$. Given a room $(\mathcal{P}, d)$, $\mathcal{G}$ is the
intersection of these feasible intervals for all combinations of attics and cc-pairs.
However, it is not necessary to compute the intersection for all the combinations. We have only to consider the essential cc-pairs which make the narrowest
intersections with the dominated chains of attics, that is, compute the interval
a constant number of times for each attic. Note that we compute $\mathcal{G}$ only when
there are at least one attic and at least one cc-pair.

By Lemma 1, Corollary 1 and Lemma 3, we obtain the following statement.

**Theorem 2.** *If a room $(\mathcal{P}, d)$ has an aa-pair or $\mathcal{G}$ is an empty set, then $(\mathcal{P}, d)$
is unsearchable.*

### 3.2   Necessary and Sufficient Condition

In this section, we suggest the necessary and sufficient condition for unsearchable
rooms, which is equivalent to the condition stated in Theorem 2. For examples
satisfying $C1$, $C2$, $C3$ and $C4$, refer to Figure 5.

- ($C1$) $(\mathcal{P}, d)$ has an aa-pair $\langle v_i, v_j \rangle$.
- ($C2$) $(\mathcal{P}, d)$ has a cc-pair $\langle v_i, v_j \rangle$ and an attic $v_p$ such that $\mathcal{ND}(v_i, v_p)$ and
  $\mathcal{ND}(v_j, v_p)$.
- ($C3$) There are cc-pairs $\langle v_i, v_j \rangle$, $\langle v_l, v_m \rangle$, and attics $v_p, v_q$ such that
  $\mathcal{ND}(v_i, v_p), \mathcal{ND}(v_m, v_q)$, and $v_l \prec v_j$.
- ($C4$) In the same configuration as $C3$ except $v_l \prec v_j$, each point $x$ in
  $C(v_j, v_l)$ has a cc-pair.

To show the equivalence between these four conditions and the condition stated
in Theorem 2, we have only to prove Lemma 4.

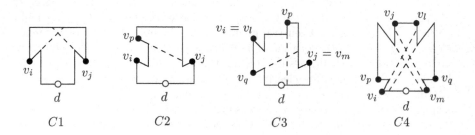

**Fig. 5.** Examples satisfying $C1$, $C2$, $C3$ and $C4$

**Lemma 4.** *Assume that a room $(\mathcal{P}, d)$ has at least one attic and at least one
cc-pair but no aa-pair. Then $(\mathcal{P}, d)$ has an empty $\mathcal{G}$ iff it satisfies one of $C2$, $C3$
and $C4$.*

*Proof.* By Corollary 1 and Lemma 3, each room satisfying $C2$, $C3$ or $C4$ has empty $\mathcal{G}$. Let us show that any room with $\mathcal{G} = \emptyset$ satisfies one of $C2$, $C3$ and $C4$.

As shown in Lemma 3, each combination of an attic and a cc-pair defines the feasible interval of $\mathcal{G}$. A cc-pair $\langle v_i, v_j \rangle$ excludes $C(v_{i+1}, v_{j-1})$ from $\mathcal{G}$, an $l$-attic $v_p$ does $C(v_{p+1}, d)$ and an $r$-attic $v_q$ does $C(d, v_{q-1})$ from $\mathcal{G}$.

Let $\langle v_A, v_B \rangle$ be the cc-pair whose $l$-cellar precedes the $l$-cellar of any other cc-pair. Let $\langle v_Y, v_Z \rangle$ be the cc-pair whose $r$-cellar does not precede the $r$-cellar of any other cc-pair. To exclude $C(d, v_{A+1})$ from $\mathcal{G}$, we need an attic $v_C$ such that $\mathcal{ND}(v_A, v_C)$. Similarly, to exclude $C(v_{Z-1}, d)$ from $\mathcal{G}$, we need an attic $v_X$ such that $\mathcal{ND}(v_Z, v_X)$.

First suppose $v_A$ and $v_Z$ are non-dominating each other. If $v_C = v_X$, then $\{v_C, \langle v_A, v_Z \rangle\}$ satisfies $C2$. If $v_C \neq v_X$, then $\{v_C, v_X, \langle v_A, v_Z \rangle\}$ satisfies $C3$. Now, suppose that $\langle v_A, v_Z \rangle$ is not an ND-pair. Then there are two cases for these two cc-pairs $\langle v_A, v_B \rangle$ and $\langle v_Y, v_Z \rangle$: one is for $v_A \prec v_Y \prec v_B \prec v_Z$, and the other is for $v_A \prec v_B \prec v_Y \prec v_Z$. For the former case, $\{v_C, v_X, \langle v_A, v_B \rangle, \langle v_Y, v_Z \rangle\}$ satisfies $C3$. For the latter case, the current feasible interval is $C[v_{B-1}, v_{Y+1}]$.

Thus, we need new attics or cc-pairs to exclude $C[v_{B-1}, v_{Y+1}]$ from $\mathcal{G}$. Suppose that attics exclude the interval. If there is an $l$-attic $v_s$ in $C[d, v_{B-1}]$, then $\{\langle v_A, v_B \rangle, v_s, v_C\}$ satisfies $C3$. Similarly, an $r$-attic in $C[v_{Y+1}, d]$ will satisfy $C3$. Suppose that an $l$-attic $v_t$ in $C[v_{B-1}, v_{Y+1}]$ and a cc-pair $\langle v_x, v_y \rangle$ whose $r$-cellar is in $C[v_{t+1}, v_{Y+1}]$ exclude the interval $C[v_{B-1}, v_{Y+1}]$. Then $\{\langle v_A, v_B \rangle, \langle v_x, v_y \rangle, v_C, v_t\}$ satisfies $C3$. Similarly, other attics that make $\mathcal{G}$ empty will satisfy $C2$ or $C3$. Thus, suppose that only cc-pairs exclude the interval $C[v_{B-1}, v_{Y+1}]$, Then it satisfies $C4$. Therefore, a room has an empty $\mathcal{G}$ if and only if it satisfies $C2$, $C3$ or $C4$. □

Let us briefly check the time complexity to test $C1$, $C2$, $C3$ and $C4$ for a given room. While scanning the boundary of $\mathcal{P}$, we can identify attics, cellars and dominated chains using the ray shooting query that takes $O(\log n)$ time [3]. As mentioned in Section 3.1, in order to test if a given room satisfies $\mathcal{G} = \emptyset$, it is not necessary to check all the cc-pairs. We have only to check a constant number of cc-pairs for each attic. Similarly, we maintain the data structure for attics whose dominated chains are maximal. Therefore, after the preprocessing, $C1$, $C2$, $C3$ and $C4$ can be tested during a scan of sorted lists of the attics and the cc-pairs in linear time. Thus, we can test if a given room is searchable in $O(n \log n)$ time. Details can be found in the full paper.

### 3.3   Necessity

To show the necessity of the condition, we revisit the corridor problem. When two guards walk in the corridor, it can be necessary that one guard moves backwards (towards $d$) while the other advances towards $g$. This type of motion is called a *counter-walk*. Icking and Klein [6] gave the necessary and sufficient condition for the corridor to admit a counter-walk, which is rewritten using our notations as follows:

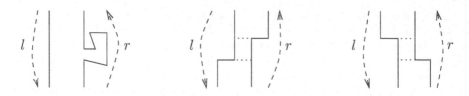

**Fig. 6.** Examples of corridor subchains that cannot have a counter-walk

**Theorem 3.** [6] *Let $L$ be a chain where $l$ moves towards $d$, and $R$ be a chain where $r$ moves towards $g$. Then $L$ and $R$ cannot have a counter-walk if:*

(a) *$L$ and $R$ are not weakly visible from each other, or*
(b) *$L$ has an $l$-cellar non-dominating with an $l$-attic in $R$, or*
(c) *$L$ has an $r$-attic non-dominating with an $r$-cellar in $R$.*

The typical examples that cannot have a counter-walk are depicted in Figure 6. Whenever two guards have to move by a counter-walk, two chains where two guards move must satisfy none of (a), (b) and (c) in Theorem 3.

For each cc-pair $\langle v_i, v_j \rangle$, let the *left-interval* denote $C[d, v_{i+1}]$ and the *right-interval* denote $C[v_{j-1}, d]$. Now let us show that a room that satisfies none of $C1, C2, C3$ and $C4$ is searchable by two guards.

**Lemma 5.** *If a room $(\mathcal{P}, d)$ satisfies none of $C1, C2, C3$ and $C4$, then $(\mathcal{P}, d)$ is searchable.*

*Proof.* Suppose that $(\mathcal{P}, d)$ satisfies none of $C1, C2, C3$ and $C4$. There are three cases for such rooms.

**A1** $(\mathcal{P}, d)$ has no attics.
**A2** $(\mathcal{P}, d)$ has neither aa-pair nor cc-pair.
**A3** $(\mathcal{P}, d)$ has a nonempty $\mathcal{G}$.

**A1:** If a room has no attic, then every point in $\mathcal{P}$ is visible from the door $d$. Thus, $l$ stands at $d$ while $r$ traverses $\partial \mathcal{P}$. When $r$ returns to $d$, the searching is done.

**A2:** First, we compute the feasible range of the final point, $\mathcal{G}' = \bigcap_{x \in \mathcal{N}_{attic}} \mathcal{D}(x)$.

Let $g'$ be an arbitrary point in $\mathcal{G}'$. Second, we transform the room $(\mathcal{P}, d)$ to the corridor $(\mathcal{P}, d, g')$, and then search $(\mathcal{P}, d, g')$ using the well-known corridor search algorithm. Because $(\mathcal{P}, d)$ has neither aa-pair nor cc-pair, $\mathcal{G}'$ is not empty and $(\mathcal{P}, d, g')$ satisfies the conditions of Theorem 1. Thus any room satisfying A2 is always searchable.

**A3:** Assume that a given room $(\mathcal{P}, d)$ has at least one attic and at least one cc-pair but no aa-pair. If $\mathcal{G}$ is not connected, that is, consists of several disjoint chains, then choose a maximal connected chain as $\mathcal{G}$. Let $\mathcal{G} = C[v_{g-1}, v_{h+1}]$. Then $\mathcal{G}$ has three cases as follows:

**B1** $\mathcal{G}$ has no intersection with the right-interval of any cc-pair.

**B2** $\mathcal{G}$ has no intersection with the left-interval of any cc-pair.

**B3** $\mathcal{G}$ intersects with a left-interval and a right-interval.

**B1:** First, we will move $r$ to reach $v_{h+1}$. Second, we will clear $C[d, v_{h+1}]$. There are no $r$-attics in $C(v_{h+1}, d)$ due to Lemma 3(b). $r$ is able to clear all the $l$-attics in $C(v_{h+1}, d)$ visible from $C[d, v_{h+1}]$. Suppose that there is an $l$-attic $v_p$ invisible from $C[d, v_{h+1}]$. If $v_h$ is an $l$-attic, then $v_h$ and $v_p$ will form an aa-pair. So $v_h$ must be an $l$-cellar of a cc-pair. Let $\langle v_h, v_f \rangle$ be a cc-pair. Then $v_f$ must precede $v_p$ ; otherwise $v_p$ and $\langle v_h, v_f \rangle$ would make $\mathcal{G}$ empty. Thus, we do not violate Lemma 2 when $l$ goes outside $C[d, v_{h+1}]$ to see $r$ at $v_p$. Also, $v_h$ should dominate $v_p$ ; otherwise $\mathcal{G}$ would be empty by Lemma 3(c). Now we will show that $l$ is always able to go back to $C[d, v_{h+1}]$. In other words, a counter-walk where $l$ moves back to $v_{h+1}$ and $r$ moves from $v_p$ toward $v_f$ should not satisfy the conditions in Theorem 3. Let $L$ be $C[v_{h+1}, shot(v_p)]$ and $R$ be $C[v_{f-1}, v_p]$. Then $L$ has no $r$-attic invisible from $v_f$ ; otherwise the $r$-attic would make $\mathcal{G}$ empty with $\langle v_h, v_f \rangle$. And an $l$-cellar or $l$-attic in $L$ non-dominating with $v_p$ will make an aa-pair or make $\mathcal{G}$ empty. Thus, $L$ and $R$ are weakly visible each other. If this counter-walk satisfies Theorem 3(b), then an $l$-attic is non-dominating with $v_h$, so $\mathcal{G}$ will become empty. If it satisfies Theorem 3(c), then an $r$-attic non-dominating with $v_h$ will make $\mathcal{G}$ empty by Lemma 3(c). Therefore, we can always move $r$ finally to $v_{h+1}$. Clearing $C[d, v_{h+1}]$ is always possible because $C[d, v_{h+1}]$ has no cc-pair and no aa-pair.

**B2:** Symmetric to **B1**.

**B3:** Let $L$ be $C[d, v_{g-1}]$ and $R$ be $C[v_{h+1}, d]$. By Lemma 3(a) and (b), $L$ has no $l$-attics and $R$ has no $r$-attics. An $l$-cellar in $L$ and an $r$-cellar in $R$ do not make a cc-pair ; otherwise $\mathcal{G}$ would be empty. To avoid an aa-pair, $L$ cannot have an attic invisible from $R$ when $L$ has an attic invisible from $R$, and vice versa. If there are no such attics, we can move $l$ from $d$ to $v_{g-1}$ and move $r$ from $d$ to $v_{h+1}$, which does not violate the conditions in Theorem 1. Otherwise, assume that $R$ has an $l$-attic $v_p$ invisible from $L$, without loss of generality. Then $v_p$ should be visible from a point in $\mathcal{G}$, say $\bar{v}_p$. Let us move $l$ from $d$ to $v_{g-1}$ and move $r$ from $d$ to $v_{h+1}$. When $r$ passes $v_p$, $l$ moves up to $\bar{v}_p$. However, if there is an $r$-cellar $v_j \in C(v_{h+1}, v_p)$ that is invisible from $\bar{v}_p$, then $l$ should move back. Let us show that this counter-walk does not satisfy the conditions in Theorem 3. Let $L'$ be the chain where $l$ should move down and $R'$ be the chain where $r$ should move up. First, suppose that this counter-walk satisfies Theorem 3(b). Then an $l$-cellar $v_i$ in $L'$ invisible from $v_j$ will make a cc-pair with $v_j$. By Corollary 1, $C(v_{i+1}, v_{j-1})$ should be excluded from $\mathcal{G}$, which is a contradiction. If this counter-walk satisfies Theorem 3(c), then an $r$-attic in $L'$ will make an aa-pair with $v_p$. The weak-visibility between $L'$ and $R'$ can be shown by a similar way. Therefore, we can always move both $l$ and $r$ up to $\mathcal{G}$. Finally, we can always clear the inside of $\mathcal{G}$ because $\mathcal{G}$ has no cc-pair and no aa-pair. ☐

By Theorem 2, Lemma 4 and Lemma 5, we have the following conclusion.

**Theorem 4.** *A room is unsearchable by two guards if and only if it satisfies one of C1, C2, C3 and C4. To test these conditions for a given room can be done in $O(n \log n)$ time.*

## 4    Conclusion

In this paper, the problem of searching a room by two mobile guards in the presence of mobile intruders is considered. We have suggested and proven the necessary and sufficient condition for two guards to search a room, and showed that to test whether a given room is searchable by two guards can be done in $O(n \log n)$ time. We expect that this results will lead to insights into the problem of searching a polygon without a door.

## References

1. D. Avis and G. T. Toussaint. An Optimal algorithm for determining the visibility of a polygon from an Edge, *IEEE Transactions on Computers* 30:910–914, 1981.
2. D. Crass, I. Suzuki and M. Yamashita. Searching for a mobile intruder in a corridor - The open edge variant of the polygon search problem, *International Journal of Computational Geometry an Applications*, 5(4):397–412, 1995.
3. L. J. Guibas, J. Hershberger, D. Leven, M. Sharir, and R. Tarjan. Linear-time algorithm for visibility and shortest path problems inside triangulated simple polygons. *Algorithmica*, 2:209–233, 1987.
4. L. J. Guibas, J.-C. Latombe, S. M. Lavalle, D. Lin and R. Motwani. A visibility-based pursuit-evasion problem, *International Journal of Computational Geometry an Applications*, 9(4):471–493, 1999.
5. P. J. Heffernan. An optimal algorithm for the two-guard problem, *International Journal of Computational Geometry an Applications*, 6(1):15–44, 1996.
6. C. Icking and R. Klein. The two guards problem, *International Journal of Computational Geometry an Applications*, 2(3):257–285, 1992.
7. S. M. Lavalle, B. H. Simov, and G. Slutzki. An algorithm for searching a polygonal region with a flashlight. In *Proceedings, ACM Symposium on Computational Geometry*, pages 260–269, Hong Kong, June 2000.
8. J.-H. Lee, S.-M. Park and K.-Y. Chwa. Searching a polygonal room with one door by a 1-searcher, *International Journal of Computational Geometry an Applications*, 10(2):201–220, 2000.
9. J.-H. Lee, S. Y. Shin and K.-Y. Chwa. Visibility-based pursuit-evasion in a polygonal room with a door, In *Proceedings, ACM Symposium on Computational Geometry*, pages 281–290, FL, USA, June 1999.
10. G. Narashimhan. On hamiltonian triangulations in simple polygons, *International Journal of Computational Geometry an Applications*, 9(3):261–275, 1999.
11. I. Suzuki and M. Yamashita. Searching for a mobile intruder in a polygonal region, *SIAM Journal on Computing*, 21(5):863–888, 1992.
12. L. H. Tseng, P. Heffernan, and D. T. Lee. Two-guard walkability of simple polygons, *International Journal of Computational Geometry an Applications*, 8:85–116, 1998.

# Improved Phylogeny Comparisons: Non-shared Edges, Nearest Neighbor Interchanges, and Subtree Transfers

Wing-Kai Hon[*][1], Ming-Yang Kao[**][2], and Tak-Wah Lam[1]

[1] Department of Computer Science and Information Systems, The University of Hong Kong, Hong Kong, {wkhon,twlam}@csis.hku.hk

[2] Department of Computer Science, Yale University, New Haven, CT 06520, U.S.A. kao-ming-yang@cs.yale.edu

**Abstract.** The number of the non-shared edges of two phylogenies is a basic measure of the distance (dissimilarity) between the phylogenies. The non-shared edges are also the building block for approximating a more sophisticated metric called the NNI distance. In this paper we give the first sub-quadratic time algorithm for finding the non-shared edges, which are then used to speed up the existing approximation algorithm for the NNI distance. The time is improved from $O(n^2)$ to $O(n \log n)$. Another popular distance metric for phylogenies is the STT distance. Previous work on computing the STT distance focused on degree-3 trees only. We show that the STT distance can be applied in a broader sense, allowing us to cover degree-$d$ trees, where $d \geq 3$. In particular, we give a new approximation algorithm for the STT distance.

## 1 Introduction

Phylogenetic trees or phylogenies are trees whose leaves are labeled with distinct species. Different theories about the evolutionary relationship of the same species often result in different phylogenies. This paper is concerned with several well-known metrics for measuring the distance (or dissimilarity) between two phylogenies, namely, the non-shared edges [1,12,9], the nearest neighbor interchange distance [11,10] and the subtree transfer distance [5,6]. Basically, the first metric is relatively primitive and it simply compares the phylogenies according to some structure criteria; the other two metrics measure the minimum number of some kind of tree operations required to transform one phylogeny to the other. The NNI distance is based on the operation that swaps two subtrees over an internal edge; for the STT distance, we allow in one operation to detach a subtree from a node and re-attach it to another part of the tree. The non-shared edges can be found in quadratic time using a brute-force approach, while computing the NNI or STT distance is NP-hard.

---

[*] Research supported in part by Hong Kong RGC Grant HKU-7027/98E.
[**] Research supported in part by NSF Grant 9531028.

D.T. Lee and S.-H. Teng (Eds.): ISAAC 2000, LNCS 1969, pp. 527–538, 2000.

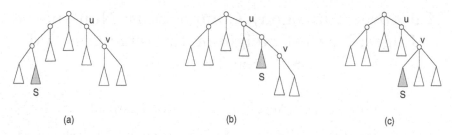

**Fig. 1.** Examples of restricted-STT and STT operations: (a) is transformed to (b) by a restricted-STT operation, while (a) is transformed to (c) by an STT operation

In this paper we consider phylogenies whose nodes have arbitrary degrees, say, at most $d \geq 3$, and whose edges may carry weights.[1] Our first result is a faster algorithm for finding the non-shared (also known as bad) edges of two weighted degree-$d$ phylogenies $T$ and $T'$, which are defined as follows: An edge $e$ in $T$ is said to be *shared* if for some edge $e'$ in $T'$, $e$ and $e'$ induce the same partition of leaf labels, internal node degrees, and edge weights; otherwise, $e$ is *non-shared*. Prior to our work, non-shared edges could only be found using a brute-force approach in $O(n^2)$ time, where $n$ is the number of leaves. If we restrict our attention to the partition of leaf labels only, Day [4] showed that the time for finding non-shared edges can be reduced to $O(n)$. The improvement stems from the fact that leaf labels are distinct but node degrees and edge weights are not. In this paper we show an $O(n \log n)$ time algorithm for finding the general non-shared edges.

The problem of finding non-shared edges is a key step, as well as the most time consuming step, for approximating the NNI distance. In particular, for weighted degree-3 or unweighted/weighted degree-$d$ phylogenies, existing approximation algorithms take $O(n^2)$ time [3,8]. With our new non-shared edge algorithm, the time complexity of these approximation algorithms can all be improved to $O(n \log n)$. Note that for unweighted degree-3 trees, an $O(n \log n)$-time algorithm has already been obtained [9], which makes use of Day's linear-time algorithm [4] to identify the non-shared edges.

Previous work on the subtree transfer (STT) distance focuses on degree-3 trees only [7,2]. In particular, in the course of transforming a degree-3 tree to another degree-3 tree, it is assumed that all intermediate trees are also of degree 3. In other words, the STT operation is *restricted* in the sense that the subtree detached can only be re-attached to the middle of an edge, producing a new internal node with degree 3. See Figure 1 for an example. In this paper we study the STT distance in a broader sense, covering degree-$d$ phylogenies for $d \geq 3$ and allowing an STT operation to re-attach the subtree to either an internal node or the middle of an edge.

---

[1] The magnitude of an edge weight, also known as branch length in genetics, could represent the number of mutations or the time required by the evolution along the edge.

An STT operation is charged by how far the subtree is transferred. More specifically, depending on whether the trees are unweighted or weighted, we count respectively the number or total weight of the edges between the nodes where detachment and re-attachment take place.[2] Define the STT (resp. restricted-STT) distance between two phylogenies as the minimum cost of transforming one to the other using STT (resp. restricted-STT) operations. Unlike many other graph or tree problems, the unweighted version of the STT distance problem is not a special case of the weighted version. In particular, Figure 2 shows two phylogenies whose unweighted STT distance is $\Omega(n)$, yet when we consider these phylogenies with every edge assigned a unit weight, their weighted STT distance is only $O(1)$. On the other hand, the unweighted STT distance is not necessarily bigger than the weighted one; Figure 3 shows two phylogenies whose unweighted STT distance is indeed smaller than the weighted one.

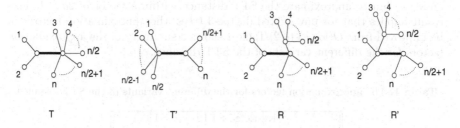

**Fig. 2.** The unweighted STT distance between $T$ and $T'$ is $\Omega(n)$. Let us consider $T$ and $T'$ as weighted trees such that every internal edge has a unit weight (i.e., the highlighted edges in the figures). The weighted STT distance between $T$ and $T'$ is 1. In particular, the cost of transforming $T$ to $R$, then to $R'$, and finally to $T'$ is $0+1+0=1$

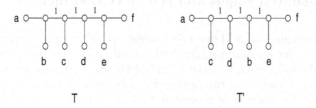

**Fig. 3.** $T$ and $T'$ are degree-3 phylogenies. The unweighted STT distance between $T$ and $T'$ (which is 3) is smaller than the weighted STT distance (which is 4)

---

[2] This charging model is referred to as the linear cost model in the literature. It is preferred to the unit cost model as the latter does not reflect the evolutionary distance.

For degree-3 phylogenies, when they are weighted, we can prove that the STT distance is the same as the restricted-STT distance, and DasGupta et al. have shown that the latter can be approximated within a factor of 2 [2]. For unweighted phylogenies, deriving a tight approximation algorithm is more difficult; the restricted-STT distance can be approximated within only a factor of $O(\log n)$ [2]. The result on restricted-STT distance implies an approximation algorithm for the STT distance with the same performance. However, there are examples in which the STT distance is much smaller than restricted-STT distance. It is natural to ask whether the STT distance can be approximated within a better factor.

Let us look at degree-$d$ phylogenies. First of all, it is worth-mentioning that the restricted-STT distance is $\infty$ as a restricted-STT operation can only produce an internal node of degree 3. For weighted phylogenies, the STT distance can be approximated by adapting the algorithm by DasGupta for degree-3 trees [2], achieving the approximation factor of 2. For unweighted phylogenies, we derive an algorithm to approximate the STT distance within a factor of $2d - 4$. This result implies that for unweighted degree-3 trees, the approximation factor can be improved from $O(\log n)$ to 2. Table 1 shows a summary of the approximation factors for the different variants of the STT distance.

**Table 1.** The approximation factors for the different variants of the STT distance

|  | restricted-STT (degree-3 trees) | STT (degree-$d$ trees) |
|---|---|---|
| weighted | 2 | 2 |
| unweighted | $O(\log n)$ | $2d - 4$ |

## 2   Non-shared Edges and the NNI Distance

Given a phylogeny, an NNI operation swaps two subtrees over an internal edge. See Figure 4 for an example. An NNI operation is charged a cost of one for unweighted phylogenies, and the weight of the internal edge for weighted phylogenies. Let $T$ and $T'$ be two phylogenies labeled with the same set of species, and let $n$ be the number of species in $T$. The NNI distance between $T$ and $T'$ is defined to be the minimum cost of transforming $T$ to $T'$ using NNI operations (see [8] for the necessary and sufficient conditions for the existence of such transformations).

The problem of computing the NNI distance is NP-hard [3]. For weighted degree-3 phylogenies, or unweighted/weighted degree-$d$ phylogenies, existing approximation algorithms for the NNI distance [3,8] have the same bottleneck of finding the non-shared edges of the phylogenies, and other computations take

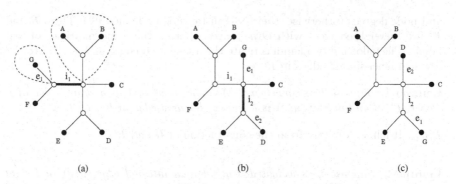

**Fig. 4.** An NNI operation swaps two subtrees over an internal edge. (b) is transformed from (a) using an NNI operation over the edge $i_1$, and (c) from (b) over the edge $i_2$. The NNI distance between phylogeny in (a) and phylogeny in (c) is 2

only $O(n \log n)$ time. In this section, we present an algorithm for finding non-shared edges in $O(n \log n)$ time, thus improving the running time of these approximation algorithms to $O(n \log n)$ time. Below, we first show that the non-shared edge problem of two weighted phylogenies $T$ and $T'$ can be transformed in linear time to a simpler problem of two unweighted trees $R$ and $R'$ with leaves labeled by non-distinct symbols. The simpler problem is to find the non-leaf-label-shared edges which are defined as follows:

**Definition 1.** *Consider two trees $R$ and $R'$ with leaves labeled with the same multi-set of symbols. An edge $e$ in $T$ is said to be a leaf-label-shared edge if there exists an edge $e'$ in $T'$ such that $e$ and $e'$ partition the leaf labels into the same multi-sets. Otherwise, $e$ is a non-leaf-label-shared edge.*

We will give an $O(n \log n)$-time algorithm for finding non-leaf-label-shared edges, thus solving the original non-shared edge problem in $O(n \log n)$ time.

## 2.1   Non-leaf-Label-Shared Edges

In this section we show that two weighted phylogenies $T$ and $T'$ can be transformed to two unweighted trees $R$ and $R'$ with leaves labeled with non-distinct symbols such that if we have found the non-leaf-label-shared edges of $R$ and $R'$, the non-shared edges of $T$ and $T'$ can be identified in extra $O(n)$ time.

The construction of $R$ and $R'$ is as follows. First of all, $R$ is made identical to $T$. We attach a new leaf to every internal node in $R$, and nodes with the same degree each recieve a new leaf with the same label. Each internal edge in $R$ is then split into two edges sharing a common node, to which a new labeled leaf is attached. Labels of such new leaves are the same if the original edges have the same weight in $T$. Finally, we remove the edge weights in $R$ to make it unweighted. $R'$ is constructed from $T'$ in a similar way. We assume that $T$ and $T'$ have the same set of leaf labels and the same multi-sets of edge weights and node degrees (otherwise, their NNI distance is undefined [8]). Thus, $R$ and $R'$ are unweighted trees with $O(n)$ leaves, sharing the same multi-set of leaf labels. The following two lemmas relate the non-shared edges of $T$ and $T'$ to the non-leaf-label-shared edges in $R$.

**Lemma 1.** *Suppose $T$ is unweighted. An edge $(u, v)$ in $T$ is a shared edge of $T$ (w.r.t. $T'$) if and only if $(u, v)$ is a leaf-label-shared edge of $R$ (w.r.t. $R'$).*

*Proof.* It follows directly from the construction of $R$ and $R'$.

**Lemma 2.** *Suppose $T$ is weighted. Consider an internal edge $(u, v)$ in $T$ that is split into two edges $(u, s)$ and $(v, s)$ in $R$. Then $(u, v)$ is a shared edge of $T$ (w.r.t. $T'$) if and only if $(u, s)$ and $(v, s)$ are leaf-label-shared edges of $R$ (w.r.t. $R'$).*

*Proof.* If $(u, v)$ is a shared edge in $T$, it is obvious that $(u, s)$ and $(v, s)$ are leaf-label-shared. Conversely, if $(u, s)$ and $(v, s)$ are leaf-label-shared, then there are some edges $e$ and $e'$ in $R'$ that give the same partitioning of leaf labels as $(u, s)$ and $(v, s)$, respectively. The partitioning defined by $(u, s)$ and $(v, s)$ differ only by one leaf label (the label of the leaf attaching to $s$), therefore, $e$ and $e'$ must be adjacent edges in $R'$. Moreover, only one leaf is attached to the common node of $e$ and $e'$ and the label is the same as the label of the leaf attached to $s$. This implies that $e$ and $e'$ are split from a weighted edge in $T'$ which has the same partitioning (of leaf labels, edge weights and node degrees) as $(u, v)$ in $T$. In other words, $(u, v)$ is a shared edge and this completes the proof.

We arrive at the following conclusion.

**Lemma 3.** *Suppose the non-leaf-label-shared edges of $R$ and $R'$ are given. Then the non-shared edges between $T$ and $T'$ can be identified in $O(n)$ time.*

*Proof.* By Lemma 1 and Lemma 2, once the non-leaf-label-shared edges in $R$ and $R'$ are known, we can use $O(n)$ time to identify all the non-shared edges of $T$ and $T'$.

In the following subsection, we show that the non-leaf-label-shared edges of $R$ and $R'$ can be found in $O(n \log n)$ time. Therefore, we claim the following theorem.

**Theorem 1.** *The non-shared edges of $T$ and $T'$ can be identified in $O(n \log n)$ time.*

## 2.2   An $O(n \log n)$-Time Algorithm

Let $R$ and $R'$ be two unweighted trees with the same multi-set of leaf labels, and let $n$ be the number of leaves in either tree. In this subsection, we show that the non-leaf-label-shared edges of $R$ and $R'$ can be found in $O(n \log n)$ time.

We have the following observation: Suppose that $R$ and $R'$ are rooted to become $X$ and $X'$ respectively, so that every proper subtree of $X$ and $X'$ contains less than $\frac{n}{2}$ leaves. (When no such root can be found, there must be an edge in $R$ which partitions the leaves evenly. In that case, we insert a new node between the edge to make a root for $X$.) Let $(u, v)$ be an edge in $R$, with $v$ being the child of $u$ in $X$. It is easy to see that $(u, v)$ is leaf-label-shared if and only if there is some node $v'$ in $X'$, such that the subtrees rooted at $v$ and $v'$ share the same the multi-set of leaf labels.

Making use of the observation, we identify the non-leaf-labeled-shared edges of $R$ and $R'$ as follows.

Step 1. Root $R$ and $R'$ to become $X$ and $X'$.

Step 2. Identify nodes in $X$ and $X'$ whose subtrees contain the same multi-set of leaf labels. Afterwards, report non-leaf-labeled-shared edges of $R$ and $R'$.

Finding the root for $X$ (Step 1) is rather simple and can be done in linear time: We arbitrarily root $R$ at some node, traverse $R$ in a post-order traversal, and count the number of leaves in the subtree rooted at each node. The first node which has more than $\frac{n}{2}$ leaves becomes the root for $X$.

To achieve an $O(n \log n)$ running time for the overall algorithm, Step 2 needs to be handled in $O(n \log n)$ time. Our method is to apply a bottom-up algorithm on $X$ and $X'$ with relabeling technique. In the remaining parts, we first describe some lemmas related to the relabeling technique and finally present the bottom-up algorithm which runs in $O(n \log n)$ time.

## Preliminaries

**Definition 2.** *To relabel a (multi-)set of objects, we mean that objects are assigned the same label whenever the objects are the same, and are assigned different labels whenever the objects are different.*

**Lemma 4.** Let $A$ and $B$ be two sets of consecutive integers starting from 0. Suppose we are given $t$ objects, each corresponds to a 2-tuple in the form of $(a, b)$, where $a \in A$ and $b \in B$. Then we can relabel the objects (2-tuples) with integers in the range $[1, t]$ using $O(|A| + |B| + t)$ time.

*Proof.* First, we sort the $t$ 2-tuples by radix sort. This can be done in $O(|A| + |B| + t)$ time. We then traverse the sorted list of 2-tuples, compare consecutive ones and assign a new integer (starting from 1) to every distinct 2-tuple encountered. This can be done in $O(t)$ time. Finally, observe that at most $t$ integers are used for the relabeling, since there are at most $t$ distinct 2-tuples.

We next describe the relabeling technique used by the bottom-up algorithm. Let $S$ be the multi-set of leaf labels in $X$ (or $X'$). Let $A$ be a subset of $S$.

**Definition 3.** *Define $X_A$ to be an induced subtree of $X$ with leaves labeled by $A$.*

**Definition 4.** *For each internal node $v$ in a tree, define $L(v)$ be the multi-set of leaf labels in the subtree rooted at $v$. Moreover, define $L(v|A)$ to be the multi-set of labels formed by retaining only the labels in $L(v)$ which is in $A$, while deleting all the others.*

**Lemma 5.** Let $A$ and $B$ be disjoint subsets of $S$. Let $v$ be an internal node in $X_{A \cup B}$. Then either $L(v|A) = \phi$ or $L(v|A) = L(u)$ for some internal node $u$ in $X_A$.

*Proof.* Suppose on the contrary that there is such $v$ with $L(v|A) \neq \phi$ nor $L(v|A) \neq L(u)$ for all internal node $u$ in $X_A$. Without loss of generality, let this $v$ be the first one visited by post-order traversal of $X_{A \cup B}$. $v$ cannot be in $X_A$, so $v$ has at most 1 child whose subtree contains some leaf labels in $A$. If $v$ has 1 such child $s$, then $L(v|A) = L(s|A)$ which contradicts the choice of $v$. If $v$ has no such child, $L(v|A) = \phi$. Thus, no such $v$ exists and Lemma 5 follows.

**Lemma 6.** Let $A$ and $B$ be disjoint subsets of $S$. Suppose the internal nodes in $X_A$ are relabeled with consecutive integers from 1, such that the integers for internal nodes $u$ and $u'$ are the same if and only if $L(u) = L(u')$. Then in linear time, we can relabel every internal nodes $v$ in $X_{A \cup B}$ according to $X_A$, such that if $L(v|A) = \phi$, $v$ is relabeled with 0 and if $L(v|A) = L(u)$ for some internal node $u$ in $X_A$, $v$ is relabeled by the same integer as $u$.

*Proof.* The relabeling can be done by traversing $X_{A \cup B}$ using post-order traversal. For every internal node $v$ encountered,

– if $v$ is also in $X_A$, assign the integer of $v$ in $X_A$ to $v$ in $X_{A \cup B}$.
– if $v$ is not in $X_A$, at most one child of $v$ can be assigned a non-zero integer. Since the children of $v$ is traversed before $v$, we can examine the relabeling of all those children. If all of them are 0, assign 0 to $v$. Otherwise, exactly one child is assigned non-zero and we assign that integer to $v$.

Using the above relabeling, an internal node $v$ in $X_{A \cup B}$ is assigned the same label as an internal node $u$ in $X_A$ if and only if $L(v|A) = L(u)$. Since each internal node is traversed once and examined once, the algorithm runs in linear time.

**Corollary 1.** All the internal nodes $v$ in $X_{A \cup B}$ can be associated with 2-tuples $(a, b)$ in linear time, such that $a$ and $b$ are the relabelings of $v$ according to $X_A$ and $X_B$ respectively.

The next part describes our bottom-up algorithm on $X$ and $X'$.

**The bottom-up algorithm.** First of all, we give the definition of matched nodes and unmatched nodes as follows.

**Definition 5.** *An internal node $u$ in $X_A$ is* matched *if there is some internal node $v$ in $X'_A$ such that $L(u|A) = L(v|A)$. Otherwise, $u$ is* unmatched.

To identify the nodes in $X$ whose subtree contains the same multi-set of leaf labels as some node in $X'$, is therefore equivalent to identify the *matched* nodes in $X_S$. The following presents an algorithm that finds all the *unmatched* internal nodes for $X_S$ and $X'_S$.

Step 1. For each distinct label $i$ in $S$, compute $L(v)$ for every internal node $v$ in $X_{\{i\}}$ and $X'_{\{i\}}$. Relabel the internal nodes by consecutive integers starting from 1, such that two nodes $v_1$ and $v_2$ shares the same integer if and only if $L(v_1) = L(v_2)$. Moreover, we check for any *unmatched* nodes.

Step 2. Pair up the labels in $S$. For each pair of labels $i$ and $j$, associate 2-tuples to internal nodes of $X_{\{i,j\}}$ according to $X_{\{i\}}$ and $X_{\{j\}}$, as described in Corollary 1. Similarly, associate 2-tuples to internal nodes of $X'_{\{i,j\}}$. Relabel the 2-tuples in both trees with consecutive integers starting from 1 (Lemma 4). Moreover, we check for any *unmatched* nodes.

Step 3. Pair up the pairs of labels (say, $\{i,j\}$ and $\{k,l\}$) from Step 2. We associate 2-tuples to internal nodes of $X_{\{i,j,k,l\}}$ according to $X_{\{i,j\}}$ and $X_{\{k,l\}}$. Similarly, we associate 2-tuples to internal nodes of $X'_{\{i,j,k,l\}}$ according to $X'_{\{i,j\}}$ and $X'_{\{k,l\}}$. Relabel the 2-tuples in both trees with consecutive integers starting from 1. Moreover, we check for any *unmatched* nodes.

Step 4 to Step $\log |S|$. Similar to Step 3. Continue pair up the labels until the size become $|S|$.

Note that the unmatched nodes in $X_S$ or $X'_S$ must be unmatched in one of the steps. Therefore, the above algorithm identifies all the unmatched nodes (and also the matched nodes) in $X_S$ and $X'_S$.

Observe that relabeling of internal nodes can be done in time proportional to the number of internal nodes involved, whereas the checking for unmatched nodes can be done along with the relabeling (because unmatched nodes in one tree is relabeled by an integer not appearing in the other tree). Since a total of at most $2n$ internal nodes are involved in each step, we thus need $O(n)$ time to complete one step. Finally, we have the following lemma and corollary.

**Lemma 7.** The unmatched nodes in $X$ and $X'$ can be identified in $O(n \log |S|)$ time.

**Corollary 2.** The nodes in $X$ whose subtree contains the same multi-set of leaf labels as some node in $X'$, can be identified in $O(n \log n)$ time.

## 3    The STT Distance between Degree-$d$ Phylogenies

In this section we investigate the subtree-transfer (STT) distance between degree-$d$ phylogenies, where $d \geq 3$. Recall that an STT operation allows us to detach a subtree and re-attach it to either an internal node or the middle of an edge. For weighted phylogenies, it is again NP-hard to compute the STT distance; we can prove it by directly adapting the proof of the NP-hardness of the restricted-STT distance between degree-3 trees [2]. Also, we can use the approximation algorithm for the restricted-STT distance between degree-3 phylogenies [2] to approximate the STT distance between two degree-$d$ phylogenies within a factor of 2. Details will be shown in the full paper.

The rest of this section devotes to unweighted phylogenies. We discuss the NP-hardness and a new approximation algorithm for finding the STT distance between unweighted degree-$d$ phylogenies. We achieve an approximation factor of $2d - 4$. An implication of our result is that, if we allow intermediate trees to be of non-uniform degrees, the STT distance between two degree-3 phylogenies can be approximated within a factor of 2.

We believe that it is NP-hard to compute the STT distance between two degree-$d$ phylogenies, but we can only prove the NP-hardness of a slightly more general problem. See the following lemma.

**Lemma 8.** Let $T_1$ and $T_2$ be two degree-$d$ trees whose leaves are labeled with the same multi-set of symbols. Then computing the STT distance between them is NP-hard.

*Proof (Proof (sketch):).* We make use of the ideas in [3]. Our proof is based on the reduction from a well-known NP-complete problem called Exact Cover by 3-sets (X3C), which is defined as follows. Given a set $S = \{s_1, \ldots, s_{3q}\}$ elements and $n$ 3-sets $C_1, \ldots, C_n$ where $C_i = \{s_{i_1}, s_{i_2}, s_{i_3}\}$, determine whether there is an exact cover of $S$ (by $q$ disjoint sets of $C_i$). We can argue that for any instance of the X3C problem (with sufficiently large $n$), we can construct two non-uniquely labeled trees $T$ and $T'$ (see Figure 5) such that there is an exact cover of $S$ if and only if the STT distance between $T$ and $T'$ is less than $3n^3 + o(n^2)$. The details are as follows.

- if there is an exact cover of $S$, then $T$ can be transformed to $T'$ with cost $= 3n^3 + o(n)$, by transforming (i) $q$ long arms (which corresponds the $q$ cover-set) in $T$ to $3q$ short arms in $T'$ and (ii) the remaining $n - q$ long arms in $T$ to $n - q$ long arms in $T'$.
- if there is no exact cover of $S$, then at least $3n^3 + n^2$ cost is needed to transform $T$ to $T'$. This is because at least $q + 1$ long arms are needed in the production of the $3q$ short arms, which requires an extra cost of $n^2$.

The following lemma gives a useful lower bound on the STT distance between two phylogenies.

**Lemma 9.** Let $T$ and $T'$ be two degree-$d$ phylogenies with the same multi-set of leaf labels. Let $b$ and $b'$ denote the number of non-leaf-label-shared edges in

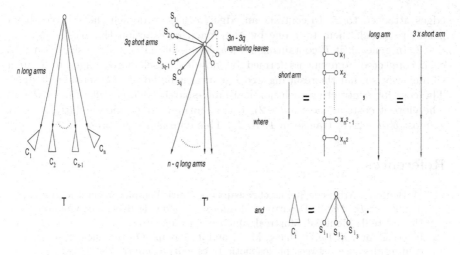

**Fig. 5.** Trees $T$ and $T'$ in the proof of Lemma 8

$T$ and $T'$ respectively (see Section 2 for the definition of non-leaf-label-shared edges). Then the STT distance between $T$ and $T'$ is at least $max(b, b')$.

*Proof.* By viewing an edge as a partitioning of leaves, a sequence of STT operations with cost $k$ can create at most $k$ new edges and delete at most $k$ edges. To transform $T$ to $T'$, we must either delete or create at least $max(b, b')$ edges, because any non-leaf-label-shared edge of one tree is not contained in another. Thus, the STT distance is at least $max(b, b')$.

The following lemma gives an approximation algorithm that transforms an degree-$d$ phylogeny to another. The approximation factor is $2d - 4$, which is independent of the number of leaves, $n$.

**Lemma 10.** Let $T$ and $T'$ be degree-$d$ phylogenies with the same set of leaf labels. Then the STT distance between them can be approximated within a ratio of $2(d - 2)$, where $d$ is the maximum degree of internal nodes in $T$ and $T'$.

*Proof.* We give an algorithm that transforms $T$ into $T'$ with cost bounded by $b(d - 2) + b'(d - 2)$, where $b$ and $b'$ are the number of non-leaf-label-shared edges in $T$ and $T'$ respectively. Then by Lemma 9, we prove Lemma 10.

The algorithm is as follows. We first contract all the non-leaf-label-shared edges in $T$ to become $T_c$. Then we contract all the non-leaf-label-shared edges in $T'$ to become $T'_c$. $T_c$ and $T'_c$ are isomorphic, because they contain leaf-label-shared edges only (Theorem 4, [12]). Since an STT operation is reversible, we have essentially found a way to transform $T$ to $T'$. It remains to show that the required cost is at most $b(d - 2) + b'(d - 2)$. For ease of discussion, suppose $T$ contains non-leaf-label-shared edges only. To transform $T$ into $T_c$, we arbitrary choose an internal node $x$ in $T$, and then repeatedly contract all the internal edges attached to $x$. To contract an edge $\{x, y\}$, we detach the subtrees from $y$ and re-attach them to $x$ one by one. Each contraction thus costs at most $d - 2$. In general, if $T$ contains some leaf-label-shared edges, we shall contract each connected components formed by non-leaf-label-shared edges in $T$ in a similar way, so that the resulting tree $T_c$ contains no non-leaf-label-shared edges. The cost for contracting each non-leaf-label-shared edge is still at most $d - 2$. Therefore it costs at most $b(d - 2)$ to transform $T$ to $T_c$ and similarly, it costs at most $b'(d - 2)$ to transform $T'$ to $T_c'$. This completes the proof.

# References

1. M. Bourque. Arbres de Steiner et reseaux dont varie l'emplagement de certain somments. *Ph.D. Thesis*, Department l'Informatique et de Recherche Operationelle, Université de Montréal, Montréal, Québec, Canada, 1978.
2. B. DasGupta, X. He, T. Jiang, M. Li and J. Tromp. On the linear-cost subtree-transfer distance between phylogenetic trees. *Algorithmica*, 25:2 (1999), pp. 176-195.
3. B. DasGupta, X. He, T. Jiang, M. Li, J. Tromp and L. Zhang. On distances between phylogentic trees. In *Proceedings of the 8th Annual ACM-SIAM Symposium on Discrete Mathematics*, 1997, pp. 427-436.
4. W.H.E. Day. Optimal algorithms for comparing trees with labeled leaves. *Journal of Classification*, 2 (1985), pp. 7-28.
5. J. Hein. Reconstructing evolution of sequences subject to recombination using parsimony. *Mathematical Biosciences*, 98 (1990), pp. 185-200.
6. J. Hein. A heuristic method to reconstruct the history of sequences subject to recombination. *Journal of Molecular Evolution*, 36 (1993), pp. 396-405.
7. J. Hein, T. Jaing, L. Wang and K. Zhang. On the complexity of comparing evolutionary trees. *Discrete Applied Mathematics*, 71 (1996), pp. 153-169.
8. W.K. Hon and T.W. Lam. Approximating the nearest neighbor interchange distance for evolutionary trees with non-uniform degrees. In *Proceedings of Computing and Combinatorics*, 1999, pp. 61-70.
9. M. Li, J. Tromp, and L.X. Zhang. Some notes on the nearest neighbour interchange distance. *Journal of Theoretical Biology*, 182 (1996), pp. 463-467.
10. G.W. Moore, M. Goodman and J. Barnabas. An iterative approach from the standpoint of the additive hypothesis to the dendrogram problem posed by molecular data sets. *Journal of Theoretical Biology*, 38 (1973), pp. 423-457.
11. D.F. Robinson. Comparison of labeled trees with valency three. *Journal of Combinatorial Theory*, 11 (1971), pp. 105-119.
12. D.F. Robinson and L.R. Foulds. Comparison of phylogenetic trees. *Mathematical Biosciences*, 53 (1981), pp. 131-147.

# Phylogenetic $k$-Root and Steiner $k$-Root

Guo-Hui Lin[1,2] *, Paul E. Kearney[1] **, and Tao Jiang[2,3] * * *

[1] Department of Computer Science, University of Waterloo,
Waterloo, Ontario N2L 3G1, Canada.
[2] Department of Computing and Software, McMaster University,
Hamilton, Ontario L8S 4L7, Canada.
[3] Department of Computer Science, University of California,
Riverside, CA 92521.

**Abstract.** Given a graph $G = (V, E)$ and a positive integer $k$, the PHYLOGENETIC $k$-ROOT PROBLEM asks for a (unrooted) tree $T$ without degree-2 nodes such that its leaves are labeled by $V$ and $(u, v) \in E$ if and only if $d_T(u, v) \leq k$. If the vertices in $V$ are also allowed to be internal nodes in $T$, then we have the STEINER $k$-ROOT PROBLEM. Moreover, if a particular subset $S$ of $V$ are required to be internal nodes in $T$, then we have the RESTRICTED STEINER $k$-ROOT PROBLEM. Phylogenetic $k$-roots and Steiner $k$-roots extend the standard notion of GRAPH ROOTS and are motivated by applications in computational biology. In this paper, we first present $O(n + e)$-time algorithms to determine if a (not necessarily connected) graph $G = (V, E)$ has an $S$-restricted 1-root Steiner tree for a given subset $S \subset V$, and to determine if a connected graph $G = (V, E)$ has an $S$-restricted 2-root Steiner tree for a given subset $S \subset V$, where $n = |V|$ and $e = |E|$. We then use these two algorithms as subroutines to design $O(n + e)$-time algorithms to determine if a given (not necessarily connected) graph $G = (V, E)$ has a 3-root phylogeny and to determine if a given connected graph $G = (V, E)$ has a 4-root phylogeny.

**Keywords:** Graph power, graph root, tree power, tree root, phylogeny, computational biology, maximal clique, critical clique, efficient algorithm

## 1 Introduction

A fundamental problem in computational biology is the reconstruction of the evolutionary history of a set of species from biological data. This evolutionary history is typically modeled by an evolutionary tree or *phylogeny*. A phylogeny is a tree where the leaves are labeled by species and each internal node represents a special event whereby an ancestral species gives rise to two or more child species.

* Supported in part by NSERC Research Grant OGP0046613 and a CITO grant.
Email: `ghlin@math.uwaterloo.ca`.
** Supported in part by NSERC Research Grant 160321 and a CITO grant. Email:
`pkearney@math.uwaterloo.ca`.
* * * Supported in part by NSERC Research Grant OGP0046613 and a UCR startup
grant. Email: `jiang@cs.ucr.edu`.

D.T. Lee and S.-H. Teng (Eds.): ISAAC 2000, LNCS 1969, pp. 539–551, 2000.
© Springer-Verlag Berlin Heidelberg 2000

Both rooted and unrooted trees have been used to describe phylogenies in the literature; but here we will only consider unrooted trees. The internal nodes of a phylogeny usually have degrees (in the sense of unrooted trees) at least three. Proximity within the phylogeny corresponds to evolutionary similarity.

In this paper we investigate the computational feasibility of constructing phylogenies from species similarity data. Specifically, interspecies similarity is represented by a graph where the vertices are the species and adjacencies represent evidence of evolutionary similarity. A phylogeny is then constructed from the graph such that the leaves of the phylogeny are labeled by vertices of the graph and two vertices are adjacent in the graph if and only if the corresponding leaves in the tree are connected by a path of length at most $k$, where $k$ is a chosen proximity threshold. Recall that the length of the path connecting two nodes $u$ and $v$ in tree $T$ is the distance between $u$ and $v$, and is denoted by $d_T(u, v)$. This gives rise to the following algorithmic problem:

> PHYLOGENETIC $k$-ROOT PROBLEM (P$k$RP):
> Given a graph $G = (V, E)$, find a phylogenetic tree $T$ such that its leaves are labeled by $V$ and for each pair of vertices $u, v \in V$, $(u, v) \in E$ if and only if $d_T(u, v) \leq k$.

Such a tree $T$ (if exists) is called a $k$-root phylogeny of $G$ and $G$ is called the $k$th phylogenetic power of $T$.

It is useful to extend P$k$RP to allow the vertices in $V$ to appear as internal nodes in the output tree $T$. Let us call such a tree $T$ a Steiner tree of $V$. The nodes of $T$ that are not vertices in $V$ are termed Steiner points. Observe that a phylogenetic tree of $V$ is a Steiner tree of $V$ where all internal nodes are Steiner points and have degree at least 3. We will be interested in the following extension of P$k$RP.

> STEINER $k$-ROOT PROBLEM (S$k$RP):
> Given a graph $G = (V, E)$, find a Steiner tree $T$ of $V$ such that all Steiner points have degree at least 3 and for each pair of vertices $u, v \in V$, $(u, v) \in E$ if and only if $d_T(u, v) \leq k$.

If $T$ exists then it is called a $k$-root Steiner tree of $G$ and $G$ the $k$th Steiner power of $T$.

Phylogenetic power and Steiner power might be thought of as Steiner extensions of the standard notion of graph power. A graph $G$ is the $k$th power of a graph $H$ (or equivalently, $H$ is a $k$-root of $G$) if vertices $u$ and $v$ are adjacent in $G$ if and only if the length of the shortest path from $u$ to $v$ in $H$ is at most $k$. An important special case of graph power/root problems is the following:

> TREE $k$-ROOT PROBLEM (T$k$RP):
> Given a graph $G = (V, E)$, find a tree $T$ on $V$ such that $(u, v) \in E$ if and only if $d_T(u, v) \leq k$.

If $T$ exists then it is called a $k$-root tree of $G$.

It is NP-complete to recognize a graph power [5], but it is possible to determine if a graph has a $k$-root tree, for any fixed $k$, in $O(n^3)$ time, where $n$ is the number of vertices in the input graph [3]. For the special case $k = 2$, determining if a graph has a 2-root tree takes $O(n + e)$ time [4], where $e$ is the number of edges in the input graph. There is rich literature on graph roots and powers (see [1] for an overview) but few results on phylogenetic roots/powers and Steiner roots/powers. Recently, Nishimura, Ragde, and Thilikos [6] presented an $O(n^3)$-time algorithm for a variant of P$k$RP, for $k = 3$ and $k = 4$, where internal nodes (Steiner points) are allowed to have degree 2. This algorithm does not work directly for P$k$RP, as we will see later that eliminating degree-2 Steiner points is not an easy task. Moreover, it is assumed in [6] that each connected component of the input graph can be dealt with separately and the resulting trees joined together via paths of length $k$, on which all Steiner points have degree 2. We see that this is not true when degree-2 Steiner points are not allowed.

In this paper, we investigate P$k$RP and a restricted version of S$k$RP that has applications in the solution of P$k$RP. In this restricted version, we are given an input graph $G = (V, E)$ and a subset $S \subseteq V$ and we need to find a $k$-root Steiner tree $T$ for $G$ with the further constraint that every vertex in $S$ must have degree at least 2 (*i.e.*, they must be internal nodes in $T$). If such a Steiner tree $T$ exists, it is called an *S-restricted $k$-root Steiner tree*. This restricted version of S$k$RP will be referred to as the RESTRICTED STEINER $k$-ROOT PROBLEM (RS$k$RP).

As in the practice of computational biology where the set of species under consideration are related, we are interested in connected graphs. Nonetheless, whenever possible, we will extend our results to disconnected graphs. Notice that problem P1RP is not interesting and problem P2RP can be trivially answered by checking whether or not the input graph $G$ is a complete graph (for $G$ being disconnected, checking whether or not every connected component of $G$ is complete and if there are at least two non-singleton connected components). Therefore, we will assume that $k \geq 3$ in P$k$RP.

The main contributions in this paper are

1. an $O(n + e)$-time algorithm to determine if a (not necessarily connected) graph $G = (V, E)$ has a 3-root phylogeny, and if so, demonstrate one such phylogeny;
2. an $O(n + e)$-time algorithm to determine if a connected graph $G = (V, E)$ has a 4-root phylogeny, and if so, demonstrate one such phylogeny;
3. an $O(n)$-time algorithm to determine if a (not necessarily connected) graph $G = (V, E)$ has an $S$-restricted 1-root Steiner tree for a given subset $S \subseteq V$, and if so, demonstrate one such Steiner tree; and
4. an $O(n + e)$-time algorithm to determine if a connected graph $G = (V, E)$ has an $S$-restricted 2-root Steiner tree for a given subset $S \subseteq V$, and if so, demonstrate one such Steiner tree.

The results (3) and (4) are essential to the construction of our algorithms for results (1) and (2). We also characterize some properties for graphs that have a $k$-root phylogeny for general $k \geq 3$ and some structural properties for $k$-root phylogenies. These characterizations may be useful in discovering algorithms for general $k$.

We assume throughout the paper that in P$k$RP, $G$ is not a complete graph, since otherwise it always has a $k$-root phylogeny. We introduce some notations and definitions, as well as some existing related results, in Section 2. Section 3 is devoted to S$k$RP and RS$k$RP, where we give the two $O(n + e)$-time algorithms. P$k$RP is studied in Section 4. We first present some properties of graphs having a $k$-root phylogeny for general $k$ and some structural properties of $k$-root phylogenies. We then reduce P3RP and P4RP to RS1RP and RS2RP, respectively, in $O(n + e)$ time. We conclude our paper in Section 5 with several possible future research topics.

## 2    Definitions

For an induced subgraph $S$ of $G$, we abuse $S$ to denote its vertex set. Fixing a subset $U$ of $V$, let $N_U(v)$ (where $v \in U$) denote the set of neighbors of $v$ in $V \setminus U$. If all the $N_U(v)$ are identical, we call it the set of neighbors of $U$ (in $V$) and denote it by $N(U)$. Note that by definition, $U \cap N(U) = \emptyset$.

Suppose $G$ has a $k$-root phylogeny $T$, then for a Steiner point $s$ in $T$, $N(s)$ denotes the set of vertices in $V$ that are adjacent to $s$ in $T$. $|N(s)|$ is the $V$-degree, denoted by V-deg$(s)$, of $s$; the number of Steiner points adjacent to $s$ is the $S$-degree, denoted by S-deg$(s)$, of $s$. The degree of $s$ in $T$, denoted by deg$(s)$, is the sum of V-deg$(s)$ and S-deg$(s)$, which should be greater than or equal to 3. A Steiner point $s$ with S-deg$(s) = 1$ is called a *leaf Steiner point*, otherwise an *internal Steiner point*.

A graph is *chordal* if it contains no induced subgraph which is a cycle of size greater than 3.

**Lemma 1.** *If $G$ has a $k$-root phylogeny, then $G$ is chordal.*

**Lemma 2.** *If $G$ has a $k$-root Steiner tree, then $G$ is chordal.*

**Corollary 1.** *If $G$ has an $S$-restricted $k$-root Steiner tree for a subset $S$, then $G$ is chordal.*

**Lemma 3.** [7,8] *Checking if a graph $G$ is chordal can be carried out in $O(n+e)$ time.*

**Lemma 4.** [2,7] *Computing all maximal cliques in a chordal graph can be carried out in $O(n+e)$ time.*

# 3    Restricted Steiner $k$-Root Problem

In this section, we present efficient algorithms for RS1RP and RS2RP. These results have applications in the solutions of P3RP and P4RP discussed in the next section. We first note that RS$k$RP is actually more general than S$k$RP since the given subset $S$ of vertices can be empty.

## 3.1    $k = 1$

Problem S1RP, for a graph $G = (V, E)$, simply asks if $G$ is a forest containing one tree or more than two trees. That is, if $G$ is a tree, then it is a 1-root Steiner tree for itself and if $G$ is a forest containing more than 2 trees, then connecting one vertex from each tree to a common Steiner point forms a 1-root Steiner tree.

In the following, we concentrate on RS1RP where the given subset $S$ is nonempty. An easy observation is that an $S$-restricted 1-root Steiner tree for $G$ must include $G$ as an induced subgraph. It follows that $G$ is a forest. If $G$ is connected, thus a tree, and every vertex in $S$ has degree at least 2 in $G$, then $G$ is an $S$-restricted 1-root Steiner tree for itself. Otherwise, we conclude that $G$ has no $S$-restricted 1-root Steiner tree. Thus, we assume in the following that $G$ is disconnected.

Let us consider how to *optimally* connect the components of $G$ into a tree via Steiner points so that every vertex in $S$ has degree at least 2. We may simplify set $S$ by excluding vertices with degree at least 2 in $G$, and assume that the vertices in $S$ are either leaves or isolated vertices in $G$. Call a (component) tree in $G$ containing at least two vertices of $S$ a $Z$-tree. A vertex in $S$ appearing in some $Z$-tree is called a $Y$-vertex. Suppose that there are $z$ $Z$-trees and $y$ $Y$-vertices. Assume that $S$ contains $w$ isolated vertices in $G$, each corresponding to a singleton component tree of $G$. Call these vertices $W$-vertices. For each of the remaining component trees of $G$, which either has more than one vertex and contains at most one vertex of $S$ or consists of single isolated vertex outside $S$, we choose a vertex to be connected to a Steiner point, as follows: if it contains a vertex of $S$, we choose this vertex; otherwise we choose an arbitrary vertex. These chosen vertices are called $X$-vertices. Suppose that we have $x$ $X$-vertices.

We want to interconnect the $Y$- and $X$- vertices via Steiner points into a tree with the maximum number of internal edges (so that the $W$-vertices can be inserted). Therefore, every Steiner point has degree exactly 3. Three $Y$-vertices from different $Z$-trees can be interconnected into a bigger tree via a Steiner point. This new tree has at least 3 $Y$-vertices that do not yet satisfy the degree requirement, and can thus be thought of as a $Z$-tree. It follows that by introducing $(z - 1)/2$ Steiner points we can interconnect all the $Z$-trees into a single $Z$-tree, when $z$ is odd. This will make $3(z - 1)/2$ $Y$-vertices satisfy the degree requirement, that is, have degree 2. Each of the other $y - 3(z - 1)/2$ $Y$-vertices needs 2 $X$-vertices to satisfy its degree requirement (if an $X$-vertex belonging to $S$ is used here, the connection gives it degree 2 as well). Therefore, if $x < 2y - 3(z - 1)$ then we can conclude that $G$ has no $S$-restricted 1-root Steiner tree. The same conclusion can be made when $z$ is even. If $x \geq 2y - 3(z - 1)$, we can use $2y - 3(z - 1) - 2$ $X$-vertices to make $y - 3(z - 1)/2 - 1$ $Y$-vertices have degree 2. This leaves us with $x - 2y + 3(z - 1) + 3 = x - 2y + 3z$ vertices to be interconnected into a tree, among them one is $Y$-vertex and all the others are $X$-vertices. Since a full Steiner tree interconnecting $x - 2y + 3z$ vertices can contain up to $x - 2y + 3z - 3$ internal edges, on which those $W$-vertices may be inserted (to satisfy their degree requirements). If $w > x - 2y + 3z - 3$ then it is impossible to insert these $W$-vertices to produce an $S$-restricted 1-root Steiner tree of $G$. Therefore if this is the case, $G$ has no $S$-restricted 1-root Steiner tree. If $w \leq x - 2y + 3z - 3$, then putting one $W$-vertex on an internal edge would result in an $S$-restricted 1-root Steiner tree of $G$.

Consider the final case that $z = 0$, which implies that $y = 0$. If $x = 2$, then $G$ has no $S$-restricted 1-root Steiner tree. If $x \geq 3$, we interconnect the $x$ $X$-vertices into a full Steiner tree with $x - 3$ internal edges. If $w \leq x - 3$, we can construct an $S$-restricted 1-root Steiner tree by inserting one $W$-vertex on an internal edge of the full Steiner tree; Otherwise $G$ has no $S$-restricted 1-root Steiner tree. A high-level description of the overall algorithm, Algorithm *Restricted 1-Root Steiner Tree*, is depicted in Figure 1. Note that whenever **No** is returned, we may stop and conclude that $G$ has no $S$-restricted 1-root Steiner tree. The time complexity is linear in $n$ since Step 1 guarantees that $e < n$.

**Theorem 1.** *Given a graph $G = (V, E)$ and a subset $S$ of vertices, there is an $O(n)$-time algorithm that determines if $G$ has an $S$-restricted 1-root Steiner tree, and if so, demonstrates one such Steiner tree.*

In the instance illustrated in Figure 2, nodes in circle are vertices and those shaded are in subset $S$ and nodes in square are Steiner points added for the sake of interconnection. For this instance, $(z, y, x, w) = (2, 5, 9, 2)$. Therefore $G$ has an $S$-restricted 1-root Steiner tree, as shown in Figure 2(c). The tree shown in Figure 2(b) is the full Steiner tree obtained before Step 5.3.4, which has 2 internal edges on which the 2 $W$-vertices are going to be inserted respectively.

## 3.2   $k = 2$

We assume in this subsection that $G$ is connected. We prove some structural properties of 2-root Steiner trees first, and then design the $O(n + e)$-time algorithm for RS2RP. Due to the space constraint, proofs of lemmas are not provided. The interested reader may refer to the full paper available at URL http://www.math.uwaterloo.ca/~ghlin.

**Lemma 5.** *Suppose that $G$ has a 2-root Steiner tree $T$. The vertices in a maximal clique $K$ of $G$ either are adjacent to a common Steiner point implying that $|K| \geq 3$, or form a claw rooted at some vertex in $K$, in tree $T$.*

We also say in the above situation that maximal clique $K$ is adjacent to a Steiner point, or maximal clique $K$ forms a claw, in $T$.

**Corollary 2.** *Suppose that $G$ has a 2-root Steiner tree $T$.*

| | |
|---|---|
| 1. | If $G$ contains a cycle, return **No**. |
| 2. | Modify set $S$; |
| 3. | Determine the $z$ $Z$-trees, $y$ $Y$-vertices, $x$ $X$-vertices, and $w$ $W$-vertices. |
| 4. | If $z = 0$: |
| 4.1 | If $w = 0$: |
| 4.1.1 | If $x = 1$ ($G$ is connected): |
| 4.1.1.1 | If the $X$-vertex is in $S$, return **No**; |
| 4.1.1.2 | Otherwise the tree is a solution. |
| 4.1.2 | If $x = 2$, return **No**. |
| 4.1.3 | If $x \geq 3$, interconnect the $X$-vertices into a full Steiner tree. |
| 4.2 | If $w > 0$: |
| 4.2.1 | If $w > x - 3$, return **No**; |
| 4.2.2 | Otherwise, interconnect the $X$-vertices into a full Steiner tree with $x - 3$ internal edges, and insert one $W$-vertex on an internal edge. |
| 5. | If $z > 0$: |
| 5.1 | If $x < 2y - 3z + 3$, return **No**. |
| 5.2 | Else if $w > x - 2y + 3z - 3$, return **No**. |
| 5.3 | Else, output the following tree: |
| 5.3.1 | Use a Steiner point to interconnect 3 $Y$-vertices, one from a $Z$-tree; if necessary, use a Steiner point to interconnect 2 $Y$-vertices, from the last two $Z$-trees and one $X$-vertex. |
| 5.3.2 | Use a Steiner point to interconnect one $Y$-vertex and two $X$-vertices, if there is more than one $Y$-vertex; |
| 5.3.3 | Interconnect the last $Y$-vertex and the remaining $X$-vertices into a full Steiner tree with $x - 2y + 3z - 3$ internal edges; |
| 5.3.4 | Insert one $W$-vertex on an internal edge. |

**Fig. 1.** Algorithm *Restricted 1-Root Steiner Tree*.

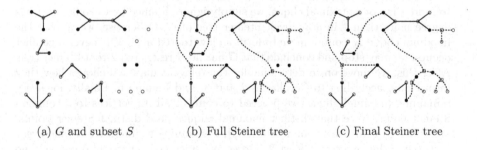

(a) $G$ and subset $S$      (b) Full Steiner tree      (c) Final Steiner tree

**Fig. 2.** An instance of RS1RP.

1. *Two maximal cliques in $G$ cannot form claws rooted at a same vertex.*
2. *If there is a maximal clique $K$ of size 2, then the two vertices in $K$ are adjacent in $T$. We say that $K$ forms a claw, rooted at either vertex, in $T$.*

3. If vertex $v$ belongs to $c$ distinct maximal cliques in $G$, then $v$ has degree at least $c$ in $T$.
4. If a vertex $v$ belongs to a unique maximal clique $K$ of $G$ and the degree of $v$ is greater than 1 in $T$, then $K$ forms a claw in $T$ rooted at $v$ and $|K| \geq 3$.
5. If vertices $v_1$ and $v_2$ both belong to a unique maximal clique $K$ in $G$, then one of them must be a leaf in $T$.

**Lemma 6.** If $G$ has a 2-root Steiner tree $T$, then two maximal cliques $K_1$ and $K_2$ in $G$ can overlap by at most two vertices; and if they overlap by two vertices, say $v_1$ and $v_2$, then $K_1$ and $K_2$ form claws in $T$ rooted at $v_1$ and $v_2$ (or, $v_2$ and $v_1$), respectively.

**Corollary 3.** Suppose that $G$ has a 2-root Steiner tree $T$.

1. No three distinct maximal cliques can overlap by two vertices.
2. For every maximal clique $K$ of $G$, there is at most one vertex $v$ in $K$ such that if $|K \cap K_1| = 2$ and $|K \cap K_2| = 2$, then $\{v\} = K \cap K_1 \cap K_2$. If such a vertex exists in $K$, then $K$ forms a claw in $T$ rooted at this vertex.

**Theorem 2.** Given a connected graph $G = (V, E)$ and a subset $S$ of vertices, there is an $O(n + e)$ time algorithm that determines if $G$ has an $S$-restricted 2-root Steiner tree, and if so, demonstrates one such Steiner tree.

*Proof.* We spend $O(n + e)$ time to check if $G$ is chordal, and if so, to compute all the maximal cliques in $G$. For every vertex $v$ in $S$, if we find that it belongs to more than one maximal clique, we simply ignore it since by Corollary 2 it has degree more than 1 in any 2-root Steiner tree of $G$; Otherwise, we restrict the maximal clique $K$ containing $v$ to form a claw rooted at $v$. Whenever a conflict occurs, we may stop and conclude that $G$ has no $S$-restricted 2-root Steiner tree. After this, we move on to determine for the relevant maximal cliques how they form claws, according to Corollaries 2 and 3, and Lemma 6. Finally, for every remaining maximal clique, we proceed to connect all its vertices to a common Steiner point. Note that distinct maximal cliques need distinct Steiner points. We will get in this way a connected graph $T$ spanning a superset of $V$ and every vertex in $S$ has degree at least 2. Moreover, since $G$ is chordal, $T$ contains no cycle and thus is a tree. By Lemma 5 and Corollary 2, nonadjacent vertices in $G$ has a distance at least 3 in $T$. Therefore, $T$ is an $S$-restricted 2-root Steiner tree for $G$.

Notice that handling these maximal cliques takes time in $O(e)$. In fact, we may record for each edge in $E$ which maximal clique contains it, and use this information to determine which maximal clique should form a claw in the Steiner tree. The overall algorithm thus runs in $O(n + e)$ time. $\qquad\square$

# 4  Phylogenetic $k$-Root Problem

## 4.1  Preliminaries

In this subsection, we present some preliminary results for problem P$k$RP as well as some structural properties of the $k$-root phylogenies of a graph $G$. Graph $G$ could be disconnected.

**Lemma 7.** *If $G$ has a $k$-root phylogeny $T$, then for any Steiner point $s$, the induced subgraph on $N(s)$ is a clique in $G$ and vertices in $N(s)$ have a same set of neighbors in $V \setminus N(s)$.*

Given a graph $G = (V, E)$, let $K$ denote a clique in $G$ such that the vertices in $K$ have a same set of neighbors in $V \setminus K$, which is denoted as $N(K)$. The number of vertices in $K$ is $|K|$ and we let $n(K)$ denote the size of $N(K)$. We say that $K$ is *maximal* if either $n(K) = 0$, meaning that $K$ is a complete connected component of $G$, or $n(K) \geq 1$ such that in $N(K)$ there is no vertex which is adjacent to all other vertices in $N(K)$ but no other vertex outside $K \cup N(K)$, meaning that $K$ is not expandable. This kind of maximal cliques are called *critical cliques* of $G$. Note that a critical clique is not necessarily a maximal clique, but it is always completely contained in some maximal clique(s).

**Corollary 4.** *If $G$ has a $k$-root phylogeny $T$, then for any Steiner point $s$, $N(s) \subseteq K$ for some critical clique $K$.*

**Lemma 8.** *If $G$ has a $k$-root phylogeny $T$ in which vertices in a critical clique $K$ are adjacent to Steiner points $s_1, s_2, \cdots, s_l$, then $d_T(s_i, s_j) \leq k - 2$ for any pair $i$ and $j$, and no vertices in other critical cliques can be adjacent to Steiner points in the minimal induced subtree in $T$ containing $s_1, s_2, \cdots, s_l$.*

We also say in this case that $K$ is *adjacent* to Steiner points $s_1, s_2, \cdots, s_l$. Obviously, if $l \geq 2$ and S-deg$(s_1) \geq 3$, then we may move the vertices adjacent to $s_1$ to be adjacent to $s_2$. The resultant tree is still a $k$-root phylogeny, and thus we may assume that when $l \geq 2$, S-deg$(s_i) \leq 2$ for all $i$, $1 \leq i \leq l$.

**Lemma 9.** *For two critical cliques $K_1$ and $K_2$ in $G$, if $K_1 \cap N(K_2) \neq \emptyset$ then $K_1 \subseteq N(K_2)$.*

Notice that for two critical cliques $K_1$ and $K_2$ in $G$, $K_1 \subseteq N(K_2)$ if and only if $K_2 \subseteq N(K_1)$ (but it is impossible that $K_1 = N(K_2)$ and $K_2 = N(K_1)$ hold simultaneously). And if $K_1 \subseteq N(K_2)$, then $K_1$ and $K_2$ are *adjacent*.

**Lemma 10.** *Every vertex of $G$ belongs to exactly one critical clique.*

From the above two lemmas we see that graph $G$ induces a *critical clique graph*, denoted as $CC(G)$, in which a node is a critical clique in $G$ and two nodes are adjacent whenever the two corresponding critical cliques are adjacent. Let $\mathcal{K}$ denote the node set in $CC(G)$, and $\mathcal{E}$ the edge set. If $G$ is chordal and we have all the maximal cliques at hand, we may spend $O(e)$ time to partition (if necessary) every maximal clique into critical cliques. In fact, vertices belonging to a same set of maximal cliques form a critical clique. Therefore, we have

**Theorem 3.** *There is an $O(n + e)$ time algorithm to check if a graph $G$ is chordal and, if so, to construct the critical clique graph $CC(G) = (\mathcal{K}, \mathcal{E})$.*

### 4.2   $k = 3$

**Lemma 11.** *If $G$ has a 3-root phylogeny, then it has a 3-root phylogeny in which every critical clique of $G$ is adjacent to exactly one Steiner point.*

In the following we will only consider 3-root phylogenies $T$ where every critical clique $K$ of $G$ is adjacent to exactly one Steiner point in $T$. Such a Steiner point is called the *representing Steiner point* of $K$ and is denoted by $s(K)$.

**Lemma 12.** *If $G$ has a 3-root phylogeny $T$ and two critical cliques $K_1$ and $K_2$ are adjacent, then $s(K_1)$ and $s(K_2)$ are adjacent in $T$.*

**Theorem 4.** *Problem P3RP is solvable in $O(n + e)$-time.*

*Proof.* By Theorem 3, given a graph $G$, we can spend $O(n+e)$ time to determine if $G$ is chordal, and if so, to compute the graph $CC(G) = (\mathcal{K}, \mathcal{E})$. For a node $K \in \mathcal{K}$, if $|K| = 1$ and it is a leaf or an isolated node in $CC(G)$, it is included into subset $S$. We then apply the Algorithm *Restricted 1-Root Steiner Tree* to compute an $S$-restricted 1-root Steiner tree for $CC(G)$. If the Algorithm returns **No**, then we conclude that $G$ has no 3-root phylogeny. Otherwise, we substitute node $K$ by the representing Steiner point $s(K)$ for $K$ in the $S$-restricted 1-root Steiner tree, and then attach the vertices in $K$ to $s(K)$. The resultant tree is a 3-root phylogeny for $G$. Notice that $|\mathcal{K}| \leq n$ and $|\mathcal{E}| \leq e$. Therefore, we can determine if $G$ has a 3-root phylogeny in $O(n + e)$ time, and if so, demonstrate one such phylogeny.                                        $\square$

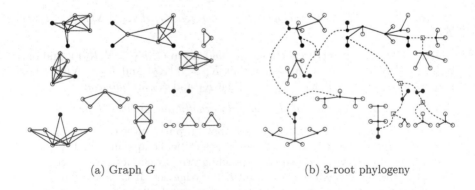

(a) Graph $G$                                    (b) 3-root phylogeny

**Fig. 3.** An instance of P3RP.

Graph $G$ illustrated in Figure 3(a) has 13 connected components. It is easy to check that those shaded vertices each forms a critical clique having degree 0 or 1 in $CC(G)$, which is isomorphic to the graph shown in Figure 2(a). It follows that we have a 3-root phylogeny for $G$, as shown in Figure 3(b).

## 4.3   $k = 4$

Unlike the fact that if $CC(G)$ has a cycle then $G$ has no 3-root phylogeny, $CC(G)$ may contain cycles for graph $G$ that has a 4-root phylogeny, but such cycles are limited to have size 3, as we shall see below.

**Lemma 13.** *If $G$ has a 4-root phylogeny, then there is a 4-root phylogeny in which every critical clique is*

- *either adjacent to one Steiner point,*
- *or adjacent to two non-adjacent leaf Steiner points,*
- *or adjacent to two adjacent internal Steiner points.*

**Corollary 5.** *There is a 4-root phylogeny in which,*

1. *suppose that critical clique $K$ is adjacent to two non-adjacent leaf Steiner points $s_1$ and $s_2$ and they are adjacent to $s_3$, then $\mathsf{S\text{-}deg}(s_3) = 3$ and $\mathsf{V\text{-}deg}(s_3) = 0$. We call $s_3$ the representing Steiner point of $K$.*
2. *suppose that critical clique $K$ is adjacent to two adjacent internal Steiner points $s_1$ and $s_2$, then $\mathsf{S\text{-}deg}(s_1) = \mathsf{S\text{-}deg}(s_2) = 2$. We call $s_1$ and $s_2$ the representing Steiner points of $K$.*

From Lemma 13 and Corollary 5, we arrive at a similar situation as in the case $k = 3$. However, rather than having one representing structure for a critical clique $K$, this time we have three R(epresenting-)S(tructure)s, namely,

(RS1) all vertices are adjacent to a Steiner point,
(RS2) vertices are (arbitrarily) partitioned into two (non-empty) parts each adjacent to a Steiner point and the two Steiner points are adjacent,
(RS3) vertices are (arbitrarily) partitioned into two (non-empty, non-singular) parts each adjacent to a Steiner point and the two Steiner points are both adjacent to a third Steiner point.

We say that the critical clique is in RS1, RS2, and RS3, respectively. We only consider 4-root phylogenies of $G$ in which every critical clique is in one of RS1, RS2, and RS3.

**Lemma 14.** *If two critical cliques are adjacent then in any 4-root phylogeny one of them must be in RS1.*

**Lemma 15.** *Suppose $G$ is connected and it has a 4-root phylogeny, and a degree-1 critical clique $K_1$ $(|K_1| \geq 4)$ is adjacent to critical clique $K_2$, then there is a 4-root phylogeny in which $K_1$ is in RS3 and its representing Steiner point is adjacent to the representing Steiner point of $K_2$, which is in RS1.*

**Lemma 16.** *Suppose $G$ is connected and it has a 4-root phylogeny, then there is a 4-root phylogeny in which a critical clique is in RS2 if and only if its degree is 2, its two neighboring critical cliques are not adjacent, and none of them is in RS3.*

**Theorem 5.** *Suppose $G$ is connected, then there is an $O(n+e)$ algorithm which determines if $G$ has a 4-root phylogeny, and if so, demonstrates one such phylogeny.*

## 5   Concluding Remarks

We considered in this paper the problems P$k$RP for $k \leq 4$ and RS$k$RP for $k \leq 2$. By examining the interconnecting structures of $k$-root phylogenies and Steiner trees, we presented linear time algorithms to determine if a given graph $G = (V, E)$ has a $k$-root phylogeny for $k \leq 4$ (or an $S$-restricted $k$-root Steiner tree for $k \leq 2$), and if so, demonstrate one such phylogeny (or Steiner tree, respectively). We also characterized some properties for graphs having a $k$-root phylogeny for general $k$, and some structural properties of $k$-root phylogenies. The definition of critical clique is crucial in the designing of algorithms for P$k$RP when $k = 3$ and $k = 4$. We believe that it will continue to play an important role in the discussions for large $k$.

Notice that P$k$RP and RS$(k-2)$RP are closely related, for $k \leq 4$. Does this relation exist for larger $k$? A key step towards establishing this relation would be to eliminate critical cliques in RS2. Understanding similar representing structures for larger $k$ would be very important.

Since there may be errors in the input graph, one may consider the approximation version of P$k$RP: Given a graph $G$, find a $k$-root phylogeny $T$ whose $k$th phylogenetic power differs from $G$ by the smallest number of edges. The approximation version of T$k$RP has been shown to be NP-hard [3]. We suspect that the approximation version of P$k$RP, as well as that of S$k$RP and RS$k$RP, are also NP-hard. The next natural question is then how well can we approximate these problems.

## References

1. A. Brandstadt, V.B. Le, and J.P. Spinrad. Graph classes: a survey. *SIAM Monographs on Discrete Mathematics and Applications*, 1999.
2. F. Gavril. Algorithms for minimum coloring, maximum clique, minimum covering by cliques, and maximum independent set of a chordal graph. *SIAM Journal on Computing*, 1:180–187, 1972.
3. P.E. Kearney and D.G. Corneil. Tree powers. *Journal of Algorithms*, 29:111–131, 1998.
4. Y.-L. Lin and S.S. Skiena. Algorithms for square roots of graphs. *SIAM Journal on Discrete Mathematics*, 8:99–118, 1995.

5. R. Motwani and M. Sudan. Computing roots of graphs is hard. *Discrete Applied Mathematics*, 54:81–88, 1994.
6. N. Nishimura, P. Ragde, and D.M. Thilikos. On graph powers for leaf-labeled trees. In *Proceedings of the Seventh Scandinavian Workshop on Algorithm Theory (SWAT 2000)*, 2000. To appear.
7. D.J. Rose, R.E. Tarjan, and G.S. Lueker. Algorithmic aspects of vertex elimination on graphs. *SIAM Journal on Computing*, 5:266–283, 1976.
8. R.E. Tarjan and M. Yannakakis. Simple linear-time algorithms to test chordality of graphs, test acyclicity of hypergraphs, and selectively reduce acyclic hypergraphs. *SIAM Journal on Computing*, 13:566–579, 1984.

# Maintenance of a Piercing Set for Intervals with Applications

Matthew J. Katz[1]*, Frank Nielsen[2], and Michael Segal[3]**

[1] Ben-Gurion University of the Negev, CS Dept., Israel
[2] SONY Computer Science Laboratories Inc., FRL, Japan
[3] University of British Columbia, CS Dept., Canada

**Abstract.** We show how to efficiently maintain a minimum piercing set for a set $\mathcal{S}$ of intervals on the line, under insertions and deletions to/from $\mathcal{S}$. A linear-size dynamic data structure is presented, which enables us to compute a new minimum piercing set following an insertion or deletion in time $O(c(\mathcal{S}) \log |\mathcal{S}|)$, where $c(\mathcal{S})$ is the size of the new minimum piercing set. We also show how to maintain a piercing set for $\mathcal{S}$ of size at most $(1 + \varepsilon)c(\mathcal{S})$, for $0 < \varepsilon \leq 1$, in $\bar{O}(\frac{\log |\mathcal{S}|}{\varepsilon})$ amortized time per update. We then apply these results to obtain efficient (sometimes improved) solutions to the following three problems: (i) the shooter location problem, (ii) computing a minimum piercing set for arcs on a circle, and (iii) dynamically maintaining a box cover for a $d$-dimensional point set.

## 1 Introduction

Let $\mathcal{S} = \{s_1 = [l_1, r_1], \ldots, s_n = [l_n, r_n]\}$ be a set of $n$ intervals on the real line. An *independent subset* of $\mathcal{S}$ is a set of pairwise non-intersecting intervals of $\mathcal{S}$. Let $b(\mathcal{S})$ be the maximum size of an independent subset of $\mathcal{S}$. A *piercing set* for $\mathcal{S}$ is a set $\mathcal{P}$ of points on the real line, such that, for each interval $s_i \in \mathcal{S}$, $s_i \cap \mathcal{P} \neq \emptyset$. Let $c(\mathcal{S})$, the *piercing number* of $\mathcal{S}$, be the size of a minimum piercing set for $\mathcal{S}$. (In graph theory terminology, we are dealing with the *interval graph* defined by $\mathcal{S}$ that is obtained by associating a node with each of the intervals in $\mathcal{S}$, and by drawing edges between nodes whose corresponding intervals intersect. The number $b(\mathcal{S})$ is also called the *packing number* of $\mathcal{S}$, a piercing set is also called a *cut set*, and the number $c(\mathcal{S})$ is also called the *transversal number of $\mathcal{S}$*.)

Clearly $c(\mathcal{S}) \geq b(\mathcal{S})$, since $b(\mathcal{S})$ piercing points are needed in order to pierce all intervals in a maximum independent subset of $\mathcal{S}$. It is not difficult to see though that $b(\mathcal{S})$ piercing points are also sufficient in order to pierce all intervals in $\mathcal{S}$, thus $c(\mathcal{S}) = b(\mathcal{S})$, and a minimum piercing set for $\mathcal{S}$ can be found in time $O(n \log c(\mathcal{S}))$ (see [11]).

In this paper we deal with the problem where the set of intervals $\mathcal{S}$ is dynamic (i.e., from time to time a new interval is inserted into $\mathcal{S}$ or an interval is deleted

* Supported by the Israel Science Foundation founded by the Israel Academy of Sciences and Humanities, and by an Intel research grant.
** Supported by the Pacific Institute for Mathematical Studies and by the NSERC research grant.

D.T. Lee and S.-H. Teng (Eds.): ISAAC 2000, LNCS 1969, pp. 552–563, 2000.

from $\mathcal{S}$), and we wish to efficiently maintain a minimum (or nearly minimum) piercing set for $\mathcal{S}$. Assuming the size of $\mathcal{S}$ never exceeds $n$, we present two solutions: an exact solution and an approximate solution (which is based on the exact solution). In the exact solution, a new minimum piercing set for $\mathcal{S}$ is computed from the current minimum piercing set, following an insertion/deletion of an interval to/from $\mathcal{S}$. The computation time is $O(c \log n)$, where $c$ is the size of the new minimum piercing set (which differs from the size of the current set by at most 1). More precisely, a linear-size data structure, representing the current set of intervals and its minimum piercing set, is used to compute the new minimum piercing set, following an insertion/deletion of an interval. The data structure is updated during the computation.

In the approximate solution, a piercing set for $\mathcal{S}$ of size at most $(1+\varepsilon)c(\mathcal{S})$ is maintained, for a given approximation factor $\varepsilon$, $0 < \varepsilon \leq 1$. The amortized cost of an update (for any sequence of updates following a preprocessing stage that requires $O(n \log n)$ time) is $\bar{O}(\frac{\log n}{\varepsilon})$. (Notice that the update cost varies from $O(\log n)$, for $\varepsilon = 1$ (i.e., a 2-approximation), to $O(c(\mathcal{S}) \log n)$, for $\varepsilon < 1/c(\mathcal{S})$ (i.e., an exact solution).) Both the exact and approximate solutions are presented in Section 2. In Section 3, we apply the above exact and approximate solutions to obtain efficient solutions to the problems below.

**The shooter location problem.** Given a set of $n$ disjoint segments in the plane, find a location $p$ in the plane, for which the number of shots needed to hit all segments is minimal, where a shot is a ray emanating from $p$. This problem was first introduced by Nandy et al. [10], who observed that solving the problem for a given location $p$ is equivalent to finding a minimum piercing set for a set of $n$ arcs on a circle. The latter problem can be solved in time $O(n \log n)$, see below. They also presented an $O(n^3)$-time algorithm for the case where the shooter is allowed to move along a given line, and left open the general problem. Wang and Zhu [15] obtained an $O(n^5 \log n)$-time solution for the general problem. They also gave an $O(n^5)$-time algorithm for computing a 2-approximation, that is, a location for which the number of required shots is at most twice the optimal number of shots. Recently, Chaudhuri and Nandy [1] presented an improved solution for the general problem; its worst-case running time is $O(n^5)$, but it is expected to perform better in practice. Actually, the general problem can be solved by applying the solution for a shooter on a line to the $O(n^2)$ lines defined by the endpoints of the segments, thus obtaining an alternative $O(n^5)$-time solution.

Here we obtain an $O(\frac{1}{\varepsilon}n^4 \log n)$-time algorithm for computing a $(1 + \varepsilon)$-approximation for the general problem (with possibly one extra shot), significantly improving the $O(n^5)$ 2-approximation of [15]. We can also find a location for which the number of shots is at most $r^* + 1$, where $r^*$ is the optimal number of shots, in (output-sensitive) $O(n^4 r^* \log n)$ time. Finally, we describe another, more complicated, method for computing a $(1+\varepsilon)$-approximation. This method uses cuttings to compute a $(1 + \varepsilon)$-approximation in $O(\frac{1}{\varepsilon^3} \frac{n^4 \log n}{r^*})$ time, thus breaking the $O(n^4)$ barrier for most values of $r^*$, assuming $\varepsilon$ is a constant (and improving the previously best known 2-approximation [15] by up to a quadratic factor).

**A minimum piercing set for arcs on a circle.** Let $\mathcal{A} = \{a_1, ..., a_n\}$ be a set of $n$ arcs on the unit circle centered at the origin. As for intervals on the line, a set $\mathcal{P}$ of points on the circle is a *piercing set* for $\mathcal{A}$, if for each arc $a_i \in \mathcal{A}$, $a_i \cap \mathcal{P} \neq \emptyset$. We wish to compute a minimum piercing set for $\mathcal{A}$. (In graph theory terminology, we are dealing with the *circular-arc graph* for $\mathcal{A}$ that is obtained by associating a node with each of the circular arcs in $\mathcal{A}$, and by drawing edges between nodes whose corresponding circular arcs intersect. We denote this graph by $G(\mathcal{A})$.)

Observe that now, unlike in the case of intervals on the line, the packing number $b(\mathcal{A})$ and the piercing number $c(\mathcal{A})$ may differ. (Assume, for example, that $\mathcal{A}$ consists of three arcs, each of length $2\pi/3$, that together cover the circle, then $b(\mathcal{A}) = 1$ while $c(\mathcal{A}) = 2$.) However, it is easy to see (Claim 3.2) that in this case either $c(\mathcal{A}) = b(\mathcal{A})$ or $c(\mathcal{A}) = b(\mathcal{A}) + 1$.

A point $p$ on the unit circle induces a clique $\{a_i \in \mathcal{A} \mid p \in a_i\}$ of the graph $G(\mathcal{A})$. Notice that $G(\mathcal{A})$ might also have cliques whose arcs do not share a point (as in the example above). Cliques of the former type are called *linear* cliques. Assume we wish to find a minimum number of cliques of $G(\mathcal{A})$ whose union is $\mathcal{A}$ (the clique covering problem). Hsu and Tsai [7] and Rao and Rangan [12] showed that if $\mathcal{A}$ itself is not a clique, then it suffices to consider only linear cliques. Thus, if $\mathcal{A}$ is not a clique, the problem of finding a minimum piercing set for $\mathcal{A}$ is essentially equivalent to the problem of finding a minimum number of cliques of $G(\mathcal{A})$ whose union is $\mathcal{A}$.

Golumbic and Hammer [5], Hsu and Tsai [7], Lee et al. [8], and Masuda and Nakajima [9] gave $O(n \log n)$-time algorithms for computing a maximum independent set of a circular-arc graph with $n$ arcs. Gupta et al. [6] gave an $\Omega(n \log n)$ lower bound for this problem (actually, for the simpler problem of computing a maximum independent set of an interval graph with $n$ intervals). Lee et al. [8] gave an $O(n \log n)$-time algorithm for the minimum cut set (i.e., piercing set) problem together with an application to a facility location problem, and Hsu and Tsai [7] gave an $O(n \log n)$-time algorithm for the minimum number of cliques problem. More recently, Tsai and Lee [14] investigated the problem of finding $k$ best cuts (i.e., $k$ cuts for which the number of different arcs that are cut is maximal). They showed how this problem is related to a facility location problem. Daniels and Milenkovic [3] use piercing sets (which they call *hitting sets*) in connection with generating layouts for the clothing industry.

We provide yet another optimal $\Theta(n \log n)$-time algorithm for computing a minimum piercing set for $\mathcal{A}$. We believe that our algorithm is (at least conceptually) simpler than the previous algorithms. Moreover, we can maintain a piercing set for $\mathcal{A}$ of size at most $(1 + \varepsilon)c(\mathcal{A}) + 1$ in amortized update time $\bar{O}(\frac{\log n}{\varepsilon})$.

**Maintenance of a box cover.** Let $\mathcal{Q}$ be a set of $n$ points in $\mathbb{R}^d$. A *cover* for $\mathcal{Q}$ is a set of (axis-parallel) unit hypercubes whose union contains $\mathcal{Q}$. The problem of computing a minimum cover is known to be NP-complete [4], and is dual to the following piercing problem. Given a set $\mathcal{B}$ of $n$ unit hypercubes in $\mathbb{R}^d$, compute a minimum piercing set for $\mathcal{B}$. We present several efficient algorithms for dynamically maintaining a small piercing set for a set of arbitrary (axis-parallel) boxes in $\mathbb{R}^d$. We obtain an $O(c^* \log^d n)$ update-time algorithm for maintaining a piercing set of size $c$ for arbitrary boxes, where $c \leq (1 + \log_2 n)^{d-1} c^*$ and $c^*$ denotes the optimal size, and an $O(2^{d-1} c^* \log n)$ update-time algorithm for maintaining a piercing set of size $c$ for congruent boxes, where $c \leq 2^{d-1} c^*$. We can also obtain (in both cases) a trade-off between the update time and the approximation factor. These algorithms are based both on our dynamic data structures for intervals on the line, and on ideas from [11]. The full description of this part is omitted due to lack of space.

## 2    Maintenance of a Piercing Set for Intervals

### 2.1    Exact Maintenance

Let $S$ be a set of $m \leq n$ intervals on the line. We assume that from time to time a new interval is added to $S$ or an existing interval is removed from $S$. However, we require that at any moment $|S| \leq n$. We show how to maintain a minimum piercing set for $S$ under insertions and deletions in $O(c \log n)$ time, where $c$ is the size of the new piercing set. We actually maintain a certain minimum piercing set which we call the *right-to-left piercing set* and which is defined as follows. Find the rightmost among the left endpoints of the intervals in $S$. Let $s \in S$ be the interval to which this endpoint belongs. Clearly the best location for a piercing point $p$ in $s$ is at its left endpoint. Remove all intervals that are pierced by $p$ and reiterate. In this way we obtain a minimum piercing set for $S$. The right-to-left piercing set can be computed easily in $O(n \log n)$ time. (Actually it can be computed in $O(n \log c(S))$ time, see [11]). Initially, we compute the right-to-left piercing set $\mathcal{P}$ of $S$.

We now construct a data structure of size $O(n)$ that will allow us to update the right-to-left piercing set within the claimed bound. For each piercing point $p \in \mathcal{P}$, let $S_p$ be the subset of intervals of $S$ that were pierced by $p$ during the right-to-left piercing process. These subsets are computed during the computation of $\mathcal{P}$. Notice that an interval $s \in S$ is associated with the rightmost piercing point of $\mathcal{P}$ that lies in it. Construct a balanced binary search tree $T$ on the piercing points in $\mathcal{P}$. For each node $v$ in $T$ representing a piercing point $p$, construct a balanced binary search tree $T_p$ on the right endpoints of the intervals in $S_p$, and let $v$ point to the root of $T_p$. With each node $w$ in $T_p$ we store the point $l_w$ which is the rightmost among the left endpoints corresponding to the right endpoints in the subtree rooted at $w$. Notice that $l_{\text{root}} = p$. The overall construction time is $O(n \log n)$, and the resulting data structure is of size $O(n)$. We now describe the updating procedures for insertion and deletion of an interval.

**Insertion.** Let $s = [s_l, s_r]$ be a new segment to be added to $S$. We first check, using the tree $T$, whether $s$ is already pierced by the current piercing set $\mathcal{P}$. If it is, then $\mathcal{P}$ is also the right-to-left piercing set of $S \cup \{s\}$. We insert $s$ into the tree $T_p$, where $p$ is the rightmost point in $\mathcal{P}$ that lies in $s$, and update the values $l_w$ in the relevant nodes of $T_p$. All these operations can be done in $O(\log n)$ time.

Assume now that $s \cap \mathcal{P} = \emptyset$. Notice that all the piercing points of $\mathcal{P}$ that lie to the right of $s$ are also present in the right-to-left piercing set of $S \cup \{s\}$ and their corresponding trees do not change. We first insert $s_l$ as a new piercing point to the main tree $T$. Next we need to create its corresponding tree $T_{s_l}$. $T_{s_l}$ should consist of the new segment $s$ together with all segments in $S$ that are pierced by $s_l$, but not by any other piercing point to the right of $s_l$. All these segments, however, must belong to $S_p$, where $p$ is the rightmost piercing point

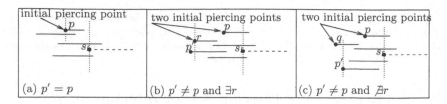

**Fig. 1.** Three different cases that may occur during the insertion process. The dashed segment is the one being inserted.

to the left of $s_l$. So we locate $p$ in $O(\log n)$ time using $T$, and search in $T_p$ in $O(\log n)$ time for the leftmost right endpoint $e$ that lies to the right of $s_l$. All the intervals in $T_p$ whose right endpoint is to the right of $e$, including $e$, should be removed from $T_p$ and added to $T_{s_l}$. We must also update the values $l_w$ in the relevant nodes of both trees. Below, we describe how to perform this transfer and update in a more general setting.

It is possible that the interval defining the point $p$ has been transfered to $T_{s_l}$. Let $p'$ be the value that is currently stored in the root of $T_p$, i.e., $l_{\text{root}} = p'$. (If $p'$ does not exist, i.e., if $T_p$ is empty, we simply delete $p$ from $T$ and stop.) If $p' = p$, then we are done, otherwise the interval defining $p$ has been transfered and we replace the piercing point $p$ by $p'$ (see Figure 1).

We now have to check whether there is a piercing point (perhaps several of them) in $T$ that lies to the right of $p'$ and to the left of $s_l$. If the answer is positive, we consider the rightmost piercing point $r$ in $T$ that lies between $p'$ and $s_l$. All right endpoints of the intervals that are currently stored in $T_r$ are to the left of all right endpoints of the intervals currently stored in $T_{p'}$. Thus, we can remove the point $p'$ from $T$ and transfer the intervals in the tree $T_{p'}$ to the tree $T_r$, by applying the *join* operation described below. We update the values $l_w$ in $T_r$ and stop. Otherwise, if the answer is negative, we need to locate the piercing point $q$ that lies immediately to the left of $p'$, and transfer the intervals of $T_q$ that are pierced by $p'$ to $T_{p'}$. As before we search in $T_q$ for the leftmost right endpoint $e$ that lies to the right of $p'$. We need to transfer the intervals in $T_q$ whose right endpoint is to the right of $e$, including $e$, to $T_{p'}$. Observe that if $s'$ is an interval in $T_q$ whose right endpoint $e'$ is to the right of $e$, including $e$, then $e'$ lies to the left of all right endpoints in $T_{p'}$, since otherwise $p \in s'$ and $s'$ should already be in $T_{p'}$ (which was obtained from $T_p$). This property allows us to apply the standard *split* and *join* operations, see below, for first removing the intervals whose right endpoint $e'$ is to the right of $e$, including $e$, from $T_q$ (split) and then adding them to $T_{p'}$ (join) in $O(\log n)$ time. We update the values $l_w$ in both trees.

We continue in this way until we either reach a step in which the piercing point does not change (Figure 1(a)), or the case of Figure 1(b) occurs, or there are no more piercing points to the left of the piercing point. Clearly the whole insertion process takes only $O(c \log n)$ time, i.e., $O(\log n)$-time for the at most $c$ cascading steps. A more careful analysis yields $O(c \log \frac{n}{c})$. (We apply Hölder's inequality to $\sum_{i=1}^{c} \log n_i$, where $\sum_i n_i = n$.)

**Deletion.** Let $s = [s_l, s_r]$ be an interval to be deleted from $S$. We locate the rightmost piercing point $p$ of $\mathcal{P}$ that lies in $s$. We distinguish between two cases. If $p \neq s_l$, then we remove $s$ from $T_p$, update the necessary $l_w$ values and stop. This can be done in $O(\log n)$ time. The more difficult case is when $p = s_l$. In this case, we first remove $s$ from $T_p$ and update the necessary $l_w$ values. We then replace $p$ (in $T$) by the value $p'$ that is stored in the root of $T_p$, which now becomes $T_{p'}$. (If $p'$ does not exist, we simply delete $p$ from $T$ and stop.) We proceed as described in the insertion procedure, that is, we either locate the rightmost piercing point $r$ which lies to the right of $p'$ and to the left of $s_l$ (if such a point exists) and transfer the intervals of $T_{p'}$ to $T_r$ thus removing $p'$, or we locate the piercing point $q$ that lies immediately to the left of $p'$, and transfer the intervals of $T_q$ that are pierced by $p'$ to $T_{p'}$, and so on. The overall time spent on a deletion operation is thus $O(c \log n)$.

**Theorem 1.** *Let $S$ be a set of intervals on a line, and assume that the size of $S$ never exceeds $n$. It is possible to construct, in time $O(n \log n)$, a data structure of size $O(n)$, that enables us to maintain a minimum piercing set for $S$, under insertions and deletions of intervals to/from $S$, in time $O(c \log \frac{n}{c})$ per update, where $c$ is the size of the current minimum piercing set for $S$.*

Notice that we can use the data-structure above to maintain a maximum independent subset of $S$.

**Theorem 2.** *Let $S$ be a set of intervals on a line, and assume that the size of $S$ never exceeds $n$. It is possible to construct, in time $O(n \log n)$, a data structure of size $O(n)$, that enables us to maintain a maximum independent set of $S$, under insertions and deletions of intervals to/from $S$, in time $O(b \log \frac{n}{b})$ per update, where $b$ is the size of the current maximum independent set of $S$.*

**Joining and splitting trees.** We now describe how to implement the split and join operations that are used by the algorithms for insertion and deletion above.

**Joining trees.** Let $A_1$ and $A_2$ be two sets of keys, such that all the keys in $A_1$ are smaller than $i$, and all the keys in $A_2$ are greater than $i$, for some key $i$. Let $T_{A_1}$ and $T_{A_2}$ be the balanced binary search (red-black) trees for the sets $A_1$ and $A_2$, respectively. The *join* operation $join(A_1, i, A_2)$, described by Tarjan [13], takes $T_{A_1}$, the key $i$, and $T_{A_2}$, and returns the balanced binary search tree $T_{(A_1 \cup \{i\} \cup A_2)}$ for the set $A_1 \cup \{i\} \cup A_2$. In our case, $i$ stands for the smallest value in the tree $T_{p'}$. The cost of Tarjan's join operation is $O(\log n)$. Moreover, within the same time bound we can update the values $l_w$ wherever needed.

**Splitting trees.** Let $A$ be a set of keys, $i$ some key that belongs to $A$, and $T_A$ a balanced binary search (red-black) tree for $A$. The *split* operation $split(A, i)$, described in [13], takes $T_A$ and $i$ and returns two balanced binary search trees: $T_{A_1}$ for all members of $A$ that are smaller than $i$, and $T_{A_2}$ for all members of $A$ that are greater than $i$. In our case, $i$ stands for the right endpoint $e$ in the description of the algorithms for insertion and deletion. The cost of Tarjan's split operation is $O(\log n)$. Moreover, within the same time bound we can update the values $l_w$ wherever needed.

## 2.2   Approximate Maintenance

We now show how to maintain a piercing set $\mathcal{P}'$ for $\mathcal{S}$, where $\mathcal{S}$ is as above, such that $|\mathcal{P}'| \leq (1 + \varepsilon)c(\mathcal{S})$, for any fixed $0 < \varepsilon \leq 1$. The amortized cost per update is $\bar{O}(\frac{\log n}{\varepsilon})$, for any sequence of insertions and deletions, which begins immediately after a preprocessing stage in which the right-to-left (minimum) piercing set $\mathcal{P}$, $|\mathcal{P}| = c_0$, for $\mathcal{S}$ is computed and some additional work, that does not affect the time bound for this stage, is done. (Of course, we continue to assume that at any time $|\mathcal{S}| \leq n$.)

The key idea is to avoid long cascades by fixing stopping points, which are points in $\mathcal{P}'$, such that, a cascade cannot continue beyond a stopping point. Initially, we set $\mathcal{P}' = \mathcal{P} = (p_1, \ldots, p_{c_0})$, and $p_1, p_{1+\lceil \frac{2}{\varepsilon} \rceil}, p_{1+2\lceil \frac{2}{\varepsilon} \rceil}, \ldots$ are the stopping points. The stopping points partition the sequence of piercing points into at most $\lceil \frac{\varepsilon}{2} c_0 \rceil$ groups, each of size at most $\lceil \frac{2}{\varepsilon} \rceil$. (The first group begins with $p_{c_0}$ and ends with the first stopping point from the right, the second group begins with the point immediately to the left of this stopping point and ends with the second stopping point from the right, and so on.) Roughly, at any time, each of the groups consists of the right-to-left piercing set for the subset of intervals associated with the points in the group. An insertion or a deletion of an interval can only affect a single group, which now has to adapt to the change in the subset of intervals associated with its points.

A stopping point is never deleted (in between clean-up stages, see below), even if it is not needed as a piercing point any more. One can think of a stopping point as a degenerate (dummy) interval. But, whenever the size of a group reaches twice its initial size, i.e. $2\lceil \frac{2}{\varepsilon} \rceil$, it is split into two, by making the point in position $\lceil \frac{2}{\varepsilon} \rceil$ in the group a new stopping point. This guarantees an update cost of $\bar{O}(\frac{\log n}{\varepsilon})$ time.

In this way, we can ensure for a while that $\mathcal{P}'$ is a $(1 + \varepsilon)$-approximation. However, after performing a sequence of $\frac{\varepsilon}{4} c_0$ insertions and deletions, we need to perform a clean-up stage (see below), in which we reset $\mathcal{P}'$ to the current right-to-left piercing set of $\mathcal{S}$. This stage requires $O(c_0 \log n)$ time, which is divided among the updates in the sequence. Below, we describe the insertion and deletion operations and then analyze our approximation scheme.

**Insertion.** Let $s = [s_l, s_r]$ be a new interval to be added to $\mathcal{S}$. We check in $O(\log n)$ time whether $s$ is already pierced by a point in $\mathcal{P}'$. If yes, we insert $s$ in $O(\log n)$ time, associating it with the rightmost point in $\mathcal{P}'$ that lies in it, as in the exact scheme. If not, we add $s_l$ as a new piercing point to $\mathcal{P}'$, and begin the iterative process (which we call a cascade) that was described in Section 2.1. This process can either end naturally, before the group's stopping point is encountered, or artificially, upon reaching this stopping point. The number of points in the group may increase by 1, and if it has reached $2\lceil \frac{2}{\varepsilon} \rceil$, we split it into two equal size groups by making the point in position $\lceil \frac{2}{\varepsilon} \rceil$ in the group a new stopping point. The length of the cascade is thus less than $2\lceil \frac{2}{\varepsilon} \rceil$, and therefore the cost of an insertion is $O(\frac{\log n}{\varepsilon})$.

**Deletion.** Let $s = [s_l, s_r]$ be an interval to be deleted from $\mathcal{S}$, and let $p$ be the rightmost point in $\mathcal{P}'$ that lies in $s$. If $p \neq s_l$, we simply remove the segment $s$ in $O(\log n)$ time from $p$'s tree, as in the exact scheme. If, however, $p = s_l$, we begin the iterative process described in Section 2.1, which either stops naturally, or when the group's stopping point is encountered. The cost of a deletion is thus $O(\frac{\log n}{\varepsilon})$. In both cases, if $p$ is a stopping point, we simply remove $s$ without replacing or deleting $p$, even if $p$'s tree is empty.

**The clean-up stage.** In order to ensure that we remain with a $(1 + \varepsilon)$-approximation after each update, we need to perform a clean-up stage following a sequence of $\frac{\varepsilon}{4}c_0$ updates. The clean-up stage brings us back to the initial state, where $\mathcal{P}'$ is the right-to-left piercing set for $\mathcal{S}$, and the stopping points are the points of $\mathcal{P}'$ in position $1, 1 + \lceil\frac{2}{\varepsilon}\rceil, 1 + 2\lceil\frac{2}{\varepsilon}\rceil, \ldots$ The clean-up requires only $O(c_0 \log n)$ time (unlike the initial preprocessing stage which requires $O(n \log n)$ time), so if we divide it over the last sequence of updates, we obtain the claimed $\bar{O}(\frac{\log n}{\varepsilon})$ amortized cost per update.

The situation just before the clean-up is that each interval is stored with the rightmost point in $\mathcal{P}'$ that lies in it. However, there may be piercing points (among the stoppers) whose corresponding set of intervals is empty, and there may be piercing points (among the stoppers) for which the value $l_{\text{root}}$ at the root of their tree is different from the piercing point itself.

In the clean-up stage we perform a right-to-left traversal, beginning at the rightmost stopper in $\mathcal{P}'$. During the traversal the various cases which are described in Section 2.1 occur, and we handle them accordingly.

If $p$ is of the first type above, then we delete it, and jump to the next stopper $q$. Otherwise, let $p'$ be the value stored at the root of $p$'s tree. If $p' = p$, then we jump to $q$, and if $p' \neq p$, then we proceed as follows. If $p'$ is to the left of $r$, the point immediately to the left of $p$, then we transfer the intervals in $p$'s tree to $r$'s tree, delete $p$, and jump to $q$. Otherwise, we replace $p$ with $p'$, and start a cascade as in Section 2.1. We then jump to the first stopper following the cascade.

At the end of this process $\mathcal{P}'$ is again the right-to-left minimum piercing set for $\mathcal{S}$ and we update the value of $c_0$. The whole process requires only $O(c_0 \log n)$ time.

**The analysis.** We have to show that $\mathcal{P}'$ is a $(1 + \varepsilon)$-approximation after each update. At time $t$ (i.e., after the $t$'th update), the size $c_t$ of the minimum piercing set and the size $c'_t$ of $\mathcal{P}'$ are surely in between $c_0 - \frac{\varepsilon}{4}c_0$ and $c_0 + \frac{\varepsilon}{4}c_0$. Thus, even in the worst case, where $c_t$ is equal to the minimum value and $c'_t$ is equal to the maximum value, we have $c'_t \doteq (1 + \frac{\varepsilon}{4})c_0 \leq (1 + \frac{3\varepsilon}{4} - \frac{\varepsilon^2}{4})c_0 = (1 + \varepsilon)c_t$, so $\mathcal{P}'$ is indeed a $(1 + \varepsilon)$-approximation.

We obtain the following theorem:

**Theorem 3.** *For any $0 < \varepsilon \leq 1$, we can maintain a $(1 + \varepsilon)$-approximation of a minimum piercing set for $\mathcal{S}$ in amortized update time $\bar{O}(\frac{\log n}{\varepsilon})$.*

As a corollary, we obtain the following theorem concerning the size $b(\mathcal{S})$ of a maximum independent subset of $\mathcal{S}$.

**Theorem 4.** *For any $0 < \varepsilon \leq 1$, we can maintain a $(1 + \varepsilon)$-approximation of the size $b(\mathcal{S})$ of a maximum independent subset of $\mathcal{S}$ in amortized update time $\bar{O}(\frac{\log n}{\varepsilon})$. (That is, at time $t$, $\frac{c'_t}{1+\varepsilon} \leq b(\mathcal{S}) \leq c'_t$.)*

# 3   Applications

In this section we present the three applications that were mentioned in Section 1. See Section 1 for a survey of related previous results.

## 3.1   Shooter Location Problem

In the *Shooter Location Problem* (SLP for short), we are given a set $\mathcal{S} = \{s_1, \ldots, s_n\}$ of $n$ disjoint segments in the plane, and we seek a point $p$ from which the number of shots needed to hit all segments in $\mathcal{S}$ is minimal, where a shot is a ray emanating from $p$.

**A $(1 + \varepsilon)$-approximation.** Let $\mathcal{L}$ be the set of $O(n^2)$ lines defined by the endpoints of the segments in $\mathcal{S}$. Consider any cell $f$ of the arrangement $\mathcal{A}(\mathcal{L})$, and let $p$ be a point in the interior of $f$. The number of shots from $p$ needed to hit all segments in $\mathcal{S}$ is equal to the size of a minimum piercing set for the set of circular arcs obtained by projecting each of the segments in $\mathcal{S}$ on a circle enclosing all the segments in $\mathcal{S}$ and centered at $p$. For any other point $p'$ in the interior of $f$, the number of shots from $p'$ is equal to the number of shots from $p$, since the circular-arc graphs for $p$ and for $p'$ are identical. Moving from one cell of $\mathcal{A}(\mathcal{L})$ to an adjacent cell corresponds to a swap in the locations of two adjacent arc endpoints.

We traverse the arrangement $\mathcal{A}(\mathcal{L})$, dynamically maintaining an approximation of the minimum number of rays required to intersect all the segments from a point in the current cell. At each cell of $\mathcal{A}(\mathcal{L})$, we shoot a vertical ray directed upwards, allowing us to deal with the interval graph obtained by unrolling the cell's circular-arc graph (after removing the arcs that are intersected by the vertical ray). We use the data structure of Section 2.2 to maintain in amortized time $\bar{O}(\frac{\log n}{\varepsilon})$ a $(1+\varepsilon)$-approximation of the size of the minimum piercing set for this interval graph. At the end, we choose the cell for which the number computed is the smallest. (Actually, this scheme will also work for segments that are not necessarily disjoint.)

**Theorem 5.** *For any fixed $0 < \varepsilon \leq 1$, a $(1 + \varepsilon)$-approximation (with possibly one extra shot) for the shooter location problem can be found in $O(\frac{1}{\varepsilon} n^4 \log n)$ time.*

**Towards an exact solution.** We showed how to obtain a $(1+\varepsilon)$-approximation, that is, how to find a number $r$ such that $r^* \leq r \leq (1 + \varepsilon)r^* + 1$, where $r^*$ is the optimal number of shots. Therefore, if $\varepsilon r^* < 1$, we obtain a location for which the number of rays is either optimal or optimal plus one. Since we need to choose $\varepsilon < \frac{1}{r^*}$ without knowing $r^*$, we first run the algorithm with, say, $\varepsilon = 1$, and obtain a number of rays $r^* \leq r' \leq 2r^* + 1$. Then we choose $\varepsilon = \frac{1}{r'} < \frac{1}{r^*}$ and run the algorithm to obtain the optimal, or optimal with one extra shot, solution in $O(n^4 r^* \log n)$ output-sensitive time (single bootstrapping).

**Theorem 6.** *The optimal number of shots $r^*$ (with possibly one extra shot) of the shooter location problem can be computed in $O(n^4 r^* \log n)$ time.*

**Avoiding the complete arrangement traversal.** We now describe another method for obtaining a $(1 + \varepsilon)$-approximation, which is often more efficient than the method described above. Let $\mathcal{L}'$ be a $\frac{1}{c}$-cutting of $\mathcal{L}$ (see [2]). That is, $\mathcal{L}'$ is a set of $O(c)$ lines, and each cell of the (vertical decomposition of the) arrangement $\mathcal{A}(\mathcal{L}')$ is cut by at most $\frac{|\mathcal{L}|}{c} \leq \frac{2n^2}{c}$ lines of $\mathcal{L}$. For each of these lines $l$, we dynamically compute a $(1 + \delta)$-approximation for a shooter moving along $l$ (in the original environment $S$). The total computation time is $O(n^2 c \frac{\log n}{\delta})$. Let $r_{min}$ be the best score obtained during the computation. We have $r^* \leq r_{min} \leq (1 + \delta)(r^* + \frac{2n^2}{c})$. (The right inequality holds since if $C \in \mathcal{A}(\mathcal{L})$ is the cell from which only $r^*$ shots are needed, then there exists a cell $C' \in \mathcal{A}(\mathcal{L})$ that is supported by a line in $\mathcal{L}'$, such that, $C$ can be reached from $C'$ by passing through at most $\frac{2n^2}{c}$ cells of $\mathcal{A}(\mathcal{L})$.) By setting $c = \frac{2n^2}{\gamma r^*}$, for some $0 < \gamma < 1$, we obtain $r^* \leq r_{min} \leq (1 + \delta)(1 + \gamma) r^*$ in $O(\frac{1}{\delta \gamma} \frac{n^4 \log n}{r^*})$ time. We choose $\delta = \gamma = \frac{\varepsilon}{3}$ to ensure a $(1 + \varepsilon)$-approximation scheme in $O(\frac{1}{\varepsilon^2} \frac{n^4 \log n}{r^*})$ time.

However, we do not know $r^*$, the size of the optimal solution, beforehand. We are going to approximate it by $r'$ as follows. We first demonstrate the method for the special case where a 4-approximation is desired, and then present it for the general case.

For a 4-approximation, assume $\delta = \gamma = \frac{1}{4}$, and set $r' \leftarrow \frac{n}{2}$. Let $c = \frac{2n^2}{\gamma r'} = 16n$, and, as above, first compute a $\frac{1}{c}$-cutting of $\mathcal{L}$ and then, for each of the $O(c)$ lines in the cutting, compute a $(1 + \delta)$-approximation for a shooter moving along the line. The total computation time is $O(n^3 \log n)$. By taking the minimum score $r_{min}$ along the lines of the cutting, we have $r^* \leq r_{min} \leq (1 + \frac{1}{4})(r^* + \frac{n}{8})$. Therefore, if $r_{min} \geq \frac{n}{2}$, then $r^* \geq \frac{11n}{40} \geq \frac{n}{4}$ and we return $r_{min}$ and stop. This gives $\frac{r_{min}}{r^*} \leq \frac{n}{n/4} = 4$. Otherwise, we set $r' \leftarrow \frac{r'}{2}$ and repeat. We continue halving $r'$ until at some stage $r_{min} \geq r'$ (and $r_{min} < 2r'$). At this stage we have $r^* \geq \frac{11r'}{20} \geq \frac{r'}{2}$, and $\frac{r_{min}}{r^*} \leq \frac{2r'}{r'/2} = 4$. The overall cost of this algorithm is bounded by $O(n^4 \log n) \sum_{r'} \frac{1}{r'}$ with $r' = \frac{n}{2^i}$ for $i \leq \log \frac{n}{r^*}$. Thus we end up with a 4-approximation in $O(\frac{n^4 \log n}{r^*})$ time.

For the general case, where a $(1 + \varepsilon)$-approximation is desired, we set $r' = \beta n$, for an appropriate $0 < \beta < 1$, as our current estimate of $r^*$, and let $c = \frac{2n^2}{\gamma r'} = \frac{2n^2}{\gamma \beta n}$. After computing a $\frac{1}{c}$-cutting and $r_{min}$ as before, we have $r^* \leq r_{min} \leq (1 + \delta)(r^* + \frac{2n^2}{c}) = (1 + \delta)(r^* + \gamma \beta n)$. Now, if $r_{min} \geq r'$ (i.e., if $r_{min} \geq \beta n$), then $(1 + \delta)(r^* + \gamma \beta n) \geq \beta n$, which implies that $r^* \geq \frac{\beta n (1 - (1 + \delta)\gamma)}{1 + \delta}$. Thus, our first equation is $\frac{r_{min}}{r^*} \leq \frac{1 + \delta}{\beta(1 - (1 + \delta)\gamma)}$, since $r_{min} \leq n$.

If, however, $r_{min} < r'$, we set $r' \leftarrow \beta r'$, and repeat until at some stage $r_{min} \geq r'$. At this stage we have $\beta^i n \leq r_{min} < \beta^{i-1} n$, for some $i \geq 2$, and the ratio between $r_{min}$ and $r^*$ is as in the first stage (our first equation), this time using $r_{min} < \beta^{i-1} n$.

Therefore, we must pick $\delta, \gamma$ and $\beta$ in order to satisfy our second equation: $\frac{1 + \delta}{\beta(1 - (1 + \delta)\gamma)} \leq 1 + \varepsilon$. The running time is $\frac{n^4 \log n}{\gamma \delta} \sum_i \frac{1}{\beta^i n}$, with $i$ ranging from 1 to $\log_{\frac{1}{\beta}} \frac{n}{r^*}$. That is, $\frac{n^3 \log n}{\gamma \delta} \sum_{i=1}^{\log_{\frac{1}{\beta}} \frac{n}{r^*}} (\frac{1}{\beta})^i$. But $\sum_{i=1}^{\log_{\frac{1}{\beta}} \frac{n}{r^*}} (\frac{1}{\beta})^i$ is less than $\frac{n}{(1-\beta)r^*}$. Therefore the running time for a $(1+\varepsilon)$-approximation is $O(\frac{n^4 \log n}{\delta \gamma (1-\beta) r^*})$. It is easy to verify that by picking $\gamma = \delta = \frac{\varepsilon}{5}$ and $\beta = 1 - \frac{\varepsilon}{5}$, our second equation is satisfied (assuming $\varepsilon \leq 1$), and thus the running time becomes $O(\frac{1}{\varepsilon^3} \frac{n^4 \log n}{r^*})$. Comparing this method with the first method, we see that this method is more efficient than the first method whenever $r^* \geq \frac{1}{\varepsilon^2}$.

**Theorem 7.** *A $(1+\varepsilon)$-approximation for the shooter location problem can be found in $O(\frac{1}{\varepsilon^3} \frac{n^4 \log n}{r^*})$ time.*

## 3.2   Minimum Piercing Set for Circular Arcs

Let $\mathcal{A} = \{a_1, \ldots, a_n\}$ be a set of $n$ arcs on the unit circle $C$ centered at the origin. Our goal is to compute a minimum piercing set $\mathcal{P} \subseteq C$ for $\mathcal{A}$.

Let $c$ denote the size of a minimum piercing set for $\mathcal{A}$, and let $b$ denote the maximum size of an independent subset of $\mathcal{A}$, that is, a subset of $\mathcal{A}$ whose arcs are pairwise disjoint. Clearly $c \geq b$, since we need $b$ piercing points in order to pierce all arcs in a maximum independent subset of $\mathcal{A}$. For a set $\mathcal{S}$ of intervals on a line, it is easy to see ([11]) that $b(\mathcal{S})$ piercing points are also sufficient in order to pierce all intervals in $\mathcal{S}$. In our case, however, $b$ piercing points may not be enough. For example, if $\mathcal{A}$ consists of three arcs obtained by cutting the circle $C$ into three parts, then $b = 1$ while $c = 2$. It is easy to see though that the difference between $b$ and $c$ can never exceed 1. Place a piercing point $p$ anywhere on the circle $C$ and remove all arcs that are pierced by $p$. We can think of the remaining arcs as intervals on a line. The size of a maximum independent subset of these intervals is either $b$ or $b-1$. Thus, in view of the remark above concerning intervals on a line, either $c = b + 1$, or $c = b$. Therefore, we have:

*Claim.* $b \leq c \leq b + 1$, and there exists sets of arcs that require $b + 1$ piercing points.

For an arc $a \in \mathcal{A}$, let $f(a)$ be the number of arc endpoints that lie in $a$, including $a$'s two endpoints. Let $a^*$ be an arc in $\mathcal{A}$ such that $f(a^*) \leq f(a)$ for any other arc $a \in \mathcal{A}$. Clearly $f(a^*) \leq \lfloor \frac{2n}{b} \rfloor$, by the pigeon hole principle. We can find $a^*$ in $O(n \log n)$ time: After sorting the endpoints by their polar angle, one can determine the number of endpoints lying in an arc $a$ in $O(\log n)$ time.

The endpoints that lie in the interior of $a^*$ together with $a^*$'s two endpoints divide $a^*$ into $O(n/b)$ subarcs. Since $a^*$ must be pierced, we traverse $a^*$ from end to end moving from one subarc to an adjacent subarc. For each of these subarcs, we place in it a piercing point $p$, and compute a minimum piercing set for the remaining set of arcs that are not pierced by $p$ (which can be viewed as a set of intervals on a line). The subarc whose corresponding minimum piercing set is the smallest, is then chosen as the subarc in which $p$ is eventually placed, and the final piercing set is composed of $p$ and the piercing set that was computed for this subarc. (Of course, if there exists a point of $C$ that is not covered by $\mathcal{A}$, then we can simply treat the set $\mathcal{A}$ as a set of intervals on the line.)

During the traversal, when moving from one subarc to an adjacent subarc we either enter or leave an arc of $\mathcal{A}$. We can therefore use our data structure for maintaining a minimum piercing set for a set $S$ of intervals on a line (see Section 2.1). Initially $S$ is obtained from the arcs in $A$ that are not pierced by a point lying in the first subarc of $a^*$. We construct our data structure for $S$ in $O(n \log n)$ time. When moving from one subarc to an adjacent subarc, an interval is either inserted or deleted to/from $S$. For any subarc of $a^*$, the number of intervals in $S$ is at most $n-1$, the size of the minimum piercing set that is computed is at most $b+1$ (by Claim 3.2), and the computation time is $O(b \log n)$. Since there are $O(n/b)$ subarcs, we conclude that the total running time of our algorithm (for computing a minimum piercing set for $A$) is $O(n \log n)$.

**Theorem 8.** *Let $A$ be a set of $n$ arcs on a circle. It is possible to compute a minimum piercing set for $S$ in $O(n \log n)$ time.*

**Remark:** We can apply the approximation scheme of Section 2.2 in order to maintain a small piercing set for $A$, under insertions and deletions of arcs to/from $A$. If $c(A)$ is the piercing number of $A$, then we can maintain a piercing set for $A$ of size at most $(1 + \varepsilon)c(A) + 1$ in amortized $\bar{O}(\frac{\log n}{\varepsilon})$ time per update.

# References

1. J. Chaudhri and S.C. Nandy "Generalized shooter location problem", in *Lecture Notes in Computer Science* 1627, pp. 389–401, 1999.
2. B. Chazelle "Cutting hyperplanes for divide-and-conquer", *Discrete Comput. Geom.* 9 (1993), pp. 145–158.
3. K. Daniels and V. Milenkovic "Limited Gaps", in *Proc. 6th Canad. Conf. Comput. Geom.*, pp. 225–231, 1994.
4. R. J. Fowler and M. S. Paterson and S. L. Tanimoto "Optimal packing and covering in the plane are NP-complete", *Info. Processing Letters* 12(3) (1981), pp. 133–137.
5. M. C. Golumbic and P. L. Hammer "Stability in circular arc graphs", *J. of Algorithms* 9 (1988), pp. 314–320.
6. U. Gupta, D. T. Lee and Y.-T. Leung "Efficient algorithms for interval graphs and circular-arc graphs", *Networks* 12 (1982), pp. 459–467.
7. W.-L. Hsu and K.-H. Tsai "Linear time algorithms on circular-arc graphs", *Information Processing Letters* 40 (1991), pp. 123–129.
8. D. T. Lee, M. Sarrafzadeh and Y. F. Wu "Minimum cuts for circular-arc graphs", *SIAM J. Computing* 19(6) (1990), pp. 1041–1050.
9. S. Masuda and K. Nakajima "An optimal algorithm for finding a maximum independent set of a circular-arc graph", *SIAM J. Computing* 17(1) (1988), pp. 41–52.
10. S. C. Nandy and K. Mukhopadhyaya and B. B. Bhattacharya "Shooter location problem", in *Proc. 8th Canad. Conf. Comput. Geom.*, pp. 93–98, 1996.
11. F. Nielsen "Fast stabbing of boxes in high dimensions", in *Proc. 8th Canad. Conf. Comput. Geom.*, pp. 87–92, 1996. *Theo. Comp. Sci.*, Elsevier Sci., Sept. 2000.
12. A. S. Rao and C. P. Rangan "Optimal parallel algorithms on circular-arc graphs", *Information Processing Letters* 33 (1989), pp. 147-156.
13. R. E. Tarjan "Data Structures and Network Algorithms", *Regional Conference Series in Applied Mathematics* 44, SIAM, 1983.
14. K. H. Tsai and D. T. Lee "$k$-best cuts for circular-arc graphs", *Algorithmica* 18(2) (1997), pp. 198–216.
15. C. A. Wang and B. Zhu "Shooter location problems revisited", in *Proc. 9th Canad. Conf. Comput. Geom.*, pp. 223–228, 1997.

# Optimal Polygon Cover Problems and Applications*

Danny Z. Chen, Xiaobo (Sharon) Hu, and Xiaodong Wu**

Department of Computer Science and Engineering, University of Notre Dame, Notre
Dame, IN 46556, USA, {chen,shu,xwu}@cse.nd.edu

**Abstract.** Polygon cover problems arise in computational geometry and
in a number of applied areas, such as material layout, layered manufacturing, radiation therapy and radiosurgery, etc. In this paper, we study
three optimal polygon cover problems: monotone polygon cover with
obstacles, star-shaped polygon cover with obstacles, and rectangular cover. Based on useful geometric observations, we develop efficient algorithms for solving these problems.
Either our algorithms improve the quality of the previously best known
solutions for these polygon cover problems, or our complexity bounds are
comparable to those of the previously best known algorithms for simpler
cases of the problems.

## 1   Introduction

Polygon cover problems arise in computational geometry and in a number of
applied areas. In this paper, we study three polygon cover problems: monotone
polygon cover with obstacles, star-shaped polygon cover with obstacles, and
rectangular cover. The first two problems appear in applications such as material
layout [2,8] (e.g., apparel manufacturing) and layered manufacturing [18]. The
third problem is applicable to radiation therapy and radiosurgery [20].

Arkin *et al.* [2] studied the problem of computing a minimum-area monotone (resp., star-shaped) polygon cover $P^*$ for an $n$-vertex polygon $P$ (with no
obstacles). They transformed in $O(n \log n)$ (resp., $O(n^2)$) time the optimal monotone (resp., star-shaped) polygon cover problem to solving $O(n)$ (resp., $O(n^2)$)
instances of a special optimization problem [2]. Chen *et al.* [6] simplified the form
of the optimization problems used in [2] and improved the space bound of the
star-shaped cover algorithm. In this paper, we generalize these two problems
to the setting scattering with obstacles, i.e., we seek an optimal polygon cover
$P^*$ that contains $P$ and avoids all obstacles. Taking obstacles into consideration
for these problems is well motivated by practical applications. For example, in
apparel manufacturing, the layout problem involves placing 2-D polygonal apparel pattern pieces inside a rectangular sheet of stock material (e.g., cloth) of
a fixed width and minimum length. Daniels, Li, and Milenkovic [9] showed that

* The first and the third author were supported in part by the National Science Foundation under Grants CCR-9623585 and CCR-9988468. The second author was
supported in part by the National Science Foundation under Grants MIP-9701416
and CCR-9988468, and by HP Labs, Bristol, England, under an external research
program grant.
** Corresponding author.

D.T. Lee and S.-H. Teng (Eds.): ISAAC 2000, LNCS 1969, pp. 564–576, 2000.
© Springer-Verlag Berlin Heidelberg 2000

a promising approach is to place the large pieces first; regions of unused cloth between the large pieces are then used for smaller pieces. In this case, the placed large pieces can be viewed as obstacles, and we seek to use star-shaped or monotone polygons to approximate the shapes of the small pieces and to reduce the material waste. Similar situations also occur in layered manufacturing and other applications, in which the obstacles represent either defective regions or modules that have been placed on the material in previous manufacturing.

The third polygon cover problem we consider is rectangular cover, motivated by beam shaping in radiation therapy and radiosurgery. Radiation therapy and radiosurgery use radiation beams to eradicate localized benign and malignant tumors [21]. The beam shaping problem is important since poor shape matching between the beams and the tumor can greatly compromise the treatment quality (e.g., not meeting the prescribed dose homogeneity or falloff rate). Several studies have found that conformal beam collimation techniques substantially improve treatment quality and reduce treatment time in many cases [20]. A common technique is to use a *jaw collimator* to obtain beams of rectangular cylinder shape. A jaw collimator consists of two pairs of parallel, independent jaws; the height and width of the rectangular cross-section of the beam are set by moving the jaws (see Figure 1(a)). It can be used to produce a rectangular cover as shown in Figure 1(b). Schweikard, Tombropoulos, and Adler [20] presented robotic and geometric methods for computing two types of rectangular covers (definitions and discussions of these covers are in Section 4). They choose the "best" cover by checking the quality of the covers generated based on a set of fixed rectangle orientations; but this cannot guarantee the optimality of their solution.

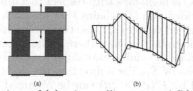

(a)　　(b)

**Fig. 1.** The cross-sections of (a) a jaw collimator, and (b) a rectangular cover.

There are other geometric algorithms for problems related to polygon covers. Majhi *et al.* [18] studied several geometric optimization problems in layered manufacturing, such as minimizing the stair-step error on the manufactured object surface, minimizing the volume of the support structure used, and minimizing the contact area between the supports and the manufactured object. Chang and Yap [4] studied the optimal inclusion and enclosure problems of a polygon, and obtained polynomial time algorithms for finding a maximum-area convex region of a polygon, a minimum-area enclosing convex $k$-gon, and a minimum enclosing $k$-gon of a fixed shape. Fleischer *et al.* [12] considered the problems of simultaneous inner and outer approximation of shapes.

Let $n = |P|$ and $m$ be the total number of obstacle vertices. Our main results are summarized as follows. (Note that the complexity bounds of our algorithms for the obstacle cases are comparable to those of the previous results on the (simpler) obstacle-free cases.)

1. An $O((n+m)\log n+n*f(n))$ time algorithm for computing a minimum-area monotone polygon cover of $P$ among obstacles, where $f(n)$ is the time for optimizing the sum of $O(n)$ 1-D linear fractional functions over an interval.

2. An $O((n+m)^2 * g(n))$ time algorithm for computing a minimum-area star-shaped polygon cover of $P$ among obstacles, where $g(n)$ is the time for optimizing the sum of $O(n)$ linear fractional functions subject to $O(n+m)$ linear constraints in 2-D.

3. An $O((n+|E|)\log n)$ time algorithm for computing a minimum rectangular cover of $P$ and its penumbra polygon $P'$, where $E$ is the edge set of the visibility graph $G$ of $P$.

Our overall approach, like those in [2,6,18], transforms a polygon cover problem to solving a number of instances of a certain special optimization problem. However, unlike the previous algorithms, we must judiciously characterize and partition the feasible domains on which our optimization problems are defined. Infeasible regions to our problems that occur due to the presence of obstacles must be excluded. We are able to do that by exploiting a set of geometric observations.

## 2    Minimum Monotone Polygon Cover with Obstacles

In this section, we consider the following problem: Given a simple polygon $P$ of $n$ vertices and a set of polygonal obstacles $R = \{R_1, R_2, \ldots, R_k\}$ with a total of $m$ vertices, compute a monotone polygon $P^*$, such that: (i) $P \subseteq P^*$; (ii) $intr(P^*) \cap intr(R_i) = \varnothing$ for every $R_i \in R$, where $intr(Q)$ denotes the interior of a polygon $Q$; (iii) the area of $P^*$ is minimized. Without loss of generality (WLOG), we assume that $intr(P) \cap intr(R_i) = \varnothing$ for every $R_i \in R$.

A simple polygon $Q$ is *monotone* with respect to a direction $\boldsymbol{d}$ if the boundary $B(Q)$ of $Q$ can be divided into two chains that are both monotone with respect to $\boldsymbol{d}$. The two common end vertices of these two chains are the *extreme vertices* of $Q$. A direction $\boldsymbol{d}$ is said to be *feasible* if there exists a monotone polygon $P'$ with respect to $\boldsymbol{d}$ that contains $P$ and avoids the obstacles in $R$. We denote the set of all feasible directions by $S_f$. For a direction $\boldsymbol{d} \in S_f$, the minimum monotone cover of $P$ is denoted by $P'(\boldsymbol{d})$. $P'(\boldsymbol{d})$ can be obtained as follows [2]. Consider each vertex $v$ of $P$ such that the two incident edges of $v$ form a non-monotone chain with respect to the direction $\boldsymbol{d}$ and such that $v$ sees infinity in exactly one of the two directions orthogonal to $\boldsymbol{d}$ (by treating $P$ as the only "opaque" object in the plane). We perform a ray shooting from $v$ along the direction orthogonal to $\boldsymbol{d}$ and towards the interior of $P$. Denote the first intersection between this ray and the boundary $B(P)$ of $P$ by $v'$. Then, $P'$ is obtained by traversing $B(P)$ starting from an extreme vertex with respect to $\boldsymbol{d}$, and "short-cutting" the tour by edges $(v, v')$. We call the vertices $v'$ of $P'(\boldsymbol{d})$ that are not vertices of $P$ the *augmented* vertices, and the other vertices $v$ of $P'(\boldsymbol{d})$ the *original* vertices.

The first key issue to our algorithm is to compute $S_f$. Once $S_f$ is known, one might attempt to compute $P'(\boldsymbol{d})$ for each $\boldsymbol{d} \in S_f$ and then choose the one with the minimum area as $P^*$. But, $S_f$ is normally an infinite set, and we must explore further the structure of $S_f$. We make use of the relation of *topological equivalence* [2]: For two directions $\boldsymbol{d_1}$ and $\boldsymbol{d_2}$ in $S_f$, $P'(\boldsymbol{d_1})$ and $P'(\boldsymbol{d_2})$ are *topologically equivalent* if $P'(\boldsymbol{d_1})$ and $P'(\boldsymbol{d_2})$ have the same sequence of original vertices and their corresponding augmented vertices lie on the same edge of $P$. Clearly, the topological equivalence relation partitions $S_f$ into a number of equivalence classes $\Pi_1, \Pi_2, \ldots, \Pi_l$, such that for any $i = 1, 2, \ldots, l$, $\boldsymbol{d_1}, \boldsymbol{d_2} \in \Pi_i$ implies that $P'(\boldsymbol{d_1})$ and $P'(\boldsymbol{d_2})$ are topologically equivalent. We will show later that $l = O(n)$ and for each equivalence class $\Pi_i$, it is possible to compute the minimum monotone cover (denoted by $P^*(\Pi_i)$) among all $\boldsymbol{d} \in \Pi_i$. This is the second key issue to our algorithm: compute the equivalence classes $\Pi_i$ of $S_f$ and compute $P^*(\Pi_i)$ for every $i = 1, 2, \ldots, l$.

## 2.1  Computing Feasible Directions in $S_f$

Let $H = \{x\mathbf{i} + y\mathbf{j} : x^2 + y^2 = 1, x \geq 0\}$ be a set of unit directions in 2-D. Clearly, it is sufficient to consider the directions of $H$ for the feasible directions in $S_f$, i.e., $S_f \subseteq H$. We illustrate our idea by first considering the set of feasible directions for one obstacle $R_q$, denoted by $S_{R_q}$ (i.e., $\forall \boldsymbol{d} \in S_{R_q}$, there exists a monotone polygon with respect to $\boldsymbol{d}$ that contains $P$ and avoids $R_q$). Note that $S_f = \bigcap_{R_i \in R} S_{R_i}$. Obviously, if $R_q$ lies outside the convex hull $CH(P)$ of $P$, then $S_{R_q} = H$ (i.e., $R_q$ does not affect $S_f$ and thus we can ignore $R_q$). Further, even if $R_q$ intersects the boundary of $CH(P)$, we can ignore the part of $R_q$ outside $CH(P)$ (e.g., see $R_2$ in Figure 2(a)). Hence, we only consider the part of each obstacle $R_q$ inside $CH(P)$. WLOG, we assume $R_q$ is inside $CH(P)$.

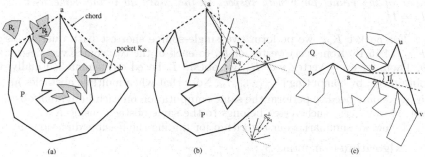

**Fig. 2.** (a) Convex hull and pockets of $P$. (b) Visible angular interval $S_{R_q}^{\perp}$ of an obstacle $R_q$. (c) The funnel of a point inside a polygon.

We call the edges of $CH(P)$ that are not edges of $P$ the *chords* of $CH(P)$. Each chord $\overline{ab}$ of $CH(P)$, together with a chain on $B(P)$ from vertex $a$ to vertex $b$, defines a simple polygon $K_{ab}$ such that $intr(P) \cap intr(K_{ab}) = \varnothing$. We call $K_{ab}$ a *pocket* of $P$ (e.g., see Figure 2(a)). WLOG, we assume that obstacle $R_q$ lies completely in the pocket $K_{ab}$.

**Lemma 1.** *A direction $\boldsymbol{d}$ is feasible for an obstacle $R_q$ if and only if $R_q$ can be moved away from $P$ by translating $R_q$ along an orthogonal direction $\boldsymbol{d}^{\perp}$ of $\boldsymbol{d}$ without intersecting $intr(P)$.*

Denote by $S_{R_q}^{\perp}$ the set of all directions along each of which $R_q$ can be moved away from $P$ by a translation as defined in Lemma 1. Note that once $S_{R_q}^{\perp}$ is available, $S_{R_q}$ can be easily obtained. Hence we focus on computing $S_{R_q}^{\perp}$.

**Lemma 2.** *$R_q$ can be moved away from $P$ by translating along a direction $\boldsymbol{d}$ iff each vertex $v$ of $R_q$ can be moved away from $P$ by translating $v$ along $\boldsymbol{d}$.*

Lemma 2 implies that it is sufficient to consider each individual vertex of $R_q$ (with respect to the pocket $K_{ab}$ that contains $R_q$). For each vertex $v$ of $R_q$, all directions along each of which $v$ can be translated away from $P$ form an angular interval $I_v$. We call $I_v$ the *visible angular interval* of $v$ since $v$ can "see" infinity along each direction $\boldsymbol{d} \in I_v$ without being blocked by the (only) "opaque" object $P$. Further, Lemma 2 implies that $S^{\perp}_{R_q} = \bigcap_{v \in V(R_q)} I_v$, where $V(R_q)$ denotes the vertex set of $R_q$ (see Figure 2(b)). Thus, we need to compute the visible angular interval $I_v$ for each $v \in V(R_q)$.

To compute $I_v$, we use the concept of funnel defined by Lee and Preparata [17]. For a simple polygon $Q$, let $p$ be a point in $Q$ and $\overline{uv}$ be an edge of $Q$. The shortest paths in $Q$ from $p$ to $u$ and from $p$ to $v$ may travel together for a while; then at some point $a$, the two shortest paths diverge and go to $u$ and $v$ respectively in a concave fashion, as illustrated in Figure 2(c). The region bounded by $\overline{uv}$ and the two concave chains from $a$ is called a *funnel*, with $a$ being the *apex* of the funnel. Extending away from $a$ the two funnel edges incident to $a$ defines an angular interval for $p$, denoted by $I^f_p$. Obviously, for each $\boldsymbol{d} \in I^f_p$, $a$ can see infinity along $\boldsymbol{d}$ without being blocked by the "opaque" $B(Q) - \overline{uv}$. Hence, if $a \neq p$, $p$ cannot be translated away from $B(Q) - \overline{uv}$, i.e., $I_p = \varnothing$.

**Lemma 3.** *Given a pocket $K_{ab}$ of polygon $P$ and a point $v$ inside $K_{ab}$, if the apex of the funnel for $v$ with respect to the chord $\overline{ab}$ is the same as $v$, then $I_v = I^f_v$.*

For pocket $K_{ab}$, we perform two single-source shortest path queries inside $K_{ab}$ [14,15,16] from every vertex of $R_q$ to each of the two source vertices $a$ and $b$. Then, for every vertex $v$ of $R_q$, we obtain $I_v$ based on Lemma 3. Finally, we obtain $S^{\perp}_{R_q}$ by computing $\bigcap_{v \in V(R_q)} I_v$. Note that when multiple obstacles are in $K_{ab}$, we only need to perform the same computation on each individual obstacle vertex as if every such vertex belongs to the same obstacle inside $K_{ab}$.

Below we summarize our algorithm for finding the feasible directions in $S_f$:

**Algorithm** Computing-$S_f$;
**Input:**     A simple polygon $P$ and a set of obstacles $R = \{R_1, R_2, \ldots, R_k\}$.
**Output:**    The set $S_f$ of all feasible directions.
**Begin**

    (1) compute the convex hull $CH(P)$ of $P$;
    (2) perform planar point location queries to determine which obstacle vertex is contained in which pocket of $P$;
    (3) for each pocket $K_{ab}$ of $P$, perform single-source shortest path queries for every vertex of each obstacle $R_i$ in $K_{ab}$ to compute $S^{\perp}_i$;
    (4) compute the intersection of the $S^{\perp}_i$'s to obtain $S_f$;

**end**

Step (1) takes $O(n)$ time [19]. Step (2) needs $O(n + m \log n)$ time and $O(n)$ space, since each point location query takes $O(\log n)$ time [19]. Single-source shortest path queries in a simple polygon need $O(n)$ time and space to create the data structure, and each query takes $O(\log n)$ time [15]. Thus, Step (3) takes totally $O(n + m \log n)$ time. Step (4) clearly uses $O(k) = O(m)$ time.

**Lemma 4.** *Given a simple polygon $P$ of $n$ vertices and a set of polygonal obstacles $R = \{R_1, R_2, \ldots, R_k\}$ with a total of $m$ vertices, the set $S_f$ of all feasible directions can be computed in $O(n + m \log n)$ time.*

## 2.2  Computing Equivalence Classes of $S_f$

Recall that, for two directions $d_1$ and $d_2$ in $S_f$, $P'(d_1)$ and $P'(d_2)$ are topologically equivalent if $P'(d_1)$ and $P'(d_2)$ have the same sequence of original vertices and their corresponding augmented vertices lie on the same edge of $P$. Arkin *et al.* [2] presented an $O(n \log n)$ time algorithm for computing the equivalence classes of $S_f$ without considering obstacles; in that case, $S_f = [0, \pi]$, the number of equivalence classes is $O(n)$, and each equivalence class is an angular interval. In our algorithm, we first ignore the obstacles in $R$ and run the algorithm of [2] to obtain $l$ equivalence classes $E_1, E_2, \ldots, E_l$, with $l = O(n)$. Next, we compute $S_f$, which is one angular interval. Finally, we compute the intersection of each $E_i$ and $S_f$, which is an equivalence class of $S_f$. We denote the set of equivalence classes of $S_f$ by $\Pi = \{\Pi_1, \Pi_2, \ldots, \Pi_l\}$. Thus, we have the following lemma.

**Lemma 5.** *The equivalence classes, $\Pi = \{\Pi_1, \Pi_2, \ldots, \Pi_l\}$, of $S_f$ can be computed in $O((n + m) \log n)$ time, with $l = O(n)$. $\Pi$ is a partition of $S_f$ with each $\Pi_i$ being an angular interval.*

## 2.3  Computing Minimum Monotone Cover $P^*$

We now discuss how to compute the minimum monotone cover $P^*$ of $P$. Lemmas 4 and 5 state that $\Pi$ consists of $l = O(n)$ consecutive angular intervals. Thus, there are at most $l$ events corresponding to the topological changes of $P'(d)$. Our overall strategy is to first determine, for every $\Pi_i$, the feasible direction $d_i^* \in \Pi_i$ such that its corresponding monotone polygon $P'(d_i^*)$ (denoted by $P^*(\Pi_i)$) is of the minimum area among all $d \in \Pi_i$. Then, we find the minimum monotone cover $P^*$ and $d^*$ for $P$ among the $P^*(\Pi_i)$'s, with $i = 1, 2, \ldots, l$.

For each angular interval $\Pi_i \in \Pi$, we are able to formulate the problem of computing $P^*(\Pi_i)$ to solving an optimization problem instance that minimizes the sum of $O(n)$ 1-D linear fractional functions over an interval. This optimization problem can be handled efficiently by the algorithm of Falk and Palocsay[11]. We leave the details of our transformation to the full paper.

Now, while $d$ rotates from $\Pi_i$ to $\Pi_{i+1}$, the topology of $P'(d)$ has only $O(1)$ changes. We can identify these changes and update the function $F(d)$ incrementally in $O(1)$ time. Initially, we can easily compute $F(d)$ for $d \in \Pi_1$ in $O(n \log n)$ time. Each successive $F(d)$ for $d \in \Pi_j$ is then obtained in $O(1)$ time, for $j = 2, 3, \ldots, l$. The total time for generating $F(d)$ for all $\Pi_j$'s is $O(n \log n)$.

**Theorem 1.** *Given a simple polygon $P$ of $n$ vertices and a set of obstacles $R = \{R_1, \ldots, R_k\}$ with a total of $m$ vertices, the minimum monotone cover $P^*$ of $P$ can be computed in $O((n+m) \log n + n * f(n))$ time, where $f(n)$ is the time for optimizing the sum of $O(n)$ 1-D linear fractional functions over an interval.*

# 3   Minimum Star-Shaped Polygon Cover with Obstacles

In this section, we consider the following problem: Given a simple polygon $P$ of $n$ vertices and a set of obstacles $R = \{R_1, R_2, \ldots, R_k\}$ with a total of $m$ vertices, find a star-shaped polygon $P^*$ such that: (i) $P \subseteq P^*$; (ii) $intr(P^*) \cap intr(R_i) = \varnothing$ for every $R_i \in R$; (iii) the area of $P^*$ is minimized. WLOG, we assume that $intr(P) \cap intr(R_i) = \varnothing$ for every $R_i \in R$.

A simple polygon $Q$ is *star-shaped* [19] if there exists a point $z$ in $Q$ such that for every point $p \in Q$, the line segment $\overline{zp}$ lies entirely in $Q$; $z$ is called a *kernel point* of $Q$. A point $z$ on the plane is a *feasible point* if there exists a star-shaped polygon $P'$ containing $P$ such that $z$ is a kernel point of $P'$ and $P'$ avoids all obstacles in $R$. All feasible points on the plane form the *feasible region*, denoted by $S_f$. For a point $z \in S_f$, the (obstacle-avoiding) minimum star-shaped cover of $P$ is denoted by $P'(z)$. $P'(z)$ can be obtained as follows [2]. For each vertex $v$ of $P$, let a ray $r(z, v)$ emanate from $z$ and pass through $v$. Suppose that ray $r(z, v)$ crosses the boundary $B(P)$ of $P$, at a point $v'$, for the last time before reaching $v$ (note that $v'$ may not exist). After passing through $v$, if $r(z, v)$ can reach infinity along the same direction without being blocked by $P$, then $v$ is a vertex of $P'(z)$. The point $v'$ on $B(P)$ is also a vertex of $P'(z)$ if the segment $\overline{v'v}$ does not intersect $intr(P)$. Besides, $z$ itself is a vertex of $P'(z)$ if $z \notin P$. Then we build $P'(z)$ by traversing along $B(P)$ and making "shortcuts" through segments $\overline{vv'}$. Again, we call the vertices, such as $v'$ and possibly $z$, of $P'(z)$ that are not vertices of $P$ the *augmented* vertices, and other vertices of $P'(z)$ the *original* vertices. For two points $z_1$ and $z_2$, $P'(z_1)$ and $P'(z_2)$ are said to be *topologically equivalent* if they have the same sequence of original vertices, and their corresponding augmented vertices lie on the same edge of $P$.

Arkin *et al.* [2] studied a special case of this problem (with no obstacle). The key steps of their algorithm are as follows. (i) Compute the *visibility cone* $Cone(v)$ with its apex at $v$ for each vertex $v$ of $P$. (ii) Extend the two rays of $Cone(v)$ into two lines for each vertex $v$, and build a 2-D arrangement $A_1$ of $O(n^2)$ cells using the $O(n)$ lines thus obtained, in $O(n^2)$ time. (The cells of $A_1$ cover the whole plane, and for all points $z$ in the same cell, the polygons $P'(z)$ are all topologically equivalent.) (iii) For each cell $C$ of $A_1$, compute the polygon (denoted by $\hat{P}^*(C)$) whose area is the minimum among all polygons $P'(z)$ with $z \in C$, and choose the one with the minimum area over all the cells of $A_1$ as the minimum star-shaped cover $P^*$ of $P$.

Our generalized problem takes the obstacles of $R$ into account. A key difference with the presence of obstacles is that a point $z$ on the plane may be *infeasible* (i.e., no $P'(z)$ can avoid all obstacles in $R$). Thus, we need to characterize and compute the feasible region $S_f$.

It would be nice if we could, like in Section 2 for computing the monotone polygon cover, use only the vertices of the obstacles *individually* (instead of treating an obstacle as a whole) to characterize the feasible region $S_f$. This turns out to remain true for the portions of obstacles that are inside the interior of the convex hull $CH(P)$ of $P$.

**Lemma 6.** *For the portions of obstacles in $intr(CH(P))$, it is sufficient to use their vertices individually to characterize the feasible region $S_f$.*

In fact, each obstacle vertex $u$ in $intr(CH(P))$ defines a feasible region (with respect to $u$) bounded by two lines passing through $u$ (e.g., the region associated with $I'_u$ in Figure 3(a)). More precisely, let two rays $r(u, a)$ and $r(u, b)$ define the visible angular interval $I_u$ of $u$, as in Section 2. Actually, $I_u$ defines the visibility cone $Cone(u)$ with its apex at $u$ (see Figure 3(a)). If $I_u = \varnothing$, then clearly the whole plane is infeasible. If $I_u \neq \varnothing$, then the cone defined by $u$ and the two opposite rays of $r(u, a)$ and $r(u, b)$ is the feasible region with respect to $u$. Further, the overall impact on $S_f$ generated by all the obstacle vertices in $intr(CH(P))$ is the *intersection* of the feasible regions with respect to all such vertices in $intr(CH(P))$ (see Figure 3(a)). Note that this intersection is simply the common intersection of $O(m)$ half-planes, which can be obtained easily in $O(m \log m)$ time [19]. We denote by $A_2$ the (convex) feasible region for this common intersection.

However, for the portions of obstacles that are *not* in $intr(CH(P))$, things become significantly different. In fact, we can no longer use only the obstacle vertices outside $intr(CH(P))$ individually to characterize the feasible region $S_f$. Instead, not only we must use each portion of the obstacles outside $intr(CH(P))$ as a whole to characterize $S_f$, but also we must consider the intersections between the obstacles and $CH(P)$.

**Lemma 7.** *For the portions of obstacles outside* $intr(CH(P))$*, it is* insufficient *to use their vertices* individually *to characterize the feasible region* $S_f$.

Based on Lemma 7, we need to consider the impact of each obstacle *point* (vertex or not) outside $intr(CH(P))$ on $S_f$. To obtain a description of all the obstacle points outside $intr(CH(P))$, we first need to compute the intersections between the obstacles and $CH(P)$.

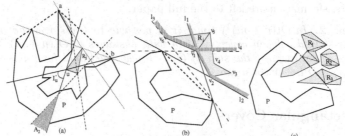

**Fig. 3.** (a) The feasible region $S_1$ for an obstacle inside $CH(P)$; (b) the feasible region for an obstacle outside $CH(P)$; (c) the portions of obstacles outside $CH(P)$.

**Lemma 8.** *Every obstacle edge can intersect at most one edge of* $CH(P)$.

By Lemma 8, the total number of intersections between the obstacle edges and the edges of $CH(P)$ is $O(m)$. Hence, we can compute all such intersections between the obstacle edges and the edges of $CH(P)$ in $O((n + m) \log(n + m))$ time by using an optimal output-sensitive algorithm for computing the intersections between line segments (e.g., [1]). Once these intersections are available, we can compute the portions of each obstacle outside $intr(CH(P))$ (i.e., $R_i - intr(CH(P))$). This can be done in $O(m \log m)$ time by performing $O(m)$ ray shooting operations.

Assume now we have obtained the portions of obstacles outside $intr(CH(P))$, which we treat as a set of polygons (see Figure 3(c)). We triangulate each such outside polygon in linear time [5]. Let $Tri(Q)$ be the resulting triangulation of such a polygonal obstacle $Q$ outside $intr(CH(P))$. Note that to consider the impact of each point of $Q$ on $S_f$, it is sufficient to consider the impact of each triangle $tri_i(Q)$ of $Tri(Q)$ on $S_f$. Since both $CH(P)$ and $tri_i(Q)$ are convex and they are disjoint with each other, it is easy to compute, in $O(\log n)$ time, the two tangent lines between $CH(P)$ and $tri_i(Q)$ each of which separates $CH(P)$ and $tri_i(Q)$ (see Figure 3(b)). These two tangent lines and some edge of $tri_i(Q)$ together bound the infeasible region with respect to $tri_i(Q)$ (e.g., the chain $(l_3, v_6, v_1, l_4)$ in Figure 3(b)). Further, with respect to all such triangles of the portions of obstacles outside $intr(CH(P))$, the infeasible region is simply the *union* of the infeasible regions associated with all these triangles. Note that the union of all such infeasible regions can be obtained by computing the arrangement of $O(m)$ line segments (which bound the $O(m)$ triangles outside $intr(CH(P))$). This can be done in $O(m^2)$ time using [1]. We denote by $A_3$ the set of cells for the infeasible region captured by this arrangement.

As in [2], we compute the arrangement $A_1$ of the whole plane (as if there is no obstacle) such that for each cell $C$ of $A_1$, the polygons $P'(z)$ are topologically equivalent for all points $z \in C$. This takes $O(n^2)$ time [3,7]. Finally, we compute the overall feasible region $S_f = (A_1 \cap A_2) - A_3$. This can be done by overlaying the arrangements $A_1$, $A_2$, and $A_3$, in $O((m+n)^2)$ time. The cells of $S_f$ are all convex and represent the sets of topologically equivalent polygons $P'(z)$ in $S_f$.

For each feasible cell $C$ of $S_f$, we are able to transform the problem of computing $P^*(C)$ to solving an optimization problem instance that minimizes the sum of $O(n)$ linear fractional functions on $C$ (note that $C$ is associated with a set of $O(m+n)$ 2-D linear constraints). This optimization problem can be handled efficiently by using the SOLF algorithm of Chen *et al.* [6]. The details of our transformation are left to the full paper.

**Theorem 2.** *In $O((n+m)^2)$ time, it is possible to transform the minimum-area star-shaped polygon cover problem with obstacles to $O((n+m)^2)$ problem instances of minimizing the sum of $O(n)$ linear fractional functions subject to $O(n+m)$ 2-D linear constraints.*

## 4    Rectangular Covers

We discuss here the rectangular cover problem [20]. Let $P$ be an $n$-vertex polygon possibly with holes. For an edge $e_i$ of $P$, let $e_i'$ be a segment that is parallel to $e_i$, on the side of $e_i$ that is in the exterior of $P$, and at a distance $\epsilon_i \geq 0$ away from $e_i$, where the value $\epsilon_i$ may depend on $e_i$. The polygonal region enclosed by all such segments $e_i'$ is called the *penumbra polygon* $P'$ of $P$ (see Figure 4). $P'$ can be computed efficiently in sub-quadratic time[10]. But we do not need to compute $P'$ explicitly. In radiosurgery, $P$ is the projection of the 3D tumor volume onto a plane that is orthogonal to the beams, and $P'$ represents the *tolerance zone* on the plane that the beams are allowed to intersect (outside $P'$ are possibly some critical organs that the beams should avoid). We seek a set of rectangles to cover $P$ such that: (i) the union of the rectangles contains $P$, (ii) the rectangles are mutually parallel and may overlap with each other only at their vertical boundary edges, (iii) the rectangles are confined to $P'$, and (iv) for a trapezoid $t$ of $P$ (with respect to a given direction $\boldsymbol{d}$), the widths of the rectangles covering $t$ are the same (the width is determined by the penumbra above and below $t$ and by the height of $t$). Two somewhat conflicting criteria are important: the area of $P'$ and the total number of rectangles used. The rectangle number is related to the treatment time in radiosurgery and $area(P')$ is related to the cover error. A large penumbra may need a small set of rectangles to cover. We thus consider two problems: (1) For a given penumbra $P'$, minimize the total number of rectangles for covering $P$, and (2) for a given rectangle number $k$, minimize $area(P')$ (assume that the relationship among the $\epsilon_i$'s is described by a function).

Observe that for Problem (1), once a direction $d$ is given, it is easy to compute the number of covering rectangles. Let $n_i$ be the unit vector normal to the edge $e_i$ of $P$, and $\epsilon_i$ be the distance between $e_i$ and its corresponding edge $e'_i$ of $P'$. We do a trapezoidal decomposition on $P$ with respect to $d$ and denote the set of resulting trapezoids by $T(d)$. Let $f_{t_i}(d)$ be the number of rectangles for covering the trapezoid $t_i$ with respect to $d$. Then the total number of rectangles for covering $P$ is $F(d) = \sum_{t_i \in T(d)} f_{t_i}(d)$. Our problem is to find a direction $d^*$ such that $F(d^*)$ is minimized. For each trapezoid $t_i \in T(d)$, we assume that $t_i$ is bounded by edges $e_{i1}$ and $e_{i2}$ of $P$ (see Figure 4). Note that the rectangles covering $t_i$ have the same width $w_i(d)$ which is determined by $\epsilon_{i1}$ and $\epsilon_{i2}$. Let $w'_{i1}(d)$ (resp., $w'_{i2}(d)$) be the maximum width of the rectangles that are allowed to cover $t_i$ based on $\epsilon_{i1}$ (resp., $\epsilon_{i2}$). Then $w'_{i1}(d) = \frac{\epsilon_{i1}}{|n_{i1} \cdot d|}$ and $w'_{i2}(d) = \frac{\epsilon_{i2}}{|n_{i2} \cdot d|}$. If $n_{i1} \cdot d = 0$ (resp., $n_{i2} \cdot d = 0$), we let $w'_{i1}(d)$ (resp., $w'_{i2}(d)$) be the height of $t_i$. Let $w_i(d) = \min\{w'_{i1}(d), w'_{i2}(d)\}$. Denote by $v_i(d)$ and $u_i(d)$ respectively the highest and lowest vertices of $P$ on the trapezoid $t_i$ with respect to $d$. Then the height of $t_i$, denoted by $h_i(d)$, is $v_i \cdot d - u_i \cdot d$, where $v_i$ (resp., $u_i$) is the vector from the origin to the point $v_i(d)$ (resp., $u_i(d)$). Therefore, $f_{t_i}(d) = \frac{h_i(d)}{w_i(d)}$.

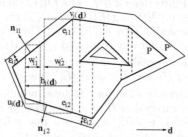

**Fig. 4.** Computing the number of rectangles covering $P$ with respect to direction $d$.

As $d$ rotates continuously, the topological structure of the trapezoidal decomposition $T(d)$ of $P$ changes. Our idea is to obtain a partition $\Pi$ of the direction space $H$ (as did in Section 2) with the following properties: If $I$ is an angular interval of $\Pi$, then for all directions $d \in I$, each trapezoid $t_i \in T(d)$ uses the same highest and lowest vertices of $P$ to determine the height $h_i(d)$ of $t_i$ (called the *height property*), and the same edge $e_j$ of $P$ to determine the width $w_i(d)$ of the rectangles for covering $t_i$ (called the *width property*). We compute $\Pi$ by overlaying two partitions, $\Pi_1$ and $\Pi_2$, of $H$, herein $\Pi_1$ (resp., $\Pi_2$) captures the height property (resp., width property).

First, we construct the partition $\Pi_1$ of $H$. For any two directions $d_1$ and $d_2$, we say that $T(d_1)$ and $T(d_2)$ are *topologically equivalent* if they have the same number of trapezoids and their corresponding trapezoids are bounded by the same two edges and same two vertices of $P$. Clearly, as $d$ rotates across the normal of a line passing through any two visible vertices of $P$, $T(d)$ changes topologically. Hence, we can obtain the topologically equivalent partition $\Pi_1$ of $H$ by computing the orthogonal unit-direction of the vector defined by each edge of the visibility graph $G = (V, E)$ of $P$, which can be computed in $O(|E|+n \log n)$ time[13]. Then, we sort these $O(|E|)$ unit-directions, in $O(|E| \log |E|)$ time. Thus, $\Pi_1$ consists of $O(|E|)$ angular intervals in sorted order.

Note that $w_i'(d)$ on edge $e_i$ depends on the sign of $n_i \cdot d$. If $n_i \cdot d > 0$, $w_i'(d) = \frac{\epsilon_i}{n_i \cdot d}$, while if $n_i \cdot d < 0$, $w_i'(d) = \frac{\epsilon_i}{-n_i \cdot d}$. Thus, the unit-directions of the vectors defined by all edges of $P$ together partition $H$ into $O(n)$ angular intervals. For any two directions $d_1$ and $d_2$ in such an interval, if it is the normal (resp., the negation) of edge $e_i$ of $P$ that determines $w_i'(d_1)$ on $e_i$, then it is also the normal (resp., the negation) of $e_i$ that determines $w_i'(d_2)$ on $e_i$. We denote this partition of $H$ by $\Pi_{21}$. Furthermore, for any trapezoid $t_i \in T(d)$, to decide which edge of $P$ on $t_i$ determines $w_i(d)$, we compute another partition $\Pi_{22}$ of $H$. Obviously, it may be computed in $O(n^2)$ time, but we can handle it in $O(|E|)$ time, where $E$ is the edge set of the visibility graph $G$ of $P$. As note that we are interested in the pairs of edges that bound the trapezoids in $T(d)$ for each $d \in H$. Let $I$ be an angular interval of $\Pi_1$. For each $d \in I$, the $O(n)$ pairs of edges that bound the trapezoids in $T(d)$ are the same. When $d$ rotates from $I$ to the adjacent angular interval $I'$ in $\Pi_1$, only $O(1)$ pairs of edges that bound the trapezoids in $T(d)$ change. Hence, there are totally $O(|E|)$ pairs of edges we need to consider. For every such pair of edges $e_i$ and $e_j$, we compute the angular interval such that $w_i'(d) \leq w_j'(d)$ (similarly, the interval for $w_i'(d) > w_j'(d)$ is computed). This defines the partition $\Pi_{22}$ which consists of $O(|E|)$ angular intervals. For an interval $I \in \Pi_{22}$, $w_i'(d) \leq w_j'(d)$ (say) holds for an edge pair of $e_i$ and $e_j$ of $P$ over all directions $d \in I$. The $O(|E|)$ intervals of $\Pi_{22}$, in sorted order, can be computed in $O(|E| \log |E|)$ time. $\Pi_2$ is the overlapping of $\Pi_{21}$ and $\Pi_{22}$, which can be obtained in $O(n + |E|)$ time. Thus, $w_i(d)$ is determined over each angular interval of $\Pi_2$ for any trapezoid $t_i \in T(d)$.

Once $\Pi_1$ and $\Pi_2$ are available, we compute the desired partition $\Pi$ of size $O(|E|)$ as the overlay of $\Pi_1$ and $\Pi_2$, in $O(|E|)$ time.

Now consider the formula $F(d)$ for the total number of rectangles covering $P$. Let $I$ be an angular interval of $\Pi$, and $d = x\mathbf{i} + y\mathbf{j}$ be a unit direction in $I$. Then for each trapezoid $t_i \in T(d)$, $w_i(d)$ is a linear fractional function of the form $\frac{c}{a_i x + b_i y}$, and $h_i(d)$ is a linear function $a_i' x + b_i' y$. Hence, $f_{t_i}(d) = \frac{h_i(d)}{w_i(d)}$ is a quadratic function, and $F(d) = \sum_{t_i \in T(d)} f_{t_i}(d)$ is also a quadratic function, both of the form $Ax^2 + By^2 + Cxy$. Therefore, finding the optimal direction $d \in I$ involves solving the problem of minimizing $F(d) = Ax^2 + By^2 + Cxy$ on $I$, which takes $O(1)$ time.

Note that when moving from $I$ to a neighboring interval $I'$ of $I$, the objective function $F(d)$ may change due to three factors: (i) $w_i'(d)$ on an edge $e_i$ of $P$ that changes from its normal to its negation, or *vice versa*, (ii) $w_i(d)$ of a trapezoid that changes from one edge of $P$ to another edge, and (iii) the changes of the trapezoidal decomposition $T(d)$ of $P$ ($O(1)$ changes per event). We can detect these changes and update $F(d)$ incrementally from $I$ to $I'$ in $O(1)$ time. Thus, the total time for solving the $O(|E|)$ optimization problem instances over all the intervals of $\Pi$ is $O(|E|)$.

**Theorem 3.** *Given an n-vertex polygon P and its penumbra polygon P′, a rectangular cover of P with the minimum number of rectangles can be computed in* $O((n + |E|) \log n)$ *time, where E is the edge set of the visibility graph G of P.*

For Problem (2) (i.e., given polygon $P$ and a rectangle number $k$, minimize the area of the penumbra $P'$ of $P$), we use a binary search approach. Each "comparison" operation of the binary search is a call to the algorithm for Theorem 3 for Problem (1). Depending on the outcome of a "comparison", we adjust the values $\epsilon_i$ for the penumbra $P'$, until a certain specified tolerance is met. The total number of "comparisons" is logarithmic depending on the $\epsilon_i$'s and the tolerance.

# References

1. N.M. Amato, M.T. Goodrich, and E.A. Ramos, Computing the Arrangement of Curve Segments: Divide-and-Conquer Algorithms via Sampling, *Proc. 11th Annual ACM-SIAM Symposium on Discrete Algorithms*, 2000, pp. 705-706.
2. E.M. Arkin, Y.-J. Chiang, M. Held, J.S.B. Mitchell, V. Sacristan, S.S. Skiena, and T.-C. Yang, On Minimum-Area Hulls, *Algorithmica*, 21(1998), 119-136.
3. T. Asano, L.J. Guibas, and T. Tokuyama, Walking in an Arrangement Topologically, *Int. J. of Comput. Geom. & Appl.*, 4(2)(1994), 123-151.
4. J.S. Chang and C.K. Yap, A Polynomial Solution for the Potato-Peeling Problem, *Discrete Comput. Geom.*, 1(1986), 155-182.
5. B. Chazelle, Triangulating a Simple Polygon in Linear Time, *Discrete Comput. Geom.*, 6(1991), 485-524.
6. D.Z. Chen, O. Daescu, Y. Dai, N. Katoh, X. Wu, and J. Xu, Optimizing the Sum of Linear Fractional Functions and Applications, *Proc. 11th ACM-SIAM Symposium on Discrete Algorithms*, 2000, pp. 707-716.
7. D.Z. Chen and J. Xu, Peeling an Arrangement Topologically, *Proc. 4th CGC Workshop on Comput. Geom.*, 1999.
8. K.M. Daniels, The Restrict/Evaluate/Subdivide Paradigm for Translational Containment, *Proc. 5th MSI Stony Brook Workshop on Comput. Geom.*, 1995.
9. K.M. Daniels, Z. Li, and V.J. Milenkovic, Multiple Containment Methods, Technical Report TR-12-94, Division of Applied Sciences, Harvard University.
10. D. Eppstein and J. Erickson, Raising Roofs, Crashing Cycles, and Playing Pool: Applications of a Data Structure for Finding Pairwise Interactions, *Discrete Comput. Geom.*, 22(1999), 569-592.
11. J.E. Falk and S.W. Palocsay, Optimizing the Sum of Linear Fractional Functions, *Collection: Recent Advances in Global Optimization*, C.A. Floudas and P.M. Pardalos (eds.), 1992, 221-258.
12. R. Fleischer, K. Mehlhorn, G. Rote, E. Welzl, and C.K. Yap, Simultaneous Inner and Outer Approximation of Shapes, *Algorithmica*, 8(1992), 365-389.
13. S.K. Ghosh and D.M. Mount, An Output-Sensitive Algorithm for Computing Visibility Graphs, *SIAM J. Comput.*, 20(1991), 888-910.
14. M.T. Goodrich, Geometric Data Structures, *Handbook of Computational Geometry*, J.-R. Sack and J. Urrutia (editors), Elsevier Science Publishers B.V., North-Holland, Amsterdam, 1998.
15. L.J. Guibas, J. Hershberger, D. Leven, M. Sharir, and R.E. Tarjan, Linear-Time Algorithms for Visibility and Shortest Path Problems inside Triangulated Simple Polygons, *Algorithmica*, 2(1987), 209-233.
16. J. Hershberger and J. Snoeyink, Computing Minimum Length Paths of a Given Homotopy Class, *Comput. Geom. Theory Appl.*, 9(1994), 63-98.
17. D.T. Lee and F.P. Preparata, Euclidean Shortest Paths in the Presence of Rectilinear Barriers, *Networks*, 14(1984), 393-410.

18. J. Majhi, R. Janardan, M. Smid, and P. Gupta, On Some Geometric Optimization Problems in Layered Manufacturing, *Comput. Geom.: Theory Appl.*, 12(1999), 219-239.
19. F.P. Preparata and M.I. Shamos, *Computational Geometry: An Introduction*, Springer-Verlag, Berlin, 1985.
20. A. Schweikard, R. Tombropoulos, and J.R. Adler, Robotic Radiosurgery with Beams of Adaptable Shapes, *Proc. 1st Int. Conf. on Computer Vision, Virtual Reality and Robotics in Medicine, Lecture Notes in Computer Science*, Vol. 905, Springer, 1995, pp. 138-149.
21. R. Tombropoulos, J.R. Adler, and J.C. Latombe, CARABEAMER: A Treatment Planner for a Robotic Radiosurgical System with General Kinematics, *Medical Image Analysis, Medical Image Analysis*, 3(1999), 1–28.

# Author Index

# Lecture Notes in Computer Science

For information about Vols. 1–1875
please contact your bookseller or Springer-Verlag

Vol. 1911: D.G. Feitelson, L. Rudolph (Eds.), Job Scheduling Strategies for Parallel Processing. VII, 209 pages. 2000.

Vol. 1912: Y. Gurevich, P.W. Kutter, M. Odersky, L. Thiele (Eds.), Abstract State Machines. Proceedings, 2000. X, 381 pages. 2000.

Vol. 1913: K. Jansen, S. Khuller (Eds.), Approximation Algorithms for Combinatorial Optimization. Proceedings, 2000. IX, 275 pages. 2000.

Vol. 1914: M. Herlihy (Ed.), Distributed Computing. Proceedings, 2000. VIII, 389 pages. 2000.

Vol. 1915: S. Dwarkadas (Ed.), Languages, Compilers, and Run-Time Systems for Scalable Computers. Proceedings, 2000. VIII, 301 pages. 2000.

Vol. 1916: F. Dignum, M. Greaves (Eds.), Issues in Agent Communication. X, 351 pages. 2000. (Subseries LNAI).

Vol. 1917: M. Schoenauer, K. Deb, G. Rudolph, X. Yao, E. Lutton, J.J. Merelo, H.-P. Schwefel (Eds.), Parallel Problem Solving from Nature – PPSN VI. Proceedings, 2000. XXI, 914 pages. 2000.

Vol. 1918: D. Soudris, P. Pirsch, E. Barke (Eds.), Integrated Circuit Design. Proceedings, 2000. XII, 338 pages. 2000.

Vol. 1919: M. Ojeda-Aciego, I.P. de Guzman, G. Brewka, L. Moniz Pereira (Eds.), Logics in Artificial Intelligence. Proceedings, 2000. XI, 407 pages. 2000. (Subseries LNAI).

Vol. 1920: A.H.F. Laender, S.W. Liddle, V.C. Storey (Eds.), Conceptual Modeling – ER 2000. Proceedings, 2000. XV, 588 pages. 2000.

Vol. 1921: S.W. Liddle, H.C. Mayr, B. Thalheim (Eds.), Conceptual Modeling for E-Business and the Web. Proceedings, 2000. X, 179 pages. 2000.

Vol. 1922: J. Crowcroft, J. Roberts, M.I. Smirnov (Eds.), Quality of Future Internet Services. Proceedings, 2000. XI, 368 pages. 2000.

Vol. 1923: J. Borbinha, T. Baker (Eds.), Research and Advanced Technology for Digital Libraries. Proceedings, 2000. XVII, 513 pages. 2000.

Vol. 1924: W. Taha (Ed.), Semantics, Applications, and Implementation of Program Generation. Proceedings, 2000. VIII, 231 pages. 2000.

Vol. 1925: J. Cussens, S. Džeroski (Eds.), Learning Language in Logic. X, 301 pages 2000. (Subseries LNAI).

Vol. 1926: M. Joseph (Ed.), Formal Techniques in Real-Time and Fault-Tolerant Systems. Proceedings, 2000. X, 305 pages. 2000.

Vol. 1927: P. Thomas, H.W. Gellersen, (Eds.), Handheld and Ubiquitous Computing. Proceedings, 2000. X, 249 pages. 2000.

Vol. 1928: U. Brandes, D. Wagner (Eds.), Graph-Theoretic Concepts in Computer Science. Proceedings, 2000. X, 315 pages. 2000.

Vol. 1929: R. Laurini (Ed.), Advances in Visual Information Systems. Proceedings, 2000. XII, 542 pages. 2000.

Vol. 1931: E. Horlait (Ed.), Mobile Agents for Telecommunication Applications. Proceedings, 2000. IX, 271 pages. 2000.

Vol. 1658: J. Baumann, Mobile Agents: Control Algorithms. XIX, 161 pages. 2000.

Vol. 1766: M. Jazayeri, R.G.K. Loos, D.R. Musser (Eds.), Generic Programming. Proceedings, 1998. X, 269 pages. 2000.

Vol. 1791: D. Fensel, Problem-Solving Methods. XII, 153 pages. 2000. (Subseries LNAI).

Vol. 1799: K. Czarnecki, U.W. Eisenecker, Generative and Component-Based Software Engineering. Proceedings, 1999. VIII, 225 pages. 2000.

Vol. 1812: J. Wyatt, J. Demiris (Eds.), Advances in Robot Learning. Proceedings, 1999. VII, 165 pages. 2000. (Subseries LNAI).

Vol. 1932: Z.W. Raś, S. Ohsuga (Eds.), Foundations of Intelligent Systems. Proceedings, 2000. XII, 646 pages. (Subseries LNAI).

Vol. 1933: R.W. Brause, E. Hanisch (Eds.), Medical Data Analysis. Proceedings, 2000. XI, 316 pages. 2000.

Vol. 1934: J.S. White (Ed.), Envisioning Machine Translation in the Information Future. Proceedings, 2000. XV, 254 pages. 2000. (Subseries LNAI).

Vol. 1935: S.L. Delp, A.M. DiGioia, B. Jaramaz (Eds.), Medical Image Computing and Computer-Assisted Intervention – MICCAI 2000. Proceedings, 2000. XXV, 1250 pages. 2000.

Vol. 1937: R. Dieng, O. Corby (Eds.), Knowledge Engineering and Knowledge Management. Proceedings, 2000. XIII, 457 pages. 2000. (Subseries LNAI).

Vol. 1938: S. Rao, K.I. Sletta (Eds.), Next Generation Networks. Proceedings, 2000. XI, 392 pages. 2000.

Vol. 1939: A. Evans, S. Kent, B. Selic (Eds.), «UML» – The Unified Modeling Language. Proceedings, 2000. XIV, 572 pages. 2000.

Vol. 1940: M. Valero, K. Joe, M. Kitsuregawa, H. Tanaka (Eds.), High Performance Computing. Proceedings, 2000. XV, 595 pages. 2000.

Vol. 1941: A.K. Chhabra, D. Dori (Eds.), Graphics Recognition. Proceedings, 1999. XI, 346 pages. 2000.

Vol. 1942: H. Yasuda (Ed.), Active Networks. Proceedings, 2000. XI, 424 pages. 2000.

Vol. 1943: F. Koornneef, M. van der Meulen (Eds.), Computer Safety, Reliability and Security. Proceedings, 2000. X, 432 pages. 2000.

Vol. 1945: W. Grieskamp, T. Santen, B. Stoddart (Eds.), Integrated Formal Methods. Proceedings, 2000. X, 441 pages. 2000.

Vol. 1948: T. Tan, Y. Shi, W. Gao (Eds.), Advances in Multimodal Interfaces – ICMI 2000. Proceedings, 2000. XVI, 678 pages. 2000.

Vol. 1952: M.C. Monard, J. Simão Sichman (Eds.), Advances in Artificial Intelligence. Proceedings, 2000. XV, 498 pages. 2000. (Subseries LNAI).

Vol. 1954: W.A. Hunt, Jr., S.D. Johnson (Eds.), Formal Methods in Computer-Aided Design. Proceedings, 2000. XI, 539 pages. 2000.

Vol. 1968: H. Arimura, S. Jain, A. Sharma (Eds.), Algorithmic Learning Theory. Proceedings, 2000. XI, 335 pages. 2000. (Subseries LNAI).

Vol. 1969: D.T. Lee, S.-H. Teng (Eds.), Algorithms and Computation. Proceedings, 2000. XIV, 578 pages. 2000.